SIMON DIFFORD

IS PROUD TO PRESENT

DIFFORDSGUIDE

~~~

COCKTAILS

~~~

AN ENCYCLOPAEDIA

OF MORE THAN

3000 ILLUSTRATED COCKTAIL RECIPES

Please enjoy cocktails responsibly

- This guide is intended for adults of legal drinking age
- Consumption of alcohol in excess can be harmful to your health
- The sugar levels in some cocktails may mask their alcohol content
- Do not consume cocktails and drive or operate machinery
- Great care should be exercised when combining flames and alcohol
- Consumption of raw and unpasteurised eggs may be harmful to health
- Please follow the alcohol content guidelines included in this guide where a shot is equal to 30ml at most. A 25ml measure of spirit at 40% alc./vol. is equal to 1 unit of alcohol. Most men can drink up to three to four units of alcohol a day and most women can drink up to two to three units of alcohol a day without significant risks to their health.
- Women who are trying to conceive or who are pregnant are advised to avoid alcohol

We recommend you visit: www.drinkaware.co.uk

Publisher & Author Simon Difford
Art Direction Dan Malpass
Design Gavin Yam
Cocktail Photography Rob Lawson

Published by Odd Firm of Sin Limited
1 Futura House, 169 Grange Road, London, SE1 3BN, England.
www.diffordsguide.com

Don't blame us
The views expressed in this publication are not necessarily the view of Odd Firm of Sin Limited. While every effort is made to ensure the accuracy of information contained in this publication at the time of going to press, no responsibility can be accepted for errors or omissions and Odd Firm of Sin Limited specifically disclaims any implied warranties of merchantability or fitness for a particular purpose. The advice and strategies contained herein may not be suitable for your situation.

ISBN: 978-0-9556276-9-9

SIMON DIFFORD

IS PROUD TO PRESENT

DIFFORDSGUIDE

COCKTAILS

AN ENCYCLOPAEDIA

OF MORE THAN

3000 ILLUSTRATED COCKTAIL RECIPES

11th EDITION

WRITTEN BY

SIMON DIFFORD

Welcome

This 11th edition of diffordsguide Cocktails contains 3,100 recipes. As I continue my quest to create the world's ultimate cocktail guide I've added scores of drinks to an already bulging collection. Some are new additions, perhaps the latest creations from cocktail competitions held in 2013, or modern classics inspired by the new golden age of mixed drinks we are living in. Others are far older, hidden gems found secreted in long-forgotten tomes. As ever, I have sampled, photographed and scored every recipe.

I've been doing this job for 16 years and, while there's never a dull moment, I certainly couldn't continue such a search without the help of the many cocktail aficionados and professional bartenders who share their recipes with me. Thanks to them I have accumulated hundreds more recipes which I have still yet to sample. I owe you all a huge debt of gratitude.

I always love to hear what fellow discerning drinkers think of the recipes in this book. Do you have a better version of a classic cocktail? Do you think one of your own creations is worth including? Do please email me. There's also a chance that we might include your recipe in an edition of our magazine, published weekly on diffordsguide.com – to receive our weekly email alerts for free, sign up at diffordsguide.com

In this digital age, it's on the diffordsguide.com website that you'll find our most recently updated cocktail recipes and the results of the huge numbers of cocktail competitions that are held each year. These are often the source for inspired new concoctions from today's talented mixologists – though only those I think should stand the test of time make it into print here.

If you're only just beginning an immersion into the world of cocktails it can be pretty overwhelming to face such a collection as this. But that's when I like to remind readers that anyone starting out should begin with the 14 Key Ingredients featured in the opening pages. These are the most frequently used ingredients and by combining them with fruit juices and common household items you will be able to make over 500 cocktails. Look for the 'key' symbol throughout this guide for drinks made using just these ingredients.

Cheers,
Simon Difford.
simon@diffordsguide.com

Bartending basics

Equipment and techniques you can't do without

By definition, any drink which is described as a cocktail contains more than one ingredient. So if you are going to make cocktails, you first have to know how to combine these various liquids precisely. Firstly, as in cooking, there is a correct order in which to prepare things and, with few exceptions, it runs as follows:

1. Select glass and chill or pre-heat (if required) 2. Prepare garnish 3. Pour ingredients 4. Add ice 5. Mix ingredients (shake, stir etc.) 6. Add pre-prepared garnish 7. Consume or serve to guest

Essentially, there are four different ways to mix a cocktail: shake, stir, blend and build. Building a drink refers to simply combining the ingredients within the glass in which the cocktail will be served. A further construction method, layering, isn't strictly mixing. The idea here is to float each ingredient on its predecessor without the ingredients merging at all. At the heart of every cocktail lies at least one of these five methods, so understanding these terms is fundamental.

SHAKERS & SHAKING

When you see the instruction "shake with ice and strain" or a similar phrase in a method, you should place all the necessary ingredients with cubed ice in a cocktail shaker and shake briskly. Don't be shy about it – imagine how you might agitate the metal ball in a can of spray paint. Shake for around fifteen seconds, then strain the liquid into the glass, leaving the ice behind in the shaker.

Shaking not only mixes a drink, it also chills, dilutes and aerates it. The dilution achieved by shaking is just as important to the resulting cocktail as using the right proportions of each ingredient. If you use too little ice it will melt too quickly in the shaker, producing an over-diluted drink – so always fill your shaker at least two-thirds full with fresh ice.

Losing your grip while shaking is likely to make a mess and a flying shaker could injure a bystander, so always hold the shaker firmly with two hands and never shake fizzy ingredients

(unless in a minute proportion to the rest of drink). Although shakers come in many shapes and sizes there are two basic types, though confusingly each of the two types has at least three different names:

Three-Piece/Standard/Cobbler Shakers
These consist of three parts:
1. A flat-bottomed, conical base or can
2. A top with a built-in strainer
3. A cap

In 1872, the first patent for a cobbler-style shaker was granted in the United States. Three-piece shakers are preferred by Japanese bartenders due to their small capacity and the limited travel of the ingredients and ice inside the shaker. Japanese bartenders are famous for their 'Hard Shake' which, perversely, is actually more gentle on the ingredients and ice and aims to end up with some fine fragments of ice being poured from the shaker into the drink, rather than larger and more uneven ice shards. Three-piece shakers with built-in strainers are slower to use and pour more slowly than two-piece shakers, especially if the drink being poured contains muddled fruit. However, we recommend this style of shaker for home or non-professional use due to its ease.

To use:
1. Combine all ingredients in the base of the shaker.
2. Fill two-thirds full with ice.
3. Place the top and cap firmly on the base.
4. Pick up the closed shaker with one hand on the top, securing the cap, and the other gripping the bottom, and shake vigorously. The cap should always be on the top when shaking and should point away from guests.
5. After shaking briskly for around 15 seconds, lift off the cap, hold the shaker by its base with one finger securing the top and pour the drink through the built-in strainer.

Two-Piece/Boston/French Shakers
In contrast to most Japanese bartenders, for professional use we recommend two-piece shakers with a capacity of at

least one pint. These comprise two flat-bottomed cones, one larger than the other. The large cone, or 'can', is made of stainless steel or silver-plated steel while the smaller cone can be either glass, stainless steel or even plastic. If the smaller cone is glass the pair are collectively known as a 'Boston Shaker', and if metal then you have what's known as a French Shaker.

Two-piece or two-part shakers tend to have a larger capacity than three-piece shakers, so allow for a lot more movement of the ingredients inside from one end to the other. As the name Boston and French may suggest, two-piece shakers are very popular amongst European and American bartenders. Avoid Boston shakers that rely on a rubber ring to seal.

I use Alessi Boston and WMF tins as I find these seal without a thump and open with the lightest tap. However good your Boston shaker, these devices demand an element of skill and practice is usually required for a new user to become proficient.

To use:
1. Combine ingredients in the glass (or smaller of the two cans).
2. Fill the large can with ice and briskly up-end over the smaller can (or glass), quickly enough to avoid spilling any ice. Lightly tap the top with the heel of your hand to create a seal between the two parts.
3. Lift shaker with one hand on the top and the other gripping the base and shake vigorously. The smaller can (or glass) should always be on the top when shaking and should point away from guests.
4. After shaking for around 15 seconds, hold the larger can in one hand and break the seal between the two halves of the shaker by tapping the base can with the heel of your other hand at the point where it meets the upper can (or glass).
5. Before pouring, place a strainer with a coiled rim (also known as a Hawthorne strainer) over the top of the can and strain the mixture into the glass, leaving the ice behind.
6. The ice used during shaking is now spent and should simply be dumped. The used empty shaker should be

rinsed with cold water before making the next drink. I recommend always shaking with cubed ice. However, if shaking with large chunks of ice hacked off an ice block (block ice) then a longer shake will be required to achieve the same dilution due to the reduced service area of the ice. Conversely, if shaking with crushed ice then the extra surface area will result in increased dilution.

DRY SHAKE

When making drinks containing cream and eggs it is common practice among some bartenders to first shake the mixture in a shaker without ice, before shaking the drink a second time with ice. This practice is known as dry shaking and the theory is that shaking first without ice, and so at a higher temperature, better allows the drink to emulsify. Some bartenders also place a spring from a Hawthorne strainer in the shaker during the first dry shake as this acts as a whisk inside the shaker when the drink is shaken.

STIRRING

Stirring is the most basic way of mixing a cocktail. You might not give much thought to a technique used to stir everything from a cup of tea to a pot of paint, but somehow cocktails deserve a little more reverence.

There is much debate among bartenders as to the best vessel to use for stirring, with some preferring glass to metal. Scientific experiments by the New York-based director of the French Culinary Institute, Dave Arnold, prove that metal heats up and cools down quickly, and in doing so uses minimal energy, so having little effect on the temperature of the finished cocktail. In contrast, heavy stirring glasses have more thermal heat capacity, so absorb more energy from the drink being mixed. The heavier they are, the more energy they will absorb. Pre-chilling or freezing such glasses mitigates this effect and, according to Dave, "makes them as good as, or better than, an un-chilled metal shaker".

Mixing glasses come in a multitude of shapes and sizes and, bearing in mind the above, heavy Japanese cut-glass stirring glasses stored in a refrigerator or freezer

are now favoured in many high-end bars. If a specially designed lipped mixing glass is not available, a Boston glass (the glass half of a Boston shaker) or even the base of a standard shaker, will suffice.

There are almost as many different styles of bar spoon on the market as there are stirring glasses. Some have spiralling stems, some have flat ends and others three-pronged fork ends. The key thing is for your spoon to have a long stem so it will reach down to the base of the glass while allowing you to comfortably hold the stem high above the glass.

If a cocktail recipe calls for you to "stir with ice and strain" then you should:

1. Ideally pre-chill both your mixing glass and serving glass in a refrigerator or freezer. However, if this is not possible, you will need to chill them by first filling with ice and then topping with water. Stir the ice and water in the glass as if mixing a drink before dumping the contents.

2. Measure your ingredients into your chilled mixing glass and then fill two-thirds with ice. Bartending myth used to have it that adding ice last would better control dilution, as the ice would not be melting as you measured in the ingredients. However, science (again, it was Dave Arnold at the French Culinary Institute in New York) has shown that leaving the ingredients on ice for as much as a minute has little effect on either dilution or the temperature of the finished cocktail.

3. Hold the bar spoon between your thumb and the first two fingers of your dominant hand with the spoon's shaft running between your middle finger and ring finger.

4. Slide the bowl of the spoon down the inside edge of the glass until it almost touches the base of the glass.

5. Keeping your arm, and to an extent your wrist still, use your fingers to pull the spoon towards and then away from you, aiming to hit the quarter hour marks on an imaginary clock-face inside your mixing glass. As the spoon runs around it will spin the ice and liquid in the glass, while spinning on its own axis in your fingers.

6. Stir briskly for about 30-45 seconds – this should account for at least 50 revolutions.

7. Place your strainer into or over the mixing glass and strain into your chilled serving glass. If the recipe calls for the drink to be served over ice then you should ice your glass first. Never use the ice from the mixing glass in the drink itself.

8. The ice used during stirring is now spent and should be dumped, or alternatively can be left in the mixing glass to keep it chilled ready for the next drink. If the latter, remember to dump the ice and rinse the glass with cold water before making the next drink.

STIRRING VS. SHAKING

Stirring and shaking obviously result in the various ingredients being mixed together, but both actions also cool and dilute the cocktail being mixed.

The key difference between the two mixing methods is that the violent action of shaking achieves the same results quicker. The same degree of cooling and dilution can be achieved with 15 to 20 seconds of shaking as 90 to 120 seconds of stirring. With few exceptions, (most notably the Old Fashioned) drinks are not stirred for longer than 30 to 45 seconds, so do not end up as cold or as diluted as if they had been shaken.

Why stir then? Stirring merely chills and dilutes a cocktail whereas shaking additionally changes its texture. The ice, being violently shaken about inside the shaker, aerates the drink with tiny air bubbles, which are held in suspension in the liquid, giving the cocktail a cloudy appearance.

Stirring, on the other hand, has the benefit of delivering a crystal-clear cocktail.

Bartending 'law' has it that drinks made with only clear ingredients should be stirred and drinks with cloudy ingredients such as citrus juice, milk or cream should be shaken. Laws are, of course, made to be broken, and while it is true that any drink which can be stirred can also be shaken – and occasionally might even be better for it – drinks containing egg white, cream and, to an extent, milk, should always be shaken.

STRAINING

When straining a shaken drink, a Hawthorn strainer tends to be used, but when straining a stirred drink it is traditional to use a Julep strainer. Both strainers allow the liquid to be poured from the shaker/mixing glass while retaining the spent ice.

Hawthorn strainers have a spring which runs around their circumference to help catch particles of ice and fruit created by the violent act of shaking.

They also often have 'lugs' which rest on the rim of the shaker to hold the strainer in position when being used. Most designs of Hawthorn strainer incorporate a ridge or finger rest, which when pushed serves to secure the sprung-loaded gap between the strainer and the side of the shaker, so allowing finer particles to be caught.

Julep strainers are best described as being perforated metal spoons which fit inside the mixing glass. They are said to take their name from Kentucky gentlemen who would historically hold them over a Mint Julep to keep the ice and mint from their moustaches.

Julep strainers are not as efficient at catching small fragments of ice as Hawthorn strainers but are more pleasing to use in conjunction with a mixing glass.

FINE/DOUBLE-STRAINING

Most cocktails that are served straight up – without ice – benefit from an additional strain, over and above the standard Hawthorn strain.

This fine strain (sometimes also called a double strain) removes even the smallest fragments of fruit and fine flecks of ice which can float to the surface and spoil the appearance of a drink. This is not usually necessary when a drink has been stirred (or rolled).

Fine straining is achieved by simply holding a fine sieve, like a tea strainer, between the shaker and the glass. Some misguided souls believe that double straining a shaken drink removes air trapped in the liquid, so affecting mouth-feel and reducing the thickness of any foamy head. Rest assured, the holes in the strainer are small enough to capture ice crystals but not air, so please always fine strain when shaking.

SWIZZLING

To swizzle a drink is simply to stir it using a particular tool and action. This style of drink mixing originated in the Caribbean and originally a special twig with particular forked branches was used. Today swizzle sticks are usually made of metal or plastic and have several blades or fingers attached to the base at right angles to the shaft, though some suppliers still sell Caribbean swizzle sticks.

To swizzle, simply immerse the blades of your swizzle stick into the drink. Swizzled drinks are served with crushed ice. Hold the shaft between the palms of both hands and rotate the stick rapidly by sliding your hands back and forth against it. If you do not have a bona fide swizzle stick, use a bar spoon in the same manner.

BLENDING

When a cocktail recipe calls for you to 'blend with ice', place all ingredients and ice into a blender and blend until a smooth, even consistency is achieved. Ideally you should use crushed ice, as this lessens wear on the blender. Place liquid ingredients in the blender first, adding the ice last. If you have a variable speed blender always start slowly and build up speed.

ROLLING

Sometimes also referred to as the Cuban Roll after the origin of this method of mixing, rolling offers more dilution and aeration than stirring, but is more gentle than shaking. It is achieved by simply pouring the ingredients from one container to another.

To do this, assemble your ingredients in a mixing glass or base of your shaker. Add ice and strain into a second mixing glass with a large diameter-lipped rim increasing the distance between the two vessels as you pour. Then pour the partially mixed cocktail back into the first ice-filled container and strain into the second again. Repeat this several times.

The best-known example of a drink which benefits from being rolled rather than shaken is a Bloody Mary. Rolling maintains the thick mouth-feel of the tomato juice while shaking produces a very thin drink.

LAYERING

As the name suggests, layered drinks include layers of different ingredients, often with contrasting colours. This effect is achieved by carefully pouring each ingredient into the glass so that it floats on its predecessor.

The success of this technique is dependent on the density of the liquids used. As a rule of thumb, the less alcohol and the more sugar an ingredient contains, the heavier it is. The heaviest ingredients should be poured first and the lightest last. Syrups are non-alcoholic and contain a lot of sugar so are usually the heaviest ingredient. Liqueurs, which are high in sugar and lower in alcohol than spirits, are generally the next heaviest ingredient. The exception to this rule is cream and cream liqueurs, which can float.

One brand of a particular liqueur may be heavier or lighter than another. The relative temperatures of ingredients may also affect their ability to float or sink. Hence, a degree of experimentation is inevitable when creating layered drinks.

Layering can be achieved in one of two ways. The first involves pouring liquid down the spiral handle of a bar spoon, keeping the flat, disc-shaped end of the spoon over the surface of the drink. Alternatively you can hold the bowl end of a bar spoon (or a soup spoon) in contact with the side of the glass and over the surface of the drink and pour slowly over it. The term float refers to layering the final ingredient of a cocktail on to its surface.

MUDDLING

Muddling means pummelling fruits, herbs and/or spices with a muddler (a blunt tool similar to a pestle) so as to crush them and release their flavour. You can also use a rolling pin. Just as you would use a pestle and mortar, push down on the muddler with a twisting action.

Only attempt to muddle in the base of a shaker or a suitably sturdy glass. Never attempt to muddle hard, unripe fruits in a glass as the pressure required could break the glass. I've witnessed a bartender slash his hand open on a broken glass while muddling and can't over-emphasize how careful you should be.

MEASURING (SHOTS & SPOONS)

Balancing each ingredient within a cocktail is key to making a great drink. Therefore the accuracy with which ingredients are measured is critical to the finished cocktail.

In this guide we've expressed the measures of each ingredient in shots. Ideally a shot is 25ml or one US fluid ounce (29.6ml), measured in a standard jigger. (You can also use a clean medicine measure or even a small shot glass.) Whatever your chosen measure, it should have straight sides to enable you to accurately judge fractions of a shot. Look out for measures which are graduated in ounces and marked with quarter and half ounces.

The measure 'spoon' refers to a bar spoon, which is slightly larger than a standard teaspoon. Personally, I measure in ounces and count a slightly under-filled flat bar spoon as ⅛ of an ounce.

Some bartenders attempt to measure shots by counting time and estimating the amount of liquid flowing through a bottle's spout. This is known as free-pouring and in unskilled hands can be terribly inaccurate. I strongly recommend the use of a physical measure and a great deal of care. Fellow Europeans who find shots and fluid ounces decidedly imperial should work to the following rough conversion table (1 US fluid ounce is actually 29.574ml but the below rule-of-thumbs are much simpler to follow):

2 shots (2oz) = 60ml
1½ shots (1½oz) = 52.5ml
1 shot (1oz) = 30ml
¾ shot (¾oz) = 22.5ml
½ shot (½oz) = 15ml
⅓ shot (⅓oz) = 10ml
¼ shot (¼oz) = 7.5ml
⅛ shot (⅛oz) = 3.75ml

ICE

A plentiful supply of fresh ice is essential to making good cocktails. When buying bagged ice, avoid the hollow, tubular kind and thin wafers. Instead, look for large, solid cubes of ice. I recommend a Kold Draft (kolddraft.com) or Hoshizaki (hoshizaki.com) ice machine to produce large (1 inch/25mm) solid cubes.

When filling ice cube trays, use bottled or filtered water to avoid the taste of chlorine often apparent in municipal water supplies. Your ice should be dry, almost sticky to the touch. Avoid 'wet' ice that has started to thaw.

Whenever serving a drink over ice, always fill the glass right up with ice, rather than just adding a few cubes. This not only makes the drink much colder, but the ice lasts longer and so does not dilute into the drink.

Never use ice in a cocktail shaker twice, even if it's to mix the same drink as before. You should always discard ice after straining the drink and use fresh ice to fill the glass if so required. Pouring shaken ice straight into the glass with the liquid will result in an overly diluted drink which will not be as cold as one where the drink is strained over fresh ice.

Unless otherwise stated, all references to ice in this guide mean cubed ice. If crushed ice is required for a particular recipe, the recipe will state crushed ice. This is available commercially. Alternatively, you can crush cubed ice in an ice-crusher or simply bash a Lewis bag or tea towel of cubed ice with a rolling pin.

If a glass is broken near your ice stocks, melt the ice with warm water, clean the container and re-stock with fresh ice. If this occurs in a busy bar and you are not immediately able to clean the ice chest, mark it as being contaminated with a liberal coating of red grenadine syrup and draw ice from another station.

FLAMING

The terms ignite, flame or flambé mean that a drink should be set alight. Please exercise extreme care when setting fire to drinks. Be particularly careful not to knock over a lit drink and never attempt to carry a drink which is still alight. Before drinking, cover the glass so as to suffocate the flame and be aware that the rim of the glass may be hot.

INFUSION/MACERATION

Alcohol's ability to draw out flavoursome substances from herbs and spices by infusion and then preserve those flavours has been used since the middle ages – originally by monks to produce potions with perceived health benefits. Today infusion/maceration is used to flavour spirits.

Infusion simply involves immersing herbs, spices, nuts or fruit in alcohol and leaving them to soak until the desired flavours have leached out. The same applies to macerating, but as the name implies, in this case the botanicals being infused are first broken up/sliced/diced to expose a larger surface area, so allowing the alcohol to leach flavour from more of the botanical's cells.

Motion, heat and pressure can be used to increase the rate of extraction. Motion can be as simple as shaking a bottle in which something is being infused every few hours, or in commercial applications infusion often takes place in revolving tanks. Heating (leaving in a warm place) helps break open the botanical's cells, so allowing the alcohol to more easily extract flavour while pressure forces the alcohol into the botanical being infused.

Beware of the speed and degree of extraction. A common mistake is to allow over extraction by adding too much of the flavouring substance or leaving it in the alcohol for too long. Tea, for example, infuses very quickly and starts releasing unwanted bitter tannins after just five minutes while vanilla pods can be left for days and hard substances such as nuts left for weeks.

FOAMS

Some cocktails benefit from being served with a foam float, the aroma and flavour of which usually contrasts with that of the drink beneath, so adding complexity. Foams are usually made in and dispensed from cream whipping siphons.

Gelatin, egg white or another form of protein such as Hy-foamer is added to the flavoured mixture so when the siphon is charged with nitrous oxide this reacts with the protein to produce a foam. Popular base ingredients include cold tea, fruit juice and champagne, but the foam can be made using pretty much any liquid provided it is not oily and the alcohol content is below 20%, and ideally under 10% alc./vol.. Both the ingredients and the charged siphon should be stored in a refrigerator as the colder the foam, the thicker it will be when discharged and the longer it will last on the drink.

When making your foam mixture allow one egg white per 200ml of liquid or one sheet of gelatin leaf per 500ml. Some advocate adding a small amount of gelatin leaf even

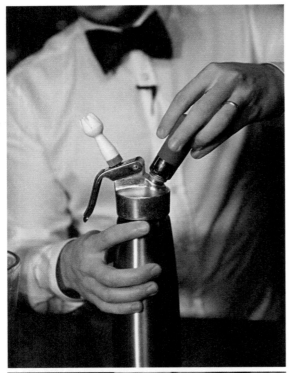

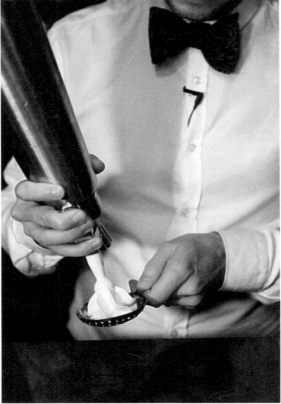

if using egg as it produces a finer, longer lasting foam. Sugar syrup (possibly flavoured) or another sweetener such as honey should be used in your foam recipe as this amplifies the flavour of the foam. If using fruit juice then strain out any pulp with a fine strainer or cheesecloth.

Only fill your siphon two-thirds its capacity to ensure room for the gas to react, then screw closed to seal. Charge with one nitrous oxide cartridge for a 500ml siphon and two cartridges if a litre capacity. Store in the refrigerator and leave for the nitrous oxide to react with the protein for at least 30 minutes before dispensing.

Nitrous oxide (N2O), the key to these foams, is commonly known as laughing gas and is a colourless non-flammable gas with a pleasant, slightly sweet smell. Its nickname refers to the stimulating effects of inhaling it, which include spontaneous laughter, slight hallucinations and an analgesic effect. It is used in motorsport to boost power (nitrous oxide kit), and in surgery and dentistry as an analgesic. A 50/50 mixture of nitrous oxide and oxygen ('gas and air') is commonly used during childbirth. Nitrous oxide is a powerful greenhouse gas and you add to its global warming effect when opening a bag of potato chips as the gas is used to displace staleness-inducing oxygen in snack food packaging.

WARNING
Inhaling nitrous oxide directly from a whipped cream charger or tank poses very serious health risks. These include potential lung collapse due to the high pressure and frostbite since the gas is very cold when released. Nitrous oxide can also cause mild nausea or dizziness and is unsafe to inhale while standing as you are likely to fall over. I should also add that the possession of and recreational use of nitrous oxide is a criminal offence in much of the US and other areas of the world.

SMOKES & SMOKERS
Originally used as a preservative, chefs commonly use smoke to flavour food and a chef's smoker can also be used to flavour cocktails. Resembling a battery-powered bong, chef's smokers use an electric fan to draw air through a fire chamber with a gauze base and expel the smoke created

through a plastic tube which can be bubbled through your cocktail or dispensed into a vessel containing the cocktail.

A large range of fine wood shavings cut for use in smokers are available with maple, apple and hickory wood the most popular. Dried spices, leaf teas and even essential oil soaked cotton wool can also be burnt.

Be warned, the flavour of smoke is very pervasive and over exposure can ruin a good drink in the same manner as over-use of bitters. Turn on the motor before attempting to light your combustible material as the fan will help draw the flame into the chamber and aid ignition. Once lit, chef's smokers produce a lot of smoke so have your drink ready to be smoked, ensure adequate ventilation of the room and beware of smoke alarms. It's essential to clean smokers regularly to prevent the resins generated during burning clogging up the device and also impairing the flavours emitted by the smoke.

FAT-WASHING
Made famous by the Benton's Old Fashioned, created by Don Lee at PDT in New York City, which uses bourbon flavoured by smoky bacon fat, fat-washing is a method of flavouring any spirit with a variety of fatty foods including meats, fish, cheeses and butter.

Grill or melt the food with heat, drain off the fat emitted and pour it into a bottle of spirit via a fine strainer to remove unwanted particulates. Seal the bottle, shake and place in a refrigerator to solidify the fat, shaking occasionally. Leave for a week to allow the fat's flavour to infuse into the spirit.

Lastly, clarify by straining first through a fine strainer and then a cheesecloth. The spirit will have taken on the flavour of the fat and also acquired a silky mouth-feel.

TOASTING & CARAMELISATION
Natural sugars in foods can be caramelised by heating with a chef's blow-torch (also called a crème brûlée burner). Caramelisation changes the flavour of foods such as fruit and nuts which can be used as a garnish or muddled into the drink.

Bartender's kit

Everything you need, all in one place

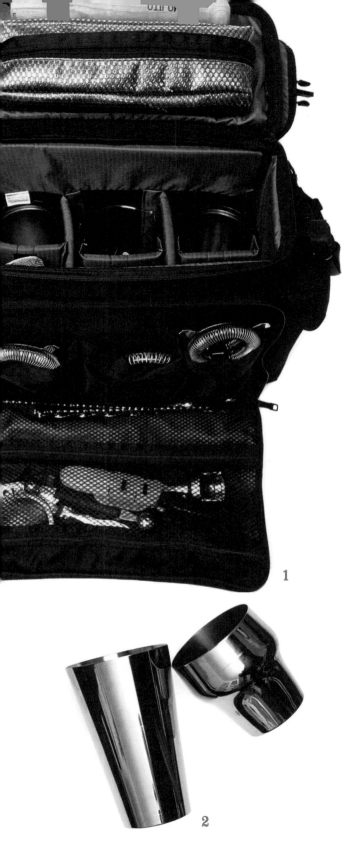

1. THE BAG

Professional photographer's equipment bags are perfect for storing and carrying bar equipment. The one pictured by Tamrac (tamrac.com) is the one I use and features padded sections originally designed to house camera lenses but which are deep enough to accommodate shakers, mixing glasses and glassware. An abundance of front and side pockets, designed for holding films or other paraphernalia, snugly house bar spoons, measures, strainers and smaller bar tools. Visit any camera store and you'll find an abundance of such bags in all shapes and sizes.

2. SHAKER

There are numerous shapes and sizes of shaker. Personally I now favour a 'tin & tin' two-piece and some years ago, with the help of some German bartending friends, I found a WMF Boston tin designed to be used with a glass and a mismatched smaller tin designed to be part of a three-piece shaker. One tin is made of polished stainless steel and the other has a dull brushed finish but this unlikely combination of relatively cheap mismatched tins works for me, and soon after I discovered this, I purchased another ten pairs so I'd be sure of always having my personal favourite shaker set to hand.

Having checked WMF's website I'm not sure the tins I use are still available (just as well I bought ten) so I recommend you purchase an Alessi shaker (alessi.com). In my experience, this widely available Italian designer brand makes expensive but reliably well-functioning cocktail shakers, be that a two or three-piece.

That said, Alessi's Boston Shaker (glass and tin set) comes with an elegant but also delicate glass which you're almost bound to break. If you do break it, you'll find that most regular cheap Boston glasses can be substituted and work just as well. The sides of an Alessi tin are firm yet flexible enough to make a tight seal against a Boston glass with the lightest of taps. Consequently, opening is effortless.

For home use, I recommend you use a three-piece shaker, but whichever design of shaker you decide to use, the most important thing is you feel comfortable using it. Before buying, be sure to repeatedly try closing and opening your chosen shaker. Ideally, also fill it with

water and give it a trial shake. At the end of the day, be it designer, antique or plain cheap, if it holds liquid without leaking, is easy to seal, to hold when shaking and to open, then it is perfect for the task in hand. Sadly, this is more than can be said of many shakers branded by drinks companies which I've come across. Whatever you do, avoid plastic shakers as they never seem to work properly. Stainless steel is the most practical while silver is the most luxurious.

4.MUDDLERS

David Nepove's Mojitos are renowned in San Francisco and this is one of two shapes of muddler he has designed for his signature drink (mistermojito.com). I'm also very fond of Tony Abou-Ganim's 'Tag Bar' muddler (themodernmixologist.com). I also use more contemporary looking and robust stainless steel and plastic muddlers.

3.BAR SPOONS

Like most items of bar equipment, bar spoons come in a myriad of designs and lengths. The UK-made Bonzer bar spoon (mitchellcooper.com) is the most versatile with its flat, disc-shaped end which can be used as a muddler (although I've met bartenders who have stabbed themselves through the hand by breaking similar spoons), for layering drinks and for stirring. Of course, the spoon end also comes in handy for measuring or lifting maraschino cherries out of jars as well as stirring. As mentioned, many top bartenders choose to use a Japanese stirring glass so it's understandable that they also often opt for a matching Japanese stirring spoon. These are available with forked or rounded ends and in different lengths (from cocktailkingdom.com) and I'd recommend you buy a long one.

5.MIXING GLASS

Heavy, Japanese-style 'Yarai' cut-glass mixing glasses (available from cocktailkingdom.com) are the preferred choice of many bartenders, but whatever style of stirring glass you choose, be sure it is large enough (500ml) to hold plenty of ice, making for a colder, less-diluted drink.

6. SPRUNG STRAINER BY URBAN BAR

Hawthorn is to strainers what Hoover is to vacuum cleaners. Whoever makes them, sprung strainers with two or more prongs, designed to be used with Boston shakers, tend to be called Hawthorns. This one by Urban Bar (urbanbar.com) is well made with a tightly coiled spring.

7. JULEP STRAINER

These bowl-shaped colander-like spoons are designed to fit inside shakers and mixing glasses as opposed to pronged Hawthorn strainers which sit on top of shakers. Most professional bartenders I know favour Cocktail Kingdom's spoon (cocktailkingdom.com).

8. MEASURE

This measure by Oxo (oxo.com) may not look as slick as a stainless steel thimble measure but, with graduations from ¼oz to 2oz (perfect for shots and fractions of a shot) and with a millilitre scale on the side, it's more practical, not to mention being easier to read from above. The only downside, evident when tested using a laboratory cylinder measure, is its accuracy. However, it beats guessing (and many would argue free-pouring, but that's another argument).

9. FINE STRAINER

The challenge with fine strainers is to find one that is not so fine that liquid takes ages to flow through and that also has sufficient capacity to hold a decent volume. Fresh fruit Martinis tend to quickly clog most strainers. Cocktail Kingdom (cocktailkingdom.com) sell the only perfect strainer I know of.

10. SWIVEL PEELER

I like to cut generously sized long twists rather than the coin-sized circular variety and find a peeler such as this one by Oxo (oxo.com) infinitely better and safer than a knife for cutting twists without too much pith.

11. PARING KNIFE

You'll need a sharp knife and cutting board, and when it comes to really sharp knives you have to look to Japan. Tanaka by Kin Knives (kinknives.com) boast thirty-two layers of

alternating nickel and stainless steel surround a cutting core of powdered steel. Something that beautiful deserves real respect – sharpen with ceramic rather than steel. On the subject of ceramic, I'm also a fan of ceramic knives as, unlike Japanese carbon steel, they are not corroded by citrus juice. (Prolonged contact with citrus quickly turns carbon steel black and this can stain cutting boards and garnishes).

12. CUTTING BOARD

Food hygiene used to point towards the use of polyethylene plastic boards, but while these will stand up to sanitising in hot temperatures and harsh cleaning products, the thin grooves left in these boards is a harbourer of bacteria. It is not uncommon to see white cutting boards turned black in bars.

Avoid glass cutting boards or indeed any such hard surface which will blunt your knives. Properly cared-for wooden boards are a traditional but practical choice. Wipe them regularly with antibacterial cleaner and rub the board with coarse salt at the end of a bar shift before a thorough clean. Revive the wood with regular doses of food-grade mineral oil (poppyseed oil or linseed oil, not vegetable or olive oils).

Many chefs are now using rubber cutting boards as they are durable enough to withstand cleaning in hot water and yet are kind to knives. Unlike wooden or plastic boards they also have the advantage of not needing to be placed on a damp cloth to stop them slipping. Rubber cutting boards are more expensive than wood but last much longer, so are worth the investment.

13. JUICER

An industrial lever-action citrus press is strongly recommended for bar use as the combination of the leverage and ratchet action allows quick and effortless juicing of citrus fruit. Alternatively, many bars favour the use off hand-held hinged "Mexican elbow" juicers. For domestic use, a simple juicer of the glass bowl variety should suffice.

14. CITRUS ZESTER & CANAL KNIFE

I have a number of zesters and canal knives, none of

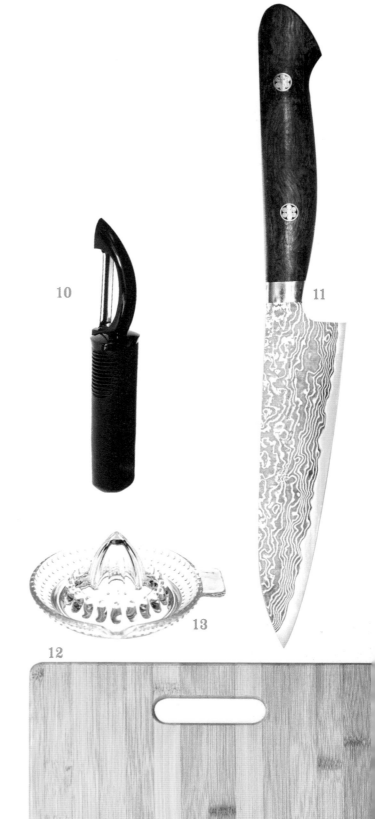

14

16

which seem particularly sharp even when new. This one by Oxo combines both tools.

15. BAR BLENDER
You'll need a blender for all those Frozen Daiquiris and Piña Coladas so choose one with a large capacity and a powerful motor. Vitamix (www.vitamix.com) may not be the best-looking but they are certainly powerful and tough. Judge your blender by the power (wattage) of its electric motor rather than how slick the stainless steel design looks on your countertop.

16. ICE SCOOP
I use three ice scoops: one monster-size plastic one for taking ice from the machine; a 12oz aluminium scoop for cubed ice; and a 6oz aluminium scoop for crushed ice – the latter chosen because its small size is better for channelling crushed ice into the glass.

17. NUTMEG GRATER
When selecting a nutmeg grater look for the type which also has a compartment for storing your nutmeg. That way you'll always know where your nutmeg is.

18. POWDER SHAKER
A shaker with a fine mesh of the type used in coffee shops to dust cappuccinos is perfect for applying powdered chocolate and cinnamon over cocktails.

19. WAITER'S FRIEND CORK SCREW
I would love to claim that I use a Chateau Laguiole Master Sommelier but like so many others, I actually own, and have lost, numerous cheap Waiter's Friends which double as cork screw and bottle opener (Model 60 – double lever at www.waitersfriend.com).

20. EGG SEPARATOR
I'm a fan of using fresh egg whites in my cocktails and tend to use the shells to separate the white from the yolk where required. However, some may prefer this nifty tool from Oxo (oxo.com).

17

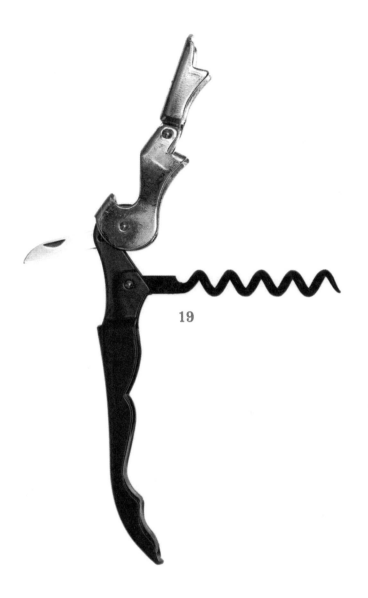

19

18

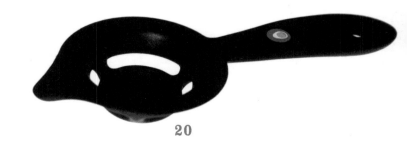

20

Glassware

What you serve your cocktail in is just as important as the liquid it contains

Cocktails are something of a luxury. You don't just ping a cap or pop a cork and pour. These drinks take a degree of time and skill to mix, so deserve a decent glass. Before you start, check your glassware is clean and free from chips and marks such as lipstick. Always handle glasses by the base or the stem to avoid leaving finger marks and never put your fingers inside a glass.

Ideally, glassware should be chilled in a freezer prior to use. This is particularly important for Martini and Flute glasses, in which drinks are usually served without ice. It takes about half an hour to sufficiently chill a glass in the freezer. If time is short, you can chill a glass by filling it with ice (ideally crushed, not cubed) and topping it up with water. Leave the glass to cool while you prepare the drink, then discard the ice and water once you are ready to pour. This method is quicker than chilling in the freezer but not nearly as effective.

To warm a glass, ready for a hot cocktail, place a bar spoon in the glass and fill it with hot water. Then discard the water and pour in the drink. Only then should you remove the spoon, which is there to help disperse the shock of the heat. There are thousands of differently shaped glasses, but if you own those mentioned here you will have a glass to suit practically every drink and occasion. Failing that, a set of Collins, Martini and Old-fashioned or Rocks glasses, and possibly Flutes if you fancy champagne cocktails, will allow you to serve the majority of drinks in this guide. Use a Martini in place of a Coupette and a Collins as a substitute for Hurricane and Sling glasses.

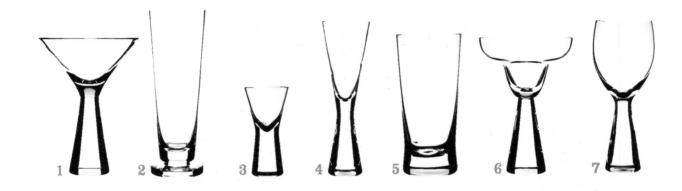

1. COUPETTE/MARTINI

Those in the old guard of bartending insist on calling this style of glass a 'cocktail glass'. It may once have been, but to most of us today a V-shaped glass is a Martini glass. The recent resurgence in vintage cocktails has also led to a vogue for using a champagne saucer or Coupette to serve straight-up drinks. Whatever your glassware preference, when choosing either a Martini or a 'Coupe' it should be no bigger than 7oz, as a true Martini warms up too much in the time it takes to drink a larger one. I'd suggest keeping your glasses in the refrigerator or even the freezer so they are chilled before use.

Capacity to brim: 7oz / 20cl

2. SLING

This elegant glass is perfect for tall drinks served over crushed ice such as the Russian Spring Punch.

Capacity to brim: 11oz / 32cl

3. SHOT

Shot glasses come in all shapes and sizes. You'll need small ones if you're sensible and big ones if you're not. If you are serving layered shots then choose tall, thin glasses to accentuate the thickness of each layer.

Capacity to brim (pictured glass): 2oz / 6cl

4. FLUTE

Flutes are perfect for serving champagne cocktails as their tall, slim design helps maintain the wine's fizz. Chill before use.

Capacity to brim: 6oz / 17cl

5. COLLINS

In this guide I refer to a tall glass as a Collins. A high-ball is slightly squatter than a Collins but has the same capacity. A 12oz Collins glass will suffice for cocktails and is ideal for a standard 330ml bottle of beer. However, many favour the use of larger 14oz glasses with the occasional smaller 8oz for drinks such as Fizzes which are served tall but not very long.

Capacity to brim: 14oz / 40cl or 8oz / 24cl

6. MARGARITA

Named after the cocktail with the same name, this glass is still used predominately for the Mexican cocktail – the rim cries out for salt.

Capacity to brim: 8oz / 24cl

7. GOBLET

Not often used for cocktails, but worth having, if for no other reason than to enjoy your wine. An 11oz glass is big enough to be luxurious.

Capacity to brim: 11oz / 32cl

8. BOSTON

A tall, heavy conical glass with a thick rim, which depending on how you view it, is either designed for serving beer or to be combined with a Boston tin to form a shaker. It can also be used as a mixing glass for stirred drinks

Capacity to brim: 17oz / 48cl

9. HURRICANE

Sometimes referred to as a 'poco grande' or 'Piña Colada' glass, this big-bowled glass is commonly used for frozen drinks. It screams out for a pineapple wedge, a cherry and possibly a paper parasol as well.

Capacity to brim: 15oz / 43cl

10. OLD-FASHIONED

Another glass whose name refers to the best-known drink served in it, it is also great for enjoying spirits such as whisky. Choose a luxuriously large glass with a thick, heavy base. Alternatively, the similarly shaped 'Rocks' glass has a thick rim and is usually made from toughened glass so better suited to drinks that require muddling in the glass.

Capacity to brim: 11oz / 32cl

11. SNIFTER

Sometimes referred to as a brandy balloon. The bigger the bowl, the more luxurious the glass appears. Use to enjoy cocktails and deluxe aged spirits such as cognac.

Capacity to brim: 12oz / 35cl

12. TODDY

Frequently referred to as a 'liqueur coffee glass', which is indeed its main use, this glass was popularised by the Irish Coffee. Toddy glasses are designed to withstand heat and usually have a handle on the side, allowing you to comfortably hold hot drinks.

Capacity to brim: 8.5oz / 25cl

13. SOUR

This small glass is narrow at the stem and tapers out to a wider lip. As the name would suggest, it is used for serving Sours straight-up. I favour serving Sours over ice in an Old-fashioned but any of the Sour recipes in this guide can be strained and served 'up' in this glass.

Capacity to brim: 4oz / 12cl

14. ROCKS

Like an Old-fashioned with a thick rim, this is usually made from toughened glass - perfect for drinks that require muddling in the glass. A hardy glass, if there is such a thing.

Capacity to brim: 9oz / 27cl

Garnishes

The finishing touch should enhance the look, smell and flavour of a drink

Garnishes are used to decorate cocktails and are often anchored to the rim of the glass. Strictly speaking, garnishes should be edible and can comprise anything from banana chunks, strawberries or redcurrants to coffee beans, confectionery, basil leaves and slices of fresh ginger. The correct garnish will often enhance the aroma and flavour, as well as the look, of a drink.

When deciding on what to garnish your cocktail with, use the ingredients within the drink as inspiration. For example, if a drink is made using lime juice, then a lime wedge is a safe option.

Fruit selected for high juice yields may not be ideal for garnishes. For example, larger limes juice well but smaller limes make more attractive garnishes. Whatever fruit you use, it should be unblemished and washed prior to use. Cut citrus fruits have a maximum shelf life of 24 hours when refrigerated.

APPLE SLICE

Apple wedges can easily be secured to the rim of a glass – cut a wedge that is a maximum ¾in thick and slice diagonally to centre to allow placement on glass rim. Alternatively, just drop the garnish into the drink – this is particularly effective in tall drinks. The fruit should be firm and fresh, not brown or bruised, and the skin should be left on.

APPLE WEDGE

Apple wedges can easily be secured to the rim of a glass – cut a wedge that is a maximum ¾in thick and slice diagonally to centre to allow placement on glass rim. Alternatively, just drop the garnish into the drink – this is particularly effective in tall drinks. The fruit should be firm and fresh, not brown or bruised, the skin left on.

APPLE CHEVRON

Using a quarter of an apple, cut wafer-thin slices down into the fruit, but not all the way through – stop about a centimetre from the end of the apple wedge. Cut 5 or 6 slices into the fruit and then ease out these slices into a fan. Leave the skin of the apple on.

APPLE DISCS (CARAMELISED)

These are more time-consuming but worth the effort. Slice an apple finely using a mandolin. Then either coat the slices in sugar syrup or blanch them by dipping them into a simmering pan containing three parts granulated sugar and two parts water.

Whichever option you choose, drain off the excess liquid and lay the slices on a baking tray lined with greaseproof paper. Place the tray in an oven set to 85ºC (185ºF) and bake for about three hours, until the discs are crisp and golden. You can store these in an air-tight container in the refrigerator for up to a fortnight.

APRICOT SLICE

Use either whole dried apricots or a slice of apricot and cut a slit into centre of fruit (rather than the skin side) to allow placement on the glass rim.

BANANA SLICE

Fruit should not be either green, bruised or overripe. Some like to remove the skin, whereas others prefer to leave on for both appearance and ease of use. Cut a slit into the centre of fruit to allow placement on glass rim.

BERRY SKEWERS

Berries such as blackberries, raspberries, strawberries and blueberries make an attractive and tasty garnish. Use fruit that is ripe but firm and not mushy. Berries can either be floated on the top of a drink or skewered (usually in threes) kebab-style on a cocktail stick and placed across the top of the glass.

CELERY STICKS

Celery sticks may be placed in drinks as stirring rods, as is typical in a Bloody Mary. Choose firm sticks without bruises and cut to a length several inches longer than your glass, so when placed inside it protrudes over the rim. Angled cuts tend to be more attractive than simply chopping at 90° to the stem. I like to leave a little of the leaf on, if possible.

CHERRIES

Fresh cherries make a tasty and attractive garnish and are less syrupy and sweet than maraschino cherries, but have the same visual effect. Use fruit that is ripe but firm and not mushy. Cut a slit in cherries to secure to the glass rim.

CHOCOLATE DUST

The instruction 'dust with chocolate' refers to a fine coating of cocoa powder on the surface of a drink. The chocolate layer needs to remain very fine so as not to sink into the drink. Use cocoa powder, rather than grated chocolate.

CHOCOLATE RIM

Wipe a cut orange slice around the outside rim of a glass to leave a line of juice with which to stick chocolate powder to glass (rather than lime juice when using salt). Also see 'salt rim'.

CINNAMON DUST

The instruction 'dust with cinnamon' refers to a fine coating of the spice on the surface of a drink. If using powdered cinnamon, use sparingly so the layer does not become too thick and sink into the drink. I prefer to use a whole cinnamon stick and a fine grater.

CINNAMON & SUGAR RIM

Wipe a thin strip of sugar syrup around the outside rim of your glass and then roll this in a saucer containing a mixture of cinnamon powder and caster sugar. Also see 'salt rim'.

CINNAMON STICKS

These are often placed whole into hot drinks and toddies. There are several lengths of dried cinnamon stick available, so ensure that cinnamon is longer than the glass you are serving in.

CHILLI

A small red eye chilli, with a diagonal slice to allow it to sit firmly on the rim of the glass, looks good, smells good but is probably best not consumed – each to their own. Take the usual precautions when handling chillies.

COFFEE BEANS

Simply float three coffee beans on the surface of the drink. Why three? The number signifies health, wealth and happiness and is said to bestow good luck on the drinker.

CUCUMBER SLICE

Use fresh, moist, crisp cucumber as either a slice or stick. Slices can be cut thin enough to float on the surface of the drink, or, cut thicker, slit and secured to the glass rim.

CUCUMBER STICK

To make a stick, cut a length of cucumber to suit the glass (it should either sit *an inch* above the rim of the glass or fit exactly) then cut lengthways into ⅛ segments leaving the skin on. These can be used as a stirrer, much like a celery stick.

FLAMING ZEST BOAT

Not only does this potentially dangerous garnish add to the theatrical style of Tiki drinks, but my inner child finds floating fire boats irresistible.

Make a zest boat by chopping a lime or lemon lengthwise into four and scraping away the flesh from one wedge. Float your boat on top of the drink and carefully pour in its cargo of high-strength dark rum – for example Woods 100 or Pusser's Navy rum. Lastly, and very carefully, ignite the rum.

This is almost certainly against nanny state rules and definitely constitutes a fire hazard. All the same, dear readers, I trust you to be responsible and careful.
To prevent carnage I should add:

1. Only use a fraction of a shot of rum or it will burn for ages.
2. Be aware that the flame may be blue and so almost invisible.
3. Don't move the glass, let alone drink from it, until the flame is out.
4. Don't blame us if your bar/home/life goes up in smoke.

FLAMED ZEST TWIST

A flamed zest twist is a dramatic variation on the usual wide-cut zest twist and involves burning the aromatic oils emitted from citrus fruit zest as they are expressed over the surface of a drink. Lemons and limes are sometimes treated in this way but oranges are most popular and give the best results. Firm, thick-skinned navel oranges are best.

You will need to cut as wide a strip of zest as you can, wider than you would for a standard twist. Hold the cut zest, peel side down, between the thumb and forefinger about four inches above the drink. In your other hand, ignite a match or lighter, then pinch the peel by its edges so that its oils squirt through the flame towards the surface of the drink – there should be a flash as the oils ignite.

Some then like to wipe the zest around the rim of the glass, while others maintain this merely makes the edge of the glass taste bitter. You also have the option to discard the spent zest or drop it onto the surface of the drink. There is no wrong or right answer to these options and I'd recommend you go with whatever pleases you or your guest.

FLOWERS & PETALS

Edible flowers and petals set afloat on a drink make for an attractive garnish. Ensure the flowers used are edible and have not been sprayed. Suitable varieties include Dendrobium Orchids, Pansies, certain Rose varieties, Nasturtiums, Marigolds and Violets.

FRUIT STICK

A fruit stick consists of one or more pineapple cubes and a maraschino cherry skewered kebab-style on a cocktail stick or specially designed plastic or wooden pick. Popularly used to garnish Tiki-style drinks, the creation of the fruit stick is credited to Victor Jules Bergeron (A.K.A. Trader Vic) in the early 1930s.

Cut pineapple into quarters from top to bottom and remove woody core. Further cut into ½inch or 1cm cubes. Do not use overripe or mushy fruit. Cut pineapple kept refrigerated (in a sealed box with a moist paper towel) will stay fresh for up to a day but it is of course preferable to cut to order.

GRAPES

Grapes can be a simple and effective garnish. Either drop them into the drink or push three onto a cocktail stick and balance across the rim of the glass.

GRAPEFRUIT ZEST TWIST

Treat it as you would an oversized lemon and 'twist' a zest of the flavoursome oils over your drink.

GRATED CHOCOLATE

To sprinkle chocolate on the surface of a drink you can either shave chocolate using a vegetable peeler or dust with powder using a chocolate shaker with a fine mesh. Alternatively, crumble a Cadbury's Flake, in which case ensure fragments are small enough to prevent them sinking into drink.

HORSE'S NECK PEEL

This is usually used to garnish the drink of the same name and is basically a long ½inch wide strip of peel cut in a continuous spiral and placed so as to overhang the rim of the glass. Lemon is most commonly used but a Horse's Neck can also be made from oranges and limes.

To achieve this hold a lemon horizontally in your hand with one end facing you. Use a canal knife to cut into the far end of the fruit and pull towards you ¼inch. Then turn the cut 90 degrees and start cutting around the lemon so that a ½inch wide strip is left between the channels you cut. The strip left spiralling around the lemon that will form your Horse's Neck. Using a small knife, carefully cut this strip from the lemon leaving as much of the white pith behind. This is placed in the glass spiralling up from the bottom to the top with the 'head' hooked over the rim of the glass. Place ice inside the spiral before pouring your drink.

KIWI SLICE

Kiwi fruit slices prettily. Clean the fruit, peel and slice using a slit in the side to secure to the rim of the glass.

LEMON SLICE

Sometimes referred to as a 'lemon wheel', this is one of

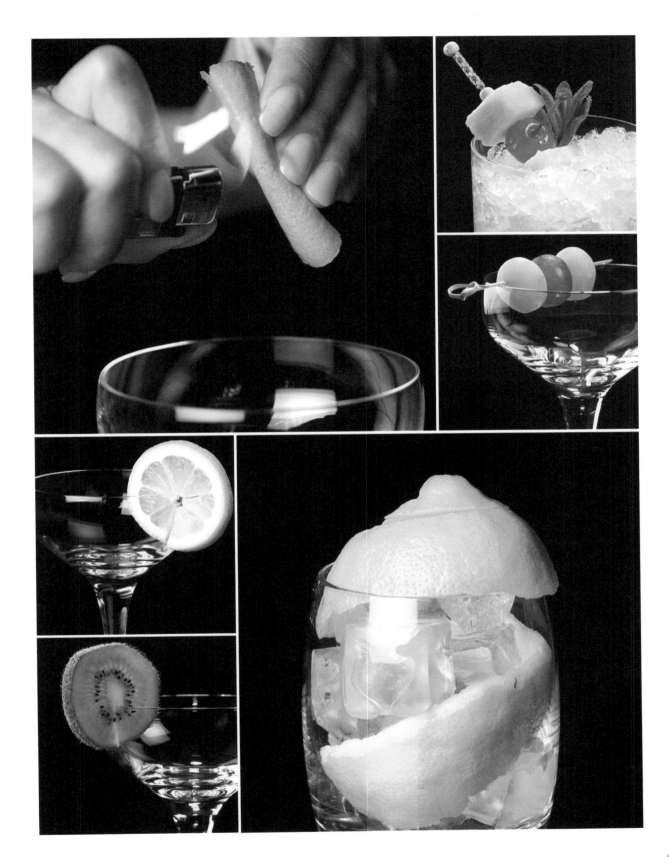

the truly classic garnishes. Wash fruit thoroughly and preferably use un-waxed lemons with uniform yellow skin (without green or brown discolouration). Cut 3/8 inch thick slices across the width of the fruit discarding both ends (poles). Slice to centre for placement on glass rim. Preferably cut to order or store cut fruit for a maximum of six hours.

LEMON WEDGE

Wedges of lemons are often squeezed into drinks or fixed to the side of the glass as a garnish. A lemon wedge is a one eighth segment of the fruit.

Wash fruit thoroughly and preferably use un-waxed lemons with uniform yellow skin (without green or brown discolouration). Cut the tips from either end of the fruit, slice the fruit in half lengthwise, then cut each half into four equal wedges lengthwise. Cut a slit into the pointed flesh of each wedge to enable placement on glass rim. Preferably cut as required or store cut fruit for a maximum of six hours.

LIME SLICE

Sometimes referred to as a 'lime wheel'. Wash fruit thoroughly and preferably use un-waxed limes with uniform green skin (without yellow or brown discolouration). Cut 3/8 inch thick slices across the width of the fruit having discarded both ends. Slice to centre for placement on glass rim. Preferably cut as required or store cut fruit for a maximum of six hours.

LIME WEDGE

Fix lime wedge on side of glass or squeeze and drop into drink. A wedge is a sixth, or with large limes, a one eighth segment of the fruit. The lime should have green skin without yellow or brown discolouration. Cut the 'knobs' from the top and bottom tips of the fruit, slice the fruit in half lengthwise, then cut each half into three (or for eighths, four) equal wedges lengthwise.

There are numerous ways to cut a slit into the fruit to fix onto glass but the most popular is by cutting into the pointed flesh at an angle. Lime wedges should be used within six hours of being cut and preferably cut as required.

MANGO

Fresh mango is not generally used as a garnish. However, you can cut the flesh into cubes and skewer them on a cocktail stick or fix long thin wedge on the glass rim. Alternatively garnish mango cocktails with slices of dried mango on a stick.

MARASCHINO CHERRIES

Maraschino cherries were originally fresh cherries marinated in maraschino liqueur and such cherries are still available from producers such as Luxardo. However, nowadays the term typically refers to preserved, sweetened cherries dyed bright red with food colouring and usually almond-flavoured.

Blue and yellow dyed maraschino cherries are also available and typically the green ones are peppermint-flavoured (think green crème de menthe) while the blue ones are orange-flavoured (think blue curaçao). That said, in the US, it would appear they all have the same almond-maraschino flavour regardless of the colour. Shame.

Opies stemmed maraschino cherries, as the name suggests, retain their stems to make a more attractive garnish (those with dexterous tongues can amaze their friends by tying said stems in a knot).

Maraschino cherries should be refrigerated and left in their own syrup/liqueur which should be saved as it is often used in recipes such as a Sweet Manhattan. Drop cherry into drink.

MINT LEAF

A simple leaf or mint sprig atop a cocktail adds colour and a wonderful fresh fragrance. Boost the olfactory effect by smacking the mint lightly between your hands before you drop onto the surface of the drink or drape over the rim.

MINT SPRIG

When selecting a mint sprig for garnish, look for the tips of the sprig and use the top two inches or 50mm. There should be at least six leaves that push together and sit within drink.

NUTMEG DUST

The instruction 'dust with nutmeg' refers to a fine coating of the spice on the surface of a drink. It is preferable to

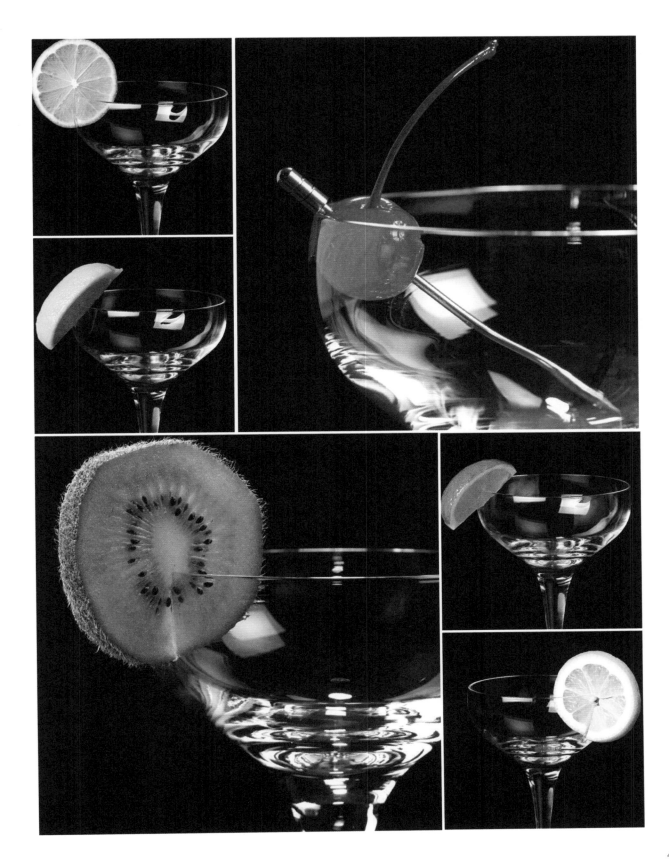

grate fresh nutmeg as the powdered kind lacks flavour. Use a very fine grater and ensure that no one area becomes too heavily covered and so sinks into the drink.

OLIVES

The 'Oliver' from the 'Oliver Twist' duo classically graces a Dry Martini. It is essential to wash olives thoroughly to prevent oil from spoiling the appearance of a drink. Only remove sufficient olives required for a particular session from the jar. Olives should be refrigerated and left in the oil or brine in which they were packaged. This brine may be used in a Dirty Martini.

ONIONS

Onions should be stored and left in the oil or brine in which they were packaged and only removed from the jar when required. Small white cocktail onions are most notably used to garnish a Gibson Martini.

ORANGE SLICE

Orange slices (or wheels) can be used whole in the drink or speared with cocktail sticks and cherries to make sails. It's also common to cut the slices in half. Select (preferably un-waxed) fruit without brown discolouration and wash thoroughly. Cut 3/8 inch thick slices and store for a maximum of six hours. Even better, cut as required.

ORANGE ZEST TWIST

The fruit's bright skin adds flavoursome aromatic oils to a drink when used as a twist. If you are making twists, however, it is best to buy organically grown oranges, which are not sprayed with chemicals. See 'Zest Twist' below.

PARASOL (UMBRELLA)

A cocktail parasol is a miniature paper umbrella with cardboard ribs and a toothpick stem. It tends to be used to garnish rum-based or Tiki cocktails and is thought to have originally been introduced in the early 1930s by Don the Beachcomber at his Beachcomber restaurant in Hollywood, USA. Their purpose is ostensibly to shield delicate ice cubes from the rays of the sun, but they have attained a kitsch, iconic status.

PASSION FRUIT BOAT

Despite its name, the fruit of love is remarkably ugly and garnishing can be a challenge. The two best garnishes utilising this fruit I know are 1) to float half a fruit like a boat on the surface of your drink, or 2) if your cocktail uses crushed ice, cut a quarter of passion fruit and place it on the surface of the ice

PEACH SLICE/WEDGE

Peaches should be firm but not mushy and the skin should remain on. Cut wedges a maximum ¾ inch thick and slice diagonally to allow placement on glass rim.

PEAR SLICE/WEDGE

Slices of pear can look great on the rim of a Martini glass. However, they oxidise very quickly, and should be rubbed with lemon juice to prevent this.

PHYSALIS

Leave fruit whole with leaves and stalks but wash before use. Carefully open the leaves and gently fold back against the stem and turn the stem and leaves in the opposite direction of the fruit half-a-turn. Then make a diagonal incision across the bottom of the fruit to facilitate placement on glass rim.

PINEAPPLE WEDGE

No Piña Colada or truly tropical cocktail is properly dressed without a wedge of pineapple, preferably with a maraschino cherry spiked into it. Cut the pineapple into ½ inch or 1 cm thick rings and cut each ring into wedges as if cutting a cake, avoiding the woody core. A knife slit in the side of the wedge allows you to anchor it to the rim of a glass. The skin adds to the appearance of this garnish so should remain on, but golden is preferable to green. Do not use overripe or mushy fruit and either cut as required or store for a maximum of one day.

SAIL

A sail is a whole slice (or wheel) of citrus fruit, usually orange, served on a cocktail stick 'mast' and so known as

a sail. Usually the circular slice of fruit is folded around a maraschino cherry and the cocktail stick is skewered through both pieces of fruit.

SALT/SUGAR RIM

Some recipes call for the rim of a glass to be coated with salt, sugar or other ingredients: you will need to moisten the rim before so the ingredient will hold. When using salt, wipe a cut wedge of lime around the outside edge of the rim, then roll the outside edge through a saucer of salt. (Use sea salt rather than iodised salt.) For sweet ingredients like sugar, either use an orange slice or moisten a sponge or paper towel with a suitable liqueur.

Whatever you are using to rim the glass should cling to the outside edge only. Remember, garnishes are not a cocktail ingredient but an optional extra to be consumed by choice. They should not contaminate your cocktail.

It is good practice to salt or sugar only half or two-thirds of the rim of a glass. This allows drinkers the option of avoiding the salt or sugar. If you rim glasses some hours prior to use, the lime juice or liqueur will dry, leaving a crust of salt or sugar crystals around the rim. The glasses can then be placed in a refrigerator to chill ready for use. If not kept ice cold, the juice and sugar can run down the glass.

A professional piece of equipment known as a 'rimmer' has three sections: one with a sponge for water or lime juice; one containing sugar; and a third containing salt. Beware, as this encourages dipping the glass onto a moist sponge and then into the garnish, and so contaminating the inside of the glass.

SPICY BEANS

Canadian readers will be well aware of these long, thin pickled beans. They are a popular alternative to celery in those parts as a garnish for 'Caesar' cocktails, a Canadian twist on the Bloody Mary. They originate with Blaze Denoon, who started picking beans in Vancouver in 1995. For more information, see blazesbeans.com.

STAR ANISE

Star anise is the star-shaped pericarp of Illicium verum,

a small native evergreen tree of southwest China. This dried spice is frequently floated on the surface of anise-flavoured drinks (so those who dislike this flavour should consider themselves warned).

STAR FRUIT

Star fruit can be floated on the top of the drink and a wafer-thin slice should be cut to ensure the fruit does not sink. Otherwise a thicker slice can also be placed on the rim of the glass. Cut a slice of star fruit about ¼inch or ½cm thick and cut a slit diagonally to centre to allow placement on glass rim.

STRAWBERRY FAN

Cut wafer-thin slices into strawberry and spear with a cocktail stick. Spread the slices apart to create a fan.

ZEST TWIST

This term refers to affecting the aroma and perceived flavour of a drink by releasing the aromatic oils from a strip of citrus zest (lemon, lime, orange, grapefruit).

Using a knife or peeler, cut a ½inch (12mm) wide length of zest from an un-waxed, cleaned fruit so as to leave just a little of the white pith. Hold it over the glass with the thumb and forefinger of each hand, coloured side down. Twist the peel and force some of its oils over the surface of the drink.

You may then opt to deposit any flavoursome oils left on the surface of the peel by wiping the coloured side around the rim of the glass. Some prefer to dispose of the spent twist but most drop the peel onto the surface of the drink as a garnish.

Citrus twists can also be thin, string-like lengths of zest cut with a canal knife and wrapped around a stirring rod to make a spring-like garnish, which is then slid off the stirrer and into the drink. Such thinly cut string-like twists can also be tied into a knot.

Ideally, zests should be cut fresh for each drink but if this is not possible then kept pre-cut refrigerated. Store in a sealed plastic box with some moist paper towel, but once cut their shelf life is little more than one day.

Key ingredients

Staying fully stocked makes for a versatile bartender

THE 14 KEY INGREDIENTS

VODKA

GIN

RUM

TEQUILA

SCOTCH WHISKY

COGNAC

BOURBON

TRIPLE SEC

ORANGE LIQUEUR

APRICOT LIQUEUR

BERRY LIQUEUR

DRY VERMOUTH

SWEET VERMOUTH

CHAMPAGNE

With just the 14 Key Ingredients above, a few mixers, some fresh fruit, copious amounts of ice and a handful of kitchen basics you will be able to make more than 500 cocktails in this guide. Look for the

FRIDGE & PANTRY ESSENTIALS

CRANBERRY
JUICE

ORANGE
JUICE

PRESSED APPLE
JUICE

GRAPEFRUIT
JUICE (PINK)

PINEAPPLE
JUICE

TOMATO
JUICE

COLA

SODA
WATER

GINGER ALE &
GINGER BEER

TONIC
WATER

LEMONADE

LIME
CORDIAL

ANGOSTURA
BITTERS

MILK

FRESH
LEMONS

FRESH
LIMES

FRESH
MINT

STRAWBERRIES

RASPBERRIES

MARASCHINO
CHERRIES

EGGS

BLUEBERRIES

BANANAS

WHITE
GRAPES

RED
GRAPES

RUNNY
HONEY

EARL GREY
TEA

HEAVY
CREAM

Our Recipes Explained

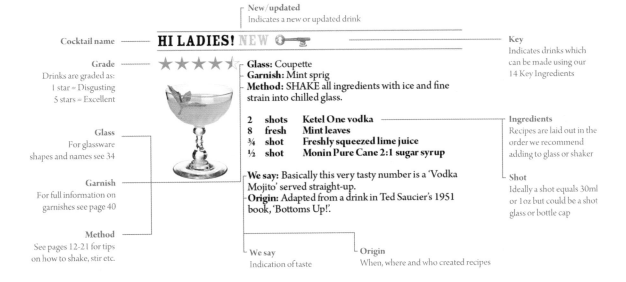

New/updated
Indicates a new or updated drink

Cocktail name ——— **HI LADIES! NEW** 🔑

Key
Indicates drinks which can be made using our 14 Key Ingredients

Grade
Drinks are graded as:
1 star = Disgusting
5 stars = Excellent

★★★★⯪

Glass: Coupette
Garnish: Mint sprig
Method: SHAKE all ingredients with ice and fine strain into chilled glass.

2	shots	Ketel One vodka
8	fresh	Mint leaves
¾	shot	Freshly squeezed lime juice
½	shot	Monin Pure Cane 2:1 sugar syrup

Ingredients
Recipes are laid out in the order we recommend adding to glass or shaker

Glass
For glassware shapes and names see 34

Garnish
For full information on garnishes see page 40

We say: Basically this very tasty number is a 'Vodka Mojito' served straight-up.
Origin: Adapted from a drink in Ted Saucier's 1951 book, 'Bottoms Up!'.

Shot
Ideally a shot equals 30ml or 1oz but could be a shot glass or bottle cap

Method
See pages 12-21 for tips on how to shake, stir etc.

We say
Indication of taste

Origin
When, where and who created recipes

1862

★★★★☆

Glass: Martini
Garnish: Orange zest twist (discarded) & maraschino cherry
Method: DRY SHAKE (without ice) all ingredients to emulsify. Add ice, SHAKE again and fine strain into a chilled glass.

2½	**shots**	**Bacardi Superior rum**
¾	**shot**	**Tio Pepe fino sherry**
¼	**shot**	**Luxardo Maraschino liqueur**
¼	**shot**	**Freshly squeezed lemon juice**
¼	**shot**	**Monin Pure Cane 2:1 sugar syrup**
1	**dash**	**Angostura aromatic bitters**
½	**fresh**	**Egg white**

We say: Fantastically complex with notes of rum, maraschino, sherry and orange.
Origin: Adapted from a drink created in 2008 by Scott Ingram at MC Bar, Abode Hotel, Glasgow, Scotland. The name is a reference to the year when Facundo M. Bacardi established his first distillery.

57 T-BIRD SHOT

★★★★☆

Glass: Shot
Garnish: None
Method: SHAKE all ingredients with ice and fine strain into chilled glass.

½	**shot**	**Ketel One vodka**
½	**shot**	**Grand Marnier liqueur**
½	**shot**	**Amaretto liqueur**

Variant: With California Plates add ½ shot orange juice; with Cape Cod Plates add ½ shot cranberry juice; with Florida Plates add ½ shot grapefruit juice; with Hawaiian Plates add ½ shot pineapple juice.
Origin: A 57 T-bird, or 1957 Ford Thunderbird to give it its full title, immortalised in the Beach Boys' song 'Fun Fun Fun', was the classic car for any 1950s teenager. Top down, radio up, girl next to you...

8TH DAY (MOCKTAIL) NEW

★★★½☆

Glass: Collins
Garnish: Lime wedge & ginger slice
Method: SHAKE all ingredients with ice and fine strain into ice-filled glass.

2½	**shots**	**Cold jasmine tea**
¾	**shot**	**Freshly squeezed lime juice**
¼	**shot**	**Monin Ginger syrup**
Top up with		**Lemonade/Sprite/7-Up**

We say: Jasmine, lime, ginger and lemon – refreshing and complex.
Origin: Discovered in 2009 at Cloud 23, Manchester, England.

THE 75

★★★★½

Glass: Martini
Garnish: Star anise
Method: SHAKE all ingredients with ice and fine strain into chilled glass.

2	**shots**	**Calvados/Applejack brandy**
1	**shot**	**Tanqueray London dry gin**
¼	**shot**	**Absinthe**
¼	**shot**	**Pomegranate (grenadine) syrup**
½	**shot**	**Chilled mineral water**

We say: Hardened palates will appreciate this fantastically dry, aromatic and complex cocktail.
Origin: Like the French 75, this was named after the celebrated 75, a French 75mm field gun developed during the 1890s and used by the French army during the First World War and beyond. The gun was unusually lethal due to its fast rate of fire.

A.B.C.

★★★½☆

Glass: Shot
Garnish: None
Method: Refrigerate ingredients then LAYER in chilled glass by carefully pouring in the following order.

½	**shot**	**Amaretto liqueur**
½	**shot**	**Baileys Irish cream liqueur**
½	**shot**	**Cognac VSOP**

We say: A stripy shooter with almond, whiskey, cream and cognac.

A.B.C. COCKTAIL

★★★★½

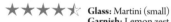

Glass: Martini (small)
Garnish: Lemon zest twist & maraschino cherry
Method: TEAR mint and place in shaker. Add other ingredients, SHAKE with ice and fine strain into chilled glass.

7	**fresh**	**Mint leaves**
1	**shot**	**Warre's Otima tawny port**
1	**shot**	**Cognac VSOP**
¼	**shot**	**Luxardo Maraschino liqueur**
⅛	**shot**	**Monin Pure Cane 2:1 sugar syrup**

We say: Wonderfully delicate. Mint gives subtle freshness to the classic port and brandy combo.
Origin: Vintage cocktail of unknown origin.

A.J.

★★★★☆

Glass: Martini
Garnish: Dust with cinnamon powder
Method: SHAKE all ingredients with ice and fine strain into chilled glass.

2	**shots**	**Calvados/Applejack brandy**
2	**shots**	**Freshly squeezed grapefruit juice**
½	**shot**	**Monin Pure Cane 2:1 sugar syrup**

We say: Amazingly simple and beautifully balanced. I hope you like apple brandy as much as I do.
Origin: The initials in the name stand for 'applejack', the American-style of apple brandy this drink was originally based upon.

A1 COCKTAIL UPDATED

★★★★½☆

Glass: Martini
Garnish: Orange zest twist
Method: SHAKE all ingredients with ice and fine strain into chilled glass.

1½	shots	Tanqueray London dry gin
1	shot	Grand Marnier liqueur
¼	shot	Freshly squeezed lemon juice
⅛	shot	Pomegranate (grenadine) syrup

We say: The richness of Grand Marnier balances lemon juice in this classic gin-led drink. A dash of grenadine provides the pink hue.
Origin: In W.J. Tarling's 1937 *Café Royal Cocktail Book* this cocktail is accompanied by the notation, 'Invented by Albert'. The recipe stated is '1 dash lemon juice, ⅓ Grand Marnier, ⅔ Dry Gin, Dash Grenadine.'

A STOUT FELLOW NEW

★★★★☆

Glass: Coupette
Garnish: Dust with grated 85% cacao chocolate
Method: SHAKE all ingredients with ice and fine strain into chilled glass.

2	shots	Guinness
1	shot	Myer's dark Jamaican rum
1	shot	Kahlúa coffee liqueur
⅛	shot	Bols Cacao Brown

We say: Made in a similar style to an Espresso Martini but with very different ingredients, including Guinness stout and coffee liqueur in place of espresso coffee.
Origin: Created in 2013 by Matthew Coates at Jake's Bar and Still Room, Leeds. Matthew was one of five finalists in the diffordsguide Beer-tail Competition for London Cocktail Week 2013 held in August 2013 at Simon Difford's Cabinet Room in London.

Matthew told us: "The inspiration behind my cocktail comes from my love of all of its components – rum, Guinness and coffee. I call my drink 'A Stout Fellow' because it's strong and hearty but also warming and friendly. It also refers to the old advertising slogan 'Guinness for strength', encompassing more than one meaning of the word stout."

ABACAXI RICAÇO

★★★★☆

Glass: Pineapple shell (frozen)
Garnish: Cut a straw sized hole in the top of the pineapple shell & replace it as a lid
Method: Cut the top off a small pineapple and carefully scoop out the flesh from the base to leave a shell with 12mm (½ inch) thick walls. Place the shell in a freezer to chill. Remove the hard core from the pineapple flesh and discard; roughly chop the remaining flesh, add other ingredients and BLEND with one 12oz scoop of crushed ice. Pour into the pineapple shell and serve with straws. (The flesh of one pineapple blended with the following ingredients will fill at least two shells).

1	whole	Pineapple (fresh)
3	shots	Bacardi Oro golden rum
¾	shot	Freshly squeezed lime juice
½	shot	Granulated sugar

AKA: Burner
We say: Looks and tastes great but a load of hassle to make.
Origin: Adapted from David Embury's 1948 'The Fine Art of Mixing Drinks'. Pronounced 'Ah-bah-Kah-shee Rich-kah-So', the Portuguese name of this Brazilian drink literally translates as 'Extra Delicious Pineapple'

ABBEY MARTINI

★★★★½☆

Glass: Martini
Garnish: Orange zest twist
Method: SHAKE all ingredients with ice and fine strain into chilled glass.

2	shots	Tanqueray London dry gin
1	shot	Martini Rosso sweet vermouth
1	shot	Freshly squeezed orange juice
3	dashes	Angostura aromatic bitters

We say: A dry, orangey, herbal, gin-laced concoction.
Origin: This 1930s classic cocktail is closely related to the better known Bronx

ABSINTHE COCKTAIL #1

★★★½☆

Glass: Martini
Garnish: Mint leaf
Method: SHAKE all ingredients with ice and fine strain into chilled glass.

1	shot	Absinthe
1	shot	Chilled mineral water
¼	shot	Monin Pure Cane 2:1 sugar syrup

Variant: If grenadine (pomegranate syrup) is substituted for the sugar syrup this becomes a Tomate.
We say: Absinthe tamed and served up.
Origin: Dr. Ordinaire perfected his recipe for absinthe in 1792 and from day one it required the addition of water and sugar to make it palatable

ABSINTHE COCKTAIL #2

★★★½☆

Glass: Martini
Garnish: Lemon zest twist
Method: SHAKE all ingredients with ice and fine strain into chilled glass.

1	shot	Absinthe
¼	shot	Monin Almond (orgeat) syrup
¼	shot	Marie Brizard anisette liqueur
1	dash	Angostura aromatic bitters
¾	shot	Chilled mineral water

Variant: Absinthe Frappe – served over crushed ice.
We say: This aniseed flavoured mix tastes surprisingly tame but includes a shot of the notorious green fairy.
Origin: Simon Difford's adaptation of a classic recipe

STAR RATINGS EXPLAINED

★★★★★ **Excellent**

★★★★½ Recommended	★★★★☆ Praiseworthy
★★★½☆ Commended	★★★☆☆ Mediocre
★★½☆☆ Disappointing	★★☆☆☆ Pretty awful
★½☆☆☆ Shameful	★☆☆☆☆ Disgusting

ABSINTHE DRIP COCKTAIL #1
(FRENCH METHOD)

Glass: Absinthe glass or old-fashioned
Garnish: None
Method: POUR absinthe into glass. PLACE cube of sugar on a slotted absinthe spoon resting across the top of the glass. Using a bottle of chilled mineral water with a small hole in the cap, DRIP water over the sugar so it dissolves and drips into the glass. Traditionally the same amount of sugar is added as water but I find full strength absinthe requires more dilution. Add ice, stir and serve.

1½	shots	La Fée Parisienne (68%) absinthe
2	shots	Chilled mineral water
1	cube	Granulated sugar

We say: Patience is a virtue. Slow dripping of the water is essential to dissolve the entire sugar cube and give the drink enough sweetness to balance the absinthe.
Origin: This is the traditional method of serving absinthe. It was common until shortly before the First World War, when the drink was banned in most countries.

ABSINTHE DRIP COCKTAIL #2
(CZECH METHOD)

Glass: Absinthe glass or old-fashioned
Garnish: None
Method: PLACE sugar cube on a slotted absinthe spoon resting across the top of the glass. POUR the absinthe over the sugar cube into the glass. LIGHT the absinthe soaked cube and leave to burn and caramelise. Using a bottle of chilled mineral water with a small hole in the cap, DRIP water over what's left of the sugar so it dissolves and drips into the glass. Add ice, stir and serve.

1½	shots	Absinthe
2	shots	Chilled mineral water
1	cube	Granulated sugar

We say: More about the theatrics involved in its making than the taste of the finished drink.
Origin: This supposedly bohemian method of serving absinthe came back in to being in 1998 with the UK launch of Hill's Absinthe.

ABSINTHE DROP

Glass: Old-fashioned
Garnish: None
Method: STIR all ingredients and strain into ice-filled glass.

1	shot	Absinthe
¼	shot	Marie Brizard Anisette
2	shots	Chilled mineral water

We say: A fix for aniseed addicts.
Origin: Vintage cocktail of unknown origin.

STAR RATINGS EXPLAINED

★★★★★ Excellent

★★★★⯪ Recommended	★★★★☆ Praiseworthy
★★★⯪☆ Commended	★★★☆☆ Mediocre
★★⯪☆☆ Disappointing	★★☆☆☆ Pretty awful
★⯪☆☆☆ Shameful	★☆☆☆☆ Disgusting

ABSINTHE FRAPPÉ

Glass: Old-fashioned
Garnish: Mint sprig
Method: SHAKE all ingredients with ice and fine strain into glass filled with crushed ice. CHURN (stir) and serve with straws.

1½	shots	Absinthe
½	shot	Marie Brizard anisette liqueur
1½	shots	Chilled mineral water
¼	shot	Monin Pure Cane 2:1 sugar syrup

We say: Aniseed and the fire of absinthe moderated by sugar and ice but still a dangerous combination.
Origin: Created in 1874 by Cayetano Ferrer at Aleix's Coffee House, New Orleans, which consequently became known as The Absinthe Room. Today the establishment is fittingly known as the Old Absinthe House but sadly US law prevents it from actually serving absinthe.

ABSINTHE GIMLET NEW

Glass: Coupette
Garnish: Lime wedge
Method: SHAKE all ingredients with ice and fine strain into chilled glass.

1½	shots	Tanqueray London dry gin
½	shot	La Fée Parisienne (68%) absinthe
½	shot	Rose's lime cordial
¼	shot	Freshly squeezed lime juice
½	shot	Chilled mineral water

We say: A herbal riff on Charles Schumann's Gimlet (see Gimlet #2)
Origin: Created by Tara Garnell at The Cabinet Room, London, England after making Charles Vexenat's Green Beast.

ABSINTHE ITALIANO COCKTAIL

Glass: Martini
Garnish: Lemon zest twist
Method: SHAKE all ingredients with ice and fine strain into chilled glass.

1	shot	Absinthe
½	shot	Marie Brizard anisette liqueur
¼	shot	Luxardo Maraschino liqueur
1½	shots	Chilled mineral water

We say: Liqueurs sweeten and tame the absinthe burn in this milky green concoction.
Origin: A long lost classic.

ABSINTHE MARTINI

Glass: Martini
Garnish: Star anise
Method: STIR all ingredients with ice and strain into chilled glass.

2½	shots	Tanqueray London dry gin
½	shot	Martini Extra Dry vermouth
⅛	shot	Absinthe

We say: A classic Gin Martini made aniseed fresh with a dash of absinthe.

ABSINTHE SOUR

★★★⯪☆

Glass: Old-fashioned
Garnish: Lemon zest twist
Method: DRY SHAKE (without ice) all ingredients to emulsify. Add ice, SHAKE again and strain into ice-filled glass.

1	shot	La Fée Parisienne (68%) absinthe
1	shot	Monin Pure Cane 2:1 sugar syrup
1	shot	Freshly squeezed lemon juice
½	fresh	Egg white

Variant: Served 'up' in sour glass.
We say: A touch of the sours for absinthe lovers.

ABSINTHE SPECIAL COCKTAIL

★★★☆☆

Glass: Martini
Garnish: Lemon zest twist
Method: SHAKE all ingredients with ice and fine strain into chilled glass.

1	shot	Absinthe
¼	shot	Tanqueray London dry gin
¼	shot	Marie Brizard anisette liqueur
2	dashes	Angostura aromatic bitters
1	dash	Orange bitters
1½	shots	Chilled mineral water

We say: Tongue-numbingly strong in flavour and alcohol.
Origin: A long lost classic.

ABSINTHE SUISESSE

★★★☆☆

Glass: Old-fashioned
Garnish: Mint sprig
Method: SHAKE all ingredients with ice and strain into glass filled with crushed ice.

1½	shots	Absinthe
½	shot	Monin Almond (orgeat) syrup
1	fresh	Egg white
½	shot	Milk
½	shot	Double (heavy) cream

Variant: Also spelt 'Suissesse' and sometimes made with absinthe, vermouth, sugar, crème de menthe and egg white shaken and topped with sparkling water.
We say: Absinthe smoothed with cream and sweet almond.
Origin: New Orleans 1930s.

ABSINTHE WITHOUT LEAVE

★★⯪☆☆

Glass: Shot
Garnish: None
Method: Refrigerate ingredients then LAYER in chilled glass by carefully pouring in the following order.

¾	shot	Pisang Ambon liqueur
¾	shot	Baileys Irish cream liqueur
½	shot	Absinthe

We say: This green and brown stripy shot is easy to layer but not so easy to drink.
Origin: Discovered in 2003 at Hush, London, England.

ABSOLUTELY FABULOUS

★★★★☆

Glass: Flute
Garnish: Strawberry
Method: SHAKE first two ingredients with ice and strain into glass. TOP with champagne.

1	shot	Ketel One vodka
2	shots	Ocean Spray cranberry juice
Top up with		Brut champagne

We say: Easy to quaff – Patsy would love it.
Origin: Created in 1999 at Monte's Club, London, England, and named after the Absolutely Fabulous television series where Patsy consumed copious quantities of Stoli and Bolly–darlings.

ACAPULCO

★★★⯪☆

Glass: Collins
Garnish: Pineapple wedge
Method: SHAKE all ingredients with ice and strain into ice-filled glass.

1	shot	Tequila 100% Agave
1	shot	Bacardi Oro golden rum
1	shot	Freshly squeezed grapefruit juice
2½	shots	Fresh pressed pineapple juice
½	shot	Monin Pure Cane 2:1 sugar syrup

We say: An innocuous, fruity mixture laced with tequila and rum.

BARTENDER'S TIP ORDER OF PREPARATION

As in cooking, there is a correct order in which to prepare a drink which, with a few exceptions, runs as follows:

1. Select glass and chill or pre-heat (if required) 2. Prepare garnish (if required) 3. Pour ingredients. 4. Add ice (if required - add last to minimise melt) 5. Combine ingredients (shake, stir etc.) 6. Add garnish (if required) 7. Consume or serve to guest

ACAPULCO DAIQUIRI

★★★★☆

Glass: Martini
Garnish: Lime wedge
Method: DRY SHAKE (without ice) all ingredients to emulsify. Add ice, SHAKE again and fine strain into chilled glass.

1½	shots	**Rum light white/blanco**
½	shot	**Cointreau triple sec**
¾	shot	**Freshly squeezed lemon juice**
¾	shot	**Rose's lime cordial**
½	fresh	**Egg white**

We say: A smooth, yet citrus-rich Daiquiri.

ACE

★★★½☆

Glass: Martini
Garnish: Maraschino cherry
Method: DRY SHAKE (without ice) all ingredients to emulsify. Add ice, SHAKE again and fine strain into chilled glass.

2	shots	**Tanqueray London dry gin**
½	shot	**Pomegranate (grenadine) syrup**
½	shot	**Double (heavy) cream**
½	shot	**Milk**
½	fresh	**Egg white**

We say: Pleasant, creamy, sweetened gin. Add more pomegranate syrup to taste.

ACE OF CLUBS DAIQUIRI

★★★★½

Glass: Martini
Garnish: Dust with chocolate powder
Method: SHAKE all ingredients with ice and fine strain into chilled glass.

½	shot	**White Crème de Cacao**
2	shots	**Bacardi Oro golden rum**
½	shot	**Freshly squeezed lime juice**
⅛	shot	**Monin Pure Cane 2:1 sugar syrup**

We say: A Daiquiri with a hint of chocolate.
Origin: Created in the 1930s at a Bermudian nightclub of the same name.

ACHILLES HEEL

★★★★☆

Glass: Collins
Garnish: Apple slice
Method: SHAKE all ingredients with ice and strain into ice-filled glass.

2	shots	**Żubrówka bison vodka**
¼	shot	**Chambord black raspberry liqueur**
¼	shot	**Peachtree peach schnapps**
1	shot	**Pressed apple juice**
½	shot	**Freshly squeezed lemon juice**

We say: If you like French Martinis you'll love this semi-sweet Tatanka.
Origin: Created in 2005 at Koba, Brighton, England.

ACT OF VIOLETS

★★★½☆

Glass: Coupette
Garnish: Dust with grated nutmeg
Method: DRY SHAKE all ingredients (without ice). SHAKE again with ice and fine strain into chilled glass.

2	shots	**Tanqueray London dry gin**
⅓	shot	**Martini Extra dry vermouth**
⅔	shot	**Benoit Serres créme de violette**
⅔	shot	**Freshly squeezed lemon juice**
2	dashes	**Angostura aromatic bitters**
½	fresh	**Egg white**

We say: Silky berry fruit fortified with gin and balanced with lemon juice and dry vermouth.
Origin: Created in 2009 by Ryan Chetiyawardana at Bramble Bar and Lounge, Edinburgh, Scotland. Originally based on Martin Miller's gin, this cocktail won the brand's UK Lost and Stolen competition.

ADAM & EVE

★★★★☆

Glass: Old-fashioned
Garnish: Lemon zest twist
Method: SHAKE all ingredients with ice and strain into ice filled glass.

2	shots	**Maker's Mark bourbon**
½	shot	**Galliano L'Autentico liqueur**
¼	shot	**Monin Pure Cane 2:1 sugar syrup**
3	dashes	**Angostura aromatic bitters**

We say: Lovers of the Sazerac will appreciate this herbal, bourbon-laced concoction.

ADAM & EVE #2

★★★½☆

Glass: Martini
Garnish: Raspberries & lemon zest twist
Method: SHAKE all ingredients with ice and fine strain into chilled glass.

1	shot	**Tanqueray London dry gin**
1	shot	**Cognac VSOP**
1	shot	**Freshly squeezed lemon juice**
1	shot	**Crème de cassis liqueur**

We say: Fruity but not too sweet.

ADDINGTON

★★★★★

Glass: Martini
Garnish: Orange zest twist
Method: SHAKE first two ingredients with ice and fine strain into chilled glass. TOP with just the merest squirt of soda from chilled siphon.

2	shots	**Martini Rosso sweet vermouth**
1	shot	**Martini Extra Dry vermouth**
Top up with		**Soda from siphon**

We say: Substitute vermouths such as Antica Formula by Giuseppe B. Carpano dramatically alter the character of this cocktail.
Origin: Vintage cocktail of unknown origin

ADDISON

★★★⯪☆

Glass: Martini
Garnish: Maraschino cherry
Method: STIR all ingredients with ice and fine strain into chilled glass.

| 1½ | shots | Tanqueray London dry gin |
| 1½ | shots | Martini Rosso sweet vermouth |

We say: Basically a very wet, sweet Martini.

ADELAIDE SWIZZLE

★★★★☆

Glass: Collins
Garnish: Lime slice
Method: POUR all ingredients into glass filled with crushed ice and SWIZZLE.

2	shots	Bacardi Superior rum
¾	shot	Taylor's Velvet Falernum liqueur
½	shot	Freshly squeezed lime juice
2	dashes	Peychaud's aromatic bitters

We say: A slightly pink, dry, spicy long drink with rum and a hint of cloves and lime.
Origin: This is the signature cocktail at Café Adelaide's Swizzle Stick Bar, New Orleans, USA. There it is made with a liquid poured from a plain bottle marked 'top secret' but, having tried a drop, we think it is Falernum.

ADIOS

★★★⯪☆

Glass: Shot
Garnish: None
Method: Refrigerate ingredients then LAYER in chilled glass by carefully pouring in the following order.

| ¾ | shot | Kahlúa coffee liqueur |
| ¾ | shot | Tequila 100% Agave |

We say: Surprisingly tasty with a potent agave reminder of what you've just knocked back.

ADIOS AMIGOS #2

★★★☆☆

Glass: Martini
Garnish: Lemon zest twist
Method: SHAKE all ingredients with ice and fine strain into chilled glass.

1	shot	Tanqueray London dry gin
½	shot	Cognac VSOP
½	shot	Bacardi Superior rum
½	shot	Martini Rosso sweet vermouth
½	shot	Freshly squeezed lemon juice
⅛	shot	Monin Pure Cane 2:1 sugar syrup

We say: I have added a dash of sugar to what was originally a bone dry recipe.

ADIOS AMIGOS COCKTAIL

★★★⯪☆

Glass: Martini
Garnish: Lemon zest twist
Method: SHAKE all ingredients with ice and fine strain into chilled glass.

1	shot	Bacardi Superior rum
½	shot	Cognac VSOP
½	shot	Tanqueray London dry gin
½	shot	Martini Extra Dry vermouth
¼	shot	Freshly squeezed lime juice
¼	shot	Monin Pure Cane 2:1 sugar syrup
½	shot	Chilled mineral water

We say: To quote Vic, "You know that adios means good-bye. You drink two or three of these, and it's adios, believe me, it's adios."
Origin: Adapted from Victor Bergeron's *'Trader Vic's Bartender's Guide'* (1972 revised edition).

ADONIS

★★★★☆

Glass: Martini
Garnish: Orange zest twist
Method: STIR all ingredients with ice and strain into chilled glass.

2	shots	Tio Pepe fino sherry
1	shot	Martini Rosso sweet vermouth
2	dashes	Orange bitters

We say: A Surprisingly delicate, dry, aromatic oldie.
Origin: Thought to have been created in 1886 to celebrate the success of a Broadway musical.

AFFINITY

★★★★☆

Glass: Martini
Garnish: Lemon zest twist
Method: STIR all ingredients with ice and strain into chilled glass.

1	shot	Dewar's White label Scotch
1	shot	Martini Rosso sweet vermouth
1	shot	Martini Extra Dry vermouth
1	dash	Angostura aromatic bitters

AKA: Scotch Manhattan
Variant: Rob Roy & Violet Affinity
We say: Aperitif-style cocktail which when shaken has an almost creamy, soft, mouth feel. Stir, as the recipe originally intended and the Scotch notes are more pronounced. I prefer mine shaken.
Origin: Fashionable in the 1920s

AFTER EIGHT

★★★☆☆

Glass: Shot
Garnish: None
Method: SHAKE all ingredients with ice and fine strain into chilled glass.

½	shot	Ketel One vodka
½	shot	White Crème de Cacao
½	shot	Green crème de menthe liqueur

We say: Looks like mouthwash but tastes like liquid After Eight chocolates.

AFTER SIX SHOT

Glass: Shot
Garnish: None
Method: Refrigerate ingredients then LAYER in chilled glass by carefully pouring in the following order.

½	shot	Kahlúa coffee liqueur
½	shot	Giffard Menthe Pastille liqueur
½	shot	Baileys Irish cream liqueur

We say: A layered, creamy, coffee and mint shot.

AFTERBURNER

Glass: Snifter
Garnish: None
Method: POUR all ingredients into glass, swirl to mix, Flambé and then extinguish flame. Please take care and beware of hot glass rim.

1	shot	Giffard Menthe Pastille liqueur
½	shot	Wray & Nephew overproof rum
1	shot	Kahlúa coffee liqueur

We say: A surprisingly smooth and moreish peppermint-laced drink.

AGED HONEY DAIQUIRI

Glass: Martini
Garnish: Lime wedge
Method: STIR honey with rum in base of shaker until honey dissolves. Add lime juice and water, SHAKE with ice and fine strain into chilled glass.

2	shots	Bacardi Superior rum
1½	spoon	Runny honey
½	shot	Freshly squeezed lime juice
½	shot	Chilled mineral water

We say: Sweet honey replaces sugar syrup in this natural Daiquiri. Try experimenting with different honeys. We favour orange blossom honey.

AGENT ORANGE

Glass: Old-fashioned
Garnish: Orange zest twist
Method: SHAKE all ingredients with ice and strain into ice-filled glass.

1	shot	Ketel One vodka
½	shot	Grand Marnier liqueur
½	shot	Triple Sec
2	shots	Freshly squeezed orange juice

We say: Fresh orange is good for you. This has all of the flavour but few of the health benefits.

AGGRAVATION

Glass: Old-fashioned
Garnish: Dust with grated nutmeg
Method: SHAKE all ingredients with ice and strain into ice-filled glass.

2	shots	Dewar's White label Scotch
¾	shot	Kahlúa coffee liqueur
¾	shot	Double (heavy) cream
¾	shot	Milk
¼	shot	Monin Pure Cane 2:1 sugar syrup

We say: If you like Scotch and enjoy creamy drinks, you'll love this.

AGUA DE CUBA NEW

Glass: Flute
Garnish: Watermelon wedge
Method: MUDDLE watermelon in base of shaker. Add other ingredients, SHAKE with ice and fine strain into chilled glass.

2	slices	Fresh watermelon
2	shots	Rum light white/blanco
⅔	shot	Taylor's Velvet Falernum liqueur
⅔	shot	Freshly squeezed lemon juice

We say: A light summery rum-based drink with fresh watermelon and subtle clove spice.
Origin: Adapted from a drink created in 2010 by Joey Medrington at Tigerlily, Edinburgh, Scotland.

AIR MAIL

Glass: Collins
Garnish: Mint sprig
Method: SHAKE first four ingredients with ice and fine strain into ice-filled glass. TOP with champagne.

2	shots	Bacardi Oro golden rum
¼	shot	Monin Honey syrup
½	shot	Freshly squeezed lime juice
½	shot	Freshly squeezed orange juice
Top up with		Brut champagne

We say: This old classic is basically a Honeysuckle served long and topped with champagne, rum, honey and a touch of citrus freshness make this one of the better champagne cocktails.
Origin: Adapted from a classic recipe, which first appears in the 1949 *Esquire's Handbook for Hosts*.

STAR RATINGS EXPLAINED

★★★★★ Excellent

★★★★⯪ Recommended	★★★★☆ Praiseworthy
★★★⯪☆ Commended	★★★☆☆ Mediocre
★★⯪☆☆ Disappointing	★★☆☆☆ Pretty awful
★⯪☆☆☆ Shameful	★☆☆☆☆ Disgusting

AKU AKU

★★★★★⯪☆

Glass: Martini
Garnish: ineapple wedge, maraschino cherry and mint sprig
Method: BLEND all ingredients with 12oz scoop of crushed ice. Serve with short straws.

1	shot	Rum light white/blanco
½	shot	Peach Tree peach schnapps
1½	shots	Fresh pressed pineapple juice
½	shot	Monin Pure Cane 2:1 sugar syrup
¾	shot	Freshly squeezed lime juice
10	fresh	Mint leaves

We say: This Tiki classic looks a little like frozen stagnant pond water but tastes minty fresh and rather good.
Origin: Adapted from Victor Bergeron's '*Trader Vic's Bartender's Guide*' (1972 revised edition)

ALABAMA SLAMMER #1

★★★☆☆

Glass: Martini
Garnish: Orange zest twist
Method: SHAKE all ingredients with ice and fine strain into chilled glass.

1½	shots	Ketel One vodka
¾	shot	Southern Comfort liqueur
1	shot	Freshly squeezed orange juice
¼	shot	Pomegranate (grenadine) syrup

We say: None of the ingredients come from Alabama and the drink is served too long to slam. However, it's a good, rhythmic, rhyming name, if a little naff these days.

ALABAMA SLAMMER #2

★★★☆☆

Glass: Old-fashioned
Garnish: Peach slice
Method: SHAKE all ingredients with ice and strain into ice-filled glass.

1½	shots	Southern Comfort liqueur
½	shot	Amaretto liqueur
½	shot	Sloe Gin liqueur
2	shots	Freshly squeezed orange juice
¾	shot	Freshly squeezed lemon juice

We say: Rich in flavour and quite sweet with a citrus bite. Surprisingly peachy!

ALABAZAM

★★★⯪☆

Glass: Collins
Garnish: Lemon slice
Method: SHAKE first five ingredients with ice and strain into ice-filled glass. TOP with soda.

2	shots	Cognac VSOP
1	shot	Grand Marnier liqueur
1	shot	Freshly squeezed lemon juice
½	shot	Monin Pure Cane 2:1 sugar syrup
1	dash	Orange bitters
Top up with		Soda (club soda)

We say: Beware – this long fruity number packs a cognac charged punch.
Origin: Recipe adapted from William Schmidt's 1892 '*The Flowing Bowl*'.

THE ALAMAGOOZLUM COCKTAIL UPDATED

★★★★⯪

Glass: Martini
Garnish: Pineapple wedge
Method: DRY SHAKE (without ice) all ingredients to emulsify. Add ice, SHAKE again and fine strain into glass.

1	shot	Bols Genever
¾	shot	Chartreuse Yellow liqueur
¾	shot	Wray & Nephew overproof rum
¼	shot	Grand Marnier liqueur
¾	shot	Monin Pure Cane 2:1 sugar syrup
1	shot	Chilled mineral water
¼	shot	Angostura aromatic bitters
¼	fresh	Egg white

We say: Even Mr Embury would approve of this version. Overproof Jamaican rum and copious amounts of bitters make this drink.
Origin: Adapted from David A. Embury's 1948 '*Fine Art of Mixing Drinks*', where he writes, "This cocktail is supposed to have been a speciality of the elder Morgan of the House of Morgan, which goes to prove as a bartender he was an excellent banker."

ALAN'S APPLE BREEZE

★★★⯪☆

Glass: Collins
Garnish: Apple wedge
Method: SHAKE all ingredients with ice and strain into ice-filled glass.

2	shots	Bacardi Superior rum
½	shot	De Kuyper Apricot Brandy liqueur
1½	shots	Pressed apple juice
1½	shots	Ocean Spray cranberry juice
½	shot	Freshly squeezed lime juice
¼	shot	Monin Pure Cane 2:1 sugar syrup

We say: A sweet, tangy version of the Apple Breeze.
Origin: Created in 2002 by Alan Johnston at Metropolitan, Glasgow, Scotland.

BARTENDER'S TIP FINE STRAIN

Most cocktails that are served 'straight up' without ice benefit from an additional finer strain, over and above the standard strain.

This 'fine strain' removes small fragments of fruit and fine flecks of ice which can spoil the appearance of a drink and is particularly beneficial if the drink has been shaken. Fine straining is achieved by simply holding a fine sieve, like a tea strainer, between the shaker and the glass.

ALASKA #1 (SAVOY RECIPE)

★★★★☆

Glass: Martini
Garnish: Orange zest twist
Method: SHAKE all ingredients with ice and fine strain into chilled glass.

2½	shots	**Tanqueray London dry gin**
¾	shot	**Chartreuse Yellow liqueur**
1	shot	**Tio Pepe fino sherry**
3	dashes	**Orange bitters**

AKA: Nome
Origin: In his 1930 '*The Savoy Cocktail Book*', Harry Craddock writes, "so far as can be ascertained this delectable potion is NOT the staple diet of the Esquimaux. It was probably first thought of in South Carolina – hence its name." The addition of dry sherry is recommended in David Embury's 1948 '*Fine Art of Mixing Drinks*'.

ALASKA #2

★★★☆☆

Glass: Martini
Garnish: Maraschino cherry
Method: SHAKE all ingredients with ice and fine strain into chilled glass.

2	shots	**Tanqueray London dry gin**
1½	shots	**Freshly squeezed lemon juice**
½	shot	**Monin Pure Cane 2:1 sugar syrup**
¼	shot	**Crème de cassis liqueur**

We say: The original recipe suggests adding the cassis separately after the drink is strained into the glass so it sinks. Looks great but the resulting drink is very sour until the cassis is stirred in.

ALASKAN MARTINI

★★★★☆

Glass: Martini
Garnish: Lemon zest twist (discarded) & mint leaf
Method: STIR all the ingredients with ice and strain into a chilled glass.

2½	shots	**Tanqueray London dry gin**
¾	shot	**Chartreuse Yellow liqueur**

We say: Stir long and well – this needs dilution. The result will appeal to gin and Chartreuse fans.
Origin: Modern version of the Alaska.

ALBERTO MARTINI

★★★★☆

Glass: Coupette
Garnish: Orange zest twist
Method: STIR all ingredients with ice and strain into chilled glass.

1¼	shots	**Tanqueray London dry gin**
1¼	shots	**Martini Extra Dry vermouth**
1	shot	**Tio Pepe fino sherry**
½	shot	**Triple Sec**

We say: Dry, complex and aromatic. An equal parts gin and vermouth Martini with a good dose of fino sherry and a splash of triple sec.
Origin: In W.J. Tarling's 1937 *Café Royal Cocktail Book* the invention of this cocktail iscredited to A.J. Smith.

ALESSANDRO

★★★☆☆

Glass: Martini
Garnish: Lemon zest twist
Method: SHAKE all ingredients with ice and fine strain into chilled glass.

¾	shot	**Tanqueray London dry gin**
¾	shot	**Opal Nera black sambuca**
¾	shot	**Milk**
¾	shot	**Double (heavy) cream**

We say: Hints of aniseed, elderflower and gin emerge from this grey, creamy drink.

ALEXANDER UPDATED

★★★★½

Glass: Martini
Garnish: Dust with grated nutmeg
Method: SHAKE all ingredients with ice and fine strain into chilled glass.

2	shots	**Tanqueray London dry gin**
1	shot	**White Crème de Cacao**
½	shot	**Double (heavy) cream**

AKA: Gin Alexander or Princess Mary
We say: This gin-based Alexander has sadly slipped from popularity, partly knocked by its successors, particularly the Brandy Alexander. Predictably, I've doubled the amount of gin used from the original recipe.
Origin: The original Alexander, equal parts gin, crème de cacao and cream, is thought to have originated in the twentieth century, certainly before 1915, evidenced by an equal parts recipe appearing in Hugo Ensslin's 1916 'Recipes for Mixed Drinks.'
Historian Barry Popik's website lists several plausible origins for this drink. The first being a cutting from page 11 of news section of the 3rd October 1915 Philadelphia (PA) Inquirer. "The head bartender has even gone so far as to invent an Alexander cocktail, which he is reserving to be served during the World Series." This referred to The Racquet Club and the 1915 World Series which was won by Boston beating Philadelphia. The bartender created the drink in honour of Philadelphia pitcher Grover Cleveland Alexander (1887-1950).

Alternatively, a newspaper column dated 21-March 1929 by New York columnist Walter Winchell links the origin of the Alexander cocktail to Troy Alexander, a bartender at a New York pre-Prohibition lobster restaurant called Rector's and claims that Troy created his eponymously named cocktail for a dinner celebrating a successful advertising campaign.

The advertisement depicted Phoebe Snow, a fictitious railway traveller, wearing a snow-white dress featured in an advertising campaign for the Delaware, Lackawanna and Western Railroad (DL&W) to promote the company's use of clean-burning anthracite to fuel its locomotives.

Coal-fuelled trains frequently covered travellers with black soot but DL&W owned vast anthracite mines in Pennsylvania so could legitimately claim that their passengers' clothes would arrive clean after a long journey. The first advertisement depicted an image of Phoebe Snow, supposedly a young New York socialite who frequently travelled to Buffalo, New York wearing a white dress and a short poem:

Says Phoebe Snow
about to go
upon a trip to Buffalo
"My gown stays white
from morn till night
Upon the Road of Anthracite"

The popular advertisements first appeared at the turn of the 20th century and ran for nearly seventy years. Phoebe became one of America's most recognised advertising mascots. The Alexander became a Prohibition favourite as the cream and nutmeg garnish helped disguise the rough taste of homemade 'bathtub' gin.

ALEXANDER THE GREAT

★★★★½☆

Glass: Martini
Garnish: Dust with grated nutmeg
Method: SHAKE all ingredients with ice and fine strain into chilled glass.

1½ shots	Ketel One vodka
½ shot	Kahlúa coffee liqueur
½ shot	White Crème de Cacao
¾ shot	Double (heavy) cream
¾ shot	Milk

We say: A tasty combination of coffee, chocolate and cream, laced with vodka.

ALEXANDER'S BIG BROTHER

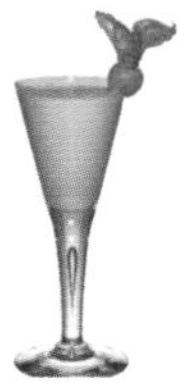

★★★★½☆

Glass: Martini
Garnish: Physalis (cape gooseberry)
Method: SHAKE all ingredients with ice and fine strain into chilled glass.

1½ shots	Tanqueray London dry gin
¼ shot	Triple Sec
¾ shot	Bols Blue Curaçao liqueur
¾ shot	Milk
¾ shot	Double (heavy) cream

We say: Orangey in taste and creamy blue in colour - mildly better than pink for the macho out there.

ALEXANDER'S SISTER

★★½☆☆

Glass: Martini
Garnish: Dust with grated nutmeg
Method: SHAKE all ingredients with ice and fine strain into chilled glass.

1½ shots	Tanqueray London dry gin
¾ shot	Green crème de menthe liqueur
¾ shot	Double (heavy) cream
⅛ shot	Monin Pure Cane 2:1 sugar syrup

We say: A green minty thing for dairy lovers.

ALEXANDRA

★★★★½☆

Glass: Martini
Garnish: Dust with grated nutmeg
Method: SHAKE all ingredients with ice and fine strain into chilled glass.

1½ shots	Pusser's Navy rum
1 shot	Kahlúa coffee liqueur
¾ shot	Milk
¾ shot	Double (heavy) cream

We say: Surprisingly potent and spicy, despite the ladylike name.

ALFONSO

★★★★½☆

Glass: Flute
Garnish: Lemon zest twist
Method: Coat sugar cube with bitters and drop into glass. POUR Dubonnet and then champagne into chilled glass.

1 cube	Granulated sugar
4 dashes	Angostura aromatic bitters
½ shot	Dubonnet Red (French made)
Top up with	Brut champagne

We say: Herbal variation on the classic Champagne Cocktail
Origin: Named after the deposed Spanish king Alfonso XIII, who first tasted this drink while exiled in France.

ALFONSO MARTINI

★★★★☆

Glass: Martini
Garnish: Orange zest twist
Method: SHAKE all ingredients with ice and fine strain into a chilled glass.

½ shot	Tanqueray London dry gin
1 shot	Grand Marnier liqueur
½ shot	Martini Extra Dry vermouth
¼ shot	Martini Rosso sweet vermouth
2 dashes	Angostura aromatic bitters
½ shot	Chilled mineral water

We say: Dry yet slightly sweet with hints of orange, gin and warm spice.
Origin: Adapted from Victor Bergeron's '*Trader Vic's Bartender's Guide*' (1972 revised edition).

ALGERIA

★★★★½

Glass: Martini
Garnish: Orange zest twist
Method: SHAKE all ingredients with ice and fine strain into chilled glass.

2 shots	Macchu pisco
½ shot	Triple Sec
½ shot	De Kuyper Apricot Brandy liqueur
¾ shot	Chilled mineral water

We say: Pisco, apricot and orange combine wonderfully in this medium dry, balanced cocktail with a tangy bite.
Origin: Modern adaptation of a classic.

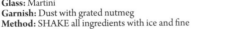

BARTENDER'S TIP LAYER

As the name would suggest, layered drinks include layers of different ingredients, often with contrasting colours.

This effect is achieved by carefully pouring each ingredient into the glass so that it floats on its predecessor. The success of this technique is dependent on the density (specific gravity) of the liquids used. As a rule of thumb, the less alcohol and the more sugar an ingredient contains, the heavier it is. The heaviest ingredients should be poured first and the lightest last.

ALGONQUIN UPDATED

★★★★☆

Glass: Old-fashioned
Garnish: Pineapple wedge & maraschino cherry
Method: MUDDLE pineapple in base of shaker. Add other ingredients, SHAKE with ice and fine strain into ice-filled glass.

½	ring	Pineapple (fresh)
1½	shots	Straight rye whiskey
¾	shot	Martini Extra Dry vermouth
1	dash	Peychaud's aromatic bitters

We say: A dry aromatic aperitif-style of cocktail. If you don't want this drink frothy then stir instead of shake.
Origin: One of several classic cocktails accredited to New York City's Algonquin Hotel in the 1930s. Its true origins are lost in time.

ALICE FROM DALLAS

★★★☆☆

Glass: Shot
Garnish: None
Method: Refrigerate ingredients then LAYER in chilled glass by carefully pouring in the following order.

½	shot	Kahlúa coffee liqueur
½	shot	Grand Marnier liqueur
½	shot	Tequila 100% Agave

We say: Coffee and orange spiked with tequila.

ALICE IN WONDERLAND 🗝️

★★★☆☆

Glass: Shot
Garnish: Lime wedge
Method: Refrigerate ingredients then LAYER in chilled glass by carefully pouring in the following order.

| 1 | shot | Grand Marnier liqueur |
| ½ | shot | Tequila 100% Agave |

We say: Brings a whole new dimension to tequila and orange.

ALICE MINE 🗝️

★★★★☆

Glass: Martini
Garnish: Orange zest twist
Method: STIR all ingredients with ice and strain into chilled glass.

1	shot	Grand Marnier liqueur
½	shot	Tanqueray London dry gin
½	shot	Martini Extra Dry vermouth
¼	shot	Martini Rosso sweet vermouth
1	dash	Angostura aromatic bitters

We say: A Medium Dry Martini with luscious orange notes.
Origin: Vintage cocktail of unknown origin.

ALIEN SECRETION

★★★☆☆

Glass: Collins
Garnish: Pineapple wedge & maraschino cherry
Method: SHAKE all ingredients with ice and strain into ice-filled glass.

2	shots	Ketel One vodka
½	shot	Midori green melon liqueur
½	shot	Malibu coconut rum liqueur
3	shots	Fresh pressed pineapple juice

We say: Lime green and fruity but all too drinkable, with a distinct bite despite its mild sweetness.
Origin: One of many 80s cocktails with a dodgy name.

ALL FALL DOWN

★★★☆☆

Glass: Shot
Garnish: None
Method: Refrigerate ingredients then LAYER in chilled glass by carefully pouring in the following order.

½	shot	Kahlúa coffee liqueur
½	shot	Tequila 100% Agave
½	shot	Pusser's Navy rum

We say: Too many of these and you will.

ALL WHITE FRAPPÉ

★★★☆☆

Glass: Old-fashioned
Garnish: Lemon zest twist
Method: BLEND ingredients with 6oz scoop of crushed ice. Pour into glass and serve with short straws.

1	shot	Luxardo Sambuca dei Cesari
1	shot	White Crème de Cacao
1	shot	Giffard Menthe Pastille liqueur
1	shot	Freshly squeezed lemon juice

We say: Aniseed, chocolate, peppermint and lemon juice are an unlikely but tasty combination for summer afternoons.

ALLEGROTTINI

★★★☆☆

Glass: Martini
Garnish: Orange zest twist
Method: SHAKE all the ingredients with ice and fine strain into chilled glass.

1½	shots	Ketel One Citroen vodka
¾	shot	Triple Sec
¼	shot	Martini Extra Dry vermouth
¾	shot	Freshly squeezed orange juice
¼	shot	Freshly squeezed lime juice

We say: Strongly citrus but dry rather than bitter.
Origin: Discovered in 2005 at the Four Seasons Hotel, Prague, Czech Republic.

ALMOND MARTINI #1

★★★★☆

Glass: Martini
Garnish: Sink three almonds
Method: SHAKE all ingredients with ice and fine strain into chilled glass.

2	shots	**Ketel One vodka**
½	shot	**Freshly squeezed lemon juice**
½	shot	**Monin Almond (orgeat) syrup**
1	shot	**Pressed apple juice**
2	dashes	**Peach bitters**

We say: Almond inspired with hints of apple and lemon juice.
Origin: Created in 2004 by Matt Pomeroy at Baltic, London, England.

ALMOND MARTINI #2

★★★★☆

Glass: Martini
Garnish: Sink three almonds
Method: SHAKE all ingredients with ice and fine strain into chilled glass.

2	shots	**Ketel One vodka**
¾	shot	**Amaretto liqueur**
¼	shot	**Martini Extra Dry vermouth**
¾	shot	**Chilled mineral water**

We say: A delicate, almond flavoured Vodka Martini.
Origin: Created in 2005 by Simon Difford.

ALMOND OLD FASHIONED

★★★★½

Glass: Old-fashioned
Garnish: Orange zest twist
Method: STIR one shot of tequila with two ice cubes in a glass. Add amaretto, agave syrup, bitters and two more ice cubes. Stir some more then add another two ice cubes and the remaining tequila. Stir lots more so as to melt ice then add more ice. The melting and stirring in of ice cubes is essential to the dilution and taste of the drink.

2	shots	**Tequila 100% Agave**
¼	shot	**Amaretto liqueur**
¼	shot	**Agave nectar**
3	dashes	**Orange bitters**

We say: One to please fans of both tequila and the Old Fashioned drinks genre.
Origin: Created in 2005 by Mark Prat at Maze, London, England.

THE AMALFI

★★★½☆

Glass: Coupette
Garnish: Grated lemon zest
Method: DRY SHAKE (without ice) all ingredients. Add ice, SHAKE again and fine strain into chilled glass.

2	shots	**Bacardi Superior rum**
¾	shot	**Limoncello liqueur**
¾	shot	**Martini Extra Dry vermouth**
¼	shot	**Luxardo Maraschino liqueur**
½	shot	**Egg white**

We say: A flavour reminiscent of lemon meringue charged with light rum and enhanced with a dash of maraschino.
Origin: Adapted from a drink created in 2010 by Andy Pearson, London, England for Barack Obama.

AMALIA

★★★★☆

Glass: Coupette
Garnish: Pineapple foam
Method: SHAKE all ingredients with ice and fine strain into chilled glass.

2	shots	**Bacardi Superior rum**
¾	shot	**Freshly squeezed lemon juice**
¼	shot	**Monin Pure Cane 2:1 sugar syrup**
1	shot	**Sauvignon blanc wine**
⅛	shot	**Gooseberry & mint cordial**

We say: Sip a gooseberry and mint influenced lemon Daiquiri though a foam topping.
Origin: Created in 2008 by Sam Dean, Mobar, Nottingham England.

AMANTE PICANTE

★★★½☆

Glass: Martini
Garnish: Cucumber slices
Method: MUDDLE cucumber and coriander (cilantro). ADD other ingredients, SHAKE with ice and fine strain into chilled glass.

2	slices	**Cucumber (chopped & peeled)**
2	sprig	**Coriander (cilantro)**
1½	shots	**Tequila 100% Agave**
1	shot	**Freshly squeezed lime juice**
½	shot	**Agave nectar**
2	dashes	**Green Tabasco Sauce**

We say: So green and fresh that it must be good for you as well as tasting great.
Origin: Created in 2008 by Francesco Lafranconi of Southern Wine & Spirits USA.

AMARETTO SOUR

★★★½☆

Glass: Old-fashioned
Garnish: Lemon slice & cherry on stick (sail)
Method: DRY SHAKE (without ice) all ingredients to emulsify. Add ice, SHAKE again and strain into ice-filled glass.

2	shots	**Luxardo Amaretto di Saschira**
1	shot	**Freshly squeezed lemon juice**
½	fresh	**Egg white**
3	dashes	**Angostura aromatic bitters**

We say: Sweet 'n' sour – frothy with an almond buzz. Three dashes (12 drops) of Angostura bitters help balance the drink and add an extra burst of flavour.

STAR RATINGS EXPLAINED

★★★★★ Excellent

★★★★½	Recommended	★★★★☆	Praiseworthy
★★★½☆	Commended	★★★☆☆	Mediocre
★★½☆☆	Disappointing	★★☆☆☆	Pretty awful
★½☆☆☆	Shameful	★☆☆☆☆	Disgusting

AMARETTO SOUR II NEW
(MORGENTHALER FORMULA)

★★★★☆

Glass: Old fashioned
Garnish: Cherry and lemon zest twist
Method: DRY SHAKE all ingredients without ice. SHAKE again with ice and strain into ice-filled glass.

1½	shots	Luxardo Amaretto di Saschira
1	shot	Maker's Mark bourbon
1	shot	Freshly squeezed lemon juice
½	fresh	Egg white

We say: As the name suggests, this drink is dominated by amaretto, with lemon juice providing the sour balancing element and a slug of bourbon giving backbone.
Origin: Adapted from a drink created in 2012 by Jeffrey Morgenthaler in Oregon, USA. Jeffrey's original formula called for 3/4 shot cask-strength bourbon and additionally used 1 spoon of sugar syrup.

AMARITA

★★★☆☆

Glass: Martini
Garnish: Length of lime peel
Method: SHAKE all ingredients with ice and fine strain into chilled glass.

1½	shots	Tequila 100% Agave
¾	shot	Aperol
½	shot	Freshly squeezed lime juice
3	shots	Grapefruit bitters

We say: Tequila predominates in this fairly bitter drink.
Origin: Created in 2007 by Neyah White, San Francisco USA.

AMATITAN TWIST UPDATED

★★★★☆

Glass: Coupette
Garnish: Grapefruit zest twist
Method: STIR all ingredients with ice and strain into chilled glass.

2	shot	Tequila 100% Agave (añejo)
¼	shot	Luxardo maraschino liqueur
¼	shot	Chartreuse Yellow liqueur
1	dash	Grapefruit bitters
½	shot	Chilled water (omit if wet ice)

We say: The sublime taste of great añejo tequila mellowed and delicately flavoured with maraschino, chartreuse and grapefruit bitters.
Origin: Created in 2010 by Dave West at Trio Bar and Grill, Leeds, England.

STAR RATINGS EXPLAINED

★★★★★ Excellent

★★★★☆ Recommended
★★★☆☆ Commended
★★☆☆☆ Disappointing
★☆☆☆☆ Shameful

★★★★☆ Praiseworthy
★★★☆☆ Mediocre
★★☆☆☆ Pretty awful
★☆☆☆☆ Disgusting

AMBER

★★★★☆

Glass: Collins
Garnish: Dust with grated nutmeg & apple wedge
Method: MUDDLE ginger in base of shaker. Add other ingredients, SHAKE with ice and strain into glass filled with crushed ice.

4	slice	Fresh root ginger (thumbnail sized)
1½	shots	Żubrówka bison vodka
4	shots	Pressed apple juice
½	shot	Monin Pure Cane 2:1 sugar syrup
½	shot	Berentzen Apple schnapps

We say: A fantastic combination of adult flavours in a long, thirst-quenching drink. Also great served up.
Origin: Created in 2001 by Douglas Ankrah for Akbar at the Red Fort, Soho, London, England.

AMBER NECTAR NEW

★★★★☆

Glass: Coupette
Garnish: Lemon zest twist
Method: STIR honey with scotch in base of shaker until honey dissolves. ADD other ingredients, SHAKE with ice and strain into ice-filled glass.

2	shots	Dewar's White Label Scotch
¼	shot	Lagavulin 16yo malt whisky
2	spoons	Runny honey
1	shot	Martini Extra dry vermouth

We say: Honey lifts and enhances this blend of scotch, single Islay malt and dry vermouth.
Origin: Adapted by Simon Difford from a cocktail promoted in 2013 by Bols, the Dutch liqueur producer. Originally based on vodka with Bols honey liqueur, the honey cried out for scotch and then some Islay single malt. It's called the Amber Nectar after all.

AMBER ROOM #1

★★★★☆

Glass: Martini
Garnish: Lemon zest twist (discarded) & maraschino cherry
Method: SHAKE all ingredients with ice and fine strain into chilled glass.

1½	shots	Tanqueray London dry gin
½	shot	Chartreuse Green liqueur
½	shot	Martini Rosso sweet vermouth
2	dashes	Orange bitters
½	shot	Chilled mineral water

AKA: Golden Glow
We say: Serious and packed with bold flavours. Fellow Chartreuse fans will approve.
Origin: This vintage cocktail originated from a layered or 'pousse-café'-style drink called a Bijou. This original drink was so named after the French word meaning 'jewel' due to its trio of ingredients being coloured after the three most precious jewels: diamond (gin), ruby (sweet vermouth) and emerald (Green Chartreuse). Shaken rather than layered and the colours combine to make this aptly named amber coloured drink.

AMBER ROOM #2

★★★★☆

Glass: Martini
Garnish: Lemon zest twist
Method: STIR all ingredients with ice and strain into chilled glass.

1½	shots	Tanqueray London dry gin
1	shot	Martini Extra Dry vermouth
¼	shot	St~Germain elderflower liqueur
1	dash	Orange bitters

We say: A subtle, delicately floral Martini.
Origin: Created in 2007 by Stephan Berg, Munich, Germany.

AMBROSIA

★★★★☆

Glass: Flute
Garnish: None
Method: SHAKE first 4 ingredients with ice and strain into glass, TOP with champagne.

1	shot	Cognac VSOP
1	shot	Calvados/Applejack brandy
¼	shot	Triple Sec
¼	shot	Freshly squeezed lemon juice
Top up with		Brut champagne

We say: Dry, fortified champers with a hint of apple.

AMBROSIA COCKTAIL

★★★★☆

Glass: Martini
Garnish: Dust with grated nutmeg
Method: SHAKE all ingredients with ice and fine strain into chilled glass.

¾	shot	Cognac VSOP
2	shots	Advocaat liqueur
1	shot	Cuarenta y Tres (Licor 43) liqueur
½	shot	Chartreuse Yellow liqueur

We say: Easy-drinking but complex with a herbal edge.
Origin: I created this drink and named it after the Greek for 'elixir of life, the food of the gods.' In Britain Ambrosia is a brand of custard, so advocaat seemed appropriate, while, if there is a God, he/she/it surely drinks Chartreuse.

AMERICAN BEAUTY #1

★★★★☆

Glass: Martini
Garnish: Rose petal
Method: SHAKE first six ingredients with ice and fine strain into chilled glass. Use the back of a soup spoon to FLOAT red wine over drink.

2½	shots	Cognac VSOP
½	shot	Martini Extra Dry vermouth
½	shot	Giffard Menthe Pastille liqueur
½	shot	Freshly squeezed orange juice
½	shot	Pomegranate (grenadine) syrup
1	shot	Chilled mineral water
¼	shot	Shiraz red wine

Variant: When served in a tall glass with crushed ice this is called an American Beauty Punch.
We say: Both fresh and refreshing - a subtle hint of peppermint gives zing to this cognac cocktail.
Origin: Adapted from a recipe found in David A. Embury's 'The Fine Art Of Mixing Drinks'.

AMERICAN BEAUTY #2

★★★☆☆

Glass: Martini
Garnish: Mint leaf
Method: SHAKE first five ingredients with ice and fine strain into chilled glass. Use the back of a soup spoon to FLOAT port over drink.

1	shot	Cognac VSOP
1	shot	Martini Extra Dry vermouth
¼	shot	Giffard Menthe Pastille liqueur
1	shot	Freshly squeezed orange juice
½	shot	Pomegranate (grenadine) syrup
½	shot	Warre's Otima tawny port

We say: Invigorating and peppermint-fresh yet sophisticated and complex.
Origin: Adapted from Victor Bergeron's 'Trader Vic's Bartender's Guide' (1972 revised edition).

AMERICAN BREAKFAST

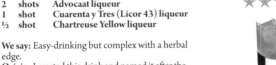

★★★☆☆

Glass: Old-fashioned
Garnish: Grapefruit zest twist
Method: SHAKE all ingredients with ice and strain into ice-filled glass.

½	shot	Maple syrup
2	shots	Maker's Mark bourbon
½	shot	Freshly squeezed pink grapefruit juice

We say: This citrus fresh bourbon-laced drink would be great with your morning muesli.

BARTENDER'S TIP DRY SHAKE

It is common practice to first shake drinks containing cream and eggs without ice, then to shake the drink a second time with ice added.

This practice is known as 'dry shaking' and the theory is that first shaking without ice, and so at a higher temperature, better allows the drink to emulsify.

AMERICAN PIE MARTINI

★★★★☆

Glass: Martini
Garnish: Apple wedge
Method: SHAKE all ingredients with ice and fine strain into chilled glass.

1½	shots	Maker's Mark bourbon
½	shot	Berentzen Apple schnapps
½	shot	Crème de myrtille liqueur
¾	shot	Ocean Spray cranberry juice
½	shot	Pressed apple juice
¼	shot	Freshly squeezed lime juice

We say: This berry and apple pie has a tangy bite.
Origin: Adapted from a recipe discovered at Oxo Tower Restaurant & Bar, London, England.

AMERICANA

★★★☆☆

Glass: Flute
Garnish: Peach slice
Method: Coat sugar cube with bitters and drop into glass. POUR bourbon and then champagne into chilled glass.

1	cube	Granulated sugar
4	dashes	Angostura aromatic bitters
½	shot	Maker's Mark bourbon
Top up with		Brut champagne

We say: The Wild West take on the classic Champagne Cocktail.

AMERICANO

★★★★☆

Glass: Collins
Garnish: Orange slice
Method: POUR Campari and vermouth into ice-filled glass and TOP with soda. Stir and serve with straws.

2	shots	Campari Bitter
2	shots	Martini Rosso sweet vermouth
Top up with		Soda (club soda)

We say: A bitter, fizzy, long refreshing drink, which you'll love if you like Campari.
Origin: First served in the 1860s in Gaspare Campari's bar in Milan, this was originally known as the 'Milano-Torino' as Campari came from Milano (Milan) and Cinzano from Torino (Turin). It was not until Prohibition that the Italians noticed an influx of Americans who enjoyed the drink and so dubbed it Americano.

STAR RATINGS EXPLAINED

★★★★★ Excellent

★★★★⯪ Recommended	★★★★☆ Praiseworthy
★★★⯪☆ Commended	★★★☆☆ Mediocre
★★⯪☆☆ Disappointing	★★☆☆☆ Pretty awful
★⯪☆☆☆ Shameful	★☆☆☆☆ Disgusting

AMPERSAND

★★★★⯪

Glass: Martini
Garnish: Orange zest twist
Method: STIR all ingredients with ice and strain into chilled glass.

1	shot	Old Tom gin
1	shot	Cognac VSOP
1	shot	Martini Rosso sweet vermouth
¼	shot	Grand Marnier liqueur
1	dash	Orange bitters

We say: A brandy influenced wet, sweet Martini with a hint of orange.
Origin: First published in A. S. Crockett's 1935 '*The Old Waldorf-Astoria Bar Book*'. The name may be a reference to the '&' in Martini & Rossi, likely the brand of vermouth originally used.

AMSTERDAM COCKTAIL

★★★★☆

Glass: Martini
Garnish: Orange zest twist
Method: Shake all ingredients with ice and fine strain into chilled glass.

2	shots	Bols Genever
1	shot	Triple Sec
1	shot	Freshly squeezed orange juice
3	dashes	Orange bitters

We say: Very orange, dry but wonderfully smooth.
Origin: Adapted from Victor Bergeron's '*Trader Vic's Bartender's Guide*' (1972 revised edition).

THE ANCIENT DAIQUIRI

★★★☆☆

Glass: Martini
Garnish: None
Method: SHAKE all ingredients with ice and fine strain into chilled glass.

1	shot	Bacardi Superior rum
½	shot	Drambuie
½	shot	Chartreuse Green liqueur
¾	shot	Freshly squeezed lime juice
¼	shot	Monin Vanilla sugar syrup

We say: Herbal liqueurs heavily influence this Daiquiri twist.
Origin: Created in 2008 by Lewis Jaffrey, Drambuie's Global Brand Ambassador and according to Lewis it is so named due to the ingredients having a combined age over 650 years

AÑEJO HIGHBALL

★★★★☆

Glass: Collins
Garnish: Orange & lime slices
Method: SHAKE first four ingredients with ice and strain into ice-filled glass.

2	shots	Bacardi 8yo aged rum
1	shot	Curaçao orange liqueur
1	shot	Freshly squeezed lime juice
1	dash	Angostura aromatic bitters
Top up with		Ginger beer

We say: Orange and rum with a hint of ginger spice. Long and thirst-quenching.
Origin: Created in the late 1990s by Dale DeGroff, New York City, USA.

AÑEJO MANHATTAN

★★★½☆

Glass: Martini
Garnish: Salami wrapped cherry on a pick
Method: STIR all ingredients with ice and strain glass.

2	shots	Tequila 100% Agave
½	shot	Martini Rosso sweet vermouth
¼	shot	Cuarenta y Tres (Licor 43) liqueur
1	dash	Angostura aromatic bitters
1	dash	Orange bitters

We say: Tequila dominates this dry, serious Manhattan-like cocktail
Origin: Created by Ryan Magarian, Seattle, USA.

ANGEL FACE

★★★★½

Glass: Martini
Garnish: Apple wedge
Method: SHAKE all ingredients with ice and fine strain into a chilled glass.

1	shot	Tanqueray London dry gin
1	shot	Calvados/Applejack brandy
1	shot	De Kuyper Apricot Brandy liqueur

We say: Rich apricot and apple with a backbone of botanical gin. Balanced rather than dry or sweet.
Origin: Adapted from Harry Craddock's 1930 'The Savoy Cocktail Book'.

ANGEL JUICE

★★★½☆

Glass: Martini
Garnish: Apple fan
Method: DRY SHAKE (without ice) all ingredients to emulsify. Add ice, SHAKE again and fine strain into glass.

1	shot	Pear flavoured vodka
½	shot	St-Germain elderflower liqueur
½	shot	Sauvignon blanc wine
½	shot	Pressed apple juice
¼	shot	Monin Pure Cane 2:1 sugar syrup
½	shot	Freshly squeezed lime juice
½	fresh	Egg white

We say: Pear and elderflower lead this fruity drink.
Origin: Created in 2008 by Jay Decker at Paramount, London, England.

ANGEL'S DRAFT NEW

★★★★½

Glass: Coupette
Garnish: Grapefruit zest twist (discarded) & mint leaf
Method: DRY SHAKE all ingredients (without ice), SHAKE again with ice and fine strain into chilled glass.

1½	shots	Bacardi Superior rum
¼	shot	Chartreuse Yellow liqueur
½	shot	Freshly squeezed lime juice
¼	shot	Agave nectar
1	dash	Grapefruit bitters
3	fresh	Mint leaves
¼	fresh	Egg white

We say: A refreshing, minty, light cocktail with herbal complexity.
Origin: Adapted from the Bacardi legacy UK winning drink of 2010 by Matthew Dakers. He created this drink in 2009 at The Hoxton Pony, London, England.

ANGEL'S SHARE #1

★★★★½

Glass: Martini
Garnish: Orange zest twist
Method: STIR heaped spoon if orange marmalade with cognac in base of shaker until marmalade dissolves. Add other ingredients, SHAKE with ice and fine strain into chilled glass.

1	spoon	Orange marmalade
2	shots	Cognac VSOP
¼	shot	Cuarenta y Tres (Licor 43) liqueur
½	shot	Freshly squeezed lemon juice
¼	shot	Monin Pure Cane 2:1 sugar syrup

We say: Tangy citrus fruit and cognac smoothed with a hint of vanilla.
Origin: Created in 2005 by Milo Rodriguez, London.

ANGEL'S SHARE #2

★★★★½

Glass: Snifter
Garnish: None
Method: POUR the Chartreuse into glass and coat the inside of the glass with the liqueur by tilting and rotating it. DISCARD excess liqueur. Carefully set the liqueur on the inside of the glass alight and allow it to BURN for a few seconds. Extinguish flame by placing a saucer over the glass, add other ingredients and SWIRL to mix. Beware of hot glass rim.

¼	shot	Chartreuse Green liqueur
1½	shots	Cognac VSOP
¾	shot	Nocello walnut liqueur
½	shot	Warre's Otima tawny port

We say: A fabulous drink, especially when VEP Chartreuse, family reserve cognac and 20 year old tawny port are used as per the original Starlight Room recipe.
Origin: Adapted from a recipe created in 2005 by Jacques Bezuidenhout at Harry Denton's Starlight Room, San Francisco, USA.

ANIS'TINI

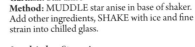

★★★★☆

Glass: Martini
Garnish: Star anise
Method: MUDDLE star anise in base of shaker. Add other ingredients, SHAKE with ice and fine strain into chilled glass.

2	dried	Star anise
1	shot	Ketel One vodka
¾	shot	Opal Nera black sambuca
½	shot	Pernod anise
1½	shots	Chilled mineral water

We say: Specs of star anise are evident in this aniseedy Martini.
Origin: Discovered in 2002 at Lot 61, New York City, USA

THE ANIS-THETIC NEW

★★★★½☆

Glass: Old-fashioned
Garnish: Mint sprig & absinthe mist from atomiser
Method: SHAKE all ingredients and fine strain into an empty chilled glass.

12	fresh	Mint leaves
2	shots	Maker's Mark bourbon
¼	shot	Giffard Menthe Pastille liqueur
¼	shot	Bénédictine D.O.M.
⅛	shot	Marie Brizard anisette liqueur
⅛	shot	Monin Pure Cane 2:1 sugar syrup
3	dashes	Angostura aromatic bitters
3	dashes	Peychaud's aromatic bitters
¼	shot	Chilled mineral water

We say: As the name suggests, this bourbon-based drink is fresh breath-tastic.
Origin: Adapted from a drink created in 2009 by Danny Murphy at the Met Bar, London, England. Originally made with homemade anis syrup and without crème de menthe.

ANITA'S ATTITUDE ADJUSTER ⚷

★★★☆☆

Glass: Sling
Garnish: Lemon slice & cherry on stick (sail)
Method: SHAKE first seven ingredients with ice and strain into ice-filled glass. TOP with champagne and gently stir.

½	shot	Triple Sec
½	shot	Tequila 100% Agave
½	shot	Bacardi Superior rum
½	shot	Tanqueray London dry gin
½	shot	Ketel One vodka
½	shot	Freshly squeezed lime juice
½	shot	Monin Pure Cane 2:1 sugar syrup
Top up with		Brut champagne

We say: Anita has a problem - she's indecisive when it comes to choosing base spirits.

THE ANSONIA NEW

★★★★☆

Glass: Coupette
Garnish: Maraschino cherry
Method: STIR all ingredients with ice and strain into chilled glass.

2	shots	Dewar's White Label Scotch
½	shot	Martini Rosso sweet vermouth
¼	shot	Luxardo maraschino liqueur
⅛	shot	La Fée Parisienne (68%) absinthe

We say: Scotch with delicate notes of sweet vermouth, maraschino and absinthe. Subtle and refined.
Origin: Adapted from a recipe by Charles Christopher in his 1934 Pioneers of Mixing at Elite Bars and named after a luxurious residential hotel on Manhattan's Upper West Side. The Ansonia was built in 1904 and was the permanent home of the rich and famous including baseball player Babe Ruth, composer Igor Stravinsky, writer Theodore Dreiser and operatic tenor Enrico Caruso. The first air-conditioned hotel in New York, the hotel's opulence was legendary and included a lobby pool and fountain which was home to a family of live seals.

The original recipe called for dashes of Ojen bitters rather than absinthe. However, absinthe was banned in the USA at the time and Ojen was a Spanish brand of absinthe, so this was a way to communicate use of absinthe to other bartenders without highlighting the fact to authorities.

ANTE

★★★★☆

Glass: Martini
Garnish: Orange zest twist
Method: STIR all ingredients with ice and strain glass.

2	shots	Calvados/Applejack brandy
½	shot	Triple Sec
1	shot	Dubonnet Red (French made)
2	dashes	Angostura aromatic bitters

We say: Medium dry, complex spiced apple with hints of orange.
Origin: Recipe adapted from one discovered in 2006 on drinkboy.com

APACHE

★★★☆☆

Glass: Shot
Garnish: None
Method: Refrigerate ingredients then LAYER in chilled glass by carefully pouring in the following order.

¾	shot	Kahlúa coffee liqueur
½	shot	Midori green melon liqueur
½	shot	Baileys Irish cream liqueur

AKA: Quick F.U.
We say: A coffee, melon and whiskey cream layered shot.

APEROL SPIRTZ NEW

★★★★½

Glass: Old-fashioned
Garnish: Orange slice
Method: POUR ingredients into ice-filled glass in the following order and lightly stir.

3	shots	Soave wine
2	shots	Aperol
Top up with		Soda (club soda)

Variant: Sometimes Prosecco is substituted for the wine and soda water.
We say: Slightly sweetened, herbal flavoured and diluted wine. Those of you with a sweet tooth may like to try equal parts wine and Aperol with a splash of soda. Surprisingly it's the wine that dries this drink. Aperol is relatively sweet – it may be red but it's not Campari.
Origin: Popular in northern Italy, especially in Venice and the Veneto region where it is pronounced "Spriss". (From the German verb Spritzen, meaning spray or splash). This aperitif cocktail's origins date back to the end of the 19th century when Venice was still part of the Austrian Empire, and is based on the Austrian Spritzer, a combination of equal parts white wine and soda water. It is made with the traditional white wines of the Veneto region, Pinot Grigio or Soave and sometimes with Prosecco.

APHRODISIAC

★★★☆☆

Glass: Collins
Garnish: Apple slice
Method: MUDDLE ginger in base of shaker. Add other ingredients, SHAKE with ice and fine strain into ice-filled glass.

2	slices	Fresh root ginger (thumbnail sized)
2	shots	Vanilla-infused Ketel One vodka
½	shot	Chartreuse Green liqueur
2½	shots	Pressed apple juice
1½	shots	Sauvignon blanc wine

We say: As strong in flavour as it is high in alcohol.
Origin: Created in 2002 by Yannick Miseriaux at The Fifth Floor Bar, London, England.

APPILY MARRIED

★★★★⯪

Glass: Martini
Garnish: Cinnamon & sugar rim
Method: STIR honey with vodka in base of shaker until honey dissolves. Add apple juice, SHAKE with ice and fine strain into chilled glass.

2	spoons	Runny honey
2½	shots	Ketel One vodka
½	shot	Pressed apple juice

We say: Apple and honey are indeed a marriage made in heaven, especially when laced with grainy vodka notes.
Origin: Created in 2005 by Simon Difford.

APPLE & BLACKBERRY PIE

★★★⯪☆

Glass: Martini
Garnish: Dust with cinnamon powder & blackberry
Method: MUDDLE blackberries in base of shaker. Add vodka and apple juice, SHAKE all ingredients with ice and fine strain into chilled glass. FLOAT cream on the surface of the drink by pouring over the back of a spoon and swirl to form a thin layer. Depending on the sweetness of your blackberries, you may need to add a touch of sugar syrup.

7	fresh	Blackberries
2	shots	Ketel One vodka
1	shot	Pressed apple juice
Float		Double (heavy) cream

We say: A dessert in a glass, but not too sweet.
Origin: Created in 2005 by Simon Difford.

APPLE & CRANBERRY PIE

★★★⯪☆

Glass: Martini
Garnish: Dust with cinnamon powder
Method: SHAKE first three ingredients with ice and fine strain into chilled glass. FLOAT cream on surface of drink by pouring over back of spoon and swirl to form a thin layer.

1½	shots	Ketel One vodka
¾	shot	Berentzen Apple schnapps
1	shot	Ocean Spray cranberry juice
Float		Double (heavy) cream

We say: Sip apple and cranberry through a creamy cinnamon layer.
Origin: Created in 2003 by Simon Difford.

APPLE & CUSTARD COCKTAIL

★★★⯪☆

Glass: Martini
Garnish: Apple wedge
Method: SHAKE all ingredients with ice and fine strain into chilled glass.

2	shots	Advocaat liqueur
1½	shots	Calvados/Applejack brandy
½	shot	Berentzen Apple schnapps
¼	shot	Monin Vanilla sugar syrup

We say: Smooth, creamy and authentically flavoured.
Origin: Created by Simon Difford in 2002 after discovering advocaat on a trip to Amsterdam.

APPLE & ELDERFLOWER COLLINS

★★★★☆

Glass: Collins
Garnish: Lemon slice
Method: SHAKE first 4 ingredients with ice and strain into ice-filled glass. TOP with soda, stir and serve with straws.

1½	shots	Tanqueray London dry gin
1	shot	St~Germain elderflower liqueur
1	shot	Berentzen Apple schnapps
1	shot	Freshly squeezed lime juice
Top up with		Soda (club soda)

We say: A John Collins with lime in place of lemon and sweetened with apple and elderflower liqueurs.
Origin: Formula by Simon Difford in 2004.

APPLE & ELDERFLOWER MARTINI

★★★★☆

Glass: Martini
Garnish: Apple slice
Method: SHAKE all ingredients with ice and fine strain into chilled glass.

1¾	shots	Ketel One vodka
1	shot	St~Germain elderflower liqueur
1¼	shots	Pressed apple juice

We say: Light and easy – apple and elderflower laced with vodka.
Origin: Created in 2006 by Simon Difford.

APPLE & MELON MARTINI

★★★⯪☆

Glass: Martini
Garnish: Apple wedge
Method: SHAKE all ingredients with ice and fine strain into chilled glass.

2	shots	Ketel One vodka
1	shot	Sour apple liqueur
½	shot	Midori green melon liqueur
½	shot	Freshly squeezed lime juice

We say: The ubiquitous Green Apple Martini with extra colour and flavour thanks to a dash of melon liqueur.

APPLE & SPICE

★★★☆☆

Glass: Shot
Garnish: Dust with cinnamon powder
Method: Refrigerate ingredients then LAYER in chilled glass by carefully pouring in the following order.

| ¾ | shot | Calvados/Applejack brandy |
| ¾ | shot | Double (heavy) cream |

We say: A creamy apple shot

APPLE BLOSSOM

★★★☆☆

Glass: Martini
Garnish: Orange zest twist
Method: SHAKE all ingredients with ice and strain into chilled glass.

2	shots	Tanqueray London dry gin
¼	shot	Boulard Grand Solage calvados
1	shot	Freshly squeezed orange juice
⅛	shot	Monin Pure Cane 2:1 sugar syrup
⅛	shot	Chilled mineral water

We say: A Gin & Juice with a little extra interest courtesy of a dash of apple brandy. I've added the merest hint of sugar to lift Buckby's rather flat original recipe.
Origin: In W.J. Tarling's 1937 '*Café Royal Cocktail Book*' the invention of this cocktail is credited to one R.G. Buckby.

APPLE BLOSSOM COCKTAIL

★★★★½

Glass: Martini
Garnish: Apple wedge
Method: SHAKE all ingredients with ice and fine strain into chilled glass.

2	shots	Boulard Grand Solage calvados
2	shots	Martini Rosso sweet vermouth

We say: Stupidly simple to mix but complex to taste - spiced and concentrated apple.
Origin: Adapted from Victor Bergeron's '*Trader Vic's Bartender's Guide*' (1972 revised edition).

APPLE BRANDY SOUR

★★★★½

Glass: Old-fashioned
Garnish: Lemon slice & cherry on stick (sail)
Method: DRY SHAKE (without ice) all ingredients to emulsify. Add ice, SHAKE again and strain into ice-filled glass.

2	shots	Boulard Grand Solage calvados
1	shot	Freshly squeezed lemon juice
¾	shot	Monin Pure Cane 2:1 sugar syrup
3	dashes	Angostura aromatic bitters
½	fresh	Egg white

We say: Sour by name - balanced sweet and sour apple by nature.

APPLE BREEZE

★★★★☆

Glass: Collins
Garnish: Apple wedge
Method: SHAKE all ingredients with ice and strain into ice-filled glass.

2	shots	Żubrówka bison vodka
2½	shots	Pressed apple juice
1½	shots	Ocean Spray cranberry juice

We say: A lot more interesting than the better known Sea Breeze.

APPLE BUCK

★★★★☆

Glass: Collins
Garnish: Apple wedge
Method: SHAKE first four ingredients with ice and strain into ice-filled glass. TOP with ginger ale.

1½	shots	Calvados/Applejack brandy
½	shot	Sour apple liqueur
1	shot	Pressed apple juice
½	shot	Freshly squeezed lime juice
Top up with		Ginger ale

We say: A refreshing long number with a taste reminiscent of cider.
Origin: Adapted from a drink created in 2004 by Wayne Collins.

APPLE CART

★★★★☆

Glass: Martini
Garnish: Apple wedge
Method: SHAKE all ingredients with ice and fine strain into chilled glass.

1½	shots	Calvados/Applejack brandy
1	shot	Triple Sec
1	shot	Freshly squeezed lemon juice
½	shot	Chilled mineral water

AKA: Calvados Sidecar
Variant: Deauville
We say: A serious combination of apple with orange and sweet with sour.
Origin: This classic cocktail is an adaptation of the even older Sidecar.

APPLE CRUMBLE MARTINI #1

★★★½☆

Glass: Martini
Garnish: Apple wedge
Method: SHAKE all ingredients with ice and fine strain into chilled glass.

2	shots	Dewar's White label Scotch
¼	shot	Butterscotch schnapps
1	shot	Pressed apple juice
½	shot	Freshly squeezed lemon juice
¼	shot	Monin Pure Cane 2:1 sugar syrup

We say: That's the way the apple crumbles - in this case enhancing the flavour of the Scotch.

APPLE CRUMBLE MARTINI #2

★★★★☆

Glass: Martini
Garnish: Dust with cinnamon powder
Method: SHAKE all ingredients with ice and fine strain into chilled glass.

2	shots	Tuaca liqueur
½	shot	Freshly squeezed lemon juice
2	shots	Pressed apple juice

We say: Easy to make and equally easy to drink.
Origin: Created in 2002 by Eion Richards at Bond's Bar, London, England.

APPLE DAIQUIRI

★★★★☆

Glass: Martini
Garnish: Apple wedge
Method: SHAKE all ingredients with ice and fine strain into chilled glass.

2	shots	Bacardi Superior rum
1½	shots	Pressed apple juice
½	shot	Freshly squeezed lime juice
¼	shot	Monin Pure Cane 2:1 sugar syrup

We say: A classic Daiquiri with a very subtle hint of apple.
Origin: Formula by Simon Difford in 2004.

APPLE FOOL

★★★★☆

Glass: Coupette
Garnish: Apple slice
Method: Shake all ingredients with ice and fine strain into chilled glass.

5	fresh	Basil leaves
1½	shots	Tequila 100% Agave (blanco)
½	shot	Green Chartruese liqueur
1	shot	Squeezed red grapefruit juice
¾	shot	Freshly squeezed lime juice
½	shot	Monin Pure Cane 2:1 sugar syrup

We say: This drink looks like it is going to be good for you and it sure tastes good - fresh and enlivening.
Origin: Adapted from a drink created by Aisha Sharpe, New York City, USA

APPLE MAC

★★★★☆

Glass: Martini
Garnish: Apple slice
Method: SHAKE all ingredients with ice and fine strain into chilled glass.

2	shots	Dewar's White label Scotch
1½	shots	Pressed apple juice
½	shot	Stone's green ginger wine

Variant: Also suits being served over ice in an old-fashioned glass.
We say: Scotch, ginger and apple are a threesome made in heaven.
Origin: A twist on the classic Whisky Mac created in 2004 by Simon Difford.

APPLE MANHATTAN #1

★★★★☆

Glass: Martini
Garnish: Apple wedge
Method: SHAKE all ingredients with ice and fine strain into chilled glass.

2	shots	Maker's Mark bourbon
1½	shots	Berentzen Apple schnapps
½	shot	Martini Rosso sweet vermouth

We say: Rusty gold in colour, this is a flavoursome number for bourbon lovers.
Origin: My take on a drink created by David Marsden at First on First in New York City and latterly popularised by Dale DeGroff. Traditionalists may want to stir it.

APPLE MANHATTAN #2

★★★★☆

Glass: Martini
Garnish: Apple wedge
Method: STIR all ingredients with ice and strain into chilled glass.

2	shots	Maker's Mark bourbon
¾	shot	Berentzen Apple schnapps
¼	shot	Triple Sec
½	shot	Martini Rosso sweet vermouth

We say: Exactly as billed - a Manhattan with a hint of apple.
Origin: Created in Sweden by Asa Nevestveit and Robert Sorman at Grill, Stockholm, Sweden.

APPLE MARTINI # 2

★★★★☆

Glass: Martini
Garnish: Apple wedge
Method: SHAKE all ingredients with ice and fine strain into chilled glass.

1½	shots	Ketel One vodka
1	shot	Berentzen Apple schnapps
2	shots	Pressed apple juice

We say: There are as many different recipes for this drink as there are varieties of apple and brands of apple liqueur: this one was popular in the UK during the Noughties.

APPLE MARTINI #1 (SIMPLE VERSION)

★★★★☆

Glass: Martini
Garnish: Maraschino cherry
Method: SHAKE all ingredients with ice and fine strain into chilled glass.

2	shots	Ketel One vodka
2	shots	Pressed apple juice
¼	shot	Monin Pure Cane 2:1 sugar syrup

Variant: Sour Apple Martini, Caramelised Apple Martini
We say: This is subtitled the simple version for good reason but, if freshly pressed juice is used, it's as good if not better than other Apple Martini recipes.
Origin: Formula by Simon Difford in 2004.

APPLE MARTINI #3 (IBA SPEC)

★★★☆☆

Glass: Martini
Garnish: Apple slice
Method: STIR all ingredients with ice and fine strain into chilled glass.

2	shots	Ketel One vodka
¾	shot	Berentzen Apple schnapps
¾	shot	Triple Sec

We say: Not really a Martini and not really much good.
Origin: This recipe is formulated according to International Bartender's Association 2008 proportions.

APPLE MOJITO

★★★★☆

Glass: Collins
Garnish: Mint sprig
Method: Lightly MUDDLE (just to bruise) mint in base of glass. Add other ingredients, half fill glass with crushed ice and CHURN (stir) with bar spoon. Fill glass to brim with more crushed ice and CHURN some more. Serve with straws.

12	fresh	Mint leaves
2	shots	Bacardi Superior rum
1	shot	Berentzen Apple schnapps
1	shot	Freshly squeezed lime juice

We say: An enduring classic given a touch of apple. Those with a sweet tooth may want to add more apple liqueur or even a dash of sugar syrup.
Origin: Recipe by Simon Difford in 2005.

APPLE OF ONE'S EYE

★★★☆☆

Glass: Collins
Garnish: Apple wedge
Method: SHAKE first three ingredients with ice and strain into ice-filled glass. TOP with ginger beer.

2	shots	Cognac VSOP
½	shot	Freshly squeezed lime juice
1½	shots	Pressed apple juice
Top up with		Ginger beer

We say: This spicy concoction is long and refreshing.

THE APPLE ONE

★★★★☆

Glass: Collins
Garnish: Apple slice & mint leaf
Method: SHAKE all ingredients with ice and fine strain into glass filled with crushed ice.

2	shots	Maker's Mark bourbon
¾	shot	St~Germain elderflower liqueur
¾	shot	Pressed apple juice
½	shot	Freshly squeezed lime juice

We say: Whiskey, elderflower and apple with a refreshing burst of citrus.
Origin: Adapted from a recipe created in 2008 by Vincenzo Marianella at Doheny, Los Angeles, USA.

APPLE PIE MARTINI

★★★★☆

Glass: Martini
Garnish: Apple wedge
Method: SHAKE all ingredients with ice and fine strain into chilled glass.

1½	shots	Żubrówka bison vodka
½	shot	Goldschläger cinnamon schnapps
2	shots	Pressed apple juice
1	shot	Ocean Spray cranberry juice

We say: There's a good hit of cinnamon in this apple pie.
Origin: Created in 2000 by Alexia Pau Barrera at Sand Bar, Clapham, England.

APPLE PIE SHOT

★★★⯪☆

Glass: Shot
Garnish: Dust with cinnamon powder
Method: SHAKE first two ingredients with ice and strain into chilled glass. FLOAT cream on drink by carefully pouring over the back of a spoon.

1	shot	Berentzen Apple schnapps
½	shot	Hazelnut liqueur
¼	shot	Double (heavy) cream

We say: Nuts, apple, cinnamon and cream - pudding, anyone?

APPLE SPRITZ

★★★★☆

Glass: Flute
Garnish: Peach slice
Method: POUR first two ingredients into glass and TOP with champagne.

¾	shot	Berentzen Apple schnapps
¼	shot	Peachtree peach schnapps
Top up with		Brut champagne

We say: Sweet, fruity champagne – oh yeah, baby.
Origin: Discovered in 2003 at Paramount Hotel, New York City, USA.

APPLE STRUDEL #1

★★★☆☆

Glass: Martini
Garnish: Dust with cinnamon powder
Method: SHAKE first 5 ingredients with ice and fine strain into chilled glass. Carefully FLOAT cream by pouring over the back of a spoon.

1	shot	Berentzen Apple schnapps
½	shot	Bols Cacao Brown
½	shot	Bols Cacao White
½	shot	Goldschläger cinnamon schnapps
1	shot	Pressed apple juice
¾	shot	Double (heavy) cream

Variant: May also be served as a shot.
We say: This sweet dessert cocktail tastes just like mum's home-made apple pie with cream.
Origin: Created in 1999 by Alex Kammerling, London, England.

APPLE STRUDEL #2

Glass: Martini
Garnish: Cinnamon & sugar rim
Method: SHAKE all ingredients with ice and fine strain into chilled glass.

1½	shots	Ketel One vodka
½	shot	Dewar's White label Scotch
½	shot	Berentzen Apple schnapps
½	shot	Martini Extra Dry vermouth
1	shot	Pressed apple juice

We say: Apple, vanilla and a hint of Scotch – reminiscent of the dessert but a good deal drier.
Origin: Recipe by Simon Difford in 2006.

APPLE SUNRISE

Glass: Collins
Garnish: Apple slice
Method: SHAKE all ingredients with ice and strain into ice-filled glass.

2	shots	Calvados/Applejack brandy
3½	shots	Freshly squeezed orange juice
½	shot	Crème de cassis liqueur

We say: A pleasing blend of fruits with the apple punch of Calvados.
Origin: Created in 1980 by Charles Schumann, Munich, Germany.

APPLE VIRGIN MOJITO (MOCKTAIL)

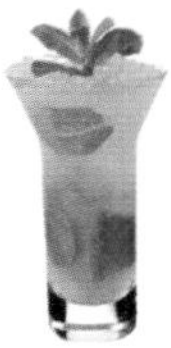

Glass: Collins
Garnish: Mint sprig
Method: PLACE mint, lemon, lime and sugar in glass. Half fill glass with crushed ice and CHURN (stir). Add more crushed ice to fill glass. Add apple juice, top with soda and CHURN some more. Serve with straws.

12	fresh	Mint leaves
½	shot	Freshly squeezed lemon juice
½	shot	Freshly squeezed lime juice
¾	shot	Monin Pure Cane 2:1 sugar syrup
3	shots	Pressed apple juice
Top up with		Soda (club soda)

We say: A very refreshing driver's option.
Origin: Created in 2002 by Tony Conigliaro at Isola, London, England.

APPLE, CUCUMBER & ELDERFLOWER CUP

Glass: Martini
Garnish: Cucumber slices
Method: MUDDLE cucumber in base of shaker. Add other ingredients, SHAKE with ice and fine strain into chilled glass.

1	inch	Cucumber (chopped & peeled)
2	shots	Żubrówka bison vodka
½	shot	St~Germain elderflower liqueur
½	shot	Pressed apple juice

We say: Apple and Żubrówka is a magic combination, as is and apple and elderflower. Here these flavoursome blends are enhanced and freshened by cucumber.
Origin: Discovered in 2007 at Public Restaurant, New York City, USA.

APPLEISSIMO

Glass: Collins
Garnish: Apple slice
Method: SHAKE first three ingredients with ice and strain into ice-filled glass. TOP with anis and serve with straws.

1½	shots	Berentzen Apple schnapps
2	shots	Pressed apple juice
1½	shots	Ocean Spray cranberry juice
1½	shots	Pernod anise

We say: Stir the anis in with straws before drinking. Anis is best added last as it reacts on contact with ice

APPLEJACK RABBIT #2 UPDATED

Glass: Jam jar
Garnish: Cinnamon stick & dust with freshly grated cinnamon
Method: SHAKE all ingredients with ice and strain into ice-filled jar.

1½	shots	Laird's Applejack brandy
½	shot	Maple syrup
1	shot	Freshly squeezed orange juice
¾	shot	Freshly squeezed lemon juice

We say: Apple brandy sweetened by maple syrup, soured by lemon and lengthened with orange.
Origin: This on the rocks and jarred version of the Savoy book's classic is adapted from a drink discovered in 2009 by Dino Koletsas at Bourne & Hollingsworth, London, England.

APPLEJACK RABBIT COCKTAIL NEW

Glass: Coupette
Garnish: Lemon zest twist
Method: SHAKE all ingredients with ice and fine strain into chilled glass.

1¾	shots	Calvados/Applejack brandy
¼	shot	Maple syrup
¾	shot	Freshly squeezed orange juice
½	shot	Freshly squeezed lemon juice

We say: Stewed apple with citrus and a faint toffee apple finish.
Origin: This drink is usually credited to Harry Craddock's 1930 'The Savoy Cocktail Book' which specifies: one hooker of applejack, the juice of one lemon, the juice of one orange and one hooker of maple syrup. In his 1948 'Fine Art of Mixing Drinks', David A. Embury writes, "This drink is also sometimes, for no reason at all, called the Applejack Dynamite. The same cocktail made with a gin base plus a dash of Angostura is called the Old Vermont." Incidentally, Embury's recipe is: 6 part applejack (1 ½ shots), 1 part lemon juice (¼ shot), 1 part orange juice (¼ shot) and 1 part maple syrup (¼ shot).

APPLES 'N' PEARS

★★★★☆

Glass: Martini
Garnish: Apple or pear slice
Method: SHAKE all ingredients with ice and fine strain into chilled glass.

1	shot	Ketel One vodka
1	shot	Calvados/Applejack brandy
¾	shot	Belle de Brillet pear liqueur
1½	shots	Pressed apple juice

We say: 'Apples and pears' means stairs in cockney rhyming slang. Well worth climbing.
Origin: Created in 2005 by Simon Difford.

APPLESINTH

★★★★☆

Glass: Old-fashioned
Garnish: Apple wedge
Method: SHAKE all ingredients with ice and strain into glass filled with crushed ice.

1	shot	Absinthe
1	shot	Berentzen Apple schnapps
2	shots	Pressed apple juice
¾	shot	Freshly squeezed lime juice
½	shot	Monin Pure Cane 2:1 sugar syrup

We say: Hints of apple and liquorice combine to make a very moreish cocktail.
Origin: Created in 1999 by Alex Kammerling, London, England.

APRICOT COSMO

★★★★½

Glass: Martini
Garnish: Apricot slice
Method: STIR apricot preserve with vodka until preserve dissolves. Add other ingredients, SHAKE with ice and fine strain into chilled glass.

2	shots	Ketel One vodka
1	spoon	Apricot jam (preserve)
1	shot	Ocean Spray cranberry juice
¼	shot	Monin Pure Cane 2:1 sugar syrup
½	shot	Freshly squeezed lime juice
2	dashes	Orange bitters

We say: The apricot preserve adds a flavoursome tang to the contemporary classic.
Origin: Created in 2004 at Aura Kitchen & Bar, London, England.

APRICOT FIZZ

★★★½☆

Glass: Collins
Garnish: Lemon wedge
Method: SHAKE first three ingredients with ice and strain into ice-filled glass. TOP with soda water.

2	shots	De Kuyper Apricot Brandy liqueur
1	shot	Freshly squeezed orange juice
½	shot	Freshly squeezed lime juice
Top up with		Soda from siphon

We say: This low-alcohol, refreshing cocktail is perfect for a summer afternoon.

APRICOT LADY SOUR

★★★½☆

Glass: Old-fashioned
Garnish: Lemon slice & cherry on stick (sail)
Method: DRY SHAKE (without ice) all ingredients to emulsify. Add ice, SHAKE again and strain into ice-filled glass.

1½	shots	Rum light white/blanco
1	shot	De Kuyper apricot brandy liqueur
1	shot	Freshly squeezed lemon juice
¼	shot	Monin Pure Cane 2:1 sugar syrup
½	fresh	Egg white

We say: This seemingly soft and fluffy, apricot flavoured drink hides a most unladylike rum bite.

APRICOT MANGO MARTINI

★★★★☆

Glass: Martini
Garnish: Mango slice
Method: MUDDLE mango in base of shaker. Add other ingredients, SHAKE with ice and fine strain into glass.

1	cupful	Fresh diced mango
2	shots	Tanqueray London dry gin
1	shot	De Kuyper Apricot Brandy liqueur
¾	shot	Freshly squeezed lemon juice
½	shot	Monin Pure Cane 2:1 sugar syrup

Variant: Use one-and-a-half shots of Boiron mango purée in place of fresh mango and halve amount of sugar syrup.
We say: A simple, great tasting variation on the fresh fruit Martini.

APRICOT MARTINI

★★★☆☆

Glass: Martini
Garnish: Lemon zest twist
Method: SHAKE all ingredients with ice and fine strain into chilled glass.

1½	shots	Tanqueray London dry gin
1	shot	De Kuyper Apricot Brandy liqueur
⅛	shot	Pomegranate (grenadine) syrup
¼	shot	Freshly squeezed lemon juice
3	dashes	Angostura aromatic bitters
¾	shot	Chilled mineral water

We say: This scarlet cocktail combines gin, apricot and lemon juice.

APRICOT RICKEY

★★★★☆

Glass: Collins (small 8oz)
Garnish: Length of lime peel
Method: SHAKE first three ingredients with ice and strain into ice-filled glass. TOP with soda.

1	shot	Tanqueray London dry gin
1	shot	De Kuyper Apricot Brandy liqueur
½	shot	Freshly squeezed lime juice
Top up with		Soda (club soda)

We say: Light, fruity and refreshing, if a little on the sweet side.

APRICOT SOUR

★★★★☆

Glass: Old-fashioned
Garnish: Lemon zest twist
Method: STIR apricot jam (preserve) with bourbon until it dissolves. Add other ingredients, SHAKE with ice and fine strain into ice-filled glass.

2	spoons	Apricot jam (preserve)
1½	shots	Maker's Mark bourbon
½	shot	De Kuyper Apricot Brandy liqueur
1	shot	Pressed apple juice
½	shot	Freshly squeezed lemon juice

We say: Short and fruity.
Origin: Created in 2005 by Wayne Collins for Maxxium UK.

APRIL SHOWER

★★★★☆

Glass: Martini
Garnish: Orange zest twist
Method: SHAKE all ingredients with ice and fine strain into chilled glass.

2	shots	Cognac VSOP
½	shot	Bénédictine D.O.M.
1½	shots	Freshly squeezed orange juice

We say: This mustard coloured, medium dry, cognac-based drink harnesses the uniquely herbal edge of Bénédictine.

AQUARIUS

★★★★⯪☆

Glass: Old-fashioned
Garnish: Lemon slice & cherry sail
Method: SHAKE all ingredients with ice and strain into ice-filled glass.

2	shots	Dewar's White label Scotch
1	shot	De Kuyper Cherry Brandy liqueur
1½	shots	Ocean Spray cranberry juice

We say: A sweet cherry edge is balanced by the dryness of cranberry and Scotch.

ARBUZ

★★★☆☆

Glass: Martini
Garnish: Watermelon wedge
Method: MUDDLE watermelon and lemon grass in base of shaker. Add other ingredients, SHAKE with ice and fine strain into chilled glass.

⅛	fresh	Fresh watermelon
1	inch	Lemongrass stem (chopped)
1½	shots	Żubrówka bison vodka
½	shot	Triple Sec
¼	shot	Pressed apple juice

We say: Summery watermelon with herbal grassy notes.
Origin: Created in 2008 by Andreas Cortes at Maze bar & Restaurant, London, England.

ARCHIBALD PERISCOPE NEW

★★★★☆

Glass: Collins
Garnish: Long bendy straw
Method: SHAKE first three ingredients with ice and fine strain into chilled glass. TOP with soda and then carefully FLOAT Rioja wine.

2	shots	Tanqueray London dry gin
1	shot	Peach Tree peach schnapps
¾	shot	Sauvignon blanc wine
¾	shot	Chilled mineral water
½	shot	Rioja Red Wine

We say: Slightly sweet, long and refreshing. To quote the menu at Albert & Pearl where we discovered this cocktail, "a sight for sore eyes".
Origin: Adapted (considerably) from a drink discovered in 2009 at Albert & Pearl, Islington, London, England.

ARGENTINA COCKTAIL

★★★★☆

Glass: Martini
Garnish: Orange zest twist
Method: STIR all ingredients with ice and strain into chilled glass.

1	shot	Tanqueray London dry gin
1	shot	Martini Extra Dry vermouth
¼	shot	Triple Sec
¼	shot	Bénédictine D.O.M.
1	dash	Orange bitters
1	dash	Angostura aromatic bitters

We say: A wet martini softened by liqueur and given a hint of citrus and spice.

ARGHA NOAH

★★★★☆

Glass: Old-fashioned
Garnish: Orange zest twist
Method: STIR all ingredients with ice and strain into ice-filled glass.

2	shots	Bacardi 8yo aged rum
⅛	shot	Monin Honey syrup
¼	shot	Drambuie
⅛	shot	Matusalem Oloroso sherry
½	shot	Ocean Spray cranberry juice

We say: Delicately spiced, honeyed and sherried aged rum.
Origin: Created in January 2009 by Simon Difford at the Cabinet Room, London, England.

THE ARGYLL

★★★☆☆

Glass: Martini
Garnish: Orange zest twist
Method: STIR all ingredients with ice and strain into chilled glass.

2	shots	Southern Comfort liqueur
1	shot	Martini Rosso sweet vermouth
1	dash	Orange bitters

We say: Southern Comfort lovers only need apply.

ARIZONA BREEZE

★★★★☆

Glass: Collins
Garnish: Grapefruit wedge
Method: SHAKE all ingredients with ice and strain into ice-filled glass.

2½	shots	Tanqueray London dry gin
3	shots	Ocean Spray cranberry juice
2	shots	Freshly squeezed grapefruit juice

We say: A tart variation on the Sea Breeze – as dry as Arizona.

ARMILLITA CHICO

★★★☆☆

Glass: Martini (large 10oz)
Garnish: Lime wedge
Method: BLEND all ingredients with 12oz scoop crushed ice.

2	shots	Tequila 100% Agave
1	shot	Freshly squeezed lime juice
½	shot	Pomegranate (grenadine) syrup
2	dashes	Orange flower water

We say: Similar to a frozen Margarita but more subtle and dry.

ARMY & NAVY

★★★★☆

Glass: Martini
Garnish: Lemon zest twist
Method: SHAKE all ingredients with ice and fine strain into chilled glass.

2	shots	Tanqueray London dry gin
½	shot	Freshly squeezed lemon juice
¼	shot	Monin Almond (orgeat) syrup
½	shot	Chilled mineral water

We say: Almond and lemon flavoured gin. Subtle, citrusy and dry.
Origin: This old classic was originally made to an 8:4:4 formula but we have borrowed this 8:2:1 formula from David A. Embury's 1948 'Fine Art of Mixing Drinks' (he describes the original formulation as "horrible"). The addition of water is a Difford touch.

ARMY MARTINI

★★★★☆

Glass: Martini
Garnish: Mint leaf
Method: SHAKE all ingredients with ice and fine strain into chilled glass.

2½	shots	Tanqueray London dry gin
¼	shot	Martini Rosso sweet vermouth
¼	shot	Pomegranate (grenadine) syrup

Variant: Served 'dry' without the grenadine.
We say: This rosé Martini is harder than it looks - perhaps why the name?

ARNAUD MARTINI

★★★★☆

Glass: Martini
Garnish: Blackberries
Method: STIR all ingredients with ice and strain into chilled glass.

1	shot	Tanqueray London dry gin
1	shot	Martini Extra Dry vermouth
1	shot	Crème de cassis liqueur

We say: An interesting balance of blackcurrant, vermouth and gin. Sweet palate and dry finish.
Origin: A classic cocktail named after the pre-war stage actress Yvonne Arnaud.

ARNOLD PALMER (MOCKTAIL)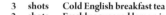

★★★★☆

Glass: Collins
Garnish: Lemon slice
Method: SHAKE all ingredients with ice and strain into ice-filled glass.

3	shots	Cold English breakfast tea
2	shots	Freshly squeezed lemon juice
1	shot	Monin Pure Cane 2:1 sugar syrup

Variant: Tom Arnold, John Daly
We say: Real lemon iced tea. Balanced and wonderfully refreshing.
Origin: A popular drink throughout the United States. Named after and said to be a favourite of the legendary golfer.

ARTLANTIC

★★★☆☆

Glass: Collins
Garnish: Orange wedge
Method: SHAKE all ingredients with ice and strain into ice-filled glass.

1	shot	Spiced rum
½	shot	Amaretto liqueur
½	shot	Bols Blue Curaçao liqueur
½	shot	Freshly squeezed lime juice
3	shots	Pressed apple juice

We say: This sea green cocktail tastes much better than it looks.
Origin: Atlantic Bar & Grill, London, England.

ASIAN GINGER MARTINI

★★★★☆

Glass: Martini
Garnish: Fresh ginger slice
Method: MUDDLE ginger in base of shaker. Add other ingredients, SHAKE with ice and fine strain into chilled glass.

2	slices	Fresh root ginger (thumbnail sized)
2¼	shots	Sake
1½	shots	Ketel One vodka
¼	shot	Monin Pure Cane 2:1 sugar syrup

We say: Lightly spiced with ginger, distinctly oriental in character.
Origin: Adapted from a recipe created in 2004 by Chris Langan of Barnomadics.

ASIAN MARY

★★★★☆

Glass: Collins
Garnish: Lemongrass
Method: MUDDLE ginger in base of shaker and add vodka. Squeeze wasabi paste onto bar spoon and STIR with vodka and ginger until dissolved. Add other ingredients, SHAKE with ice and fine strain into ice-filled glass.

3	slice	Fresh root ginger (thumbnail sized)
3	pea	Wasabi paste
3	shots	Ketel One Citroen vodka
1	spoon	Soy sauce
½	shot	Freshly squeezed lemon juice
4	shots	Tomato juice

We say: An aptly named Bloody Mary with plenty of Asian spice.

ASIAN PEAR MARTINI

★★★★☆

Glass: Martini
Garnish: Pear slice
Method: SHAKE all ingredients with ice and fine strain into chilled glass.

2	shots	Sake
¼	shot	Belle de Brillet pear liqueur
½	shot	Poire William eau de vie
1½	shots	Pressed pear juice
¼	shot	Freshly squeezed lemon juice

We say: Sake and pear juice with a kick.
Origin: Created in 2002 by Simon Difford.

ASSISTED SUICIDE

★★★½☆

Glass: Shot
Garnish: None
Method: SHAKE first 2 ingredients with ice and strain into chilled glass. TOP with Coca-Cola.

1	shot	Bacardi Superior rum
½	shot	Jägermeister
Top up with		Coca-Cola

We say: Not for the faint-hearted.

ASTOR

★★★★☆

Glass: Martini
Garnish: Lemon zest twist
Method: SHAKE all ingredients with ice and fine strain into chilled glass.

1¼	shots	Tanqueray London dry gin
1	shot	Swedish Punch liqueur
¼	shot	Freshly squeezed lemon juice
¼	shot	Freshly squeezed orange juice

Variant: Waldorf Cocktail No.2
We say: Citrus and the tang of Swedish punch add a distinctive flavour to gin in this tasty vintage cocktail.
Origin: Recipe adapted from Albert Stevens Crockett's 1931 'The Old Waldorf-Astoria Bar Book' where the drink was accompanied by the following notation, "Perhaps [named] after William Waldorf, who built the original Waldorf. However, chances are, it was originated either at the old Astor House or the Astor Hotel, and took its name from its bar of nativity."

ASTORIA

★★★★☆

Glass: Martini
Garnish: Lemon zest twist
Method: STIR all ingredients with ice and strain into chilled glass.

1	shot	Old Tom gin
2	shots	Martini Extra dry vermouth
2	dashes	Orange bitters

We say: An Old Tom based super wet (two-thirds vermouth to one-third gin) Martini with a slug of orange bitters and served with a twist.
Origin: Recipe adapted from Albert Stevens Crockett's 1931 'The Old Waldorf-Astoria Bar Book' where the drink was accompanied by the following notation, "After the big annex to the Old Waldorf, which at its opening, in 1897, became the main part of the establishment."

William Waldorf Astor built the original Waldorf Hotel, which opened in 1893, next door to his aunt's home, on the site of his father's mansion and today's Empire State Building. John Astor persuaded his aunt to move uptown and then built the Astor Hotel. The two hotels were connected and the combined Waldorf-Astoria became the largest hotel in the world at the time.

BARTENDER'S TIP LAYER

As the name would suggest, layered drinks include layers of different ingredients, often with contrasting colours.

This effect is achieved by carefully pouring each ingredient into the glass so that it floats on its predecessor. The success of this technique is dependent on the density (specific gravity) of the liquids used. As a rule of thumb, the less alcohol and the more sugar an ingredient contains, the heavier it is. The heaviest ingredients should be poured first and the lightest last.

ASYLUM COCKTAIL

★★★☆☆

Glass: Old-fashioned
Garnish: None
Method: POUR ingredients into glass without ice and STIR. Gently add ice and do NOT stir again. Consume once drink has turned cloudy.

1½	shots	Tanqueray London dry gin
1½	shots	Pernod anise
¼	shot	Pomegranate (grenadine) syrup

We say: Seabrook said of this drink, "look like rosy dawn, taste like the milk of Paradise, and make you plenty crazy." He must have been a Pernod lover.
Origin: Created by William Seabrook, famous for his account of eating human flesh, and first published in a 1935 book, 'So Red the Nose, or Breath in the Afternoon'.

ATHOLL BROSE

★★★★☆

Glass: Martini
Garnish: Dust with grated nutmeg
Method: Prepare oatmeal water by soaking three heaped tablespoons of oatmeal in half a mug of warm water. Stir and leave to stand for fifteen minutes. Then strain to extract the creamy liquid and discard what's left of the oatmeal.

To make the drink, STIR honey with Scotch until honey dissolves. Add other ingredients, SHAKE with ice and fine strain into chilled glass.

2	spoons	Runny honey
2	shots	Dewar's White label Scotch
1½	shots	Oatmeal water
¼	shot	Drambuie
¼	shot	Amaretto liqueur
½	shot	Double (heavy) cream

We say: Forget the porridge and kick start your day with a Atholl Brose.
Origin: My adaptation of a Scottish classic. Legend has it that Atholl Brose was created by the Earl of Atholl in 1475 when he was trying to capture Iain MacDonald, Lord of the Isles and leader of a rebellion against the king. Hearing rumours that MacDonald was drawing his drinking water from a small well, the Earl ordered it to be filled with honey, whisky and oatmeal. MacDonald lingered at the well enjoying the concoction and was captured.

ATLANTIC BREEZE

★★★☆☆

Glass: Collins
Garnish: Orange slice
Method: SHAKE all ingredients with ice and strain into ice-filled glass.

1½	shots	Bacardi Superior rum
½	shot	De Kuyper Apricot Brandy liqueur
¼	shot	Galliano L'Autentico liqueur
2½	shots	Fresh pressed pineapple juice
½	shot	Freshly squeezed lemon juice

We say: A fruity, tropical cocktail finished with herbal and citrus notes.

ATOMIC COCKTAIL

★★★☆☆

Glass: Martini
Garnish: Orange zest twist
Method: SHAKE first 3 ingredients with ice and fine strain into chilled glass. TOP with champagne.

1¼	shots	Ketel One vodka
1¼	shots	Cognac VSOP
½	shot	Amontillado sherry
Top up with		Brut champagne

We say: Golden and flavoursome - handle with care.
Origin: Created in the early 50s in Las Vegas. A-bomb tests were being conducted in Nevada at the time.

ATOMIC DOG

★★★★☆

Glass: Collins
Garnish: Pineapple wedge & maraschino cherry
Method: SHAKE all ingredients with ice and strain into ice-filled glass.

1½	shots	Bacardi Superior rum
¾	shot	Midori green melon liqueur
¾	shot	Malibu coconut rum liqueur
2½	shots	Fresh pressed pineapple juice
¾	shot	Freshly squeezed lemon juice

We say: A long, refreshing tropical drink with melon, coconut and pineapple juice.

ATTITUDE ADJUSTER

★★★☆☆

Glass: Hurricane
Garnish: Orange slice & cherry on stick (sail)
Method: SHAKE first 3 ingredients with ice and strain into ice-filled glass. TOP with Coca-Cola then DRIZZLE orange and coffee liqueurs.

2	shots	Tanqueray London dry gin
1	shot	Triple Sec
¾	shot	Freshly squeezed lime juice
Top up with		Coca-Cola
¼	shot	Grand Marnier liqueur
¼	shot	Kahlúa coffee liqueur

We say: We've simplified and tried to improve this somewhat dodgy but popular cocktail.

THE ATTY COCKTAIL

★★★★☆

Glass: Martini
Garnish: Lemon zest twist
Method: SHAKE all ingredients with ice and fine strain into chilled glass.

2¼	shots	Tanqueray London dry gin
¾	shot	Martini Extra Dry vermouth
¼	shot	Benoit Serres créme de violette
¼	shot	Absinthe

We say: Dry and aromatic with floral hints and aniseed notes.
Origin: Adapted from Harry Craddock's 1930 'The Savoy Cocktail Book'.

AULD ALLIANCE UPDATED

★★★½☆

Glass: Collins
Garnish: Lemon slice
Method: SHAKE first 4 ingredients with ice and strain into ice-filled glass. TOP with lemonade.

1½	shots	Dewar's White Label Scotch
¾	shot	Freshly squeezed lemon juice
½	shot	Cointreau triple sec
¼	shot	Monin Pure Cane 2:1 sugar syrup
Top up with		Lemonade (English-style)

We say: An orange-influenced whisky sour served long and refreshing.

AUNT AGATHA

★★★½☆

Glass: Old-fashioned
Garnish: Orange zest twist
Method: SHAKE first 3 ingredients with ice and strain into glass filled with crushed ice. DASH bitters over surface.

1½	shots	Pusser's Navy rum
2	shots	Freshly squeezed orange juice
1	shot	Fresh pressed pineapple juice
3	dashes	Angostura aromatic bitters

We say: A most unusual looking, tropical tasting concoction.
Origin: Aunt Agatha was Bertie Wooster's terrifying aunt in P.G. Wodehouse's books.

AUNT EMILY

★★★★☆

Glass: Martini
Garnish: Apricot slice
Method: SHAKE all ingredients with ice and fine strain into chilled glass.

1½	shots	Tanqueray London dry gin
1½	shots	Calvados/Applejack brandy
¾	shot	De Kuyper Apricot Brandy liqueur
¾	shot	Freshly squeezed orange juice
⅛	shot	Pomegranate (grenadine) syrup

We say: Aunt Emily is onto something as these ingredients combine to make a stylish fruity Martini.
Origin: A forgotten classic.

AUNTIE'S HOT XMAS PUNCH

★★★★☆

Glass: Toddy
Garnish: Cinnamon stick
Method: POUR all ingredients into glass and stir. MICROWAVE for a minute (vary time depending on your microwave oven), stir again and serve.

1½	shots	Pedro Ximénez sherry
2¼	shots	Cognac VSOP
¾	shot	Freshly squeezed lemon juice
3	shots	Pressed apple juice
4	dashes	Peychaud's aromatic bitters

We say: A fruity seasonal warmer.
Origin: I created this drink to serve live on Christmas Eve 2002 during a broadcast on BBC radio. 'Auntie' is a nickname for the BBC and the drink uses the traditional punch proportions of 1 sour, 2 sweet, 3 strong and 4 weak.

AUTUMN LEAVES

★★★★½

Glass: Old-fashioned
Garnish: Orange zest twist
Method: STIR all ingredients with ice and strain into ice-filled glass.

1	shot	Straight rye whiskey
1	shot	Calvados/Applejack brandy
1	shot	Martini Rosso sweet vermouth
¼	shot	Strega liqueur
2	dashes	Angostura aromatic bitters

We say: Jeffrey's original recipe calls for Carpano Antica sweet vermouth in this whiskey, apple brandy, vermouth and herbal liqueur delightful old-school combos. Serious drinkers need only apply.
Origin: Created in 2008 by Jeffrey Morgenthaler at Bel Ami Lounge, Oregon, USA.

AUTUMN MARTINI

★★★★☆

Glass: Martini
Garnish: Orange zest twist
Method: Cut passion fruit in half and scoop out flesh into shaker. Add other ingredients, SHAKE with ice and fine strain into chilled glass.

1	fresh	Passion fruit
2	shots	Żubrówka bison vodka
1	shot	Pressed apple juice
½	shot	Passion fruit syrup
½	fresh	Egg white

We say: An easy drinking, smooth, fruity cocktail with grassy hints courtesy of bison vodka.
Origin: Created in 2004 by Simon Difford, inspired by Max Warner's excellent Autumn Punch.

AUTUMN PUNCH

★★★★½

Glass: Sling
Garnish: Physalis (cape gooseberry)
Method: Cut passion fruit in half and scoop out flesh into shaker. Add vodka, passion fruit sugar syrup, pear and lemon juice, SHAKE with ice and strain into ice-filled glass. TOP with champagne.

1	fresh	Passion fruit
2	shots	Żubrówka bison vodka
¼	shot	Passion fruit syrup
1	shot	Pressed pear juice
½	shot	Freshly squeezed lemon juice
Top up with		Brut champagne

We say: Autumnal in colour with a wonderful meld of complementary flavours.
Origin: Created in 2001 by Max Warner at Baltic Bar, London, England.

STAR RATINGS EXPLAINED

★★★★★ Excellent

★★★★½ Recommended ★★★★☆ Praiseworthy
★★★½☆ Commended ★★★☆☆ Mediocre
★★½☆☆ Disappointing ★★☆☆☆ Pretty awful
★½☆☆☆ Shameful ★☆☆☆☆ Disgusting

AVALANCHE

★★★☆☆

Glass: Collins
Garnish: Banana chunk
Method: BLEND ingredients with 12oz scoop of crushed ice. Pour into glass and serve with straws.

2	shots	Bols Banana liqueur
1	shot	White Crème de Cacao
½	shot	Amaretto liqueur
1	shot	Double (heavy) cream
1	shot	Milk
½	fresh	Banana (peeled)

We say: Creamy, rich and smooth. Fluffy but lovely.
Origin: Created in 1979 at Maudes Bar, New York City, USA.

AVALANCHE SHOT

★★☆☆☆

Glass: Shot
Garnish: None
Method: Refrigerate ingredients then LAYER in chilled glass by carefully pouring in the following order.

½	shot	Kahlúa coffee liqueur
½	shot	White Crème de Cacao
½	shot	Southern Comfort liqueur

We say: Rich, smooth and sticky – peculiarly, this has an almost nutty taste.

AVENUE

★★★★☆

Glass: Martini
Garnish: Orange zest twist
Method: Cut passion fruit in half and scoop flesh into shaker. Add other ingredients, SHAKE with ice and fine strain into chilled glass.

1	fresh	Passion fruit
1	shot	Maker's Mark bourbon
1	shot	Calvados/Applejack brandy
¼	shot	Pomegranate (grenadine) syrup
⅛	shot	Orange flower water
1	dash	Orange bitters
½	shot	Chilled mineral water

We say: Passion fruit and orange flavours, laced with apple brandy and Bourbon. Fruity yet dry.
Origin: Adapted from the 1937 'Café Royal Bar Book'.

AVIATION NO.1

★★★★☆

Glass: Martini
Garnish: Lemon zest twist (& optional sugar rim)
Method: SHAKE all ingredients with ice and fine strain into chilled glass.

1¾	shots	Tanqueray London dry gin
½	shot	Luxardo Maraschino liqueur
¼	shot	Benoit Serres créme de violette
½	shot	Freshly squeezed lemon juice
¼	shot	Chilled mineral water

Variant: Blue Moon
We say: Benefits from a long shake. Citrus, floral gin with a slightly sour finish.
Origin: Simon Difford's adaptation of Hugo R. Esslinn's Aviation in his 1916 'Recipes for Mixed Drinks'.

AVIATION NO.2

★★★★☆

Glass: Martini
Garnish: Maraschino cherry (& optional sugar rim)
Method: SHAKE all ingredients with ice and fine strain into chilled glass.

1¾	shots	Tanqueray London dry gin
¾	shot	Luxardo Maraschino liqueur
½	shot	Freshly squeezed lemon juice
¼	shot	Chilled mineral water

We say: This is a fantastic, tangy cocktail and dangerously easy to drink – too many of these and you really will be flying.
Origin: A well-established vintage cocktail, although the original formulation is thought to be as listed here under Aviation #1. This adaptation by Simon Difford.

AVIATOR #1

★★★★☆

Glass: Martini
Garnish: Lemon zest twist
Method: SHAKE first 4 ingredients with ice and fine strain into chilled glass. POUR cassis into to centre of drink (it should sink).

2	shots	Tanqueray London dry gin
½	shot	Luxardo Maraschino liqueur
½	shot	Freshly squeezed lemon juice
½	fresh	Egg white
¼	shot	Crème de cassis liqueur

We say: An Aviation with egg white and a dash of cassis in the bottom but is actually better and more balanced when the cassis is shaken with the other ingredients.

AVIATOR #2

★★★☆☆

Glass: Martini
Garnish: Lemon zest twist
Method: STIR all ingredients with ice and strain into chilled glass.

1	shot	Tanqueray London dry gin
1	shot	Martini Extra Dry vermouth
1	shot	Martini Rosso sweet vermouth
1	shot	Dubonnet Red (French made)

We say: Bittersweet herbal notes of vermouth with a subtle hint of gin.
Origin: A classic cocktail of unknown origin.

AWOL

★★★★☆

Glass: Shot
Garnish: None
Method: LAYER in chilled glass by carefully pouring ingredients in the following order. Then FLAME drink and allow to burn for no more than ten seconds before extinguishing flame and consuming. Take extreme care and beware of hot glass.

½	shot	Midori green melon liqueur
½	shot	Ketel One vodka
½	shot	Fresh pressed pineapple juice
½	shot	Wray & Nephew overproof rum

We say: A strong but surprisingly palatable shot.
Origin: Created in 1993 by Lane Zellman at Louis XVI Restaurant, St. Louis Hotel, New Orleans, USA.

AZTEC

★★★★½☆

Glass: Martini
Garnish: Orange zest twist (flamed)
Method: STIR all ingredients with ice and strain
into chilled glass.

1¾	shots	Maker's Mark bourbon
½	shot	Bénédictine D.O.M.
¼	shot	White Crème de Cacao
1	drop	Tabasco hot pepper sauce

We say: Whiskey with the merest touch of herbal
and chocolate liqueurs spiced with a wisp of pepper.
Origin: Adapted from a recipe created in 2007 by
Neyah White, Nopa, San Francisco, USA.

AZURE MARTINI

★★★★☆

Glass: Martini
Garnish: Apple slice
Method: SHAKE all ingredients with ice and fine
strain into chilled glass.

2	shots	Leblon cachaça
¼	shot	Goldschläger cinnamon schnapps
1	shot	Pressed apple juice
½	shot	Freshly squeezed lime juice
¼	shot	Monin Pure Cane 2:1 sugar syrup

We say: A tangy cocktail - reminiscent of a
cinnamon laced apple pie. Shame it's not blue.
Origin: Created in 1998 by Ben Reed at the Met Bar,
London, England, and originally made with muddled
fresh apple.

B & B #1

★★★★½

Glass: Coupette
Garnish: Lime wedge
Method: SHAKE all ingredients with ice and fine
strain into chilled glass.

1	shot	42 Below Manuka honey vodka
1	shot	Tequila 100% Agave (blanco)
¾	shot	Agave nectar
½	shot	Freshly squeezed lime juice
3	drops	Difford's Margarita Bitters

We say: A Margarita with a touch of honey vodka
and agave enriched orange liqueur.
Origin: Created in 2010 by Simon Difford at The
Cabinet Room, London, England and named after
Julio Bermejo & Jacob Briars.

B & B #2 NEW

★★★★☆

Glass: Old-fashioned
Garnish: Lemon zest twist
Method: STIR ingredients with ice and strain into
ice-filled glass.

2	shots	Bénédictine D.O.M.
2	shots	Cognac VSOP

We say: Honeyed and spiced cognac.
Origin: Created in 1937 by a bartender at New York's
famous 21 Club.

B & T

★★★★☆

Glass: Martini
Garnish: Lime zest twist
Method: SHAKE all ingredients with ice and fine
strain into chilled glass.

2	shots	Tequila 100% Agave
1	shot	Bénédictine D.O.M.

We say: Delicately spiced and slightly
sweetened tequila.
Origin: Adapted from a drink created in 2007 by
Neyah White, San Francisco, USA. Originally this
consisted of equal parts served unchilled in a brandy
glass and using anejo tequila.

B-52 FROZEN

★★★★½☆

Glass: Old-fashioned
Garnish: Crumbled Cadbury's Flake bar
Method: BLEND ingredients with 6oz scoop of
crushed ice. Pour into glass and serve with straws.

1	shot	Baileys Irish cream liqueur
1	shot	Grand Marnier liqueur
1	shot	Kahlúa coffee liqueur

We say: The classic shot blended with ice.

B-52 SHOT

★★★★½☆

Glass: Shot
Garnish: None
Method: Refrigerate ingredients then LAYER
in chilled glass by carefully pouring in the
following order.

½	shot	Kahlúa coffee liqueur
½	shot	Baileys Irish cream liqueur
½	shot	Grand Marnier liqueur

We say: Probably the best-known and most popular
shot.
Origin: Named after B-52 bombers in Vietnam.

B-53 SHOT

★★★☆☆

Glass: Shot
Garnish: None
Method: Refrigerate ingredients then LAYER in
chilled glass by carefully pouring in the following
order.

½	shot	Kahlúa coffee liqueur
½	shot	Baileys Irish cream liqueur
½	shot	Ketel One vodka

We say: Why settle for a 52 when you can go
one better?

B-54 SHOT

★★★☆☆

Glass: Shot
Garnish: None
Method: Refrigerate ingredients then LAYER in chilled glass by carefully pouring in the following order.

½	shot	Amaretto liqueur
½	shot	Kahlúa coffee liqueur
½	shot	Baileys Irish cream liqueur

We say: Layered and sticky - but nice.

B-55 SHOT

★★★☆☆

Glass: Shot
Garnish: None
Method: Refrigerate ingredients then LAYER in chilled glass by carefully pouring in the following order.

½	shot	Kahlúa coffee liqueur
½	shot	Baileys Irish cream liqueur
½	shot	Absinthe

We say: The latest and scariest of the B-something range of layered shots.

B.J. SHOT

★★★☆☆

Glass: Shot
Garnish: Thin layer of single cream
Method: Refrigerate ingredients then LAYER in chilled glass by carefully pouring in the following order.

| ½ | shot | Grand Marnier liqueur |
| ½ | shot | Baileys Irish cream liqueur |

We say: A classic but lewdly named shooter. Proceed with caution.

B2C2

★★★★☆

Glass: Martini
Garnish: Orange zest twist
Method: SHAKE first 3 ingredients with ice and strain into ice-filled glass. TOP with champagne.

1	shot	Cognac VSOP
1	shot	Bénédictine D.O.M.
1	shot	Triple Sec
Top up with		Brut champagne

We say: Strong and sweet. This wartime drink can still be deadly if not handled with care.
Origin: Named after the four ingredients and created in France during World War II by American soldiers using ingredients liberated from retreating Germans.

B5200

★★★★☆

Glass: Shot
Garnish: None
Method: Refrigerate ingredients then LAYER in chilled glass by carefully pouring in the following order.

½	shot	Kahlúa coffee liqueur
½	shot	Baileys Irish cream liqueur
½	shot	Wood's 100 rum

We say: Layering this drink is as easy as inflating a life jacket - drink a few and you'll need one.
Origin: Discovered in 2003 at Circus Bar, London, England.

BABO NATALE

★★★★☆

Glass: Martini
Garnish: Mint sprig
Method: SHAKE all ingredients with ice and fine strain into chilled glass.

5	fresh	Mint leaves
2	shots	Warre's Otima tawny port
1	shot	Crème de framboise liqueur

We say: Richly flavoured and on the sweet side. One to chase a hearty dinner.

BABY BLUE MARTINI

★★★★☆

Glass: Martini
Garnish: Orange zest twist
Method: SHAKE all ingredients with ice and fine strain into chilled glass.

2	shots	Tanqueray London dry gin
¾	shot	Bols Blue Curaçao liqueur
¾	shot	Freshly squeezed grapefruit juice
¾	shot	Fresh pressed pineapple juice

We say: Turquoise blue, easy drinking, fruity gin.

BABY GUINNESS

★★★★☆

Glass: Shot
Garnish: None
Method: Refrigerate ingredients then LAYER in chilled glass by carefully pouring in the following order.

| 1 | shot | Kahlúa coffee liqueur |
| ½ | shot | Baileys Irish cream liqueur |

We say: Looks like a miniature pint of Guinness stout.

BABY WOO WOO

★★★☆☆

Glass: Shot
Garnish: Lime wedge
Method: SHAKE all ingredients with ice and fine strain into chilled glass.

½	shot	Ketel One vodka
½	shot	Peachtree peach schnapps
½	shot	Ocean Spray cranberry juice

We say: Pink, sweet and all too easy to shoot

BACARDI COCKTAIL

★★★★½

Glass: Martini
Garnish: Maraschino cherry
Method: SHAKE all ingredients with ice and fine strain into chilled glass.

2	shots	Rum light white/blanco
½	shot	Freshly squeezed lime juice
¼	shot	Pomegranate (grenadine) syrup
½	shot	Chilled mineral water
⅛	shot	Monin Pure Cane 2:1 sugar syrup

We say: This classic salmon pink drink perfectly combines and balances the subtle blue cheese notes we love in Bacardi with the rich sourness of lime juice and the sweetness of pomegranate syrup.
Origin: The Bacardi Cocktail originated in Cuba in 1917 and quickly grew in popularity as cocktail culture boomed in the USA after Prohibition, so much so that it became known simply as 'the Bacardi'.

There are two schools of thought over the original ingredients - some believe it was simply a Daiquiri, containing rum, lime juice, and sugar but made using Bacardi rum, and that the now ubiquitous grenadine version originated in New York after Prohibition. However, others hold that grenadine was there at the moment of conception - after all, there is no doubt that the Daiquiri was originally made with Bacardi rum. However, the number of vintage cocktails books listing a Bacardi Cocktail without grenadine would seem to confirm the inclusion of grenadine as a later addition.

Like the Daiquiri, The Bacardi Cocktail was sometimes served frozen and talking about this special iced version, Jack Doyle, former barman at Sloppy Joe's in Key West, Florida, and later a barman in New York, explained, "The secret to the iced version was to shake the flaked iced until it looked like sherbet." This technique became known as 'frappé'.

As the Bacardi Cocktail soared in popularity a small number of establishments neglected to use Bacardi rum as the base ingredient, despite the brand being fundamental to the drink's name and taste. In 1936 this led the Bacardi Company to take the Barbizon-Plaza Hotel and the Wivel Restaurant in West Fifty-Fourth Street to court in New York City to ensure that when a customer asked for 'Bacardi' by name they were given Bacardi Rum.

Bacardi's case centred around the premise that theirs was a unique rum and Bacardi family members travelled from Cuba to appear as witnesses - even Enrique Schueg, the third President of the Bacardi Company, took to the witness stand. When asked by Justice Walsh, "Well, how is this Bacardi Rum of yours made?" he replied, "Oh! That is my secret." Despite this secrecy, after deliberation, Justice John L. Walsh eventually affirmed that "Bacardi Rum is unique and uncopyable" and issued a ruling that a Bacardi Cocktail must legally be made with rum manufactured by the Compania Ron Bacardi.

BACARDI SPECIAL

★★★★★

Glass: Coupette
Garnish: Maraschino cherry
Method: SHAKE all ingredients with ice and fine strain into chilled glass.

1½	shots	Bacardi Superior rum
¾	shot	Tanqueray London dry gin
½	shot	Freshly squeezed lime juice
¼	shot	Pomegranate (grenadine) syrup
⅛	shot	Monin Pure Cane 2:1 sugar syrup
½	shot	Chilled mineral water

We say: Hit the perfect proportions and you will strike a wondrous balance of flavoursome rum, gin botanicals, limey sourness and fruity sweetness.
Origin: Adapted from Harry Craddock's 1930 'The Savoy Cocktail Book' which also has the following notation to this vintage adaptation of the 'Bacardi Cocktail' - "Made famous by Karl K. Kitchen, the well-known New York Newspaper Columnist."

BACCIO PUNCH

★★★☆☆

Glass: Collins
Garnish: Orange & lemon slices
Method: SHAKE first three ingredients with ice and strain into ice-filled glass. TOP with champagne and soda water. Lightly stir and serve with straws.

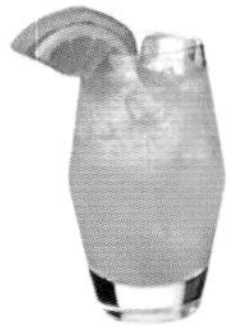

1½	shots	Tanqueray London dry gin
¾	shot	Marie Brizard Anisette
1½	shots	Freshly squeezed grapefruit juice
1½	shots	Brut champagne
¾	shot	Soda (club soda)

We say: A classic for aniseed lovers.
Origin: The origin of this vintage cocktail is unknown but it in Italian its name means 'kiss'.

BAHAMA MAMA

★★★★☆

Glass: Collins
Garnish: Pineapple wedge & maraschino cherry
Method: SHAKE all ingredients with ice and strain into ice-filled glass.

¾	shot	Pusser's Navy rum
¾	shot	Bacardi 8yo aged rum
1	shot	Malibu coconut rum liqueur
1¾	shots	Freshly squeezed orange juice
2½	shots	Fresh pressed pineapple juice
3	dashes	Angostura aromatic bitters

We say: A tropical, fruity number laced with flavoursome rum.

BAHAMAS DAIQUIRI

★★★★½

Glass: Martini
Garnish: Pineapple wedge
Method: SHAKE all ingredients with ice and fine strain into chilled glass.

1½	shots	Myer's dark Jamaican rum
¾	shot	Malibu coconut rum liqueur
¼	shot	Kahlúa coffee liqueur
1½	shots	Fresh pressed pineapple juice
½	shot	Freshly squeezed lime juice

We say: Totally tropical with a sweet tangy edge.
Origin: Adapted from the Bahamas Martini created in 2002 by Yannick Miseriaux at the Fifth Floor Bar, Harvey Nichols, London, England.

BAHIA

★★★½☆

Glass: Collins
Garnish: Pineapple wedge, maraschino cherry & mint sprig
Method: BLEND all ingredients with 12oz scoop crushed ice and serve with straws.

2½	shots	Bacardi Superior rum
½	shot	Coco López cream of coconut
3	shots	Fresh pressed pineapple juice

We say: If you like Piña Coladas but are too embarrassed to order one then this drink is for you.
Origin: Bahia is one of the 26 states of Brazil. It is also a pre-Prohibition drink containing dry vermouth, sherry, absinthe and bitters. This more recent Piña Colada-style offering has more mass market appeal.

BAJAN DAIQUIRI

★★★★☆

Glass: Coupette
Garnish: Lime wedge
Method: SHAKE all ingredients with ice and fine strain into chilled glass.

2	shots	Bacardi Oro golden rum
½	shot	Taylor's Velvet Falernum liqueur
¾	shot	Freshly squeezed lime juice
½	shot	Chilled mineral water

We say: A full-flavoured Daiquiri with clove spice.
Origin: Created in 2006 by Simon Difford.

BAJAN MOJITO

★★★★☆

Glass: Collins
Garnish: Passion fruit & mint sprig
Method: Cut passion fruit in half and scoop flesh into glass. Add mint and gently MUDDLE (just to bruise mint). Add rum, lime juice and crushed ice. CHURN (stir) drink in glass to mix. DRIZZLE passion fruit liqueur and serve with straws.

1	fresh	Passion fruit
8	fresh	Mint leaves
2	shots	Bacardi Oro golden rum
½	shot	Freshly squeezed lime juice
½	shot	Monin Pure Cane 2:1 sugar syrup
¼	shot	Passoã passion fruit liqueur

We say: A laid-back fruity, slightly sweet Mojito.
Origin: Adapted from a recipe by Wayne Collins, London, England

BAJAN PASSION

★★★★☆

Glass: Martini
Garnish: Passion fruit
Method: Cut passion fruit in half and scoop flesh into shaker. Add other ingredients, SHAKE with ice and fine strain into chilled glass.

1	fresh	Passion fruit
1½	shots	Bacardi Oro golden rum
½	shot	De Kuyper Apricot Brandy liqueur
1	shot	Freshly squeezed lime juice
¼	shot	Monin Pure Cane 2:1 sugar syrup
¼	shot	Monin Vanilla sugar syrup

We say: A Daiquiri laced with fruit and spice.
Origin: Created in 2004 by Wayne Collins for Maxxium UK.

BAJITO

★★★★☆

Glass: Collins
Garnish: Mint sprig
Method: Lightly MUDDLE mint and basil. Add rum, sugar and lime juice. Half fill glass with crushed ice and CHURN with bar spoon. Add more crushed ice and CHURN again. Continue adding crushed ice and churning until glass is full.

6	fresh	Mint leaves
6	fresh	Torn basil leaves
2	shots	Bacardi Superior rum
1	shot	Freshly squeezed lime juice
¼	shot	Monin Pure Cane 2:1 sugar syrup

We say: Basically a Mojito with basil as well as mint.
Origin: Discovered in 2004 at Excelsior Bar, Boston, USA.

BALABUSHKA

★★★★☆

Glass: Martini
Garnish: Apple slice
Method: SHAKE all ingredients with ice and fine strain into chilled glass.

1½	shots	Ketel One vodka
½	shot	Triple Sec
½	shot	Freshly squeezed lemon juice
1	shot	Pressed apple juice
⅛	shot	Monin Almond (orgeat) syrup

We say: This vodka-based cocktail has flavours of apple, lemon, orange and almond.
Origin: Created in 2001 by Julien Escot at Langdon Hall Hotel, Cambridge, Ontario, Canada. Named in homage to George Balabushka, the legendary billiards cue maker.

BALALAIKA

★★★★☆

Glass: Martini
Garnish: Orange zest twist
Method: SHAKE all ingredients with ice and fine strain into chilled glass.

1¼	shots	Ketel One vodka
1¼	shots	Triple Sec
1¼	shots	Freshly squeezed lemon juice

We say: Richly flavoured with orange and lemon.

BALD EAGLE

★★★★☆

Glass: Martini
Garnish: Salt rim
Method: SHAKE all ingredients with ice and fine strain into chilled glass.

2	shots	Tequila 100% Agave
¾	shot	Freshly squeezed grapefruit juice
½	shot	Ocean Spray cranberry juice
¼	shot	Freshly squeezed lime juice
¼	shot	Freshly squeezed lemon juice
¼	shot	Monin Pure Cane 2:1 sugar syrup

We say: If you like tequila and you like your drinks on the sour side, this is for you.
Origin: Created for me in 2001 by Salvatore Calabrese at The Lanesborough Hotel's Library Bar, London, England.

BALD EAGLE SHOT

★★☆☆☆

Glass: Shot
Garnish: None
Method: Refrigerate ingredients then LAYER in chilled glass by carefully pouring in the following order.

½	shot	Giffard Menthe Pastille liqueur
¾	shot	Tequila 100% Agave

We say: Minty tequila – fresh breath tastic

BALI TRADER

★★★☆☆

Glass: Martini
Garnish: Banana chunk
Method: SHAKE all ingredients with ice and fine strain into chilled glass.

2	shots	Ketel One vodka
1	shot	Pisang Ambon liqueur
1	shot	Fresh pressed pineapple juice

We say: A tasty Caribbean combination of banana and pineapple.

BALLET RUSSE

★★★☆☆

Glass: Martini
Garnish: Lime wedge
Method: SHAKE all ingredients with ice and fine strain into chilled glass.

2	shots	Ketel One vodka
1	shot	Freshly squeezed lime juice
¼	shot	Monin Pure Cane 2:1 sugar syrup
¾	shot	Crème de cassis liqueur

We say: Intense sweet blackcurrant balanced by lime sourness.

BALM COCKTAIL

★★★☆☆

Glass: Martini
Garnish: Olive on stick
Method: SHAKE all ingredients with ice and fine strain into chilled glass.

3	shots	Manzanilla Sherry
½	shot	Triple Sec
⅛	shot	Berry Hill pimento allspice liqueur
½	shot	Freshly squeezed orange juice
1	dash	Orange bitters

We say: Medium dry sherry flavoured with orange and subtle spice.
Origin: Adapted from Harry Craddock's 1930 'The Savoy Cocktail Book'.

BALTIC SPRING PUNCH

★★★★☆

Glass: Collins
Garnish: Mint sprig
Method: MUDDLE peach in base of shaker. Add other ingredients, SHAKE with ice and fine strain into ice-filled glass.

1	fresh	Ripe peach (skinned and diced)
1½	shots	Lanique rose petal liqueur
½	shot	Freshly squeezed lemon juice
¼	shot	Monin Pure Cane 2:1 sugar syrup
Top up with		Brut champagne

Variant: If using peach purée omit the sugar.
We say: Just peachy.
Origin: Created in 2002 at Baltic, London, England.

BALTIMORE EGG NOG

★★★☆☆

Glass: Wine
Garnish: Dust with grated nutmeg
Method: Vigorously SHAKE all ingredients with ice and fine strain into chilled glass.

1	shot	Cognac VSOP
1	shot	Gosling's Black Seal rum
½	shot	Blandy's Alvada madeira
1	fresh	Egg
½	shot	Monin Pure Cane 2:1 sugar syrup
½	shot	Double (heavy) cream
½	shot	Milk

We say: A rich meal of a drink with a whole egg and cream - fortified with cognac, rum and madeira.
Origin: One of the most famous flip-style drinks.

BAMBOO #1

★★★★☆

Glass: Martini
Garnish: Orange zest twist
Method: STIR all ingredients with ice and strain into chilled glass.

2	shots	Tio Pepe fino sherry
2	shots	Martini Extra Dry vermouth
¼	shot	Triple Sec
3	dashes	Orange bitters

Variant: Add two dashes of Angostura aromatic bitters in place of triple sec. Also see East Indian'
We say: For sophisticated palates only.
Origin: A classic and all but forgotten cocktail from the 1940s.

BAMBOO #2

★★★★☆

Glass: Martini
Garnish: Toasted almonds
Method: STIR all ingredients with ice and strain into ice-filled glass.

2	shots	Tio Pepe fino sherry
1	shot	Martini Extra Dry vermouth
1	shot	Martini Rosso sweet vermouth

We say: The combination of vermouth and fino makes for a fabulously complex cocktail.
Origin: Adapted from Harry Craddock's 1930 'The Savoy Cocktail Book'.

BANANA ALCOHOLIC SMOOTHIE NEW

★★★★☆

Glass: Sling
Garnish: Banana chunk
Method: BLEND ingredients with 12oz scoop of crushed ice. Pour into glass and serve immediately with straws.

2	shots	Ketel One vodka
1½	shots	Bols Natural Yoghurt liqueur
3	spoons	Runny honey
½	fresh	Banana (peeled)
½	shot	Bols Banana liqueur
1	shot	Pressed apple juice

We say: Packed with fruit, this creamy banana flavoured shake is 'hardened' with a double measure of vodka.
Origin: Created in 2011 by Simon Difford at the Cabinet Room, London, England.

BANANA BLISS

★★★⯪☆

Glass: Martini
Garnish: Orange zest twist
Method: STIR all ingredients with ice and strain into chilled glass.

2	shots	Cognac VSOP
1	shot	Bols Banana liqueur
½	shot	Chilled mineral water
2	dashes	Orange bitters

AKA: Golden Brown
We say: Crème de banane and cognac go shockingly well together.

BANANA BOOMER

★★★★☆

Glass: Martini
Garnish: Banana chunk
Method: SHAKE all ingredients with ice and strain into chilled glass.

1	shot	Ketel One vodka
1	shot	Bols Banana liqueur
½	shot	De Kuyper Apricot Brandy liqueur
½	shot	De Kuyper Cherry Brandy liqueur
¾	shot	Freshly squeezed orange juice
¾	shot	Fresh pressed pineapple juice

We say: Fortified bubble gum for the young at heart.

BANANA COLADA

★★★★☆

Glass: Hurricane
Garnish: Banana chunk
Method: BLEND ingredients with 12oz scoop of crushed ice. Pour into glass and serve with straws.

2	shots	Bacardi Superior rum
½	shot	Bols Banana liqueur
4	shots	Fresh pressed pineapple juice
1	fresh	Banana (peeled)
1	shot	Coco López cream of coconut

We say: Don't skimp, use a whole banana per drink for real flavour.

BANANA COW

★★★☆☆

Glass: Collins
Garnish: Banana chunk
Method: BLEND all ingredients with 12oz scoop crushed ice and serve with straws.

1	shot	Bacardi Superior rum
3	shots	Milk
½	shot	Monin Pure Cane 2:1 sugar syrup
1	dash	Angostura aromatic bitters
1	dash	Vanilla extract
1	fresh	Banana (peeled)

We say: The Trader writes of his drink, "the world's finest, greatest, oh-so good peachy hangover special. This'll do when nothing else will." We think Vic is somewhat overselling this malty banana meal of a drink.
Origin: Created by Victor J. Bergeron. This recipe is adapted from his '*Trader Vic's Bartender's Guide*' (1972 revised edition)

BANANA DAIQUIRI

★★★⯪☆

Glass: Hurricane
Garnish: Banana chunk
Method: BLEND ingredients with 12oz scoop of crushed ice. Pour into glass and serve with straws.

2	shots	Bacardi Superior rum
1	shot	Bols Banana liqueur
½	shot	Freshly squeezed lime juice
1	fresh	Banana (peeled)

Variant: Add a dash of maraschino liqueur.
We say: A tangy banana disco drink that's not too sweet.

BANANA FLAMBÉ

★★★★☆

Glass: Old-fashioned
Garnish: Cinnamon stick
Method: In a shallow dish flambé half a split banana with orange juice, sugar and cinnamon. FLAMBÉ until the banana softens completely and the orange juice reduces. Add cognac and flambé further. MUDDLE banana in the base of shaker, add other ingredients, SHAKE with ice and fine strain into chilled glass.

½	fresh	Banana (peeled)
1	shot	Freshly squeezed orange juice
1	spoon	Granulated sugar
2	pinch	Ground cinnamon
½	shot	Cognac VSOP
1½	shots	Ketel One vodka
½	shot	Leblon cachaça
½	shot	Freshly squeezed lemon juice
¼	shot	Monin Pure Cane 2:1 sugar syrup

Variant: Substitute the vodka for cachaça for a Banana Flambé Caipirinha.
We say: As Tony says "it's worth it".
Origin: Created in 2008 by Mauricio 'Tony' Harion from Mixing Bar Consulting, Belo Horizonte, Brazil.

BANANA SMOOTHIE (MOCKTAIL)

★★★★⯪

Glass: Hurricane
Garnish: Banana chunk
Method: BLEND ingredients with 12oz scoop of crushed ice. Pour into glass and serve immediately with straws.

7	spoon	Natural yoghurt
3	spoons	Runny honey
1	fresh	Banana (peeled)
3	shots	Pressed apple juice

We say: Serve with breakfast cereal and you'll be set up for the day. The high fresh banana content means this drink will quickly turn brown if left. This can be countered by adding fresh lemon juice and balancing with more honey but this detracts from the fresh banana flavour.
Origin: Created in 2005 by Lisa Ball, London, England.

BANANAS & CREAM

★★★★☆

Glass: Collins
Garnish: Banana chunk
Method: BLEND ingredients with 12oz scoop of crushed ice. Pour into glass and serve with straws.

2	shots	**Bols Banana liqueur**
1	shot	**Amaretto liqueur**
1	shot	**Baileys Irish cream liqueur**
1	shot	**Double (heavy) cream**
2	shots	**Milk**

We say: Banana and cream frappé with hints of almond - one for a summer afternoon.

BANDERA

★★★★☆

Glass: Shot
Garnish: None
Method: POUR tequila and lime juice into separate shot (caballitos) glasses. To make Sangrita to fill third glass, SHAKE rest of ingredients with ice and fine strain into glass. Instruct drinker to sip from all three glasses alternatively.

2	shots	**Tequila 100% Agave**
2	shots	**Freshly squeezed lime juice**
½	shot	**Tomato juice**
½	shot	**Pomegranate juice**
¼	shot	**Freshly squeezed orange juice**
½	shot	**Freshly squeezed lime juice**
⅛	shot	**Pomegranate (grenadine) syrup**
2	drops	**Tabasco hot pepper sauce**
2	dashes	**Worcestershire sauce**
1	pinch	**Salt**
1	grind	**Black pepper**

We say: In Mexico the quality of the homemade Sangrita can make or break a bar. The Sangrita in this trio is spicy and slightly sweet.
Origin: A popular and classic way of serving tequila in Mexico. Sangrita means 'little blood' in Spanish and the drink is served with tequila in practically every bar in Mexico.

BANOFFEE MARTINI

★★★★☆

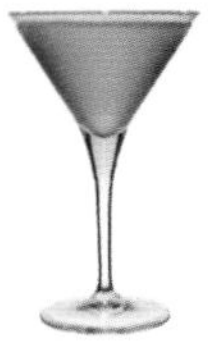

Glass: Martini
Garnish: Dust with chocolate powder
Method: MUDDLE banana in base of shaker. Add other ingredients, SHAKE with ice and fine strain into chilled glass.

¼	fresh	**Banana (peeled)**
1½	shots	**Vanilla-infused Ketel One vodka**
¾	shot	**Butterscotch schnapps**
¾	shot	**Bols Banana liqueur**
1	spoon	**Maple syrup**
½	shot	**Milk**
½	shot	**Double (heavy) cream**

We say: Thick and rich, one for after the cheese course.
Origin: Adapted from a recipe created in 2002 by Barrie 'Snood' Wilson, Zinc Bar & Grill, Edinburgh, Scotland.

BANSHEE

★★★☆☆

Glass: Shot
Garnish: None
Method: SHAKE all ingredients with ice and fine strain into chilled glass.

½	shot	**Bols Banana liqueur**
½	shot	**White Crème de Cacao**
½	shot	**Double (heavy) cream**

We say: Creamy chocolate banana.

BARBARA

★★★☆☆

Glass: Martini
Garnish: Dust with grated nutmeg
Method: SHAKE all ingredients with ice and fine strain into chilled glass.

1½	shots	**Ketel One vodka**
¾	shot	**White Crème de Cacao**
¾	shot	**Double (heavy) cream**
¾	shot	**Milk**

We say: Quite neutral and subtle - the nutmeg garnish is as important to the flavour as cacao.

BARBARA WEST

★★★½☆

Glass: Martini
Garnish: Lemon zest twist
Method: SHAKE all ingredients with ice and fine strain into chilled glass.

2	shots	**Tanqueray London dry gin**
1	shot	**Amontillado sherry**
½	shot	**Freshly squeezed lemon juice**
¼	shot	**Monin Pure Cane 2:1 sugar syrup**
2	dashes	**Angostura aromatic bitters**

We say: Well balanced but for serious gin and sherry drinkers only.
Origin: A classic from the 1930s.

BARBARY COAST

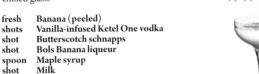

★★★½☆

Glass: Martini
Garnish: Dust with grated nutmeg
Method: SHAKE all ingredients with ice and fine strain into chilled glass.

1	shot	**Dewar's White label Scotch**
1	shot	**Tanqueray London dry gin**
1	shot	**White Crème de Cacao**
½	shot	**Double (heavy) cream**
½	shot	**Milk**

We say: Creamy and smooth without smothering the spirits.
Origin: A Prohibition era cocktail (1920-1933) of unknown origin.

BARBARY COAST HIGHBALL

★★★☆☆

Glass: Collins
Garnish: None
Method: SHAKE all but soda with ice and strain into ice-filled glass. TOP with soda and stir.

1	shot	Maker's Mark bourbon
1	shot	Tanqueray London dry gin
1	shot	Dark Crème de Cacao
½	shot	Double (heavy) cream
½	shot	Milk
Top up with		Soda (club soda)

Variant: Omit soda and serve straight-up in a Martini glass.
We say: Looks like a glass of frothy weak tea - bourbon and chocolate predominate.

BARNACLE BILL

★★★☆☆

Glass: Old-fashioned
Garnish: Mint sprig
Method: SHAKE all ingredients with ice and strain into glass filled with crushed ice.

½	shot	Chartreuse Yellow liqueur
½	shot	Parfait Amour liqueur
½	shot	Pernod anise
½	shot	Chilled mineral water

We say: This sweet drink is great after a meal on a warm night.
Origin: Adapted from Victor Bergeron's *'Trader Vic's Bartender's Guide'* (1972 revised edition).

BARNAMINT

★★★☆☆

Glass: Hurricane
Garnish: Oreo cookie
Method: BLEND ingredients with 12oz scoop of crushed ice. Pour into glass and serve with straws.

2	shots	Baileys Irish cream liqueur
1½	shots	Green crème de menthe liqueur
1	shot	Double (heavy) cream
1	shot	Milk
2	scoop	Häagen Dazs vanilla ice cream
3	whole	Oreo cookies

We say: If you're after a drinkable dessert, then this TGI classic may be the cocktail for you.
Origin: This original TGI Friday's cocktail is named after the Barnum & Bailey Circus, which also inspired the red and white awnings outside Friday's restaurants.

BARNEY BARNATO COCKTAIL

★★★★☆

Glass: Martini
Garnish: Lemon zest twist
Method: STIR all ingredients with ice and strain into chilled glass.

1½	shots	Dubonnet Red (French made)
1½	shots	Cognac VSOP
¼	shot	Grand Marnier liqueur
1	dash	Angostura aromatic bitters

We say: Orange always works when mixed with cognac and here Dubonnet also tames and adds an aromatic wine complexity.
Origin: This cocktail is named after Barney Barnato, who was born Barnett Issacs in 1852 in the then Whitechapel slum of London and traded on his Jewish-Cockney wit and humour. With only a box of cigars to his name, in 1873 Barney fled poverty to join his brother in the South African diamond rush and changed his name. He formed the Barnato Diamond Mining Company and within ten years he had become a millionaire.

He and his brother were eventually forced to sell out to Cecil John Rhodes for $5,338,650, then the single largest cheque that had been written. The fortune was little compensation for being beaten in the battle to control the Cape diamond mines - Rhodes went on to form the now mighty De Beers.

After a brief spell in South African politics Barnato died in 1897 when he was lost overboard near the island of Madeira, whilst on a passage home to England. It is still questioned as to whether he jumped, fell or was pushed. His body was recovered but the mysterious circumstances of his death were never resolved. He is buried at Willesden Jewish Cemetery, London.

His vast fortune was divided between his family, including his sister Sarah and her husband Abraham Rantzen.

This recipe is adapted from Harry Craddock's 1930 *'The Savoy Cocktail Book'* which calls for a now defunct South African product called Caperitif. We have used Dubonnot Red in its place, but some consider white vermouth or aromatised wine a better substitute

BARNUM (WAS RIGHT)

★★★½☆

Glass: Martini
Garnish: Lemon zest twist
Method: SHAKE all ingredients with ice and fine strain into chilled glass.

2	shots	Tanqueray London dry gin
1	shot	De Kuyper Apricot Brandy liqueur
½	shot	Freshly squeezed lemon juice
2	dashes	Angostura aromatic bitters
½	shot	Chilled mineral water

We say: A classic cocktail flavour combination that still pleases.
Origin: A 1930s classic resurrected by Ted Haigh in his 2004 book *'Vintage Spirits & Forgotten Cocktails'.*

BARRANQUILLA GREEN JADE

★★★☆☆

Glass: Martini
Garnish: Maraschino cherry & mint sprig
Method: SHAKE all ingredients with ice and fine strain into chilled glass.

2	shots	Tanqueray London dry gin
1	shot	Green crème de menthe liqueur
½	shot	Double (heavy) cream
½	shot	Milk
½	fresh	Egg white

We say: Lime green in colour, a tad minty and creamy smooth.

BARTENDER'S MARTINI

★★★★☆

Glass: Martini
Garnish: Orange zest twist
Method: SHAKE all ingredients with ice and fine strain into chilled glass.

1	shot	Tanqueray London dry gin
1	shot	Tio Pepe fino sherry
1	shot	Dubonnet Red (French made)
1	shot	Martini Extra Dry vermouth
½	shot	Grand Marnier liqueur

We say: This classic cocktail resembles an aromatic Martini. Hints of sherry and orange are followed by a dry finish.

BARTENDER'S MUM

★★★½☆

Glass: Shot
Garnish: None
Method: Carefully LAYER ingredients in the following order.

| ¾ | shot | Butterscotch schnapps |
| ¾ | shot | Baileys Irish cream liqueur |

We say: A sweet shot but as shots go...

BARTENDER'S ROOT BEER

★★★★☆

Glass: Collins
Garnish: Lime wedge
Method: POUR first three ingredients into ice-filled glass and TOP with cola.

1	shot	Galliano L'Autentico liqueur
1	shot	Kahlúa coffee liqueur
¼	shot	Freshly squeezed lime juice
Top up with		Coca-Cola

We say: Not quite the root of all evil, but tasty all the same.

BARTON SPECIAL COCKTAIL

★★★☆☆

Glass: Martini
Garnish: Lemon zest twist
Method: STIR all ingredients with ice and fine strain into chilled glass.

1½	shots	Tanqueray London dry gin
¾	shot	Calvados/Applejack brandy
¾	shot	Dewar's White label Scotch

We say: Dry and hardcore - gin, apple brandy and Scotch, tamed only by a little dilution and being chilled.
Origin: Thought to be named after the noted 'all American' Advertising guru and political publicist, Bruce Fairchild Barton, who in 1919 co-founded the Barton, Durstine & Osborn advertising agency.

BASIL & HONEY DAIQUIRI

★★★★★

Glass: Martini
Garnish: Basil leaf
Method: STIR honey and rum in base of shaker until honey dissolves. Add other ingredients, SHAKE with ice and fine strain into chilled glass.

2	spoons	Runny honey
2½	shots	Bacardi Superior rum
3	fresh	Torn basil leaves
½	shot	Freshly squeezed lime juice

We say: Basil adds dry vegetable notes to this outstanding classic drink.
Origin: Formula by Simon Difford in 2005.

BASIL BEAUTY

★★★★☆

Glass: Martini
Garnish: Pineapple wedge
Method: Cut passion fruit in half and scoop flesh into shaker. Add other ingredients, SHAKE with ice and fine strain into chilled glass.

1	whole	Passion fruit
3	fresh	Torn basil leaves
2	shots	Ketel One Citroen vodka
2	shots	Fresh pressed pineapple juice
¼	shot	Freshly squeezed lime juice
½	shot	Monin Pure Cane 2:1 sugar syrup

We say: Pineapple and passion fruit laced with citrus vodka and infused with hints of lime, basil and coconut.
Origin: Created in 1999 by Wayne Collins, London, UK

BASIL BRAMBLE SLING

★★★★☆

Glass: Sling
Garnish: Mint sprig
Method: MUDDLE basil in base of shaker. Add rest of ingredients, SHAKE with ice and strain into ice-filled glass. Serve with straws.

7	fresh	Torn basil leaves
2	shots	Tanqueray London dry gin
1½	shots	Freshly squeezed lemon juice
½	shot	Monin Pure Cane 2:1 sugar syrup
½	shot	Crème de Mûre liqueur

We say: Wonderfully refreshing and balanced.
Origin: Created in 2003 by Alexandra Fiot at Lonsdale House, London, UK.

BASIL CRUSH

★★★⯪☆

Glass: Collins
Garnish: Basil leaf
Method: SHAKE all ingredients with ice and fine strain into ice-filled glass.

2	fresh	Torn basil leaves
1	shot	Tanqueray London dry gin
¾	shot	Cynar
1½	shots	Pressed apple juice
1	shot	Cold green tea
½	shot	Freshly squeezed lime juice
¼	shot	Monin Honey syrup

We say: Green and herbal to the extent of almost being healthy. Bitter sweet and fruity.
Origin: This drink for Basil Brush fans is adapted from a recipe by Fabio Raffaelli, Restaurante Tristan, Mallorca.

BASIL GIMLET

★★★★⯪

Glass: Martini
Garnish: Lime wedge
Method: SHAKE all ingredients with ice and fine strain into chilled glass.

2½	shots	Tanqueray London dry gin
¼	shot	Freshly squeezed lime juice
1½	shots	Rose's lime cordial
3	shots	Torn basil leaves

We say: Tangy, citrus fresh and balanced.
Origin: Adapted from a drink discovered in 2006 at Stella, Boston, USA

BASIL GRANDE NEW

★★★★☆

Glass: Martini
Garnish: Strawberry
Method: MUDDLE strawberries and basil leaves in shaker base. Add other ingredients, SHAKE with ice and fine strain into glass. Dust with black pepper.

4	fresh	Strawberries (hulled)
4	fresh	Torn basil leaves
¾	shot	Ketel One vodka
¾	shot	Chambord liqueur
¾	shot	Grand Marnier liqueur
1½	shots	Ocean Spray cranberry juice

We say: Fruity, and interesting thanks to the basil and grind of pepper.
Origin: Created in 2001 by Jamie Wilkinson at Living Room, Manchester, England.

STAR RATINGS EXPLAINED

★★★★★ Excellent

★★★★⯪ Recommended	★★★★☆ Praiseworthy
★★★⯪☆ Commended	★★★☆☆ Mediocre
★★⯪☆☆ Disappointing	★★☆☆☆ Pretty awful
★⯪☆☆☆ Shameful	★☆☆☆☆ Disgusting

BASIL MARY

★★★★☆

Glass: Collins
Garnish: Basil leaf
Method: SHAKE all ingredients with ice and fine strain into ice-filled glass.

7	fresh	Torn basil leaves
2	shots	Pepper-infused Ketel One vodka
4	shots	Tomato juice
8	drops	Tabasco hot pepper sauce
½	shot	Warre's Otima tawny port
4	dashes	Worcestershire sauce
½	spoon	Horseradish sauce
2	pinch	Celery salt
2	grind	Black pepper
½	shot	Freshly squeezed lemon juice

We say: A particularly spicy Mary with a herbal twist.
Origin: Discovered in 2004 at Indigo Yard, Edinburgh, Scotland.

BASILIAN

★★★⯪☆

Glass: Collins
Garnish: Lime slice & basil leaf
Method: MUDDLE cucumber and basil in base of shaker. Add next four ingredients, SHAKE with ice and fine strain into ice-filled glass. TOP with ginger ale.

1	inch	Cucumber (chopped & peeled)
5	fresh	Torn basil leaves
2	shots	Leblon cachaça
¾	shot	Grand Marnier liqueur
½	shot	Freshly squeezed lime juice
¼	shot	Monin Pure Cane 2:1 sugar syrup
Top up with		Ginger ale

We say: Vegetable notes with hints of orange and ginger. Healthy tasting!
Origin: Created in 2005 by Duncan McRae at Dragonfly, Edinburgh, Scotland.

BASILICO

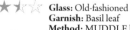

★★★⯪☆

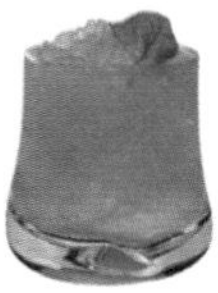

Glass: Old-fashioned
Garnish: Basil leaf
Method: MUDDLE basil in base of shaker. Add other ingredients, SHAKE with ice and strain into glass filled with crushed ice.

7	fresh	Torn basil leaves
2	shots	Ketel One vodka
½	shot	Limoncello liqueur
½	shot	Freshly squeezed lemon juice
½	shot	Monin Pure Cane 2:1 sugar syrup

We say: A lemon Caipirovska with basil.
Origin: Discovered in 2004 at Atlantic Bar & Grill, London, England.

BAT BITE

★★★⯨☆☆

Glass: Collins
Garnish: Lime wedge
Method: SHAKE all ingredients with ice and strain into ice-filled glass.

2	shots	Bacardi Superior rum
1	shot	Crème de framboise liqueur
2	shots	Ocean Spray cranberry juice
½	shot	Freshly squeezed lime juice

We say: All too easy - light and fruity, lightly fortified with rum character.
Origin: Adapted from a cocktail promoted by Bacardi.

BATANGA UPDATED 🔑

★★★★☆

Glass: Collins
Garnish: Salt rim
Method: POUR ingredients into ice-filled glass, stir and serve with straws.

2	shots	Tequila 100% Agave
½	shot	Freshly squeezed lime juice
Top up with		Coca-Cola

We say: Basically a Cuba Libre made with tequila in place of rum - an improvement.
Origin: Created in 1961 by the now legendary Don Javier Delgado Corona, the owner/bartender of La Capilla (The Chapel) in Tequila, Mexico. Still mixing, even in his eighties, Don Javier is noted for ritualistically stirring his drinks with a huge knife. The Batanga is a very popular drink in Mexico, helped by being featured in an advertising campaign by El Tequileño, a tequila distilled close to Don Javier's bar and still the house-pour to this day.

BATIDA DE ABACAXI

★★★★☆

Glass: Collins
Garnish: Pineapple wedge
Method: SHAKE all ingredients with ice and strain into ice-filled glass.

2	shots	Leblon cachaça
2½	shots	Fresh pressed pineapple juice
1	shot	Condensed milk
½	shot	Monin Pure Cane 2:1 sugar syrup

We say: This easy crowd pleaser is creamy, fruity and to taste - only vaguely alcoholic.
Origin: The Batida (meaning 'shake') is a traditional Brazilian drink and 'Abacaxi' means pineapple in Portuguese, the official language of Brazil.
Batida is a broad term for a drink usually containing fresh fruit, sugar and/or sweetened condensed milk (leite condensado). They are often blended with crushed ice or shaken and served over crushed ice.

BATIDA DE BANANA

★★★★⯨☆

Glass: Collins
Garnish: Banana chunk
Method: BLEND ingredients with 12oz scoop of crushed ice. Pour into glass and serve with straws.

2	shots	Leblon cachaça
1	fresh	Banana (peeled)
1	shot	Condensed milk

We say: So thick that this is something of a liquid dessert - surprisingly yummy.
Origin: The Batida (meaning 'shake') is a traditional Brazilian drink.

BATIDA DE CARNEVAL

★★★★⯨☆☆

Glass: Collins
Garnish: Mango slice
Method: BLEND all ingredients with 12oz scoop crushed ice and serve with straws.

2	shots	Leblon cachaça
2	shots	Boiron mango purée
1	shot	Freshly squeezed orange juice
1	shot	Condensed milk

We say: So thick and fruity this easy, smoothie-style drink is something of a meal in itself - a three-course dessert that is.
Origin: The Batida (meaning 'shake') is a traditional Brazilian drink and 'Carneval' means mango in Portuguese, the official language of Brazil.

BATIDA DE COCO

★★★☆☆

Glass: Collins
Garnish: Dust with grated nutmeg
Method: BLEND ingredients with 12oz scoop of crushed ice. Pour into glass and serve with straws.

2	shots	Leblon cachaça
2	shots	Coco López cream of coconut
1	shot	Condensed milk

We say: As the name would suggest this is literally an alcoholic coconut-flavoured shake.
Origin: Literally meaning a shake of coconut, this is a traditional Brazilian drink.

BARTENDER'S TIP SWIZZLE

To 'swizzle' a drink is simply to stir it using a particular tool and action.

To swizzle simply immerse the blades of your swizzle stick into the drink, hold the shaft between the palms of both hands and rotate the stick rapidly by sliding your hands back and forth against it. If you do not have a bona fide swizzle stick, use a barspoon in the same manner.

BATIDA DE GOIBA

★★★☆☆

Glass: Collins
Garnish: Mango slice
Method: SHAKE all ingredients with ice and strain into glass filled with crushed ice.

2	shots	Leblon cachaça
2½	shots	Guava juice
1	shot	Condensed milk

We say: An alcoholic guava-flavoured shake.
Origin: The Batida (meaning 'shake') is a traditional Brazilian drink and "Goiba" means guava in Portuguese, the official language of Brazil.

BATIDA DE MILHO VERDE

★★★½☆

Glass: Collins
Garnish: Dust with cinnamon powder
Method: BLEND all ingredients with 12oz scoop crushed ice. Serve with straws.

2½	shots	Leblon cachaça
70	gram	Sweetcorn (canned)
1½	shots	Condensed milk

We say: Quite possibly your first sweetcorn cocktail.
Origin: A classic Brazilian drink.

BATIDA DE MORANGO

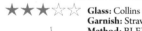

★★★☆☆

Glass: Collins
Garnish: Strawberry
Method: BLEND all ingredients with 12oz scoop crushed ice. Serve with straws.

2	shots	Leblon cachaça
12	fresh	Strawberries (hulled)
1	shot	Crème de fraise liqueur
½	shot	Condensed milk

We say: Strawberry milkshake laced with cachaça.
Origin: The Batida (meaning 'shake') is a traditional Brazilian drink and 'Morango' means strawberry in Portuguese, the official language of Brazil.

BATIDA ROSA

★★★½☆

Glass: Large wine glass
Garnish: Pineapple wedge
Method: SHAKE first three ingredients with ice and strain into ice-filled glass. TOP with soda.

2	shots	Leblon cachaça
1	shot	Freshly squeezed lemon juice
1	shot	Fresh pressed pineapple juice
½	shot	Pomegranate (grenadine) syrup
Top up with		Soda (club soda)

We say: Cachaça pleasantly shines in this balanced fruity, Daiquiri-style drink.
Origin: Adapted from a drink created in 2008 by Jeffrey Morgenthaler at Bel Ami Lounge, Oregon, USA.

BAY BREEZE

★★★½☆

Glass: Collins
Garnish: Pineapple wedge
Method: SHAKE all ingredients with ice and strain into ice-filled glass.

2	shots	Ketel One vodka
1½	shots	Ocean Spray cranberry juice
2½	shots	Fresh pressed pineapple juice

We say: Pink, fluffy, sweet and easy to drink.

BAZOOKA

★★½☆☆

Glass: Shot
Garnish: None
Method: SHAKE all ingredients with ice and fine strain into chilled glass.

¾	shot	Southern Comfort liqueur
½	shot	Bols Banana liqueur
⅛	shot	Pomegranate (grenadine) syrup
¼	shot	Double (heavy) cream

We say: A sticky, pink shot.

BAZOOKA JOE

★★½☆☆

Glass: Shot
Garnish: None
Method: Refrigerate ingredients then LAYER in chilled glass by carefully pouring in the order listed.

½	shot	Bols Blue Curaçao liqueur
½	shot	Bols Banana liqueur
½	shot	Baileys Irish cream liqueur

We say: Banana and orange topped with whiskey cream.

BÉNÉDICTINE CONVERSION NEW

★★★★½

Glass: Martini
Garnish: None
Method: STIR all ingredients with ice and strain into chilled glass.

1	shot	Tequila 100% Agave
½	spoon	Mezcal
¼	shot	Bénédictine D.O.M.
¼	shot	White Crème de Cacao
¾	shot	Chilled mineral water

We say: A Mexican flavour trio (chocolate is an important Mexican export) converted by a herbal French liqueur.
Origin: Created in 2011 by Ian Cameron at the Cabinet Room, London, England.

BBC

★★★⯪☆

Glass: Martini
Garnish: Dust with grated nutmeg
Method: SHAKE all ingredients with ice and fine strain into chilled glass.

1¼ shots	Cognac VSOP
1 shot	Bénédictine D.O.M.
¾ shot	Double (heavy) cream
¾ shot	Milk

We say: Brandy and Bénédictine (a classic combo) smoothed with cream. Drier than you might expect.
Origin: Thought to have originated in the UK in the late 1970s and named, not after the British Broadcasting Company, but brandy, Bénédictine and cream.

BBC COCKTAIL

★★★★☆

Glass: Old-fashioned
Garnish: Apple fan
Method: STIR all ingredients with ice and strain into ice-filled glass.

2 shots	Bacardi 8yo aged rum
½ shot	Becherovka liqueur
1 dash	Wormwood bitters

We say: Based on the classic BandB cocktail with Bacardi rum replacing brandy and Becherovka in place of Bènèdictine.
Origin: Created in 2009 by Marian Beke at the Artesian Bar, London, England. The Artesian Bar sits in the Langham Hotel opposite the BBC's Broadcasting House. Indeed, the BBC moved into the Langham after the Broadcasting House was bombed during the Second World War ...they stayed almost 20 years.

BE-TON

★★★⯪☆

Glass: Collins
Garnish: Lime wedge
Method: POUR Becherovka into ice-filled glass, then TOP with tonic water and stir.

2 shots	Becherovka liqueur
Top up with	Tonic water

We say: This spicy drink is the Czech Republic's answer to the Gin 'n' Tonic.
Origin: Becherovka (or Carlsbad Becher as it's sometimes known) is the Czech national liqueur. Matured in oak, it contains cinnamon, cloves, nutmeg and other herbs.

BEACH BLONDE

★★★★☆

Glass: Collins
Garnish: Banana chunk
Method: BLEND ingredients with 12oz scoop of crushed ice. Pour into glass and serve with straws.

½ fresh	Banana (peeled)
3 shots	Advocaat liqueur
1 shot	Wray & Nephew overproof rum
3 shots	Freshly squeezed orange juice

We say: Fruity, creamy holiday drinking.
Origin: Created in 2002 by Alex Kammerling, London, England.

BEACH ICED TEA

★★★⯪☆

Glass: Sling
Garnish: Lemon slice
Method: SHAKE all ingredients with ice and strain into ice-filled glass.

½ shot	Bacardi Superior rum
½ shot	Tanqueray London dry gin
½ shot	Ketel One vodka
½ shot	Tequila 100% Agave
½ shot	Triple Sec
1 shot	Freshly squeezed lemon juice
½ shot	Monin Pure Cane 2:1 sugar syrup
3 shots	Ocean Spray cranberry juice

We say: A Long Island Iced Tea with cranberry juice instead of cola.

BEACHCOMBER

★★★★☆

Glass: Martini
Garnish: Lime wedge
Method: SHAKE all ingredients with ice and fine strain into chilled glass.

2 shots	Bacardi Superior rum
½ shot	Triple Sec
¾ shot	Freshly squeezed lime juice
¼ shot	Luxardo Maraschino liqueur
½ shot	Chilled mineral water

We say: A Daiquiri with the addition of a dash of triple sec and maraschino.
Origin: Adapted from Patrick Gavin Duffy's 'The Official Mixer's Manual' (1956 James A. Beard edition).

BEACHCOMBER'S DAIQUIRI

★★★★☆

Glass: Martini
Garnish: Lime slice
Method: BLEND all ingredients with one 6oz scoop crushed ice and serve with straws.

2 shots	Bacardi Superior rum
1 shot	Triple Sec
¾ shot	Freshly squeezed lime juice

We say: Basically a frozen rum margarita.
Origin: Created by Ernest Raymond Beaumont-Gantt, A.K.A. Don The Beachcomber at his bar in Hollywood, California, USA.

STAR RATINGS EXPLAINED

★★★★★ Excellent

★★★★⯪ Recommended	★★★★☆ Praiseworthy
★★★⯪☆ Commended	★★★☆☆ Mediocre
★★⯪☆☆ Disappointing	★★☆☆☆ Pretty awful
★⯪☆☆☆ Shameful	★☆☆☆☆ Disgusting

BEACHCOMBER'S RUM BARREL

★★★½☆

Glass: Rum barrel mug or pint glass
Garnish: Pineapple wedge, maraschino cherry & mint sprig
Method: BLEND all ingredients with 12oz scoop crushed ice and serve with straws.

2	shots	**Bacardi Superior rum**
2	shots	**Myer's Planter's Punch rum**
1	shot	**Freshly squeezed orange juice**
1	shot	**Fresh pressed pineapple juice**
1	shot	**Freshly squeezed grapefruit juice**
¾	shot	**Freshly squeezed lime juice**
½	shot	**Monin Honey syrup**
¼	shot	**Pomegranate (grenadine) syrup**
¼	shot	**Berry Hill pimento allspice liqueur**
¼	shot	**Taylor's Velvet Falernum liqueur**
⅛	shot	**Absinthe**
1	dash	**Angostura aromatic bitters**

We say: A foamy head hides a tasty (and be warned) rum laced, tangy fruity drink.
Origin: Created by Ernest Raymond Beaumont-Gantt, A.K.A. Don The Beachcomber at his bar in Hollywood, California, USA.

BEAM-ME-UP SCOTTY

★★½☆☆

Glass: Shot
Garnish: None
Method: Refrigerate ingredients then LAYER in chilled glass by carefully pouring in the following order.

½	shot	**Kahlúa coffee liqueur**
½	shot	**Bols Banana liqueur**
½	shot	**Baileys Irish cream liqueur**

We say: Very sweet but not too offensive and easy to layer.

BEARSKIN MARTINI

★★★★☆

Glass: Martini
Garnish: Two Kalamata olives
Method: STIR all ingredients with ice and strain into chilled glass.

2½	shots	**Ketel One vodka**
⅛	shot	**Kümmel**
⅛	shot	**Martini Extra Dry vermouth**

We say: A caraway influenced Martini.

BEAUTIFUL LADY NEW

★★★★☆

Glass: Martini
Garnish: Grated chocolate
Method: STIR first 2 ingredients with ice and strain into chilled glass. FLOAT thin layer of lightly whipped cream.

1½	shots	**Mozart Dry chocolate spirit**
¾	shot	**Cherry brandy liqueur**
Float		**Double (heavy) cream**

We say: This dessert-style drink with cherry and chocolate combined under a layer of cream may be reminiscent of a black forest gateau, but the use of chocolate spirit rather than liqueur means it's not too sweet.
Origin: Created in 2010 by Klaus St. Rainer at Schumann's Bar Munich, Germany.

THE BEAUTY BENEATH

★★★★☆

Glass: Martini
Garnish: Orange zest twist
Method: STIR all ingredients with ice and strain into a chilled glass.

1¾	shots	**Bacardi 8yo aged rum**
½	shot	**Martini Rosso sweet vermouth**
½	shot	**Campari Bitter**
½	shot	**Triple Sec**
1	dash	**Angostura aromatic bitters**

We say: Orange dominates this bitter-sweet Manhattan, come Daiquiri, come Negroni.
Origin: Created in 2008 by Jeffrey Morgenthaler at Bel Ami Lounge, Oregon, USA.

BEBBO

★★★★☆

Glass: Martini
Garnish: Lemon zest twist
Method: STIR honey with gin in base of shaker until honey dissolves. Add other ingredients, SHAKE with ice and fine strain into chilled glass.

2	spoons	**Runny honey**
1½	shots	**Tanqueray London dry gin**
1	shot	**Freshly squeezed lemon juice**
½	shot	**Freshly squeezed orange juice**
¼	shot	**Chilled mineral water**

We say: Fresh, clean and fruity with honeyed notes. Choose your honey wisely.
Origin: A long lost relation of the Bee's Knees. This recipe is based on one from Ted Haigh's 2004 book *'Vintage Spirits & Forgotten Cocktails'.*

BEE STING

★★★★☆

Glass: Collins
Garnish: Apple slice
Method: STIR honey with whiskey in base of shaker until honey dissolves. Add tequila and apple juice, SHAKE with ice and strain into ice-filled glass. TOP with a splash of ginger ale

1	shot	**Straight rye whiskey**
1	spoon	**Runny honey**
1	shot	**Tequila 100% Agave**
2	shots	**Pressed apple juice**
Top up with		**Ginger ale**

We say: A delicately spiced, long, refreshing drink.
Origin: Discovered in 2005 at The Royal Exchange Grand Café & Bar, London, England.

STAR RATINGS EXPLAINED

★★★★★ Excellent

★★★★½	Recommended	★★★★☆	Praiseworthy
★★★½☆	Commended	★★★☆☆	Mediocre
★★½☆☆	Disappointing	★★☆☆☆	Pretty awful
★½☆☆☆	Shameful	★☆☆☆☆	Disgusting

BEE'S KNEES #1

★★★★☆

Glass: Martini
Garnish: Orange zest twist
Method: STIR honey with rum until honey dissolves. Add other ingredients, SHAKE with ice and fine strain into chilled glass.

1¼	shots	Bacardi Superior rum
1¼	shots	Pusser's Navy rum
2	spoons	Runny honey
1	shot	Freshly squeezed orange juice
½	shot	Milk
½	shot	Double (heavy) cream

We say: Smooth and orangey to start, with a rum and honey finish.

BEE'S KNEES #2 🔑

★★★★★

Glass: Martini
Garnish: Orange zest twist
Method: In base of shaker STIR honey with gin until honey dissolves. Add lemon and orange juice, SHAKE with ice and fine strain into chilled glass.

2	shots	Tanqueray London dry gin
3	spoons	Runny honey
1	shot	Freshly squeezed lemon juice
1	shot	Freshly squeezed orange juice

Variant: Made with light rum in place of gin this drink becomes a Honeysuckle Martini.
We say: This honeyed citrus concoction really is the bee's knees.
Origin: Adapted from David Embury's 1948 'The Fine Art Of Mixing Drinks'.

BEE'S KNEES #3 🔑

★★★★★

Glass: Martini
Garnish: Lemon zest twist
Method: In base of shaker STIR honey with gin until honey dissolves. Add lemon juice, SHAKE with ice and fine strain into chilled glass.

2	shots	Tanqueray London dry gin
3	spoons	Runny honey
¾	shot	Freshly squeezed lemon juice

We say: The combination of honey and lemon suggests flu relief but don't wait for an ailment before trying this soothing concoction.

BEETLE JEUSE

★★★★☆

Glass: Collins
Garnish: Mint sprig
Method: Lightly MUDDLE mint in base of shaker just enough to bruise. Add other ingredients, SHAKE with ice and strain into ice-filled glass.

7	fresh	Mint leaves
1	shot	Chartreuse Green liqueur
1	shot	Żubrówka bison vodka
3½	shots	Pressed apple juice
¼	shot	Passion fruit syrup

We say: Long and refreshing with a flavour reminiscent of caramelised apple.
Origin: Created in 2003 by Milo Rodriguez at Raoul's Bar, Oxford, and named after Beetlejuice, the Tim Burton black comedy about a young couple whose premature death leads them to a series of bizarre afterlife exploits.

BEGGAR'S BANQUET NEW

★★★★☆

Glass: Collins
Garnish: Orange slice
Method: SHAKE first four ingredients with ice and strain into ice-filled glass. TOP with beer.

2	shots	Maker's Mark bourbon
1	shot	Freshly squeezed lemon juice
¾	shot	Maple syrup
2	dashes	Angostura aromatic bitters
Top up with		British cask conditioned ale

We say: If using a 12oz glass you'll know you have great ice if when strained onto glass you have sufficient room for a good 1-2 shots of beer.
Origin: Created in 2010 by Aisha Sharpe, New York City, USA.

BEHEMOTH

★★★★☆

Glass: Martini
Garnish: Lemon zest twist
Method: SHAKE all ingredients with ice and fine strain into chilled glass.

1½	shots	Maker's Mark bourbon
¾	shot	White Crème de Cacao
1	shot	Martini Rosso sweet vermouth
¾	shot	Freshly squeezed lemon juice
½	shot	Monin Pure Cane 2:1 sugar syrup
½	fresh	Egg white
2	dashes	Peychaud's aromatic bitters

We say: Tangy, citrus bourbon with a hint of chocolate.
Origin: This monstrous beast was created in 2004 by Simon Difford.

BARTENDER'S TIP FLAME

The term ignite, flame or flambé means that the drink should be set alight.

Please exercise extreme care when setting fire to drinks. Be particularly careful not to knock over a lit drink and never attempt to carry a drink which is still alight. Before drinking, cover the glass so as to suffocate the flame and be aware that the rim of the glass may be hot.

BEJA FLOR

★★★★☆

Glass: Martini
Garnish: Banana chunk
Method: SHAKE all ingredients with ice and fine strain into chilled glass.

2	shots	Leblon cachaça
1	shot	Triple Sec
1	shot	Bols Banana liqueur
½	shot	Freshly squeezed lemon juice

We say: Sharp and quite dry but with a sweet banana twang.

BELLA DONNA DAIQUIRI

★★★★⯪

Glass: Martini
Garnish: Cinnamon powder rim
Method: SHAKE all ingredients with ice and fine strain into chilled glass.

1½	shots	Gosling's Black Seal rum
1½	shots	Amaretto liqueur
½	shot	Freshly squeezed lemon juice
¼	shot	Monin Pure Cane 2:1 sugar syrup
½	shot	Chilled mineral water

We say: This was the hit cocktail for diffordsguide staff at the Bellagio, Las Vegas, after working at the Nightclub & Bar Beverage Convention. Try one and see why.
Origin: Adapted from a drink discovered in 2003 at Bellagio, Las Vegas, USA.

BELLINI (DIFFORD'S FORMULA)

★★★★⯪

Glass: Flute
Garnish: Peach slice
Method: SHAKE first three ingredients with ice and fine strain into chilled glass. Add prosecco and gently stir.

2	shots	Boiron peach purée
½	shot	Crème de pêche de vigne liqueur
¼	shot	Freshly squeezed lemon juice
Top up with		Prosecco sparkling wine

We say: It's hard not to like this blend of peaches and sparkling wine.
Origin: It has long been traditional in Italy to marinade fresh peaches in wine and the Bellini draws on this tradition, combining prosecco wine with puréed white peaches. Giuseppe Cipriani created this drink at Harry's Bar, Venice, in 1945, fourteen years after he opened his tiny place on the edge of the Grand Canal, not far from St. Mark's Square. Cipriani named his cocktail after the 15th-century Venetian painter Giovanni Bellini due to the drink's pink hue and the painter's penchant for using rich pinks on his canvases.

Like many other legendary bars around the world, Harry's owes some of its notoriety to being patronised by probably the world's greatest drinker, Ernest Hemingway. It was also the haunt of Sinclair Lewis, Orson Welles, F. Scott Fitzgerald and Dorothy Parker, and continues to attract celebrities to this day. But you don't have to be a celebrity to go to Harry's Bar. Cocktail aficionados from around the world make pilgrimages to the birthplace of the Bellini to sample the original recipe.

White peaches are in season in Italy from May to September, so in Venice those bars that insist on only using fresh peaches rather than frozen purée sell the drink between May and October.

BELLINI-TINI

★★★★☆

Glass: Martini
Garnish: Peach slice
Method: SHAKE all ingredients with ice and fine strain into chilled glass.

2	shots	Ketel One vodka
½	shot	Peachtree peach schnapps
2	shots	Boiron peach purée
3	dashes	Peach bitters

We say: Peachy! Based on the Bellini, funnily enough.

BELLISSIMO

★★★☆☆

Glass: Old-fashioned
Garnish: Orange slice
Method: SHAKE all ingredients with ice and fine strain into chilled glass.

1	shot	Hazelnut liqueur
1	shot	Campari Bitter
1	shot	Limoncello liqueur
½	shot	Freshly squeezed lemon juice

We say: An unusual meld of flavours, but Campari lovers should give this a try.
Origin: Adapted from drink created in 2003 by Ben Davidson at Posh Lounge, Sydney, Australia.

BÉNÉDICTINE CONVERSION UPDATED

★★★★⯪

Glass: Martini
Garnish: None
Method: STIR all ingredients with ice and strain into chilled glass.

2	shots	Olmeca Altos 100% agave tequila
½	spoon	Del Maguey Mezcal
¼	shot	Bénédictine D.O.M.
¼	shot	Bols Cacao White
¾	shot	Chilled mineral water

We say: A Mexican flavour trio (chocolate is an important Mexican export) converted by a herbal French liqueur.
Origin: Created in 2011 by Ian Cameron at the Cabinet Room, London, England.

STAR RATINGS EXPLAINED

★★★★★ Excellent

★★★★⯪ Recommended	★★★★☆ Praiseworthy
★★★⯪☆ Commended	★★★☆☆ Mediocre
★★⯪☆☆ Disappointing	★★☆☆☆ Pretty awful
★⯪☆☆☆ Shameful	★☆☆☆☆ Disgusting

BENNY & HOT NEW

★★★★☆

Glass: Toddy
Garnish: Lemon slice
Method: POUR ingredients into warmed glass.

| 2 | shots | Bénédictine D.O.M. |
| 4 | shots | Boiling water |

We say: Make this winter warmer to the classic 'Burnley' 50:50 proportions and it can be a tad rich, hence the 1:2 proportions used here.
Origin: Burnley Miner's Club in North West England is, you might think somewhat bizarrely, thought to be the world's biggest single account for sales of Bénédictine. Its 700-odd members consume around 48 bottles each week. This conspicuous liqueur consumption dates back to after the Second World War when the men of the 11th battalion of the East Lancashire regiment were based in Normandy. They discovered the local liqueur, Bénédictine, which they drunk as a grog with hot water. This firm favourite of the regiment became known as a 'Benny and Hot' and its popularity travelled home with the troops to Lancashire towns such as Accrington and Burnley. At Burley Miner's Club the Benny & Hot is served 50/50 Bénédictine liqueur and hot water with a squeeze of lemon juice. We have not visited the club myself and it was Ludovic Miazga, Bénédictine's charismatic French brand ambassador, who recounted the serve he discovered while visiting the club. We must have looked sceptical because he was emphatic. "No bullshit," he said, before adding: "Excuse my French". It's not every day you hear an actual Frenchman say "Excuse my French" – so it must be true.

BENSONHURST

★★★★☆

Glass: Martini
Garnish: Maraschino cherry
Method: STIR all ingredients with ice and strain into chilled glass.

2	shots	Straight rye whiskey
¼	shot	Luxardo Maraschino liqueur
1	shot	Martini Extra Dry vermouth
⅛	shot	Cynar

We say: This Manhattan-like drink is one of many to emerge since 2006 taking their inspiration from the Brooklyn cocktail.
Origin: Adapted from a drink created in 2006 by Chad Solomon and named after a neighbourhood close to his home in Brooklyn, New York City, USA.

BENTLEY

★★★★☆

Glass: Old-fashioned
Garnish: Orange zest twist
Method: STIR all ingredients with ice and strain into empty glass

1½	shots	Calvados/Applejack brandy
1½	shots	Dubonnet Red (French made)
2	dashes	Peychaud's aromatic bitters

Variant: Originally served straight-up.
We say: Dry, spiced wine impregnated with apple - pretty damn good.
Origin: Adapted from Harry Craddock's 1930 'The Savoy Cocktail Book'.

BENTON'S OLD-FASHIONED UPDATED

★★★★★★

Glass: Old-fashioned
Garnish: Orange zest twist
Method: STIR bourbon and maple syrup in base of mixing glass until syrup dissolves. Add other ingredients, STIR with ice and strain into ice-filled glass.

2	shots	Maker's Mark bourbon (bacon fat washed)
¼	shot	Maple syrup (Grade B)
2	dash	Angostura aromatic bitters

We say: Even vegetarians like bacon and everybody likes Old Fashioneds.
Origin: Created in 2008 by Don Lee at PDT, New York City, USA. To make the fat washed bourbon: Grill 4 slices bacon to obtain 30ml/1oz of warm fat (originally Benton's bacon was used but any extra-smoky bacon will suffice) and pour this into a 75cl bottle so room. Leave to infuse at room temperature for a day before placing bottle in freezer to solidify to fat. Clarify the bourbon by straining into a clean bottle.

BERLIN SOUR

★★★★☆

Glass: Sour or Martini/Coupette
Garnish: Lemon slice & cherry on stick (sail)
Method: SHAKE all ingredients with ice and fine strain into chilled glass.

2	shots	Kümmel
½	shot	Luxardo Maraschino liqueur
1	shot	Freshly squeezed lemon juice
¼	shot	Monin Pure Cane 2:1 sugar syrup

We say: The sweet powerful flavours of kummel and maraschino liqueurs are tamed and harnessed in this sour.
Origin: Created in 2009 by Thorsten Pannek at Hilton, Frankfurt, Germany.

BERMONDSEY BREEZE

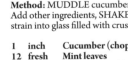

★★★★☆

Glass: Collins
Garnish: Cucumber slices
Method: MUDDLE cucumber in base of shaker. Add other ingredients, SHAKE with ice and fine strain into glass filled with crushed ice.

1	inch	Cucumber (chopped & peeled)
12	fresh	Mint leaves
2	shots	St–Germain elderflower liqueur
2	shots	Pinot Grigio white wine
1	shot	Freshly squeezed lime juice
¼	shot	Monin Pure Cane 2:1 sugar syrup

We say: Light and summery.
Origin: Created in 2008 by Scott Wallace at Village East, London, England.

BERMUDA COCKTAIL

★★★★☆
Glass: Martini
Garnish: Orange zest twist
Method: SHAKE all ingredients with ice and fine strain into chilled glass.

2	shots	Tanqueray London dry gin
½	shot	Peachtree peach schnapps
½	shot	Freshly squeezed orange juice
¼	shot	Pomegranate (grenadine) syrup

We say: Gin with a sweetening touch of peach, orange and pomegranate.
Origin: Adapted from Victor Bergeron's '*Trader Vic's Bartender's Guide*' (1972 revised edition).

BERMUDA ROSE COCKTAIL

★★★★☆
Glass: Martini
Garnish: Apricot slice
Method: SHAKE all ingredients with ice and fine strain into chilled glass.

2	shots	Tanqueray London dry gin
½	shot	De Kuyper Apricot Brandy liqueur
¼	shot	Pomegranate (grenadine) syrup
½	shot	Chilled mineral water

We say: Delicate, floral and aromatic. A hint of sweetness but not so as to offend.
Origin: Adapted from Victor Bergeron's '*Trader Vic's Bartender's Guide*' (1972 revised edition).

BERMUDA RUM SWIZZLE

★★★★☆
Glass: Collins
Garnish: Pineapple wedge & maraschino cherry
Method: Swizzle, or better and easier: SHAKE all ingredients with ice and strain into glass filled with crushed ice.

1	shot	Bacardi Oro golden rum
1	shot	Gosling's Black Seal rum
¾	shot	Taylor's Velvet Falernum liqueur
1	shot	Fresh pressed pineapple juice
1	shot	Freshly squeezed orange juice
½	shot	Freshly squeezed pink grapefruit juice
½	shot	Freshly squeezed lime juice
¼	shot	Freshly squeezed lemon juice
2	dashes	Angostura aromatic bitters

We say: Your five-a-day fruits in a glass, laced with pungent rums and clove infused Falernum.
Origin: This recipe is adapted from one by Del Pedro, originally from Bermuda but now resident in New York City. It came my way (in 1997) courtesy of the dangerously sexy LeNell Smothers, and apparently it originally heralds from the Swizzle Inn in Bermuda where their rather appropriate slogan is "Swizzle Inn, Swagger Out".

STAR RATINGS EXPLAINED

★★★★★ Excellent

★★★★⯪ Recommended	★★★★☆ Praiseworthy
★★★⯪☆ Commended	★★★☆☆ Mediocre
★★⯪☆☆ Disappointing	★★☆☆☆ Pretty awful
★⯪☆☆☆ Shameful	★☆☆☆☆ Disgusting

BERNICE NEW

★★★⯪☆
Glass: Coupette
Garnish: Mint sprig
Method: SHAKE all ingredients with ice and fine strain into chilled glass.

2	shots	Ketel One vodka
¾	shot	Freshly squeezed lime juice
¼	shot	Galliano L'Autentico liqueur
½	shot	Monin Pure Cane 2:1 sugar syrup

We say: Vodka and lime with sweet herbal peppermint courtesy of Galliano.
Origin: Adapted from a drink in Ted Saucier's 1951 book, "Bottoms Up!".

BERRY CAIPIRINHA

★★★★☆
Glass: Old-fashioned
Garnish: None
Method: MUDDLE lime and berries in base of glass. Add other ingredients and fill glass with crushed ice. CHURN drink with bar spoon and serve with short straws.

¾	fresh	Lime
3	fresh	Raspberries
3	fresh	Blackberries
2	shots	Leblon cachaça
¾	shot	Monin Pure Cane 2:1 sugar syrup

Variant: Black 'N' Blue Caipirovska
We say: A fruity version of the popular Brazilian drink.

BERRY NICE

★★★⯪☆
Glass: Collins
Garnish: Blackberries
Method: MUDDLE blackberries in base of shaker. Add next three ingredients, SHAKE with ice and strain into ice-filled glass. TOP with ginger beer.

5	fresh	Blackberries
2	shots	Ketel One vodka
¼	shot	Chambord black raspberry liqueur
½	shot	Freshly squeezed lemon juice
Top up with		Ginger beer

We say: Rich blackberry flavour with a strong ginger finish.
Origin: Adapted from a drink created in 2001 in the UK's The Living Room chain of bars.

BERRY SMASH (MOCKTAIL)

★★★★☆
Glass: Old-fashioned
Garnish: Seasonal berries
Method: SHAKE all ingredients with ice and strain into glass filled with crushed ice.

7	fresh	Raspberries
3	fresh	Blackberries
2	shots	Ocean Spray cranberry juice
1	shot	Pressed apple juice
½	shot	Freshly squeezed lemon juice
¼	spoon	Monin Honey syrup

We say: Red berries with a splash of apple juice and honey served over crushed ice.

BESSIE & JESSIE

★★★⯪☆

Glass: Collins
Garnish: Orange slice
Method: SHAKE all ingredients with ice and strain into ice-filled glass.

2	shots	Dewar's White label Scotch
2	shots	Advocaat liqueur
3½	shots	Milk

We say: Malty, creamy and eggy, but tasty.

BETSY ROSS NEW

★★★★⯪

Glass: Coupette
Garnish: Orange zest twist
Method: STIR all ingredients with ice and strain into chilled glass.

1½	shots	Courvoisier VSOP Exclusif
1½	shots	Ruby port
½	shot	Orange Curaçao liqueur
2	dashes	Angostura aromatic bitters

We say: Deep burgundy red and boozy and based in the classic combination of port and brandy, this is a drink to finish a night with. (Benefits from some dilution so stir well.)

BETWEEN DECKS ⛝

★★★⯪☆

Glass: Collins
Garnish: Pineapple wedge, maraschino cherry & mint sprig
Method: SHAKE all ingredients with ice and strain into ice-filled glass.

2½	shots	Tanqueray London dry gin
1	shot	Freshly squeezed orange juice
1	shot	Ocean Spray cranberry juice
½	shot	Freshly squeezed lime juice
¼	shot	Monin Pure Cane 2:1 sugar syrup
½	shot	Chilled mineral water

We say: I've upped the ante on this drink with more gin and less fruit than the original - so beware.
Origin: Adapted from Victor Bergeron's '*Trader vic's Bartender's Guide*' (1972 revised edition).

BETWEEN THE SHEETS #1 ⛝
(DIFFORD'S FORMULA)

★★★★⯪

Glass: Martini
Garnish: Lemon zest twist
Method: SHAKE all ingredients with ice and fine strain into chilled glass.

¾	shot	Bacardi Superior rum
¾	shot	Cognac VSOP
¾	shot	Triple Sec
¼	shot	Freshly squeezed lemon juice
⅛	shot	Monin Pure Cane 2:1 sugar syrup
½	shot	Chilled mineral water

We say: Classic proportions to this drink are most often quoted as being: 1 rum, 1 cognac, 1 triple sec and 1/4 lemon juice but three shots of 40% alcohol and a splash of lemon juice make for a tart drink which should not be undertaken lightly. The formula above maintains the essential flavour and ingredients of the classic recipe but is a little more approachable.
Origin: Created in the early 1930s (during Prohibition) by Harry MacElhone of Harry's New York Bar in Paris, and derived from the Sidecar.

BETWEEN THE SHEETS #2
(WONDRICH'S FORMULA)

★★★★★

Glass: Martini
Garnish: Orange zest twist (flamed)
Method: SHAKE all ingredients with ice and fine strain into chilled glass.

1	shot	Cognac VSOP
½	shot	Bénédictine D.O.M.
½	shot	Triple Sec
¼	shot	Freshly squeezed lemon juice
½	shot	Chilled mineral water

We say: Bènèdictine takes the place of rum in this variation on a classic.
Origin: Formula adapted from recipe by David Wondrich. We've cut the lemon by a third, and when using fresh ice added a splash of water.

BEVERLY HILLS HOTEL MARTINI

★★★★☆

Glass: Martini
Garnish: Rosemary sprig
Method: SHAKE all ingredients with ice and fine strain into chilled glass.

2	shots	Tanqueray London dry gin
1	shot	St~Germain elderflower liqueur
1	shot	Freshly squeezed pink grapefruit juice

We say: Dry, but not oppressively so. Zingy grapefruit with gin complexity and delicate floral notes.
Origin: Adapted from a drink created in 2007 by Philip Spee at The Beverly Hills Hotel, California, USA.

BARTENDER'S TIP THROWING

Sometimes also referred to as the 'Cuban Roll' after the origin of this method of mixing, 'throwing' offers greater dilution and aeration than stirring but is more gentle than shaking. It is achieved by simply pouring the ingredients from one container to another. To do this, assemble your ingredients in a mixing glass or base of your shaker. Add ice and strain into a second mixing glass with a large diameter lipped rim increasing the distance between the two vessels as you pour. Then pour the partially mixed cocktail back into the first ice-filled container and strain into the second once again. Repeat this process several times and you will have 'thrown' your drink.

BEVERLY HILLS ICED TEA

★★★⯪☆

Glass: Sling
Garnish: Lime zest twist
Method: SHAKE first five ingredients with ice and strain into ice-filled glass. TOP with champagne and gently stir.

¾	shot	Tanqueray London dry gin
¾	shot	Ketel One vodka
1	shot	Triple Sec
½	shot	Freshly squeezed lime juice
½	shot	Monin Pure Cane 2:1 sugar syrup
Top up with		Brut champagne

We say: Very strong and refreshing.

BG3 NEW

★★★⯪☆

Glass: Collins
Garnish: Lemon wedge
Method: SHAKE first 3 ingredients with ice and strain into ice-filled glass. Top up with bitter lemon and lightly stir.

2	shots	Bols Genever
1	shot	Cointreau triple sec
2	dashes	Orange bitters
Top up with		Bitter lemon

We say: A long, refreshing drink combining the full-bodied flavours of genever with sweet orange and bitter lemon.
Origin: A drink promoted by Bols.

BIARRITZ

★★★⯪☆

Glass: Old-fashioned
Garnish: Orange slice & cherry on stick (sail)
Method: SHAKE all ingredients with ice and strain into ice-filled glass.

2	shots	Cognac VSOP
1	shot	Grand Marnier liqueur
¾	shot	Freshly squeezed lemon juice
3	dashes	Angostura aromatic bitters
½	fresh	Egg white

We say: Basically a brandy sour with a little something extra from the orange liqueur.

BIBLICAL SIDECAR NEW

★★★★☆

Glass: Coupette
Garnish: Orange zest twist
Method: MUDDLE cloves in base of shaker glass. Add other ingredients, SHAKE with ice and fine strain into chilled glass.

1	dried	Clove
2	shots	Courvoisier Exclusif VSOP cognac
½	shot	Grand Marnier liqueur
¼	shot	Domain de Canton ginger liqueur
¾	shot	Freshly squeezed orange juice

We say: Cognac and freshly squeezed orange juice warmed with ginger and clove spice.
Origin: A Christmas cocktail created in October 2011 by Simon Difford at the Cabinet Room, London, England.

BICARDAR

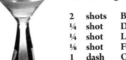

★★★★☆

Glass: Martini
Garnish: Lemon zest twist
Method: STIR all ingredients with ice and strain into chilled glass.

2	shots	Bacardi Superior rum
¼	shot	De Kuyper Apricot Brandy liqueur
¼	shot	Luxardo Maraschino liqueur
⅛	shot	Freshly squeezed lemon juice
1	dash	Orange bitters
¼	shot	Chilled mineral water

We say: Subtle and delicate with hints of apricot, cherry, lemon and orange.
Origin: Created in 2008 by Kashi Forootani at Seattle Hotel, Brighton, England.

BIG APPLE MARTINI

★★★⯪☆

Glass: Martini
Garnish: Apple wedge
Method: SHAKE all ingredients with ice and fine strain into chilled glass.

2½	shots	Ketel One vodka
1	shot	Berentzen Apple schnapps
1	shot	Sour apple liqueur

AKA: Apple Martini, Sour Apple Martini
We say: There's no apple juice in this Martini, but it has an appealing light minty green hue.

THE BIG EASY

★★★★☆

Glass: Collins
Garnish: Orange slice
Method: SHAKE first three ingredients with ice and strain into ice-filled glass. TOP with ginger ale.

¾	shot	Triple Sec
1¾	shots	Southern Comfort liqueur
2	shots	Freshly squeezed orange juice
Top up with		Ginger ale

We say: Fruity and refreshing with a hint of spice.

BIG JUICY (MOCKTAIL)

★★★⯪☆

Glass: Collins
Garnish: Lime wedge
Method: SHAKE first five ingredients with ice and strain into ice-filled glass. TOP with soda, stir and serve with straws.

2½	shots	Ocean Spray cranberry juice
1½	shots	Fresh pressed pineapple juice
1	shot	Freshly squeezed lime juice
¼	shot	Monin Pure Cane 2:1 sugar syrup
¼	shot	Pomegranate (grenadine) syrup
Top up with		Soda (club soda)

We say: Everything about this drink is juicy, even its creator. A tasty way to top up your vitamin C levels.
Origin: Created in 2006 by Jose 'Juice' Miranda at Wd-50, New York City, USA.

BIGGLES AVIATION

★★★★☆

Glass: Martini
Garnish: Fresh ginger & lime slices
Method: SHAKE all ingredients with ice and strain into ice-filled glass.

2	shots	**Tanqueray London dry gin**
½	shot	**Domaine de Canton ginger liqueur**
½	shot	**Freshly squeezed lemon juice**
¼	shot	**Monin Pure Cane 2:1 sugar syrup**
¼	shot	**Chilled mineral water**

We say: A ginger influenced Aviation named after fictional flying heroes. The ginger used in Canton's liqueur is also sourced from Borneo. How neat.
Origin: Created in 2008 by Simon Difford at the Cabinet Room, London, England.

BIGGLES SIDECAR

★★★★½

Glass: Martini
Garnish: Fresh ginger & lemon slices
Method: SHAKE all ingredients with ice and fine strain into chilled glass.

2	shots	**Cognac VSOP**
½	shot	**Domaine de Canton ginger liqueur**
½	shot	**Freshly squeezed lemon juice**
¼	shot	**Monin Pure Cane 2:1 sugar syrup**
1	dash	**Peychaud's aromatic bitters**
½	shot	**Chilled mineral water**

We say: I set out to make an Aviation - but ginger cries out for cognac so I also ended up with this Sidecar twist.
Origin: Created in 2008 by Simon Difford, The Cabinet Room, London, England.
As a kid I was a Biggles reader and fan and I was working on a theme (see Biggles Aviation).

BIJOU #1 (AKA AMBER DREAM) NEW

★☆☆☆☆

Glass: Coupette
Garnish: Lemon zest twist (discarded) and olive
Method: STIR all ingredients with ice and strain into chilled glass.

1½	shot	**Tanqueray London dry gin**
½	shot	**Green Chartreuse liqueur**
1½	shot	**Martini Rosso sweet vermouth**
4	drops	**Orange bitters**
½	shot	**Chilled water (omit if wet ice)**

We say: It is not uncommon to see this drink stipulated with equal parts gin, Chartreuse and sweet vermouth, as called for in Harry Johnson's 1882 *Bartender's Manual.* It's also not uncommon to see this shaken rather than stirred. Both variations work, but equal parts is strong enough to drop a rhinoceros and shaken ruins the amber appearance. The level of booze in this drink makes dilution key to its success, so don't be scared to up the amount of water if using huge chunks of ice fresh out the freezer.
Origin: Recipe adapted from Harry Johnson's 1882 *Bartender's Manual* which calls for "⅓ wine glass Chartreuse (green); ⅓ wine glass vermouth (Italian); ⅓ wine glass of Plymouth gin; 1 dash orange bitters".

BIJOU #2 UPDATED

★★★☆☆

Glass: Shot
Garnish: None
Method: Carefully LAYER ingredients in the following order.

½	shot	**Martini Rosso sweet vermouth**
½	shot	**Chartreuse Green liqueur**
½	shot	**Tanqueray London dry gin**

We say: A shot loaded with bold flavours best suited to fans of Chartreuse.
Origin: This vintage layered, or 'pousse-café'-style drink is named after the French for 'jewel', apparently a reference to its trio of ingredients having the colours of the three most precious jewels: diamond (gin), ruby (sweet vermouth) and emerald (Green Chartreuse). If all the ingredients, and so the colours, are mixed together the result is a rather better 'Bijou #1', also aptly named Amber Dream due to its colour. If I were you I wouldn't bother with this layered drink, grab a stirring glass and enjoy an Amber Dream.

BIKINI MARTINI

★★★★☆

Glass: Martini
Garnish: Orange zest twist
Method: SHAKE all ingredients with ice and fine strain into chilled glass.

2	shots	**Tanqueray London dry gin**
¼	shot	**Peachtree peach schnapps**
¾	shot	**Bols Blue Curaçao liqueur**
¼	shot	**Freshly squeezed lemon juice**
½	shot	**Chilled mineral water**

We say: A vivid blue combination of lemon, orange and peach laced with gin.
Origin: Adapted from a cocktail created in 1999 by Dick Bradsell for an Agent Provocateur swimwear launch. The bikini swimsuit was named after Bikini Atoll, where A-bombs were tested after World War II, on the basis that such a revealing garment would cause as much shock as a thermonuclear device.

BINGO

★★★☆☆

Glass: Collins
Garnish: Lemon slice
Method: SHAKE first four ingredients with ice and strain into ice-filled glass. TOP with soda water.

1	shot	**Ketel One vodka**
1	shot	**Grand Marnier liqueur**
1	shot	**De Kuyper Apricot Brandy liqueur**
½	shot	**Freshly squeezed lemon juice**
Top up with		**Soda (club soda)**

We say: Refreshing, fruity long drink.

STAR RATINGS EXPLAINED

★★★★★ Excellent

★★★★½	Recommended	★★★★☆	Praiseworthy
★★★½☆	Commended	★★★☆☆	Mediocre
★★½☆☆	Disappointing	★★☆☆☆	Pretty awful
★½☆☆☆	Shameful	★☆☆☆☆	Disgusting

THE BIRD IS THE WORD NO.1

★★★★☆

Glass: Coupette
Garnish: Lemon zest twist
Method: SHAKE all ingredients with ice and fine strain into chilled glass.

1½	shots	Tequila 100% Agave
1	shot	Chartreuse Yellow liqueur
½	shot	De Kuyper Apricot Brandy liqueur
1	shot	Freshly squeezed lemon juice

We say: To quote Fraser Campbell, the drink's creator, "influenced primarily by "The Last Word" with hints of "Yellow Parrot" ...and a tequila base."
Origin: Adapted from a drink created in May 2010 by Fraser Campbell at Tony Starr's Kitten Club, Melbourne, Australia.

THE BIRD IS THE WORD NO.2 NEW

★★★★☆

Glass: Coupette
Garnish: Maraschino cherry
Method: SHAKE all ingredients with ice and fine strain into chilled glass.

¾	shot	Grappa di Moscato
¾	shot	Chartreuse Green liqueur
½	shot	Luxardo Maraschino liqueur
½	shot	Freshly squeezed lime juice
½	shot	Chilled mineral water
1	dash	Chocolate bitters

We say: A grappa based *'Last Word'* by way of Denmark.
Origin: Adapted from a drink discovered at Salon 39, Copenhagen, Denmark.

BIRD OF PARADISE

★★★☆☆

Glass: Martini
Garnish: Dust with grated nutmeg
Method: SHAKE all ingredients with ice and fine strain into chilled glass.

1¼	shots	Tequila 100% Agave
¾	shot	White Crème de Cacao
½	shot	Amaretto liqueur
1	shot	Double (heavy) cream
¾	shot	Milk

We say: If you like tequila and creamy drinks, the two don't mix much better than this.

BISHOP

★★★★☆

Glass: Toddy
Garnish: Dust with grated nutmeg
Method: MUDDLE cloves in base of shaker. Add boiling water and STIR in honey and other ingredients. Fine strain into glass and MICROWAVE for 20 seconds. STIR and garnish.

7	dried	Cloves
2	spoons	Runny honey
3	shots	Boiling water
2½	shots	Warre's Otima tawny port
1	shot	Freshly squeezed orange juice

We say: A flavoursome variation on mulled wine.
Origin: Our quick 'n' easy take on this variation of the 18th century Negus. The traditional recipe begins with studding an orange with cloves and roasting it.

BISON SOUR

★★★☆☆

Glass: Old-fashioned
Garnish: Lemon zest twist
Method: SHAKE all ingredients with ice and strain into ice-filled glass.

2	shots	Żubrówka bison vodka
1	shot	Freshly squeezed lemon juice
½	shot	Monin Pure Cane 2:1 sugar syrup
1	pinch	Ground cinnamon
½	fresh	Egg white

We say: A flavour-enhanced vodka sour.

THE BISTRO SIDECAR

★★★★☆

Glass: Martini
Garnish: Lemon zest twist
Method: SHAKE all ingredients with ice and fine strain into chilled glass.

1½	shots	Cognac VSOP
½	shot	Tuaca liqueur
½	shot	Hazelnut liqueur
¼	shot	Freshly squeezed lemon juice
¼	shot	Freshly squeezed orange juice

We say: Although significantly twisted from the classic, this is still recognisably a Sidecar in style.
Origin: Adapted from a recipe by chef Kathy Casey Food Studios, Seattle, USA. Kathy's original recipe called for a sugar rim and tangerine juice.

BIT-O-HONEY

★★★☆☆

Glass: Shot
Garnish: None
Method: Refrigerate ingredients then LAYER in chilled glass by carefully pouring in the following order.

¾	shot	Butterscotch schnapps
¾	shot	Baileys Irish cream liqueur

Variant: Layered with butterscotch, then honey liqueur and an Irish cream float.
We say: A sweet but pleasant tasting shot.

BITCHES BREW

★★★★☆

Glass: Sour or Martini/Coupette
Garnish: Dust with grated nutmeg
Method: DRY SHAKE all ingredients without ice. Add ice, SHAKE again and fine strain into chilled glass.

1	shot	Martinique agricole rum
1	shot	Bacardi 8yo aged rum
1	shot	Freshly squeezed lime juice
½	shot	Berry Hill pimento allspice liqueur
½	shot	Monin Pure Cane 2:1 sugar syrup
1	shot	Egg

We say: This flavoursome flip-style drink comes served with a hint of Caribbean spice.
Origin: Created in 2008 by Daniel Eun at PDT, New York City, USA.

BITTER AND TWISTED NAIL

★★★☆☆

Glass: Old-fashioned
Garnish: Orange zest twist
Method: STIR all ingredients with ice and fine strain into ice-filled glass.

1½ shots	Dewar's White label Scotch
½ shot	Drambuie
½ shot	Campari Bitter

We say: A Nail that will appeal to Negroni lovers.
Origin: Created in 2010 by Simon Difford at the Cabinet Room, London, England.

BITTER ELDER

★★★☆☆

Glass: Collins
Garnish: Lemon wedge
Method: SHAKE all ingredients with ice and strain into ice-filled glass.

2 shots	Tanqueray London dry gin
1 shot	St~Germain elderflower liqueur
2 shots	Pressed apple juice
¾ shot	Freshly squeezed lemon juice
3 dashes	Angostura aromatic bitters

We say: The eponymous elderflower is well balanced with the other ingredients to make a dry refreshing long drink.
Origin: Adapted from a short drink created in 2005 by Tonin Kacaj at Maze, London, England.

BITTER GRAPEFRUIT

★★★☆☆

Glass: Martini
Garnish: Grapefruit zest twist
Method: SHAKE all ingredients with ice and fine strain into chilled glass.

1½ shots	Ketel One vodka
½ shot	Aperol
1 shot	Martini Rosso sweet vermouth
½ shot	Freshly squeezed pink grapefruit juice

We say: Grapefruit influenced and Negroni in style.
Origin: Discovered in 2007 at Public Restaurant, New York City, USA.

BITTER LADY

★★★★☆

Glass: Martini
Garnish: Grapefruit zest twist
Method: SHAKE all ingredients with ice and fine strain into chilled glass.

1½ shots	Tanqueray London dry gin
1 spoon	Runny honey
¼ shot	Campari Bitter
½ shot	Freshly squeezed lemon juice
½ fresh	Egg white

We say: We have dramatically cut the Campari and lemon in Mickael's original recipe to make a much lighter drink.
Origin: Adapted from a drink created by Mickael Perron from Bar Now On.

BITTER SWEET SYMPHONY ⚷

★★★☆☆

Glass: Martini
Garnish: Apricot slice
Method: SHAKE all ingredients with ice and fine strain into chilled glass.

½ shot	Ketel One vodka
1 shot	Triple Sec
1 shot	De Kuyper Apricot Brandy liqueur
½ shot	Freshly squeezed lime juice
1½ shots	Freshly squeezed grapefruit juice

We say: This roller coaster ride of bitter and sweet mainly features apricot and grapefruit.
Origin: Adapted from a drink created in 2003 by Wayne Collins for Maxxium UK.

BITTEREST PILL

★★★☆☆

Glass: Shot
Garnish: None
Method: Refrigerate ingredients then LAYER in chilled glass by carefully pouring in the following order.

½ shot	Ketel One vodka
½ shot	Campari Bitter
½ shot	Passion fruit syrup

We say: The bitterness of Campari, toned down by passion fruit sugar syrup.
Origin: Created by Alex Kammerling, London, England.

BLACK & TAN

★★★☆☆

Glass: Pint
Garnish: None
Method: POUR lager into chilled glass then FLOAT Guinness on top.

| ½ pint | Lager |
| ½ pint | Guinness |

We say: Lager downstairs, Guinness upstairs.

BLACK & VELVET

★★★☆☆

Glass: Boston
Garnish: None
Method: POUR cider into chilled glass then FLOAT Guinness on top.

| ½ pint | Dry cider |
| ½ pint | Guinness |

We say: Cider downstairs, Guinness upstairs

BLACK & WHITE DAIQUIRI

★★★★⯪ **Glass:** Martini
Garnish: Blackberries
Method: MUDDLE berries in base of shaker. Add other ingredients, SHAKE with ice and fine strain into chilled glass.

12	fresh	Blackberries
2	shots	Malibu coconut rum liqueur
1	shot	Bacardi Superior rum
¾	shot	Crème de Mûre liqueur
½	shot	Freshly squeezed lime juice
½	shot	Chilled mineral water

We say: Blackberries and coconut add depth to the classic Daiquiri.
Origin: Created by Simon Difford, named after the blackberries and the white Malibu bottle.

BLACK 'N' BLUE CAIPIROVSKA

★★★★☆ **Glass:** Old-fashioned
Garnish: None
Method: MUDDLE berries in base of glass. Add other ingredients. Fill glass with crushed ice and CHURN (stir) with bar spoon. Serve with straws.

6	fresh	Blackberries
10	fresh	Blueberries
2	shots	Ketel One vodka
½	shot	Freshly squeezed lime juice
¾	shot	Monin Pure Cane 2:1 sugar syrup

We say: A great fruity twist on the regular Caipirovska.

BLACK BEARD

★★★☆☆ **Glass:** Pint
Garnish: None
Method: POUR ingredients in glass and serve.

2	shots	Bacardi Superior rum
½	pint	Guinness
Top up with		Coca-Cola

We say: Something of a student drink, this tastes better than it sounds.
Origin: Thought to have originated in Stirling, Scotland, during the late 1990s.

BLACK BISON MARTINI

★★★★⯪ **Glass:** Martini
Garnish: Apple wedge
Method: SHAKE all ingredients with ice and fine strain into chilled glass.

2	shots	Tanqueray London dry gin
½	shot	Berentzen Apple schnapps
1½	shots	Pressed apple juice
¼	shot	Martini Extra Dry vermouth

We say: A fragrant cocktail with a dry finish. As the name suggests, also works well with Zubrowka Bison vodka in place of gin.
Origin: Adapted from a drink discovered in 2001 at Oxo Tower Bar, London, England.

BLACK CHERRY MARTINI

★★★★☆ **Glass:** Martini
Garnish: Maraschino cherry
Method: SHAKE all ingredients with ice and fine strain into chilled glass.

| 2½ | shots | Ketel One vodka |
| 1 | shot | Chambord black raspberry liqueur |

We say: Subtle berry fruit tames vodka's sting.

BLACK DREAM

★★★☆☆ **Glass:** Shot
Garnish: None
Method: Refrigerate ingredients then LAYER in chilled glass by carefully pouring in the following order.

| ½ | shot | Opal Nera black sambuca |
| ½ | shot | Baileys Irish cream liqueur |

We say: Slippery Nipple with black sambuca.

BLACK EYE

★★★⯪☆ **Glass:** Old-fashioned
Garnish: Seasonal berries & mint sprig
Method: MUDDLE first three ingredients in base of shaker. Add other ingredients, SHAKE with ice and strain into ice-filled glass.

2	fresh	Blackberries
5	fresh	Raspberries
5	fresh	Mint leaves
2	shots	Jameson Irish whiskey
¾	shot	Drambuie
¼	shot	Crème de cassis liqueur

We say: A fruity Rusty Nail variation.
Origin: Created in 2008 by Simon Lamont at Jardine, Cape Town, South Africa.

BLACK FEATHER

★★★★☆ **Glass:** Martini
Garnish: Lemon zest twist
Method: STIR all ingredients with ice and strain into chilled glass.

2	shots	Cognac VSOP
½	shot	Triple Sec
1	shot	Martini Extra Dry vermouth
1	dash	Angostura aromatic bitters

We say: Rounded cognac notes with a hint of orange. For dry, adult palates.
Origin: Adapted from a drink created in 2000 by Robert Hess and published on drinkboy.com

BLACK FOREST GATEAU MARTINI

★★★★★ (4½)

Glass: Martini
Garnish: Dust with chocolate powder
Method: SHAKE first four ingredients with ice and strain into chilled glass. FLOAT cream on drink.

2	shots	Ketel One vodka
¾	shot	Chambord black raspberry liqueur
¾	shot	Crème de fraise du bois liqueur
1	shot	Double (heavy) cream
¼	shot	Crème de cassis liqueur

We say: Dessert by name and dessert by nature. Wonderfully moreish, naughty but very nice.
Origin: Created in 2002 at Hush, London, England.

BLACK IRISH

★★★☆☆

Glass: Hurricane
Garnish: Dust with chocolate powder
Method: BLEND ingredients with 12oz scoop of crushed ice. Pour into glass and serve with straws.

1	shot	Ketel One vodka
1	shot	Baileys Irish cream liqueur
1	shot	Kahlúa coffee liqueur
2	scoops	Häagen Dazs vanilla ice cream

AKA: Frozen Black Irish
We say: Like a very sweet, alcoholic, frozen caffé latte.

BLACK JACK COCKTAIL

★★★★☆

Glass: Martini
Garnish: Lemon zest twist
Method: STIR all ingredients with ice and strain into chilled glass.

1½	shots	Tanqueray London dry gin
½	shot	Kirschwasser eau de vie
½	shot	Crème de cassis liqueur
¾	shot	Chilled mineral water

We say: More burgundy than black but dark fruits of the forest dominate this medium dry cocktail.
Origin: The name Black Jack traditionally refers to a water bottle made from air dried leather. When the leather was dried it tended to turn black.

BLACK JACK SHOT

★★★☆☆

Glass: Shot
Garnish: None
Method: Refrigerate ingredients then LAYER in chilled glass by carefully pouring in the following order.

| ¾ | shot | Opal Nera black sambuca |
| ¾ | shot | Jack Daniels Tennessee whiskey |

We say: Whiskey sweetened with sambuca.

BLACK JAPAN

★★½☆☆

Glass: Collins
Garnish: None
Method: POUR melon liqueur into chilled glass then float Guinness on top.

| 1½ | shots | Midori green melon liqueur |
| Float | | Guinness |

We say: This student-style drink will appeal to those with youthful exuberance and a sweet tooth.
Origin: Black Japan is the name of a protective lacquer applied to metal.

BLACK MAGIC

★★★★☆

Glass: Flute
Garnish: Black grapes
Method: MUDDLE grapes in base of shaker. Add liqueur, SHAKE with ice and fine strain into chilled glass. TOP with champagne.

12	fresh	Red grapes
½	shot	Grand Marnier liqueur
Top up with		Brut champagne

We say: More peachy in colour than black but balanced and tasty. Not sweet.

BLACK MARTINI

★★★★½

Glass: Martini
Garnish: Dust with grated white chocolate
Method: SHAKE all ingredients with ice and fine strain into chilled glass.

1½	shots	Bacardi Superior rum
1½	shots	Dark Crème de Cacao
1½	shots	Hot espresso coffee

We say: This flavoursome mix of coffee and chocolate is further enhanced if vanilla-infused rum is used.
Origin: Created in March 2004 by Simon Difford.

BLACK MUSSEL

★★★½☆

Glass: Flute
Garnish: Orange zest twist (discarded)
Method: POUR first two ingredients into glass and TOP with champagne.

½	shot	Bols Blue Curaçao liqueur
¼	shot	Crème de cassis liqueur
Top up with		Brut champagne

We say: Blue curaçao adds a hint of orange to a Kir Royale.

BLACK NAIL #1

★★★★½ **Glass:** Old-fashioned
Garnish: Lemon zest twist
Method: STIR all ingredients with ice and fine strain into chilled glass.

½	shot	Lagavulin 16yo malt whisky
½	shot	Drambuie
1	shot	Dewar's White Label Scotch
1	shot	Honey flavoured vodka

We say: A suitably hardened nail variation with a full three measures of spirit.
Origin: Created in 2010 by Simon Difford at The Cabinet Room, London, England and named after the New Zealand's Rugby team, the All Blacks – the folk that get fed to the British Lions.

BLACK NAIL #2 NEW

★★★½☆ **Glass:** Collins
Garnish: Lemon slice
Method: POUR all ingredients into glass, lightly STIR and serve with straws.

1	shot	Jack Daniel's Tennessee whiskey
1	shot	Drambuie
Top up with		Coca-Cola

We say: A nail (Drambuie and Whiskey) served long with cola.
Origin: Created in 2010 by Simon Difford at the Cabinet Room, London, England during a meeting with Drambuie's Tim Dewey, Vicki Wonders and Jamie Stephenson.

BLACK NUTS

★★½☆☆ **Glass:** Shot
Garnish: None
Method: LAYER in chilled glass by carefully pouring ingredients in the following order.

¾	shot	Opal Nera black sambuca
¾	shot	Hazelnut liqueur

We say: It's something of a challenge to get the Frangelico to float on the black sambuca. If you store the Opal Nera in a freezer and the Frangelico at room temperature, this helps.

BLACK ROSE

★★★★½ **Glass:** Old-fashioned
Garnish: Lemon zest twist
Method: STIR all ingredients with ice and strain into (empty - no ice) chilled glass.

1	shot	Maker's Mark bourbon
1	shot	Cognac VSOP
¼	shot	Pomegranate (grenadine) syrup
3	dashes	Peychaud's aromatic bitters
1	dash	Angostura aromatic bitters

We say: Sazerac-like but easier for the uninitiated.

BLACK RUSSIAN

★★★½☆ **Glass:** Old-fashioned
Garnish: Lemon slice & cherry on stick (sail)
Method: STIR all ingredients with ice and strain into ice-filled glass.

2	shots	Ketel One vodka
¾	shot	Kahlúa coffee liqueur

Variant: 1/ Served straight-up in a Martini glass. 2/ Topped with cola and served over ice in a Collins glass. 3/ Made into a White Russian.
We say: Most popularly served with cola. With or without, this drink is not that interesting.
Origin: Thought to have been created circa 1949 by Gustav Tops, a hotel bartender in Brussels. Set against the start of the Cold War, the drink is said to have been inspired by Perle Skirvin Mesta, the US ambassador to Luxembourg (1949-1953) and rich American socialite who the term 'hostess with the mostess' was coined for due to her lavish parties. As well as this cocktail, Perle was the inspiration for Irving Berlin's musical 'Call Me Madam' and several books.

BLACK STRAP

★★★★☆ **Glass:** Martini
Garnish: Orange zest twist
Method: STIR all ingredients with ice and strain into chilled glass.

2	shots	Gosling's Black Seal rum
½	shot	Bénédictine D.O.M.
½	shot	Dark Crème de Cacao
2	drops	Tabasco hot pepper sauce

We say: This drink benefits from the dilution, which comes with a lengthy stir.
Origin: Adapted from a recipe created in 2007 by Neyah White, San Francisco, USA.

BLACK TIE

★★★★☆ **Glass:** Old-fashioned
Garnish: Physalis (cape gooseberry)
Method: SHAKE all ingredients with ice and strain into ice-filled glass.

1	shot	Bacardi 8yo aged rum
½	shot	Bacardi Superior rum
½	shot	Triple Sec
¼	shot	Monin Almond (orgeat) syrup
½	spoon	Black strap molasses
¾	shot	Freshly squeezed lime juice
⅛	shot	Monin Pure Cane 2:1 sugar syrup

We say: Depending on the sweetness of your molasses, you may not need to add sugar syrup.
Origin: Adapted from a drink created by Mark Lynch at Green 19, Dublin, Ireland.

STAR RATINGS EXPLAINED

★★★★★ Excellent

★★★★½ Recommended	★★★★☆ Praiseworthy
★★★½☆ Commended	★★★☆☆ Mediocre
★★½☆☆ Disappointing	★★☆☆☆ Pretty awful
★½☆☆☆ Shameful	★☆☆☆☆ Disgusting

BLACK VELVET

★★★☆☆

Glass: Flute
Garnish: Shamrock (or mint leaf)
Method: Slowly POUR ingredients into chilled glass and gently stir.

3½ shots   Guinness
Top up with Brut champagne

AKA: Bismark
Variant: If porter is used instead of stout, this drink becomes simply a Velvet. If beer is used, it is known as the Halstead Street Velvet.

We say: Full-flavoured stout and delicate champagne are an unlikely combination but this classic has stood the test of time. Some may wish to add a barspoon of sugar syrup.
Origin: Thought to have originated in 1861 at Brook's Club, London although some credit some credit the Shelbourne Hotel, Dublin, Ireland. What is certain is that this drink was created at the time when Britain was mourning the death of HRH Prince Albert, husband of Queen Victoria.

The Black Velvet is often served to commemorate Saint Patrick's Day but is more fittingly served on 14 December as this is the day Prince Albert died of typhoid fever 1861. Devastated, the Queen wore black for the rest of her life so this drink's shrouding of champagne is most appropriate.

In his 1948 '*Fine Art of Mixing Drinks*', David A. Embury writes of this drink, "I was first introduced to Black Velvet at the home of a very dear friend of mine in Montreal and I received one of the greatest of all the drinking surprises of my whole life. The combination of champagne and stout sounds terrifying - something like molasses and horseradish. Actually, its excellent. The champagne cuts the heavy, syrupy consistency of the stout, and the stout takes the sharp, tart edge off the champagne. Each is the perfect complement of the other. Be sure, however, that you use (a) a good bottle of stout, (b) an extra-dry champagne - preferably a brut or nature."

BLACK WIDOW

★★★☆☆

Glass: Martini
Garnish: Liquorice
Method: SHAKE all ingredients with ice and fine strain into chilled glass.

1   shot   Crème de fraise du bois liqueur
1   shot   Opal Nera black sambuca
1   shot   Malibu coconut rum liqueur
½   shot   Milk
½   shot   Double (heavy) cream

We say: This sticky, fruity, liquorice cocktail tastes a little like an Allsort sweet.

BLACKTHORN COCKTAIL

★★★★☆

Glass: Martini
Garnish: Lemon zest twist
Method: STIR all ingredients with ice and strain into chilled glass.

1½ shots   Tanqueray London dry gin
¾   shot   Kirschwasser eau de vie
¾   shot   Dubonnet Red (French made)

We say: This drink benefits from a long, chilling and diluting stir. The result is a Martini-style, fruity but dry.

BLACKTHORN ENGLISH

★★★★☆

Glass: Martini
Garnish: Orange zest twist
Method: SHAKE all ingredients with ice and fine strain into chilled glass.

1½ shots   Sloe Gin liqueur
1   shot   Tanqueray London dry gin
¾   shot   Martini Rosso sweet vermouth
3   dashes Orange bitters
½   shot   Chilled mineral water

We say: A fruit influenced yet dry and classic Martini.
Origin: A vintage classic whose origins are unknown

BLACKTHORN IRISH

★★★★☆

Glass: Martini
Garnish: Lemon zest twist (flamed)
Method: SHAKE all ingredients with ice and fine strain into chilled glass.

1½ shots   Jameson Irish whiskey
¼   shot   Pernod anise
1   shot   Martini Extra Dry vermouth
4   dashes Angostura aromatic bitters
½   shot   Chilled mineral water

We say: A dry and aromatic Martini with hints of anise. Some may prefer to add a dash of sugar syrup.
Origin: A classic cocktail whose origins are unknown.

BLADE RUNNER

★★★★☆

Glass: Collins
Garnish: Pineapple wedge & maraschino cherry
Method: SHAKE all ingredients with ice and strain into ice-filled glass.

2   shots   Bacardi Superior rum
½   shot   Myer's dark Jamaican rum
2½ shots   Fresh pressed pineapple juice
¼   shot   Monin Pure Cane 2:1 sugar syrup
2   dashes Angostura aromatic bitters
½   shot   Freshly squeezed lime juice

We say: Tangy and fruity but not too sweet.
Origin: Discovered in 2005 at Zoulou Bar, Berlin, Germany.

BLIMEY

★★★★☆

Glass: Old-fashioned
Garnish: Blackberries
Method: MUDDLE blackberries in base of shaker. Add other ingredients, SHAKE with ice and fine strain into glass filled with crushed ice. Serve with straws.

2   shots   Ketel One vodka
7   fresh   Blackberries
1   shot   Freshly squeezed lime juice
⅛   shot   Monin Pure Cane 2:1 sugar syrup
¾   shot   Crème de cassis liqueur

We say: This blackberry and lime blend is both fruity and aptly named.
Origin: Created in 2002 by Simon Difford.

BLING! BLING!

★★★★★☆

Glass: Shot 
Method: MUDDLE raspberries in base of shaker. Add vodka, lime and sugar, SHAKE with ice and fine strain into glass. TOP with champagne.

7	fresh	Raspberries
½	shot	Ketel One vodka
½	shot	Freshly squeezed lime juice
¼	shot	Monin Pure Cane 2:1 sugar syrup
Top up with		Brut champagne

We say: An ostentatious little number.
Origin: Created in 2001 by Phillip Jeffrey at the GE Club, London, England.

BLINKER

★★★★☆

Glass: Martini
Garnish: Lemon zest twist
Method: SHAKE all ingredients with ice and fine strain into chilled glass.

2	shots	Maker's Mark bourbon
¼	shot	Pomegranate (grenadine) syrup
1	shot	Freshly squeezed grapefruit juice

We say: Back in the 1930s David Embury wrote of this drink, "One of a few cocktails using grapefruit juice. Not particularly good but not too bad." How times have changed!
Origin: A 1930s classic revisited.

BLOOD & SAND #1 (CLASSIC FORMULA)

★★★★☆

Glass: Martini
Garnish: Orange zest twist
Method: SHAKE all ingredients with ice and fine strain into chilled glass.

¾	shot	Dewar's White Label Scotch
¾	shot	Cherry brandy liqueur
¾	shot	Martini Rosso sweet vermouth
¾	shot	Freshly squeezed orange juice

We say: One of the best classic Scotch cocktails but a little sweet.
Origin: Created for the premiere of the 1922 Rudolph Valentino movie, Blood and Sand – the bloos is represented by the red cherry liqueur while the orange represents the sand. This equal parts formula comes from the 1930 edition of '*The Savoy Cocktail Book*'.

BLOOD & SAND #2 (DIFFORD'S FORMULA)

★★★★★☆

Glass: Martini
Garnish: Orange zest twist
Method: SHAKE all ingredients with ice and fine strain into chilled glass.

1½	shots	Dewar's White Label Scotch
¾	shot	Cherry brandy liqueur
¾	shot	Martini Rosso sweet vermouth
¾	shot	Freshly squeezed orange juice

We say: The equal parts (scotch, cherry brandy, sweet vermouth and orange juice) formula from the 1930 edition of '*The Savoy Cocktail Book*' is the excepted classic Blood & Sand recipe but results in a cocktail that's a tad sweet for hardened whisky drinkers. This is a dryer, more spirited Blood & Sand for those who like their Scotch.
Origin: This Scotch forward formula by Simon Difford in 2006.

BLOOD ORANGE

★★★★☆

Glass: Martini
Garnish: Orange zest twist
Method: SHAKE all ingredients with ice and fine strain into chilled glass.

2	shots	Tanqueray London dry gin
½	shot	Campari Bitter
½	shot	Martini Extra Dry vermouth
1	shot	Freshly squeezed orange juice

We say: Bone-dry but with full-on tangy fresh orange.
Origin: Created in 2008 by Jeffrey Morgenthaler at Bel Ami Lounge, Oregon, USA.

BLOOD SAGE

★★★★★☆

Glass: Martini
Garnish: Sage leaf
Method: MUDDLE orange and sage in base of shaker. Add other ingredients, SHAKE with ice and fine strain into chilled glass.

½	shot	Freshly squeezed orange juice
2	fresh	Sage leaves
2	shots	Tanqueray London dry gin
¾	shot	Freshly squeezed lime juice
½	shot	Monin Pure Cane 2:1 sugar syrup
½	fresh	Egg white

We say: Sage combines wonderfully with gin and orange in this beautifully balanced drink.
Origin: Adapted from a drink created by Ryan Magarian, Seattle, USA.

BLOODHOUND #1

★★★½☆

Glass: Martini
Garnish: Raspberries
Method: MUDDLE raspberries in base of shaker. Add other ingredients, SHAKE with ice and fine strain into chilled glass.

6	fresh	Raspberries
2	shots	Tanqueray London dry gin
¾	shot	Martini Extra Dry vermouth
¾	shot	Martini Rosso sweet vermouth
¼	shot	Luxardo Maraschino liqueur

Variant: Made with strawberries in place of raspberries.
We say: Looks like fruity disco drink fodder but is actually surprising dry and strong.
Origin: Unknown but in his 1922 'Mixing Cocktails', Harry McElhone credits the Duke of Manchester with this drinks creation. However, in his 1907 'World Drinks', William Boothby lists a Bloodhound, as does Tom Bullock in his 1917 'The Ideal Bartender'.

BLOODHOUND #2

★★★★☆

Glass: Collins
Garnish: Lime wedge
Method: SHAKE all ingredients with ice and strain into ice-filled glass.

1	shot	Ketel One vodka
2	shots	Campari Bitter
3	shots	Freshly squeezed grapefruit juice

We say: A dry, tart, refreshing long drink.

BLOODY BRONX

★★★★☆

Glass: Martini
Garnish: Maraschino cherry
Method: SHAKE all ingredients with ice and fine strain into chilled glass.

2	shots	Tanqueray London dry gin
¼	shot	Martini Extra Dry vermouth
¼	shot	Martini Rosso sweet vermouth
1	shot	Freshly squeezed orange juice

We say: A Bronx made 'bloody' by the use of blood oranges.
Origin: A vintage cocktail adapted from the classic Bronx Cocktail, created in 1906 by Johnny Solon, a bartender at New York's Waldorf-Astoria Hotel, and named after the newly opened Bronx Zoo.

BLOODY CAESAR UPDATED

★★★★☆

Glass: Collins
Garnish: Pickled bean
Method: ROCK, rather than shake, all ingredients in a shaker with ice and fine strain into ice-filled glass.

2	shots	Ketel One vodka
4	shots	Mott's Clamato juice
½	shot	Freshly squeezed lemon juice
7	drops	Tabasco hot pepper sauce
3	dashes	Worcestershire sauce
2	pinch	Celery salt
2	grind	Black pepper

We say: A peculiarly Canadian fishy twist on the classic Bloody Mary.
Origin: Created by Walter Chell in 1969 to celebrate the opening of Marco's Italian restaurant at the Calgary Inn, Canada. Walter was inspired by the flavours of Spaghetti Vongole (spaghetti with clams) and named the drink after the Roman emperor.

BLOODY JOSEPH UPDATED

★★★★☆

Glass: Collins
Garnish: Celery stick
Method: ROCK, rather than shake, all ingredients in a shaker with ice and fine strain into ice-filled glass.

2	shots	Dewar's White label Scotch
4	shots	Tomato juice
½	shot	Freshly squeezed lemon juice
8	drops	Tabasco hot pepper sauce
4	dashes	Worcestershire sauce
½	spoon	Horseradish sauce
2	pinch	Celery salt
2	grind	Black pepper

We say: A Bloody Mary with whisky.

BLOODY MARIA UPDATED

★★★★☆

Glass: Collins
Garnish: ROCK, rather than shake, all ingredients in a shaker with ice and fine strain into ice-filled glass.

2	shots	Tequila 100% Agave
4	shots	Tomato juice
½	shot	Freshly squeezed lemon juice
8	dropss	Tabasco hot pepper sauce
4	dashes	Worcestershire sauce
½	spoon	Horseradish sauce
½	shot	Warre's Otima tawny port
2	pinch	Celery salt
2	grind	Black pepper

We say: Tequila adds a very interesting kick to the classic Bloody Mary.

BLOODY MARU UPDATED

★★★★☆

Glass: Collins
Garnish: Lemongrass
Method: ROCK, rather than shake, all ingredients in a shaker with ice and fine strain into ice-filled glass.

4	shots	Sake
½	shot	Freshly squeezed lemon juice
8	drops	Tabasco hot pepper sauce
4	dashes	Worcestershire sauce
2	pinch	Celery salt
2	grind	Black pepper

We say: A Bloody Mary based on sake.

BLOODY MARY #1 (1930s RECIPE)

★★★☆☆

Glass: Old-fashioned
Garnish: Salt & pepper rim
Method: ROCK all ingredients with ice and strain into empty glass.

2½	shots	Ketel One vodka
2	shots	Tomato juice
¼	shot	Freshly squeezed lemon juice
5	dashes	Worcestershire sauce
4	pinch	Salt
2	pinch	Black pepper
2	pinch	Cayenne pepper

Variant: Red Snapper
We say: Originally made with 2.5 shots 50% alc/vol. vodka this drink is fiery. The modern version is more user friendly.
Origin: A 1933 version of the classic commomly attibuted to Fernand Petiot at Harry's New York Bar, Paris, France.

STAR RATINGS EXPLAINED

★★★★★ Excellent

★★★★☆ Recommended	★★★★☆ Praiseworthy
★★★☆☆ Commended	★★★☆☆ Mediocre
★★☆☆☆ Disappointing	★★☆☆☆ Pretty awful
★☆☆☆☆ Shameful	★☆☆☆☆ Disgusting

BLOODY MARY #2 (MODERN RECIPE) UPDATED

★★★★☆

Glass: Collins
Garnish: Salt & pepper rim plus celery stick
Method: ROCK, rather than shake, all ingredients in a shaker with ice and fine strain into ice-filled glass.

2	shots	Ketel One vodka
4	shots	Tomato juice
½	shot	Freshly squeezed lemon juice
7	drops	Tabasco hot pepper sauce
4	dashes	Worcestershire sauce
2	grind	Black pepper
⅔	pinch	Celery salt

We say: The classic brunch cocktail.
Origin: The creation of The Bloody Mary is a matter of some dispute, but is generally credited to Fernand Petiot. Whether this was in 1920 (or 1921), when Petiot was a young bartender at Harry's New York Bar in Paris, or in America, during the 1940s, after the comedian George Jessel had first popularised the unspiced combination of vodka and tomato juice, is not clear.

If you believe that Petiot first created it around 1920, then you will believe that the name is borrowed not from the English Queen Mary I, whose persecution of Protestants gave her that name, or for the silent movie actress Mary Pickford, but from one of Petiot's customers, apparently the entertainer Roy Barton. He had worked at a nightclub (or knew a bar) called the Bucket of Blood in Chicago, where there was a waitress known as 'Bloody Mary', and he said the drink reminded him of her.

If you believe Petiot invented it in New York, where he worked at the St. Regis Hotel certainly from the end of Prohibition, then he may have had assistance in its creation from Serge Obolansky, the manager of the hotel, who asked him to spice up his 50-50 blend of vodka and tomato juice. According to this version, he attempted to rename the drink Red Snapper, after Vincent Astor, who owned the hotel, found the name too crude for his clientele. (now days a Red Snapper is a Bloody Mary made with gin.)

The celery stick garnish apparently dates back to 1960 when a bartender at the Ambassador Hotel in Chicago noticed a lady stirring her drink with a celery stick.

Whatever the precise story behind this fantastic drink, Bloody Mary recipes are as personal as Martinis. Purists will only use Tabasco, Worcestershire sauce, salt and lemon to spice up tomato and vodka but everything from oysters to V8 can be added. Variations include:

Asian Mary (with wasabi, ginger & soy sauce)
Bloody Bull (with beef consommé)
Bloody Caesar (with clam juice)
Bloody Joseph (with Scotch whisky)
Bloody Maria (with tequila)
Bloody Maru (with sake)
Bloody Shame (without alcohol)
Bullshot (with beef bouillon)
Cubanita (with rum)
Red Snapper (with gin)

BLOODY MARY #3 (DIFFORD'S RECIPE)

★★★★☆

Glass: Collins
Garnish: Salt & pepper rim plus celery stick
Method: MUDDLE pepper in base of shaker. Add other ingredients, ROCK, rather than shake, with ice and fine strain into ice-filled glass.

2	ring	Yellow bell pepper (chopped)
2	shots	Ketel One vodka
3	shots	Tomato juice
¾	shot	Harvey's Bristol Cream sherry
8	drops	Tabasco hot pepper sauce
4	dashes	Worcestershire sauce
2	pinch	Celery salt
2	grind	Black pepper

We say: My take on the Bloody Mary benefits from extra pepper spice and is sweetened and flavoured with sweet sherry.
Origin: Created in 2007 by Simon Difford at the Cabinet Room, London, England.

BLOODY SHAME (MOCKTAIL) UPDATED

★★★☆☆

Glass: Collins
Garnish: Celery stick
Method: ROCK, rather than shake, all ingredients in a shaker with ice and fine strain into ice-filled glass.

5	shots	Tomato juice
½	shot	Freshly squeezed lemon juice
8	drops	Tabasco hot pepper sauce
4	dashes	Worcestershire sauce
½	spoon	Horseradish sauce
2	pinch	Celery salt
2	grind	Black pepper

AKA: Virgin Mary
We say: Somehow missing something.

BLOOMSBURY MARTINI

★★★★☆

Glass: Martini
Garnish: Lemon zest twist
Method: STIR all ingredients with ice and strain into chilled glass.

2	shots	Tanqueray London dry gin
½	shot	Cuarenta y Tres (Licor 43) liqueur
½	shot	Martini Extra Dry vermouth
2	dashes	Peychaud's aromatic bitters

We say: This pinky/rusty drink benefits from a good long stir but the result is an aromatic, medium dry, spicy vanilla Martini.
Origin: Adapted from a drink created in 2003 by Robert Hess and published on drinkboy.com

BARTENDER'S TIP MUDDLE

Muddling means pummelling fruits, herbs and/or spices with a muddler (a blunt tool similar to a pestle) so as to crush them and release their flavour. (You can also use a rolling pin.)

As when using a pestle and mortar, push down on the muddler with a twisting action. Never attempt to muddle hard, unripe fruits in a glass as the pressure required could break the glass.

BLOW JOB

★★★★☆

Glass: Shot
Garnish: None
Method: SHAKE all ingredients with ice and fine strain into chilled glass.

½	shot	**Grand Marnier liqueur**
½	shot	**Bols Banana liqueur**
½	shot	**Kahlúa coffee liqueur**

We say: A juvenile but pleasant tasting sweet shot.

BLUE ANGEL

★★☆☆☆

Glass: Martini
Garnish: Orange zest twist
Method: SHAKE all ingredients with ice and fine strain into chilled glass.

¾	shot	**Cognac VSOP**
¾	shot	**Parfait Amour liqueur**
¾	shot	**Bols Blue Curaçao liqueur**
¾	shot	**Freshly squeezed lemon juice**
¾	shot	**Double (heavy) cream**

We say: This baby blue cocktail is sweet, creamy and floral.

BLUE BIRD

★★★☆☆

Glass: Martini
Garnish: Orange zest twist
Method: SHAKE all ingredients with ice and fine strain into chilled glass.

2	shots	**Tanqueray London dry gin**
1	shot	**Bols Blue Curaçao liqueur**
¾	shot	**Freshly squeezed lemon juice**
¼	shot	**Monin Almond (orgeat) syrup**

We say: A blue rinsed, orange washed, gin based 'tini' that benefits from being sweetened with almond rather than plain syrup.
Origin: Thought to have been created in the late 1950s in Montmartre, Paris, France.

BLUE BLAZER UPDATED

★★★★☆

Glass: Snifter
Garnish: Lemon zest twist
Method: The drink involves setting whisky alight and pouring it between to silver tankards, creating an arc of flame.

WARNING - please practice with water first to perfect your method. Stand on a non-flammable floor and have suitable fire-fighting equipment nearby. The following recipe makes two drinks.

You will need two large silver-plated tankards with handles. Preheat these with boiling water and warm the whisky. POUR the whisky into one tankard and fresh boiling water into the other. Ignite the whiskey using a long match and while still blazing pour the whisky into the other tankard. Then mix ingredients by pouring them from one tankard to the other. The foolhardy increase the distance between the tankards as they pour, thus creating a spectacular long blue flame between the two. Jerry Thomas is said to have held the tankards at a meter's distance from each other. Extinguish flame by covering flaming tankard with base of the other tankard, pour into glass and sweeten to taste by stirring in powdered sugar.

4	shots	**Dewar's White Label Scotch**
4	shots	**Boiling water**
1	spoon	**Powdered sugar**

We say: The showy way to make a simple hot whisky punch.
Origin: This spectacular serve was created by 'Professor' Jerry Thomas, author of the first bartending book and travelling performance bartender. Thomas was a master of showmanship; he used solid silver bar tools and cups embellished with precious stones and metals. He understood the importance of putting on a show when making drinks and people travelled to see his 'act' as much as they did to try his legendary cocktails.

Nicknamed the 'Professor' due to his ability to deal "with the fanciest orders imaginable", Thomas developed his signature 'Blue Blazer' drink whilst working at the El Dorado, a gambling saloon in San Francisco. President Ulysses S. Grant was apparently so impressed by this spectacular display that he gave Thomas a cigar.

Legend has it that Thomas would only make the drink if the outside temperature was 50F (10C) or below, making an exception to this rule if the person ordering was suffering with a cold or the flu, whose symptoms the drink was to alleviate.

BLUE CHAMPAGNE

★★★☆☆

Glass: Flute
Garnish: None
Method: SHAKE first four ingredients with ice and strain into glass. TOP with champagne.

¾	shot	**Ketel One vodka**
⅛	shot	**Triple Sec**
¼	shot	**Bols Blue Curaçao liqueur**
¼	shot	**Freshly squeezed lemon juice**
Top up with		**Brut champagne**

Variant: With gin in place of vodka.
We say: Fortified, citrussy champagne.

BARTENDER'S TIP MEASURING - SHOTS & SPOONS

In this guide measures of each ingredient are expressed in 'shots'. Ideally a shot is 25ml or one US fluid ounce (29.6ml), measured in a standard jigger. (You can also use a clean medicine measure or even a small shot glass.)

Whatever your chosen measure, it should have straight sides to enable you to accurately judge fractions of a shot. Look out for measures which are graduated in ounces and marked with quarter and half ounces.

BLUE COSMO

★★★⯪☆

Glass: Martini
Garnish: Orange zest twist
Method: SHAKE all ingredients with ice and fine strain into chilled glass.

2	shots	Ketel One vodka
1½	shots	Ocean Spray cranberry juice
¾	shot	Bols Blue Curaçao liqueur
¼	shot	Freshly squeezed lime juice

Variant: Purple Cosmo
We say: This blue rinsed drink may have sales appeal but sadly is not quite as good as a traditional red Cosmo.

BLUE EYED MARTINI

★★★⯪☆

Glass: Martini
Garnish: Lemon zest twist
Method: STIR all ingredients with ice and strain into chilled glass.

1½	shots	Ketel One vodka
½	shot	Tanqueray London dry gin
⅛	shot	Bols Blue Curaçao liqueur
¼	shot	Martini Extra Dry vermouth

We say: Blue drinks are no longer confined to the 80s. They're back in a big way and this is one of the best.

BLUE FIN

★★★⯪☆

Glass: Martini
Garnish: Gummy Fish sweet
Method: SHAKE all ingredients with ice and fine strain into chilled glass.

2	shots	Ketel One vodka
1	shot	Hpnotiq liqueur
1½	shots	Ocean Spray cranberry juice

We say: Citrussy, reminiscent of a blue Cosmo.
Origin: Created in 2003 at The Blue Fin, W Hotel, Times Square, New York, USA.

BLUE HAWAII

★★★⯪☆

Glass: Collins
Garnish: Pineapple wedge, maraschino cherry & paper parasol
Method: POUR blue curaçao into ice-filled glass. SHAKE the sugar syrup, pineapple and lime juice with ice and strain into ice filled glass so it forms a LAYER (carefully pour so floats on previous layer) over blue curaçao. Lastly FLOAT rum on top of drink.

½	shot	Bols Blue Curaçao liqueur
3	shots	Fresh pressed pineapple juice
1	shot	Freshly squeezed lime juice
½	shot	Monin Pure Cane 2:1 sugar syrup
1½	shots	Bacardi Superior rum

We say: Aloha!
Origin: Created in 1957 by Harry Yee at Henry Kaiser's Hawaiian Village Hotel (latterly the Hilton) in Waikiki, Oahu, Hawaii. The drink is named after the hit song from the 1937 Bing Crosby film, Waikiki Wedding, and not after what is generously described as a "musical-comedy" Elvis Presley 1961 film of the same name.

BLUE HAWAIIAN

★★★☆☆

Glass: Hurricane
Garnish: Pineapple wedge & maraschino cherry
Method: BLEND ingredients with 12oz scoop of crushed ice. Pour into glass and serve with straws.

2	shots	Bacardi Superior rum
1	shot	Bols Blue Curaçao liqueur
1½	shots	Coco López cream of coconut
3	shots	Fresh pressed pineapple juice
¼	shot	Freshly squeezed lemon juice

We say: A blue rinsed Piña Colada.
Origin: Probably created by Don the Beachcomber in Los Angeles, USA.

BLUE HEAVEN

★★⯪☆☆

Glass: Collins
Garnish: Pineapple wedge & maraschino cherry
Method: SHAKE all ingredients with ice and strain into ice-filled glass.

2	shots	Bacardi Superior rum
½	shot	Amaretto liqueur
1	shot	Bols Blue Curaçao liqueur
½	shot	Rose's lime cordial
4	shots	Fresh pressed pineapple juice

We say: Actually more aqua than blue, this sweet concoction includes orange, almond, lime cordial and pineapple.

BLUE KAMIKAZE

★★★⯪☆

Glass: Shot
Garnish: None
Method: SHAKE all ingredients with ice and fine strain into chilled glass.

½	shot	Ketel One vodka
½	shot	Bols Blue Curaçao liqueur
½	shot	Freshly squeezed lime juice

We say: Tangy orange - except it's blue.

BLUE LADY

★★★☆☆

Glass: Martini
Garnish: Orange zest twist
Method: SHAKE all ingredients with ice and fine strain into chilled glass.

1	shot	Tanqueray London dry gin
2	shots	Bols Blue Curaçao liqueur
1	shot	Freshly squeezed lemon juice
½	fresh	Egg white

We say: Quite sweet with an orange, citrus finish.

BLUE LAGOON 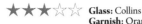 UPDATED

★★★☆☆

Glass: Collins
Garnish: Orange slice
Method: BLEND ingredients with 12oz scoop of crushed ice. Pour into glass and serve with straws.

1	shot	Tanqueray London dry gin
1	shot	Ketel One vodka
1	shot	Bols Blue Curaçao liqueur
1	shot	Freshly squeezed lime juice
1	shot	Monin Pure Cane 2:1 sugar syrup

Variant: Vodka, blue curaçao and lemonade on the rocks.
We say: Better than the film - not hard!
Origin: Created in 1960 by Andy MacElhone (son of Harry) at Harry's New York Bar, Paris, France.

BLUE LASSI NEW

★★★★☆

Glass: Coupette
Garnish: Orange zest twist (discarded) & mint leaf
Method: SHAKE all ingredients with ice and fine strain into chilled glass.

1½	shots	Vanilla-infused Ketel One vodka
1½	shots	Bols Natural Yoghurt liqueur
½	shot	Bols Blue Curaçao liqueur
2	dashes	Rose water

We say: Baby blue creamy yoghurt with vanilla infused vodka, orange liqueur and aromatic rose water.
Origin: Created in 2011 by Simon Difford at the Cabinet Room, London, England.

BLUE MARGARITA

★★★½☆

Glass: Coupette
Garnish: Lime slice
Method: BLEND all ingredients with one 12oz scoop crushed ice. Serve with straws.

2	shots	Tequila 100% Agave
1	shot	Bols Blue Curaçao liqueur
1	shot	Freshly squeezed lime juice
½	shot	Monin Pure Cane 2:1 sugar syrup

We say: As the name suggests, a Margarita, only blue. This 'Disco Drink' look scary but tastes pretty good.

BLUE MONDAY

★★★½☆

Glass: Old-fashioned
Garnish: Orange zest twist
Method: SHAKE all ingredients with ice and fine strain into chilled glass.

1½	shots	Ketel One Citroen vodka
¾	shot	Bols Blue Curaçao liqueur
½	shot	Triple Sec
½	shot	Martini Extra Dry vermouth
2	dashes	Orange bitters

AKA: Caucasian
We say: Disco blue but medium dry with a bittersweet orange taste.
Origin: Simon Difford's adaptation of Patrick Gavin Duffy's classic. The original consisted of ¾ vodka, ¼ triple sec, 1 dash blue food colouring.

BLUE MOON

★★★★☆

Glass: Coupette
Garnish: Raspberries
Method: SHAKE all ingredients with ice and fine strain into chilled glass.

2	shots	Tanqueray London dry gin
¾	shot	Benoit Serres crème de violette
½	shot	Freshly squeezed lemon juice
½	fresh	Egg white

AKA: Blue Devil
Variant: Aviation.
We say: More red than blue with a flavour that is reminiscent of a berry flavoured Aviation.
Origin: Said to have been made circa 1940 by "Oscar of the Waldorf", this drink featured on the back label of the Créme Yvette bottles of the same era. This cocktail was lost for decades, due to production of Créme Yvette ceasing in 1969, but thanks to Créme Yvette's 2010 relaunch, has been rediscovered. Incidentally, *"Blue Moon"* is an astronomical term for the second of two full moons to occur in the same calendar months.

BLUE MOON COCKTAIL NEW

★★★★☆

Glass: Coupette
Garnish: Sage leaf & blueberry
Method: Lightly MUDDLE blueberry in base of shaker (just to break skin). ADD vodka and one heaped spoon of oolong tea and stir in base of shaker for 60 seconds (or better still, leave to steep for ten minutes). Add other ingredients, SHAKE with ice and fine strain into chilled glass.

1	fresh	Blueberries
2	shots	Ketel One vodka
1	spoon	Oolong tea
½	shot	St~Germain elderflower liqueur
¾	shot	Freshly squeezed lemon juice
½	shot	Agave nectar
1	fresh	Sage leaves

We say: A hint of blueberry fruit with oolong tea, elderflower, sage and lemon – a seriously complex cocktail.
Origin: Adapted from a recipe created in 2010 by Dale DeGroff, New York, USA. Incidentally, *"Blue Moon"* is an astronomical term for the second of two full moons to occur in the same calendar month.

STAR RATINGS EXPLAINED

★★★★★ Excellent

★★★★⯪ Recommended ★★★★☆ Praiseworthy
★★★½☆ Commended ★★★☆☆ Mediocre
★★⯪☆☆ Disappointing ★★☆☆☆ Pretty awful
★⯪☆☆☆ Shameful ★☆☆☆☆ Disgusting

BLUE MOUNTAIN COCKTAIL

★★★★☆

Glass: Martini
Garnish: Orange zest twist (discarded) & coffee beans
Method: Lightly MUDDLE blueberry in base of shaker (just to break skin). ADD vodka and one heaped spoon of oolong tea and stir in base of shaker for 60 seconds (or better still, leave to steep for ten minutes). Add other ingredients, SHAKE with ice and fine strain into chilled glass.

1	fresh	Blueberries
2	shots	Ketel One vodka
1	spoon	Oolong tea
½	shot	St-Germain elderflower liqueur
¾	shot	Freshly squeezed lemon juice
½	shot	Agave nectar
1	fresh	Sage leaves

We say: A hint of blueberry fruit with oolong tea, elderflower, sage and lemon - a seriously complex cocktail.
Origin: Adapted from a recipe created in 2010 by Dale DeGroff, New York, USA. Incidentally, "Blue Moon" is an astronomical term for the second of two full moons to occur in the same calendar months.

BLUE PASSION

★★★★☆

Glass: Old-fashioned
Garnish: Orange zest twist
Method: SHAKE all ingredients with ice and strain into glass.

1	shot	Bacardi Superior rum
1	shot	Bols Blue Curaçao liqueur
1¾	shots	Freshly squeezed lime juice
1	shot	Monin Pure Cane 2:1 sugar syrup

We say: This sweet and sour tangy drink is surprisingly good.

BLUE RIBAND

★★★☆☆

Glass: Coupette
Garnish: Maraschino cherry
Method: STIR all ingredients with ice and strain into chilled glass.

2	shots	Tanqueray London dry gin
1	shot	Triple Sec
1	shot	Bols Blue Curaçao liqueur

We say: A sweetened, blue rinsed, orange and gin Martini.
Origin: The 'Blue Riband' was awarded to the liner that made the fastest Atlantic crossing. This cocktail is thought to have been created on one of these ships

BLUE SKY

★★★☆☆

Glass: Martini
Garnish: Orange zest twist
Method: SHAKE all ingredients with ice and fine strain into chilled glass.

¾	shot	Tanqueray London dry gin
¾	shot	Freshly squeezed lime juice
¾	shot	Bols Blue Curaçao liqueur
¼	shot	Luxardo Maraschino liqueur

We say: Orange and lime predominate.

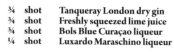

BLUE STAR

★★★☆☆

Glass: Martini
Garnish: Orange zest twist
Method: SHAKE all ingredients with ice and fine strain into chilled glass.

1½	shots	Tanqueray London dry gin
¾	shot	Bols Blue Curaçao liqueur
¾	shot	Martini Extra Dry vermouth
¾	shot	Freshly squeezed orange juice

We say: Gin, orange and a kick.

BLUE TRAIN NEW

★★★⯪☆

Glass: Coupette
Garnish: Orange wedge on rim
Method: SHAKE all ingredients with ice and fine strain into chilled glass.

2	shots	Tanqueray London dry gin
¾	shot	Cointreau triple sec
½	shot	Bols blue curaçao liqueur
¾	shot	Freshly squeezed lemon juice

We say: Yup, it's blue, slightly sweet and orange flavoured.

BLUE VELVET MARGARITA

★★★★☆

Glass: Coupette
Garnish: Lime wedge
Method: SHAKE all ingredients with ice and fine strain into chilled glass.

2	shots	Tequila 100% Agave
½	shot	Triple Sec
½	shot	Bols Blue Curaçao liqueur
1	shot	Freshly squeezed lime juice

We say: May look lurid but is a surprisingly tasty Margarita.
Origin: Discovered in 2005 at Velvet Margarita Cantina, Los Angeles, USA.

BLUE WAVE

★★★☆☆

Glass: Hurricane
Garnish: Pineapple wedge
Method: SHAKE ingredients with ice and strain into ice-filled glass.

1	shot	Tanqueray London dry gin
1	shot	Bacardi Superior rum
½	shot	Bols Blue Curaçao liqueur
3	shots	Fresh pressed pineapple juice
1¾	shots	Freshly squeezed lime juice
¾	shot	Monin Pure Cane 2:1 sugar syrup

We say: A fruity holiday drink.

BLUEBERRY DAIQUIRI

★★★★☆

Glass: Martini
Garnish: Blueberries
Method: MUDDLE blueberries in base of shaker.
Add other ingredients, SHAKE with ice and fine
strain into chilled glass.

20	fresh	Blueberries
2	shots	Bacardi Superior rum
½	shot	Crème de myrtille liqueur
¼	shot	Freshly squeezed lime juice

We say: Blueberry juice and liqueur lengthens and
sweetens an otherwise classic Daiquiri.
Origin: Created in 2002 by Simon Difford.

BLUEBERRY MARTINI #1

★★★½☆

Glass: Martini
Garnish: Lemon zest twist (discarded) &
blueberries
Method: MUDDLE blueberries in base of shaker.
Add other ingredients, SHAKE with ice and fine
strain into chilled glass.

20	fresh	Blueberries
2	shots	Ketel One vodka
¼	shot	Crème de myrtille liqueur
⅛	shot	Monin Pure Cane 2:1 sugar syrup

We say: Rich blueberry fruit fortified with grainy
vodka. Not too sweet.

BLUEBERRY MARTINI #2

★★★★☆

Glass: Martini
Garnish: Blueberries
Method: MUDDLE blueberries in base of shaker.
Add other ingredients, SHAKE with ice and fine
strain into chilled glass.

30	fresh	Blueberries
2	shots	Ketel One vodka
¼	shot	Monin Pure Cane 2:1 sugar syrup
¾	shot	Sauvignon blanc wine

We say: Rich blueberry fruit fortified with vodka - much
more interesting with the additional splash of wine.

BLUEBERRY TEA

★★★★☆

Glass: Toddy
Garnish: Lemon wedge & cinnamon stick
Method: POUR first two ingredients into glass, top
up with tea and stir.

¾	shot	Amaretto liqueur
¾	shot	Grand Marnier liqueur
Top up with		Hot English breakfast tea

We say: This does indeed taste just as described on the tin.

BLUEGRASS

★★★★☆

Glass: Martini
Garnish: Cucumber peel
Method: MUDDLE cucumber in base of shaker
Add other ingredients, SHAKE with ice and fine
strain into chilled glass.

2	inch	Cucumber (chopped & peeled)
1½	shots	Maker's Mark bourbon
¾	shot	Aperol
⅛	shot	Monin Pure Cane 2:1 sugar syrup
1	dash	Angostura aromatic bitters
1	dash	Orange bitters

We say: Cucumber and Bourbon with a hint of
bitter sweet orange.
Origin: Created in 2008 by Hayden Lambert at
Merchant Hotel, Belfast, Northern Ireland and named
after the bluegrass that grows in Bourbon County
where some of the best horses in the world are bred.

BLUSH MARTINI

★★★½☆

Glass: Martini
Garnish: Dust with cinnamon powder
Method: SHAKE all ingredients with ice and fine
strain into chilled glass.

1	shot	Ketel One vodka
¾	shot	Vanilla schnapps
½	shot	Amaretto liqueur
¾	shot	Double (heavy) cream
¾	shot	Milk
¼	shot	Ocean Spray cranberry juice

We say: Drier than it looks, but still one to follow
the dessert trolley.
Origin: Created by Colin William Crowden, Mashed
Bar, Leicester, England

BLUSHIN' RUSSIAN

★★★★☆

Glass: Martini
Garnish: Coffee beans
Method: SHAKE all ingredients with ice and fine
strain into chilled glass.

1	shot	Ketel One vodka
½	shot	Amaretto liqueur
1	shot	Kahlúa coffee liqueur
¾	shot	Milk
¾	shot	Double (heavy) cream

We say: White Russian with a hint of almond.

STAR RATINGS EXPLAINED

★★★★★ Excellent

★★★★½ Recommended	★★★★☆ Praiseworthy
★★★½☆ Commended	★★★☆☆ Mediocre
★★½☆☆ Disappointing	★★☆☆☆ Pretty awful
★½☆☆☆ Shameful	★☆☆☆☆ Disgusting

BOBBY BURNS #1 (CRADDOCK'S VERSION)

★★★★½

Glass: Martini
Garnish: Lemon zest twist & side of shortbread
Method: STIR all ingredients with ice and strain into chilled glass.

2	shots	**Dewar's White label Scotch**
1	shot	**Martini Rosso sweet vermouth**
¼	shot	**Bénédictine D.O.M.**

We say: Rich and slightly sweet, laced with spice liqueur and a good dram. The ritualistic serving of haggis and a dram or two.
Origin: Recipe adapted from Harry Craddock's 1930, *'The Savoy Cocktail Book'* which calls for equal parts vermouth and Scotch with three dashes of Bénédictine. Craddock writes of this drink, "One of the very best Whisky Cocktails. A very fast mover on Saint Andrew's Day."

This drink is named after and commemorates Robert Burns (1759-1796): poet, balladeer and Scotland's favourite son. On the 25th January Scots honour the great man's presumed birthday on what has become known as Burns Night with poem readings, the ritualistic serving of haggis and a few drams.

BOBBY BURNS #2 (CROCKETT'S VERSION)

★★★★½

Glass: Old-fashioned
Garnish: Maraschino cherry
Method: POUR absinthe into ice-filled glass. TOP with water and leave to stand. Separately STIR Scotch, vermouth and bitters with ice. DISCARD contents of glass (absinthe, water and ice) and fill with fresh ice. STRAIN contents of mixing glass into ice-filled absinthe-coated glass.

2	shots	**Dewar's White label Scotch**
1	shot	**Martini Rosso sweet vermouth**
1	dash	**Orange bitters**
½	shot	**Absinthe**

AKA: Robert Burns
We say: Scotch and vermouth with added interest courtesy of absinthe and orange bitters.
Origin: Recipe adapted from Albert Stevens Crockett's 1935 *'The Old Waldorf-Astoria Bar Book'* where the drink is listed as "Robert Burns" accompanied by the following notation, "It may have been named after the celebrated Scotsman. Chances are, however, that it was christened in honour of a cigar salesman, who 'bought' in the Old Bar [at the Waldorf-Astoria]."It was cocktail historian, Gaz Regan who discovered a street scene on the corner of 42nd Street and Broadway dating back to 1880, in the 1923 edition of 'Valentine's Manuel of Old New York', edited by Henry Collins Brown.

The scene includes billboards advertising Bergen Beach, the Castle Square Opera Company, and the Lyceum Theatre, which was playing The Moth and the Flame at the time but as Gaz points out, "Most interesting, though, is the shop that stands in the foreground of the picture. The words on the awning proclaim, Robert Burns Cigars."

As Gaz explained in his Drinks Bulletin, "Albert Stevens Crockett might well have been correct when he said that the drink could have been named for a cigar salesman, but 'Robert Burns' was the name of a brand of cigar, and although it's very possible that the guy who owned this shop went by the same name, it's more likely that The Robert Burns cocktail that was created at the old Waldorf was named for the shop, as a nod to the owner. The old Waldorf Astoria [which stood on the site of today's Empire State Building] didn't open until 1893, some 13 years after the aforementioned picture was taken, but it's not a big stretch to think that the cigar vendor was still in business when the hotel opened, and the Robert Burns brand of cigars was still on the market in the 1960s, or maybe later."
Thanks Gaz.

BOBBY BURNS #3 (EMBURY'S VERSION)

★★★★½

Glass: Coupette
Garnish: Lemon zest twist
Method: STIR all ingredients with ice and strain into chilled cocktail glass

2	shots	**Dewar's White label Scotch**
1	shot	**Martini Rosso sweet vermouth**
¼	shot	**Drambuie**
2	dashes	**Peychaud's aromatic bitters**

We say: As Embury says, there would seem to be some sense in using a Scotch based liqueur and although this version of the Bobby Burns is rarely seen, it is worthy of a trial.
Origin: Recipe adapted from David A. Embury's 1953 *'Fine Art of Mixing Drinks'*, in which he writes of this drink, "Peychaud, somehow seems to blend better than Angostura with the Scotch. Benedictine is sometimes used in place of Drambuie. However, the Drambuie is preferable because it is made with a Scotch whisky base."

BOBBY DE NIRO

★★★½☆

Glass: Martini
Garnish: Apricot slice
Method: STIR jam with gin until jam is dissolved. Add other ingredients, SHAKE with ice and fine strain into chilled glass.

1	spoon	**Apricot jam (preserve)**
2	shots	**Tanqueray London dry gin**
¼	shot	**De Kuyper Apricot Brandy liqueur**
½	shot	**Freshly squeezed lemon juice**
1	dash	**Orange bitters**

We say: An apricot flavoured twist on the classic Casino cocktail.
Origin: Adapted from a drink discovered in 2008 at Westbourne House, London, England.

BOHEMIAN ICED TEA

★★★★½

Glass: Old-fashioned
Garnish: Lemon zest twist
Method: STIR all ingredients with ice and strain into ice-filled glass.

1½	shots	**Becherovka liqueur**
½	shot	**Ketel One vodka**
½	shot	**Krupnik spiced honey liqueur**
½	shot	**Peachtree peach schnapps**
2½	shots	**Cold earl gray tea**

We say: A fruity and refreshing drink with surprising flavours.
Origin: Created by Alex Kammerling at Detroit, London, England. Originally stirred in a tea pot and served in tea cups.

STAR RATINGS EXPLAINED

★★★★★ Excellent

★★★★½ Recommended	★★★★☆ Praiseworthy
★★★½☆ Commended	★★★☆☆ Mediocre
★★½☆☆ Disappointing	★★☆☆☆ Pretty awful
★½☆☆☆ Shameful	★☆☆☆☆ Disgusting

BOHEMIAN MARTINI

★★★★★½

Glass: Martini
Garnish: Caperberry
Method: STIR all ingredients with ice and strain into chilled glass.

| 2½ shots | Tanqueray London dry gin |
| ½ shot | Martini Extra Dry vermouth |

We say: A regular gin Martini garnished with a caperberry.
Origin: Created at LAB Bar, London, England. The name comes from Cafe Boheme, the restaurant practically opposite, where the LAB crew would go for sustenance after a shift.

BOHEMIAN MULE

★★★☆☆

Glass: Collins
Garnish: Lime wedge
Method: POUR all ingredients into ice-filled glass and lightly stir.

1 shot	Absinthe
½ shot	Freshly squeezed lime juice
Top up with	Ginger beer

We say: Ginger beer and the length of this drink tame the absinthe within but its presence is most evident.
Origin: Created in 1990s by Giovanni Burdi, London, England.

BOILERMAKER

★★★★★

Glass: Shot
Garnish: None
Method: POUR whiskey to brim of shot glass and then manoeuvre shot glass so it is held tight up against the inside base of an upturned Boston glass. Then quickly flip the Boston glass over so that the bourbon is trapped in the now upside-down shot glass. Now pour beer into Boston glass over the whiskey filled shot glass.d

| 1 shot | Maker's Mark bourbon |
| 1 pint | Lager |

We say: When you get to the end of the beer the shot glass lifts and the whiskey is released as a chaser.
Origin: Unknown but in his book 'The Joy of Mixology' Gary Regan credits steelworkers in western Pennsylvania.

BOLERO

★★★★½☆

Glass: Martini
Garnish: Apple slice
Method: STIR all ingredients with ice and strain into chilled glass.

1½ shots	Bacardi Superior rum
¾ shot	Calvados/Applejack brandy
¼ shot	Martini Rosso sweet vermouth

We say: A dry, challenging drink for modern palates. Be sure to stir well as dilution is key.
Origin: A classic of unknown origins.

BOLERO SOUR

★★★★★★

Glass: Old-fashioned
Garnish: Orange & lime zest twists (discarded)
Method: SHAKE all ingredients with ice and fine strain into an ice-filled glass.

1 shot	Bacardi Superior rum
1 shot	Cognac VSOP
½ shot	Freshly squeezed orange juice
1 shot	Freshly squeezed lime juice
½ shot	Monin Pure Cane 2:1 sugar syrup
½ fresh	Egg white

We say: A beautifully balanced, flavoursome medley of sweet and sour.
Origin: Adapted from David A. Embury's 1948 'The Fine Art of Mixing Drinks'.

BOLSHOY PUNCH

★★★★☆

Glass: Old-fashioned
Garnish: None
Method: SHAKE all ingredients with ice and strain into glass filled with crushed ice.

1½ shots	Wray & Nephew overproof rum
¾ shot	Freshly squeezed lime juice
½ shot	Monin Pure Cane 2:1 sugar syrup
1 shot	Crème de cassis liqueur

We say: An innocuous-seeming pink classic - richly flavoured and easy to drink.

BOMBAY LASSI COCKTAIL NEW

★★★★☆

Glass: Martini
Garnish: Mint sprig
Method: MUDDLE cardamom in base of shaker. ADD other ingredients, SHAKE with ice and fine strain into chilled glass.

1 whole	Cardamom pods
1½ shots	Vanilla-infused Ketel One vodka
1½ shots	Bols Natural Yoghurt liqueur
½ shot	Domaine de Canton ginger liqueur
¼ shot	Freshly squeezed lemon juice

We say: Creamy vanilla yet balanced rather than sweet with hints of cardamom, ginger and lemon.
Origin: Created in 2011 by Simon Difford at the Cabinet Room, London, England.

BOMBAY NO. 2

★★★★★½

Glass: Coupette
Garnish: Orange zest twist
Method: STIR all ingredients with ice and fine strain into chilled glass.

1½ shots	Cognac VSOP
¼ shot	Triple Sec
¾ shot	Martini Extra Dry vermouth
¾ shot	Martini Rosso sweet vermouth
⅛ shot	Absinthe

We say: A smooth, complex, Sazerac-style Martini.
Origin: My 2006 adaptation of a recipe from Harry Craddock's 1930 'The Savoy Cocktail Book'.

BOMBER

★★★★☆

Glass: Collins
Garnish: Lime wedge
Method: SHAKE first three ingredients with ice and strain into ice-filled glass. TOP with ginger beer, stir and serve with straws.

1	shot	Bacardi Superior rum
1	shot	Spiced rum
1	shot	Freshly squeezed lime juice
Top up with		Ginger beer

We say: Cross between a Moscow Mule and a Cuba Libre.
Origin: Created in 1998 by the B. Bar crew at The Reading Festival, England

BON BON

★★★★☆

Glass: Martini
Garnish: Lemon zest twist
Method: SHAKE all ingredients with ice and fine strain into chilled glass.

1	shot	Ketel One vodka
½	shot	Butterscotch schnapps
¾	shot	Limoncello liqueur
¾	shot	Freshly squeezed lemon juice
¼	shot	Monin Pure Cane 2:1 sugar syrup
½	shot	Chilled mineral water

We say: Relive your youth and the taste of those big round sweets in this bitter-sweet, lemony cocktail.
Origin: Adapted from a drink discovered in 2001 at LAB Bar, London, England.

BONNIE PRINCE CHARLES

★★★★☆

Glass: Martini
Garnish: Lime wedge
Method: SHAKE all ingredients with ice and fine strain into chilled glass.

2¼	shots	Cognac VSOP
¾	shot	Drambuie
¾	shot	Freshly squeezed lime juice

We say: Honeyed, spiced cognac with a touch of citrus. But is it fit for a Prince?
Origin: Recipe to proportions found in Victor Bergeron's '*Trader Vic's Bartender's Guide*' (1972 revised edition).

BONSONI

★★★☆☆

Glass: Coupette
Garnish: Orange zest twist
Method: STIR all ingredients with ice and strain into chilled glass.

2	shots	Martini Rosso sweet vermouth
½	shot	Fernet Branca
¾	shot	Chilled mineral water

We say: Vermouth tames Fernet but will still only appeal to those with suitably old-school palates.
Origin: Vintage cocktail of unknown origin.

BOOMERANG

★★★☆☆

Glass: Martini
Garnish: Maraschino cherry
Method: SHAKE all ingredients with ice and fine strain into chilled glass.

1½	shots	Maker's Mark bourbon
¼	shot	Luxardo Maraschino liqueur
¾	shot	Martini Extra Dry vermouth
¾	shot	Martini Rosso sweet vermouth
½	shot	Freshly squeezed lemon juice
½	shot	Monin Pure Cane 2:1 sugar syrup
2	dashes	Angostura aromatic bitters

We say: A very Sweet Manhattan with lemon juice.

BORA BORA BREW (MOCKTAIL)

★★☆☆☆

Glass: Collins
Garnish: Pineapple wedge
Method: SHAKE all ingredients with ice and strain into ice-filled glass.

3	shots	Fresh pressed pineapple juice
⅛	shot	Pomegranate (grenadine) syrup
Top up with		Ginger ale

We say: Fruity and frothy ginger beer.

BORDERLINE

★★★☆☆

Glass: Martini
Garnish: Orange zest twist
Method: SHAKE all ingredients with ice and fine strain into chilled glass.

2	shots	Maker's Mark bourbon
½	shot	Freshly squeezed lemon juice
½	shot	Maple syrup
¾	shot	Carpano Punt E Mes

We say: Bourbon sweetened with maple syrup, soured by lemon and made more complex by vermouth.
Origin: Created in 2004 by James Mellor at Mint Leaf, London, England.

BOSOM CARESSER

★★★★☆

Glass: Martini
Garnish: Orange zest twist (discarded)
Method: SHAKE all ingredients with ice and fine strain into chilled glass.

2	shots	Cognac VSOP
½	shot	Grand Marnier liqueur
½	shot	Blandy's Alvada madeira
¼	shot	Pomegranate (grenadine) syrup
1	fresh	Egg yolk

We say: An oddly-named but smooth and creamy drink.

BOSSA NOVA #1

★★★★☆

Glass: Collins
Garnish: Lime slice
Method: SHAKE all ingredients with ice and strain into ice-filled glass.

2	shots	Bacardi Superior rum
¾	shot	De Kuyper Apricot Brandy liqueur
¾	shot	Galliano L'Autentico liqueur
2	shots	Pressed apple juice
¾	shot	Freshly squeezed lime juice

We say: Apple with the added zing of rum, Galliano, apricot and lime juice.
Origin: Named after the Brazilian dance which in turn comes from the Portuguese 'bossa', meaning 'tendency', and 'nova', meaning 'new'.

BOSSA NOVA #2

★★★½☆

Glass: Collins
Garnish: None
Method: SHAKE all ingredients with ice and strain into ice-filled glass.

2	shots	Bacardi Superior rum
½	shot	De Kuyper Apricot Brandy liqueur
½	shot	Galliano L'Autentico liqueur
2	shots	Fresh pressed pineapple juice
½	shot	Freshly squeezed lemon juice

We say: Long and frothy with fruity rum and subtle anis notes. Not too sweet.

BOSSA

BOSTON

★★★½☆

Glass: Martini
Garnish: Apricot slice
Method: SHAKE all ingredients with ice and fine strain into chilled glass.

1¾	shots	Tanqueray London dry gin
1	shot	De Kuyper Apricot Brandy liqueur
1	shot	Freshly squeezed lemon juice
¼	shot	Monin Pure Cane 2:1 sugar syrup
⅛	shot	Pomegranate (grenadine) syrup

We say: Gin laced tangy fruit.

BOSTON DELUXE NEW

★★★★☆

Glass: Coupette
Garnish: Saffron fronds
Method: DRY SHAKE all ingredients (without ice). SHAKE with ice and fine strain into chilled glass.

1½	shots	Maker's Mark bourbon
¾	shot	Freshly squeezed lemon juice
¾	shot	Freshly squeezed orange juice
½	shot	Saffron syrup (2:1 sugar syrup heated with saffron fronds)
2	dashes	Orange bitters
½	fresh	Egg white

We say: A citrusy take on a bourbon sour, spiced with saffron.
Origin: Created in 2012 by Nicolas Kröger at the Rivoli Bar at the Ritz Hotel, London, England

BOSTON FLIP

★★★★☆

Glass: Goblet
Garnish: Dust with grated nutmeg
Method: SHAKE all ingredients with ice and fine strain into chilled glass.

2	shots	Maker's Mark bourbon
2	shots	Blandy's Alvada madeira
¼	shot	Monin Pure Cane 2:1 sugar syrup
1	fresh	Egg

We say: A good dusting of freshly grated nutmeg makes this old school drink.

BOSTON TEA PARTY

★★★☆☆

Glass: Collins
Garnish: Orange slice
Method: SHAKE first ten ingredients with ice and strain into ice-filled glass. TOP with cola and serve with straws.

½	shot	Ketel One vodka
½	shot	Dewar's White label Scotch
½	shot	Triple Sec
½	shot	Pusser's Navy rum
½	shot	Tanqueray London dry gin
½	shot	Tequila 100% Agave
½	shot	Martini Extra Dry vermouth
½	shot	Freshly squeezed orange juice
1	shot	Freshly squeezed lime juice
½	shot	Monin Pure Cane 2:1 sugar syrup
Top up with		Coca-Cola

Origin: Named after the revolt by early US settlers against the imposition of tax by the British Crown, which became the War of Independence.

BOULEVARD

★★★★☆

Glass: Martini
Garnish: Orange zest twist (discarded) & maraschino cherry
Method: STIR all ingredients with ice and strain into chilled glass.

2½	shots	Maker's Mark bourbon
½	shot	Grand Marnier liqueur
1	shot	Martini Extra Dry vermouth
2	dashes	Orange bitters

We say: A Manhattan-style cocktail which takes no prisoners.
Origin: A classic of unknown origins.

STAR RATINGS EXPLAINED

★★★★★ Excellent

★★★★⯪ Recommended   ★★★★☆ Praiseworthy
★★★⯪☆ Commended   ★★★☆☆ Mediocre
★★⯪☆☆ Disappointing   ★★☆☆☆ Pretty awful
★⯪☆☆☆ Shameful   ★☆☆☆☆ Disgusting

THE BOULEVARDIER NEW

★★★★½

Glass: Old-fashioned
Garnish: Lemon or orange zest twist
Method: STIR all ingredients with ice and strain into glass.

1½	shots	**Maker's Mark bourbon**
1	shot	**Martini Rosso sweet vermouth**
1	shot	**Campari Bitter**

We say: Basically a Negroni with bourbon replacing gin. A combo which Negroni lovers should try.
Origin: This Prohibition cocktail first appeared in Harry McElhone's 1927 bar guide, 'Barflies and Cocktails'. According to cocktail historian, Ted Haigh, it was the signature drink of Erskine Gwynne, a Parisian-based expat writer and socialite who was the nephew of American railroad tycoon Alfred Vanderbilt. The drink takes its name from The Boulevardier, a monthly Parisian magazine which Gwynne edited.

BOUQUET

★★★½☆

Glass: Martini
Garnish: Lemon zest twist
Method: SHAKE all ingredients with ice and fine strain into chilled glass.

1	spoon	**Runny honey**
2	shots	**Tanqueray London dry gin**
½	shot	**Freshly squeezed lemon juice**
¼	shot	**Rose syrup**
½	shot	**Chilled mineral water**

We say: Rose delicately flavours gin with a sweet and sour balance provided by honey and lemon.
Origin: Adapted from a drink created in 2005 by Alex Pacumbo at Cocoon, London, England.

BOURBON BLUSH UPDATED

★★★★½

Glass: Martini
Garnish: Strawberry
Method: MUDDLE strawberries in base of shaker. Add other ingredients, SHAKE with ice and fine strain into chilled glass.

3	fresh	**Strawberries (hulled)**
2	shots	**Maker's Mark bourbon**
¾	shot	**Crème de framboise liqueur**
¼	shot	**Maple syrup**

We say: Strawberry and maple syrup combine brilliantly with bourbon in this drink.
Origin: Created in 2003 by Simon King at MJU at Millennium Hotel, London, England.

BOURBON COOKIE

★★★★☆

Glass: Old-fashioned
Garnish: Dust with cinnamon powder
Method: SHAKE all ingredients with ice and strain into ice-filled glass.

2	shots	**Maker's Mark bourbon**
½	shot	**Double (heavy) cream**
½	shot	**Milk**
½	shot	**Passion fruit syrup**
½	shot	**Butterscotch schnapps**

We say: Looks tame but packs a flavoursome punch.
Origin: Created in 2002 by Andres Masso, London, England.

BOURBON CRUSTA

★★★★½

Glass: Flute
Garnish: Find a lemon which fits into a small wineglass tightly enough to act as a watertight extension to the glass. Cut off both ends of the fruit and carefully remove the pulp to leave a barrel-shaped shell of skin. Place in the top of the glass. Wet the edge of the glass and exposed fruit shell with sugar syrup and dip in caster sugar to frost the edge of both peel and glass. Leave for a couple of hours to form a hard crust.
Method: SHAKE all ingredients with ice and fine strain into pre-prepared glass.

2	shots	**Maker's Mark bourbon**
¼	shot	**Cointreau triple sec**
⅛	shot	**Luxardo maraschino liqueur**
½	shot	**Freshly squeezed lemon juice**
¼	shot	**Monin Pure Cane 2:1 sugar syrup**
2	dashes	**Orange bitters**
½	shot	**Chilled mineral water**

Variant: Brandy Crusta
We say: Beautifully balanced bourbon and fresh lemon.

BOURBON MILK PUNCH UPDATED

★★★★½

Glass: Collins
Garnish: Dust with grated nutmeg
Method: SHAKE all ingredients with ice and strain into ice-filled glass.

1½	shots	**Maker's Mark bourbon**
¼	shot	**Monin Pure Cane 2:1 sugar syrup**
4	shots	**Milk**
⅛	shot	**Vanilla extract**

Variant: Brandy Milk Punch
We say: Truly the milk of the Gods! Delicate bourbon with a touch of vanilla. Balanced rather than sweet and milky rather than creamy.
Origin: This classic was popular during America's Prohibition era and is still widely served in New Orleans where it is commonly consumed with Sunday brunch.

BOURBON RENEWAL

★★★½☆

Glass: Old-fashioned
Garnish: Seasonal berries
Method: SHAKE all ingredients with ice and strain into ice-filled glass.

2	shots	**Maker's Mark bourbon**
1	shot	**Freshly squeezed lemon juice**
¼	shot	**Monin Pure Cane 2:1 sugar syrup**
1	dash	**Angostura aromatic bitters**
½	shot	**Crème de cassis liqueur**

We say: Fruit supplements rather than dominates Bourbon in this easy long drink.
Origin: Created in 2008 by Jeffrey Morgenthaler at Bel Ami Lounge, Oregon, USA.

STAR RATINGS EXPLAINED

★★★★★ Excellent

★★★★½	Recommended	★★★★☆	Praiseworthy
★★★½☆	Commended	★★★☆☆	Mediocre
★★½☆☆	Disappointing	★★☆☆☆	Pretty awful
★½☆☆☆	Shameful	★☆☆☆☆	Disgusting

BOURBON SKIN NEW

★★★★☆

Glass: Toddy
Garnish: Large orange zest twist
Method: Place barspoon in warmed glass. POUR all ingredients into warmed glass and STIR.

2	shots	Maker's Mark bourbon
3	shots	Boiling water
¼	shot	Monin Pure Cane 2:1 sugar syrup

We say: Hot, watered down bourbon stirred with orange oils. Simple but very tasty.
Origin: The only difference between a 'skin' and a 'toddy' is the addition of citrus peel to a skin.

BOURBON SMASH

★★★⯪☆

Glass: Collins
Garnish: Lime slice
Method: MUDDLE raspberries in base of shaker. Add other ingredients, SHAKE with ice and fine strain into ice-filled glass.

12	shots	Raspberries
4	fresh	Mint leaves
2½	shots	Maker's Mark bourbon
3	shots	Ocean Spray cranberry juice
1	shot	Freshly squeezed lime juice
½	shot	Monin Pure Cane 2:1 sugar syrup
2	dashes	Angostura aromatic bitters

We say: This refreshing long drink has a sharp edge that adds to its appeal.

BOURBONELLA

★★★★☆

Glass: Martini
Garnish: Maraschino cherry
Method: STIR all ingredients with ice and fine strain into chilled glass.

1¾	shots	Maker's Mark bourbon
¾	shot	Triple Sec
¾	shot	Martini Extra Dry vermouth
¼	shot	Pomegranate (grenadine) syrup
3	dashes	Peychaud's aromatic bitters

We say: If you like bourbon, you'll love this fruity Manhattan.

BOXCAR

★★★⯪☆

Glass: Martini
Garnish: Sugar rim
Method: SHAKE all ingredients with ice and fine strain into chilled glass.

2	shots	Tanqueray London dry gin
½	shot	Triple Sec
¾	shot	Freshly squeezed lime juice
⅛	shot	Pomegranate (grenadine) syrup
½	fresh	Egg white

We say: A White Lady in a sugar-rimmed glass with the addition of a dash of grenadine and substituting lemon juice for lime.

BRADFORD

★★★★☆

Glass: Martini
Garnish: Chilled olive on stick or lemon zest twist
Method: SHAKE all ingredients with ice and fine strain into chilled glass.

2½	shots	Tanqueray London dry gin
½	shot	Martini Extra Dry vermouth
3	dashes	Orange bitters

We say: More approachable than a stirred Traditional Dry Martini and downright soft compared to a Naked Martini.
Origin: A Bradford is a Martini which is shaken rather than stirred. Like the Martini itself, the origin of the Bradford is lost in time.

BRAINSTORM

★★★★⯪

Glass: Martini
Garnish: Orange zest twist
Method: STIR all ingredients with ice and strain into chilled glass.

1½	shots	Maker's Mark bourbon
¾	shot	Bénédictine D.O.M.
1	shot	Martini Extra Dry vermouth
½	shot	Chilled mineral water

We say: Spiced and slightly sweetened bourbon.
Origin: Another long lost classic.

BRAKE TAG

★★★⯪☆

Glass: Old-fashioned
Garnish: Orange zest twist
Method: SHAKE all ingredients with ice and strain into ice-filled glass.

½	shot	Amaretto liqueur
1½	shots	Southern Comfort liqueur
1	shot	Ocean Spray cranberry juice
1	shot	Freshly squeezed orange juice
3	dashes	Peychaud's aromatic bitters

Origin: Discovered in 2005 at Café Adelaide's Swizzle Stick Bar, New Orleans, USA.

BRAMBLE

★★★★☆

Glass: Old-fashioned
Garnish: Blackberries & lemon slice
Method: SHAKE first three ingredients with ice and strain into glass filled with crushed ice. DRIZZLE liqueur over drink to create a 'bleeding' effect in the glass. Serve with short straws.

2	shots	Tanqueray London dry gin
1	shot	Freshly squeezed lemon juice
½	shot	Monin Pure Cane 2:1 sugar syrup
½	shot	Crème de Mûre liqueur

We say: One of the best and most popular drinks created in the 1980s.
Origin: Created in the mid-80s by Dick Bradsell at Fred's Club, Soho, London, England.

BRAMBLETTE

★★★½☆

Glass: Martini
Garnish: Orange zest twist
Method: SHAKE all ingredients with ice and fine strain into chilled glass.

2	**shots**	**Tanqueray London dry gin**
1	**shot**	**Benoit Serres créme de violette**
¾	**shot**	**Freshly squeezed lemon juice**
¼	**shot**	**Monin Pure Cane 2:1 sugar syrup**

We say: A martini-style drink with a floral, gin-laced palate.

BRANDY ALEXANDER UPDATED

★★★★½

Glass: Martini
Garnish: Dust with grated nutmeg
Method: SHAKE all ingredients with ice and fine strain into chilled glass.

2	**shots**	**Cognac VSOP**
½	**shot**	**Dark Crème de Cacao**
½	**shot**	**White Crème de Cacao**
½	**shot**	**Double (heavy) cream**

AKA: The Panama
We say: This after dinner classic is rich, creamy and spicy.
Origin: Originally known as 'Alexander #2', the Brandy Alexander is thought to have been created sometime during the 1930s, certainly prior to 1941 when it first appears in print. This classic blend of brandy and chocolate smoothed with cream is based on the original Alexander calling for gin as its base. As to whom substituted brandy in place of gin is lost in time.

BRANDY BLAZER

★★★½☆

Glass: Snifter
Garnish: Lemon & orange zest twists
Method: POUR cognac into a warmed glass and rest the bowl of the glass on an old-fashioned glass so it lies on its side supported by the rim. FLAME the cognac and carefully move the glass back to an upright position sitting normally on your work surface. POUR in hot water (this will extinguish any remaining flame) and sugar. Stir, garnish and serve.

2	**shots**	**Cognac VSOP**
2	**shots**	**Boiling water**
¼	**shot**	**Monin Pure Cane 2:1 sugar syrup**

We say: One way to warm your winter nights.
Origin: A variation on 'Professor' Jerry Thomas' Blue Blazer which involved theatrically pouring ignited brandy between two mugs. Please don't try this at home, kids.

STAR RATINGS EXPLAINED

★★★★★ Excellent

★★★★½ Recommended	★★★★☆ Praiseworthy
★★★½☆ Commended	★★★☆☆ Mediocre
★★½☆☆ Disappointing	★★☆☆☆ Pretty awful
★½☆☆☆ Shameful	★☆☆☆☆ Disgusting

BRANDY BUCK

★★★½☆

Glass: Collins
Garnish: Lemon wedge
Method: SHAKE first 3 ingredients with ice and strain into ice-filled glass. TOP with ginger ale and serve with straws.

2½	**shots**	**Cognac VSOP**
¼	**shot**	**Grand Marnier liqueur**
¼	**shot**	**Freshly squeezed lemon juice**

Top up with Ginger ale

We say: Lemon juice adds balance to the sweet ginger ale. Cognac provides the backbone.

BRANDY COCKTAIL

★★★★☆

Glass: Martini
Garnish: Lemon zest twist
Method: SHAKE all ingredients with ice and fine strain into chilled glass.

5	**fresh**	**Mint leaves**
2	**shots**	**Cognac VSOP**
¼	**shot**	**Grand Marnier liqueur**
¼	**shot**	**Monin Pure Cane 2:1 sugar syrup**
1	**dash**	**Angostura aromatic bitters**

We say: Subtle mint and citrus lightly flavour the cognac.
Origin: Vintage cocktail of unknown origin.

BRANDY CRUSTA

★★★★½

Glass: Flute
Garnish: Find a lemon which fits into a small wineglass tightly enough to act as a watertight extension to the glass. Cut off both ends of the fruit and carefully remove the pulp to leave a barrel-shaped shell of skin. Place in the top of the glass. Wet the edge of the glass and exposed fruit shell with sugar syrup and dip in caster sugar to frost the edge of both peel and glass. Leave for a couple of hours to form a hard crust.
Method: SHAKE all ingredients with ice and fine strain into pre-prepared glass.

2	**shots**	**Courvoisier VSOP Exclusif**
¼	**shot**	**Cointreau triple sec**
⅛	**shot**	**Luxardo maraschino liqueur**
½	**shot**	**Freshly squeezed lemon juice**
¼	**shot**	**Monin Pure Cane 2:1 sugar syrup**
2	**dashes**	**Angostura aromatic bitters**
¾	**shot**	**Chilled mineral water**

Variant: Bourbon Crusta
We say: This old classic zings with fresh lemon and is beautifully balanced by the cognac base.
Origin: Created in the 1840s - 50s by Joseph Santina at Jewel of the South, Gravier Street, New Orleans, USA. The name refers to the crust of sugar around the rim. This recipe is adapted from the David A. Embury's 1948 *'the Fine Art of Mixing Drinks'.*

BRANDY DAISY

★★★☆☆

Glass: Martini
Garnish: Mint sprig & maraschino cherry
Method: STIR all ingredients with ice and fine strain into chilled glass.

1½	shots	Cognac VSOP
½	shot	Chartreuse Yellow liqueur
½	shot	Freshly squeezed lemon juice
1	dash	Angostura aromatic bitters
½	shot	Chilled mineral water

We say: Dry, and to be honest, a tad flat. A vintage cocktail for vintage palates.
Origin: Vintage cocktail of unknown origin.

BRANDY FIX

★★★★½

Glass: Old-fashioned
Garnish: Lemon zest twist
Method: SHAKE all ingredients with ice and strain into ice-filled glass.

2	shots	Cognac VSOP
½	shot	Fresh pressed pineapple juice
½	shot	Freshly squeezed lemon juice
¼	shot	Monin Pure Cane 2:1 sugar syrup
⅛	shot	Chartreuse Yellow liqueur

We say: This wonderful classic is on the tart side of well balanced.

BRANDY FIZZ

★★★★☆

Glass: Collins (small 8oz)
Garnish: Lemon slice
Method: SHAKE first three ingredients with ice and fine strain into chilled glass (without ice). TOP with soda.

2	shots	Cognac VSOP
½	shot	Freshly squeezed lemon juice
¼	shot	Monin Pure Cane 2:1 sugar syrup
Top up with		Soda from siphon

We say: A refreshing and tasty dry drink: cognac and lemon balanced with a little sugar and lengthened with soda.

BRANDY FLIP

★★★★½

Glass: Martini
Garnish: Dust with grated nutmeg
Method: SHAKE all ingredients with ice and fine strain into chilled glass.

1½	shots	Cognac VSOP
¼	shot	Monin Pure Cane 2:1 sugar syrup
¼	shot	Double (heavy) cream
1	fresh	Egg

We say: A serious alternative to Advocaat for those without raw egg inhibitions.
Origin: A forgotten classic.

BRANDY MILK PUNCH UPDATED

★★★★☆

Glass: Collins
Garnish: Dust with grated nutmeg
Method: SHAKE all ingredients with ice and strain into ice-filled glass.

1½	shots	Courvoisier VSOP Exclusif
4	shots	Milk
¼	shot	Monin Pure Cane 2:1 sugar syrup
⅛	shot	Vanilla extract

Variant: Bourbon Milk Punch
We say: This traditional New Orleans hangover cure beats your bog-standard vanilla milkshake.
Origin: A classic which was popular during America's Prohibition era and dates back to colonial times. It is still widely served in New Orleans where it is commonly consumed with Sunday brunch.

BRANDY SMASH

★★★★☆

Glass: Old-fashioned
Garnish: Mint sprig
Method: Lightly MUDDLE mint in base of shaker just enough to bruise. Add other ingredients, SHAKE with ice and fine strain into ice-filled glass.

7	fresh	Mint leaves
2	shots	Cognac VSOP
¼	shot	Monin Pure Cane 2:1 sugar syrup

We say: Sweetened cognac flavoured with mint. Simple but beautiful.
Origin: A classic from the 1850s.

BRANDY SOUR

★★★★½

Glass: Old-fashioned
Garnish: Lemon slice & cherry on stick (sail)
Method: SHAKE all ingredients with ice and strain into ice-filled glass.

2	shots	Cognac VSOP
1	shot	Freshly squeezed lemon juice
½	shot	Monin Pure Cane 2:1 sugar syrup
3	dashes	Angostura aromatic bitters
½	fresh	Egg white

We say: After the Whisky Sour, this is the most requested sour. Try it and you'll see why - but don't omit the egg white.

BRASS MONKEY

★★★½☆

Glass: Collins
Garnish: Lemon slice
Method: SHAKE all ingredients with ice and strain into ice-filled glass.

1	shot	Bacardi Superior rum
1	shot	Ketel One vodka
2½	shots	Freshly squeezed lemon juice
1	shot	Monin Pure Cane 2:1 sugar syrup

We say: Tangy, alcoholic, almost sherberty lemonade. Packed with Vitamin C.

BRASS RAIL

★★★★⯪ **Glass:** Martini
Garnish: Physalis (cape gooseberry)
Method: SHAKE all ingredients with ice and fine strain into chilled glass.

2	shots	Bacardi Superior rum
½	shot	Bénédictine D.O.M.
½	shot	Freshly squeezed lemon juice
2	shots	Monin Pure Cane 2:1 sugar syrup
½	fresh	Egg white
1	dash	Orange bitters
½	shot	Chilled mineral water

We say: Rather like a Daiquiri, yet subtly sweetened and spiced.
Origin: Adapted from a recipe by Tony Abou-Ganim. He was inspired by his late cousin Helen David's penchant for a nightcap after a special occasion; her favourite was Bénédictine. This drink is named after Helen's bar the Brass Rail in Port Huron. Helen's memory is commemorated in the 'Helen David Spirit Award' which is given for lifetime achievement at the annual Tales of the Cocktail.

BRAZEN MARTINI

★★★★☆ **Glass:** Martini
Garnish: Orange zest twist
Method: STIR all ingredients with ice and strain into chilled glass.

2½	shots	Żubrówka bison vodka
¼	shot	Parfait Amour liqueur

We say: Not for the faint hearted - a great combination of grassy bison vodka with violet Parfait Amour.

BRAZILIAN BERRY

★★★★☆ **Glass:** Old-fashioned
Garnish: Mint sprig
Method: MUDDLE fruit in base of shaker. Add other ingredients, SHAKE with ice and fine strain into glass filled with crushed ice. Serve with straws.

4	fresh	Blackcurrants
3	fresh	Raspberries
1½	shots	Sauvignon blanc wine
1	shot	Leblon cachaça
1	shot	Crème de cassis liqueur

We say: This drink combines wine, cachaça and rich berry fruits.
Origin: Created in 2002 by Dan Spink at Browns, St Martin's Lane, London, England.

BRAZILIAN COFFEE

★★★★⯪☆ **Glass:** Toddy
Garnish: Coffee beans
Method: BLEND ingredients with 6oz scoop of crushed ice. Pour into glass and serve with straws.

1	shot	Leblon cachaça
1	shot	Double (heavy) cream
2	shots	Hot espresso coffee
¾	shot	Monin Pure Cane 2:1 sugar syrup

We say: Strong coffee and plenty of sugar are essential in this Brazilian number.

BRAZILIAN COSMOPOLITAN

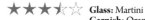

★★★⯪☆ **Glass:** Martini
Garnish: Orange zest twist
Method: SHAKE all ingredients with ice and fine strain into chilled glass.

1	shot	Leblon cachaça
1	shot	Triple Sec
1½	shots	Ocean Spray cranberry juice
½	shot	Freshly squeezed lime juice

We say: The distinctive character of cachaça bursts through the fruit in this twist on the contemporary classic.

BRAZILIAN MONK

★★★⯪☆ **Glass:** Hurricane
Garnish: Crumbled Cadbury's Flake bar
Method: BLEND ingredients with 12oz scoop of crushed ice. Pour into glass and serve with straws.

1	shot	Hazelnut liqueur
1	shot	Kahlúa coffee liqueur
1	shot	Dark Crème de Cacao
3	scoop	Häagen Dazs vanilla ice cream

We say: Nutty and rich dessert in a glass.

BRAZILIAN NAIL

★★★★☆ **Glass:** Old-fashioned
Garnish: Lime zest twist
Method: STIR all ingredients with ice and strain into ice-filled glass.

1½	shots	Leblon cachaça
½	shot	Dewar's White label Scotch
¾	shot	Drambuie

We say: A rift on the classic Nail using cachaca as the main base spirit with a hint of Scotch maintaining its lineage to the Drambuie Nail family.
Origin: Created in 2010 by Jamie Stephenson, Manchester, England.

BREAKFAST AT TERRELL'S

★★★★☆ **Glass:** Flute
Garnish: Kumquat
Method: SHAKE first four ingredients with ice and strain into chilled glass. TOP with champagne.

¾	shot	Double (heavy) cream
¾	shot	Mandarine Napoléon liqueur
¾	shot	Freshly squeezed orange juice
⅛	shot	Monin Pure Cane 2:1 sugar syrup
Top up with		Brut champagne

We say: This creamy orange champagne cocktail is almost as smooth as a Sgroppino.
Origin: Created by Jamie Terrell for Philip Holzberg at Vinexpo, Bordeaux, France, 1999.

BREAKFAST CLUB

★★★★★

Glass: Martini
Garnish: Lemon zest twist
Method: STIR honey and marmalade with rum until dissolved. Add tea, SHAKE with ice and fine strain into chilled glass.

1	spoon	Orange marmalade
1	spoon	Runny honey
2	shots	Bacardi Superior rum
1	shot	Cold Lapsang Souchong tea

We say: Slightly smoky with incredible depth of flavour. A perfectly balanced delight.
Origin: Recipe discovered in 2008 courtesy of DrinkBoy.com.

BREAKFAST GIMLET

★★★★☆

Glass: Martini
Garnish: Basil leaf
Method: STIR marmalade with gin in base of shaker to dissolve marmalade. Add lemon juice and lime cordial, SHAKE with ice and fine strain into chilled glass.

2½	shots	Tanqueray London dry gin
¼	shot	Rose's lime cordial
2	spoons	Orange marmalade
¼	shot	Freshly squeezed lemon juice

We say: Orange marmalade both justifies the 'breakfast' prefix and adds complexity to this gimlet.
Origin: Created by Simon Difford at the Cabinet Room, London, England.

BREAKFAST IN MANHATTAN NEW

★★★★⯪

Glass: Coupette
Garnish: Orange zest twist
Method: STIR marmalade with bourbon to dissolve marmalade. Add other ingredients, STIR with ice and fine strain into chilled glass.

1	spoon	Orange marmalade
2	shots	Maker's Mark bourbon
½	shot	Martini Rosso sweet vermouth
1	dash	Orange bitters

We say: The British Breakfast Martini comes to Manhattan.
Origin: Discovered in 2009 at Bentley's, Dublin, Ireland.

STAR RATINGS EXPLAINED

★★★★★ Excellent

★★★★⯪ Recommended	★★★★☆ Praiseworthy
★★★⯪☆ Commended	★★★☆☆ Mediocre
★★⯪☆☆ Disappointing	★★☆☆☆ Pretty awful
★⯪☆☆☆ Shameful	★☆☆☆☆ Disgusting

BREAKFAST MARTINI

★★★★★

Glass: Martini
Garnish: Orange zest twist & slice of toast on rim
Method: STIR marmalade with gin in base of shaker until it dissolves. Add other ingredients, SHAKE with ice and fine strain into chilled glass.

1	spoon	Orange marmalade
2	shots	Tanqueray London dry gin
½	shot	Triple Sec
½	shot	Freshly squeezed lemon juice

We say: The success or failure of this tangy drink is partly reliant on the quality of marmalade used.
Origin: Created in the late 1990s by Salvatore Calabrese at the Library Bar, London, England. It is very similar to the *'Marmalade Cocktail'* created in the 1920s by Harry Craddock and published in his 1930 *'The Savoy Cocktail Book'*, or you could describe the Breakfast Martini as being White Lady with marmalade in it.

Salvatore came up with the idea for this drink after his wife insisted he have breakfast one morning and served up toast and marmalade. He took the jar to work with him and this contemporary classic was the result. This drink was the inspiration for the many variations on the preserve (jam/marmalade) theme that have followed in the decade since Salvatore stopped for 'proper' breakfast rather than just his usual swift espresso.

BRIDGETOWN DAIQUIRI NEW

★★★★☆

Glass: Coupette
Garnish: Grapefruit wedge
Method: SHAKE all ingredients with ice and fine strain into chilled glass.

2	shots	Rum Golden
½	shot	Luxardo maraschino liqueur
½	shot	Monin Pure Cane 2:1 sugar syrup
½	shot	Ruby grapefruit juice
½	shot	Freshly squeezed lime juice

We say: Delicate and very slightly sweet with maraschino liqueur brilliantly balancing grapefruit juice.
Origin: Unknown.

BRIGHTON PUNCH

★★★★☆

Glass: Collins
Garnish: Pineapple wedge
Method: SHAKE all ingredients with ice and fine strain into chilled glass.

1½	shots	Maker's Mark bourbon
1½	shots	Bénédictine D.O.M.
1½	shots	Cognac VSOP
2½	shots	Fresh pressed pineapple juice
2	shots	Freshly squeezed lemon juice

Variant: With orange juice in place of pineapple juice
We say: Don't bother trying the version with orange juice but do try halving the quantities and serving up. Served long or short this is beautifully balanced.
Origin: Popular in the bars of Berlin, Germany.

THE BROADMOOR

★★★★½

Glass: Martini
Garnish: Orange zest twist (flamed)
Method: SHAKE all ingredients with ice and fine strain into chilled glass.

2	shots	Dewar's White label Scotch
½	shot	Chartreuse Green liqueur
½	shot	Monin Pure Cane 2:1 sugar syrup
4	dashes	Orange bitters

We say: Beautifully simple and seriously complex.
Origin: Created in 2001 by Swedish bartender Andreas Noren at The Player, London, England and popularised at Milk & Honey, London, England. Named after the infamous British mental institution.

BROKEN SPUR

★★★☆☆

Glass: Martini
Garnish: Dust with grated nutmeg
Method: SHAKE all ingredients with ice and fine strain into chilled glass.

3	shots	Taylor's chip dry white port
¼	shot	Tanqueray London dry gin
¼	shot	Martini Rosso sweet vermouth
⅛	shot	Marie Brizard anisette liqueur
1	fresh	Egg yolk

We say: Smooth rather than creamy and only lightly alcoholic. Perhaps one after a boozy dinner?
Origin: Vintage cocktail of unknown origin.

BRONX #1 (ORIGINAL)

★★★★☆

Glass: Martini
Garnish: Orange zest twist (discarded) & maraschino cherry
Method: SHAKE all ingredients with ice and fine strain into chilled glass.

1½	shots	Tanqueray London dry gin
¾	shot	Martini Extra Dry vermouth
¾	shot	Martini Rosso sweet vermouth
1	shot	Freshly squeezed orange juice

Variant: 1/ Bloody Bronx - made with the juice of a blood orange. 2/ Golden Bronx - with the addition of an egg yolk. 3/ Silver Bronx - with the addition of egg white. 4/ Income Tax Cocktail - with two dashes Angostura bitters. Also see the Abbey Martini and Satan's Whiskers.
We say: A serious, dry, complex cocktail - less bitter than many of its era, but still challenging to more tender modern palates.
Origin: Created in 1906 by Johnny Solon, a bartender at New York's Waldorf-Astoria Hotel (the Empire State Building occupies the site today), and named after the newly opened Bronx Zoo. This is reputedly the first cocktail to use fruit juice.

In his 1935, *'The Old Waldorf-Astoria Book'*, A.S. Crockett says "Solon's own story of the Creation - of the Bronx: We had a cocktail in those days called the Duplex, which had a pretty fair demand. One day, I was making one for a customer when in came Traverson, head waiter of the Empire Room - the main dining room in the original Waldorf. A Duplex was composed of equal parts of French [dry] and Italian [sweet] Vermouth, shaken up with squeezed orange peel, or two dashes of Orange Bitters. Traverson said, "Why don't you get up a new cocktail? I have a customer who says you can't do it." "Can't I?" I replied. "Well," I finished the Duplex I was making, and a thought came to me. I poured into a mixing glass the equivalent of two jiggers of Gordon Gin. Then I filled the jigger with orange juice, so that it made one-third of orange and two-thirds of gin. Then into the mixture I put a dash of each Italian and French Vermouth, shaking the thing up. I didn't taste it myself, but I poured it into a cocktail glass and handed it to Traverson and said: "You are a pretty good judge. (He was.) See what you think of that." Traverson tasted it. Then he swallowed it whole.

" 'By God!' he said, 'you've really got something new! That will make a big hit. Make me another and I will take it back to that customer in the dining room. Bet you'll sell a lot of them. Have you got plenty of oranges? If you haven't, you had better stock up, because I'm going to sell a lot of those cocktails during lunch.'

"The demand for Bronx cocktails started that day. Pretty soon we were using a whole case of oranges a day. And then several cases.

"The name? No, it wasn't really named directly after the borough or the river so-called. I had been at the Bronx Zoo a day or so before, and saw, of course, a lot of beasts I had never known. Customers used to tell me of the strange animals they saw after a lot of mixed drinks. So when Traverson said to me, as he started to take the drink in to the customer, "What'll I tell him is the name of this drink?" I thought of those animals, and said: "Oh, you can tell him it is a 'Bronx.'"

BRONZE ADONIS

★★★★☆

Glass: Martini
Garnish: Lemon zest twist
Method: STIR all ingredients with ice and strain into a chilled glass.

1½	shots	Tio Pepe fino sherry
1½	shots	Noilly Ambre vermouth
½	shot	Manzanilla Sherry
2	dashes	Orange bitters

We say: A simple yet fabulous twist on the Adonis.
Origin: Created in 2008 by Julian de Feral at The Player, London, England.

BROOKLYN #1

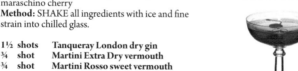

★★★★☆

Glass: Martini
Garnish: Maraschino cherry
Method: STIR all ingredients with ice and strain into chilled glass.

2½	shots	Maker's Mark bourbon
¼	shot	Luxardo Maraschino liqueur
½	shot	Martini Extra Dry vermouth
½	shot	Martini Rosso sweet vermouth
3	dashes	Angostura aromatic bitters

We say: A Perfect Manhattan with maraschino liqueur.
Origin: Thought to have originated at the St George Hotel, Brooklyn, New York City, USA.

BROOKLYN #2

★★★★☆

Glass: Martini
Garnish: Maraschino cherry
Method: STIR all ingredients with ice and strain into chilled glass.

2	shots	Maker's Mark bourbon
½	shot	Amaretto liqueur
¾	shot	Martini Extra Dry vermouth

We say: A simple, very approachable Manhattan.

BROOKLYN COCKTAIL

★★★★★½

Glass: Coupette
Garnish: Maraschino cherry
Method: STIR all ingredients with ice and strain into chilled glass.

1½	shots	Straight rye whiskey
½	shot	Martini Extra Dry vermouth
¼	shot	Amer Picon
¼	shot	Luxardo Maraschino liqueur

Variant: Manhattan
We say: One of the Manhattan variations named after New York's many neighbourhoods.

BROWN DERBY NEW

★★★★★★

Glass: Coupette
Garnish: Grapefruit zest twist
Method: SHAKE all ingredients with ice and fine strain into chilled glass.

1½	shots	Maker's Mark bourbon
1	shot	Freshly squeezed grapefruit juice
¼	shot	Maple syrup

We say: Maple syrup combines wonderfully with bourbon and balances grapefruit sourness to make a short drink that's equally as enticing at the beginning or end of a night.
Origin: Named after The Brown Derby chain of restaurants in Los Angeles, California. The original restaurant opened in 1926 at 3427 Wilshire Boulevard and was iconic due to the building being shaped like a man's derby hat. The chain was started by Robert H. Cobb and Herbert Somborn (a former husband of film star Gloria Swanson).

BRUBAKER OLD-FASHIONED

★★★★☆

Glass: Old-fashioned
Garnish: Lemon zest twist
Method: STIR malt extract in glass with Scotch until malt extract dissolves. Add ice and one shot of Scotch and stir. Add remaining Scotch, sugar and Angostura and stir some more. Add more ice and keep stirring so that ice dilutes the drink.

2	spoons	Malt Extract
2	shots	Dewar's White label Scotch
¼	shot	Monin Pure Cane 2:1 sugar syrup
3	dashes	Angostura aromatic bitters

We say: If you like Scotch you should try this extra malty dram. After all that stirring you'll deserve one.
Origin: Created in 2003 by Shelim Islam at the GE Club, London, England. Shelim named this drink after a horse in the sports section of a paper (also a film made in the seventies starring Robert Redford).

STAR RATINGS EXPLAINED

★★★★★ Excellent

★★★★½ Recommended	★★★★☆ Praiseworthy
★★★½☆ Commended	★★★☆☆ Mediocre
★★½☆☆ Disappointing	★★☆☆☆ Pretty awful
★½☆☆☆ Shameful	★☆☆☆☆ Disgusting

BRUNSWICK

★★★★★½

Glass: Old-fashioned
Garnish: Orange slice & cherry on stick (sail)
Method: SHAKE first 3 ingredients with ice and fine strain into ice-filled glass. FLOAT claret on drink.

2	shots	Straight rye whiskey
¾	shot	Freshly squeezed lemon juice
½	shot	Monin Pure Cane 2:1 sugar syrup
¾	shot	Claret red wine

We say: Has the good looks and also the flavour profile to back them up.
Origin: Recipe adapted from the 1935 '*The Old Waldorf-Astoria Bar Book*' in which Albert S. Crocket writes of this drink, "Invented at the Old Hotel Brunswick, once a resort for Fashion, and situated on the north side of Madison Square."

BUBBLEGUM SHOT

★★★☆☆

Glass: Shot
Garnish: None
Method: SHAKE all ingredients with ice and fine strain into chilled glass.

½	shot	Midori green melon liqueur
½	shot	Amaretto liqueur
¼	shot	Double (heavy) cream

We say: As the name suggests, this tastes a little like bubblegum.

THE BUCK/GIN BUCK UPDATED ⚷

★★★★½☆

Glass: Collins
Garnish: Lemon wedge
Method: POUR first two ingredients into ice-filled glass and TOP with ginger ale. Stir and serve with straws.

2½	shots	Tanqueray London dry gin
½	shot	Freshly squeezed lemon juice
Top up with		Ginger ale

Variant: The recipe above is for a Gin Buck, but this drink can also be based on brandy, calvados, rum, whiskey, vodka etc.
We say: The Buck can be improved by adding a dash of liqueur appropriate to the spirit base. E.g. add a dash of Grand Marnier to a Brandy Buck.

BUCK'S FIZZ ⚷

★★★☆☆

Glass: Flute
Garnish: None
Method: POUR ingredients into chilled glass and gently stir.

| 2 | shots | Freshly squeezed orange juice |
| Top up with | | Brut champagne |

AKA: Mimosa
We say: Not really a cocktail and not that challenging, but great for brunch.
Origin: Created in 1921 by Mr McGarry, first bartender at the Buck's Club, London.

BUCKEYE

★★★★½

Glass: Martini
Garnish: Black olive
Method: STIR all ingredients with ice and strain into chilled glass.

| 2½ | shots | Tanqueray London dry gin |
| ½ | shot | Martini Extra Dry vermouth |

We say: A standard Dry Martini - but a Buckeye is always garnished with a black olive instead of a green one.

BUENA VIDA UPDATED

★★★★☆

Glass: Old-fashioned
Garnish: Pineapple wedge on rim
Method: SHAKE all ingredients with ice and strain into ice-filled glass.

2	shots	Tequila 100% Agave (reposado)
1¾	shots	Freshly squeezed grapefruit juice
¾	shot	Fresh pressed pineapple juice
¼	shot	Monin Vanilla sugar syrup
3 dashes Angostura aromatic bitters		

We say: Pineapple and grapefruit combine charged with tequila, sweetened with vanilla and spiced with Angostura bitters.
Origin: Adapted from a drink created in 2011 by Lee Clinton.

BULL SHOT

★★★½☆

Glass: Collins
Garnish: Celery salt rim
Method: SHAKE all ingredients with ice and strain into ice-filled glass.

2	shots	Ketel One vodka
4	shots	Cold beef bouillon
½	shot	Freshly squeezed lemon juice
3	dashes	Worcestershire sauce
3	dashes	Tabasco hot pepper sauce
1	pinch	Salt
1	grind	Black pepper

We say: Beef broth replaces tomato in this Mary for carnivorous drinkers.

BULL'S BLOOD

★★★½☆

Glass: Martini
Garnish: Orange zest twist
Method: SHAKE all ingredients with ice and fine strain into chilled glass.

½	shot	Bacardi Superior rum
1	shot	Cognac VSOP
1	shot	Grand Marnier liqueur
1½	shots	Freshly squeezed orange juice

We say: This beautifully balanced fruity cocktail has a dry finish.

BULL'S MILK

★★★½☆

Glass: Collins
Garnish: None
Method: SHAKE all ingredients with ice and strain into ice-filled glass.

1	shot	Bacardi Superior rum
1½	shots	Cognac VSOP
4	shots	Milk
½	shot	Maple syrup

We say: Dark spirits tamed by thick maple syrup and milk.

BULLDOG

★★★½☆

Glass: Collins
Garnish: None
Method: SHAKE first 4 ingredients with ice and strain into ice-filled glass. TOP with cola, stir and serve with straws.

1	shot	Bacardi Superior rum
1	shot	Kahlúa coffee liqueur
1½	shots	Milk
1½	shots	Double (heavy) cream
Top up with Coca-Cola		

We say: Surprisingly nice - cola cuts through the cream.

BULLDOG HIGHBALL

★★★☆☆

Glass: Collins
Garnish: Orange slice
Method: SHAKE first two ingredients with ice and strain into ice-filled glass. TOP with ginger ale and lightly stir. Serve with straws.

2	shots	Tanqueray London dry gin
1½	shots	Freshly squeezed orange juice
Top up with Ginger ale		

We say: Light and easy drinking. Gin and orange lightly spiced with ginger.

BULLFROG #1

★★★☆☆

Glass: Collins
Garnish: Maraschino cherry
Method: SHAKE all ingredients with ice and strain into glass filled with crushed ice.

1½	shots	Ketel One vodka
¾	shot	Giffard Menthe Pastille liqueur
1	shot	Double (heavy) cream
1	shot	Milk

We say: Tastes of mint ice cream.

BULLFROG #2

★★★☆☆

Glass: Collins
Garnish: Lime wedge
Method: POUR vodka and lime into ice-filled glass and TOP with lemonade.

2	shots	Ketel One vodka
½	shot	Freshly squeezed lime juice
Top up with		Lemonade/Sprite/7-Up

We say: Long, dry and fresh.

BUMBLE BEE

★★★★☆

Glass: Shot
Garnish: None
Method: Refrigerate ingredients then LAYER in chilled glass by carefully pouring in the following order.

½	shot	Kahlúa coffee liqueur
½	shot	Luxardo Sambuca dei Cesari
½	shot	Baileys Irish cream liqueur

We say: A B-52 with a liquorice kick.

BUONA SERA SHOT

★★★★☆

Glass: Shot
Garnish: None
Method: SHAKE all ingredients with ice and fine strain into chilled glass.

½	shot	Amaretto liqueur
½	shot	Bacardi Superior rum
½	shot	Kahlúa coffee liqueur

We say: A popular sweet shot

BURNING BUSH SHOT(S)

★★☆☆☆

Glass: Shot
Garnish: None
Method: POUR tequila into chilled glass and then drop Tabasco over the top. This will sink through the tequila.

| 1 | shot | Tequila 100% Agave |
| 4 | drops | Tabasco hot pepper sauce |

AKA: Prairie Dog, Prairie Fire
We say: The Mexicans are fans of hot pepper sauce, although they probably would not condone this way of drinking tequila.

BURNT TOASTED ALMOND

★★★☆☆

Glass: Martini
Garnish: Dust with grated nutmeg
Method: SHAKE all ingredients with ice and fine strain into chilled glass.

1	shot	Ketel One vodka
½	shot	Baileys Irish cream liqueur
1	shot	Amaretto liqueur
½	shot	Kahlúa coffee liqueur
1	shot	Milk
1	shot	Double (heavy) cream

Variant: Toasted Almond
We say: There's more than just almond to this sweety.

THE BUSINESS NEW

★★★★☆

Glass: Coupette
Garnish: Lime zest twist
Method: SHAKE all ingredients with ice and fine strain into chilled glass.

2	shots	Tanqueray London dry gin
½	shot	Acacia honey syrup (2 honey : 1 water)
½	shots	Freshly squeezed lime juice

We say: A Bee's Knees made snappier with lime instead of lemon.
Origin: Adapted from a drink discovered at Milk & Honey, London, England

BUSHRANGER NEW

★★★★☆

Glass: Martini or Coupette
Garnish: Orange zest twist
Method: STIR all ingredients with ice and stain into ice-filled glass.

1½	shots	Rum light white/blanco
1½	shots	Dubonnet Red (French made)
2	dashes	Angostura aromatic bitters

We say: Slightly sweet, this complex cocktail combines flavours of red wine with subtle herbal notes and is fortified with light rum.
Origin: Unknown. Originally, in the early years of the British settlement of Australia, Bushrangers where runaway convicts who had the survival skills necessary to use the Australian bush as a refuge from the authorities. He term then evolved as the Australian term for a highwaymen.

BARTENDER'S TIP CONVERTING 'SHOTS'

To covert 'shots' into and fluid ounces simply treat one shot as one ounce. To convert 'shots' into metric measures use the following conversions:

2 shot(s) = 60ml, 1¾ shot(s) 52.5ml, 1½ shot(s) = 45ml, 1 shot(s) = 30ml, ¾ shot(s) = 22.5ml, ⅔ hot = 20ml, ½ shot(s) =15ml, ⅓ shot(s) = 10ml, ¼ shot(s) = 7.5ml, ⅙ shot(s) = 5ml, ⅛ shot(s) = 4ml

BUSHWICK

★★★★½

Glass: Coupette
Garnish: None
Method: STIR all ingredients with ice and strain into a chilled glass.

2	shots	Straight rye whiskey
¾	shot	Martini Rosso sweet vermouth
¼	shot	Luxardo Maraschino liqueur
¼	shot	Amer Picon

We say: This Italian-American blend is better and even more gripping than Godfather II.
Origin: Created in 2009 by Phil Ward at Mayahuel New York City, USA. This twist on the classic Brooklyn is named after Bushwick, a neighbourhood in the north east of the New York City borough of Brooklyn.

BUTTERFLY COCKTAIL

★★★★☆

Glass: Martini
Garnish: Lemon zest twist
Method: MUDDLE grapes in base of shaker. Add other ingredients and fine strain into chilled glass.

8	fresh	Seedless white grapes
3	fresh	Torn basil leaves
3	fresh	Mint leaves
1½	shots	Ketel One vodka
¼	shot	St-Germain elderflower liqueur
¼	shot	Freshly squeezed lemon juice

We say: Light and refreshing but with citrus complexity.
Origin: Created by Alex Kammerling, London, England.

BUTTERFLY'S KISS

★★★☆☆

Glass: Martini
Garnish: Cinnamon stick
Method: STIR all ingredients with ice and strain into chilled glass.

2	shots	Ketel One vodka
1	shot	Hazelnut liqueur
½	shot	Goldschläger cinnamon schnapps
½	shot	Monin Pure Cane 2:1 sugar syrup
½	shot	Chilled mineral water

We say: Golden coloured Martini-style drink complete with the odd gold flake and a hazelnut cinnamon twang.
Origin: Adapted from a drink discovered in 2003 at Bar Marmont, Los Angeles, USA.

BUTTERSCOTCH DAIQUIRI

★★★★½

Glass: Martini
Garnish: Butterscotch sweet
Method: SHAKE all ingredients with ice and fine strain into chilled glass.

2	shots	Bacardi Superior rum
1	shot	Butterscotch schnapps
½	shot	Freshly squeezed lime juice
½	shot	Chilled mineral water

We say: A candified Daiquiri.

BUTTERSCOTCH DELIGHT

★★★½☆

Glass: Shot
Garnish: None
Method: Refrigerate ingredients then LAYER in chilled glass by carefully pouring in the following order.

¾	shot	Butterscotch schnapps
¾	shot	Baileys Irish cream liqueur

We say: Sweet connotations!
Origin: The origin of this drink is unknown but it is very popular in the bars in and around Seattle, USA.

BUTTERSCOTCH MARTINI

★★★★☆

Glass: Martini
Garnish: Butterscotch sweet
Method: SHAKE all ingredients with ice and fine strain into chilled glass.

2	shots	Bacardi Superior rum
¾	shot	Butterscotch schnapps
¾	shot	White Crème de Cacao
⅛	shot	Monin Pure Cane 2:1 sugar syrup
½	shot	Chilled mineral water

We say: Sweet and easy to sip.

BUZZARD'S BREATH

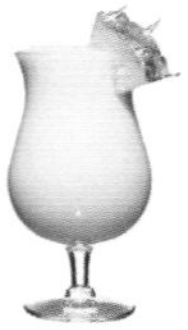

★★★½☆

Glass: Hurricane
Garnish: Pineapple wedge
Method: BLEND ingredients with 12oz scoop of crushed ice. Pour into glass and serve with straws.

2½	shots	Leblon cachaça
1	shot	Coco López cream of coconut
2	shots	Fresh pressed pineapple juice
¼	shot	Double (heavy) cream

We say: A Piña Colada made with cachaça.

BYCULLA

★★★★☆

Glass: Martini
Garnish: Fresh ginger slice
Method: SHAKE all ingredients with ice and fine strain into chilled glass.

1	shot	Tio Pepe fino sherry
1	shot	Warre's Otima tawny port
½	shot	Grand Marnier liqueur
½	shot	Domaine de Canton ginger liqueur
½	shot	Chilled mineral water

We say: Claret-cum-mulled wine, but hold out for the warming ginger finish.
Origin: An adaptation of a vintage cocktail recipe of unknown origin. Believed to be named after a neighbourhood in South Mumbai, India.

BYZANTINE

★★★★☆

Glass: Collins
Garnish: Basil leaf
Method: MUDDLE basil in base of shaker. Add other ingredients apart from tonic water, SHAKE with ice and strain into ice-filled glass. TOP with tonic water.

6	fresh	**Torn basil leaves**
1½	shots	**Tanqueray London dry gin**
½	shot	**Passion fruit syrup**
½	shot	**Lime & lemongrass cordial**
2	shots	**Fresh pressed pineapple juice**
Top up with		**Tonic water**

We say: This fruity, herbal drink is even better made the way Douglas originally intended, with basil infused gin instead of muddled leaves.
Origin: Created in 2001 by Douglas Ankrah for Akbar, Soho, London, England.

C C KAZI

★★★★☆

Glass: Martini
Garnish: Lime wedge
Method: SHAKE all ingredients with ice and fine strain into chilled glass.

1¾	shots	**Tequila 100% Agave**
1¾	shots	**Ocean Spray cranberry juice**
½	shot	**Freshly squeezed lime juice**
¼	shot	**Monin Pure Cane 2:1 sugar syrup**

We say: A Rude Cosmo without the liqueur.

THE C&C

★★★☆☆

Glass: Shot
Garnish: None
Method: LAYER by carefully pouring ingredients in the following order.

¾	shot	**Triple Sec**
¾	shot	**Cognac VSOP**

We say: The initial heat of brandy is chased and extinguished by sweet orange liqueur.

STAR RATINGS EXPLAINED

★★★★★ Excellent

★★★★½ Recommeded	★★★★☆ Praiseworthy
★★★½☆ Commended	★★★☆☆ Mediocre
★★½☆☆ Disappointing	★★☆☆☆ Pretty awful
★½☆☆☆ Shameful	★☆☆☆☆ Disgusting

CABLE CAR UPDATED

★★★★☆

Glass: Coupette
Garnish: Sugar-cinnamon rim
Method: SHAKE all ingredients with ice and fine strain into chilled glass.

1½	shots	**Spiced rum**
1	shot	**Triple Sec**
¾	shot	**Freshly squeezed lemon juice**
¼	shot	**Monin Pure Cane 2:1 sugar syrup**

We say: Slightly sweet balance between the Christmas spices and refreshing citrus.
Origin: Created in 1996 by Tony Abou-Ganim at the Starlight Room, a nightclub and cocktail lounge atop San Francisco's Sir Francis Drake Hotel. The Nob Hill cable cars pass by the bar, hence its catchphrase 'between the stars and the cable cars'. Some say that Cory Reistad created the Cable Car but this is what Tony says of such claims: "Cory Reistad did indeed work at the Starlight Room with me although not as a member of the opening team. All the menus were created by me, and yes, other bartenders were encouraged to participate, but the Cable Car was one of my creations which did indeed go on the menu and was created in 1996."
Tony's original 1996 recipe: 1½ oz Captain Morgan Spiced Rum, ¾4oz Marie Brizard orange curaçao and 1½ oz fresh lemon sour mix (which is made with 2 parts fresh squeezed, filtered lemon juice with 1 part simple syrup).

CABLEGRAM

★★★★☆

Glass: Collins
Garnish: Candied ginger
Method: SHAKE all ingredients with ice and fine strain into ice-filled glass. TOP with soda.

2	shots	**Straight rye whiskey**
¾	shot	**Monin Ginger syrup**
½	shot	**Freshly squeezed lime juice**
Top up with		**Soda (club soda)**

We say: Whiskey and ginger with a fresh zing of lime.
Origin: Adapted from a drink created in 2009 by Eric Alperin at The Varnish, Los Angeles, USA.

CACHAÇA DAIQUIRI

★★★½☆

Glass: Martini
Garnish: Lime wedge
Method: SHAKE all ingredients with ice and fine strain into chilled glass.

2	shots	**Leblon cachaça**
½	shot	**Freshly squeezed lime juice**
¼	shot	**Monin Pure Cane 2:1 sugar syrup**
½	shot	**Chilled mineral water**

We say: Might be in a Martini glass but it tastes like a Caipirinha.

CACTUS BANGER

★★★★☆

Glass: Martini
Garnish: Lime wedge
Method: SHAKE all ingredients with ice and fine strain into chilled glass.

1	shot	**Tequila 100% Agave**
1	shot	**Grand Marnier liqueur**
2	shots	**Freshly squeezed orange juice**
½	shot	**Freshly squeezed lime juice**

We say: A golden, sunny looking and sunny tasting drink.

CACTUS JACK

★★★½☆

Glass: Martini
Garnish: Pineapple leaf
Method: SHAKE all ingredients with ice and fine strain into chilled glass.

1	shot	**Tequila 100% Agave**
¾	shot	**Bols Blue Curaçao liqueur**
1¼	shots	**Freshly squeezed orange juice**
1	shot	**Fresh pressed pineapple juice**
½	shot	**Freshly squeezed lemon juice**

We say: Vivid in colour, this orange led, Tequila based drink has a balanced sweet and sourness.

CAFÉ GATES

★★★½☆

Glass: Toddy
Garnish: Coffee beans
Method: Place bar spoon in glass, POUR first three ingredients and top up with coffee, then float cream by pouring over the back of a spoon.

¾	shot	**Grand Marnier liqueur**
¾	shot	**Kahlúa coffee liqueur**
¾	shot	**Dark Crème de Cacao**
Top up with		**Hot filter coffee**
¾	shot	**Double (heavy) cream**

We say: Chocolate orange with coffee and cream.

CAIPI

★★★☆☆

Glass: Old-fashioned
Garnish: None
Method: MUDDLE lime in base of shaker. Add rest of ingredients, SHAKE with 6oz scoop of crushed ice and pour without straining into glass.

¾	fresh	**Lime**
2	shots	**Campari Bitter**
½	shot	**Monin Pure Cane 2:1 sugar syrup**

We say: Bittersweet Campari and lime.

CAIPIGINGER

★★★½☆

Glass: Old-fashioned
Garnish: Lime zest twist (discarded) & lime wedge
Method: MUDDLE ginger in base of shaker. Add other ingredients, SHAKE with ice and strain into glass filled with crushed ice. Serve with straws.

2	shots	**Leblon cachaça**
2	slices	**Fresh root ginger (thumbnail sized)**
1	shot	**Freshly squeezed lime juice**
¾	shot	**Monin Pure Cane 2:1 sugar syrup**

We say: A ginger spiced take on the Caipirinha

CAIPIRINHA #1 (BRAZILIAN SERVE)

★★★★½

Glass: Old-fashioned
Garnish: None
Method: MUDDLE lime in the base of a robust glass to release the juices and oils in its skin. Pour cachaça and sugar into glass, add ice and STIR. Serve with straws.

¾	fresh	**Lime**
2	shots	**Leblon cachaça**
½	shot	**Monin Pure Cane 2:1 sugar syrup**

We say: You are probably used to this drink being served with crushed ice but until you have tried it with cubed ice you have not really tried a Caipirinha.
Origin: Pronounced 'Kie-Pur-Reen-Yah', the name of this traditional Brazilian cocktail literally translates as 'little countryside drink'. It is made by muddling green lemons known as 'limon subtil', which are native to Brazil (limes are the best substitute when these are not available), and mixing with sugar and cachaça. Be sure to muddle in a sturdy, non-breakable glass. In Britain and other 'new' cachaça markets it is common practice to serve this drink with crushed ice but in Brazil it is usually served with cubed ice. Capirinhas and variations on the theme are staples in cachaçarias, traditional Brazilian bars which specialise in cachaça.

CAIPIRINHA #2 (CONTEMPORARY SERVE)

★★★★☆

Glass: Old-fashioned
Garnish: Serve with 2 short straws
Method: MUDDLE lime wedges in the base of shaker to release juice and oils in its skin. Add cachaça and sugar. SHAKE with 6oz scoop crushed ice and pour all without straining into glass.

¾	fresh	**Lime**
2	shots	**Leblon cachaça**
½	shot	**Monin Pure Cane 2:1 sugar syrup**

We say: There is much debate among bartenders as to whether granulated sugar or sugar syrup and if brown or white sugar should be used when making this drink. Those who favour granulated sugar argue that muddling with the abrasive crystals helps extract the oils from the lime's skin. Personally, I hate the crunch of sugar as inevitably not all the granulated sugar dissolves. Whether you should use brown or white sugar to make your syrup is another question. I prefer mine made the way it is in its native Brazil, with white sugar.
Origin: In its native Brazil it is usual to serve this drink with cubed ice but the drink travelled to the UK at a time when the use of crushed ice was fashionable and so in this and other 'new' cachaça markets use of crushed ice has become the norm.

CAIPIRISSIMA

★★★★⯪

Glass: Old-fashioned
Garnish: Serve with 2 short straws
Method: MUDDLE lime wedges in the base of shaker to release juice and oils in its skin. Add rum and sugar. SHAKE with a scoop of crushed ice and pour all without straining into glass.

¾	fresh	Lime
2	shots	Bacardi Superior rum
½	shot	Monin Pure Cane 2:1 sugar syrup

We say: A Daiquiri-like drink made in the style of a Caipirinha.

CAIPIROVSKA

★★★★☆

Glass: Old-fashioned
Garnish: Serve with 2 short straws
Method: MUDDLE lime wedges in the base of shaker to release juice and oils in its skin. Add vodka and sugar. SHAKE with a scoop of crushed ice and pour all without straining into glass.

¾	fresh	Lime
2	shots	Ketel One vodka
½	shot	Monin Pure Cane 2:1 sugar syrup

We say: Vodka replaces cachaça in this Caipirinha-style drink.
w

CAIPIRUVA

★★★★☆

Glass: Old-fashioned
Garnish: None
Method: MUDDLE lime wedges and grapes in base of shaker to release juices. Add cachaça and sugar. SHAKE with a scoop of crushed ice and pour all without straining into glass.

½	fresh	Lime
4	fresh	Seedless white grapes
2	shots	Leblon cachaça
½	shot	Demerara sugar syrup (2:1)

Variant: Use pitted cherries instead of grapes.
We say: A grape juice laced twist on the Caipirinha.
Origin: Created by Dale DeGroff, New York, USA.

CAIPIRUVA BACCHANALIA

★★★★⯪☆

Glass: Old-fashioned
Garnish: None
Method: MUDDLE lime and grapes in base of shaker to release juices. Add other ingredients, SHAKE with a scoop of crushed ice and pour all without straining into glass.

½	fresh	Lime
5	fresh	Red grapes
2	shots	Leblon cachaça
1	shot	Monin Honey syrup
¾	shot	Sauternes dessert wine
3	dashes	Grapefruit bitters

We say: This twist on Dale's Caipiruva is sweetened by honey and dessert wine.
Origin: Created in 2008 by Julian de Feral at The Player, London, England.

CAJUN MARTINI

★★★☆☆

Glass: Martini
Garnish: Chilli pepper slice
Method: STIR vermouth with ice. Strain, discard vermouth to leave only a coating on the ice. Pour vodka over ice, STIR and strain into chilled glass.

| 2½ | shots | Pepper-infused Ketel One vodka |
| ½ | shot | Martini Extra Dry vermouth |

We say: A very hot vodka Martini. Be brave!

CAJUN NAIL

★★★★★

Glass: Old-fashioned
Garnish: Lemon zest twist (discarded)
Method: POUR absinthe into ice-filled glass, TOP with water and leave to stand. Separately STIR bourbon, cognac, sugar and bitters with ice. DISCARD contents of glass (absinthe, water and ice) and STRAIN contents of shaker into absinthe-coated glass.

½	shot	Absinthe
1½	shots	Jack Daniels Tennessee whiskey
1½	shots	Drambuie
3	dashes	Peychaud's aromatic bitters
3	dashes	Angostura aromatic bitters

We say: A riff on the classic Sazerac.
Origin: Created in 2010 by Simon Difford at the Cabinet Room, London, England.

CAJUN THUNDER NEW

★★☆☆☆

Glass: Shot
Garnish: None
Method: POUR ingredients into glass and serve.

| 1 | shot | Southern Comfort liqueur |
| 4 | dropss | Tabasco hot pepper sauce |

We say: Sweet southern comfort followed by hot chilli pepper finish.

CALIFORNIA ROOT BEER

★★★⯪☆

Glass: Sling
Garnish: Lime wedge
Method: SHAKE first 3 ingredients with ice and strain into ice-filled glass. TOP with soda.

1	shot	Ketel One vodka
½	shot	Kahlúa coffee liqueur
¾	shot	Galliano L'Autentico liqueur
Top up with		Soda (club soda)

Variant: Bartender's Root Beer
We say: Does indeed taste like root beer.

STAR RATINGS EXPLAINED

★★★★★ Excellent

★★★★⯪ Recommended   ★★★★☆ Praiseworthy
★★★⯪☆ Commended   ★★★☆☆ Mediocre
★★⯪☆☆ Disappointing   ★★☆☆☆ Pretty awful
★⯪☆☆☆ Shameful   ★☆☆☆☆ Disgusting

CALIFORNIAN MARTINI

★★★★☆

Glass: Martini
Garnish: Orange zest twist
Method: STIR all ingredients with ice and strain into chilled glass.

2	shots	Ketel One vodka
1	shot	Grand Marnier liqueur
½	shot	Martini Extra Dry vermouth
2	dashes	Orange bitters

We say: A medium dry, fragrant orange Martini

CALL ME OLD-FASHIONED

★★★★⯪

Glass: Old-fashioned
Garnish: Orange zest twist
Method: STIR sugar syrup and bitters with two ice cubes in a glass. Add one shot of cognac and two more ice cubes. Stir some more and add another two ice cubes and another shot of cognac. Stir lots more and add more ice.

2	shots	Cognac VSOP
¼	shot	Monin Pure Cane 2:1 sugar syrup
2	dashes	Angostura aromatic bitters

We say: An Old-Fashioned made with cognac instead of whiskey - works well.
Origin: Created in 2001 by Simon Difford.

CALVADOS COCKTAIL

★★★★⯪

Glass: Martini
Garnish: Orange zest twist
Method: SHAKE all ingredients with ice and fine strain into chilled glass.

1½	shots	Calvados/Applejack brandy
¾	shot	Triple Sec
1½	shots	Freshly squeezed orange juice
2	dashes	Orange bitters

We say: Tangy orange with an alcoholic apple bite.
Origin: Adapted from Harry Craddock's 1930 'The Savoy Cocktail Book'.

CAMERON'S KICK

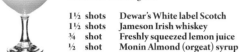

★★★★☆

Glass: Martini
Garnish: Lemon zest twist
Method: SHAKE all ingredients with ice and fine strain into chilled glass.

1½	shots	Dewar's White label Scotch
1½	shots	Jameson Irish whiskey
¾	shot	Freshly squeezed lemon juice
½	shot	Monin Almond (orgeat) syrup

We say: Peaty, honeyed whisky with a cleansing hint of lemon rounded off by almond.
Origin: Adapted form Harry Craddock's 1930 'The Savoy Cocktail Book'.

CAMOMILE & BLACKTHORN BREEZE

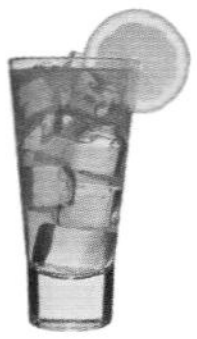

★★★⯪☆

Glass: Collins
Garnish: Lemon slice
Method: SHAKE all ingredients with cubed ice and strain into ice-filled glass.

2	shots	Ketel One vodka
3	shots	Cold camomile tea
1	shot	Chambord black raspberry liqueur

We say: Adult, clean and subtle in flavour with a twang of fruit.
Origin: Created in 2002 by Simon Difford.

CAMPIRINHA

★★★★☆

Glass: Old-fashioned
Garnish: None
Method: MUDDLE lime and grapefruit in base of shaker to release juices. Add other ingredients, SHAKE with a scoop of crushed ice and pour all without straining into glass.

½	fresh	Lime
¼	fresh	Ruby red grapefruit
2	shots	Campari Bitter
½	shot	Monin Pure Cane 2:1 sugar syrup

We say: This bright red fruit laden drink has the looks to appeal to all but its bitter-sweet flavour is specific to Campari convertees.
Origin: Adapted from a drink created in 2006 by Jamie Lawton at Orchid, Auckland, New Zealand.

BARTENDER'S TIP CONVERTING 'SHOTS'

To covert 'shots' into and fluid ounces simply treat one shot as one ounce. To convert 'shots' into metric measures use the following conversions:

2 shot(s) = 60ml, 1¾ shot(s) 52.5ml, 1½ shot(s) = 45ml, 1 shot(s) = 30ml, ¾ shot(s) = 22.5ml, ⅔ hot = 20ml, ½ shot(s) = 15ml, ⅓ shot(s) = 10ml, ¼ shot(s) = 7.5ml, ⅙ shot(s) = 5ml, ⅛ shot(s) = 4ml

CANADIAN APPLE (MOCKTAIL)

★★★★☆

Glass: Collins
Garnish: Apple slice
Method: SHAKE all ingredients with ice and fine strain into ice-filled glass.

3½	shots	Pressed apple juice
1½	shots	Freshly squeezed lemon juice
¾	shot	Maple syrup

We say: Refreshing and balanced with just the right amount of citrus acidity.
Origin: Adapted from a drink discovered in 2005 at the Four Seasons Hotel, Prague, Czech Republic.

CANARIE

★★★☆☆

Glass: Collins
Garnish: None
Method: POUR pastis and lemon syrup into glass. Serve iced water separately in a small jug (known in France as a 'broc') so the customer can dilute to their own taste (I recommend five shots). Lastly, add ice to fill glass.

1	shot	Ricard Pastis
½	shot	Monin Glasco Citron (Lemon) Syrup
Top up with		Chilled mineral water

We say: The traditional French café drink with a twist of lemon sweetness.
Origin: Very popular throughout France, this drink is fittingly named after the bird, which is typically bred for its bright yellow plumage.

CANARIES

★★★☆☆

Glass: Hurricane
Garnish: Pineapple leaf
Method: SHAKE ingredients with ice and strain into ice-filled glass.

¾	shot	Bacardi Superior rum
¾	shot	Triple Sec
¾	shot	Bols Banana liqueur
¾	shot	De Kuyper Cherry Brandy liqueur
2	shots	Fresh pressed pineapple juice
2	shots	Freshly squeezed orange juice

We say: A long, fruity sweet drink that's only fit for consumption on a tropical beach.

CANARY FLIP

★★★★☆

Glass: Martini
Garnish: Lemon zest twist
Method: SHAKE all ingredients with ice and fine strain into chilled glass.

2	shots	Advocaat liqueur
2	shots	Sauvignon blanc wine
¾	shot	Freshly squeezed lemon juice

We say: A delightful balance of egg, brandy and wine.
Origin: Created in 2002 by Alex Kammerling, London, England.

CANCHANCHARA

★★★☆☆

Glass: Old-fashioned
Garnish: Lemon slice
Method: STIR honey with rum in the glass drink is to be served in. Add lemon juice and ice. STIR and serve.

3	spoons	Runny honey
2	shots	Bacardi Superior rum
1½	shots	Freshly squeezed lemon juice

We say: Achieve the perfect balance between sweet honey and sour lemon and this is a great drink.
Origin: The Cuban forerunner of the Daiquiri, as drunk by Cuban revolutionaries fighting off the Spanish at the end of the nineteenth century. To be really authentic omit the ice. Origin and the recipe from Christine Sismondo's 2005 'Mondo Cocktail'.

CANTARITOS NEW

★★★★☆

Glass: Cantaritos clay pot
Garnish: Lime wedge
Method: Submerge pot in cold water to clean the inside and wet the outside clay. This improves appearance and keeps pot cold. POUR ingredients into ice-filled pot, STIR and serve with straws.

2	shots	Olmeca Altos Reposado tequila
2	shot	Freshly squeezed orange juice
1	shot	Ruby red grapefruit juice
¾	shot	Freshly squeezed lime juice
1	spoon	Sea salt
Top up with		Mexican 'Squirt' or Caribbean 'Ting' grapefruit soda

We say: Juicy (freshly squeezed orange, grapefruit and lime) and refreshing slightly salty tequila invigorated with sparkling grapefruit soda.
Origin: A cocktail commonly made in the bars, cafés and even road side stalls of Jalisco, Mexico. The simple 'cantaritos' clay pot is often used as a disposable take away container.

CANTEEN MARTINI

★★★☆☆

Glass: Martini
Garnish: Maraschino cherry
Method: SHAKE all ingredients with ice and fine strain into chilled glass.

1½	shots	Bacardi Superior rum
½	shot	Amaretto liqueur
1½	shots	Southern Comfort liqueur
½	shot	Freshly squeezed lime juice

We say: Tangy, sweet and sour - Southern Comfort drinkers will love this.
Origin: Originally created by Joey Guerra at Canteen, New York City, and adapted by author and columnist Gary Regan.

THE CAPPA COCKTAIL  NEW

★★★★½☆

Glass: Coupette
Garnish: Lemon zest twist
Method: STIR all ingredients with ice and strain into chilled glass.

2	shots	Tanqueray London dry gin
1½	shots	Pineau des Charentes
½	shot	Luxardo maraschino liqueur

We say: Dry, balanced and delicate with a balanced marriage of gin, fortified wine and maraschino.
Origin: Adapted created in 2012 by Franky Marshall at 15 Romolo, San Francisco, USA.

CAPE CODDER

★★★★½☆

Glass: Old-fashioned
Garnish: Lime wedge
Method: SHAKE all ingredients with ice and strain into ice-filled glass.

2	shots	Ketel One vodka
3	shots	Ocean Spray cranberry juice
¼	shot	Freshly squeezed lime juice

Variant: Without lime juice this is a Cape Cod. Lengthened with soda becomes the Cape Cod Cooler.
We say: Dry and refreshing but not particularly interesting.
Origin: Named after the resort on the Massachusetts coast. This fish shaped piece of land is where some of the first Europeans settled in the US. Here they found cranberries, the indigenous North American berry on which this drink is based.

CAPITANO

★★★☆☆

Glass: Martini
Garnish: Orange zest twist
Method: SHAKE all ingredients with ice and fine strain into chilled glass.

1½	shots	Campari Bitter
1½	shots	Carpano Antica Formula
½	shot	Freshly squeezed lemon juice
⅛	shot	Monin Pure Cane 2:1 sugar syrup

We say: This bitter-sweet drink is one for Campari converts only.
Origin: Created in 2008 by Bernhard List.

CAPPERCAILLE

★★★★☆

Glass: Martini
Garnish: Pineapple wedge
Method: STIR honey with whisky until honey dissolves. Add other ingredients, SHAKE with ice and fine strain into chilled glass.

2	shots	Dewar's White label Scotch
½	shot	Triple Sec
½	shot	De Kuyper Apricot Brandy liqueur
2	spoons	Runny honey
1	shot	Fresh pressed pineapple juice
½	shot	Freshly squeezed lemon juice

We say: Wonderfully tangy, fruity Scotch.
Origin: Created by Wayne Collins for Maxxium UK.

CAPRICE

★★★★☆

Glass: Martini
Garnish: Orange zest twist
Method: STIR all ingredients with ice and strain into chilled glass.

1½	shots	Tanqueray London dry gin
½	shot	Bénédictine D.O.M.
½	shot	Martini Extra Dry vermouth
1	dash	Orange bitters

We say: A long stir delivers the dilution necessary for this aromatic, spiced Wet Martini.

CAPTAIN COLLINS

★★★★½☆

Glass: Collins
Garnish: Orange slice & cherry on stick (sail)
Method: SHAKE first 3 ingredients with ice and strain into ice-filled glass. TOP with soda, stir and serve with straws.

2	shots	Canadian whisky
1	shot	Freshly squeezed lemon juice
½	shot	Monin Pure Cane 2:1 sugar syrup
Top up with		Soda (club soda)

We say: Sweetened, soured and diluted whiskey.
Origin: Classic Collins variation.

CARAMEL MANHATTAN

★★★★½

Glass: Martini
Garnish: Lemon zest twist (discarded) & pineapple wedge
Method: SHAKE all ingredients with ice and fine strain into chilled glass.

1½	shots	Maker's Mark bourbon
¾	shot	Giffard caramel liqueur
½	shot	Martini Rosso sweet vermouth
1	shot	Fresh pressed pineapple juice
2	dashes	Peychaud's aromatic bitters

We say: Flavours combine harmoniously with the character of the bourbon still evident.
Origin: Adapted from a drink created in 2002 by Nick Strangeway, London, England.

CARAVAN

★★★☆☆

Glass: Collins
Garnish: Cherries
Method: POUR ingredients into ice-filled glass. Stir and serve with straws.

3	shots	Shiraz red wine
½	shot	Grand Marnier liqueur
Top up with		Coca-Cola

We say: A punch-like long drink.
Origin: Popular in the French Alpine ski resorts.

CARDINAL PUNCH

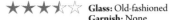

★★★½☆

Glass: Old-fashioned
Garnish: None
Method: POUR cassis into ice-filled glass and top up with wine. Stir and serve with straws.

1 shot Crème de cassis liqueur
Top up with Shiraz red wine

We say: A particularly fruity red.

CARDINALE

★★★★☆

Glass: Old-fashioned
Garnish: Orange slice
Method: SHAKE all ingredients with ice and fine strain into chilled glass.

2 shots Tanqueray London dry gin
1½ shots Campari Bitter
1 shot Martini Extra Dry vermouth

Variant: Negroni
We say: An extra dry Negroni for hardcore fans. We have to admit to being one.
Origin: A variation on the classic equal parts Negroni.

CARIBBEAN BREEZE

★★★★☆

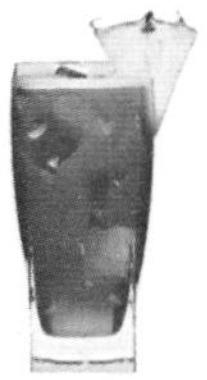

Glass: Collins
Garnish: Pineapple wedge
Method: SHAKE all ingredients with ice and strain into ice-filled glass.

1¼ shots Bacardi Superior rum
½ shot Bols Banana liqueur
2½ shots Fresh pressed pineapple juice
2 shots Ocean Spray cranberry juice
½ shot Rose's lime cordial

We say: A long drink with bags of tangy fruit flavours.

CARIBBEAN CRUISE

★★★½☆

Glass: Collins
Garnish: Pineapple wedge
Method: SHAKE all ingredients with ice and strain into ice-filled glass.

1½ shots Bacardi Superior rum
1½ shots Malibu coconut rum liqueur
4 shots Fresh pressed pineapple juice
1 spoon Pomegranate (grenadine) syrup

We say: Long, frothy and fruity - one for the beach bar.

CARIBBEAN PIÑA COLADA

★★★½☆

Glass: Hurricane
Garnish: Pineapple wedge & maraschino cherry
Method: BLEND ingredients with a scoop of crushed ice. Pour into glass and serve with straws.

2 shots Bacardi Superior rum
3 shots Fresh pressed pineapple juice
½ shot Coco López cream of coconut
4 dashes Angostura aromatic bitters
1 pinch Salt

We say: Angostura and salt make this a less sticky Colada.

CARIBBEAN PUNCH

★★★★☆

Glass: Collins
Garnish: Lime zest twist
Method: SHAKE all ingredients with ice and strain into glass filled with crushed ice.

2¼ shots Wray & Nephew overproof rum
½ shot Amaretto liqueur
½ shot Malibu coconut rum liqueur
¼ shot Galliano L'Autentico liqueur
¾ shot Freshly squeezed lemon juice
3 shots Fresh pressed pineapple juice
¼ shot Pomegranate (grenadine) syrup

We say: Red in colour and innocent looking, this flavoursome drink sure packs a punch.

CARIBE DAIQUIRI

★★★★☆

Glass: Martini
Garnish: Lemon wedge
Method: SHAKE all ingredients with ice and fine strain into chilled glass.

2 shots Bacardi Superior rum
1 shot Fresh pressed pineapple juice
½ shot Freshly squeezed lemon juice
¼ shot Taylor's Velvet Falernum liqueur

We say: A dry, fruity spicy Daiquiri

CARIBEÑO NEW

★★★☆☆

Glass: Collins
Garnish: Lime wedge
Method: SHAKE all the ingredients with ice and strain into a ice-filled glass.

2 shots Bacardi Superior rum
3 shots Coconut water
¼ shot Freshly squeezed lime juice
¼ shot Monin Pure Cane 2:1 sugar syrup

We say: Rum and coconut served long with a dash of lime juice.
Origin: Created in 2009 by Martin Cate, Forbidden Island, San Francisco, USA.

CAROL CHANNING

★★★☆☆

Glass: Flute
Garnish: Raspberries
Method: SHAKE first 3 ingredients with ice and strain into chilled glass. TOP with champagne.

¼	shot	Crème de framboise liqueur
⅛	shot	Monin Pure Cane 2:1 sugar syrup
Top up with		Brut champagne

We say: Fortified raspberry and champagne.
Origin: Created by Dick Bradsell in 1984 with the milliner Stephen Jones. Named after the famously large mouthed American comedienne Carol Channing because of her appearance in the film 'Thoroughly Modern Milly', where, for some unknown reason, she spends much of the time running around shouting 'raspberries'.

CARROL COCKTAIL ⚷

★★★★☆

Glass: Martini
Garnish: Pickled walnut or onion
Method: STIR all ingredients with ice and strain into chilled glass.

| 2 | shots | Cognac VSOP |
| 1 | shot | Martini Rosso sweet vermouth |

We say: Aromatic wine and cognac - dry yet easy.
Origin: Adapted form Victor Bergeron's 'Trader Vic's Bartender's Guide' (1972 revised edition).

CARROLL GARDENS

★★★★☆

Glass: Coupette
Garnish: Maraschino cherry
Method: STIR ingredients over ice and strain into a cocktail glass. Squeeze lemon twist over the drink, wipe the rim with the peel and discard.

2	shots	Straight rye whiskey
½	shot	Averna Amaro
⅛	shot	Luxardo Maraschino liqueur
½	shot	Carpano Punt E Mes

We say: This delightful twist on the Brooklyn is the most Italian American of drinks.
Origin: Created in 2009 by Joaquin Simo at Death and Company, New York City, USA in honour of his neighbourhood, Brooklyn's Carroll Gardens.

CARROT CAKE

★★★☆☆

Glass: Martini
Garnish: Dust with cinnamon powder
Method: SHAKE all ingredients with ice and fine strain into chilled glass.

2	shots	Baileys Irish cream liqueur
¾	shot	Goldschläger cinnamon schnapps
1½	shots	Kahlúa coffee liqueur

We say: Tastes nothing like carrot cake - surely that's a good thing.

CARTHUSIAN NAIL

★★★★☆

Glass: Old-fashioned
Garnish: Mint sprig
Method: STIR all ingredients with ice and strain into ice-filled glass.

1½	shots	Dewar's White label Scotch
¾	shot	Drambuie
¼	shot	Chartreuse Green liqueur

We say: Sweet and yet bone dry. The monastic liqueurs, Drambuie and Chartreuse battle to be the most righteous in this Humanist's cocktail.
Origin: Created in 2010 by Simon Difford at the Cabinet Room, London, England.

CARUSO MARTINI

★★★☆☆

Glass: Martini
Garnish: Mint leaf
Method: SHAKE all ingredients with ice and fine strain into chilled glass.

1	shot	Tanqueray London dry gin
1	shot	Martini Extra Dry vermouth
1	shot	Green crème de menthe liqueur

We say: Emerald Green with full-on mint. Good as a digestif after a tenor-sized meal.
Origin: This recipe was adapted form Harry Craddock's 1930 'The Savoy Cocktail Book'. The drink was created at The Savoy for the tenor Enrico Caruso in the early 20th century.

CASABLANCA #1

★★★★☆

Glass: Martini
Garnish: Orange zest twist
Method: SHAKE all ingredients with ice and fine strain into chilled glass.

2	shots	Bacardi Superior rum
¾	shot	Triple Sec
¾	shot	Freshly squeezed lime juice
½	shot	Luxardo Maraschino liqueur
½	fresh	Egg white

We say: A rum based variation on the White Lady, with zingy citrus and sweet maraschino.
Origin: Named after Michael Curtiz's 1942 classic starring Bogie and Ingrid Bergman.

CASABLANCA #2

★★★☆☆

Glass: Martini
Garnish: Dust with grated nutmeg
Method: SHAKE all ingredients with ice and fine strain into chilled glass.

1	shot	Ketel One vodka
1	shot	Advocaat liqueur
¼	shot	Galliano L'Autentico liqueur
¼	shot	Freshly squeezed lemon juice
1	shot	Freshly squeezed orange juice
½	shot	Double (heavy) cream

We say: Creamy, fruity, alcoholic custard. Different!

CASANOVA

★★★★☆

Glass: Martini
Garnish: Crumbled Cadbury's Flake bar
Method: SHAKE all ingredients with ice and fine strain into chilled glass.

1½	shots	Maker's Mark bourbon
¾	shot	Kahlúa coffee liqueur
¾	shot	Blandy's Alvada madeira
¾	shot	Milk
¾	shot	Double (heavy) cream
⅛	shot	Monin Pure Cane 2:1 sugar syrup

We say: Rich, medium-sweet and creamy with a mocha coffee finish.

CASCADE MARTINI

★★★½☆

Glass: Martini
Garnish: Raspberries
Method: SHAKE all ingredients with ice and fine strain into chilled glass.

8	fresh	Raspberries
2	shots	Ketel One vodka
1	shot	Ocean Spray cranberry juice
¾	shot	Freshly squeezed lemon juice
¼	shot	Chambord black raspberry liqueur
¼	shot	Monin Vanilla sugar syrup

We say: Rich raspberry with hints of citrus and vanilla.

CASINO #1

★★★★★

Glass: Martini
Garnish: Maraschino cherry
Method: SHAKE all ingredients with ice and fine strain into chilled glass.

1½	shots	Tanqueray London dry gin
¾	shot	Luxardo Maraschino liqueur
½	shot	Freshly squeezed lemon juice
¼	shot	Chilled mineral water
1	dash	Orange bitters

Variant: Bee's Knees, Blue Moon
We say: Basically an Aviation dried and made more complex with a dash of orange bitters.
Origin: Recipe adapted from Harry Craddock's 1930 'The Savoy Cocktail Book'.

CASINO #2

★★★★½

Glass: Martini
Garnish: Maraschino cherry
Method: SHAKE all ingredients with ice and fine strain into chilled glass.

2	shots	Tanqueray London dry gin
¾	shot	Luxardo Maraschino liqueur
½	shot	Freshly squeezed lemon juice
½	shot	Freshly squeezed orange juice
1	dash	Orange bitters

Variant: Bee's Knees, Blue Moon
We say: Basically an Aviation but with a dash of orange juice and orange bitters.
Origin: Recipe adapted from David A. Embury's 1948 'Fine Art of Mixing Drinks'.

CASSE NOISSETTE

★★★½☆

Glass: Martini
Garnish: Dust with grated nutmeg
Method: SHAKE first 3 ingredients with ice and strain into chilled glass. FLOAT thin layer of cream over drink.

1½	shots	Ketel One vodka
¾	shot	Kahlúa coffee liqueur
¾	shot	Hazelnut liqueur
¾	shot	Double (heavy) cream

We say: Sip hazelnut and coffee through a creamy topping. A dessert of a drink.
Origin: Adapted from a drink created in 2001 by Julien Escot at Hotel du Cap-Eden Roc in Cap d'Antibes (France). Casse Noisette won the overall contest at London, Drinks International Bartender's Challenge 2004.

CASSINI

★★★½☆

Glass: Martini
Garnish: Blackberries
Method: SHAKE all ingredients with ice and fine strain into chilled glass.

2	shots	Ketel One vodka
1½	shots	Ocean Spray cranberry juice
¼	shot	Crème de cassis liqueur

We say: A simple but pleasant berry drink.
Origin: Created in 1998 by Simon Difford.

CASTRO

★★★½☆

Glass: Martini
Garnish: Lime wedge
Method: SHAKE all ingredients with ice and fine strain into chilled glass.

1½	shots	Bacardi 8yo aged rum
¾	shot	Calvados/Applejack brandy
¼	shot	Freshly squeezed orange juice
½	shot	Freshly squeezed lime juice
¼	shot	Rose's lime cordial
¼	shot	Monin Pure Cane 2:1 sugar syrup

We say: Tangy and fruity.
Origin: Named after the Cuban.

CAUSEWAY

★★★½☆

Glass: Collins
Garnish: None
Method: SHAKE first 5 ingredients with ice and strain into ice-filled glass, TOP with ginger ale.

2	shots	Jameson Irish whiskey
1	shot	Drambuie
2	dashes	Orange bitters
4	dashes	Angostura aromatic bitters
¼	shot	Freshly squeezed lemon juice
Top up with		Ginger ale

We say: Dry, aromatic long whiskey drink.
Origin: Created by David Myers at Titanic, London, England.

THE CELERY GIMLET NEW

★★★★☆

Glass: Coupette
Garnish: Celery tip & leaf
Method: SHAKE all ingredients with ice and fine strain into chilled glass.

1½	shots	Tanqueray London dry gin
1	shot	Freshly extracted celery juice
¼	shot	Green Chartreuse liqueur
⅓	shot	Freshly squeezed lime juice
⅛	shot	Rose's lime cordial
⅛	shot	Chardonnay vinegar
2	dashes	Celery bitters

We say: Occupying the ground between the Gimlet and a Shrub with pleasing savoury celery notes adding interest.
Origin: Created in 2010 by Naren Young at Saxon & Parole, New York City, USA.

CELERY MARTINI

★★★★☆

Glass: Martini
Garnish: Salt rim & celery stick
Method: SHAKE all ingredients with ice and fine strain into chilled glass.

2	shots	Ketel One vodka
¼	shot	Monin Pure Cane 2:1 sugar syrup
1¾	shots	Freshly extracted celery juice

We say: I only usually like celery when loaded with blue cheese - but I love this Martini.
Origin: Created by Andreas Tsanos at Momos, London, England in 2001.

CELTIC MARGARITA

★★★★½

Glass: Coupette
Garnish: Salt rim & lemon wedge
Method: SHAKE all ingredients with ice and fine strain into chilled glass.

2	shots	Dewar's White label Scotch
1	shot	Triple Sec
1	shot	Freshly squeezed lemon juice

We say: A Scotch Margarita - try it, it works.
Origin: Discovered in 2004 at Milk & Honey, London, England.

CEMENT MIXER NEW

★☆☆☆☆

Glass: Shot
Garnish: None
Method: POUR cream liqueur into glass and carefully LAYER lime juice so it floats on cream liqueur. Instruct drinker to hold and swirl the drink around in their mouth before swallowing.

| ¾ | shot | Baileys Irish cream liqueur |
| ¾ | shot | Freshly squeezed lime juice |

We say: When mixed in the mouth, the acid in the lime juice will curdle the cream liqueur causing it to rapidly gain viscosity and stick to the drinkers' teeth, like cement.

CHAM 69 #1

★★★½☆

Glass: Sling
Garnish: Seasonal berries
Method: SHAKE first four ingredients with ice and strain into ice-filled glass. TOP with lemonade, stir and serve with straws.

2	shots	Ketel One vodka
¾	shot	Amaretto liqueur
¾	shot	Freshly squeezed lime juice
¾	shot	Chambord black raspberry liqueur
Top up with		Lemonade/Sprite/7-Up

We say: Medium sweet, long and fruity.
Origin: I created this drink back in 1998 and I've noticed it on cocktail menus across Europe. I was something of a beginner with a sweet tooth at the time but this new formulation is better balanced.

CHAM 69 #2

★★★½☆

Glass: Sling
Garnish: Seasonal berries
Method: SHAKE first four ingredients with ice and strain into ice-filled glass. TOP with champagne, stir and serve with straws.

1	shot	Ketel One vodka
½	shot	Amaretto liqueur
½	shot	Chambord black raspberry liqueur
¼	shot	Freshly squeezed lime juice
Top up with		Brut champagne

We say: Long, fruity and refreshing.
Origin: While re-examining my old creation in 2005 I decided champagne would be more appropriate considering the name.

CHAM CHAM

★★★½☆

Glass: Flute
Garnish: Seasonal berries
Method: POUR liqueur into chilled glass and TOP with champagne.

| ½ | shot | Chambord black raspberry liqueur |
| Top up with | | Brut champagne |

Variant: Kir Royale
We say: A pleasant blend of fruit and champagne to rival the Kir Royale.

STAR RATINGS EXPLAINED

★★★★★ Excellent

★★★★½ Recommended	★★★★☆ Praiseworthy
★★★½☆ Commended	★★★☆☆ Mediocre
★★★½☆☆ Disappointing	★★☆☆☆ Pretty awful
★★½☆☆☆ Shameful	★☆☆☆☆ Disgusting

CHAMPAGNE COCKTAIL

★★★☆☆

Glass: Flute
Garnish: Orange zest twist (discarded)
Method: COAT sugar cube with bitters and drop into glass. POUR cognac over soaked cube, then TOP with champagne.

1	cube	**Brown sugar**
3	dashes	**Angostura aromatic bitters**
1	shot	**Courvoisier VSOP Exclusif**
Top up with		**Brut champagne**

Variant: Chicago, Prince of Wales
We say: An over hyped classic cocktail that gets sweeter as you reach the dissolving cube at the bottom.
Origin: First recorded in Jerry Thomas's 1862 book *'How To Mix Drinks'*, or *'The Bon Vivant's Companion'*, where he almost certainly mistakenly specifies this as a shaken drink – that would be explosive. Another early reference to Champagne cocktails is in Mark Twain's 1869 novel, Innocents Abroad. It is thought the drink found popularity after a bartender named John Dougherty won an 1899 New York cocktail competition with a similar drink named Business Brace.

CHAMPAGNE CUP

★★★★☆

Glass: Flute
Garnish: Maraschino cherry
Method: STIR first 3 ingredients with ice and strain into chilled glass. TOP with champagne and gently stir.

¾	shot	**Cognac VSOP**
½	shot	**Grand Marnier liqueur**
¼	shot	**Maraschino syrup (from cherry jar)**
Top up with		**Brut champagne**

We say: Sweet maraschino helps balance this dry drink.

CHAMPAGNE DAISY

★★★☆☆

Glass: Flute
Garnish: Pomegranate wedge
Method: SHAKE first 3 ingredients with ice and fine strain into chilled glass, TOP with champagne.

1	shot	**Chartreuse Yellow liqueur**
⅛	shot	**Pomegranate (grenadine) syrup**
1	shot	**Freshly squeezed lemon juice**
Top up with		**Brut champagne**

We say: You'll need to like Chartreuse and citrus champagne to appreciate this drink.

CHAMPAGNE PICK-ME-UP

★★★★☆

Glass: Flute
Garnish: Orange zest twist (discarded)
Method: SHAKE first three ingredients with ice and fine strain into chilled glass. TOP with champagne.

1	shot	**Cognac VSOP**
1½	shots	**Freshly squeezed orange juice**
¼	shot	**Pomegranate (grenadine) syrup**
Top up with		**Brut champagne**

We say: A subtle hint of biscuity champagne shines through this very quaffable drink.
Origin: There are many versions of this classic cocktail but I have taken this one from Dale DeGroff's 2008 *'The Essential Cocktail'* where Dale credits this recipe to the Ritz Bar Paris circa 1936.

CHAMPINO

★★★★☆

Glass: Flute
Garnish: Orange zest twist
Method: SHAKE first 2 ingredients with ice and fine strain into chilled glass. TOP with champagne.

1	shot	**Campari Bitter**
1	shot	**Martini Rosso sweet vermouth**
Top up with		**Brut champagne**

AKA: Americano Royale
We say: A champagne option for Negroni lovers.

CHAMPS-ELYSÉES

★★★★½

Glass: Martini
Garnish: Lemon zest twist
Method: SHAKE all ingredients with ice and fine strain into chilled glass.

1¾	shots	**Cognac VSOP**
¼	shot	**Chartreuse Green liqueur**
½	shot	**Freshly squeezed lemon juice**
½	shot	**Monin Pure Cane 2:1 sugar syrup**
3	dashes	**Angostura aromatic bitters**
¾	shot	**Chilled mineral water**
½	fresh	**Egg white**

We say: A great after dinner drink for lovers of cognac and Chartreuse.
Origin: Named after the touristy Parisian boulevard where (coincidentally) Rémy Cointreau have their offices.

BARTENDER'S TIP LAYER

As the name would suggest, layered drinks include layers of different ingredients, often with contrasting colours.

This effect is achieved by carefully pouring each ingredient into the glass so that it floats on its predecessor. The success of this technique is dependent on the density (specific gravity) of the liquids used. As a rule of thumb, the less alcohol and the more sugar an ingredient contains, the heavier it is. The heaviest ingredients should be poured first and the lightest last.

CHANCELLOR

★★★★½

Glass: Martini
Garnish: Orange zest twist
Method: SHAKE all ingredients with ice and fine strain into chilled glass.

2	shots	**Dewar's White label Scotch**
1	shot	**Warre's Otima tawny port**
½	shot	**Martini Extra Dry vermouth**
¼	shot	**Monin Pure Cane 2:1 sugar syrup**
2	dashes	**Orange bitters**

We say: Complex and sophisticated Scotch with fruity notes.
Origin: A classic of unknown origins.

CHANTICLEER COCKTAIL

★★★★★

Glass: Coupette
Garnish: Orange zest twist
Method: STIR all ingredients with ice and fine strain into a chilled glass.

1	shot	**Tanqueray London dry gin**
1½	shots	**Martini Extra Dry vermouth**
½	shot	**Triple Sec**
½	fresh	**Egg white**

We say: Wonderfully aromatic orange with a complex balance of gin and vermouth.
Origin: Recipe adapted from A.S. Crockett's 1935, *The Old Waldorf-Astoria Bar Book* which originally calls for 'orange gin' rather than using an orange liqueur. Crockett handily says of this drink, "Add a Cock's Comb if desired." He also explains that the drink "celebrated the local opening of Edmond Rostand's Chanticler".

Edmond Rostand was a French poet and dramatist, best-known for his play Cyrano de Bergerac. First released in 1910, Chantecler (correct spelling) is a story where the characters are based on barnyard animals, and whose eponymous protagonist is a rooster who believes that his song makes the sun rise.

By all accounts the cocktail is rather better than the play. Incidentally, the 'Chantecler' is actually a breed of chicken developed in the early 20th century by Brother Wilfred Chantelain, a Trappist monk at the Abbey of Notre-Dame du Lac in Canada.

CHARENTE COLLINS

★★★★☆

Glass: Collins
Garnish: Mint sprig & orange zest twist
Method: Lightly MUDDLE mint in base of shaker (just to bruise). Add other ingredients, SHAKE with ice and strain into glass filled with crushed ice. Serve with straws.

5	fresh	**Mint leaves**
2	shots	**Grand Marnier liqueur**
1	shot	**St~Germain elderflower liqueur**
1	shot	**Freshly squeezed lemon juice**

We say: Created in 2005 by Kieran Bailey, The Light Bar, London, England.
Origin: Refreshing orange and lemon with a hint of elderflower.

CHARLES DAIQUIRI

★★★★½

Glass: Martini
Garnish: Lime wedge
Method: SHAKE all ingredients with ice and fine strain into chilled glass.

1	shot	**Bacardi Superior rum**
1	shot	**Pusser's Navy rum**
½	shot	**Triple Sec**
½	shot	**Freshly squeezed lime juice**
⅛	shot	**Monin Pure Cane 2:1 sugar syrup**
½	shot	**Chilled mineral water**

We say: Navy rum and triple sec add special interest to this Daiquiri.

CHARLIE

★★★★½

Glass: Coupette
Garnish: Maraschino cherry
Method: STIR all ingredients with ice and strain into chilled glass.

2	shots	**Maker's Mark bourbon**
½	shot	**Martini Rosso sweet vermouth**
¼	shot	**Chambord black raspberry liqueur**
1	dash	**Angostura aromatic bitters**

We say: A sweet Manhattan-style cocktail.
Origin: Created in 2009 by Simon Difford for Charlotte Ashburner, the Chambord brand manager.

CHARLIE CHAPLIN COCKTAIL UPDATED

★★★★☆

Glass: Coupette
Garnish: Apricot wedge
Method: SHAKE all ingredients with ice and fine strain into chilled glass.

¾	shot	**De Kuyper apricot brandy liqueur**
¾	shot	**Sloe Gin liqueur**
¾	shot	**Freshly squeezed lime juice**
¾	shot	**Chilled mineral water**

We say: Dilution is key to this fruity bitter-sweet cocktail, hence the possible need to add some water depending on your ice.
Origin: Created and originally served at New York's old Waldorf-Astoria prior to 1920. This recipe is adapted from Albert Stevens Crocketts 1935 '*The Old Waldorf-Astoria Bar Book*'. The drink is named after Sir Charles Spencer's '*Charlie Chaplin* (1889-1977), the English slapstick comic actor of the silent film era, who was at the height of his career when this eponymous cocktail was created.

STAR RATINGS EXPLAINED

★★★★★ Excellent

★★★★½	Recommended	★★★★☆	Praiseworthy
★★★½☆	Commended	★★★☆☆	Mediocre
★★½☆☆	Disappointing	★★☆☆☆	Pretty awful
★½☆☆☆	Shameful	★☆☆☆☆	Disgusting

CHARTREUSE SWIZZLE

★★★½☆

Glass: Collins
Garnish: Pineapple wedge & maraschino cherry
Method: POUR ingredients into glass filled with crushed ice and SWIZZLE. (Or SHAKE all ingredients with ice and strain into glass filled with crushed ice).

1¼ shots	Chartreuse Green liqueur
½ shot	Taylor's Velvet Falernum liqueur
1 shot	Fresh pressed pineapple juice
½ shot	Freshly squeezed lime juice

We say: A drink for people like me - Chartreuse lovers.
Origin: Created by Marco Dionysos at Tres Agaves, San Francisco, USA.

CHAS

★★★★☆

Glass: Martini
Garnish: Orange zest twist
Method: SHAKE all ingredients with ice and fine strain into chilled glass.

1¾ shots	Maker's Mark bourbon
½ shot	Bénédictine D.O.M.
½ shot	Amaretto liqueur
½ shot	Triple Sec
½ shot	Grand Marnier liqueur

We say: A wonderfully tangy cocktail with great bourbon personality and hints of almond and orange.
Origin: Created in 2003 by Murray Stenson at Zig Zag Café, Seattle, USA.

CHATHAM HOTEL SPECIAL

★★★★☆

Glass: Martini
Garnish: Dust with grated nutmeg
Method: SHAKE all ingredients with ice and fine strain into chilled glass.

2 shots	Cognac VSOP
¾ shot	Warre's Otima tawny port
½ shot	Dark Crème de Cacao
¼ shot	Double (heavy) cream
¼ shot	Milk

We say: We've slightly changed the proportions and replaced the original lemon zest garnish with a little extra spice.
Origin: This mid-1900s classic from New York's Chatham Hotel was resurrected by Ted Haigh in his 2004 book '*Vintage Spirits & Forgotten Cocktails*'.

CHE'S REVOLUTION

★★★★½

Glass: Martini
Garnish: Pineapple wedge
Method: MUDDLE mint with rum in base of shaker. Add other ingredients, SHAKE with ice and fine strain into chilled glass.

4 fresh	Mint leaves
2 shots	Bacardi Superior rum
2 shots	Fresh pressed pineapple juice
¼ shot	Maple syrup

We say: Complex and smooth with hints of maple syrup and mint amongst the pineapple and rum.
Origin: Created in 2003 by Ben Reed for the launch party of MJU Bar @ Millennium Hotel, London, England

CHEEKY MONKEY

★★★★☆

Glass: Martini
Garnish: Orange zest twist
Method: SHAKE all ingredients with ice and fine strain into chilled glass.

1 shot	Ketel One vodka
1 shot	Chartreuse Yellow liqueur
1½ shots	Freshly squeezed orange juice
1 dash	Orange bitters

We say: Fire yellow in colour, this drink features the distinctive flavour of Chartreuse with a citrus supporting cast.
Origin: Created in 2001 by Tony Conigliaro at Isola, Knightsbridge, London, England.

CHEEKY VIMTO NEW

★★½☆☆

Glass: Boston
Garnish: Don't bother
Method: Pour port into glass and TOP with WKD Blue.

| 2 shots | Ruby port |
| 1 bottle | WKD Original Blue |

Variant: To make an 'Extra Cheeky Vimto' add 1 shot of vodka prior to topping with WKD Blue.
We say: A sickly sweet blackcurrant and berry fruit flavoured drink for the undiscerning.
Origin: So named as this cocktail's flavour resembles the soft drink of the same name. The Cheeky Vimto emerged in Britain in the early-noughties.

Despite the name, the soft drink Vimto is not an ingredient in this drink, but for the record, it is a sweet purple coloured soft drink containing grape, raspberry and blackcurrant juices and flavoured with herbs and spices.

Vimto was created in 1908 in Timperley, Cheshire, England by John Noel Nichols, a wholesaler of spices and medicines.

CHELSEA SIDECAR

★★★★☆

Glass: Martini
Garnish: Lemon zest twist
Method: SHAKE all ingredients with ice and fine strain into chilled glass.

1½ shots	Tanqueray London dry gin
1 shot	Triple Sec
1 shot	Freshly squeezed lemon juice
¼ shot	Monin Pure Cane 2:1 sugar syrup

Variant: Sidecar
We say: Gin replaces cognac in this variation on the classic Sidecar.

CHERRUTE

★★★★☆

Glass: Martini
Garnish: Grapefruit zest twist (discarded) & maraschino cherry
Method: SHAKE all ingredients with ice and fine strain into chilled glass.

2	shots	Ketel One vodka
½	shot	De Kuyper Cherry Brandy liqueur
1½	shots	Freshly squeezed grapefruit juice

We say: Sweet cherry brandy balanced by the fruity acidity of grapefruit, laced with vodka.
Origin: Created in the early Noughties by Nicholas P J Snape at Mojo, Leeds, England.

CHERRY ALEXANDER

★★★★☆

Glass: Martini
Garnish: Maraschino cherry
Method: SHAKE all ingredients with ice and fine strain into chilled glass.

1	shot	Vanilla-infused Ketel One vodka
½	shot	De Kuyper Cherry Brandy liqueur
½	shot	White Crème de Cacao
1	shot	Double (heavy) cream
1	shot	Milk

Variant: Alexander
We say: A fruity twist on the creamy classic.
Origin: Created by Wayne Collins for Maxxium UK.

CHERRY BLOSSOM

★★★½☆

Glass: Martini
Garnish: Maraschino cherry
Method: SHAKE all ingredients with ice and fine strain into chilled glass.

¾	shot	De Kuyper Cherry Brandy liqueur
¾	shot	Kirschwasser eau de vie
½	shot	Triple Sec
¼	shot	Maraschino syrup (from cherry jar)
1¼	shots	Freshly squeezed lemon juice

We say: Bundles of flavour - tangy and moreish.

CHERRY DAIQUIRI

★★★★☆

Glass: Martini
Garnish: Maraschino cherry
Method: MUDDLE cherries in base of shaker. Add other ingredients, SHAKE with ice and fine strain into chilled glass.

8	fresh	Stoned cherries
2	shots	Vanilla-infused Bacardi rum
1	shot	De Kuyper Cherry Brandy liqueur
⅛	shot	Maraschino syrup (from cherry jar)
½	shot	Freshly squeezed lime juice
½	shot	Chilled mineral water

We say: Cherry sweetness paired with Daiquiri sharpness.
Origin: Created in 2003 by Simon Difford.

CHERRY MARINER

★★★★☆

Glass: Martini
Garnish: Maraschino cherry
Method: SHAKE all ingredients with ice and fine strain into chilled glass.

2	shots	Tanqueray London dry gin
1	shot	De Kuyper Cherry Brandy liqueur
¼	shot	Luxardo Maraschino liqueur
2	dashes	Orange bitters

We say: Rich cherry liqueurs fortified by gin and bittered with a hint of orange.
Origin: Adapted from a drink created by Mickael Perron from Bar Now On.

CHERRY MARTINI

★★★★☆

Glass: Martini
Garnish: Lemon zest twist
Method: SHAKE all ingredients with ice and fine strain into chilled glass.

2	shots	Ketel One Citroen vodka
¾	shot	De Kuyper Cherry Brandy liqueur
½	shot	Martini Extra Dry vermouth
½	shot	Chilled mineral water

We say: A hint of cherry is balanced by citrus freshness, and dried and deepened by vermouth.
Origin: Created in 2005 by Simon Difford.

CHERRY MASH SOUR

★★★½☆

Glass: Old-fashioned
Garnish: Lemon zest twist & maraschino cherry
Method: SHAKE all ingredients with ice and strain into ice-filled glass.

2	shots	Jack Daniels Tennessee whiskey
½	shot	De Kuyper Cherry Brandy liqueur
¾	shot	Freshly squeezed lemon juice
½	shot	Monin Pure Cane 2:1 sugar syrup

We say: The rich flavour of Tennessee whiskey soured with lemon and sweetened with cherry liqueur.
Origin: Created by Dale DeGroff when Beverage Manager at the Rainbow Room Promenade Bar, New York City, USA.

CHICLET DAIQUIRI

★★★½☆

Glass: Martini
Garnish: Banana chunk
Method: BLEND ingredients with a a scoop of crushed ice and serve in large chilled glass.

2½	shots	Bacardi Superior rum
½	shot	Bols Banana liqueur
⅛	shot	Giffard Menthe Pastille liqueur
½	shot	Freshly squeezed lime juice
¼	shot	Monin Pure Cane 2:1 sugar syrup

We say: A wonderfully refreshing drink on a summer's day with surprisingly subtle flavours.
Origin: Often found on Cuban bar menus, this was created at La Floridita, Havana.

CHIHUAHUA MARGARITA

Glass: Martini
Garnish: None
Method: SHAKE all ingredients with ice and fine strain into chilled glass.

2	shots	Tequila 100% Agave
2	shots	Freshly squeezed grapefruit juice
⅛	shot	Agave nectar
3	dashes	Angostura aromatic bitters

We say: Tequila and grapefruit juice pepped up with Angostura.

CHILL-OUT MARTINI

Glass: Martini
Garnish: Pineapple wedge
Method: SHAKE all ingredients with ice and fine strain into chilled glass.

1¼	shots	Ketel One Oranje vodka
¾	shot	Baileys Irish cream liqueur
1	shot	Malibu coconut rum liqueur
1	shot	Freshly squeezed orange juice

We say: Smooth, creamy sweet orange and surprisingly strong.

CHIMAYO

Glass: Martini
Garnish: Apple slice
Method: SHAKE all ingredients with ice and fine strain into chilled glass.

2	shots	Tequila 100% Agave
½	shot	Crème de cassis liqueur
¾	shot	Pressed apple juice
¼	shot	Freshly squeezed lemon juice

We say: Apple juice and cassis take the sting off tequila.
Origin: Named after El Potrero de Chimayo in northern New Mexico, USA

CHIN CHIN

Glass: Flute
Garnish: None
Method: STIR honey with Scotch in base of shaker. Add apple juice, SHAKE with ice and strain into chilled glass. TOP with champagne.

½	spoon	Runny honey
1	shot	Dewar's White label Scotch
½	shot	Pressed apple juice
Top up with		Brut champagne

We say: Golden honey in colour and also in flavour. An unusual and great tasting Champagne cocktail.
Origin: Created in 2002 by Tony Conigliaro at Isola, Knightsbridge, London, England.

CHINA BEACH

Glass: Martini
Garnish: Fresh ginger slice
Method: SHAKE all ingredients with ice and fine strain into chilled glass.

1	shot	Ketel One vodka
1	shot	Domaine de Canton ginger liqueur
2	shots	Ocean Spray cranberry juice

We say: Dry and lightly spiced.

CHINA BLUE

Glass: Collins
Garnish: Orange slice
Method: SHAKE all ingredients with ice and strain into ice-filled glass.

1	shot	Kwai Feh lychee liqueur
1	shot	Bols Blue Curaçao liqueur
4	shots	Freshly squeezed grapefruit juice

We say: Looks sweet, but due to a generous splash of grapefruit is actually balanced and refreshing.
Origin: Emerged in Japan in the late 1990s and still popular along the Pacific Rim.

CHINA BLUE MARTINI

Glass: Martini
Garnish: Lychee
Method: SHAKE all ingredients with ice and fine strain into chilled glass.

1	shot	Kwai Feh lychee liqueur
1	shot	Bols Blue Curaçao liqueur
2	shots	Freshly squeezed grapefruit juice
¼	shot	Freshly squeezed lemon juice

Variant: China Blue
We say: This simple cocktail with its turquoise colour tastes more adult and interesting than its colour might suggest.
Origin: An almost inevitable short adaptation of the original long drink.

STAR RATINGS EXPLAINED

★★★★★ Excellent

★★★★⯪ Recommended
★★★⯪☆ Commended
★★⯪☆☆ Disappointing
★⯪☆☆☆ Shameful

★★★★☆ Praiseworthy
★★★☆☆ Mediocre
★★☆☆☆ Pretty awful
★☆☆☆☆ Disgusting

CHINA MARTINI

★★★½☆☆

Glass: Martini
Garnish: Orange zest twist & lychee
Method: STIR all ingredients with ice and fine strain into chilled glass.

1½	shots	Tanqueray London dry gin
½	shot	Kwai Feh lychee liqueur
¼	shot	Triple Sec
½	shot	Martini Extra Dry vermouth

We say: A complex, not too sweet lychee Martini.
Origin: Created in 2004 by Wayne Collins for Maxxium UK.

CHINATO NAIL NEW

★★★★☆

Glass: Old Fashioned
Garnish: Lemon zest twist
Method: STIR all ingredients with ice and strain into ice-filled glass.

2½	shots	Dewar's White Label Scotch
½	shot	Drambuie
½	shot	Barolo Chinato

We say: A riff on the Rusty Nail using Barolo Chinato. Perhaps one for whisky and Negroni fans.
Origin: Created in 2012 by Simon Difford at the Cabinet Room, London, England.

CHINESE COSMOPOLITAN

★★★★☆

Glass: Martini
Garnish: Orange zest twist (flamed)
Method: SHAKE all ingredients with ice and fine strain into chilled glass.

2	shots	Krupnik spiced honey liqueur
¾	shot	Kwai Feh lychee liqueur
½	shot	Freshly squeezed lime juice
1	shot	Ocean Spray cranberry juice

We say: Oriental in name and style - perhaps a tad sweeter than your standard Cosmo.
Origin: Discovered in 2003 at Raoul's Bar, Oxford, England.

CHINESE WHISPER MARTINI

★★★★☆

Glass: Martini
Garnish: Lemon zest twist
Method: MUDDLE ginger in base of shaker. Add other ingredients, SHAKE with ice and fine strain into chilled glass.

2	slices	Fresh root ginger (thumbnail sized)
2	shots	Ketel One Citroen vodka
1	shot	Kwai Feh lychee liqueur
½	shot	Freshly squeezed lime juice
¼	shot	Monin Ginger syrup

We say: There's more than a whisper of ginger in this spicy Martini.
Origin: Adapted from a recipe discovered in 2003 at Oxo Tower Bar, London, England.

CHOC & NUT MARTINI

★★★½☆☆

Glass: Martini
Garnish: Chocolate powder rim
Method: SHAKE all ingredients with ice and fine strain into chilled glass.

2	shots	Ketel One vodka
1	shot	Hazelnut liqueur
1	shot	White Crème de Cacao
¼	shot	Chilled mineral water

We say: Surprise, surprise - it's chocolate and hazelnut.

CHOCOLARITA

★★★★☆

Glass: Coupette
Garnish: Chocolate powder rim
Method: SHAKE all ingredients with ice and fine strain into chilled glass.

2	shots	Tequila 100% Agave
¼	shot	Dark Crème de Cacao
¼	shot	Kahlúa coffee liqueur
1	shot	Freshly squeezed lime juice
¼	shot	Monin Pure Cane 2:1 sugar syrup

We say: As the name suggests - a Margarita with chocolate and coffee.
Origin: Adapted from a recipe discovered in 2005 at Agave, Hong Kong.

CHOCOLATE & CRANBERRY MARTINI

★★★★☆

Glass: Martini
Garnish: Chocolate powder rim
Method: SHAKE all ingredients with ice and fine strain into chilled, rimmed glass.

2	shots	Vanilla-infused Ketel One vodka
½	shot	White Crème de Cacao
½	shot	Martini Extra Dry vermouth
1	shot	Ocean Spray cranberry juice

We say: The chocolate rim sounds naff but makes this drink. Surprisingly dry.
Origin: Created in 2003 by Simon Difford.

CHOCOLATE BISCUIT

★★★½☆☆

Glass: Martini
Garnish: Bourbon biscuit
Method: SHAKE all ingredients with ice and fine strain into chilled glass.

2	shots	Cognac VSOP
1	shot	Dark Crème de Cacao
1	shot	Kahlúa coffee liqueur

We say: Sweet and rich, with coffee and chocolate - one to chase dessert.
Origin: Created in 1999 by Gillian Stanfield at The Atlantic Bar & Grill, London, England.

CHOCOLATE MARTINI

★★★★☆

Glass: Martini
Garnish: Chocolate powder rim
Method: SHAKE all ingredients with ice and fine strain into chilled glass.

2	shots	Ketel One vodka
1	shot	White Crème de Cacao
1	shot	Martini Extra Dry vermouth

We say: Vodka and chocolate made more interesting with a hint of vermouth.

CHOCOLATE MINT MARTINI

★★★★☆

Glass: Martini
Garnish: Chocolate powder rim
Method: STIR all ingredients with ice and strain into chilled glass.

2	shots	Ketel One vodka
½	shot	Giffard Menthe Pastille liqueur
½	shot	White Crème de Cacao
½	shot	Martini Extra Dry vermouth

We say: An after dinner sweety that tastes of chocolate mints.

CHOCOLATE PUFF

★★★★☆

Glass: Old-fashioned
Garnish: Crumbled Cadbury's Flake bar
Method: SHAKE all ingredients with ice and fine strain into chilled glass.

1	shot	Bacardi Oro golden rum
1	shot	Dark Crème de Cacao
6	spoon	Natural yoghurt
2	twist	Fresh orange
¼	shot	Monin Pure Cane 2:1 sugar syrup

We say: Smooth as you like. The orange is surprisingly evident.
Origin: Created by Wayne Collins in 2002 for Maxxium UK.

CHOCOLATE SAZERAC

★★★★☆

Glass: Old-fashioned
Garnish: Lemon zest twist (discarded) & apple wedge
Method: Fill glass with ice, POUR in absinthe, top up with water and leave the mixture to stand in the glass. Separately SHAKE bourbon, cacao, sugar and bitters with ice. Finally discard contents of glass (absinthe, water and ice) and strain contents of shaker into empty absinthe-coated glass.

½	shot	Absinthe
2	shots	Maker's Mark bourbon
½	shot	White Crème de Cacao
¼	shot	Monin Pure Cane 2:1 sugar syrup
2	dashes	Peychaud's aromatic bitters

We say: This twist on the classic Sazerac pairs absinthe, bourbon and chocolate to great effect.
Origin: Created in 2005 by Tonin Kacaj at Maze, London, England.

CHOCOLATE SIDECAR

★★★★☆

Glass: Martini
Garnish: Chocolate powder rim
Method: SHAKE all ingredients with ice and fine strain into chilled glass.

1	shot	Cognac VSOP
1	shot	Dark Crème de Cacao
1	shot	Warre's Otima tawny port
1	shot	Freshly squeezed lime juice
½	shot	Monin Pure Cane 2:1 sugar syrup

Origin: Created in 2005 by Wayne Collins for Maxxium UK.

CHOCOLATE STINGER NEW

★★★★☆

Glass: Old-fashioned
Garnish: Mint sprig
Method: STIR all ingredients with ice and strain into glass filled with crushed ice.

| 2 | shots | Mozart Dry chocolate spirit |
| ¾ | shot | Giffard Menthe Pastille liqueur |

We say: Chocolate and mint served frappé.
Origin: Adapted from a drink created in 2010 by Klaus St. Rainer at Schumann's Bar, Munich, Germany

CHRISTMAS PUDDING & CUSTARD COCKTAIL NEW

★★★★☆

Glass: Coupette
Garnish: Serve a shot of chilled Pedro Ximenez sherry on the side
Method: SHAKE all ingredients with ice and fine strain into chilled glass.

1½	shots	Warnink's Advocaat liqueur
1½	shots	Courvoisier VSOP Exclusif
¾	shot	Tio Pepe fino sherry

We say: This cocktail tastes like alcoholic custard and Pedro Ximenez (PX) sherry-like liquid Christmas pudding.
Origin: A Christmas cocktail created in October 2011 by Simon Difford at the Cabinet Room, London, England.

CHRISTMAS VELVET ALEXANDER NEW

★★★★☆

Glass: Coupette
Garnish: Orange zest twist
Method: SHAKE all ingredients with ice and fine strain into chilled glass.

1½	shots	Advocaat liqueur
1½	shots	Tanqueray London dry gin
¾	shot	Tio Pepe fino sherry

We say: Combining advocaat, gin and fino sherry, this is the ultimate stereotypical Christmas English granny's cocktail.
Origin: A Christmas cocktail created in October 2011 by Simon Difford at the Cabinet Room, London, England.

CHRISTMOPOLITAN NEW

★★★½☆

Glass: Coupette
Garnish: Orange zest twist (discarded) and string red currants
Method: SHAKE all ingredients with ice and fine strain into chilled glass.

1½	shots	**Ketel One vodka**
1½	shots	**Ocean Spray cranberry juice**
½	shot	**Luxardo Amaretto di Saschira**
½	shot	**Freshly squeezed lime juice**

We say: A suitably Christmassy amaretto influenced Cosmopolitan.
Origin: A Christmas cocktail created in October 2011 by SImon Difford at the Cabinet Room, London, England.

CHRISTMAS MARGARITA NEW

★★★½☆

Glass: Coupette
Garnish: Orange zest twist
Method: SHAKE all ingredients with ice and fine strain into chilled glass.

1½	shots	**Tequila 100% Agave (blanco)**
1½	shots	**Ocean Spray cranberry juice**
½	shot	**Freshly squeezed lime juice**
½	shot	**Grand Marnier liqueur**

We say: The Cosmopolitan meets the Margarita in this gloriously pink cocktail.
Origin: A Christmas cocktail created in October 2011 by Simon Difford at the Cabinet Room, London, England.

CHRYSANTHEMUM

★★★★☆

Glass: Martini
Garnish: Orange zest twist
Method: STIR all ingredients with ice and strain into chilled glass.

2	shots	**Martini Extra Dry vermouth**
1	shot	**Bénédictine D.O.M.**
⅛	shot	**Absinthe**

We say: Herbal and aromatic, this benefits from the dilution that comes with a good long stir.
Origin: In his 1930 *'The Savoy Cocktail Book'*, Harry Craddock writes of this drink: 'Well-known and very popular in the American Bar of the S.S. Europa'.

STAR RATINGS EXPLAINED

★★★★★ Excellent

★★★★½ Recommeded
★★★½☆ Commended
★★½☆☆ Disappointing
★½☆☆☆ Shameful
★★★★☆ Praiseworthy
★★★☆☆ Mediocre
★★☆☆☆ Pretty awful
★☆☆☆☆ Disgusting

CHUBACABRAS DAIQUIRI

★★★☆☆

Glass: Martini
Garnish: Maraschino cherry
Method: SHAKE all ingredients with ice and fine-strain into chilled glass.

2	shots	**Bacardi Superior rum**
¾	shot	**Freshly squeezed lime juice**
¼	shot	**Monin Almond (orgeat) syrup**
⅛	shot	**Luxardo Maraschino liqueur**
⅛	shot	**Absinthe**
⅛	shot	**Orange flower water**

We say: Absinthe, almond, maraschino and orange flower blossom water make for a highly flavoured daiquiri.
Origin: Created in 2008 by Marcis Dzelzainis, Quo Vadis, London, England. The name literally translates as 'goat sucker' and is the name given to a mythical Latin American creature that is said to kill goats and other small animals to then suck the blood out of them. The first reported incidences ocurred in Puerto Rico in 1995 .

CHURCHILL MARTINI

★★★☆☆

Glass: Martini
Garnish: Olive
Method: STIR gin with ice while glancing at an unopened bottle of dry vermouth. Strain into chilled glass.

2½	shots	**Tanqueray London dry gin**

We say: Gin served chilled and neat, other than with a little dilution courtesy of melting ice. A great man but not necessarily a great drink.
Origin: Legend has it that Sir Winston Churchill liked his Martinis served without the vermouth actually being added to the drink, just present in the same room. He is quoted as saying of the drink, 'Glance at the vermouth bottle briefly while pouring the juniper distillate freely'.

CICADA COCKTAIL

★★★½☆

Glass: Martini
Garnish: Dust with grated nutmeg
Method: SHAKE all ingredients with ice and fine strain into chilled glass.

2	shots	**Maker's Mark bourbon**
1	shot	**Amaretto liqueur**
½	shot	**Double (heavy) cream**
¾	shot	**Monin Pure Cane 2:1 sugar syrup**

We say: Smoothed whiskey with more than a hint of almond.
Origin: Those familiar with the Grasshopper cocktail (named for its green colour) will understand why this one is called the Cicada (they're a bit browner).

CIDER APPLE COOLER

★★★★☆

Glass: Collins
Garnish: None
Method: SHAKE all ingredients with ice and strain into ice-filled glass.

2	shots	Calvados/Applejack brandy
1	shot	Berentzen Apple schnapps
4½	shots	Pressed apple juice

We say: Not unlike the taste of strong dry cider.

CIDER APPLE MARTINI

★★★★☆

Glass: Martini
Garnish: Apple wedge
Method: SHAKE all ingredients with ice & fine strain into chilled glass.

1½	shots	Calvados/Applejack brandy
¾	shot	Berentzen Apple schnapps
¾	shot	Freshly squeezed lemon juice
1	shot	Pressed apple juice
¼	shot	Monin Pure Cane 2:1 sugar syrup

We say: As the name suggests, rich cider flavours with a sharp finish.
Origin: Created in 1998 by Jamie Terrell at Lab, London, England.

CIDER HOUSE RULES

★★★★☆

Glass: Old-fashioned
Garnish: Apple wedge
Method: SHAKE all ingredients with ice & fine strain into ice-filled glass.

2	shots	Tequila 100% Agave
1½	shots	Pressed apple juice
½	shot	Freshly squeezed lemon juice
¼	shot	Agave nectar
½	spoon	Ground cinnamon

We say: Margarita-style drink with tequila, lemon and apple juice.
Origin: Created by New York-based Brian Van Flandern, of Creative Cocktail Consultants Corp and named after the double Academy Award winning 1999 film and 1985 novel by John Irving of the same name.

CINDERELLA

★★☆☆☆

Glass: Collins
Garnish: Lemon slice
Method: SHAKE first 5 ingredients with ice & strain into ice-filled glass.
TOP with soda water.

2	shots	Freshly squeezed orange juice
1½	shots	Fresh pressed pineapple juice
¾	shot	Freshly squeezed lemon juice
⅛	shot	Pomegranate (grenadine) syrup
3	dashes	Angostura aromatic bitters
Top up with		Soda (club soda)

We say: Long, fresh and fruity.

CINNAMON DAIQUIRI

★★★☆☆

Glass: Martini
Garnish: Dust with cinnamon powder
Method: SHAKE all ingredients with ice and fine strain into chilled glass.

2	shots	Bacardi Superior rum
½	shot	Goldschläger cinnamon schnapps
½	shot	Freshly squeezed lime juice

We say: A subtle spicy cinnamon taste with tangy length.
Origin: Created in 1999 by Porik at Che, London, England.

CITRUS CAIPIROVSKA

★★★★☆

Glass: Old-fashioned
Garnish: None
Method: MUDDLE lemon in base of glass. Add other ingredients and fill glass with crushed ice. CHURN drink with bar spoon and serve with short straws.

¾	fresh	Lemon cut into wedges
2	shots	Ketel One Citroen vodka
¾	shot	Monin Pure Cane 2:1 sugar syrup

We say: Superbly refreshing balance of sweet and citrus sourness.

CITRUS MARTINI

★★★★☆

Glass: Martini
Garnish: Orange zest twist
Method: SHAKE all ingredients with ice & fine strain into chilled glass.

1½	shots	Ketel One Citroen vodka
¼	shot	Triple Sec
1	shot	Freshly squeezed lemon juice
¼	shot	Monin Pure Cane 2:1 sugar syrup
3	dashes	Orange bitters

AKA: Lemon Martini
We say: Orange undertones add citrus depth to the lemon explosion.
Origin: Created by Dick Bradsell at Fred's, London, England, in the late 80s.

CITRUS RUM COOLER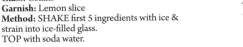

★★★★☆

Glass: Collins
Garnish: Orange slice
Method: SHAKE first three ingredients with ice and strain into ice-filled glass. TOP with lemonade. Lightly stir and serve with straws.

1	shot	Bacardi Superior rum
½	shot	Grand Marnier liqueur
2	shots	Freshly squeezed orange juice
Top up with		Lemonade/Sprite/7-Up

We say: Light, fruity, easy and very refreshing.

CLAIRVOYANT

Glass: Martini
Garnish: Orange zest twist
Method: STIR all ingredients with ice & fine strain into chilled glass.

1½	shots	Tio Pepe fino sherry
1½	shots	Martini Extra Dry vermouth
¾	shot	Hazelnut liqueur
1	dash	Orange bitters

Variant: Coronation Cocktail
We say: A hazelnut flavoured variation on the classic Coronation Cocktail.
Origin: Created in 2008 by Simon Difford in Jerez, Spain and named after Claire Hu, a fellow drinks hack on the same trip who was a fan of hazelnut liqueur.

CLARA ASTIÉ COCKTAIL

Glass: Martini
Garnish: Grapefruit zest twist (discarded) & dried apricot
Method: STIR jam with rum until jam dissolves. Add other ingredients, SHAKE with ice and fine strain into chilled glass.

2	shots	Bacardi Superior rum
1	spoon	Apricot jam (preserve)
1	shot	Martini Extra Dry vermouth
⅛	shot	Luxardo Maraschino liqueur
1	dash	Grapefruit bitters
½	shot	Chilled mineral water

We say: Tangy apricot with hints of maraschino, dried by vermouth and fortified by light rum.
Origin: Adapted from a drink created in 2008 by Ian McLaren of Bacardi Brown-Forman Brands, UK. The name is in tribute to Doña Amalia's Godmother whose bequest revived the fortunes of Don Facundo Bacardi Massó allowing him to establish the rum brand we know today.

CLARET COBBLER

Glass: Goblet
Garnish: Mint sprig
Method: SHAKE all ingredients with ice & fine strain into glass filled with crushed ice. Serve with straws.

1½	shots	Cognac VSOP
1	shot	Grand Marnier liqueur
2½	shots	Shiraz red wine

We say: Fortified and slightly sweetened wine cooled and lengthened by ice.
Origin: Simon Difford's version of an old classic.

STAR RATINGS EXPLAINED

★★★★★ Excellent

★★★★☆ Recommended
★★★☆☆ Commended
★★☆☆☆ Disappointing
★☆☆☆☆ Shameful

★★★★☆ Praiseworthy
★★★☆☆ Mediocre
★★☆☆☆ Pretty awful
★☆☆☆☆ Disgusting

CLARIDGE COCKTAIL

Glass: Martini
Garnish: Lemon zest twist
Method: SHAKE all ingredients with ice and fine strain into chilled glass.

1½	shots	Tanqueray London dry gin
1½	shots	Martini Extra Dry vermouth
½	shot	Triple Sec
½	shot	De Kuyper Apricot Brandy liqueur

AKA: Frankenjack
We say: Gin for strength, vermouth for dryness and liqueur to sweeten - an interesting combination.
Origin: Adapted from Harry Craddock's 1930 'The Savoy Cocktail Book'

CLASSIC COCKTAIL

Glass: Martini
Garnish: Lemon zest twist (and optional sugar rim)
Method: SHAKE all ingredients with ice and fine strain into chilled glass.

2	shots	Cognac VSOP
½	shot	Grand Marnier liqueur
½	shot	Luxardo Maraschino liqueur
½	shot	Freshly squeezed lemon juice
½	shot	Chilled mineral water

We say: Reminiscent of a Sidecar with Maraschino.
Origin: Adapted form Harry Craddock's 1930 'The Savoy Cocktail Book'

CLEMENTINE

Glass: Shot
Garnish: Sugar coated orange wedge
Method: Refrigerate ingredients then LAYER in chilled glass by carefully pouring in the following order. Instruct drinker to down in one and bite into the wedge.

| ½ | shot | Limoncello liqueur |
| ½ | shot | Mandarine Napoléon liqueur |

We say: Short, sweet and very fruity

CLIPPER COCKTAIL

Glass: Martini
Garnish: Lemon zest twist
Method: SHAKE all ingredients and fine strain into glass filled with crushed ice.

2	shots	Bacardi Superior rum
2	shots	Martini Extra Dry vermouth
½	shot	Pomegranate (grenadine) syrup

We say: Light, easy drinking and very refreshing.
Origin: Peggy Guggenheim's biography mentions that this cocktail was served during the 1940s on the Boeing flying boats known as Clippers.

CLOCKWORK ORANGE

★★★½☆

Glass: Collins
Garnish: Orange slice
Method: SHAKE all ingredients with ice and strain into ice-filled glass.

1½	shots	Cognac VSOP
1½	shots	Grand Marnier liqueur
3	shots	Freshly squeezed orange juice

We say: Neither as memorable nor as controversial as the film but a pleasant orange drink all the same.

CLOVER CLUB (HOUSE-MADE)

★★★★½

Glass: Martini
Garnish: Lemon zest twist
Method: SHAKE all ingredients with ice and fine strain into chilled glass.

1½	shots	Tanqueray London dry gin
1½	spoon	Raspberry syrup (1 juice to 1 sugar)
½	shot	Martini Extra Dry vermouth
¾	shot	Freshly squeezed lemon juice

Variant: Substitute vodka or tequila for gin. Different flavours of jam may also be used.
We say: Fruity, light, well-balanced and easy-drinking.
Origin: Created by Julie Reiner at Clover Club, New York City, USA.

CLOVER CLUB COCKTAIL NO.3 #1
(LOWE'S RECIPE)

★★★★☆

Glass: Martini
Garnish: None
Method: SHAKE all ingredients with ice & fine strain into chilled glass.

1	shot	Tanqueray London dry gin
1	shot	Martini Extra dry vermouth
1	shot	Freshly squeezed lemon juice
1	shot	Raspberry syrup (1 juice to 1 sugar)
½	fresh	Egg white

Variant: With a mint leaf garnish this drink called a 'Clover Leaf'.
We say: Balanced and complex with a fruity blast of raspberry - made interesting due to its inclusion of vermouth.
Origin: Recipe from '1909 Drinks - How to Mix and Serve, by Paul E. Lowe' and courtesy of Dave Wondrich who says this is the earliest Clover Club recipe he has discovered. Lowe omits the lemon juice in his original recipe but this is thought to be a mistake. Albert Stevens Crockett credits the creation of this cocktail to the Bellevue-Stratford Hotel, Philadelphia in his 1931 '*Old Waldorf Bar Days*'.

CLOVER CLUB COCKTAIL NO.3 #2 UPDATED
(DIFFORD'S RECIPE)

★★★★½

Glass: Martini
Garnish: Lemon zest twist (sprayed & discarded)
Method: SHAKE all ingredients with ice and fine strain into chilled glass.

5	fresh	Raspberries
1¾	shots	Tanqueray London dry gin
¼	shot	Martini Extra dry vermouth
¼	shot	Martini Rosso sweet vermouth
¼	shot	Freshly squeezed lemon juice
¼	shot	Monin Pure Cane 2:1 sugar syrup
½	fresh	Egg white

We say: Creamy and easy – with notes of raspberry, gin, citrus and delicate spice.
Origin: Version of a vintage classic by Simon Difford at the Cabinet Room, London, England.

CLOVER LEAF COCKTAIL NO.1
(CLASSIC FORMULA)

★★★★☆

Glass: Martini
Garnish: Mint leaf
Method: SHAKE all ingredients with ice & fine strain into chilled glass.

2	shots	Tanqueray London dry gin
½	shot	Freshly squeezed lemon juice
¼	shot	Pomegranate (grenadine) syrup
½	fresh	Egg white

AKA: Without the mint garnish this drink is called a 'Clover Club'.
Variant: With raspberry syrup in place of pomegranate syrup.
We say: Smooth, aromatic, fruity and medium sweet.

CLOVER LEAF MARTINI NO.2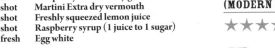
(MODERN FORMULA)

★★★★☆

Glass: Martini
Garnish: Mint leaf
Method: MUDDLE raspberries in base of shaker. Add other ingredients, SHAKE with ice and fine strain into chilled glass.

7	fresh	Raspberries
3	fresh	Mint leaves
2	shots	Tanqueray London dry gin
¾	shot	Freshly squeezed lemon juice
½	shot	Pomegranate (grenadine) syrup
½	fresh	Egg white

AKA: With a mint leaf garnish this drink is called a 'Clover Leaf'.
We say: Carpet scaring red, this fruity adaptation perhaps has a wider appeal than the original Clover Leaf.

CLOYSTERS

★★★★☆

Glass: Martini
Garnish: Grapefruit zest twist
Method: SHAKE all ingredients with ice & fine strain into chilled glass.

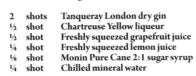

2	shots	Tanqueray London dry gin
½	shot	Chartreuse Yellow liqueur
½	shot	Freshly squeezed grapefruit juice
¼	shot	Freshly squeezed lemon juice
⅛	shot	Monin Pure Cane 2:1 sugar syrup
¼	shot	Chilled mineral water

We say: There's a suitable subtle monastic influence to this complex, gin based, most learned of cocktails.
Origin: Adapted from a drink created in 2007 by John Deragon at PDT, New York City, USA.

CLUB COCKTAIL #1

★★★★☆

Glass: Martini
Garnish: Orange zest twist
Method: STIR all ingredients with ice and strain into chilled glass.

1½	shots	Tio Pepe fino sherry
1½	shots	Warre's Otima tawny port
1	dash	Orange bitters

We say: Dry and incredibly aromatic. A perfect aperitif.
Origin: In his 1948 'The Fine Art of Mixing Drinks', David A. Embury writes, "Perhaps it would not be too much of an exaggeration to say there are as many Club Cocktails as there are clubs." This example is adapted form the same book.

CLUB COCKTAIL #2

★★★★☆

Glass: Martini
Garnish: Chilled olive on stick
Method: SHAKE all ingredients with ice and strain into chilled glass.

2	shots	Tanqueray London dry gin
1	shot	Martini Rosso sweet vermouth
⅛	shot	Chartreuse Yellow liqueur

We say: A sweet Martini with a hint of Chartreuse.
Origin: Adapted form Harry Craddock's 1930 'The Savoy Cocktail Book'.

CLUB COCKTAIL #3

★★★★☆

Glass: Martini
Garnish: Maraschino cherry
Method: STIR all ingredients with ice & fine strain into chilled glass.

2	shots	Bacardi Oro golden rum
½	shot	Martini Rosso sweet vermouth
½	shot	Martini Extra Dry vermouth
½	shot	Maraschino syrup (from cherry jar)
3	dashes	Angostura aromatic bitters
¾	shot	Chilled mineral water

We say: An aromatic, spirited, classical cocktail.
Origin: Adapted from a drink created in 2002 by Michael Butt at Milk & Honey, London, England.

CLUBLAND COCKTAIL

★★★★☆

Glass: Coupette
Garnish: Orange zest twist
Method: STIR all ingredients with ice & fine strain into chilled glass.

1½	shots	Ketel One vodka
1½	shots	Taylor's chip dry white port
1	dash	Angostura aromatic bitters

We say: Go easy on the bitters and this is a complex and rewarding Martini-style drink.
Origin: In W.J. Tarling's (Bill Tarling) 1937 Café Royal Cocktail Book Coronation edition, the creation of this drink is credited to one A. Mackintosh. Originally made with a brand of port called Clubland, hence this drink's name.

COBBLE HILL

★★★★☆

Glass: Coupette
Garnish: Lemon zest twist (discarded) & cucumber slice
Method: MUDDLE cucumber in base of stirring glass. Add other ingredients, STIR with ice and fine strain into chilled glass.

2	slices	Cucumber (chopped & peeled)
2	shots	Straight rye whiskey
½	shot	Martini Extra Dry vermouth
½	shot	Averna Amaro

We say: Sam describes this drink as "a summertime Manhattan" - it is.
Origin: Created in 2009 by Sam Ross at Milk and Honey, New York City, USA.

COBBLED RASPBERRY MARTINI

★★★★⯪

Glass: Martini
Garnish: Raspberries
Method: MUDDLE raspberries in base of shaker. Add other ingredients, SHAKE with ice and fine strain into chilled glass.

2	shots	Ketel One vodka
1	shot	Shiraz red wine
¼	shot	Monin Pure Cane 2:1 sugar syrup
12	fresh	Raspberries

We say: The addition of a splash of wine to a simple Raspberry Martini adds another level of complexity.
Origin: Created by Simon Difford in 2004.

COBBLERS

★★★★☆

Glass: Goblet
Garnish: Mint sprig
Method: SHAKE all ingredients with ice and fine strain into glass filled with crushed ice. Serve with straws.

1½	shots	Cognac VSOP
1	shot	Grand Marnier liqueur
2½	shots	Shiraz red wine

We say: Fortified and slightly sweetened wine cooled and lengthened by ice.
Origin: Cobblers emerged in the mid 1800s and circa 1880 the bartender Harry Johnson said of the Sherry Cobbler 'This drink is without doubt the most popular beverage in this country, with ladies as well as with

gentlemen. It is a very refreshing drink for old and young.'

Cobblers are served with straws in a goblet filled with crushed ice and decorated with fruit and a sprig or two of mint. They are based on spirits and/or wine sweetened with sugar syrup or sweet liqueur. Classically Cobblers contain little or no citrus but modern variations often call for citrus and other fruits to be muddled. Personally I believe it's the lack of citrus that sets Cobblers apart. The best examples of these use the tannin and acidity in the wine to bitter and so balance.

Cobblers are also classically built in the glass. I prefer to shake mine to properly cool and mix them before straining over fresh crushed ice and stirring. I've taken to calling neo-Martinis which use wine in place of citrus 'Cobbled Martinis' (see Cobbled Raspberry Martini) although I understand that the name actually refers to the ice and not the fruit.

Interestingly, this drink is often cited for heralding in the paper straw which wasn't patented until 1888. Prior to that straws were just that, 'straw', usually rye, or even hollow pasta (macaroni or vermicelli).
Our version of an old classic.

COCO CABANA

★★★½☆

Glass: Martini
Garnish: Pineapple wedge
Method: SHAKE all ingredients with ice and fine strain into chilled glass.

½	**shot**	**Midori green melon liqueur**
1½	**shots**	**Malibu coconut rum liqueur**
2	**shots**	**Fresh pressed pineapple juice**
¾	**shot**	**Milk**
¾	**shot**	**Double (heavy) cream**

We say: A sweet, creamy tropical number for Barry Manilow fans.

COCO NAUT

★★½☆☆

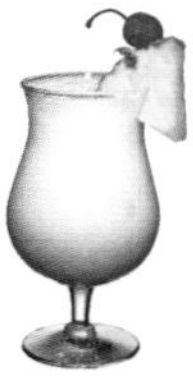

Glass: Hurricane
Garnish: Pineapple wedge & maraschino cherry
Method: BLEND ingredients with 12oz scoop of crushed ice. Pour into glass and serve with straws.

2	**shots**	**Wray & Nephew overproof rum**
1½	**shots**	**Coco López cream of coconut**
1	**shot**	**Freshly squeezed lime juice**

We say: This snow-white drink is hardly innocent with a double shot of overproof rum masked by the sweet coconut.

COCONUT DAIQUIRI

★★★★☆

Glass: Martini
Garnish: Lime wedge
Method: SHAKE all ingredients with ice & fine strain into chilled glass.

2	**shots**	**Bacardi Superior rum**
1	**shot**	**Malibu coconut rum liqueur**
½	**shot**	**Freshly squeezed lime juice**
½	**shot**	**Monin Coconut syrup**
¾	**scoop**	**Chilled mineral water**

Variant: Blend with a 6oz scoop of crushed ice and a tad more coconut syrup.
We say: Classic Daiquiri flavour with a pleasing tropical touch.

COCONUT WATER

★★★★☆

Glass: Martini
Garnish: None
Method: STIR all ingredients with ice and fine strain into chilled glass.

1	**shot**	**Ketel One vodka**
2¼	**shots**	**Malibu coconut rum liqueur**
⅛	**shot**	**Monin Coconut syrup**
1¼	**shots**	**Chilled mineral water**

We say: Have you ever drunk from a fresh coconut in the Caribbean? Well, this is the alcoholic equivalent.
Origin: Created in 2003 by Simon Difford.

COFFEE & VANILLA DAIQUIRI

★★★★☆

Glass: Martini
Garnish: Coffee beans
Method: SHAKE all ingredients with ice & fine strain into chilled glass.

2	**shots**	**Vanilla-infused Bacardi rum**
1	**shot**	**Kahlúa coffee liqueur**
½	**shot**	**Freshly squeezed lime juice**
⅛	**shot**	**Monin Pure Cane 2:1 sugar syrup**
¾	**shot**	**Chilled mineral water**

We say: Coffee, vanilla, sweetness and sourness all in harmony.
Origin: Created in 2002 by Simon Difford.

COESSENTIAL NEW

★★★★½

Glass: Coupette
Garnish: Float mint leaf
Method: SHAKE all ingredients with ice and fine strain into chilled glass.

8	**fresh**	**Mint leaves**
2	**shots**	**Ketel One vodka**
½	**shot**	**White Crème de Cacao**
⅛	**shot**	**Absinthe**

We say: To quote the Oxford English Dictionary, "This is done with the help of the hands of consciousness that extend from the spiritual heart and are coessential to it." This delicate but aromatic drink is dedicated to my long term supporter and friend John Coe.
Origin: Created in 2011 by Simon Difford at the Cabinet Room, London, England.

COFFEE BATIDA

★★★☆☆

Glass: Old-fashioned
Garnish: Coffee beans
Method: BLEND all ingredients with crushed ice and serve with straws

2	**shots**	**Leblon cachaça**
1	**shot**	**Kahlúa coffee liqueur**
1	**shot**	**Hot espresso coffee**
½	**shot**	**Monin Pure Cane 2:1 sugar syrup**

We say: Fortunately this caffeine and cachaça laced cocktail tastes a good deal better than it looks.

COFFEE COCKTAIL

★★★★½

Glass: Wine
Garnish: Dust with grated nutmeg
Method: SHAKE all ingredients with ice and fine strain into chilled glass.

2	shots	Warre's Otima tawny port
1	shot	Cognac VSOP
½	shot	Monin Pure Cane 2:1 sugar syrup
1	fresh	Egg

We say: As the anonymous writer of the 1887 edition of the Professor's book comments, "The name of this drink is a misnomer, as coffee and bitters are not to be found among its ingredients, but it looks like coffee when it has been properly concocted."
Origin: Recipe adapted from Jerry 'The Professor' Thomas's 1887 'The Bartender's Guide, or How to Mix All Kinds of Plain and Fancy Drinks'.

COGNAC JULEP NEW

★★★★★

Glass: Julep Tin
Garnish: Mint sprig
Method: SHAKE all ingredients with ice and fine strain into julep cup half filled with crushed ice. CHURN (stir) the drink with the crushed ice using a bar spoon. Top up the cup with more crushed ice and CHURN again. Repeat this process until the drink fills the cup and serve.

12	fresh	Mint leaves
2½	shots	Cognac VSOP
¾	shot	Monin Pure Cane 2:1 sugar syrup

We say: A truly deliciously refreshing cocktail. Woody rancio notes in the cognac are freshened by the mint. Those with a dry palate may want to reduce the sugar a touch.
Origin: Although bourbon is now most commonly associated with the Julep it is probable that it was first made with cognac.

COLA DE MONO

★★★★½

Glass: Martini
Garnish: Dust with cinnamon powder
Method: MUDDLE cinnamon stick and pisco in base of shaker. Add other ingredients, SHAKE with ice and fine strain into a chilled glass.

1	inch	Cinnamon stick
2	shots	Macchu pisco
1	shot	Hot espresso coffee
1	shot	Kahlúa coffee liqueur

We say: Coffee and cinnamon - a drink to be savoured.
Origin: Based on a Chilean drink traditionally consumed at Christmas, the name of which literally translates as 'Tail of Monkey'. The original uses milk and sugar instead of coffee liqueur.

COLD BLOODED

★★★½☆

Glass: Old-fashioned
Garnish: Rosemary sprig
Method: MUDDLE rosemary in base of shaker. Add other ingredients, SHAKE with ice & fine strain into ice-filled glass.

1	fresh	Rosemary sprig
1½	shots	Grand Marnier liqueur
2	shots	Ocean Spray cranberry juice
½	shot	Freshly squeezed lemon juice
½	shot	Monin Pure Cane 2:1 sugar syrup

We say: Red berry, orange and pine.
Origin: Adapted from a drink discovered in 2008 on Steve Olson's akawinegeek.com site.

COLD COMFORT

★★★★☆

Glass: Old-fashioned
Garnish: None
Method: SHAKE all ingredients with ice and strain into ice-filled glass.

2	shots	Wray & Nephew overproof rum
6	spoon	Runny honey
1	shot	Freshly squeezed lime juice

We say: Take at the first sign of a cold, and then retreat under your bed covers. Repeat dose regularly while symptoms persist. Warning - do not consume with other forms of medication.
Origin: Discovered in Jamaica in 2001.

COLD WINTER WARMER SOUR

★★★★☆

Glass: Old-fashioned
Garnish: Orange slice & cherry on stick (sail)
Method: STIR honey with vodka in base of shaker until honey dissolves. Add other ingredients, SHAKE with ice and strain into ice-filled glass.

1	spoon	Runny honey
1	shot	Ketel One Citroen vodka
½	shot	Bénédictine D.O.M.
1	shot	Freshly squeezed lemon juice
½	fresh	Egg white

We say: Flavours reminiscent of a hot toddy but served in a cold sour.
Origin: Created in 2006 by Simon Difford.

COLLAR & CUFF

★★★★☆

Glass: Toddy
Garnish: Lemon slice
Method: PLACE bar spoon in glass, add ingredients & STIR.

2	spoons	Runny honey
1	shot	Dewar's White label Scotch
1	shot	Domaine de Canton ginger liqueur
1	shot	Freshly squeezed lemon juice
Top up with		Boiling water

We say: A ginger infused riff on a toddy.
Origin: Created in 2003 by Simon Difford.

COLLECTION MARTINI

★★★☆☆

Glass: Martini
Garnish: Lime wedge
Method: SHAKE all ingredients with ice & fine strain into chilled glass.

¾	shot	Ketel One vodka
¾	shot	Ketel One Citroen vodka
¾	shot	Bénédictine D.O.M.
¾	shot	Crème de Mûre liqueur
½	shot	Freshly squeezed lime juice

We say: Honey, spice and vodka enhanced by blackberries, with a very alcoholic edge.
Origin: Originally created by Matthew Randall whilst at The Collection, London, England.

COLLINS

★★★★½

Glass: Collins
Garnish: Orange slice & cherry on stick (sail)
Method: SHAKE first 3 ingredients with ice & strain into ice-filled glass. TOP with soda, stir & serve with straws.

2	shots	Bols Genever
1	shot	Freshly squeezed lemon juice
½	shot	Monin Pure Cane 2:1 sugar syrup
Top up with		Soda (club soda)

We say: Some say the John/Tom Collins was originally made with genever. So is this the original or an adaptation on the Tom Collins. We will probably never know, but it tastes great.
Origin: In England, this drink is traditionally credited to John Collins, a bartender who worked at Limmer's Hotel, Conduit Street, London. The 'coffee house' of this hotel, a true dive bar, was popular with sporting types during the 19th century, and famous, according to the 1860s memoirs of a Captain Gronow, for its gin-punch as early as 1814.

Others say that the Tom Collins originated in New York, and takes its name from the Great Tom Collins Hoax of 1874, a practical joke which involved telling a friend that a man named Tom Collins had been insulting them, and that he could be found in a bar some distance away, and took the city by storm. This is supported by the fact that the first known written occurrence of a Tom Collins cocktail recipe is found in the 1876 edition of Jerry Thomas' 'The Bartender's Guide'.

An alternative story attributes the drink to a Collins who started work at a New York tavern called the Whitehouse in 1873 and started pouring a thirst quencher made with gin. Another identifies a different Tom Collins, who worked as a bartender in New Jersey and New York area.
There are apparently also versions of its creation in San Francisco and Australia, and it is not impossible that the drink evolved in two or more places independently.

There is also debate as to whether Old Tom gin, Tanqueray London dry gin or Dutch genever was the original spirit base. Other spirits have since spawned an entire family of Collins' variants as follows:

Captain Collins (with Canadian whiskey)
Colonel Collins (with Bourbon)
Jack Collins (with vodka)
Jock or Sandy Collins (with Scotch whisky)

Joe Collins (with vodka)
John Collins (with Tanqueray London dry gin)
Mike Collins (with Irish whiskey)
Pedro Collins (with light white rum)
Pepito Collins (with tequila)
Pierre Collins (with cognac/brandy)
Tom Collins (with old tom gin)
Vodka Collins (AKA Joe Collins)

COLONEL COLLINS 🔑

★★★★☆

Glass: Collins
Garnish: Orange slice & cherry on stick (sail)
Method: SHAKE first three ingredients with ice and strain into ice-filled glass. TOP with soda, stir and serve with straws.

2	shots	Maker's Mark bourbon
1	shot	Freshly squeezed lemon juice
½	shot	Monin Pure Cane 2:1 sugar syrup
Top up with		Soda (club soda)

We say: Classic Collins variation.
Origin: Sweetened, soured and diluted bourbon.

COLONEL T 🔑

★★★½☆

Glass: Sling
Garnish: Pineapple leaf
Method: SHAKE all ingredients with ice and strain into ice-filled glass.

2	shots	Maker's Mark bourbon
1	shot	De Kuyper Apricot Brandy liqueur
2½	shots	Fresh pressed pineapple juice

We say: Mellow and long with pineapple, apricot and bourbon.

COLONEL'S BIG OPU

★★★½☆

Glass: Collins
Garnish: Orange slice & cherry on stick (sail)
Method: SHAKE first 3 ingredients with ice and strain into ice-filled glass. TOP up with champagne and serve with straws.

1	shot	Tanqueray London dry gin
1	shot	Triple Sec
½	shot	Freshly squeezed lime juice
1	dash	Orange bitters
Top up with		Brut champagne

We say: A long, fruity yet dry drink charged with champagne.
Origin: Adapted from Victor J. Bergeron's and taken from his 'Trader Vic's Bartender's Guide' (1972 revised edition), where he writes "This is one of our old drinks. The colonel's big opu: the colonel's big belly."

BARTENDER'S TIP ROLLING

This is a gentle way of mixing a drink using a shaker and is most commonly used when making a Bloody Mary.

To do this charge your shaker with ingredients and ice as normal but rather than shaking, simply gently roll the shaker over and an over by holding the top and bottom of the shaker in each hand and then rotating your hand one over the other so tuning the shaker in a circular motion. Rolling should not be confused with the 'Cuban Roll' which is a term for mixing a drink using the throwing method.

THE COLONIAL COOLER NEW

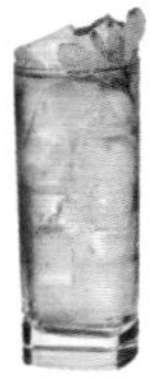

★★★★☆
Glass: Collins
Garnish: Mint sprig and pineapple wedge
Method: STIR first 5 ingredients with ice and strain into ice-filled glass. TOP with soda water.

1½	shots	Tanqueray London dry gin
1½	shots	Martini Rosso sweet vermouth
⅛	shot	Grand Marnier liqueur
⅛	shot	Amer Picon
1	dash	Angostura aromatic bitters
		Top up with Soda water

We say: Basically a 'Gin and It' lengthened with soda and spiced with dashes of Amer Picon, Angostura bitters and orange Curaçao.

Origin: This recipe is adapted from Charles H. Baker's 1939 The Gentlemen's Companion in which Baker writes that he encountered this drink in the mid-1920s in the Sandakan Club, North Borneo, during an excursion from the SS Resolute, a round-the-world steamer. The steamer anchored some 14 miles off shore and Baker and his companions set ashore in two lifeboats, both of which failed to make dry land due to engine trouble. A Borneo prahu "with a sail like a striped butterfly and a gent in a G-string and a headdress" raised the alarm and the adventurers were eventually towed ashore by a British North Borneo Company tug.

"We first went out to the Sandakan Club – there'd be a British Club on Mount Everest if 2 Britishers could stand the cold there! – and had these Coolers, through the courtesy of an American who was sentimental enough to fetch a mint root out with him."

"To 1 jigger of dry gin add the same of Italian vermouth. To this base donate 1 dash of each Angostura and Amer Picon, and 1 tsp of orange Curaçao. Stir with a goodly lump of ice in a small highball or sour glass, and top off with a squirt of soda, garnished with 2 sprigs of mint and a stick of ripe pineapple."

COLONIAL ROT

★★★☆☆
Glass: Collins
Garnish: Mint sprig
Method: Lightly MUDDLE mint in base of shaker just enough to bruise. Add next 4 ingredients, SHAKE with ice and fine strain into ice-filled glass. TOP with half soda and half lemonade.

7	fresh	Mint leaves
½	shot	Absinthe
1	shot	Ketel One Citroen vodka
½	shot	Monin Pure Cane 2:1 sugar syrup
½	shot	Freshly squeezed lime juice
		Top up with Half soda and half lemonade

We say: Long and green with more than a touch of the green fairy.

COLONY

★★★★☆
Glass: Martini
Garnish: Grapefruit zest twist
Method: SHAKE all ingredients with ice and fine strain into chilled glass.

1½	shots	Tanqueray London dry gin
¾	shot	Freshly squeezed grapefruit juice
¼	shot	Luxardo Maraschino liqueur

We say: Grapefruit and maraschino balance each other in the gin based classic.
Origin: Created during the Prohibition period at New York's Colony speakeasy, possibly by bartender Marco Hattem. The Colony attracted an upmarket Clientele, including the Vanderbilts and Windsors. The liquor was kept in an elevator which would be sent to either that attic or the basement if federal agents raided.

COLORADO BULLDOG

★★☆☆☆
Glass: Collins
Garnish: None
Method: SHAKE first 4 ingredients with ice and strain into ice-filled glass. TOP with cola.

1½	shots	Ketel One vodka
1	shot	Kahlúa coffee liqueur
1	shot	Double (heavy) cream
1	shot	Milk
		Top up with Coca-Cola

Variant: Colorado Mother (with tequila in place of vodka).
We say: This dog's bite is hidden by cream.

COLUMBUS DAIQUIRI

★★★☆☆
Glass: Martini
Garnish: Lime wedge
Method: SHAKE all ingredients with ice and fine strain into chilled glass.

1	shot	Bacardi Oro golden rum
1	shot	De Kuyper Apricot Brandy liqueur
1	shot	Freshly squeezed lime juice
½	shot	Chilled mineral water

We say: A tangy, apricot flavoured Daiquiri.

THE COMET

★★★★☆
Glass: Martini
Garnish: Lemon zest twist
Method: MUDDLE grapes in base of shaker. Add other ingredients, SHAKE with ice and fine strain into chilled glass.

7	fresh	Seedless white grapes
2	shots	Cognac VSOP
¾	shot	Grand Marnier liqueur
1	dash	Angostura aromatic bitters

We say: Cognac with freshly extracted grape juice and a splash of orange liqueur.
Origin: Created by Eddie Clark at the Albany Club, Albermarle Street, London, to celebrate the launch of the Comet jetliner in 1952.

COMET COCKTAIL

★★★★☆
Glass: Coupette
Garnish: Lemon zest twist
Method: SHAKE all ingredients with ice and fine strain into chilled glass.

2	shots	Cognac VSOP
½	shot	Drambuie
¼	shot	Freshly squeezed lime juice
¼	shot	Chilled mineral water

We say: Something of a cross between a Sidecar and a Rusty Nail. A successful hybrid.

COMMODORE #1

★★★★☆

Glass: Martini
Garnish: Maraschino cherry
Method: SHAKE all ingredients with ice and fine strain into chilled glass.

2	shots	Bacardi Oro golden rum
½	shot	Freshly squeezed lemon juice
¼	shot	Monin Pure Cane 2:1 sugar syrup
⅛	shot	Pomegranate (grenadine) syrup
½	fresh	Egg white

We say: A smooth, sweet Daiquiri with flavoursome rum.
Origin: Adapted from David A. Embury's 1948 '*The Fine Art of Mixing Drinks*', where he writes, "Another version of the Commodore calls for whisky instead of rum, omits the egg white, and uses orange bitters in place of the grenadine. Obviously, the two Commodores command two different fleets."

COMMODORE #2

★★★★☆

Glass: Old-fashioned
Garnish: Maraschino cherry
Method: SHAKE all ingredients with ice and fine strain into ice-filled glass.

2	shots	Maker's Mark bourbon
¾	shot	White Crème de Cacao
¼	shot	Pomegranate (grenadine) syrup
½	shot	Freshly squeezed lemon juice
2	dashes	Angostura aromatic bitters

We say: Fruity, tangy Bourbon, surprisingly dry despite its sweet ingredients.
Origin: Recipe adapted from Albert S. Crockett's 1935 '*Old Waldorf Bar Days*'. The original recipe calls for equal parts lemon juice, bourbon and crème de cacao with a dash of grenadine, and for the drink to be served 'straight-up' - we believe it better suited to being served on the rocks.

CONAN DOYLE NEW

★★★★★★

Glass: Old-fashioned
Garnish: Lemon zest twist
Method: STIR ingredients with ice and strain into-filled glass.

2	shots	Talisker single malt whisky
¼	shot	Taylor's Velvet Falernum 'liqueur
3	dashes	Bitters (whiskey barrel aged)

We say: A literary riff on a Corn 'n' Oil – elementary but tasty.
Origin: Discovered in 2008 at Tonic Bar, Edinburgh, Scotland.

STAR RATINGS EXPLAINED

★★★★★ Excellent

★★★★⯪ Recommended   ★★★★☆ Praiseworthy
★★★⯪☆ Commended   ★★★☆☆ Mediocre
★★⯪☆☆ Disappointing   ★★☆☆☆ Pretty awful
★⯪☆☆☆ Shameful   ★☆☆☆☆ Disgusting

CONCEALED WEAPON

★★★☆☆

Glass: Old-fashioned
Garnish: Lemon zest twist
Method: SHAKE all ingredients with ice and strain into ice-chilled glass.

1	shot	Absinthe
1	shot	Chambord black raspberry liqueur
¾	shot	Freshly squeezed lemon juice
½	shot	Monin Pure Cane 2:1 sugar syrup
1	dash	Angostura aromatic bitters
1	dash	Peychaud's aromatic bitters
½	fresh	Egg white

We say: Absinthe is the 'weapon' in this full-on short berry drink.
Origin: Created in 2000 by Danny Smith at Che, London, England.

CONGO BLUE

★★★⯪☆

Glass: Martini
Garnish: Lemon zest twist
Method: SHAKE all ingredients with ice and fine strain into chilled glass.

1¼	shots	Żubrówka bison vodka
½	shot	Midori green melon liqueur
½	shot	Crème de Mûre liqueur
1	shot	Pressed apple juice
¼	shot	Freshly squeezed lemon juice

We say: Flavoursome and sweet.
Origin: Created in 1999 by Marc Dietrich at Atlantic Bar & Grill, London and apparently named after the beauty of the Congo sunset.

CONTINENTAL SOUR NEW

★★★★☆

Glass: Old-fashioned
Garnish: None
Method: SHAKE first five ingredients with ice and fine strain into ice-filled glass. Finish with port float.

2	shots	Maker's Mark bourbon
1	shot	Freshly squeezed lemon juice
½	fresh	Monin Pure Cane 2:1 sugar syrup
1	dash	Angostura aromatic bitters
½	shot	Egg white
¼	shot	Warre's Otima tawny port

We say: A Whiskey Sour made 'continental' by the addition of a splash of port.
Origin: Discovered in May 2010 at Stagger Lee, Berlin, Germany

COOL MARTINI

★★★⯪☆

Glass: Martini
Garnish: Apple fan
Method: SHAKE all ingredients with ice and fine strain into chilled glass.

1½	shots	Midori green melon liqueur
1	shot	Tequila 100% Agave
1½	shots	Ocean Spray cranberry juice

We say: Tastes nothing like the ingredients - which include melon, tequila and cranberry juice. Try it and see if you taste toffee.

COOL ORCHARD

★★★★☆

Glass: Old-fashioned
Garnish: Pineapple wedge & maraschino cherry
Method: MUDDLE ginger in base of shaker. Add other ingredients, SHAKE with ice and fine strain into ice-filled glass.

2	slices	**Fresh root ginger (thumbnail sized)**
1½	shots	**Bacardi 8yo aged rum**
½	shot	**Monin Ginger syrup**
¼	shot	**Monin Almond (orgeat) syrup**
1	shot	**Fresh pressed pineapple juice**
¼	shot	**Freshly squeezed lime juice**
½	shot	**Vanilla schnapps**

We say: An unusual line up of ingredients combine to make a great drink.
Origin: Created in 2001 by Douglas Ankrah for Akbar, Soho, London, England

COOLMAN MARTINI

★★★★½

Glass: Martini
Garnish: Orange zest twist
Method: SHAKE all ingredients with ice and fine strain into chilled glass.

1¾	shots	**Ketel One vodka**
½	shot	**Triple Sec**
2	shots	**Pressed apple juice**
¼	shot	**Freshly squeezed lemon juice**

We say: Fragrant and complex. Integrated hints of apple and orange are laced with grassy vodka.
Origin: Created in 2001 by Jack Coleman at The Library Bar, Lanesborough Hotel, London, England.

COOPERSTOWN

★★★☆☆

Glass: Coupette
Garnish: Orange zest twist (discarded) & mint sprig
Method: STIR all ingredients (including mint) with ice and fine strain into chilled glass.

8	fresh	**Mint leaves**
2½	shots	**Tanqueray London dry gin**
¼	shot	**Martini Extra Dry vermouth**
¼	shot	**Martini Rosso sweet vermouth**

We say: A minty Perfect Martini which is made more widely appreciable by the addition of half a barspoon of sugar syrup.

STAR RATINGS EXPLAINED

★★★★★ Excellent

★★★★½ Recommeded	★★★★☆ Praiseworthy
★★★½☆ Commended	★★★☆☆ Mediocre
★★½☆☆ Disappointing	★★☆☆☆ Pretty awful
★½☆☆☆ Shameful	★☆☆☆☆ Disgusting

COPPER ILLUSION

★★★★☆

Glass: Old-fashioned
Garnish: Orange zest twist
Method: STIR all ingredients with ice and strain into ice-filled glass.

1½	shots	**Tanqueray London dry gin**
¾	shot	**Triple Sec**
¾	shot	**Campari Bitter**

Variant: Negroni
We say: Basically a Negroni with liqueur replacing sweet vermouth. Like the Italian classic this is both bitter and sweet.
Origin: Unknown but brought to my attention in 2005 courtesy of Angus Winchester and alconomics.com.

COQUETAIL AU VANILLA

★★★★½

Glass: Old-fashioned
Garnish: Maraschino cherry
Method: SHAKE all ingredients with ice and strain into glass filled with crushed ice. Serve with straws.

2	shots	**Vanilla-infused Bacardi rum**
¼	shot	**Taylor's Velvet Falernum liqueur**

We say: This drink may look fluffy and sweet but it's dry and lightly spiced. Perfect for a sunny afternoon.
Origin: An adaptation of a classic by Simon Difford.

CORDLESS SCREWDRIVER

★★★☆☆

Glass: Shot
Garnish: Sugar coated orange slice
Method: POUR vodka and champagne into glass and serve. Instruct drinker to down in one and then bite into the orange wedge.

1 shot	**Ketel One Oranje vodka**
Top up with	**Brut champagne**

We say: A slammer-style drink for those looking for a fruity alternative to tequila.

CORN'N'OIL NEW

★★★★☆

Glass: Old-fashioned
Garnish: Lime zest twist (discarded) & lime slice
Method: STIR all ingredients with ice and strain into-filled glass.

2	shots	**Bacardi Oro golden rum**
½	shot	**Taylor's Velvet Falernum liqueur**
2	dashes	**Angostura aromatic bitters**

AKA: Corning Oil
We say: Rum slightly sweetened and flavoured with the lime and clove flavours of falernum.
Origin: Popular in the Caribbean, particularly Barbados and Jamaica, the origins of the Corn'n'Oil are lost in time.

CORNWALL NEGRONI

★★★★⯪

Glass: Coupette
Garnish: Orange zest twist (flamed)
Method: STIR all ingredients with ice and strain into chilled glass.

2	shots	Tanqueray London dry gin
½	shot	Campari Bitter
½	shot	Carpano Punt E Mes
½	shot	Martini Rosso sweet vermouth
1	dash	Regan's Orange #6

We say: A Negroni-style cocktail served up. Heavy on the gin and relatively light on Campari and vermouth. It's a formula that works but like us, you may prefer yours served on the rocks.
Origin: Created in 2006 by Philip Ward, New York, USA after attending Gaz Regan's Cocktails in the Country workshop in Cornwall-on-Hudson.

CORONATION

★★★☆☆

Glass: Collins
Garnish: Maraschino cherry
Method: STIR first 5 ingredients with ice and strain into ice-filled glass. TOP with soda, stir and serve with straws.

1	shot	Tio Pepe fino sherry
2	shots	Sauvignon blanc wine
¼	shot	Luxardo Maraschino liqueur
1	shot	Martini Extra Dry vermouth
2	dashes	Angostura aromatic bitters
Top up with		Soda (club soda)

We say: Light and aromatic.

CORONATION COCKTAIL NO.1

★★★★⯪

Glass: Martini
Garnish: Orange zest twist
Method: STIR all ingredients with ice and strain into chilled glass.

1½	shots	Tio Pepe fino sherry
¼	shot	Luxardo Maraschino liqueur
1½	shots	Martini Extra Dry vermouth
2	dashes	Orange bitters

We say: Medium dry and wonderfully aromatic.
Origin: Adapted from Harry Craddock's 1930 '*The Savoy Cocktail Book*'.

CORPSE REVIVER NO.BLUE

★★★★☆

Glass: Coupette
Garnish: Lemon zest twist
Method: SHAKE all ingredients with ice and fine strain into chilled glass.

1	shot	Tanqueray London dry gin
1	shot	Lillet Blanc
1	shot	Bols Blue Curaçao liqueur
1	shot	Freshly squeezed lemon juice
⅛	shot	Absinthe

We say: "Considering it's blue, I quite like it," was the general opinion from across the Cabinet Room bar.
Origin: Created by Jacob Briars as a reaction to a Facebook group called 'A Jihad on all Blue Drinks'.

CORPSE REVIVER NO.1 #1

★★★⯪☆

Glass: Martini
Garnish: Orange zest twist
Method: STIR ingredients with ice and strain into chilled glass.

1½	shots	Cognac VSOP
¾	shot	Calvados/Applejack brandy
¾	shot	Martini Rosso sweet vermouth
½	shot	Chilled mineral water

We say: Dry and potent. A 'pick-me-up' hangover cure - or possibly put-you-right-back-down-again!
Origin: Created by Frank Meier, Ritz Bar, Paris, France. This recipe was adapted from Harry Craddock's 1930 '*The Savoy Cocktail Book*', where he writes, "To be taken before 11am, or whenever steam or energy are needed."

CORPSE REVIVER NO.1 #2 (GILBERG'S RECIPE)

★★★⯪☆

Glass: Martini
Garnish: Lemon zest twist
Method: STIR all ingredients with ice and strain into chilled glass.

2	shots	Calvados/Applejack brandy
¾	shot	Cognac VSOP
¾	shot	Martini Rosso sweet vermouth

We say: Strong enough to awaken the dead.
Origin: In his book 'The *Joy of Mixology*', Gary Regan recommends this version of the Corpse Reviver, which he writes was originally created in 2001 by Steve Gilberg, publisher of happyhours.com

CORPSE REVIVER NO.2 #1 (SAVOY RECIPE)

  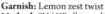

★★★★☆

Glass: Martini
Garnish: Lemon zest twist
Method: SHAKE all ingredients with ice and fine strain into chilled glass.

¾	shot	Tanqueray London dry gin
¾	shot	Cointreau triple sec
¾	shot	Lillet Blanc
¾	shot	Freshly squeezed lemon juice
⅛	shot	La Fée Parisienne (68%) absinthe

We say: Well-balanced with zesty lemon and absinthe just shinning above other ingredients.
Origin: Adapted from 1930 *Savoy Cocktail Book* where Harry Craddock says of this drink, "Four of these taken in swift succession will unrevive the corpse again". Harry originally stipulated Kina Lillet as the dry vermouth..

CORPSE REVIVER NO.2 #2

★★★★☆

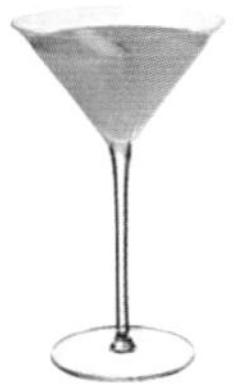

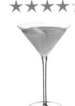

Glass: Martini
Garnish: Lemon zest twist
Method: SHAKE all ingredients with ice and fine strain into chilled glass.

¾	shot	**Tanqueray London dry gin**
¾	shot	**Chartreuse Yellow liqueur**
¾	shot	**Martini Extra dry vermouth**
¾	shot	**Freshly squeezed lemon juice**
⅛	shot	**La Fée Parisienne (68%) absinthe**

We say: If a mouthwash tasted great and kicked you in the balls, then this would be it.
Origin: We've noticed this version is popular with modern day bartenders, who, where possible follow Harry Craddock's original stipulation for Kina Lillet as dry vermouth.

CORPSE REVIVER #3

★★★★☆

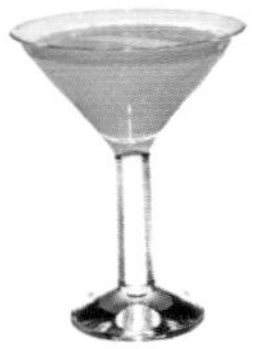

Glass: Martini
Garnish: Lemon zest twist
Method: SHAKE all ingredients with ice and fine strain into chilled glass.

¾	shot	**Tanqueray London dry gin**
¾	shot	**Swedish Punch liqueur**
¾	shot	**Cointreau triple sec**
⅛	shot	**La Fée Parisienne (68%) absinthe**
¾	shot	**Freshly squeezed lemon juice**

We say: Adapted from Victor Bergeron's '*Trader Vic's Bartender's Guide*' (1972 revised edition).
Origin: Perhaps a touch sweet but the kill or cure alcohol is well masked.

COSMOGRONI

★★★½☆

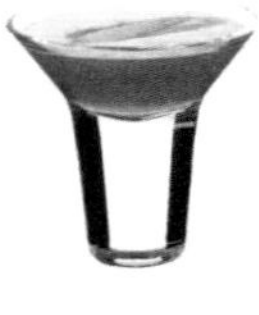

Glass: Martini
Garnish: Orange zest twist
Method: SHAKE all ingredients with ice and fine strain into chilled glass.

½	shot	**Tanqueray London dry gin**
1	shot	**Campari Bitter**
¼	shot	**Martini Rosso sweet vermouth**
1½	shots	**Ocean Spray cranberry juice**

We say: One for Campari lovers.
Origin: Recipe adapted from one discovered on DrinkBoy.com in February 2008. If this is your drink, please let us know.

STAR RATINGS EXPLAINED

★★★★★ Excellent

★★★★½ Recommeded	★★★★☆ Praiseworthy
★★★½☆ Commended	★★★☆☆ Mediocre
★★½☆☆ Disappointing	★★☆☆☆ Pretty awful
★½☆☆☆ Shameful	★☆☆☆☆ Disgusting

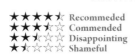

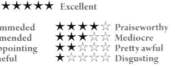

COSMOPOLITAN #1 (DIFFORD'S FORMULA)

★★★★½

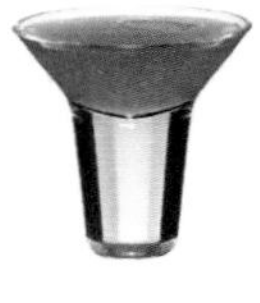

Glass: Martini
Garnish: Orange zest twist (flamed)
Method: SHAKE all ingredients with ice and fine strain into chilled glass.

1	shot	**Ketel One vodka**
1	shot	**Triple Sec**
1½	shots	**Ocean Spray cranberry juice**
½	shot	**Freshly squeezed lime juice**
1	dash	**Orange bitters**

We say: An authentic Cosmopolitan should be made with citrus vodka and this formula also works well if flavoured vodka is substituted. However, I prefer the simplicity of this recipe which when quality juice with at least 24% cranberry is used, the balance of vodka, citrus, berry fruit and sweetness is perfect.
Origin: The Cosmopolitan is one of those drinks that has had various incarnations through the ages - some of them, quite probably, independent of one another. And during the 1990s, the familiar blend of cranberry, citrus and vodka was one of the most popular cocktails in London and New York.

Most people agree a Cosmopolitan appeared on the West Coast of America at some point during the 1980s, and travelled from there to New York and beyond. Cheryl Cook has a claim to have invented the drink during the latter half of the 1980s while head bartender at The Strand on Washington Avenue, South Beach, Miami. She apparently based her drink on the newly available Absolut Citron vodka and added a splash of triple sec, a dash of Rose's lime and, in her own words, "just enough cranberry to make it oh so pretty in pink".

Her version is believed to have travelled by way of San Francisco to Manhattan where Toby Cecchini is credited with first using fresh lime juice in place of Rose's at his Passerby bar.

A likely early ancestor of the Cosmopolitan is the Harpoon, a drink promoted by Ocean Spray during the 1960s which consisted of vodka, cranberry juice and a squeeze of fresh lime. And a long-forgotten 1934 book of gin recipes, '*Pioneers of Mixing Gin at Elite Bars*', contains a recipe for a Cosmopolitan that is very similar to today's drink, only with lemon in place of lime, gin in place of vodka, and raspberry in place of cranberry.

Whatever the origin, however, it was *Sex And The City's* Carrie Bradshaw who popularised the drink when she swapped Martinis for Cosmos. And New York's Dale DeGroff played a large part in refining today's popular recipe.

COSMOPOLITAN #2 (DEGROFF'S FORMULA)

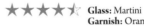

★★★★½

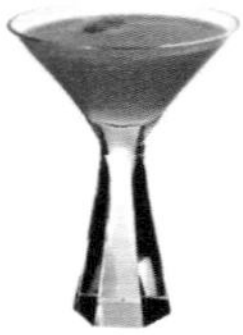

Glass: Martini
Garnish: Orange zest twist (flamed)
Method: SHAKE all ingredients with ice and fine strain into chilled glass.

1½	shots	**Ketel One Citroen vodka**
½	shot	**Triple Sec**
1	shot	**Ocean Spray cranberry juice**
¼	shot	**Freshly squeezed lime juice**

We say: This is the definitive Cosmo recipe from the man most associated with the drinks development and popularity.
Origin: . Although it is generally agreed that the Cosmopolitan originated on America's West Coast sometime during the 1980s, this drink is most closely identified with New York City where bar legend, Dale DeGroff, and HBO's '*Sex and the City*' perfected the drink and made it stylish.

This recipe is from Dale's 2002 'The Craft of the Cocktail' where he also explains that while he did not invent the Cosmopolitan, in his own words, "What I did do was popularize a definitive recipe that became widely accepted as the standard."Dale put the drink on his menu at New York's Rainbow Room in 1996 and shortly after it was reported that Madonna had enjoyed one. As a result Dale received calls from all over the world asking for the recipe, which he had perfected by adding a dash of Cointreau and a flamed orange peel twist. New York Magazine credited Dale with the drinks' invention, other publications followed this and he was asked to present it on several television stations.When the HBO television series, '*Sex and the City*', debuted in 1998, its creators decided the Cosmopolitan would be the perfect accompaniment to Carrie Bradshaw's fashionista Manhattan lifestyle.

COSMOPOLITAN #3 (1934 RECIPE)

★★★★☆

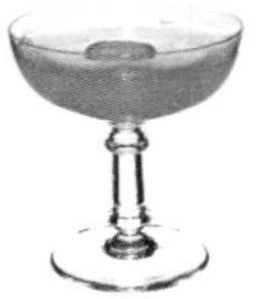

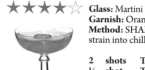

Glass: Martini
Garnish: Orange zest twist
Method: SHAKE all ingredients with ice and fine strain into chilled glass.

2	shots	**Tanqueray London dry gin**
½	shot	**Triple Sec**
¾	shot	**Freshly squeezed lemon juice**
¼	shot	**Raspberry syrup (1 juice to 1 sugar)**

We say: Reminiscent of a Sidecar and, depending on your syrup, well balanced. Thanks to drinkboy.com forum for first bringing this drink to my attention.
Origin: Recipe adapted from 1934 '*Pioneers of Mixing Gin at Elite Bars*'.

COSMOPOLITAN DELIGHT UPDATED

★★★★☆

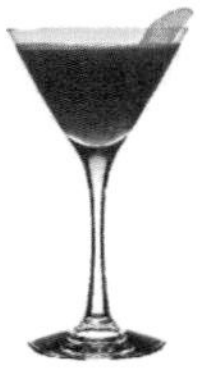

Glass: Martini
Garnish: Orange zest twist (flamed)
Method: SHAKE all ingredients with ice and fine strain into chilled glass.

1½	shots	**Cognac VSOP**
½	shot	**Grand Marnier liqueur**
1¼	shots	**Shiraz red wine**
¼	shot	**Monin Almond (orgeat) syrup**
¾	shot	**Freshly squeezed lemon juice**
¼	shot	**Monin Pure Cane 2:1 sugar syrup**

We say: No relation to the modern Cosmopolitan, this is a mellow, balanced blend of citrus, brandy and red wine.
Origin: Adapted from Dale DeGroff's book, 'The Craft of the Cocktail'. He credits the original recipe to a 1902 book by Charlie Paul.

COUNTRY BREEZE

★★★½☆

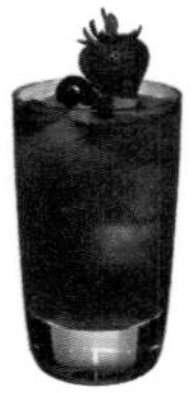

Glass: Collins
Garnish: Seasonal berries
Method: SHAKE all ingredients with ice and strain into ice-filled glass.

2	shots	**Tanqueray London dry gin**
3½	shots	**Pressed apple juice**
½	shot	**Crème de cassis liqueur**

We say: Not too sweet. The gin character shines through the fruit.

COVADONGA

★★★☆☆

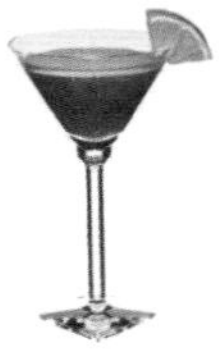

Glass: Martini
Garnish: Orange slice
Method: SHAKE all ingredients with ice and fine strain into chilled glass.

1½	shots	**Campari Bitter**
1	shot	**Martini Rosso sweet vermouth**
1	shot	**Freshly squeezed orange juice**
½	shot	**Pomegranate (grenadine) syrup**
5	dashes	**Angostura aromatic bitters**

We say: Sweet, tart and fruity.
Origin: Adapted form Victor Bergeron's '*Trader Vic's Bartender's Guide*' (1972 revised edition).

COWBOY HOOF MARTINI

★★★½☆

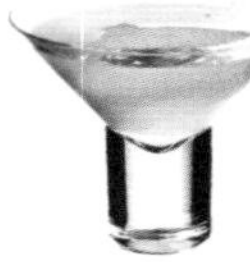

Glass: Martini
Garnish: Orange zest twist
Method: SHAKE all ingredients (including mint) with ice and fine strain into chilled glass.

7	fresh	**Mint leaves**
3	shots	**Tanqueray London dry gin**
½	shot	**Monin Pure Cane 2:1 sugar syrup**
3	dashes	**Orange bitters**

Variant: Detroit Martini
We say: Sweetened gin shaken with fresh mint.
Origin: Created in the early 90s by Dick Bradsell at Detroit, London, England.

COX'S DAIQUIRI

★★★★★

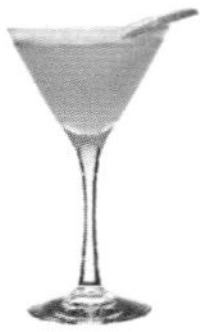

Glass: Martini
Garnish: Cox's apple ring (in memory of Jennings Cox)
Method: SHAKE all ingredients with ice and fine strain into chilled glass.

2½	shots	**Vanilla-infused Bacardi rum**
½	shot	**Freshly squeezed lime juice**
1	shot	**Fresh pressed pineapple juice**
¼	shot	**Monin Vanilla sugar syrup**

We say: Vanilla and pineapple bring out the sweetness of the rum against a citrus background.
Origin: One of two cocktails with which Simon Difford won 'The Best Daiquiri in London Competition' in 2002. It is named after Jennings Cox, the American mining engineer credited with first creating the Daiquiri.

CRANAPPLE BREEZE

★★★½☆

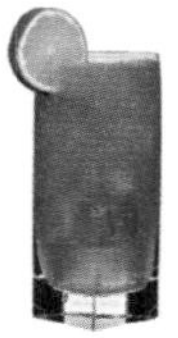

Glass: Collins
Garnish: Lime slice
Method: SHAKE first five ingredients with ice and strain into ice-filled glass. TOP with ginger ale and stir.

1	shot	**Ketel One Citroen vodka**
1	shot	**Triple Sec**
1	shot	**Ocean Spray cranberry juice**
1	shot	**Pressed apple juice**
½	shot	**Freshly squeezed lime juice**
Top up with		**Ginger ale**

We say: A refreshing cooler for a hot day by the pool.
Origin: Created in 2002 by Wayne Collins.

CRANBERRY & MINT MARTINI

★★★½☆

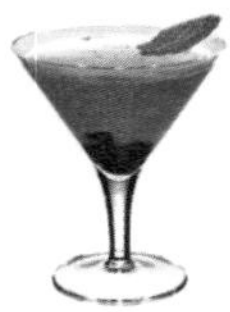

Glass: Martini
Garnish: Cranberries & mint leaf
Method: Lightly MUDDLE mint in base of shaker just enough to bruise. Add other ingredients, SHAKE with ice and fine strain into chilled glass.

8	fresh	**Mint leaves**
2	shots	**Ketel One vodka**
1½	shots	**Ocean Spray cranberry juice**
¼	shot	**Pomegranate (grenadine) syrup**

We say: This little red number combines the dryness of cranberry, the sweetness of grenadine and the fragrance of mint.
Origin: Created in 2003 by Simon Difford.|

CRANBERRY COOLER

★★★☆☆

Glass: Collins
Garnish: Orange slice
Method: SHAKE all ingredients with ice and strain into ice-filled glass.

2	shots	Amaretto liqueur
2	shots	Ocean Spray cranberry juice
2	shots	Freshly squeezed orange juice

We say: Easy drinking for those with a sweet tooth.

CRANBERRY DELICIOUS (MOCKTAIL)

★★★☆☆

Glass: Collins
Garnish: Mint sprig
Method: MUDDLE mint in base of shaker. Add other ingredients, SHAKE with ice and strain into ice-filled glass.

12	fresh	Mint leaves
1	shot	Freshly squeezed lime juice
½	shot	Monin Pure Cane 2:1 sugar syrup
4	shots	Ocean Spray cranberry juice
3	dashes	Angostura aromatic bitters

We say: Cranberry juice given more interest with mint, lime and bitters. This drink contains trace amounts of alcohol but remains an effective driver's option.
Origin: Adapted from a drink created in 2006 by Damian Windsor at Bin 8945 Wine Bar & Bistro, West Hollywood, USA.

CRANBERRY SAUCE

★★★½☆

Glass: Martini
Garnish: Lime wedge
Method: SHAKE all ingredients with ice and fine strain into chilled glass.

2	shots	Ketel One vodka
¾	shot	Lapponia cranberry liqueur
2½	shots	Ocean Spray cranberry juice
¼	shot	Freshly squeezed lime juice

We say: Rich, fruity flavour but with that customary dry cranberry finish.
Origin: Created in 2003 by Simon Difford.

CRAPPLE (MOCKTAIL)

★★★½☆

Glass: Collins
Garnish: Lime wedge
Method: SHAKE all ingredients with ice and strain into ice-filled glass. Serve with straws.

2½	shots	Ocean Spray cranberry juice
2	shots	Pressed apple juice
1	shot	Freshly squeezed lime juice
½	shot	Monin Pure Cane 2:1 sugar syrup

We say: Cranberry, apple and lime. Simple but refreshing and decidedly fruity.

CRÈME ANGLAISE MARTINI

★★★★☆

Glass: Martini
Garnish: Dust with chocolate powder
Method: SHAKE all ingredients with ice and fine strain into chilled glass.

1	shot	Vanilla-infused Ketel One vodka
2	shots	Advocaat liqueur
1	shot	Milk

We say: Very reminiscent of alcoholic crème anglaise.
Origin: Created in 2004 by Simon Difford.

CRÈME BRÛLÉE MARTINI

★★★½☆

Glass: Martini
Garnish: Dust with cinnamon powder
Method: SHAKE all ingredients with ice and fine strain into chilled glass.

2	shots	Vanilla-infused Ketel One vodka
½	unit	Giffard caramel liqueur
¾	shot	Cuarenta y Tres (Licor 43) liqueur
1	shot	Double (heavy) cream
½	fresh	Egg yolk

We say: OK, so there's no crust, but this does contain egg yolk, caramel, vanilla, sugar and cream. Due to the cinnamon, it even has a brown top.
Origin: Adapted from a drink created in 2002 by Yannick Miseriaux at the Fifth Floor Bar, London, England.

CRÈME DE CAFÉ

★★★½☆

Glass: Old-fashioned
Garnish: None
Method: SHAKE ingredients with ice and strain into ice-filled glass.

¾	shot	Bacardi Oro golden rum
1	shot	Kahlúa coffee liqueur
¾	shot	Luxardo Sambuca dei Cesari
1	shot	Double (heavy) cream
1	shot	Milk

We say: Coffee predominates over the creaminess with hints of aniseed and rum.

CREAM CAKE

★★★★½☆

Glass: Martini
Garnish: Crumbled Cadbury's Flake bar
Method: SHAKE all ingredients with ice and fine strain into chilled glass.

1¼	shots	Baileys Irish cream liqueur
1¼	shots	Peachtree peach schnapps
1¼	shots	Amaretto liqueur
1	shot	Double (heavy) cream

We say: Creamy pleasure for the sweet of tooth.

CREAM SODA

★★★½☆

Glass: Collins
Garnish: Lemon slice
Method: SHAKE first 3 ingredients with ice and strain into ice-filled glass. TOP with lemonade and serve with straws.

1½	shots	Vanilla-infused Ketel One vodka
1	shot	Bacardi Superior rum
½	shot	Cuarenta y Tres (Licor 43) liqueur
Top up with		Lemonade/Sprite/7-Up

We say: An alcoholic cream soda created for Debbie Rizzo who expressed a desire for just such a thing.
Origin: Created in 2008 by Simon Difford at The Cabinet Room, London, England.

CREAMSICLE

★★★½☆

Glass: Martini
Garnish: Orange zest twist
Method: SHAKE all ingredients with ice and fine strain into chilled glass.

1	shot	Ketel One Oranje vodka
1	shot	Grand Marnier liqueur
½	shot	Double (heavy) cream
½	shot	Milk
¼	shot	Monin Pure Cane 2:1 sugar syrup

We say: A creamy orange number with a surprisingly pleasant taste.

CREAMY BEE

★★★★☆

Glass: Martini
Garnish: Cinnamon & sugar rim with raspberry
Method: SHAKE all ingredients with ice and fine strain into chilled glass

1½	shots	Krupnik spiced honey liqueur
½	shot	Baileys Irish cream liqueur
½	shot	Chambord black raspberry liqueur
½	shot	Hazelnut liqueur
¼	shot	Goldschläger cinnamon schnapps

We say: Creamy cinnamon with hints of honey, nuts and berries.
Origin: Created in 2002 at Hush, London, England and originally made with cinnamon syrup in place of Goldschläger.

CREAMY CREAMSICLE

★★★½☆

Glass: Martini
Garnish: None
Method: SHAKE all ingredients with ice and fine strain into chilled glass.

½	shot	Ketel One Oranje vodka
1¼	shots	Amaretto liqueur
1	shot	Freshly squeezed orange juice
¾	shot	Milk
¾	shot	Double (heavy) cream

We say: Ultra smooth and creamy. Dessert, anyone

CREAMY VANILLA COLADA NEW

★★★★½

Glass: Coupette
Garnish: Dust with chocolate powder
Method: SHAKE all ingredients with ice and fine strain into chilled glass.

2	shots	Rum Aged
1½	shots	Bols Natural Yoghurt liqueur
6	drops	Vanilla extract

AKA: White Christmas
We say: Creamy yoghurt married with aged rum and richly flavoured with vanilla.
Origin: Created in 2011 by Simon Difford at the Cabinet Room, London, England.

CREOLE CONTENTMENT NEW

★★★★☆

Glass: Coupette
Garnish: Maraschino cherry
Method: STIR all ingredients with ice and strain into chilled glass.

1½	shots	Courvoisier VSOP Exclusif
1	shot	Sercial (dry) Madeira wine
¼	shot	Luxardo maraschino liqueur
1	dash	Orange bitters
½	shot	Chilled mineral water

We say: If using a sweeter Madeira such as Verdelho/Rainwater (medium dry) or Bual (medium sweet) you'll need to adjust this finely balanced cocktail. Even Baker himself says says it "needs a little trimming". However, dry Sercial Madeira works best to produce a finely balanced complex cocktail.
Origin: This recipe is adapted from Charles H. Baker's 1939 'The Gentlemen's Companion' in which Baker writes, "Creole Contentment, an Insidious Pleasantry from the Charming-Hot-Bed of Intrigue and Culture which is the Pulse of the Great Delta Country - New Orleans.

"This hazard and liability to consistent maidenhood came to out desk through office of a friend whose father once was Episcopal Bishop of Washington, and who writes books about pirates. Don't treat this one lightly, mes amis....

"Of Cognac, Madeira wine and maraschino, take 1 pony; turn this into a bar glass with ice; toss in 1 dash of orange bitters, stir well, pour into a big Manhattan glass or saucer type champagne, and garnish with 3 maraschino cherries; red, green and white... Our personal experience is that it is better to cut the maraschino down by half, stepping up the cognac in that ratio. The business of the 3 cherries, while no doubt a pretty and chivalrous gesture of the feminine victim is, of course, sheerest swank. It is a good drink and needs a little trimming."

CREOLE COSMO

★★★★½

Glass: Martini
Garnish: Lime zest twist
Method: SHAKE all ingredients with ice and fine strain into chilled glass.

1	shot	Martinique agricole rum
1	shot	Clément Creole Shrubb liqueur
1	shot	Ocean Spray cranberry juice
½	shot	Freshly squeezed lime juice

We say: Dry tangy and more sophisticated than your bog-standard Cosmo.

CREOLE GIMLET NEW

★★★★☆

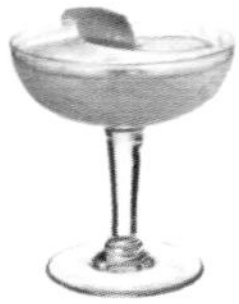

Glass: Coupette
Garnish: Lime zest twist
Method: STIR all ingredients with ice and strain into chilled glass.

2½	shots	**Tanqueray London dry gin**
½	shot	**Taylor's Velvet Falernum liqueur**
¼	shot	**Rose's lime cordial**
1	dash	**Peychaud's aromatic bitters**

We say: Falernum adds a touch of Caribbean spice to this Gimlet.
Origin: Created in 2009 by Gonçalo de Sousa Monteiro, Berlin, Germany.

CRIMEA

★★★☆☆

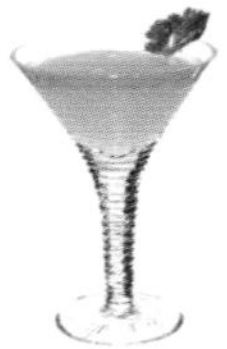

Glass: Martini
Garnish: Coriander leaf
Method: MUDDLE coriander in base of shaker. Add other ingredients, SHAKE with ice and fine strain into chilled glass.

5	fresh	**Coriander (cilantro)**
2	shots	**Tanqueray London dry gin**
1	shot	**Pressed apple juice**
¼	shot	**Freshly squeezed lemon juice**
⅛	shot	**Monin Pure Cane 2:1 sugar syrup**
½	shot	**Chilled mineral water**

We say: Fragrant, herbal gin with a hint of citrus.
Origin: Adapted from a drink discovered in 2006 at Ballroom, London, England.

CRIMSON BLUSH

★★★★☆

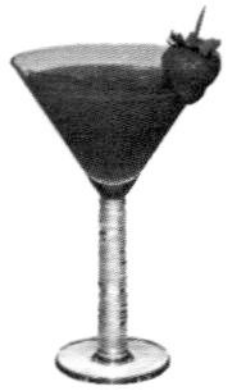

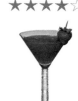

Glass: Martini
Garnish: Seasonal berries
Method: SHAKE all ingredients with ice and fine strain into chilled glass.

2	shots	**Ketel One Citroen vodka**
½	shot	**Chambord black raspberry liqueur**
2	shots	**Freshly squeezed grapefruit juice**
¼	shot	**Monin Pure Cane 2:1 sugar syrup**

We say: Well balanced, fruity sweet and sour.
Origin: Created in 2004 by Jonathan Lamm at The Admirable Crichton, London, England.

CROSSBOW

★★★☆☆

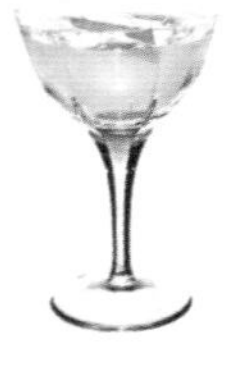

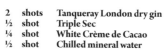

Glass: Martini
Garnish: Orange zest twist
Method: SHAKE all ingredients with ice and fine strain into chilled glass.

2	shots	**Tanqueray London dry gin**
½	shot	**Triple Sec**
¼	shot	**White Crème de Cacao**
½	shot	**Chilled mineral water**

We say: Surprisingly dry orange and chocolate laced with gin.
Origin: Adapted from a drink discovered in 2005 at Bar Opiume, Singapore.

CROUCHING TIGER

★★★☆☆

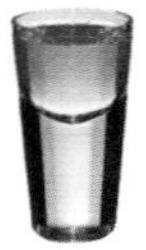

Glass: Shot
Garnish: None
Method: SHAKE all ingredients with ice and fine strain into chilled glass.

¾	shot	**Tequila 100% Agave**
½	shot	**Kwai Feh lychee liqueur**

We say: Tequila and lychee combine harmoniously in this semi - sweet shot.

THE CROW COCKTAIL

★★★☆☆

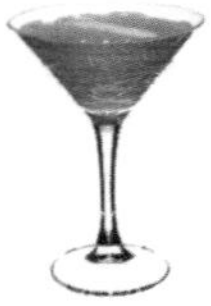

Glass: Martini
Garnish: Lemon zest twist
Method: SHAKE all ingredients with ice and fine strain into chilled glass.

2	shots	**Dewar's White label Scotch**
1	shot	**Freshly squeezed lemon juice**
½	shot	**Pomegranate (grenadine) syrup**

We say: If you use great syrup and have a penchant for Scotch then you could be pleasantly surprised by this drink.
Origin: Adapted from Harry Craddock's 1930 '*The Savoy Cocktail Book*'.

CROWN STAG

★★★½☆

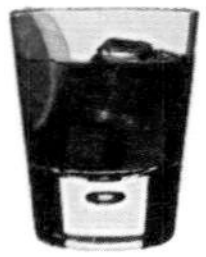

Glass: Old-fashioned
Garnish: Lemon slice
Method: SHAKE ingredients with ice and strain into ice-filled glass.

1½	shots	**Ketel One vodka**
1½	shots	**Jägermeister**
1	shot	**Chambord black raspberry liqueur**

We say: A surprisingly workable combination.

CRUEL INTENTION

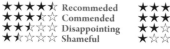

★★★½☆

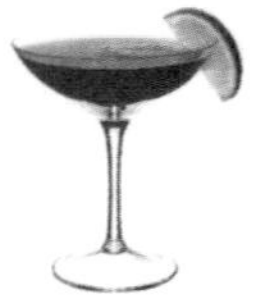

Glass: Martini
Garnish: Lime wedge
Method: SHAKE all ingredients with ice and fine strain into chilled glass.

2	shots	**Maker's Mark bourbon**
¼	shot	**De Kuyper Apricot Brandy liqueur**
¼	shot	**Amaretto liqueur**
1	shot	**Fresh pressed pineapple juice**
½	shot	**Freshly squeezed lime juice**

We say: Bourbon with a hint of apricot, almond, pineapple and lime. Hardly cruel!
Origin: Discovered in 2005 at The Mansion, Amsterdam, The Netherlands.

STAR RATINGS EXPLAINED

★★★★★ Excellent

★★★★½	Recommended	★★★★☆	Praiseworthy
★★★½☆	Commended	★★★☆☆	Mediocre
★★½☆☆	Disappointing	★★☆☆☆	Pretty awful
★½☆☆☆	Shameful	★☆☆☆☆	Disgusting

CRUSHED STRAWBERRY FIZZ

Glass: Collins (small 8oz)
Garnish: Strawberry
Method: MUDDLE strawberries in base of shaker. Add other ingredients apart from soda, SHAKE with ice and fine strain into chilled glass (without ice). TOP with soda.

3	fresh	Strawberries (hulled)
2	shots	Old Tom gin
1	shot	Freshly squeezed lemon juice
½	shot	Monin Pure Cane 2:1 sugar syrup
Top up with		Soda from siphon

We say: Fruity and all too easy to drink. Don't hold back, the lack of ice in this tall drink requires you consume while still cold. But responsibly, of course.
Origin: This Gin Fizz adaptation was created circa 1880 at the St. Nicholas Hotel, New York City.

CRUSTAS (GENERIC NAME)

Glass: Wine
Garnish: Find a lemon which fits into a small wineglass tightly enough to act as a watertight extension to the glass. Cut off both ends of the fruit and carefully remove the pulp to leave a barrel-shaped shell of skin. Place in the top of the glass. Wet the edge of the glass and exposed fruit shell with sugar syrup and dip in caster sugar to frost the edge of both peel and glass. Leave for a couple of hours to form a hard crust.
Method: SHAKE all ingredients with ice and fine strain into pre-prepared glass.

2	shots	Brandy, whisk(e)y, gin, rum etc.
½	shot	Freshly squeezed lemon juice
¼	shot	Monin Pure Cane 2:1 sugar syrup
1	dash	Angostura aromatic bitters

We say: Some cocktail historians, Ted Haigh included, consider the Crusta the forerunner of the Sidecar and in turn the Margarita. It's a very logical argument.
Origin: The invention of the Crusta is credited to a Joseph Santina at the Jewel of the South or a Joseph Santini at the City Exchange in New Orleans sometime during the 1840s or 1850s. It first appeared in print as 'The Brandy Crusta' in Jerry Thomas' 1862 bartender's guide.

Crustas always contain a spirit, lemon juice and sugar - sometimes in the form of a liqueur or liqueurs. They are so named due to their sugar rim, which should be applied hours before the drink is made so that it is dried hard, or indeed crusty, when the drink is served. Crustas are also distinguished by being garnished with a band of orange or lemon zest, and are drunk from the rim of the fruit, rather than the rim of the glass.

As David A. Embury writes in his 1948 'The Fine Art of Mixing Drinks', "The distinguishing feature of the Crusta is that the entire inside of the glass is lined with lemon or orange peel. The drink may be served in either a wineglass or an Old-Fashioned glass, although it is much harder to make the peel fit in the Old-Fashioned glass."

Embury goes on to say, "While the 'Brandy Crusta' is the most common form of this drink, it is, after all, merely a Sour-type drink served in fancy-style. Substitution of a different liquor as a base will give a Gin Crusta, a Rum Crusta, an Applejack Crusta, A Whisky Crusta, and so on."

CRUX

Glass: Martini
Garnish: Orange zest twist
Method: SHAKE all ingredients and fine strain into chilled glass.

1	shot	Cognac VSOP
1	shot	Triple Sec
1	shot	Dubonnet Red (French made)
1	shot	Freshly squeezed lemon juice

We say: The 'crux' of the matter is rarely as tasty as this fruity and none too sweet cognac.

CUBA LIBRE

Glass: Collins
Garnish: Lime wedge
Method: POUR ingredients into ice-filled glass, stir and serve with straws.

2	shots	Bacardi Superior rum
½	shot	Freshly squeezed lime juice
Top up with		Coca-Cola

Variant: Cuba Pintada and Cuba Campechana
We say: Basically a rum and coke with a squeeze of lime - but Cuba Libre has much more of a ring about it. And it is much more of a drink - the squeeze of lime adds layers of complexity and balances the sweetness of the cola.
Origin: The Cuba Libre was born out of Cuba's War of Independence with the Spanish, a war in which, like most Cubans, the Bacardi family were involved. In the late 1890s, Cuba's anti-colonial fighters were called the Mambí. Emilito Bacardi, eldest son of Emilio Bacardi, was one of them. He began his military service as aide de camp to Major General Antonio Maceo, Cuba's 'Bronze Titan', fighting the Spanish from Cuba's dense forests, or 'manigua'. During the war he was promoted to colonel, and became known as 'El Coronel'.

The war was scarcely over when, in late 1898 Warren Candler (brother of Asa Candler, then owner of Coca-Cola) sailed for Cuba, the first of twenty such trips. As a result of Warren's visits to Cuba, there in May 1899 the company hired a sales merchant to sell Coca-Cola syrup for use in soda fountains and appointed Jose Parejo, a Havana wine merchant as the Cuban distributor for Coca-Cola.

By 1900 Coco-Cola was both popular and widely available in Cuba so it is not surprising that American solders still garrisoned there started ordering Bacardi Cuban Rum and Coke with a squeeze of the ubiquitous lime. One solider in particular, Captain Russell of the US Signal Corp, is credited with starting this trend when one day in August 1900 he ordered the combination in a Havana bar. Naturally his drink sparked interest from the soldiers around him and before long the entire bar was drinking it. The Captain proposed a toast, 'Por Cuba libre!' in celebration of a 'free Cuba'. Fortunately for posterity, the event is supported by an affidavit from a witness, Fausto Rodriguez.

Rodriguez was a personal messenger to General Wood, appointed the military governor of Cuba after entering Santiago de Cuba on 17th July 1898, after Roosevelt's victory at the battle of San Juan Hill. After the Republic of Cuba was born on 20th May 1902, General Wood left Cuba and Fausto Rodriguez returned to Santiago de Cuba. Sixty-five years later, on 21st December 1964, Rodriguez told Emilito Bacardi the following story, affirmed under oath:

During the period of military intervention, two Americans opened and operated a bar called The American Bar on Neptuno Street, between Consulado and Prado in Havana. It was patronized almost exclusively by American soldiers and by American civilians who worked in the various government offices in Havana.

"While I was employed at the office of the Signal Corps, I became quite friendly with an American whose last name was Russell (I do not remember his given name). He worked in the office of the Chief Signal Officer. Mr Russell frequently took me to The American Bar where we used to drink Bacardi Rum and Coca-Cola."

"One afternoon in August 1900, I went to The American Bar with Mr

Russell, and he drank his usual Bacardi Rum and Coca-Cola. I just drank Coca-Cola, being only 14 years old. On that occasion, there was a group of American soldiers at the bar, and one of them asked Mr Russell what he was drinking. He told them it was Bacardi Rum and Coca-Cola and suggested they try it, which they did."

"The soldiers who drank the Bacardi Rum and Coca-Cola said they liked it, and wanted to know what the drink was called. When Mr Russell told them that the drink did not have a name, one of the soldiers said, "Let's give it a name". Another said, "How about calling it 'Cuba Libre'?" They all agreed and ordered another round of Bacardi Rum and Coca-Cola, calling it a Cuba Libre. To my best knowledge, this is the first time this phrase 'Cuba Libre' has been applied to a drink. Thus, the first Cuba Libre consisted of Bacardi Rum and Coca-Cola.

"During the American intervention, the words Cuba Libre - meaning Free Cuba - had a special political significance, and were used a great deal by the Cubans and Americans in Cuba. It seemed quite natural that the American soldiers selected and applied this popular slogan to this drink, which they considered indigenous to Cuba, consisting of Bacardi Rum and Coca-Cola. The name caught on quickly, and has remained popular to the present time." (sic)

The Cuba Libre peaked in popularity during the 1940s, partly aided by the Andrews Sisters who in 1945 had a hit with 'Rum and Coca-Cola', named after the drink's ingredients. During the war, all spirits production went over to industrial alcohol - in the absence of whiskey and gin, Americans turned to imported rum. The Cuba Libre is an enduring classic, still made with Bacardi rum and still enjoyed the world.

CUBA PINTADA

★★★☆☆

Glass: Collins
Garnish: Lime wedge
Method: POUR ingredients in to ice-filled glass, STIR and serve with straws.

2	shots	Bacardi Superior rum
1	shot	Coca-Cola
Top up with		Soda (club soda)

Variant: Cuba Campechana - rum with half soda and half cola; Cuba Libre - rum, cola and a dash of lime juice.
Origin: The name of this popular Cuban drink literally means 'stained Cuba' and there is just enough cola in this rum and soda to stain the drink brown.

CUBAN COCKTAIL NO.2 #1

★★★★☆

Glass: Martini
Garnish: Lemon zest twist
Method: SHAKE all ingredients with ice and fine strain into chilled glass.

1½	shots	Bacardi Superior rum
⅛	shot	Luxardo Maraschino liqueur
⅛	shot	Pomegranate (grenadine) syrup
¼	shot	Freshly squeezed lemon juice
1	dash	Orange bitters
½	shot	Chilled mineral water

We say: Perfumed yet not sweetened rum.
Origin: Adapted from Victor Bergeron's 'Trader Vic's Bartender's Guide' (1972 revised edition).

CUBAN COCKTAIL NO.3 #2

★★★★☆☆

Glass: Martini
Garnish: Lemon zest twist
Method: SHAKE all ingredients with ice and fine strain into chilled glass.

1½	shots	Bacardi Oro golden rum
¼	shot	Cognac VSOP
½	shot	De Kuyper Apricot Brandy liqueur
½	shot	Freshly squeezed lime juice
1	dash	Orange bitters
½	shot	Chilled mineral water

We say: Like much of the caribbean, this drink has French influences. Thank goodness for Admiral Rodney.
Origin: Adapted from Victor Bergeron's 'Trader Vic's Bartender's Guide' (1972) revised edition).

CUBAN HEAL

★★★★☆

Glass: Martini
Garnish: Lemon zest twist
Method: STIR all ingredients with ice and strain into chilled glass.

2½	shots	Bacardi Superior rum
¼	shot	Cynar
¼	shot	Limoncello liqueur
¼	shot	Monin Honey syrup
2	dashes	Peychaud's aromatic bitters

We say: Honey-ed and initially sweet with herbal spirity rum notes adding depth.
Origin: Created in 2008 by Matthew Keegan at Blanch House, Brighton, England. The ingredients were chosen due to their historically being believed to be remedies.

CUBAN ISLAND

★★★★☆☆

Glass: Martini
Garnish: Orange zest twist
Method: SHAKE all ingredients with ice and fine strain into chilled glass.

2	shots	Bacardi Superior rum
½	shot	Martini Extra Dry vermouth
½	shot	Freshly squeezed lemon juice
¼	shot	Monin Pure Cane 2:1 sugar syrup

We say: The Daiquiri meets the Wet Martini. Interesting!
Origin: Adapted from a drink discovered in 2005 at DiVino's, Hong Kong.

CUBAN LIBERAL

★★★★★

Glass: Coupette
Garnish: Orange zest twist
Method: SHAKE all ingredients with ice and fine strain into chilled glass.

1½	shots	Bacardi Superior rum
1	shot	Martini Rosso sweet vermouth
½	spoon	Amer Picon
2	dashes	Orange bitters

Origin: Adapted from a drink featured in bar La Florida (El Floridita) Cocktails of 1935.

CUBAN MASTER

★★★☆☆

Glass: Collins
Garnish: None
Method: SHAKE all ingredients with ice and fine strain into chilled glass.

1½	shots	Bacardi Superior rum
1	shot	Cognac VSOP
1½	shots	Freshly squeezed orange juice
1½	shots	Fresh pressed pineapple juice
½	shot	Freshly squeezed lemon juice
¼	shot	Monin Pure Cane 2:1 sugar syrup

We say: Well balanced, wonderfully fruity.
Origin: A classic cocktail discovered in 1999 during a trip to in Cuba.

CUBAN SPECIAL

★★★☆☆

Glass: Old-fashioned
Garnish: Orange zest twist
Method: SHAKE ingredients with ice and strain into ice-filled glass.

1½	shots	Bacardi Superior rum
¾	shot	Triple Sec
2	shots	Fresh pressed pineapple juice
¼	shot	Freshly squeezed lime juice

We say: Not that special, but certainly OK.

CUBANITA

★★★★☆

Glass: Collins
Garnish: Lime wedge
Method: SHAKE all ingredients with ice and strain into ice-filled glass.

2	shots	Bacardi Superior rum
3½	shots	Tomato juice
½	shot	Freshly squeezed lemon juice
7	dash	Tabasco hot pepper sauce
4	dashes	Worcestershire sauce
½	spoon	Horseradish sauce
2	pinch	Celery salt
2	pinch	Black pepper

We say: The Bloody Mary returns - this time with rum.

CUBATA

★★★★☆

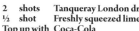

Glass: Collins
Garnish: Lime wedge
Method: SHAKE gin and lime with ice and strain into ice-filled glass. TOP with cola and serve with straws.

2	shots	Tanqueray London dry gin
½	shot	Freshly squeezed lime juice
Top up with		Coca-Cola

We say: Hard to hate but the cola and lime dominate the subtle gin flavours.
Origin: The gin-based equivalent to the rum-based Cuba Libre. This drink is popular in Spain where gin is the dominant spirit.

CUCUMBER & MINT MARTINI

★★★★☆

Glass: Martini
Garnish: Cucumber slices
Method: MUDDLE cucumber and mint in base of shaker. Add other ingredients, SHAKE with ice and fine strain into chilled glass.

2	inch	Cucumber (chopped & peeled)
7	fresh	Mint leaves
2	shots	Ketel One vodka
1	shot	Pressed apple juice
¼	shot	Monin Pure Cane 2:1 sugar syrup

We say: A well balanced fortified salad in a glass - almost healthy.
Origin: Created in 2004 by David Ramos in the Netherlands.

CUCUMBER MARTINI

★★★★½

Glass: Martini
Garnish: Cucumber peel
Method: MUDDLE cucumber in base of shaker. Add other ingredients, SHAKE with ice and strain into glass.

1	shot	Ketel One vodka
1	shot	Żubrówka bison vodka
2	inch	Cucumber (chopped & peeled)
½	shot	Monin Pure Cane 2:1 sugar syrup

We say: Cucumber has never tasted so good.
Origin: There are many different Cucumber Martini recipes; this is mine.

CUCUMBER SAKE-TINI

★★★★☆

Glass: Martini
Garnish: Cucumber slices
Method: MUDDLE cucumber in base of shaker. Add other ingredients, SHAKE with ice and fine strain into chilled glass.

1½	inch	Cucumber (chopped & peeled)
1½	shots	Ketel One vodka
1½	shots	Sake
¼	shot	Monin Pure Cane 2:1 sugar syrup

We say: Subtle and dry. Cucumber and sake are made for each other.
Origin: Created in 2004 by Lisa Ball, London, England.

CULROSS COCKTAIL

★★★★☆

Glass: Coupette
Garnish: Orange zest twist
Method: SHAKE all ingredients with ice and fine strain into chilled glass.

1	shot	Bacardi Superior rum
1	shot	De Kuyper Apricot Brandy liqueur
1	shot	Martini Extra Dry vermouth
¾	shot	Freshly squeezed lemon juice

We say: Light rum, aromatic wine served 'up' with the marzipan and almond notes of apricot liqueur. Originally made with Lillet Blanc in place of dry vermouth.

CUMBERSOME

★★★★☆

Glass: Martini
Garnish: Physalis (cape gooseberry)
Method: MUDDLE cucumber in base of shaker. Add other ingredients, SHAKE with ice and strain into a chilled Martini glass.

4	inch	**Cucumber (chopped & peeled)**
2	shots	**Tanqueray London dry gin**
½	shot	**Campari Bitter**
1	shot	**Freshly squeezed orange juice**
½	shot	**Monin Pure Cane 2:1 sugar syrup**

We say: Interesting and fresh as you like with a pleasant bitterness.
Origin: Created in 2002 by Shelim Islam at the GE Club, London, England.

CUNNINGHAM

★★★★½

Glass: Martini
Garnish: Cherries & orange zest twist (flamed)
Method: SHAKE all ingredients with ice and fine strain into a chilled glass.

1½	shots	**Dewar's White label Scotch**
½	shot	**Freshly squeezed lemon juice**
½	shot	**Freshly squeezed orange juice**
¼	shot	**Bénédictine D.O.M.**
¼	shot	**De Kuyper Cherry Brandy liqueur**

We say: Tangy citrus fruit and Scotch with a herbal and cherry liqueur garnish makes for a damn tasty, fruity dram.
Origin: Created by Marco Dionysos at Tres Agaves, San Francisco, USA and in memory of Johnny Cunningham (1957 - 2003), one of the world's all-time great Scottish fiddlers.

CUPPA JOE

★★★★☆

Glass: Martini
Garnish: Lemon zest twist
Method: SHAKE all ingredients with ice and fine strain into chilled glass.

1½	shots	**Ketel One vodka**
1½	shots	**Hot espresso coffee**
1½	shots	**Hazelnut liqueur**

We say: Nutty coffee fortified with vodka - well balanced.
Origin: Created in 2003 at Cellar Bar, New York City, USA.

CURDISH MARTINI

★★★★☆

Glass: Martini
Garnish: Lemon zest twist
Method: STIR lemon curd with gin in base of shaker until curd dissolves. Add other ingredients, SHAKE with ice and fine strain into chilled glass.

2	shots	**Tanqueray London dry gin**
2	spoons	**Lemon curd**
½	shot	**Sour apple liqueur**
½	shot	**Freshly squeezed lime juice**

We say: Beautifully balanced with the tang of lemon curd.
Origin: Created in 2001 by Tadgh Ryan at West Street, London, England.

THE CURRIER

★★★★☆

Glass: Martini
Garnish: Mint leaf
Method: SHAKE all ingredients with ice and fine strain into chilled glass.

1½	shots	**Maker's Mark bourbon**
½	shot	**Kümmel**
¼	shot	**Freshly squeezed lime juice**
¼	shot	**Rose's lime cordial**

We say: A wonderfully cleansing after dinner cocktail with bourbon and lime plus hints of caraway and fennel courtesy of Kümmel.
Origin: Recipe submitted in July 2006 by Murray Stenson at ZigZag Café, Seattle, USA.

CUSTARD TART

★★★★☆

Glass: Shot
Garnish: Physalis (cape gooseberry)
Method: MUDDLE physalis fruits in base of shaker can. Add other ingredients, SHAKE with ice and strain.

3	fresh	**Physalis fruits**
¾	shot	**Bacardi Superior rum**
½	shot	**Advocaat liqueur**
½	shot	**Peachtree peach schnapps**
¼	shot	**Freshly squeezed lime juice**

We say: Custardy, strangely enough.
Origin: Created by Alex Kammerling in 2001.

CVO FIREVAULT

★★★★☆

Glass: Martini
Garnish: Orange zest twist
Method: SHAKE all ingredients with ice and fine strain into chilled glass.

1½	shots	**Ketel One vodka**
¾	shot	**Campari Bitter**
¾	shot	**Freshly squeezed orange juice**
¾	shot	**Fresh pressed pineapple juice**

We say: Fruity yet slightly bitter. Orange predominates with strong bursts of Campari.
Origin: Discovered in 2005 at CVO Firevault, London, England.

CYDER PRESS

★★★★☆

Glass: Martini
Garnish: Apple slice
Method: SHAKE all ingredients with ice and fine strain into chilled glass.

2	shots	**Calvados/Applejack brandy**
1	shot	**Dry cider**
½	shot	**St~Germain elderflower liqueur**
¾	shot	**Pressed apple juice**

We say: Fresh, fermented and distilled apple juice with a hint of elderflower.
Origin: Created in 2006 by Simon Difford.

D'ARTAGNAN

★★★½☆

Glass: Martini
Garnish: Lemon zest twist
Method: SHAKE first four ingredients with ice and fine strain into chilled glass. TOP with champagne.

½	shot	**Armagnac**
½	shot	**Grand Marnier liqueur**
2	shots	**Freshly squeezed orange juice**
¼	shot	**Monin Pure Cane 2:1 sugar syrup**
Top up with		**Brut champagne**

We say: Use genuine freshly pressed juice and you'll have a tasty Mimosa-style drink.

DAIQUIRI AUTHENTICO

★★★★½

Glass: Martini
Garnish: Lime wedge
Method: SHAKE all ingredients with ice and fine strain into chilled glass.

2	shots	**Bacardi Superior rum**
¼	shot	**Galliano L'Autentico liqueur**
½	shot	**Freshly squeezed lime juice**
¼	shot	**Monin Pure Cane 2:1 sugar syrup**

We say: A lightly peppermint spiced influenced daiquiri.
Origin: A simplification of a drink created in 2008 by Erik Lorincz at Purple Bar, Sanderson Hotel, London, England.

DAIQUIRI DE LUXE

★★★★☆

Glass: Martini
Garnish: Lime wedge
Method: SHAKE all ingredients with ice and fine strain into chilled glass.

2	shots	**Bacardi Superior rum**
¼	shot	**Rose's lime cordial**
½	shot	**Freshly squeezed lime juice**
¼	shot	**Monin Almond (orgeat) syrup**
¼	shot	**Chilled mineral water**

We say: A classic Daiquiri but with lime cordial and almond syrup replacing sugar as the sweetener.

DAIQUIRI ELIXIR

★★★★★

Glass: Martini
Garnish: Lime wedge
Method: SHAKE all ingredients with ice and fine strain into chilled glass.

2	shots	**Bacardi Superior rum**
½	shot	**Freshly squeezed lime juice**
¼	shot	**Martinique cane sugar syrup**
⅛	shot	**Chartreuse Green liqueur**
½	shot	**Chilled mineral water**

We say: Freshly pressed sugar cane syrup and the French elixir Chartreuse add complexity to the classic Daiquiri.
Origin: Another Daiquiri variation from Simon Difford.

DAIQUIRI NATURAL NO.1 #1 (DIFFORD'S 10:3:2 FORMULA)

★★★★★

Glass: Martini
Garnish: Lime wedge
Method: SHAKE all ingredients with ice and fine strain into chilled glass.

2½	shots	**Bacardi Superior rum**
¾	shot	**Freshly squeezed lime juice**
½	shot	**Monin Pure Cane 2:1 sugar syrup**
½	shot	**Chilled mineral water**
3	drops	**Difford's Daiquiri Bitters**

We say: Crisp, light and refreshing. Perfectly balanced complexity of flavours.
Origin: Pronounced 'Dye-Ker-Ree', this drink bears a close relationship to the Canchanchara, a 19th century Cuban blend of rum, lemon, honey and water, but the Daiquiris creation is credited Jennings Stockton Cox, an American engineer.

In 1898, after Roosevelt's victory at the Battle of San Juan Hill, the Americans began to exploit Cuba's iron-ore mines and Cox led one of the initial exploratory expeditions. Cox and his team worked in the Sierra Maestra Mountains on the south-eastern shore of Cuba where the small town of Daiquirí lies and it was while there that he created his classic drink.

The engineers received substantial salaries and generous tobacco rations, after all there had to be some inducements for these qualified engineers to leave secure positions in the USA and brave the threat of yellow fever in Cuba. Thankfully our hero also requested they each received a monthly ration of the local rum, Bacardi Carta Blanca, and noticing that the Cuban workers often mixed Bacardi with their evening coffee, he began to experiment himself.

Drinks legend has it that another engineer called Pagliuchi was viewing mines in the region and met with Cox. During their meeting they set about making a drink from the ingredients Cox had to hand: rum, limes and sugar. Cox's granddaughter recounts a slightly different tale; namely that Cox ran out of gin when entertaining American guests. Wary of serving them straight rum, he added lime and sugar. However Cox came to concoct the drink, the result was sublime.

On page 38 of his 1928 book, *'When it's Cocktail Time in Cuba'*, Basil Woon writes that this drink was popular with a group who used to meet in Santiago's Venus bar every morning at eight o'clock. "The boys used to have three or four every morning. Most of them worked in the Daiquiri mines, the superintendent of which was a gentleman named Cox - Jennings Cox. One morning in the Venus Cox said: "Boys, we've been drinking this delicious little drink for some time, but we've never named it. Let's christen it now!" The boys milled around a bit and finally Cox said: "I'll tell you what, lads - we all work at Daiquiri and we all drank this drink first there. Let's call it a Daiquiri."

Basil Woon's account documents the origin and naming of the Daiquiri and unlike many other cocktails where there creation is lost in time, that of the Daiquiri is well substantiated, including the original recipe, recorded by Jennings Cox in his personal diary.
The Daiquiri seems to have travelled back to America with US Admiral Lucius Johnson, who fought in the Spanish-American war of 1898. He introduced the drink to the Army & Navy Club in Washington DC and a plaque in their Daiquiri Lounge records his place in cocktail history.

The Perfect Daiquiri Recipe
In his seminal 1948 *'Fine Art of Mixing Drinks'*, David A. Embury writes, "The Daiquiri, like the Old-Fashioned, deserves an even greater popularity than it now enjoys. For example, it is in my opinion, a vastly superior cocktail to the Manhattan, yet most bars sell more Manhattans than Daiquiris. So far as I can ascertain there are two main reasons why more Daiquiris are not sold: the use of inferior rums and the use of improper proportions."

To address those two points...
In his personal diary Jennings Cox records his original Daiquiri recipe (to serve six) as follows: "The juice of six lemons; Six teaspoons full of sugar; Six Bacardi cups ('Carta Blanca'); Two small cups of mineral water; Plenty of crushed ice"

This original recipe and other such historical references specify 'Bacardi Carta Blanca' (now known as Bacardi Superior) as the rum used

to make a Daiquiri. Thus to make a truly authentic Daiquiri you should use this rum as it purports to be made using the same strain of cultured yeast and recipe so maintains its original flavour profile. Bacardi Superior has a delicate mushroom/blue cheese note, which adds a distinctive character to the finished drink.

Although Cox's recipe records the use of lemons it is most likely that he is actually referring to limes which are native to Cuba and that the confusion arises due to the common Cuban term for lime being 'limón.' Again to quote from Embury, "Actually lemons are almost unknown in Cuba, whereas lime trees grow in everyone's own yard."

Embury's own recipe calls for sugar syrup and this is something with which I whole-heartedly agree as granulated or caster sugar does not as readily dissolve in cold liquid. If you must insist in 'spooning' rather than pouring your sugar please use a mortar and pestle to first crush caster sugar to a fine powder, often termed 'bar sugar' or 'powdered sugar'.

Better still, make your own sugar syrup by pouring one mug of filtered water into a saucepan and over a very low heat, so as not to even come close to boiling, stir in two mugs of caster sugar. Allow to cool, bottle and store in a refrigerator where it will last for a couple of months.

Thus we have our ingredients: Bacardi Superior, freshly squeezed lime juice and 2-to-1 (double strength) sugar syrup. Now to the perfect proportions.

London's most famous bartender, Dick Bradsell, originally taught me David Embury's 8:2:1 Daiquiri formula and I used to believe this was the best (I still do when making Daiquiris with aged rum. Embury's 8:2:1 Daiquiri consists: 8 parts (2 shots) white label Cuban rum, 2 parts (½ shot) lime juice and 1 part (¼ shot) sugar syrup.

Some bartenders make Daiquiris according to the classic Margarita formula with twice as much lime and sugar as Embury. I have experimented with this but found that while tequila is robust enough to shine above the citrus flavour such a large proportion of lime tends to overpower the more delicate flavours of light rum. However, I do prefer a small increase in lime but in proportion to a simular small increase in the rum. After all a mere two measures of rum would hardly satisfy great Daiquiri drinkers such as Hemingway. Thus I have now settled on the 10:3:2 formula show in the recipe here.

Embury's mixing instructions are, "Shake vigorously with plenty of finely crushed ice and strain into chilled cocktail glasses." This is to add dilution, a crucial aspect to perfecting the Daiquiri. As crushed ice is so variable in its wetness and so also the amount of dilution it adds to a drink, instead I prefer to shake with large cubes of double frozen ice taken from a freezer with the addition of ½ hot iced water. (I 'double freeze' cubed ice produced by ice machine). I shake with such vigour that there is indeed crushed ice left in the shaker when I strain the drink. This makes for an ice-cold Daiquiri with the controlled dilution essential to great straight-up Daiquiris.

What's in the Name
I first visited Cuba with Jamie Terrell back in the days when he was still working behind the stick at London's Atlantic Bar & Grill and not living a cachaça laced jet-set lifestyle in New York. Fortunately Jamie spoke reasonable Spanish thanks to a sun-drenched season bartending on the Costa del Sol so as we toured Havana's bars in search of the perfect Daiquiri we were able to question the bartenders.
Our first lesson was that asking for a mere "Daiquiri" would result in being handed a blended Daiquiri. We quickly learnt that in Cuba you need to ask for a "Natural Daiquiri" when seeking a Daiquiri shaken rather than blended.

Wherever you are in the world, when ordering a Daiquiri you need to convey to the bartender exactly what Daiquiri you desire. It is essential to be specific otherwise ordering just a 'Daiquiri' could result in your being asked, "What flavour would you like - strawberry, banana, mango or pineapple?" In such cases answering "just lime please" often leaves the questioner perplexed.

To further confuse the ordering of a Daiquiri, the great Ribalagua listed his Daiquiri adaptations as Daiquiri No.2, No.3, No.4 and No.5. Thus a simple 'original' or 'classic' Daiquiri should properly be termed 'Daiquiri No.1' and this can be served either 'Natural' (straight-up), 'On-The-Rocks' (over cubed ice) or 'Frozen' (blended with crushed ice).

DAIQUIRI NATURAL NO.1 #2
(EMBURY'S 8:2:1 FORMULA)

★ ★ ★ ★ ★

Glass: Martini
Garnish: Lime wedge
Method: SHAKE all ingredients with ice and fine strain into chilled glass.

2	shots	Bacardi 8yo aged rum
½	shot	Freshly squeezed lime juice
¼	shot	Monin Pure Cane 2:1 sugar syrup
½	shot	Chilled mineral water

We say: Traditionally a Natural Daiquiri should always be based on light rum but if I should feel like breaking with tradition and using aged rum, I find Embury's 8:2:1 formula works particularly well.
Origin: According to David A. Embury's 1948 'Fine Art of Mixing Drinks' the classic proportions of a daiquiri are: 8 parts (2 shots) white label Cuban rum, 2 parts (1/2 shot) lime juice and 1 part (1/4 shot) sugar syrup. I have added the optional addition of water for increased dilution.

DAIQUIRI NATURAL NO.1 #3 NEW
(COUNTDOWN 3:2:1 FORMULA)

★ ★ ★ ★ ½

Glass: Martini
Garnish: Lime wedge
Method: SHAKE all ingredients with ice and fine strain into chilled glass.

2¼	shots	Bacardi Superior rum
1½	shots	Freshly squeezed lime juice
¾	shot	Monin Pure Cane 2:1 sugar syrup
½	shot	Chilled mineral water
3	drops	Difford's Daiquiri Bitters

We say: Made to the easy-to-remember 3:2:1 Daiquiri (or countdown) formula this balanced but limey daiquiri lacks the pose of our preferred 10:3:2 formula.
Origin: We are indebted to Roger Vilalta who in 2010 at Banker's Bar in Barcelona, Spain made Simon Difford an excellent daiquiri using this formula.

DAIQUIRI NO.1 FROZEN
(DIFFORD'S 16:6:6:1 FORMULA)

★ ★ ★ ★ ★

Glass: Martini
Garnish: Maraschino cherry
Method: BLEND well all ingredients with 6oz scoop of crushed ice. STRAIN blended drink through a fine strainer to remove ice fragments.

2	shots	Bacardi Superior rum
¾	shot	Freshly squeezed lime juice
¾	shot	Monin Pure Cane 2:1 sugar syrup
⅛	shot	Luxardo Maraschino liqueur

Variant: Floridita Daiquiri or with fruit and/or fruit liqueurs.
We say: Blend with too much ice and you will have a tasteless slushy drink that will give you brain-ache if you drink it too fast. However, made correctly and fine strained this is a superbly refreshing drink on a hot day.
Origin: Daiquiris were originally shaken and served 'straight-up' or 'on-the-rocks'. The frozen, blended version is said to have first been produced by Emilio Gonzalez at the Plaza Hotel in Cuba. However, it was made famous by Constantino (Constante) Ribalagua Vert who presided over the bar at Havana's La Florida (later renamed Floridita to distinguish it from the restaurant of the same name) for some forty years until his death in early December 1952.

In his 1948 'The Fine Art of Mixing Drinks', David A. Embury writes of Havana's Floridita, "This restaurant, at the corner of Obispo and Monserrate streets in Havana, became known as 'La Catedral del Daiquiri'

(The Temple of the Daiquiri) and Ribalagua as the Cocktail King - 'El Rey de los Coteleros'". The title was, indeed, well deserved. His limes were gently squeezed with his fingers lest even a drop of the bitter oil from the peel get into the drink; the cocktails were mixed (but not over mixed) in a Waring Blender; the stinging cold drink was strained through a fine sieve into the glass so that not one tiny piece of the ice remained in it. No smallest detail was overlooked in achieving the flawless perfection of the drink.

Ernest Hemingway, the hard-drinking, Nobel prize-winning author, lived in Cuba for years, indulging his passions for fishing, shooting and boozing. In the 30s and the 40s he would often work his way through twelve of the Floridita's frozen Daiquiris - often doubles, renamed 'Papa Dobles' in his honour. The Hemingway Special Daiquiri, which includes grapefruit, was created for him.

In his book 'Islands in the Stream', Hemingway's hero stares deep into his frozen Daiquiri, and Hemingway writes, "It reminded him of the sea. The frappéd part of the drink was like the wake of a ship and the clear part was the way the water looked when the bow cut it when you were in shallow water over marl bottom. That was almost the exact colour."

DAIQUIRI NO.1 ON-THE-ROCKS (DIFFORD'S 10:3:2 FORMULA)

★★★★★

Glass: Old-fashioned
Garnish: Lime slice & maraschino cherry
Method: SHAKE all ingredients with ice and fine strain into ice-filled glass.

2½	shots	**Bacardi Superior rum**
¾	shot	**Freshly squeezed lime juice**
½	shot	**Monin Pure Cane 2:1 sugar syrup**

We say: Light and refreshing. No one flavour predominates - sweet and sour are in harmony with the rum.
Origin: In my formative Daiquiri drinking years I followed the convention that a Daiquiri No.1 should be served 'straight-up'. However, I have now reverted to drinking my Daiquiris 'on-the-rocks' and interestingly Cox's original recipe (see Daiquiri No.1 Natural) suggests that this may also be the way he originally intended the drink to be served. In his diary Cox stipulates, "Put all ingredients in a cocktail shaker and shake well. Do not strain as the glass may be served with some ice." And as Albert S. Crockett notes of this drink in his 1935 "*The Old Waldorf-Astoria Bar Book*", "Personal preference dictates serving the cocktail with finely shaved ice in the glass."
Obviously serving a drink over ice will add dilution so rendering the additional dash of water to my 10:3:2 Daiquiri formula superfluous. Having tried 'up' and 'on-the-rocks' Daiquiris made to the same 'No.1' formula next to each other I have to admit that more nuances are found in the 'up' when compared to 'on-the-rocks'. However, I prefer holding and drinking from a big heavy old-fashioned glass rather than a delicate V-shaped Martini or curvaceous Coupette. Thus I now vary my serve according to mood but with 1/2 shot of water added when served 'up' and omitted when served 'on-the-rocks'.

DAIQUIRI NO.2

★★★★½

Glass: Martini
Garnish: Lime wedge
Method: SHAKE all ingredients with ice and fine strain into chilled glass.

2	shots	**Bacardi Superior rum**
⅛	shot	**Triple Sec**
½	shot	**Freshly squeezed orange juice**
½	shot	**Freshly squeezed lime juice**
¼	shot	**Monin Pure Cane 2:1 sugar syrup**

We say: A Daiquiri with subtle orange notes, but far from being a mere Orange Daiquiri.
Origin: Created circa 1915 by Constantino (Constante) Ribalaigua Vert at Floridita bar in Havana, Cuba.

DAIQUIRI NO.3

★★★★★

Glass: Old-fashioned
Garnish: Lime wedge
Method: SHAKE all ingredients with ice and fine strain into chilled glass.

2	shots	**Bacardi Superior rum**
½	shot	**Freshly squeezed lime juice**
½	shot	**Monin Pure Cane 2:1 sugar syrup**
¼	shot	**Freshly squeezed pink grapefruit juice**
⅛	shot	**Luxardo Maraschino liqueur**

We say: A Daiquiri No.1 with a tang of grapefruit and hint of maraschino. Essentially a Hemingway Special Daiquiri (Papa Doble Daiquiri) for folk without the great author's constitution or love of the sours.
Origin: Thought to have been created by Constantino (Constante) Ribalaigua Vert at the Floridita bar in Havana, Cuba, circa 1915. If this was invented as early as 1915, then this was the predecessor of the Hemingway Daiquiri, since Hemingway did not arrive in Cuba until 1928.

DAIQUIRI NO.4 (FLORIDA STYLE)

★★★★☆

Glass: Martini
Garnish: Lime wedge
Method: SHAKE all ingredients with finely crushed ice and strain into chilled glass.

2	shots	**Bacardi Oro golden rum**
½	shot	**Lime**
¼	shot	**Monin Pure Cane 2:1 sugar syrup**
¼	shot	**Luxardo Maraschino liqueur**
½	shot	**Chilled mineral water**

We say: Maraschino cherry liqueur flavours this finely balanced golden rum based Daiquiri.
Origin: Created by Constantino (Constante) Ribalaigua Vert at the Floridita bar in Havana, Cuba. This recipe is adapted from a 1937 Bar Florida (later renamed Floridita) menu, also in Havana, Cuba.

DAIQUIRI NO.5 (PINK DAIQUIRI)

★★★★½

Glass: Martini
Garnish: Lime wedge
Method: SHAKE all ingredients with ice and fine strain into chilled glass.

2	shots	**Bacardi Superior rum**
⅛	shot	**Luxardo Maraschino liqueur**
¼	shot	**Pomegranate (grenadine) syrup**
½	shot	**Freshly squeezed lime juice**
¼	shot	**Monin Pure Cane 2:1 sugar syrup**

We say: Classically tangy Daiquiri but sweetened with pomegranate syrup and a splash of maraschino.
Origin: Created by Constantino (Constante) Ribalaigua Vert at the Floridita bar in Havana, Cuba.

DAIQUIRI NOIR

★★★★⯪

Glass: Martini
Garnish: Mint sprig
Method: Lightly MUDDLE mint in base of shaker. Add other ingredients, SHAKE with ice and fine strain into chilled glass.

7	fresh	Mint leaves
2	shots	Bacardi 8yo aged rum
½	shot	Drambuie
½	shot	Freshly squeezed lime juice
¼	shot	Monin Pure Cane 2:1 sugar syrup

We say: Discovered in 2008 at Hugos Bar Pizza, Sydney, Australia.
Origin: Drambuie adds herbal consistency to this minty fresh aged rum Daiquiri.

DAISY CUTTER MARTINI

★★★★⯪

Glass: Martini
Garnish: Mint leaf
(just to bruise). Add other ingredients, SHAKE with ice and fine strain into chilled glass.

3	fresh	Mint leaves
1½	shots	Ketel One vodka
1	shot	St-Germain elderflower liqueur
1	shot	Martini Extra dry vermouth
¼	shot	Chartreuse Yellow liqueur

We say: Floral, minty and herbal with a dry finish.
Origin: Created in 2006 by Simon Difford, named not for the bomb but after the cricketing term for a ball bowled so incompetently that it skims along the ground.

DAISY DUKE

★★★⯪☆

Glass: Old-fashioned
Garnish: Seasonal berries
Method: SHAKE all ingredients with ice and strain into glass filled with crushed ice. Serve with straws.

2	shots	Maker's Mark bourbon
½	shot	Pomegranate (grenadine) syrup
1	shot	Freshly squeezed lemon juice

We say: This bright red drink tastes more adult than it looks.
Origin: Created in 2002 by Jake Burger at Townhouse, Leeds, England.

DAMN IT JIMMY

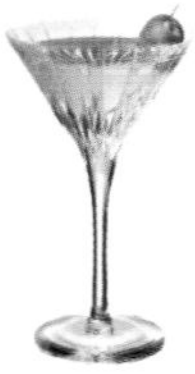

★★★★⯪

Glass: Martini
Garnish: Blue cheese-stuffed olives
Method: STIR all ingredients with ice and fine strain into chilled glass.

1½	shots	Sake
1½	shots	Bacardi Superior rum
¼	shot	Tio Pepe fino sherry
¼	shot	Martini Extra Dry vermouth
¼	shot	Monin Pure Cane 2:1 sugar syrup

We say: Delicately flavoured and ever so slightly sweet.
Origin: Created in August 2008 by Simon Difford at The Cabinet Room, London, England.

DAMN-THE WEATHER

★★★⯪☆

Glass: Martini
Garnish: Orange zest twist
Method: SHAKE all ingredients with ice and fine strain into chilled glass.

1	shot	Tanqueray Tanqueray London dry gin
½	shot	Triple Sec
1	shot	Martini Rosso sweet vermouth
1½	shots	Freshly squeezed orange juice

We say: Gin and herbal notes emerge in this predominantly orange drink.

DAMSON IN DISTRESS

★★★★☆

Glass: Shot
Garnish: None
Method: SHAKE all ingredients with ice and fine strain into chilled glass.

1½	shots	Damson gin liqueur
½	shot	Amaretto liqueur
¼	shot	Freshly squeezed lemon juice

We say: Damson and amaretto sharpened by lemon juice.
Origin: Discovered in 2003 at Hush, London, England.

DANDY COCKTAIL

★★★★⯪

Glass: Martini
Garnish: Lemon & orange zest twists
Method: STIR all ingredients with ice and strain into chilled glass.

1½	shots	Maker's Mark bourbon
½	shot	Triple Sec
1½	shots	Dubonnet Red (French made)
1	dash	Angostura aromatic bitters

We say: This complex Manhattan variant is a well balanced combo of spirit, liqueur and aromatic wine.
Origin: Adapted from Harry Craddock's 1930 'The Savoy Cocktail Book'.

DARK 'N' STORMY

★★★★☆

Glass: Collins
Garnish: Lime wedge
Method: SHAKE first three ingredients with ice and strain into ice-filled glass. TOP with ginger beer, stir and serve with straws.

2	shots	Gosling's Black Seal rum
1	shot	Freshly squeezed lime juice
½	shot	Monin Pure Cane 2:1 sugar syrup
Top up with		Ginger beer

We say: This deliciously spicy drink is part of the Mule family - but is distinctive due to the strong flavour of the rum.
Origin: The national drink of Bermuda, where ginger beer and Gosling's rum are produced.

DARK AND STORMY SHOT NEW

★★★½☆

Glass: Shot
Method: POUR the first 3 ingredients into the glass in the following order. Then carefully FLOAT rum on surface of drink.

¼	shot	**Freshly squeezed lime juice**
¾	shot	**Ginger beer**
¼	shot	**Canton ginger liqueur**
½	shot	**Gosling's Black Seal rum**

We say: Tastes just like a bite-sized Dark and Stormy and as 'shots' go is both tasty and relatively restrained on its alcoholic punch.
Origin: Adapted from a drink created by Simon Fraser and Andrew Holmes at Rumbar, Hamilton, Bermuda home of the Dark and Stormy. In September 2011 Simon emailed us to say, "About a year or so ago we received a bottle of Canton Ginger Liqueur. My part time co-worker Andrew Holmes, who works full time for Goslings as brand rep for Black Seal, Goslings Gold and Old Family Reserve, and I looked at each other and said right away, "Dark and Stormy Shots?!"

DARK DAIQUIRI

★★★★½

Glass: Martini
Garnish: Lime wedge
Method: SHAKE all ingredients with ice and fine strain into chilled glass.

1½	shots	**Bacardi 8yo aged rum**
½	shot	**Pusser's Navy rum**
½	shot	**Freshly squeezed lime juice**
½	shot	**Monin Pure Cane 2:1 sugar syrup**
¾	shot	**Chilled mineral water**

We say: The fine sweet and sour balance of a great Daiquiri with hints of molasses.

DARLINGTON

★★★☆☆

Glass: Martini
Garnish: Orange zest twist
Method: SHAKE all ingredients with ice and fine strain into chilled glass.

2	shots	**Tanqueray London dry gin**
½	shot	**Calvados/Applejack brandy**
½	shot	**Bols Blue Curaçao liqueur**
1	shot	**Martini Extra Dry vermouth**
1	shot	**Freshly squeezed lemon juice**
¼	shot	**Monin Pure Cane 2:1 sugar syrup**

We say: Gin, orange and lemon made Martini-like by a drying splash of vermouth.
Origin: In W.J. Tarling's 1937 *Café Royal Cocktail Book* (Coronation Edition), the invention of this cocktail is credited to J.B. O'Brien.

STAR RATINGS EXPLAINED

★★★★★ Excellent

★★★★½ Recommended	★★★★☆ Praiseworthy
★★★½☆ Commended	★★★☆☆ Mediocre
★★½☆☆ Disappointing	★★☆☆☆ Pretty awful
★½☆☆☆ Shameful	★☆☆☆☆ Disgusting

DARTH JÄGER

★★★½☆

Glass: Shot/Old-fashioned
Method: POUR Jägermeister into shot glass. Place old-fashioned glass over shot glass and UPEND to leave full shot glass now upside down in old-fashioned glass. Slowly POUR cider into old fashioned glass.

1	shot	**Jägermeister**
3	shots	**Dry cider**

We say: This riff on a Jägerbomb leaves the 'Dark Lord' sitting in 'Ciderspace'
Origin: Created in 2012 by Darren Warburton at Buddha on the Beach bar on Koh Tao island, Thailand.

DC MARTINI

★★★★☆

Glass: Martini
Method: STIR all ingredients with ice and strain glass.

2	shots	**Bacardi Superior rum**
¼	shot	**Hazelnut liqueur**
¼	shot	**White Crème de Cacao**
¼	shot	**Monin Pure Cane 2:1 sugar syrup**
½	shot	**Chilled mineral water**

We say: Vanilla, chocolate and a hint of nut.
Origin: Discovered in 2000 at Teatro, London, England.

DE BEAUVOIR NEW

★★★★★

Glass: Coupette
Garnish: Orange zest twist
Method: SHAKE all ingredients with ice and fine strain into chilled glass.

1	shot	**Straight rye whiskey**
⅔	shot	**Hazelnut liqueur**
½	shot	**Freshly squeezed lemon juice**
1¾	shots	**Smoked porter beer**
1	spoon	**Brown sugar**
1	dash	**Bitters (whiskey barrel-aged)**

We say: Richly flavoured and lusciously bittersweet with rye whisky, bitter porter and sour lemon juice balancing hazelnut liqueur and brown sugar.
Origin: Created in 2013 by Andrea Montague from London. Andrea beat four other finalists with this drink in the diffordsguide Beer-tail Competition for London Cocktail Week 2013, held in August 2013 at Simon Difford's Cabinet Room bar in London.

This cocktail is named after De Beauvoir Town, an area of north London bordered by Kingsland Road to the east, Southgate Road to the west, the Regent's Canal to the south and Tottenham Road to the north. The cockney name for the area, Beaverstown, is also the name of the brewery in Hackney whose Smog Rocket porter Andrea used in her winning cocktail.

DE LA LOUISIANE #1

★★★★☆

Glass: Martini
Garnish: Lemon zest twist
Method: STIR all ingredients with ice and strain into chilled glass.

2	shots	**Maker's Mark bourbon**
¼	shot	**Bénédictine D.O.M.**
1	dash	**Angostura aromatic bitters**
½	shot	**Chilled mineral water**

We say: Whiskey with hints of honey and spice.
Origin: The signature cocktail of the Restaurant de la Louisiane in New Orleans which opened in 1881.

DE LA LOUISIANE #2 (EQUAL PARTS BORBON)

★★★★☆

Glass: Martini
Garnish: Maraschino cherry
Method: STIR all ingredients with ice and strain into chilled glass.

1	shot	Maker's Mark bourbon
1	shot	Bénédictine D.O.M.
1	shot	Martini Rosso sweet vermouth
⅛	shot	La Fée Parisienne (68%) absinthe
3	dashes	Peychaud's aromatic bitters

We say: Full flavoured and complex, yet fairly sweet, with herbal notes and a touch of absinthe.
Origin: This bourbon rather than rye take on this cocktail is adapted from Stanley Clisby Arthur's 1937 book 'Famous New Orleans Drinks and How to Mix 'Em' in which he wrote, This is the special cocktail served at Restaurant de la Louisiane, one of the famous French restaurants of New Orleans, long the rendezvous of those who appreciate the best in Creole cuisine.

DE LA LOUISIANE #3

★★★★☆

Glass: Martini
Garnish: Orange zest twist
Method: STIR all ingredients with ice and strain into chilled glass.

1½	shots	Maker's Mark bourbon
1	shot	Dubonnet Red (French made)
¼	shot	Cointreau triple sec
2	dashes	Peychaud's aromatic bitters
½	shot	Chilled mineral water

We say: Beautifully balanced. This fruity whiskey drink manages to be both approachable and serious.
Origin: Another variation on this New Orleans classic first served in the early 1930s at Restaurant de la Louisiane in New Orleans.

DE LA LOUISIANE #4 NEW

★★★★★

Glass: Coupette
Garnish: Maraschino cherry
Method: STIR all ingredients with ice and strain into chilled glass.

1	shot	Straight rye whiskey
½	shot	Bénédictine D.O.M.
1	shot	Martini Rosso sweet vermouth
⅛	shot	La Fée Parisienne (68%) absinthe
2	dashes	Peychaud's aromatic bitters
¾	shot	Chilled mineral water

We say: A rye-based Sweet Manhattan made even sweeter with herbal Bènèdictine liqueur and bittered with Peychaud's and absinthe.
Originally made with equal parts rye whiskey, Bénédictine DOM and sweet vermouth, unless you have a sweet tooth reducing the liqueur as per this recipe makes for a more balanced drink. This is our favoured version of this famous New Orleans cocktail.
Origin: Recipe adapted from Stanley Clisby Arthur's 1937 book 'Famous New Orleans Drinks and How to Mix 'Em' in which he wrote, This is the special cocktail served at Restaurant de la Louisiane, one of the famous French restaurants of New Orleans, long the rendezvous of those who appreciate the best in Creole cuisine. La Louisiane cocktail is as out-of-the-ordinary as the many distinctive dishes that grace its menu.

DEAD MAN'S MULE

★★★½☆

Glass: Collins
Garnish: Lime wedge
Method: SHAKE first four ingredients with ice and strain into ice-filled glass. TOP with ginger beer.

¾	shot	Absinthe
¾	shot	Goldschläger cinnamon schnapps
¾	shot	Monin Almond (orgeat) syrup
½	shot	Freshly squeezed lime juice
Top up with		Ginger beer

We say: Strong in every respect. Big, full-on flavours of aniseed, cinnamon and ginger.
Origin: Discovered in 2003 at the Met bar, London, England.

DEAN'S GATE MARTINI

★★★½☆

Glass: Martini
Garnish: Orange zest twist
Method: SHAKE all ingredients with ice and fine strain into chilled glass.

2	shots	Ketel One vodka
1	shot	Drambuie
1	shot	Rose's lime cordial
¾	scoop	Chilled mineral water

We say: Rich and strong with a warm, honeyed citrus flavour.

DEATH BY CHOCOLATE

★★★★☆

Glass: Hurricane
Garnish: Crumbled Cadbury's Flake bar
Method: BLEND all ingredients with two 12oz scoops of crushed ice and serve with straws.

1	shot	Ketel One vodka
1½	shots	Baileys Irish cream liqueur
1	shot	Dark Crème de Cacao
3	scoops	Chocolate ice cream

We say: Unsophisticated but delicious. Don't be cheap - use deluxe ice cream.

DEATH FLIP

★★★★½

Glass: Coupette
Garnish: Grated Nutmeg
Method: DRY SHAKE all ingredients (without ice). SHAKE again with ice and fine strain into chilled glass.

1	shot	Olmeca Altos 100% agave tequila
1	shot	Jägermeister
1	shot	Chartreuse Yellow liqueur
¼	shot	Monin Pure Cane 2:1 sugar syrup
1	whole	Egg

We say: With a whole egg a shot of tequila, Jägermeister and Chartreuse, this is both a Death Flip and your last meal. Challenging herbal and bitter complexity yet with endearing sweet creaminess.
Origin: Created in 2010 by Chris (Hasselhoff) Hysted the Black Pearl, Melbourne, Australia.

DEATH IN THE AFTERNOON UPDATED

★★★☆☆

Glass: Flute
Garnish: Rose petal
Method: SHAKE first three ingredients with ice and fine strain into chilled glass. TOP with champagne.

¼	shot	Absinthe
½	shot	Freshly squeezed lemon juice
¼	shot	Monin Pure Cane 2:1 sugar syrup
Top up with		Brut champagne

We say: Bravado (absinthe) dominates this drink, alongside hints of citrus and biscuity champagne.
Origin: Created by Ernest Hemingway (not just named after his book), this recipe was the author's contribution to a 1935 cocktail book titled "So Red the Nose, or Breath in the Afternoon". We've toned down the maestro's original recipe a little, as it included a whopping ounce-and-a-half of absinthe.

DEATH IN THE GULF STREAM

★★★★☆

Glass: Collins
Garnish: Lime wedge
Method: SHAKE all ingredients with ice and strain into glass filled with crushed ice. CHURN (stir) and add more ice until glass is filled.

2	shots	Bols Genever
1	shot	Freshly squeezed lime juice
½	shot	Monin Pure Cane 2:1 sugar syrup
4	dashes	Angostura aromatic bitters
Grated zest of 1 Lime		

We say: Remembering that Hemingway was a diabetic so has a very sour tooth, I believe this drink needs more than 'one teaspoon' of sugar. Thus I have added half a shot of syrup to the original recipe. It also needs dilution, so be sure to shake well and churn in the glass.
Origin: According to 'Gentleman's Companion' this libation was a favourite of Ernest Hemingway. "We got Hemingway's other picker-upper, and liked it. Take a tall thin water tumbler and fill it with finely cracked ice. Lace this broken debris with four good purple splashes of Angostura, add the juice and crushed peel of one green lime, and fill the glass almost full with Holland gin . . . No sugar, no fancying. It's strong, it's bitter - but so is English ale strong and bitter, in many cases. We don't add sugar to ale, and we don't need sugar in a Death In The Gulf Stream - or at least not more than one teaspoon. Its tartness and its bitterness are its chief charm. It is reviving and refreshing; cools the blood and inspires renewed interest in food, companions and life."

DEATH IN VENICE NEW

★★★★☆

Glass: Flute
Garnish: Orange zest twist
Method: POUR Campari and grapefruit bitters into chilled glass and TOP with Prosecco.

½	shot	Campari Bitter
2	dashes	Grapefruit bitters
Top up with		Prosecco sparkling wine

We say: Something of a cross between the Italian Spritz and Ernest Hemingway's Death in the Afternoon.
Origin: Created in 2010 by Tony Conigliaro at 69 Colebrooke Row, London, England.

DEAUVILLE #1

★★★★☆

Glass: Martini
Garnish: Lemon zest twist
Method: SHAKE all ingredients with ice and fine strain into chilled glass.

1	shot	Calvados/Applejack brandy
1	shot	Cognac VSOP
¾	shot	Triple Sec
½	shot	Freshly squeezed lemon juice
⅛	shot	Monin Pure Cane 2:1 sugar syrup
½	shot	Chilled mineral water

Variant: Apple Cart, Calvados Sidecar.
We say: A well-balanced appley twist on the classic Sidecar.
Origin: A classic drink of unknown origin.

DEAUVILLE #2

★★★½☆

Glass: Martini
Garnish: Lemon zest twist
Method: SHAKE all ingredients with ice and fine strain into chilled glass.

1	shot	Calvados/Applejack brandy
1	shot	Cognac VSOP
1	shot	Triple Sec
1	shot	Freshly squeezed lemon juice
¼	shot	Monin Pure Cane 2:1 sugar syrup

We say: The classic recipe omits the sugar syrup, which makes this drink too sour for my taste. Duly sweetened, it is very much in the Sidecar vein.
Origin: A classic drink of unknown origin.

THE DEBONAIR

★★★★½

Glass: Coupette
Garnish: Lemon zest twist
Method: STIR all ingredients with ice and strain into chilled glass.

| 2½ | shots | Spey malt whisky |
| 1 | shot | Domaine de Canton ginger liqueur |

We say: Rich and sophisticated, this Scotch based drink has a zing of ginger spice and citrus from the garnish.
Origin: Created in the 1990s by Gaz Regan who in his San Francisco Chronicle 'The Cocktailian' column wrote of this drink, "I gave the formula a series of silly names, and eventually I got really frustrated with it so I looked up "sophisticated" in Roget's Thesaurus. The Debonair was born."

DEEP SOUTH

★★★☆☆

Glass: Old-fashioned
Garnish: Lime wedge
Method: MUDDLE ginger in base of shaker. Add other ingredients, SHAKE with ice and fine strain into glass filled with crushed ice.

2	slices	Fresh root ginger (thumbnail sized)
1½	shots	Tanqueray London dry gin
1½	shots	Freshly squeezed orange juice
¾	shot	Freshly squeezed lime juice

We say: Citrussy with delicate orange and ginger flavours.
Origin: Discovered in 1999 at AKA Bar, London, England.

THE DEFENDER

★★★★★★

Glass: Coupette
Garnish: Orange zest twist
Method: STIR all ingredients with ice and strain into chilled glass.

1½	shots	Old Tom gin
1½	shots	Martini Rosso sweet vermouth
¼	shot	Benoit Serres créme de violette
2	dashes	Orange bitters

We say: One of those drinks where the bitter oils from the orange zest twist is crucial to its fine balance.
Origin: Recipe adapted from '*Old Waldorf Bar Days*' published 1931, which said of this drink, "The name of an American yacht which took care of one of Sir Thomas Lipton's early but seemingly endless Shamrocks'". (Shamrock being the name of Sir Thomas Lipton's fleet of America's Cup racing yachts.)

THE DELICIOUS SOUR

★★★★★½

Glass: Old-fashioned
Garnish: Lemon slice & cherry on stick (sail)
Method: SHAKE all ingredients with ice and strain into ice-filled glass.

2	shots	Calvados/Applejack brandy
1	shot	Crème de pêche de vigne liqueur
1	shot	Freshly squeezed lemon juice
¼	shot	Monin Pure Cane 2:1 sugar syrup
½	fresh	Egg white
Top up with		Soda (club soda)

We say: Tis rather.
Origin: Adapted from William Schmidt's 1892 book, '*The Flowing Bowl*'.

DELMARVA COCKTAIL NO.1

★★★★★½

Glass: Martini
Garnish: Mint sprig
Method: SHAKE all ingredients with ice and fine strain into chilled glass.

2	shots	Maker's Mark bourbon
½	shot	Martini Extra Dry vermouth
½	shot	Giffard Menthe Pastille liqueur
½	shot	Freshly squeezed lemon juice

We say: A minty fresh, dry, whiskey-based palate cleanser.
Origin: Created by Ted 'Dr. Cocktail' Haigh, who hails from America's Delmarva Peninsula.

DELMARVA COCKTAIL NO.2

★★★★★¼

Glass: Martini
Garnish: Lemon zest twist
Method: SHAKE all ingredients with ice and fine strain into chilled glass.

2	shots	Maker's Mark bourbon
½	shot	Martini Extra Dry vermouth
½	shot	White Crème de Cacao
½	shot	Freshly squeezed lemon juice

We say: Whiskey's distinctive character shines through but is softened and flavoured by chocolate and a hint of citrus.
Origin: Gary Regan adapted Ted Haigh's original Delmarva Cocktail and published this version in his '*Joy of Mixology*'.

DELMONICO

★★★★☆

Glass: Martini
Garnish: Orange zest twist
Method: STIR all ingredients with ice and strain into chilled glass.

1¼	shots	Cognac VSOP
1½	shots	Martini Rosso sweet vermouth
1¼	shots	Martini Extra Dry vermouth
3	dashes	Angostura aromatic bitters

Variant: If orange bitters are used in place of Angostura this becomes a Harvard.
We say: A perfect Manhattan with cognac substituted for the whiskey.
Origin: A classic from the 1930s.

DELMONICO SPECIAL

★★★½☆

Glass: Martini
Garnish: Orange zest twist
Method: STIR all ingredients with ice and strain into chilled glass.

2¼	shots	Tanqueray London dry gin
¼	shot	Cognac VSOP
¾	shot	Martini Extra Dry vermouth
3	dashes	Angostura aromatic bitters

We say: A Wet Martini dried with a splash of cognac.
Origin: A classic from the 1930s.

THE DEMOCRAT

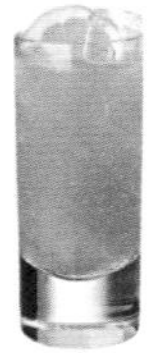

★★★½☆

Glass: Collins
Garnish: Lemon slice
Method: SHAKE with ice and strain into glass filled with crushed ice.

2	shots	Maker's Mark bourbon
½	shot	Crème de pêche de vigne liqueur
½	shot	Monin Honey syrup
1½	shots	Freshly squeezed lemon juice

We say: The base spirit is inspired by Harry Truman, 33rd President, who only drank bourbon and is considered by many to be the last great Democrat.
Origin: Created in 2007 by Jon Santer at Bourbon & Branch, San Francisco, USA as 'a kind of ode to the south - a democratic stronghold for so long'.

DEMPSEY

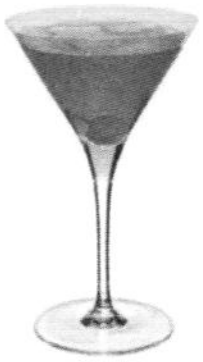

★★★★☆

Glass: Martini
Garnish: Maraschino cherry
Method: SHAKE all ingredients with ice and fine strain into chilled glass.

1½	shots	Tanqueray London dry gin
1½	shots	Calvados/Applejack brandy
⅛	shot	Absinthe
½	shot	Pomegranate (grenadine) syrup

We say: Just on the right side of sweet but as hard as nails.
Origin: A vintage cocktail of unknown origins.

DEPTH BOMB

★★★½☆

Glass: Old-fashioned
Garnish: Lime wedge
Method: SHAKE all ingredients with ice and strain into glass filled with crushed ice.

1	shot	**Calvados/Applejack brandy**
1	shot	**Cognac VSOP**
¼	shot	**Pomegranate (grenadine) syrup**
¾	shot	**Freshly squeezed lime juice**
½	shot	**Monin Pure Cane 2:1 sugar syrup**

We say: Brandy and apple brandy benefit from a sour hint of lemon, balanced by grenadine.

DEPTH CHARGE

★★☆☆☆

Glass: Boston & shot
Garnish: None
Method: POUR lager into Boston glass. POUR vodka into shot glass. DROP shot glass into lager and consume.

1½	shots	**Ketel One vodka**
1	pint	**Lager**

Variant: Boilermaker.
We say: One way to ruin a good beer.

DERBY DAIQUIRI

★★★★½

Glass: Martini
Garnish: Orange zest twist
Method: SHAKE all ingredients with ice and fine strain into chilled glass.

2	shots	**Bacardi Superior rum**
¾	shot	**Freshly squeezed orange juice**
½	shot	**Freshly squeezed lime juice**
¼	shot	**Monin Pure Cane 2:1 sugar syrup**

We say: A fruity twist on the Classic Daiquiri.

DERBY FIZZ

★★★★☆

Glass: Collins (small 8oz)
Garnish: Lemon slice
Method: SHAKE first six ingredients with ice and strain into chilled glass. TOP with soda.

1¾	shots	**Maker's Mark bourbon**
1½	shots	**Bacardi Superior rum**
¼	shot	**Grand Marnier liqueur**
1	shot	**Freshly squeezed lemon juice**
½	shot	**Monin Pure Cane 2:1 sugar syrup**
½	fresh	**Egg white**
Top up with		**Soda from siphon**

We say: An elongated sour with perfectly balanced strength, sweetness and sourness.

DESERT COOLER

★★★½☆

Glass: Collins
Garnish: Orange slice
Method: SHAKE first three ingredients with ice and strain into ice-filled glass. TOP with ginger beer.

2	shots	**Tanqueray London dry gin**
¾	shot	**De Kuyper Cherry Brandy liqueur**
1½	shots	**Freshly squeezed orange juice**
Top up with		**Ginger beer**

We say: Sandy in colour - as its name suggests - with a refreshing bite.

DETOX

★★★☆☆

Glass: Shot
Garnish: Lime wedge
Method: Refrigerate ingredients then LAYER in chilled glass by carefully pouring in the following order.

½	shot	**Peachtree peach schnapps**
½	shot	**Ocean Spray cranberry juice**
½	shot	**Ketel One vodka**

We say: Hardly a detox but tasty all the same.

DETROIT ATHLETIC CLUB NEW

★★★★½

Glass: Coupette
Garnish: Float thin lemon wheel on surface
Method: SHAKE all ingredients with ice and fine strain into chilled glass.

2	shots	**Jameson Irish whiskey**
¼	shot	**Chartreuse Green liqueur**
¼	shot	**Martini Rosso sweet vermouth**
¼	shot	**Taylor's Velvet Falernum liqueur**
¾	shot	**Chilled mineral water**

We say: Irish whisky with a splash of sweet vermouth, clove rich falernum and the all-important monastic liqueur.
Origin: Adapted from a drink created in 2010 by Donovan Sornig, Bar Manager at Bol Restaurant, Vail, Colorado. The drink was inspired by The Last Word created at the Detroit Athletic Club Donovan grew up just four miles away.

DETROIT MARTINI

★★★★☆

Glass: Martini
Garnish: Mint sprig
Method: SHAKE all ingredients (including mint) with ice and fine strain into chilled glass.

7	fresh	**Mint leaves**
3	shots	**Ketel One vodka**
½	shot	**Monin Pure Cane 2:1 sugar syrup**
⅛	shot	**Freshly squeezed lime juice**

Variant: Cowboy Hoof Martini
We say: Vodka doused mint with the merest hint of lime. Clean and flavoursome.
Origin: Created by Dick Bradsell in the mid 90s and based on his Cowboy Hoof Martini.

DETROPOLITAN

★★★★☆

Glass: Martini
Garnish: Orange zest twist (flamed)
Method: SHAKE all ingredients with ice and fine strain into chilled glass.

1	shot	Ketel One vodka
½	shot	Triple Sec
1½	shots	Ocean Spray cranberry juice
½	shot	Freshly squeezed lime juice
¼	shot	Crème de cassis liqueur

We say: Yet another twist on the Cosmopolitan.
Origin: Created at Detroit, London, England.

DEVIL

★★★⯪☆

Glass: Martini
Garnish: Lemon zest twist
Method: SHAKE all ingredients with ice and fine strain into chilled glass.

2	shots	Warre's Otima tawny port
1½	shots	Martini Extra Dry vermouth
¼	shot	Freshly squeezed lemon juice

We say: A devil to get out of your carpet but quite dry and aromatic on the palate.

DEVIL'S COCKTAIL

★★★⯪☆

Glass: Martini
Garnish: Lemon zest twist
Method: SHAKE all ingredients with ice and fine strain into a chilled glass.

2	shots	Warre's Otima tawny port
1½	shots	Martini Extra Dry vermouth
¼	shot	Freshly squeezed lemon juice

We say: Lemon predominates with the richness of port fighting to be heard.
Origin: Vintage cocktail of unknown origin.

DEVIL'S HORN NEW

★★★★☆

Glass: Coupette
Garnish: Two chillies on rim as devil's horns
Method: MUDDLE chilli in base of shaker. Add other ingredients, SHAKE with ice and fine strain into chilled glass.

1	ring	Red chilli (thin slice)
3	fresh	Raspberries
2	shots	Rum Aged
¾	shot	Ocean Spray cranberry juice
1	shot	Monin Honey syrup
1	shot	Freshly squeezed lime juice

We say: A great balance of sweetness, sourness and spice.
Origin: Created in 2010 by Roger Vilalta at Banker's Bar, Mandarin Oriental, Barcelona, Spain.

DEVIL'S MANHATTAN

★★★★☆

Glass: Martini
Garnish: Lemon zest twist
Method: STIR all ingredients with ice and strain into chilled glass.

2	shots	Maker's Mark bourbon
1	shot	Southern Comfort liqueur
½	shot	Martini Rosso sweet vermouth
3	dashes	Peychaud's aromatic bitters

We say: A sweet Manhattan with a hint of the south.

DEVIL'S SHARE

★★★★☆

Glass: Old-fashioned
Garnish: Orange zest twist
Method: MUDDLE ginger in base of shaker. Add other ingredients, SHAKE with ice and fine strain into ice-filled glass.

2	slices	Fresh root ginger (thumbnail sized)
2	shots	Maker's Mark bourbon
¾	shot	Freshly squeezed orange juice
1	shot	Freshly squeezed lemon juice
½	shot	Maple syrup

We say: Ginger, bourbon and lemon makes for a spicy and tasty little devil.
Origin: Created in 2006 by Pete Kendall at Match Bar, London, England.

DIABLE ROUGE

★★★⯪☆

Glass: Martini
Garnish: Seasonal berries
Method: SHAKE all ingredients with ice and fine strain into chilled glass.

2	shots	Ketel One vodka
2	shots	Fresh pressed pineapple juice
¼	shot	Crème de cassis liqueur

We say: Not quite as rouge as the name would suggest. Hard to hate.

DIAMOND DOG

★★★⯪☆

Glass: Old-fashioned
Garnish: Orange slice
Method: SHAKE all ingredients with ice and strain into ice-filled glass.

1	shot	Campari Bitter
1	shot	Martini Extra Dry vermouth
1	shot	Rose's lime cordial
1	shot	Freshly squeezed orange juice

We say: Bittersweet and refreshingly different.
Origin: Discovered in 2005 at Four Seasons George V, Paris, France.

DIAMOND FIZZ

★★★★☆

Glass: Collins (small 8oz)
Garnish: Lemon slice
Method: SHAKE first three ingredients with ice and strain into chilled glass (without ice). TOP with champagne.

2	shots	**Tanqueray London dry gin**
1	shot	**Freshly squeezed lemon juice**
½	shot	**Monin Pure Cane 2:1 sugar syrup**
Top up with		**Brut champagne**

We say: Why top a Fizz with soda when you can use champagne?
Origin: A long lost classic.

DIAMONDBACK NEW

★★★★½

Glass: Coupette
Garnish: Maraschino cherry
Method: STIR all ingredients with ice and strain unto chilled glass.

1½	shots	**Straight rye whiskey**
¾	shot	**Laird's Applejack brandy**
¾	shot	**Chartreuse Yellow liqueur**

We say: This potent cocktail marries apple spirit with rye whiskey and rich herbal Chartreuse. A great after dinner tipple.
Origin: Adapted from Ted Saucier's 1951 *Bottoms UP* book in which the author calls for two parts rye whiskey, one part applejack and one part yellow Chartreuse.

DIANA'S BITTER

★★★☆☆

Glass: Martini
Garnish: Lime wedge
Method: SHAKE all ingredients with ice and fine strain into chilled glass.

2	shots	**Tanqueray London dry gin**
1	shot	**Campari Bitter**
1	shot	**Freshly squeezed lime juice**
½	shot	**Monin Pure Cane 2:1 sugar syrup**

We say: A drink for the Campari aficionado: bittersweet and strong.

DICKENS' DRY MARTINI

★★★★½

Glass: Martini
Garnish: None
Method: STIR all ingredients with ice and strain into chilled glass.

2½	shots	**Tanqueray London dry gin**
½	shot	**Martini Extra Dry vermouth**

We say: A 5:1 Dry Martini served with out any garnish (i.e. no olive or twist). The names is a reference to Charles Dicken's novel Oliver Twist.

DIKI-DIKI

★★★★½

Glass: Martini
Garnish: Sugar rim
Method: SHAKE all ingredients with ice and fine strain into chilled glass.

2	shots	**Calvados/Applejack brandy**
½	shot	**Swedish Punch liqueur**
½	shot	**Freshly squeezed grapefruit juice**

We say: Fruity yet tart. The sourness is a challenge initially but very rewarding.
Origin: Adapted from Harry Craddock's 1930 '*The Savoy Cocktail Book*'.

DIMI-TINI

★★★★☆

Glass: Martini
Garnish: Grapefruit zest twist
Method: SHAKE all ingredients with ice and fine strain into chilled glass.

7	fresh	**Raspberries**
2	shots	**Ketel One vodka**
¼	shot	**De Kuyper Cherry Brandy liqueur**
½	shot	**Freshly squeezed lime juice**
⅛	shot	**Monin Pure Cane 2:1 sugar syrup**

We say: Like Dimi - this drink's easy to like.
Origin: Adapted from a recipe by Dimitri Lezinska, the Grey Goose Ambassador, originally using Grey Goose vodka.

DINGO

★★★☆☆

Glass: Collins
Garnish: Orange slice
Method: SHAKE all ingredients with ice and strain into ice-filled glass.

1	shot	**Bacardi Superior rum**
1	shot	**Maker's Mark bourbon**
½	shot	**Amaretto liqueur**
2	shots	**Freshly squeezed orange juice**
1	shot	**Freshly squeezed lemon juice**
¼	shot	**Pomegranate (grenadine) syrup**
¼	shot	**Monin Pure Cane 2:1 sugar syrup**

We say: Very fruity but with a rum and whiskey kick.

DINO SOUR

★★★★½

Glass: Old-fashioned
Garnish: Lemon slice & cherry on stick (sail)
Method: SHAKE all ingredients with ice and fine strain into chilled glass.

1	shot	**Bacardi Superior rum**
1	shot	**Gosling's Black Seal rum**
1	shot	**Freshly squeezed lemon juice**
½	shot	**Monin Pure Cane 2:1 sugar syrup**
½	fresh	**Egg white**

We say: Two diverse rums combine brilliantly in this classic sour.

DIPLOMAT

★★★½☆

Glass: Old-fashioned
Garnish: Orange zest twist
Method: STIR all ingredients with ice and strain into ice-filled glass.

2	shots	**Martini Extra Dry vermouth**
1	shot	**Martini Rosso sweet vermouth**
⅛	shot	**Luxardo Maraschino liqueur**
2	dashes	**Orange bitters**

We say: Wonderfully aromatic and dry. Too good to waste on diplomats.
Origin: Adapted from Harry Craddock's 1930 '*The Savoy Cocktail Book*'.

DIRTY BANANA

★★★★☆

Glass: Collins
Garnish: Banana chunk
Method: BLEND all ingredients with 12oz scoop crushed ice. Serve with straws.

1½	shots	**Bacardi Superior rum**
1	shot	**Kahlúa coffee liqueur**
1	shot	**Bols Banana liqueur**
1	shot	**Double (heavy) cream**
1	shot	**Milk**
1	fresh	**Banana (peeled)**

We say: Long, creamy and filling banana drink with a 'dirty' flavour and colour courtesy of coffee liqueur.
Origin: A popular cocktail in Jamaica.

DIRTY DRY MARTINI

★★★½☆

Glass: Martini
Garnish: Olive on stick
Method: STIR all ingredients with ice and strain into a chilled glass.

2½	shots	**Tanqueray London dry gin**
¼	shot	**Olive brine (from jarred olive)**
¼	shot	**Martini Extra dry vermouth**

AKA: F.D.R. Martini after the American president Frankin Delano Roosevelt.
Variant: Substitute vodka for gin.
We say: This drink varies from delicious to disgusting, depending on the liquid in your jar of olives. Oil will provide a revolting emulsion: make sure that your olives are packed in brine.

DIRTY SANCHEZ

★★★★☆

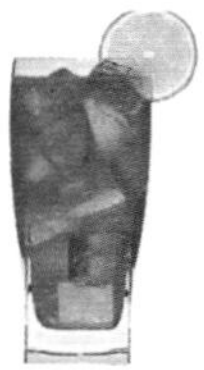

Glass: Collins
Garnish: Lime slice
Method: SHAKE first four ingredients with ice and strain into ice-filled glass. TOP with ginger beer.

2	shots	**Tequila 100% Agave**
¾	shot	**Agavero liqueur**
½	shot	**Chambord black raspberry liqueur**
½	shot	**Freshly squeezed lime juice**
Top up with		**Ginger beer**

We say: A wonderfully refreshing and complex long summer drink.
Origin: Created in 2001 by Phillip Jeffrey and Ian Baldwin at the GE Club, London, England.

DIVINO'S

★★★★☆

Glass: Martini
Garnish: Dust with grated white chocolate
Method: SHAKE all ingredients with ice and fine strain into chilled glass.

½	shot	**Ketel One vodka**
2½	shots	**Barolo wine**
1	shot	**Dark Crème de Cacao**

We say: The chocolate liqueur takes the acidity off the wine without masking its flavour.
Origin: Discovered in 2005 at DiVino, Hong Kong.

DIXIE COSMOPOLITAN

★★★☆☆

Glass: Martini
Garnish: Cinnamon & sugar rim with orange zest twist (flamed)
Method: Brake up section of cinnamon and drop into shaker. Add other ingredients, SHAKE with ice and fine strain into chilled glass.

2	inch	**Cinnamon stick**
1	shot	**Southern Comfort liqueur**
1	shot	**Triple Sec**
¼	shot	**Rose's lime cordial**
1½	shots	**Ocean Spray cranberry juice**

We say: Slightly sweet and somewhat reminiscent of jellybean sweets.
Origin: Created circa 2005 by Matthew Dakers, a globetrotting professional bartender.

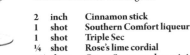

DIXIE DEW

★★★★½

Glass: Martini
Garnish: Orange zest twist
Method: SHAKE all ingredients with ice and fine strain into chilled glass.

2	shots	**Maker's Mark bourbon**
½	shot	**Giffard Menthe Pastille liqueur**
½	shot	**Triple Sec**
¾	shot	**Chilled mineral water**

We say: A peppermint fresh, bourbon laced drink.

DNA #1

★★★½☆

Glass: Martini
Garnish: Orange zest twist
Method: SHAKE all ingredients with ice and fine strain into chilled glass.

1½	shots	**Tanqueray London dry gin**
¾	shot	**De Kuyper Apricot Brandy liqueur**
1	shot	**Freshly squeezed lemon juice**
¼	shot	**Monin Pure Cane 2:1 sugar syrup**
2	dashes	**Orange bitters**

We say: Slightly sharp and very fruity, but pleasantly so.
Origin: Created by Emmanuel Audermatte at The Atlantic Bar and Grill, London, England, 1999.

DNA #2

★★★☆☆

Glass: Martini
Garnish: Lemon zest twist
Method: SHAKE all ingredients with ice and fine strain into chilled glass.

1	shot	Tanqueray London dry gin
1	shot	Damson gin liqueur
¾	shot	De Kuyper Apricot Brandy liqueur
½	shot	Freshly squeezed lime juice
2	dashes	Angostura aromatic bitters
½	shot	Chilled mineral water

We say: Tangy, fruity and gin laced.
Origin: Created in 2005 by Tonin Kacaj at Maze, London, England.

DOCTOR #1

★★★★⯪

Glass: Martini
Garnish: Lime zest twist
Method: SHAKE all ingredients with ice and fine strain into chilled glass.

1½	shots	Bacardi 8yo aged rum
1½	shots	Swedish Punch liqueur
¾	shot	Freshly squeezed lime juice

We say: Retitled 'Swedish Daiquiri', this could be a hit.
Origin: In David Embury's classic, 'The Fine Art of Mixing Drinks', my hero lists four wildly different drinks using Swedish Punch. 'Trader Vic's 'Bartender's Guide' lists two variations of a single drink, for which the above is my own recipe.

DOCTOR #2

★★★★⯪

Glass: Martini
Garnish: Lime zest twist
Method: SHAKE all ingredients with ice and fine strain into chilled glass.

| 2 | shots | Swedish Punch liqueur |
| 1 | shot | Freshly squeezed lime juice |

We say: Lime combines wells with the aromatics spices in Swedish Punch.
Origin: Vintage cocktail of unknown origin.

DOCTOR FUNK

★★★⯪☆

Glass: Sling
Garnish: Lime wedge
Method: SHAKE first 6 ingredients with ice and strain into glass filled with crushed ice. TOP with soda and serve with straws.

2½	shots	Gosling's Black Seal rum
¼	shot	Pernod anise
½	shot	Freshly squeezed lemon juice
¼	shot	Freshly squeezed lime juice
¼	shot	Monin Pure Cane 2:1 sugar syrup
¼	shot	Pomegranate (grenadine) syrup
Top up with		Soda (club soda)

We say: Too many and you'll need your very own doctor.
Origin: A Tiki drink adapted from one created circa 1937 by Don the Beachcomber.

DOHENY PISCO PUNCH

★★★★☆

Glass: Collins
Garnish: Mint sprig & pineapple slice
Method: Lightly MUDDLE (just to bruise) mint in base of shaker. Add next five ingredients, SHAKE with ice and strain into ice-filled glass. TOP with ginger beer.

12	fresh	Mint fresh sprigs
1½	shots	Fresh pressed pineapple juice
2	shots	Macchu pisco
¾	shot	Freshly squeezed lemon juice
¼	shot	Monin Vanilla sugar syrup
1	dash	Angostura aromatic bitters
Top up with		Ginger beer

We say: Vincenzo's twist on the San Franciscan classic.
Origin: Adapted from a drink created in 2007 by Vincenzo Marianello at Doheny, Los Angeles, USA.

DOLCE HAVANA

★★★★☆

Glass: Martini
Garnish: None
Method: SHAKE all ingredients with ice and fine strain into chilled glass.

1¼	shots	Bacardi Superior rum
½	shot	Triple Sec
½	shot	Campari Bitter
1¼	shots	Freshly squeezed orange juice
1¼	shots	Freshly squeezed lime juice
⅛	shot	Monin Pure Cane 2:1 sugar syrup

We say: A melange of Mediterranean fruit.
Origin: Created by Fabrizio Musorella in 2000 at the Library Bar, Lanesborough Hotel, London, England.

DOLCE-AMARO

★★★⯪☆

Glass: Martini
Garnish: Orange zest twist
Method: STIR all ingredients with ice and strain into chilled glass.

¾	shot	Amaretto liqueur
1½	shots	Campari Bitter
1½	shots	Martini Extra Dry vermouth

We say: The very apt name translates as 'bittersweet'.

DOLORES #1

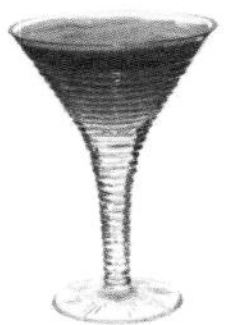

★★★★☆

Glass: Martini
Garnish: Lemon zest twist
Method: SHAKE all ingredients with ice and fine strain into chilled glass.

2	shots	Bacardi 8yo aged rum
2	shots	Dubonnet Red (French made)
1	shot	Tio Pepe fino sherry

We say: Aromatic and well balanced, provided you use French-made Dubonnet.
Origin: A classic. Some recipes include a splash of orange juice.

DOLORES #2

★★★½☆

Glass: Martini
Garnish: Dust with grated nutmeg
Method: SHAKE all ingredients with ice and fine strain into chilled glass.

1½	shots	Cognac VSOP
¾	shot	De Kuyper Cherry Brandy liqueur
¾	shot	White Crème de Cacao
1	fresh	Egg white

We say: A chocolaty after dinner libation.

DON DAISY

★★★★☆

Glass: Martini
Garnish: Lemon zest twist
Method: SHAKE all ingredients with ice and fine strain into chilled glass.

1½	shots	Bacardi Superior rum
½	shot	St-Germain elderflower liqueur
½	shot	Martini Extra Dry vermouth
¼	shot	Freshly squeezed lemon juice
¼	shot	Monin Pure Cane 2:1 sugar syrup
½	fresh	Egg white

We say: A zesty, silky smooth and easy drink..
Origin: Created in 2008 by James Tait, UK.

DON JUAN

★★★½☆

Glass: Martini
Garnish: Orange zest twist
Method: SHAKE all ingredients with ice and fine strain into chilled glass.

1¾	shots	Cognac VSOP
1	shot	Cuarenta y Tres (Licor 43) liqueur
1	shot	Freshly squeezed orange juice
½	shot	Milk
½	shot	Double (heavy) cream

We say: A lightly creamy orange affair with vanilla spice.

DON'S DELIGHT

★★★★½

Glass: Martini
Garnish: Lime wedge
Method: SHAKE all ingredients with ice and fine strain into chilled glass.

2	shots	Tequila 100% Agave
½	shot	Maker's Mark bourbon
⅛	shot	Amaretto liqueur
1¼	shots	Lime
½	shot	Monin Pure Cane 2:1 sugar syrup
1	fresh	Egg white

We say: When made with Don Julio 1942, as this drink originally was, this is another memorable trick by the affable Brian Van Flandern.
Origin: Created in 2008 by Brian Van Flandern (Don Julio Global Brand Ambassador) in New York, USA.

DON'S PASSION

★★★½☆

Glass: Coupette
Garnish: Passion fruit
Method: Cut passion fruit in half and scoop out flesh and seeds into shaker. Add next 4 ingredients, SHAKE with ice and fine strain into chilled glass. Pour grenadine into centre of drink (should sink to bottom).

1	fresh	Passion fruit
2	shots	Bacardi Superior rum
½	shot	Galliano L'Autentico liqueur
1	shot	Freshly squeezed lime juice
½	shot	Freshly squeezed orange juice
¼	shot	Pomegranate (grenadine) syrup

We say: Passion fruit and Galliano influence this Bacardi Cocktail-style drink.
Origin: Created in 2008 by Symeon White at Avon Gorge Hotel, Bristol, UK.

DONEGAL

★★★★☆

Glass: Martini
Garnish: Orange zest twist
Method: SHAKE all ingredients with ice and fine strain into chilled glass.

1½	shots	Jameson Irish whiskey
½	shot	Luxardo Maraschino liqueur
½	shot	Mandarine Napoléon liqueur
1¼	shots	Martini Extra Dry vermouth

We say: Aromatised Irish whiskey with cherry and orange.

DONNA'S CREAMY'TINI

★★★★☆

Glass: Martini
Garnish: Maraschino cherry
Method: SHAKE all ingredients with ice and fine strain into chilled glass.

1	shot	Amaretto liqueur
1	shot	De Kuyper Cherry Brandy liqueur
1	shot	Dark Crème de Cacao
1	shot	Double (heavy) cream

We say: A fine example of an alcoholic liquid pudding.
Origin: Adapted from a drink created in 2002 by Yannick Miseriaux at the Fifth Floor Bar, London, England.

DOPO CENA NEW

★★★★☆

Glass: Coupette
Garnish: Cherry
Method: DRY SHAKE all ingredients (without ice). SHAKE again with ice and fine strain into chilled glass.

1	shot	Luxardo Amaretto di Saschira
1	shot	Kirsch eau-de-vie
½	shot	Luxardo maraschino liqueur
1	shot	Freshly squeezed lemon juice
1	spoon	Monin Pure Cane 2:1 sugar syrup
1	dash	Egg white
1	dash	Angostura aromatic bitters

We say: Under the white head lies a desert cocktail with aromatic cherry and marzipan flavours.
Origin: Created by Adrian Gomes, 10 Dollar Shake, Aberdeen, Scotland.

DORIAN GRAY

★★★½☆

Glass: Martini
Garnish: Orange zest twist
Method: SHAKE all ingredients with ice and fine strain into chilled glass.

1½	shots	**Bacardi Superior rum**
¾	shot	**Grand Marnier liqueur**
1	shot	**Freshly squeezed orange juice**
¾	shot	**Ocean Spray cranberry juice**

We say: Fruity and rum laced, not overly sweet.
Origin: Discovered in 1999 at One Aldwych, London, England. This cocktail takes its name from Oscar Wilde's novel, in which a socialite's wish to remain as young and charming as his own portrait is granted. Allured by his depraved friend Lord Henry Wotton, Dorian Gray assumes a life of perversion and sin. But every time he sins the painting ages, while Gray stays young and healthy.

DOROTHY PARKER

★★★½☆

Glass: Martini
Garnish: Sugar rim
Method: SHAKE first 4 ingredients with ice and fine strain into chilled glass. TOP with champagne.

1½	shots	**Ketel One Citroen vodka**
½	shot	**Triple Sec**
¼	shot	**Chambord black raspberry liqueur**
½	shot	**Freshly squeezed lemon juice**
Top up with		**Brut champagne**

We say: Light, fruity and easy to drink.
Origin: Discovered in 2007 at Town Hall, San Francisco, USA, and named for the wit and drinker.

DOUBLE GRAPE MARTINI

★★★★½

Glass: Martini
Garnish: White grapes
Method: MUDDLE grapes in base of shaker. Add other ingredients, SHAKE with ice and fine strain into chilled glass.

12	fresh	**Seedless white grapes**
2	shots	**Ketel One vodka**
¾	shot	**Sauvignon blanc wine**
½	shot	**Monin Pure Cane 2:1 sugar syrup**

We say: The wine adds complexity to a simple Grape Martini.
Origin: Created by Simon Difford in 2004.

STAR RATINGS EXPLAINED

★★★★★ Excellent

★★★★½ Recommended	★★★★☆ Praiseworthy
★★★½☆ Commended	★★★☆☆ Mediocre
★★½☆☆ Disappointing	★★☆☆☆ Pretty awful
★½☆☆☆ Shameful	★☆☆☆☆ Disgusting

DOUBLE VISION

★★★☆☆

Glass: Martini
Garnish: Blackcurrants
Method: SHAKE all ingredients with ice and fine strain into chilled glass.

1	shot	**Ketel One Citroen vodka**
1	shot	**Raspberry flavoured vodka**
1	shot	**Pressed apple juice**
½	shot	**Freshly squeezed lime juice**
¼	shot	**Monin Pure Cane 2:1 sugar syrup**
3	dashes	**Angostura aromatic bitters**

We say: Citrus fresh with strong hints of apple and red berries.

DOUGHNUT MARTINI

★★★½☆

Glass: Martini
Garnish: Doughnut segment
Method: SHAKE all ingredients with ice and fine strain into chilled glass.

1½	shots	**Bacardi Superior rum**
¾	shot	**Maker's Mark bourbon**
½	shot	**Vanilla schnapps**
½	shot	**Cuarenta y Tres (Licor 43) liqueur**
½	shot	**Butterscotch schnapps**
¾	shot	**Chilled mineral water**

We say: My attempt at mimicking the taste of a Krispy Kreme Original Glazed doughnut without ending up with an overly sweet cocktail.
Origin: Created in 2003 by Simon Difford.

DOWA

★★★★☆

Glass: Old-fashioned
Garnish: Lime wedge
Method: STIR honey and vodka in base of shaker until honey dissolves. Add lime juice, SHAKE with ice and strain into glass filled with crushed ice. Serve with straws.

2½	shots	**Ketel One vodka**
4	spoons	**Runny honey**
¼	shot	**Freshly squeezed lime juice**

We say: Very similar to the Caipirovska in its use of vodka, lime and crushed ice: the honey makes the difference.
Origin: This cocktail is particularly popular in upscale hotel bars in Kenya where it is enjoyed by the safari set. The name translates as 'medicine'.

DOWNHILL RACER

★★★★☆

Glass: Martini
Garnish: Pineapple wedge
Method: SHAKE all ingredients with ice and fine strain into chilled glass.

1¾	shots	**Bacardi Superior rum**
¾	shot	**Amaretto liqueur**
1¾	shots	**Fresh pressed pineapple juice**

We say: Aged rum sweetened, softened and flavoured with pineapple and amaretto.

DR ZEUS

★★★★⯪☆

Glass: Old-fashioned
Garnish: None
Method: POUR Fernet Branca into ice-filled glass. Separately MUDDLE raisins in base of shaker, add other ingredients and SHAKE with ice. Finally DISCARD contents of glass and strain contents of shaker into the Fernet Branca coated glass.

1	shot	Fernet Branca
20	dried	Raisins
2	shots	Cognac VSOP
¼	shot	Monin Pure Cane 2:1 sugar syrup
⅛	shot	Kahlúa coffee liqueur
1	dash	Orange bitters

We say: Not that far removed from a Sazerac cocktail, this is innovative and great tasting.
Origin: Created by Adam Ennis in 2001 at Isola, Knightsbridge, London, England.

DRAGON BLOSSOM

★★★☆☆

Glass: Martini
Garnish: Maraschino cherry
Method: SHAKE all ingredients with ice and fine strain into chilled glass.

1¾	shots	Lanique rose petal liqueur
¼	shot	Kwai Feh lychee liqueur
¼	shot	Maraschino syrup (from cherry jar)
1¾	shots	Ocean Spray cranberry juice

We say: Light, aromatic, semi-sweet and distinctly oriental in style.

DRAMATIC MARTINI

★★★⯪☆

Glass: Martini
Garnish: Dust with grated nutmeg
Method: SHAKE all ingredients with ice and fine strain into chilled glass.

1	shot	Tuaca liqueur
1	shot	Grand Marnier liqueur
1	shot	Baileys Irish cream liqueur
1	shot	Milk

We say: Creamy and sweet with orangey, herbal notes.

DREAM COCKTAIL UPDATED

★★★★☆

Glass: Martini
Garnish: Orange zest twist
Method: SHAKE all ingredients with ice and fine strain into chilled glass.

1½	shots	Courvoisier VSOP Exclusif
¾	shot	Cointreau triple sec
⅛	shot	Marie Brizard anisette liqueur
½	shot	Chilled mineral water

Variant: Made with orange curaçao and absinthe - if you reduce the strength of the liqueur then up the anti on the aniseed.
We say: An after-dinner drink with brandy, orange liqueur and a refreshing burst of aniseed. Double the measure of anisette liqueur if a tad on the sweet side.

DREAMSICLE

★★★⯪☆

Glass: Martini
Garnish: None
Method: SHAKE first 3 ingredients with ice and fine strain into chilled glass. FLOAT cream.

1½	shots	Kahlúa coffee liqueur
¾	shot	Triple Sec
1	shot	Freshly squeezed orange juice
¾	shot	Double (heavy) cream

We say: Sweet coffee and orange smoothed by a creamy top. A veritable dessert in a glass.

DREAMY DORINI SMOKING MARTINI

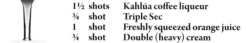

★★★★☆

Glass: Coupette
Garnish: Lemon zest twist
Method: STIR all ingredients with ice and strain into chilled glass.

2	shots	Ketel One vodka
½	shot	Laphroaig 10yo single malt
½	spoon	Pernod anise

We say: As the name implies, this Martini is a good helping of smoky peat. If you like that kind of thing, it's equally dreamy.
Origin: Adapted from a recipe created by Audrey Saunders in 2003 at Beacon restaurant, New York, USA

DREIKLANG (THREE OF A KIND)

★★★★☆

Glass: Old-fashioned
Garnish: Orange zest twist
Method: STIR sugar syrup with two ice cubes, add xoxolate mole and stir again. Add more ice plus tequila and STIR some more.

2	shots	Tequila 100% Agave
½	shot	Monin Pure Cane 2:1 sugar syrup
5	drops	Xocolatl Mole bitters

We say: Named after the German word for 'three of a kind' due to the trio of flavours encountered in this drink; orange, agave and chocolate.
Origin: Created in 2007 by Heiko Tagawa, Germany.

DROWNED OUT

★★★⯪☆

Glass: Collins
Garnish: Lime wedge
Method: POUR ingredients into ice-filled glass, stir and serve with straws.

2	shots	Pernod anise
1	shot	Freshly squeezed lime juice
Top up with		Ginger ale

We say: Ginger combines with aniseed rather than drowning it.

DRY DAIQUIRI

★★★½☆

Glass: Martini
Garnish: Lime wedge
Method: SHAKE all ingredients with ice and fine strain into chilled glass.

2	shots	Bacardi 8yo aged rum
½	shot	Freshly squeezed lime juice
¼	shot	Monin Pure Cane 2:1 sugar syrup
⅛	shot	Campari Bitter
⅛	shot	Passion fruit syrup

We say: Passion fruit syrup is powerful stuff and a little goes a long way in this drink.
Origin: Created in 2007 by Kevin Armstrong, Match Group, London.

DRY ICE MARTINI

★★★★½

Glass: Martini
Garnish: Lemon zest twist
Method: STIR all ingredients with ice and strain into chilled glass.

2	shots	Ketel One vodka
½	shot	Martini Extra Dry vermouth
¾	shot	Icewine

We say: Despite the name, this is slightly honeyed rather than dry.
Origin: Created by Simon Difford in 2004

DRY MARTINI #1 UPDATED
(PREFERRED 5:1 RATIO)

★★★★★

Glass: Martini
Garnish: Chilled olive on stick or lemon zest twist
Method: STIR all ingredients with ice and strain into chilled glass.

2½	shots	Tanqueray London dry gin
½	shot	Martini Extra Dry vermouth
4	drops	Orange bitters

Variant: The following are some of the most popular variations on the classic Dry Martini:

Dickens' Martini - without a twist.
Dirty Martini - with the brine from an olive jar.
Franklin Martini - named after Franklin Roosevelt and served with two olives.
Gibson Martini - with two cocktail onions.
Vesper Martini - James Bond's Martini, made with gin and vodka.
Vodkatini - very dry, vodka based Martini.
Wet Martini - heavy on the vermouth.

We say: We have chosen a 5:1 ratio as our 'preferred' Dry Martini specification in deference to David Embury who writes of this drink in his "*The Fine Art of Mixing Drinks*", "After extensive experimentation I have arrived at the ratio of 5 to 1 as the proportion most pleasing to the average palate. Personally I like a ratio of about 7 to 1 even better, and I know some who prefer a ratio as high as 10 to 1."

The proportion of gin to vermouth is a matter of taste; some say 5 to 1, others that one drop is sufficient. I recommend you ask the drinker how they would like their Martini, in the same manner that you might ask how they have their steak.

DRY MARTINI #2 UPDATED
(NAKED 10:1 RATIO)

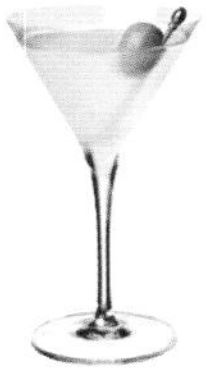

★★★★☆

Glass: Martini
Garnish: Chilled olive on stick or lemon zest twist
Method: POUR water into glass, swirl around to coat and place in freezer for at least two hours, alongside the bottle of gin, until the inside of the glass is covered in a thin layer of ice and the gin is frozen. POUR vermouth into icy glass and swirl to coat the ice with vermouth. POUR frozen gin into glass and serve immediately.

2½	shots	The Bombay Original dry gin
¼	shot	Chilled mineral water
⅛	shot	Martini Extra dry vermouth

AKA: Diamond Martini
We say: Dilution is achieved as the water you have frozen in the glass begins to melt. Both glass and gin must be freezing cold so that the temperature masks the strength of the alcohol. Thus the drink does not taste nearly as strong as it is – you have been warned.
Origin: After the Second World War, vermouth proportions in the classic Dry Martini dropped rapidly, and this 'Naked'-style of serve began to appear. Traditionally both vermouth and gin had been stirred with ice. In a Naked Martini the merest hint of vermouth is swirled around a well-chilled glass and then frozen gin is poured into the vermouth-coated glass.

The trick to a good Naked Martini is still achieving some dilution by the addition of a splash of water in the glass before freezing. I learnt this from Salvatore Calabrese, who once tended bar at London's Duke's Hotel – famous for its Dry Martinis.

DRY MARTINI #3 NEW
(3:1 RATIO)

★★★★½

Glass: Martini
Garnish: Chilled olive on stick or lemon zest twist
Method: STIR all ingredients with ice and strain into chilled glass.

| 2¼ | shots | London Dry vermouth |
| ¾ | shot | Martini Extra Dry vermouth |

We say: Unfair odds in a fight but vermouth shines in this off-dry Martini.

DRY MARTINI #4 NEW
(EMBURY'S 7:1 RATIO)

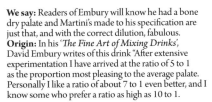

★★★★★

Glass: Martini
Garnish: Chilled olive on stick or lemon zest twist
Method: STIR all ingredients with ice and strain into chilled glass.

| 2½ | shots | London Dry vermouth |
| ⅓ | shots | Martini Extra Dry vermouth |

We say: Readers of Embury will know he had a bone dry palate and Martini's made to his specification are just that, and with the correct dilution, fabulous.
Origin: In his '*The Fine Art of Mixing Drinks*', David Embury writes of this drink "After extensive experimentation I have arrived at the ratio of 5 to 1 as the proportion most pleasing to the average palate. Personally I like a ratio of about 7 to 1 even better, and I know some who prefer a ratio as high as 10 to 1.

DRY MARTINI #5 UPDATED
(MONTGOMERY'S 15:1 RATIO)

★★★★☆

Glass: Martini
Garnish: Lemon zest twist
Method: SHAKE all ingredients with ice and fine strain into chilled glass.

2	shots	Tanqueray London dry gin
	shot	Martini Extra dry vermouth
1	dash	Orange bitters

We say: Bone dry - a superbly cleansing Martini. Through experimentation we have found that 15:1 Martinis are better shaken rather than stirred. Conversely 3:1 Martinis are better stirred rather than shaken.
Origin: Unknown but this 15:1 gin-to-vermouth Martini was said to be Ernest Hemingway's favourite formula and is named after British Field Marshall Bernard Montgomery, who it is said, liked the gin in his Martini to outnumber the vermouth in roughly the same ratio as he liked to outnumber his opponents in battle.

Nicknamed 'Monty', Field Marshal Bernard Law Montgomery (1887-1976) fought and was seriously wounded in the First World War and was one of the most notorious British commanders in the Second World War. He commanded allied troops at the Battle of El Alamein and was a key planner of the Normandy D-Day invasion. On 4 May 1945 he took the German surrender at Luneburg Heath in northern Germany.

DRY MARTINI #5 UPDATED
(MONTGOMERY'S 15:1 RATIO)

★★★★☆

Glass: Martini
Garnish: Lemon zest twist
Method: STIR all ingredients with ice and fine strain into chilled glass.

2	shots	Tanqueray London dry gin
⅓	shot	Martini Extra Dry vermouth
1	dash	Orange bitters

We say: Bone dry - a superbly cleansing Martini.
Origin: Unknown but this 15:1 gin to vermouth Martini was said to be Ernest Hemingway's favourite formula and is named after British Field Marshall Bernard Montgomery, who it is said, liked the gin in his Martini to outnumber the vermouth in roughly the same ratio as he liked to outnumber his opponents in battle.
Nicknamed 'Monty', Field Marshal Bernard Law Montgomery (1887-1976) fought and was seriously wounded in the First World War and was one of the most notorious British commanders in the Second World War. He commanded allied troops at the Battle of El Alamein and was a key planner of the Normandy D-Day invasion. On 4 May 1945 he took the German surrender at Luneburg Heath in northern Germany.

DRY MARTINI #6 UPDATED
(SERVED WET 2:1 RATIO)

★★★★☆

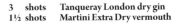

Glass: Martini
Garnish: Chilled olive on stick or lemon zest twist
Method: STIR all ingredients with ice and strain into chilled glass.

| 3 | shots | Tanqueray London dry gin |
| 1½ | shots | Martini Extra Dry vermouth |

AKA: Wet Martini
We say: Reputed to be a favourite of HRH Prince Charles.
Origin: A generous measure of vermouth to two of gin, hence the name 'Wet' Martini.

DRY MARTINI #7 UPDATED
(SOPPING WET 2:1.5 RATIO)

★★★★☆

Glass: Martini
Garnish: Chilled olive on stick or lemon zest twist.
Method: STIR all ingredients with ice and strain into chilled glass.

| 2½ | shots | The Bombay Original dry gin |
| ⅓ | shot | Martini Extra dry vermouth |

We say: Readers of Embury will know he had a bone dry palate and Martinis made to his specification are just that, and with the correct dilution, fabulous.
Origin: In his *Fine Art of Mixing Drinks*, David Embury writes of this drink: "After extensive experimentation I have arrived at the ratio of 5 to 1 as the proportion most pleasing to the average palate. Personally, I like a ratio of about 7 to 1 even better, and I know some who prefer a ratio as high as 10 to 1.

DRY ORANGE MARTINI

★★★★☆

Glass: Martini
Garnish: Grapefruit zest twist
Method: STIR all ingredients with ice and strain into chilled glass.

2	shots	Tanqueray London dry gin
¼	shot	Triple Sec
¾	shot	Martini Extra Dry vermouth
2	dashes	Orange bitters

We say: Bone dry, orangey, aptly named Martini.
Origin: Created in 2003 by Wayne Collins for Maxxium UK.

DUBLINER

★★★★☆

Glass: Martini
Garnish: Maraschino cherry
Method: STIR all ingredients with ice and strain into chilled glass.

2	shots	Jameson Irish whiskey
½	shot	Grand Marnier liqueur
½	shot	Martini Rosso sweet vermouth
1	dash	Orange bitters

We say: Irish whiskey shines through the spicy orange.
Origin: Adapted from a recipe by Gary Regan and discovered in 2007 at Death & Company, New York City, USA.

THE DUBONNET COCKTAIL #1

Glass: Old-fashioned
Garnish: Lemon zest twist
Method: STIR all ingredients with ice and strain into ice-filled glass.

1½	shots	Tanqueray London dry gin
1½	shots	Dubonnet Red (French made)
¼	shot	Freshly squeezed lemon juice

We say: Simple yet complex. Dry and aromatic.
Origin: A classic that was popular in Britain during the 1920s.

THE DUBONNET COCKTAIL #2

Glass: Martini
Garnish: Lemon zest twist
Method: SHAKE all ingredients with ice and fine strain into chilled glass.

1½	shots	Tanqueray London dry gin
1½	shots	Dubonnet Red (French made)
¼	shot	Freshly squeezed lemon juice

We say: Gin and Dubonnet with a hint of citrus. Be sure your Dubonnet is the French stuff.
Origin: Vintage cocktail of unknown origin.

DULCHIN

Glass: Martini
Garnish: Orange zest twist
Method: SHAKE all ingredients with ice and fine strain into chilled glass.

2	shots	Macchu pisco
½	shot	Grand Marnier liqueur
½	shot	De Kuyper Apricot Brandy liqueur
¼	shot	Rose's lime cordial
¼	shot	Pomegranate (grenadine) syrup
¾	shot	Chilled mineral water

We say: This dry, amber coloured, fruity cocktail carries a pisco punch.

THE DUNAWAY NEW

Glass: Coupette
Garnish: Lemon zest twist (discarded)
Method: STIR all ingredients with ice and strain into chilled glass.

2¼	shots	Tio Pepe fino sherry
½	shot	Cynar
¼	shot	Luxardo maraschino liqueur
2	dashes	Angostura aromatic bitters

We say: A dry sherry-rich aperitif cocktail.
Origin: Created in 2010 by Misty Kalkofen at Drink, Boston, USA.

DURANGO

Glass: Collins
Garnish: Orange slice
Method: SHAKE first three ingredients with ice and strain into ice-filled glass. TOP with soda.

2	shots	Tequila 100% Agave
¾	shot	Amaretto liqueur
1	shot	Freshly squeezed grapefruit juice
Top up with		Soda (club soda)

We say: This sandy coloured drink makes tequila, amaretto and grapefruit into unlikely but harmonious bedfellows.

DUTCH BREAKFAST MARTINI

Glass: Martini
Garnish: Orange zest twist
Method: SHAKE all ingredients with ice and fine strain into chilled glass.

1½	shots	Advocaat liqueur
1½	shots	Tanqueray London dry gin
1	shot	Freshly squeezed lemon juice
¼	shot	Monin Pure Cane 2:1 sugar syrup
⅛	shot	Galliano L'Autentico liqueur

We say: A tasty, aromatic, almost creamy alternative to a fry-up.
Origin: Created in 2002 by Alex Kammerling, London, England.

DUTCH BLOOD AND SAND NEW

Glass: Coupette
Garnish: Orange zest twist
Method: SHAKE all ingredients with ice and fine strain into chilled glass.

1	shot	Bols Genever
¾	shot	Martini Rosso sweet vermouth
¾	shot	De Kuyper Cherry Brandy liqueur
¾	shot	Freshly squeezed orange juice

We say: A light fragrant-style of the classic cocktail usually Scotch whisky based.

DUTCH COUNT NEGRONI UPDATED

Glass: Old-fashioned
Garnish: Orange slice
Method: POUR ingredients into ice-filled glass and STIR.

1	shot	Bols Genever
1	shot	Campari Bitter
1	shot	Martini Rosso sweet vermouth

We say: Genever's flavoursome character adds malty notes to an otherwise traditional Negroni.
Origin: Discovered in 2011 at Vesper Bar, Amsterdam, The Netherlands and a drink promoted by Bols Genever.

DUTCH COURAGE

★★★★☆

Glass: Collins
Garnish: Lemon slice
Method: SHAKE all ingredients with ice and strain into ice-filled glass.

1	shot	Tanqueray London dry gin
1	shot	Advocaat liqueur
¾	shot	Freshly squeezed lemon juice
3	shots	Pressed apple juice

We say: A refreshing alternative to a traditional English lemonade.
Origin: Created in 2002 by Alex Kammerling, London, England.

DUTCH WORD NEW

★★★★☆

Glass: Martini
Garnish: Lime wedge
Method: SHAKE all ingredients with ice and fine strain into chilled glass.

2	shots	Bols Genever
½	shot	Chartreuse Green liqueur
½	shot	Luxardo maraschino liqueur
½	shot	Freshly squeezed lime juice

We say: A genever-based variation to the classic Last Word cocktail.
Origin: Created in December 2010 by Simon Difford at The Cabinet Room, London, England.

DUTCH MARTINI

★★★★☆

Glass: Martini
Garnish: Olive on stick
Method: STIR all ingredients with ice and strain into chilled glass.

2	shots	Ketel One vodka
¼	shot	Bols Genever
⅛	shot	Orange curaçao liqueur (or Grand Marnier)
⅛	shot	Martini Extra Dry vermouth

We say: A modern twist on the classic Dr Martini inspired by a vintage bartender. In his 1882 'New and Improved *Bartender's Manual*' Harry Johnson's Martini Cocktail recipe calls for "a dash of curaçao or absinthe, if required."

DYEVITCHKA

★★★★☆

Glass: Martini
Garnish: Orange zest twist
Method: SHAKE all ingredients with ice and fine strain into chilled glass.

1	shot	Ketel One vodka
1	shot	Triple Sec
½	shot	Freshly squeezed lime juice
¼	shot	Monin Pure Cane 2:1 sugar syrup
1½	shots	Fresh pressed pineapple juice

We say: Pineapple replaces cranberry in this Cosmo-like cocktail.

DUTCH MASTER

★★★★☆

Glass: Martini
Garnish: White grapes
Method: STIR all ingredients with ice and strain into chilled glass.

2	shots	Ketel One vodka
⅛	shot	Tio Pepe fino sherry
⅛	shot	St~Germain elderflower liqueur
1	shot	Tonic water

We say: It's a vodka and tonic but not like you know it.
Origin: Created in 2007 by Bruce Borthwick in Fife, Scotland.

E.T.

★★★★☆

Glass: Shot
Garnish: None
Method: Refrigerate ingredients and LAYER in chilled glass by carefully pouring in the following order.

½	shot	Midori green melon liqueur
½	shot	Baileys Irish cream liqueur
½	shot	Ketel One vodka

We say: Fortified creamy melon.

BARTENDER'S TIP ORDER OF PREPARATION

As in cooking, there is a correct order in which to prepare a drink which, with a few exceptions, runs as follows:

1. Select glass and chill or pre-heat (if required) 2. Prepare garnish (if required) 3. Pour ingredients. 4. Add ice (if required - add last to minimise melt) 5. Combine ingredients (shake, stir etc.) 6. Add garnish (if required) 7. Consume or serve to guest

EARL GREY FIZZ

★★★★☆

Glass: Flute
Garnish: Lemon zest twist
Method: SHAKE first three ingredients with ice and strain into chilled glass. TOP with champagne.

1	shot	**Ketel One vodka**
½	shot	**Cold earl gray tea**
¼	shot	**Monin Pure Cane 2:1 sugar syrup**
Top up with		**Brut champagne**

We say: Looks like a glass of champagne but has a well judged little extra something.
Origin: Created in 2002 by Henry Besant at Lonsdale House, London, England.

EARL GREY MAR-TEA-NI

★★★★½

Glass: Martini
Garnish: Lemon zest twist
Method: SHAKE all ingredients with ice and fine strain into chilled glass.

2	shots	**Tanqueray London dry gin**
¾	shot	**Freshly squeezed lemon juice**
½	fresh	**Egg white**
½	shot	**Monin Pure Cane 2:1 sugar syrup**

We say: A fantastic and very English drink created by a New Yorker. The gin botanicals combine wonderfully with the flavours and tannins of the tea.
Origin: Adapted from a drink created in 2000 by Audrey Saunders at Bemelmans Bar at the Carlyle, New York City.

EAST INDIA #1

★★★★★

Glass: Martini
Garnish: Orange zest twist
Method: SHAKE all ingredients with ice and fine strain into chilled glass.

2½	shots	**Cognac VSOP**
⅛	shot	**Grand Marnier liqueur**
⅛	shot	**Luxardo Maraschino liqueur**
¼	shot	**Pomegranate (grenadine) syrup**
1	dash	**Angostura aromatic bitters**

We say: Wonderfully complex and rounded - a serious drink for serious drinkers.
Origin: An old classic. This recipe is adapted from one in Ted Haigh's book 'Vintage Spirits & Forgotten Cocktails'.

EAST INDIA #2

★★★★½

Glass: Martini
Garnish: Orange zest twist & dust with grated nutmeg
Method: SHAKE all ingredients with ice and fine strain into chilled glass.

1½	shots	**Cognac VSOP**
¾	shot	**Grand Marnier liqueur**
1½	shots	**Fresh pressed pineapple juice**
2	dashes	**Angostura aromatic bitters**

We say: A rich but bitter short drink based on cognac.
Origin: Another version of the East India classic, thought to originate with Frank Meier at the Ritz Bar, Paris.

EAST INDIA HOUSE

★★★★☆

Glass: Martini
Garnish: Lemon zest twist
Method: SHAKE all ingredients with ice and fine strain into chilled glass.

2	shots	**Cognac VSOP**
½	shot	**Bacardi 8yo aged rum**
½	shot	**Triple Sec**
½	shot	**Fresh pressed pineapple juice**
2	dashes	**Orange bitters**

We say: Dry and challenging - rewarding for some.
Origin: I've adapted this recipe from a classic cocktail which is thought to have been created in the 19th century by Harry Johnson: I've doubled the quantities of everything but cognac.

EAST INDIAN

★★★★½

Glass: Martini
Garnish: Olive on stick
Method: STIR all ingredients with ice and strain into chilled glass.

2	shots	**Tio Pepe fino sherry**
2	shots	**Martini Extra Dry vermouth**
¼	shot	**Monin Pure Cane 2:1 sugar syrup**
3	dashes	**Orange bitters**

Variant: Bamboo
We say: Dry and pretty flat (like much of India) but perfectly balanced with subtle hints of orange zest.

EAST MEETS WEST JULEP

★★★½☆

Glass: Old-fashioned
Garnish: Mint sprig & pomegranate seeds
Method: SHAKE all ingredients with ice and fine strain into glass filled with crushed ice.

¾	shot	**Pomegranate juice**
7	fresh	**Mint leaves**
2	shots	**Maker's Mark bourbon**
½	shot	**Monin Honey syrup**
¼	shot	**Pomegranate (grenadine) syrup**

We say: Reminiscent of honeyed Mint Julep with pomegranate fruit.
Origin: Adapted from a drink created in 2008 by Nidal Ramini at Montgomery Place, London, England.

EAST VILLAGE ATHLETIC CLUB

★★★★☆

Glass: Martini
Garnish: Lime wedge
Method: SHAKE all ingredients with ice and fine strain into chilled glass.

¾	shot	**Tequila 100% Agave**
¾	shot	**Chartreuse Yellow liqueur**
¾	shot	**Grand Marnier liqueur**
¾	shot	**Freshly squeezed lemon juice**

We say: Essentially a Last Word with tequila instead of gin.
Origin: The Last Word, a vintage cocktail classic, was first documented in Ted Saucier's Bottoms Up in 1951 where its creation was attributed to the Detroit Athletic Club. In 2008 the folk at New York's PDT tinkered with the recipe to create this drink named after their own hood.

EASTER MARTINI

★★★★½

Glass: Martini
Garnish: Crumbled Cadbury's Flake bar
Method: MUDDLE cardamom pods in base of shaker. Add other ingredients, SHAKE with ice and fine strain into chilled glass.

4	whole	Cardamom pods
2	shots	Vanilla-infused Ketel One vodka
1	shot	White Crème de Cacao
¼	shot	Monin Pure Cane 2:1 sugar syrup
½	shot	Chilled mineral water
½	fresh	Egg white

We say: A standard Chocolate Martini with extra interest thanks to the clever use of vanilla and cardamom. The egg white was my own addition. It seemed appropriate given the Easter in the title.
Origin: Created in 2003 by Simon King at MJU Bar, Millennium Hotel, London, England.

EASTERN PROMISES NEW

★★★★☆

Glass: Coupette
Garnish: Mandarin zest
Method: SHAKE all ingredients with ice and fine strain into chilled glass.

2	shots	Rum light white/blanco
½	shot	Martini Rosso sweet vermouth
1	shot	Freshly squeezed orange juice
⅓	shot	Freshly squeezed lime juice
⅓	shot	Monin Pure Cane 2:1 sugar syrup
2	dashes	Peychaud's aromatic bitters

We say: This rum-based drink was apparently inspired by the golden age of the cocktail, with aromatic mandarin, tart lime, bittersweet vermouth resulting in an elegant cocktail with a complex finish.
Origin: Created in 2011 by Simone Caporale at Artesian at the Langham Hotel, London, England.

EASTERN MARTINI

★★★★½

Glass: Martini
Garnish: Japanese ume plum
Method: SHAKE all ingredients with ice and fine strain into chilled glass.

2	shots	Ketel One vodka
1½	shots	Choya Umeshu plum liqueur
1	shot	Pressed apple juice

We say: Light, fragrant and fruity – distinctly oriental.
Origin: Created in 2003 by Chris Langan, Barnomadics, Scotland.

EASTERN RASPBERRY SIDECAR

★★★★☆

Glass: Martini
Garnish: Sugar rim & raspberry
Method: MUDDLE raspberries in base of shaker. Add other ingredients, SHAKE with ice and fine strain into chilled glass.

7	fresh	Raspberries
1	shot	Cognac VSOP
1	shot	Sake
½	shot	Triple Sec
½	shot	Monin Pure Cane 2:1 sugar syrup
½	shot	Freshly squeezed lemon juice

We say: Refreshing, fruity, easy drinking.
Origin: Created by Ryan Magarian, Seattle, USA.

EASTERN PROMISE

★★★★☆

Glass: Martini
Garnish: Lemon zest twist
Method: SHAKE all ingredients with ice and fine strain into chilled glass.

2	shots	Ketel One vodka
¼	shot	De Kuyper Apricot Brandy liqueur
½	shot	Rose syrup
½	shot	Freshly squeezed lemon juice
½	shot	Chilled mineral water

We say: Citrus dominates this drink but the result is floral rather than tart.
Origin: Adapted from a drink discovered in 2004 at Oxo Tower Bar, London, England.

EASTERN SIN

★★★½☆

Glass: Martini
Garnish: Pineapple wedge
Method: SHAKE all ingredients with ice and fine strain into chilled glass.

1½	shots	Dewar's White label Scotch
1½	shots	De Kuyper Cherry Brandy liqueur
½	shot	Triple Sec
½	shot	Martini Rosso sweet vermouth
½	shot	Fresh pressed pineapple juice

We say: Fruity, slightly sweet but toned by a hint of Scotch.
Origin: In W.J. Tarling's 1937 *Café Royal Cocktail Book* the invention of this cocktail is credited to J. Stoneham. I have cut the amount of cherry brandy by a third compared to the Café Royal formula

BARTENDER'S TIP FINE STRAIN

Most cocktails that are served 'straight up' without ice benefit from an additional finer strain, over and above the standard strain.

This 'fine strain' removes small fragments of fruit and fine flecks of ice which can spoil the appearance of a drink and is particularly beneficial if the drink has been shaken. Fine straining is achieved by simply holding a fine sieve, like a tea strainer, between the shaker and the glass.

EASY SPEAK  NEW

★★★★☆

Glass: Old-fashioned
Garnish: Lemon zest twist
Method: STIR all ingredients with ice and strain into chilled glass (without ice).

2	shots	Maker's Mark bourbon
¾	shot	Cynar
¼	shot	Monin Pure Cane 2:1 sugar syrup

We say: Originally with a few dashes if chocolate bitters but this drink has enough complexity without the extra bitterness.
Origin: Created in 2012 by Scott Diaz, Beverage & Cafe Manager at Elliott's Oyster House & Seafood Café, Seattle, USA.

EASY TIGER

★★★★☆

Glass: Martini
Garnish: Orange zest twist
Method: MUDDLE ginger in base of shaker. Add honey and tequila, and STIR until honey is dissolved. Add other ingredients, SHAKE with ice and fine strain into chilled glass.

2	slices	Fresh root ginger (thumbnail sized)
2	spoons	Runny honey
2	shots	Tequila 100% Agave
1	shot	Freshly squeezed lime juice
¾	shot	Chilled mineral water

We say: Tangy and zesty with rich honey and ginger.
Origin: Created in 1999 by Alex Kammerling.

ECLIPSE

★★★★☆

Glass: Collins
Garnish: Raspberries & mint sprig
Method: MUDDLE raspberries in base of shaker. Add other ingredients, SHAKE with ice and strain into glass filled with crushed ice. Serve with straws.

12	fresh	Raspberries
2	shots	Maker's Mark bourbon
1	shot	Chambord black raspberry liqueur
½	shot	Freshly squeezed lime juice
2	shots	Ocean Spray cranberry juice

We say: A fruity summer cooler which I challenge anyone not to like.
Origin: Signature cocktail at the chain of Eclipse Bars, London, England.

EDEN

★★★★☆

Glass: Collins
Garnish: Orange zest twist
Method: SHAKE first three ingredients with ice and strain into ice-filled glass. TOP with tonic water.

2	shots	Ketel One vodka
½	shot	St–Germain elderflower liqueur
1½	shots	Pressed apple juice
Top up with		Tonic water

We say: Orange zest predominates in a long, refreshing drink that's perfect for warm days.
Origin: Created in 2003 by Sylvian Solignac at Citrus, London, England.

EDEN MARTINI

★★★★☆

Glass: Martini
Garnish: Orange zest twist
Method: SHAKE all ingredients with ice and fine strain into chilled glass.

2½	shots	Tanqueray London dry gin
½	shot	Parfait Amour liqueur
¼	shot	Freshly squeezed lemon juice
¼	shot	Rose water
¼	shot	Chilled mineral water

We say: Rich purple in colour with rose, vanilla, almond, citrus and gin.
Origin: Adapted from a recipe discovered in 2003 at Oxo Tower Bar, London, England.

EGG CUSTARD MARTINI

★★★★☆

Glass: Martini
Garnish: Dust with grated nutmeg
Method: SHAKE all ingredients with ice and fine strain into chilled glass.

1½	shots	Ketel One vodka
1	shot	Advocaat liqueur
½	shot	Vanilla-infused Ketel One vodka
½	shot	Maker's Mark bourbon
¼	shot	Monin Pure Cane 2:1 sugar syrup

We say: As custardy as the name would suggest but surprisingly potent.
Origin: Created in 2002 by Alex Kammerling, London, England.

EGGNOG #1 (COLD)

★★★☆☆

Glass: Collins
Garnish: Dust with grated nutmeg
Method: SHAKE all ingredients with ice and strain into ice-filled glass.

2½	shots	Cognac VSOP
½	shot	Monin Pure Cane 2:1 sugar syrup
1	fresh	Egg
½	shot	Double (heavy) cream
2	shots	Milk

We say: Lightly flavoured alcoholic egg custard. Also try swapping dark rum for the cognac.

EGGNOG #2 (HOT)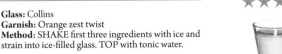

★★★★☆

Glass: Toddy
Garnish: Dust with grated nutmeg
Method: POUR ingredients into heatproof glass and STIR thoroughly. HEAT in microwave oven for a minute (adjust time as appropriate to your oven) and STIR again. Alternatively, mix and warm in pan over heat - do not boil.

2½	shots	Cognac VSOP
½	shot	Monin Pure Cane 2:1 sugar syrup
1	fresh	Egg
½	shot	Double (heavy) cream
2	shots	Milk

We say: A warming, spicy and filling meal in a glass.

EIGHTEEN '97

★★★★½

Glass: Martini
Garnish: Orange zest twist (discarded) & white grapes
Method: MUDDLE kumquats in base of shaker. Add next three ingredients, shake and fine strain into a chilled glass. FLOAT wine.

5	fresh	Kumquats (chopped)
1½	shots	Grappa di Moscato
1¼	shots	St~Germain elderflower liqueur
¼	shot	Monin Pure Cane 2:1 sugar syrup
¼	shot	Merlot red wine

We say: Looks great and, with the citrus freshness of kumquat combined with the oily character of grappa, it also tastes great.
Origin: Created in 2008 by Raffaello Dante at Salvatore's at FIFTY, London, England.

EL BURRO

★★★★☆

Glass: Collins
Garnish: Lime slice
Method: SHAKE first 4 ingredients with ice and strain into ice-filled glass. TOP with ginger beer.

2	shots	Tequila 100% Agave
½	shot	Freshly squeezed lime juice
¼	shot	Monin Pure Cane 2:1 sugar syrup
3	dashes	Angostura aromatic bitters
Top up with		Ginger beer

AKA: Mexican Mule
We say: Ginger spice and tequila soured with lime.
Origin: Created by Henry Besant and Andres Masso, London, England. The name of this Mexican version of the Moscow Mule translates from Spanish as 'The Donkey'.

EL COCO

★★★★☆

Glass: Martini
Garnish: Lime zest twist
Method: STIR all ingredients with ice and fine strain into chilled glass.

2	shots	Bacardi Superior rum
1	shot	Coconut water
¼	shot	Monin Pure Cane 2:1 sugar syrup
⅛	shot	Freshly squeezed lime juice

We say: Rum and coconut water with the merest hint of lime.
Origin: Created in 2008 by Richard Hunt at Mahiki, London, England and named after the coconut palm outside the original Bacardi distillery in Santiago de Cuba.

EL DIABLO

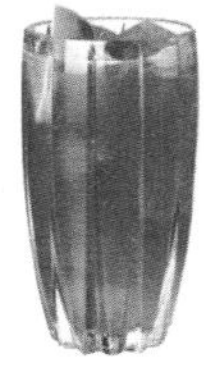

★★★★☆

Glass: Collins
Garnish: Lime wedge
Method: SHAKE first 3 ingredients with ice and strain into ice-filled glass. TOP with ginger beer.

2	shots	Olmeca Altos 100% agave tequila
¾	shot	Crème de cassis liqueur
1	shot	Freshly squeezed lime juice
Top up with		Ginger beer

We say: The tequila, red fruit and ginger aren't exactly a subtle combination but it is one that has proved both popular and enduring.
Origin: Thought to have originated in California during the 1940s. The name translates as 'The Devil'.

EL ESTRIBO

★★★☆☆

Glass: Martini
Garnish: Seasonal berries
Method: SHAKE all ingredients with ice and fine strain into chilled glass.

2	shots	Tequila 100% Agave
1	shot	Fresh pressed pineapple juice
½	shot	Double (heavy) cream
½	shot	Milk
¼	shot	Crème de cassis liqueur

We say: Pink and creamy but with a tequila kick.
Origin: The signature drink at El Estribo, Mexico City, which sadly closed in 2005. The drink and this once legendary tequila bar's name 'estribo' is used to say "one for the road" in Mexico... before you get into the stirrups and ride away.

EL FLORIDITA DAIQUIRI NO.1

★★★★☆

Glass: Martini
Garnish: Maraschino cherry
Method: BLEND all ingredients with 6oz scoop of crushed ice. Pour into glass and serve.

2	shots	Bacardi Superior rum
⅛	shot	Luxardo Maraschino liqueur
½	shot	Freshly squeezed lime juice
¼	shot	Freshly squeezed grapefruit juice
½	shot	Monin Pure Cane 2:1 sugar syrup

Variant: With fruit.
We say: Great on a hot day, but the coldness masks much of the flavour evident when this drink is served 'up' or natural.
Origin: Emilio Gonzalez is said to have first adapted the Natural Daiquiri into this frozen version at the Plaza Hotel in Cuba. However, Constantino Ribalaigua Vert of Havana's Floridita bar made the drink famous in 1912 and today the Floridita is known as 'the cradle of the Daiquiri'.

BARTENDER'S TIP DRY SHAKE

It is common practice to first shake drinks containing cream and eggs without ice, then to shake the drink a second time with ice added.

This practice is known as 'dry shaking' and the theory is that first shaking without ice, and so at a higher temperature, better allows the drink to emulsify.

EL FLORIDITA DAIQUIRI NO.2

★★★★½☆

Glass: Martini
Garnish: Lime wedge
Method: SHAKE all ingredients with ice and fine strain into chilled glass.

2	shots	Bacardi Superior rum
½	shot	Martini Rosso sweet vermouth
½	shot	Freshly squeezed lime juice
¼	shot	White Crème de Cacao
⅛	shot	Pomegranate (grenadine) syrup

Variant: With fruit.
We say: Like other Daiquiris, this complex version benefits from dilution so consider adding a dash of water.

EL MOMENTO PERFECTO NEW

★★★★☆

Glass: Old-fashioned
Garnish: Lemon zest twist
Method: STIR over cubed ice and julep strain into heavy old fashioned glass over fresh ice.

1½	shots	Rum light white/blanco
⅔	shot	Lillet Blanc
⅔	shot	Byrrh aperitif
⅓	shot	Campari Bitter
1	spoon	Orange marmalade

We say: A rum and marmalade Negroni-like drink.
Origin: Adapted from a drink created in 2011 by Daniel Bovey at Sahara Bar, Reading, England.

EL PEDRONI

★★★½☆

Glass: Old-fashioned
Garnish: Orange zest twist
Method: POUR ingredients into ice-filled glass and stir.

1½	shots	Tequila 100% Agave
1½	shots	Campari Bitter
1½	shots	Carpano Punt E Mes

We say: Tequila replaces gin in this Negroni variation. Not an easy option.
Origin: Created by Teddy Joseph, UK.

EL PRESIDENTE #2

★★★★½☆

Glass: Martini
Garnish: Lime zest twist
Method: SHAKE all ingredients with ice and fine strain into chilled glass.

2	shots	Bacardi Superior rum
1	shot	Martini Extra Dry vermouth
1	dash	Angostura aromatic bitters

We say: Bone dry. Rather like a rum based, old school Martini.

EL PRESIDENTE #3

★★★☆☆

Glass: Martini
Garnish: Orange zest twist
Method: SHAKE all ingredients with ice and fine strain into chilled glass.

2	shots	Bacardi Superior rum
1	shot	Martini Extra Dry vermouth
½	shot	Triple Sec
¼	shot	Pomegranate (grenadine) syrup

We say: A sweeter version of El Presidente #2
Origin: Adapted from Victor Bergeron's '*Trader Vic's Bartender's Guide*' (1972 revised edition). Vic writes of this drink, "This is the real recipe".

EL PRESIDENTE #4

★★★★☆

Glass: Martini
Garnish: Orange zest twist
Method: STIR all ingredients with ice and strain into chilled glass.

1½	shots	Bacardi Superior rum
½	shot	Triple Sec
¾	shot	Martini Extra Dry vermouth

We say: Dry, but not bone dry, with balanced fruit from the triple sec and vermouth.

EL PRESIDENTE NO.1 #1

★★★★½

Glass: Martini
Garnish: Lime wedge
Method: SHAKE all ingredients with ice and fine stain into chilled glass.

2	shots	Bacardi Superior rum
¾	shot	Fresh pressed pineapple juice
½	shot	Freshly squeezed lime juice
¼	shot	Pomegranate (grenadine) syrup

We say: Rum and pineapple combine wonderfully and the Daiquiri is the king of cocktails.
Origin: Classic variation on the Daiquiri, of unknown origin.

EL PRESIDENTE NO.1 #2 NEW

★★★★☆

Glass: Coupette/Martini
Garnish: Orange zest twist
Method: SHAKE all ingredients with ice and fine strain into chilled glass.

2	shots	Bacardi Superior rum
1	shot	Martini Extra Dry vermouth
¼	shot	Pomegranate (grenadine) syrup

We say: This rose tinted drink harnesses a delicate balance between light rum and vermouth with a touch of pomegranate fruity sweetness.

EL TORADO

★★★★½

Glass: Martini
Garnish: Apple slice
Method: SHAKE all ingredients with ice and fine strain into chilled glass.

2	shots	**Tequila 100% Agave**
½	shot	**Martini Extra Dry vermouth**
1½	shots	**Pressed apple juice**

We say: Dry, sophisticated and fruity, with tequila body.
Origin: Popular throughout Mexico.

ELDER & WISER

★★★★☆

Glass: Old-fashioned
Garnish: Lemon zest twist
Method: SHAKE all ingredients with ice and fine strain into ice-filled glass.

2	shots	**Maker's Mark bourbon**
1	shot	**St~Germain elderflower liqueur**
1	shot	**Pressed apple juice**

We say: Apple and elderflower combine wonderfully with bourbon.
Origin: Created in 2006 by Simon Difford and named for its original base, Wiser's Canadian whisky.

THE ELDER AVIATOR

★★★★½

Glass: Martini
Garnish: Lemon zest twist
Method: SHAKE all ingredients with ice and fine strain into chilled glass.

2	shots	**Tanqueray London dry gin**
½	shot	**St~Germain elderflower liqueur**
¼	shot	**Luxardo Maraschino liqueur**
½	shot	**Freshly squeezed lemon juice**
½	shot	**Chilled mineral water**

We say: Fans of the classic Aviation may appreciate this floral twist.
Origin: Created in 2006 by Simon Difford.

ELDER FASHIONED

★★★★☆

Glass: Old-fashioned
Garnish: Orange zest twist
Method: STIR one shot of bourbon with two ice cubes in a glass. ADD elderflower liqueur, orange bitters and two more ice cubes. STIR some more and add another two ice cubes and the rest of the bourbon. STIR lots more and add more ice.

2	shots	**Maker's Mark bourbon**
¾	shot	**St~Germain elderflower liqueur**
1	dash	**Angostura aromatic bitters**

We say: Whiskey and elderflower served in the Old-Fashioned style. The elderflower liqueur smooths the bourbon.
Origin: Created in 2006 by Simon Difford.

ELDER SOUR

★★★★½

Glass: Old-fashioned
Garnish: Lemon slice & cherry on stick (sail)
Method: SHAKE all ingredients with ice and strain into ice-filled glass.

2	shots	**St~Germain elderflower liqueur**
1	shot	**Freshly squeezed lime juice**
½	fresh	**Egg white**
1	dash	**Orange bitters**

Variant: Served 'up' in a sour glass.
We say: So smooth it's almost fluffy. A great after-dinner drink.
Origin: Created in 2006 by Simon Difford.

ELDERFLOWER COLLINS #1

★★★★☆

Glass: Collins
Garnish: Physalis (cape gooseberry)
Method: SHAKE first 4 ingredients with ice and strain into ice-filled glass. TOP with soda.

2	shots	**Tanqueray London dry gin**
½	shot	**St~Germain elderflower liqueur**
1	shot	**Freshly squeezed lemon juice**
⅛	shot	**Monin Pure Cane 2:1 sugar syrup**
Top up with		**Soda (club soda)**

We say: A hint of elderflower adds interest to the classic Collins cocktail - long, balanced and refreshing.

ELDERFLOWER COLLINS #2

★★★★☆

Glass: Collins
Garnish: Lemon slice
Method: SHAKE first four ingredients with ice and strain into ice-filled glass. TOP with soda.

2	shots	**Ketel One Citroen vodka**
⅛	shot	**Luxardo Maraschino liqueur**
¼	shot	**St~Germain elderflower liqueur**
¾	shot	**Freshly squeezed lemon juice**
Top up with		**Soda (club soda)**

We say: Long and refreshing with a floral, cherry and citrus flavour.

ELDERFLOWER COSMO

★★★★½

Glass: Martini
Garnish: Lime zest twist
Method: SHAKE all ingredients with ice and fine strain into chilled glass.

1½	shots	**Ketel One vodka**
1	shot	**St~Germain elderflower liqueur**
½	shot	**Fresh pressed pineapple juice**
¼	shot	**Freshly squeezed lime juice**

We say: Despite the absence of citrus vodka, orange liqueur and cranberry, this delicate blend is still Cosmopolitan in style.
Origin: Created in 2006 by Simon Difford.

ELDERFLOWER DAIQUIRI

★★★★☆

Glass: Martini
Garnish: Lime wedge
Method: SHAKE all ingredients with ice and fine strain into chilled glass.

2	shots	Bacardi Superior rum
1	shot	St~Germain elderflower liqueur
½	shot	Freshly squeezed lime juice

We say: Elderflower liqueur adds floral interest to the classic Daiquiri.
Origin: Created in 2006 by Simon Difford.

ELDERFLOWER GIN FIZZ NEW

★★★★☆

Glass: Collins (small 8oz)
Garnish: Lemon slice & mint sprig
Method: SHAKE first three ingredients with ice and fine strain into chilled glass (without ice). TOP with soda.

2	shots	Tanqueray London dry gin
¾	shot	Freshly squeezed lemon juice
1	shot	St-Germain elderflower liqueur
Top up with		Soda from siphon

We say: Go easy with the size of Collins glass you use or this drink with become over diluted. Due to the lack of ice in the serve also ensure the soda is well chilled and preferably use a frozen bottle of gin.

ELDERFLOWER MANHATTAN

★★★★½

Glass: Martini
Garnish: Maraschino cherry
Method: SHAKE all ingredients with ice and fine strain into chilled glass.

2	shots	Maker's Mark bourbon
1	shot	St~Germain elderflower liqueur
½	shot	Martini Extra Dry vermouth
2	dashes	Angostura aromatic bitters

We say: Elderflower replaces sweet vermouth in this 'perfect' and aromatic Manhattan.
Origin: Created in 2006 by Simon Difford.

ELDERFLOWER MARTINI #1

★★★★☆

Glass: Martini
Garnish: Lime zest twist
Method: SHAKE all ingredients with ice and fine strain into chilled glass.

2	shots	Żubrówka bison vodka
1	shot	St~Germain elderflower liqueur
½	shot	Martini Extra Dry vermouth

We say: This veritable shrubbery is both floral and grassy with dry borders.

ELDERFLOWER MARTINI #2

★★★★½

Glass: Martini
Garnish: Lemon zest twist
Method: SHAKE all ingredients with ice and fine strain into chilled glass.

1	shot	Żubrówka bison vodka
1	shot	Ketel One vodka
1	shot	St~Germain elderflower liqueur
½	shot	Martini Extra Dry vermouth

We say: Dry but not bone dry with aromatic hints of grass and elderflower.

ELDERFLOWER MOJITO

★★★★½

Glass: Collins
Garnish: Mint sprig
Method: Lightly MUDDLE (just to bruise) mint in base of glass. Add other ingredients, half fill glass with crushed ice and CHURN (stir) with bar spoon. Fill glass to brim with more crushed ice and churn some more. Serve with straws.

12	fresh	Mint leaves
2	shots	Bacardi Superior rum
1	shot	St~Germain elderflower liqueur
1	shot	Freshly squeezed lime juice

We say: The enduring classic benefits from a touch of elderflower.

ELEGANTE MARGARITA

★★★★½

Glass: Coupette
Garnish: Lime wedge & salt rim (optional)
Method: SHAKE all ingredients with ice and fine strain into chilled glass.

1½	shots	Tequila 100% Agave
½	shot	Triple Sec
½	shot	Rose's lime cordial
¾	shot	Freshly squeezed lime juice
½	shot	Monin Pure Cane 2:1 sugar syrup

We say: One of the best Margarita recipes around. Richly endowed with flavour.
Origin: Created in 1999 by Robert Plotkin and Raymon Flores of BarMedia, USA.

ELIXIR

★★★★☆

Glass: Collins
Garnish: Mint sprig
Method: Lightly MUDDLE mint in base of shaker. Add next 3 ingredients, SHAKE with ice and strain into ice-filled glasses. TOP with soda, stir and serve with straws.

7	fresh	Mint leaves
1½	shots	Chartreuse Green liqueur
1	shot	Monin Pure Cane 2:1 sugar syrup
¾	shot	Freshly squeezed lime juice
Top up with		Soda (club soda)

We say: A minty, herbal, refreshing summer drink.
Origin: Created in 2003 by Gian Franco Pola for Capannina in Cremona and Coconuts in Rimini, Italy.

ELIXIR 66

★★★½☆

Glass: Martini
Garnish: Coriander leaf
Method: Lightly MUDDLE coriander in base of shaker. Add other ingredients, SHAKE with ice and fine strain into chilled glass.

1	fresh	**Coriander (cilantro)**
1	shot	**Chartreuse Green liqueur**
¼	shot	**Absinthe**
⅛	shot	**Berentzen Apple schnapps**
½	shot	**Freshly squeezed lime juice**
1	shot	**Pressed apple juice**
¼	shot	**Monin Pure Cane 2:1 sugar syrup**
½	shot	**Chilled mineral water**

We say: Bright green and intensely flavoured but considering it is flavoured with absinthe and chartreuse, it is surprisingly subtle.
Origin: Created in 2003 by Ben Davidson of Elixir Group, Australia.

ELIXIRITA

★★★★☆

Glass: Martini
Garnish: None
Method: SHAKE all ingredients with ice and fine strain into chilled glass.

2	shots	**Tequila 100% Agave**
1	shot	**Lime**
½	shot	**Agave nectar**
¼	shot	**Cognac VSOP**

We say: Basically a Tommy's Margarita with a splash of cognac served straight-up.
Origin: Created in 2007 by H. Joseph Ehrmann, this is the signature Margarita at his bar 'Elixir' in San Francisco, USA. He dedicated it to the Boston College Eagles.

ELK MARTINI

★★★½☆

Glass: Martini
Garnish: Lemon zest twist
Method: STIR all ingredients with ice and fine strain into chilled glass.

1	shot	**Tanqueray London dry gin**
1	shot	**La Vieille Prune plum brandy**
¼	shot	**Martini Extra Dry vermouth**

We say: Craddock calls for this drink to be shaken, but in this instance stirring seems more in order.
Origin: Adapted from Harry Craddock's 1930 *'The Savoy Cocktail Book'*.

STAR RATINGS EXPLAINED

★★★★★ Excellent

★★★★½	Recommended	★★★★☆	Praiseworthy
★★★½☆	Commended	★★★☆☆	Mediocre
★★½☆☆	Disappointing	★★☆☆☆	Pretty awful
★½☆☆☆	Shameful	★☆☆☆☆	Disgusting

ELLE FOR LEATHER

★★★★½

Glass: Collins
Garnish: Vanilla pod
Method: SHAKE first 4 ingredients with ice and strain into glass filled with crushed ice. TOP with champagne.

1½	shots	**Dewar's White label Scotch**
1	shot	**Vanilla schnapps**
¼	shot	**Freshly squeezed lemon juice**
⅛	shot	**Monin Pure Cane 2:1 sugar syrup**
Top up with		**Brut champagne**

We say: A long, cool champagne cocktail pepped up with Scotch whisky and vanilla schnapps. Easy drinking - yet adult.
Origin: Created in 2001 by Reece Clark at Hush Up, London, England.

ELYSIAN

★★★★☆

Glass: Martini
Garnish: Apple slice
Method: STIR all ingredients with ice and strain into chilled glass.

2	shots	**Calvados/Applejack brandy**
½	shot	**Martini Rosso sweet vermouth**
½	shot	**Martini Extra Dry vermouth**
¼	shot	**Maple syrup**
3	dashes	**Angostura aromatic bitters**
3	dashes	**Peychaud's aromatic bitters**

We say: Dry and aromatic, although not for all tastes.
Origin: Created in 2004 by Mickael Perron at Millbank Lounge Bar, London, England.

EMBASSY COCKTAIL

★★★☆☆

Glass: Martini
Garnish: Orange zest twist
Method: SHAKE all ingredients with ice and fine strain into chilled glass.

1	shot	**Cognac VSOP**
1	shot	**Bacardi Superior rum**
1	shot	**Triple Sec**
¾	shot	**Freshly squeezed lime juice**
1	dash	**Angostura aromatic bitters**

We say: Bone dry - one for hardened palates.
Origin: Created in 1930 at the famous Embassy Club speakeasy in Hollywood, USA.

EMBASSY ROYAL

★★★½☆

Glass: Martini
Garnish: Orange zest twist
Method: SHAKE all ingredients with ice and fine strain into chilled glass.

1¾	shots	**Maker's Mark bourbon**
1	shot	**Drambuie**
1	shot	**Martini Rosso sweet vermouth**
1	shot	**Freshly squeezed orange juice**

We say: An aromatic, herbal and altogether pleasant concoction.

EMERALD MARTINI

★★★★☆

Glass: Martini
Garnish: Lemon & lime zest twists (discarded) & mint leaf
Method: STIR all ingredients with ice and strain into chilled glass.

1	shot	Chartreuse Green liqueur
1	shot	Chilled mineral water
2	shots	Lime flavoured vodka

We say: A serious drink that's rammed with alcohol and flavour.
Origin: Discovered in 2005 at Bugsy's Prague, Czech Republic.

EMERSON NEW

★★★½☆

Glass: Coupette
Garnish: Maraschino cherry on stick
Method: SHAKE all ingredients with ice and fine strain into chilled glass.

2	shots	Old Tom gin
1	shot	Martini Rosso sweet vermouth
¾	shot	Freshly squeezed lemon juice
⅓	shot	Luxardo maraschino liqueur

We say: The botanical notes of old tom with herbal vermouth, zesty lime and sweet maraschino. Balanced but old-school.
Origin: Recipe adapted from Albert Stevens Crockett's 1931 *The Old Waldorf-Astoria Bar Book*.

EMPEROR'S MEMOIRS

★★★★☆

Glass: Collins
Garnish: Orange & lemon zest twists
Method: SHAKE first 4 ingredients with ice and strain into ice-filled glass. TOP with ginger beer.

1	shot	Tanqueray London dry gin
½	shot	Carpano Punt E Mes
¼	shot	Ginger cordial (non-alcoholic)
¼	shot	Freshly squeezed lemon juice
Top up with		Ginger beer

We say: Not particularly alcoholic, but strong in a gingery, spicy way.
Origin: Created in 2001 by Douglas Ankrah for Akbar, Soho, London, England.

EMPIRE COCKTAIL

★★★☆☆

Glass: Martini
Garnish: Apricot slice
Method: SHAKE all ingredients with ice and fine strain into chilled glass.

1½	shots	Tanqueray London dry gin
¾	shot	Calvados/Applejack brandy
¾	shot	De Kuyper Apricot Brandy liqueur

We say: Apricot dried by gin and apple brandy.
Origin: Adapted from Harry Craddock's 1930 "*The Savoy Cocktail Book*".

ENCANTADO

★★★★☆

Glass: Martini
Garnish: Mint sprig
Method: SHAKE all ingredients with ice and fine strain into chilled glass.

1½	shots	Tequila 100% Agave
½	shot	Cognac VSOP
½	shot	Peachtree peach schnapps
½	shot	Chambord black raspberry liqueur
½	shot	Freshly squeezed lime juice

We say: Essentially a Margarita with a hint of peach and raspberry. Not too sweet.

ENCHANTED

★★★½☆

Glass: Collins
Garnish: Mint sprig
Method: MUDDLE grapes in base of shaker. Add next three ingredients, SHAKE with ice and fine strain into ice-filled glass. TOP with ginger ale.

7	fresh	Seedless white grapes
1½	shots	Courvoisier VSOP Exclusif
½	shot	Kwa Feh lychee liqueur
½	shot	Freshly squeezed lime juice
Top up with		Ginger ale

We say: Light, fruity and easy drinking with lychee and ginger dominating.
Origin: Created by Wayne Collins, UK.

ENGLISH BREAKFAST MARTINI

★★★★½

Glass: Martini
Garnish: Orange zest twist
Method: SHAKE all ingredients with ice and fine strain into chilled glass.

1	shot	Tanqueray London dry gin
1	shot	St~Germain elderflower liqueur
1	shot	Cold English breakfast tea
½	shot	Freshly squeezed lemon juice

We say: Light and fragrant, thanks to tea, elderflower and the botanicals in the gin.
Origin: Created in 2006 by Simon Difford.

ENGLISH CHANNEL

★★★★½

Glass: Martini
Garnish: Lemon zest twist
: SHAKE all ingredients with ice and fine strain into chilled glass.

¾	shot	Grand Marnier liqueur
¾	shot	Bénédictine D.O.M.
2	shots	Cold earl grey tea

We say: The earl grey tannins balance the spice and orange in the liqueurs to make a harmonious aperitif.
Origin: Adapted from a drink discovered in 2005 at Bellini, Auckland, New Zealand.

ENGLISH GARDEN

★★★★☆

Glass: Collins
Garnish: Cucumber slices
Method: SHAKE all ingredient with ice and fine strain into ice-filled glass.

2	shots	Tanqueray London dry gin
2½	shots	Pressed apple juice
1	shot	St~Germain elderflower liqueur
½	shot	Freshly squeezed lime juice

We say: Quintessentially English in flavour - anyone for tennis?

ENGLISH MARTINI

★★★★½

Glass: Martini
Garnish: Rosemary sprig
Method: Strip rosemary leaves from stem and MUDDLE in base of shaker. Add other ingredients, SHAKE with ice and fine strain into chilled glass.

1	fresh	Rosemary sprig
2½	shots	Tanqueray London dry gin
1	shot	St~Germain elderflower liqueur

We say: Rosemary and sweet elderflower combine wonderfully with the gin botanicals to make an interesting and approachable Martini.
Origin: Adapted from a drink created in 2003 at MJU, Millennium Hotel, London, England.

ENGLISH ROSE

★★★★☆

Glass: Martini
Garnish: Maraschino cherry
Method: STIR all ingredients with ice and strain into chilled glass.

1¾	shots	Tanqueray London dry gin
½	shot	Parfait Amour liqueur
¾	shot	Martini Extra Dry vermouth
¼	shot	Freshly squeezed lemon juice
⅛	shot	Pomegranate (grenadine) syrup

We say: A dry, complex, gin laced drink. Stir well.

THE ENTWISTLE NEW

★★★★½☆

Glass: Coupette
Garnish: Dust with cinnamon powder
Method: STIR calvados with maple syrup to dissolve syrup. Add other ingredients, STIR with ice and strain into chilled glass.

1	spoon	Maple syrup
2	shots	Calvados/Applejack brandy
½	shot	Campari Bitter
½	shot	Berentzen Apple schnapps

We say: Complex and bitter-sweet with a cidery base courtesy of apple spirit and apple liqueur with sweet maple syrup balancing bitter Campari.
Origin: Updated from a drink discovered in 2010 at Rye, San Francisco, USA.

ENTWISTLE'S ERROR NEW

★★★★☆

Glass: Collins
Garnish: Lemon slice
Method: SHAKE first two ingredients with ice and strain into ice-filled glass. TOP with tonic water.

2	shots	Bacardi 8yo aged rum
½	shot	Freshly squeezed lemon juice
Top up with		Tonic water

We say: Richly flavoured - an elongated long aged daiquiri-like cocktail.

ENVY

★★★★☆

Glass: Martini
Garnish: Star fruit
Method: SHAKE all ingredients with ice and fine strain into chilled glass.

½	shot	Ketel One vodka
2	shots	Midori green melon liqueur
1	shot	Peachtree peach schnapps
¾	shot	Hazelnut liqueur
¼	shot	Freshly squeezed lime juice

We say: Green with melon, oh, and a hint of hazelnut. A tad on the sweet side.

EPESTONE DAIQUIRI

★★★★☆

Glass: Martini
Garnish: Lime wedge
Method: SHAKE all ingredients with ice and fine strain into chilled glass.

2	shots	Bacardi Superior rum
½	shot	Freshly squeezed lime juice
½	shot	Chilled mineral water
½	shot	Crème de cassis liqueur

We say: A pleasant, maroon coloured, blackcurrant flavoured Daiquiri.

EPIPHANY

★★★★½☆

Glass: Martini
Garnish: Seasonal berries
Method: SHAKE all ingredients with ice and fine strain into chilled glass.

1¾	shots	Maker's Mark bourbon
½	shot	Crème de Mûre liqueur
2	shots	Pressed apple juice

We say: Not sure what a fruity bourbon drink has to do with the manifestation of Christ.
Origin: Created in 2004 by Naomi Young at Match, London, England.

EPISCOPAL

★★★★½

Glass: Old-fashioned
Garnish: None
Method: STIR ingredients with ice and fine strain into chilled glass.

1½	shots	**Chartreuse Green liqueur**
¾	shot	**Chartreuse Yellow liqueur**

We say: My favourite way to enjoy Chartreuse. Especially good when made with V.E.P Chartreuse.
Origin: A well-established drink promoted by the marketeers at Chartreuse and named due to the combining of the clerical colours of yellow and green.

ESCALATOR MARTINI

★★★★★

Glass: Martini
Garnish: Pear slice
Method: SHAKE all ingredients with ice and fine strain into chilled glass.

1	shot	**Poire William eau de vie**
½	shot	**Żubrówka bison vodka**
2	shots	**Pressed apple juice**
⅛	shot	**Monin Pure Cane 2:1 sugar syrup**

We say: This orchard-fresh concoction was originally made with Korte Palinka (Hungarian pear schnapps) - if using that or Poire William eau de vie, little or no sugar is necessary.
Origin: Created in 2002 by Kevin Connelly, England. It's called an escalator because the 'apples and pears', rhyming slang for 'stairs', are shaken.

ESPECIAL DAY

★★★★½

Glass: Martini
Garnish: Blackberries & lemon zest twist (discarded)
Method: MUDDLE blackberries in base of shaker. Add other ingredients, SHAKE with ice and fine strain into chilled glass.

3	fresh	**Blackberries**
2	shots	**Bacardi Superior rum**
½	shot	**Martini Rosso sweet vermouth**
¾	shot	**Crème de Mûre liqueur**
½	shot	**Fresh pressed pineapple juice**
3	dashes	**Peychaud's aromatic bitters**

We say: Beautifully balanced, aromatic, rum laced and fruity.
Origin: Created in 2005 by Tonin Kacaj at Maze, London, England.

STAR RATINGS EXPLAINED

★★★★★ Excellent

★★★★½ Recommeded
★★★★☆ Praiseworthy
★★★½☆ Commended
★★★☆☆ Mediocre
★★½☆☆ Disappointing
★★☆☆☆ Pretty awful
★½☆☆☆ Shameful
★☆☆☆☆ Disgusting

ESPECIE

★★★½☆

Glass: Martini
Garnish: Lime zest twist
Method: SHAKE all ingredients with ice and fine strain into chilled glass.

2½	shots	**Bacardi Superior rum**
1	shot	**Taylor's Velvet Falernum liqueur**
¾	shot	**Chilled mineral water**
2	dashes	**Angostura aromatic bitters**

We say: Rum laced and rust coloured with hints of clove and jasmine. A touch syrupy.
Origin: Created in 2008 by Juraj Ivan at Coq D'Argent, London, England.

ESPRESSO DAIQUIRI

★★★★☆

Glass: Martini
Garnish: Coffee beans
Method: SHAKE all ingredients with ice and fine strain into chilled glass.

2	shots	**Bacardi Superior rum**
1¾	shots	**Hot espresso coffee**
½	shot	**Monin Pure Cane 2:1 sugar syrup**

Variant: Espresso Martini
We say: Rum based twist on the ubiquitous Espresso Martini.

ESPRESSO MARTINI UPDATED

★★★★★

Glass: Martini
Garnish: Float 3 coffee beans
Method: SHAKE all ingredients with ice and fine strain into chilled glass.

2	shots	**Ketel One vodka**
1½	shots	**Hot espresso coffee**
½	shot	**Monin Pure Cane 2:1 sugar syrup**
¼	shot	**Kahlúa coffee liqueur**

Variant: Pharmaceutical Stimulant, Vodka Espresso, Espresso Daquiri, Insomniac, Irish Coffee Martini, Jalisco Espresso, Jolt'ini.
We say: Forget the 'Vodka Red Bull', this is the cocktail connoisseur's way of combining caffeine and vodka.
Origin: Created by Dick Bradsell and adapted from his 1983 'Vodka Espresso' invented at the Soho Brasserie, London, England.

ESQUIRE #1

★★★★☆

Glass: Martini
Garnish: Orange zest twist
Method: SHAKE all ingredients with ice and fine strain into chilled glass.

2	shots	**Maker's Mark bourbon**
¾	shot	**Grand Marnier liqueur**
¾	shot	**Freshly squeezed orange juice**
1	dash	**Angostura aromatic bitters**
½	shot	**Chilled mineral water**

We say: Spicy bourbon laden with orange fruit.

ESQUIRE #2

★★★½☆

Glass: Martini
Garnish: Blackberries
Method: STIR all ingredients with ice and strain into chilled glass.

1½	**shots**	**Ketel One vodka**
¾	**shot**	**Raspberry flavoured vodka**
¾	**shot**	**Parfait Amour liqueur**

We say: One for hardened Martini drinkers.
Origin: Created in the 1990s by Dick Bradsell for *Esquire* magazine.

ESTES

★★★★☆

Glass: Collins
Garnish: Raspberries & lime zest strips
Method: MUDDLE raspberries in base of shaker. Add other ingredients, SHAKE with ice and fine strain into glass filled with crushed ice.

1¾	**shots**	**Tequila 100% Agave**
½	**shot**	**Chambord black raspberry liqueur**
1¾	**shots**	**Ocean Spray cranberry juice**
½	**shot**	**Agave nectar**
¾	**shot**	**Freshly squeezed lime juice**
7	**fresh**	**Raspberries**

We say: This rich, fruity long drink is a real crowd pleaser.
Origin: Created in 2005 by Henry Besant and Andres Masso, London, England, and named in honour of Tomas Estes, the official Tequila Ambassador in Europe.

ESTILO VIEJO

★★★★½

Glass: Old-fashioned
Garnish: Lime zest twist
Method: STIR half of the tequila with two ice cubes in a glass. Add agave syrup and Angostura and two more ice cubes. Stir some more and add another two ice cubes and the rest of the tequila. Stir lots more and add more ice. The melting and stirring of the ice is essential to the dilution and taste of the drink.

2½	**shots**	**Tequila 100% Agave**
½	**shot**	**Agave nectar**
3	**dashes**	**Angostura aromatic bitters**

We say: Even better when made with añejo tequila.
Origin: The name of this drink literally translates from Spanish as 'Old Style'. It is basically a Tequila Old-fashioned.

STAR RATINGS EXPLAINED

★★★★★ Excellent

★★★★½	Recommended	★★★★☆	Praiseworthy
★★★½☆	Commended	★★★☆☆	Mediocre
★★½☆☆	Disappointing	★★☆☆☆	Pretty awful
★½☆☆☆	Shameful	★☆☆☆☆	Disgusting

EUREKA COCKTAIL

★★★☆☆

Glass: Martini
Garnish: Lemon zest twist
Method: SHAKE all ingredients with ice and fine strain into chilled glass.

1	**shot**	**Calvados/Applejack brandy**
¾	**shot**	**Sloe Gin liqueur**
½	**shot**	**De Kuyper Cherry Brandy liqueur**
½	**shot**	**Freshly squeezed lemon juice**
½	**shot**	**Chilled mineral water**

We say: A punchy, full-flavoured, veritable basket of fruit.
Origin: Recipe adapted from a 1937 Bar Florida (later renamed Floridita) menu, Havana, Cuba.

EVERY-BODY'S IRISH COCKTAIL

★★★☆☆

Glass: Martini
Garnish: Green maraschino cherry
Method: SHAKE all ingredients with ice and fine strain into chilled glass.

2	**shots**	**Jameson Irish whiskey**
½	**shot**	**Chartreuse Green liqueur**
¼	**shot**	**Green crème de menthe liqueur**

We say: Like the Incredible Hulk, this drink packs a dangerous green punch.
Origin: In his 1930 '*The Savoy Cocktail Book*', Harry Craddock writes of this drink, "Created to mark, and now in great demand on, St. Patrick's Day."

EVITA

★★★½☆

Glass: Martini
Garnish: Orange zest twist
Method: SHAKE all ingredients with ice and fine strain into chilled glass.

2	**shots**	**Ketel One vodka**
½	**shot**	**Midori green melon liqueur**
1	**shot**	**Freshly squeezed orange juice**
½	**shot**	**Freshly squeezed lime juice**

We say: A tangy, lime green, medium-sweet combination of melon, orange and lime.

EXOTIC PASSION

★★★½☆

Glass: Collins
Garnish: Pineapple wedge & strawberry
Method: SHAKE all ingredients with ice and strain into ice-filled glass.

1½	**shots**	**Ketel One vodka**
¾	**shot**	**Crème de fraise du bois liqueur**
¾	**shot**	**Passoã passion fruit liqueur**
1½	**shots**	**Fresh pressed pineapple juice**
1½	**shots**	**Freshly squeezed grapefruit juice**

We say: Bittersweet and floral - one for the poolside.

EXTRADITION

★★★★☆

Glass: Old-fashioned
Garnish: Strawberry
Method: MUDDLE strawberries in base of shaker. Add other ingredients, SHAKE with ice and fine strain into ice-filled glass.

3	fresh	**Strawberries (hulled)**
2	shots	**Macchu pisco**
2	shots	**Pressed apple juice**
¾	shot	**Passion fruit syrup**

We say: A light, fruity drink for a summer afternoon.
Origin: Created in 2001 by Francis Timmons at Detroit, London, England.

F-16 SHOT

★★★☆☆

Glass: Shot
Garnish: Maraschino cherry
Method: Refrigerate ingredients then LAYER in chilled glass by carefully pouring in the order listed.

½	shot	**Baileys Irish cream liqueur**
½	shot	**Bacardi Superior rum**
½	shot	**Kahlúa coffee liqueur**

We say: May not break the sound barrier but at least it layers well.
Origin: Named for the F-16 jet and closely related to the B-52.

F. WILLY SHOT

★★★½☆

Glass: Shot
Garnish: None
Method: SHAKE all ingredients with ice and fine stain into chilled glass.

½	shot	**Ketel One vodka**
½	shot	**Bacardi Superior rum**
½	shot	**Amaretto liqueur**
½	shot	**Triple Sec**
¼	shot	**Rose's lime cordial**

We say: Not as bad as it looks or sounds.

FACUNDO'S FLARE

★★★½☆

Glass: Martini
Garnish: None
Method: SHAKE all ingredients with ice and fine strain into chilled glass.

1½	shots	**Bacardi Superior rum**
½	shot	**Aperol**
1	shot	**Freshly squeezed orange juice**
½	shot	**Monin Vanilla sugar syrup**
2	dashes	**Peach bitters**
½	fresh	**Egg white**

We say: So smooth this drink is almost creamy. Vanilla dominates with fruity hints of rum.
Origin: Created by Bruce Hamilton at Tigerlily, Edinburgh, Scotland.

FAIR & WARMER COCKTAIL

★★★☆☆

Glass: Martini
Garnish: Orange zest twist
Method: SHAKE all ingredients with ice and fine strain into chilled glass.

2	shots	**Bacardi Superior rum**
½	shot	**Triple Sec**
1	shot	**Martini Rosso sweet vermouth**

We say: Sure to warm and fairly good.
Origin: Adapted from Harry Craddock's 1930 '*The Savoy Cocktail Book*'.

FAIRBANKS COCKTAIL NO.1

★★★☆☆

Glass: Martini
Garnish: Maraschino cherry
Method: SHAKE all ingredients with ice and fine strain into chilled glass.

1	shot	**Tanqueray London dry gin**
1	shot	**De Kuyper Apricot Brandy liqueur**
1	shot	**Martini Extra Dry vermouth**
¼	shot	**Freshly squeezed lemon juice**
¼	shot	**Pomegranate (grenadine) syrup**
½	shot	**Chilled mineral water**

We say: Apricot liqueur dominates this cocktail but the Martini Extra Dry vermouth and dilution save from excessive sweetness.
Origin: Adapted from Harry Craddock's 1930 '*The Savoy Cocktail Book*'.

FALCONI

★★★★☆

Glass: Martini
Garnish: Orange zest twist
Method: STIR all ingredients with ice and strain into chilled glass.

2	shots	**Straight rye whiskey**
1	shot	**Martini Extra Dry vermouth**
1	shot	**Warre's Otima tawny port**
1	dash	**Orange bitters**

We say: Dry and subtly aromatic.

FALLEN ANGEL

★★★☆☆

Glass: Martini
Garnish: Mint leaf
Method: SHAKE all ingredients with ice and fine strain into chilled glass.

2	shots	**Tanqueray London dry gin**
1	shot	**Freshly squeezed lemon juice**
¼	shot	**Green crème de menthe liqueur**
¼	shot	**Monin Pure Cane 2:1 sugar syrup**

We say: Gin laced lime and fresh mint. A somewhat acquired taste.
Origin: Vintage cocktail of unknown origin.

FALLEN LEAVES

Glass: Martini
Garnish: Lemon zest twist
Method: STIR all ingredients with ice and strain into chilled glass.

1½ shots	**Calvados/Applejack brandy**
1½ shots	**Martini Rosso sweet vermouth**
½ shot	**Martini Extra Dry vermouth**
¼ shot	**Cognac VSOP**

We say: Suitably autumnal in colour. The vermouths and brandies are in harmony.
Origin: Created in 1982 by Charles Schumann in Munich, Germany, and first published in his book 'American Bar'.

FANCY BRANDY

Glass: Martini
Garnish: Lemon zest twist
Method: SHAKE all ingredients with ice and fine strain into chilled glass.

2 shots	**Cognac VSOP**
¼ shot	**Triple Sec**
⅛ shot	**Monin Pure Cane 2:1 sugar syrup**
1 dash	**Angostura aromatic bitters**
½ shot	**Chilled mineral water**

We say: The appropriately named brandy based drink benefits from dilution, hence my addition of a splash of water.
Origin: Adapted from a recipe by Charles Schumann, Munich, Germany, and published in his 'American Bar'. Very similar to Jerry Thomas' Fancy Brandy Cocktail, published in his 1862 edition.

FANCY DRINK

Glass: Sling
Garnish: Lemon slice & kumquat
Method: SHAKE first three ingredients with ice and strain into ice-filled glass. TOP with bitter lemon.

1 shot	**Grand Marnier liqueur**
1 shot	**Bacardi Superior rum**
2 shots	**Freshly squeezed grapefruit juice**
Top up with	**Bitter lemon**

We say: Tasty tart! Refreshingly sour.

FANCY FREE

Glass: Martini
Garnish: Maraschino cherry
Method: SHAKE all ingredients with ice and fine strain into chilled glass.

2 shots	**Maker's Mark bourbon**
½ shot	**Luxardo Maraschino liqueur**
2 dashes	**Angostura aromatic bitters**
2 dashes	**Orange bitters**
½ shot	**Chilled mineral water**

We say: Aromatised, tamed bourbon.

FANDANGO NEW

Glass: Coupette
Garnish: Mint sprig
Method: STIR all ingredients with ice and fine strain into ice-filled glass.

1¼ shots	**Tanqueray London dry gin**
1¼ shots	**Ketel One vodka**
1 shot	**Chartreuse Yellow liqueur**
½ shot	**Chilled mineral water**

We say: A heady mix of gin, vodka and the distinctive herbal flavour of Chartreuse.
Origin: Recipe adapted from a book titled 'Cocktails de Paris RIP' which was published in Paris in 1929.

FANHATTAN NEW

Glass: Martini
Garnish: Fig wedge
Method: STIR all ingredients with ice and fine strain into chilled glass.

2 shots	**Maker's Mark bourbon**
½ shot	**Carpano Punt E Mes**
½ shot	**Crème de Figue (fig) liqueur**
1 dash	**Angostura aromatic bitters**

We say: Twist on a Manhattan for fig lovers.
Origin: Created in 2010 by Dan Richards of Host Academy, UK.

FANTASIA (MOCKTAIL)

Glass: Collins
Garnish: Lime wedge
Method: SHAKE first four ingredients with ice and strain into ice-filled glass. TOP with lemonade, stir and serve with straws.

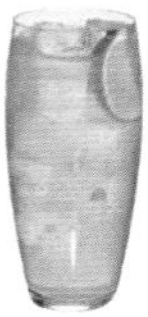

¼ shot	**Freshly squeezed lime juice**
¼ shot	**Freshly squeezed lemon juice**
¼ shot	**Monin Pure Cane 2:1 sugar syrup**
5 dashes	**Angostura aromatic bitters**
Top up with	**Lemonade/Sprite/7-Up**

We say: A Spanish twist on the popular Australian LLB.
Origin: Discovered in 2004 at Claris Hotel, Barcelona, Spain.

FAT SAILOR

Glass: Old-fashioned
Garnish: Lime wedge
Method: SHAKE all ingredients with ice and strain into glass filled with crushed ice.

1½ shots	**Bacardi Oro golden rum**
¾ shot	**Pusser's Navy rum**
¼ shot	**Kahlúa coffee liqueur**
½ shot	**Freshly squeezed lime juice**
1 shot	**Rose's lime cordial**

We say: A tasty, suitably calorie laden, rum concoction.
Origin: Tiki-style drink of unknown origin.

FAT TIRE

★★★★☆

Glass: Old-fashioned
Garnish: Orange zest twist
Method: SHAKE all ingredients with ice and fine strain into ice-filled glass.

1½	shots	Bacardi 8yo aged rum
1	shot	Averna Amaro
½	shot	Freshly squeezed orange juice
½	shot	Fresh pressed pineapple juice

We say: This flavourful, bittersweet aperitif won't be to everyone's taste.
Origin: Discovered in San Francisco in 2006, hence the American spelling of 'tyre'.

FBI

★★★★☆

Glass: Collins
Garnish: Crumbled Cadbury's Flake bar
Method: BLEND all ingredients with 18oz scoop of crushed ice and serve with straws.

2	shots	Ketel One vodka
1	shot	Baileys Irish cream liqueur
1	shot	Kahlúa coffee liqueur
3	scoop	Häagen Dazs vanilla ice cream

We say: Yummy alcoholic milkshake with coffee and whiskey cream.

FEATHER DUSTER CRUSTA

★★★★☆

Glass: Martini
Garnish: Find a lemon which fits into a small wineglass tightly enough to act as a watertight extension to the glass. Cut off both ends of the fruit and carefully remove the pulp to leave a barrel-shaped shell of skin. Place in the top of the glass. Wet the edge of the glass and exposed fruit shell with sugar syrup and dip in caster sugar to frost the edge of both peel and glass. Leave for a couple of hours to form a hard crust.
Method: SHAKE all ingredients with ice and fine strain into chilled glass.

1½	shots	Boulard Grand Solage calvados
½	shot	Luxardo maraschino liqueur
¾	shot	Freshly squeezed grapefruit juice
½	shot	Freshly squeezed lemon juice
¼	shot	Passion fruit syrup
¼	shot	Pomegranate (grenadine) syrup
2	dashes	Peychaud's aromatic bitters

We say: In Gregor's own words, Based on the father of the Sidecar, the granddad of the Margarita, Laydeez an' Gennulmen! The Brandy Crusta.
Origin: Created in 2006 by Gregor de Gruyther at Ronnie Scott's, London, England. It is 'quite a light Crusta', hence the name.

STAR RATINGS EXPLAINED

★★★★★ Excellent

★★★★⯪ Recommended   ★★★★☆ Praiseworthy
★★★⯪☆ Commended   ★★★☆☆ Mediocre
★★⯪☆☆ Disappointing   ★★☆☆☆ Pretty awful
★⯪☆☆☆ Shameful   ★☆☆☆☆ Disgusting

FEN ELLA NEW

★★★★☆

Glass: Old-fashioned
Garnish: Fresh fennel
Method: MUDDLE fennel in stirring glass. Add other ingredients, STIR with ice and fine strain into ice-filled glass.

15	dried	Fennel seeds
2	shots	Dewar's White Label Scotch
½	shot	Berentzen Apple schnapps
⅛	shot	Monin Pure Cane 2:1 sugar syrup
⅛	shot	Ricard Pastis
½	shot	Chilled mineral water

We say: Fennel and pastis freshen and delicately flavour Scotch with the merest hint of apple. Best made by infusing the fennel with the scotch whisky for a week or so rather than muddling.
Origin: Created in July 2013 by Simon Difford at the Cabinet Room, London, England.

FERNANDO

★★★★☆

Glass: Coupette
Garnish: None
Method: STIR all ingredients with ice and strain into chilled glass.

1	shot	Martini Extra Dry vermouth
1	shot	Martini Rosso sweet vermouth
¼	shot	Galliano L'Autentico liqueur
	shot	Fernet Branca

We say: An unusually vermouth based herbal cocktail - very fresh and aromatic.
Origin: Drink adapted from one discovered in 2010 at Employees Only, New York City, USA. Originally based only on bianco vermouth with no dry vermouth.

FIBBER MCGEE UPDATED 🔑

★★★⯪☆

Glass: Coupette
Garnish: Grapefruit zest twist
Method: SHAKE all ingredients with ice and fine strain into chilled glass.

2	shots	Tanqueray London dry gin
1	shot	Martini Rosso sweet vermouth
1	shot	Freshly squeezed pink grapefruit juice
2	dashes	Angostura aromatic bitters

We say: Delicately flavoured, bitter-sweet grapefruit and sweet vermouth fortified with gin.

FIENDTINI 🔑

★★★★☆

Glass: Martini
Garnish: Gherkin
Method: STIR all ingredients with ice and strain into chilled glass.

2½	shots	Tanqueray London dry gin
½	shot	Martini Extra Dry vermouth
¼	shot	Chilled mineral water

We say: A gin Martini 'dirtied' with pickled gherkin brine and garnished with a pickled gherkin.

FIESTA

★★★★☆

Glass: Martini
Garnish: Pomegranate seeds
Method: SHAKE all ingredients with ice and fine strain into chilled glass.

1	shot	Bacardi Superior rum
1	shot	Calvados/Applejack brandy
1	shot	Martini Extra Dry vermouth
⅛	shot	Freshly squeezed lime juice
⅛	shot	Pomegranate (grenadine) syrup

We say: With the right amount of quality pomegranate syrup, this is a great drink.

FIFTH AVENUE SHOT

★★☆☆☆

Glass: Shot
Garnish: None
Method: Refrigerate ingredients then LAYER in chilled glass by carefully pouring in the following order.

½	shot	Bols crème de cacao brown
½	shot	De Kuyper Apricot Brandy liqueur
½	shot	Double (heavy) cream

We say: A sweet, apricot and chocolate creamy shot.

FIFTH DEGREE

★★★★☆

Glass: Martini
Garnish: Lemon zest twist
Method: STIR Campari with ice (to coat ice and glass) and then strain to discard excess. Add other ingredients, STIR with coated ice and strain into chilled glass.

⅛	shot	Campari Bitter
2	shots	Ketel One vodka
1	shot	Martini Rosso sweet vermouth
¼	shot	Luxardo Maraschino liqueur

We say: Bitter sweet.
Origin: Created in 2008 and promoted by Diageo's Reserve Brands division. Apparently this drink was inspired by the classic Martinez.

FIFTY-FIFTY DRY MARTINI #8
(1:1 RATIO)

★★★★☆

Glass: Martini
Garnish: Olive on stick
Method: SHAKE all ingredients with ice and fine strain into chilled glass.

1½	shots	Tanqueray London dry gin
1½	shots	Martini Extra Dry vermouth

We say: A very 'wet' but wonderfully dry Martini which demands an olive, not a twist. Before you start - Craddock calls for it to be shaken.
Origin: Adapted from Harry Craddock's 1930 'The Savoy Cocktail Book'.

FIG SUPREME

★★★☆☆

Glass: Old-fashioned
Garnish: Fig wedge
Method: Scoop out the flesh of figs and MUDDLE in base of shaker. Add other ingredients, SHAKE with ice and fine strain into glass filled with crushed ice.

2	fresh	Figs
2	shots	Tequila 100% Agave
½	shot	Freshly squeezed lime juice
¼	shot	Grand Marnier liqueur
¼	shot	Pomegranate (grenadine) syrup

We say: Fig and pomegranate add an extra dimension to this Margarita-style cocktail.
Origin: Created by Salvatore Calabrese at Salvatore At Fifty, London, England.

FILTHY DIRTY DRY MARTINI

★★★☆☆

Glass: Martini
Garnish: Chilled olives on stick & lemon zest twist
Method: STIR all ingredients with ice and fine strain into chilled glass.

2	shots	Tanqueray London dry gin
¼	shot	Martini Extra Dry vermouth
⅛	shot	Freshly squeezed lime juice
⅛	shot	Olive brine (from jarred olive)

AKA: Dirty-Dry-Dirty Martini
We say: However hard you think you are, this one is harder.

FINAL WARD NEW

★★★★☆

Glass: Martini
Garnish: Lemon zest twist
Method: SHAKE all ingredients with ice and fine strain into chilled glass.

¾	shot	Straight rye whiskey
¾	shot	Chartreuse Green liqueur
¾	shot	Luxardo Maraschino liqueur
¾	shot	Freshly squeezed lemon juice

We say: The Last Word is classically made with gin, maraschino, Chartreuse and lime juice. In this twist, whiskey replaces the gin, and Mr Ward switches citrus fruits from lime to lemon.
Origin: Adapted from a drink created in 2007 by Phil Ward at Death & Co., New York City, USA.

FINE & DANDY

★★★★☆

Glass: Martini
Garnish: Lemon zest twist
Method: SHAKE all ingredients with ice and fine strain into chilled glass.

1¾	shots	Tanqueray London dry gin
¾	shot	Triple Sec
½	shot	Freshly squeezed lemon juice
¼	shot	Monin Pure Cane 2:1 sugar syrup
½	shot	Chilled mineral water
1	dash	Angostura aromatic bitters

We say: A gin based drink that's soured with lemon and sweetened with orange liqueur.

FINITALY

★★★★☆

Glass: Martini
Garnish: Raspberries
Method: SHAKE all ingredients with ice and fine strain into chilled glass.

1½	shots	Ketel One vodka
½	shot	Chambord black raspberry liqueur
½	shot	Martini Rosso sweet vermouth
¾	shot	Chilled mineral water

We say: A simple, berry led Martini.
Origin: Created by Michael Mahe at Hush, London, England.

FINN ROUGE

★★★☆☆

Glass: Martini
Garnish: Lemon zest twist
Method: MUDDLE raspberries in base of shaker. Add other ingredients, SHAKE with ice and fine strain into chilled glass.

5	fresh	Raspberries
1¾	shots	Cranberry flavoured vodka
½	shot	Crème de framboise liqueur
¾	shot	Ocean Spray cranberry juice
¼	shot	Freshly squeezed lemon juice
⅛	shot	Monin Pure Cane 2:1 sugar syrup
1	grind	Black pepper

We say: A rather red, rasping, berry rich drink.
Origin: Adapted from a drink created in 2005 by Jamie Stephenson, Manchester, England.

FINNBERRY MARTINI

★★★★☆

Glass: Martini
Garnish: Cranberries
Method: SHAKE all ingredients with ice and fine stain into chilled glass.

2	shots	Ketel One vodka
2	shots	Ocean Spray cranberry juice
1	shot	Lapponia cloudberry liqueur

We say: This rich berry Martini can be varied by using other berry liqueurs in the Lapponia range - try using two with half a shot of each.
Origin: Created by Simon Difford in 2002 after a trip to Finland.

FINO FLIP NEW

★★★★☆

Glass: Coupette
Garnish: Three drops angostura bitters
Method: SHAKE all ingredients with ice and fine strain into chilled glass.

3	shots	Tio Pepe fino sherry
½	shot	Monin Pure Cane 2:1 sugar syrup
3	dash	Angostura aromatic bitters
1	fresh	Egg yolk

We say: Salty tang of fino balanced and given extra richness by the egg.
Origin: Unknown.

FIREBALL

★★☆☆☆

Glass: Shot
Garnish: None
Method: SHAKE all ingredients with ice and fine strain into chilled glass.

2	drops	Tabasco hot pepper sauce
1	shot	Goldschläger cinnamon schnapps

We say: Down this in one and be prepared for a sweet cinnamon palate quickly followed by a hot, spicy finish.

FIREMAN'S SOUR

★★★★☆

Glass: Old-fashioned
Garnish: Orange slice & cherry on stick (sail)
Method: SHAKE all ingredients with ice and strain into ice-filled glass.

2	shots	Bacardi Superior rum
1	shot	Freshly squeezed lime juice
½	shot	Pomegranate (grenadine) syrup
½	fresh	Egg white

We say: Smooth and balanced with great rum character. Lime fresh and fruity sweet.
Origin: Circa 1930s, USA

FIRST OF JULY

★★★★☆

Glass: Martini
Garnish: Apple slice & blackberry
Method: MUDDLE blackberries in base of shaker. Add other ingredients, SHAKE with ice and fine strain into chilled glass.

4	fresh	Blackberries
2	shots	Calvados/Applejack brandy
1	shot	Chambord black raspberry liqueur
2	shots	Freshly squeezed grapefruit juice

We say: Rich blackberry fruit with a hint of grapefruit acidity.
Origin: Created on 1st of July by David Guidi at Morton's, London, England.

STAR RATINGS EXPLAINED

★★★★★ Excellent

★★★★⯪ Recommeded	★★★★☆ Praiseworthy
★★★⯪☆ Commended	★★★☆☆ Mediocre
★★⯪☆☆ Disappointing	★★☆☆☆ Pretty awful
★⯪☆☆☆ Shameful	★☆☆☆☆ Disgusting

FISH HOUSE PUNCH #1 UPDATED

★★★★★ **Glass:** Collins
Garnish: Lemon slice
Method: SHAKE all ingredients with ice and strain into ice-filled glass.

1	shot	Cognac VSOP
1	shot	Bacardi Oro golden rum
¾	shot	Crème de pêche de vigne liqueur
¾	shot	Freshly squeezed lemon juice
¼	shot	Monin Pure Cane 2:1 sugar syrup
2	shots	Chilled mineral water

We say: This fruit laced mix is neither too sweet, nor too strong. It is perfect.
Origin: Probably the most famous of all punch recipes this believed to have originated at a Philadelphia fishing and social club called the 'State in Schuylkill Fishing Corporation' which was established in 1732 with a club house built on the banks of Pennsylvania's Schuylkill River (pronounced Skoo-kul). When the drink was first made here is unknown but drinks historian David Wondrich says the first written reference to the Fish House Punch appeared in 1794.

Others say it was first made in 1848 by Shippen Willing of Philadelphia to celebrate women being allowed into the Fish House for the first time for a Christmas Party. Whatever the origin, as with all traditional punch recipes, this would have originally been mixed in larger quantities and served from a punch bowl. Many modern variations use soda water (club soda) in place of mineral water. The inclusion of peach liqueur is a modern substitute for the traditional barrel-aged peach brandy. However, some believe the Schuylkill original omitted peach entirely. The following poem may be recited when serving a Fish House Punch.

There's a little place just out of town,
Where, if you go to lunch,
They'll make you forget your mother-in-law
With a drink called Fish-House Punch.

FISH HOUSE PUNCH #2

★★★★½ **Glass:** Collins
Garnish: Lemon slice & dust with grated nutmeg
Method: SHAKE all ingredients with ice and strain into ice-filled glass.

1	shot	Cognac VSOP
1	shot	Bacardi Superior rum
1	shot	Crème de pêche de vigne liqueur
1½	shots	Cold English breakfast tea
1	shot	Freshly squeezed lemon juice
¼	shot	Monin Pure Cane 2:1 sugar syrup

We say: Over the decades the recipe the Fish House Punch has constantly morphed. The inclusion of cold tea is the latest adaptation.
Origin: Formula by Simon Difford.

FITZGERALD

★★★★☆ **Glass:** Old-fashioned
Garnish: Lemon wedge
Method: SHAKE all ingredients with ice and strain into ice-filled glass.

2	shots	Tanqueray London dry gin
½	shot	Monin Pure Cane 2:1 sugar syrup
1	shot	Freshly squeezed lemon juice
2	dashes	Angostura aromatic bitters

We say: A gin sour without the egg white.
Origin: Adapted from a drink created in the early 1990s by Dale DeGroff at the Rainbow Room, New York City, USA.

FIX (GENERIC NAME)

★★★★☆ **Glass:** Old-fashioned
Garnish: Seasonal fruit
Method: SHAKE all ingredients with ice and strain into ice-filled glass.

2	shots	Brandy, whisk(e)y, gin, rum etc.
1	shot	Freshly squeezed lemon juice
1	shot	Sweet fruit juice
½	shot	Monin Pure Cane 2:1 sugar syrup

We say: Match the juice and spirit and this formula works every time.
Origin: A Fix is a classic style of drink that constitutes of a spirit, lemon juice, and some kind of sweet fruit served short.

FIZZ (GENERIC NAME) UPDATED

★★★★☆ **Glass:** Collins (small 8oz)
Garnish: None
Method: SHAKE first four ingredients with ice and strain into chilled glass (no ice in glass). TOP with soda dispensed from a siphon.

2	shots	Brandy, whisk(e)y, gin, rum etc.
1	shot	Freshly squeezed lemon or lime juice
½	shot	Monin Pure Cane 2:1 sugar syrup
½	fresh	Egg white
Top up with		Soda from siphon

We say: I recommend the Derby Fizz with its combination of liqueur and spirits over these more traditional versions.
Origin: Like the Collins, this mid-19th century classic is basically a sour lengthened with carbonated water and at first glance there is little difference between a Fizz and a Collins. However, there are several distinguishing features. A Collins should be served in at least a twelve ounce, and ideally a fourteen ounce tall glass, while that used for a Fizz should be no bigger than eight ounces. A Collins should be served in an ice-filled glass, while a Fizz should be served in a chilled glass without ice.

A Fizz should also be made using carbonated water from a siphon in preference to soda from bottles or cans. The burst of pressure from the siphon helps build a bubbly head while the tiny bubbles generated give off carbonic acid, benefiting the flavour and the mouth-feel of the drink.

For the correct proportions I have turned to David A. Embury's seminal '*The Fine Art of Mixing Drinks*'. He recommends: "1 - or a little less sweet (sugar, fruit syrup, or liqueur), 2 sour (lime or lemon juice), 3 - or a little more - strong (spirituous liquor), and 4 weak (charged water and ice). I interpret this as follows: 2 shots spirit (gin, whiskey, vodka, brandy), 1 shot lemon or lime juice, ½ shot sugar syrup, topped up with soda. I also like to add half a fresh egg white, which technically makes the drink a 'Silver Fizz.'"

STAR RATINGS EXPLAINED

★★★★★ Excellent

★★★★⯪ Recommended	★★★★☆ Praiseworthy
★★★⯪☆ Commended	★★★☆☆ Mediocre
★★⯪☆☆ Disappointing	★★☆☆☆ Pretty awful
★⯪☆☆☆ Shameful	★☆☆☆☆ Disgusting

FIZZ Á LA VIOLETTE

★★★★☆

Glass: Collins (small 8oz)
Garnish: None
Method: 1/ Flash BLEND first 6 ingredients without ice (to emulsify mix). Then pour contents of blender into shaker and SHAKE with ice. Strain into chilled glass (no ice in glass) and TOP with soda from siphon.
ALTERNATIVELY: 2/ Vigorously DRY SHAKE first 6 ingredients WITHOUT ice until bored/tired. Add ice to shaker, SHAKE again and strain into chilled glass (no ice). TOP with soda water from siphon.

1½ shots	Old Tom gin
¼ shot	Benoit Serres créme de violette
1 shot	Freshly squeezed lemon juice
½ shot	Monin Pure Cane 2:1 sugar syrup
1 shot	Double (heavy) cream
1 shot	Egg white
Top up with	Soda from siphon

Variant: Blend rather than shake.
We say: Note: The so called 'dry shake' allows the cream and egg white to emulsify thus giving this drink its legendary silky mouth feel without the over dilution which would result from such a prolonged shake with ice. A delicate floral drink that is so creamy smooth that it is almost fluffy.
Origin: An adaptation of the Ramos Fizz. In his 1939 'The Gentleman's Companion', Charles H. Baker Jr. credits this drinks creation to Ahmed Soliman a manufacturer and seller of Perfume Essences in the Khan el Kalili Bazaar, Cairo.

FLAME OF LOVE MARTINI

★★★★½☆

Glass: Martini
Garnish: Orange zest twist (flamed)
Method: Pour sherry into chilled glass, swirl to coat inside and discard excess. Using a match or lighter, express and ignite the oils from the orange peel so the burn oil coats the inside of the sherry-coated glass. SHAKE the vodka with ice and fine strain into the coated glass.

3 twist	Orange peel
2 shots	Ketel One vodka
¼ shot	Tio Pepe fino sherry

We say: Bone dry but fresh and most definitely citrussy.
Origin: Created at Chasen's, a legendary Hollywood restaurant that opened in 1936 and was a haunt of movie stars and even royalty until its eventual demise in 1995. The memorabilia that decorated the restaurant was held in storage and in 1997 Maud and Dave Chasen's grandson opened another Chasen's on Beverly Hills' Cañon Drive which sadly failed due to a lack of patrons.

During the original Chasen's heyday its star-studded clientele enjoyed drinks created by its noted bartender Pepe Ruiz. Of these the Flame of Love is his most famous creation, partly due to its originally being made for Dean Martin. The legend of this drink is further embellished by Dean dragging his old pal Frank Sinatra to Chasen's to try the drink. The story goes that Frank was so impressed that he ordered one for everyone in the place.

FLAMING DR PEPPER

★★☆☆☆

Glass: Boston & shot
Garnish: None
Method: POUR beer into Boston glass. Layer amaretto and rum in chilled shot glass by carefully pouring amaretto and then rum. IGNITE the rum and carefully lift shot glass then drop (bottom first) into Boston glass.

1 pint	Lager
½ shot	Amaretto liqueur
½ shot	Wray & Nephew overproof rum

We say: Please consider the likelihood of burning yourself while attempting to lift the flaming shot into the beer.
Origin: So named as the end result resembles the taste of the proprietary Dr Pepper soft drink. This drink inspired an episode of The Simpsons featuring a similar drink titled the 'Flaming Homer' and later the 'Flaming Moe' (after the programme's bartender).

FLAMING FERRARI

★★☆☆☆

Glass: Shot
Garnish: Assistant to help the drinker consume the concoction
Method: Step 1: LAYER the first four ingredients by carefully pouring in order into a Martini glass.
Step 2: In two shot glasses POUR the remaining two ingredients separately.
Step 3: IGNITE the contents of the Martini glass. Give two long straws to the drinker and instruct them to drink the contents of the Martini glass in one go. As they do so, slowly POUR the contents of the two shot glasses into the flaming Martini glass.

½ shot	Pomegranate (grenadine) syrup
1 shot	Galliano L'Autentico liqueur
1 shot	Opal Nera black sambuca
1 shot	Chartreuse Green liqueur
1 shot	Grand Marnier liqueur
1 shot	Pusser's Navy rum

Variant: Flaming Lamborghini with coffee liqueur and blue curaçao in the shot glasses.
We say: Not recommended if you want to remember the rest of the evening and please be careful - alcohol and fire is a risky combination.

FLAMING HENRY

★★★★½☆

Glass: Shot
Garnish: None
Method: LAYER by carefully pouring ingredients in the order below. IGNITE bourbon. Extinguish flame prior to drinking and beware of hot glass rim.

½ shot	Amaretto liqueur
½ shot	Baileys Irish cream liqueur
½ shot	Maker's Mark bourbon

We say: Flaming good shot.
Origin: Created by Henry Smiff and friends in the South of France and popularised by one of their number, John Coe, the successful London drinks retailer.

FLAMINGO #1

Glass: Martini
Garnish: Banana chunk
Method: SHAKE all ingredients with ice and fine strain into chilled glass.

1	shot	Maker's Mark bourbon
¾	shot	Bols Banana liqueur
1½	shots	Freshly squeezed orange juice
¾	shot	Freshly squeezed lemon juice
½	fresh	Egg white

We say: It's not pink but it has bourbon, banana, orange and lemon smoothed with egg white.

FLAMINGO #2

Glass: Martini
Garnish: Star fruit
Method: SHAKE all ingredients with ice and fine strain into chilled glass.

2	shots	Bacardi 8yo aged rum
1½	shots	Fresh pressed pineapple juice
½	shot	Freshly squeezed lime juice
⅛	shot	Pomegranate (grenadine) syrup

We say: A tasty, pink drink with a frothy top.
Origin: Classic of unknown origins.

FLATLINER

Glass: Shot
Method: POUR sambuca into chilled glass. LAYER tequila by carefully pouring over sambuca. Lastly DRIP pepper sauce onto drink. This will sink through the tequila to form an orange line on top of the sambuca.

¾	shot	Luxardo Sambuca dei Cesari
¾	shot	Tequila 100% Agave
8	drops	Tabasco hot pepper sauce

We say: A serious combination of sweetness, strength and heat. Looks weird and tastes weirder.

FLIP (GENERIC NAME) 🔑

Glass: Sour or Martini/Coupette
Garnish: Dust with grated nutmeg
Method: SHAKE all ingredients with the ice and fine strain into chilled glass.

2	shots	Brandy, whisk(e)y, gin, rum etc.
1	shot	Monin Pure Cane 2:1 sugar syrup
1	fresh	Egg
½	shot	Double (heavy) cream

Variant: Served hot in a toddy glass - heat in a microwave oven or mix in a pan over heat.
We say: I favour creamy, spicy, bourbon based Flips.
Origin: Flips basically consist of any fortified wine or liquor shaken with a whole egg and sweetened with sugar. They can also contain cream and are typically garnished with a dusting of nutmeg and served in a sour glass or small Martini glass. They can be served hot or cold.

The very first Flips, which emerged as early as the late 1600s, consisted of tankard of ale to which a mixture made from sugar, eggs and spices was added before being heated with a red-hot iron poker from the fire.

FLIP WILLIAMS

Glass: Sour or Martini/Coupette
Garnish: Dust with grated nutmeg
Method: SHAKE all ingredients with ice and fine strain into chilled glass.

1½	shots	Maker's Mark bourbon
¾	shot	Poire William pear liqueur
¼	shot	Monin Pure Cane 2:1 sugar syrup
½	shot	Double (heavy) cream
2	dashes	Angostura aromatic bitters
1	fresh	Egg yolk

We say: Velvety smooth with hints of whiskey and pear.
Origin: Created in 2007 by Julian de Feral at Milk & Honey, London, England.

FLIPPING GOOD

Glass: Sour or Martini/Coupette
Garnish: Dust with grated nutmeg
 Dust with grated nutmeg
Method: DRY SHAKE all ingredients (without ice). SHAKE again with ice and fine strain into chilled glass.

2	shots	Rum Aged
½	shot	Monin Pure Cane 2:1 sugar syrup
½	shot	Double (heavy) cream
1	fresh	Egg yolk

We say: Basically an aged rum flip with the sugar level reduced and egg white omitted.
Origin: Created in December 2008 by Simon Difford at the Cabinet Room, London, England.

THE FLIRT 🔑

Glass: Martini
Garnish: Lipstick on rim
Method: SHAKE all ingredients with ice and fine strain into chilled glass.

2	shots	Tequila 100% Agave
¾	shot	De Kuyper Apricot Brandy liqueur
¾	shot	Freshly squeezed lime juice
1	shot	Ocean Spray cranberry juice

We say: A fruity drink to upset glass washers throughout the land.
Origin: Created in 2002 by Dick Bradsell at Lonsdale House, London, England

FLIRTINI #1 🔑

Glass: Martini
Garnish: Pineapple wedge
Method: SHAKE all ingredients with ice and fine strain into chilled glass.

2	shots	Ketel One vodka
¼	shot	Chambord black raspberry liqueur
1½	shots	Fresh pressed pineapple juice

AKA: French Martini
We say: It's a French Martini - hard not to like.
Origin: Made famous on television's Sex and the City. Said to have been created in 2003 for Sarah Jessica Parker at Guastavinos, New York City, USA.

FLIRTINI #2

★★★★☆

Glass: Martini
Garnish: Maraschino cherry
Method: SHAKE first 3 ingredients with ice and fine strain into chilled glass. TOP with champagne.

¾	shot	Ketel One vodka
¾	shot	Triple Sec
2	shots	Fresh pressed pineapple juice
Top up with		Brut champagne

We say: A flirtatious little number that slips down easily.
Origin: Adapted from a recipe by the New York bartender Dale DeGroff.

THE FLO ZIEGFELD

★★★⯪☆

Glass: Martini
Garnish: Pineapple wedge
Method: SHAKE all ingredients with ice and fine strain into chilled glass.

2	shots	Tanqueray London dry gin
1	shot	Fresh pressed pineapple juice
¼	shot	Monin Pure Cane 2:1 sugar syrup

We say: The original recipe omits sugar but was probably made with sweetened pineapple juice.
Origin: Named after Florenz Ziegfeld, the Broadway Impresario, who's widow released the recipe for the 1946 'Stork Club Bar Book'.

FLORAL MARTINI

★★★★☆

Glass: Martini
Garnish: Edible flower
Method: STIR all ingredients with ice and fine strain into chilled glass.

2	shots	Tanqueray London dry gin
½	shot	St~Germain elderflower liqueur
½	shot	Martini Extra Dry vermouth
¼	shot	Rose water
½	shot	Chilled mineral water

We say: This aptly named gin Martini is soft but dry.
Origin: Adapted from a drink created in 2003 at Zander Bar, London, England.

FLORIDA COCKTAIL (MOCKTAIL)

★★★☆☆

Glass: Collins
Garnish: Orange slice & cherry on stick (sail)
Method: SHAKE first 4 ingredients with ice and strain into ice-filled glass, TOP with soda.

1	shot	Freshly squeezed grapefruit juice
2	shots	Freshly squeezed orange juice
½	shot	Freshly squeezed lemon juice
¼	shot	Monin Pure Cane 2:1 sugar syrup
Top up with		Soda (club soda)

We say: The Florida sun shines through this fruity, refreshing drink.

FLORIDA DAIQUIRI

★★★★⯪

Glass: Martini
Garnish: Maraschino cherry
Method: SHAKE all ingredients with ice and fine strain into chilled glass.

2	shots	Bacardi Superior rum
½	shot	Freshly squeezed lime juice
¼	shot	Monin Pure Cane 2:1 sugar syrup
½	shot	Freshly squeezed grapefruit juice
⅛	shot	Luxardo Maraschino liqueur
¾	shot	Chilled mineral water

We say: This classic blend of rum, lime and sugar, but with a hint of freshly squeezed grapefruit juice and maraschino. A user-friendly version of a Hemingway Special.

FLORIDA SLING

★★★☆☆

Glass: Sling
Garnish: Redcurrants
Method: SHAKE all ingredients with ice and strain into ice-filled glass.

2	shots	Tanqueray London dry gin
¼	shot	De Kuyper Cherry Brandy liqueur
2	shots	Fresh pressed pineapple juice
¾	shot	Freshly squeezed lemon juice
¼	shot	Pomegranate (grenadine) syrup

We say: A tall, pink, dumbed down Singapore Sling.

FLORIDITA MARGARITA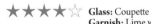

★★★★☆

Glass: Coupette
Garnish: Lime wedge & salt rim (optional)
Method: SHAKE all ingredients with ice and fine strain into chilled glass.

1½	shots	Tequila 100% Agave
½	shot	Triple Sec
½	shot	Ocean Spray cranberry juice
¼	shot	Rose's lime cordial
1½	shots	Freshly squeezed grapefruit juice
¾	shot	Freshly squeezed lime juice
½	shot	Monin Pure Cane 2:1 sugar syrup

We say: A blush coloured, Margarita-style drink with a well-matched amalgamation of flavours.
Origin: Created in 1999 by Robert Plotkin and Raymon Flores or BarMedia, USA.

FLOWER POWER MARTINI

★★★★⯪

Glass: Martini
Garnish: Orange zest twist
Method: SHAKE all ingredients with ice and fine strain into chilled glass.

2	shots	Tanqueray London dry gin
½	shot	St~Germain elderflower liqueur
½	shot	Martini Extra Dry vermouth
¼	shot	Benoit Serres crème de violette

We say: A Dry Martini served super-wet with more flower power than the 1960s.
Origin: Created in 2007 by Simon Difford.

FLUFFY DUCK

★★★½☆

Glass: Collins
Garnish: Orange slice
Method: SHAKE first 4 ingredients with ice and strain into ice-filled glass. TOP with soda.

1½ shots	Tanqueray London dry gin
1½ shots	Advocaat liqueur
1 shot	Triple Sec
1 shot	Freshly squeezed orange juice
Top up with	Soda (club soda)

We say: Light, creamy and easy drinking. The gin's character prevents it from being too fluffy.

FLUTTER

★★★★½

Glass: Martini
Garnish: Orange zest twist
Method: SHAKE all ingredients with ice and fine strain into chilled glass.

2 shots	Tequila 100% Agave
1 shot	Kahlúa coffee liqueur
1¼ shots	Fresh pressed pineapple juice

We say: The three ingredients combine brilliantly.
Origin: Created in 2003 by Tony Coningliaro at Lonsdale House, London, England.

FLY LIKE A BUTTERFLY

★★★★☆

Glass: Martini
Garnish: Orange zest twist
Method: SHAKE all ingredients with ice and fine strain into chilled glass.

1½ shots	Martini Extra Dry vermouth
1½ shots	Martini Rosso sweet vermouth
¾ shot	Dubonnet Red (French made)
¾ shot	Freshly squeezed orange juice

We say: This light, aromatic, sweet and sour beauty has a grown-up, quinine-rich flavour but lacks the 'sting like a bee' finish.
Origin: My take on a classic called a 'Lovely Butterfly'.

FLYING DUTCHMAN MARTINI

★★★★☆

Glass: Martini
Garnish: Orange zest twist
Method: STIR all ingredients with ice and strain into chilled glass.

2½ shots	Bols Genever
¼ shot	Triple Sec
2 dashes	Orange bitters
¾ shot	Chilled mineral water

We say: A Martini with more than a hint of orange.

FLYING GRASSHOPPER

★★★½☆

Glass: Martini
Garnish: Chocolate powder rim & mint leaf
Method: SHAKE all ingredients with ice and fine strain into chilled glass.

1 shot	Ketel One vodka
¾ shot	White Crème de Cacao
¾ shot	Double (heavy) cream
¾ shot	Milk
½ shot	Green crème de menthe liqueur

We say: A Grasshopper with vodka - tastes like a choc mint ice cream.

FLYING SCOTSMAN

★★★★☆

Glass: Old-fashioned
Garnish: Orange zest twist
Method: STIR all ingredients with ice and strain into ice-filled glass.

2 shots	Dewar's White label Scotch
2 shots	Martini Rosso sweet vermouth
¼ shot	Monin Pure Cane 2:1 sugar syrup
3 dashes	Angostura aromatic bitters

We say: Sweetened Scotch with plenty of spice: like a homemade whisky liqueur.

FLYING TIGRE COCTEL

★★★★☆

Glass: Martini
Garnish: Orange zest twist
Method: SHAKE all ingredients with ice and fine strain into chilled glass.

1¾ shots	Bacardi Superior rum
¾ shot	Tanqueray London dry gin
¼ shot	Monin Pure Cane 2:1 sugar syrup
⅛ shot	Pomegranate (grenadine) syrup
3 dashes	Angostura aromatic bitters
¾ shot	Chilled mineral water

We say: Light, aromatic and complex - one to sip.
Origin: Adapted from a recipe in the 1949 edition of Esquire's *Handbook for Hosts*. Credited to an unnamed Captain serving in the US Marines in 1942.

FOG CUTTER #1

★★★★☆

Glass: Collins
Garnish: Orange slice
Method: SHAKE first 6 ingredients with ice and strain into ice-filled glass. FLOAT sherry on top of drink and serve without straws.

1½ shots	Bacardi Superior rum
¾ shot	Cognac VSOP
½ shot	Tanqueray London dry gin
1½ shots	Freshly squeezed orange juice
½ shot	Freshly squeezed lemon juice
½ shot	Monin Almond (orgeat) syrup
½ shot	Amontillado sherry

We say: This long, fruity drink packs a serious kick.
Origin: A version of what became a Tiki classic, sometimes credited to Trader Vic and/or Don the Beachcomber. In his 'Bartender's Guide' (1972 revised edition) Vic remarks, Fog Cutter, hell. After two of these, you won't even see the stuff.

FOG CUTTER #2 UPDATED

★★★★⯪

Glass: Old-fashioned
Garnish: Orange slice
Method: SHAKE first 5 ingredients with ice and strain into glass filled with crushed ice. DRIZZLE cherry brandy over drink and serve with straws.

1	shot	Bacardi Superior rum
½	shot	Cognac VSOP
½	shot	Tanqueray London dry gin
½	shot	Freshly squeezed lime juice
¼	shot	Monin Pure Cane 2:1 sugar syrup
¼	shot	De Kuyper Cherry Brandy liqueur

We say: A well balanced (neither too strong nor to sweet), short, fruity drink which is reminiscent of the modern day Bramble.

FOG HORN

★★★⯪☆

Glass: Old-fashioned
Garnish: Lime wedge
Method: POUR ingredients into ice-filled glass and stir.

2	shots	Tanqueray London dry gin
½	shot	Rose's lime cordial
Top up with		Ginger ale

We say: Different! Almost flowery in taste with the spice of ginger beer.

FOGERTY NEW

★★★★☆

Glass: Coupette
Garnish: Orange zest twist
Method: STIR all ingredients with ice and strain into chilled glass.

2	shots	Straight rye whiskey
½	shot	Campari Bitter
¼	shot	Crème de cassis liqueur
2	dashes	Regan's Orange #6

We say: This well-balanced cocktail was originally based on straight rye but we prefer with bourbon.
Origin: Adapted from a drink created in 2010 by Ryan 'Jesus' Fitzgerald at Beretta San Francisco, USA.

FONTAINEBLEAU SPECIAL

★★★⯪☆

Glass: Martini
Garnish: Star anise
Method: SHAKE all ingredients with ice and fine strain into chilled glass.

1½	shots	Cognac VSOP
1½	shots	Marie Brizard anisette liqueur
¾	shot	Martini Extra Dry vermouth

We say: Cognac, aniseed and vermouth combine in this pleasant after dinner drink which has a taste reminiscent of liquorice.

FORBIDDEN FRUITS

★★★★☆

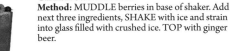

Glass: Collins
Garnish: Seasonal berries
Method: MUDDLE berries in base of shaker. Add next three ingredients, SHAKE with ice and strain into glass filled with crushed ice. TOP with ginger beer.

4	fresh	Blueberries
4	fresh	Blackberries
4	fresh	Raspberries
4	fresh	Strawberries (hulled)
2	shots	Bacardi Superior rum
1	shot	Freshly squeezed lime juice
½	shot	Monin Pure Cane 2:1 sugar syrup
Top up with		Ginger beer

We say: Long and fruity with something of a bite.
Origin: Created in 2001 by Andres Masso at Lab Bar, London, England.

THE FORMOSA

★★★⯪☆

Glass: Martini
Garnish: Orange zest twist
Method: STIR all ingredients with ice and strain into chilled glass.

2	shots	Sake
2	shots	Taylor's chip dry white port

We say: Light and easy to drink. Wine-like.

FORT LAUDERDALE

★★★☆☆

Glass: Martini
Garnish: Orange zest twist
Method: SHAKE all ingredients with ice and fine strain into chilled glass.

1½	shots	Bacardi Superior rum
½	shot	Martini Rosso sweet vermouth
1	shot	Freshly squeezed orange juice
¼	shot	Freshly squeezed lime juice

We say: Rum, vermouth, lime and orange form a challenging combination in this golden drink.

STAR RATINGS EXPLAINED

★★★★★ **Excellent**

★★★★⯪ Recommended	★★★★☆ Praiseworthy
★★★⯪☆ Commended	★★★☆☆ Mediocre
★★⯪☆☆ Disappointing	★★☆☆☆ Pretty awful
★⯪☆☆☆ Shameful	★☆☆☆☆ Disgusting

FOSBURY FLIP  UPDATED

★★★★★ (4½)
Glass: Collins
Garnish: Apricot slice
Method: SHAKE all ingredients with ice and strain into ice-filled glass.

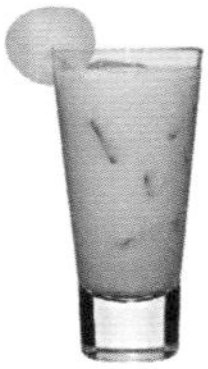

2	shots	Rum Aged
¾	shot	De Kuyper apricot brandy liqueur
¾	shot	Hazelnut liqueur
2	shots	Freshly squeezed orange juice
⅔	shot	Freshly squeezed lime juice
⅛	shot	Pomegranate (grenadine) syrup
1	fresh	Egg yolk

We say: This richly flavoured, velvety drink is almost custardy in consistency but a refreshing hint of lime.
Origin: Adapted from a drink created in 2002 by Salvatore Calabrese at the Library Bar, Lanesborough Hotel, London, England, for Kirsten Fosbury. The Fosbury Flop is the style of high jump used by almost all successful high jumpers today and introduced by the American Dick Fosbury, who won the Gold Medal at the 1968 Olympic Games.

FOUR ACES

★★★★★ (4½)
Glass: Old-fashioned
Garnish: Basil leaf
Method: MUDDLE grapes in base of shaker. Add next five ingredients, SHAKE with ice and fine strain into ice-filled glass. TOP with soda water, stir and serve with straws.

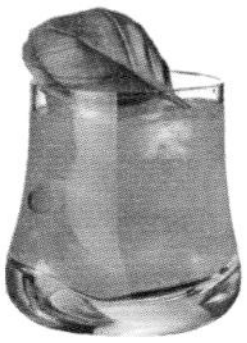

6	fresh	Seedless white grapes
1½	shots	Ketel One vodka
½	shot	Freshly squeezed lime juice
½	shot	Domaine de Canton ginger liqueur
¼	shot	Monin Pure Cane 2:1 sugar syrup
4	fresh	Torn basil leaves

We say: A summery, light, superbly balanced herbal fruit cocktail. Origionally made with Luksusowa.
Origin: Created in 2009 by Damian Windsor at The Roger Room, Los Angeles, USA. Inspired by Table 8, Los Angeles.

FOUR LEAF CLOVER

★★★★★ (4½)
Glass: Martini
Garnish: Physalis (cape gooseberry)
Method: MUDDLE clove in base of shaker. Add other ingredients, SHAKE with ice and fine strain into chilled glass.

1	dried	Clove
2	shots	Bacardi Superior rum
1	shot	Pressed apple juice
¾	shot	Freshly squeezed lime juice
½	shot	Monin Honey syrup

We say: Originally based on vodka but seemed a shame not to try it as a Daiquiri.
Origin: Created in 2008 by Denis Broci at Maze bar & Restaurant, London, England.

FOUR W DAIQUIRI

★★★★☆
Glass: Martini
Garnish: Grapefruit wedge
Method: SHAKE all ingredients with ice and fine strain into chilled glass.

2	shots	Bacardi Oro golden rum
1½	shots	Freshly squeezed grapefruit juice
2	dashes	Angostura aromatic bitters
¾	shot	Maple syrup
½	shot	Chilled mineral water

We say: The oomph of rum, the sourness of grapefruit and the richness of maple syrup, all aromatised by bitters.
Origin: Our version of an old brick drink created by Herb Smith and popularised by his friend Oscar at the Waldorf, New York City. The drink was named in honour of the Duke of Windsor and his bride, formerly Wallis Warfield Simpson. The four 'W's stand for Wallis Warfield Windsor Wallop

FOURTH OF JULY COCKTAIL

★★★☆☆
Glass: Martini
Garnish: Dust with cinnamon powder
Method: POUR bourbon and Galliano into warm glass, IGNITE and sprinkle cinnamon while flaming. SHAKE last three ingredients with ice and strain into glass over extinguished bourbon and Galliano base.

1	shot	Maker's Mark bourbon
1	shot	Galliano L'Autentico liqueur
1	pinch	Ground cinnamon
1	shot	Kahlúa coffee liqueur
1	shot	Freshly squeezed orange juice
1	shot	Double (heavy) cream

We say: More a stage show than a cocktail but rich and tasty all the same.

FOURTH OF JULY SHOT

★★½☆☆ 
Glass: Shot
Garnish: None
Method: Refrigerate ingredients then LAYER in chilled glass by carefully pouring in the following order.

¼	shot	Pomegranate (grenadine) syrup
½	shot	Bols Blue Curaçao liqueur
½	shot	Ketel One vodka

We say: Looks cool... tastes less so!

STAR RATINGS EXPLAINED

★★★★★ **Excellent**

★★★★½ Recommeded	★★★★☆ Praiseworthy
★★★½☆ Commended	★★★☆☆ Mediocre
★★½☆☆ Disappointing	★★☆☆☆ Pretty awful
★½☆☆☆ Shameful	★☆☆☆☆ Disgusting

FOXY LADY NEW

★★★★☆

Glass: Coupette
Garnish: Strawberry
Method: DRY SHAKE all ingredients (without ice). SHAKE again with ice and strain to chilled cocktail glass.

1½	shots	Tanqueray London dry gin
½	shot	Crème de fraise du bois liqueur
¾	shot	Freshly squeezed lemon juice
⅓	shot	Monin Pure Cane 2:1 sugar syrup
½	fresh	Egg white

We say: Best described as a strawberry gin sour, the herbal botanicals in the gin combine well with the sweet strawberry.
Origin: Adapted from a drink created in 2005 by Nicolas Skovgaard at Fox Hotelbar, Copenhagen, Denmark. Nicolas revised this recipe in 2013 to use chamomile tea infused gin.

FRANCOPHILE MARTINI NEW

★★★★⯪

Glass: Martini
Garnish: Pineapple wedge
Method: SHAKE all ingredients with ice and fine strain into chilled glass.

1	shot	Tanqueray London dry gin
1	shot	Ketel One vodka
½	shot	Chambord black raspberry liqueur
½	shot	Martini Extra Dry vermouth
1	shot	Fresh pressed pineapple juice

We say: A simple variation on the vodka-based 'French Martini' adding gin and dry vermouth to help justify its 'martini' name.
Origin: Created in June 2011 by Simon Difford at The Cabinet Room, London, England.

FRANK SULLIVAN COCKTAIL

★★★☆☆

Glass: Martini
Garnish: Lemon zest twist & sugar rim
Method: SHAKE all ingredients with ice and fine strain into chilled glass.

1	shot	Cognac VSOP
1	shot	Triple Sec
1	shot	Martini Extra Dry vermouth
1	shot	Freshly squeezed lemon juice

We say: A Sidecar made dry with the vermouth. It needs the sweet rim.
Origin: Adapted from Harry Craddock's 1930 'The Savoy Cocktail Book'.

FRANKENJACK COCKTAIL

★★★★☆

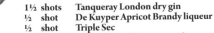

Glass: Martini
Garnish: Orange zest twist
Method: SHAKE all ingredients with ice and fine strain into chilled glass.

1½	shots	Tanqueray London dry gin
½	shot	De Kuyper Apricot Brandy liqueur
½	shot	Triple Sec
1½	shots	Martini Extra Dry vermouth

AKA: Claridge Cocktail
We say: Dry and sophisticated.
Origin: Adapted from Harry Craddock's 1930 'The Savoy Cocktail Book'.

FRANKLIN DRY MARTINI

★★★★★★

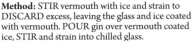

Glass: Martini
Garnish: Two olives on stick
Method: STIR vermouth with ice and strain to DISCARD excess, leaving the glass and ice coated with vermouth. POUR gin over vermouth coated ice, STIR and strain into chilled glass.

| 2½ | shots | Tanqueray London dry gin |
| ½ | shot | Martini Extra Dry vermouth |

We say: A Dry Martini named after Franklin Roosevelt and garnished with two olives.

FREDDY FUDPUCKER

★★★☆☆

Glass: Collins
Garnish: Orange slice
Method: SHAKE all ingredients with ice and strain into ice-filled glass.

2	shots	Tequila 100% Agave
½	shot	Galliano L'Autentico liqueur
3½	shots	Freshly squeezed orange juice

Variant: Harvey Wallbanger
We say: A Harvey Wallbanger made with tequila in place of vodka. It's usual to build this drink and 'float' Galliano over the top. However, as the Galliano sinks anyway it is better shaken.

FREE TOWN

 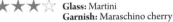
★★★★☆

Glass: Martini
Garnish: Maraschino cherry
Method: SHAKE all ingredients with ice and fine strain into chilled glass.

2	shots	Bacardi Superior rum
1	shot	Warre's Otima tawny port
½	shot	Monin Pure Cane 2:1 sugar syrup
2	dashes	Peychaud's aromatic bitters

We say: Great for sipping after dinner.
Origin: Created in 2004 by Alexandra Fiot Fiot at Lonsdale, London, England.

STAR RATINGS EXPLAINED

★★★★★ Excellent

★★★★⯪ Recommended	★★★★☆ Praiseworthy
★★★⯪☆ Commended	★★★☆☆ Mediocre
★★⯪☆☆ Disappointing	★★☆☆☆ Pretty awful
★⯪☆☆☆ Shameful	★☆☆☆☆ Disgusting

FRENCH 75

★★★★☆

Glass: Flute
Garnish: Lemon zest twist
Method: SHAKE first three ingredients with ice and strain into chilled glass. TOP with champagne.

1½ shots	Tanqueray London dry gin
½ shot	Freshly squeezed lemon juice
¼ shot	Monin Pure Cane 2:1 sugar syrup
Top up with	Brut champagne

We say: Fresh, clean, sophisticated - very drinkable and hasn't dated.
Origin: Legend has it that the drink was created by Harry MacElhone at his Harry's American Bar, Paris, in 1925 and was named after the 75mm Howitzer field gun used by the French army during the First World War (1914 to 1918). However, like other drinks in the first (1919) edition of Harry's own book, 'The ABC of Mixing Drinks', he credits the drink to Macgarry of Buck's Club, London, England.

However, its creation is now commonly attributed to the USA during the Prohibition era (1920-1933). Although the Howitzer was mounted on American tanks my issues with the American origin theory are that the Great War was well over by the time Prohibition started and I question whether an American, now or then, would name a drink after a metric measurement. Being a Brit, I favour The French 75 being an English drink that gained in popularity in France during the Prohibition era and found its way to the US with returning officers.

FRENCH 76

★★★★☆

Glass: Flute
Garnish: Maraschino cherry
Method: SHAKE first 3 ingredients with ice and strain into chilled glass. TOP with champagne.

1 shot	Ketel One vodka
½ shot	Freshly squeezed lemon juice
¼ shot	Monin Pure Cane 2:1 sugar syrup
Top up with	Brut champagne

Variant: Diamond Fizz.
We say: A Vodka Sour topped with champagne. Works well.

FRENCH 77

★★★★☆

Glass: Flute
Garnish: Lemon zest twist
Method: POUR first two ingredients into chilled glass, and TOP with champagne.

1 shot	St~Germain elderflower liqueur
¼ shot	Freshly squeezed lemon juice
Top up with	Brut champagne

We say: Elderflower liqueur adds flavour to champagne while a splash of lemon juice balances the sweetness.
Origin: I created this twist on the classic French 75 in 2006.

FRENCH BISON-TINI

★★★★☆

Glass: Martini
Garnish: Raspberries
Method: SHAKE all ingredients with ice and fine strain into chilled glass.

2 shots	Żubrówka bison vodka
¼ shot	Chambord black raspberry liqueur
2 shots	Fresh pressed pineapple juice

We say: A French Martini with the distinctive taste of Żubrówka.

FRENCH COCKTAIL NEW

★★★★½

Glass: Martini
Garnish: Pineapple wedge
Method: SHAKE all ingredients with ice and fine strain into chilled glass.

2 shots	Cognac VSOP
1½ shots	Fresh pressed pineapple juice
½ shot	Chambord black raspberry liqueur

We say: A simple rift on the 'French Martini' swapping the usual vodka for the more French cognac. Fruity and easy drinking.
Origin: Created in June 2011 by Simon Difford at The Cabinet Room, London, England.

FRENCH CONNECTION

★★★½☆

Glass: Old-fashioned
Garnish: Lemon zest twist
Method: STIR all ingredients with ice and strain into ice-filled glass.

| 2 shots | Cognac VSOP |
| 1 shot | Amaretto liqueur |

We say: The apricot and almond notes in amaretto combine perfectly with cognac in this simple drink.

FRENCH DAIQUIRI

★★★★½

Glass: Martini
Garnish: Pineapple wedge
Method: SHAKE all ingredients with ice and fine strain into chilled glass.

2½ shots	Bacardi Superior rum
½ shot	Chambord black raspberry liqueur
½ shot	Freshly squeezed lime juice
1½ shots	Fresh pressed pineapple juice
3 dashes	Difford's Daiquiri Bitters

We say: A classic Daiquiri made fruity with the addition of black raspberry liqueur and pineapple juice.
Origin: Created in 2009 by Simon Difford at The Cabinet Room, London, England for Charlotte Ashburner, Chambord's UK brand manager.

FRENCH DAISY

★★★½☆

Glass: Martini
Garnish: Lemon zest twist
Method: SHAKE first four ingredients with ice and fine strain into chilled glass. TOP with champagne.

1 shot	Cognac VSOP
½ shot	St~Germain elderflower liqueur
1 shot	Freshly squeezed lemon juice
Top up with	Brut champagne
½ shot	Crème de cassis liqueur

We say: Rich blackcurrant with hints of elderflower, citrus and champagne. Slightly sweet.
Origin: Adapted from a drink created by Wayne Collins, London, England.

FRENCH KISS #1

★★★☆☆

Glass: Martini
Garnish: Star anise
Method: SHAKE first 3 ingredients with ice and fine strain into chilled glass. POUR grenadine into centre of drink. (It should sink.)

1	shot	Ketel One vodka
¾	shot	Pernod anise
2	shots	Freshly squeezed orange juice
⅛	shot	Pomegranate (grenadine) syrup

We say: Looks like a Tequila Sunrise but tastes of anis and orange.

FRENCH KISS #2

★★★★☆

Glass: Martini
Garnish: Raspberries
Method: SHAKE all ingredients with ice and fine strain into chilled glass.

1½	shots	Ketel One vodka
½	shot	Chambord black raspberry liqueur
½	shot	White Crème de Cacao
½	shot	Double (heavy) cream
½	shot	Milk

We say: Smooth creamy chocolate and raspberry.

FRENCH LETTER NEW

★★★★★

Glass: Champagne flute
Garnish: Cherry tomato on a cocktail spike
Method: MUDDLE cherry tomato in base of shaker. ADD other ingredients, SHAKE with ice and fine strain into chilled glass. TOP with sparkling water.

1	whole	Cherry tomato
1½	shots	Pear flavoured vodka
⅔	shot	Trivento Argentinean Viognier
½	shot	Monin Pure Cane syrup (2:1)
½	shot	Freshly squeezed lemon juice
½	shot	Sparkling mineral water

We say: This cocktail relies on the fine balance between the sugar and the acidity in the tomato and white wine. When this balance is hit then the French Letter is a harmonious mix.
Origin: Created in 2010 by Joey Medrington, Edinburgh, Scotland who won CLASS Bartender of the Year 2010 with this cocktail.

FRENCH LEAVE

★★★☆☆

Glass: Collins
Garnish: Orange slice
Method: SHAKE all ingredients with ice and strain into ice-filled glass.

1½	shots	Ketel One vodka
½	shot	Pernod anise
3½	shots	Freshly squeezed orange juice

We say: An easy drinking blend of vodka, anise and orange juice.

FRENCH MAID NEW

★★★★☆

Glass: Collins
Garnish: Mint sprig speared cucumber slice
Method: MUDDLE cucumber in base of shaker. Add next 5 ingredients, SHAKE with ice and fine strain into ice-filled glass. TOP with ginger beer.

3	slice	Cucumber (chopped & peeled)
8	fresh	Mint leaves
1½	shots	Courvoisier VSOP Exclusif
½	shot	Taylor's Velvet Falernum liqueur
¾	shot	Freshly squeezed lime juice
⅓	shot	Monin Pure Cane 2:1 sugar syrup
1	shot	Ginger beer

We say: As Jim Meeham said when he gave us this recipe, "This hybrid of Audrey Saunders Gin Gin Mule substitutes cognac for gin and adds falernum and cucumber. Milk & Honey barman Sam Ross has a similar drink made with Bourbon dubbed the Kentucky Maid: consider this her spicy French sister."
Origin: Created in autumn 2008 by Jim Meehan at PDT, New York, USA.

FRENCH MARTINI

★★★★☆

Glass: Martini
Garnish: Pineapple wedge
Method: SHAKE all ingredients with ice and fine strain into chilled glass.

2	shots	Ketel One vodka
½	shot	Chambord liqueur
1½	shots	Fresh pressed pineapple juice

AKA: Flirtini
We say: Raspberry and pineapple laced with vodka. Easy drinking and very fruity.
Origin: The origin of the French Martini is unknown although we discovered the drink in the late 1990s at London's Quo Vadis where it was made by Dick Bradsell. Obviously named for its use of French liqueur this is not actually a 'Martini' as it does not contain vermouth and is a touch on the fruity sweet side (depending on how much liqueur you add). During the 1990s cocktail renaissance pretty much any drink served in a V-shaped glass became a Martini.

FRENCH MOJITO

★★★★☆

Glass: Collins
Garnish: Raspberries & mint sprig
Method: Lightly MUDDLE mint in base of glass (just to bruise). Add rum, liqueur and lime juice. Half-fill glass with crushed ice and CHURN (stir) with bar spoon. Continue to add crushed ice and churn until drink is level with glass rim.

12	fresh	Mint leaves
2	shots	Bacardi Superior rum
½	shot	Chambord black raspberry liqueur
1	shot	Freshly squeezed lime juice
¼	shot	Monin Pure Cane 2:1 sugar syrup

We say: A classic Mojito with a hint of berry fruit.

FRENCH MONKEY

★★★½☆

Glass: Old-fashioned
Garnish: Lemon zest twist
Method: SHAKE first three ingredients with ice and strain into ice-filled glass. TOP with just a splash of soda.

2	shots	Dewar's White label Scotch
½	shot	St~Germain elderflower liqueur
½	shot	Pressed apple juice
1	shot	Soda (club soda)

We say: Apple, Scotch and elderflower, honeyed and floral.
Origin: Created in 2006 for my French friend, Xavier Padovani.

FRENCH MULE ☞

★★★★☆

Glass: Collins
Garnish: Mint sprig
Method: SHAKE first four ingredients with ice and strain into ice-filled glass. TOP with ginger beer, stir and serve with straws.

2	shots	Cognac VSOP
1	shot	Freshly squeezed lime juice
1	shot	Monin Pure Cane 2:1 sugar syrup
3	dashes	Angostura aromatic bitters
Top up with		Ginger beer

We say: This French answer to the vodka based Moscow Mule uses cognac to make a more flavoursome, long, refreshing drink.

FRENCH SHERBERT ☞

★★★½☆

Glass: Martini
Garnish: Orange zest twist
Method: SHAKE all ingredients with ice and fine strain into chilled glass.

1	shot	Tanqueray London dry gin
1	shot	Triple Sec
1	shot	Freshly squeezed orange juice
1	shot	Freshly squeezed lime juice

We say: Not particulary French or sherbety - just a fresh orange wake up call.

FRENCH SPRING PUNCH

★★★★☆

Glass: Sling
Garnish: Strawberry
Method: SHAKE first 4 ingredients with ice and strain into ice-filled glass. TOP with champagne and serve with straws.

1	shot	Courvoisier VSOP Exclusif
½	shot	Crème de framboise liqueur
½	shot	Freshly squeezed lemon juice
¼	shot	Monin Pure Cane 2:1 sugar syrup
Top up with		Brut champagne

We say: Not as popular as the Russian Spring Punch but still a modern day London classic.
Origin: Created by Dick Bradsell and Rodolphe Sorel at Match EC1, London, England, during the late 1990s.

FRENCH TEAR #1 ☞

★★★★☆

Glass: Martini
Garnish: Pineapple wedge
Method: SHAKE all ingredients with ice and fine strain into chilled glass.

1¾	shots	Bacardi Superior rum
¾	shot	Grand Marnier liqueur
2	shots	Fresh pressed pineapple juice

We say: Light, flavoursome, easy drinking. Altogether very gluggable.
Origin: Discovered in 2000 at Quo Vadis, London, England.

FRENCH WHISKY SOUR

★★★★½

Glass: Old-fashioned
Garnish: Lemon slice & cherry on stick (sail)
Method: SHAKE all ingredients with ice and strain into ice-filled glass.

2	shots	Dewar's White label Scotch
½	shot	Ricard Pastis
1	shot	Freshly squeezed lemon juice
½	shot	Monin Pure Cane 2:1 sugar syrup
½	fresh	Egg white
3	dashes	Angostura aromatic bitters

We say: Pastis adds a pleasing hint of anise and liquorice to the classic Whisky Sour.
Origin: Created in 2006 by Simon Difford and inspired by Tony Conigliaro's Liquorice Whisky Sour.

FRESA BATIDA

★★★½☆

Glass: Collins (small 8oz)
Garnish: Strawberry
Method: MUDDLE strawberries in base of shaker. Add other ingredients, SHAKE with ice and strain into glass filled with crushed ice.

2½	shots	Leblon cachaça
½	shot	Freshly squeezed lemon juice
½	shot	Monin Pure Cane 2:1 sugar syrup
7	fresh	Strawberries (hulled)

We say: A long, very refreshing strawberry drink laced with cachaça.
Origin: The Batida is a traditional Brazilian-style of drink and 'Fresa' means strawberry in Portuguese, the official language of Brazil.

FRESCA

★★★½☆

Glass: Martini
Garnish: Lemon zest twist
Method: SHAKE first 4 ingredients with ice and fine strain into chilled glass. TOP with lemonade.

1½	shots	Ketel One Citroen vodka
½	shot	Chambord black raspberry liqueur
1	shot	Freshly squeezed grapefruit juice
½	shot	Freshly squeezed lemon juice
Top up with		Lemonade/Sprite/7-Up

We say: The sweet, fizzy topping is essential to lengthen and balance this drink.

FRESCA NOVA

★★★½☆

Glass: Flute
Garnish: Orange slice
Method: SHAKE first four ingredients with ice and fine strain into chilled glass. Slowly TOP with champagne.

1½	shots	Grand Marnier liqueur
¾	shot	Freshly squeezed orange juice
¼	shot	Monin Pure Cane 2:1 sugar syrup
1	shot	Double (heavy) cream
Top up with		Brut champagne

We say: Cream, orange and champagne work surprisingly well.
Origin: Created by Jamie Terrell for Phillip Holzberg at Vinexpo 1999.

FRIAR TUCK

★★★½☆

Glass: Martini
Garnish: Dust with grated nutmeg
Method: SHAKE all ingredients with ice and fine strain into chilled glass.

1	shot	Dark Crème de Cacao
1	shot	Hazelnut liqueur
1	shot	Milk
1	shot	Double (heavy) cream

Variant: With amaretto and ice cream.
We say: Round, jolly and creamy with chocolate and hazelnut.

FRIDA'S BROW

★★★★☆

Glass: Martini
Garnish: Dust with cinnamon powder
Method: SHAKE all ingredients with ice and fine strain into chilled glass.

2	shots	Tequila 100% Agave
½	shot	White Crème de Cacao
¼	shot	Pomegranate (grenadine) syrup
½	shot	Double (heavy) cream
½	shot	Milk

We say: Creamy, sweetened tequila with hints of chocolate.
Origin: Discovered in 2005 at Velvet Margarita Cantina, Los Angeles, USA.

FRISCO SOUR

★★★★☆

Glass: Old-fashioned
Garnish: Orange slice & cherry on stick (sail)
Method: SHAKE all ingredients and strain into ice-filled glass.

2	shots	Maker's Mark bourbon
½	shot	Bénédictine D.O.M.
½	shot	Freshly squeezed lemon juice
¼	shot	Monin Pure Cane 2:1 sugar syrup
½	fresh	Egg white

We say: A bourbon rich sour with monastic herbal notes.

FRISKY BISON

★★★★½

Glass: Martini
Garnish: Apple slice
Method: Lightly MUDDLE mint in base of shaker (just to bruise). Add other ingredients, SHAKE with ice and fine strain into chilled glass.

7	fresh	Mint leaves
2	shots	Żubrówka bison vodka
1	shot	Berentzen Apple schnapps
1	shot	Pressed apple juice
½	shot	Freshly squeezed lime juice
¼	shot	Monin Pure Cane 2:1 sugar syrup

We say: Sweet 'n' sour, fruity, minty and fresh.
Origin: Created by Tony Kerr in 1999 at Mash & Air in Manchester, England.

FRISKY LEMONADE

★★★½☆

Glass: Collins
Garnish: Lime wedge
Method: POUR ingredients into ice-filled glass and stir.

2	shots	Lime flavoured vodka
½	shot	Martini Extra Dry vermouth
Top up with		Lemonade/Sprite/7-Up

We say: Reminiscent of alcoholic lemon barley water.
Origin: Created by Aaron Rudd in 2002 at Home, London, England.

FROTH BLOWER COCKTAIL

★★★★½

Glass: Martini
Garnish: Lemon zest twist (discarded)
Method: SHAKE all ingredients with ice and fine strain into chilled glass.

2	shots	Tanqueray London dry gin
¼	shot	Pomegranate (grenadine) syrup
1	fresh	Egg white

We say: Salmon-pink and very frothy but surprisingly complex and tasty.
Origin: Adapted from Harry Craddock's 1930 'The Savoy Cocktail Book'.

FROUPE COCKTAIL

★★★★☆

Glass: Martini
Garnish: Orange zest twist
Method: STIR all ingredients with ice and strain into chilled glass.

1½	shots	Cognac VSOP
1½	shots	Martini Rosso sweet vermouth
¼	shot	Bénédictine D.O.M.

We say: A bittersweet, herbal old-school drink that's in line for rediscovery.
Origin: Adapted from Harry Craddock's 1930 'The Savoy Cocktail Book'.

FROZEN MARGARITA

★★★★☆
Glass: Martini
Garnish: Maraschino cherry
Method: BLEND all ingredients with 6oz scoop of crushed ice. Serve heaped in the glass and with straws.

1½	shots	Tequila 100% Agave
¾	shot	Triple Sec
¾	shot	Freshly squeezed lime juice
½	shot	Monin Pure Cane 2:1 sugar syrup

Variant: With fruit and/or fruit liqueurs.
We say: Citrus freshness with the subtle agave of tequila served frozen.

FRU FRU

★★★☆☆
Glass: Flute
Garnish: Strawberry
Method: SHAKE first three ingredients with ice and strain into glass. TOP with champagne.

¾	shot	Crème de fraise du bois liqueur
¾	shot	Passoã passion fruit liqueur
¾	shot	Freshly squeezed grapefruit juice
Top up with		Brut champagne

We say: Dry, bitter grapefruit complimented by passion fruit and strawberry.

FRUIT & NUT MARTINI

★★★★☆
Glass: Martini
Garnish: Orange zest twist & almond flakes
Method: SHAKE all ingredients with ice and fine strain into chilled glass.

1	shot	Ketel One vodka
½	shot	Pedro Ximénez sherry
1	shot	Hazelnut liqueur
1	shot	Ocean Spray cranberry juice
½	shot	Freshly squeezed orange juice

We say: A rich Christmas pudding of a Martini.
Origin: Created by Simon Difford in 2004.

FRUIT AND NUT CHOCOLATE MARTINI

★★★★☆
Glass: Martini
Garnish: Crumbled Cadbury's Flake bar
Method: SHAKE all ingredients with ice and fine strain into chilled glass.

1	shot	Raspberry flavoured vodka
½	shot	White Crème de Cacao
½	shot	Baileys Irish cream liqueur
½	shot	Hazelnut liqueur
½	shot	Chambord black raspberry liqueur
¾	shot	Double (heavy) cream
¾	shot	Milk

We say: Naughty but nice - one for confectionery lovers.

FRUIT CUP

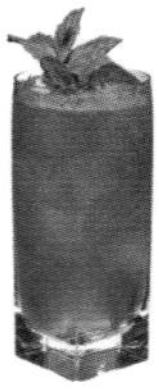

★★★★☆
Glass: Collins
Garnish: Lemon, orange & strawberry slices, mint sprig & borage in drink
Method: SHAKE first 3 ingredients with ice and strain into ice-filled glass. Add garnish. TOP with ginger ale and lightly stir.

1½	shots	Tanqueray London dry gin
½	shot	Triple Sec
1	shot	Martini Rosso sweet vermouth
Top up with		Ginger ale

We say: A refreshing fruity long summery drink, reminiscent of home-made Pimms.

FRUIT PASTEL UPDATED

★★★☆☆
Glass: Martini
Garnish: Fruit Pastille sweet
Method: SHAKE all ingredients with ice and fine strain into chilled glass.

1½	shots	Ketel One Citroen vodka
½	shot	Parfait Amour liqueur
½	shot	Berentzen Apple schnapps
¼	shot	Freshly squeezed lime juice
⅛	shot	Monin Pure Cane 2:1 sugar syrup

We say: Tastes distinctly like a Fruit Pastille sweet.
Origin: Created in late October 2005 by Darren Thrush at the fourth floor Cafe and Bar at Harvey Nichols, Leeds, England. To quote Darren, "The martini glass must have a sugared rim to enhance the presentation and the sweet concept. What's amazing about this concept is that the colour represents what is probably everybody's favourite flavour fruit pastille - the blackcurrant one."

FRUIT SALAD

★★★☆☆
Glass: Martini
Garnish: Fruit Salad sweet (or banana chunk)
Method: SHAKE all ingredients with ice and strain into chilled glass.

2	shots	Ketel One vodka
½	shot	Bols Banana liqueur
½	shot	Galliano L'Autentico liqueur
2½	shots	Freshly squeezed orange juice
¼	shot	Pomegranate (grenadine) syrup

We say: This variation on the Harvey Wallbanger tastes like Fruit Salad 'penny chew' sweets.

FRUIT SOUR

★★★★☆
Glass: Old-fashioned
Garnish: Lemon zest twist
Method: SHAKE all ingredients with ice and strain into ice-filled glass.

1	shot	Maker's Mark bourbon
1	shot	Triple Sec
1	shot	Freshly squeezed lemon juice
½	shot	Egg white

We say: An orange influenced, sweet and sour whiskey cocktail.

FRUIT TREE DAIQUIRI

★★★★☆

Glass: Martini
Garnish: Grapefruit wedge & maraschino cherry
Method: SHAKE all ingredients with ice and fine strain into chilled glass.

2	shots	Bacardi Superior rum
¾	shot	De Kuyper Apricot Brandy liqueur
¾	shot	Freshly squeezed grapefruit juice
¾	shot	Freshly squeezed lime juice
¼	shot	Maraschino syrup (from cherry jar)
½	shot	Chilled mineral water

We say: A restrained Papa Doble with apricot liqueur.

FRUITS OF THE FOREST

★★★½☆

Glass: Martini
Garnish: Raspberries
Method: SHAKE first 5 ingredients with ice and fine strain into chilled glass. POUR Chambord into the centre of the drink: it should sink to the bottom.

2	shots	Żubrówka bison vodka
½	shot	St~Germain elderflower liqueur
1	shot	Freshly squeezed orange juice
½	shot	Freshly squeezed lime juice
½	fresh	Egg white
¼	shot	Chambord black raspberry liqueur

We say: Grassy, floral, citrus and smooth, but look out for the fruity bottom.
Origin: Adapted from a drink created in 2004 by Stuart Barnett at TGI Friday's, Reading, England.

FU MANCHU DAIQUIRI

★★★★☆

Glass: Collins
Garnish: Pineapple wedge
Method: SHAKE all ingredients with ice and fine strain into chilled glass.

2	shots	Bacardi Superior rum
1	shot	Freshly squeezed lime juice
½	shot	Monin Pure Cane 2:1 sugar syrup
¼	shot	Triple Sec
¼	shot	Giffard Menthe Pastille liqueur
¾	shot	Chilled mineral water

We say: A natural Daiquiri with a refreshing, clean, citrussy, minty edge.
Origin: Adapted from a recipe by David Embury.

STAR RATINGS EXPLAINED

★★★★★ Excellent

★★★★½ Recommended	★★★★☆ Praiseworthy
★★★½☆ Commended	★★★☆☆ Mediocre
★★★½☆ Disappointing	★★☆☆☆ Pretty awful
★★½☆☆ Shameful	★☆☆☆☆ Disgusting

FUEGO MANZANA NO.2

★★★★☆

Glass: Martini
Garnish: Small red chilli
Method: MUDDLE chilli in base of shaker. Add other ingredients, SHAKE with ice and fine strain into chilled glass.

1	inch	Red chilli (thin slice)
2	shots	Tequila 100% Agave
½	shot	Berentzen Apple schnapps
1	shot	Pressed apple juice
½	shot	Freshly squeezed lime juice
⅛	shot	Monin Pure Cane 2:1 sugar syrup

We say: A hint of chilli heat adds interest to an Apple Margarita, creating a full flavoured contemporary classic.
Origin: Created by Danny Smith at Che, London, England, initially using rum instead of tequila. 'Fuego Manzana' is Spanish for Fire Apple.

FULL CIRCLE

★★★★☆

Glass: Collins
Garnish: Pineapple wedge
Method: Cut pomegranate in half and juice with a spinning citrus juicer. SHAKE all ingredients with ice and fine strain into ice-filled glass.

3	shots	Pomegranate juice
2	shots	Tanqueray London dry gin
¾	shot	Fresh pressed pineapple juice

We say: Fruity and easy drinking, yet with complexity from the gin.
Origin: Adapted from a drink discovered in 2004 at Mandarin Oriental, New York City, USA. The name is a reference to the bar's location - Columbus Circle, where the world's first one-way rotary system (roundabout) was implemented in 1904.

FULL MONTE

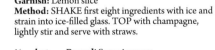

★★★★☆

Glass: Sling
Garnish: Lemon slice
Method: SHAKE first eight ingredients with ice and strain into ice-filled glass. TOP with champagne, lightly stir and serve with straws.

½	shot	Bacardi Superior rum
½	shot	Tanqueray London dry gin
½	shot	Ketel One vodka
½	shot	Tequila 100% Agave
½	shot	Luxardo Maraschino liqueur
1	shot	Freshly squeezed lemon juice
¼	shot	Monin Pure Cane 2:1 sugar syrup
2	dashes	Angostura aromatic bitters
Top up with		Brut champagne

Variant: Beverly Hills Iced Tea
We say: Champagne replaces cola and maraschino liqueur replaces triple sec in this sophisticated adaptation of a Long Island Iced Tea.
Origin: Created by Audrey Saunders at Pegu Club, New York City, USA.

FUMIGATOR FLIP

★★★★½☆

Glass: Sour or Martini/Coupette
Garnish: Dust with grated nutmeg & maraschino cherry
Method: Wash chilled glass with whisky 9swirl to coat inside and shake to discard excess). SHAKE other ingredients with ice and fine strain into whisky coated chilled glass.

¼	shot	Lagavulin 16yo malt whisky
2	shots	Bacardi 8yo aged rum
1	shot	De Kuyper Cherry Brandy liqueur
⅛	shot	Monin Pure Cane 2:1 sugar syrup
½	shot	Double (heavy) cream
1	fresh	Egg yolk

We say: Subtle notes, smoky malt with rum and cherry, smoothed by egg and cream.
Origin: Created in 2008 by Julian de Feral at Bureau, London, England.

FUNKY MONKEY

★★★★☆

Glass: Coconut shell
Garnish: Toasted coconut strips
Method: BLEND all ingredients with 12oz scoop of crushed ice and serve with straws.

1	shot	Bacardi Oro golden rum
¾	shot	Bols Banana liqueur
¾	shot	White Crème de Cacao
1	shot	Coco López cream of coconut
1	shot	Double (heavy) cream
1	shot	Milk
1	fresh	Banana (peeled)

We say: Be sure to use a ripe or even over-ripe banana in this tropical-style drink.
Origin: Created in 1998 by Tony Abou-Ganim, Las Vegas, USA.

FUR COLLAR NEW

★★★★☆

Glass: Coupette
Garnish: Orange zest twist
Method: SHAKE all ingredients with ice and fine strain into chilled glass.

2	shots	Ketel One vodka
½	shot	De Kuyper Apricot Brandy liqueur
¾	shot	Freshly squeezed orange juice

We say: Apricot brandy adds fruity zingyness to what otherwise would be a Screwdriver served 'up'.
Origin: Adapted from a drink in Ted Saucier's 1951 book, 'Bottoms Up!'

STAR RATINGS EXPLAINED

★★★★★ Excellent

★★★★½ Recommended   ★★★★☆ Praiseworthy
★★★½☆ Commended   ★★★☆☆ Mediocre
★★½☆☆ Disappointing   ★★☆☆☆ Pretty awful
★½☆☆☆ Shameful   ★☆☆☆☆ Disgusting

FUZZY NAVEL

★★½☆☆

Glass: Collins
Garnish: Lemon slice
Method: SHAKE all ingredients with ice and strain into ice-filled glass.

| 2 | shots | Peachtree peach schnapps |
| 4 | shots | Freshly squeezed orange juice |

Variant: Hairy Navel with the addition of a shot of vodka.
We say: The hairy version is a slightly more interesting, drier, less fluffy concoction. So why have a fluffy navel when you can have a hairy one?
Origin: A not very well regarded but extremely well known cocktail whose origins are lost.

G & TEA

★★★★☆

Glass: Collins
Garnish: Lemon slice
Method: SHAKE first 3 ingredients with ice and strain into ice-filled glass. TOP with tonic water.

1½	shots	Tanqueray London dry gin
1	shot	St~Germain elderflower liqueur
1	shot	Cold English breakfast tea
Top up with		Tonic water

We say: Dry, floral, long and refreshing.
Origin: Created in 2006 by Simon Difford.

G. G AND G

★★★★☆

Glass: Old-fashioned
Garnish: Grapefruit zest twist
Method: SHAKE all ingredients with ice and fine strain into an ice-filled rocks glass.

1½	shots	Tanqueray London dry gin
1	shot	Galliano L'Autentico liqueur
1	shot	Freshly squeezed pink grapefruit juice
2	dashes	Orange bitters

We say: Pine fresh gin notes combine with aniseed and herbal notes, freshened by pink grapefruit and toned by dashes of orange bitters.
Origin: Adapted from a recipe by Ago Perrone, Connaught Hotel, London, England.

GALVANISED NAIL

★★★★☆

Glass: Martini
Garnish: Lemon zest twist
Method: SHAKE all ingredients with ice and fine strain into chilled glass.

2	shots	Dewar's White label Scotch
½	shot	Drambuie
¼	shot	St~Germain elderflower liqueur
½	shot	Pressed apple juice
¼	shot	Freshly squeezed lemon juice

We say: Scotch and honeyed spice with a hint of apple and elderflower plus some lemon freshness.
Origin: Created in 2003 by Simon Difford, taking inspiration from the Rusty Nail.

GAMBLE

★★★★☆☆

Glass: Old-fashioned
Garnish: Grapefruit slice
Method: SHAKE all ingredients with ice and fine strain into glass filled with crushed ice.

1	shot	Sloe Gin liqueur
1	shot	Tanqueray London dry gin
1	shot	Freshly squeezed pink grapefruit juice
¼	shot	Monin Pure Cane 2:1 sugar syrup
½	shot	De Kuyper Cherry Brandy liqueur

We say: An easy drinking, gin-laced, fruity summery drink.
Origin: Created in April 2011 by Matt Donnelly at the Bacchus Pub and Kitchen, London. To quote Matt, "The drink is called 'A Gamble' due to the fact I gambled on changing 'The Bramble.'"

GARIBALDI

★★★☆☆

Glass: Collins
Garnish: Orange slice
Method: POUR Campari into ice-filled glass. TOP with orange juice, stir and serve with straws.

2	shots	Campari Bitter
Top up with		Freshly squeezed orange juice

We say: Reminiscent of red grapefruit juice.
Origin: Appears on cocktail lists throughout Italy. Named after the famous revolutionary general who helped liberate and reunify Italy.

GANSEVOORT FIZZ

★★★★☆☆

Glass: Collins
Garnish: Lemon slice
Method: SHAKE first 4 ingredients with ice and strain into ice-filled glass. TOP with soda.

2	shots	Bacardi 8yo aged rum
1	shot	Drambuie
1	shot	Freshly squeezed lemon juice
2	dashes	Peychaud's aromatic bitters
Top up with		Soda (club soda)

We say: A potent, flavoursome herbal cooler based on aged rum.
Origin: Created for 5 Ninth in Manhattan and originally published in David Wondrich's 2005 'Killer Cocktails'.

GATOR BITE

★★★★☆☆

Glass: Coupette
Garnish: Salt rim
Method: SHAKE all ingredients with ice and fine strain into chilled glass.

1	shot	Chartreuse Green liqueur
1½	shots	Triple Sec
1	shot	Freshly squeezed lime juice
¾	shot	Monin Pure Cane 2:1 sugar syrup

We say: Looks like a Margarita, but instead of tequila features the unique taste of Chartreuse. Yup, it bites.

GARDEN, GRAIN & GRAPE NEW

★★★★★

Glass: Coupette
Garnish: Mint sprig
Method: MUDDLE grapes in base of shaker. Add other ingredients, DRY SHAKE (without ice). SHAKE again with ice and fine strain into chilled glass.

5	fresh	Seedless white grapes
1½	shots	Ketel One vodka
¾	shot	Sauvignon blanc wine
1	dash	Egg white

We say: Pale green lime with frothy white head, this delicate wine and grape flavoured drink is laced with a large splash of vodka.
Origin: Adapted from a drink created in 2012 by Mal Spence at Blythswood Square Hotel, Glasgow, Scotland.

GAUGUIN

★★★☆☆

Glass: Old-fashioned
Garnish: Maraschino cherry
Method: BLEND all ingredients with 6oz crushed ice and serve with straws.

2	shots	Bacardi Superior rum
½	shot	Freshly squeezed lime juice
½	shot	Freshly squeezed lemon juice
½	shot	Passion fruit syrup

We say: The passion fruit shines through in this drink, which is very much a frozen Daiquiri in style.

BARTENDER'S TIP DRY SHAKE

It is common practice to first shake drinks containing cream and eggs without ice, then to shake the drink a second time with ice added.

This practice is known as 'dry shaking' and the theory is that first shaking without ice, and so at a higher temperature, better allows the drink to emulsify.

GE BLONDE

★★★★⯪

Glass: Martini
Garnish: Apple wedge
Method: SHAKE all ingredients with ice and fine strain into chilled glass.

1¾	shots	Dewar's White label Scotch
1¼	shots	Sauvignon blanc wine
1	shot	Pressed apple juice
½	shot	Monin Pure Cane 2:1 sugar syrup
¼	shot	Freshly squeezed lemon juice

We say: This delicate drink demands freshly pressed apple juice and flavoursome Scotch with subtle peat.
Origin: A combined effort by the staff of London's GE Club in January 2002, this was named by Linda, a waitress at the club who happens to be blonde. She claimed the name was inspired by the cocktail's straw colour.

GEISHA MAR-TEA-KNEE

★★★★☆

Glass: Martini
Garnish: Open tea pearl
Method: SHAKE all ingredients with ice and fine strain into chilled glass.

1½	shots	Tanqueray London dry gin
¾	shot	Zen green tea liqueur
1	shot	Cold jasmine tea

We say: Surprisingly fresh and light, this starts slightly sweet but finishes with refreshing bitter tannins. Tea pearls - hand-rolled balls of tea leaves -make a wonderful garnish.
Origin: Created in the USA in 2006.

GENEVER PUNCH NEW

★★★★⯪

Glass: Goblet
Garnish: Nutmeg
Method: SHAKE first 4 ingredients with ice and strain into ice-filled glass. TOP with soda.

1½	shots	Bols Genever
1	shots	Freshly squeezed lemon juice
½	shot	Demerara 2:1 sugar syrup
2	dashes	Luxardo Maraschino liqueur
½	shot	Soda water (club soda)

We say: A more complex riff of a Collins with malty genever and brown sugar flavours considerably adding to the drink.

GENERAL HARRISON'S NOGG NEW

★★★★★

Glass: Old-fashioned
Garnish: Dust with freshly grated nutmeg
Method: Using an especially designed 'fizz' shaker (such as Perlini) that's designed to be carbonated. SHAKE all ingredients with ice and strain into glass (without ice). Be sure to shake well to completely emulsify the egg.

1½	shots	Boulard Grand Solage calvados
2	shots	Medium dry cider
½	shot	Monin Pure Cane 2:1 sugar syrup
2	dashes	Dale DeGroff's Pimento Bitters
1	fresh	Egg

We say: A whole raw egg contributes body to this filling, flavoursome, wintry, delicate cocktail. The retained CO2 fizz of the cider adds essential body and balancing acidy but demands the use of a specialised shaker.
Origin: We were sent this recipe by Dale DeGroff in December 2012 who said: "A personal favourite, adapted from a recipe from Jerry Thomas' 1862 edition of *How to Mix Drinks*: a totally different take on eggnog – made as a single-serve drink it includes a raw egg, so you need to shake the hell out of it. The bourbon and bitters are my addition."
This cocktail is named after General William Henry Harrison, the American president to hold office for the shortest period. He was elected 4th March 1841 and died a month to the day later of pneumonia. Harrison was known for his drinking and cider was one of his preferred tipples. It is said that this eggnog was his favourite drink.

GENTLE BREEZE (MOCKTAIL)

★★★☆☆

Glass: Collins
Garnish: Lime wedge
Method: POUR ingredients into ice-filled glass, stir and serve with straws.

4	shots	Ocean Spray cranberry juice
2	shots	Freshly squeezed grapefruit juice

We say: A Seabreeze without the hard stuff.

GENTLEMAN'S AGREEMENT NEW

★★★★☆

Glass: Collins
Garnish: Orange zest twist
Method: SHAKE first 3 ingredients with ice and strain into ice-filled glass. TOP with soda.

2½	shots	Gentleman Jack Whiskey
½	shot	Monin Almond (orgeat) syrup
½	shot	Freshly squeezed lemon juice
Top up with		Soda (club soda)

We say: Amaretto-like almond flavours with Tennessee whiskey balanced with fresh lemon juice and lengthened with refreshing soda.
Origin: A cocktail used by Brown-Forman to promote Gentleman Jack.

BARTENDER'S TIP LAYER

As the name would suggest, layered drinks include layers of different ingredients, often with contrasting colours.

This effect is achieved by carefully pouring each ingredient into the glass so that it floats on its predecessor. The success of this technique is dependent on the density (specific gravity) of the liquids used. As a rule of thumb, the less alcohol and the more sugar an ingredient contains, the heavier it is. The heaviest ingredients should be poured first and the lightest last.

GEORGETOWN PUNCH

★★★★☆

Glass: Collins
Garnish: Pineapple wedge
Method: SHAKE all ingredients with ice and fine strain into ice-filled glass.

1	shot	Bacardi Superior rum
¾	shot	Gosling's Black Seal rum
1½	shots	Malibu coconut rum liqueur
1	shot	Ocean Spray cranberry juice
1	shot	Fresh pressed pineapple juice
¾	shot	Freshly squeezed lime juice

We say: A Tiki-style, fruity rum punch.
Origin: Adapted from a drink discovered in 2005 at Degrees, Washington DC, USA.

GEORGIA MINT JULEP

★★★★½

Glass: Collins
Garnish: Mint sprig
Method: Lightly MUDDLE (only to bruise) mint in base of shaker. Add other ingredients, SHAKE with ice and strain into chilled glass half filled with crushed ice. CHURN (stir) the drink using a bar spoon. Top up the glass with more crushed ice and churn again. Continue adding crushed ice and churning until the drink meets the rim of the glass. Serve with two long straws.

12	fresh	Mint leaves
2½	shots	Maker's Mark bourbon
1	shot	Peachtree peach schnapps
⅛	shot	Monin Pure Cane 2:1 sugar syrup
3	dashes	Angostura aromatic bitters

We say: Bourbon, peach and mint are flavours that combine harmoniously.
Origin: This classic was originally made with peach brandy in place of peach liqueur. It is also sometimes made with apricot brandy.

THE GETAWAY (AKA CYNAR DAIQUIRI) NEW

★★★★☆

Glass: Coupette
Garnish: Lime wedge on rim
Method: SHAKE all ingredients with ice and fine strain into chilled glass.

1½	shots	Rum Aged
½	shot	Cynar
¼	shot	Freshly squeezed lemon juice
¼	shot	Freshly squeezed lime juice
¼	shot	Monin Pure Cane 2:1 sugar syrup

We say: The bitter vegetal taste of Cynar turns this Daiquiri into a digestif.
Origin: Adapted from a drink created in 2012 by Wayne Curtis at The Passenger, Washington D.C., USA.

GIBSON DRY MARTINI

★★★★½

Glass: Martini
Garnish: Two cocktail onions on stick
Method: STIR all ingredients with ice and strain into chilled glass.

2½	shots	Tanqueray London dry gin
½	shot	Martini Extra Dry vermouth

We say: A classic Dry Martini with cocktail onions in place of an olive or a twist.
Origin: Today a Gibson is a Dry Martini served with two onions. Charles Dana Gibson produced hugely popular pen-and-ink drawings between the 1890s and 1930s. His illustrations of girls were as iconic as modern-day supermodels, and it is said this drink was named after the well-endowed Gibson Girls – hence the two onions. Gibson was a member of New York's The Players Club and a bartender there by the name of Charley Connolly is credited for at least adding the garnish, if not actually creating the drink.

However, a cocktail book published in 1917 includes a Martini-like drink named Gibson but without the onions, and a separate Onion cocktail which we might today call a Gibson.

GIMLET #1

★★★★☆

Glass: Martini
Garnish: Lime wedge
Method: STIR all ingredients with ice and strain into chilled glass.

2½	shots	Tanqueray London dry gin
¾	shot	Rose's lime cordial

Variant: Other spirits, particularly vodka, may be substituted for gin.
We say: A simple blend of gin and sweet lime.
Origin: In 1747, James Lind, a Scottish surgeon, discovered that consumption of citrus fruits helped prevent scurvy, one of the most common illnesses on board ship. (We now understand that scurvy is caused by a Vitamin C deficiency and that it is the vitamins in citrus fruit which help ward off the condition.) In 1867, the Merchant Shipping Act made it mandatory for all British ships to carry rations of lime juice for the crew.

Lauchlin Rose, the owner of a shipyard in Leith, Scotland, had been working to solve the problem of how to keep citrus juice fresh for months on board ship. In 1867 he patented a process for preserving fruit juice without alcohol. To give his product wider appeal he sweetened the mixture, packaged it in an attractive bottle and named it 'Rose's Lime Cordial'.

Once the benefits of drinking lime juice became more broadly known, British sailors consumed so much of the stuff, often mixed with their daily ration of rum and water ('grog'), that they became affectionately known as 'Limeys'. Naval officers mixed Rose's lime cordial with gin to make Gimlets.

A 'gimlet' was originally the name of a small tool used to tap the barrels of spirits which were carried on British Navy ships: this could be the origin of the drink's name. Another story cites a naval doctor, Rear-Admiral Sir Thomas Desmond Gimlette (1857-1943), who is said to have mixed gin with lime 'to help the medicine go down'. Although this is a credible story it is not substantiated in his obituary in The Times, 6 October 1943.

BARTENDER'S TIP SWIZZLE

To 'swizzle' a drink is simply to stir it using a particular tool and action.

To swizzle simply immerse the blades of your swizzle stick into the drink, hold the shaft between the palms of both hands and rotate the stick rapidly by sliding your hands back and forth against it. If you do not have a bona fide swizzle stick, use a barspoon in the same manner.

GIMLET #2 (SCHUMANN'S RECIPE)

★★★★⯪☆

Glass: Martini
Garnish: Maraschino cherry
Method: SHAKE all ingredients with ice and fine strain into chilled glass.

2½	shots	Tanqueray London dry gin
¼	shot	Freshly squeezed lime juice
1¼	shots	Rose's lime cordial

We say: Generously laced with gin and wonderfully tart.
Origin: A shaken twist on an already established drink by the famous bartender and cocktail author Charles Schumann of Munich, Germany.

GIN BASIL SMASH/GIN PESTO NEW

★★★★⯪☆

Glass: Old-fashioned
Garnish: 3 Basil sprigs
Method: SHAKE all ingredients with ice and fine strain into ice-filled glass.

2	shots	Tanqueray London dry gin
2	shots	Freshly squeezed lemon juice
1	shot	Monin Pure Cane 2:1 sugar syrup
12	fresh	Torn basil leaves

We say: Jörg says: better too much, than not enough, basil in this drink. He also specifies that the basil is muddled rather than just broken by the action of shaking as this produces a greener drink. Lazily, I prefer them just shaken as this seems to produce a fresher-tasting drink. Whichever method you employ, you'll find the flavours of basil combine wonderfully in this gin sour.
Origin: Adapted from a drink created in July 2008 by Jörg Meyer at Bar Le Lion, Hamburg, Germany. Jörg originally blogged that his new creation was called a Gin Pesto but it quickly became better known as the Gin Basil Smash.

GIN & FRENCH

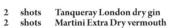

★★★★⯪☆

Glass: Old-fashioned
Garnish: Lemon slice
Method: STIR all ingredients with ice and strain into ice-filled glass.

| 2 | shots | Tanqueray London dry gin |
| 2 | shots | Martini Extra Dry vermouth |

We say: Bone dry but botanically rich.
Origin: Traditionally Italian vermouth was sweet while French vermouth was dry. Hence this drink is simply gin and dry vermouth.

GIN & IT

★★★⯪☆

Glass: Old-fashioned
Garnish: Orange slice
Method: STIR all ingredients with ice and strain into ice-filled glass.

2	shots	Tanqueray London dry gin
2	shots	Martini Rosso sweet vermouth
1	dash	Angostura aromatic bitters

We say: Simple but tasty combination of botanicals, wine and spirit.
Origin: The name is short for "Gin and Italian", a reference to the sweet vermouth, which was traditionally Italian while French vermouth was dry. In his 'Craft of the Cocktail', Dale DeGroff states that this drink was originally known as a 'Sweet Martini' and as such was a popular drink during the 1880s and 1890s at the Hoffman House and other New York bars. Later it became known as "Gin & Italian", until during/ post Prohibition it was shortened to "Gin & It".

GIN & JUICE

★★★☆☆

Glass: Collins
Garnish: Orange slice
Method: SHAKE all ingredients with ice and strain into ice-filled glass.

2	shots	Tanqueray London dry gin
2½	shots	Freshly squeezed orange juice
1½	shots	Freshly squeezed pink grapefruit juice

We say: Gin and fruit juice. OK, but nothing to sing about.
Origin: Possibly the inspiration behind the Top 10 single 'Gin and Juice' by rapper Snoop Doggy Dogg, from his debut album 'Doggystyle'.

GIN & SIN

★★★★☆

Glass: Martini
Garnish: Orange zest twist
Method: SHAKE all ingredients with ice and fine strain into chilled glass.

2	shots	Tanqueray London dry gin
1	shot	Freshly squeezed orange juice
½	shot	Freshly squeezed lemon juice
¼	shot	Pomegranate (grenadine) syrup
½	shot	Chilled mineral water

We say: This is one of those drinks that benefits from a little dilution to prevent the citrus and gin becoming too aggressive.

BARTENDER'S TIPS ROLLING

This is a gentle way of mixing a drink using a shaker and is most commonly used when making a Bloody Mary.

To do this charge your shaker with ingredients and ice as normal but rather than shaking, simply gently roll the shaker over and an over by holding the top and bottom of the shaker in each hand and then rotating your hand one over the other so tuning the shaker in a circular motion. Rolling should not be confused with the 'Cuban Roll' which is a term for mixing a drink using the throwing method.

GIN & TONIC

★★★★★½

Glass: Collins
Garnish: Lime wedge
Method: POUR ingredients into ice-filled glass, stir and serve without straws.

| 2 | shots | Tanqueray London dry gin |
| Top up with | | Tonic water |

We say: This might not be considered a cocktail by most, but it is actually classified as a Highball. Whatever, it's one of the simplest and best drinks ever devised, hence its lasting popularity.
Origin: The precise origin of the G&T is lost in the mists of time. Gin (or at least a grain based juniper spirit) was drunk for medicinal reasons from the 1600s onwards. Quinine, the pungent bark extract which gives tonic its distinctive bitterness, had been used against malaria for even longer. The first known quinine-based tonics were marketed during the 1850s.

The popularity of tonic in the British colonies, especially India, is clear. Schweppes launched their first carbonated quinine tonic in 1870, branding it Indian Tonic Water. The ladies and gentlemen of the Raj also drank phenomenal quantities of gin. It is therefore accepted that gin and tonic emerged in India during the second half of the nineteenth century and was drunk partly to ward off malaria.

GIN ATOMIC

★★★½☆

Glass: Collins
Garnish: Lemon zest twist
Method: Lightly MUDDLE (just to bruise) basil in base of shaker. Add other ingredients apart from tonic, SHAKE with ice and strain into ice-filled glass. TOP with tonic water and serve with straws.

3	fresh	Torn basil leaves
2	shots	Tanqueray London dry gin
1	shot	St~Germain elderflower liqueur
½	shot	Freshly squeezed lemon juice
2	dashes	Fee Brothers lemon bitters
Top up with		Tonic water

We say: A nuclear gin and tonic - or at least, one that simply radiates flavour.
Origin: Created in 2007 by Brendan Mainini at The Ambassador Bar, San Francisco, USA.

GIN BERRY

★★★½☆

Glass: Martini
Garnish: Lime zest twist
Method: SHAKE all ingredients with ice and fine strain into chilled glass.

1½	shots	Tanqueray London dry gin
½	shot	Chambord black raspberry liqueur
½	shot	Freshly squeezed lime juice
1½	shots	Ocean Spray cranberry juice

We say: Berry flavours combine harmoniously with gin - what an appropriate name.
Origin: Adapted from a drink created in 2004 by Chris Lacey, UK.

GIN COCKTAIL

★★★★☆

Glass: Martini
Garnish: Lemon zest twist
Method: STIR all ingredients with ice and fine strain into chilled glass.

2½	shots	Tanqueray London dry gin
⅛	shot	Triple Sec
⅛	shot	Monin Pure Cane 2:1 sugar syrup
2	dashes	Angostura aromatic bitters

We say: A pink gin made more approachable by a splash of triple sec and sugar syrup.
Origin: A classic that was already well-established when Jerry Thomas recorded his version of the recipe in 1862.

GIN DAISY

★★★★☆

Glass: Goblet
Garnish: Maraschino cherry
Method: SHAKE all ingredients with ice and strain into glass filled with crushed ice. CHURN (stir) drink with ice and serve with straws.

2	shots	Tanqueray London dry gin
¼	shot	Chartreuse Yellow liqueur
¼	shot	Freshly squeezed lemon juice
¼	shot	Pomegranate (grenadine) syrup

We say: If correctly made this serious, gin dominated cocktail should be blush, not pink.
Origin: A classic Daisy variation.

GIN DAISY #2 UPDATED (JERRY THOMAS STYLE)

★★★★☆

Glass: Martini
Garnish: Seasonal berries
Method: SHAKE first four ingredients with ice and fine strain into chilled glass. TOP with a splash of soda from a siphon.

1½	shots	Bols Genever
½	shot	Grand Marnier liqueur
¾	shot	Freshly squeezed lemon juice
¼	shot	Monin Pure Cane 2:1 sugar syrup
1	Splash	Soda from siphon

Variant: Use almond (orgeat) syrup in place of sugar.
We say: The rich style of genever combines wonderfully with orange liqueur in this balanced classic.
Origin: The origins of the Daisy are lost in time but the first written reference to it is in an 1866 novel called 'Gay Life in New York, or Fast Men and Grass Widows' by Henry Llewellyn Williams. This recipe is adapted from Jerry Thomas' 1876 'How to Mix Drinks'

GIN DAISY #3 (MODERN LONG STYLE)

★★★★☆

Glass: Collins
Garnish: Seasonal berries
Method: SHAKE first 3 ingredients with ice and strain into ice-filled glass. TOP with soda and serve with straws.

2	shots	Tanqueray London dry gin
1	shot	Freshly squeezed lemon juice
½	shot	Pomegranate (grenadine) syrup
Top up with		Soda (club soda)

We say: Fruit and botanicals served long and refreshing.
Origin: Daisies can be served in a goblet filled with crushed ice, straight-up or as in this case in a Collins glass.

GIN FIX

★★★★☆
Glass: Goblet
Garnish: Lemon slice
Method: SHAKE all ingredients with ice and strain into glass with crushed ice. CHURN (stir) drink with ice and serve with straws.

2	shots	Tanqueray London dry gin
1	shot	Freshly squeezed lemon juice
½	shot	Monin Pure Cane 2:1 sugar syrup

We say: A Gin Sour served over crushed ice in a goblet.
Origin: The fix is an old classic that's very similar to the Daisy.

GIN FIXED

★★★★☆
Glass: Martini
Garnish: Lemon slice
Method: SHAKE all ingredients with ice and strain into glass with crushed ice. CHURN (stir) drink with ice and serve with straws.

2	shots	Tanqueray London dry gin
¼	shot	Triple Sec
1	shot	Fresh pressed pineapple juice
½	shot	Freshly squeezed lemon juice
¼	shot	Monin Pure Cane 2:1 sugar syrup

We say: Sweet and sour with a spirity pineapple twang.

GIN FIZZ UPDATED

★★★★☆
Glass: Collins (small 8oz)
Garnish: Lemon slice & mint sprig
Method: SHAKE first three ingredients with ice and strain into chilled glass (without ice). TOP with soda.

2	shots	Tanqueray London dry gin
1	shot	Freshly squeezed lemon juice
½	shot	Monin Pure Cane 2:1 sugar syrup

Top up with Soda from siphon

Variations: With the addition of egg white this drink becomes a Silver Fizz; with egg yolk it becomes a Golden Fizz. A Royal Fizz includes one whole egg; a Diamond Fizz uses champagne instead of carbonated water; a Green Fizz has a dash of green crème de menthe; and a Purple Fizz uses equal parts of sloe gin and grapefruit juice in place of gin and lemon juice.

STAR RATINGS EXPLAINED

★★★★★ Excellent

★★★★⯪ Recommended	★★★★☆ Praiseworthy
★★★⯪☆ Commended	★★★☆☆ Mediocre
★★⯪☆☆ Disappointing	★★☆☆☆ Pretty awful
★⯪☆☆☆ Shameful	★☆☆☆☆ Disgusting

GIN GARDEN

★★★★☆
Glass: Martini
Garnish: Cucumber slices
Method: MUDDLE cucumber in base of shaker. Add other ingredients, SHAKE with ice and fine strain into chilled glass.

1	inch	Cucumber (chopped & peeled)
2	shots	Tanqueray London dry gin
1	shot	St~Germain elderflower liqueur
1	shot	Pressed apple juice

We say: A veritable English shrubbery with flowers, fruit and vegetables flourishing in harmony.
Origin: Adapted from a drink that Dan Warner at Zander and Tobias Blazquez Garcia at Steam collaborated on in London, England, in 2001.

GIN GENIE

★★★★☆
Glass: Collins
Garnish: Mint sprig
Method: Lightly MUDDLE mint in base of shaker (just to bruise). Add other ingredients, SHAKE with ice and strain into glass filled with crushed ice.

8	fresh	Mint leaves
1½	shots	Tanqueray London dry gin
1	shot	Sloe Gin liqueur
1	shot	Freshly squeezed lemon juice
½	shot	Monin Pure Cane 2:1 sugar syrup

We say: A fruit-led long drink for gin-loving Bowie fans.
Origin: Adapted from a drink created in 2002 by Wayne Collins, UK.

GIN GIN

★★★⯪☆
Glass: Old-fashioned
Garnish: Lemon zest twist
Method: STIR all ingredients with ice and strain into ice-filled glass.

| 2 | shots | Tanqueray London dry gin |
| 1 | shot | Stone's green ginger wine |

We say: Gin and ginger - as simple as that. Surprisingly good.

GIN GIN MULE

★★★★☆
Glass: Collins
Garnish: Lime wedge
Method: MUDDLE ginger in base of shaker. Add next 4 ingredients, SHAKE with ice and fine strain into ice-filled glass. TOP with ginger beer.

2	slices	Fresh root ginger (thumbnail sized)
2	unit	Tanqueray London dry gin
½	shot	Freshly squeezed lime juice
¼	shot	Monin Pure Cane 2:1 sugar syrup
3	dashes	Angostura aromatic bitters

Top up with Ginger beer

We say: Fresh ginger and the herbal notes from gin make this much more than another take on the Moscow Mule.
Origin: Adapted from a drink created in 2004 by Audrey Saunders, New York City, USA.

GIN PUNCH #1

★★★★⯪

Glass: Collins
Garnish: Lemon slice
Method: SHAKE all ingredients with ice and strain into ice-filled glass.

2	shots	Tanqueray London dry gin
¾	shot	Freshly squeezed lemon juice
¾	shot	Monin Pure Cane 2:1 sugar syrup
2	shots	Chilled mineral water
1	dash	Angostura aromatic bitters

We say: Light and refreshing - akin to alcoholic real lemonade.
Origin: This is a version of the drink for which Limmer's Hotel in London was most famed: a Captain Gronow recalled it in his 1860s memoirs as one of the top, if filthy and seedy, sporting hangouts of 1814, thanks in part to its 'famous gin-punch'. A bartender named John Collins worked there later in the 19th century, and was famous enough to inspire a limerick, so many believe he created the Collins, which is similar to gin punch, although the drink is not named in the rhyme which goes as follows:

My name is John Collins,
head waiter at Limmer's,
Corner of Conduit Street,
Hanover Square,
My chief occupation is filling brimmers
For all the young gentlemen frequenters there.

GIN PUNCH #2

★★★★☆

Glass: Collins
Garnish: Seasonal berries
Method: SHAKE all ingredients with ice and strain into ice-filled glass. Serve with straws.

3	shots	Bols Genever
½	shot	Freshly squeezed lemon juice
¼	shot	Raspberries
¼	shot	Monin Pure Cane 2:1 sugar syrup
¼	shot	Freshly squeezed orange juice
⅛	shot	Fresh pressed pineapple juice
⅛	shot	Luxardo Maraschino liqueur
2	shots	Chilled mineral water

We say: Easy on the palate yet incredibly complex. Linseed oil notes of genever shine through.
Origin: Adapted from Hebert Asbury's 1928 reprint of Jerry Thomas' 1862 How to Mix Drink, or *The Bon Vivant's Companion*.

STAR RATINGS EXPLAINED

★★★★★ Excellent

★★★★⯪ Recommended	★★★★☆ Praiseworthy
★★★⯪☆ Commended	★★★☆☆ Mediocre
★★⯪☆☆ Disappointing	★★☆☆☆ Pretty awful
★⯪☆☆☆ Shameful	★☆☆☆☆ Disgusting

GIN RICKEY

★★★★☆

Glass: Collins (small 8oz)
Garnish: Length of lime peel
Method: SHAKE first three ingredients with ice and strain into ice-filled glass. TOP with soda.

2	shots	Brandy, whisk(e)y, gin, rum etc.
½	shot	Freshly squeezed lime juice
¼	shot	Monin Pure Cane 2:1 sugar syrup
Top up with		Soda (club soda)

Variant: Vodka Rickey, Apricot Rickey
We say: Clean, sharp and refreshing.
Origin: Believed to have been created by bartender George A. Williamson in 1880 at Shoomaker's Bar in Washington DC and named after Colonel Joe Rickey, who it is said Williamson witnessed squeeze lime into his whisky before topping his drink with soda. Coincidentally or not, Colonel Rickey went on to be-come a major importer of limes into the US. The Gin Rickey cocktail first appeared in print in Harry Johnson's 1882 'Bartenders Manual' where Harry calls for a "medium size fizz glass" to be used with "1 or 2 pieces of ice; Squeeze the juice of 1 good-sized lime or 2 small ones; 1 wine glass of Tom or Holland gin if required; Fill up glass with club soda, carbonic or selters if required, and serve with a spoon."

Many confuse the Rickey and the Collins. For the record a Rickey is made with lime juice and a Collins with lemon juice. A Rickey is also usually served in a shorter glass than a Collins but that differ-ence is secondary.

GIN SALAD DRY MARTINI UPDATED

★★★★★

Glass: Martini
Garnish: 3 chilled Olives and 2 Cocktail onions
Method: STIR all ingredients with ice and strain into chilled glass.

2½	shots	The Bombay Original dry gin
½	shot	Martini Extra dry vermouth
1 dash Orange bitters (optional)		

We say: A Gin Salad is made like a regular Dry Martini but with three olives and two cocktail onions as garnish. They should be pushed onto the stick in the following order: olive-onion-olive-onion-olive.

GIN SLING

★★★★☆

Glass: Sling
Garnish: Lemon slice
Method: SHAKE first 3 ingredients with ice and fine strain into ice-filled glass. TOP with soda water.

2	shots	Tanqueray London dry gin
½	shot	Freshly squeezed lemon juice
¼	shot	Monin Pure Cane 2:1 sugar syrup
Top up with		Soda (club soda)

We say: Sugar balances the citrus juice, the spirit fortifies and the carbonate lengthens.
Origin: 'Sling' comes from the German word 'schlingen', meaning 'to swallow' and is a style of drink which was popular from the late 1700s.

GIN SOUR

★★★★⯪

Glass: Old-fashioned
Garnish: Lemon slice & cherry on stick (sail)
Method: SHAKE all ingredients with ice and strain into ice-filled glass.

2	shots	Tanqueray London dry gin
1	shot	Freshly squeezed lemon juice
½	shot	Monin Pure Cane 2:1 sugar syrup
½	fresh	Egg white
3	dashes	Angostura aromatic bitters

We say: This 4:2:8 formula is a tad sourer than the classic sour proportions of 3:4:8: three quarter part of the sour ingredient (lemon juice), one part of the sweet ingredient (sugar syrup) and two parts of the strong ingredient (gin).

GIN TWIST NEW

★★★★⯪

Glass: Toddy
Garnish: Lemon zest twist
Method: POUR ingredients into pre-warmed glass and STIR.

1½	shots	Tanqueray London dry gin
¾	shot	Freshly squeezed lemon juice
½	shot	Monin Pure Cane 2:1 sugar syrup
Top up with		Boiling water

We say: Gin botanicals flavour this delicate citrusy, warming drink.
Origin: This classic English cocktail dates back to at least the early 1800s and was so popular at the time that it is frequently referred to in novels and periodicals from the time. In Sir Walter Scott's 1823 novel St Ronan's Well, the character Captain MacTurk says, "Sir Binco, I will beg the favour of your company to the smoking-room, where we may have a cigar and a glass of gin-twist; and we will consider how the honour of the company must be supported and upholden upon the present conjuncture."

William Makepeace Thackeray mentions the Gin Twist in his 1869 'Miscellanies: The Book of Snobs. Sketches and Travels in London'. "About eleven men in white neckcloths drop in from dinner-parties, and show their lacquered boots and shirt-studs with a little complacency - and at midnight, after the theatres, the young rakes and viveurs come swaggering in, and call loudly for Gin-Twist."

GIN-GER & TONIC

★★★★☆

Glass: Collins
Garnish: Lime wedge
Method: MUDDLE ginger in base of shaker, add gin and sugar, SHAKE with ice and strain into icefilled glass. TOP with tonic water.

2	slices	Fresh root ginger (thumbnail sized)
2	shots	Tanqueray London dry gin
¼	shot	Monin Pure Cane 2:1 sugar syrup
Top up with		Tonic water

We say: A dry, refreshing long drink for those that like their G&Ts gingered.

GIN-GER TOM

★★★★☆

Glass: Collins
Garnish: Orange slice & cherry on stick (sail)
Method: MUDDLE ginger in base of shaker. Add other ingredients, SHAKE with ice and fine strain into ice filled glass.

2	slices	Fresh root ginger (thumbnail sized)
2	shots	Tanqueray London dry gin
1	shot	Freshly squeezed lime juice
½	shot	Monin Pure Cane 2:1 sugar syrup
Top up with		Soda (club soda)

We say: A Tom Collins with lime and ginger - very refreshing.
Origin: Adapted from a drink created in 2003 by Jamie Terrell at Lab, London, England.

GINA

★★★☆☆

Glass: Sling
Garnish: Seasonal berries
Method: SHAKE first three ingredients with ice and strain into ice-filled glass. TOP with soda.

2	shots	Tanqueray London dry gin
½	shot	Freshly squeezed lemon juice
Top up with		Soda (club soda)
½	shot	Crème de cassis liqueur

AKA: Cassis Collins
We say: The lemon and blackcurrant mask the character of the gin.

GINGER & LEMONGRASS MARTINI

★★★★☆

Glass: Martini
Garnish: Apple slice
Method: MUDDLE ginger and lemongrass in base of shaker. Add other ingredients and STIR until honey dissolves. SHAKE with ice and fine strain into chilled glass.

1	slice	Fresh root ginger (thumbnail sized)
½	fresh	Lemongrass stem (chopped)
2	spoons	Runny honey
2	shots	Tanqueray London dry gin
¼	shot	Martini Extra Dry vermouth
¼	shot	Pressed apple juice
¾	shot	Chilled mineral water

We say: Consider infusing the lemongrass in gin instead of muddling.
Origin: Created in 2005 by Simon Difford.

GINGER BEER DAIQUIRI (MOCKTAIL)

★★★☆☆

Glass: Old-fashioned
Garnish: Lime wedge
Method: SHAKE all ingredients with ice and strain into ice-filled glass.

1	shot	Freshly squeezed lime juice
½	shot	Monin Pure Cane 2:1 sugar syrup
2	shots	Ginger beer
2	dashes	Angostura aromatic bitters

We say: *Note: Angostura aromatic bitters contain alcohol but in the finished drink the alcohol level is negligible. Audrey, we love you but where's the rum?
Origin: Created in 2006 by Audrey Saunders, New York, USA.

GINGER COSMO

★★★★☆

Glass: Martini
Garnish: Fresh ginger slice
Method: SHAKE all ingredients with ice and fine strain into glass.

2	shots	Ketel One Citroen vodka
¾	shot	Domaine de Canton ginger liqueur
1¼	shots	Ocean Spray cranberry juice
¼	shot	Freshly squeezed lime juice
⅛	shot	Monin Pure Cane 2:1 sugar syrup

We say: Just what it says on the tin - your everyday Cosmo given extra vitality courtesy of a hint of ginger spice.
Origin: Emerged during 2002 in New York City.

GINGER COSMOS

★★★☆☆

Glass: Collins
Garnish: Basil leaf
Method: MUDDLE ginger and basil in base of shaker. Add other ingredients, SHAKE with ice and fine strain into glass filled with crushed ice. Stir and serve with straws.

2	slices	Fresh root ginger (thumbnail sized)
5	fresh	Torn basil leaves
2	shots	Tanqueray London dry gin
1½	shots	Fresh pressed pineapple juice
1½	shots	Pressed apple juice
¼	shot	Freshly squeezed lime juice
¼	shot	Monin Pure Cane 2:1 sugar syrup

We say: Warming ginger spice in a very cooling, fruity drink.
Origin: Created in 2003 by Massilimiliano Greco at Zander, London, England. 'Cosmos' is a reference to the botanical name for pineapple, Ananas comosus.

GINGER FROST

★★★☆☆

Glass: Coupette
Garnish: Fresh ginger slice
Method: DRY SHAKE (without ice) all ingredients. SHAKE again with ice and strain into chilled glass.

1½	shots	Ketel One vodka
½	shot	Freshly squeezed lemon juice
¼	shot	Monin Pure Cane 2:1 sugar syrup
¾	shot	Freshly squeezed orange juice
½	fresh	Egg white
¾	shot	Domaine de Canton ginger liqueur

We say: Freshly squeezed lemon and orange juices, spiced with ginger and laced with vodka.

GINGER MARGARITA

★★★★☆

Glass: Coupette
Garnish: Lime wedge
Method: SHAKE all ingredients with ice and fine strain into chilled glass.

2	shots	Tequila 100% Agave
1	shot	Domaine de Canton ginger liqueur
1	shot	Freshly squeezed lime juice

We say: A Margarita spiced with ginger.

GINGER MARTINI

★★★★☆

Glass: Martini
Garnish: Brandy Snap biscuit
Method: MUDDLE ginger in base of shaker. Add other ingredients, SHAKE with ice and fine strain into chilled glass.

2	slices	Fresh root ginger (thumbnail sized)
2	shots	Ketel One vodka
¾	shot	Stone's green ginger wine
¾	shot	Pressed apple juice
½	shot	Freshly squeezed lime juice
¼	shot	Monin Pure Cane 2:1 sugar syrup

We say: This Martini may be served chilled but its flavour is distinctly warming.
Origin: Discovered in 2003 at Hurricane Bar and Grill, Edinburgh, Scotland.

GINGER MOJITO

★★★★☆

Glass: Collins
Garnish: Mint sprig
Method: MUDDLE ginger in base of shaker. Add mint and lightly MUDDLE (just to bruise). Add next three ingredients, SHAKE with ice and fine strain into glass filled with crushed ice. TOP with ginger ale.

3	slice	Fresh root ginger (thumbnail sized)
12	fresh	Mint leaves
2	shots	Bacardi Superior rum
½	shot	Freshly squeezed lime juice
½	shot	Monin Pure Cane 2:1 sugar syrup
Top up with		Ginger ale

We say: A spiced variation on the classic Mojito.

GINGER NUT

★★★☆☆

Glass: Collins
Garnish: Lemon wedge
Method: POUR ingredients into ice-filled glass and stir.

1½	shots	Ketel One Citroen vodka
1½	shots	Hazelnut liqueur
Top up with		Ginger beer

We say: A long, refreshing meld of strong flavours.

GINGER PUNCH

★★★☆☆

Glass: Collins
Garnish: Lime wedge
Method: MUDDLE ginger in base of shaker. Add honey and rum and STIR until honey is dissolved. Add lime juice and sugar, SHAKE with ice and fine strain into ice-filled glass. TOP with ginger ale.

2	slices	Fresh root ginger (thumbnail sized)
2	spoons	Runny honey
2½	shots	Bacardi Oro golden rum
¾	shot	Freshly squeezed lime juice
¼	shot	Monin Pure Cane 2:1 sugar syrup
Top up with		Ginger ale

We say: A ginger spiced rum punch.

GINGER SNAP

★★★★☆

Glass: Collins
Garnish: Lemon zest twist
Method: SHAKE first five ingredients with ice and strain into an ice-filled glass. TOP with soda and serve with straws.

1½	shots	**Tanqueray London dry gin**
½	shot	**Domaine de Canton ginger liqueur**
½	shot	**Triple Sec**
½	shot	**Freshly squeezed lemon juice**
1	dash	**Angostura aromatic bitters**
Top up with		**Soda (club soda)**

We say: This balanced Gin Collins is sweetened by ginger and orange liqueurs.
Origin: Created in 2007 by Gary Regan, New York, USA.

GINGERBREAD MARTINI

★★★★☆

Glass: Martini
Garnish: Fresh ginger slice
Method: SHAKE all ingredients with ice and fine strain into into chilled glass.

1½	shots	**Maker's Mark bourbon**
¾	shot	**Butterscotch schnapps**
¾	shot	**Stone's green ginger wine**
2	shots	**Pressed apple juice**

We say: Sticky, warming and spicy.
Origin: Created by Simon Difford in 2004.

GINGERTINI

★★★★☆

Glass: Martini
Garnish: Orange zest twist
Method: SHAKE all ingredients with ice and fine strain into chilled glass.

2	shots	**Tanqueray London dry gin**
½	shot	**Domaine de Canton ginger liqueur**
¼	shot	**Martini Extra Dry vermouth**
¼	shot	**Monin Pure Cane 2:1 sugar syrup**
½	shot	**Chilled mineral water**

We say: A delicate Martini with a warming hint of ginger.
Origin: Created by Simon Difford in 2002.

GIUSEPPE'S HABIT

★★★★☆

Glass: Martini
Garnish: Star anise
Method: Spray the oils from the two lemon zest twists into the cocktail shaker, wipe them around the rim of the glass and drop them into the shaker, SHAKER with ice and fine strain into chilled glass.

2	fresh	**Lemon zest twist**
1½	shots	**Galliano L'Autentico liqueur**
¾	shot	**Hazelnut liqueur**
¾	shot	**Triple Sec**
1¼	shots	**Pressed apple juice**

We say: An intriguing drink that combines hazelnut, orange, apple, aniseed and peppermint.
Origin: Created in 2002 by Leon Stokes at Zinc Bar & Grill, Birmingham, England,

GIVE ME A DIME

★★★★☆

Glass: Martini
Garnish: Crumbled Cadbury's Flake bar
Method: SHAKE all ingredients with ice and fine strain into chilled glass.

1½	shots	**White Crème de Cacao**
1½	shots	**Butterscotch schnapps**
1½	shots	**Double (heavy) cream**

We say: Creamy, sweet and tasty.

GLAD EYE COCKTAIL

★★★☆☆

Glass: Martini
Garnish: Star anise
Method: SHAKE all ingredients with ice and fine strain into chilled glass.

1½	shots	**Absinthe**
1	shot	**Giffard Menthe Pastille liqueur**
1	shot	**Chilled mineral water**

We say: This minty aniseed cocktail takes more than its colour from the green fairy.
Origin: Adapted from Harry Craddock's 1930 '*The Savoy Cocktail Book*'.

GLASS TOWER

★★★☆☆

Glass: Collins
Garnish: None
Method: SHAKE first 5 ingredients with ice and strain into ice-filled glass. TOP with lemonade and stir.

1	shot	**Ketel One vodka**
1	shot	**Bacardi Superior rum**
½	shot	**Triple Sec**
½	shot	**Peachtree peach schnapps**
Top up with		**Lemonade/Sprite/7-Up**

We say: A heady, slightly sweet combination of spirits and liqueurs.

GLENN'S BRIDE

★★★★½

Glass: Martini
Garnish: Orange zest twist
Method: SHAKE all ingredients with ice and fine strain into chilled glass.

2	shots	**Maker's Mark bourbon**
1	shot	**St~Germain elderflower liqueur**
2	dashes	**Angostura aromatic bitters**
¼	shot	**Rose water**

We say: This serious, bourbon based cocktail ranks alongside the Sazerac in its aromatic complexity.
Origin: Adapted from a drink created in 2005 by Julian Gibbs, England.

GLOOM CHASER COCKTAIL #1

★★★½☆

Glass: Martini
Garnish: Orange zest twist
Method: SHAKE all ingredients with ice and strain into chilled glass.

¾	shot	Grand Marnier liqueur
¾	shot	Triple Sec
1	shot	Freshly squeezed lemon juice
¼	shot	Pomegranate (grenadine) syrup
1	shot	Chilled mineral water

We say: A sunny coloured drink for happy souls. And sweet orange and pomegranate soured with lemon would make anyone happy.
Origin: Adapted from Harry Craddock's 1930 'The Savoy Cocktail Book'.

GLOOM CHASER COCKTAIL #2

★★★½☆

Glass: Martini
Garnish: Seasonal berries
Method: SHAKE all ingredients with ice and strain into chilled glass.

¾	shot	Grand Marnier liqueur
¾	shot	Triple Sec
1	shot	Freshly squeezed lemon juice
¼	shot	Pomegranate (grenadine) syrup
1	shot	Chilled mineral water

We say: A sunny coloured drink for happy souls. And sweet orange and pomegranate soured with lemon would make anyone happy.
Origin: Adapted from Harry Craddock's 1930 'The Savoy Cocktail Book'.

GLOOM LIFTER UPDATED

★★★★☆

Glass: Martini
Garnish: Lemon wedge
Method: DRY SHAKE all ingredients (without ice). SHAKE again with ice and fine strain into chilled glass.

1½	shots	Jameson Irish whiskey
½	shot	Courvoisier VSOP Exclusif
⅓	shot	Pomegranate (grenadine) syrup
1	shot	Freshly squeezed lemon juice
¼	shot	Monin Pure Cane 2:1 sugar syrup
½	fresh	Egg white

We say: An Irish whiskey and cognac sour served straight-up.

GLORIA

★★★½☆

Glass: Flute
Garnish: Lemon zest twist
Method: SHAKE first 3 ingredients with ice and fine strain into chilled glass. TOP with champagne.

1	shot	Tequila 100% Agave
½	shot	Freshly squeezed lemon juice
½	shot	Monin Pure Cane 2:1 sugar syrup
Top up with		Brut champagne

We say: A tequila sour topped with champagne or a tequila French 75.

GODFATHER

★★★½☆

Glass: Old-fashioned
Garnish: None
Method: STIR all ingredients with ice and strain into ice-filled glass.

2	shots	Dewar's White label Scotch
1	shot	Amaretto liqueur

Variant: Based on vodka, this drink becomes a Godmother and when made with cognac it's known as a Godchild.
We say: Scotch diluted and sweetened with almond - simple but good.

GODFREY

★★★★☆

Glass: Old-fashioned
Garnish: Blackberries
Method: MUDDLE blackberries in base if shaker. Add other ingredients, SHAKE with ice and fine strain into glass filled with crushed ice.

6	fresh	Blackberries
1½	shots	Cognac VSOP
½	shot	Grand Marnier liqueur
¼	shot	Crème de Mûre liqueur
¼	shot	Freshly squeezed lemon juice
¼	shot	Monin Pure Cane 2:1 sugar syrup

We say: Well balanced with a rich blackberry flavour.
Origin: Created by Salvatore Calabrese at the Library Bar, Lanesborough Hotel, London, England.

GOLD

★★★☆☆

Glass: Martini
Garnish: Orange zest twist
Method: SHAKE all ingredients with ice and fine strain into chilled glass.

1½	shots	Dewar's White label Scotch
1	shot	Triple Sec
1	shot	Bols Banana liqueur
¾	shot	Chilled mineral water

We say: Sweet, ripe banana, Scotch and a hint of orange.

GOLD MEDALION

★★★½☆

Glass: Martini
Garnish: Orange zest twist (flamed)
Method: SHAKE all ingredients with ice and fine strain into chilled glass.

1½	shots	Cognac VSOP
1	shot	Galliano L'Autentico liqueur
1½	shots	Freshly squeezed orange juice
¼	shot	Freshly squeezed lime juice
½	fresh	Egg white

We say: Gold by name and golden in colour. Frothy, orange fresh and cognac based.

GOLD MEMBER

★★★★☆ **Glass:** Martini
Garnish: Apple slice
Method: SHAKE all ingredients with ice and fine strain into chilled glass.

¾	shot	**Goldschläger cinnamon schnapps**
¾	shot	**Butterscotch schnapps**
¾	shot	**Berentzen Apple schnapps**
2¼	shots	**Pressed apple juice**

We say: Hints of cinnamon and apple - an interesting tipple, if a tad sweet.

THE GOLD RUSH NEW

★★★★☆ **Glass:** Coupette
Garnish: Maraschino cherry
Method: SHAKE all ingredients with ice and fine strain into chilled glass.

1½	shots	**Domaine de Canton ginger liqueur**
1	shot	**Maker's Mark bourbon**
¼	shot	**Freshly squeezed lime juice**
¼	shot	**Freshly squeezed lemon juice**

We say: The name refers to this slightly sweet, zesty ginger drinks golden hue. Bourbon provides the base while lemon and lime balance the flavoursome ginger liqueur

GOLD RUSH ON-THE-ROCKS NEW

★★★½☆ **Glass:** Old-fashioned
Garnish: Lemon wedge
Method: DRY SHAKE all ingredients (without ice). SHAKE with ice and strain into ice-filled glass.

2	shots	**Maker's Mark bourbon**
¾	shot	**Freshly squeezed lemon juice**
½	shot	**Maple syrup (B-grade)**
½	fresh	**Egg white**

We say: Rich bourbon notes highlighted by maple syrup (particularly charcoal) in an otherwise classic sour. A tad rich for those with a dry palate.

GOLD RUSH SLAMMER

★★★☆☆ **Glass:** Shot
Garnish: None
Method: SHAKE first 2 ingredients with ice and fine strain into chilled glass. TOP with champagne.

½	shot	**Tequila 100% Agave**
½	shot	**Goldschläger cinnamon schnapps**
Top up with		**Brut champagne**

We say: Flakes of gold dance with the champagne's bubbles.
Origin: Discovered in 2003 at Oxo Tower Bar, London, England.

GOLDEN IVY NEW

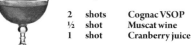

★★★★☆ **Glass:** Coupette/Martini
Garnish: Orange zest twist
Method: STIR all ingredients with ice and strain into chilled glass.

2	shots	**Cognac VSOP**
½	shot	**Muscat wine**
1	shot	**Cranberry juice**

We say: Cognac stirred with rich berry and dried berry flavours.
Origin: A Christmas cocktail created in October 2011 by Simon Difford at the Cabinet Room, London, England.

GOLDEN BIRD

★★★½☆ **Glass:** Martini
Garnish: Orange 'beak' on rim
Method: SHAKE all ingredients with ice and fine strain into chilled glass.

1	shot	**Bacardi Superior rum**
1	shot	**Grand Marnier liqueur**
½	shot	**Bols Banana liqueur**
1½	shots	**Freshly squeezed orange juice**
1	shot	**Fresh pressed pineapple juice**

We say: Fruity and sweet - an after dinner cocktail.

GOLDEN BRONX

★★★½☆ **Glass:** Martini
Garnish: Maraschino cherry
Method: SHAKE all ingredients with ice and fine strain into chilled glass.

2	shots	**Tanqueray London dry gin**
¼	shot	**Martini Extra Dry vermouth**
¼	shot	**Martini Rosso sweet vermouth**
1	shot	**Freshly squeezed orange juice**
⅛	shot	**Monin Pure Cane 2:1 sugar syrup**
1	fresh	**Egg yolk**

We say: A Bronx made 'golden' by the addition of egg yolk.
Origin: A vintage cocktail adapted from the classic Bronx Cocktail, created in 1906 by Johnny Solon, a bartender at New York's Waldorf-Astoria Hotel, and named after the newly opened Bronx Zoo.

STAR RATINGS EXPLAINED

★★★★★ Excellent

★★★★½	Recommeded	★★★★☆	Praiseworthy
★★★½☆	Commended	★★★☆☆	Mediocre
★★½☆☆	Disappointing	★★☆☆☆	Pretty awful
★½☆☆☆	Shameful	★☆☆☆☆	Disgusting

GOLDEN CADILLAC

★★★★⯪☆

Glass: Martini
Garnish: Dust with grated nutmeg
Method: SHAKE all ingredients with ice and fine strain into chilled glass.

1	shot	White Crème de Cacao
½	shot	Galliano L'Autentico liqueur
1½	shots	Freshly squeezed orange juice
½	shot	Double (heavy) cream
½	shot	Milk
2	dashes	Orange bitters

We say: A silky smooth but not very potent cocktail.
Origin: To quote the bar's own website (poorredsbbq.com), "Poor Red's is world famous for its Golden Cadillacs. Cadillacs are a blended drink of Galliano liqueur, half and half, white créme de cacao and ice, most delicious! We are the largest consumer of Galliano in the world. Also famous for our award winning barbecued ribs."

The above shaken recipe also includes orange juice and this gives the otherwise anaemic looking drink its namesake golden hue. The addition of orange bitters helps balance the drink and boost the orange flavour.

GOLDEN DAWN

★★★★☆

Glass: Martini
Garnish: Orange zest twist
Method: SHAKE first five ingredients with ice and fine strain into chilled glass. Carefully POUR grenadine into centre of drink so that it sinks to create a sunrise effect.

¾	shot	Tanqueray London dry gin
1	shot	Calvados/Applejack brandy
1	shot	De Kuyper Apricot Brandy liqueur
1	shot	Freshly squeezed orange juice
2	dashes	Angostura aromatic bitters
⅛	shot	Pomegranate (grenadine) syrup

We say: Although it spoils the sunrise effect, this drink is less tart if the syrup lying on the bottom is stirred into the drink (or, better, included when shaking).
Origin: Created in September 1930 by Tom Buttery at the Berkeley Hotel, London, England. There are now many versions of this classic drink (David Embury's 'The Fine Art of Mixing Drinks' lists three) but this is my favourite.

GOLDEN DRAGON

★★★⯪☆

Glass: Collins
Garnish: Apple wedge
Method: SHAKE all ingredients with ice and strain into ice-filled glass.

2	shots	Tequila 100% Agave
¾	shot	Pisang Ambon liqueur
2	shots	Pressed apple juice
1	shot	Freshly squeezed lime juice
½	shot	Passion fruit syrup

We say: Bright green, tangy and tropical.

GOLDEN DREAM

★★★★☆

Glass: Martini
Garnish: Sponge biscuit
Method: SHAKE all ingredients with ice and fine strain into chilled glass.

1	shot	Triple Sec
1	shot	Galliano L'Autentico liqueur
2	shots	Freshly squeezed orange juice
1	shot	Double (heavy) cream

We say: Tastes remarkably like syllabub.

GOLDEN FIZZ #1

★★★⯪☆

Glass: Collins (small 8oz)
Garnish: Lemon slice & mint sprig
Method: SHAKE first four ingredients with ice and fine strain into chilled glass. TOP with soda.

2	shots	Tanqueray London dry gin
1	shot	Freshly squeezed lemon juice
½	shot	Monin Pure Cane 2:1 sugar syrup
1	fresh	Egg yolk
Top up with		Soda from siphon

Variant: Gin Fizz
We say: You may have some raw egg inhibitions to conquer before you can enjoy this drink.
Origin: Mid-19th Century classic.

GOLDEN FIZZ #2

★★★★☆

Glass: Collins
Garnish: Orange slice & mint sprig
Method: STIR honey with gin in base of shaker until honey dissolves. Add next three ingredients, SHAKE with ice and strain into ice-filled glass. TOP with lemonade.

2	spoons	Runny honey
1½	shots	Tanqueray London dry gin
1	shot	Triple Sec
1	shot	Freshly squeezed grapefruit juice
¼	shot	Freshly squeezed lemon juice
Top up with		Lemonade/Sprite/7-Up

We say: More cloudy white than golden but a pleasant, refreshing long drink all the same.
Origin: Adapted from a drink created by Wayne Collins, UK.

GOLDEN GIRL

★★★★☆

Glass: Martini
Garnish: Grated orange zest
Method: SHAKE all ingredients with ice and fine strain into chilled glass.

1¼	shots	Bacardi 8yo aged rum
1	shot	Fresh pressed pineapple juice
1	shot	Warre's Otima tawny port
¼	shot	Monin Pure Cane 2:1 sugar syrup
1	fresh	Egg

We say: This appropriately named velvety drink is a refined dessert in a glass.
Origin: Created in Dale DeGroff, New York City, USA. I've slightly increased the proportions of rum and port from Dale's original recipe.

GOLDEN MAC

★★★⯪☆

Glass: Old-fashioned
Garnish: Orange zest twist
Method: MUDDLE ginger in base of shaker. Add honey and Scotch and STIR until honey dissolves. Add other ingredients, SHAKE with ice and fine strain into ice-filled glass.

2	slices	Fresh root ginger (thumbnail sized)
2	spoons	Runny honey
2	shots	Dewar's White label Scotch
¼	shot	Hazelnut liqueur
¼	shot	Butterscotch schnapps

We say: Looks, and even tastes golden.
Origin: Adapted from a drink discovered in 2003 at Golden Mac, Glasgow, Scotland.

GOLDEN NAIL

★★★★☆

Glass: Old-fashioned
Garnish: Orange zest twist
Method: STIR all ingredients with ice and strain into ice-filled glass.

1½	shots	Maker's Mark bourbon
¾	shot	Southern Comfort liqueur
2	dashes	Peychaud's aromatic bitters

We say: A warming taste of southern hospitality.

GOLDEN REIGN

★★★☆☆

Glass: Martini
Garnish: Orange zest twist
Method: SHAKE all ingredients with ice and fine strain into chilled glass.

1½	shots	Bacardi Oro golden rum
½	shot	Galliano L'Autentico liqueur
½	shot	Grand Marnier liqueur
1	shot	Double (heavy) cream
⅛	shot	Monin Pure Cane 2:1 sugar syrup

We say: A lightly creamy, after dinner drink.
Origin: Adapted from a drink created in 2002 by Peter Dorelli at The American Bar at The Savoy Hotel, London, England to celebrate the Queen's golden jubilee.

GOLDEN RETRIEVER

★★★★⯪

Glass: Martini
Garnish: Orange zest twist
Method: STIR all ingredients with ice and strain into chilled glass.

1	shot	Bacardi Superior rum
1	shot	Chartreuse Green liqueur
1	shot	Cuarenta y Tres (Licor 43) liqueur

We say: This powerful straw yellow cocktail offers a myriad of flavours. Benefits from the dilution of a long stir.
Origin: Created in 2002 by Dick Bradsell at Alfred's, London, England.

GOLDEN SCREW

★★★⯪☆

Glass: Flute
Garnish: Physalis (cape gooseberry)
Method: POUR all ingredients into chilled glass and lightly stir.

½	shot	Cognac VSOP
½	shot	De Kuyper Apricot Brandy liqueur
1	shot	Freshly squeezed orange juice
Top up with		Brut champagne

Variant: With gin in place of brandy.
We say: A favourite with the Midas and others whose budgets extend beyond a Buck's Fizz or a Mimosa.

GOLDEN SHOT

★★★☆☆

Glass: Shot
Garnish: None
Method: Refrigerate ingredients then LAYER in chilled glass by carefully pouring in the following order.

½	shot	Drambuie
½	shot	Baileys Irish cream liqueur
½	shot	Dewar's White label Scotch

We say: A whiskey based layered shot with plenty of character.

GOLDEN SLIPPER

★★★★⯪

Glass: Martini
Garnish: Apricot slice
Method: SHAKE all ingredients with ice and fine strain into chilled glass.

1½	shots	Chartreuse Yellow liqueur
1½	shots	De Kuyper Apricot Brandy liqueur
1	fresh	Egg yolk

We say: Rich in colour and equally rich in flavour. A dessert with a punch.

GOLDEN WAVE

★★★⯪☆

Glass: Sling
Garnish: Pineapple wedge
Method: BLEND all ingredients with a 12oz scoop of crushed ice and serve with straws.

1	shot	Bacardi Superior rum
½	shot	Triple Sec
½	shot	Taylor's Velvet Falernum liqueur
1	shot	Fresh pressed pineapple juice
¾	shot	Freshly squeezed lemon juice

We say: Rum laced fruit served long and cold with crushed ice.
Origin: A Tiki drink created in 1969 by Jose 'Joe' Yatco at China Trader, California, USA.

GOLF COCKTAIL

★★★★☆

Glass: Martini
Garnish: Orange zest twist
Method: STIR all ingredients with ice and strain into chilled glass.

2	shots	Tanqueray London dry gin
1	shot	Martini Extra Dry vermouth
1	dash	Angostura aromatic bitters

We say: A 'wet' Martini with bitters.

GOOD HOPE PLANTATION RUM PUNCH

★★★★☆

Glass: Old-fashioned
Garnish: Maraschino cherry
Method: SHAKE first four ingredients with ice and strain into glass filled with crushed ice. TOP with soda.

1	shot	Myer's dark Jamaican rum
1	shot	Triple Sec
1	shot	Grand Marnier liqueur
1	shot	Freshly squeezed lime juice
Top up with		Soda (club soda)

We say: A classic citrus laced, big flavoured, punch.
Origin: Originally made at the Good Hope Hotel, Falmouth, Jamaica. The Good Hope is an 18th Century country house set in a 2,000-acre plantation high in the lush landscape of Cockpit Country near Montego Bay.

GOODY-GOODY

★★★☆☆

Glass: Martini
Garnish: Orange zest twist
Method: SHAKE all ingredients with ice and fine strain into chilled glass.

2	shots	Tanqueray London dry gin
1	shot	Dubonnet Red (French made)
¼	shot	Freshly squeezed lemon juice
½	shot	Chartreuse Yellow liqueur

We say: Gin, lemon and Chartreuse. Not to everybody's taste.
Origin: In W.J. Tarling's 1937 *Café Royal Cocktail Book* Coronation Edition' the invention of this cocktail is credited to G. Bongarzoni.

GOOMBAY SMASH

★★★★☆

Glass: Collins
Garnish: Lime wedge
Method: SHAKE all ingredients with ice and strain into ice-filled glass.

2	shots	Pusser's Navy rum
½	shot	Triple Sec
¾	shot	Malibu coconut rum liqueur
3	shots	Fresh pressed pineapple juice
¼	shot	Freshly squeezed lime juice

We say: Smashes are usually short drinks that include muddled mint, but this potent Tiki-style drink features rum, coconut and fruit.
Origin: The Goombay Smash is a speciality of Miss Emily's Blue Bee Bar in the Bahamas. Mrs Emily Cooper is now deceased but her daughter, Violet Smith, presides over her secret recipe.

GRAND 'O' NEW

★★★★☆

Glass: Collins
Garnish: Lemon wedge & seasonal berries
Method: POUR soda water into ice-filled glass to half fill. ADD lemon juice, orange juice and Grand Marnier. TOP with soda.

2¼	shots	Soda (club soda)
2¼	shots	Freshly squeezed orange juice
1	dash	Freshly squeezed lemon juice
1½	shots	Grand Marnier liqueur
1	wedge	Lemon

We say: A fruity, zesty, light summery cocktail. Tip - pouring the soda first makes this refreshingly juicy drink easier to mix due to the specific gravities of the ingredients.

GRAND BERRY NEW

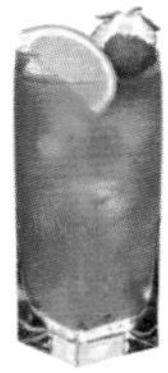

★★★☆☆

Glass: Collins
Garnish: Lime wedge & seasonal berries
Method: POUR cranberry juice into ice-filled glass to half fill. ADD lime juice and Grand Marnier.

4½	shots	Ocean Spray cranberry juice
¼	shot	Freshly squeezed lime juice
1½	shots	Grand Marnier liqueur

We say: Pouring the cranberry before the liqueur makes this drink easier to mix due to the ingredients specific gravities. The liqueur falls through the juice.

GRAND COSMOPOLITAN UPDATED

★★★★☆

Glass: Martini
Garnish: Orange zest twist (flamed)
Method: SHAKE all ingredients with ice and fine strain into chilled glass.

1	shot	Ketel One vodka
1	shot	Grand Marnier liqueur
1½	shots	Ocean Spray cranberry juice
½	shot	Freshly squeezed lime juice
1	dash	Angostura aromatic bitters

We say: The rich flavours of Grand Marnier shine through what is indeed a 'grand' Cosmopolitan.

GRAND DESIGNS

★★★★☆

Glass: Martini
Garnish: Rosemary sprig
Method: MUDDLE rosemary in base of shaker. Add other ingredients, SHAKE with ice and fine strain into chilled glass.

1	inch	Rosemary sprig
1½	shots	Tanqueray London dry gin
1	shot	St~Germain elderflower liqueur
¼	shot	Martini Extra Dry vermouth
¾	shot	Fresh pressed pineapple juice

We say: Easy drinking and slightly sweet, dried and made altogether grander by the rosemary.
Origin: Created in 2008 for Grand Designs Live exhibition by Simon Difford at the Cabinet Room, London, England.

GRAND ESPRIT NEW

★★★★☆☆

Glass: Collins
Garnish: Orange & strawberry slices
Method: POUR soda into ice-filled glass to half fill. ADD garnish, Grand Marnier and elderflower. TOP with more soda water.

3½	shots	Soda (club soda)
1	shot	Grand Marnier liqueur
¾	shot	Elderflower cordial

We say: A long, refreshing orange and elderflower summery drink.

GRAND MARGARITA UPDATED

★★★★☆

Glass: Coupette
Garnish: Lime wedge & salt rim (optional)
Method: SHAKE all ingredients with ice and fine strain into chilled glass.

1½	shots	Tequila 100% Agave
1	shot	Grand Marnier liqueur
¾	shot	Freshly squeezed lime juice
3	drops	Difford's Margarita Bitters

We say: A balanced and flavoursome Margarita with the rich cognac and orange notes of Grand Marnier adding to this drinks depth of flavour.

GRAND MIMOSA

★★★★☆☆

Glass: Flute
Garnish: Strawberry
Method: SHAKE first two ingredients with ice and strain into chilled glass. TOP with champagne.

1	shot	Grand Marnier liqueur
2	shots	Freshly squeezed orange juice
Top up with		Brut champagne

We say: As the name suggests, the orange of Grand Marnier heavily influences this drink. Basically a Buck's Fizz with more oomph.
Origin: The Mimosa was created in 1925 at the Ritz Hotel, Paris, and named after the Mimosa plant - probably because of its trembling leaves, rather like the gentle fizz of this mixture. The Grand Mimosa as shown here benefits from the addition of Grand Marnier liqueur.

GRAND MOJITO NEW

★★★★☆☆

Glass: Collins
Garnish: Lime wedge
Method: POUR ingredients into glass and half fill with crushed ice. CHURN (stir) with bar spoon. Fill glass with more crushed ice and CHURN some more. Keep adding ice and churning until drink fills glass. Serve with straws.

1½	shots	Grand Marnier liqueur
½	shot	Freshly squeezed lime juice
8	fresh	Mint leaves

We say: Grand Marnier adds its distinctive rich orange flavour to this twist on a Mojito.

GRAND PASSION

★★★☆☆

Glass: Martini
Garnish: Passion fruit
Method: Cut passion fruit in half and scoop out flesh into shaker. Add other ingredients. SHAKE with ice and fine strain into chilled glass.

1	fresh	Passion fruit
2	shots	Bacardi Superior rum
1	shot	Pressed apple juice
½	shot	Monin Pure Cane 2:1 sugar syrup
3	dashes	Angostura aromatic bitters
½	fresh	Egg white

We say: Are you lacking passion in your life? There's plenty in this fruity little number.

GRAND SAZERAC

★★★★☆

Glass: Old-fashioned
Method: POUR absinthe into ice-filled glass and TOP with water. Leave the mixture to stand in the glass. Separately, SHAKE liqueur, bourbon and bitters with ice. Finally discard contents of absinthe-coated glass and fine strain contents of shaker into absinthe washed glass. (Note that there is no ice in the finished drink.)

½	shot	Absinthe
1½	shots	Grand Marnier liqueur
1½	shots	Maker's Mark bourbon
2	dashes	Angostura aromatic bitters
3	dashes	Peychaud's aromatic bitters
Top up with		Chilled mineral water

We say: An orange twist on the classic Sazerac.
Origin: Created in 2004 by Simon Difford.

GRAND SIDECAR UPDATED

★★★★☆

Glass: Martini
Garnish: Half sugar rim and orange zest twist
Method: SHAKE all ingredients with ice and fine strain into chilled glass.

2	shots	Grand Marnier liqueur
1	shot	Freshly squeezed lemon juice
½	shot	Chilled mineral water

We say: A twist on the classic Sidecar that's even simpler to make but equally tasty. Grand Marnier Cordon Rouge consists of 55 per cent cognac so there is no need to add cognac to make a great Sidecar, simply add lemon juice. This drink benefits from a touch of dilution so also works well served, strained over ice in an old-fashioned glass.
Origin: Created June 2005 by Simon Difford, London, England.

GRAND SLAM

★★★★☆

Glass: Martini
Garnish: Strawberry
Method: SHAKE all ingredients with ice and fine strain into chilled glass.

2	shots	Swedish Punch liqueur
1	shot	Martini Extra Dry vermouth
1	shot	Martini Rosso sweet vermouth

We say: This after dinner libation is slightly sweet but incredibly aromatic.
Origin: Vintage cocktail of unknown origin.

GRAND SOUR NEW

★★★★☆

Glass: Old-fashioned
Garnish: Orange slice
Method: DRY SHAKE all ingredients (without ice). SHAKE again with ice and fine strain into ice-filled glass.

2	shots	Grand Marnier liqueur
1	shot	Freshly squeezed lemon juice
½	shot	Freshly squeezed orange juice
½	fresh	Egg white

We say: The rich cognac and oranges flavours of Grand Marnier shine in this balanced and flavoursome sour.

GRANDE CHAMPAGNE COSMO

★★★★½

Glass: Martini
Garnish: Orange zest twist
Method: SHAKE all ingredients with ice and fine strain into chilled glass.

1½	shots	Cognac VSOP
¾	shot	Grand Marnier liqueur
½	shot	Freshly squeezed lemon juice
1	shot	Ocean Spray cranberry juice
½	fresh	Egg white

We say: 'Grande Champagne' refers to the top cru of the Cognac region: this drink is suitably elite.

GRANNY'S

★★★★☆

Glass: Martini
Garnish: Apple wedge
Method: SHAKE all ingredients with ice and fine strain into chilled glass.

1¾	shots	Bacardi Superior rum
½	shot	Berentzen Apple schnapps
¼	shot	Goldschläger cinnamon schnapps
1½	shots	Pressed apple juice

We say: Apple, rum and cinnamon were made for each other.

GRANNY'S MARTINI

★★★½☆

Glass: Martini
Garnish: Dust with grated nutmeg
Method: SHAKE all ingredients with ice and fine strain into chilled glass.

1	shot	Tanqueray London dry gin
½	shot	Tio Pepe fino sherry
2	shots	Advocaat liqueur

We say: Creamy, Christmassy drink just for nana.
Origin: I have to own up to creating and naming this drink after three drink categories often identified with a stereotypical English granny. Sorry mum.

GRAPE DELIGHT

★★★★☆

Glass: Martini
Garnish: Red grapes
Method: MUDDLE grapes in base of shaker. Add rest of ingredients, SHAKE with ice and fine strain into chilled glass.

12	fresh	Red grapes
2	shots	Tanqueray London dry gin
½	shot	Sloe Gin liqueur
½	shot	Pressed apple juice
¼	shot	Monin Pure Cane 2:1 sugar syrup
¼	shot	Freshly squeezed lime juice
1	dash	Angostura aromatic bitters

We say: This rust coloured drink is fruity and delicate.

GRAPE EFFECT

★★★★☆

Glass: Martini
Garnish: Red & white grapes
Method: MUDDLE grapes in base of shaker. Add other ingredients, SHAKE with ice and fine strain into chilled glass.

12	fresh	Seedless white grapes
2	shots	Bacardi Superior rum
1	shot	St~Germain elderflower liqueur

We say: Delicately flavoured and heavily laced with rum.

GRAPE ESCAPE

★★★★½

Glass: Collins
Garnish: Mint sprig
Method: MUDDLE grapes and mint in base of shaker. Add cognac and sugar, SHAKE with ice and strain into glass filled with crushed ice. TOP with champagne, stir and serve with straws.

8	fresh	Seedless white grapes
5	fresh	Mint leaves
2	shots	Cognac VSOP
½	shot	Monin Pure Cane 2:1 sugar syrup
Top up with		Brut champagne

We say: A cracking drink - subtle and refreshing.
Origin: Created in 2000 by Brian Lucas and Max Warner at Long Bar at The Sanderson, London, England.

GRAPE MARTINI #1

★★★★☆

Glass: Martini
Garnish: White grapes
Method: MUDDLE grapes in base of shaker. Add other ingredients, SHAKE with ice and fine strain into chilled glass.

12	fresh	Seedless white grapes
2	shots	Ketel One vodka
¼	shot	Monin Pure Cane 2:1 sugar syrup

We say: Simple but remarkably tasty.
Origin: Formula by Simon Difford in 2004.

GRAPE MARTINI #2

★★★★☆

Glass: Martini
Garnish: Red grapes
Method: MUDDLE grapes in base of shaker. Add other ingredients, SHAKE with ice and fine strain into chilled glass.

12	fresh	Seedless white grapes
2	shots	Ketel One vodka
¼	shot	Chartreuse Green liqueur

We say: Green Chartreuse adds extra complexity to what would otherwise be simply be vodka laced grape juice.

GRAPEFRUIT DAIQUIRI #1

★★★★☆

Glass: Martini
Garnish: Maraschino cherry
Method: SHAKE all ingredients with ice and fine strain into chilled glass.

2	shots	Bacardi Superior rum
1½	shots	Freshly squeezed grapefruit juice
¾	shot	Monin Pure Cane 2:1 sugar syrup

We say: The flavours of rum and grapefruit combine perfectly - clean and fresh.

GRAPEFRUIT DAIQUIRI #2 (MOCKTAIL)

★★★☆☆

Glass: Old-fashioned
Garnish: Lime wedge
Method: SHAKE all ingredients with ice and fine strain into chilled glass.

2	shots	Freshly squeezed pink grapefruit juice
1	shot	Freshly squeezed lime juice
½	shot	Monin Pure Cane 2:1 sugar syrup
2	dashes	Angostura aromatic bitters

We say: *Note: Angostura aromatic bitters contain alcohol but in the finished drink the alcohol level is negligible. Balanced and adult but cries out for rum. Take a cab instead.
Origin: Created in 2006 by Audrey Saunders, New York, USA.

GRAPEFRUIT JULEP

★★★★★

Glass: Collins
Garnish: Mint sprig
Method: STIR honey with vodka in base of shaker until honey dissolves. Add other ingredients, SHAKE with ice and strain into glass filled with crushed ice.

1	spoon	Runny honey
2	shots	Ketel One vodka
4	fresh	Mint leaves
½	shot	Freshly squeezed lime juice
¾	shot	Freshly squeezed grapefruit juice
½	shot	Pomegranate (grenadine) syrup

We say: Wonderfully refreshing. Bring on the sun.
Origin: Created by Dale DeGroff, New York City, USA.

GRAPPACINO

★★★☆☆

Glass: Martini
Garnish: Coffee beans
Method: SHAKE all ingredients with ice and fine strain into chilled glass.

2	shots	Grappa di Moscato
½	shot	Amaretto liqueur
½	shot	Monin Pure Cane 2:1 sugar syrup
1	shot	Hot espresso coffee

We say: The character of the grappa shines through and is complimented by the amaretto and coffee.
Origin: Adapted from a drink created in 2006 by George Sinclair.

GRAPPARITA

★★★☆☆

Glass: Coupette
Garnish: Lime wedge
Method: SHAKE all ingredients with ice and fine strain into chilled glass.

2	shots	Grappa di Moscato
1	shot	Limoncello liqueur
1	shot	Freshly squeezed lemon juice
½	fresh	Egg white

We say: Grappa replaces tequila and lemon liqueur triple sec in this Italian twist in the classic Margarita.
Origin: Adapted from a drink discovered in 2005 at Alfredo's of Rome, New York City, USA. The original called for a sour mix.

GRAPPLE MARTINI

★★★★☆

Glass: Martini
Garnish: White grapes
Method: MUDDLE grapes in base of shaker. Add other ingredients, SHAKE with ice and fine strain into chilled glass.

7	fresh	Seedless white grapes
2	shots	Ketel One vodka
¾	shot	Sauvignon blanc wine
1	shot	Pressed apple juice
¼	shot	Monin Pure Cane 2:1 sugar syrup

We say: A rounded, fruity Martini-style drink.
Origin: Adapted from a recipe created in 2003 by Chris Setchell at Las Iguanas, UK.

GRASSHOPPER

★★★☆☆

Glass: Martini
Garnish: Mint leaf
Method: SHAKE all ingredients with ice and fine strain into chilled glass.

1	shot	Green crème de menthe liqueur
1	shot	White Crème de Cacao
1	shot	Double (heavy) cream
1	shot	Milk

We say: It's hard not to like this creamy, minty after dinner treat.
Origin: Created at Tujague's, the second oldest restaurant in New Orleans, opened in 1856 by Guillaume Tujague. Guillaume sold the restaurant to Philibert Guichet, who won second prize in a New York cocktail competition for this drink.

GRASSY FINNISH

★★★★☆

Glass: Martini
Garnish: Lemongrass
Method: MUDDLE lemongrass in base of shaker. Add other ingredients, SHAKE with ice and fine strain into chilled glass.

1	fresh	Lemongrass stem (chopped)
2	shots	Lime flavoured vodka
1	shot	Krupnik spiced honey liqueur
¼	shot	Monin Pure Cane 2:1 sugar syrup

We say: Like Finland, this drink is clean, green, wooded and safe, but deep down there's plenty of spice.
Origin: Created in 2003 by Gerard McCurry at Revolution, UK.

GRATEFUL DEAD UPDATED

★★★½☆

Glass: Sling
Garnish: Lime wedge
Method: SHAKE first 7 ingredients with ice and strain into ice-filled glass. TOP with soda and serve with straws.

½	shot	Ketel One vodka
½	shot	Tanqueray London dry gin
½	shot	Rum light white/blanco
½	shot	Cointreau triple sec
½	shot	Midori green melon liqueur
1	shot	Freshly squeezed lime juice
½	shot	Monin Pure Cane 2:1 sugar syrup
Top up with		Soda (club soda)

We say: Don't be put off by the lime green colour. This fruity, sweet 'n' sour drink is actually quite pleasant.
Origin: An LA Iced Tea with Midori in place of berry liqueur.

GREAT MUGHAL MARTINI

★★★★☆

Glass: Martini
Garnish: Lemon zest twist
Method: MUDDLE raisins in base of shaker. Add other ingredients, SHAKE with ice and fine strain into chilled glass.

20	dried	Raisins
1½	shots	Maker's Mark bourbon
¼	shot	Monin Pure Cane 2:1 sugar syrup
¾	shot	Passion fruit syrup
¼	shot	Freshly squeezed lime juice
3	drops	Rose water
1	shot	Lime & lemongrass cordial

We say: Douglas' original recipe called for raisin infused boubon and I'd recommend you make this drink that way if time permits.
Origin: Created in 2001 by Douglas Ankrah for Red Fort, Soho, London, England.

GREEK PIÑA COLADA NEW

★★★★☆

Glass: Pineapple shell (frozen)
Garnish: Lime wedge
Method: BLEND ingredients with 12oz scoop of crushed ice. Pour into glass and serve immediately with straws.

2	shots	Bacardi Oro golden rum
1½	shots	Bols Natural Yoghurt liqueur
2	wedges	Pineapple (fresh)
½	shot	Ananas (pineapple) liqueur
1	shot	Malibu coconut rum liqueur

We say: A yoghurt and rum based pineapple and coconut drink, and if your blender is sufficiently powerful, with tiny fragments of pineapple shrapnel.
Origin: Created in 2011 by Simon Difford at the Cabinet Room, London, England.

GREEN APPLE & CUCUMBER MARTINI

★★★★☆

Glass: Martini
Garnish: Cucumber slices
Method: MUDDLE cucumber in base of shaker. Add other ingredients, SHAKE with ice and fine strain into chilled glass.

1	inch	Cucumber (chopped & peeled)
2	shots	Cucumber flavoured vodka
½	shot	Sour apple liqueur
½	shot	Pressed apple juice
⅛	shot	Monin Pure Cane 2:1 sugar syrup

We say: Archetypal English flavours. Clean, green and refreshing.
Origin: Adapted from a recipe discovered in 2003 at Oxo Tower Bar, London, England.

GREEN BEAST (FRESH VERSION) NEW

★★★☆☆

Glass: Collins
Garnish: Cucumber slice
Method: MUDDLE cucumber in base of shaker. Add other ingredients, SHAKE with ice and strain into glass.

3	slices	Cucumber
1	shot	Absinthe
½	shot	Monin Pure Cane 2:1 sugar syrup)
1	shot	Freshly squeezed lime juice
2¼	shot	Chilled water

We say: A whole shot of absinthe, tamed by lime, sugar and plenty of water. The cucumber is an essential freshening element.
Origin: Adapted from a drink created in 2010 for Pernod Absinthe by Charles Vexenat, Paris, France.

GREEN BEAST (PUB VERSION) NEW

★★★½☆

Glass: Collins
Garnish: Thin cucumber slices
Method: POUR ingredients into ice-filled glass and STIR.

1	shot	Absinthe
3½	shots	Chilled water
1	shots	Rose's lime cordial

We say: Absinthe loves to combine with lime, sugar and water. .
Origin: Adapted from a drink created in 2010 for Pernod Absinthe by Charles Vexenat, Paris, France

GREEN BEETLE

★★★★½☆

Glass: Martini
Garnish: Lemon zest twist
Method: POUR absinthe into ice-filled glass, TOP with water and leave to stand. Separately SHAKE other ingredients with ice. DISCARD contents of glass (absinthe, water and ice) and STRAIN contents of shaker into absinthe-coated glass.

½	shot	Absinthe
Top up with		Chilled mineral water
2	shots	Tequila 100% Agave
½	shot	Agave nectar
½	shot	Limoncello liqueur

We say: Tequila and lemon aromatized by absinthe.
Origin: Created by Alex Richer at Bar Red, London, England.

GREEN DEACON

★★★★½☆☆

Glass: Martini
Garnish: Grapefruit zest twist (discarded)
Method: MIST glass with spray or rinse of absinthe. Separately SHAKE all other ingredients with ice and STRAIN into absinthe-coated glass.

½	shot	Absinthe
1½	shots	Tanqueray London dry gin
¾	shot	Sloe Gin liqueur
1	shot	Freshly squeezed grapefruit juice

We say: Red not green, this is an unusual combination.
Origin: Created in 2009 by Jim Meehan at PDT, New York City, USA.

GREEN DESTINY

★★★★½☆

Glass: Old-fashioned
Garnish: Kiwi slice
Method: MUDDLE cucumber and kiwi in base of shaker. Add other ingredients, SHAKE with ice and fine strain into glass filled with crushed ice.

1	inch	Cucumber (chopped & peeled)
½	fresh	Kiwi fruit
2	shots	Żubrówka bison vodka
1½	shots	Pressed apple juice
¼	shot	Monin Pure Cane 2:1 sugar syrup

We say: Even tastes green, but pleasantly so.
Origin: Created in 2001 by Andrew Tiunos at Hakk, Warsaw, Poland.

GREEN DRAGON

★★★★½☆

Glass: Martini
Garnish: Mint sprig
Method: SHAKE all ingredients with ice and fine strain into chilled glass.

2	shots	Tanqueray London dry gin
½	shot	Green crème de menthe liqueur
¼	shot	Kümmel
¼	shot	Freshly squeezed lemon juice
3	dashes	Peach bitters
½	shot	Chilled mineral water

We say: An unusual cocktail that's conducive to fresh breath.
Origin: Adapted from Harry Craddock's 1930 'The Savoy Cocktail Book'.

GREEN EYES

★★★★½☆

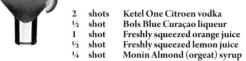

Glass: Martini
Garnish: Lime wedge
Method: SHAKE all ingredients with ice and fine strain into chilled glass.

2	shots	Ketel One Citroen vodka
½	shot	Bols Blue Curaçao liqueur
1	shot	Freshly squeezed orange juice
½	shot	Freshly squeezed lemon juice
¼	shot	Monin Almond (orgeat) syrup

We say: A cross between a Blue Cosmo and a short Screwdriver.

GREEN FAIRY

★★★★☆

Glass: Martini
Garnish: Lemon zest twist
Method: SHAKE all ingredients with ice and fine strain into chilled glass.

1	shot	Absinthe
1	shot	Freshly squeezed lemon juice
1	shot	Chilled mineral water
¾	shot	Monin Pure Cane 2:1 sugar syrup
1	dash	Angostura aromatic bitters
½	fresh	Egg white

We say: An Absinthe Sour-style drink served straight-up.
Origin: Created in the 1990s by Dick Bradsell, London, England.

GREEN FIZZ

★★★☆☆

Glass: Collins
Garnish: Lemon slice & mint sprig
Method: SHAKE first four ingredients with ice and strain into chilled glass. TOP with soda.

2	shots	Tanqueray London dry gin
½	shot	Giffard Menthe Pastille liqueur
1	shot	Freshly squeezed lemon juice
¼	shot	Monin Pure Cane 2:1 sugar syrup
Top up with		Soda (club soda)

Variant: Gin Fizz
We say: Fresh, cleansing and refreshing - as only a minty Fizz can be.
Origin: A mid-19th century classic.

GREEN FLY

★★★★½☆

Glass: Shot
Garnish: None
Method: Refrigerate ingredients then LAYER in chilled glass by carefully pouring in the following order.

½	shot	Midori green melon liqueur
½	shot	Giffard Menthe Pastille liqueur
½	shot	Chartreuse Green liqueur

We say: A strong shot comprising three layers of different green liqueurs.
Origin: Created by Alex Turner at Circus, London, England.

GREEN GLAZIER

★★★★☆

Glass: Martini
Garnish: Lime zest twist
Method: STIR all ingredients with ice and strain into chilled glass.

2	shots	Cognac VSOP
¾	shot	Chartreuse Green liqueur
¼	shot	White Crème de Cacao
2	dashes	Angostura aromatic bitters

We say: This Martini-style drink doesn't take any prisoners. Go easy.
Origin: Created in 2008 by Jamie Boudreau at Vessel, Seattle, USA.

GREEN HORN

★★★⯪☆

Glass: Martini
Garnish: Pineapple wedge & maraschino cherry
Method: SHAKE all ingredients with ice and fine strain into chilled glass.

1½	shots	Bacardi 8yo aged rum
1	shot	Fresh pressed pineapple juice
1	shot	Midori green melon liqueur
½	fresh	Egg white

We say: Far more interesting and serious than the green hue from the melon liqueur would suggest.

GREEN HORNET

★★★★☆

Glass: Shot
Garnish: None
Method: SHAKE all ingredients with ice and fine strain into chilled glass.

¾	shot	Ketel One vodka
⅛	shot	Absinthe
¾	shot	Pisang Ambon liqueur
½	shot	Rose's lime cordial

We say: A surprisingly palatable and balanced shot.

GREEN MELON SOUR

★★★☆☆

Glass: Old-fashioned
Garnish: Lemon slice & cherry on stick (sail)
Method: SHAKE all ingredients with ice and strain into ice-filled glass.

2	shots	Midori green melon liqueur
1	shot	Freshly squeezed lemon juice
1	dash	Angostura aromatic bitters

We say: Neon green in colour and a tad on the sweet side, but each to their own.

STAR RATINGS EXPLAINED

★★★★★ Excellent

★★★★⯪ Recommended	★★★★☆ Praiseworthy
★★★⯪☆ Commended	★★★☆☆ Mediocre
★★⯪☆☆ Disappointing	★★☆☆☆ Pretty awful
★⯪☆☆☆ Shameful	★☆☆☆☆ Disgusting

GREEN PARK NEW

★★★★☆

Glass: Martini
Garnish: Basil leaf
Method: DRY SHAKE all ingredients (without ice). SHAKE again with ice and fine strain into chilled glass.

2	shots	Tanqueray London dry gin
1	shot	Freshly squeezed lemon juice
¾	shot	Monin Pure Cane 2:1 sugar syrup
1	dash	Celery bitters
4	fresh	Torn basil leaves
½	fresh	Egg white

We say: Lime green in colour under a frothy head, lemon fresh and botanical with gin, basil and a hint of celery.
Origin: Created in 2011 by Erik Lorincz at the American Bar, The Savoy, London, England.

GREEN SWIZZLE

★★★★☆

Glass: Old-fashioned
Method: POUR all ingredients into glass. Fill glass with crushed ice and SWIZZLE (stir) with bar spoon or swizzle stick to mix. Serve with straws.

2	shots	Bacardi Superior rum
¼	shot	Giffard Menthe Pastille liqueur
½	shot	Freshly squeezed lime juice
¼	shot	Monin Pure Cane 2:1 sugar syrup
1	dash	Angostura aromatic bitters

Variant: With gin in place of rum
We say: A Daiquiri-like drink with a hint of peppermint.
Origin: This 1940s classic features in *The Rummy Affair of Old Biffy* by P.G. Wodehouse. Bertie Wooster sings its praises after enjoying a few at the Panter's Bar of the West Indian stand at the 1924 Empire Exhibition.

GREEN TEA MARTINI #1

★★★★☆

Glass: Martini
Garnish: Banana chunk
Method: SHAKE all ingredients with ice and fine strain into chilled glass.

2	shots	Żubrówka bison vodka
¼	shot	Pisang Ambon liqueur
⅛	shot	Giffard Menthe Pastille liqueur
2	shots	Pressed apple juice

We say: It's green and, although it doesn't actually contain any tea, has something of the flavour of alcoholic peppermint tea.

GREEN TEA MARTINI #2

★★★★☆

Glass: Martini
Garnish: Shiso (or mint leaf)
Method: SHAKE all ingredients with ice and strain into chilled glass

2	shots	Tanqueray London dry gin
1	shot	Zen green tea liqueur
¼	shot	Martini Extra Dry vermouth
¾	shot	Cold green tea

We say: Exactly what it says on the tin: as subtle and delicate as green tea itself.
Origin: Created in 2006 by Simon Difford.

GREENBELT

★★★★☆☆

Glass: Collins
Garnish: White grapes
Method: MUDDLE grapes in base of shaker. Add other ingredients, SHAKE with ice and fine strain into ice-filled glass.

12	fresh	Seedless white grapes
2	shots	Macchu pisco
1	shot	St~Germain elderflower liqueur
Top up with		Brut champagne

We say: This tastes as green as it looks - aromatic and refreshing.
Origin: Created in 2007 by Simon Difford.

GRETA GARBO

★★★★☆

Glass: Martini
Garnish: Star anise
Method: SHAKE all ingredients with ice and fine strain into chilled glass.

2	shots	Bacardi Superior rum
¼	shot	Luxardo Maraschino liqueur
½	shot	Monin Pure Cane 2:1 sugar syrup
1	shot	Freshly squeezed lime juice
⅛	shot	Pernod anise

We say: A most unusual Daiquiri.

GREY MOUSE

★★★☆☆

Glass: Shot
Garnish: None
Method: SHAKE all ingredients with ice and fine strain into chilled glass.

1	shot	Baileys Irish cream liqueur
½	shot	Opal Nera black sambuca

We say: Aniseed and whiskey cream.

GREYHOUND

★★★☆☆

Glass: Collins
Garnish: Orange slice
Method: POUR ingredients into ice-filled glass and stir.

2	shots	Ketel One vodka
Top up with		Freshly squeezed grapefruit juice

We say: A sour Screwdriver

STAR RATINGS EXPLAINED

★★★★★ Excellent

★★★★☆ Recommended	★★★★☆ Praiseworthy
★★★☆☆ Commended	★★★☆☆ Mediocre
★★☆☆☆ Disappointing	★★☆☆☆ Pretty awful
★☆☆☆☆ Shameful	★☆☆☆☆ Disgusting

GREYHOUND'S TOOTH UPDATED

★★★★★

Glass: Coupette
Garnish: Lemon zest twist
Method: SHAKE all ingredients with ice and fine strain into chilled glass.

¾	shot	Bénédictine D.O.M.
1½	shots	Ketel One vodka
¾	shot	Freshly squeezed pink grapefruit juice
¼	shot	Freshly squeezed lemon juice
2	dashes	Grapefruit bitters

We say: Fresh grapefruit flavours form the backbone of this summer-fresh cocktail.
Origin: Created in 2010 by Brandon Clements, San Francisco, USA.

GROG UPDATED

★★★★★

Glass: Old-fashioned
Garnish: Lime wedge
Method: SHAKE all ingredients with ice and strain into ice-filled glass.

2	shots	Pusser's Navy rum
½	shot	Freshly squeezed lime juice
½	shot	Muscovado sugar syrup (2 sugar to 1 water)
2	shots	Chilled mineral water
2	dashes	Angostura aromatic bitters

Variant: Grogs were probably originally sweetened with honey and you may want to try substituting three spoons of runny honey in place of the sugar syrup. We've tried both and prefer Demerara sugar to honey in this drink.
We say: Strong, flavoursome navy rum with a splash of scurvy-inhibiting lime. Properly mixed at the right dilution, this is a great drink. However, too many and you'll be groggy in the morning.
Origin: For over 300 years the British Navy issued a daily 'tot' of rum, sometimes with double issues before battle. In 1740, as an attempt to combat drunkenness, Admiral Vernon gave orders that the standard daily issue of half a pint of neat, high-proof rum be replaced with two servings of a quarter of a pint, diluted 4:1 with water.

The Admiral was nicknamed 'Old Grogram' due to the waterproof grogram cloak he wore, so the mixture he introduced became known as 'grog'. Lime juice was often added to the grog in an attempt to prevent scurvy, lending British sailors their 'limey' nickname.

The 'tot' tradition, which started in Jamaica in 1665, was finally broken on 31st July 1970, a day now known as 'Black Tot Day' - although by then the 'tot' had been reduced to a meagre two ounces. This all sounds plausible but drinks historians now say that grog emanates from an earlier period than Old Grogram.

GROUNDS FOR DIVORCE UPDATED

★★★★☆☆

Glass: Coupette
Method: MUDDLE pineapple in base of shaker. Add other ingredients, SHAKE with ice and fine stain into chilled glass.

4	wedge	Pineapple (fresh)
2	shots	Olmeca Altos 100% agave tequila
½	shot	Cuarenta y Tres (Licor 43) liqueur
½	shot	Freshly squeezed lime juice

We say: Vanilla and herbal notes with pineapple and tequila.
Origin: Adapted from a recipe created by Jasper de Graaf.

THE GTO COCKTAIL

★★★½☆

Glass: Collins
Garnish: Pineapple wedge
Method: SHAKE all ingredients with ice and strain into ice-filled glass.

2	shots	Maker's Mark bourbon
½	shot	Amaretto liqueur
½	shot	Freshly squeezed lemon juice
3	shots	Fresh pressed pineapple juice

We say: A fruity punch-like drink.
Origin: Adapted from a recipe discovered in 2004 at Jones, Los Angeles, USA

GUARD'S COCKTAIL

★★★★☆

Glass: Martini
Garnish: Orange zest twist
Method: SHAKE all ingredients with ice and fine strain into chilled glass.

1½	shots	Tanqueray London dry gin
¾	shot	Martini Rosso sweet vermouth
⅛	shot	Grand Marnier liqueur
1	dash	Orange bitters

We say: Old Guard but this Sweet Martini made sweeter with a dash of orange liqueur well deserves a place on modern cocktail lists.
Origin: Vintage cocktail of unknown origins.

GUARDABOSQUES

★★★½☆

Glass: Old-fashioned
Garnish: Pineapple wedge
Method: SHAKE ingredients with ice and strain into ice-filled glass.

1½	shots	Tanqueray London dry gin
1	shot	Midori green melon liqueur

We say: Don't let the lime-green hue of this drink put you off. It tastes considerably more adult than it looks.
Origin: A popular cocktail in Mexico.

GUILLOTINE

★★★½☆

Glass: Flute
Garnish: Seasonal berries
Method: POUR first two ingredients into glass and TOP with champagne.

½	shot	Poire William eau de vie
½	shot	Crème de cassis liqueur
Top up with		Brut champagne

We say: Add some life to your bubbly.

GULF COAST SEX ON THE BEACH

★★★★☆

Glass: Collins
Method: SHAKE all ingredients with ice and strain into ice-filled glass.

1½	shots	Bacardi Superior rum
¾	shot	Midori green melon liqueur
¾	shot	Bols Banana liqueur
1½	shots	Fresh pressed pineapple juice
1½	shots	Ocean Spray cranberry juice
¼	shot	Freshly squeezed lime juice

We say: Golden tan in colour and tropical in flavour, complete with frothy top.
Origin: Created in 1997 by Roberto Canino and Wayne Collins at Navajo Joe, London, England.

GUN CLUB PUNCH NO.1

★★★★½

Glass: Cartridge mug or Collins
Garnish: Pineapple wedge, maraschino cherry & mint sprig
Method: BLEND all ingredients with 12oz scoop crushed ice. Serve with straws.

1	shot	Bacardi Superior rum
1	shot	Pusser's Navy rum
1	shot	Freshly squeezed lime juice
1½	shots	Fresh pressed pineapple juice
¼	shot	Triple Sec
¼	shot	Pomegranate (grenadine) syrup

We say: This Trader Vic classic is balanced rather than sweet. Fruit juice and ice tone down rum's powerful blast.
Origin: Victor Bergeron specified that this drink should be served in one of his bespoke green cartridge mugs (pictured here). This recipe comes from 'Trader Vic's Bartender's Guide' (1972 revised edition).

GUSTO

★★★★☆

Glass: Collins
Garnish: Apple slice
Method: MUDDLE grapes in base of shaker. Add other ingredients, SHAKE with ice and fine strain into ice-filled glass.

7	fresh	Seedless white grapes
2	shots	Tequila 100% Agave
¾	shot	Agavero liqueur
2	shots	Pressed apple juice

We say: A pleasing long drink flavoured with apple, grape and tequila.
Origin: Created in 2003 by Thomas Gillgren at The Kingly Club, London, England.

BARTENDER'S TIP THROWING

Sometimes also referred to as the 'Cuban Roll' after the origin of this method of mixing, 'throwing' offers greater dilution and aeration than stirring but is more gentle than shaking. It is achieved by simply pouring the ingredients from one container to another. To do this, assemble your ingredients in a mixing glass or base of your shaker. Add ice and strain into a second mixing glass with a large diameter lipped rim increasing the distance between the two vessels as you pour. Then pour the partially mixed cocktail back into the first ice-filled container and strain into the second once again. Repeat this process several times and you will have 'thrown' your drink.

GYPSY #1

★★★★☆

Glass: Martini
Garnish: Lime zest twist
Method: SHAKE all ingredients with ice and fine strain into chilled glass.

1½	shots	Tanqueray London dry gin
¾	shot	St~Germain elderflower liqueur
¼	shot	Chartreuse Green liqueur
½	shot	Freshly squeezed lime juice

We say: Dominic describes this drink as "a little homage to the 'Last Word' cocktail".
Origin: Created in 2007 by Dominic Venegas at Bourbon & Branch, San Francisco, USA.

GYPSY MARTINI

★★★★☆

Glass: Martini
Garnish: Rosemary sprig
Method: MUDDLE rosemary and raisins in base of shaker. Add other ingredients, SHAKE with ice and fine strain into chilled glass.

1	sprig	Rosemary sprig
10	dried	Raisins
2	shots	Tanqueray London dry gin
½	shot	Monin Pure Cane 2:1 sugar syrup
1	shot	Chilled mineral water

We say: Jason's original recipe called for raisin infused gin and I'd recommend you make this drink that way if time permits.
Origin: Adapted from a recipe created by Jason Fendick in 2002 for Steam, London, England.

GYPSY QUEEN #1 UPDATED

★★★★☆

Glass: Coupette
Garnish: Lemon zest twist (discarded)
Method: STIR all ingredients with ice and strain into chilled glass.

1½	shots	Ketel One vodka
½	shot	Bénédictine D.O.M.
½	shot	Courvoisier VSOP Exclusif
1	dash	Angostura aromatic bitters

Variant: With 1 shot of Bénédictine B&B replacing D.O.M. and cognac.
We say: Vodka both fortifies and adds cereal notes to this complexly spiced cocktail.
Origin: This recipe is adapted from one by drinks historian, David Wondrich (thanks Dave). The Gypsy originated in New York City's famed Russian Tea Room, which in 1938 published a vodka cocktail booklet which included this cocktail.

GYPSY QUEEN #2 UPDATED

★★★★☆

Glass: Martini
Garnish: Orange zest twist
Method: STIR all ingredients with ice and strain into chilled glass.

1½	shots	Ketel One vodka
¾	shot	Bénédictine D.O.M.
¾	shot	Freshly squeezed orange juice
¼	shot	Freshly squeezed lemon juice

We say: Tangy, herbal, predominantly orange and not overly sweet.
Origin: A long lost classic.

HABERDASHER NEW

★★★★★

Glass: Small wine
Garnish: Cocoa & mint leaf
Method: STIR first 3 ingredients with ice and strain into chilled glass. DRY SHAKE Chartreuse and cream (without ice) and LAYER by carefully pouring over surface of drink. (Whip cream to ensure it floats.)

1½	shots	Maker's Mark bourbon
1	shot	Bols Cacao Brown
¼	shot	Fernet Branca
¾	shot	Chartreuse Green liqueur
¾	shot	Double (heavy) cream
¾	shot	Milk

We say: Chocolaty bourbon with a freshening herbal blast of Fernet Branca, smoothed by sipping through a Chartreuse cream head. The ultimate after-dinner drink.
Origin: Discovered in January 2013 at Pouring Ribbons, New York City, USA.

HABANERO

★★★★☆

Glass: Martini
Garnish: Orange zest twist
Method: MUDDLE ginger and chilli in base of shaker. Add other ingredients, SHAKE with ice and fine-strain into chilled glass.

1	slice	Red chilli (thin slice)
1	slice	Fresh root ginger (thumbnail sized)
2	shots	Bacardi Superior rum
1	shot	Drambuie
¾	shot	Freshly squeezed lime juice
2	spoons	Monin Honey syrup
2	dashes	Orange bitters
½	fresh	Egg white

We say: A Daiquiri-style drink with honey, ginger and chilli.
Origin: Created in 2008 by Giuliano Morandin at The Bar at The Dorchester Hotel, Hotel, London, England.

BARTENDER'S TIP FLAME

The term ignite, flame or flambé means that the drink should be set alight.

Please exercise extreme care when setting fire to drinks. Be particularly careful not to knock over a lit drink and never attempt to carry a drink which is still alight. Before drinking, cover the glass so as to suffocate the flame and be aware that the rim of the glass may be hot.

THE HAC

★★★★½

Glass: Coupette
Garnish: Pineapple wedge
Method: MUDDLE cardamom in base of shaker. Add other ingredients, SHAKE with ice and fine strain into chilled glass.

1	fresh	**Cardamom pods**
1½	shots	**Tequila 100% Agave**
½	shot	**Fresh pressed pineapple juice**
½	shot	**Freshly squeezed lime juice**
¼	shot	**Agave nectar**
1	dash	**Orange bitters**

We say: Perhaps better billed as being a 'Pineapple and Cardamom Margarita'.
Origin: Discovered in 2009 at Cloud 23, Manchester, England.

HAIR OF THE DOG

★★★★☆

Glass: Martini
Garnish: Dust with grated nutmeg
Method: STIR honey with Scotch until honey dissolves. Add other ingredients, SHAKE with ice and fine strain into chilled glass.

3	spoons	**Runny honey**
2	shots	**Dewar's White label Scotch**
1	shot	**Double (heavy) cream**
1	shot	**Milk**

We say: This drink's name and reputation as a hangover cure may lead you to assume it tastes unpleasant. In fact, honey, whisky and cream combine wonderfully.
Origin: Traditionally drunk as a pick-me-up hangover cure.

HAKKATINI

★★★★☆

Glass: Martini
Garnish: Orange zest twist
Method: SHAKE all ingredients with ice and fine strain into chilled glass.

1	shot	**Ketel One vodka**
1	shot	**Grand Marnier liqueur**
¼	shot	**Campari Bitter**
¾	shot	**Pressed apple juice**

We say: Balanced bitter sweet orange and apple.
Origin: Adapted from a drink discovered in 2003 at Hakkasan, London, England.

STAR RATINGS EXPLAINED

★★★★★ Excellent

★★★★½	Recommeded	★★★★☆	Praiseworthy
★★★½☆	Commended	★★★☆☆	Mediocre
★★½☆☆	Disappointing	★★☆☆☆	Pretty awful
★½☆☆☆	Shameful	★☆☆☆☆	Disgusting

HAMMER OF THE GODS

★★½☆☆

Glass: Boston & shot
Garnish: None
Method: LAYER ingredients by carefully pouring into shot glass in the following order. IGNITE and hold pint glass upside down a few inches above the flame. Allow the drink to burn for thirty seconds or so before killing the flame, being sure to keep the pint glass in place. Instruct your subject to suck the alcohol vapour from the inverted pint glass using a bendy straw. Finally, remove the pint glass and let your subject consume the drink through the straw.

1	shot	**Tuaca liqueur**
½	shot	**Absinthe**

We say: Killjoys would point out the dangers of fire and alcohol and observe that this is hardly 'responsible drinking'.
Origin: Created by Dick Bradsell at The Player, London, UK.

HAND GRENADE

★★★☆☆

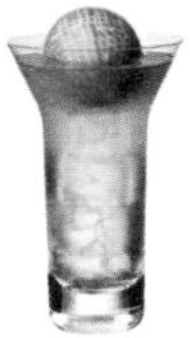

Glass: Collins
Garnish: Whole lime with scored skin
Method: SHAKE all ingredients with ice and strain into glass filled with crushed ice.

1½	shots	**Tanqueray London dry gin**
1½	shots	**Bacardi Superior rum**
1½	shots	**Ketel One vodka**
1½	shots	**Midori green melon liqueur**

We say: A blend of white spirits sweetened and melon flavoured by the addition of green-coloured liqueur. Classy!
Origin: This recipe bares little similarity to the notorious Hand Grenade served by the three Tropical Isle Bars and the Funky Pirate bar in New Orleans, USA. Marketed as 'New Orleans' most powerful drink' and served in long plastic half-yard hand-grenade shaped vessels this green melon flavoured proprietary drink is available as a pre-mix by mail order from www.tropicalisle.com. In the USA the operators of Tropical Isle have trademarked Hand Grenade so preventing other establishments not licensed by Tropical Isle from selling cocktails of this name.

HANKY-PANKY MARTINI UPDATED

★★★★☆

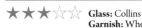

Glass: Martini
Garnish: Orange zest twist
Method: STIR all ingredients with ice and strain into chilled glass.

1¾	shots	**Tanqueray London dry gin**
1¾	shots	**Martini Rosso sweet vermouth**
⅛	shot	**Fernet Branca**
¼	shot	**Freshly squeezed orange juice**

We say: A Sweet Martini made bitter and aromatic by Fernet Branca and clouded by a squeeze of orange.
Origin: Created in the early 1900s by Ada 'Coley' Coleman at The Savoy's American Bar, London, for actor Sir Charles Hawtrey.

Ada was quoted in a 1925 edition of 'The People' newspaper as saying, "The late Charles Hawtrey... was one of the best judges of cocktails that I knew. Some years ago, when he was overworking, he used to come into the bar and say, "Coley, I am tired. Give me something with a bit of punch in it." It was for him that I spent hours experimenting until I had invented a new cocktail. The next time he came in, I told him I had a new drink for him. He sipped it, and, draining the glass, he said, "By Jove! That is the real hanky-panky!" And Hanky Panky it has been called ever since."

Coley was the first Bar Manager of the Savoy's famous American Bar and the Hanky-Panky is her most famous creation. She perfected her craft at Claridge's Hotel and left to start at the Savoy in July 1903, where she stayed until her retirement in December 1924. During her tenure at the Savoy she served drinks to the likes of Mark Twain, the Prince of Wales and Prince Wilhelm of Sweden.

HAPPY NEW YEAR

★★★☆☆

Glass: Flute
Garnish: Orange slice
Method: SHAKE first three ingredients with ice and fine strain into chilled glass. TOP with champagne.

¼	shot	Cognac VSOP
¾	shot	Warre's Otima tawny port
¾	shot	Freshly squeezed orange juice
Top up with		Brut champagne

We say: Reminiscent of fizzy, fruity claret.
Origin: Created in 1981 by Charles Schumann, Munich, Germany.

HARD LEMONADE

★★★★☆

Glass: Collins
Garnish: Lemon slice
Method: SHAKE first three ingredients with ice and strain into ice-filled glass. TOP with soda and serve with straws.

2	shots	Ketel One vodka
2	shots	Freshly squeezed lemon juice
1	shot	Monin Pure Cane 2:1 sugar syrup
Top up with		Soda (club soda)

Variant: Vodka Collins, Ray's Hard Lemonade
We say: Refreshing lemonade with a kick. Great for a hot afternoon.
Origin: Discovered in 2004 at Spring Street Natural Restaurant, New York City, USA.

THE HARLEM

★★★★☆

Glass: Martini
Garnish: Maraschino cherry
Method: SHAKE all ingredients with ice and fine strain into chilled glass.

2	shots	Tanqueray London dry gin
¼	shot	Luxardo Maraschino liqueur
2	shots	Fresh pressed pineapple juice

We say: Soft and fruity. Careful, it's harder than you think.
Origin: Thought to date back to the Prohibition era and the Cotton Club in Harlem

HAROLD AND MAUDE

★★★★½

Glass: Coupette
Garnish: Orange zest twist
Method: SHAKE all ingredients with ice and fine strain into ice-filled glass.

1	shot	Dewar's White label Scotch
1	shot	Bacardi 8yo aged rum
½	shot	Freshly squeezed lemon juice
¼	shot	Rose syrup
⅛	shot	Monin Lavender sugar syrup

We say: Balanced, complex and very, very serious.
Origin: Adapted from a drink created in 2009 by Chase Mallen at Raines Lay Rooms, New York City, USA.

HARPOON

★★★½☆

Glass: Old-fashioned
Garnish: Lime wedge
Method: POUR ingredients into ice-filled glass and stir.

1½	shots	Ketel One vodka
2	shots	Ocean Spray cranberry juice
¼	shot	Freshly squeezed lime juice

We say: Innocuously light in both flavour and alcohol. Add a shot of triple sec and you are well on your way to making a Cosmopolitan.
Origin: Though to be the forerunner to the Cosmopolitan. A 1968 bottle label from Ocean Spray's archives lists the Harpoon as a "new cocktail". It was originally launched as being 2 ounces Ocean Spray cranberry and 1 ounce vodka or light rum served "over the rocks or tall with soda. Suggested garnish: a splash of lime or lemon optional." In 1970, it was updated to also list gin as a possible base spirit.

HARVARD

★★★★☆

Glass: Martini
Garnish: Lemon zest twist
Method: STIR all ingredients with ice and strain into chilled glass. TOP with a shot or so of chilled soda.

1½	shots	Cognac VSOP
2	shots	Martini Rosso sweet vermouth
2	dashes	Orange bitters
Top up with		Soda from siphon

AKA: New Orleans Manhattan
Variant: Delmonico (with Angostura in place of orange bitters).
We say: Old-school, but approachable so. Dry and herbal. A great aperitif.
Origin: Recipe adapted from George J. Kappeler's 1895 'Modern American Drinks'. In his 1931 book 'Old Waldorf Bar Days', Albert Stevens Crockett notes of this drink, "Named after a school for young men, whose site is contiguous to the Charles River, in a suburb of Boston. Alumni who drunk it sometimes lost the 'Harvard accent.'"

HARVARD COOLER

★★★★½

Glass: Collins
Garnish: Lime wedge
Method: SHAKE first 3 ingredients with ice and strain into ice-filled glass. TOP with soda, stir and serve with straws.

2	shots	Calvados/Applejack brandy
1	shot	Freshly squeezed lime juice
½	shot	Monin Pure Cane 2:1 sugar syrup
Top up with		Soda (club soda)

We say: Refreshing and not too sweet. Lime and sugar enhance the appley spirit.

HARVEY WALLBANGER

★★★★⯪
Glass: Collins
Garnish: Orange slice
Method: POUR all ingredients into ice-filled glass.

2	shots	Ketel One vodka
½	shot	Galliano L'Autentico liqueur
3½	shots	Freshly squeezed orange juice

Variant: Freddie Fudpucker
We say: Like the Screwdriver, the Harvey Wallbanger has sadly waned in popularity in recent years, probably due to it being served with packaged orange juice. When made with freshly squeezed orange juice and recently revived Galliano L'Autentico this is worthy of a renaissance.
Origin: Legend has it that 'Harvey' was a surfer at Manhattan beach, California. His favourite drink was a Screwdriver with added Galliano. One day in the late sixties, while celebrating winning a surfing competition, he staggered from bar to bar, banging his surfboard on the walls, and so a contemporary classic gained its name.

However, an article in Bartender Magazine credits the creation to Bill Donner, the host of a house party held in the mid-sixties in Newport Beach, California. One of the guests, Harvey, was found banging his head the next morning, complaining of the hangover this drink induced.

HAVANA COBBLER

★★★★☆
Glass: Old-fashioned
Garnish: Lime zest twist
Method: SHAKE all ingredients with ice and strain into glass filled with crushed ice.

2	shots	Bacardi Superior rum
1	shot	Warre's Otima tawny port
½	shot	Stone's green ginger wine
¼	shot	Monin Pure Cane 2:1 sugar syrup

We say: An unusual, spiced, Daiquiri-like drink.

HAVANA SPECIAL

★★★★☆
Glass: Old-fashioned
Garnish: Lemon zest twist
Method: SHAKE all ingredients with ice and strain into glass filled with crushed ice.

2	shots	Bacardi Superior rum
½	shot	Luxardo Maraschino liqueur
1¾	shots	Fresh pressed pineapple juice

We say: Daiquiri-like without the sourness. Fragrant and all too easy to drink.

HAVANATHEONE

★★★★★
Glass: Martini
Garnish: Mint leaf
Method: Lightly MUDDLE mint (just to bruise) in base of shaker. Add rum and honey and STIR until honey dissolves. Add other ingredients, SHAKE with ice and fine strain into chilled glass.

10	fresh	Mint leaves
2	spoons	Runny honey
2	shots	Bacardi Superior rum
½	shot	Freshly squeezed lime juice
1	shot	Pressed apple juice

We say: A flavoursome Daiquiri featuring honey, apple and mint.
Origin: Discovered in 2003 at Hush, London, England.

HAWAIIAN

★★★☆☆
Glass: Hurricane
Garnish: Pineapple wedge & maraschino cherry
Method: BLEND all ingredients with two 12oz scoops crushed ice and serve with straws.

½	shot	Triple Sec
½	shot	Bacardi Superior rum
2	shots	Malibu coconut rum liqueur
1½	shots	Freshly squeezed orange juice
1½	shots	Fresh pressed pineapple juice
1	shot	Freshly squeezed lime juice
½	shot	Monin Pure Cane 2:1 sugar syrup
1	shot	Coco López cream of coconut

We say: Coconut, rum and fruit juice. Aloha.

HAWAIIAN COCKTAIL

★★★★☆
Glass: Martini
Garnish: Pineapple wedge & maraschino cherry
Method: SHAKE all ingredients with ice and fine strain into chilled glass.

1½	shots	Bacardi Superior rum
½	shot	Amaretto liqueur
½	shot	Southern Comfort liqueur
¾	shot	Freshly squeezed orange juice
1½	shots	Fresh pressed pineapple juice

We say: Sweet, tangy and fruity.
Origin: Discovered in Las Vegas in 2004.

HAWAIIAN COSMOPOLITAN

★★★★☆
Glass: Martini
Garnish: Pineapple wedge
Method: SHAKE all ingredients with ice and fine strain into chilled glass.

2	shots	Ketel One vodka
1	shot	Sour apple liqueur
1	shot	Pressed apple juice
½	shot	Freshly squeezed lime juice

We say: Fresh, tangy and distinctly tropical.
Origin: Created in 2002 by Wayne Collins, UK.

HAWAIIAN EYE

★★★★✭☆

Glass: Collins
Garnish: Pineapple wedge & maraschino cherry
Method: BLEND all ingredients with two 12oz scoops of crushed ice. Serve with straws.

1	shot	Bacardi Superior rum
1	shot	Bacardi Oro golden rum
½	shot	Taylor's Velvet Falernum liqueur
½	shot	Freshly squeezed lime juice
½	shot	Monin Pure Cane 2:1 sugar syrup

We say: Tropical, rum laced cooler.
Origin: A Tiki drink created in 1963 by Tony Ramos at China Trader, California, USA, fr the cast of the TV series of the same name.

HAWAIIAN MARTINI ⚷

★★★★☆

Glass: Martini
Garnish: Pineapple wedge & maraschino cherry
Method: SHAKE all ingredients with ice and fine strain into chilled glass.

1½	shots	Tanqueray London dry gin
½	shot	Martini Extra Dry vermouth
½	shot	Martini Rosso sweet vermouth
1½	shots	Fresh pressed pineapple juice

We say: An aptly named fruity twist on the classic Martini.
Origin: Adapted from a drink discovered in 2005 at the Four Seasons, Milan, Italy.

HAWAIIAN SEABREEZE ⚷

★★★★✭☆

Glass: Collins
Garnish: Pineapple wedge
Method: SHAKE all ingredients with ice and strain into ice-filled glass.

2	shots	Ketel One vodka
2½	shots	Ocean Spray cranberry juice
1½	shots	Fresh pressed pineapple juice

Variant: Bay Breeze
We say: Easygoing, foam topped relative of the Seabreeze.

HAWAIIAN STONE SOUR NEW

★★★★☆

Glass: Old-fashioned
Garnish: Pineapple slice and cherry.
Method: SHAKE all ingredients with ice and fine strain into ice-filled glass.

1½	shots	Maker's Mark bourbon
¾	shot	Freshly squeezed lemon juice
1	shot	Fresh pressed pineapple juice
½	shot	Monin Pure Cane 2:1 sugar syrup

We say: The thinking man's Piña Colada.
Origin: Created in 2000 by Dale DeGroff at Blackbird Bar, New York City, USA.

HAYDENISTIC

★★★★☆

Glass: Martini
Garnish: Lime zest twist
Method: STIR all ingredients with ice and strain into chilled glass.

2	shots	Ketel One vodka
⅛	shot	St~Germain elderflower liqueur
⅛	shot	Taylor's Velvet Falernum liqueur

We say: Extremely subtle, like a very complex Wet Vodkatini.
Origin: Created in 2007 by Hayden Lambert at The Merchant Hotel, Belfast, Northern Ireland.

HAZEL'ITO

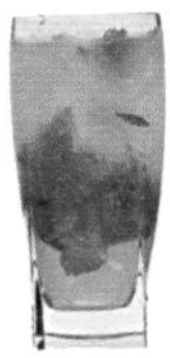

★★★★✭

Glass: Collins
Garnish: None
Method: Lightly MUDDLE mint in base of glass (just to bruise). Add other ingredients, fill glass with crushed ice and CHURN (stir) with bar spoon to mix.

12	fresh	Mint leaves
2	shots	Bacardi Superior rum
2	shots	Hazelnut liqueur
1	shot	Freshly squeezed lime juice
½	shot	Monin Pure Cane 2:1 sugar syrup

We say: Looks like a Mojito but has a nutty twang courtesy of the hazelnut liqueur.
Origin: Created in January 2002 by Adam Wyartt, London, England.

HAZELNUT ALEXANDER

★★★★☆

Glass: Martini
Garnish: Dust with chocolate powder
Method: SHAKE all ingredients and fine strain into chilled glass.

1¾	shots	Cognac VSOP
½	shot	Dark Crème de Cacao
¾	shot	Hazelnut liqueur
½	shot	Milk
½	shot	Double (heavy) cream
2	dashes	Angostura aromatic bitters

We say: Great twist on a classic - the use of bitters is inspired.
Origin: Created in 2005 by James Mellnor at Maze, London, England.

HAZELNUT MARTINI

★★★★✭☆

Glass: Martini
Garnish: Hazelnut
Method: STIR all ingredients with ice and strain into chilled glass.

2	shots	Ketel One vodka
½	shot	Hazelnut liqueur
½	shot	White Crème de Cacao
¾	shot	Chilled mineral water

We say: A hazelnut Vodkatini with a hint of chocolate

HE'S AT HOME

★★★½☆☆

Glass: Collins
Garnish: Lime zest twist
Method: SHAKE all ingredients with ice and fine strain into glass filled with crushed ice.

½	shot	Freshly squeezed lime juice
2	shots	Chartreuse Green liqueur
1	dash	Fee Brothers mint bitters

We say: LeNell's kind of drink and accompanying story. Other Chartreuse lover's should experiment.
Origin: This recipe is adapted from one by Del Pedro, Alexander's, New York City. It came to me (in 1997) courtesy of the infamous LeNell Smothers. To quote from Del, "I used to call this a 'Gatsby cooler' at one time, because there seems something kinda evilly 'Hampton-ish' about this drink, but I also called it 'He's At Home' which was the name given to porcelain dildos that Nantucket ship's captain's wives kept stashed in the flue of their fireplaces for the lonely winter nights when the old dog was chasing whales."

HEAD SHOT

★★½☆☆☆

Glass: Shot
Garnish: None
Method: Refrigerate ingredients then LAYER in chilled glass by carefully pouring in the following order.

| ¾ | shot | Opal Nera black sambuca |
| ¾ | shot | Chartreuse Green liqueur |

We say: Please drink responsibly.

HEARST MARTINI

★★★★☆

Glass: Martini
Garnish: Orange zest twist
Method: STIR all ingredients with ice and strain into chilled glass.

2	shots	Tanqueray London dry gin
1	shot	Martini Rosso sweet vermouth
1	dash	Orange bitters
1	dash	Angostura aromatic bitters

We say: A fantastically wet, sweet and aromatic Martini.
Origin: This was supposedly a favourite of hacks who worked for the American newspaper magnate, William Randolph Hearst, and is believed to have been created at New York's Waldorf-Astoria. It is nicknamed 'The Disgruntled Journalist' and indeed, is not dissimilar to a Journalist with extra bitters.

HEATHER JULEP

★★★★½

Glass: Collins
Garnish: Mint sprig
Method: Lightly MUDDLE mint in base of shaker (just to bruise). Add other ingredients, SHAKE with ice and strain into glass filled with crushed ice. CHURN (stir) the drink using a bar spoon. Top the glass with more crushed ice so as to fill it and churn again. Serve with straws.

12	fresh	Mint leaves
2½	shots	Dewar's White label Scotch
½	shot	Drambuie
¾	shot	Monin Pure Cane 2:1 sugar syrup

We say: A Scottish twist on the classic bourbon based Mint Julep.
Origin: Adapted from a drink discovered in 2001 at Teatro, London, England.

HEAVEN SCENT

★★★½☆

Glass: Martini
Garnish: Orange zest twist
Method: SHAKE all ingredients with ice and fine strain into chilled glass.

1½	shots	Vanilla-infused Ketel One vodka
1½	shots	Krupnik spiced honey liqueur
½	shot	Freshly squeezed lemon juice
¾	shot	Chilled mineral water

We say: Honey, vanilla and lemon - reminiscent of a chilled, straight-up toddy.
Origin: Discovered in 2003 at Oxo Tower Bar, London, England.

HEAVENS ABOVE

★★★★½☆

Glass: Collins
Garnish: Pineapple wedge
Method: SHAKE all ingredients with ice and strain into glass filled with crushed ice.

2	shots	Bacardi Superior rum
¼	shot	Dark Crème de Cacao
¼	shot	Kahlúa coffee liqueur
3	shots	Fresh pressed pineapple juice

We say: Slightly sweet, fruity rum - hard not to like.
Origin: A Tiki-style drink adapted from a drink featured in Jeff Berry's 'Intoxica' and originally created circa 1970 at Top of Toronto, CN Tower, Toronto, Canada.

HEDGEROW SLING

★★★★½☆

Glass: Sling
Garnish: Lemon slice & seasonal berries
Method: SHAKE first ingredients with ice and strain into glass filled with crushed ice. TOP with soda and then DRIZZLE blackberry liqueur over drink. Serve with straws.

1	shot	Tanqueray London dry gin
1	shot	Sloe Gin liqueur
1	shot	Freshly squeezed lemon juice
½	shot	Monin Pure Cane 2:1 sugar syrup
Top up with		Soda (club soda)
¼	shot	Crème de Mûre liqueur

We say: Rich, long, berry drink.
Origin: Created by Brian Duell at Detroit, London, England.

HEMINGWAY

★★★☆☆

Glass: Flute
Garnish: Star anise
Method: POUR anis into chilled glass. TOP with champagne.

1 shot Pernod anise
Top up with Brut champagne

AKA: Corpse Reviver #2
We say: Why dilute your anis with water when you can use champagne.
Origin: Created at Cantineros' Club, the famous Cuban bar school.

HEMINGWAY MARTINI

★★★★☆

Glass: Martini
Garnish: Maraschino cherry
Method: SHAKE all ingredients with ice and fine strain into chilled glass.

2 shots Ketel One Oranje vodka
¼ shot Vanilla schnapps
1 shot Freshly squeezed grapefruit juice
¼ shot Martini Extra Dry vermouth
¼ shot Maraschino syrup (from cherry jar)

We say: A fresh and refreshing orange and vanilla influenced Vodkatini.
Origin: Created in 2005 by Claire Smith, London, England.

HEMINGWAY SPECIAL DAIQUIRI

★★★★½

Glass: Martini
Garnish: Lime wedge
Method: SHAKE all ingredients with ice and fine strain into chilled glass.

3½ shots Bacardi Superior rum
1 shot Freshly squeezed grapefruit juice
¾ shot Luxardo Maraschino liqueur
1 shot Freshly squeezed lime juice
½ shot Monin Pure Cane 2:1 sugar syrup

AKA: Papa Doble Daiquiri
We say: A true Hemingway Special should be served without the addition of sugar. However, Hemingway had a hardened palate and more delicate drinkers may prefer the recipe above.
Origin: Created by Constantino (Constante) Ribalaigua Vert, the legendary head bartender of La Floridita, Havana, Cuba for Ernest Hemingway, after the great man wandered into the bar to use the toilet. When Hemingway tried the Floridita's standard frozen Daiquiri, he is quoted as saying, "That's good but I prefer it without sugar and with double rum" - so the Hemingway Special was born.

Hemingway suffered from haemochromotosis, a rare and hereditary form of diabetes from which his father also suffered, hence his aversion to sugar. The original version was exactly as Hemingway requested a Daiquiri without sugar and heavy on the rum, basically rum shaken with a splash of lime juice. Years later after he took over the position of Head Bartender at La Floridita, Antonio Meilan added maraschino and grapefruit juice into the drink. Today sugar is commonly also added to balance this drink and make it more palatable to people with less sour palates than Hemingway.

Hemingway was affectionately known as 'Papa' in Cuba and this drink was originally named 'Daiquiri Like Papa' and then later 'Papa Doble'. After Meilan added maraschino and grapefruit the drink changed its name again to the Hemingway Special we recognise today.

HENRY VIII

★★★½☆

Glass: Flute
Garnish: Orange zest twist
Method: Soak sugar cube with absinthe and drop into chilled glass. POUR other ingredients over sugar cube and serve.

1 cube Granulated sugar
⅛ shot Absinthe
½ shot Ketel One Citroen vodka
½ shot Pepper-infused Ketel One vodka
Top up with Brut champagne

We say: A contemporary twist in the classic Champagne cocktail.
Origin: Created in 2004 by Henry Besant, London, UK

HESITATION

★★★½☆

Glass: Martini
Garnish: Lemon zest twist
Method: SHAKE all ingredients with ice and fine strain into chilled glass.

2 shots Swedish Punch liqueur
1 shot Maker's Mark bourbon
¼ shot Freshly squeezed lemon juice
½ shot Chilled mineral water

We say: Lightly spiced and slightly on the sweet side.
Origin: Vintage cocktail of unknown origin.

HEUSER & ANGUS SPECIAL UPDATED

★★★★☆

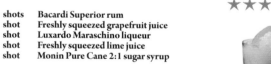

Glass: Old-fashioned
Garnish: Orange zest twist
Method: SHAKE all ingredients with ice and fine strain into glass filled with crushed ice.

1¾ shots Chartreuse Green liqueur
¾ shot Freshly squeezed lime juice
½ shot Luxardo Maraschino liqueur
⅛ shot Monin Pure Cane 2:1 sugar syrup
1 whole Egg
3 dashes Orange flower water

We say: A floral, aromatic and herbal Chartreuse flip.
Origin: Created by Gonçalo de Sousa Monteiro of Berlin, Germany who was inspired to make this drink for two fellow 'Travelling Mixologists', Bastian Heuser and Angus Winchester.

STAR RATINGS EXPLAINED

★★★★★ Excellent

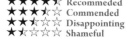

★★★★½ Recommended	★★★★☆ Praiseworthy
★★★½☆ Commended	★★★☆☆ Mediocre
★★½☆☆ Disappointing	★★☆☆☆ Pretty awful
★½☆☆☆ Shameful	★☆☆☆☆ Disgusting

HEY HEY COCKTAIL NEW

★★★★☆

Glass: Coupette
Garnish: Lemon zest twist
Method: SHAKE all ingredients with ice and fine strain into chilled glass.

1	shot	Cognac VSOP
1	shot	Triple Sec
1	shot	Lillet Blanc
1	shot	Freshly squeezed lemon juice

We say: A sidecar-like cocktail with a good balance between sweet (triple sec) and sour (lemon juice), fortified by cognac and smoothed by Lillet Blanc.
Origin: Hey Hey is a song by Eric Clapton and also a long-running variety television program on Australian television. However, this cocktail is thought to predate both. The origin of the Hey Hey cocktail is unknown but its original calling for 'Kina Lillet' dates the drink before 1986 as this is when the product's name was changed to Lillet Blanc.

HI FALUTIN NEW

★★★★★

Glass: Coupette
Garnish: Lemon zest twist
Method: STIR all ingredients with ice and strain into chilled glass.

1½	shots	Maker's Mark bourbon
1	shot	Swedish Punch liqueur
1	shot	Byrrh aperitif

We say: Forceful and Manhattan-like in style but with sweet delicate influences from France and Sweden.
Origin: Adapted from a drink created in 2012 at Tooker Alley Bar, Brooklyn, USA by owner Del Pedro. To quote the menu, "This brash American Whippersnapper has been nattily clad by a classy old-world tailor. A puttin'-on-aits, high-steppin', diamond-pink-ed, cane-twirlin' dandy of a cocktail. Whippersnapper American Whiskey, Swedish Punsch, Byrrh and lemon essence."

HI LADIES! NEW 🗝

★★★★☆

Glass: Coupette
Garnish: Mint sprig
Method: SHAKE all ingredients with ice and fine strain into chilled glass.

2	shots	Ketel One vodka
8	fresh	Mint leaves
¾	shot	Freshly squeezed lime juice
½	shot	Monin Pure Cane 2:1 sugar syrup

We say: Basically this very tasty number is a 'Vodka Mojito' served straight-up.
Origin: Adapted from a drink in Ted Saucier's 1951 book, 'Bottoms Up!'.

STAR RATINGS EXPLAINED

★★★★★ Excellent

★★★★⯪ Recommended	★★★★☆ Praiseworthy
★★★⯪☆ Commended	★★★☆☆ Mediocre
★★⯪☆☆ Disappointing	★★☆☆☆ Pretty awful
★⯪☆☆☆ Shameful	★☆☆☆☆ Disgusting

HIBISCUS KISS

★★★⯪☆

Glass: Flute
Garnish: Lemon zest twist (discarded)
Method: Place hibiscus flower in base of chilled glass. Add rest of ingredients and gently stir.

1	candied	Wild Hibiscus flower (jarred)
¾	shot	Pear flavoured vodka
¾	shot	St~Germain elderflower liqueur
Top up with		Brut champagne

We say: Pear and elderflower champagne over a candied hibiscus flower.
Origin: Created in 2008 by Francesco Lafranconi of Southern Wine & Spirits, USA.

HIBISCUS MARGARITA

★★★★☆

Glass: Martini
Garnish: Wild hibiscus flower
Method: SHAKE all ingredients with ice and fine strain into chilled glass.

2	shots	Tequila 100% Agave
1	shot	Freshly squeezed lime juice
1	shot	Homemade hibiscus tea syrup

We say: Hibiscus combines wonderfully with tequila in this flavoursome Margarita.

HIGHBALL (GENERIC NAME) 🗝

★★★★⯪

Glass: Collins
Garnish: Orange, lime or lemon slice (as appropriate to the spirit or the carbonate)
Method: POUR spirit into ice-filled glass and TOP with a carbonated soft drink (ginger ale, soda or tonic water). Stir gently so as not to kill the fizz.

| 2 | shots | Brandy, whisk(e)y, gin, rum etc. |
| Top up with | | Ginger ale, soda, tonic water or other carbonated mixer |

We say: Simple, but simplicity can be beautiful.
Origin: Scotch & Soda, Gin & Tonic, Whiskey & Ginger, Vodka & Tonic and Rum & Coke are all examples of Highball cocktails. Highballs are a type of simple cocktail with only two ingredients, normally a spirit and a carbonate, served in a tall ice-filled glass (often referred to as a highball glass). Unlike Rickeys, Collinses and Fizzes, Highballs do not contain citrus fruit juice.

In his 1934 'The Official Mixer's Guide', Patrick Gavin Duffy writes, "It is one of my fondest hopes that the highball will again take its place as the leading American Drink. I admit to being prejudiced about this - it was I who first brought the highball to America, in 1895. Although the distinction is claimed by the Parker House in Boston, I was finally given due credit for this innovation in the New York Times of not many years ago."

That New York Times reference appears to be a letter written by Duffy on 22 October 1927 to the Editor in response to an editorial piece in the paper. He starts, "An editorial in The Times says that the Adams House, Boston, claims to have served the first Scotch highball in this country. This claim is unfounded." He goes on to tell of how in 1894 he opened a little café next the old Lyceum in New York City and that in the Spring of that year, an English actor and regular patron, E. J. Ratcliffe, one day asked for a Scotch and soda. At that time Duffy did not carry Scotch but this request and the growing number of English actors frequenting his bar led Duffy to order five cases of Usher's from Park & Tilford. Duffy claims that when the shipment arrived he "sold little but Scotch highballs", consisting of 'Scotch, a lump of ice and a bottle of club soda'. His letter finishes, "Shortly afterward every actor along Broadway, and consequently every New Yorker who frequented the popular bars, was drinking Scotch highballs. In a few years other Scotch distillers introduced their brands and many were enriched by the quantity consumed in this country. Actors on tour, and members of the Ancient and

Honorable Artillery of Boston, who came here annually to attend the Old Guard Ball, brought the new drink to the Adams House. Duffy's letter to The New York Times mentions Adam House in Boston while the reference in his subsequent book talks of 'Parker House'. Both are plausible Boston locations but does this confusion mean we should not take any of Duffy's claims for being the first to make Scotch Highballs in America seriously? The Times merely published Duffy's letter to the editor, the paper did not substantiate or even 'give credit' to his claims. In his 2003 'The Joy of Mixology', Gary Regan explains that "Highball is an old railroad term for the ball indicator connected to a float inside a steam train's water tank which told the conductor that there was enough water in the tank and so the train could proceed. Apparently when the train was set to depart, the conductor would give the highball - two short whistle blows and one long". Gary explains that this term was apt as the drinks consist of 2 shots of liquor and a long pour of mixer.

HIGHLAND DRUM

★★★½☆

Glass: Coupette
Garnish: Orange zest twist
Method: SHAKE all ingredients with ice and fine strain into chilled glass.

2	shots	Spey malt whisky
1	shot	Martini Extra Dry vermouth
¾	shot	Drambuie
¼	shot	Freshly squeezed orange juice
1	spoon	Monin Honey syrup
2	dashes	Angostura aromatic bitters

We say: The classic blend of Scotch and Drambuie with fresh orange and vermouth complexity.
Origin: Created by Salvatore Calabrese at Salvatore at Fifty, London, England.

HIGHLAND SAZERAC NEW

★★★★½

Glass: Old-fashioned
Garnish: Lemon zest twist
Method: POUR Chartreuse into glass and twirl to coat inside with liqueur, fill glass with ice and stand to one side. Separately, STIR other ingredients with ice in mixing glass. DISCARD contents of glass (Chartreuse and ice), fill with fresh ice and strain contents of mixing glass.

½	shot	Chartreuse Green liqueur
1½	shots	Courvoisier VSOP Exclusif
½	shot	Spey malt whisky
¼	shot	Monin Pure Cane 2:1 sugar syrup
3	dashes	Peychaud's aromatic bitters
2	dashes	Angostura aromatic bitters

We say: A dash of malt gives a Highland influence to the Sazerac, also given a herbal note due to a generous splash of Chartreuse.
Origin: Adapted from a recipe by Don Lee, PDT, New York, USA. Don's original recipe called for yellow Chartreuse.

HIGHLAND SLING

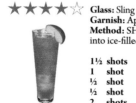

★★★★☆

Glass: Sling
Garnish: Apple wedge
Method: SHAKE all ingredients with ice and strain into ice-filled glass.

1½	shots	Dewar's White label Scotch
1	shot	Chambord black raspberry liqueur
½	shot	De Kuyper Apricot Brandy liqueur
½	shot	Galliano L'Autentico liqueur
2	shots	Pressed apple juice

We say: A surprisingly good combination of diverse flavours.

HIGHLANDER NEW

★★★★½

Glass: Coupette
Garnish: Orange zest twist
Method: STIR all ingredients with ice and fine strain into chilled glass.

2	shots	Dewar's White label Scotch
1	shot	Martini Rosso sweet vermouth
1	dash	Orange bitters

We say: A sweet Manhattan with orange bitters.
Origin: Adapted from a drink discovered in 2010 at Campbell Apartment, New York City, USA.

THE HIVE

★★★★☆

Glass: Martini
Garnish: Orange zest twist
Method: STIR honey with vodka until honey dissolves. Add other ingredients, SHAKE with ice and fine strain into chilled glass.

2	spoons	Runny honey
1	shot	Ketel One vodka
1	shot	Krupnik spiced honey liqueur
2	shots	Freshly squeezed grapefruit juice

We say: Sour grapefruit balanced by sweet honey.
Origin: Discovered in 2004 at Circus, London, England.

HOA SUA

★★★★☆

Glass: Martini
Garnish: Pineapple wedge
Method: SHAKE all ingredients with ice and fine strain into chilled glass.

1½	shots	Pomegranate juice
1½	shots	Bacardi Superior rum
¾	shot	Sake
⅛	shot	Monin Pure Cane 2:1 sugar syrup
1	dash	Angostura aromatic bitters

We say: Light and easy drinking - the rum flavour shines through.
Origin: Created in 2005 by Simon Difford for Hoa Sua catering school in Vietnam using locally available products.

HOBSON

★★★☆☆

Glass: Old-fashioned
Garnish: Orange slice
Method: SHAKE all ingredients with ice and strain into glass filled with crushed ice.

2	shots	Sloe Gin liqueur
1	shot	Triple Sec
¼	shot	Absinthe

We say: Unbalanced towards sweetness. With drinks like this you can see why Hobson chose to be an abstainer. Originally served 'straight-up' but better over crushed ice.
Origin: Named after Richmond Pearson Hobson (1870-1937) the United States Navy Rear Admiral and not Thomas Hobson (1545 - 1631) from Cambridge, England who gave rise to the term 'Hobson's choice'. R.P. Hopson was a hero of the American-Spanish war of 1898 who went on to became a Congressman. An ardent abstainer, Hobson has been called 'The Father of American Prohibition' due of his advocacy for criminalizing alcohol and other drugs and was a prolific author on this subject.

HOBSON'S CHOICE (MOCKTAIL)

★★★☆☆

Glass: Collins
Garnish: Lime wedge
Method: SHAKE all ingredients with ice and strain into ice-filled glass.

2½	shots	Freshly squeezed orange juice
2½	shots	Pressed apple juice
1	shot	Freshly squeezed lime juice
¼	shot	Pomegranate (grenadine) syrup

We say: A fruity, non-alcoholic cocktail.

HOCUS POCUS NEW

★★★★☆

Glass: Coupette/Martini
Garnish: Orange zest twist
Method: STIR all ingredients with ice and strain into chilled glass.

2	shots	Tanqueray London dry gin
¾	shot	Carpano Antica Formula
¾	shot	Orange Curaçao liqueur
⅛	shot	Fernet Branca

We say: Bittersweet with gin's botanical complexity and orange zest freshness.
Origin: Adapted from a drink discovered in 2010 at Forty Four, New York City, USA. Hocus Pocus by the Dutch rock band Focus was a chart-topper both sides of the Atlantic in 1971. Famous for its yodelling, whistling, accordion and flute this is a tune that has to heard to be believed.

HOFFMAN HOUSE

★★★★☆

Glass: Martini
Garnish: Lemon zest twist
Method: SHAKE all ingredients with ice and fine strain into chilled glass.

2½	shots	Tanqueray London dry gin
½	shot	Martini Extra Dry vermouth
2	dashes	Orange bitters

We say: A shaken Wet (5:1) Martini with orange bitters.
Origin: Apparently the house cocktail at Manhattan's Hoffman House in the 1880s

THE HOLLAND HOUSE #1 NEW
(KAPPELER'S RYE BASED)

★★★½☆

Glass: Coupette
Garnish: Orange zest twist
Method: STIR all ingredients with ice and fine strain into chilled glass.

2	shots	Straight rye whiskey
½	shot	Triple Sec
2	dashes	Peychaud's bitters
½	shot	Chilled water (omit if wet ice)

We say: Spicy rye whiskey sweetened and given an orange accent by a splash or triple sec and heightened with a couple of dashes of Peychaud's bitters.
Origin: Recipe adapted from George J. Kappeler's 1895 book, 'Modern American Drinks: How to Mix and Serve All Kinds of Cups and Drinks' published by The Merriam Company, New York. In this Kappeler stipulates, "Mixing-glass half-full fine ice, two dashes Peychaud bitters, one-half pony Eau de Vie d'Oranges, one and a half pony old rye whiskey, a piece lemon-peel. Mix. Moisten the edge of cocktail glass with lemon, dip in sugar. Strain the

cocktail into prepared glass." There are numerous versions of the Holland House but Kappeler was head barman at the Holland House Hotel so was well placed to recount how the hotel's signature cocktail was made. Orange eau de vie, or distillate of oranges is not readily available but clear sweetened orange distillate in the shape of triple sec is, hence we have used as a substitute in this drink.

THE HOLLAND HOUSE #2 NEW
(CRADDOCK'S LONDON DRY BASED)

★★★★☆

Glass: Coupette
Garnish: Lemon zest twist
Method: MUDDLE pineapple in base of shaker. Add other ingredients, SHAKE with ice and fine strain into chilled glass.

4	wedges	Pineapple (fresh) (cored, skinned and chopped)
2	shots	Tanqueray London dry gin
¾	shot	Martini Extra Dry vermouth
¼	shot	Luxardo Maraschino liqueur
½	shot	Freshly squeezed lemon juice

We say: Pineapple, maraschino, gin and vermouth makes for a dry fruit Aviation-style drink.
Origin: Recipe adapted from Harry Craddock's 1930 book, 'The Savoy Cocktail Book' published by Constable & Co. Ltd, London. Prior to heading up the American Bar at the Savoy Hotel in London, Craddock worked at New York's Holland House Hotel where this was the signature cocktail. Craddock's Holland House recipe is very different to that of George J. Kappeler, who preceded Craddock at The Holland House and wrote his cocktail book 35 years earlier.

THE HOLLAND HOUSE #3 NEW
(MODERN JENEVER BASED)

★★★★☆

Glass: Coupette
Garnish: Lemon zest twist
Method: SHAKE all ingredients with ice and fine strain into chilled glass.

1¾	shot	Bols Genever
¾	shot	Martini Extra Dry vermouth
¼	shot	Luxardo Maraschino liqueur
½	shot	Freshly squeezed lemon juice

We say: Genever adds its own complexity to this Dutch version of the classic Holland House.
Origin: This genever (jenever) based version of The Holland House was practically unknown before the 2008 launch of Bols Genever. Bols rescued The Holland House from obscurity by making it one of its promotional cocktails.

THE HOLLAND HOUSE COCKTAIL

★★★★☆

Glass: Martini
Garnish: Lemon zest twist
Method: SHAKE all ingredients with ice and fine strain into chilled glass.

1¾	shots	Bols Genever
¾	shot	Martini Extra Dry vermouth
½	shot	Freshly squeezed lemon juice
¼	shot	Luxardo Maraschino liqueur

We say: Dry and reminiscent of an Aviation but with genever personality.
Origin: A forgotten classic which is rightly being championed by the House of Bols, Amsterdam, The Netherlands.

HOLLYWOOD

★★★★★★

Glass: Flute
Garnish: Dust with grated nutmeg
Method: DRY SHAKE all ingredients without ice to emulsify. SHAKE again with ice and fine strain into chilled glass.

1½	shots	Bacardi Superior rum
½	shot	Freshly squeezed pink grapefruit juice
½	shot	Pomegranate (grenadine) syrup
½	fresh	Egg white

We say: This drink is deliciously different. Rum, grapefruit and pomegranate smoothed with egg white and spice with nutmeg.

HONEY & MARMALADE DRAM

★★★★½

Glass: Martini
Garnish: Orange zest twist
Method: STIR honey with Scotch in base of shaker until honey dissolves. Add other ingredients, SHAKE with ice and fine strain into chilled glass.

2	shots	Dewar's White label Scotch
4	spoons	Runny honey
1	shot	Freshly squeezed lemon juice
1	shot	Freshly squeezed orange juice

We say: This citrussy drink seems to enrich and enhance the flavour of Scotch.
Origin: Recipe adapted from the Honeysuckle Daiquiri.

HONEY APPLE MARTINI

★★★★☆

Glass: Martini
Garnish: Lemon zest twist
Method: SHAKE all ingredients with ice and fine strain into chilled glass.

1½	shots	Żubrówka bison vodka
¾	shot	Krupnik spiced honey liqueur
1¼	shots	Pressed apple juice
¼	shot	Freshly squeezed lemon juice

Variant: Polish Martini
We say: A classically Polish blend of flavours.

HONEY BEE

★★★★☆

Glass: Martini
Garnish: Lemon zest twist
Method: STIR honey with rum in base of shaker until honey dissolves. Add other ingredients, SHAKE with ice and fine strain into chilled glass.

2	shots	Bacardi Superior rum
3	spoons	Runny honey
½	shot	Freshly squeezed lemon juice
¾	shot	Chilled mineral water

We say: Honey balances lemon juice in this vodka cocktail.
Origin: Adapted from 1949 copy of Esquire's 'Handbook for Hosts'.

HONEY BERRY SOUR #1

★★★★☆

Glass: Old-fashioned
Garnish: Lemon wedge
Method: SHAKE all ingredients with ice and strain into ice-filled glass.

1½	shots	Krupnik spiced honey liqueur
¾	shot	Crème de cassis liqueur
1	shot	Freshly squeezed lemon juice
¼	shot	Monin Pure Cane 2:1 sugar syrup
½	fresh	Egg white

We say: More sweet than sour but berry nice.
Origin: Created by Tim Hallilaj.

HONEY BLOSSOM

★★★☆☆

Glass: Old-fashioned
Garnish: Pineapple wedge
Method: SHAKE all ingredients with ice and fine strain into ice-filled glass.

3	shots	Fresh pressed pineapple juice
1	shot	Freshly squeezed lemon juice
¼	shot	Monin Vanilla sugar syrup
½	fresh	Egg white
3	dashes	Angostura aromatic bitters

We say: Soft, fruity, yet adult.
Note: contains trace amounts of alcohol.
Origin: Created in 2003 by Tim Phillips at the GE Club, London, England.

HONEY BUBBLE NEW

★★★★½

Glass: Flute
Garnish: Mint sprig in top of hulled strawberry
Method: STIR honey with gin in base of shaker until honey dissolves. ADD other ingredients, SHAKE with ice and strain into ice-filled glass.

2	spoons	Runny honey
1	shot	Tanqueray London dry gin
Top up with		Prosecco sparkling wine

We say: Light and delicate, a great aperitif cocktail.
Origin: Adapted from a cocktail promoted in 2013 by Bols, the Dutch liqueur producer, to promote their honey liqueur which can be used in place of runny honey.

HONEY COBBLER NEW

★★★★½

Glass: Goblet
Garnish: Mint sprig and berries
Method: STIR honey with Scotch in base of shaker until honey dissolves. ADD other ingredients, SHAKE with ice and strain into ice-filled glass.

2	spoons	Runny honey
1½	shots	Dewar's White Label Scotch
1	shot	Claret red wine
¼	shot	Crème de cassis liqueur

We say: Dry wine tannins and smoky scotch balance rich honey and blackcurrant liqueur.

HONEY DAIQUIRI

★★★★⯪

Glass: Martini
Garnish: Lime wedge
Method: STIR honey with rum in base of shaker until honey dissolves. Add other ingredients, SHAKE with ice and fine strain into chilled glass.

2	spoons	Runny honey
2	shots	Bacardi Superior rum
½	shot	Freshly squeezed lime juice
½	shot	Chilled mineral water

We say: Sweet honey replaces sugar syrup in this natural Daiquiri. Try experimenting with different honeys. I favour orange blossom honey.

HONEY LIMEAID (MOCKTAIL)

★★★★☆

Glass: Collins
Garnish: Lime wedge
Method: Stir honey with lime juice in base of shaker until honey dissolves. SHAKE with ice and strain into ice-filled glass. TOP with soda.

7	spoon	Runny honey
1½	shots	Freshly squeezed lime juice
Top up with		Soda (club soda)

We say: A refreshing Mexican variation on Real Lemonade.
Origin: Discovered in 2005 at Hotel Quinta Real, Guadalajara, Mexico.

HONEY VODKA COLLINS NEW

★★★★☆

Glass: Collins
Garnish: Lemon slice
Method: STIR honey with rum in base of shaker until honey dissolves. ADD other ingredients, SHAKE with ice and strain into ice-filled glass.

2	spoons	Runny honey
2	shots	Ketel One vodka
1	shot	Freshly squeezed lemon juice
Top up with		Soda (club soda)

We say: The honey and lemon combo are reminiscent of a toddy but here served long and iced with cleansing vodka.

HONEY VODKA SOUR

★★★★☆

Glass: Old-fashioned
Garnish: Lime wedge
Method: SHAKE all ingredients with ice and strain into ice-filled glass.

2	shots	Krupnik spiced honey liqueur
1½	shots	Freshly squeezed lemon juice
½	shot	Monin Pure Cane 2:1 sugar syrup
½	fresh	Egg white
3	dashes	Angostura aromatic bitters

We say: A vodka sour with true honey character.

HONEY WALL

★★★★☆

Glass: Martini
Garnish: Orange zest twist (flamed)
Method: STIR all ingredients with ice and strain into chilled glass.

1¼	shots	Bacardi Superior rum
1¼	shots	Tuaca liqueur
1¼	shots	Dark Crème de Cacao

We say: Strong, rich and chocolatey.
Origin: Adapted from a drink created in 2002 by Dick Bradsell at Downstairs at Alfred's, London, England.

HONEYMOON UPDATED

★★★★⯪

Glass: Martini
Garnish: Orange zest twist
Method: SHAKE all ingredients with ice and fine strain into chilled glass.

¾	shot	Bénédictine D.O.M.
1½	shots	Calvados/Applejack brandy
¼	shot	Triple Sec
½	shot	Freshly squeezed lemon juice
½	fresh	Egg white

AKA: Farmer's Daughter
We say: A romantic combination of apple, orange, lemon and herbs.
Origin: A 1930s classic created in a long since departed New York bar called Brown Derby.

HONEYSUCKLE DAIQUIRI

★★★★★

Glass: Martini
Garnish: Mint leaf
Method: STIR honey with rum in base of shaker until honey dissolves. Add lemon and orange juice, SHAKE with ice and fine strain into chilled glass.

2	shots	Bacardi Superior rum
4	spoons	Runny honey
1	shot	Freshly squeezed lemon juice
1	shot	Freshly squeezed orange juice

Variant: Made with gin in place of rum this drink becomes the 'Bee's Knees Martini'.
We say: Honey - I love it!
Origin: Adapted from a recipe in David Embury's 'The Fine Art of Mixing Drinks'.

THE HONEYSUCKLE ORCHARD

★★★★☆

Glass: Martini
Garnish: Lemon wedge
Method: STIR honey with vodka in base of shaker until honey dissolves. Add other ingredients, SHAKE with ice and fine strain into chilled glass.

1	spoon	Runny honey
2	shots	Żubrówka bison vodka
1½	shots	Pressed apple juice
¼	shot	Freshly squeezed lemon juice

We say: A back to nature Polish Martini - all the better for it.
Origin: Discovered in 2005 at The Stanton Social, New York City, USA.

HONG KONG FUEY

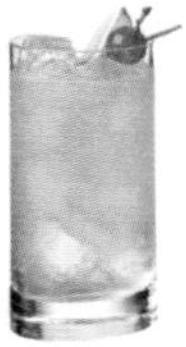

★★★⯪☆

Glass: Collins
Garnish: Lime wedge & maraschino cherry
Method: SHAKE first eight ingredients with ice and strain into ice-filled glass. TOP with lemonade, stir and serve with straws.

½	shot	Ketel One vodka
½	shot	Tanqueray London dry gin
½	shot	Bacardi Superior rum
½	shot	Tequila 100% Agave
¾	shot	Midori green melon liqueur
¼	shot	Chartreuse Green liqueur
¼	shot	Freshly squeezed lemon juice
¼	shot	Rose's lime cordial
Top up with		Lemonade/Sprite/7-Up

Variant: 'Reloaded' with champagne in place of lemonade.
We say: You may recall Hong Kong Phooey, the 1970s Hanna-Barbera animated children's TV series featuring the mild-mannered janitor Penry and his superhero alter ego. This party drink is little better than Penry's kung fu but deadly all the same.

HONI HONI

★★★⯪☆

Glass: Old-fashioned
Garnish: Pineapple wedge, maraschino cherry & mint sprig
Method: SHAKE all ingredients with ice and fine strain into glass filled with crushed ice.

2	shots	Maker's Mark bourbon
½	shot	Triple Sec
¾	shot	Freshly squeezed lime juice
½	shot	Monin Almond (orgeat) syrup
¼	shot	Monin Pure Cane 2:1 sugar syrup

We say: A Mai Tai based on whiskey rather than rum.
Origin: Adapted from Victor Bergeron's '*Trader Vic's Bartender's Guide*' (1972 revised edition). The name of this vintage Tiki drink means 'Kiss Kiss'.

HONOLULU

★★★★☆

Glass: Old-fashioned
Garnish: Pineapple wedge & maraschino cherry
Method: BLEND all ingredients with 12oz scoop of crushed ice and serve with straws.

1½	shots	Bacardi Superior rum
1	shot	Fresh pressed pineapple juice
½	shot	Freshly squeezed lemon juice
¼	shot	Monin Pure Cane 2:1 sugar syrup
¼	shot	Pomegranate (grenadine) syrup

We say: Cooling, fruity and pretty light on alcohol - perfect for a hot afternoon in Honolulu.
Origin: Adapted from Victor Bergeron's '*Trader Vic's Bartender's Guide*' (1972 revised edition).

HONOLULU COCKTAIL NO.1

★★★⯪☆

Glass: Martini
Garnish: Pineapple wedge & maraschino cherry
Method: SHAKE all ingredients with ice and fine strain into chilled glass.

2	shots	Tanqueray London dry gin
¼	shot	Freshly squeezed orange juice
¼	shot	Fresh pressed pineapple juice
¼	shot	Freshly squeezed lemon juice
¼	shot	Monin Pure Cane 2:1 sugar syrup

We say: Gin is hardly Hawaiian, but its bite works well in this tropically fruity cocktail.
Origin: Adapted from Harry Craddock's 1930 '*The Savoy Cocktail Book*'.

HONOLULU COCKTAIL NO.2

★★★⯪☆

Glass: Martini
Garnish: Maraschino cherry
Method: STIR all ingredients with ice and strain into chilled glass.

¾	shot	Tanqueray London dry gin
¾	shot	Bénédictine D.O.M.
¾	shot	Luxardo Maraschino liqueur
¾	shot	Chilled mineral water

We say: Spicy maraschino dominates this old-school after dinner cocktail.
Origin: Adapted from Harry Craddock's 1930 '*The Savoy Cocktail Book*'.

HONOLULU JUICER

★★★⯪☆

Glass: Collins
Garnish: Pineapple wedge & maraschino cherry
Method: SHAKE all ingredients with ice and strain into glass filled with crushed ice.

1	shot	Bacardi Superior rum
1½	shots	Southern Comfort liqueur
2	shots	Fresh pressed pineapple juice
¾	shot	Rose's lime cordial
¾	shot	Freshly squeezed lemon juice
¼	shot	Monin Pure Cane 2:1 sugar syrup

We say: A practically tropical, rum laced, fruity number.
Origin: A classic Tiki drink.

HOOPLA

★★★★☆

Glass: Martini
Garnish: Orange zest twist
Method: SHAKE all ingredients with ice and fine strain into chilled glass.

1	shot	Cognac VSOP
1	shot	Triple Sec
¾	shot	Martini Extra Dry vermouth
¾	shot	Freshly squeezed lemon juice
½	fresh	Egg white

We say: Not far removed from a Sidecar.

HOP TOAD #1

★★★★☆

Glass: Martini
Garnish: Apricot slice
Method: SHAKE all ingredients with ice and fine strain into chilled glass.

1¼	shots	Bacardi Superior rum
1¼	shots	De Kuyper Apricot Brandy liqueur
1¼	shots	Freshly squeezed lime juice
½	shot	Chilled mineral water

Variant: Made with brandy this is sometimes known as a Bullfrog.
We say: Resembles an apricot Daiquiri that's heavy on the lime yet balanced.
Origin: First published in Tom Bullock's 'Ideal Bartender', circa 1917

HOP TOAD #2

★★★★☆

Glass: Martini
Garnish: Apricot slice
Method: SHAKE all ingredients with ice and fine strain into chilled glass.

1¾	shots	Bacardi 8yo aged rum
1	shot	De Kuyper Apricot Brandy liqueur
¾	shot	Freshly squeezed lime juice
½	shot	Chilled mineral water

We say: Alcoholic apricot jam with a lovely twang of aged rum.

HOP TOAD #3

★★★★☆

Glass: Martini
Garnish: Lemon zest twist
Method: SHAKE all ingredients with ice and fine strain into chilled glass.

1½	shots	De Kuyper Apricot Brandy liqueur
¾	shot	Freshly squeezed lemon juice
¾	shot	Chilled mineral water

We say: Fresh apricot dessert - all it lacks is a dollop of whipped cream.
Origin: Adapted from Harry Craddock's 1930 'The Savoy Cocktail Book'.

HORNITOS LAU

★★★★☆

Glass: Collins
Garnish: Mint sprig
Method: Lightly MUDDLE mint (just to bruise) in base of shaker. Add other ingredients, SHAKE with ice and strain into glass filled with crushed ice. CHURN (stir) drink and add more crushed ice so drink meets rim of glass.

12	fresh	Mint leaves
2	shots	Tequila 100% Agave
1½	shots	Cuarenta y Tres (Licor 43) liqueur
½	shot	Freshly squeezed lime juice

We say: Jaspar recommends making a batch in their glasses and refreezing them with the straws already in the glass, like the old colonels and their julep freezers in Kentucky.
Origin: Created in 2005 by Jaspar Eyears at Bar Tiki, Mexico City, Mexico.

HORSE'S NECK WITH A KICK

★★★☆☆

Glass: Collins
Garnish: Lemon peel (whole)
Method: POUR ingredients into ice-filled glass and stir.

2	shots	Maker's Mark bourbon
3	dashes	Angostura aromatic bitters
Top up with		Ginger ale

We say: Whiskey and ginger with added shrubbery.
Origin: A Horse's Neck without a kick is simply ginger ale and bitters.

THE HORSESHOE SLING

★★★★☆

Glass: Collins
Garnish: Seasonal fruit
Method: SHAKE first five ingredients with ice and strain into ice-filled glass. TOP with champagne.

2	shots	Tequila 100% Agave
¾	shot	Freshly squeezed lime juice
½	shot	Bénédictine D.O.M.
½	shot	De Kuyper Cherry Brandy liqueur
1½	shots	Fresh pressed pineapple juice
Top up with		Brut champagne

We say: Like its creator, this is upfront and refreshingly different.
Origin: Adapted from a drink created by Gary Regan, New York, USA.

HOT BUTTERED RUM

★★★★☆

Glass: Toddy
Garnish: Cinnamon stick & lemon slice (studded with cloves)
Method: Place bar spoon loaded with honey in warmed glass. Add other ingredients and STIR until honey and butter are dissolved.

2	spoons	Runny honey
1	knob	Unsalted butter
2	shots	Bacardi Oro golden rum
1	spoon	Freshly grated nutmeg
Top up with		Boiling water

We say: In 'The Fine Art of Mixing Drinks', David Embury says, "The Hot Spiced Rum is bad enough, but the lump of butter is the final insult. It blends with the hot rum just about as satisfactorily as warm olive oil blends with champagne!"
It's rare for me to question Embury but I rather like this slightly oily, warming, spicy toddy. It's even better with dry cider instead of boiling water.

HOT BUTTERED WHISKEY

★★★★☆

Glass: Toddy
Garnish: Dust with grated nutmeg
Method: Place bar spoon in warmed glass. Add ingredients and STIR until butter dissolves.

1	knob	Unsalted butter
2	shots	Maker's Mark bourbon
¾	shot	Monin Pure Cane 2:1 sugar syrup
Top up with		Boiling water

We say: Warming and smooth - great on a cold day or whenever you fancy a warming treat.

HOT GROG

★★★★☆

Glass: Toddy
Garnish: Lemon zest twist
Method: Place bar spoon loaded with honey in warmed glass. Add other ingredients and STIR until honey dissolves.

3	spoons	Runny honey
1	shot	Pusser's Navy rum
¼	shot	Freshly squeezed lime juice
2½	shots	Boiling water

Variant: Black Stripe, with molasses replacing the honey.
We say: Warming, honeyed, pungent rum with a hint of lime.

HOT PASSION

★★★☆☆

Glass: Collins
Garnish: Maraschino cherry
Method: SHAKE all ingredients with ice and strain into ice-filled glass.

1	shot	Ketel One vodka
1	shot	Passoã passion fruit liqueur
2	shots	Ocean Spray cranberry juice
2	shots	Freshly squeezed orange juice

We say: A fruity, slightly sweet twist on a Madras.

HOT RED BLOODED FRENCHMAN

★★★★☆

Glass: Toddy
Garnish: Orange zest twist
Method: Place bar spoon in warmed glass. Add other ingredients and STIR.

1	shot	Grand Marnier liqueur
2	shots	Claret red wine
½	shot	Freshly squeezed orange juice
½	shot	Freshly squeezed lemon juice
¼	shot	Monin Pure Cane 2:1 sugar syrup
Top up with	Boiling water	

We say: Warm, fruity red wine - great on a cold night.

HOT RUM PUNCH

★★★★☆

Glass: Toddy
Garnish: Dust with grated nutmeg
Method: Place bar spoon in warmed glass. Add ingredients and STIR.

1	shot	Bacardi Oro golden rum
1	shot	Cognac VSOP
½	shot	Tio Pepe fino sherry
¼	shot	Monin Pure Cane 2:1 sugar syrup
1	shot	Freshly squeezed lime juice
Top up with	Boiling water	

We say: A great winter warmer.
Origin: Punch was one of the many rum-based drinks popular in the 18th century when taverns would serve cold punch and warm it upon request by dunking a red-hot iron in it. This version is said to have been a favourite drink of Mozart the composer.

HOT SHOT

★★★☆☆

Glass: Shot
Garnish: None
Method: LAYER by carefully pouring ingredients in the following order.

¾	shot	Galliano L'Autentico liqueur
¾	shot	Hot espresso coffee
½	shot	Double (heavy) cream

We say: The Scandinavian answer to Irish coffee.
Origin: A huge drink in Scandinavia during the early 90s
.

HOT TODDY #1

★★★★⯨

Glass: Toddy
Garnish: Lemon wedge & cinnamon stick
Method: Place bar spoon loaded with honey in warmed glass. Add other ingredients and STIR until honey dissolves.

1	spoon	Runny honey
2	shots	Dewar's White label Scotch
½	shot	Freshly squeezed lemon juice
½	shot	Monin Pure Cane 2:1 sugar syrup
3	dried	Cloves
Top up with	Boiling water	

We say: The smoky flavours in the Scotch add spice to this warming drink that's great when you're feeling down with a cold or the flu.
Origin: Lost in time but Dickens refers to a "Whisky Toddy" in 'The Pickwick Papers'.

HOT TODDY #2

★★★★⯨

Glass: Toddy
Garnish: Lemon zest twist
Method: Place bar spoon loaded with honey in warmed glass. Add other ingredients and STIR until honey dissolves.

1	spoon	Runny honey
2	shots	Dewar's White label Scotch
3	dried	Cloves
¼	spoon	Freshly grated nutmeg
Top up with	Hot English breakfast tea	

We say: Tea and Scotch combine wonderfully in this hot and spicy winter warmer.

HOT TODDY #3 ⚷

★★★★☆

Glass: Toddy
Garnish: Lemon wedge & cinnamon stick
Method: Place bar spoon in warmed glass. Add ingredients and STIR.

2	shots	Cognac VSOP
½	shot	Freshly squeezed lemon juice
¼	shot	Monin Pure Cane 2:1 sugar syrup
Top up with	Boiling water	

We say: Warms the cockles with cognac with cognac and a good dose of citrus.

HOT TOMMY

★★★★☆

Glass: Toddy
Garnish: Lime zest twist
Method: Place spoon in glass. POUR first 3 ingredients into glass. TOP up with boiling water and STIR until agave nectar dissolves.

2	shots	Tequila 100% Agave
½	shot	Freshly squeezed lime juice
½	shot	Agave nectar
Top up with		Boiling water

We say: A Mexican twist on the original winter pick-me-up.
Origin: Created in December 2009 by Alan Brown of Menzel's Bar, who says of this drink "Over the busy festive period, feeling full of flu and cold I decided to make a hot toddy to soothe my symptoms. Having no honey to hand I tried using agave nectar instead. This led me to the idea of using tequila and lime instead of lemon (to complement the tequila) with the agave and boiling water. The name for the drink is a Hot Tommy, a nod to the Tommy's Margarita, which makes use of both tequila and agave."

HOT TUB

★★★★☆

Glass: Martini
Garnish: Pineapple wedge
Method: SHAKE first three ingredients with ice and fine strain into chilled glass. TOP with prosecco.

1½	shots	Ketel One vodka
1	shot	Fresh pressed pineapple juice
¼	shot	Chambord black raspberry liqueur
Top up with		Prosecco sparkling wine

We say: Basically a French Martini with bubbles.
Origin: Adapted from a drink discovered in 2004 at Teatro Boston, USA.

HOT WINE LEMONADE NEW

★★★☆☆

Glass: Toddy
Garnish: Lemon zest twist
Method: POUR first three ingredients into warmed glass and top up with boiling water.

2	shots	Claret red wine
1½	shots	Freshly squeezed lemon juice
¾	shot	Monin Pure Cane 2:1 sugar syrup
Top up with		Boiling water

We say: This citrusy mulled wine is simply made with hot red wine and freshly squeezed lemon juice.
Origin: Rediscovered classic.

HOULA HOULA COCKTAIL

★★★☆☆

Glass: Martini
Garnish: Orange zest twist
Method: SHAKE all ingredients with ice and fine strain into chilled glass.

2	shots	Tanqueray London dry gin
½	shot	Triple Sec
1	shot	Freshly squeezed orange juice
½	shot	Chilled mineral water

We say: Orange generously laced with gin.
Origin: Adapted from Harry Craddock's 1930 '*The Savoy Cocktail Book*'.

HOYT'S DAIQUIRÍ

★★★★☆

Glass: Martini
Garnish: Lime slice (seared)
Method: Sear two halves of lime with a chef's blow torch and squeeze into a shaker. SHAKE all remaining ingredients with ice and fine strain into chilled glass.

2	shots	Bacardi Superior rum
1	shot	Burnt lime juice
¼	shot	Jägermeister
½	shot	Monin Vanilla sugar syrup
½	fresh	Egg white

We say: Most unusual and interesting. Recognisably a Daiquiri but with creamy mouth-feel and great depth of flavour.
Origin: Created in 2008 by Meimi Sanchez at Bramble, Edinburgh, Scotland.

HUAPALA

★★★★☆

Glass: Martini
Garnish: Lemon wedge
Method: SHAKE all ingredients with ice and fine strain into chilled glass.

1	shot	Bacardi Superior rum
1	shot	Tanqueray London dry gin
½	shot	Freshly squeezed lemon juice
¼	shot	Pomegranate (grenadine) syrup
½	shot	Chilled mineral water

We say: In his book Vic prefaces this cocktail with the comment, "Nice, easy drink". It's basically a lemon Daiquiri with gin and grenadine.
Origin: Adapted from Victor Bergeron's '*Trader Vic's Bartender's Guide*' (1972 revised edition).

BARTENDERS TIPS SWIZZLE

To 'swizzle' a drink is simply to stir it using a particular tool and action.

To swizzle simply immerse the blades of your swizzle stick into the drink, hold the shaft between the palms of both hands and rotate the stick rapidly by sliding your hands back and forth against it. If you do not have a bona fide swizzle stick, use a barspoon in the same manner.

HUCKLE-MY-BUFF NEW

★★★★★

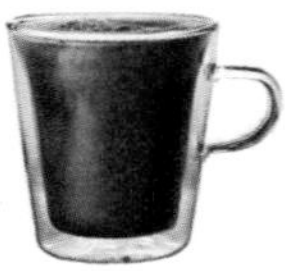

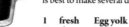

Glass: Toddy
Garnish: Freshly grated nutmeg
Method: Gently BLEND all ingredients on a slow speed (without ice) then warm in a saucepan, gently stirring with a whisk, before pouring into a warmed glass. This recipe makes one drink but due to preparation time it is best to make several drinks at a time.

1	fresh	**Egg yolk**
⅔	shot	**Muscovado sugar syrup (2:1)**
1	shot	**Courvoisier VSOP Exclusif**
5	shots	**Harvey's Porter**
¼	shot	**Domaine de Canton ginger liqueur**

We say: To quote Jamie Oliver, "the Huckle-my-buff is not a Dodo but a Phoenix."
Origin: Our adaptation of a recipe presented by Jamie Oliver and Jimmy Doherty in August 2013 at Simon Difford's Cabinet Room bar in London as their entry to the diffordsguide Beer-tail Competition for London Cocktail Week 2013. The competition was filmed for the Channel 4 series 'Jamie and Jimmy's Food Fight'. Huckle-my-buff was joint second to Andrea Montague's De Beauvoir cocktail.

Also known as Huckle-my-butt and Huckle-and-buff, this is a hot drink dating from the early 18th century combining gin or cognac and beer. Long forgotten, Jamie and Jimmy resurrected the Huckle-my-buff and gave it a modern twist with the use of nitrous oxide and a sous-vide immersion in place of the traditional red-hot poker.

The recipe Jamie and Jimmy presented used: 1 fresh egg yolk, 20 grams muscovado sugar, 35ml cognac, 150ml Harvey's Porter beer and 0.8ml ginger juice. The method they used is as follows: whisk egg yolk in mixing bowl and slowly add sugar, cognac, beer and ginger juice while continuing to whisk. Pour mixture into a soda syphon, close and charge with nitrous oxide (laughing gas/N2O). Gently warm the filled cream whipper to 60°C in a sous-vide (water bath). Discharge warmed syphon into glass and then finish with freshly grated nutmeg.

HULA HULA

★★★½☆

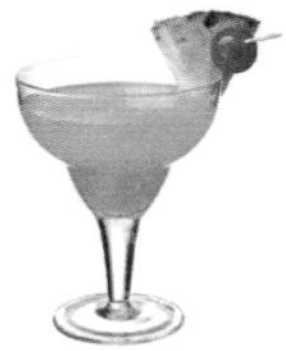

Glass: Martini
Garnish: Pineapple wedge and maraschino cherry
Method: SHAKE all ingredients with ice and fine strain into chilled glass.

1½	shots	**Tanqueray London dry gin**
1	shot	**Triple Sec**
1½	shots	**Freshly squeezed orange juice**

We say: Gin and juice - orange with a splash of orange liqueur.
Origin: Adapted from a drink created by Ray Buhen, one of Don The Beachcomber's original bartenders. In 1961 Ray opened his own Tiki-Ti Bar in Los Angeles, which today is run by his son and grandson.

HULK

★★½☆☆

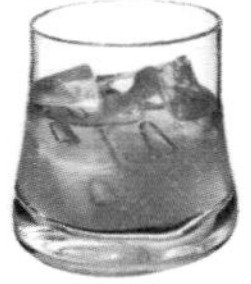

Glass: Old-fashioned
Garnish: None
Method: LAYER ingredients in ice-filled glass by carefully pouring in the following order.

2	shots	**Hpnotiq liqueur**
1	shot	**Cognac VSOP**

We say: Turns green. A waste of good cognac.

HUMMINGBIRD

★★★☆☆

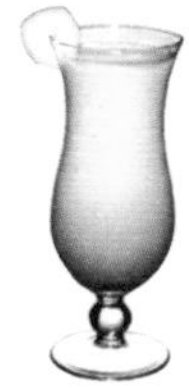

Glass: Hurricane
Garnish: Banana chunk
Method: BLEND all ingredients with a 12oz scoop of crushed ice and serve with straws.

1½	shots	**Bacardi Superior rum**
½	shot	**Kahlúa coffee liqueur**
1	shot	**Bols Banana liqueur**
1	shot	**Coco López cream of coconut**
1	fresh	**Banana (peeled)**

We say: This tall, frozen drink tastes like dessert.
Origin: The house cocktail at the Hummingbird Beach Resort, Soufriere, St. Lucia.

HUNK MARTINI

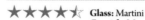

★★★★½

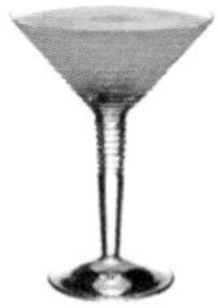

Glass: Martini
Garnish: Maraschino cherry
Method: SHAKE all ingredients with ice and fine strain into chilled glass.

2	shots	**Ketel One vodka**
1¾	shots	**Fresh pressed pineapple juice**
½	shot	**Freshly squeezed lime juice**
¼	shot	**Monin Pure Cane 2:1 sugar syrup**

We say: Pineapple and vanilla combine wonderfully. American readers may notice more than a passing resemblance to a Key Lime Pie.
Origin: The drink Carrie Bradshaw from Sex and the City discovered in the summer of 2003.

HUNTER COCKTAIL NEW

★★★★☆

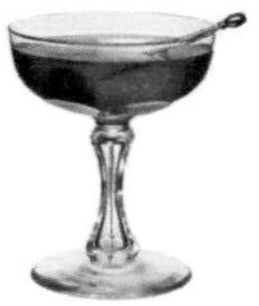

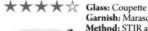

Glass: Coupette
Garnish: Maraschino cherry
Method: STIR all ingredients with ice and strain into chilled glass.

2½	shots	**Maker's Mark bourbon**
½	shot	**De Kuyper Cherry Brandy liqueur**
⅛	shot	**Luxardo Maraschino liqueur**
3	drops	**Orange bitters**

We say: An after-dinner cocktail with a good slug of bourbon sweetened by rich cherry.
Origin: Unknown but the popularity of the Hunter Cocktail has been helped by being recommended by the famous bartender Hidetsugu Ueno San to visitors at his High Five bar in Ginza, Tokyo, Japan.

HURRICANE #1

★★★★☆

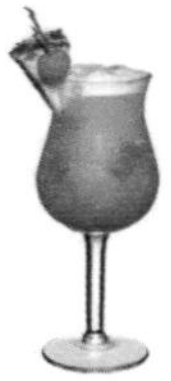

Glass: Hurricane
Garnish: Pineapple wedge and maraschino cherry
Method: SHAKE all ingredients with ice and strain into ice-filled glass.

1½	shots	**Bacardi Superior rum**
1	shot	**Pusser's Navy rum**
1	shot	**Freshly squeezed orange juice**
1	shot	**Fresh pressed pineapple juice**
½	shot	**Freshly squeezed lime juice**
¼	shot	**Passion fruit syrup**
¾	shot	**Rose's lime cordial**

We say: A strong, tangy, refreshing drink packed with fruit and laced with rum.
Origin: Thought to have originated in 1939 at The Hurricane Bar, New York City, but made famous at Pat O'Brien's in New Orleans. Some old cocktail books list a much earlier Hurricane made with cognac, absinthe and vodka.

HURRICANE #2

★★★☆☆

Glass: Hurricane
Garnish: Orange slice & cherry on stick (sail)
Method: Cut passion fruit in half and scoop flesh into shaker. Add other ingredients, SHAKE with ice and strain into ice-filled glass.

1	fresh	Passion fruit
1½	shots	Gosling's Black Seal rum
1½	shots	Bacardi Superior rum
1	shot	Freshly squeezed orange juice
1	shot	Fresh pressed pineapple juice
½	shot	Freshly squeezed lime juice
¼	shot	Passion fruit syrup
¼	shot	Pomegranate (grenadine) syrup

We say: Sweet, tangy and potentially dangerous.

HURRICANE #3

★★★☆☆

Glass: Hurricane
Garnish: Pineapple wedge and maraschino cherry
Method: Cut passion fruit in half and scoop flesh into shaker. Add other ingredients, SHAKE with ice and strain into ice-filled glass.

1	shot	Gosling's Black Seal rum
1	shot	Bacardi Superior rum
½	shot	Galliano L'Autentico liqueur
2	shots	Fresh pressed pineapple juice
2	shots	Freshly squeezed orange juice
¾	shot	Freshly squeezed lime juice
¾	shot	Passion fruit syrup
2½	dash	Angostura aromatic bitters

We say: A veritable tropical fruit salad laced with rum.
Origin: Adapted from a 2006 recipe by Chris McMillian, New Orleans, USA.

HURRICANE NO.1 (ORIGINAL RECIPE)

★★★☆☆

Glass: Hurricane
Garnish: Pineapple wedge and maraschino cherry
Method: SHAKE all ingredients with ice and strain into ice-filled glass.

4	shots	Myer's Planter's Punch rum
2	shots	Passion fruit syrup
2	shots	Freshly squeezed lemon juice

We say: Passion fruit syrup predominates.
Origin: Recipe adapted from Jeff Berry's 1998 'Beachbum Berry's Grog Log' and purported to be the 1960s recipe used at Pat O'Brien's in New Orleans. The recipe was adapted to a rum and juice combination where it was served in 1939 at the World's Fair in New York at the Hurricane bar.

THE HYPNOTIC MARGARITA

★★★★☆

Glass: Coupette
Garnish: Lime wedge
Method: SHAKE all ingredients with ice and fine strain into chilled glass.

1½	shots	Tequila 100% Agave
½	shot	Triple Sec
½	shot	Hpnotiq liqueur
½	shot	Freshly squeezed lime juice

We say: A tangy, fruity Margarita.
Origin: Created in 2005 by Gary Regan at Painter's, Cornwall-on-Hudson, New York, USA.

I B DAMM'D

★★★★☆

Glass: Martini
Garnish: Peach slice
Method: SHAKE all ingredients with ice and fine strain into chilled glass.

2	shots	Bols Genever
½	shot	St~Germain elderflower liqueur
¼	shot	Peachtree peach schnapps
1¾	shots	Pressed apple juice

We say: Subtle combination of fruit and floral flavours.
Origin: Discovered in 2003 at Oxo Tower Bar, London, England.

I'LL TAKE MANHATTAN

★★★★☆

Glass: Martini
Garnish: Maraschino cherry
Method: STIR all ingredients with ice and strain into chilled glass.

2	shots	Maker's Mark bourbon
½	shot	De Kuyper Cherry Brandy liqueur
1	shot	Martini Rosso sweet vermouth
2	dashes	Angostura aromatic bitters

We say: Cherry is more than a garnish in this twist on the classic Manhattan.
Origin: Adapted from a drink discovered in 2005 at The Stanton Social, New York City, USA.

I.V.F MARTINI

★★★★☆

Glass: Martini
Garnish: Coffee beans
Method: SHAKE first four ingredients with ice and strain into glass. FLOAT cream on drink.

1	shot	Absinthe
½	shot	Kahlúa coffee liqueur
½	shot	Tuaca liqueur
2	shots	Hot espresso coffee
1	shot	Double (heavy) cream

We say: Creamy, sweetened absinthe and coffee - hardcore but tasty.
Origin: Created by Giovanni Burdi, London, England. In this case I.V.F stands for 'Italy v France', not 'in vitro fertilisation'.

ICE 'T' KNEE

★★★★☆

Glass: Martini
Garnish: Orange zest twist
Method: STIR all ingredients with ice and strain into chilled glass.

2	shots	Ketel One vodka
1½	shots	Cold jasmine tea
¾	shot	Icewine

We say: Honeyed palate topped off with tannin and jasmine.
Origin: Created by Simon Difford in 2004.

ICE MAIDEN MARTINI

★★★★☆

Glass: Martini
Garnish: Orange zest twist
Method: STIR all ingredients with ice and strain into chilled glass.

1½	shots	Tanqueray London dry gin
1	shot	Icewine
¾	shot	Sauvignon blanc wine
¾	shot	Chilled mineral water

We say: A subtle Martini with the honeyed flavours of icewine melding with botanicals in the gin and balanced by the acidity of the white wine.
Origin: Created in 2004 by Simon Difford.

ICE WHITE COSMO

★★★★☆

Glass: Martini
Garnish: Orange zest twist (flamed)
Method: SHAKE all ingredients with ice and fine strain into chilled glass.

2	shots	Ketel One vodka
¾	shot	Icewine
1¼	shots	Ocean Spray cranberry juice
¼	shot	Freshly squeezed lime juice

We say: Recognisably from the Cosmo family but wonderfully different.
Origin: Created by Simon Difford in 2004.

ICED SAKE MARTINI

★★★★☆

Glass: Martini
Garnish: Cucumber slices
Method: STIR all ingredients with ice and strain into chilled glass.

2	shots	Ketel One vodka
2	shots	Sake
¼	shot	Icewine

We say: The icewine adds interest and wonderfully honeyed notes to this Sake Martini.
Origin: Created in 2004 by Simon Difford.

ICED TEA

★★★★☆

Glass: Collins
Garnish: Lime wedge
Method: SHAKE first six ingredients with ice and strain into glass filled with crushed ice. TOP with cola.

½	shot	Cognac VSOP
½	shot	Gosling's Black Seal rum
½	shot	Triple Sec
½	shot	Freshly squeezed lime juice
½	shot	Freshly squeezed orange juice
2	shots	Cold English breakfast tea
Top up with		Coca-Cola

We say: Sweetened and fortified fruity cola.
Origin: Created in 1990 by Charles Schumann, Munich, Germany.

ICED TEA MARTINI

★★★★☆

Glass: Martini
Garnish: Lemon zest twist
Method: SHAKE all ingredients with ice and strain into chilled glass.

2	shots	Tanqueray London dry gin
1	shot	Cold earl gray tea
½	shot	Martini Extra Dry vermouth
½	shot	Monin Pure Cane 2:1 sugar syrup

We say: Tannic and bittersweet - a very refreshing after dinner drink.
Origin: Created in 2006 by Simon Difford.

ICEWINE MARTINI

★★★★☆

Glass: Martini
Garnish: Orange zest twist
Method: STIR all ingredients with ice and strain into chilled glass.

1½	shots	Ketel One vodka
1½	shots	Icewine
1½	shots	Pressed apple juice

We say: Delicate with subtle flavours.
Origin: Created in 2004 by Simon Difford.

ICY PINK LEMONADE

★★★★☆

Glass: Collins
Garnish: Lemon slice
Method: SHAKE first 4 ingredients with ice and strain into ice-filled glass. TOP with soda.

2	shots	Ketel One vodka
½	shot	Chambord black raspberry liqueur
2	shots	Freshly squeezed lemon juice
½	shot	Monin Pure Cane 2:1 sugar syrup
Top up with		Soda (club soda)

We say: Tangy, citrussy, fruity and refreshing - just not that butch.

IDEAL

★★★★☆

Glass: Martini
Garnish: Almonds
Method: SHAKE all ingredients with ice and fine strain into chilled glass.

1	shot	Tanqueray London dry gin
1	shot	Martini Extra Dry vermouth
1	shot	Martini Rosso sweet vermouth
¼	shot	Freshly squeezed grapefruit juice
⅛	shot	Luxardo Maraschino liqueur

We say: Aromatic and herbal with grapefruit sourness balancing sweeter notes.
Origin: Recipe adapted from a 1937 Bar Florida menu (later renamed Floridita), Havana, Cuba.

IGNORANCE IS BLISS

★★★½☆

Glass: Collins
Garnish: Passion fruit
Method: SHAKE all ingredients with ice and strain into ice-filled glass.

1	shot	Campari Bitter
1	shot	Ketel One Citroen vodka
1	shot	Pressed apple juice
½	shot	Passion fruit syrup

We say: Passion fruit syrup dominates.
Origin: Adapted from a drink created in the mid 1990s by Alex Kammerling, from whom I quote the following words of wisdom, "I once described Campari to a girl - It is like anal sex, it takes a few goes before you actually start liking it." Tsk.

IGUANA

★★★½☆

Glass: Shot
Garnish: None
Method: SHAKE all ingredients with ice and fine stain into chilled glass.

½	shot	Ketel One vodka
½	shot	Tequila 100% Agave
½	shot	Kahlúa coffee liqueur

We say: Coffee and tequila's successful relationship is enhanced by the introduction of vodka.

IGUANA WANA

★★★☆☆

Glass: Old-fashioned
Garnish: Orange slice
Method: SHAKE all ingredients with ice and strain into ice-filled glass.

1	shot	Ketel One vodka
¾	shot	Peachtree peach schnapps
2½	shots	Freshly squeezed orange juice

We say: Orange juice and peach schnapps, laced with vodka.

ILLICIT AFFAIR

★★★½☆

Glass: Old-fashioned
Garnish: Orange slice
Method: SHAKE all ingredients with ice and strain into ice-filled glass.

2	shots	Ketel One vodka
1¾	shots	Freshly squeezed orange juice
1¾	shots	Ocean Spray cranberry juice

We say: Fruity, easy drinking.

ILLUSION

★★★★☆

Glass: Collins
Garnish: Watermelon wedge
Method: SHAKE all ingredients with ice and strain into ice-filled glass.

2	shots	Ketel One vodka
¾	shot	Triple Sec
¾	shot	Midori green melon liqueur
2½	shots	Fresh pressed pineapple juice

We say: This medium-sweet, lime green drink is one for a summer's day by the pool.

IMPERIAL MARTINI

★★★☆☆

Glass: Martini
Garnish: Maraschino cherry
Method: STIR all ingredients with ice and strain into chilled glass.

1½	shots	Tanqueray London dry gin
1½	shots	Martini Extra Dry vermouth
3	dashes	Angostura aromatic bitters
⅛	shot	Luxardo Maraschino liqueur

We say: This rust coloured Martini is very dry despite the inclusion of maraschino liqueur - not for everyone.

IMPROVED HOLLAND GIN COCKTAIL UPDATED

★★★★☆

Glass: Coupette
Garnish: Lemon zest twist
Method: STIR all ingredients with ice and strain into chilled glass.

2	shots	Bols Genever
¼	shot	Luxardo maraschino liqueur
2	dashes	Angostura aromatic bitters
¼	spoon	La Fée Parisienne (68%) absinthe
½	spoon	Monin Pure Cane 2:1 sugar syrup
½	shot	Chilled mineral water

We say: Salmon-pink with subtle juniper, rounded by maraschino liqueur, Angostura bitters and absinthe.
Origin: The classic Holland House "improved" due to the use of genever. This version promoted by the House of Bols also has a hint of absinthe and Angostura bitters.

IN-AND-OUT MARTINI UPDATED

★★★½☆

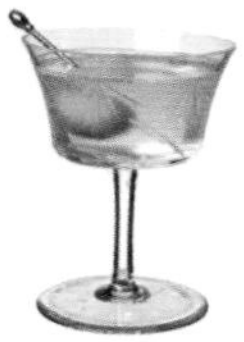

Glass: Martini
Garnish: Chilled olive on stick or lemon zest twist
Method: Gently SHAKE vermouth with ice. Strain and discard vermouth to leave the ice in the shaker coated with vermouth. Add gin, SHAKE again with coated ice and strain into chilled glass.

½	shot	**Martini Extra Dry vermouth**
2½	shots	**Tanqueray London dry gin**

We say: A well-diluted shaken Dry Martini. However, seems like a waste of good vermouth.
Origin: This drinks origin is unknown but former U.S. President Richard Nixon is said to have preferred his Martini made this way.

IN-SEINE

★★★★★

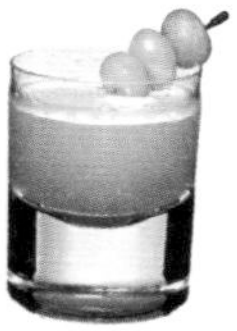

Glass: Old-fashioned
Garnish: White grapes
Method: SHAKE all ingredients with ice and fine strain into chilled glass.

1	shot	**Cognac VSOP**
1	shot	**Maker's Mark bourbon**
1	shot	**St~Germain elderflower liqueur**
	shot	**Absinthe**
½	fresh	**Egg white**

We say: Elderflower liqueur mellows and boosts floral notes in the cognac with the merest dash of absinthe dries and adds a robust hint of aniseed.
Origin: Created in 2006 by Simon Difford at The Cabinet Room, London, England. The name references the fact that St-Germain is a district of Paris on the left bank of the River Seine and absinthe was banned in Paris, partly because it was believed to induce insanity.

INCOGNITO

★★★½☆

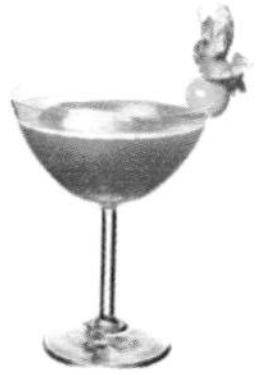

Glass: Martini
Garnish: Apricot slice
Method: SHAKE all ingredients with ice and fine strain into chilled glass.

1½	shots	**Cognac VSOP**
1	shot	**De Kuyper Apricot Brandy liqueur**
1½	shots	**Martini Extra Dry vermouth**
3	dashes	**Angostura aromatic bitters**

We say: Dry with hints of sweet apricot - unusual.

INCOME TAX COCKTAIL UPDATED

★★★★☆

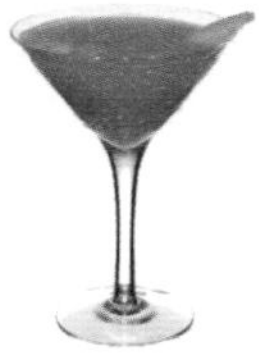

Glass: Martini
Garnish: Orange zest twist
Method: SHAKE all ingredients with ice and fine strain into chilled glass.

2	shots	**Tanqueray London dry gin**
¼	shot	**Martini Extra dry vermouth**
¼	shot	**Martini Rosso sweet vermouth**
1	shot	**Freshly squeezed orange juice**
2	dashes	**Angostura aromatic bitters**

We say: A Bronx with the addition of two dashes of Angostura.
Origin: A vintage cocktail adapted from the classic Bronx Cocktail, created in 1906 by Johnny Solon, a bartender at New York's Waldorf-Astoria Hotel.

INDIAN ROSE

★★★★☆

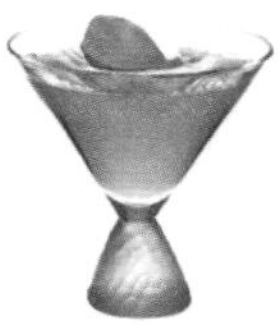

Glass: Martini
Garnish: Rose petal
Method: SHAKE all ingredients with ice and fine strain into chilled glass.

2½	shots	**Tanqueray London dry gin**
¼	shot	**De Kuyper Apricot Brandy liqueur**
¼	shot	**Rose water**
¼	shot	**Rose syrup**
½	shot	**Chilled mineral water**

We say: Subtle rose hue and flavour
Origin: Adapted from a drink discovered in 2005 at Mie N Yu, Washington DC, USA

INDIAN SUNSET

★★★½☆

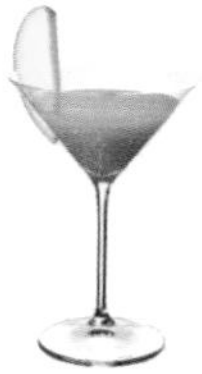

Glass: Martini
Garnish: Mango slice
Method: MUDDLE cardamom in base of shaker. Add other ingredients, SHAKE with ice and fine strain into chilled glass.

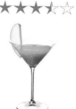

2	whole	**Cardamom pods**
2	shots	**Ketel One vodka**
½	shot	**Domaine de Canton ginger liqueur**
1	shot	**Boiron mango purée**
½	shot	**Freshly squeezed lime juice**
⅛	shot	**Monin Pure Cane 2:1 sugar syrup**

We say: Mango, ginger and cardamom are all classic Indian flavours and here are rum laced with a splash of lime juice.
Origin: Created in 2008 by Simon Difford with David Furnish for Grey Goose's 'Character & Cocktails'.

INDOCHINE

★★★★☆

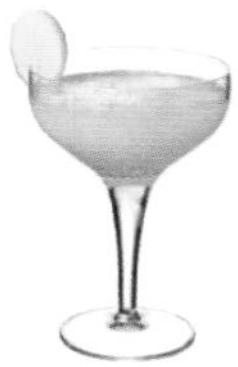

Glass: Martini
Garnish: Fresh ginger slice
Method: SHAKE all ingredients with ice and fine strain into chilled glass.

2	shots	**Ketel One vodka**
1	shot	**Domaine de Canton ginger liqueur**
¾	shot	**Fresh pressed pineapple juice**

We say: Slightly sweet and very frothy. Easy drinking with a ginger kick.
Origin: Adapted from a drink promoted at the end of 2007 by the makers of Canton ginger liqueur.

INGA FROM SWEDEN

★★★★☆

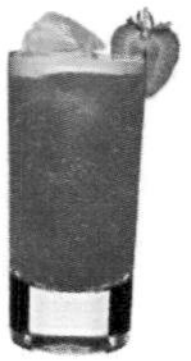

Glass: Collins
Garnish: Strawberry
Method: MUDDLE strawberries in base of shaker. Add other ingredients, SHAKE with ice and fine strain into ice-filled glass.

1½	shots	**Belle de Brillet pear liqueur**
½	shot	**Campari Bitter**
2	shots	**Ocean Spray cranberry juice**
¼	shot	**Monin Pure Cane 2:1 sugar syrup**
¼	shot	**Freshly squeezed lime juice**
2	fresh	**Strawberries (hulled)**

We say: Inga must be a girl who likes a touch of bitter Italian with her fruit.

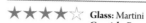

INK MARTINI #1

★★★½☆

Glass: Martini
Garnish: Orange zest twist
Method: SHAKE all ingredients with ice and fine strain into chilled glass.

1¼	shots	Tanqueray London dry gin
½	shot	Peachtree peach schnapps
½	shot	Bols Blue Curaçao liqueur
2	shots	Ocean Spray cranberry juice

We say: This simple, appropriately named drink is surprisingly quaffable.
Origin: Created in 2002 by Gentian Naci at Bar Epernay, Birmingham, England.

INK MARTINI #2

★★★★☆

Glass: Martini
Garnish: Orange zest twist
Method: SHAKE all ingredients with ice and fine strain into chilled glass.

2	shots	Ketel One vodka
½	shot	Bols Blue Curaçao liqueur
1½	shots	Ocean Spray cranberry juice

We say: Surprisingly subtle and pleasant in flavour.
Origin: Discovered in 2005 at Halo, Atlanta, USA.

INSOMNIAC

★★★★½

Glass: Martini
Garnish: Coffee beans
Method: SHAKE all ingredients with ice and fine strain into chilled glass.

¾	shot	Ketel One vodka
¾	shot	Hazelnut liqueur
¾	shot	Kahlúa coffee liqueur
1	shot	Hot espresso coffee
½	shot	Double (heavy) cream
½	shot	Milk

Variant: Espresso Martini
We say: Wonderfully balanced, creamy and caffeine laced.

INTERNATIONAL INCIDENT

★★★★☆

Glass: Martini
Garnish: Dust with grated nutmeg
Method: SHAKE all ingredients with ice and fine strain into chilled glass.

¾	shot	Ketel One vodka
¾	shot	Amaretto liqueur
1½	shots	Baileys Irish cream liqueur
¾	shot	Kahlúa coffee liqueur
¾	shot	Hazelnut liqueur

We say: Rich and creamy.

INTIMATE MARTINI

★★★★☆

Glass: Martini
Garnish: Orange zest twist
Method: STIR all ingredients with ice and strain into chilled glass.

2	shots	Ketel One vodka
1	shot	De Kuyper Apricot Brandy liqueur
½	shot	Martini Extra Dry vermouth
3	dashes	Orange bitters

We say: Sweet apricot dried and balanced by vermouth and bitters. Surprisingly complex and pleasant.

IRISH ALEXANDER

★★★½☆

Glass: Martini
Garnish: Crumbled Cadbury's Flake bar
Method: SHAKE all ingredients with ice and fine strain into chilled glass.

1½	shots	Baileys Irish cream liqueur
1½	shots	Cognac VSOP
1	shot	Double (heavy) cream

We say: Rich, thick, creamy and yummy.

IRISH CHARLIE

★★★☆☆

Glass: Shot
Garnish: None
Method: SHAKE all ingredients with ice and fine strain into chilled glass.

| ¾ | shot | Baileys Irish cream liqueur |
| ¾ | shot | Giffard Menthe Pastille liqueur |

Variant: Float Bailey's on crème de menthe.
We say: The ingredients go surprisingly well together.

IRISH CHOCOLATE ORANJ'TINI

★★★★½☆

Glass: Martini
Garnish: Crumbled Cadbury's Flake bar
Method: SHAKE all ingredients with ice and fine strain into chilled glass.

1½	shots	Baileys Irish cream liqueur
1½	shots	Kahlúa coffee liqueur
1½	shots	Grand Marnier liqueur

We say: A B-52 served 'up'.

IRISH COFFEE

Glass: Toddy
Garnish: Coffee beans
Method: Place bar spoon in glass. POUR whiskey into glass, top with coffee and stir. FLOAT cream.

1	shot	Jameson Irish whiskey
Top up with		Hot filter coffee

AKA: Gaelic Coffee
Variant: Sweeten with sugar syrup or liqueur to taste before floating cream.
We say: Like most great ideas, this one is very simple. Coffee with a whiskey kick. Tip: To ensure a good float, lightly whip or simply shake cream in before pouring over the bowl of a spoon. It also helps if the cream is gently warmed.
Origin: This now ubiquitous cocktail was created in 1942 by Joe Sheridan, a bartender at Foynes airport (near the present-day Shannon airport). The majority of transatlantic flights used to stop to refuel in Ireland and in 1947 an American journalist, Stan Delaphane, found himself at Joe Sheridan's bar and tried his Irish Coffee. Delaphane was so impressed that on returning home he passed the recipe on to the bartender at his local bar, the Buena Vista Café in San Francisco. The recipe spread and the drink became a classic.

IRISH COFFEE MARTINI

Glass: Martini
Garnish: Coffee beans
Method: SHAKE all ingredients with ice and fine strain into chilled glass.

1½	shots	Jameson Irish whiskey
2	shots	Hot espresso coffee
½	shot	Monin Pure Cane 2:1 sugar syrup
1	shot	Double (heavy) cream

We say: Forget sipping warm java through a cold head of cream. This Martini version of the classic Irish Coffee offers all the flavour without the moustache.
Origin: Created in 2003 by Simon Difford.

IRISH ESPRESSO'TINI

Glass: Martini
Garnish: Coffee beans
Method: SHAKE all ingredients with ice and fine strain into chilled glass.

2	shots	Baileys Irish cream liqueur
1¼	shots	Vanilla-infused Ketel One vodka
1¼	shots	Hot espresso coffee

We say: Richly flavoured with a pleasantly bitter finish.

STAR RATINGS EXPLAINED

★★★★★ Excellent

★★★★⯪ Recommended	★★★★☆ Praiseworthy
★★★⯪☆ Commended	★★★☆☆ Mediocre
★★⯪☆☆ Disappointing	★★☆☆☆ Pretty awful
★⯪☆☆☆ Shameful	★☆☆☆☆ Disgusting

IRISH FLAG

Glass: Shot
Garnish: None
Method: Refrigerate ingredients then LAYER in chilled glass by carefully pouring in the following order.

½	shot	Green crème de menthe liqueur
½	shot	Baileys Irish cream liqueur
½	shot	Grand Marnier liqueur

We say: Tricoloured orange and mint smoothed with cream liqueur.
Origin: The Irish tricolour is the national flag of the Republic of Ireland. Its three equal stripes represent the political landscape. Orange stands for the Protestants because of William of Orange, the Protestant king of England who defeated the Roam Catholic James II in 1690. Green stands for the Catholic nationalists of the south and white for the the hope of peace between Catholics and Protestants.

IRISH FRAPPÉ

Glass: Hurricane
Garnish: Coffee beans
Method: BLEND all ingredients with two 12oz scoops of crushed ice and serve with straws.

3	shots	Baileys Irish cream liqueur
2	shots	Hot espresso coffee
2	scoops	Coffee ice cream

We say: A tasty frappé with coffee, cream and a hint of whiskey.

IRISH LATTE

Glass: Toddy
Garnish: None
Method: POUR ingredients into warmed glass in the following order.

1	shot	Hot espresso coffee
1½	shots	Baileys Irish cream liqueur
Top up with		Milk

We say: A latte with extra interest and flavour courtesy of Irish cream liqueur.

IRISH MANHATTAN

Glass: Martini
Garnish: Shamrock (or mint leaf)
Method: STIR all ingredients with ice and strain into chilled glass.

1½	shots	Maker's Mark bourbon
1	shot	Tuaca liqueur
½	shot	Grand Marnier liqueur
¼	shot	Monin Vanilla sugar syrup

We say: There's nothing Irish about this drink, but its good all the same.
Origin: Adapted from a drink discovered in 2001 at Detroit, London, England.

IRRESISTIBLE

★★★☆☆

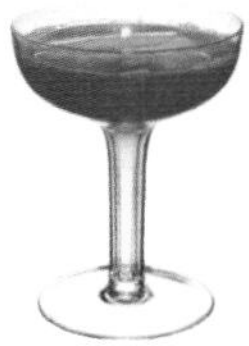

Glass: Martini
Garnish: Lemon zest twist
Method: SHAKE all ingredients with ice and fine strain into chilled glass.

1½	**shots**	**Bacardi Superior rum**
½	**shot**	**Martini Rosso sweet vermouth**
¼	**shot**	**Bénédictine D.O.M.**
¼	**shot**	**Freshly squeezed lemon juice**
¾	**shot**	**Chilled mineral water**

We say: Herbal yet delicate with hints of citrus.

ISLAND BREEZE

★★★½☆

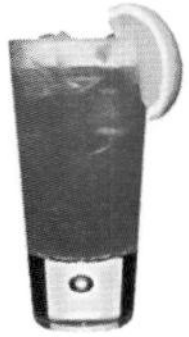

Glass: Collins
Garnish: Grapefruit wedge
Method: SHAKE all ingredients with ice and strain into ice-filled glass.

2	**shots**	**Malibu coconut rum liqueur**
2½	**shots**	**Ocean Spray cranberry juice**
1½	**shots**	**Freshly squeezed grapefruit juice**

We say: Great balance of sweet and sour flavours.
Origin: Named after the Twelve Islands Shipping Company, The Caribbean producers of Malibu.

ISLANDER

★★★★½

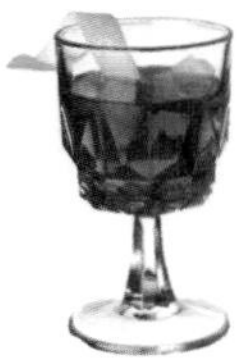

Glass: Coupette
Garnish: Lemon zest twist
Method: STIR all ingredients with ice and strain into a chilled glass.

2	**shots**	**Martini Rosso sweet vermouth**
¾	**shot**	**Dewar's White label Scotch**
¼	**dash**	**Pernod anise**

We say: Vermouth based and bitter-sweet with hints of liquorice and malty, smoky notes.
Origin: Adapted from a recipe by Gary 'Gaz' Regan, Ardent Spirits, New York.

ITALIAN JOB #1

★★★½☆

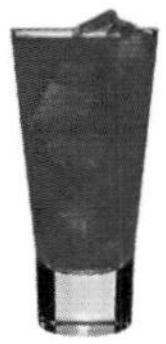

Glass: Collins
Garnish: Orange slice
Method: SHAKE first 6 ingredients with ice and fine strain into ice-filled glass. TOP with tonic water, stir and serve with straws.

¾	**shot**	**Monasterium liqueur**
¾	**shot**	**Campari Bitter**
¾	**shot**	**Mandarine Napoléon liqueur**
1½	**shots**	**Freshly squeezed grapefruit juice**
½	**shot**	**Freshly squeezed lemon juice**
¼	**shot**	**Monin Pure Cane 2:1 sugar syrup**
Top up with		**Tonic water**

We say: This orange coloured drink combines sweet and sour flavours in a most interesting and grown up way.
Origin: Created by Tony Conigliaro in 2001 at Isola, Knightsbridge, London, England.

ITALIAN JOB #2

★★★★☆

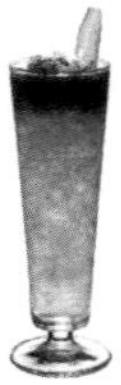

Glass: Sling
Garnish: Orange zest twist
Method: SHAKE first three ingredients with ice and strain into glass filled with crushed ice. TOP with wine and serve with straws.

1	**shot**	**Tuaca liqueur**
1	**shot**	**Amaretto liqueur**
1	**shot**	**Ocean Spray cranberry juice**
Top up with		**Shiraz red wine**

We say: Mix layers with straw prior to drinking for vanillaed, almond, fruity wine.
Origin: Discovered in 2002 at Rapscallion, London, England.

ITALIAN MARGARITA

★★★½☆

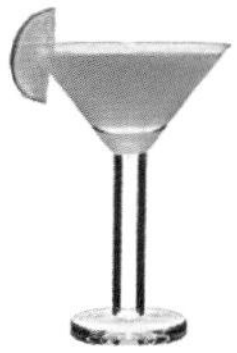

Glass: Martini
Garnish: Lime wedge
Method: SHAKE all ingredients with ice and fine strain into chilled glass.

2	**shots**	**Tequila 100% Agave**
½	**shot**	**Triple Sec**
½	**shot**	**Amaretto liqueur**
1	**shot**	**Freshly squeezed lime juice**

We say: A liberal dash of amaretto adds very Italian subtexts of apricot and almond to your classic Margarita.
Origin: Discovered in 2005 at the Club Bar, The Peninsula Beverly Hills, USA.

ITALIAN MILK PUNCH #2 NEW

★★★★☆

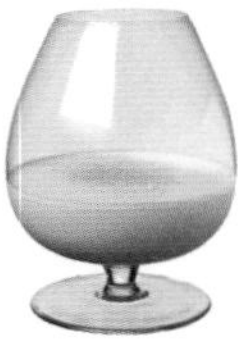

Glass: Snifter
Garnish: Dust with grated nutmeg
Method: SHAKE all ingredients and fine strain into chilled glass.

1½	**shots**	**Italian Brandy**
¼	**shot**	**Galliano L'Autentico liqueur**
½	**shot**	**Amaretto liqueur**
⅛	**shot**	**Grappa di Moscato**
3½	**shots**	**Milk**

We say: The distinctive flavour of moscato grappa shines through in this milky drink, with amaretto adding rich almond notes and Galliano a touch of peppermint and aniseed.
Origin: A riff on the classic Milk Punch created in 2011 by Simon Difford at the Cabinet Room, London, England.

ITALIAN SOUR

★★★☆☆

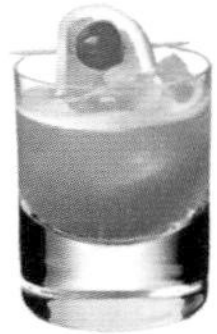

Glass: Old-fashioned
Garnish: Lemon slice & cherry on stick (sail)
Method: SHAKE all ingredients and strain into ice-filled chilled glass.

½	**shot**	**Galliano L'Autentico liqueur**
½	**shot**	**Strega liqueur**
½	**shot**	**Campari Bitter**
1	**shot**	**Freshly squeezed lemon juice**
1	**dash**	**Angostura aromatic bitters**
½	**fresh**	**Egg white**

We say: Perhaps a little too many powerful Italian flavours for one drink.

ITALIAN SUN

★★★★☆

Glass: Martini
Garnish: Lemon zest twist
Method: SHAKE all ingredients with ice and fine strain into chilled glass.

2	shots	Sauvignon blanc wine
1½	shots	Limoncello liqueur
¾	shot	Hazelnut liqueur
½	shot	Freshly squeezed lemon juice

We say: Tastes rather like a bon bon (a round, sugar coated, lemon flavoured sweet).
Origin: Created in 2002 by Dan Spink at Browns, St Martin's Lane, London, England.

ITALIAN SURFER WITH A RUSSIAN ATTITUDE

★★★☆☆

Glass: Martini
Garnish: None
Method: SHAKE all ingredients with ice and fine strain into chilled glass.

1½	shots	Ketel One vodka
½	shot	Amaretto liqueur
½	shot	Malibu coconut rum liqueur
¾	shot	Fresh pressed pineapple juice
¾	shot	Ocean Spray cranberry juice

Variant: Served as a long drink, over ice in a Collins glass.
We say: Fruity and easy drinking but a tad sweet.

IVO

★★★★½

Glass: Coupette
Garnish: Maraschino cherry
Method: STIR all ingredients with ice and strain into chilled glass.

2	shots	Maker's Mark bourbon
1	shot	Martini Extra Dry vermouth
½	shot	Chambord black raspberry liqueur
1	dash	Angostura aromatic bitters

We say: A fruity twist on the Manhattan.
Origin: Named after Quo Vadis London logo, where Simon Difford asked Emma Ramos to make this drink for Charlotte Ashburner, Chambord's UK Brand Manager in December 2009.

JA-MORA

★★★★☆

Glass: Flute
Garnish: Raspberries
Method: SHAKE first four ingredients with ice and fine strain into chilled glass. TOP with champagne.

1	shot	Ketel One vodka
½	shot	Chambord black raspberry liqueur
½	shot	Freshly squeezed orange juice
½	shot	Pressed apple juice
Top up with		Brut champagne

We say: Ja-mora of this fruity champagne cocktail you drink, ja-mora you'll like it.
Origin: Created by Jamie Terrell and Andres Masso in 1998. Named after 'mora', the Spanish for raspberry. The 'j' and 'a' stand for the names of its two creators.

JACK COLLINS

★★★★½

Glass: Collins
Garnish: Lemon slice
Method: SHAKE first 3 ingredients with ice and strain into ice-filled glass. TOP with soda, stir and serve with straws.

2	shots	Calvados/Applejack brandy
1	shot	Freshly squeezed lemon juice
½	shot	Monin Pure Cane 2:1 sugar syrup
Top up with		Soda (club soda)

We say: Apple brandy makes a great base spirit in this refreshing classic.
Origin: A Collins named after its applejack (apple brandy) base.

JACK DEMPSEY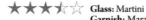

★★★★½

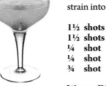

Glass: Martini
Garnish: Maraschino cherry
Method: SHAKE all ingredients with ice and fine strain into chilled glass.

1½	shots	Bacardi Superior rum
1½	shots	Tanqueray London dry gin
¼	shot	Freshly squeezed lemon juice
¼	shot	Monin Pure Cane 2:1 sugar syrup
¾	shot	Chilled mineral water

We say: Dilution makes or breaks this subtle, gin laced drink.

JACK FROST #1

★★★★½

Glass: Old-fashioned
Garnish: Orange zest twist
Method: SHAKE all ingredients with ice and strain into ice-filled glass.

2	shots	Jack Daniels Tennessee whiskey
½	shot	Drambuie
¾	shot	Freshly squeezed orange juice
½	shot	Freshly squeezed lemon juice
¼	shot	Pomegranate (grenadine) syrup

We say: Tangy and fruity with the whiskey base dominating.

JACK FROST #2

★★★★½

Glass: Coupette
Garnish: Sugar rim
Method: SHAKE all ingredients with ice and strain into ice-filled glass.

1½	shots	Cognac VSOP
1½	shots	Chambord black raspberry liqueur
1½	shots	Ocean Spray cranberry juice
½	shot	Freshly squeezed lime juice

We say: Fruits of the forest and cranberry burst forth from this cognac laced, slightly sweet drink.

JACK MAPLES

★★★⯪☆

Glass: Martini
Garnish: Dust with cinnamon powder
Method: SHAKE all ingredients with ice and fine strain into chilled glass.

2	shots	Calvados/Applejack brandy
¼	shot	Maple syrup
1	dash	Orange bitters

We say: Maple syrup smooths apple brandy, even as it enhances its character.

JACK POT NEW

★★★★⯪

Glass: Coupette
Garnish: Strawberry on rim
Method: STIR all ingredients with ice and fine strain into chilled glass.

⅓	shot	Drambuie
¼	shot	Dewar's White Label Scotch
¼	shot	Lagavulin 16yo malt whisky
¼	shot	Jameson Irish whiskey
¼	shot	Welsh single malt whisky
¾	shot	Tanqueray London dry gin
1½	shots	British bitter ale
¼	shot	Pressed apple juice

We say: A truly British beer-tail, garnish with an English strawberry. Named after the Union Jack which symbolically flies over the British Isles. And when we finally nailed the recipe for this drink I thought Jack Pot.
Origin: Created in August 2013 by Simon Difford and Paloma Alos at the Cabinet Room, London, England.

JACK PUNCH

★★★★☆

Glass: Collins
Garnish: Pineapple wedge
Method: Cut passion fruit in half and scoop flesh into shaker. Add other ingredients, SHAKE with ice and strain into ice-filled glass.

1	fresh	Passion fruit
2	shots	Jack Daniels Tennessee whiskey
½	shot	Cuarenta y Tres (Licor 43) liqueur
3	shots	Fresh pressed pineapple juice
⅛	shot	Monin Pure Cane 2:1 sugar syrup
3	dashes	Angostura aromatic bitters

We say: Vanilla hints in the whiskey and liqueur combine to dominate this fruity long drink.
Origin: Adapted from a recipe created in 2002 at Townhouse, London, England.

JACK ROSE

★★★★☆

Glass: Martini
Garnish: Lemon wedge
Method: SHAKE all ingredients with ice and fine strain into chilled glass.

2	shots	Calvados/Applejack brandy
¾	shot	Freshly squeezed lemon juice
¼	shot	Pomegranate (grenadine) syrup
¼	shot	Monin Pure Cane 2:1 sugar syrup
2	dashes	Angostura aromatic bitters
½	shot	Chilled mineral water

Variant: Made better by adding half fresh egg white (substitute for water).
We say: An apple brandy sour sweetened with grenadine. Better when shaken with egg white.
Origin: Like many great classics this drink is served with numerous plausible origins:
1. The Jack Rose is named after the Jacqueminot rose, which in turn takes its name from the French general, Jean-François Jacqueminot. According to Albert S. Crockett's 1935 "*The Old Waldorf-Astoria Bar Book*", it is so called because of its pink colour, the exact shade of a Jacqueminot rose, when properly concocted.
2. Some credit this drink's creation to the Colt's Neck inn in New Jersey, which was originally owned by a member of the Laird's family of applejack distillers. His name was Jack and 'Rose' is said to be a reference to the drink's reddish-pink hue. However, this theory has been discredited by Lisa Laird-Dunn, a ninth generation Laird family ancestor.
3. Other simply claim 'Jack' is short for 'applejack' and again hold that 'Rose' a reference to the drink's colour.
4. According to the Police Gazette of 1905, Frank J. May, better known as Jack Rose, a wrestling bartender who held bar at Gene Sullivan's Café, 187 Pavonia Avenue, Jersey City, New Jersey created this drink.
5. However, the most popular theory relates to a late 19th century New York small-time gangster called Jack Rose who was the informant in a notorious 1912 murder case. 'Bald' Jack Rose, whose favourite beverage is said to have been applejack brandy with lemon and grenadine, was heavily implicated in the 1912 the shooting of Herman Rosenthal, the owner of several New York gambling dens who was in throws of blowing the lid on police and municipal links to organised crime. Rosenthal had already squealed to the press and on the evening of July 15, after the lengthily delivery of his affidavit, left D.A. Charles Whitman's office at around midnight. Fatally he then headed to the Metropole Café at the Hotel Metropole on West 43rd Street, a favourite late night gambler's haunt, for a nightcap. As he exited the Metropole he was killed by four bullets, one to the chest and three to his head. The hit was pinned on a Lieutenant Charles Becker of the NYPD's antigambling squad and Rose was star witness in what was then the trial of the century. Becker went to the electric chair while Rose apparently went into the catering business, lending his name to his favourite drink.
6. Or, alternatively, it could be named after 'Jack Rose', an early 20th century brand of small cigars which sold for five cents a pack. Interestingly, these little cigars became known by the nickname 'squealers' after the Rosenthal case.

BARTENDER'S TIP MUDDLE

Muddling means pummelling fruits, herbs and/or spices with a muddler (a blunt tool similar to a pestle) so as to crush them and release their flavour. (You can also use a rolling pin.)

As when using a pestle and mortar, push down on the muddler with a twisting action. Never attempt to muddle hard, unripe fruits in a glass as the pressure required could break the glass.

JACK TAR NEW

Glass: Old-fashioned
Garnish: Lime wedge
Method: SHAKE all ingredients and strain into ice-filled glass.

1	shot	Pusser's Navy rum
½	shot	Maker's Mark bourbon
½	shot	Tanqueray London dry gin
¼	shot	Freshly squeezed lime juice
¼	shot	Freshly squeezed lemon juice
¼	shot	Muscovado sugar syrup (2:1)

We say: Characterful rum leads with gin and whiskey playing supporting roles with hints of citrus.
Origin: Jack is a generic name for all British sailors, derived from Jack Tar in the 18th and 19th centuries. Sailors in those years used high-grade tar in their clothing and hair for waterproofing. The term, "Jack-of-all-trades," described a sailor who could turn his hand to anything, is widely used today.

JACK-IN-THE-BOX

Glass: Martini
Garnish: Pineapple wedge
Method: SHAKE all ingredients with ice and fine strain into chilled glass.

2	shots	Calvados/Applejack brandy
2	shots	Fresh pressed pineapple juice
2	dashes	Angostura aromatic bitters

AKA: Jersey City
Variant: Pineapple blossom.
We say: Smooth 'n' easy apple and pineapple with spirity spice.
Origin: A classic cocktail of unknown origin.

JACKIE O'S ROSE

Glass: Martini
Garnish: Lime wedge
Method: SHAKE all ingredients with ice and fine strain into chilled glass.

2	shots	Bacardi Superior rum
½	shot	Triple Sec
1	shot	Freshly squeezed lime juice
½	shot	Monin Pure Cane 2:1 sugar syrup
½	spoon	Rose water

We say: In its simplest form this is a Daiquiri with added liqueur - or a Margarita with rum. Whatever, it's a good balance of sweet and sour.

JACKTINI

Glass: Martini
Garnish: None
Method: SHAKE all ingredients and fine strain into chilled glass.

1	shot	Jack Daniels Tennessee whiskey
1	shot	Mandarine Napoléon liqueur
1¾	shots	Freshly squeezed lemon juice
½	shot	Monin Pure Cane 2:1 sugar syrup

We say: A citrus bite and a smooth Tennessee draw enhanced with rich mandarin liqueur.

JACUZZI

Glass: Flute
Garnish: Orange slice
Method: SHAKE first three ingredients with ice and fine strain into chilled glass. TOP with champagne.

1	shot	Peachtree peach schnapps
½	shot	Tanqueray London dry gin
1	shot	Freshly squeezed orange juice
Top up with		Brut champagne

We say: A sweet, peachy champagne cocktail.

JADE DAIQUIRI

Glass: Martini
Garnish: Mint leaf
Method: SHAKE all ingredients with ice and fine strain into chilled glass.

2	shots	Bacardi Superior rum
¼	shot	Triple Sec
¼	shot	Giffard Menthe Pastille liqueur
½	shot	Freshly squeezed lime juice
¼	shot	Monin Pure Cane 2:1 sugar syrup

We say: A Daiquiri with a splash of orange and mint liqueurs. Fresh breath enhancing.

JADE GARDEN

Glass: Collins
Garnish: Lemon slice
Method: SHAKE all ingredients with ice and strain into ice-filled glass.

2	shots	Ketel One vodka
1	shot	St~Germain elderflower liqueur
½	shot	Cold jasmine tea
1½	shots	Pressed apple juice
½	shot	Freshly squeezed lemon juice

We say: Not too dry, nor too sweet, but tasty, balanced and refreshing.
Origin: Adapted from a drink created in 2004 by Michael Butt and Giles Looker of Soulshakers, England

JADED LADY

Glass: Martini
Garnish: Dust with grated nutmeg
Method: SHAKE first four ingredients with ice and fine strain into chilled glass. Carefully POUR blue curaçao through centre of drink (it should sink to the bottom).

1½	shots	Tanqueray London dry gin
1½	shots	Advocaat liqueur
1	dash	Orange bitters
½	shot	Freshly squeezed orange juice
⅛	shot	Bols Blue Curaçao liqueur

We say: Distinctly Dutch in style, this thick, creamy drink delivers orange, vanilla and more than a hint of gin.
Origin: First created by Simon Difford in 1996 but reinvented ten years on.

JAFFA MARTINI

★★★½☆

Glass: Martini
Garnish: Mini Jaffa Cake
Method: SHAKE all ingredients with ice and fine strain into chilled glass.

1	shot	Triple Sec
1	shot	Dark Crème de Cacao
½	shot	Ketel One Oranje vodka
½	shot	Freshly squeezed lemon juice
1	shot	Freshly squeezed orange juice
3	dashes	Orange bitters
1	fresh	Egg

We say: Sweet, dessert-style cocktail.
Origin: Created by Simon Difford in 2004. McVitie's Jaffa Cakes have a tangy orange jelly centre on a hardish sponge base, covered in dark chocolate. Back in 1991 these tasty little snacks beat off UK Customs & Excise who sought to reclassify them as chocolate biscuits, which, unlike cakes, are categorised as luxuries and so subjected to Value Added Tax.

THE JÄGERITA

★★★☆☆

Glass: Martini
Garnish: Lime wedge
Method: SHAKE all ingredients with ice and fine strain into chilled glass.

2	shots	Jägermeister
1	shot	Triple Sec
1	shot	Freshly squeezed lime juice
¼	shot	Monin Pure Cane 2:1 sugar syrup

We say: The bartender's favourite shot meets the bartender's favourite cocktail.
Origin: Created by David Cordoba and demonstrated at Difford's Cabinet Room in September 2008.

JALISCO

★★★★☆

Glass: Martini
Garnish: White grapes
Method: MUDDLE grapes in base of shaker. Add other ingredients, SHAKE with ice and fine strain into chilled glass.

12	fresh	Seedless white grapes
2½	shots	Tequila 100% Agave
½	shot	Monin Pure Cane 2:1 sugar syrup
3	dashes	Orange bitters

We say: It's amazing how well grapes combine with tequila.
Origin: Created in 2003 by Shelim Islam at GE Club, London, England. Pronounced 'Hal-is-co', this cocktail takes its name from the Mexican state that is home to the town of Tequila and the spirit of the same name.

JALISCO ESPRESSO

★★★★☆

Glass: Martini
Garnish: Coffee beans
Method: SHAKE all ingredients with ice and fine strain into chilled glass.

2	shots	Tequila 100% Agave
1	shot	Hot espresso coffee
1	shot	Kahlúa coffee liqueur

We say: A tequila laced wake up call.
Origin: Adapted from a drink created in 2005 by Henry Besant & Andres Masso, London, England, and named after the Mexican state where the tequila industry is centred.

JALISCO FLOWER

★★★★☆

Glass: Flute
Garnish: Grapefruit zest twist
Method: SHAKE first three ingredients with ice and fine strain into chilled glass. TOP with champagne. Lightly stir and serve.

½	shot	Tequila 100% Agave
¾	shot	St~Germain elderflower liqueur
1	shot	Ruby grapefruit juice
Top up with		Brut champagne

We say: Subtle, fruity and one of my favourite champagne cocktails.
Origin: Created in 2008 by Vincenzo Marianella at Doheny, Los Angeles, USA.

JAM ROLL

★★½☆☆

Glass: Shot
Garnish: None
Method: Refrigerate ingredients then LAYER in chilled glass in the following order.

½	shot	Chambord black raspberry liqueur
½	shot	Hazelnut liqueur
½	shot	Baileys Irish cream liqueur

We say: A very sweet jam roll laced with alcohol.
Origin: Created in 2003 at Liquid Lounge, Marbella, Spain.

JAMAICAN ME CRAZY

★★★★☆

Glass: Hurricane
Garnish: Passion fruit & mint sprig
Method: SHAKE all ingredients with ice and strain into glass filled with crushed ice.

1½	shots	Passion fruit juice
2	shots	Bacardi Superior rum
1	shot	Malibu coconut rum liqueur
2	shots	Freshly squeezed orange juice
2	shots	Ocean Spray cranberry juice
1½	shots	Freshly squeezed lime juice
¾	shot	Pomegranate (grenadine) syrup

We say: A rum laced (originally Jamaican), fruity, Tiki-style cocktail.

JAMAICAN MULE

★★★⯪☆

Glass: Collins
Garnish: Lime wedge
Method: POUR ingredients into ice-filled glass and lightly stir.

2	shots	Spiced rum
½	shot	Freshly squeezed lime juice
½	shot	Monin Pure Cane 2:1 sugar syrup
Top up with		Ginger beer

We say: A long, rum based drink with a spicy ginger taste.

JAMAICAN SUNSET

★★★★☆

Glass: Collins
Garnish: Orange slice
Method: SHAKE all ingredients with ice and strain into ice-filled glass.

1½	shots	Wray & Nephew overproof rum
1½	shots	Ocean Spray cranberry juice
3	shots	Freshly squeezed orange juice

We say: Made with vodka as a base this drink would be called a Madras. Overproof rum adds both strength and flavour.

JAMBALAYA

★★★⯪☆

Glass: Collins
Garnish: Orange slice & peach wedge
Method: SHAKE all ingredients with ice and strain into glass filled with crushed ice.

2	shots	Tequila 100% Agave
1	shot	Peachtree peach schnapps
2	shots	Freshly squeezed orange juice
½	shot	Freshly squeezed lime juice
¼	shot	Pomegranate (grenadine) syrup

We say: Peachy tropical fruit laced with tequila.

JAMBOUREE

★★★★☆

Glass: Martini
Garnish: Orange zest twist
Method: STIR preserve with bourbon in base of shaker until mostly dissolved. Add other ingredients, SHAKE with ice and fine strain into chilled glass.

2	spoons	Apricot jam (preserve)
2	shots	Maker's Mark bourbon
½	shot	Grand Marnier liqueur
½	shot	Freshly squeezed lemon juice
¾	shot	Chilled mineral water

We say: Rich and jammy flavours balanced by bourbon and lemon juice

JAMES JOYCE

★★★★☆

Glass: Martini
Garnish: Maraschino cherry
Method: SHAKE all ingredients with ice and fine strain into chilled glass.

1½	shots	Jameson Irish whiskey
¾	shot	Triple Sec
¾	shot	Martini Rosso sweet vermouth
½	shot	Freshly squeezed lime juice

We say: A balanced adult sour blend.
Origin: Created in 2001 by the American drinks author Gary Regan. This recipe is taken from his book, 'The *Joy of Mixology*'.

JAMMIE DODGER NEW

★★☆☆☆

Glass: Shot
Garnish: Biscuit rim
Method: POUR liqueur into glass and then float cream on top.

¾	shot	Chambord liqueur
¼	shot	Double (heavy) cream

Variant: Float Irish cream liqueur (Bailey's) in place of cream.
We say: The sugar and fat will get you before the alcohol does.
Origin: The origin of this drink is unknown but it is named after and inspired by the classic British biscuit produced by Burton's Foods. Jammie Dodgers were launched in 1960 and consist of two circular discs of shortbread biscuit with raspberry-flavoured plum jam sandwiched between with a heart-shaped hole in the upper biscuit to reveal the jam. In recent years the original heart-shaped embossing on the shortbread has been replaced by splashes.

JANIE JONES

★★★⯪☆

Glass: Collins

Garnish: Maraschino cherry
Method: SHAKE first three ingredients with ice and strain into ice-filled glass. TOP with soda.

2	shots	Tanqueray London dry gin
½	shot	Domaine de Canton ginger liqueur
2	shots	Pressed apple juice
Top up with		Soda (club soda)

We say: A long gin laced apple and ginger cocktail.
Origin: Created in 2010 by Mike Atkinson at the Badem House, Goa, India and named after the classic 1970s punk song by British band 'The Clash'. The two maraschino cherries represent Janie Jones herself who famously appeared at a London film premier in 1964 wearing a topless dress.

STAR RATINGS EXPLAINED

★★★★★ Excellent

★★★★⯪ Recommended	★★★★☆ Praiseworthy
★★★⯪☆ Commended	★★★☆☆ Mediocre
★★⯪☆☆ Disappointing	★★☆☆☆ Pretty awful
★⯪☆☆☆ Shameful	★☆☆☆☆ Disgusting

JAPANESE COCKTAIL

★★★★☆

Glass: Martini
Garnish: Lemon zest twist
Method: SHAKE all ingredients with ice and fine strain into chilled glass.

2	shots	**Cognac VSOP**
½	shot	**Monin Almond (orgeat) syrup**
¾	shot	**Chilled mineral water**
2	dashes	**Angostura aromatic bitters**

We say: Lightly sweetened and diluted cognac flavoured with almond and a hint of spice.
Origin: Adapted from a recipe first published in Jerry Thomas' 1862 'Bartender's Guide or *How To Mix Drinks*'.

JAPANESE MAPLE

★★★★½

Glass: Coupette
Garnish: Mist with Angostura
Method: DRY SHAKE (without ice) all ingredients. SHAKE again with ice and fine strain into chilled glass.

1¾	shots	**Yamazaki 12yo Japanese whisky**
¾	shot	**Freshly squeezed lemon juice**
½	shot	**Maple syrup**
½	fresh	**Egg white**

We say: This excellent Japanese whisky based sour is balanced with maple syrup.
Origin: Created in 2009 by Damian Windsor at The Roger Room, Los Angeles, USA.

JAPANESE PEAR

★★★★☆

Glass: Martini
Garnish: Pear slice
Method: SHAKE all ingredients with ice and fine strain into chilled glass.

1½	shots	**Ketel One vodka**
½	shot	**Poire William eau de vie**
1	shot	**Sake**
¼	shot	**Monin Pure Cane 2:1 sugar syrup**

We say: Originally made with Poire William liqueur, hence this version calls for a little sugar.
Origin: Adapted in 2002 from a recipe from Grand Pacific Blue Room, Sydney, Australia.

JAPANESE SLIPPER

★★★★☆

Glass: Martini
Garnish: Salt rim
Method: SHAKE all ingredients with ice and fine strain into chilled glass.

2	shots	**Tequila 100% Agave**
1	shot	**Midori green melon liqueur**
1	shot	**Freshly squeezed lime juice**

We say: A melon Margarita.

JASMINE LASSI COCKTAIL NEW

★★★★★

Glass: Coupette/Martini
Garnish: Lime zest twist
Method: MUDDLE cardamom in base of shaker. ADD other ingredients, SHAKE with ice and fine strain into chilled glass.

1	green	**Cardamom pod**
1½	shots	**Ketel One vodka**
1½	shots	**Bols Natural Yoghurt liqueur**
¾	shot	**Cold jasmine tea**

We say: Fragrant cardamom and jasmine cooled with yoghurt and ice. Best consumed with a Madras.

JASMINE & ELDERFLOWER MARTINI

★★★★☆

Glass: Martini
Garnish: Mint leaf
Method: SHAKE all ingredients with ice and fine strain into chilled glass.

2	shots	**Ketel One vodka**
1	shot	**St~Germain elderflower liqueur**
¼	shot	**Cold jasmine tea**
⅛	shot	**Martini Extra Dry vermouth**

We say: Delicate and floral yet dry and serious. The tannins in the tea compliment and balance the drink.
Origin: Created in 2006 by Simon Difford.

JAYNE MANSFIELD

★★★★☆

Glass: Flute
Garnish: Strawberry
Method: MUDDLE strawberries in base of shaker. Add next three ingredients, SHAKE with ice and fine strain into glass. TOP with champagne.

4	fresh	**Strawberries (hulled)**
1	shot	**Bacardi Superior rum**
1	shot	**Crème de fraise du bois liqueur**
¼	shot	**Monin Pure Cane 2:1 sugar syrup**

We say: Champagne is made to go with strawberries.
Origin: Named after the Hollywood actress.

BARTENDER'S TIP MEASURING - SHOTS & SPOONS

In this guide measures of each ingredient are expressed in 'shots'. Ideally a shot is 25ml or one US fluid ounce (29.6ml), measured in a standard jigger. (You can also use a clean medicine measure or even a small shot glass.)

Whatever your chosen measure, it should have straight sides to enable you to accurately judge fractions of a shot. Look out for measures which are graduated in ounces and marked with quarter and half ounces.

JÄGERBOMB 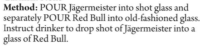 NEW

★★☆☆☆

Glass: Shot
Garnish: None
Method: POUR Jägermeister into shot glass and separately POUR Red Bull into old-fashioned glass. Instruct drinker to drop shot of Jägermeister into a glass of Red Bull.

3	shots	Red Bull
1	shot	Jägermeister

We say: Famous and infamous.
Origin: In Germany this drink is called a 'Turbojäger', a 'Flying Hirsch' with flying referencing Red Bull's marketing slogan "Red Bull gives you wings" and Hirsch (German for 'stag') the Jägermeister logo. In Mexico, it is called a Perla Negra' (Black Pearl) and in Finland, a 'Akkuhappo' (meaning 'battery acid').

A Jäger-train is a theatrical method of preparing a number of Jägerbombs at once. To do this set up a row of old-fashioned glasses with one extra glass than the number of drinkers at the end. Pour half-a-can of Red Bull into each of the old-old fashioned glasses. Pour Jägermeister into shot glasses and balance on the rims where each of the two old-fashioned glasses meet. Starting with the shot glass on the end with the empty glass, push the shot glass so it falls into the Red Bull. If the shot glasses are tall enough in relation to the old-fashioned glasses then the shot glass will knock the next shot glass as it falls so creating a domino effect. A Jäger-ring is a variation of the Jäger-train where the glasses are placed in a circle rather than a line, so eliminating the need for the empty glass at the start of the line.

JEAN GABIN

★★★★☆

Glass: Toddy
Garnish: Dust with grated nutmeg
Method: POUR first three ingredients into glass. Add maple syrup and STIR until maple syrup dissolves.

1½	shots	Gosling's Black Seal rum
¾	shot	Calvados/Applejack brandy
5	shots	Milk
1	spoon	Maple syrup

We say: Beats hot chocolate as a nightcap.
Origin: Created in 1986 by Charles Schumann, Munich, Germany.

JEAN LAFITTE COCKTAIL

★★☆☆☆

Glass:
Garnish: Orange zest twist
Method: SHAKE all ingredients with ice and fine strain into chilled glass.

2	shots	Bacardi 8yo aged rum
¼	shot	Absinthe
¼	shot	Triple Sec
⅛	shot	Monin Pure Cane 2:1 sugar syrup
1	fresh	Egg yolk
1	dash	Peychaud's aromatic bitters

We say: Not dissimilar to spicy, fortified advocaat.
Origin: My adaptation of the New Orleans classic named after the infamous privateer and hero of the Battle of New Orleans.

JEAN MARC

★★★★☆

Glass: Collins
Garnish: Mint sprig
Method: MUDDLE mint and ginger in base of shaker. Add next two ingredients, SHAKE with ice and fine strain into ice-filled glass. TOP with Appletiser, stir and serve with straws.

2	slices	Fresh root ginger (thumbnail sized)
4	fresh	Mint leaves
1½	shots	Chartreuse Green liqueur
¼	shot	Berentzen Apple schnapps
Top up with		Appletiser

We say: Chartreuse combines well with apple, ginger and mint in this summertime drink.
Origin: Created in 2003 by Simon Difford after judging a Chartreuse cocktail competition in London and realising which flavours best combine with Chartreuse. Named after my friend the President Directeur General of Chartreuse.

JELLY BELLY BEANY

★★★★☆

Glass: Martini
Garnish: Jelly Bean sweets
Method: SHAKE all ingredients with ice and fine strain into chilled glass.

1½	shots	Bacardi Superior rum
1	shot	Peachtree peach schnapps
1	shot	Malibu coconut rum liqueur
2	dashes	Orange bitters
½	shot	Chilled mineral water

We say: It's a sweetie but you're going to enjoy chewing on it.
Origin: Created in 2002 at Hush, London, England

JENEVER SOUR

★★★★☆

Glass: Old-fashioned
Garnish: Maraschino cherry
Method: SHAKE all ingredients with ice and strain into ice-filled glass.

2	shots	Bols Genever
1	shot	Freshly squeezed lemon juice
½	shot	Monin Pure Cane 2:1 sugar syrup
½	fresh	Egg white

We say: One of the more delicately flavoured sours.

JEREZ

★★★★☆

Glass: Old-fashioned
Garnish: None
Method: STIR all ingredients with ice and strain into ice-filled glass.

½	shot	Tio Pepe fino sherry
½	shot	Pedro Ximénez sherry
1	shot	Peachtree peach schnapps
1	shot	Sauvignon blanc wine
1	shot	La Vieille Prune plum brandy
1	dash	Angostura aromatic bitters

We say: Sherry depth and stoned fruit flavours.
Origin: This drink heralds from one of the noble houses in Spain - well that's what the sherry PR told us, anyway, we've changed the recipe slightly.

JERSEY SOUR

★★★★★

Glass: Old-fashioned
Garnish: Lemon zest twist
Method: SHAKE all ingredients with ice and fine strain into chilled glass.

2	shots	Calvados/Applejack brandy
1	shot	Freshly squeezed lemon juice
½	shot	Monin Pure Cane 2:1 sugar syrup
½	fresh	Egg white

We say: Apple brandy is possibly the best spirit on which to base a sour.
Origin: The classic name for an Applejack sour.

JEWEL COCKTAIL

★★★☆☆

Glass: Martini
Garnish: Maraschino cherry
Method: STIR all ingredients with ice and strain into chilled glass.

1	shot	Tanqueray London dry gin
1	shot	Chartreuse Green liqueur
1	shot	Martini Rosso sweet vermouth
1	dash	Orange bitters
½	shot	Chilled mineral water

We say: Powerful in both alcohol and flavour. An old-school drink to challenge modern palates.

JOAN BENNETT

★★★☆☆

Glass: Collins
Garnish: Pineapple wedge & maraschino cherry
Method: SHAKE all ingredients with ice and strain into glass filled with crushed ice.

2	shots	Bacardi Superior rum
1	shot	Parfait Amour liqueur
2½	shots	Fresh pressed pineapple juice

We say: Fruity and floral, but an unfortunate colour.
Origin: Adapted from a Tiki drink featured in Jeff Berry's 'Intoxica' and originally created in 1932 at Sloppy Joe's Bar, Havana, Cuba. Named after Hollywood ingénue, Joan Bennett, who starred in Fox;s Careless Lady. Years later she hit the news when her husband, producer Walter Wanger, shot her agent in the crotch after catching them in bed together.

JOCKEY CLUB

★★★★☆

Glass: Martini
Garnish: Orange zest twist
Method: SHAKE all ingredients with ice and fine strain into chilled glass.

2	shots	Tanqueray London dry gin
½	shot	Amaretto liqueur
½	shot	Freshly squeezed lemon juice
¾	shot	Chilled mineral water
1	dash	Orange bitters
1	dash	Angostura aromatic bitters

Variant: Some old books, including 'The Fine Art of Drinks', describe the Jockey Club as a Manhattan with maraschino.
We say: Peachy almond with gin.
Origin: This classic drink from the 1930s originally called for crème de noyaux.

JODI MAY

★★★½☆

Glass: Collins
Garnish: Orange slice
Method: SHAKE all ingredients with ice and fine strain into chilled glass.

1½	shots	Maker's Mark bourbon
½	shot	Triple Sec
2½	shots	Freshly squeezed orange juice
1½	shots	Ocean Spray cranberry juice
¼	shot	Freshly squeezed lime juice

We say: Long, fruity and laced with whiskey.
Origin: Adapted from a drink discovered in 2003 at World Service, Nottingham, England.

JOHN COLLINS

★★★★☆

Glass: Collins
Garnish: Orange slice & cherry on stick (sail)
Method: SHAKE first 3 ingredients with ice and strain into ice-filled glass. TOP with soda, stir and serve with straws.

2	shots	Tanqueray London dry gin
1	shot	Freshly squeezed lemon juice
½	shot	Monin Pure Cane 2:1 sugar syrup
Top up with		Soda (club soda)

We say: A refreshing balance of sour lemon and sugar, laced with gin and lengthened with soda.
Origin: In England, this drink is traditionally credited to John Collins, a bartender who worked at Limmer's Hotel, Conduit Street, London. The 'coffee house' of this hotel, a true dive bar, was popular with sporting types during the 19th century, and famous, according to the 1860s memoirs of a Captain Gronow, for its gin-punch as early as 1814.

John (or possibly Jim) Collins, head waiter of Limmer's, is immortalised in a limerick, which was apparently first printed in an 1892 book entitled 'Drinks of the World'. In 1891 a Sir Morell Mackenzie had identified John Collins as the creator of the Tom Collins, using this limerick, although both the words of the rhyme and the conclusions he drew from it were disputed. But, according to this version of the story, the special gin-punch for which John Collins of Limmer's was famous went on to become known as the Tom Collins when it was made using Old Tom gin.

The original Collins was probably based on genever gin, but there is also debate as to whether it was Old Tom or London Dry. To further complicate the issue a 'John Collins' appears to be exactly the same drink as a 'Tom Collins'. Thus I make a 'Collins' with genever gin, a 'Tom Collins' with old tom gin, and a 'John Collins' with Tanqueray London dry gin. Confused? Then you should also check out the 'Gin Punch' (which has the addition of bitters) and a 'Gin Fizz' which is topped with soda from a siphon.

JOHN DALY

★★★★☆

Glass: Collins
Garnish: Lemon slice
Method: SHAKE all ingredients with ice and strain into ice-filled glass.

1½	shots	Ketel One Citroen vodka
¼	shot	Triple Sec
1½	shots	Freshly squeezed lemon juice
¾	shot	Monin Pure Cane 2:1 sugar syrup
2	shots	Cold English breakfast tea

Variant: Arnold Palmer, Tom Palmer.
We say: Essentially an alcoholic iced tea, this is bittersweet and refreshing - perfect for a hot afternoon.
Origin: Named after the American professional golfer noted for his victory in the 1991 PGA Championship and colourful personal life.

JOL'TINI

★★★★☆

Glass: Martini
Garnish: Coffee beans
Method: SHAKE all ingredients with ice and fine strain into chilled glass.

2	**shots**	**Vanilla-infused Ketel One vodka**
½	**shot**	**Kahlúa coffee liqueur**
1	**shot**	**Hot espresso coffee**

We say: A flavoursome wake up call of espresso coffee laced with vanilla vodka.
Origin: Discovered in 2005 at Degrees, Washington DC, USA.

JOSE COLLINS

★★★★☆

Glass: Collins
Garnish: Orange slice & cherry on stick (sail)
Method: SHAKE first three ingredients with ice and strain into ice-filled glasses. TOP with soda, stir and serve with straws.

2	**shots**	**Tequila 100% Agave**
1	**shot**	**Freshly squeezed lemon juice**
½	**shot**	**Monin Pure Cane 2:1 sugar syrup**
Top up with		**Soda (club soda)**

AKA: Juan Collins
We say: The classic long balance of sweet and sour with tequila adding Mexican spirit.

JOSEPHINE BAKER UPDATED

★★★½☆

Glass: Martini
Garnish: Dust with cinnamon powder
Method: SHAKE all ingredients with ice and fine strain into chilled glass.

1½	**shots**	**Cognac VSOP**
1½	**shots**	**Warre's Otima tawny port**
1	**shot**	**De Kuyper Apricot Brandy liqueur**
¼	**shot**	**Monin Pure Cane 2:1 sugar syrup**
1	**fresh**	**Lemon zest twist**
1	**fresh**	**Egg yolk**

We say: A smooth apricot and brandy dessert-style cocktail with hints of wine and cold tea.
Origin: Recipe adapted from a 1937 Bar Florida menu, Havana, Cuba. This cocktail is named in honour of Josephine Baker (1906-1975), an American-born dancer, singer, and actress. She dropped out of school at just 12-years-old and lived as a street child amongst the slums of St. Louis until her street-corner dancing attracted attention and at 15 she was recruited for the St. Louis Chorus vaudeville show. Baker then became a hit in New York City during the Harlem Renaissance, reputedly "the highest-paid chorus girl in vaudeville".

In October 1925 she moved to Paris and stared at the Théâtre de Champs-Élysées where she appeared practically nude. Her erotic dancing earned her the nicknames Bronze Venus, Black Pearl and Créole Goddess. Baker was a staunch supporter of the Civil Rights Movement in the United States and for assisting the French Resistance during World War II which earned her French military honour, the Croix de guerre.

THE JOURNALIST

★★★★☆

Glass: Martini
Garnish: Maraschino cherry
Method: SHAKE all ingredients with ice and fine strain into chilled glass.

2	**shots**	**Tanqueray London dry gin**
¼	**shot**	**Triple Sec**
½	**shot**	**Martini Extra Dry vermouth**
½	**shot**	**Martini Rosso sweet vermouth**
¼	**shot**	**Freshly squeezed lemon juice**
2	**dashes**	**Angostura aromatic bitters**

AKA: Periodista (Journalist in Spanish).
We say: Like some journalists I've met, this gin Martini is bitter and sour.

JUBILANT

★★★★½

Glass: Martini
Garnish: Orange slice
Method: SHAKE all ingredients with ice and fine strain into chilled glass.

1½	**shots**	**Tanqueray London dry gin**
¾	**shot**	**Bénédictine D.O.M.**
½	**shot**	**Freshly squeezed lemon juice**
½	**shot**	**Freshly squeezed orange juice**
½	**fresh**	**Egg white**

We say: Wnderfully balanced, aromatic, herbal and fruity.
Origin: A long lost classic.

JUDGEMENT DAY

★★★★☆

Glass: Martini
Garnish: Spray of Pimento Dram
Method: SHAKE with ice and fine strain into chilled glass.

1	**shot**	**Macchu pisco**
⅛	**shot**	**Absinthe**
½	**shot**	**Freshly squeezed lime juice**
½	**shot**	**Freshly squeezed lemon juice**
¼	**shot**	**Monin Pure Cane 2:1 sugar syrup**
½	**fresh**	**Egg white**

We say: Charles was pretty sour about his experience when he created this very aromatic sour.
Origin: On 16th May 2008, superstar bartender Charles Vexenat was unjustly jailed in New Orleans during Tales of the Cocktail after Dre dropped a bottle in the Old Absinthe House. Fortunately for Charles he was saved a second day in the slammer by Melanie Asher, owner of Macchu Pisco who bailed them out. This cocktail, created at PDT, New York City, is Charles's tribute to Melanie.

JUDY (MOCKTAIL)

★★★½☆

Glass: Collins
Garnish: Lime wedge
Method: SHAKE all ingredients with ice and strain into ice-filled glass.

2	**shots**	**Freshly squeezed grapefruit juice**
3	**shots**	**Fresh pressed pineapple juice**
½	**shot**	**Freshly squeezed lemon juice**
½	**shot**	**Rose's lime cordial**

We say: A refreshing, not sweet, driver's option. Consider adding a couple of dashes of Angostura aromatic bitters although be aware that these contain some alcohol.

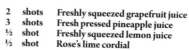

JULEP (GENERIC NAME)

★★★★★★ **Glass:** Collins
Garnish: Mint sprig
Method: Lightly MUDDLE mint leaves with spirit in base of shaker (just enough to bruise). (At this stage, if time allows, you should refrigerate the shaker, mint and spirit, and the glass in which the drink is to be served, for at least two hours.) Add other ingredients to shaker, SHAKE with ice and strain into glass filled with crushed ice. CHURN (stir) the drink with the crushed ice using a bar spoon. Top with more crushed ice to fill glass and churn again. Serve with straws.

12	fresh	Mint leaves
2½	shots	Brandy, whisk(e)y, gin, rum etc.
¾	shot	Monin Pure Cane 2:1 sugar syrup
3	dashes	Angostura aromatic bitters

We say: The key to this drink is serving it ice cold and giving the flavours in the mint time to marry with the spirit. Hence, Juleps are ideally prepared hours in advance of serving. Adjust sugar to balance if using a fortified wine in place of a spirit.
Origin: Juleps are tall drinks generally served in Collins glasses but originally served in julep cups and based on a spirit, liqueur or fortified wine. They are most often served with fresh mint over crushed ice.

The name ultimately derives from the Arabic word 'julab', meaning rosewater. Although this had been used to describe any sweetened drink, up to and including medicines. The Julep is thought to have originated in Persia, or there abouts, and it travelled to Europe (some say Southern France) where the rose petals were substituted for indigenous mint. The drink is then believed to have crossed the Atlantic where cognac was replaced with peach brandy and then whiskey - the Mint Julep we recognise today. The first known written reference to a cocktail-style Julep was by a Virginian gentleman in 1787.

JULEP MARTINI

★★★★★ **Glass:** Martini
Garnish: Mint leaf
Method: Lightly MUDDLE mint in base of shaker (just to bruise). Add other ingredients, SHAKE with ice and fine strain into chilled glass.

8	fresh	Mint leaves
2½	shots	Maker's Mark bourbon
½	shot	Monin Pure Cane 2:1 sugar syrup
¾	shot	Chilled mineral water

We say: A short variation on the classic Julep: sweetened bourbon and mint.
Origin: Adapted from a recipe created in the mid 1990s by Dick Bradsell.

JULES DELIGHT

★★★★★ **Glass:**
Garnish: Strawberry
Method: MUDDLE strawberries in base of shaker. Add other ingredients, SHAKE with ice and fine strain into chilled glass.

3	fresh	Strawberries (hulled)
2	shots	Ketel One vodka
¼	shot	White balsamic vinegar
¾	shot	Pressed apple juice
¼	shot	Freshly squeezed lemon juice
½	shot	Monin Pure Cane 2:1 sugar syrup

We say: Sweet fortified strawberries with a cleansing balsamic vinegar bite.
Origin: Created in 2005 by Julien 'Papa Jules' Gualdoni at Trailer Happiness, London, England.

JULIETTE

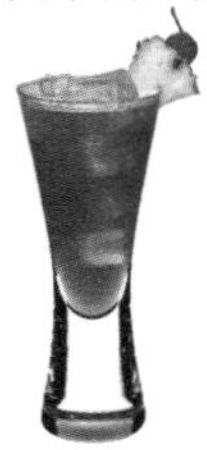

★★★☆☆ **Glass:** Collins

Garnish: Pineapple wedge & maraschino cherry
Method: SHAKE all ingredients with ice and strain into ice-filled glass.

1	shot	Cognac VSOP
1	shot	Belle de Brillet pear liqueur
¼	shot	Chambord black raspberry liqueur
2½	shots	Ocean Spray cranberry juice
1	shot	Fresh pressed pineapple juice

We say: Fruity, medium sweet, cognac laced cooler.

JUMBLED FRUIT JULEP

★★★☆☆ **Glass:** Collins
Garnish: Strawberry & mint sprig
Method: MUDDLE strawberries and then mint in base of shaker (just to bruise mint). Add other ingredients, SHAKE with ice and strain into glass filled with crushed ice.

4	fresh	Mint leaves
3	fresh	Strawberries (hulled)
2	shots	Ketel One vodka
1	shot	Pressed apple juice
½	shot	Passion fruit syrup
½	shot	Freshly squeezed lime juice

We say: A fruity twist on the classic Julep.
Origin: Created in 2005 by Michael Butt and Giles Looker of Soulshakers, England.

JUMPING JACK FLASH

★★★★☆ **Glass:** Martini
Garnish: Pineapple wedge
Method: SHAKE all ingredients with ice and fine strain into chilled glass.

1½	shots	Jack Daniels Tennessee whiskey
½	shot	Bols Banana liqueur
½	shot	Galliano L'Autentico liqueur
¾	shot	Freshly squeezed orange juice
¾	shot	Fresh pressed pineapple juice

We say: Whiskey further mellowed and sweetened by a tasty combo of liqueurs and juices.

JUNE BUG

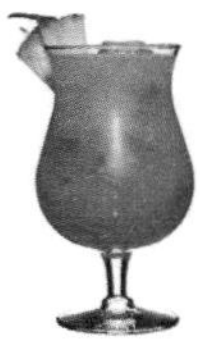

★★★★☆ **Glass:** Hurricane
Garnish: Pineapple wedge & maraschino cherry
Method: SHAKE all ingredients with ice and strain into glass filled with crushed ice. Serve with straws.

1	shot	Midori green melon liqueur
1	shot	Bols Banana liqueur
1	shot	Malibu coconut rum liqueur
4	shots	Fresh pressed pineapple juice
1	shot	Freshly squeezed lime juice

We say: Sweet & fruity.

JUNGLE BIRD

★★★★☆

Glass: Old-fashioned
Garnish: Orange slice & cherry on stick (flag)
Method: SHAKE all ingredients with ice and strain into glass filled with crushed ice.

1½	shots	Gosling's Black Seal rum
½	shot	Campari Bitter
½	shot	Freshly squeezed lime juice
½	shot	Monin Pure Cane 2:1 sugar syrup
2	shots	Fresh pressed pineapple juice

We say: Bittersweet and fruity with good rum notes.
Origin: Adapted from a drink featured in Jeff Berry's 'Intoxica' and originally created circa 1978 at the Aviary Bar, Kuala Lumpur, Malaysia.

JUNGLE FIRE SLING

★★★☆☆

Glass: Sling
Garnish: Orange slice & cherry on stick (flag)
Method: SHAKE first four ingredients with ice and strain into ice-filled glass. TOP with ginger ale, stir and serve with straws.

1	shot	Cognac VSOP
1	shot	De Kuyper Cherry Brandy liqueur
½	shot	Parfait Amour liqueur
½	shot	Bénédictine D.O.M.
Top up with		Ginger ale

We say: Hardly the most refined of drinks, but refreshing nonetheless.

JUNGLE JUICE

★★★★☆

Glass: Collins
Garnish: Orange slice
Method: SHAKE all ingredients with ice and strain into ice-filled glass.

1	shot	Ketel One vodka
1	shot	Bacardi Superior rum
½	shot	Triple Sec
1	shot	Ocean Spray cranberry juice
1	shot	Freshly squeezed orange juice
1	shot	Fresh pressed pineapple juice
¾	shot	Freshly squeezed lime juice
¼	shot	Monin Pure Cane 2:1 sugar syrup

We say: As long fruity drinks go this is not bad at all.

JUNIPORT FIZZ

★★★★☆

Glass: Collins (small 8oz)
Garnish: Mint sprig
Method: SHAKE first 4 ingredients with ice and strain into empty chilled glass. TOP with soda from a siphon.

1½	shots	Tanqueray London dry gin
½	shot	Warre's Otima tawny port
¾	shot	Freshly squeezed lemon juice
½	shot	Monin Pure Cane 2:1 sugar syrup
Top up with		Soda from siphon

We say: This straightforward fizz benefits from the unusual combination of gin and port.
Origin: Created in 2007 by Julian de Feral at Milk & Honey, London, England.

JUPITER MARTINI

★★★☆☆

Glass: Martini
Garnish: Orange zest twist
Method: SHAKE all ingredients with ice and fine strain into chilled glass.

2	shots	Tanqueray London dry gin
⅛	shot	Parfait Amour liqueur
¾	shot	Martini Extra Dry vermouth
⅛	shot	Freshly squeezed orange juice
½	shot	Chilled mineral water

We say: Bone dry and aromatic.
Origin: A classic which is thought to have originated sometime in the 1920s.

THE JUXTAPOSITION

★★★★☆

Glass: Martini
Garnish: Pineapple wedge
Method: STIR honey with vodka in base of shaker until honey dissolves. Add other ingredients, SHAKE with ice and fine strain into chilled glass.

2	spoons	Runny honey
2	shots	Cranberry flavoured vodka
1	shot	Fresh pressed pineapple juice
¾	shot	Freshly squeezed lime juice
3	dashes	Angostura aromatic bitters

We say: Tangy, complex and smoothed by foaming pineapple.
Origin: Adapted from a long drink created in 2003 by Michael Butt and Giles Looker of Soulshakers, England.

K.G.B.

★★☆☆☆

Glass: Shot
Garnish: None
Method: LAYER in glass by pouring carefully in the following order.

½	shot	Kahlúa coffee liqueur
½	shot	Galliano L'Autentico liqueur
½	shot	Cognac VSOP

We say: The initials of this simple peppermint and coffee shooter stand for Kahlúa, Galliano and brandy.

KAMANIWANALAYA

★★★☆☆

Glass: Collins
Garnish: Pineapple wedge & maraschino cherry
Method: SHAKE all ingredients with ice and strain into ice-filled glass.

1½	shots	Bacardi Superior rum
½	shot	Pusser's Navy rum
1	shot	Amaretto liqueur
3	shots	Fresh pressed pineapple juice

We say: Try saying the name after a few of these rum laced, tropical pineapple concoctions.

KAMIKAZE

★★★★☆

Glass: Shot
Garnish: None
Method: SHAKE all ingredients with ice and fine strain into chilled glass.

1	shot	Tequila 100% Agave
½	shot	Triple Sec
½	shot	Freshly squeezed lime juice

Variant: With vodka in place of tequila.
We say: A bite-sized Margarita.

KANGAROO DRY MARTINI

★★★★★

Glass: Martini
Garnish: Lemon zest twist
Method: STIR all ingredients with ice and strain into chilled glass.

2	shots	Ketel One vodka
½	shot	Martini Extra Dry vermouth

AKA: Vodkatini
We say: Temperature is key to the enjoyment of this modern classic. Consume while icy cold.
Origin: Bartending legend has it that 'Kangaroo' was the original name for a Vodkatini and the evidence usually put forward to collaborate this is the drinks listing in later editions of David A. Embury's *Fine Art of Mixing Drinks*. However, the original 1948 edition omits this drink but does list a Vodka Martini served both 'dry' and 'perfect'.

KANU-NO

★★★★☆

Glass: Old-fashioned
Garnish: Orange zest twist
Method: STIR all ingredients with ice and strain into ice-filled glass.

2¼	shots	Bacardi 8yo aged rum
¼	shot	Matusalem Oloroso sherry
⅛	shot	Harvey's Bristol Cream sherry
⅛	shot	Ruby port

We say: The rum's sherry notes are heightened by the addition of port and sherry.
Origin: Adapted from a drink created in 2007 by Mr Ueno at Star Bar, Ginza, Tokyo. Originally served straight-up.

KARAMEL SUTRA MARTINI

★★★☆☆

Glass: Martini
Garnish: Fudge
Method: SHAKE all ingredients with ice and fine strain into chilled glass.

1½	shots	Vanilla-infused Ketel One vodka
1½	shots	Tuaca liqueur
1	shot	Toffee liqueur

We say: Liquid confectionery that bites back.
Origin: Adapted from a drink discovered in 2003 at the Bellagio, Las Vegas, USA.

KATINKA

★★★★☆

Glass: Martini
Garnish: Lime wedge
Method: SHAKE all ingredients with ice and fine strain into chilled glass.

1½	shots	Ketel One vodka
½	shot	De Kuyper Apricot Brandy liqueur
1	shot	Freshly squeezed lime juice
½	shot	Monin Pure Cane 2:1 sugar syrup

We say: Medium sweet, yet also tart and tangy.

KATRINA COCKTAIL

★★★☆☆

Glass: Old-fashioned
Garnish: Dust with grated nutmeg
Method: SHAKE all ingredients with ice and fine strain into chilled glass. No ice!

2	shots	Tequila 100% Agave
¼	shot	Kahlúa coffee liqueur
⅛	shot	Absinthe
¼	shot	Chambord black raspberry liqueur
1	shot	Pressed apple juice

We say: Spicy, fruity tequila served in a style synonymous with the Crescent City - full on!
Origin: Adapted from a drink created in 2005 at Pirates Alley Café, New Orleans, and named after the hurricane which devastated the city in 2005. The name is an acronym of its original ingredients: Kahlúa, Absinthe, Tequila, Raspberry, Ice, Nutmeg and Apple juice.

KAVA

★★★★☆

Glass: Collins
Garnish: Pineapple wedge & maraschino cherry
Method: SHAKE all ingredients with ice and strain into chilled glass.

1½	shots	Bacardi Superior rum
½	shot	Bacardi Oro golden rum
1	shot	Fresh pressed pineapple juice
1	shot	Freshly squeezed lemon juice
¼	shot	Monin Pure Cane 2:1 sugar syrup
¼	shot	Pomegranate (grenadine) syrup

Variant: Multiply ingredients by a factor of four to make a Kava Bowl and serve in ice-filled Tiki bowl.
We say: A wonderfully fruity, fluffy and kitsch Tiki drink.
Origin: Adapted from a drink featured in Jeff Berry's 'Intoxica' and originally created circa 1942 by Trader Vic.

KEE-WEE MARTINI

★★★★☆

Glass: Martini
Garnish: Kiwi slice
Method: Cut kiwi fruit in half, scoop out flesh into base of shaker and MUDDLE. Add other ingredients, SHAKE with ice and fine strain into chilled glass.

1	fresh	Kiwi fruit
2	shots	Tanqueray London dry gin
¼	shot	Freshly squeezed lemon juice
½	shot	Monin Pure Cane 2:1 sugar syrup

We say: The citrus hints in the kiwi combine brilliantly with those in the gin and fresh lemon juice.
Origin: My version of this ubiquitous drink.

KENTUCKY COLONEL

★★★★☆

Glass: Old-fashioned
Garnish: Peach slice & mint sprig
Method: SHAKE all ingredients with ice and strain into glass filled with crushed ice.

1½	shots	**Maker's Mark bourbon**
¼	shot	**Triple Sec**
1	shot	**Boiron peach purée**
¼	shot	**Southern Comfort liqueur**
½	shot	**Freshly squeezed lemon juice**
½	shot	**Monin Pure Cane 2:1 sugar syrup**

We say: Peach and bourbon with hints of orange and spice.
Origin: Created by Morgan Watson of Apartment, Belfast, Northern Ireland.

KENTUCKY DREAM

★★★★☆

Glass: Old-fashioned
Garnish: Lemon zest twist
Method: STIR vanilla liqueur and bitters with two ice cubes in a glass. Add half the bourbon and two more ice cubes. Stir some more and add another two ice cubes and the rest of the bourbon. Add the last two ingredients and more ice cubes and stir lots more. Dilution is essential to the taste of the drink.

½	shot	**Vanilla schnapps**
2	shots	**Maker's Mark bourbon**
½	shot	**De Kuyper Apricot Brandy liqueur**
1	shot	**Pressed apple juice**
2	dashes	**Angostura aromatic bitters**

We say: Tames bourbon and adds hints of apricot, vanilla and apple.
Origin: Created 2002, Wayne Collins, Maxxium UK.

KENTUCKY JEWEL

★★★★☆

Glass: Martini
Garnish: Seasonal berries
Method: SHAKE all ingredients with ice and strain into chilled glass.

1½	shots	**Maker's Mark bourbon**
¼	shot	**Triple Sec**
¼	shot	**Chambord black raspberry liqueur**
2	shots	**Ocean Spray cranberry juice**

We say: Easy sipping, fruity bourbon.
Origin: Adapted from a drink created in 2004 by Jonathan Lamm, The Admirable Crichton, London, UK

KENTUCKY MAC

★★★½☆

Glass: Old-fashioned
Garnish: Mint sprig
Method: MUDDLE ginger and mint in base of shaker. Add other ingredients, SHAKE with ice and strain into glass filled with crushed ice.

2	slices	**Fresh root ginger (thumbnail sized)**
2	fresh	**Mint leaves**
1½	shots	**Maker's Mark bourbon**
1	shot	**Domaine de Canton ginger liqueur**
2	shots	**Pressed apple juice**

We say: Spicy, yet smooth and easy to sip.
Origin: Created in 1999 by Jamie Terrell, London, UK

KENTUCKY MUFFIN

★★★½☆

Glass: Old-fashioned
Garnish: Blueberries
Method: MUDDLE blueberries in base of shaker. Add other ingredients, SHAKE with ice and strain into glass filled with crushed ice. Stir and serve with straws.

12	fresh	**Blueberries**
2	shots	**Maker's Mark bourbon**
1	shot	**Pressed apple juice**
½	shot	**Freshly squeezed lime juice**
½	shot	**Monin Pure Cane 2:1 sugar syrup**

We say: Blueberries, lime and apple combine with and are fortified by bourbon.
Origin: Created in 2000 at Mash, London, England.

KENTUCKY PEAR

★★★★½

Glass: Martini
Garnish: Pear slice
Method: SHAKE all ingredients with ice and fine strain into chilled glass.

1	shot	**Maker's Mark bourbon**
1	shot	**Belle de Brillet pear liqueur**
1	shot	**Pressed pear juice**
1	shot	**Pressed apple juice**

We say: Pear, apple, vanilla and whiskey are partners in this richly flavoured drink.
Origin: Created in 2003 by Jes at The Cinnamon Club, London, England.

KENTUCKY TEA

★★★½☆

Glass: Collins
Garnish: Lime wedge
Method: SHAKE first 4 ingredients with ice and fine strain into ice-filled glass. TOP with ginger ale.

2	shots	**Maker's Mark bourbon**
1	shot	**Triple Sec**
1	shot	**Freshly squeezed lime juice**
½	shot	**Monin Pure Cane 2:1 sugar syrup**
Top up with		**Ginger ale**

We say: Spicy whiskey and ginger.

KEY LIME

★★★★☆

Glass: Coupette
Garnish: Lime wedge
Method: BLEND all ingredients without ice and serve.

1½	shots	**Vanilla-infused Ketel One vodka**
1½	shots	**Lime flavoured vodka**
½	shot	**Monin Pure Cane 2:1 sugar syrup**
½	shot	**Rose's lime cordial**
3	scoop	**Häagen Dazs vanilla ice cream**

We say: Tangy, smooth and rich! Alcoholic ice-cream for the grown-up palate.

KEY LIME PIE #1

★★★★☆

Glass: Martini
Garnish: Pie rim
Method: SHAKE first three ingredients with ice and fine strain into chilled, rimmed glass. SHAKE cream and Licor 43 without ice so as to mix and whip. FLOAT cream mix on surface of drink.

2	shots	**Malibu coconut rum liqueur**
1	shot	**Triple Sec**
1	shot	**Freshly squeezed lime juice**
2	shots	**Double (heavy) cream**
½	shot	**Cuarenta y Tres (Licor 43) liqueur**

We say: This extremely rich drink is great when served as a dessert alternative.
To make the pie rim, wipe outside edge of rim with cream mix and dip into crunched up Graham Cracker or digestive biscuits.
Origin: Created by Michael Waterhouse, owner of Dylan Prime, New York City, USA.

KEY LIME PIE #2

★★★★☆

Glass: Martini
Garnish: Pie rim
Method: Shake all ingredients with ice and fine strain into chilled, rimmed glass.

2	shots	**Vanilla-infused Ketel One vodka**
1¾	shots	**Fresh pressed pineapple juice**
½	shot	**Freshly squeezed lime juice**
¼	shot	**Rose's lime cordial**

We say: Beautiful balance of pineapple, vanilla, sweet and sour.
To make the pie rim, wipe outside edge of rim with cream mix and dip into crunched up Graham Cracker or digestive biscuits.

KEY LIME PIE #3

★★★★☆

Glass: Martini
Garnish: Pie rim
Method: SHAKE all ingredients with ice and fine strain into chilled, rimmed glass.

2	shots	**Ketel One Citroen vodka**
½	shot	**Vanilla schnapps**
1½	shots	**Fresh pressed pineapple juice**
½	shot	**Freshly squeezed lime juice**
¼	shot	**Rose's lime cordial**

We say: My favourite rendition of this dessert-in-a-glass cocktail.
To make the pie rim - wipe with cream mix and dip into crushed Graham Crackers or digestive biscuits.
Origin: Recipe adapted from one by Claire Smith in 2005, London, England.

STAR RATINGS EXPLAINED

★★★★★ Excellent

★★★★½	Recommended	★★★★☆	Praiseworthy
★★★½☆	Commended	★★★☆☆	Mediocre
★★½☆☆	Disappointing	★★☆☆☆	Pretty awful
★½☆☆☆	Shameful	★☆☆☆☆	Disgusting

KEY WEST COOLER

★★★½☆

Glass: Collins
Garnish: Lime wedge
Method: SHAKE all ingredients with ice and strain into ice-filled glass.

2	shots	**Ketel One vodka**
1	shot	**Malibu coconut rum liqueur**
1½	shots	**Ocean Spray cranberry juice**
1½	shots	**Freshly squeezed orange juice**

We say: A coconut laced Breeze that's perfectly suited to the poolside.
Origin: Named after the island near the southernmost tip of the Florida Keys in Florida, USA.

KILLER PUNCH

★★★½☆

Glass: Collins
Garnish: Lime wedge
Method: SHAKE all ingredients with ice and strain into ice-filled glass.

1	shot	**Ketel One vodka**
½	shot	**Midori green melon liqueur**
½	shot	**Amaretto liqueur**
½	shot	**Freshly squeezed lime juice**
3½	shots	**Ocean Spray cranberry juice**

We say: Pretty soft, sweet and fruity as killers go.

KING COLE COCKTAIL

★★★★☆

Glass: Martini
Garnish: Orange & pineapple slices
Method: STIR all ingredients with ice and strain into chilled glass.

2	shots	**Maker's Mark bourbon**
¼	shot	**Fernet Branca**
½	shot	**Monin Pure Cane 2:1 sugar syrup**
½	shot	**Chilled mineral water**

We say: My Fernet loving friends in San Francisco will appreciate this herbal number.
Origin: Adapted from Harry Craddock's 1930 '*The Savoy Cocktail Book*'.

KING'S JUBILEE

★★★★★

Glass: Coupette
Garnish: Lemon zest twist
Method: SHAKE all ingredients with ice and fine strain into chilled glass.

2	shots	**Bacardi Superior rum**
¾	shot	**Luxardo Maraschino liqueur**
½	shot	**Freshly squeezed lemon juice**

We say: If there is such a thing as a 'Rum Aviation', then this is surely it.
Origin: Recipe adapted from W.J. Tarling's 1937 '*Cafe Royal Cocktail Book* - Coronation Edition' in which Tarling credits this drink's creation to Harry Craddock, the then head bartender of the American Bar at London's Savoy Hotel.

KIR UPDATED

★★★⯪☆

Glass: Goblet
Garnish: None
Method: POUR cassis into glass and TOP with chilled wine.

½ shot   Crème de cassis liqueur
Top up with   Bourgogne Aligoté white wine

Variant: Kir Royale with champagne in place of Bourgogne Aligoté.
We say: Traditionally made ⅓ cassis to ⅔ wine, that's too sweet for most modern palates. Made to the above formula this blackcurrant wine concoction is clean, crisp and not too sweet. Adjust your ratio to taste.
Origin: The origins of Kir are said to date back to 1904 when a waiter named Faivre first had the idea of mixing white wine with crème de cassis at the Café Georges in Dijon, France. His new drink became known as the 'Cassis Blanc'.

The drink takes its now better known 'Kir' name from a colourful politician and WWII resistance hero by the name of Canon Félix Kir, who served as the Mayor of Dijon, France. In order to promote regional products and rescue the local 'Bourgogne Aligoté' white wines from economic doom, he served the Cassis Blanc aperitif at official functions. The Cannon popularised the concoction and it quickly became known as Canon Kir's aperitif, then Father Kir's aperitif and finally as the Kir aperitif.

Félix Kir led quite a life. He was a Catholic priest at the outbreak of the Second World War, but became a major resistance fighter against the German occupation earning him the French Honour Cross in 1946. The same year, he became a member of the French Parliament as a "député" and the mayor of Dijon, a position he retained until his death (aged 92) in 1968.

Bourgogne Aligoté is an Appellation d'Origine Contrôlée (AOC) white wine produced from the Aligoté grape variety in the France's Burgundy region. Bourgogne Aligoté tend to be light and acidic in style and are usually un-oaked. The appellation allows up to 15 per cent Chardonnay to be blended into Bourgogne Aligoté so we suggest substituting with a un-oaked Chardonnay if you are unable to source Bourgogne Aligoté.

KIR COCKTAIL UPDATED

★★★⯪☆

Glass: Martini
Garnish: Seasonal berries
Method: STIR all ingredients with ice and strain into chilled glass.

2 shots   Ketel One vodka
1 shot   Bourgogne Aligoté white wine
1 shot   Crème de cassis liqueur

We say: Canon Félix Kir traditional white wine and cassis aperitif with added vodka 'oomph'.
Origin: Created by Simon Difford in 2004. Canon Kir served as the Mayor of Dijon, France (1946-1968) and at receptions he served an aperitif made with locally made crème de cassis and Bourgogne Aligoté white wine. The concoction eventually became known as Kir aperitif.

KIR ROYALE UPDATED

★★★⯪☆

Glass: Flute
Garnish: Blackcurrants
Method: POUR cassis into glass and TOP with champagne.

½ shot   Crème de cassis liqueur
Top up with   Brut champagne

Variant: Kir
We say: Champagne replaces Bourgogne Aligoté white wine in this 'Royal' rendition of Mayor Canon Kir's classic aperitif. Easy to make, easy to drink.
Origin: As outlined in our origin for 'Kir', this drink is named after Canon Félix Kir, who served as the Mayor of Dijon, France 1945-1968 and popularised the drink by serving at official functions. In 1951, when the drink was becoming well-known, members of the Damidot family, owners of the Lejay-Lagoutte brand of cassis and the largest liqueur producer in the region, asked the mayor for his authorisation to use his (Kir) name commercially.

Probably flattered, he agreed and on 20 November 1951, on a French National Assembly letterhead, wrote: "Canon Félix Kir, Member of Parliament and Mayor of Dijon, gives exclusively to the house of Lejay Lagoute, currently represented by Roger Damidot, the right to use his name for blackcurrant liqueur advertising purposes, in the form he sees fit, and notably to designate a 'vin blanc cassis'." Armed with this letter, Lejay Lagoute patented the brand name 'KIR' in March 1952.

Years later, after seeing the increasing popularity of kir as an aperitif, the cannon sought to offer other cassis makers the same privilege but due to Lejay-Lagoutte having already registered the "Kir" trade mark he was too late. Numerous court challenges ensued propelling the case to the highest court, 'Cour de Cassation' where on 27-October 1992 it confirmed that Lejay-Lagoutte has the exclusive rights to the 'Kir' trademark.

Lejay-Lagoutte now produce a pre-mixed cassis and sparkling wine product called 'Kir Royal'.

KIRSCH COSMO NEW

★★★★⯪

Glass: Martini
Garnish: Orange zest twist
Method: SHAKE all ingredients with ice and fine strain into chilled glass.

1 shot   Kirsch eau-de-vie
1 shot   Cointreau triple sec
1½ shots   Ocean Spray cranberry juice
½ shot   Freshly squeezed lime juice

We say: As the name suggests this is riff on the classic Cosmopolitan using kirsch eau de vie in place of vodka.
Origin: Adapted from a drink created in 2013 by Hannah Lanfear at Boisdale, Canary Wharf, London.

KISS OF DEATH

★★⯪☆☆

Glass: Shot
Garnish: None
Method: Take sambuca from freezer and Galliano from refrigerator then LAYER in chilled glass by carefully pouring in the following order.

¾ shot   Luxardo Sambuca dei Cesari
¾ shot   Galliano L'Autentico liqueur

We say: Will give you fresh breath with which to apply that kiss.

KIWI BATIDA

★★★☆☆

Glass: Collins
Garnish: Kiwi slice
Method: Cut kiwi in half and scoop flesh into blender. Add other ingredients and BLEND with 18oz scoop crushed ice until smooth. Serve with straws.

2½	shots	Leblon cachaça
1	fresh	Kiwi fruit
1	shot	Monin Pure Cane 2:1 sugar syrup

We say: The kiwi fruit flavour is a little lacking so this drink is improved by using kiwi-flavoured sugar syrup.

KIWI BELLINI

★★★★☆

Glass: Flute
Garnish: Kiwi slice
Method: Cut kiwi in half, scoop out flesh into base of shaker and MUDDLE. Add next three ingredients, SHAKE with ice and fine strain into chilled glass. TOP with prosecco.

1	fresh	Kiwi fruit
1¼	shots	Ketel One vodka
¼	shot	Freshly squeezed lemon juice
¼	shot	Monin Pure Cane 2:1 sugar syrup
Top up with		Prosecco sparkling wine

We say: Lemon fresh kiwi, fortified with vodka and charged with prosecco.
Origin: Adapted from a drink discovered at Zuma, London, England, in 2004.

KIWI COLLINS 🔑

★★★★☆

Glass: Collins
Garnish: Kiwi slice
Method: Cut kiwi fruit in half, scoop out flesh into base of shaker and MUDDLE. Add next three ingredients, SHAKE with ice and fine strain into ice-filled glass. TOP with soda water.

1	fresh	Kiwi fruit
2	shots	Ketel One vodka
1½	shots	Freshly squeezed lemon juice
½	shot	Monin Pure Cane 2:1 sugar syrup
Top up with		Soda (club soda)

We say: A fruity adaptation of a Vodka Collins.
Origin: Formula by Simon Difford.

KIWI CRUSH

★★★★☆

Glass: Martini
Garnish: Kiwi slice
Method: Cut kiwi fruit in half, scoop out flesh into base of shaker and MUDDLE. Add other ingredients, SHAKE with ice and fine strain into chilled glass.

1	fresh	Kiwi fruit
2	shots	Ketel One Citroen vodka
1	shot	Pressed apple juice
½	shot	Freshly squeezed lemon juice
¼	shot	Monin Almond (orgeat) syrup

We say: Spirit laced kiwi, citrus and almond.
Origin: Adapted from a recipe by Claire Smith in 2005, London, England.

KIWI MARTINI (SIMPLE) 🔑

★★★★☆

Glass: Martini
Garnish: Kiwi slice
Method: Cut kiwi fruit in half, scoop out flesh into base of shaker and MUDDLE. Add other ingredients, SHAKE with ice and fine strain into chilled glass.

1	fresh	Kiwi fruit
2	shots	Ketel One vodka
½	shot	Monin Pure Cane 2:1 sugar syrup

We say: You may need to adjust the sugar depending on the ripeness of your fruit.
Origin: Formula by Simon Difford in 2004.

KLONDIKE 🔑

★★★½☆

Glass: Collins
Garnish: Orange slice
Method: POUR ingredients into ice-filled glass and stir.

2	shots	Maker's Mark bourbon
2	shots	Freshly squeezed orange juice
Top up with		Ginger ale

We say: A simple drink but the three ingredients combine well.
Origin: Recipe adapted from A. S. Crockett's 1935 'The Old Waldorf-Astoria Bar Book'.

KNICKER DROPPER GLORY

★★★★☆

Glass: Shot
Garnish: None
Method: SHAKE all ingredients with ice and fine strain into chilled glass.

| 1 | shot | Hazelnut liqueur |
| ½ | shot | Freshly squeezed lemon juice |

We say: Nutty sweetness sharpened with lemon.
Origin: Created circa 2000 by Jason Fendick, London, England.

KNICKERBOCKER MARTINI 🔑

★★★½☆

Glass: Martini
Garnish: Orange zest twist
Method: STIR all ingredients with ice and strain into chilled glass.

1¾	shots	Tanqueray London dry gin
¾	shot	Martini Extra Dry vermouth
½	shot	Martini Rosso sweet vermouth

We say: Aromatic vermouth dominates this flavoursome Martini variant.
Origin: Thought to have been created at the Knickerbocker Hotel, New York City, USA.

KNICKERBOCKER SPECIAL

★★★★☆

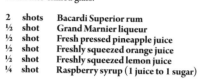

Glass: Martini
Garnish: Pineapple wedge & maraschino cherry
Method: SHAKE all ingredients with ice and fine strain into chilled glass.

2	shots	Bacardi Superior rum
½	shot	Grand Marnier liqueur
½	shot	Fresh pressed pineapple juice
½	shot	Freshly squeezed orange juice
½	shot	Freshly squeezed lemon juice
¼	shot	Raspberry syrup (1 juice to 1 sugar)

We say: Easy drinking rum and orange curaçao, flavoured with pineapple and raspberry.
Origin: Thought to have been created sometime in the mid 19th century at the Knickerbocker Hotel, New York City, USA.

KNOCKOUT MARTINI

★★★½☆

Glass: Martini
Garnish: Star anise
Method: STIR all ingredients with ice and strain into chilled glass.

1½	shots	Tanqueray London dry gin
1½	shots	Martini Extra Dry vermouth
¼	shot	Absinthe
¼	shot	Giffard Menthe Pastille liqueur

We say: A Wet Martini with hints of aniseed and mint. Stir well as it benefits from dilution.

KOI YELLOW

★★★★☆

Glass: Martini
Garnish: Rose petal
Method: SHAKE all ingredients with ice and fine strain into chilled glass.

2	shots	Raspberry flavoured vodka
½	shot	Triple Sec
1	shot	Freshly squeezed lemon juice
½	shot	Monin Pure Cane 2:1 sugar syrup

We say: Sherbet raspberry Martini with a sweet and citrus sour finish.
Origin: The signature drink at Koi Restaurant, Los Angeles, USA.

KOOL HAND LUKE UPDATED

★★★★☆

Glass: Rocks
Garnish: Lime wedge
Method: MUDDLE lime in base of glass to release juices. POUR other ingredients into glass, add crushed ice and CHURN (stir). Serve with straws.

1	fresh	Lime
2	shots	Myer's dark Jamaican rum
1	shot	Monin Pure Cane 2:1 sugar syrup
2	dashes	Angostura aromatic bitters

We say: This looks like a Caipirinha and has a similar balance of sweet, sour and spirit. The bitters bring out the spice in the rum, which is every bit as pungent as cachaça.

KOPSTOOT NEW

★★★★½

Glass: Shot and Beer
Method: POUR genever into shot glass and beer into beer glass. To enjoy, simply sip a shot of ice-cold genever from a small, tulip-shaped glass, then follow with a sip of beer.

| ½ | shot | Bols Genever |
| ½ | pint | Dark beer |

We say: In the worthy pursuit of responsible drinking I must stress that when enjoying a Kopstoot you should repeatedly take a sip from each glass – savour the combination rather than shooting the genever in one gulp.
Origin: The traditional Dutch way to drink genever, Kopstoot (pronounced 'Cop-Stout') translates as 'a blow for your head'.

KOOLAID

★★★★☆

Glass: Collins
Garnish: Lime wedge
Method: SHAKE all ingredients with ice and strain into ice-filled glass.

1½	shots	Ketel One vodka
¾	shot	Midori green melon liqueur
¾	shot	Amaretto liqueur
½	shot	Freshly squeezed lime juice
2	shots	Ocean Spray cranberry juice
1	shot	Freshly squeezed orange juice

We say: Tangy liquid marzipan with hints if melon cranberry and orange juice.
Origin: A drink with unknown origins that emerged and morphed during the 1990s.

KRAKOW TEA

★★★★☆

Glass: Collins
Garnish: Lime wedge & mint sprig
Method: Lightly MUDDLE mint in base of shaker (just to bruise). SHAKE all ingredients with ice and fine strain into ice-filled glass.

12	fresh	Mint leaves
2	shots	Żubrówka bison vodka
1	shot	Cold camomile tea
3½	shots	Pressed apple juice
¼	shot	Freshly squeezed lime juice
¼	shot	Monin Pure Cane 2:1 sugar syrup

We say: Refreshing and floral with a dry, citrus finish.
Origin: Created in 2002 by Domhnall Carlin at Apartment, Belfast, Northern Ireland

KRETCHMA

★★★½☆

Glass: Martini
Garnish: Dust with chocolate powder
Method: SHAKE all ingredients with ice and fine strain into chilled glass.

2	shots	Ketel One vodka
¾	shot	White Crème de Cacao
½	shot	Freshly squeezed lemon juice
⅛	shot	Pomegranate (grenadine) syrup

Variant: Without grenadine this is a 'Ninitchka'.
We say: Fortified Turkish Delight.
Origin: Adapted from a recipe in David Embury's 'The Fine Art of Mixing Drinks'.

KURRANT AFFAIR

★★★☆☆

Glass: Collins
Garnish: Lemon slice
Method: SHAKE all ingredients with ice and strain into ice-filled glass.

1½	shots	**Ketel One Citroen vodka**
¾	shot	**Berry flavoured vodka**
3	shots	**Pressed apple juice**

We say: Berry and citrus vodka combine with apple in this tall, refreshing and summery drink.

L'AMOUR EN FUITE

★★★★☆

Glass: Old-fashioned
Garnish: Orange zest twist
Method: POUR absinthe into ice-filled glass, TOP with water and leave to stand. Separately STIR gin, vermouth and elderflower liqueur with ice. DISCARD contents of glass (absinthe, water and ice) and STRAIN contents of mixing glass into absinthe-coated glass. No ice!

½	shot	**Absinthe**
1½	shots	**Tanqueray London dry gin**
¾	shot	**Martini Extra Dry vermouth**
¼	shot	**St~Germain elderflower liqueur**

We say: Serious yet approachably subtle with hints of vermouth and elderflower dominated by absinthe and gin.
Origin: Created in 2007 by Jamie Boudreau, Seattle, USA, originally using Lillet. The name comes from a 1979 French film.

L.A. ICED TEA UPDATED

★★★½☆

Glass: Sling
Garnish: Lime wedge
Method: SHAKE first 7 ingredients with ice and strain into ice-filled glass. TOP with soda.

½	shot	**Ketel One vodka**
½	shot	**Tanqueray London dry gin**
½	shot	**Rum light white/blanco**
½	shot	**Cointreau triple sec**
½	shot	**Chambord liqueur**
1	shot	**Freshly squeezed lime juice**
½	shot	**Monin Pure Cane 2:1 sugar syrup**
Top up with		**Soda (club soda)**

We say: Long and lime green with subtle notes of melon and fresh lime.

LA BICYCLETTE NEW

★★★½☆

Glass: Coupette
Garnish: Lemon zest twist
Method: STIR all ingredients with ice and strain.

2	shots	**Tanqueray London dry gin**
½	shot	**Martini Rosso sweet vermouth**
¼	shot	**St~Germain elderflower liqueur**
2	dashes	**Peach bitters**

We say: A light and fragrant Sweet Martini-style drink with elderflower liqueur and peach bitters.
Origin: Adapted from a drink created in 2008 by Jamie Boudreau, Seattle, USA.

LA DOLCE VITA

★★★★½

Glass: Martini
Garnish: Lemon zest twist
Method: MUDDLE grapes in base of shaker. Add vodka, honey and bitters, SHAKE with ice and fine strain into chilled glass. TOP with prosecco.

4	fresh	**Seedless white grapes**
1	shot	**Ketel One vodka**
1	spoon	**Runny honey**
1	dash	**Orange bitters**
Top up with		**Prosecco sparkling wine**

We say: Complex, yet easy to quaff with grape juice, vodka, honey and a touch of fizz.
Origin: Created in 2002 by Tony Conigliaro at Isola, London, England

LA FEUILLE MORTE

★★★½☆

Glass: Collins
Garnish: None
Method: POUR first 3 ingredients into glass. Serve iced water separately in a small jug (known in France as a 'broc') so the customer can dilute to their own taste. (I recommend five shots). Lastly, add ice to fill glass.

1	shot	**Ricard Pastis**
½	shot	**Pomegranate (grenadine) syrup**
½	shot	**Mint (menthe) syrup**
Top up with		**Chilled mineral water**

We say: A traditional French way to serve pastis.
Origin: Pronounced 'Fueel-Mort', the name literally means 'The dead leaf', a reference to its colour.

LA LOUISIANE COCKTAIL NEW

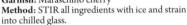

★★★★½

Glass: Coupette
Garnish: Maraschino cherry
Method: STIR all ingredients with ice and strain into chilled glass.

1	shot	**Straight rye whiskey**
½	shot	**Bénédictine D.O.M.**
1	shot	**Martini Rosso sweet vermouth**
⅛	shot	**Absinthe**
2	dashes	**Peychaud's aromatic bitters**
¾	shot	**Chilled mineral water**

We say: A rye-based Sweet Manhattan made even sweeter with herbal Bènèdictine liqueur and bittered with Peychaud's and absinthe.
Origin: Recipe adapted from Stanley Clisby Arthur's 1937 book 'Famous New Orleans Drinks and How to Mix 'Em' in which he wrote, This is the special cocktail served at Restaurant de la Louisiane, one of the famous French restaurants of New Orleans, long the rendezvous of those who appreciate the best in Creole cuisine. La Louisiane cocktail is as out-of-the-ordinary as the many distinctive dishes that grace its menu.

LA MOMIE

★★★☆☆

Glass: Shot
Garnish: None
Method: POUR pastis into chilled glass and top with chilled water.

½	shot	**Ricard Pastis**
Top up with		**Chilled mineral water**

Origin: Pronounced 'Mom-Ee', this shot is very popular in the South of France.

LA PERLA NEW

★★★★★

Glass: Coupette
Garnish: Lemon zest twist
Method: STIR ingredients with ice and strain into chilled glass.

1½	shots	**Tequila 100% Agave**
1½	shots	**Manzanilla Sherry**
¾	shot	**Belle de Brillet pear liqueur**

We say: Dry salty sherry with dry salty tequila, sweetened with pear and cognac liqueur.
Origin: Adapted from a drink created in 2010 by Jacques Bezuidenhout, San Francisco, USA.

LA ROSA MARGARITA

★★★★☆

Glass: Coupette
Garnish: Lime wedge
Method: SHAKE all ingredients with ice and fine strain into chilled glass.

2	shots	**Tequila 100% Agave**
¾	shot	**Crème de Mûre liqueur**
1	shot	**Cold hibiscus tea (strong brewed)**
½	shot	**Freshly squeezed lime juice**

We say: A fruity yet dry crimson-coloured Margarita

LA SANG

★★★★☆

Glass: Collins
Garnish: Chopped fruit
Method: SHAKE all ingredients with ice and strain into ice-filled glass.

2	shots	**Cognac VSOP**
2	shots	**Shiraz red wine**
2	shots	**Freshly squeezed orange juice**
¼	shot	**Monin Pure Cane 2:1 sugar syrup**

We say: The tannin in the wine balances the fruit and sweetness nicely.
Origin: French for 'blood', this cocktail is a twist on the classic Spanish Sangria, which also means 'blood'

LA TOUR EIFFEL NEW

★★★★☆

Glass: Flute
Garnish: Lemon zest twist
Method: STIR all ingredients with ice and fine strain into chilled glass.

2½	shots	**Courvoisier VSOP Exclusif**
½	shot	**Cointreau triple sec**
½	shot	**Suze gentaine liqueur**
1	dash	**La Fée Parisienne (68%) absinthe**

We say: Bitter sweet cognac-influenced palate with lingering flavours of liquorice root, honey, pine and eucalyptus from the Suze.
Origin: Adapted from a drink created in 2007 by Gary Regan after a Sazerac-fuelled trip to New Orleans. He was inspired by how the Sazerac might have been if it had originally been created in France rather than New Orleans.

LADY'S SIDECAR

★★★★½

Glass: Martini
Garnish: Orange zest twist
Method: SHAKE all ingredients with ice and fine strain into chilled glass.

1½	shots	**Cognac VSOP**
1	shot	**Triple Sec**
1	shot	**Freshly squeezed lemon juice**
¼	shot	**Freshly squeezed orange juice**

We say: The addition of orange juice and an orange zest twist supposedly gives this otherwise classic Sidecar a feminine twist.

THE LADY WEARS RED

★★★★☆

Glass: Martini
Garnish: Champagne foam
Method: SHAKE all ingredients with ice and fine-strain chilled glass. FLOAT champagne foam made by macerating orange zests in champagne overnight, adding gelatin and charging with N2O siphon.

1½	shots	**Bacardi Superior rum**
½	shot	**Aperol**
¼	shot	**Grand Marnier liqueur**
¼	shot	**Triple Sec**
⅛	shot	**Tio Pepe fino sherry**
⅛	shot	**Martini Extra Dry vermouth**
⅛	shot	**Taylor's Velvet Falernum liqueur**
¾	shot	**Freshly squeezed lime juice**
¼	shot	**Monin Pure Cane 2:1 sugar syrup**
1	dash	**Grapefruit bitters**
1	dash	**Orange bitters**

We say: This 'Lady' is high maintenance but she delivers a complex reward.
Origin: Adapted from a drink created in 2008 by Ben Carlotto at The Voodoo Rooms, Edinburgh, Scotland. The original recipe calls for homemade dry orange syrup made by macerating orange zests in a blend of different sugars with Lillet Blanc and fine sherry. It also calls for homemade citrus bitters, a complex mixture of kaffir lime leaves, various citrus elements, and spices like cardamom and cassia.

LAGO COSMO

★★★½☆

Glass: Martini
Garnish: Orange zest twist
Method: SHAKE all ingredients with ice and fine strain into chilled glass.

1½	shots	Cranberry flavoured vodka
¾	shot	Triple Sec
1¾	shots	Freshly squeezed orange juice
¼	shot	Freshly squeezed lime juice
½	shot	Monin Pure Cane 2:1 sugar syrup

We say: A Cosmo with cranberry vodka in place of citrus vodka and orange juice in place of cranberry juice.
Origin: Discovered in 2003 at Nectar at Bellagio, Las Vegas, USA.

LANDSLIDE

★★★☆☆

Glass: Shot
Garnish: None
Method: Refrigerate ingredients then LAYER in chilled glass by carefully pouring in the following order.

½	shot	Amaretto liqueur
½	shot	Bols Banana liqueur
½	shot	Baileys Irish cream liqueur

We say: A sweet but pleasant combination of banana, almond and Irish cream liqueur.

LARCHMONT

★★★★½

Glass: Martini
Garnish: Orange zest twist
Method: SHAKE all ingredients with ice and fine strain into chilled glass.

1½	shots	Bacardi Superior rum
½	shot	Grand Marnier liqueur
½	shot	Freshly squeezed lime juice
¼	shot	Monin Pure Cane 2:1 sugar syrup
½	shot	Chilled mineral water

We say: I share Embury's appreciation of this fine and delicate drink, although I think of it more as a type of Orange Daiquiri.
Origin: Created by David A. Embury, who in his 1948 '*Fine Art of Mixing Drinks*' writes of this drink: "As a grand finale to cocktails based on the Rum Sour, I give you one of my favorites which I have named after my favorite community".

THE LAST STRAW

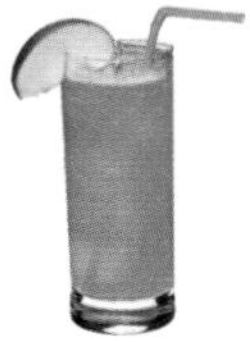

★★★★☆

Glass: Collins
Garnish: Apple wedge
Method: SHAKE all ingredients with ice and strain into ice-filled glass.

1½	shots	Calvados/Applejack brandy
1½	shots	St~Germain elderflower liqueur
1½	shots	Dry cider
1½	shots	Pressed apple juice

We say: Three stages of the apple's alcoholic journey - juice, cider and brandy - are sweetened and aromatised by elderflower liqueur.
Origin: Created in 2006 by Simon Difford. We used the last straw we had left to sample the first one.

LAVENDER & BLACK PEPPER MARTINI

★★★★☆

Glass: Martini
Garnish: None
Method: Pour the syrup into an ice filled mixing glass. Add the vodka and black pepper. STIR and super-fine strain into chilled glass.

2½	shots	Ketel One vodka
¼	shot	Monin Lavender sugar syrup
2	grind	Black pepper

We say: Subtly sweetened and lavender flavoured vodka, with a bump and grind of spicy pepper.
Origin: Adapted from a recipe created in 2006 by Richard Gillam at the Kenilworth Hotel, Warwickshire, England.

LAVENDER MARGARITA

★★★★★

Glass: Coupette
Garnish: Lime wedge
Method: SHAKE all ingredients with ice and fine strain into chilled glass.

2	shots	Tequila 100% Agave
1	shot	Freshly squeezed lime juice
½	shot	Monin Lavender sugar syrup

We say: Lavender lime and tequila combine harmoniously.
Origin: Created in 2006 by Simon Difford.

LAVENDER MARTINI

★★★★☆

Glass: Martini
Garnish: Lemon zest twist
Method: STIR all ingredients with ice and strain into chilled glass.

2½	shots	Lavender-infused Ketel One vodka
¾	shot	Parfait Amour liqueur
¼	shot	Martini Extra Dry vermouth

We say: Infusing lavender in liqueur tends to make it bitter but the Parfait Amour adds sweetness as well as flavour and colour.
Origin: Created in 2006 by Simon Difford.

LAVENDER HONEY SOUR NEW

★★★★☆

Glass: Flute
Garnish: Dried lavender
Method: STIR honey with whiskey in base of shaker to dissolve honey. Add other ingredients, SHAKE with ice and fine strain into chilled glass.

1½	shots	Jameson Irish whiskey
2	spoons	Runny honey
½	shot	Bénédictine D.O.M.
1	shot	Freshly squeezed lemon juice
½	fresh	Egg white
3	dashes	Peychaud's aromatic bitters

We say: An Irish whiskey sour sweetened with runny honey and herbal Bénédictine with Peychaud's adding aromatics.
Origin: Created by Dre Masso at Lonsdale 2006, Notting Hill, London England.

LAZARUS

★★★★★ (half)

Glass: Martini
Garnish: Coffee beans
Method: SHAKE all ingredients with ice and fine strain into chilled glass.

1	shot	Ketel One vodka
½	shot	Cognac VSOP
1	shot	Kahlúa coffee liqueur
1	shot	Hot espresso coffee

We say: A flavoursome combination of spirit and coffee.
Origin: Created in 2000 by David Whitehead at Atrium, Leeds, England.

LAZY MAN FLIP

★★★★★ (half)

Glass: Sour or Martini/Coupette
Garnish: Orange zest twist (discarded) & dust with grated nutmeg
Method: SHAKE all ingredients with ice and fine strain into chilled glass.

1½	shots	Ruby port
¾	shot	Calvados/Applejack brandy
¾	shot	Double (heavy) cream
¼	shot	Monin Pure Cane 2:1 sugar syrup
1	fresh	Egg yolk

We say: Obviously creamy but not too sweet with a great balance between the port and the calvados.
Origin: Created in 2007 by Chris Jepson at Milk and Honey, London, England.

LCB MARTINI

★★★★☆

Glass: Martini
Garnish: Lemon zest twist
Method: SHAKE all ingredients with ice and fine strain into chilled glass.

2	shots	Ketel One vodka
¾	shot	Sauvignon blanc wine
2	shots	Freshly squeezed grapefruit juice
¼	shot	Monin Pure Cane 2:1 sugar syrup

We say: A sweet and sour, citrus fresh Martini.
Origin: Created by Simon Difford in 2004 and named after Lisa Clare Ball, who loves both Sauvignon Blanc and pink grapefruit juice.

LE DIJONNAIS MARTINI

★★★★☆

Glass: Coupette
Garnish: Cocktail onion
Method: STIR all ingredients with ice and fine strain into chilled glass.

1½	shots	Galliano L'Autentico liqueur
½	shot	Martini Extra Dry vermouth
⅛	shot	Tanqueray London dry gin
½	fresh	Freshly extracted celery juice

We say: A most unusual cocktail based on a most unusual product - mustard liqueur.
Origin: Created by Gonzo de Sousa Monteiro, Berlin, Germany.

LE GRAND FEU

★★★☆☆

Glass: Martini
Garnish: Mint sprig
Method: SHAKE all ingredients with ice and fine strain into chilled glass.

1½	shots	Cognac VSOP
1½	shots	Vanilla schnapps
½	shot	Baileys Irish cream liqueur

We say: Cognac smoothed with vanilla and cream, spiced with chai tea.
Origin: Adapted from a recipe by Tony Venci, La Femme Bar, MGM Grand Hotel, Las Vegas, USA.

LE MINUIT

★★★★☆

Glass: Martini
Garnish: Orange zest twist
Method: SHAKE all ingredients with ice and fine strain into chilled glass.

½	shot	Absinthe
1	shot	Sauvignon blanc wine
1	shot	Pressed apple juice
⅛	shot	Monin Pure Cane 2:1 sugar syrup
1	dash	Orange bitters

We say: Absinthe based but incredibly subtle. Absinthe combines wonderfully with wine and apple.
Origin: Adapted from a drink created in 2001 by Tony Conigliaro at Isola, Knightsbridge, London, England.

LEAP YEAR MARTINI 🗝

★★★☆☆

Glass: Martini
Garnish: Lemon zest twist
Method: SHAKE all ingredients with ice and fine strain into chilled glass.

2	shots	Tanqueray London dry gin
½	shot	Grand Marnier liqueur
½	shot	Martini Rosso sweet vermouth
¼	shot	Freshly squeezed lemon juice

We say: This drink, which is on the dry side, needs to be served ice cold.
Origin: Harry Craddock created this drink for the Leap Year celebrations at the Savoy Hotel, London, on 29th February 1928 and recorded it in his 1930 *Savoy Cocktail Book*.

LEAVE IT TO ME MARTINI 🗝

★★★★☆ (half)

Glass: Martini
Garnish: Lemon zest twist
Method: SHAKE all ingredients with ice and fine strain into chilled glass.

1½	shots	Tanqueray London dry gin
½	shot	De Kuyper Apricot Brandy liqueur
¾	shot	Martini Rosso sweet vermouth
½	shot	Freshly squeezed lemon juice
¼	shot	Pomegranate (grenadine) syrup

We say: Gin, apricot, vermouth and lemon create an old-fashioned but well balanced drink.
Origin: Adapted from a recipe in Harry Craddock's 1930 *Savoy Cocktail Book*

THE LEAVENWORTH

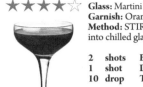

★★★★☆

Glass: Martini
Garnish: Orange zest twist
Method: STIR all ingredients with ice and strain into chilled glass.

2	shots	Bacardi 8yo aged rum
1	shot	De Kuyper Cherry Brandy liqueur
10	drop	Tiki's Falernum Bitters

We say: This great cocktail is dramatically influenced by the style of rum used. Francesco's original recipe calls for English Harbour rum.
Origin: Created in 2008 by Francesco Lafranconi of Southern Wine & Spirits, USA.

THE LAST WORD NEW

★★★★★

Glass: Martini
Garnish: Lime wedge
Method: SHAKE all ingredients with ice and fine strain into chilled glass.

1½	shots	Tanqueray London dry gin
½	shot	Chartreuse Green liqueur
½	shot	Luxardo Maraschino liqueur
½	shot	Freshly squeezed lime juice
¼	shot	Chilled mineral water

We say: Chartreuse devotees will love this balanced, tangy drink. I'm one.
Origin: This vintage classic was first documented in Ted Saucier's 'Bottoms Up' in 1951 where its creation was attributed to the Detroit Athletic Club. It was practically forgotten until championed by the team at Pegu Club, New York City in 2005.

The Detroit Athletic Club was established in 1887 by a group of privileged young men who enjoyed amateur athletics. In 1913 a group of the city's prominent automotive and industrial leaders re-established the club and commissioned architect Albert Kahn to design the magnificent six-story Clubhouse. Completed April 1915 and standing at 241 Madison Avenue in Detroit's theatre district, this still houses the exclusive club to this day. Fine dining and living sit alongside the athletics and if you'd like to join you'll need to dig deep into your wallet and also find six existing members willing to nominate you.

LE FUME NEW

Glass: Coupette
Garnish: Orange zest twist
Method: STIR all ingredients with ice and fine strain into chilled glass.

2	shots	Ketel One vodka
½	shot	Lagavulin 16yo Islay malt
¼	shot	Lapsang souchong sugar syrup
½	shot	Chilled water (omit if wet ice)

We say: Peat smoked Islay whisky meets pinewood smoked Chinese tea, fortified with vodka.
Origin: Adapted from a drink discovered in 2011 at Le Salon Bar at L'Atelier de Joël Robuchon, London, England.

LEFT BANK MARTINI UPDATED

★★★★★

Glass: Martini
Garnish: Lime zest twist
Method: SHAKE all ingredients with ice and fine strain into chilled glass.

2	shots	Tanqueray London dry gin
½	shot	St-Germain elderflower liqueur
½	shot	Chablis white wine
¼	shot	Martini Extra dry vermouth

We say: An aromatic, dry blend. Modern bartending convention would suggest that this drink should be stirred. However, it's much better shaken. Go easy with the spray of lime zest oils – this delicate drink is easily over powered with any more than a fine mist.
Origin: Created in 2006 by Simon Difford at The Cabinet Room, London, England. Updated in 2013. Older? Yes. Wiser? Perhaps. Drier palate? Definitely. Hence, seven years after creating this drink I reduced the elderflower liqueur from ¾ shot to ½ shot and I also reduced the vermouth from ½ to a ¼.

LEKKER LEKKER

★★★½☆

Glass: Martini
Garnish: Apple slice
Method: SHAKE all ingredients with ice and fine strain into chilled glass.

1	shot	Żubrówka bison vodka
¾	shot	Hazelnut liqueur
½	shot	Freshly squeezed lemon juice
2	shots	Pressed apple juice
½	shot	Monin Pure Cane 2:1 sugar syrup

We say: Most unusual with apple, hazelnut and lemon freshness.
Origin: Created by Tom Lawman at Snafu, Aberdeen. Lekker Lekker (pronounced 'Laker Laker') is Afrikaans for 'very nice', which is what Tom's South African friend exclaimed when he tasted this drink.

LEMON BEAT

★★★★☆

Glass: Rocks
Garnish: Lemon slice
Method: STIR honey with cachaça in the base of shaker to dissolve honey. Add other ingredients, SHAKE with ice and strain into ice-filled glass.

2	spoons	Runny honey
2	shots	Leblon cachaça
1	shot	Freshly squeezed lemon juice

We say: Simple but effective. Use quality cachaça and honey and you'll have a great drink.

BARTENDER'S TIP MEASURING - SHOTS & SPOONS

In this guide measures of each ingredient are expressed in 'shots'. Ideally a shot is 25ml or one US fluid ounce (29.6ml), measured in a standard jigger. (You can also use a clean medicine measure or even a small shot glass.)

Whatever your chosen measure, it should have straight sides to enable you to accurately judge fractions of a shot. Look out for measures which are graduated in ounces and marked with quarter and half ounces.

LEMON BUTTER COOKIE

★★★★☆

Glass: Old-fashioned
Garnish: Lemon zest twist
Method: SHAKE all ingredients with ice and strain into glass filled with crushed ice.

¾	shot	Żubrówka bison vodka
¾	shot	Ketel One vodka
¾	shot	Runny honey
½	shot	Monin Almond (orgeat) syrup
2	shots	Pressed apple juice
⅛	shot	Freshly squeezed lemon juice

We say: An appropriate name for a most unusually flavoured drink modelled on the Polish Martini.
Origin: Created in 2002 by Mark 'Q-Ball' Linnie and Martin Oliver at the Mixing Tin, Leeds, England.

LEMON CAIPIROVSKA

★★★★☆

Glass: Old-fashioned
Garnish: None
Method: MUDDLE lemon in base of shaker, add other ingredients and SHAKE with 6oz scoop crushed ice. Pour into glass without straining and serve with straws.

¾	fresh	Lemon
2	shots	Ketel One Citroen vodka
¾	shot	Monin Pure Cane 2:1 sugar syrup
1	dash	Angostura aromatic bitters

We say: A lemon-tastic Caipirovska.
Origin: Created in 2002 by Tony Conigliaro at Isola, London, England.

LEMON CHIFFON PIE

★★★★☆

Glass: Coupette
Garnish: Grated lemon zest
Method: BLEND all ingredients with crushed ice and serve with straws.

1	shot	Bacardi Superior rum
1	shot	White Crème de Cacao
1	shot	Freshly squeezed lemon juice
2	scoop	Häagen Dazs vanilla ice cream

We say: Creamy and tangy - like a lemon pie. Consume in place of desert.

LEMON CURD MARTINI

★★★★☆

Glass: Martini
Garnish: Lemon wedge
Method: SHAKE all ingredients with ice and fine strain into chilled glass.

2	shots	Ketel One Citroen vodka
3	spoons	Lemon curd
½	shot	Freshly squeezed lemon juice

We say: This almost creamy cocktail is named after tastes like its primary ingredient. Martini purists may justifiably balk at the absence of vermouth and the presence of fruit.
Origin: Created by Simon Difford.

LEMON DROP

★★★½☆

Glass: Shot
Garnish: Sugar coated lemon slice
Method: SHAKE all ingredients with ice and fine strain into chilled glass.

½	shot	Ketel One vodka
½	shot	Triple Sec
½	shot	Freshly squeezed lemon juice

We say: Lemon and orange combine to make a fresh tasting citrus shot.

LEMON DROP COCKTAIL UPDATED

★★★★☆

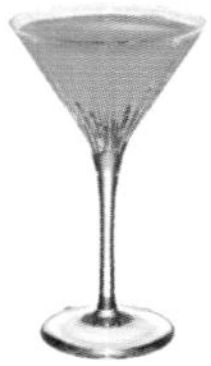

Glass: Martini
Garnish: Lemon zest twist
Method: SHAKE all ingredients with ice and fine strain into chilled glass.

2	shots	Ketel One Citroen vodka
¼	shot	Cointreau triple sec
¾	shot	Freshly squeezed lemon juice
½	shot	Monin Pure Cane 2:1 sugar syrup

We say: Sherbety lemon - well balanced and very refreshing.

LEMON LIME & BITTERS (MOCKTAIL*)

★★★½☆

Glass: Collins
Garnish: Lime wedge
Method: POUR lime and bitters into ice-filled glass. TOP with lemonade, lightly stir and serve with straws.

½	shot	Freshly squeezed lime juice
4	dashes	Angostura aromatic bitters
Top up with		Lemonade/Sprite/7-Up

AKA: LLB
We say: NOTE: Contains minute levels of alcohol due to use of Angostura bitters.
Origin: Very popular in its homeland, Australia.

LEMON MARTINI

★★★★½

Glass: Martini
Garnish: Lemon zest twist
Method: MUDDLE lemongrass in base of shaker. Add other ingredients, SHAKE with ice and fine strain into chilled glass.

2	inch	Lemongrass stem (chopped)
2¼	shots	Ketel One vodka
¼	shot	Martini Extra Dry vermouth
1	shot	Freshly squeezed lemon juice
½	shot	Monin Pure Cane 2:1 sugar syrup

We say: A complex, delicately lemon Vodkatini.
Origin: Created in 2006 by Simon Difford.

LEMON MERINGUE MARTINI

★★★★☆

Glass: Martini
Garnish: Lemon zest twist
Method: SHAKE all ingredients with ice and fine strain into chilled glass.

2	shots	Ketel One Citroen vodka
1	shot	Baileys Irish cream liqueur
1	shot	Freshly squeezed lemon juice
¼	shot	Monin Pure Cane 2:1 sugar syrup

We say: Slightly creamy in consistency, this tangy lemon drink is indeed reminiscent of the eponymous dessert.
Origin: Adapted from a drink created in 2000 by Ben Reed, London, England.

LEMON MERINGUE PIE'TINI

★★★★☆

Glass: Martini
Garnish: Pie rim
Method: SHAKE first three ingredients with ice and fine strain into chilled and rimmed glass. DRY SHAKE cream and Licor 43 (without ice) so as to mix and whip. FLOAT cream by pouring over back of spoon.

1	shot	Limoncello liqueur
1	shot	Monin Pure Cane 2:1 sugar syrup
1	shot	Freshly squeezed lemon juice
2	shots	Double (heavy) cream
½	shot	Cuarenta y Tres (Licor 43) liqueur

We say: Rich and syrupy base sipped through a vanilla cream topping.
To make the pie rim, wipe outside edge of rim with cream mix and dip into crunched up Graham Cracker or digestive biscuits.
Origin: Created by Michael Waterhouse at Dylan Prime, New York City, USA.

LEMON SORBET

★★★★☆

Glass: Martini
Garnish: Grated lemon zest
Method: Heat water in pan and add sugar. Simmer and stir until sugar dissolves, add lemon juice and grated lemon rind and continue to simmer and stir for a few minutes. Take off the heat and allow to cool. Fine strain into a shallow container and stir in liqueur and orange bitters. Beat egg whites and fold into mix. Place in freezer and store for up to 3-4 days before use.

¾	shot	Chilled mineral water
1	cupful	Granulated sugar
½	cupful	Freshly squeezed lemon juice
5	fresh	Lemon zest twist
¼	cupful	Limoncello liqueur
2	spoons	Orange bitters
2	fresh	Egg whites

Variant: To make any other citrus flavour sorbet, simply substitute the juice and peel of another fruit such as grapefruit lime or orange.
We say: My favourite recipe for this desert and occasional cocktail ingredient.

LEMONGRAD

★★★★½

Glass: Collins
Garnish: Lemon wedge
Method: SHAKE first four ingredients with ice and strain into ice-filled glass. TOP with tonic and lightly stir.

2	shots	Ketel One vodka
½	shot	Ketel One Citroen vodka
½	shot	Freshly squeezed lemon juice
½	shot	St~Germain elderflower liqueur
Top up with		Tonic water

We say: A great summer afternoon drink. Fresh lemon with elderflower and quinine.
Origin: Created in 2002 by Alex Kammerling, London, England.

LEMONGRASS COSMO

★★★★½

Glass: Martini
Garnish: Lemon zest twist
Method: MUDDLE lemongrass in base of shaker. ADD other ingredients, SHAKE with ice and fine strain into chilled glass.

1	inch	Lemongrass stem (chopped)
1	shot	Ketel One Citroen vodka
1	shot	Triple Sec
1½	shots	Ocean Spray cranberry juice
½	shot	Freshly squeezed lemon juice

We say: Lemongrass adds complexity to this balanced Cosmo.
Origin: Adapted from a drink discovered in 2005 at Opia, Hong Kong,.

LEMONY

★★★★☆

Glass: Martini
Garnish: Maraschino cherry
Method: SHAKE all ingredients with ice and fine strain into chilled glass.

2	shots	Tanqueray London dry gin
½	shot	Chartreuse Yellow liqueur
½	shot	Limoncello liqueur
½	shot	Freshly squeezed lemon juice
½	shot	Chilled mineral water

We say: Lemon subtly dominates this complex, herbal drink.

STAR RATINGS EXPLAINED

★★★★★ Excellent

★★★★✭ Recommended	★★★★☆ Praiseworthy
★★★✭☆ Commended	★★★☆☆ Mediocre
★★✭☆☆ Disappointing	★★☆☆☆ Pretty awful
★✭☆☆☆ Shameful	★☆☆☆☆ Disgusting

LENINADE UPDATED

★★★★☆

Glass: Martini
Garnish: Orange zest twist (discarded) and lemon slice
Method: SHAKE first five ingredients with ice and strain into ice-filled glass. TOP with soda.

1½	shots	**Ketel One Citroen vodka**
½	shot	**Cointreau triple sec**
1	shot	**Freshly squeezed lemon juice**
½	shot	**Monin Pure Cane 2:1 sugar syrup**
3	dashes	**Orange bitters**
Top up with		**Soda (club soda)**

We say: Orange undertones add citrus depth to the lemon explosion.
Origin: Created by Dick Bradsell at Fred's, London, England, in the late 1980s. His original recipe (1½ shots citrus vodka, ¼ shot triple sec, 1 shot lemon juice, ¼ shot sugar syrup and 3 dash orange bitters) was served short and straight-up with sugar syrup rather than grenade. Simon Difford added the grenadine and made the Leninade a long drink in July 2013 after reader feedback on diffordsguide.com.

THE LIBERTINE

★★★★☆

Glass: Old-fashioned
Garnish: Candied lime
Method: SHAKE first four ingredients with ice and fine strain into ice-filled glass. TOP with ginger beer and lightly stir.

1½	shots	**Kaffir lime flavoured vodka**
¾	shot	**Chartreuse Green liqueur**
¾	shot	**St~Germain elderflower liqueur**
½	shot	**Freshly squeezed lime juice**
1	shot	**Ginger beer**

We say: Huge flavours delicately combine in this surprisingly approachable drink.
Origin: Created in 2008 by Joe Parrilli at Bacar, San Francisco, USA.

LIFE (LOVE IN THE FUTURE ECSTASY)

★★★½☆

Glass: Old-fashioned
Garnish: Mint leaf
Method: MUDDLE mint in base of shaker. Add next three ingredients, SHAKE with ice and fine strain into glass filled with crushed ice. DRIZZLE tea liqueur over drink.

7	fresh	**Mint leaves**
1½	shots	**Ketel One vodka**
1	shot	**Freshly squeezed lime juice**
½	shot	**Monin Pure Cane 2:1 sugar syrup**
1	shot	**Zen green tea liqueur**

We say: Refreshing tea and mint.
Origin: Adapted from a drink created in 1999 by Nick Strangeway at Ché, London, England, for Martin Sexton (writer and artistic entrepreneur).

LIGHT BREEZE

★★★½☆

Glass: Collins
Garnish: Lemon slice
Method: POUR all ingredients into ice-filled glass. Stir and serve with straws.

2	shots	**Pernod anise**
3	shots	**Ocean Spray cranberry juice**
2	shots	**Freshly squeezed grapefruit juice**

We say: A Seabreeze based on anise rather than vodka, benefitting from aniseed depth and sweetness.
Origin: Created in 2000 by Simon Difford at the Light Bar, London, England (hence the name).

LIGHTER BREEZE

★★★½☆

Glass: Collins
Garnish: Apple wedge
Method: POUR all ingredients into ice-filled glass. Stir and serve with straws.

1	shot	**St~Germain elderflower liqueur**
½	shot	**Pernod anise**
3	shots	**Pressed apple juice**
½	shot	**Ocean Spray cranberry juice**

We say: Long, fragrant and refreshing.

LIMA SOUR

★★★½☆

Glass: Old-fashioned
Garnish: Lemon zest twist
Method: BLEND all ingredients with one 12oz scoop of crushed ice. Serve with straws.

2	shots	**Macchu pisco**
½	shot	**Luxardo Maraschino liqueur**
¾	shot	**Freshly squeezed grapefruit juice**
¾	shot	**Freshly squeezed lime juice**
¾	shot	**Monin Pure Cane 2:1 sugar syrup**

We say: A refreshing blend of pisco, maraschino and citrus.
Origin: Created before 1947 by Jerry Hooker.

THE LIMEY GIMLET

★★★★½

Glass: Coupette
Garnish: Lime zest twist (discarded) & lime wedge
Method: SHAKE all ingredients with ice and fine strain into chilled glass.

1	shot	**Rose's lime cordial**
1	shot	**Tanqueray London dry gin**
½	shot	**Bacardi Superior rum**
½	shot	**Freshly squeezed lime juice**

We say: The two naval spirits sit harmoniously together in this delicately flavoured Gimlet.
Origin: Created in 2010 by Simon Difford at The Cabinet Room, London, England.

LIMÓN FRESCA

★★★☆☆

Glass: Collins
Garnish: Lemon zest twist
Method: POUR ingredients into glass half filled with crushed ice and CHURN (stir). ADD more ice to fill glass, CHURN and top with soda.

2	shots	Ketel One Citroen vodka
¾	shot	Limoncello liqueur
½	shot	Freshly squeezed lemon juice
½	shot	Freshly squeezed lime juice
½	shot	Freshly squeezed orange juice
5	fresh	Mint leaves

We say: Citrus fresh palate with sharp lemon sherbet flavours.
Origin: Adapted from a drink created in 2005 by Jason Kindness at The Boat House Resturant, Tiverton R.I., USA.

LIME BLUSH (MOCKTAIL)

★★★☆☆

Glass: Old-fashioned
Garnish: Lime wedge
Method: SHAKE all ingredients with ice and strain into glass filled with crushed ice.

2	shots	Freshly squeezed lime juice
½	shot	Rose's lime cordial
½	shot	Monin Pure Cane 2:1 sugar syrup
½	shot	Pomegranate (grenadine) syrup

We say: Refreshingly sweet and sour.
Origin: Adapted from a drink discovered in 2005 at Blue Bar, Four Seasons Hotel, Hong Kong, China.

LIME BREEZE

★★★★☆

Glass: Collins
Garnish: Lime wedge
Method: SHAKE all ingredients with ice and fine strain into ice-filled glass.

2	shots	Lime flavoured vodka
3	shots	Ocean Spray cranberry juice
1½	shots	Freshly squeezed grapefruit juice

We say: A lime driven Sea Breeze.

LIME SOUR

★★★★☆

Glass: Old-fashioned
Garnish: Lime wedge
Method: SHAKE all ingredients with ice and strain into ice-filled glass.

2	shots	Lime flavoured vodka
1¼	shots	Freshly squeezed lime juice
¼	shot	Monin Pure Cane 2:1 sugar syrup
½	fresh	Egg white

We say: Fresh egg white gives this drink a wonderfully frothy top and smooths the alcohol and lime juice.

LIMEADE (MOCKTAIL)

★★★★☆

Glass: Collins
Garnish: Lime wedge
Method: SHAKE all ingredients with ice and fine strain into ice-filled glass.

2	shots	Freshly squeezed lime juice
1	shot	Monin Pure Cane 2:1 sugar syrup
3	shots	Chilled mineral water

Variant: Shake first two ingredients & top with sparkling water.
We say: A superbly refreshing alternative to lemonade.

LIMELITE

★★★☆☆

Glass: Collins
Garnish: Lime wedge
Method: SHAKE first 4 ingredients with ice and strain into ice-filled glass. TOP with lemonade.

2	shots	Lime flavoured vodka
½	shot	Triple Sec
½	shot	Freshly squeezed lime juice
¼	shot	Monin Pure Cane 2:1 sugar syrup
Top up with		Lemonade/Sprite/7-Up

We say: Long and citrussy.

LIMEOSA

★★★★☆

Glass: Flute
Garnish: None
Method: SHAKE first two ingredients with ice and fine strain into chilled glass. TOP with champagne and gently stir.

1	shot	Lime flavoured vodka
2	shots	Freshly squeezed orange juice
Top up with		Brut champagne

We say: Why settle for a plain old Buck's Fizz when you could add a shot of lime-flavoured vodka?

LIMERICK

★★★★☆

Glass: Collins
Garnish: Lime wedge
Method: SHAKE first three ingredients with ice and strain into ice-filled glass. TOP with soda water and lightly stir.

2	shots	Ketel One vodka
1	shot	Freshly squeezed lime juice
½	shot	Monin Pure Cane 2:1 sugar syrup
Top up with		Soda (club soda)

We say: A refreshing lime cooler.
Origin: This twist on the classic Vodka Rickey, created by Simon Difford in 2002.

LIMEY

★★★½☆

Glass: Martini
Garnish: Lime zest twist
Method: SHAKE all ingredients with ice and fine strain into chilled glass.

2	shots	**Lime flavoured vodka**
½	shot	**Freshly squeezed lime juice**
½	shot	**Monin Pure Cane 2:1 sugar syrup**
⅛	shot	**Rose's lime cordial**
3	dashes	**Angostura aromatic bitters**
½	shot	**Chilled mineral water**

We say: A rust coloured drink with a delicately sour flavour.
Origin: I created and named this drink after the British Naval tradition of mixing lime juice with spirits in an attempt to prevent scurvy. This practice gained British sailors the nickname 'limeys'.

LIMEY COSMO

★★★★☆

Glass: Martini
Garnish: Lime wedge
Method: SHAKE all ingredients with ice and fine strain into chilled glass.

1½	shots	**Lime flavoured vodka**
1	shot	**Triple Sec**
1¼	shots	**Ocean Spray cranberry juice**
¼	shot	**Freshly squeezed lime juice**
½	shot	**Rose's lime cordial**

We say: If you like Cosmopolitans, you'll love this zesty alternative.

LIMEY MULE

★★★★☆

Glass: Collins
Garnish: Lime wedge
Method: SHAKE first 3 ingredients with ice and strain into ice-filled glass. TOP with ginger ale, lightly stir and serve with straws.

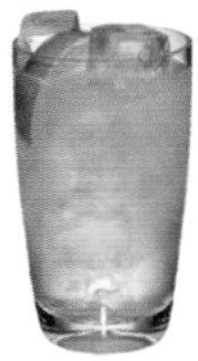

2	shots	**Lime flavoured vodka**
1	shot	**Freshly squeezed lime juice**
½	shot	**Monin Pure Cane 2:1 sugar syrup**
Top up with		**Ginger ale**

We say: Made with plain vodka this drink is a Moscow Mule. This variant uses lime flavoured vodka.

LIMINAL SHOT

★★★☆☆

Glass: Shot
Garnish: None
Method: Refrigerate ingredients then LAYER in chilled glass by carefully pouring in the following order.

½	shot	**Pomegranate (grenadine) syrup**
½	shot	**Bols Blue Curaçao liqueur**
¾	shot	**Lime flavoured vodka**

We say: The name means transitional, marginal, a boundary or a threshold. Appropriate since the layers border each other.

LIMITED LIABILITY

★★★★½

Glass: Old-fashioned
Garnish: None
Method: SHAKE all ingredients with ice and strain into ice-filled glass.

2	shots	**Lime flavoured vodka**
1	shot	**Krupnik spiced honey liqueur**
¾	shot	**Freshly squeezed lime juice**

We say: A sour and flavoursome short - honey and lime work well together.
Origin: Created in 2002 by Simon Difford.

LIMNOLOGY

★★★½☆

Glass: Martini
Garnish: Lime zest twist
Method: STIR all ingredients with ice and fine strain into chilled glass.

2	shots	**Lime flavoured vodka**
1	shot	**Rose's lime cordial**
¾	shot	**Chilled mineral water**

We say: A vodka Gimlet made with lime flavoured vodka.
Origin: The name means the study of the physical phenomena of lakes and other fresh waters - appropriate for this fresh green drink.

LIMONCELLO MARTINI

★★★½☆

Glass: Martini
Garnish: Lemon zest twist
Method: SHAKE all ingredients with ice and fine strain into chilled glass.

1½	shots	**Ketel One vodka**
1½	shots	**Limoncello liqueur**
1	shot	**Freshly squeezed lemon juice**

We say: If you like the liqueur, you'll love the cocktail.
Origin: Adapted from a drink created in 2005 by Francesco at Mix, New York City, USA.

STAR RATINGS EXPLAINED

★★★★★ Excellent

★★★★½ Recommended	★★★★☆ Praiseworthy
★★★½☆ Commended	★★★☆☆ Mediocre
★★½☆☆ Disappointing	★★☆☆☆ Pretty awful
★½☆☆☆ Shameful	★☆☆☆☆ Disgusting

LIMOUSINE

★★★★☆

Glass: Old-fashioned
Garnish: Lime wedge
Method: Place bar spoon in glass. POUR ingredients into glass and stir.

2	shots	Ketel One vodka
1	shot	Krupnik spiced honey liqueur
4	shots	Hot camomile tea

We say: In winter this hot drink is a warming treat. In summer serve cold over ice, as pictured.
Origin: Created in 2002 by Simon Difford.

LINCOLN CLUB COOLER

★★★☆☆

Glass: Collins
Garnish: Lime wedge
Method: POUR ingredients into ice-filled glass and gently stir.

| 2 | shots | Bacardi Oro golden rum |
| Top up with | | Ginger ale |

We say: Basically a rum and ginger ale Highball but Lincoln Club Cooler has mor4e of a ring to it.
Origin: Adapted from a drink originally published in George J. Kappeler's 1895 'Modern American Drinks'. Kappeler grigionally called for St. Croix rum.

LINSTEAD

★★★★★

Glass: Martini
Garnish: Lemon zest twist
Method: SHAKE all ingredients with ice and fine strain into chilled glass.

2	shots	Dewar's White label Scotch
2	shots	Fresh pressed pineapple juice
¼	shot	Monin Pure Cane 2:1 sugar syrup
⅛	shot	Absinthe

We say: Absinthe and pineapple come through first, with Scotch last. A great medley of flavours.

LIQUORICE ALL SORT

★★★★☆

Glass: Collins
Garnish: Liquorice Allsorts
Method: SHAKE first four ingredients with ice and strain into ice-filled glass. TOP with lemonade.

1	shot	Opal Nera black sambuca
1	shot	Bols Banana liqueur
1	shot	Crème de fraise du bois liqueur
1	shot	Bols Blue Curaçao liqueur
Top up with		Lemonade/Sprite/7-Up

We say: This aptly named, semi-sweet drink has a strong liquorice flavour with hints of fruit.
Origin: George Bassett (1818-1886), a manufacturer of liquorice sweets, did not invent the Liquorice Allsort that carries his name. That happened 15 years after George died when a salesman accidentally dropped a tray of sweets, they fell in a muddle and the famous sweet was born.

LIQUORICE MARTINI

★★★½☆

Glass: Martini
Garnish: Liquorice
Method: STIR all ingredients with ice and strain into chilled glass.

2	shots	Tanqueray London dry gin
¼	shot	Opal Nera black sambuca
⅛	shot	Monin Pure Cane 2:1 sugar syrup

We say: Gin tinted violet, flavoured with liquorice and slightly sweetened.
Origin: Created in 2003 by Jason Fendick, London, England.

LIQUORICE SHOT

★★★½☆

Glass: Shot
Garnish: None
Method: SHAKE all ingredients with ice and fine strain into chilled glass.

½	shot	Ketel One vodka
½	shot	Luxardo Sambuca dei Cesari
½	shot	Crème de cassis liqueur

We say: For liquorice fans.

LIQUORICE WHISKY SOUR

★★★★½

Glass: Old-fashioned
Garnish: Dust with grated liquorice
Method: SHAKE all ingredients with ice and strain into ice-filled glass.

2	shots	Dewar's White label Scotch
1	shot	Homemade liquorice syrup
½	shot	Freshly squeezed lemon juice
1	dash	Angostura aromatic bitters
½	fresh	Egg white

We say: Liquorice dramatically changes the classic Sour, working harmoniously with the Scotch. I have also tried with bourbon and the result is not nearly so pleasing.
Origin: Created in 2006 by Tony Conigliaro at Shochu Lounge, London, England.

LISA B'S DAIQUIRI

★★★★★

Glass: Martini
Garnish: Grapefruit zest twist
Method: SHAKE all ingredients with ice and fine strain into chilled glass.

2½	shots	Vanilla-infused Bacardi rum
½	shot	Freshly squeezed lime juice
½	shot	Monin Vanilla sugar syrup
1	shot	Freshly squeezed grapefruit juice

We say: Reminiscent of a Hemingway Special, this flavoursome, vanilla laced Daiquiri has a wonderfully tangy, bitter sweet finish.
Origin: Created in 2003 by Simon Difford for a gorgeous fan of both Daiquiris and pink grapefruit juice

LITTLE ITALY

★★★★★☆

Glass: Coupette
Garnish: Maraschino cherry
Method: STIR all ingredients with ice and strain into chilled glass.

2	shots	Straight rye whiskey
½	shot	Cynar
¾	shot	Martini Rosso sweet vermouth

We say: Cynar adds its characteristic bittersweet note to the Manhattan-like cocktail.
Origin: Created by Audrey Saunders at Pegu Club, New York City, USA.

LITTLE SMITH NEW

★★★★☆

Glass: Coupette
Garnish: Float dried apple slice
Method: SHAKE all ingredients with ice and fine strain into chilled glass.

1	shot	Żubrówka bison vodka
1	shot	Calvados/Applejack brandy
½	shot	Taylor's Velvet Falernum liqueur
1	shot	Pressed apple juice
1	fresh	Wasabi leaf

We say: Slightly sweet but this apple cocktail is light and delicately spiced.
Origin: Discovered in 2011 at Ubar, Copenhagen, Denmark.

LITTLE VENICE

★★★★½

Glass: Martini
Garnish: Orange zest twist (discarded) & maraschino cherry
Method: STIR all ingredients with ice and strain into chilled glass.

2	shots	Sake
1	shot	Maker's Mark bourbon
1	shot	Martini Rosso sweet vermouth

We say: Simple and yet beautiful. Just the way a great drink should be.
Origin: Discovered in 2007 at Yakitoria, London, England.

LIVINGSTONE

★★★★☆

Glass: Martini
Garnish: Lemon zest twist
Method: SHAKE all ingredients with ice and fine strain into chilled glass.

2	shots	Tanqueray London dry gin
1	shot	Martini Extra Dry vermouth
¼	shot	Monin Pure Cane 2:1 sugar syrup

Variant: Use pomegranate syrup in place of sugar and you have a Red Livingstone, named after London's 'lefty' ex-mayor, Ken.
We say: The classic gin and vermouth Martini made more approachable with a dash of sugar.
Origin: This 1930s classic was named after Doctor Livingstone, the famous African missionary.

LO MISMO

★★★★½☆

Glass: Old-fashioned
Garnish: Lime zest twist
Method: POUR ingredients into ice-filled glass.

| 2 | shots | Bacardi Superior rum |
| Top up with | | Soda (club soda) |

We say: Light rum and soda makes for a fabulously subtle and refreshing drink. Don't serve too long or the dilution will kill it.
Origin: The Mismo was a craze said to be started by a group of Americans at the Cosmopolitan Club in Santiago in 1899. When ordering drinks, one of their Cuban colleagues asked for a Bacardi rum and seltzer (soda). His friend, also Cuban, called for 'Lo mismo' - Spanish for 'the same'. Not speaking Spanish, but eager to fit in, the Americans all also asked for 'lo mismos'. The next day, the Americans returned and ordered another round of 'Mismos' from the same barman. The name stuck. "It spread with remarkable rapidity", reported the New York Tribune soon after. Now every barkeeper in Santiago knows what you are after if you ask for a 'Mismo'.

LOCH ALMOND

★★★★☆

Glass: Collins
Garnish: Amaretti biscuit
Method: POUR all ingredients into ice-filled glass, stir and serve with straws.

1½	shots	Dewar's White label Scotch
1½	shots	Amaretto liqueur
Top up with		Ginger ale

We say: If you haven't got to grips with Scotch but like amaretto, try this spicy almond combination.

LOLA

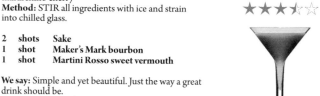

★★★★½☆

Glass: Martini
Garnish: Orange zest twist
Method: SHAKE all ingredients with ice and fine strain into chilled glass.

1½	shots	Bacardi Oro golden rum
½	shot	Mandarine Napoléon liqueur
½	shot	White Crème de Cacao
1	shot	Freshly squeezed orange juice
½	shot	Double (heavy) cream

We say: Strong, creamy orange.
Origin: Created in 1999 by Jamie Terrell, London, UK

LOLITA MARGARITA

★★★★½

Glass: Coupette
Garnish: Lime wedge
Method: STIR honey with tequila in base of shaker to dissolve honey. Add other ingredients, SHAKE with ice and fine strain into chilled glass.

2	spoons	Runny honey
2	shots	Tequila 100% Agave
1	shot	Freshly squeezed lime juice
2	dashes	Angostura aromatic bitters

We say: A fittingly seductive Margarita.
Origin: Named after the novel by Valdimir Nabokov which chronicles a middle-aged man's infatuation with a 12 year old girl. Nabokov invented the word 'nymphet' to describe her seductive qualities.

LONDON CALLING

★★★½☆

Glass: Martini
Garnish: Orange zest twist
Method: STIR all ingredients with ice and strain into chilled glass.

2	shots	Tanqueray London dry gin
1¼	shots	Sloe Gin liqueur
½	shot	Martini Rosso sweet vermouth
2	dashes	Orange bitters

We say: A traditionally styled sweet Martini with a dry, fruity finish.
Origin: Discovered in 2003 at Oxo Tower Bar & Brasserie, London, England.

LONDON COCKTAIL

★★★☆☆

Glass: Martini
Garnish: Orange zest twist
Method: SHAKE all ingredients with ice and fine strain into chilled glass.

2½	shots	Tanqueray London dry gin
⅛	shot	Absinthe
⅛	shot	Monin Pure Cane 2:1 sugar syrup
2	dashes	Orange bitters
½	shot	Chilled mineral water

We say: Chilled, diluted and sweetened gin invigorated by a hint of absinthe.
Origin: Adapted from a recipe in Harry Craddock's 1930 'Savoy Cocktail Book'.

LONDON COSMPOLITAN

★★★★☆

Glass: Martini
Garnish: Orange zest twist (discarded)
Method: SHAKE all ingredients with ice and fine strain into chilled glass.

1	shot	Tanqueray London dry gin
1	shot	Triple Sec
1½	shots	Ocean Spray cranberry juice
½	shot	Freshly squeezed lime juice

We say: Basically a Cosmopolitan but made with Tanqueray London dry gin instead of citrus vodka.
Origin: A subtle twist on the classic by Simon Difford in 2008 at The Cabinet Room, London, England.

LONDON FOG

★★½☆☆

Glass: Old-fashioned
Garnish: Orange zest twist
Method: Fill glass with ice. Add ingredients in the following order and STIR. Add more ice to fill.

1	shot	Tanqueray London dry gin
2	shots	Chilled mineral water
1	shot	Pernod anise

We say: Pernod clouds this drink and adds its distinctive aniseed flavour.

LONDON GYPSY

★★★★☆

Glass: Coupette
Garnish: Grapefruit zest twist
Method: STIR all ingredients with ice and strain into chilled glass.

2	shots	Tanqueray London dry gin
1	shot	Bénédictine D.O.M.
3	dashes	Angostura aromatic bitters

We say: The botanicals in the gin and the herbal Benedictine combine well in this drink which is balanced by the addition of bitters.

LONDON SCRAMBLE

★★★★☆

Glass: Old-fashioned
Garnish: Lemon zest twist & blackberries
Method: SHAKE first four ingredients with ice and fine strain into glass filled with crushed ice. DRIZZLE crème de mûre over drink (will slowly bleed through the cocktail).

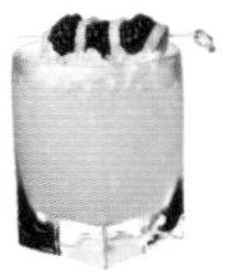

2	shots	Tequila 100% Agave
½	shot	Freshly squeezed lemon juice
½	shot	Freshly squeezed lime juice
½	shot	Agave nectar
¼	shot	Crème de Mûre liqueur

We say: A tequila Bramble of which I'm sure Dick would be most approving.
Origin: Created in 2007 by Dre Masso & Henry Besant from the Worldwide Cocktail Club, London.

THE LONE RANGER NEW

★★★★☆

Glass: Collins
Garnish: Lemon zest twist
Method: SHAKE first 3 ingredients with ice and strain into ice-filled glass. TOP with champagne.

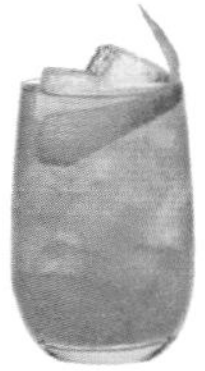

1½	shots	Olmeca Altos 100% agave tequila
¾	shot	Freshly squeezed lemon juice
½	shot	Monin Pure Cane 2:1 sugar syrup
Top up with		Brut champagne

We say: Very slightly sweet tequila and lemon, lengthened and dried with brut champagne.
Origin: Created in 2012 by Jeffrey Morgenthaler, Oregon, USA.

LONELY BULL

★★★½☆

Glass: Old-fashioned
Garnish: Dust with grated nutmeg
Method: SHAKE all ingredients with ice and strain into ice-filled glass.

1½	shots	Tequila 100% Agave
1½	shots	Kahlúa coffee liqueur
¾	shot	Double (heavy) cream
¾	shot	Milk

We say: Like a creamy iced coffee - yum.

LONG BEACH ICED TEA

★★★⯪☆

Glass: Sling
Garnish: Lemon slice
Method: SHAKE all ingredients with ice and strain into ice-filled glass. Serve with straws.

½	shot	Kahlúa coffee liqueur
½	shot	Tequila 100% Agave
½	shot	Bacardi Superior rum
½	shot	Tanqueray London dry gin
½	shot	Ketel One vodka
1	shot	Freshly squeezed lime juice
½	shot	Monin Pure Cane 2:1 sugar syrup
2	shots	Ocean Spray cranberry juice

We say: One of the more grown-up 'Iced Tea' cocktails.

LONG FLIGHT OF STAIRS

★★★★⯪

Glass: Collins
Garnish: Apple or pear slice
Method: SHAKE all ingredients with ice and strain into ice-filled glass. Serve with straws.

1	shot	Pear flavoured vodka
1	shot	Calvados/Applejack brandy
1	shot	Belle de Brillet pear liqueur
2½	shots	Pressed apple juice

We say: A seriously tasty, strong, long drink. The name is a reversal of the London rhyming slang 'apples and pears' (stairs).
Origin: Created in 2005 by Simon Difford as a homage to the G.E. Club's 'Stairs Martini'.

LONG ISLAND ICED TEA UPDATED

★★★★☆

Glass: Sling
Garnish: Lemon slice
Method: SHAKE first 7 ingredients with ice and strain into ice-filled glass. TOP with cola, stir and serve with straws.

½ shot Bacardi Superior rum
½ shot Tanqueray London dry gin
½ shot Ketel One vodka
½ shot Triple Sec
½ shot Tequila 100% Agave (blanco)
½ shot Freshly squeezed lemon juice
½ shot Freshly squeezed lime juice
½ shot Monin Pure Cane 2:1 sugar syrup (65°brix, 2:1 sugar/water)
Top up with Coca-cola

We say: A cooling, combination of five different spirits with a hint of lime and a splash of cola.
Origin: This infamous drink reached the height of its popularity in the early 1980s .Of the many stories surrounding its origin, perhaps the most credible attributes its creation to sometime in the late 1970s by Robert (Rosebud) Butt at Oak Beach Inn in Babylon, New York. This area of New York State is known as 'Long Island' and the drink looks like iced tea disguising its contents – a fact that has many claiming its true origins lie with Prohibition.

LONG ISLAND SPICED TEA

★★★⯪☆

Glass: Collins
Garnish: None
Method: SHAKE first seven ingredients with ice and strain into ice-filled glass. TOP with cola, stir and serve with straws.

½	shot	Spiced rum
½	shot	Tanqueray London dry gin
½	shot	Ketel One vodka
½	shot	Tequila 100% Agave
½	shot	Triple Sec
1	shot	Freshly squeezed lime juice
½	shot	Monin Pure Cane 2:1 sugar syrup
Top up with		Coca-Cola

We say: A contemporary spicy twist on an American classic.

THE LONG SHOT 🔑

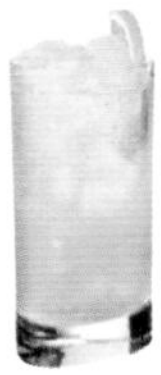

★★★★☆

Glass:
Garnish: Orange slice & lemon wedge
Method: SHAKE first five ingredients with ice and strain ice-filled glass. TOP with soda, lightly stir and serve with straws.

1½	shots	Tequila 100% Agave
½	shot	Curaçao orange liqueur
¼	shot	Monin Pure Cane 2:1 sugar syrup
¾	shot	Freshly squeezed lemon juice
1	dash	Angostura aromatic bitters
Top up with		Soda (club soda)

We say: A simple variation on William Schmidt's Alabazam.
Origin: Created in 2007 by Julian de Feral at Milk & Honey, London, England.

LONSDALE

★★★★☆

Glass: Collins
Garnish: Basil leaf & apple slice
Method: STIR honey syrup with gin until honey dissolves. TEAR basil leaves and add to shaker with all other ingredients. SHAKE with ice and fine strain into chilled glass.

2	shots	Tanqueray London dry gin
½	shot	Monin Honey syrup
3	fresh	Torn basil leaves
¾	shot	Freshly squeezed lemon juice
2½	shots	Pressed apple juice

We say: Not dry, not sweet, just balanced, long and refreshing.
Origin: Created by Alexandra Fiot at The Lonsdale, London, England.

LOOKS FAMILIAR

★★★★½

Glass: Old-fashioned
Garnish: Orange zest twist
Method: STIR malt with ice and then strain and discard excess to leave the ice and mixing glass coated. Add other ingredients and STIR with the coated ice. Strain into ice-filled glass.

½	shot	**Lagavulin 16yo malt whisky**
2	shots	**Tequila 100% Agave**
½	shot	**Agave nectar**
2	dashes	**Angostura aromatic bitters**
¼	shot	**Amer Picon**

We say: I defy you not to love this herbal bitter-sweet tequila laced concoction.
Origin: Created by Jake Burger at Jake's Bar, Leeds, England.

LORRAINE #1

★★★

Glass: Old-fashioned
Garnish: Orange zest twist
Method: STIR all ingredients with ice and strain into ice-filled glass.

1½	shots	**Tanqueray London dry gin**
1	shot	**Martini Extra Dry vermouth**
½	shot	**Grand Marnier liqueur**

We say: A Wet Martini served on the rocks, sweetened and flavoured with a slug of orange liqueur.
Origin: Created by Joe Gilmore to mark Charles de Caulle's first state visit to Britain in the 1950s and named after the Cross of Lorraine, symbol of the Order of Liberation. The original recipe called for one whole shot of Grand Marnier.

LORRAINE #2

★★★★½

Glass: Martini
Garnish: Lime zest twist
Method: SHAKE all ingredients and fine strain into chilled glass.

¾	shot	**Kirschwasser eau de vie**
¾	shot	**Ketel One vodka**
¾	shot	**Bénédictine D.O.M.**
½	shot	**Freshly squeezed lime juice**
⅛	shot	**Monin Pure Cane 2:1 sugar syrup**

We say: Sweet and sour with fruity, herbal notes.
Origin: Adaptation by Simon Difford.

LOTUS ESPRESSO

★★★★½

Glass: Martini
Garnish: Coffee beans
Method: SHAKE all ingredients with ice and fine strain into chilled glass.

2	shots	**Ketel One vodka**
½	shot	**Kahlúa coffee liqueur**
½	shot	**Maple syrup**
1	shot	**Hot espresso coffee**

We say: Coffee to the fore but with complex, earthy bitter-sweet notes.
Origin: Adapted from a drink discovered in 2005 at Lotus Bar, Sydney, Australia.

LOTUS MARTINI

★★★★

Glass: Martini
Garnish: Mint leaf
Method: Lightly MUDDLE mint (just to bruise) in base of shaker. Add other ingredients, SHAKE with ice and fine strain into chilled glass.

7	fresh	**Mint leaves**
2	shots	**Tanqueray London dry gin**
¼	shot	**Bols Blue Curaçao liqueur**
1½	shots	**Lychee syrup (from tinned fruit)**
¼	shot	**Pomegranate (grenadine) syrup**

We say: This violet coloured drink may have an unlikely list of ingredients, but definitely tastes great.
Origin: Created in 2001 by Martin Walander at Match Bar, London, England.

LOUD SPEAKER MARTINI

★★★½

Glass: Martini
Garnish: Lemon zest twist
Method: SHAKE all ingredients with ice and fine strain into chilled glass.

1½	shots	**Tanqueray London dry gin**
1½	shots	**Cognac VSOP**
½	shot	**Martini Rosso sweet vermouth**
¼	shot	**Freshly squeezed lemon juice**
¼	shot	**Monin Pure Cane 2:1 sugar syrup**

We say: I've added a dash of sugar to the original recipe which I found too dry.
Origin: Adapted from a recipe in the 1930 '*Savoy Cocktail Book*' by Harry Craddock.

LOUISIANA TRADE

★★★½

Glass: Old-fashioned
Garnish: Lime wedge
Method: SHAKE all ingredients with ice and strain into glass filled with crushed ice.

2	shots	**Southern Comfort liqueur**
1	shot	**Freshly squeezed lime juice**
¼	shot	**Monin Pure Cane 2:1 sugar syrup**
½	shot	**Maple syrup**

We say: Peach and apricot with the freshness of lime and the dense sweetness of maple syrup.
Origin: Created in 2001 by Mahdi Otmann at Zeta, London, England.

LOVE ME FLIP NEW

★★★★½

Glass: Goblet
Garnish: Grate tonka bean over drink
Method: BEAT egg yolk with sugar in base of shaker. Add other ingredients, SHAKE with ice and fine strain into chilled glass.

1	fresh	**Egg yolk**
2	shots	**Bacardi 8yo aged rum**
1	shot	**Bols Natural Yoghurt liqueur**
½	shot	**Pedro Ximénez sherry**
3	drops	**Angostura aromatic bitters**

We say: The grated Tonka bean adds a vanilla aroma to the surface of this drink.
Origin: Created in 2010 by Erik Lorincz at The Connaught Hotel, London, England.

LOVE JUNK

★★★⯨☆☆

Glass: Old-fashioned
Garnish: Apple wedge
Method: SHAKE all ingredients with ice and strain into ice-filled glass.

2	shots	Ketel One vodka
½	shot	Midori green melon liqueur
½	shot	Peachtree peach schnapps
1½	shots	Pressed apple juice

We say: A light, crisp, refreshing blend of peach, melon and apple juice, laced with vodka.

LOVE UNIT

★★★★⯨

Glass: Martini
Garnish: Basil leaf & bell pepper
Method: MUDDLE pepper in base of shaker. Add other ingredients, SHAKE with ice and fine strain glass.

2	slices	Red bell pepper
7	fresh	Torn basil leaves
1	shot	Bacardi Superior rum
1	shot	Vanilla-infused Bacardi rum
¾	shot	Freshly squeezed lime juice
½	shot	Freshly squeezed grapefruit juice
½	shot	Monin Pure Cane 2:1 sugar syrup

We say: Delicate, complex and balanced with enough fruit and veg to make your five-a-day.
Origin: Created by Ryan Magarian, Seattle, USA.

LOVED UP ⚷━

★★★⯨☆

Glass: Martini
Garnish: Seasonal berries
Method: SHAKE all ingredients with ice and fine strain into chilled glass.

1½	shots	Tequila 100% Agave
½	shot	Triple Sec
½	shot	Chambord black raspberry liqueur
½	shot	Freshly squeezed lime juice
1	shot	Freshly squeezed orange juice
¼	shot	Monin Pure Cane 2:1 sugar syrup

We say: Tequila predominates in this rusty coloured drink, which also features orange and berry fruit.
Origin: Adapted from a cocktail discovered in 2002 at the Merc Bar, New York City, where the original name was listed as simply 'Love'.

LUCIEN GAUDIN

★★★★☆

Glass: Martini
Garnish: Orange zest twist
Method: STIR all ingredients with ice and strain into chilled glass.

1½	shots	Tanqueray London dry gin
¾	shot	Triple Sec
¾	shot	Campari Bitter
¾	shot	Martini Extra Dry vermouth

We say: A must try for anyone who loves Negronis.
Origin: Recipe from 'Vintage Spirits and Forgotten Cocktails' by Ted Haigh (Dr. Cocktail). Lucien Gaudin was a French fencer who achieved gold medals with two different weapons at the 1928 Olympics in Amsterdam.

LUCKY LILY MARGARITA ⚷━

★★★★⯨

Glass: Coupette
Garnish: Pineapple wedge dusted with pepper on rim.
Method: STIR honey with tequila in base of shaker to dissolve honey. ADD other ingredients, SHAKE with ice and super-fine strain into chilled glass.

2	spoons	Runny honey
2	shots	Tequila 100% Agave
1	shot	Fresh pressed pineapple juice
¾	shot	Freshly squeezed lime juice
5	grind	Black pepper

We say: Spicy tequila and pineapple tingle with balance and flavour.
Origin: Adapted from a drink discovered in 2006 at All Star Lanes, London, England.

LUCKY LINDY

★★★⯨☆

Glass: Collins
Garnish: Lemon slice
Method: STIR honey with bourbon in base of shaker so as to dissolve honey. Add lemon juice, SHAKE with ice and strain into ice-filled glass. TOP with lemonade, lightly stir and serve with straws.

3	spoons	Runny honey
2	shots	Maker's Mark bourbon
½	shot	Freshly squeezed lemon juice
Top up with		Lemonade/Sprite/7-Up

We say: A long refreshing drink that combines whisky, citrus and honey - a long chilled toddy without the spice.
Origin: Adapted from a drink discovered in 2003 at The Grange Hall, New York City, USA.

LUSH ⚷━

★★★⯨☆

Glass: Flute
Garnish: Raspberries
Method: POUR vodka and liqueur into chilled glass, TOP with champagne and lightly stir.

1	shot	Ketel One vodka
½	shot	Chambord black raspberry liqueur
Top up with		Brut champagne

We say: It is, are you?
Origin: Created in 1999 by Spike Marchant at Alphabet, London, England.

LUTKINS SPECIAL MARTINI ⚷━

★★★⯨☆

Glass: Martini
Garnish: Orange zest twist
Method: SHAKE all ingredients with ice and fine strain into chilled glass.

1½	shots	Tanqueray London dry gin
½	shot	De Kuyper Apricot Brandy liqueur
1	shot	Martini Extra Dry vermouth
¾	shot	Freshly squeezed orange juice

We say: I've tried many variations on the above formula and none that are special.
Origin: Adapted from a recipe in Harry Craddock's 1930 'Savoy Cocktail Book'.

LUX DAIQUIRI

★★★★☆

Glass: Martini
Garnish: Maraschino cherry
Method: BLEND all ingredients with one 12oz scoop of crushed ice and serve in chilled glass.

3	shots	Bacardi Superior rum
½	shot	Luxardo Maraschino liqueur
¾	shot	Freshly squeezed lime juice
¼	shot	Maraschino syrup (from cherry jar)
¼	shot	Monin Pure Cane 2:1 sugar syrup

We say: A classic frozen Daiquiri heavily laced with maraschino cherry.
Origin: This was one of the two cocktails with which I won a Havana Club Daiquiri competition in 2002. I named it after Girolamo Luxardo, creator of the now famous liqueur, 'Luxardo Maraschino'. My educated sub also informs me Lux is Latin for light.

LUXURY COCKTAIL

★★★½☆

Glass: Martini
Garnish: None
Method: SHAKE all ingredients with ice and fine strain into chilled glass.

2	shots	Tanqueray London dry gin
¾	shot	Pimm's No.1 Cup
½	shot	Bols Banana liqueur
¾	shot	Martini Rosso sweet vermouth
¼	shot	Rose's lime cordial
3	dashes	Angostura aromatic bitters

We say: Sticky banana followed by a bitter, refined after-taste.

LUXURY MOJITO

★★★★☆

Glass: Collins
Garnish: Mint sprig
Method: MUDDLE mint in glass with sugar and lime juice. Fill glass with crushed ice, add rum, Angostura and champagne, then stir.

12	fresh	Mint leaves
¼	shot	Monin Pure Cane 2:1 sugar syrup
1	shot	Freshly squeezed lime juice
2	shots	Bacardi 8yo aged rum
3	dashes	Angostura aromatic bitters
Top up with		Brut champagne

We say: A Mojito made with aged rum and topped with champagne: more complex than the original.

LYCHEE & BLACKCURRANT MARTINI

★★★★☆

Glass: Martini
Garnish: Lychee
Method: SHAKE all ingredients with ice and fine strain into chilled glass.

2	shots	Tanqueray London dry gin
½	shot	Kwai Feh lychee liqueur
¼	shot	Rose's lime cordial
¾	scoop	Chilled mineral water
¼	shot	Crème de cassis liqueur

We say: Light, fragrant and laced with gin.
Origin: Created by Simon Difford in 2004.

LYCHEE & ROSE PETAL MARTINI

★★★★☆

Glass: Martini
Garnish: Rose petal
Method: STIR all ingredients with ice and strain into chilled glass.

2	shots	Tanqueray London dry gin
1	shot	Lanique rose petal liqueur
1	shot	Lychee syrup (from tinned fruit)
2	dashes	Peychaud's aromatic bitters

We say: Light pink in colour and subtle in flavour.
Origin: Created in 2002 by Dick Bradsell for Opium, London, England.

LYCHEE & SAKE MARTINI

★★★★☆

Glass: Martini
Garnish: Lychee
Method: STIR all ingredients with ice and strain into chilled glass.

1½	shots	Tanqueray London dry gin
¾	shot	Kwai Feh lychee liqueur
2	shots	Sake

We say: A soft, Martini-styled drink with subtle hints of sake and lychee.
Origin: Created in 2004 by Simon Difford.

LYCHEE MAC

★★★½☆

Glass: Old-fashioned
Garnish: Lychee
Method: SHAKE all ingredients with ice and strain into ice-filled glass.

2¼	shots	Dewar's White label Scotch
1	shot	Kwai Feh lychee liqueur
¾	shot	Stone's green ginger wine

We say: Peaty Scotch with sweet lychee and hot ginger.
Origin: Created by Simon Difford in 2004.

LYCHEE MARTINI

★★★★☆

Glass: Martini
Garnish: Lychee
Method: STIR all ingredients with ice and fine strain into chilled glass.

2	shots	Ketel One vodka
½	shot	Kwai Feh lychee liqueur
1	shot	Lychee syrup (from tinned fruit)
½	shot	Martini Extra Dry vermouth

We say: If you like lychee you'll love this delicate Martini.
Origin: Thought to have been first made in 2001 at Clay, a Korean restaurant in New York City, USA.

LYCHEE RICKEY

Glass: Collins (small 8oz)
Garnish: Length of lime peel
Method: SHAKE first three ingredients with ice and strain into ice-filled glass. TOP with soda water.

2	shots	Tanqueray London dry gin
1	shot	Kwai Feh lychee liqueur
½	shot	Freshly squeezed lime juice
Top up with		Soda (club soda)

We say: The Kwai Feh lychee liqueur dominates this surprisingly dry Rickey.
Origin: Adapted from a drink discovered in 2005 at Club 97, Hong Kong, China.

LYNCHBURG LEMONADE

Glass: Collins
Garnish: Lemon slice
Method: SHAKE first 3 ingredients with ice and strain into ice-filled glass. TOP with lemonade.

1½	shots	Jack Daniels Tennessee whiskey
1	shot	Triple Sec
1	shot	Freshly squeezed lemon juice
Top up with		Lemonade/Sprite/7-Up

Variant: With three dashes of Angostura aromatic bitters.
We say: Tangy, light and very easy to drink.
Origin: Created for the Jack Daniel's distillery in - yep, you guessed it - Lynchburg, Tennessee.

M.G.F.

Glass: Martini
Garnish: Orange zest twist
Method: SHAKE all ingredients with ice and fine strain into chilled glass.

1	shot	Ketel One Oranje vodka
1	shot	Ketel One Citroen vodka
1	shot	Freshly squeezed grapefruit juice
1	shot	Freshly squeezed lemon juice
½	shot	Monin Pure Cane 2:1 sugar syrup

We say: Short and sharp.
Origin: Discovered in 2003 at Claridge's Bar, London, England.

MAÇÃ

Glass: Martini
Garnish: Apple slice & mint sprig
Method: SHAKE all ingredients with ice and fine strain into chilled glass.

2	shots	Leblon cachaça
½	shot	St~Germain elderflower liqueur
1½	shots	Pressed apple juice
½	shot	Freshly squeezed lime juice

We say: Subtle combination of cachaça, fresh lime, apple juice and elderflower.
Origin: Adapted from a recipe created in 2007 by Jamie Terrell, New York, USA and originally based of Sagatiba cachaça. Maçã means apple in Portuguese.

MAÑANA DAIQUIRI

Glass: Coupette
Garnish: Apricot slice
Method: SHAKE all ingredients with ice and fine strain into chilled glass.

2	shots	Bacardi Superior rum
½	shot	De Kuyper Apricot Brandy liqueur
¼	shot	Pomegranate (grenadine) syrup
¼	shot	Freshly squeezed lemon juice
½	shot	Chilled mineral water

We say: Salmon pink in colour, the Mañana has a subtle and delicate rum laced apricot flavour.
Origin: Mañana, literally meaning 'tomorrow' in Spanish but more usually used to mean some indefinite time in the future. This recipe is adapted from David A. Embury's 1948 *"Fine Art of Mixing Drinks"*.

MAC ORANGE

Glass: Old-fashioned
Garnish: Orange zest twist
Method: SHAKE all ingredients with ice and fine strain into chilled glass.

2	shots	Dewar's White label Scotch
1	shot	Stone's green ginger wine
1	shot	Freshly squeezed orange juice
¼	shot	Monin Pure Cane 2:1 sugar syrup
3	dashes	Orange bitters

We say: A Whiskey Mac with orange topping off the ginger.

MACHINE HEAD NEW

Glass: Coupette
Garnish: Maraschino cherry & orange zest twist
Method: POUR all ingredients except tea into mixing glass. SMOKE tea using a chefs smoker and direct smoke into mixing glass. Cover to capture smoke for a minute or so. Remove cover, STIR with ice and strain into chilled glass.

1	shot	Cognac VSOP
1	shot	Bacardi Superior rum
1	shot	Maker's Mark bourbon
1	shot	Benoit Serres crème de violette
1	dash	Orange bitters
1	dash	Angostura aromatic bitters
1	dash	Xocolatl Mole bitters
3	pinch	Lychee Rose Tea

We say: Overdo the smoke and your cocktail will start to resemble a cigar. Too little and you may find a tad sweet.
Origin: Adapted from a drink created in 2010 by Jamie Boudreau at Vessel, Seattle, USA.

MACKA

Glass: Collins
Garnish: Lemon slice
Method: SHAKE first 4 ingredients with ice and strain into ice-filled glass. TOP with soda.

2	shots	Tanqueray London dry gin
½	shot	Crème de cassis liqueur
½	shot	Martini Extra Dry vermouth
½	shot	Martini Rosso sweet vermouth
Top up with		Soda (club soda)

We say: A long fruity drink for parched palates.

THE MACKINNON

★★★★☆

Glass: Martini
Garnish: Lemon zest twist
Method: SHAKE all ingredients with ice and fine strain into chilled glass.

2	shots	Bacardi Oro golden rum
1	shot	Drambuie
½	shot	Freshly squeezed lemon juice

Variant: Serve long over ice with soda.
We say: Honeyed rum with herbal and citrus nuances.
Origin: Named after the MacKinnon family, the makers of Drambuie.

MAD MONK MILKSHAKE

★★★☆☆

Glass: Collins
Garnish: Cord around glass
Method: SHAKE all ingredients with ice and strain into ice-filled glass.

1	shot	Baileys Irish cream liqueur
2	shots	Hazelnut liqueur
¼	shot	Kahlúa coffee liqueur
2	shots	Milk
1	shot	Double (heavy) cream

Variant: Blend instead of shaking and serve frozen.
We say: Long, creamy and slightly sweet with hazelnut and coffee.

MADE MAN NEW

★★★★☆

Glass: Martini
Garnish: Lemon zest twist
Method: STIR all ingredients with ice and strain into chilled glass.

1½	shots	Straight rye whiskey
¼	shot	Chartreuse Yellow liqueur
¼	shot	Cherry brandy liqueur
⅛	shot	Fernet Branca
½	shot	Chilled mineral water

We say: A Manhattanesque rye based sipper with splashes of Carthusian, cherry and Italian count influence
Origin: Adapted from a recipe created in 2012 by Ali Reynolds at Hawksmore, Spitalfields, London.

MADRAS ⚿

★★★☆☆

Glass: Collins
Garnish: Orange slice
Method: SHAKE all ingredients with ice and strain into ice-filled glass.

2	shots	Ketel One vodka
3	shots	Ocean Spray cranberry juice
2	shots	Freshly squeezed orange juice

We say: A seabreeze with orange juice in place of grapefruit, making it slightly sweeter.

MAID IN CUBA NEW

★★★★☆

Glass: Coupette
Garnish: Slice of cucumber
Method: POUR absinthe into ice-filled glass, TOP with water and leave to stand. Separately SHAKE other ingredients with ice (Don't muddle cucumber). DISCARD contents of glass (absinthe, water and ice) and STRAIN contents of shaker into absinthe-coated glass. TOP with splash of soda.

¼	shot	La Fée Parisienne (68%) absinthe
2	shots	Rum light white/blanco
¾	shot	Freshly squeezed lime juice
½	shot	Monin Pure Cane 2:1 sugar syrup
7	fresh	Mint leaves
2	slices	Cucumber (chopped & peeled)
Top up with		Soda (club soda)

We say: A classic Daiquiri shaken with mint and cucumber strained into an absinthe washed glass and spritzed with soda.
Origin: Adapted from a drink created by Tom Walker at the American Bar, Savoy Hotel, London for Bacardi Legacy 2012.

MAIDA VALE NEW

★★★★☆

Glass: Coupette
Garnish: Maraschino cherry
Method: STIR all ingredients with ice and strain into chilled glass.

2	shots	Maker's Mark bourbon
½	shot	Straight rye whiskey
½	shot	Martini Rosso sweet vermouth
½	shot	Martini Bianco vermouth
¼	shot	Grand Marnier liqueur
2	dashes	Angostura aromatic bitters

We say: Originally named the Unripe Manhattan after the website of its creator, this Manhattan-style cocktail benefits from the spice of rye whiskey with sweet and bianco vermouth and a dash of orange curaçao.
Origin: Created in January 2011 by Andy Green of Unripe, London, England.

MADROSKA ⚿

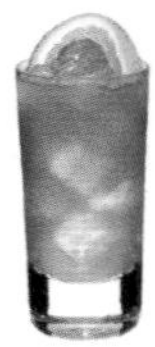

★★★☆☆

Glass: Collins
Garnish: Orange slice
Method: SHAKE all ingredients with ice and strain into ice filled glass.

2	shots	Ketel One vodka
2½	shots	Pressed apple juice
1½	shots	Ocean Spray cranberry juice
1	shot	Freshly squeezed orange juice

We say: A Madras with more than a hint of apple juice.
Origin: Created in 1998 by Jamie Terrell, London, England.

MAE WEST MARTINI

★★★★☆

Glass: Martini
Garnish: Melon slice
Method: SHAKE all ingredients with ice and fine strain into chilled glass.

2	shots	Ketel One vodka
½	shot	Amaretto liqueur
¼	shot	Midori green melon liqueur
1½	shots	Ocean Spray cranberry juice

We say: A rosé coloured, semi-sweet concoction with a cherry, chocolate flavour.

MAESTRO

★★★★☆

Glass: Martini
Garnish: Balsamic covered strawberry
Method: SHAKE all ingredients with ice and fine strain into chilled glass.

2	shots	Ketel One vodka
1	shot	Crème de fraise liqueur
1	shot	Freshly squeezed orange juice
¼	shot	Maple syrup
1	dash	Balsamic vinegar of moderna

We say: Strawberry and balsamic are a great combo - here served with orange juice, vodka and maple syrup.
Origin: Created by Salvatore Calabrese at Salvatore At Fifty, London, England.

MAGIC BUS ⚷

★★★☆☆

Glass: Martini
Garnish: Lime wedge
Method: SHAKE all ingredients with ice and fine strain into chilled glass.

1	shot	Tequila 100% Agave
1	shot	Triple Sec
1	shot	Ocean Spray cranberry juice
1	shot	Freshly squeezed orange juice

We say: Orange and cranberry laced with tequila.

MAHUKONA ⚷

★★★☆☆

Glass: Sling
Garnish: Pineapple cubes, maraschino cherry & mint sprig
Method: BLEND all ingredients with 6oz scoop crushed ice and strain into glass half-filled with crushed ice. Serve with straws.

1	shot	Bacardi Superior rum
½	shot	Triple Sec
1	shot	Fresh pressed pineapple juice
½	shot	Freshly squeezed lemon juice
¼	shot	Monin Pure Cane 2:1 sugar syrup
2	dashes	Angostura aromatic bitters

We say: Citrus fresh and refreshing, not at all a sweetie.
Origin: Adapted from Victor Bergeron's '*Trader Vic's Bartender's Guide*' (1972 revised edition).

MAI TAI #2 (BEAUMONT-GANTT'S FORMULA)

★★★★☆

Glass: Old-fashioned
Garnish: Mint sprig
Method: Lightly muddle mint in base of shaker (just to bruise). Add other ingredients, SHAKE with ice and strain glass filled with crushed ice.

12	fresh	Mint leaves
1½	shots	Myer's dark Jamaican rum
1	shot	Bacardi Superior rum
¾	shot	Triple Sec
½	shot	Taylor's Velvet Falernum liqueur
1	shot	Freshly squeezed lime juice
1	shot	Freshly squeezed grapefruit juice
2	dashes	Angostura aromatic bitters

We say: Whichever of the two created the drink; it is Trader Vic that made it famous and it is his recipe that endures.
Origin: It is claimed that Ernest Raymond Beaumont-Gantt first served this drink in 1933 at his Don The Beachcomber's bar in Hollywood, California. This is some ten years earlier than Bergeron's Mai Tai moment in cocktail history.

BARTENDER'S TIP FINE STRAIN

Most cocktails that are served 'straight up' without ice benefit from an additional finer strain, over and above the standard strain.

This 'fine strain' removes small fragments of fruit and fine flecks of ice which can spoil the appearance of a drink and is particularly beneficial if the drink has been shaken. Fine straining is achieved by simply holding a fine sieve, like a tea strainer, between the shaker and the glass.

MAI TAI (VIC'S)

★★★★☆
Glass: Old-fashioned
Garnish: Lime, mint sprig, pineapple cube & maraschino cherry
Method: SHAKE all ingredients with ice and strain into glass filled with crushed ice.

2	shots	Bacardi 8yo aged rum
½	shot	Curaçao orange liqueur
¾	shot	Freshly squeezed lime juice
¼	shot	Monin Almond (orgeat) syrup
¼	shot	Monin Pure Cane 2:1 sugar syrup

We say: I love Daiquiris and this is basically a classic Daiquiri with a few bells and whistles.
Origin: In 1934, Victor Jules Bergeron, or Trader Vic as he became known, opened his first restaurant in Oakland, San Francisco. He served Polynesian food with a mix of Chinese, French and American dishes cooked in wood-fired ovens. But he is best known for the rum based cocktails he created.

One evening in 1944 he tested a new drink on two friends from Tahiti, Ham and Carrie Guild. After the first sip, Carrie exclaimed, "Mai Tai-Roa Aé", which in Tahitian means 'Out of this world - the best!'. So Bergeron named his drink the Mai Tai. The original was based on 17 year old Jamaican J.Wray & Nephew rum which Vic in his own guide describes as being "surprisingly golden in colour, medium bodied, but with the rich pungent flavour particular to the Jamaican blends". Vic states he used "rock candy" syrup, an old term for the type of strong sugar syrup I prescribe in this guide.

The term referred to the fact that you could dangle a piece of string in it to encourage crystallisation and make rock candy. When supplies of the Jamaican 17yo rum dwindled, Vic started using a combination of dark Jamaican rum and Martinique rum to achieve the desired flavour. Sheer demand in his chain of restaurants later necessitated the introduction of a Mai Tai pre-mix (still available from www.tradervics.com).

Others, particularly Ernest Raymond Beaumont-Gantt, then owner of a Hollywood bar called Don the Beachcomber's, have also laid claim to the creation of this drink. But as Vic says in his own Bartender's Guide, "Anybody who says I didn't create this drink is a dirty stinker." This recipe is adapted from Victor Bergeron's '*Trader Vic's Bartender's Guide*' (1972 revised edition).

MAIDEN'S BLUSH

★★★★½
Glass: Martini
Garnish: Lemon zest twist
Method: SHAKE all ingredients with ice and fine strain into chilled glass.

2	shots	Tanqueray London dry gin
½	shot	Triple Sec
½	shot	Pomegranate (grenadine) syrup
¼	shot	Freshly squeezed lemon juice
½	shot	Chilled mineral water

We say: Pale pink, subtle and light.
Origin: Adapted from a recipe in Harry Craddock's 1930 '*Savoy Cocktail Book*'

MAIDEN'S PRAYER

★★★½☆
Glass: Martini
Garnish: Orange zest twist
Method: SHAKE all ingredients with ice and fine strain into chilled glass.

1½	shots	Tanqueray London dry gin
1	shot	Triple Sec
1	shot	Freshly squeezed orange juice
½	shot	Freshly squeezed lemon juice

We say: Fresh, zesty orange with a pleasing twang of alcohol.
Origin: Adapted from a recipe in Harry Craddock's 1930 '*Savoy Cocktail Book*'.

MAINBRACE

★★★★☆
Glass: Martini
Garnish: Orange zest twist
Method: SHAKE all ingredients with ice and fine strain into chilled glass.

1¼	shots	Tanqueray London dry gin
1¼	shots	Triple Sec
1¼	shots	Freshly squeezed grapefruit juice

We say: Tangy grapefruit laced with gin and a hint of orange. Tart finish.

MAISON CHARLES DAIQUIRI

★★★★☆
Glass: Martini
Garnish: Sugar & mint rim
Method: Lightly MUDDLE (just to bruise) mint in base of shaker. Add other ingredients, SHAKE with ice and fine strain into chilled glass.

8	fresh	Mint leaves
2	shots	Bacardi Superior rum
½	shot	Freshly squeezed lime juice
½	shot	Monin Pure Cane 2:1 sugar syrup
½	shot	Chilled mineral water

Variant: Substitute triple sec for sugar to make a Madison Avenue.
We say: Reminiscent of concentrated Mojito.
Origin: Pronounced 'May-Sawn Sharl', this recipe is adapted from David A. Embury's 1948 '*Fine Art of Mixing Drinks*'.

BARTENDER'S TIP DRY SHAKE

It is common practice to first shake drinks containing cream and eggs without ice, then to shake the drink a second time with ice added.

This practice is known as 'dry shaking' and the theory is that first shaking without ice, and so at a higher temperature, better allows the drink to emulsify.

MAJOR BAILEY #1

★★★★½

Glass: Sling
Garnish: Mint sprig
Method: Lightly MUDDLE (only to bruise) mint with gin in base of shaker. Add other ingredients, SHAKE with ice and fine strain into glass half filled with crushed ice. CHURN (stir) drink with ice using a barspoon. Top the glass to the brim with more crushed ice and churn again. Serve with straws.

12	fresh	**Mint leaves**
2	shots	**Tanqueray London dry gin**
¼	shot	**Freshly squeezed lime juice**
¼	shot	**Freshly squeezed lemon juice**
½	shot	**Monin Pure Cane 2:1 sugar syrup**

We say: As Victor says of this gin based Julep, "This is a hell of a drink."
Origin: Adapted from a recipe in the 1947 'Trader Vic's Bartender Guide' by Victor Bergeron.

MAJOR BAILEY #2

★★★★½

Glass: Sling
Garnish: Mint sprig
Method: BLEND all ingredients with one 12oz scoop of crushed ice and serve with straws.

2	shots	**Bacardi Superior rum**
1	shot	**Triple Sec**
1	shot	**Fresh pressed pineapple juice**
½	shot	**Freshly squeezed lemon juice**
¼	shot	**Monin Pure Cane 2:1 sugar syrup**

We say: Made well this is a long, fruity, brilliant frozen Daquiri.
Origin: Adapted from a drink created by Victor Bergeron.

MALCOM LOWRY

★★★★☆

Glass: Old-fashioned
Garnish: Lime wedge
Method: SHAKE all ingredients with ice and strain into ice-filled glass.

1	shot	**Tequila 100% Agave**
½	shot	**Wray & Nephew overproof rum**
¼	shot	**Triple Sec**
½	shot	**Freshly squeezed lime juice**
¼	shot	**Monin Pure Cane 2:1 sugar syrup**

We say: A suitably 'hard' and flavoursome Daiquiri-like drink.
Origin: Created by drinks author David Broom. Named after Malcom Lowry's 1947 novel 'Under the Volcano' which explores a man's battle with alcoholism in Mexico.

STAR RATINGS EXPLAINED

★★★★★ Excellent

★★★★½ Recommended	★★★★☆ Praiseworthy
★★★½☆ Commended	★★★☆☆ Mediocre
★★½☆☆ Disappointing	★★☆☆☆ Pretty awful
★½☆☆☆ Shameful	★☆☆☆☆ Disgusting

MAMIE TAYLOR

★★★½☆

Glass: Collins
Garnish: Lemon slice
Method: POUR all ingredients into ice-filled glass and lightly STIR.

2	shots	**Dewar's White label Scotch**
¼	shot	**Freshly squeezed lime juice**

Top up with Ginger ale

We say: A Scotch and ginger with a splash of lime juice.
Origin: Adapted from Albert Stevens Crockett's 1935 '*The Old Waldorf-Astoria Bar Book*'. The drink first appeared in the New York Herald some thirty years prior to Crockett writing his book. Who Ms. Taylor was and why this drink was dedicated to her is unknown.

MALTY DRY MARTINI

★★★★½

Glass: Martini
Garnish: Chilled olive on stick or lemon zest twist
Method: STIR all ingredients with ice and strain into chilled glass.

2½	shots	**Bols Genever**
½	shot	**Martini Extra Dry vermouth**

We say: Using a genuinely malty jenever produces a deliciously retro take on the modern Dry Martini.
Origin: A drink promoted by Bols since the launch of Bols Genever in 2008.

MAMBO

★★★½☆

Glass: Collins
Garnish: Orange slice
Method: SHAKE all ingredients with ice and strain into ice-filled glass.

1	shot	**Ketel One vodka**
1	shot	**Triple Sec**
1	shot	**De Kuyper Apricot Brandy liqueur**
¼	shot	**Campari Bitter**
3	shots	**Freshly squeezed orange juice**

We say: A slightly bitter, tangy, orange, cooling drink.
Origin: Created by Nichole Colella.

MAN-BOUR-TINI

★★★★☆

Glass: Martini
Garnish: Orange zest twist
Method: SHAKE all ingredients with ice and fine strain into chilled glass.

¾	shot	**Maker's Mark bourbon**
1	shot	**Mandarine Napoléon liqueur**
½	shot	**Freshly squeezed lime juice**
2	shots	**Ocean Spray cranberry juice**
¼	shot	**Monin Pure Cane 2:1 sugar syrup**

We say: A rounded, fruity, bourbon based drink with mandarin and lime sourness.
Origin: Created in 1999 by Simon Difford.

MANCHESTER SPECIAL RUM PUNCH

★★★☆☆

Glass: Old-fashioned
Garnish: Grapefruit slice
Method: STIR honey with rum until honey dissolves. Add other ingredients, SHAKE with ice and strain into glass filled with crushed ice.

2	shots	Myer's Planter's Punch rum
2	spoons	Runny honey
1	shot	Freshly squeezed grapefruit juice
2	dashes	Angostura aromatic bitters

We say: Fruity punch.
Origin: Originally made at the Manchester Hotel, Mandeville, Jamaica. The Manchester Hotel lies in a lush tropical setting in the centre of Jamaica high in the cool mountains of Manchester.

MANDARINE COLLINS

★★★☆☆

Glass: Collins
Garnish: Orange slice
Method: SHAKE first three ingredients with ice and strain into ice-filled glass. TOP with soda.

1½	shots	Tanqueray London dry gin
1	shot	Mandarine Napoléon liqueur
1	shot	Freshly squeezed lemon juice
Top up with		Soda (club soda)

We say: A tangy, long refreshing drink with an intense mandarin flavour.

MANDARINE SIDECAR

★★★★☆

Glass: Martini
Garnish: Sugar rim (optional) & lemon zest twist
Method: SHAKE all ingredients with ice and fine strain into chilled glass.

1½	shots	Cognac VSOP
1	shot	Mandarine Napoléon liqueur
1	shot	Freshly squeezed lemon juice
⅛	shot	Monin Pure Cane 2:1 sugar syrup
¾	shot	Chilled mineral water

We say: Wonderfully tart and strong in flavour.

MANDARINE SONGBIRD

★★★☆☆

Glass: Collins
Garnish: Orange slice
Method: SHAKE first 3 ingredients with ice and fine strain into ice-filled glass. TOP with ginger beer.

2	shots	Mandarine Napoléon liqueur
½	shot	Freshly squeezed lemon juice
¾	shot	Freshly squeezed orange juice
Top up with		Ginger beer

We say: Long, spicy orange.

MANDARINE SOUR

★★★☆☆

Glass: Old-fashioned
Garnish: Lemon slice
Method: SHAKE all ingredients with ice and strain into ice-filled glass.

2	shots	Mandarine Napoléon liqueur
1	shot	Freshly squeezed lemon juice
¼	shot	Monin Pure Cane 2:1 sugar syrup
½	fresh	Egg white

We say: Sour, but with a strong mandarin sweetness.

MANDARINTINI

★★★★★

Glass: Martini
Garnish: Orange slice
Method: SHAKE all ingredients with ice and fine strain into chilled glass.

1½	shots	Ketel One Oranje vodka
½	shot	Grand Marnier liqueur
¼	shot	Campari Bitter
1½	shots	Pressed apple juice

We say: This bittersweet palate cleanser looks like pink grapefruit juice.
Origin: Adapted from a drink discovered in 2005 at Aqua Spirit, Hong Kong, China.

MANDARITO

★★★★☆

Glass: Old-fashioned
Garnish: Mint sprig
Method: Lightly MUDDLE mint (just to bruise) in base of glass. Add next 4 ingredients, half fill glass with crushed ice and CHURN (stir). Fill glass to brim with more crushed ice and churn some more. TOP with soda, stir and serve with straws.

12	fresh	Mint leaves
1	shot	Ketel One vodka
1½	shots	Mandarine Napoléon liqueur
1	shot	Freshly squeezed lime juice
⅛	shot	Monin Pure Cane 2:1 sugar syrup
Top up with		Soda (club soda)

We say: A vodka Mojito with mandarin accents.

MANGO COLLINS

★★★★☆

Glass: Collins
Garnish: Lemon slice
Method: SHAKE first three ingredients with ice and strain into ice-filled glass. TOP with soda, stir and serve with straws.

2	shots	Tanqueray London dry gin
2	shots	Boiron mango purée
1½	shots	Freshly squeezed lemon juicew
Top up with		Soda (club soda)

We say: Lemon juice and gin combine with mango in this refreshing tall drink.
Origin: Formula by Simon Difford in 2004.

MANGO DAIQUIRI

★★★★☆

Glass: Martini
Garnish: Lime wedge
Method: SHAKE all ingredients with ice and fine strain into chilled glass.

2	shots	Bacardi Superior rum
2	shots	Boiron mango purée
½	shot	Freshly squeezed lime juice

Variant: Blended with a 12oz scoop of crushed ice and an additional half shot of sugar syrup.
We say: Tropical yet potent and refreshing.
Origin: Formula by Simon Difford in 2004.

MANGO MARGARITA #1 (SERVED 'UP')

★★★★☆

Glass: Coupette
Garnish: Lime wedge
Method: SHAKE all ingredients with ice and fine strain into chilled glass.

2	shots	Tequila 100% Agave
1	shot	Boiron mango purée
1	shot	Triple Sec
1	shot	Freshly squeezed lime juice

We say: The character of the tequila is not overwhelmed by the fruit.
Origin: Formula by Simon Difford in 2004.

MANGO MARGARITA #2 (FROZEN)

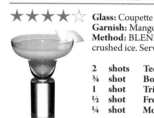

★★★★☆

Glass: Coupette
Garnish: Mango slice
Method: BLEND all ingredients with 6oz scoop of crushed ice. Serve with straws.

2	shots	Tequila 100% Agave
¾	shot	Boiron mango purée
1	shot	Triple Sec
½	shot	Freshly squeezed lime juice
¼	shot	Monin Pure Cane 2:1 sugar syrup

We say: Mango first and Margarita second.
Origin: Formula by Simon Difford in 2006.

MANGO MARTINI

★★★★☆

Glass: Martini
Garnish: Mango slice
Method: SHAKE all ingredients with ice and fine strain into chilled glass.

| 2½ | shots | Ketel One Citroen vodka |
| 2 | shots | Boiron mango purée |

We say: This drink doesn't work nearly so well with plain vodka - if citrus vodka is not available, try using gin.
Origin: Formula by Simon Difford in 2004.

MANGO PUNCH

★★★★☆

Glass: Collins
Garnish: Mango slice
Method: SHAKE all ingredients with ice and fine strain into glass filled with crushed ice.

2	shots	Wray & Nephew overproof rum
3	shots	Boiron mango purée
¾	shot	Freshly squeezed lime juice
¾	shot	Monin Pure Cane 2:1 sugar syrup

We say: A distinctly tropical cocktail flavoured with mango.
Origin: Formula by Simon Difford in 2004.

MANGO RUM COOLER

★★★½☆

Glass: Collins
Garnish: Mango slice
Method: SHAKE all ingredients with ice and strain into ice-filled glass.

2½	shots	Bacardi Superior rum
1½	shots	Boiron mango purée
1	shot	Pressed apple juice
1½	shots	Freshly squeezed lemon juice

We say: Long, fruity and cooling.
Origin: Created in 2004 by Simon Difford.

MANHATTAN DRY 🔑🍸

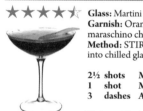

★★★★½

Glass: Martini
Garnish: Orange zest twist (discarded) & maraschino cherry
Method: STIR all ingredients with ice and strain into chilled glass.

2½	shots	Maker's Mark bourbon
1	shot	Martini Extra Dry vermouth
3	dashes	Angostura aromatic bitters

Variant: Manhattan Perfect and Manhattan Sweet. Also served over ice in an old-fashioned glass.
We say: A bone dry Manhattan for those with dry palates.
Origin: Like so many cocktails, the origins of the Manhattan are lost in time. And, as neither the name nor the ingredients are so unusual as to prevent inadvertent duplication, the mystery is likely to remain unsolved. The Democrat newspaper remarked in 1882 that, "It is but a short time ago that a mixture of whiskey, vermouth and bitters came into vogue" and observed that it had been known as a Turf Club cocktail, a Jockey Club cocktail and a Manhattan cocktail.

Until fairly recently, the most popular story was that the drink was created in November 1874 at New York City's Manhattan Club for Lady Randolph Churchill (née Jenny Jerome), while she was celebrating the successful gubernatorial campaign of Samuel Jones Tilden. (The Manhattan Club was opposite the site which now houses the Empire State Building.) However, David Wondrich has pointed out that the banquet in question was held in November 1874, when Lady C was otherwise engaged, in England, giving birth to Winston.

A 1945 article claims that a drink under the name of the Manhattan appeared in an 1860 bar guide; it certainly appears in Harry Johnson's book of 1884.

A plausible story comes from a book published in 1923, 'Valentine's Manual of New York'. In this a William F. Mulhall who was a bartender at New York's Hoffman House in the 1880s recounts, "The Manhattan cocktail was invented by a man named Black who kept a place ten doors below Houston Street on Broadway in the [eighteen] sixties - probably the most famous drink in the world in its time."

Yet another story involves a Col. Joe Walker on a yachting trip in New York but as this specifically refers to sweet vermouth I have recounted it under 'Manhattan Sweet.'

MANHATTAN ISLAND

★★★★☆

Glass: Martini
Garnish: Maraschino cherry
Method: STIR all ingredients with ice and fine strain into chilled glass.

2	shots	**Cognac VSOP**
1	shot	**Martini Rosso sweet vermouth**
3	dashes	**Angostura aromatic bitters**
⅛	shot	**Luxardo Maraschino liqueur**

We say: A twist on the classic Harvard, or brandy based Manhattan.

MANHATTAN PERFECT

★★★★★

Glass: Martini
Garnish: Orange zest twist (discarded) & maraschino cherry
Method: STIR all ingredients with ice and strain into chilled glass.

2½	shots	**Maker's Mark bourbon**
½	shot	**Martini Rosso sweet vermouth**
½	shot	**Martini Extra Dry vermouth**
3	dashes	**Angostura aromatic bitters**

Variant: Manhattan Dry and Manhattan Sweet. Also served over ice in an old-fashioned glass.
We say: The Manhattan version most popularly served - medium dry.
Origin: Whatever the truth of its invention (see Manhattan Dry), the Manhattan was probably originally made with rye whiskey, rather than bourbon, as New York was a rye-drinking city, although early bar books just state 'whiskey'. Today it is common to use bourbon, although purists are beginning to revive rye.
When Scotch is substituted for bourbon the Manhattan becomes a Rob Roy, with brandy (cognac) it becomes a Harvard and with applejack it is a Star Cocktail when made with applejack.
Some time in 2005 it became conventional in some New York bars to garnish a Manhattan with two cherries as a 9/11 tribute.

MANHATTAN SWEET

★★★★★

Glass: Martini
Garnish: Orange zest twist (discarded) & maraschino cherry
Method: STIR all ingredients with ice and strain into chilled glass.

2½	shots	**Maker's Mark bourbon**
⅛	shot	**Maraschino syrup (from cherry jar)**
1	shot	**Martini Rosso sweet vermouth**
3	dashes	**Angostura aromatic bitters**

Variant: Manhattan Dry and Manhattan Perfect. Also served over ice in an old-fashioned glass.
We say: I must confess to preferring my Manhattans served sweet, or perfect at a push. The Manhattan is complex, challenging and moreish. Best of all, it's available in a style to suit every palate.
Origin: Various origins for this drink abound. They include: in November 1874 at New York City's Manhattan Club for Lady Randolph Churchill. Sometime in the 1880s by a man named Black who kept a place ten doors below Houston Street on Broadway in the [eighteen] sixties, and by a Col. Joe Walker on a yachting trip in New York.

That last story is the most recent I have come across and comes courtesy of Barry Popik's website barrypopik.com where Barry notes an entry in the Daily Journal, Racine, Wisconsin, 8 March 1899. The article purports that Col. Joe Walker ran the then-famous Crescent Hall Saloon in New Orleans, at the corner of Canal and St. Charles Streets and that some years before he went on a little yachting trip with a party of friends while in New York.

"By some oversight the liquid refreshments in the icebox were confined to Italian vermouth and plain whisky, and it occurred to the colonel that a palatable drink might be made by mixing the two. The results were so good that he experimented a little on his return to New Orleans, and soon perfected the Manhattan cocktail, as it is known today. It was christened in honor of his friends on Manhattan island, and the fame of the decoction soon spread all over the country. The true Manhattan cocktail is always made with Italian vermouth, but at half the places where they undertake to serve them, French [dry] vermouth is substituted, and the fine flavor is altogether destroyed. French vermouth is a sort of wine, while Italian vermouth is a cordial, pure and simple. They are as different as milk and molasses. A cocktail made from the French brand is no more a Manhattan cocktail than it is a Spanish omelette."

MANICURE

★★★★☆

Glass: Coupette
Garnish: Apple wedge
Method: STIR all ingredients with ice and fine strain into chilled glass.

1	shot	**Calvados/Applejack brandy**
1	shot	**Dewar's White label Scotch**
1	shot	**Drambuie**

We say: Due to the use of Calvados this drink was going to be called 'FRENCH NAIL CARE' but thankfully this led to the name 'Manicure'.
Origin: Created in 2010 by a collaboration between Emma Ramos and Simon Difford at the Cabinet Room, London, England.

MANTINI

★★★★½

Glass: Martini
Garnish: Olive wrapped in bacon
Method: STIR all ingredients with ice and strain into chilled glass.

2½	shots	**Tanqueray London dry gin**
½	shot	**British cask conditioned ale**

We say: A gin martini-style drink made with beer in place of vermouth. A suitably manly garnish is also called for.

MAPLE LEAF

★★★★☆

Glass: Old-fashioned
Garnish: Lemon zest twist
Method: SHAKE all ingredients with ice and strain into ice-filled glass.

2	shots	**Maker's Mark bourbon**
½	shot	**Freshly squeezed lemon juice**
¼	shot	**Maple syrup**

We say: This trio combine wonderfully with maple to the fore.

MAPLE OLD-FASHIONED

★★★★☆

Glass: Martini
Garnish: Orange zest twist
Method: STIR one shot of the bourbon with two
ice cubes in a glass. Add maple syrup and Angostura
and two more ice cubes. Stir some more and add
another two ice cubes and the rest of the bourbon.
Stir lots more so as to melt the ice, then add fresh
ice to complete the drink. The melting and stirring
in of ice cubes is essential to the dilution and taste
of this drink.

2	shots	Maker's Mark bourbon
2	dashes	Angostura aromatic bitters
½	shot	Maple syrup

We say: Maple syrup replaces sugar in this
reworking of the classic Old-fashioned.
Origin: Discovered in 2004 at Indigo Yard,
Edinburgh, Scotland.

MAPLE POMME

★★★★☆

Glass: Collins
Garnish: Apple wedge
Method: SHAKE first four ingredients with ice
and strain into ice-filled glass. TOP with ginger ale,
lightly stir and serve with straws.

2	shots	Dewar's White label Scotch
½	shot	Freshly squeezed lemon juice
1	shot	Pressed apple juice
½	shot	Maple syrup
Top up with		Ginger ale

We say: Scotch based drink for warm weather.
Origin: Adapted from a short drink created in 2005
by Tonin Kacaj at Maze, London, England.

MARAMA RUM PUNCH

★★★★☆

Glass: Sling
Garnish: Mint sprig & lime wedge
Method: Lightly MUDDLE mint (just to bruise).
Add next five ingredients, SHAKE with ice and
strain into ice-filled glass. TOP with lemonade,
lightly stir and serve with straws.

12	fresh	Mint leaves
1½	shots	Wray & Nephew overproof rum
½	shot	Triple Sec
½	shot	Freshly squeezed lime juice
½	shot	Monin Almond (orgeat) syrup
3	dashes	Angostura aromatic bitters
Top up with		Lemonade/Sprite/7-Up

We say: A tangy, well-balanced punch.

STAR RATINGS EXPLAINED

★★★★★ Excellent

★★★★⯨ Recommended   ★★★★☆ Praiseworthy
★★★⯨☆ Commended   ★★★☆☆ Mediocre
★★⯨☆☆ Disappointing   ★★☆☆☆ Pretty awful
★⯨☆☆☆ Shameful   ★☆☆☆☆ Disgusting

MARGARET DUFFY

★★★★☆

Glass: Martini
Garnish: Lemon zest twist
Method: STIR all ingredients with ice and strain
into chilled glass.

2	shots	Swedish Punch liqueur
1	shot	Cognac VSOP
2	dashes	Angostura aromatic bitters
½	shot	Chilled mineral water

We say: Spiced and sweetened cognac.
Origin: Vintage cocktail of unknown origin.

MARGARITA #3 (FROZEN) ☞

★★★★☆

Glass: Martini
Garnish: Maraschino cherry
Method: BLEND all ingredients with 12oz scoop
of crushed ice. Serve heaped in the glass and with
straws.

1½	shots	Tequila 100% Agave
¾	shot	Triple Sec
¾	shot	Freshly squeezed lime juice
½	shot	Monin Pure Cane 2:1 sugar syrup

Variant: With fruit and/or fruit liqueurs.
We say: Citrus freshness with the subtle agave of
tequila served frozen.

MARGARITA ON-THE-ROCKS UPDATED
(TRADITIONAL RECIPE)

★★★★⯪

Glass: Old-fashioned
Garnish: Salt rim (optional) & lime wedge
Method: SHAKE all ingredients with ice and strain
into ice-filled glass.

2	shots	Tequila 100% Agave
1	shot	Triple Sec
1	shot	Freshly squeezed lime juice
1	spoon	Agave nectar
3	drops	Difford's Margarita Bitters

We say: Tangy citrus, tequila and salt.

MARGARITA STRAIGHT-UP UPDATED
(STANDARD RECIPE)

★★★★⯪

Glass: Margarita
Garnish: Salt rim & lime wedge
Method: SHAKE all ingredients with ice and fine
strain into chilled glass.

2	shots	Tequila 100% Agave
1	shot	Triple Sec
1	shot	Freshly squeezed lime juice
1	spoon	Agave nectar
3	drops	Difford's Margarita Bitters

Variant: Margaritas made with premium tequilas are sometimes referred
to as 'Deluxe' or 'Cadillac' Margaritas.
We say: For the perfect salt rim, liquidise sea salt to make it finer, then run
a lime wedge around the outside edge of the glass before dipping the rim
in salt. Rimming only half the glass with salt gives the drinker the option of
enjoying the cocktail with or without salt.
Origin: The Margarita can be considered a Tequila Sour, or a Tequila
Sidecar, and two variations of this classic cocktail date back to the 1930s: the

Tequila Daisy and the Picador. Both, however, lack the distinctive salt rim. There are many people who claim to have invented the Margarita, which, as Spanish for "daisy" and a popular woman's name, would have been a very common name for a drink. A brief summary of the top claimants: Francisco 'Pancho' Morales, while working in a bar called Tommy's Place in Ciudad Juarez, Mexico, was asked to make a 'Magnolia' on the 4th July 1942, but couldn't remember it so created this drink. The customer's name may even have been Margarita. Carlos 'Danny' Herrera created the cocktail either in 1947 or 1948 at his Rancho La Gloria bar in Rosarito, Mexico, for an actress called Marjorie King who drank no spirit but tequila. He added Cointreau and lime, and the unique salt rim that caught people's attention at the bar, then named his creation Margarita, the Spanish for Marjorie.

Daniel (Danny) Negrete created the drink in 1936 when he was the manager of Garci Crespo Hotel in Puebla, Mexico. His girlfriend, Margarita, apparently liked salt in her drinks and he is said to have created the drink for her as a present. In 1944 Danny moved to Tijuana, Mexico, and became a bartender at the Agua Caliente Racetrack, a place which has some claim to be the birthplace of the Margarita in the early 1930s.

Vernon Underwood was president of Young's Market Company, who in the 1930s had started distributing Cuervo tequila. He went to Johnny Durlesser, head bartender of the Tail O' The Cock in LA, and asked him to create something using his spirit, then named it after his wife Margaret (Margarita). Sara Morales, an expert in Mexican folklore, claimed the Margarita was created in 1930 by Doña Bertha, owner of Bertha's Bar in Taxco, Mexico. The socialite Margaret Sames held a Christmas party in Acapulco, Mexico, in 1948, and created the first Margarita. She thought nothing of it until, when flying home to San Antonio from Acapulco airport, she saw a bar advertising 'Margarita's Drink', a cocktail with exactly the same ingredients as her own. So, Plenty of Margarets and even Margaritas: there is also a popular holiday destination called Margarita Island, located in the Caribbean north of Venezuela, two-and-a-half hours from Miami. It could simply be a twist on the 'Daisy', a classic cocktail dating back to Victorian times and made with citrus juice, sweetened with a syrup or liqueur, and fortified with a base spirit. Margarita is the Spanish word for daisy. A British antecedent of the Margarita called a 'Picador' has recently been unearthed.

MARGARITA WITH SALT FOAM FLOAT

★★★⯪☆

Glass: Margarita
Garnish: Lime wedge
Method: Combine first three ingredients, POUR into cream whipping siphon and CHARGE with nitrous oxide. Shake and place siphon in a refrigerator for one hour prior to making drink. SHAKE next three ingredients with ice and fine strain into chilled glass. SQUIRT salt foam over surface of drink from siphon.

4	spoons	Salt
1	pint	Chilled mineral water
2	fresh	Egg white
2	shots	Tequila 100% Agave
1	shot	Freshly squeezed lime juice
1	shot	Triple Sec

We say: Classic Margarita with a salty foam topping.

MARGUERITE MARTINI

★★★★☆

Glass: Martini
Garnish: Orange zest twist
Method: SHAKE all ingredients with ice and fine strain into chilled glass.

2	shots	Tanqueray London dry gin
½	shot	Martini Extra Dry vermouth
1	dash	Orange bitters

We say: A slightly wet yet bone dry classic Martini with a hint of orange.
Origin: Adapted from a recipe in Harry Craddock's 1930 'Savoy Cocktail Book'.

MARIA THERESA MARGARITA

★★★★☆

Glass: Martini
Garnish: Lime wedge
Method: STIR honey with tequila in base of shaker to dissolve honey. ADD other ingredients, SHAKE with ice and fine strain into chilled glass.

2	spoons	Runny honey
2	shots	Tequila 100% Agave
1	shot	Ocean Spray cranberry juice
½	shot	Freshly squeezed lime juice

We say: Originally sweetened with sugar syrup, this is better smoothed with honey.
Origin: Adapted from a Tiki drink created by Victor Bergeron (Trader Vic).

MARIE ROSE

★★★★☆

Glass: Martini
Garnish: Rosemary sprig
Method: Strip leaves from rosemary and MUDDLE with grapes in base of shaker. Add other ingredients, SHAKE with ice and fine strain into chilled glass.

½	sprig	Rosemary sprig
8	fresh	Seedless white grapes
2	shots	Tanqueray London dry gin
¾	shot	St~Germain elderflower liqueur
¼	shot	Freshly squeezed lime juice

We say: Rosemary spiced gin with grape juice and elderflower: very aromatic.
Origin: Created in 2007 by Renan Lejeune at Zeta Bar, London, England.

MARKET DAIQUIRÍ

★★★★☆

Glass: Coupette
Garnish: Pear slice
Method: SHAKE all ingredients with ice and fine strain into chilled glass.

2	fresh	Mint leaves
2	shots	Bacardi Superior rum
½	shot	Boiron pear purée
¼	shot	Monin Almond (orgeat) syrup
½	shot	Freshly squeezed lime juice

We say: A classic Daiquiri influenced by the addition of pear, mint and almonds.
Origin: Created in 2008, by Dez O'Connell, London, England

MARMALADE COCKTAIL

★★★★☆

Glass: Martini
Garnish: Orange zest twist
Method: SHAKE all ingredients with ice and fine strain into chilled glass.

4	spoons	Orange marmalade
2	shots	Tanqueray London dry gin
½	shot	Freshly squeezed lemon juice

We say: Harry wrote of his own drink, "By its bitter-sweet taste this cocktail is especially suited to be a luncheon apertif."
Origin: Adapted from a recipe in the 1930 *Savoy Cocktail Book* by Harry Craddock (the original recipe serves six people).

317

MARMALADE SOUR NEW

★★★⯪☆

Glass: Coupette
Garnish: Orange zest twist
Method: SHAKE all ingredients with ice and fine strain into ice-filled glass.

2	spoons	Orange marmalade
2	shots	Leblon cachaça
½	shot	Freshly squeezed lemon juice
2	dashes	Orange bitters
½	fresh	Egg white

We say: Tangy sweet and sour marmalade flavours combine with the distinctive grassy notes of cachaça.
Origin: Adapted from a drink created in 2010 by Jamie Boudreau at Vessel, Seattle, USA.

MARMARITA ⚷

★★★★☆

Glass: Coupette
Garnish: Marmite (yeast extract) rim
Method: SHAKE all ingredients with ice and fine strain into chilled glass.

2	shots	Tequila 100% Agave
1	shot	Triple Sec
1	shot	Freshly squeezed lime juice

We say: A Margarita with a Marmite rim. After all, yeast extract is slightly salty.
Origin: Created in 2005 by Simon (Ginger) Warneford at Blanch House, Brighton, England.

MARNY COCKTAIL UPDATED

★★★★⯪

Glass: Martini
Garnish: Orange zest twist
Method: SHAKE all ingredients with ice and fine strain into chilled glass.

2	shots	Tanqueray London dry gin
1	shot	Grand Marnier liqueur
2	dashes	Orange bitters
½	shot	Chilled mineral water

We say: This appropriately named, simple drink is one of my favourite Grand Marnier cocktails.
Origin: Adapted from a recipe in Harry Craddock's 1930 *Savoy Cocktail Book*.

MARQUEE ⚷

★★★★☆

Glass: Martini
Garnish: Raspberries
Method: SHAKE all ingredients with ice and fine strain into chilled glass.

1½	shots	Maker's Mark bourbon
½	shot	Chambord black raspberry liqueur
1½	shots	Ocean Spray cranberry juice
½	shot	Freshly squeezed lemon juice
¼	shot	Monin Pure Cane 2:1 sugar syrup

We say: Raspberry and bourbon combine perfectly in this short, slightly sweet, fruity drink.
Origin: Created in 1998 by Giovanni Burdi at Match EC1, London, England.

MARTÍ'S MARTINI

★★★☆☆

Glass: Martini
Garnish: None
Method: STIR ingredients with ice and fine strain into chilled glass.

1½	shots	Bacardi Superior rum
¼	shot	Galliano L'Autentico liqueur
¼	shot	Genepi des Peres Chartreux
½	shot	Martini Extra Dry vermouth
½	shot	Chilled mineral water

We say: Herbal, medium dry, rum-based, Martini-style drink.
Origin: Created in 2008 by Oli Gillespie at Bibendum Wine Ltd, London, England and named after José Martí (1853-1895) - a leader of the Cuban independence movement, writer and renowned poet.

MARTINEZ #1 (ORIGINAL GENEVER)

★★★★★

Glass: Martini
Garnish: Orange zest twist
Method: STIR all ingredients with ice and strain into chilled glass.

1½	shots	Bols Genever
1½	shots	Martini Rosso sweet vermouth
⅛	shot	Curaçao orange liqueur
2	dashes	Angostura aromatic bitters

We say: This medium dry Martini is somewhat more approachable than a Dry Martini.
Origin: Probably the forerunner of the Martini, the first known recipe for this drink appears in O.H. Byron's 1884 "The Modern Bartender" where it is listed as a variation to the Manhattan. Its first written standalone listing in a recipe book appears in Harry Johnson's 1888 *Bartender's Manual*.

Drinks historian David Wondrich and others believe it was first made using Dutch oude genever as this was the style of exported to America long before English Old Tom gin or Tanqueray London dry gins.

Although the drink appears in his 1887 Bartenders' Guide (as a variation), there is no evidence that Jerry Thomas invented the Martinez and significantly he omits the drink from the earlier 1862 edition of his Bartender's Guide.

Many claim that one Julio Richelieu created the drink in 1874 for a goldminer and that the drink is named after the Californian town of Martinez, where that unnamed goldminer enjoyed this libation.

MARTINEZ #2 (MODERN GENEVER)

★★★★★

Glass: Martini
Garnish: Orange zest twist
Method: STIR ingredients with ice and fine strain into chilled glass.

2	shots	Bols Genever
½	shot	Martini Extra Dry vermouth
½	shot	Martini Rosso sweet vermouth
⅛	shot	Luxardo Maraschino liqueur

Origin: This modern take on the vintage classic emerged in London during early 2008 with the introduction of Antica Formula.

MARTINEZ #3 (OLD TOM)

★★★★⯪

Glass: Martini
Garnish: Orange zest twist
Method: STIR ingredients with ice and fine strain into chilled glass.

2	shots	Old Tom gin
½	shot	Martini Extra Dry vermouth
½	shot	Martini Rosso sweet vermouth
⅛	shot	Luxardo Maraschino liqueur
2	dashes	Angostura aromatic bitters

We say: Use an authentic tasting distilled with no added sugar Old Tom and this is a fabulous cocktai.

MARTINEZ #4 (LONDON DRY)

★★★★☆

Glass: Martini
Garnish: Orange zest twist
Method: STIR ingredients with ice and fine strain into chilled glass.

2	shots	Tanqueray London dry gin
½	shot	Martini Rosso sweet vermouth
¼	shot	Martini Extra Dry vermouth
⅛	shot	Luxardo Maraschino liqueur
1	dash	Angostura aromatic bitters

We say: Aromatic, complex and very dry.

MARTINEZ #5 (ORANGE)

★★★★☆

Glass: Martini
Garnish: Orange zest twist
Method: STIR ingredients with ice and fine strain into chilled glass.

2	shots	Tanqueray London dry gin
½	shot	Martini Rosso sweet vermouth
¼	shot	Curaçao orange liqueur
2	dashes	Orange bitters

We say: Stir well as dilution helps to tame this old-school classic in which bitter orange predominates.

MARTINI PERFECT

★★★⯪☆

Glass: Martini
Garnish: Orange zest twist
Method: SHAKE all ingredients with ice and fine strain into chilled glass.

1¼	shots	Tanqueray London dry gin
1¼	shots	Martini Extra Dry vermouth
1¼	shots	Martini Rosso sweet vermouth
1	dash	Orange bitters

Variant: Merry-Go-Round Martini
We say: The high proportion of vermouth makes this Martini almost sherry-like.
Origin: Adapted from a recipe in the 1930 edition of the *'Savoy Cocktail Book'* by Harry Craddock.

MARTINI ROYALE

★★★⯪☆

Glass: Martini
Garnish: Lemon zest twist
Method: STIR vodka and crème de cassis with ice and strain into chilled glass. TOP with chilled champagne.

1½	shots	Ketel One vodka
½	shot	Crème de cassis liqueur
Top up with		Brut champagne

We say: The Kir Royale meets the vodkatini in this pink but powerful drink.
Origin: Created in 2001 by Dick Bradsell at Monte's, London, England.

MARTINI SPECIAL

★★★★⯪

Glass: Martini
Garnish: Orange zest twist
Method: Fill glass with ice and POUR absinthe and Angostura over ice. TOP with chilled mineral water and leave to stand. SHAKE gin, vermouth and orange water with ice. DISCARD contents of standing glass and fine strain shaken drink into washed glass.

¼	shot	Absinthe
4	dashes	Angostura aromatic bitters
Top up with		Chilled mineral water
2	shots	Tanqueray London dry gin
¾	shot	Martini Rosso sweet vermouth
⅛	shot	Orange flower water

We say: Aromatic, very dry and very serious - yet has a frothy head.
Origin: Adapted from a recipe in Harry Craddock's 1930 *Savoy Cocktail Book*.

MARTINI THYME

★★★★☆

Glass: Martini
Garnish: Olives on thyme sprig
Method: MUDDLE thyme in base of shaker. ADD other ingredients, SHAKE with ice and fine strain into chilled glass.

2	sprig	Lemon thyme (remove stalks)
1	shot	Tanqueray London dry gin
¾	shot	Chartreuse Green liqueur
¼	shot	Monin Pure Cane 2:1 sugar syrup

We say: A wonderfully fresh herbal Martini with the distinctive taste of Chartreuse. You'll either love it or hate it.
Origin: A combination of two very similar drinks, that both originally called for thyme infused gin. The first I discovered at The Lobby Bar (One Aldwych, London) and the other came from Tony Conigliaro at Isola, London, England.

STAR RATINGS EXPLAINED

★★★★★ Excellent

★★★★⯪ Recommended	★★★★☆ Praiseworthy
★★★⯪☆ Commended	★★★☆☆ Mediocre
★★⯪☆☆ Disappointing	★★☆☆☆ Pretty awful
★⯪☆☆☆ Shameful	★☆☆☆☆ Disgusting

MARTINI WITH A SPOT

★★★☆☆

Glass: Martini
Garnish: Lemon zest twist
Method: STIR gin and vermouth with ice and strain into chilled glass. Carefully POUR 'spot' of absinthe into centre of the drink.

2½ shots	Tanqueray London dry gin
½ shot	Martini Extra Dry vermouth
1 dash	Absinthe

We say: Absinthe adds bone-dry complexity to this otherwise Wet Martini.
Origin: Discovered in 2007 at Westbourne House, London, England.

MARY PICKFORD

★★★★★

Glass: Martini
Garnish: Maraschino cherry
Method: SHAKE all ingredients with ice and fine strain into chilled glass.

2 shots	Bacardi Superior rum
1½ shots	Fresh pressed pineapple juice
¼ shot	Pomegranate (grenadine) syrup
⅛ shot	Luxardo Maraschino liqueur

We say: When made correctly, this pale pink cocktail has a perfect balance between the fruit flavours and the spirit of the rum.
Origin: Created in the 1920s (during Prohibition) by Fred Kaufman at the Hotel Nacional de Cuba, for the silent movie star and wife of Douglas Fairbanks. Mary was in Cuba filming a movie with her husband Douglas Fairbanks and Charlie Chaplin. This is recounted
on page 40 of Basil Woon's 1928 book '*When It's Cocktail Time in Cuba* - "The Mary Pickford, invented during a visit to Havana of the screen favourite by Fred Kaufman, is two-thirds pineapple-juice and one-third Bacardi, with a dash of grenadine. Both cocktails [The Presidenté is also mentioned] are sweetish and should be well shaken. The Pineapple juice must be fresh-squeezed." Thus it would appear that a dash of maraschino liqueur is a later addition.

MARY QUEEN OF SCOTS

★★★★½

Glass: Martini
Garnish: Sugar rim & maraschino cherry
Method: SHAKE all ingredients with ice and fine strain into chilled glass.

1½ shots	Dewar's White label Scotch
¾ shot	Chartreuse Green liqueur
¾ shot	Drambuie

We say: Slightly sweet but herbal, serious and strong.
Origin: Discovered in 2006 an Kyle Branch's Cocktail Hotel blog (www.cocktailhotel.blogspot.com). Mary Stuart, Mary Queen of Scots was born on December 8th 1542 at Linlithgow Place in West Lothian. On February 8th 1587, she was executed in the Great Hall of Fotheringhay.

MARY ROSE

★★★★☆

Glass: Martini
Garnish: Lime zest twist (discarded) & rosemary sprig
Method: MUDDLE rosemary in base of shaker. Add other ingredients, SHAKE with ice and fine strain into chilled glass.

1 fresh	Rosemary sprig
2 shots	Tanqueray London dry gin
1 shot	Chartreuse Green liqueur
½ shot	Monin Pure Cane 2:1 sugar syrup
½ shot	Chilled mineral water

We say: Herbal, herbal and herbal with a hint of spice.
Origin: Created in 1999 by Philip Jeffrey at the Great Eastern Hotel, London, England. Named after King Henry VIII's warship, sunk during an engagement with the French fleet in 1545 and now on display in Portsmouth.

MAT THE RAT

★★★½☆

Glass: Collins
Garnish: Lime wedge
Method: SHAKE first 4 ingredients with ice and strain into ice-filled glass. TOP with lemonade, lightly stir and serve with straws.

2 shots	Bacardi Superior rum
½ shot	Triple Sec
1½ shots	Freshly squeezed orange juice
½ shot	Freshly squeezed lime juice
Top up with	Lemonade/Sprite/7-Up

We say: Whether or not Mat was a rat, we shall never know. However, the drink that's named after him is long and thirst quenching.
Origin: A popular drink in UK branches of TGI Friday's where it was created.

MATADOR #1

★★★★☆

Glass: Collins
Garnish: Pineapple wedge
Method: SHAKE all ingredients with ice and strain into ice-filled glass.

2 shots	Tequila 100% Agave
1 shot	Triple Sec
1 shot	Freshly squeezed lime juice
2 shots	Fresh pressed pineapple juice

We say: A long Margarita-style drink. The lime and tequila work wonders with the pineapple.

MATADOR #2 (TOMMY'S STYLE)

★★★★☆

Glass: Martini
Garnish: Pineapple wedge
Method: SHAKE all ingredients with ice and fine strain into chilled glass.

2 shots	Tequila 100% Agave
1 shot	Freshly squeezed lime juice
½ shot	Agave nectar
1½ shots	Fresh pressed pineapple juice

We say: A pineapple Margarita with agave syrup in place of a sweet liqueur.

THE MATINEE NEW

★★★☆☆

Glass: Coupette
Garnish: Frozen kaffir lime leaf
Method: DRY SHAKE (without ice) all ingredients. SHAKE again with ice and fine strain into chilled glass.

4	leaf	**Kaffir lime**
2	shots	**Rum light white/blanco**
½	shot	**Martini Rosso sweet vermouth**
½	shot	**Freshly squeezed lemon juice**
¼	shot	**Monin Vanilla sugar syrup**
½	fresh	**Egg white**

We say: Created in 2010 by Metinee Kongsrivilai at The Bon Vivant, Edinburgh, Scotland.
Origin: Kaffir lime leaves add zest to this vanilla infused Rum Sour.

MAURESQUE

★★★★☆

Glass: Collins
Garnish: None
Method: POUR absinthe and almond syrup into glass. Serve iced water separately in a small jug (known in France as a 'broc') so the customer can dilute to their own taste (I recommend five shots). Lastly, add ice to fill glass.

1	shot	**Absinthe**
1	shot	**Monin Almond (orgeat) syrup**
Top up with		**Chilled mineral water**

We say: Long, refreshing aniseed, liquorice and almond.
Origin: Pronounced 'Mor-Esk', this classic drink is very popular in the South of France, where it is now commonly made with pastis in place of absinthe. It was originally created by French soldiers serving in the Bataillon d'Afrique during the Algerian campaign of the 1830s and 40s, and was alternatively known as Bureau Arabe after the military department which dealt with local affairs and was said to act like 'an iron fist in a velvet glove'.

MAURICE COCKTAIL

★★★½☆

Glass: Martini
Garnish: Orange zest twist
Method: SHAKE all ingredients with ice and fine strain into chilled glass.

1½	shots	**Tanqueray London dry gin**
¼	shot	**Absinthe**
¾	shot	**Martini Extra Dry vermouth**
¾	shot	**Martini Rosso sweet vermouth**
¾	shot	**Freshly squeezed orange juice**

We say: A Bronx Cocktail with the addition of an aromatic burst of absinthe – you'll notice the difference.
Origin: Adapted from a recipe in Harry Craddock's 1930 *Savoy Cocktail Book*.

MAXIM'S COFFEE (HOT)

★★★★☆

Glass: Toddy
Garnish: Coffee beans
Method: POUR all ingredients into warmed glass and STIR.

1	shot	**Cognac VSOP**
½	shot	**Bénédictine D.O.M.**
¼	shot	**Galliano L'Autentico liqueur**
Top up with		**Hot filter coffee**

We say: An interesting herbal cognac laced coffee.

MAYA MARGARITA NEW

★★★★☆

Glass: Coupette
Garnish: Pink river salt rim & lime wedge
Method: SHAKE all ingredients with ice and fine strain into chilled glass.

1	shot	**Olmeca Altos 100% agave tequila**
½	shot	**Agave Sec liqueur**
⅓	shot	**Grand Marnier liqueur**
1	shot	**Freshly squeezed lime juice**
½	shot	**Freshly squeezed orange juice**
1	Splash	**Calamansi juice**
¼	shot	**Calamansi juice**

We say: A tasty Margarita with Grand Marnier, Agave Sec liqueur and orange juice.
Origin: Created in 2010 by Rob Jameson at Maya Bar, Shanghai, China.

MAYAN

★★★☆☆

Glass: Old-fashioned
Garnish: Coffee beans
Method: SHAKE all ingredients with ice and strain into ice-filled glass.

1½	shots	**Tequila 100% Agave**
½	shot	**Kahlúa coffee liqueur**
2½	shots	**Fresh pressed pineapple juice**

We say: Tequila, coffee and pineapple juice combine in this medium dry short drink.

MAYAN WHORE

★★★★☆

Glass: Sling
Garnish: Pineapple wedge
Method: SHAKE first three ingredients with ice and strain into ice-filled glass. TOP with soda, DO NOT STIR and serve with straws.

2	shots	**Tequila 100% Agave**
¾	shot	**Kahlúa coffee liqueur**
1½	shots	**Fresh pressed pineapple juice**
Top up with		**Soda (club soda)**

We say: An implausible ménage à trois: coffee, tequila and pineapple, served long.

MAYFAIR COCKTAIL #1

★★★★☆

Glass: Martini
Garnish: Orange zest twist
Method: MUDDLE cloves in base of shaker. Add other ingredients, SHAKE with ice and fine strain into chilled glass.

2	**shots**	**Tanqueray London dry gin**
1	**shot**	**De Kuyper Apricot Brandy liqueur**
2	**dried**	**Clove**
1	**shot**	**Freshly squeezed orange juice**
⅛	**shot**	**Monin Pure Cane 2:1 sugar syrup**

We say: Spiced apricot laced with gin. Slightly sweet.
Origin: Adapted from a recipe in Harry Craddock's 1930 *Savoy Cocktail Book.* Apparently this drink celebrates a fair that took place in the month of May during the rein of King Charles II.

MAYFAIR COCKTAIL #2

★★★★☆

Glass: Martini
Garnish: Orange zest twist
Method: MUDDLE cloves in base of shaker. Add other ingredients, SHAKE with ice and fine strain into chilled glass.

2	**shots**	**Tanqueray London dry gin**
1	**shot**	**De Kuyper Apricot Brandy liqueur**
2	**dried**	**Clove**
1	**shot**	**Freshly squeezed orange juice**
¼	**shot**	**Berry Hill pimento allspice liqueur**

We say: Gin with spicy cloves and hints of apricot and orange.

MEDICINAL SOLUTION

★★★½☆

Glass: Collins
Garnish: Lime wedge
Method: SHAKE first 5 ingredients with ice and strain into ice-filled glass. TOP with tonic water, lightly stir and serve with straws.

1½	**shots**	**Bols Genever**
½	**shot**	**Chartreuse Green liqueur**
½	**shot**	**Freshly squeezed lime juice**
¼	**shot**	**Monin Pure Cane 2:1 sugar syrup**
3	**dashes**	**Angostura aromatic bitters**
Top up with		**Tonic water**

We say: Every ingredient, apart from the sugar, has at some time been consumed for its medicinal qualities. Even the sugar is still used to make bitter tasting medicine more palatable. Some might say that's just what I've done here.
Origin: Created in 2006 by Simon Difford.

STAR RATINGS EXPLAINED

★★★★★ Excellent

★★★★½ Recommeded	★★★★☆ Praiseworthy
★★★½☆ Commended	★★★☆☆ Mediocre
★★½☆☆ Disappointing	★★☆☆☆ Pretty awful
★½☆☆☆ Shameful	★☆☆☆☆ Disgusting

MEDITERRANEAN FIZZ NEW

★★★½☆

Glass: Collins
Garnish: Basil leaf
Method: MUDDLE grapes in base of shake. Add next four ingredients, SHAKE with ice and fine strain into ice filled glass. TOP with soda water.

8	**fresh**	**Seedless white grapes**
2	**shots**	**Ketel One vodka**
5	**fresh**	**Torn basil leaves**
½	**shot**	**Freshly squeezed lemon juice**
½	**shot**	**Monin Vanilla sugar syrup**
Top up with		**Soda (club soda)**

We say: White grapes, vanilla, basil and lemon juice fortified with vodka.
Origin: Discovered in 2010 at Mim Bar, Aberdeen, Scotland..

MEDIUM MARTINI

★★★★½

Glass: Martini
Garnish: Orange zest twist
Method: STIR all ingredients with ice and strain into chilled glass

1½	**shots**	**Tanqueray London dry gin**
¾	**shot**	**Martini Extra Dry vermouth**
¾	**shot**	**Martini Rosso sweet vermouth**

We say: A classic Martini served perfect and very wet.
Origin: Adapted from a recipe in Harry Craddock's 1930 *Savoy Cocktail Book.*

MELBA COCKTAIL

★★★★☆

Glass: Coupette
Garnish: Mint leaf
Method: SHAKE all ingredients with ice and fine strain into chilled glass.

1½	**shots**	**Bacardi Superior rum**
1	**shot**	**Swedish Punch liqueur**
½	**spoon**	**Absinthe**
½	**shot**	**Freshly squeezed lime juice**
1	**spoon**	**Pomegranate (grenadine) syrup**

We say: A dry Daiquiri-like drink with pomegranate, a touch of absinthe and pine fresh notes.

MELCHIOR NEW

★★★½☆

Glass: Coupette
Garnish: Orange zest twist
Method: STIR all ingredients with ice and strain into chilled glass.

3	**dried**	**Clove**
1½	**shots**	**Courvoisier VSOP Exclusif**
¾	**shot**	**Stone's green ginger wine**
½	**shot**	**Bénédictine D.O.M.**
1¼	**shots**	**Claret red wine**

We say: Based on cognac and named after one of the three wise men, this cocktail uses three spices – ginger, cloves and saffron (in the Bénédictine) and a good dash of red wine (after all, in later life the baby they visited reputedly turned water into wine).
Origin: A Christmas cocktail named after one of the three wise men created in 2011 by Simon Difford in Cabinet Room, London, England.

MELLOW MARTINI

★★★½☆

Glass: Martini
Garnish: Lychee
Method: SHAKE all ingredients with ice and fine strain into chilled glass.

1½	shots	Ketel One vodka
½	shot	Kwai Feh lychee liqueur
½	shot	Bols Banana liqueur
1½	shots	Fresh pressed pineapple juice

We say: A fruity, tropical drink with a frothy head. Too fluffy to be a Martini.

MELON BALL

★★★☆☆

Glass: Shot
Garnish: None
Method: SHAKE all ingredients with ice and fine strain into chilled glass.

½	shot	Ketel One vodka
½	shot	Midori green melon liqueur
¾	shot	Freshly squeezed orange juice

We say: A vivid green combination of vodka, melon and orange.

MELON COLLIE MARTINI

★★★★☆

Glass: Martini
Garnish: Crumbled Cadbury's Flake bar
Method: SHAKE all ingredients with ice and fine strain into chilled glass.

1	shot	Bacardi Superior rum
¾	shot	Midori green melon liqueur
¼	shot	White Crème de Cacao
½	shot	Malibu coconut rum liqueur
¾	shot	Milk
¾	shot	Double (heavy) cream

We say: Something of a holiday disco drink but tasty all the same.
Origin: Created in 2003 by Simon King at MJU, Millenniun Hotel, London, England.

MELON DAIQUIRI #1 (SERVED 'UP')

★★★★☆

Glass: Martini
Garnish: Melon slice or melon balls
Method: Cut melon into 8 segments and deseed. Cut cubes of flesh from skin of one segment and MUDDLE in base of shaker. Add other ingredients, SHAKE with ice and fine strain into chilled glass.

⅛	fresh	Cantaloupe melon
2	shots	Bacardi Superior rum
½	shot	Midori green melon liqueur
½	shot	Freshly squeezed lime juice
⅛	shot	Monin Pure Cane 2:1 sugar syrup

We say: A classic Daiquiri with the gentle touch of melon.

MELON DAIQUIRI #2 (SERVED FROZEN)

★★★★☆

Glass: Martini
Garnish: Melon slice or melon balls
Method: Cut melon into 8 segments and deseed. Cut cubes of flesh from skin of one segment and place in blender. Add other ingredients and BLEND with half scoop of crushed ice. Serve with straws.

⅛	fresh	Cantaloupe melon
2	shots	Bacardi Superior rum
½	shot	Midori green melon liqueur
½	shot	Freshly squeezed lime juice

We say: A cooling, fruity Daiquiri.

MELON MARGARITA #1 (SERVED 'UP')

★★★★☆

Glass: Coupette
Garnish: Melon slice or melon balls
Method: Cut melon into 8 segments and deseed. Cut cubes of flesh from skin of one segment and MUDDLE in base of shaker. Add other ingredients, SHAKE with ice and fine strain into chilled glass.

⅛	fresh	Cantaloupe melon
2	shots	Tequila 100% Agave
1	shot	Midori green melon liqueur
1	shot	Freshly squeezed lime juice

We say: Looks like stagnant pond water but tastes fantastic.

MELON MARGARITA #2 (SERVED FROZEN)

★★★½☆

Glass: Coupette
Garnish: Melon slice or melon balls
Method: Cut melon into 8 segments and deseed. Cut cubes of flesh from skin of one segment and place in blender. Add other ingredients and BLEND with 6oz scoop crushed ice. Serve with straws.

⅛	fresh	Cantaloupe melon
2	shots	Tequila 100% Agave
1	shot	Midori green melon liqueur
½	shot	Freshly squeezed lime juice

We say: Melon and tequila always combine well - here in a frozen Margarita.

MELON MARTINI #1

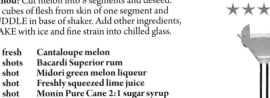

★★★☆☆

Glass: Martini
Garnish: Lime wedge
Method: SHAKE all ingredients with ice and fine strain into chilled glass.

2¼	shots	Ketel One vodka
1	shot	Midori green melon liqueur
½	shot	Freshly squeezed lime juice
¼	shot	Monin Pure Cane 2:1 sugar syrup

We say: Bright green, lime and melon with more than a hint of vodka. Do it properly - have a fresh one.

MELON MARTINI #2 (FRESH FRUIT)

★★★★☆

Glass: Martini
Garnish: Melon slice
Method: Cut melon into eight segments and deseed. Cut cubes of flesh from skin of one segment and MUDDLE in base of shaker. Add other ingredients, SHAKE with ice and fine strain into chilled glass.

⅛	fresh	Cantaloupe melon
2	shots	Ketel One vodka
¼	shot	Monin Pure Cane 2:1 sugar syrup

Variant: Substitute Midori melon liqueur for sugar syrup.
We say: Probably the most popular of all the fresh fruit martinis.

MELONCHOLY MARTINI

★★★★☆

Glass: Martini
Garnish: Mint sprig
Method: SHAKE all ingredients with ice and fine strain into chilled glass.

1	shot	Ketel One vodka
1	shot	Midori green melon liqueur
½	shot	Triple Sec
½	shot	Malibu coconut rum liqueur
1	shot	Fresh pressed pineapple juice
¼	shot	Freshly squeezed lime juice
¾	shot	Double (heavy) cream

We say: Sweet, but the flavours in this smooth, tangy, lime-green drink combine surprisingly well.
Origin: Created in 2002 by Daniel O'Brien at Ocean Bar, Edinburgh, Scotland.

MENEHUNE JUICE

★★★★☆

Glass: Old-fashioned
Garnish: Lime wedge, mint sprig & Menehune
Method: SHAKE all ingredients with ice and strain into glass filled with crushed ice. Serve with straws.

2	shots	Bacardi Superior rum
½	shot	Triple Sec
¼	shot	Monin Almond (orgeat) syrup
¾	shot	Freshly squeezed lime juice
¼	shot	Monin Pure Cane 2:1 sugar syrup

We say: Slightly sweet and strong. According to Vic, "One sip and you may see a Menehune."
Origin: Adapted from a recipe in the 1947-72 'Trader Vic's Bartender's Guide' by Victor Bergeron.

STAR RATINGS EXPLAINED

★★★★★ Excellent

★★★★⯪	Recommended	★★★★☆ Praiseworthy
★★★⯪☆	Commended	★★★☆☆ Mediocre
★★⯪☆☆	Disappointing	★★☆☆☆ Pretty awful
★⯪☆☆☆	Shameful	★☆☆☆☆ Disgusting

MERCHANT OF VENICE NEW

★★★★⯪

Glass: Flute
Garnish: Lemon zest twist
Method: STIR honey with vodka in base of shaker to dissolve. Add other ingredients and DRY SHAKE (without ice). SHAKE again with ice and fine strain into chilled glass.

2	shots	Ketel One vodka
2	spoons	Runny honey
½	shot	Aperol
½	shot	Freshly squeezed lemon juice
½	fresh	Egg white

We say: The richness and flavour of honey along with the distinctive taste of Aperol jointly balance lemon citrus notes in this majestic vodka-based drink.
Origin: Discovered in 2010 at Eclipse Bar, Barcelona, Spain. Aperol is consumed like water by Venetians hence this drink is aptly named.

MERRY WIDOW #1

★★★⯪☆

Glass: Martini
Garnish: Lemon zest twist
Method: STIR all ingredients with ice and strain into chilled glass.

1½	shots	Tanqueray London dry gin
1½	shots	Martini Extra Dry vermouth
¼	shot	Bénédictine D.O.M.
¼	shot	Absinthe
3	dashes	Angostura aromatic bitters
½	shot	Chilled mineral water

We say: Aromatic, complex, strong and bitter.
Origin: Adapted from a recipe in Harry Craddock's 1930 *Savoy Cocktail Book*.

MERRY WIDOW #2

★★★⯪☆

Glass: Martini
Garnish: Orange zest twist
Method: STIR all ingredients with ice and strain into chilled glass.

1¼	shots	Ketel One vodka
1¼	shots	Dubonnet Red (French made)
1¼	shots	Martini Extra Dry vermouth
1	dash	Fresh orange

We say: Complex, aromatic and complex - for toughened palates.

MERRY-GO-ROUND MARTINI

★★★★☆

Glass: Martini
Garnish: Chilled olive on stick or lemon zest twist
Method: STIR all ingredients with ice and fine strain into chilled glass.

2	shots	Tanqueray London dry gin
½	shot	Martini Extra Dry vermouth
½	shot	Martini Rosso sweet vermouth

We say: Stir this 'perfect' Martini around and then get merry.
Origin: Long lost classic variation on the Dry Martini.

MERYL LYNCHBURG NEW

★★★★☆

Glass: Collins
Garnish: Lemon zest twist
Method: SHAKE first four ingredients with ice and strain into ice filled glass (or mug), TOP with soda.

2	shots	Jack Daniel's Tennessee whiskey
½	shot	Agave Sec liqueur
½	shot	Freshly squeezed lemon juice
2	dashes	Bitters (whiskey barrel aged)
Top up with		Soda (club soda)

We say: A long refreshing iced tea-style drink.
Origin: Discovered in 2009 at Underdog Bar (Now closed), Clapham, London, England.

MESA FRESCA

★★★★☆

Glass: Collins
Garnish: Lime slice
Method: SHAKE all ingredient with ice and strain into ice-filled glass.

2	shots	Tequila 100% Agave
3	shots	Freshly squeezed grapefruit juice
1	shot	Freshly squeezed lime juice
½	shot	Monin Pure Cane 2:1 sugar syrup

We say: Sweet and sour tequila and grapefruit.
Origin: Mesa Grill, New York City, USA, 2005.

MESSIANIC COCKTAIL NEW

★★★★☆

Glass: Coupette
Garnish: Orange zest twist
Method: MUDDLE cloves in stirring glass. Add other ingredients, STIR with ice and fine strain into chilled glass.

1	dried	Clove
2	shots	Bacardi Oro golden rum
¼	shot	Domain de Canton ginger liqueur
¾	shot	Grand Marnier liqueur
½	shot	Chilled water (omit if wet ice)

We say: Ginger and orange delicately spiced with cloves and fortified with golden rum. You'll need to fine strain to catch the clove shrapnel or alternatively infuse cloves in your rum. Achieving the correct dilution is key to the success of this drink.
Origin: Messianic means 'of the Messiah', so how appropriate this Christmas cocktail with gold and precious spice (at least cloves were costly back in the day). Created in October 2011 by Simon Difford at the Cabinet Room, London, England.

MET MANHATTAN

★★★★☆

Glass: Martini
Garnish: Orange zest twist
Method: SHAKE all ingredients with ice and fine strain into chilled glass.

2	shots	Maker's Mark bourbon
1	shot	Grand Marnier liqueur
½	shot	Butterscotch schnapps
2	dashes	Orange bitters

We say: Smooth and rounded bourbon with a hint of orange toffee.
Origin: The Met bar, Metropolitain Hotel, London, England.

METROPOLE

★★★★☆

Glass: Martini
Garnish: Maraschino cherry
Method: STIR all ingredients with ice and strain into chilled glass.

1½	shots	Cognac VSOP
1½	shots	Martini Extra Dry vermouth
1	dash	Peychaud's aromatic bitters
1	dash	Orange bitters
¼	shot	Maraschino syrup (from cherry jar)

We say: I've added a dash of cherry syrup and changed the proportions of the original overly dry and hard classic recipe.
Origin: Named after The Hotel Metropole, located just off Times Square at 147 West 43rd Street. This was the first hotel in New York City to have running water in every room but had a less than salubrious reputation due to the clientele its all-night licensed street-level Café Metropole attracted. As Albert Stevens Crockett says in his 1935, 'The *Old Waldorf Bar Days*', Attributed to a once well known and somewhat lively hotel, whose bar was a long centre of life after dark in the Times Square district.
In the early morning hours of 16th July 1912 Herman Rosenthal, the owner of several New York gambling dens, was murdered as he left Café Metropole (a crime recounted in the story of the Jack Rose). Just one week after the murder, The Hotel Metropole went bankrupt, later to become became the Hotel Rosoff.

METROPOLITAN

★★★½☆

Glass: Martini
Garnish: Orange zest twist (flamed)
Method: SHAKE all ingredients with ice and fine strain into chilled glass.

1	shot	Raspberry flavoured vodka
1	shot	Triple Sec
1½	shots	Ocean Spray cranberry juice
½	shot	Freshly squeezed lime juice
¼	shot	Rose's lime cordial

We say: A Cosmo with more than a hint of blackcurrant.
Origin: Created in 1993 by Chuck Coggins at Marion's Continental Restaurant & Lounge, New York City. Marion's was originally opened in 1950 by fashion model Marion Nagy, who came to the States after seeking asylum while swimming for Hungary in the Paris Peace Games after WWII.

MEXICAN

★★★★☆

Glass: Martini
Garnish: Pineapple wedge
Method: SHAKE all ingredients with ice and fine strain into chilled glass.

2	shots	Tequila 100% Agave
1½	shots	Fresh pressed pineapple juice
¼	shot	Pomegranate (grenadine) syrup

Variant: Substitute sugar syrup for pomegranate syrup.
We say: Fresh pineapple makes this drink.

MEXICAN 55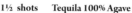

★★★★☆

Glass: Collins
Garnish: Lime wedge
Method: SHAKE first 4 ingredients with ice and strain into ice-filled glass. TOP with champagne.

1½	shots	Tequila 100% Agave
1	shot	Freshly squeezed lemon juice
½	shot	Monin Pure Cane 2:1 sugar syrup
2	dashes	Angostura aromatic bitters
Top up with		Brut champagne

Variant: Orange bitters instead of Angostura, as discovered in 2008 at the Experimental Cocktail Club, Paris.
We say: Suitably hard, yet surprisingly refreshing and sophisticated.
Origin: An adaptation of the classic French 75 created in 1988 at La Perla, Paris, France. The name comes from Fidel Castro's statement that bullets, like wine, came in vintages and Mexican 55 was a good year [for bullets].

MEXICAN COFFEE (HOT)

★★★☆☆

Glass: Toddy
Garnish: Coffee beans
Method: Place bar spoon in glass. POUR first three ingredients into glass and stir. FLOAT cream.

1	shot	Tequila 100% Agave
¼	shot	Monin Pure Cane 2:1 sugar syrup
Top up with		Hot filter coffee
Float lightly whipped		Double (heavy) cream

We say: Tequila's answer to the Irish Coffee.
Tip: Lightly whip or simply shake cream in container before pouring over the bowl of a spoon. It also helps if the cream is gently warmed.

MEXICAN MANHATTAN

★★★★☆

Glass: Martini
Garnish: Maraschino cherry
Method: STIR all ingredients with ice and strain into chilled glass.

2	shots	Tequila 100% Agave
1	shot	Martini Rosso sweet vermouth
3	dashes	Angostura aromatic bitters

We say: You've tried this with bourbon, now surprise yourself with an aged tequila.

MEXICAN MARTINI

★★★★★

Glass: Martini
Garnish: Jalapeño stuffed olives
Method: SHAKE all ingredients with ice and fine strain into chilled glass.

2	shots	Tequila 100% Agave
1	shot	Freshly squeezed lime juice
½	shot	Triple Sec
¼	shot	Agave nectar

We say: Basically a top-shelf Margarita garnished with Jalapeño stuffed olives.

MEXICAN MELON BALL

★★★☆☆

Glass: Collins
Garnish: Melon balls
Method: Cut melon into eight segments and deseed. Cut cubes of flesh from skin of one segment and MUDDLE in base of shaker. Add other ingredients, SHAKE with ice and fine strain into ice-filled glass.

⅛	fresh	Cantaloupe melon
2	shots	Tequila 100% Agave
2	shots	Freshly squeezed orange juice
¼	shot	Monin Pure Cane 2:1 sugar syrup

We say: Orange and melon laced with tequila.
Origin: Adapted from a drink discovered at the Flying V Bar & Grill, Tuscon, Arizona, USA.

MEXICAN MULE

★★★★☆

Glass: Collins
Garnish: Lime wedge
Method: SHAKE first 3 ingredients with ice and strain into ice-filled glass. TOP with ginger beer, lightly stir and serve with straws.

1½	shots	Tequila 100% Agave
¾	shot	Freshly squeezed lime juice
¼	shot	Monin Pure Cane 2:1 sugar syrup
Top up with		Ginger beer

AKA: El Burro
We say: A tequila based version of the Moscow Mule.

MEXICAN NAIL

★★★★☆

Glass: Old-fashioned
Garnish: Lime zest twist
Method: STIR all ingredients with ice and strain into ice-filled glass.

1½	shots	Tequila 100% Agave
1	shot	Drambuie
¼	shot	Lagavulin 16yo malt whisky

We say: Very complex with obvious whiskey and tequila notes made more interesting with subtle spice and chocolatey notes.
Origin: Created in 2010 by Simon Difford at the Cabinet Room, London, England.

MEXICAN SURFER

★★★★☆

Glass: Martini
Garnish: Lime wedge
Method: SHAKE all ingredients with ice and fine strain into chilled glass.

2	shots	Tequila 100% Agave
1½	shots	Fresh pressed pineapple juice
½	shot	Rose's lime cordial

We say: Frothy topped, easy to make, and all too easy to drink.

MEXICAN TEA (HOT)

★★★★⯨

Glass: Toddy
Garnish: Lime slice
Method: Place bar spoon in warmed glass. POUR all ingredients into glass and stir.

2	shots	Tequila 100% Agave
½	shot	Monin Pure Cane 2:1 sugar syrup
Top up with		Hot English breakfast tea

We say: Teatime will never be the same again.

MEXICANO (HOT)

★★★★⯨

Glass: Toddy
Garnish: Dust with grated nutmeg & cinnamon
Method: POUR tequila and liqueur into warmed glass and top with coffee. FLOAT cream over drink.

1	shot	Tequila 100% Agave
½	shot	Grand Marnier liqueur
Top up with		Hot filter coffee
Float lightly whipped Double (heavy) cream		

We say: A spicy, flavour-packed hot coffee. Lightly whip or simply shake cream in container before pouring over the bowl of a spoon. It also helps if the cream is gently warmed.

MEXICO CITY

★★★★⯨

Glass: Coupette
Garnish: Lime wedge
Method: SHAKE all ingredients with ice and fine strain into chilled glass.

1½	shots	Tequila 100% Agave
¾	shot	Grand Marnier liqueur
½	shot	Freshly squeezed lime juice
½	shot	Ocean Spray cranberry juice
¼	shot	Monin Pure Cane 2:1 sugar syrup

We say: This pinky-red Margarita benefits from a hint of cranberry.
Origin: Adapted from a cocktail discovered in 2002 at the Merc Bar, New York City.

MEZZO E MEZZO NEW

★★★★⯨

Glass: Old-fashioned
Garnish: Lemon zest twist
Method: POUR ingredients into ice-filled glass and briefly stir.

1	shot	Rabarbaro
1	shot	Soda (club soda)

We say: Slightly on the bitter side of bittersweet, this classic aperitivo is light and palate cleansing. Best made with equal parts Nardini Rosso, Nardini Rabarbaro and soda.
Origin: Originally and properly made with equal parts Nardini Rosso, Nardini Rabarbaro and soda water, we were made aware of this excellent drink by Nick Hopewell-Smith, Nardini's UK importer. The drink originates from the famous Grapperia Nardini on the Ponte Vecchio where Nardini Rosso was first served with soda water in the 1920s. In the 1970s a drinker tried it with a dash of Nardini's rhubarb liqueur. The drink, with its dash of Rabarbaro, became increasingly popular, and as its popularity grew, so did the dash increase until the mixture reached equal parts of Nardini Rosso and Rabarbaro.

MEZCAL MARGARITA

★★★★☆

Glass: Old-fashioned
Garnish: Lime wedge
Method: SHAKE all ingredients with ice and fine strain into ice-filled glass.

2	shots	Mezcal
1	shot	Triple Sec
1	shot	Freshly squeezed lime juice

We say: A smokin' Margarita.
Origin: Discovered in 2007 at Crazy Homies, London, England.

MIAMI BEACH

★★★★☆

Glass: Martini
Garnish: Pineapple wedge & maraschino cherry
Method: SHAKE all ingredients with ice and fine strain into chilled glass.

2	shots	Tanqueray London dry gin
1½	shots	Fresh pressed pineapple juice
¼	shot	Monin Pure Cane 2:1 sugar syrup

We say: Fruity and well proportioned - like the babes on Miami Beach. Sorry.

MIAMI DAIQUIRI

★★★★☆

Glass: Martini
Garnish: Mint leaf
Method: SHAKE all ingredients with ice and fine strain into chilled glass.

2	shots	Bacardi Superior rum
¼	shot	Giffard Menthe Pastille liqueur
½	shot	Freshly squeezed lime juice
⅛	shot	Monin Pure Cane 2:1 sugar syrup
¾	shot	Chilled mineral water

We say: The merest hint of mint in a refreshing Daiquiri with a dry finish.
Origin: My adaptation of a classic.

MIAMI MARTINI NEW

★★★★☆

Glass: Martini
Garnish: Watermelon Slice
Method: SHAKE all ingredients with ice and fine strain into chilled glass.

1	wedge	Fresh watermelon
2	shots	Ketel One vodka
¼	shot	Campari Bitter
½	shot	Freshly squeezed lemon juice
¾	shot	Monin Pure Cane 2:1 sugar syrup
2	dashes	Orange bitters

We say: Light, refreshing and all too quaffable. Campari and orange bitters add depth of flavour.
Origin: Adapted from a recipe by Alexandra Fiot at The Lonsdale, London, England.

MICHELADA UPDATED

★★★★☆

Glass: Collins
Garnish: Coarse salt rim
Method: SALT the rim of a chilled beer mug by rubbing it with a lime wedge and dipping rim in the coarse salt. Squeeze the lime into the mug. Add the Worcestershire sauce and Tabasco. Pour in the beer and serve.

½	shot	**Freshly squeezed lime juice**
3	dashes	**Tabasco hot pepper sauce**
2	spoons	**Worcestershire sauce**
Top up with		**Pilsner lager**

We say: On a hot day, if a beer is not refreshing enough then a Michelada may hit the spot. In Mexico Valentina is the preferred brand of hot pepper sauce.
Origin: Loosely translates as 'my beer' – 'mi' means 'my' and 'chela' is Mexican slang for pint. This drink, which is popular in Mexico, is thought to have originated there sometime in the 1940s. There are many variations of this drink. It is sometimes served with ice but usually with light Mexican lager. Even the spicy ingredients vary with soya sauce often omitted, but the hot pepper sauce is a constant.
In Mexico City itself, a Michelada almost always refers to something much simpler than this: 1 shot fresh lime juice in a glass with a salted rim, into which a light lager is poured. Very common too is the Michelato made with 2 shots Clamato (a clam-flavoured sweet tomato juice), then topped up with the beer, hot sauce (usually Valentina) and black pepper.

MIDNIGHT IN NYC NEW

★★★★☆

Glass: Coupette
Garnish: Lemon zest twist
Method: SHAKE all ingredients with ice and fine strain into chilled glass.

1	shot	**Maker's Mark bourbon**
1	shot	**Shiraz red wine**
½	shot	**Freshly squeezed lemon juice**
¼	shot	**Pomegranate (grenadine) syrup**

We say: The success of this cocktail is very dependent on the red wine you use. A lighter earthier style will work better than a big fruit red.
Origin: Adapted from a recipe by Trudy Thomas, Liquid Remedy, Inc, Phoenix, AZ.

MIDNIGHT MOON NEW

★★★½☆

Glass: Coupette
Garnish: Half apple slice to represent a crescent moon & orange zest twist (discarded)
Method: STIR first three ingredients with ice and strain into chilled glass. TOP with champagne.

½	shot	**Cognac VSOP**
½	shot	**Amaretto liqueur**
½	shot	**White Crème de Cacao**
3	shot	**Brut champagne**

We say: A slightly sweet bubbly crowd pleaser of a cocktail.
Origin: Adapted from a recipe by Colin Peter Field, Hemingway Bar, Ritz Paris, France.

MIDNIGHT OVER TENNESSEE

★★★★½

Glass: Martini
Garnish: Dust with chocolate powder
Method: SHAKE first three ingredients with ice and fine strain into chilled glass. Separately SHAKE cream and crème de menthe and carefully strain over drink to layer.

2	shots	**Jack Daniel's Tennessee whiskey**
½	shot	**Kahlúa coffee liqueur**
½	shot	**Dark Crème de Cacao**
½	shot	**Green crème de menthe liqueur**
½	shot	**Double (heavy) cream**

We say: One of the best dessert cocktails I've tried. Whiskey, coffee and chocolate sipped through a layer of minty cream.
Origin: Created in 2006 by Leon Edwards at Restaurant Bar & Grill, Manchester, England.

MIKE ROMANOFF

★★★½☆

Glass: Martini
Garnish: Orange zest twist
Method: SHAKE all ingredients with ice and fine strain into chilled glass.

2	shots	**Ketel One vodka**
⅛	shot	**Triple Sec**
⅛	shot	**De Kuyper Apricot Brandy liqueur**
¾	shot	**Freshly squeezed lime juice**
¼	shot	**Monin Pure Cane 2:1 sugar syrup**

We say: A Vodka Daisy sweetened with triple sec, apricot brandy and a touch of sugar.
Origin: Michael Romanoff (1890-1971) was a'Hollywood' impresario. Born Hershel Geguzin in Lithuania he immigrated to New York City aged ten and changed his name to Harry F. Gerguson. He moved to Hollywood where he took on the Michael Romanoff persona, claiming to be born Prince Michael Alexandrovitch Dimitri Obolensky Romanoff, nephew of Tsar Nicholas II. Scotland Yard described the former British and French convict as a 'rouge of uncertain nationality.' He was another actor in a town of actors and when a filmmaker needed a 'technical adviser' for a movie set in Europe, Romanoff was the obvious well paid expert. He was a popular Hollywood figure and he opened Romanoff's, a Beverly Hills restaurant popular with movie stars in the 1940s and 1950s.

Humphrey Bogart was a good friend of Romanoff and a regular at the restaurant. Hollywood legend has it that one day in 1955 Bogie was lunching with Frank Sinatra, Judy Garland and Jimmy Van Heusen when Mrs Bogart, A.K.A. Lauren Bacall walked into the restaurant and on seeing the group exclaimed, "I see the rat pack is all here". Thus Romanoff's became the place where the Rat Pack term was first coined and also where this drink was created.

David Niven was also a close friend and in his book "Bring on the Empty Horses" he devotes chapter eight, 'The Emperor', to the colourful Romanoff.

STAR RATINGS EXPLAINED

★★★★★ Excellent

★★★★½ Recommended	★★★★☆ Praiseworthy
★★★½☆ Commended	★★★☆☆ Mediocre
★★½☆☆ Disappointing	★★☆☆☆ Pretty awful
★½☆☆☆ Shameful	★☆☆☆☆ Disgusting

MILANESE BREAKFAST MARTINI NEW

★★★★☆

Glass: Coupette
Method: STIR marmalade with gin in base of shaker to dissolve marmalade. Add Campari and lemon juice, SHAKE with ice and fine strain into chilled glass. TOP with Prosecco.

1	shot	Tanqueray London dry gin
1	spoon	Orange marmalade
⅛	shot	Campari Bitter
½	shot	Freshly squeezed lemon juice
Top up with		Prosecco sparkling wine

We say: A fruity but dry aperitif drink served 'up' but with a hint of sparkle from prosecco.
Origin: Adapted from a drink created by Dawid Steenkamp at Jamie Oliver's Barbecoa, London, England and inspired by a Negroni and Salvatore's 'Breakfast Martini'. Originally names 'Breakfast in Milan'.

MILANO

★★★★⯪

Glass: Old-fashioned
Garnish: Orange slice
Method: STIR all ingredients with ice and strain into ice-filled glass.

1	shot	Ketel One vodka
1	shot	Campari Bitter
1	shot	Martini Rosso sweet vermouth

AKA: Negrosky
We say: A Negroni with vodka.

MILANO SOUR

★★★★☆

Glass: Old-fashioned
Garnish: Lemon slice & cherry on stick (sail)
Method: SHAKE all ingredients with ice and fine strain into ice-filled glass.

1½	shots	Tanqueray London dry gin
1	shot	Galliano L'Autentico liqueur
1	shot	Freshly squeezed lemon juice
½	fresh	Egg white

We say: Delicate anise and peppermint with citrus freshness.
Origin: Created in 2006 by Simon Difford.

MILK & HONEY MARTINI

★★★★⯪

Glass: Martini
Garnish: Dust with grated nutmeg
Method: STIR Scotch with honey in base of shaker to dissolve honey. Add other ingredients, SHAKE with ice and fine strain into chilled glass.

2	shots	Dewar's White label Scotch
3	spoons	Runny honey
½	shot	Krupnik spiced honey liqueur
¾	shot	Double (heavy) cream
¾	shot	Milk

We say: The rich flavour of Scotch is tamed by honey and cream.
Origin: Created in 2002 by Simon Difford.

MILK PUNCH

★★★★☆

Glass: Collins
Garnish: Dust with grated nutmeg
Method: SHAKE all ingredients with ice and strain into glass filled with crushed ice.

1	shot	Cognac VSOP
½	shot	Gosling's Black Seal rum
½	shot	Monin Vanilla sugar syrup
2	shots	Milk
1	shot	Double (heavy) cream

We say: The cream, vanilla and sugar tame the cognac and rum.

MILKY MOJITO

★★★⯪☆

Glass: Collins
Garnish: Mint sprig
Method: Lightly MUDDLE (just to bruise) mint in glass. Fill glass with crushed ice, add other ingredients. TOP with soda, stir and serve with straws.

12	fresh	Mint leaves
2	shots	Pernod anise
1	shot	Freshly squeezed lime juice
¾	shot	Monin Pure Cane 2:1 sugar syrup
Top up with		Soda (club soda)

We say: An anise laced alternative to a Mojito. The name refers to the opaque white colour of the drink after soda is added to the anis.

MILLENNIUM COCKTAIL NEW 🗝

★★★★⯪

Glass: Coupette
Garnish: Orange zest twist & dust with grated nutmeg
Method: SHAKE all ingredients with ice and fine strain into chilled glass.

1½	shots	Cognac VSOP
1½	shots	Fresh pressed pineapple juice
1	shot	Curaçao orange liqueur
1	dash	Angostura aromatic bitters

We say: Somewhat reminiscent of a cognac laced Hawaiian pizza. Yum!
Origin: Created by Dale DeGroff, New York City, USA.

THE MILLION DOLLAR COCKTAIL 🗝

★★★★⯪

Glass: Martini
Garnish: Lemon zest twist
Method: SHAKE all ingredients with ice and fine strain into chilled glass.

2	shots	Tanqueray London dry gin
1	shot	Martini Rosso sweet vermouth
½	shot	Fresh pressed pineapple juice
¼	shot	Pomegranate (grenadine) syrup
½	fresh	Egg white

We say: Serious, yet superbly smooth and a bit fluffy.
Origin: This classic cocktail is thought to have been created around 1910 by Ngiam Tong Boon at The Long Bar, Raffles Hotel, Singapore. Boon is more famous for the Singapore Sling.

MILLION DOLLAR MARGARITA

★★★★½

Glass: Old-fashioned
Garnish: Lime wedge
Method: SHAKE all ingredients with ice and strain into ice-filled glass.

1½	shots	**Tequila 100% Agave**
1½	shots	**Grand Marnier liqueur**
½	shot	**Freshly squeezed lime juice**

We say: The proportions of this Margarita accentuate the liqueur.
Origin: Discovered in 2006 at Maison 140 Hotel, Los Angeles, USA where I paid a mere $41.14 plus tip for the drink.

MILLIONAIRE UPDATED

★★★★☆

Glass: Coupette
Garnish: Orange slice
Method: SHAKE all ingredients with ice and fine strain into chilled glass.

2	shots	**Maker's Mark bourbon**
½	shot	**Cointreau triple sec**
½	shot	**Freshly squeezed lemon juice**
¼	shot	**Pomegranate (grenadine) syrup**
½	fresh	**Egg white**

We say: Whiskey, orange liqueur and pomegranate in sweet harmony. Depending on your grenadine, this will either look a dirty yellow or have a faint red hue.
Origin: There are numerous cocktails that go by the name Millionaire and this particular recipe is credited to London's Ritz Hotel, sometime pre 1925.

MILLIONAIRE'S DAIQUIRI

★★★½☆

Glass: Martini
Garnish: Star fruit
Method: SHAKE all ingredients with ice and fine strain into chilled glass.

1¾	shots	**Bacardi Superior rum**
¾	shot	**Sloe Gin liqueur**
¾	shot	**De Kuyper Apricot Brandy liqueur**
¾	shot	**Freshly squeezed lime juice**
¼	shot	**Pomegranate (grenadine) syrup**

We say: The colour of this cocktail, due to sloe liqueur and grenadine, belies a surprisingly dry finish.
Origin: This heralds from a classic cocktail known simply as the Millionaire. Originally Sloe gin was the main base ingredient, but David Embury once wrote, "Since the sloe gin, which is a liqueur, predominates in this drink, I do not regard it as a true cocktail." Thus above is my modern adaptation.

STAR RATINGS EXPLAINED

★★★★★ Excellent

★★★★½ Recommended	★★★★☆ Praiseworthy
★★★½☆ Commended	★★★☆☆ Mediocre
★★½☆☆ Disappointing	★★☆☆☆ Pretty awful
★½☆☆☆ Shameful	★☆☆☆☆ Disgusting

MILLY MARTINI

★★★★☆

Glass: Martini
Garnish: Pineapple wedge
Method: Lightly MUDDLE basil (just to bruise) in base of shaker. Add other ingredients, SHAKE with ice and fine strain into chilled glass.

5	fresh	**Torn basil leaves**
2	shots	**Tanqueray London dry gin**
2	shots	**Fresh pressed pineapple juice**
½	shot	**Monin Pure Cane 2:1 sugar syrup**
2	dashes	**Orange bitters**

We say: Gin and pineapple with a pleasing hint of basil.
Origin: Created in 2003 by Shelim Islam at the GE Club, London, England.

MILO

★★★½☆

Glass: Martini
Garnish: Raspberries
Method: SHAKE all ingredients with ice and fine strain into chilled glass.

4	fresh	**Raspberries**
2	shots	**Tanqueray London dry gin**
½	shot	**Triple Sec**
¼	shot	**Monin Pure Cane 2:1 sugar syrup**
1	dash	**Peychaud's aromatic bitters**

We say: Reminiscent of a Raspberry Cosmopolitan, only drier and stronger.
Origin: Created in 2002 by Tony Conigliaro at Isola, London, England.

MIMOSA

★★★½☆

Glass: Flute
Garnish: Orange zest twist
Method: POUR ingredients into chilled glass and stir.

½ shot	**Grand Marnier liqueur**
1¾ shots	**Freshly squeezed orange juice**
Top up with	**Brut champagne**

Variant: When made with mandarin juice this becomes a Puccini.
We say: A liqueur-infused take on the Buck's Fizz.
Origin: Created in 1925 at the Ritz Hotel in Paris and named after the tropical flowering shrub. In his 1948 '*Fine Art of Mixing Drinks*', David A. Embury writes of this drink, "Just another freak champagne mixture. It is not half bad and the ladies usually like it. Use a good quality domestic champagne, medium dry."

MINCEMEAT PIE

★★★½☆

Glass: Martini
Garnish: Dust with cinnamon powder
Method: SHAKE first three ingredients with ice and fine strain into chilled glass. FLOAT layer of cream on drink.

2	shots	**Bacardi 8yo aged rum**
1	spoon	**Mincemeat**
1	shot	**Pressed apple juice**
½	shot	**Double (heavy) cream**

We say: A festive tipple capturing the flavour of that Christmas staple, mince pies.
Origin: Created in 2008 by Bruce Borthwick of Inspirit Brands, Scotland.

MINT & HONEY DAIQUIRI

★★★★½

Glass: Martini
Garnish: Mint sprig
Method: STIR honey and rum in base of shaker until honey dissolves. Add other ingredients, SHAKE with ice and fine strain into chilled glass.

2	spoons	Runny honey
2	shots	Bacardi Superior rum
3	fresh	Mint leaves
½	shot	Freshly squeezed lime juice
½	shot	Chilled mineral water

We say: A fresh-breath-tastic twist on the classic Daiquiri.
Origin: Created in 2006 by Simon Difford.

MINT COCKTAIL

★★★★½

Glass: Martini
Garnish: Mint leaf
Method: Lightly MUDDLE (just to bruise) mint in base of shaker. Add other ingredients, SHAKE with ice and fine strain into chilled glass.

12	fresh	Mint leaves
2	shots	Tanqueray London dry gin
1	shot	Sauvignon blanc wine
¼	shot	Giffard Menthe Pastille liqueur
¼	shot	Monin Pure Cane 2:1 sugar syrup

We say: A great grassy, minty digestif with a good balance between acidity and sweetness.
Origin: Adapted from a recipe on Harry Craddock's 1930 *Savoy Cocktail Book*.

MINT COLLINS

★★★★☆

Glass: Collins
Garnish: Mint sprig
Method: Lightly MUDDLE (just to bruise) mint in base of shaker. Add next three ingredients, SHAKE with ice and fine strain into chilled glass. TOP with soda, lightly stir and serve with straws.

12	fresh	Mint leaves
2	shots	Tanqueray London dry gin
1	shot	Freshly squeezed lemon juice
½	shot	Monin Pure Cane 2:1 sugar syrup
Top up with		Soda (club soda)

We say: Exactly what the name promises.
Origin: Adapted from a recipe in the 1942-72 *Trader Vic's Bartender's Guide* by Victor Bergeron.

MINT DAIQUIRI

★★★★★

Glass: Martini
Garnish: Mint leaf
Method: Lightly MUDDLE (just to bruise) mint in base of shaker. Add other ingredients, SHAKE with ice and fine strain into chilled glass.

12	fresh	Mint leaves
2	shots	Bacardi Superior rum
½	shot	Freshly squeezed lime juice
¼	shot	Monin Pure Cane 2:1 sugar syrup
½	shot	Chilled mineral water

We say: A short, concentrated Mojito.
Origin: Created in 2006 by Simon Difford.

MINT FIZZ

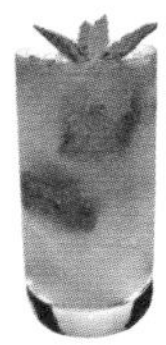

★★★½☆

Glass: Collins
Garnish: Mint sprig
Method: Lightly MUDDLE mint (just to bruise) in base of shaker. Add other ingredients apart from soda, SHAKE with ice and fine strain into ice-filled glass. TOP with soda, lightly stir and serve with straws.

7	fresh	Mint leaves
2	shots	Tanqueray London dry gin
¼	shot	Giffard Menthe Pastille liqueur
1	shot	Freshly squeezed lime juice
½	shot	Monin Pure Cane 2:1 sugar syrup
Top up with		Soda (club soda)

We say: Long, refreshing citrus and mint fizz.

MINT JULEP UPDATED

★★★★★

Glass: Julep Tin
Garnish: Mint sprig dusted with icing sugar
Method: SHAKE all ingredients with ice and fine strain into julep cup half filled with crushed ice. CHURN (stir) the drink with the crushed ice using a bar spoon. Top up the cup with more crushed ice and CHURN again. Repeat this process until the drink fills the cup and serve.

12	fresh	Mint leaves
2½	shots	Maker's Mark bourbon
¾	shot	Monin Pure Cane 2:1 sugar syrup
3	dashes	Angostura aromatic bitters

We say: This superb drink is better if the shaker and its contents are placed in the refrigerator for several hours prior to mixing with ice. This allows the mint flavours to infuse in the bourbon.
Origin: Like so many cocktails, the humble Mint Julep's origins are the subject of heated debate. Today it is closely identified with America's Deep South, famously served at the Kentucky Derby. However, the name derives from the Arabic word 'julab', meaning rosewater, and the first known written reference to a cocktail-style Julep was by a Virginia gentleman in 1787.

At that time it could be made with rum, brandy or whiskey, but by 1900 whiskey had become the preferred base spirit. Indeed in his 1862 The Bartender's Guide: How to Mix Drinks, Jerry Thomas calls for cognac, a dash of Jamaican rum and a garnish of berries and orange slices. He also lists a Julep variation made with gin and one calling for ripe pineapple as well as the now ubiquitous whiskey version.

Common perceived wisdom has it that the Julep originated in Persia, or thereabouts, and it travelled to Europe (some say Southern France) where the rose petals were substituted for indigenous mint. The drink is then believed to have crossed the Atlantic where cognac was replaced with peach brandy and then whiskey - the Mint Julep we recognise today.

The remodelled US-style mint julep reached Britain in 1837, thanks to the novelist Captain Frederick Marryat, who complained of being woken at 7am by a slave brandishing a Julep. He popularised the drink through his descriptions of American Fourth of July celebrations and praise such as the following:

"I must descant a little upon the mint julep, as it is, with the thermometer at 100?, one of the most delightful and insinuating potations that was ever invented, and may be drunk with equal satisfaction when the thermometer is as low as 70?... As the ice melts, you drink. I once overheard two ladies in the room next to me, and one of them said, 'Well, if I have a weakness for any one thing, it is for a 'mint julep!' - a very amiable weakness, and proving her good sense and taste. They are, in fact, like the American ladies, irresistible."

When making a Mint Julep it is important to only bruise the mint as crushing the leaves releases the bitter, inner juices. Also be sure to discard the stems, which are also bitter.

It is imperative that the drink is served ice cold. Cocktail etiquette dictates that the shaker containing the mint and other ingredients should be placed in a refrigerator with the serving vessel (preferably made of metal rather than glass) for at least two hours prior to adding ice, shaking and serving.

Variations on the Mint Julep include substituting the bourbon for rye whiskey, rum, gin, brandy, calvados or applejack brandy. Another variation calls for half a shot of aged rum to be floated on top of the bourbon-based julep.

MINT JULEP (MEXICAN STYLE)

★★★½☆

Glass: Martini
Garnish: Maraschino cherry
Method: PLACE lemon zest and mint in shaker. Add other ingredients, SHAKE with ice and fine strain into ice-filled glass.

1	fresh	**Lemon zest twist**
8	fresh	**Mint leaves**
1	shot	**Cognac VSOP**
1	shot	**Warre's Otima tawny port**
¼	shot	**Luxardo Maraschino liqueur**

We say: Mint, cognac, port, lemon and maraschino - all subtly contribute to this Cuban take on Mexico.
Origin: Recipe adapted from a 1937 Bar Florida (later renamed Floridita) menu, Havana, Cuba.

MINT LIMEADE (MOCKTAIL)

★★★★½

Glass: Collins
Garnish: Mint sprig
Method: Lightly MUDDLE (just to bruise) mint in base of shaker. Add next three ingredients, SHAKE with ice and fine strain into ice-filled glass. TOP with lemonade, lightly stir and serve with straws.

12	fresh	**Mint leaves**
1½	shots	**Freshly squeezed lime juice**
1	shot	**Pressed apple juice**
¾	shot	**Monin Pure Cane 2:1 sugar syrup**
Top up with		**Lemonade/Sprite/7-Up**

We say: Superbly refreshing - mint and lime served long.
Origin: Created in 2006 by Simon Difford.

MINT MARTINI

★★★★½

Glass: Martini
Garnish: Mint leaf
Method: Lightly MUDDLE (just to bruise) mint in base of shaker. Add other ingredients, SHAKE with ice and fine strain into chilled glass.

12	fresh	**Mint leaves**
1½	shots	**Ketel One vodka**
¼	shot	**Green crème de menthe liqueur**
½	shot	**Martini Extra Dry vermouth**
1½	shots	**Sauvignon blanc wine**
¼	shot	**Monin Pure Cane 2:1 sugar syrup**

We say: An after dinner palate cleanser.
Origin: Created in 2005 by Simon Difford.

STAR RATINGS EXPLAINED

★★★★★ Excellent

★★★★½	Recommeded	★★★★☆	Praiseworthy
★★★½☆	Commended	★★★☆☆	Mediocre
★★½☆☆	Disappointing	★★☆☆☆	Pretty awful
★½☆☆☆	Shameful	★☆☆☆☆	Disgusting

MISS MARTINI

★★★½☆

Glass: Martini
Garnish: Raspberries
Method: MUDDLE raspberries in base of shaker. Add other ingredients, SHAKE with ice and fine strain into chilled glass.

7	fresh	**Raspberries**
2	shots	**Ketel One vodka**
½	shot	**Chambord black raspberry liqueur**
¼	shot	**Milk**
¼	shot	**Double (heavy) cream**
⅛	shot	**Monin Pure Cane 2:1 sugar syrup**

We say: A pink, fruity, creamy concoction.
Origin: Created in 1997 by Giovanni Burdi at Match EC1, London, England.

MISSIONARY'S DOWNFALL

★★★★★

Glass: Collins
Garnish: Mint sprig
Method: Lightly MUDDLE mint (just to bruise) in base of shaker. Add other ingredients, SHAKE with ice and strain into glass filled with crushed ice.

12	fresh	**Mint leaves**
2	shots	**Bacardi Superior rum**
½	shot	**Peachtree peach schnapps**
1½	shots	**Freshly squeezed lime juice**
2	shots	**Fresh pressed pineapple juice**
½	shot	**Monin Pure Cane 2:1 sugar syrup**

We say: Superbly balanced and refreshing rum, lime, mint and a hint of peach.
Origin: Created in the 1930s by Don The Beachcomber at his restaurant in Hollywood, California, USA.

MISSISSIPPI PUNCH

★★★★☆

Glass: Collins
Garnish: Lemon slice
Method: SHAKE all ingredients with ice and strain into glass filled with crushed ice.

1½	shots	**Maker's Mark bourbon**
¾	shot	**Cognac VSOP**
¾	shot	**Freshly squeezed lemon juice**
1	shot	**Monin Pure Cane 2:1 sugar syrup**
2	shots	**Chilled mineral water**

We say: Balanced and refreshing.

MISSISSIPPI SCHNAPPER

★★★½☆

Glass: Martini
Garnish: Orange zest twist
Method: SHAKE all ingredients with ice and fine strain into chilled glass.

2	shots	**Maker's Mark bourbon**
¾	shot	**Cognac VSOP**
½	shot	**Triple Sec**
¼	shot	**Freshly squeezed lime juice**
¼	shot	**Monin Pure Cane 2:1 sugar syrup**

We say: Orange predominates with peach sweetness balanced by whiskey and lime.
Origin: Created in 1999 by Dan Cottle at Velvet, Manchester, England.

MISTER STU

★★★½☆

Glass: Collins
Garnish: Pineapple wedge
Method: SHAKE all ingredients with ice and strain into ice-filled glass. Serve with straws.

2	shots	Tequila 100% Agave
½	shot	Amaretto liqueur
½	shot	Malibu coconut rum liqueur
1½	shots	Fresh pressed pineapple juice
1½	shots	Freshly squeezed orange juice

We say: There's a touch of the disco about this foamy drink, but it is still complex and interesting.

MITCH MARTINI

★★★★☆

Glass: Martini
Garnish: Lemon zest twist
Method: SHAKE all ingredients with ice and fine strain into chilled glass.

2	shots	Żubrówka bison vodka
1	shot	Pressed apple juice
¼	shot	Peachtree peach schnapps
¼	shot	Passion fruit syrup

We say: One of London's contemporary classics. Far from a proper Martini, this is fruity and sweet, but not overly so.
Origin: Created in 1997 by Giovanni Burdi at Match EC1, London, England.

MIXED BERRY JULEP NEW

★★★★½

Glass: Collins
Garnish: Blackberries & mint sprig
Method: Lightly MUDDLE berries in base of glass. Add mint, bourbon, cognac, and sugar syrup into glass, add crushed ice and CHURN (stir) with bar spoon. Top up the glass with more crushed ice and CHURN again. Repeat this process until the drink fills the glass and serve.

12	fresh	Mint leaves
2	fresh	Blackberries
3	fresh	Raspberries
1	shot	Maker's Mark bourbon
1	shot	Cognac VSOP
¾	shot	Monin Pure Cane 2:1 sugar syrup

We say: A fruity, minty crowd pleasing Julep.
Origin: Created by Dre Masso in Colombia 2009.

MIZUWARI NEW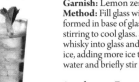

★★★★★

Glass: Collins
Garnish: Lemon zest twist (discarded) & mint sprig
Method: Fill glass with ice and STIR until water formed in base of glass. Add more ice and continue stirring to cool glass. STRAIN water from glass, pour whisky into glass and top ice to brim. STIR whisky and ice, adding more ice to keep level at brim. Lastly, add water and briefly stir some more.

| 2 | shots | Dewar's White Label Scotch |
| | | Top up with Chilled mineral water |

Variant: Shouso – a twist on a Mizuwari with lemon grass and lemon zest.
Taisho – Japanese whisky and elderflower highball.
Risshu – Japanese whisky with soda, lemon and orange peel.
Shosho – Japanese whisky with soda, rose water and fresh mint.
Shokan – Japanese whisky with cherry brandy, vanilla pod and orange zest.
Daikan – Japanese whisky with dashes of absinthe and cherry bitters.
Risshun – Japanese whisky, honey Umeshu (plum water) and ginger.
Usui – Japanese whisky with violet cordial, rosewater and orange blossom water.
Shunbun – Japanese whisky with Ume shisho (Japanese mint), angostura and orange zest.
Seimei – Japanese whisky with maraschino liqueur, absinthe and lemon zest.
Boshu – Japanese whisky with Mandarine Napoleon liqueur and orange bitters.
We say: This is simply whisky and water, but as with the Japanese tea ceremony, observing the time and care taken over it making and the prolonged anticipation contributes greatly to the finished drink. And you thought an Old Fashioned took a long time.
Origin: Pronounced "Miz-Zoo-Ware-E", this literally translates as "mizu" = water and "wari" = divide, thus the whisky is simply cut with water and served over ice. The ratio is personal to both the drinker and bartender and varies between 1:2.5 and 1:4 whisky to water. It is common in Japan for dinners to drink mizu wari in place of wine with their meals and the light whisky flavours combine excellently with Japanese food. Extremely thin, delicate glasses are used and the thickness and quality of glass is considered key to mizu wari in Japan.

MOCHA MARTINI

★★★★½

Glass: Martini
Garnish: Dust with chocolate powder
Method: SHAKE first four ingredients with ice and fine strain into chilled glass. FLOAT cream in centre of drink.

1½	shots	Maker's Mark bourbon
1	shot	Hot espresso coffee
½	shot	Baileys Irish cream liqueur
½	shot	Dark Crème de Cacao
½	shot	Double (heavy) cream

We say: Made with great espresso, this drink is a superb, richly flavoured balance of sweet and bitter.

BARTENDER'S TIP CONVERTING 'SHOTS'

To covert 'shots' into and fluid ounces simply treat one shot as one ounce. To convert 'shots' into metric measures use the following conversions:

2 shot(s) = 60ml, 1¾ shot(s) 52.5ml, 1½ shot(s) = 45ml, 1 shot(s) = 30ml, ¾ shot(s) = 22.5ml, ⅔ hot = 20ml, ½ shot(s) = 15ml, ⅓ shot(s) = 10ml, ¼ shot(s) = 7.5ml, ⅙ shot(s) = 5ml, ⅛ shot(s) = 4ml

MOCK MARGARITA

★★★½☆

Glass: Old-fashioned
Garnish: Salt rim & lime wedge
Method: SHAKE all ingredients with ice and strain into ice-filled glass.

1½ shots	Freshly squeezed lime juice
½ shot	Freshly squeezed lemon juice
1 shot	Agave nectar
Top up with	Ginger ale

We say: While this is a long way from a fine 100% agave tequila based Margarita, the flavour is surprisingly reminiscent of an alcoholic Margarita.
Origin: Adapted from a drink created in 2010 by Cheri Loughlin AKA The Intoxicologist, USA.

THE MODERN COCKTAIL NEW

★★★½☆

Glass: Coupette/Martini
Garnish: Maraschino cherry
Method: SHAKE all ingredients with ice and fine strain into chilled glass.

1½ shots	Dewar's White label Scotch
1½ shots	Sloe gin liqueur
½ shot	Freshly lemon juice
⅛ shot	Monin Pure Cane 2:1 sugar syrup)
1 dash	Absinthe
1 dash	Orange bitters

We say: A presently fruity cocktail with equal parts scotch and sloe liqueur shaken with lemon juice and a dash of absinthe.
Origin: Adapted form a drink created in the early 20th century by Charlie Mahoney, head bartender at New York's Hoffman House Hotel.

MODERNISTA

★★★½☆

Glass: Martini
Garnish: Lemon zest twist
Method: SHAKE all ingredients with ice and fine strain into chilled glass.

2 shots	Tanqueray London dry gin
½ shot	Gosling's Black Seal rum
¼ shot	Pernod anise
1 shot	Swedish Punch liqueur
¼ shot	Freshly squeezed lemon juice
1 dash	Orange bitters

We say: A massive flavour hit to awaken your taste buds.
Origin: Adapted from a drink created by Ted Haigh (AKA Dr. Cocktail) and derived from the 'Modern Cocktail'. See Ted's book, 'Vintage Spirits & Foreign Cocktails'.

STAR RATINGS EXPLAINED

★★★★★ Excellent

★★★★½ Recommended	★★★★☆ Praiseworthy
★★★½☆ Commended	★★★☆☆ Mediocre
★★½☆☆ Disappointing	★★☆☆☆ Pretty awful
★½☆☆☆ Shameful	★☆☆☆☆ Disgusting

MOJITO #1 UPDATED ⚷

★★★★★

Glass: Collins
Garnish: Mint sprig
Method: Lightly MUDDLE mint (just to bruise) in base of glass. Add rum, lime juice and sugar. Half fill glass with crushed ice and CHURN (stir) with bar spoon. Fill glass with more crushed ice and CHURN some more. TOP with soda, stir and serve with straws.

12 fresh	Mint leaves
2 shots	Rum light white/blanco
¾ shot	Freshly squeezed lime juice
½ shot	Monin Pure Cane 2:1 sugar syrup
Top up with	Soda (club soda)

Variant: Add two dashes Angostura aromatic bitters
We say: When well made, this Cuban cousin of the Mint Julep is one of the world's greatest and most refreshing cocktails.
Origin: The exact origins of the Mojito and its name are lost in the mists of time. Some trace it back to 1586 and a medicinal drink named after Sir Francis Drake. He was one of a band of privateers sponsored by England's Queen Elizabeth I to plunder Spanish cities in the New World and seize their riches.

Cuba was under Spanish rule and King Philip II of Spain had warned his governor in Cuba that he believed Drake intended to raid Havana in order to seize the Aztec gold stored in the city's royal treasury. Thus Havana was well defended but there was still surprised relief in the city when, after several days of waiting, Drake sailed away from the richest port in the West Indies after firing only a few shots.

Drake left Havana and its gold intact, but his visit was a major event - something perhaps worthy of naming a drink after.

Others say the drink was not originally Cuban and it was actually invented upon board Drake's ship which carried mint to mix with cane spirit, sugar and lime to make a drink to relieve fever and colds.

What is for certain is that the Draque, Drak or Drac was certainly drunk for its perceived medicinal value. During one of the worst cholera epidemics ever to hit Havana, the author Ramon de Paula wrote, "Every day at eleven o' clock I consume a little Drake made from aguardiente (local cane spirit) and I am doing very well."

At some time in the late 1890s the local cane spirit in the Draque was replaced with Bacardi Carta Blanca rum and over the decades the drink started to be made long. This is supported by Frederick Villoch in 1940 "... when aguardiente was replaced with rum, the Drake was to be called a Mojito."

However, some still maintain the Mojito was invented after Americans visiting Cuba's thriving bar culture between the wars, and especially during Prohibition, introduced the locals to the Mint Julep.

The origins of the name 'Mojito' are equally misty. Some say it comes from 'mojar', a Spanish verb suggesting wetness. Others claim it comes from the African word 'mojo', meaning spell.

Bodeguita del Medio bar in Havana is by urban myth credited with the first Mojito and this is apparently where Ernest Hemingway went for his." The great man wrote of Cuba's unofficial national drink, "it wasn't just a drink; it was a symbol of national pride."

MOJITO #2 (DIFFORD'S METHOD)

★★★★½

Glass: Collins
Garnish: Mint sprig
Method: SHAKE all ingredients with ice and fine strain into ice-filled glass. CHURN (stir) with bar spoon. Fill glass with more crushed ice and CHURN some more. Keep adding ice and churning until drink fills glass. Serve with straws.

12 fresh	Mint leaves
2½ shots	Bacardi Superior rum
¾ shot	Freshly squeezed lime juice
½ shot	Monin Pure Cane 2:1 sugar syrup
⅛ shot	Giffard Menthe Pastille liqueur
2 dashes	Angostura aromatic bitters

We say: All the flavour of the Mojito but without unattractive mint leaves trapped in crushed ice. This only works when fresh, cold crushed ice is used. Otherwise the drink will be overly diluted.
Origin: Recipe by Simon Difford, the man who likes his Mojito shaken and stirred.

MOJITO DE CASA

★★★★☆

Glass: Collins
Garnish: Mint sprig
Method: Lightly MUDDLE mint (just to bruise) in base of glass. Add tequila, lime juice and sugar. Half fill glass with crushed ice and CHURN (stir) with bar spoon. Fill glass with more crushed ice and churn some more. TOP with soda, stir and serve.

12	fresh	Mint leaves
2	shots	Tequila 100% Agave
¾	shot	Freshly squeezed lime juice
½	shot	Monin Pure Cane 2:1 sugar syrup
Top up with		Soda (club soda)

We say: A tequila based Mojito.
Origin: Created at Mercadito, New York City, USA.

MOJITO PARISIEN

★★★★★

Glass: Collins
Garnish: Mint sprig
Method: Lightly MUDDLE mint (just to bruise) in base of glass. Add other ingredients, half fill glass with crushed ice and CHURN (stir) with bar spoon. Fill glass to brim with more crushed ice and churn some more. Serve with straws.

12	fresh	Mint leaves
2	shots	Bacardi Superior rum
1½	shots	St~Germain elderflower liqueur
1	shot	Freshly squeezed lime juice

We say: Those with a sweet tooth may want to add a dash of sugar syrup to taste.
Origin: Recipe in 2006 by Simon Difford.

MOLLY'S MILK UPDATED

★★★★☆

Glass: Cocktail
Garnish: Dust with grated nutmeg
Method: STIR first two ingredients with ice and strain into chilled glass. FLOAT whipped cream on drink.

1½	shots	Jameson Irish whiskey
1½	shots	Irish Mist liqueur
1	shot	Whipped cream

We say: Herbal, honeyed Irish whiskey drunk through a creamy head.
Origin: Adapted from a drink created in 1997 by Dale DeGroff at Molly Malone's Pub, Prague, Czech Republic.

STAR RATINGS EXPLAINED

★★★★★ Excellent

★★★★☆ Recommended	★★★★☆ Praiseworthy
★★★☆☆ Commended	★★★☆☆ Mediocre
★★☆☆☆ Disappointing	★★☆☆☆ Pretty awful
★☆☆☆☆ Shameful	★☆☆☆☆ Disgusting

MOLOTOV COCKTAIL

★★★☆☆

Glass: Martini
Garnish: Lemon zest twist
Method: SHAKE all ingredients with ice and fine strain into chilled glass.

1½	shots	Ketel One vodka
1¼	shots	Parfait Amour liqueur
½	shot	Opal Nera black sambuca
½	shot	Freshly squeezed lemon juice

We say: The ingredients represent the four liquids used in the weapon. Vodka, stands for alcohol, parfait amour shares the purple hue of paraffin, lemon juice represents gasoline and black sambuca replaces tar.
Origin: Created after a visit to the Rajamäki distillery in Finland. At the start of WWII the plant was used to produce the inflammatory bombs with which the Finns put hundreds of Soviet tanks out of action.

MOMISETTE

★★★★☆

Glass: Collins
Method: POUR pastis and almond syrup into glass. Serve with bottle of sparkling water so the customer can dilute to their own taste. (I recommend five shots.) Lastly, add ice to fill glass.

1	shot	Ricard Pastis
¼	shot	Monin Almond (orgeat) syrup
Top up with		Sparkling mineral water

We say: Complex balance of anis, almond and liquorice.
Origin: A traditional French drink, the name of which literally translates as 'tiny mummy'.

MOMO SPECIAL

★★★★☆

Glass: Collins
Garnish: Mint sprig
Method: Lightly MUDDLE mint (just to bruise) in base of shaker. Add next 3 ingredients, SHAKE with ice and strain into ice-filled glass. TOP with soda, lightly stir and serve with straws.

12	fresh	Mint leaves
2	shots	Ketel One vodka
½	shot	Freshly squeezed lime juice
½	shot	Monin Pure Cane 2:1 sugar syrup
Top up with		Soda (club soda)

We say: Enrich the minty flavour by macerating the mint in the vodka some hours before making.
Origin: Created in 1998 by Simon Mainoo at Momo, London, England.

MONA LISA

★★★★☆

Glass: Collins
Garnish: Orange slice
Method: SHAKE first 3 ingredients with ice and strain into ice-filled glass. TOP with tonic water.

1	shot	Chartreuse Green liqueur
3	shots	Freshly squeezed orange juice
2	dashes	Angostura aromatic bitters
Top up with		Tonic water

We say: Chartreuse fans will appreciate this drink, which is also an approachable way for novices to acquire a taste for the green stuff.

MONARCH MARTINI

★★★★☆

Glass: Martini
Garnish: Lemon zest twist
Method: MUDDLE mint (just to bruise) in base of shaker. Add other ingredients, SHAKE with ice and fine strain into chilled glass.

7	fresh	Mint leaves
2	shots	Tanqueray London dry gin
½	shot	St–Germain elderflower liqueur
½	shot	Freshly squeezed lemon juice
¼	shot	Monin Pure Cane 2:1 sugar syrup
2	dashes	Peach bitters

We say: Wonderfully floral and minty - worthy of a right royal drinker.
Origin: Created in 2003 by Douglas Ankrah at Townhouse, London, England.

THE MONEY PENNY

★★★★★

Glass: Martini
Garnish: Grapefruit zest twist
Method: SHAKE all ingredients with ice and fine strain into chilled glass.

2	shots	Tanqueray London dry gin
¾	shot	Freshly squeezed grapefruit juice
½	shot	Martini Extra Dry vermouth
¼	shot	Monin Pure Cane 2:1 sugar syrup
1	dash	Grapefruit bitters

We say: Fresh grapefruit and gin soured with a splash of grapefruit and balanced with the merest touch of sugar.
Origin: Discovered in 2010 at the Blue Owl, New York City, USA.

MONET'S MOMENT NEW

★★★★☆

Glass: Wine goblet
Garnish: Orange zest twist (discarded)
Method: STIR all ingredients with ice and strain into ice-filled glass (preferably with one large hand-cracked cube)

1½	shots	Courvoisier VSOP Exclusif
1	shot	Byrrh aperitif
⅛	shot	La Fée Parisienne (68%) absinthe
¼	shot	Monin Pure Cane 2:1 sugar syrup
1	dash	Creole bitters

We say: Cognac and aromatised wine lifted with a splash of absinthe. Complex and refreshing.
Origin: Created in 2013 by Erik Lorincz, Head Bartender at the American Bar, Savoy Hotel, London. He was inspired after seeing a work by Claudio Monet that hangs in the suite where the French impressionist originally sketched the pastels piece entitled Waterloo Bridge in 1901. Erik was inspired by the moment when Monet entered his suite and decided to sketch the view from his window of the capital's iconic landmark.

MONK'S CANDY BAR

★★★☆☆

Glass: Martini
Garnish: Dust with grated nutmeg
Method: SHAKE all ingredients with ice and fine strain into chilled glass.

1	shot	Hazelnut liqueur
½	shot	Kahlúa coffee liqueur
½	shot	Butterscotch schnapps
1	shot	Double (heavy) cream
1	shot	Milk

We say: Creamy and sweet, with hazelnut, butterscotch and coffee.

MONK'S HABIT

★★★☆☆

Glass: Collins
Garnish: Orange slice
Method: SHAKE all ingredients with ice and strain into ice-filled glass.

1½	shots	Bacardi Superior rum
½	shot	Triple Sec
1	shot	Hazelnut liqueur
3	shots	Fresh pressed pineapple juice
¼	shot	Pomegranate (grenadine) syrup

We say: Fruit and nut laced with rum. Slightly sweet.

MONKEY GLAND #1

★★★★☆

Glass: Martini
Garnish: Orange zest twist
Method: SHAKE all ingredients with ice and fine strain into chilled glass.

2	shots	Tanqueray London dry gin
¼	shot	Absinthe
1½	shots	Freshly squeezed orange juice
¼	shot	Pomegranate (grenadine) syrup

We say: Approach with caution. Due diligence reveals a dangerous base of gin and absinthe.
Origin: Created in the late 1920s by Harry MacElhone at his Harry's New York Bar in Paris, France. The Monkey Gland takes its name from the work of Dr Serge Voronoff, who attempted to delay the ageing process by transplanting monkey testicles.

MONKEY GLAND #2

★★★★☆

Glass: Old-fashioned
Garnish: Orange slice
Method: SHAKE all ingredients with ice and fine strain into ice-filled glass.

2	shots	Tanqueray London dry gin
½	shot	Bénédictine D.O.M.
1¼	shots	Freshly squeezed orange juice
¼	shot	Pomegranate (grenadine) syrup

We say: A somewhat off-putting name for a very palatable cocktail.

MONKEY SHINE

★★★★☆

Glass: Martini
Garnish: Cinnamon & sugar rim
Method: SHAKE all ingredients with ice and fine strain into chilled glass.

2	shots	Bacardi Superior rum
1	shot	Malibu coconut rum liqueur
1	shot	Fresh pressed pineapple juice

We say: The sweet, tropical fruitiness of this drink is set off by the spicy rim.
Origin: An adaptation of a drink discovered in 2003 at the Bellagio Resort & Casino, Las Vegas.

MONKEY WRENCH

★★★☆☆

Glass: Collins
Garnish: None
Method: POUR rum into ice-filled glass. Top with grapefruit juice, stir and serve with straws.

2	shots	Bacardi Oro golden rum
Top up with		Freshly squeezed grapefruit juice

We say: Simple but pleasant.

MONSIEUR LECROIX NEW

★★★☆☆

Glass: Martini
Garnish: Lime zest twist
Method: STIR all ingredients with ice and strain into chilled glass.

2	shots	Mozart Dry chocolate spirit
1	shot	Cognac VSOP
½	shot	Grand Marnier liqueur
2	dashes	Orange bitters

We say: Chocolate and cognac with the merest splash of orange liqueur still leaving this drink on the dry side.
Origin: Adapted from a drink created in 2010 by Klaus St. Rainer at Schumann's Bar, Munich, Germany.

MONSTRE VERTE COCKTAIL NEW

★★★☆☆

Glass: Old-fashioned
Garnish: Basil leaf
Method: POUR aniseed into ice-filled glass and TOP with chilled water. Separately SHAKE rest of ingredients with ice. DISCARD contents of glass and refill with fresh ice. Then fine strain contents of shaker into the now absinthe coated glass.

¼	shot	Absinthe
1½	shots	Tanqueray London dry gin
½	shot	Chartreuse Green liqueur
¼	shot	Freshly squeezed lime juice
¼	shot	Monin Pure Cane 2:1 sugar syrup
4	fresh	Torn basil leaves

We say: A drink for fans of Chartreuse and aniseed.
Origin: Created in 2011 by Jamie Boudreau, Seattle, USA

MONTE CARLO #1

★★★¾☆

Glass: Collins
Garnish: Maraschino cherry
Method: POUR first 3 ingredients into empty glass. ADD soda water to half fill glass. Fill glass with ice and then top up with more soda. (This avoids 'shocking' the anis with the ice.) Serve with straws.

1	shot	Pernod anise
½	shot	Luxardo Maraschino liqueur
¾	shot	Freshly squeezed lime juice
Top up with		Soda (club soda)

We say: A long, fragrant, almost floral summer drink cooler with lots of aniseed.
Origin: An adaptation of a Martini-style drink created in 2002 by Alex Turner, London, England.

MONTE CARLO #2 (AMERICAN VERSION)

★★★½☆

Glass: Coupette
Garnish: Lemon zest twist
Method: STIR all ingredients with ice and strain into chilled glass.

2¼	shots	Maker's Mark bourbon
¾	shot	Bénédictine D.O.M.
2	dashes	Angostura aromatic bitters

We say: Spiced Bourbon.

MONTE CARLO IMPERIAL

★★★½☆

Glass: Martini
Garnish: Mint leaf
Method: SHAKE first 3 ingredients with ice and fine strain into chilled glass. TOP with champagne.

1½	shots	Tanqueray London dry gin
½	shot	Giffard Menthe Pastille liqueur
½	shot	Freshly squeezed lemon juice
Top up with		Brut champagne

We say: A classic, minty digestif.
Origin: Adapted from a recipe in Harry Craddock's 1930 *Savoy Cocktail Book*.

MONTE CASINO NEW

★★★★☆

Glass: Coupette
Garnish: Lemon zest twist
Method: SHAKE all ingredients with ice and fine strain into chilled glass.

¾	shot	Straight rye whiskey
¾	shot	Bénédictine D.O.M.
¾	shot	Chartreuse Yellow liqueur
¾	shot	Freshly squeezed lemon juice

We say: Packed with flavour and hardly short on liquor but perhaps a tad on the sweet side for some.
Origin: Adapted from a drink created in 2010 by Damon Dyer, New York City.

MONTEGO BAY

★★★½☆

Glass: Old-fashioned
Garnish: Lime wedge
Method: SHAKE all ingredients with ice and strain into ice-filled glass.

1½	shots	Martinique agricole rum
½	shot	Triple Sec
½	shot	Freshly squeezed lime juice
¼	shot	Monin Pure Cane 2:1 sugar syrup
2	dashes	Angostura aromatic bitters

We say: The name suggest Jamaica but the recipe requires agricole rum. This pungent style of rum is not Jamaican.
Origin: Adapted from a recipe in the *1947-72 Trader Vic's Bartender's Guide* by Victor Bergeron.

MONTGOMERY SLUGGER NEW

★★★★½

Glass: Coupette
Garnish: Orange zest twist
Method: POUR absinthe into ice-filled glass, TOP with water and leave to stand. Separately STIR other ingredients with ice. DISCARD contents of glass (absinthe, water and ice) and STRAIN contents of stirring glass into absinthe-coated glass.

½	shot	La Fée Parisienne (68%) absinthe
Top up with		Chilled mineral water
1½	shots	Maker's Mark bourbon
½	shot	Carpano Antica Formula
¼	shot	Kahlúa coffee liqueur
¼	shot	Taylor's Velvet Falernum liqueur
¼	shot	Nocello walnut liqueur
2	dashes	Angostura aromatic bitters
1	pinch	Salt

We say: A chocolaty nutty coffee.
Origin: Adapted from a drink discovered in January 2013 at Maison Premiere, Williamsburg, New York.

THE MONTFORD

★★★★½

Glass: Coupette
Garnish: Lemon zest twist
Method: STIR all ingredients with ice and strain into chilled glass.

2	shots	Tanqueray London dry gin
¾	shot	Lillet Blanc
½	shot	Noilly Ambre vermouth
2	dashes	Orange bitters

We say: A wonderfully wet martini with the addition of Lillet and orange bitters.
Origin: Adapted from a drink created by Dan Warner at the Beefeater Distillery, London, England.

MONTRÉAL NEW

★★★★☆

Glass: Coupette
Garnish: Orange twist
Method: STIR all ingredients with ice and fine strain into chilled glass.

1½	shots	Straight rye whiskey
¾	shot	Martini Rosso sweet vermouth
⅛	shot	Pernod anise
3	dashes	Peychaud's aromatic bitters

We say: A sweet rye Manhattan with French Creole influence.
Origin: Adapted from a recipe in Sips & Apps by Kathy Casey, Chronicle Books, Spring 2009.

MONZA

★★★★☆

Glass: Collins
Garnish: Apple slice
Method: Cut passion fruit in half and scoop flesh into shaker. Add other ingredients, SHAKE with ice and strain into ice-filled glass.

1	fresh	Passion fruit
2	shots	Ketel One vodka
2	shots	Campari Bitter
2	shots	Pressed apple juice
¼	shot	Monin Pure Cane 2:1 sugar syrup

We say: If you like Campari you'll love this.
Origin: A classic cocktail promoted by Campari and named after the Italian Grand Prix circuit.

MOO'LATA NEW

★★★★★

Glass: Martini
Garnish: Lime wedge
Method: SHAKE all ingredients with ice and fine strain into chilled glass.

2	shots	Dewar's White label Scotch
¼	shot	Dark Crème de Cacao
¼	shot	White Crème de Cacao
½	shot	Freshly squeezed lime juice
¼	shot	Monin Pure Cane 2:1 sugar syrup

We say: Scotch soured with lime (works better than lemon) and sweetened with a touch of chocolate liqueur.
Origin: Created in January 2011 by Simon Difford at the Cabinet Room, London, England after mistakenly taking a bottle of Scotch from the speed well to make a Mulata Daiquiri. It proved a tasty mistake.

BARTENDER'S TIP ROLLING

This is a gentle way of mixing a drink using a shaker and is most commonly used when making a Bloody Mary.

To do this charge your shaker with ingredients and ice as normal but rather than shaking, simply gently roll the shaker over and an over by holding the top and bottom of the shaker in each hand and then rotating your hand one over the other so tuning the shaker in a circular motion. Rolling should not be confused with the 'Cuban Roll' which is a term for mixing a drink using the throwing method.

MOOD INDIGO

★★★★☆

Glass: Martini
Garnish: Violet blossom or mint sprig
Method: SHAKE all ingredients with ice and fine strain into chilled glass.

1½	shots	**Tanqueray London dry gin**
½	shot	**Cognac VSOP**
½	shot	**Benoit Serres créme de violette**
½	fresh	**Egg white**
⅛	shot	**Monin Pure Cane 2:1 sugar syrup**
½	shot	**Chilled mineral water**

We say: Smooth, delicate and floral: the gin and brandy add just enough bite.
Origin: Named after the jazz standard that was a hit for Nat King Cole.

MOON RIVER

★★★½☆

Glass: Martini
Garnish: Mint leaf
Method: SHAKE all ingredients with ice and fine strain into chilled glass.

1½	shots	**Tanqueray London dry gin**
½	shot	**De Kuyper Apricot Brandy liqueur**
½	shot	**Triple Sec**
¼	shot	**Galliano L'Autentico liqueur**
½	shot	**Freshly squeezed lemon juice**
½	shot	**Chilled mineral water**

We say: There's a hint of aniseed in this fruity, sweet and sour drink.
Origin: Adapted from a drink discovered in 2005 at Bar Opiume, Singapore.

MOON WALK NEW

★★★★☆

Glass: Coupette
Garnish: Orange zest twist (spray & discard) & ¼ orange slice on rim.
Method: SHAKE first 3 ingredients with ice and fine strain into chilled glass. TOP with champagne.

1	shot	**Grand Marnier liqueur**
1	shot	**Freshly squeezed grapefruit juice**
⅛	shot	**Rose water**
Top up with		**Brut champagne**

We say: A Mimosa with added decadence courtesy of rose water.
Origin: Adapted from a recipe by Joe Gilmore, bartender at the Savoy Hotel, London. This drink was created to commemorate Neil Armstrong's 1969 walk on the moon.

MOONDREAM

★★★★☆

Glass: Coupette
Garnish: Peach slice
Method: STIR all ingredients with ice and strain glass.

3	shots	**Tanqueray London dry gin**
1	shot	**Manzanilla Sherry**
¼	shot	**Martini Extra Dry vermouth**
¼	shot	**Crème de pêche de vigne liqueur**

We say: Also try with subtle styles of dry vermouth such as Dolin.
Origin: Created in 2007 by Thomas Waugh at Alembic, San Francisco, USA.

MOONLIGHT COCKTAIL NEW

★★★★½

Glass: Flute
Garnish: Orange zest twist
Method: SHAKE all ingredients with ice and fine strain into chilled glass.

1½	shots	**Tanqueray London dry gin**
¾	shot	**Cointreau triple sec**
½	shot	**Benoit Serres créme de violette**
¼	shot	**Freshly squeezed lime juice**
¼	shot	**Freshly squeezed lemon juice**

We say: A twist on the Aviation, using triple sec in place of maraschino liqueur.
Origin: Adapted from a drink created in 2007 by gaz regan (then known as Gary Regan), New York. We cheekily changed the original specification of lime juice to lime and lemon juice.

MOONLIGHT MARTINI

★★★★☆

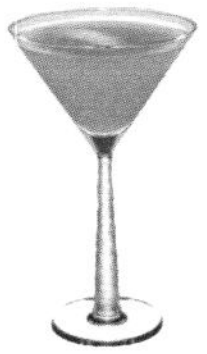

Glass: Martini
Garnish: Lemon zest twist
Method: SHAKE all ingredients with ice and fine strain into chilled glass.

1½	shots	**Tanqueray London dry gin**
¼	shot	**Kirschwasser eau de vie**
1	shot	**Sauvignon blanc wine**
1¼	shots	**Freshly squeezed grapefruit juice**

We say: Craddock describes this as 'a very dry cocktail'. It is, but pleasantly so.
Origin: Adapted from a recipe in Harry Craddock's 1930 *Savoy Cocktail Book*.

MOONRAKER

★★★½☆

Glass: Martini
Garnish: Maraschino cherry
Method: SHAKE all ingredients with ice and fine strain into chilled glass.

1½	shots	**Cognac VSOP**
¾	shot	**Peachtree peach schnapps**
¼	shot	**Pernod anise**
1½	shots	**Dubonnet Red (French made)**

We say: A diverse range of flavours come together surprisingly well.
Origin: Adapted from a recipe in the *1947-72 Trader Vic's Bartender's Guide* by Victor Bergeron.

STAR RATINGS EXPLAINED

★★★★★ Excellent

★★★★½ Recommended
★★★½☆ Commended
★★½☆☆ Disappointing
★½☆☆☆ Shameful
★★★★☆ Praiseworthy
★★★☆☆ Mediocre
★★☆☆☆ Pretty awful
★☆☆☆☆ Disgusting

MOONSHINE MARTINI

★★★★⯪

Glass: Martini
Garnish: Maraschino cherry
Method: SHAKE all ingredients with ice and fine strain into chilled glass.

1½	shots	Tanqueray London dry gin
½	shot	Luxardo Maraschino liqueur
1	shot	Martini Extra Dry vermouth
⅛	shot	Absinthe

We say: A wet Martini with balanced hints of maraschino and absinthe.
Origin: Adapted from a recipe in the 1930 *Savoy Cocktail Book* by Harry Craddock.

MORAVIAN COCKTAIL UPDATED

★★★☆☆

Glass: Old-fashioned
Garnish: Orange slice & cherry on stick (sail)
Method: STIR all ingredients with ice and strain into ice-filled glass.

¾	shot	Slivovitz plum brandy
¾	shot	Becherovka liqueur
1½	shots	Martini Rosso sweet vermouth

We say: The hardcore, Czech answer to the Italian Negroni. A drink for those who have acquired a taste for Becherovka.
Origin: Discovered in 2005 at Be Bop Bar, Prague, Czech Republic..

MORNING GLORY

★★★★☆

Glass: Old-fashioned
Garnish: Lemon zest twist
Method: SHAKE all ingredients with ice and strain into ice-filled glass.

1	shot	Cognac VSOP
¾	shot	Grand Marnier liqueur
⅛	shot	Absinthe
½	shot	Freshly squeezed lemon juice
¼	shot	Monin Pure Cane 2:1 sugar syrup
2	dashes	Angostura aromatic bitters
½	shot	Chilled mineral water

We say: Sophisticated and complex - one for sipping.
Origin: My interpretation of a classic.

MORNING GLORY FIZZ

★★★⯪☆

Glass: Collins (small 8oz)
Garnish: Lime slice
Method: Vigorously SHAKE first 6 ingredients with ice and strain into chilled glass (without ice). TOP with soda water from a siphon.

2	shots	Dewar's White label Scotch
¾	shot	Freshly squeezed lemon juice
½	shot	Monin Pure Cane 2:1 sugar syrup
½	fresh	Egg white
1	dash	Absinthe
Top up with		Soda from siphon

We say: This classic, sour and aromatic cocktail is traditionally considered a morning after pick-me-up.
Origin: Recipe adapted from George Kappeler's 1895 'Modern American Drinks'.

MOSCOW LASSI

★★★☆☆

Glass: Collins
Garnish: Cucumber slices
Method: MUDDLE cucumber in base of shaker. Add other ingredients. SHAKE with ice and fine strain into ice-filled glass.

2	inch	Cucumber (chopped & peeled)
1½	shots	Ketel One vodka
1	shot	Boiron mango purée
2	shots	Pressed apple juice
¼	shot	Monin Pure Cane 2:1 sugar syrup
3	spoons	Natural yoghurt

We say: One to serve with your Indian takeaway.
Origin: Created in 2001 by Jamie Stephenson at Graucho Grill, Manchester, England.

MOSCOW MULE

★★★★☆

Glass: Collins
Garnish: Lime wedge & mint sprig
Method: SHAKE first 3 ingredients with ice and strain into ice-filled glass. TOP with ginger beer and stir.

2	shots	Ketel One vodka
¼	shot	Freshly squeezed lime juice
1	dash	Angostura aromatic bitters
Top up with		Ginger beer

We say: A long, vodka based drink with spice provided by ginger beer and Angostura.
Origin: This classic combination was born circa 1941. John G. Martin had recently (in 1939) acquired the rights to Smirnoff vodka for Heublein, a small Connecticut based liquor and food distributor. Jack Morgan, the owner of Hollywood's famous British pub, the Cock'n'Bull Saloon, who was trying to launch his own brand of ginger beer. Legend has it that the two men met at New York City's Chatham Bar and hit on the idea of mixing Martin's vodka with Morgan's ginger beer and adding a dash of lime to create a new cocktail, the Moscow Mule. Others, most notably Eric Felton in a 2007 article in the Wall Street Journal, say the drink was invented by the Cock 'n' Bull's head bartender Wes Price.

What is sure is that the combination of vodka and ginger beer helped both men shift their products but the drinks success is greatly due to its being served in a five ounce copper mug specially engraved with a kicking mule. This intuitive was driven by a girlfriend of Morgan's recently inheriting a copper factory which made the previously poorly selling copper mugs. The success of the Moscow Mule was most fortuitous for all three friends.

By 1947 when Edwin H. Land invented the Polaroid Land Camera, the Moscow Mule was already established on the drinks menu of numerous bars. Martin, bought himself one of the instant cameras and went from bar to bar photographing bartenders holding a bottle Smirnoff Vodka in one hand and a copper mule mug in the other. He gave one photograph to the bartender and used a second to show the next neighbouring bar what they were missing out on. The Moscow Mule and the use of the Polaroid Land Camera was a stroke of marketing genius.

MOSQUITO

★★★★☆

Glass: Old-fashioned
Garnish: Mint sprig
Method: SHAKE all ingredients with ice and fine strain into ice-filled glass.

6	fresh	Mint leaves
2	shots	Macchu pisco
1	shot	Freshly squeezed lime juice
¾	shot	Monin Pure Cane 2:1 sugar syrup

We say: A short pisco based Mojito.
Origin: Adapted from a 2008 recipe created by Hans Hilburg at El Pisquerito, Cuzco, Peru.

MOTHER RUM

★★★★⯪

Glass: Old-fashioned
Garnish: Cinnamon stick
Method: STIR all ingredients with ice and strain into ice-filled glass.

2	shots	Bacardi 8yo aged rum
¼	shot	White Crème de Cacao
¼	shot	Maple syrup

We say: To quote Milo, this drink is 'warm and comforting, just like the drinks my mother made.'
Origin: Created in 2006 by Milo Rodriguez at Crazy Bear, London, England.

MOTOX

★★★★☆

Glass: Martini
Garnish: Coriander leaf
Method: MUDDLE ginger and coriander in base of shaker. Add other ingredients, SHAKE with ice and fine strain into chilled glass.

1	slice	Fresh root ginger (thumbnail sized)
10	fresh	Coriander (cilantro) leaves
1½	shots	Ketel One Citroen vodka
½	shot	Limoncello liqueur
1	shot	Fresh pressed pineapple juice
1	shot	Pressed apple juice

We say: Each sip is fruity, lemon fresh and followed by a hot ginger hit.
Origin: Adapted from a drink discovered in 2005 at Mo Bar, Landmark Mandarin Oriental Hotel, Hong Kong.

MOUNTAIN ⚷

★★★⯪☆

Glass:
Garnish: Maraschino cherry
Method: SHAKE all ingredients with ice and fine strain into chilled glass.

2	shots	Maker's Mark bourbon
¾	shot	Martini Extra Dry vermouth
¾	shot	Martini Rosso sweet vermouth
½	shot	Egg white

We say: A perfect Manhattan smoothed by egg white.

MOUNTAIN COCKTAIL ⚷

★★★⯪☆

Glass: Martini
Garnish: Maraschino cherry
Method: SHAKE all ingredients with ice and fine strain into chilled glass.

1½	shots	Maker's Mark bourbon
½	shot	Martini Extra Dry vermouth
½	shot	Martini Rosso sweet vermouth
½	shot	Freshly squeezed lemon juice
½	fresh	Egg white

We say: Bone dry - I prefer with the addition of half spoon sugar syrup.
Origin: This vintage cocktail is thought to have been originally made at New York's Hoffman House.

MOUNTAIN SIPPER ⚷

★★★⯪☆

Glass: Old-fashioned
Garnish: Orange zest twist
Method: SHAKE all ingredients with ice and strain into ice-filled glass.

2	shots	Maker's Mark bourbon
1	shot	Triple Sec
1	shot	Ocean Spray cranberry juice
1	shot	Freshly squeezed grapefruit juice
⅛	shot	Monin Pure Cane 2:1 sugar syrup

We say: Fruity citrus flavours balance the richness of the whiskey.

MR KAPPES

★★★★☆

Glass: Coupette
Garnish: Lemon zest twist
Method: STIR all ingredients with ice and fine strain into chilled glass.

2	shots	Kirschwasser eau de vie
1	shot	Lillet Blanc
1	shot	Pedro Ximénez sherry

We say: A quality Germanic brand of Kirswasser is key to this complex drink.
Origin: Created in 2009 by Diana Haider, Frankfurt, Germany.

MR PRESIDENT

Glass: Coupette
Garnish: Orange zest twist
Method: STIR all ingredients with ice and fine strain into chilled glass.

1¼	shots	Bacardi Superior rum
¾	shot	Martini Rosso sweet vermouth
½	shot	Campari Bitter

We say: A combination of the El-Presidente and Negroni. A drink Campari lovers will appreciate.
Origin: Adapted from a drink created in 2010 by Andy Pearson, London, England for Barak Obama.

MRS ROBINSON #1

Glass: Old-fashioned
Garnish: Raspberries
Method: MUDDLE raspberries in base of shaker. Add next 4 ingredients, SHAKE with ice and strain into ice-filled glass. TOP with soda, lightly stir and serve with straws.

8	fresh	Raspberries
2	shots	Maker's Mark bourbon
1	shot	Crème de framboise liqueur
¼	shot	Freshly squeezed lemon juice
¼	shot	Monin Pure Cane 2:1 sugar syrup
Top up with		Soda (club soda)

We say: Rich raspberry fruit laced with bourbon.
Origin: Created in 2000 by Max Warner at Long Bar, Sanderson, London, England.

MRS ROBINSON #2

Glass: Martini
Garnish: Orange slice
Method: SHAKE all ingredients with ice and fine strain into chilled glass.

2½	shots	Ketel One vodka
½	shot	Galliano L'Autentico liqueur
1	shot	Freshly squeezed orange juice

We say: A short Harvey Wallbanger.
Origin: Discovered in 2006 on Kyle Branch's Cocktail Hotel blog. (www.cocktailhotel.blogspot.com).

MUCKY BOTTOM

Glass: Collins
Garnish: None
Method: SHAKE first 3 ingredients with ice and strain into ice-filled glass. POUR coffee liqueur around top of drink - this will fall to the base of the glass and create a mucky bottom.

2	shots	Malibu coconut rum liqueur
1	shot	Pernod anise
¾	shot	Kahlúa coffee liqueur
3	shots	Freshly squeezed grapefruit juice

We say: Four very strong and distinctive flavours somehow tone each other down.
Origin: Created in 2003 by Simon Difford. This was formerly and more tastefully named Red Haze.

MUDDY WATER

Glass: Old-fashioned
Garnish: Coffee beans
Method: SHAKE all ingredients with ice and strain into ice-filled glass.

1	shot	Ketel One vodka
1	shot	Baileys Irish cream liqueur
1	shot	Kahlúa coffee liqueur

We say: Coffee and whiskey cream with added vodka.

MUDSLIDE

Glass: Hurricane
Garnish: Crumbled Cadbury's Flake bar
Method: BLEND all ingredients with two 12oz scoops of crushed ice and serve with straws.

1½	shots	Baileys Irish cream liqueur
1½	shots	Ketel One vodka
1½	shots	Kahlúa coffee liqueur
3	scoop	Häagen Dazs vanilla ice cream

We say: A simply scrumptious dessert drink with whiskey cream and coffee.

MUJER VERDE

Glass: Martini
Garnish: Lime zest twist
Method: SHAKE all ingredients with ice and fine strain into chilled glass.

1	shot	Tanqueray London dry gin
½	shot	Chartreuse Green liqueur
½	shot	Chartreuse Yellow liqueur
½	shot	Freshly squeezed lime juice
¼	shot	Monin Pure Cane 2:1 sugar syrup
¾	shot	Chilled mineral water

We say: The name means 'Green Lady'... and she packs a Chartreuse punch.
Origin: Discovered in 2006 at Absinthe, San Francisco, where 'D Mexican' resurrected this drink from his hometown of Guadalajara.

MULATA DAIQUIRI UPDATED

★★★★⯪ **Glass:** Martini
Garnish: Lime wedge
Method: SHAKE all ingredients with ice and fine strain into chilled glass.

2	shots	Rum Aged
¼	shot	Bols Cacao Brown
¼	shot	Bols Cacao White
½	shot	Freshly squeezed lime juice
¼	shot	Monin Pure Cane 2:1 sugar syrup

Variant: Blended with crushed ice.
We say: A classic Daiquiri with aged rum and a hint of chocolate.
Origin: Thought to have been created by Constantino (Constante) Ribalaigua Vert at Havana's Floridita bar but in the Cuban book, 'Bartender's Sixth Sense' the cocktail is said to have been created in the 1940s by one Jose Maria Vazquez.

The drink was originally made with Bacardi Elixir, a liqueur made by infusing plums in rum. Crème de cacao liqueur has been used a substitute since the 1970s. Production of Bacardi Elixir ended when Bacardi was forced to leave Cuba but a small batch of some 60m bottles were made to celebrate Bacardi Legacy Competition in April 2013..

MULATA DAISY UPDATED

★★★★☆ **Glass:** Coupette
Garnish: Chocolate powder rim
Method: MUDDLE fennel seeds in base of shaker. Add other ingredients, SHAKE with ice and fine strain into chilled glass.

1½	spoon	Fennel seeds
1¾	shots	Rum light white/blanco
1	shot	Bols Cacao Brown
¾	shot	Freshly squeezed lime juice
¼	shot	Galliano L'Autentico liqueur

We say: Delicately spiced and subtly chocolatey.
Origin: Created in 2008 by Ago Perrone at The Connaught, London, England. This drink won the 2009 Bacardi Legacy Final.

THE MULBERRY NEW

★★★★⯪ **Glass:** Old-fashioned
Garnish: Mint sprig
Method: STIR jam and gin in base of shaker to dissolve jam. Add mint, Pimm's and lemon juice, SHAKE with ice and fine strain into ice-filled glass. TOP with elderflower pressé.

1½	shots	Tanqueray London dry gin
1	spoon	Mulberry jam
7	fresh	Mint leaves
1	shot	Pimm's No.1 Cup
½	shot	Freshly squeezed lemon juice
Top up with		Elderflower pressé

We say: Jammy mulberry fruit, Pimm's and gin freshened with mint and lemon, served on the rocks.
Origin: Created in 2006 at The Manor House Hotel, Moreton-in-Marsh, Gloucestershire, England. The Manor House Hotel make their mulberry jam using fruit from the Mulberry Tree which grows in the hotels grounds and is thought to be over 350 years old.

MULE'S HIND LEG

★★★★⯪ **Glass:** Martini
Garnish: Apricot slice
Method: SHAKE all ingredients with ice and fine strain into chilled glass.

1	shot	Tanqueray London dry gin
1	shot	Bénédictine D.O.M.
1	shot	Calvados/Applejack brandy
¾	shot	De Kuyper Apricot Brandy liqueur
¼	shot	Maple syrup
½	shot	Chilled mineral water

We say: Apricot and maple syrup dominate this medium sweet drink.
Origin: My version of a classic 1920s recipe.

MULLED WINE UPDATED

★★★★☆ **Glass:** Toddy
Garnish: Cinnamon stick
Method: POUR ingredients into pre-warmed glass and stir.

5	dried	Cloves
1	wedge	Orange (squeezed)
1	pinch	Freshly grated nutmeg
1	pinch	Ground cinnamon
1½	shot	Warre's Otima tawny port
1½	shot	Shiraz red wine
½	shot	Grand Marnier liqueur
½	shot	Freshly squeezed lemon juice
2	spoons	Runny honey
Top up with		Boiling water

We say: Warming, soothing and potent. Better if several servings are made at the same time and the ingredients mixed together and warmed in a saucepan.

MY SHERRY AMORE NEW

★★★★☆ **Glass:** Cocktail
Garnish: Grapefruit zest twist
Method: SHAKE all ingredients with ice and fine strain into chilled glass.

1¾	shots	Tanqueray London dry gin
1	shot	Aperol
¾	shot	Freshly squeezed grapefruit juice
¼	shot	Tio Pepe fino sherry
2	dashes	Peychaud's aromatic bitters

We say: A bitter-sweet, salmon pink, light, delicate balance of gin, herbal complexity, grapefruit and dry sherry.
Origin: Created in 2011 by Nick Van Tiel and named after the 1969 soul classic by Motown singer-songwriter Stevie Wonder. Originally titled 'Oh My Marcia', the song was originally about Wonder's girlfriend whilst he was at the Michigan School for the Blind in Lansing, Michigan. After they broke up, the lyrics and title were changed to 'My Cherie Amour'.

MYRTLE BANK SPECIAL RUM PUNCH

★★★★⯪

Glass: Old-fashioned
Garnish: Maraschino cherry
Method: SHAKE all ingredients with ice and strain into ice-filled glass.

2	shots	Myer's Planter's Punch rum
1	shot	Freshly squeezed lime juice
⅛	shot	De Kuyper Cherry Brandy liqueur
½	shot	Monin Pure Cane 2:1 sugar syrup
½	shot	Chilled mineral water

We say: A rich fruity Daiquiri with tangy molasses.
Origin: Originally made at the Myrtle Bank Hotel, Kingston, Jamaica. Built in the mid-1800s, the Myrtle Bank, was converted from a shipyard into a select boarding house. After the hotel was destroyed in the 1907 earthquake it was reconstructed in 1918 and was then the largest hotel in Jamaica with 205 rooms and a filtered salt water pool.

MYRTLE MARTINI

★★★⯪☆

Glass: Martini
Garnish: Sugar rim
Method: SHAKE all ingredients with ice and fine strain into chilled glass.

2	shots	Ketel One vodka
½	shot	Crème de myrtille liqueur
2	shots	Pressed apple juice
¼	shot	Monin Pure Cane 2:1 sugar syrup
¼	shot	Freshly squeezed lime juice

We say: A fruity concoction to remember should you find yourself with a bottle of crème de myrtille.
Origin: Created in 2003 at Cheyne Walk Brasserie & Salon, London, England.

MYSTIQUE

★★★⯪☆

Glass: Old-fashioned
Garnish: Maraschino cherry
Method: SHAKE all ingredients with ice and strain into ice-filled glass.

2	shots	Dewar's White label Scotch
1	shot	Tuaca liqueur
1	shot	Chambord black raspberry liqueur

We say: Rust coloured and fruit charged. Not the sweetie you might expect.
Origin: Created in 2002 by Tim Halilaj, Albania.

NACIONAL DAIQUIRI #1

★★★★⯪

Glass: Martini
Garnish: Maraschino cherry
Method: SHAKE all ingredients with ice and fine strain into chilled glass.

2	shots	Bacardi Superior rum
¾	shot	De Kuyper Apricot Brandy liqueur
½	shot	Freshly squeezed lime juice
¾	shot	Chilled mineral water

We say: A sophisticated complex apricot Daiquiri.
Origin: An old classic named after the Hotel Nacional, Havana, Cuba, where it was created.

NACIONAL DAIQUIRI #2

★★★★⯪

Glass: Martini
Garnish: Maraschino cherry
Method: SHAKE all ingredients with ice and fine strain into chilled glass.

2	shots	Bacardi Superior rum
½	shot	De Kuyper Apricot Brandy liqueur
1½	shots	Fresh pressed pineapple juice
½	shot	Freshly squeezed lime juice

We say: An apricot Daiquiri with extra interest courtesy of pineapple.

NAILED

★★★⯪☆☆

Glass: Shot
Garnish: None
Method: Carefully pour so as to LAYER ingredients in the following order.

| ½ | shot | Drambuie |
| ½ | shot | Dewar's White label Scotch |

We say: A shamelessly obvious twist on the classic Rusty Nail.
Origin: Created in 2010 by Simon Difford at the Cabinet Room, London, England.

NANHI PARI  NEW

★★★⯪☆

Glass: Martini
Garnish: Rosemary sprig
Method: MUDDLE rosemary in base of mixing glass. Add other ingredients, STIR with ice and fine strain into chilled glass.

1	sprig	Rosemary
1	shot	Ketel One vodka
1½	shots	Shiraz red wine
½	shot	De Kuyper Cherry Brandy liqueur
½	shot	Kahlúa coffee liqueur

We say: Dry tannins in the red wine are balanced by cherry brandy and coffee liqueur with a slug of vodka adding the backbone.
Origin: Adapted from a drink created by Carl Anthony Brown at the Waldorf Astoria Syon Park, London, England. (Recipe originally omitted vodka.)

NANTUCKET

★★★⯪☆

Glass: Collins
Garnish: Lime wedge
Method: SHAKE all ingredients with ice and strain into ice-filled glass.

2	shots	Bacardi Superior rum
3	shots	Ocean Spray cranberry juice
2	shots	Freshly squeezed grapefruit juice

We say: Essentially a Seabreeze with rum in place of vodka.
Origin: Popularised by the Cheers bar chain, this is named after the beautiful island off Cape Cod.

NAPOLEON MARKET

★★★★⯪

Glass: Martini
Garnish: Lemon zest twist
Method: SHAKE all ingredients with ice and fine strain into chilled glass.

2	shots	Tanqueray London dry gin
¼	shot	Triple Sec
¼	shot	Fernet Branca
½	shot	Dubonnet Red (French made)
½	shot	Chilled mineral water

We say: A beautifully balanced, very approachable, rust coloured Martini.
Origin: Adapted from a recipe in Harry Craddock's 1930 'Savoy Cocktail Book'.

NARANJA

★★★★☆

Glass: Old-fashioned
Garnish: Orange zest twist
Method: STIR one shot of rum with two ice cubes in a glass. ADD sugar syrup, vermouth, bitters and two more ice cubes. STIR some more and add another two ice cubes and the rest of the rum. STIR lots more and add more ice.

2	shots	Bacardi Superior rum
⅛	shot	Cinzano Arancio
¼	shot	Monin Pure Cane 2:1 sugar syrup
2	dashes	Orange bitters

We say: Rum based twist on the classic Old-Fashioned.
Origin: Created in 2008 by Chris Edwardes at Hanbury Club, Brighton, England.

NARANJA DAIQUIRI

★★★★☆

Glass: Martini
Garnish: Orange slice
Method: SHAKE all ingredients with ice and fine strain into chilled glass.

1¾	shots	Bacardi Superior rum
¾	shot	Grand Marnier liqueur
1	shot	Freshly squeezed orange juice
½	shot	Freshly squeezed lime juice
⅛	shot	Monin Pure Cane 2:1 sugar syrup

We say: The Latino version of an orange Daiquiri.

NATHALIA

★★★⯪☆

Glass: Old-fashioned
Garnish: Orange zest twist
Method: STIR all ingredients with ice and strain into ice-filled glass.

2	shots	Cognac VSOP
¾	shot	Chartreuse Yellow liqueur
¾	shot	Bols Banana liqueur
1	dash	Orange bitters

We say: Herbal bananas and cognac. Be warned, the subtle sweetness conceals its strength.
Origin: Adapted from a drink discovered in 2006 at English Bar, Regina Hotel, Paris, France.

NAUTILUS

★★★★⯪

Glass: Collins
Garnish: Mint sprig
Method: SHAKE all ingredients with ice and strain into ice-filled glass. Serve with straws.

2	shots	Tequila 100% Agave
2	shots	Ocean Spray cranberry juice
1	shot	Freshly squeezed lime juice
½	shot	Monin Pure Cane 2:1 sugar syrup

We say: Basically a Margarita lengthened with cranberry juice.
Origin: Adapted from a drink created by Victor Bergeron (Trader Vic).

NAVIGATOR

★★★★☆

Glass: Martini
Garnish: Lemon zest twist
Method: SHAKE all ingredients with ice and fine strain into chilled glass.

2	shots	Tanqueray London dry gin
¾	shot	Limoncello liqueur
1¼	shots	Freshly squeezed grapefruit juice

We say: This fruity, grapefruit-led drink is pleasantly bitter and sour.
Origin: Created in 2005 by Jamie Terrell, London, England.

NAVY GROG

★★★★☆

Glass: Old-fashioned
Garnish: Lemon wedge
Method: STIR honey with rum in base of shaker to dissolve honey. Add next 3 ingredients, SHAKE with ice and strain into ice-filled glass.

1½	shots	Pusser's Navy rum
3	spoons	Runny honey
¼	shot	Freshly squeezed lime juice
2	dashes	Angostura aromatic bitters
2½	shots	Chilled mineral water

Variant: Also great served hot. Top with boiling water and garnish with a cinnamon stick.
We say: An extremely drinkable, honeyed cocktail.

NEAL'S BARBADOS COSMOPOLITAN

★★★★☆

Glass: Martini
Garnish: Orange zest twist
Method: SHAKE all ingredients with ice and fine strain into chilled glass.

1¼	shots	Bacardi Oro golden rum
¾	shot	Triple Sec
½	shot	Freshly squeezed lime juice
1½	shots	Ocean Spray cranberry juice

We say: Your standard Cosmo made more complex by a slug of warm Caribbean spirit.
Origin: Discovered in 2006 at Bix, San Francisco, USA.

NEGRONI

★★★★★★ **Glass:** Old-fashioned
Garnish: Orange zest twist
Method: POUR all ingredients into ice-filled glass and STIR.

1½	shots	Tanqueray London dry gin
1½	shots	Campari Bitter
1½	shots	Martini Rosso sweet vermouth

Variant: Americano
We say: Bitter and dry, but very tasty. This no namby-pamby drink is traditionally assembled and mixed directly in the glass. There is something about a Negroni that does not suit fussing about with mixing glasses and strainers. To garnish with a lemon slice is a heinous crime but I am quite partial to a fat orange wedge.
Origin: This drink takes its name from Count Camillo Negroni. Sometime between 1919 and 1921, while drinking at the Casoni Bar (later named Giacosa) on Tornabuoni Street in Florence, Italy, the Florentine Count is said to have asked for an Americano 'with a bit more kick'. He was a regular customer at the bar and bartender, Fosco Scarselli experimented with adding gin to the Count's favourite aperitif, the Americano. The combination became the Count's new regular drink and soon other patrons of the bar soon started to ask for "one of Count Negroni's drinks" and the drink quickly became known as simple 'Negroni'.

NEGRONI SBAGLIATO

★★★☆☆ **Glass:** Old-fashioned
Garnish: Orange slice
Method: POUR all ingredients into ice-filled glass and STIR.

1	shot	Martini Rosso sweet vermouth
1	shot	Campari Bitter
2	shots	Spumante (or brut champagne)

AKA: Negroni Spagliato
We say: This light-style Negroni has the bitterness but lacks the punch and character of the original.
Origin: Pronounced 'spal-yacht-oh' which in Italian means 'mistake', this drink was created in the late 1980s by Mirko Stocchetti at his Bar Basso in Milan when making a Negroni he mistakenly reached for a bottle of spumante instead of gin. They are still served at Basso today in enormous chalice like glasses with single, giant, rectangular ice cube.

NEGRONI SPUMANTE

★★★★★★ **Glass:** Old-fashioned
Garnish: Orange zest twist
Method: POUR first 3 ingredients into ice-filled glass. TOP with spumante and lightly STIR.

1	shot	Martini Rosso sweet vermouth
1	shot	Campari Bitter
1	shot	Tanqueray London dry gin
Top up with		Spumante (or brut champagne)

We say: A Negroni lengthened with sparkling wine. Every Negroni drinker should try this variation

NEGRONI TREDICI

★★★★✦ **Glass:** Old-fashioned
Garnish: Lemon zest twist (discarded) & orange wedge
Method: STIR all ingredients with ice and strain into chilled glass.

2	shots	Tanqueray London dry gin
¼	shot	Cynar
¼	shot	Campari Bitter
1	shot	Martini Rosso sweet vermouth

We say: Campari fans will love this Negroni twist.
Origin: Adapted from a drink created in 2009 by Toby Maloney of Alchemy Consulting, USA.

NEGROSKI

★★★☆☆ **Glass:** Large wine glass
Garnish: Orange slice
Method: Pour ingredients into ice-filled glass and STIR.

1½	shots	Ketel One vodka
1½	shots	Martini Rosso sweet vermouth
1½	shots	Campari Bitter

We say: A Negroni where vodka is substituted for gin. I blame Italian fashionistas.

NEGUS (HOT)

★★★★☆ **Glass:** Toddy
Garnish: Dust with grated nutmeg
Method: Place bar spoon in warmed glass. POUR all ingredients into glass and STIR.

3	shots	Warre's Otima tawny port
1	shot	Freshly squeezed lemon juice
½	shot	Monin Pure Cane 2:1 sugar syrup
Top up with		Boiling water

Variant: Bishop
We say: A tangy, citrussy hot drink.
Origin: Colonel Francis Negus was the MP for Ipswich from 1717 to 1732. He created this diluted version of the original Bishop.

NELSON'S BLOOD COCKTAIL NEW

★★★★☆ **Glass:** Coupette
Garnish: Lemon zest twist
Method: STIR all ingredients with ice and strain into chilled glass.

1½	shots	Cognac VSOP
1½	shots	Ruby port

We say: This carpet scary, appropriately named, blood red cocktail balances the rich fruitiness of port with the fortifying complexity of cognac. A popular drink in classic British pubs.
Origin: After the Battle of Trafalgar (21 October 1805) when the British Royal Navy demonstrated its navy supremacy by conquering the combined fleets of the French and Spanish Navies the Franco-Spanish fleet lost twenty-two ships without a single British vessel being lost. However, the English lost Admiral Lord Nelson who was mortally wounded during the battle aboard HMS Victory.
To preserve Nelson's body during the return voyage to England, the ship's surgeon ordered that his body be placed in a barrel of French brandy. Although this was lashed to the deck and guarded, stories abound of sailors drinking the brandy out of respect for their commander, Nelson.

NELSON'S BLOOD #2 NEW

★★★★★ **Glass:** Collins
Garnish: Lime wedge
Method: SHAKE all ingredients with ice and strain into ice.

2	shots	Pusser's Navy rum
2	shots	Ocean Spray cranberry juice
1	shot	Freshly squeezed orange juice
1	shot	Freshly squeezed lime juice
½	shot	Monin Pure Cane 2:1 sugar syrup
3	dashes	Angostura aromatic bitters

We say: The pungent flavours of naval rum contribute to this tasty, fruity rum punch with will warm your cockles – m' hearties!
Origin: A cocktail promoted by the marketers of Pusser's Rum.

NETHERLAND COCKTAIL NEW

★★★★☆ **Glass:** Coupette
Garnish: Orange zest twist
Method: SHAKE all ingredients with ice and fine strain into chilled glass.

2	shots	Cognac VSOP
⅔	shot	Curaçao orange liqueur
1	dash	Orange bitters

Variant: Dream, with dash of anisette liqueur or absinthe.
We say: There will be those that call for this cocktail to be stirred - if you are going to deviate from the original my advice would be to make frothier and add a dash of egg white.
Origin: Created in the early 1900s as the house cocktail at the New Netherland Hotel, on Fifth Avenue (at 59th Street) New York City, which was for a period the tallest hotel in the world.

THE NEUTRAL GROUND

★★★★☆ **Glass:** Coupette
Garnish: Orange zest twist
Method: STIR all ingredients with ice and strain into chilled glass.

2	shots	Straight rye whiskey
½	shot	Amontillado sherry
½	shot	Bénédictine D.O.M.
3	dashes	Angostura aromatic bitters

We say: Sweet Manhattan - like with sherry and spiced notes.
Origin: Created in 2008 by Rhiannon Enlil at Bar Tonique, New Orleans, USA and named after the area on Canal Street in New Orleans that formerly separated the American district from the Spanish/French district.

NEVADA DAIQUIRI

★★★★☆ **Glass:** Martini
Garnish: Lime wedge
Method: SHAKE all ingredients with ice and fine strain into chilled glass.

2	shots	Bacardi Superior rum
1	shot	Freshly squeezed grapefruit juice
½	shot	Freshly squeezed lime juice
½	shot	Monin Pure Cane 2:1 sugar syrup

We say: A pungent Daiquiri with the intense flavour of Navy Rum.

NEVINS COCKTAIL

★★★½☆ **Glass:** Martini
Garnish: Lemon zest twist
Method: SHAKE all ingredients with ice and fine strain into chilled glass.

1½	shots	Maker's Mark bourbon
½	shot	De Kuyper Apricot Brandy liqueur
½	shot	Freshly squeezed grapefruit juice
¼	shot	Freshly squeezed lemon juice
1	dash	Angostura aromatic bitters

We say: Whiskey and apricot combine beautifully with a light burst of citrus in this easy sipper.

NEW AMSTERDAM

★★★★½ **Glass:** Coupette
Garnish: Lemon zest twist
Method: STIR all ingredients with ice and fine strain into chilled glass.

2	shots	Bols Genever
1	shot	Kirschwasser eau de vie
1	spoon	Monin Pure Cane 2:1 sugar syrup
2	dashes	Peychaud's aromatic bitters

We say: A delicately flavoured and lightly balanced genever based drink with hints of Kirsch and aromatic Peychard's bitters.
Origin: Adapted from a drink created in 2009 by Jim Meehan at PDT, New York City, USA.

NEW ORLEANS BLACK

★★★½☆ **Glass:** Old-fashioned
Garnish: Lime wedge
Method: SHAKE first 4 ingredients with ice and strain into ice-filled glass. TOP with ginger beer.

1½	shots	Martinique agricole rum
½	shot	Freshly squeezed lime juice
⅛	shot	Monin Pure Cane 2:1 sugar syrup
2	dashes	Peychaud's aromatic bitters
Top up with		Ginger beer

We say: Agricole character bursts out of this spiced Daiquiri.
Origin: Created in 2008 by Jonny Raglin at Absinthe, San Francisco, USA.

STAR RATINGS EXPLAINED

★★★★★ Excellent

★★★★½ Recommended	★★★★☆ Praiseworthy
★★★½☆ Commended	★★★☆☆ Mediocre
★★½☆☆ Disappointing	★★☆☆☆ Pretty awful
★½☆☆☆ Shameful	★☆☆☆☆ Disgusting

NEW ORLEANS GIN FIZZ NEW

★★★★★

Glass: Collins
Garnish: Lemon slice & mint sprig
Method: 1/ Flash BLEND first 6 ingredients without ice (to emulsify mix). Then pour contents of blender into shaker and SHAKE with ice. Strain into chilled glass (no ice in glass) and TOP with soda from siphon. ALTERNATIVELY: 2/ Vigorously DRY SHAKE first 6 ingredients until bored/tired. Add ice to shaker, SHAKE again and strain into chilled glass (without ice). TOP with soda water from siphon.

2¼	shots	**Old Tom gin**
½	shot	**Freshly squeezed lemon juice**
½	shot	**Freshly squeezed lime juice**
¾	shot	**Monin Pure Cane 2:1 sugar syrup**
⅛	shot	**Orange flower water**
1	fresh	**Egg white**
1	shot	**Double (heavy) cream**
Top up with		**Soda from siphon**

We say: The full flavour of Old Tom gin adds an extra dimension to this classic Gin Fizz. Indeed, is properly the original Gin Fizz.
Origin: Said to be the original name and recipe of the Ramos Gin Fizz, created in 1888 by Henry C. Ramos at the Imperial Cabinet Saloon on the corner of Gravier and Carondelet Streets in New Orleans. Today, a New Orleans Gin Fizz is made with Old Tom gin while a Ramos Gin Fizz is made with Tanqueray London dry gin. While today's Ramos Gin Fizz always has added rose water and sometimes vanilla essence, the New Orleans Gin Fizz usually relies on the use of Old Tom gin for its flavour nuances.

NEW ORLEANS MULE

★★★½☆

Glass: Collins
Garnish: Lime wedge
Method: SHAKE first 4 ingredients with ice and fine strain into ice-filled glass. TOP with ginger beer.

2	shots	**Maker's Mark bourbon**
1	shot	**Kahlúa coffee liqueur**
1	shot	**Fresh pressed pineapple juice**
½	shot	**Freshly squeezed lime juice**
Top up with		**Ginger beer**

We say: A spicy, full-flavoured taste of the South.

NEW ORLEANS PUNCH

★★★½☆

Glass: Collins
Garnish: Lemon slice
Method: SHAKE all ingredients with ice and strain into glass filled with crushed ice. Serve with straws.

1½	shots	**Maker's Mark bourbon**
¾	shot	**Bacardi 8yo aged rum**
1½	shots	**Chambord black raspberry liqueur**
1½	shots	**Freshly squeezed lemon juice**
3	shots	**Cold camomile tea**

We say: Raspberry is the predominant flavour in this long drink

NEW PORT CODEBREAKER

★★★½☆

Glass: Collins
Garnish: None
Method: SHAKE all ingredients with ice and strain into ice-filled glass.

1	shot	**Tequila 100% Agave**
1	shot	**Pusser's Navy rum**
½	shot	**Advocaat liqueur**
½	shot	**Coco López cream of coconut**
4	shots	**Freshly squeezed orange juice**

We say: This straw yellow drink is a most unusual mix of ingredients.
Origin: Adapted from a cocktail discovered in 1999 at Perter's Bar, Covent Garden, London.

NEW YEAR'S ABSOLUTION

★★★½☆

Glass: Old-fashioned
Garnish: Mint sprig
Method: STIR honey with absinthe in base of shaker until honey dissolves. Add apple juice, SHAKE with ice and strain into ice-filled glass. TOP with ginger ale and stir.

2	spoons	**Runny honey**
1	shot	**Absinthe**
1	shot	**Pressed apple juice**
Top up with		**Ginger ale**

We say: The green fairy, tamed with honey and spiced with ginger.

NEW YORK FLIP

★★★★½

Glass: Wine
Garnish: Dust with grated nutmeg
Method: Vigorously SHAKE all ingredients with ice and fine strain into chilled glass.

1½	shots	**Maker's Mark bourbon**
½	shot	**Warre's Otima tawny port**
1	fresh	**Egg**
½	shot	**Monin Pure Cane 2:1 sugar syrup**

We say: Flipping good. Easy and light.
Origin: One of the most famous flip-style drinks.

NEW YORK, NEW YORK NEW

★★★½☆

Glass: Coupette
Garnish: Maraschino cherry
Method: STIR all ingredients with ice and strain into chilled glass.

1½	shots	**Maker's Mark bourbon**
¾	shot	**Berentzen Apple schnapps**
¾	shot	**Martini Rosso sweet vermouth**
1	shot	**Bitters (whiskey barrel aged)**

We say: This simple spirit drink is similar to an apple flavoured Sweet Manhattan.
Origin: Discovered January 2011 at the King Cole Bar & Lounge, New York City, USA.

NEW YORKER

★★★★☆

Glass: Martini
Garnish: Orange zest twist
Method: SHAKE all ingredients with ice and fine strain into chilled glass.

2	shots	Maker's Mark bourbon
1	shot	Claret red wine
½	shot	Freshly squeezed lemon juice
½	shot	Monin Pure Cane 2:1 sugar syrup

We say: Sweet 'n' sour whiskey and wine.

NIAGRA FALLS

★★★★☆

Glass: Flute
Garnish: Physalis (cape gooseberry)
Method: SHAKE first four ingredients with ice and strain into chilled glass. TOP with ginger ale and lightly stir.

1	shot	Ketel One vodka
1	shot	Grand Marnier liqueur
½	shot	Freshly squeezed lemon juice
¼	shot	Monin Pure Cane 2:1 sugar syrup
Top up with		Ginger ale

We say: Ginger ale and orange complement each other, fortified by vodka.

NICE PEAR-TINI

★★★★★

Glass: Martini
Garnish: Pear slice
Method: SHAKE all ingredients with ice and fine strain into chilled glass.

1	shot	Cognac VSOP
½	shot	Belle de Brillet pear liqueur
½	shot	Poire William eau de vie
2	shots	Pressed pear juice
¼	shot	Monin Pure Cane 2:1 sugar syrup

We say: Spirited, rich and fruity.
Origin: Created in 2002 by Simon Difford.

NICK & NORA

★★★★★

Glass: Coupette
Garnish: Olive
Method: STIR all ingredients with ice and strain into chilled glass.

| 2¼ | shots | Tanqueray London dry gin |
| ¾ | shot | Martini Extra Dry vermouth |

We say: The classic three to one Martini.
Origin: Created in the 1930s and named after Nick and Nora Charles, the flirtatious married couple at the centre the 1934 Thin Man comic detective film starring William Powell and Myrna Loy. In the film Nick is a hard drinking retired detective and Nora a wealthy heiress.

NICKY FINN

★★★★☆

Glass: Martini
Garnish: Lemon zest twist
Method: SHAKE all ingredients with ice and fine strain into chilled glass.

1	shot	Cognac VSOP
1	shot	Triple Sec
¼	shot	Pernod anise
1	shot	Freshly squeezed lemon juice

We say: Basically a Sidecar spiked with an aniseedy dash of Pernod.
Origin: Adapted from a recipe in 'Cocktail: The Drink's Bible for the 21st Century' by Paul Harrington and Laura Moorhead.

NICKY'S FIZZ

★★★★☆

Glass: Collins
Garnish: Orange slice
Method: SHAKE first two ingredients with ice and strain into ice-filled glass. TOP with soda, lightly stir and serve with straws.

2	shots	Tanqueray London dry gin
2	shots	Freshly squeezed grapefruit juice
Top up with		Soda from siphon

We say: A dry, refreshing, long drink.

NIGHT & DAY

★★★★☆

Glass: Flute
Garnish: Orange zest twist
Method: POUR ingredients into chilled glass.

½	shot	Grand Marnier liqueur
½	shot	Campari Bitter
Top up with		Brut champagne

We say: Dry, aromatic, orange champagne.

NIGHTMARE MARTINI

★★★☆☆

Glass: Martini
Garnish: Maraschino cherry
Method: SHAKE all ingredients with ice and fine strain into chilled glass.

1	shot	Tanqueray London dry gin
½	shot	De Kuyper Cherry Brandy liqueur
1	shot	Dubonnet Red (French made)
2	shots	Freshly squeezed orange juice

We say: Pleasant enough, with hints of cherry. Hardly a nightmare.

NINE-20-SEVEN

★★★★☆

Glass: Flute
Garnish: Vanilla pod
Method: POUR ingredients into chilled glass and lightly stir.

¼	shot	**Vanilla-infused Ketel One vodka**
¼	shot	**Cuarenta y Tres (Licor 43) liqueur**
Top up with		**Brut champagne**

We say: Champagne with a hint of vanilla.
Origin: Created in 2002 by Damien Caldwell at Home Bar, London, England. Damian was lost for a name until a customer asked for the time.

THE NINTH WARD

★★★★☆

Glass: Martini
Garnish: Lemon zest twist
Method: SHAKE all ingredients with ice and fine strain into chilled glass.

1½	shots	**Maker's Mark bourbon**
¼	shot	**St~Germain elderflower liqueur**
½	shot	**Taylor's Velvet Falernum liqueur**
¾	shot	**Freshly squeezed lime juice**
2	dashes	**Peychaud's aromatic bitters**

We say: Bourbon with a hint of elderflower, cloves and lime.
Origin: Adapted from a drink created by Brother Cleve, Boston, USA for Tales of the Cocktail 2008. The drink is a play on the classic Ward Eight and a homage to one of the New Orleans neighbourhoods hardest hit by Hurricane Katrina.

NIPPON MARTINI NEW

★★★½☆

Glass: Teacup or small coupette
Garnish: Orange zest
Method: STIR all ingredients with ice and strain into glass/tea cup (or alternatively use throw technique).

1½	shots	**Yamazaki 12yo Japanese whisky**
1	shot	**Martini Rosso sweet vermouth**
¼	shot	**Domaine de Canton ginger liqueur**

We say: A delicate balance of whisky, sweet vermouth and a touch of ginger spice.
Origin: Adapted from a recipe by Martini's Giuseppe Gallo, London, England.

NO.10 LEMONADE

★★★★½

Glass: Collins
Garnish: Lemon slice
Method: MUDDLE blueberries in base of shaker. Add next three ingredients, SHAKE with ice and fine strain into ice-filled glass. TOP with soda.

12	fresh	**Blueberries**
2	shots	**Bacardi Superior rum**
1½	shots	**Freshly squeezed lemon juice**
¾	shot	**Monin Pure Cane 2:1 sugar syrup**
Top up with		**Soda (club soda)**

We say: Basically a long blueberry Daiquiri.
Origin: Adapted from a drink discovered in 2006 at Double Seven, New York City, USA.

NOBLE EUROPE

★★★★½

Glass: Old-fashioned
Garnish: Orange slice
Method: SHAKE all ingredients with ice and strain into glass filled with crushed ice.

1½	shots	**Tokaji Hungarian wine**
1	shot	**Ketel One vodka**
1	shot	**Freshly squeezed orange juice**
1	dash	**Vanilla extract**

Variant: Also great served 'up' in a Martini glass.
We say: A delicious cocktail that harnesses the rich, sweet flavours of Tokaji.
Origin: Created in 2002 by Dan Spink at Brown's, St Martin's Lane, London, England.

NOBLESSE NEW

★★★★☆

Glass: Coupette
Garnish: Lime wedge
Method: SHAKE all ingredients with ice and fine strain into chilled glass.

¾	shot	**Cognac VSOP**
¾	shot	**Bénédictine D.O.M.**
½	shot	**Freshly squeezed lime juice**
1	shot	**Ocean Spray cranberry juice**

We say: A light, sweet and sour, herbal and fruity aperitif cocktail.
Origin: Recipe adapted from Gary Regan's 'Ardent Spirits', November 2010.

NOLA DAIQUIRI

★★★½☆

Glass: Old-fashioned
Garnish: Pineapple wedge
Method: SHAKE all ingredients with ice and fine strain into chilled glass.

1¾	shots	**Bacardi Superior rum**
¾	shot	**St~Germain elderflower liqueur**
⅛	shot	**Freshly squeezed lemon juice**
⅛	shot	**Orange bitters**
1	dash	**Peychaud's aromatic bitters**

We say: Light rum and elderflower with the merest hint of orange and lemon juice.
Origin: Created in 2007 by Lynnette Marrero at Freeman's, New York City, USA.

NOME

★★★★☆

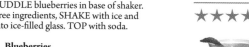

Glass: Martini
Garnish: Mint leaf
Method: STIR all ingredients with ice and strain into chilled glass.

1½	shots	**Tanqueray London dry gin**
1	shot	**Chartreuse Yellow liqueur**
1½	shots	**Tio Pepe fino sherry**

AKA: Alaska Martini
We say: This dyslexic gnome is dry and interesting.
Origin: A classic cocktail whose origin is unknown.

NOON

★★★★☆

Glass: Martini
Garnish: Orange zest twist
Method: SHAKE all ingredients with ice and strain into chilled glass.

1½	shots	Tanqueray London dry gin
¾	shot	Martini Extra Dry vermouth
¾	shot	Martini Rosso sweet vermouth
¾	shot	Freshly squeezed orange juice
2	dashes	Angostura aromatic bitters
½	fresh	Egg white

We say: This classic cocktail is smooth and aromatic

NORTH POLE MARTINI

★★★★☆

Glass: Martini
Garnish: None
Method: SHAKE first four ingredients with ice and fine strain into chilled glass. FLOAT cream over drink.

2	shots	Tanqueray London dry gin
1	shot	Luxardo Maraschino liqueur
½	shot	Freshly squeezed lemon juice
½	fresh	Egg white
Float		Double (heavy) cream

We say: An Aviation smoothed by egg white and cream.
Origin: Adapted from a recipe in the 1947-72 'Trader Vic's Bartender's Guide' by Victor Bergeron.

NORTHERN GLOW NEW

★★★★⯪

Glass: Old-fashioned
Garnish: Pink grapefruit zest
Method: SHAKE all ingredients with ice and fine strain into chilled glass.

1½	shots	Tanqueray London dry gin
½	shot	Cointreau triple sec
1	shot	Freshly squeezed pink grapefruit juice
⅓	shot	Freshly squeezed lemon juice
⅓	shot	Monin Pure Cane 2:1 sugar syrup
3	dashes	Rhubarb Bitters

We say: A White Lady with grapefruit juice and so an extra dash of sugar to balance. Tasty.
Origin: Adapted from a drink discovered in July 2013 at Plum & Split Milk, London, England.

NORTHERN LIGHTS

★★★★☆

Glass: Martini
Garnish: Star anise
Method: SHAKE all ingredients with ice and strain into chilled glass.

1½	shots	Żubrówka bison vodka
¾	shot	Berentzen Apple schnapps
½	shot	Pernod anise
1	shot	Pressed apple juice
½	shot	Freshly squeezed lime juice
½	shot	Monin Pure Cane 2:1 sugar syrup

We say: Wonderfully refreshing: apple and anis served up on a grassy vodka base.
Origin: Created in 2003 by Stuart 'Holiday' Hudson at MJU Bar, Millennium Hotel, London, England.

NORTHERN SUN

★★★★☆

Glass: Collins
Garnish: Pear slice
Method: MUDDLE ginger in base of shaker. Add other ingredients, SHAKE with ice and fine strain into ice-filled glass.

2	slices	Fresh root ginger (thumbnail sized)
2	shots	Bacardi 8yo aged rum
3	shots	Pressed pear juice
1	shot	Ocean Spray cranberry juice
¼	shot	Freshly squeezed lime juice
¼	shot	Maple syrup

We say: Subtle and easy. Hard to believe this drink contains two measures of rum.
Origin: Recipe adapted 2008 from LCBO Magazine and comes courtesy of Sean Murray, Aurora, Ontario, Canada.

NOSHINO MARTINI

★★★★☆

Glass: Martini
Garnish: Cucumber slices
Method: STIR all ingredients with ice and strain into chilled glass.

2	shots	Sake
2	shots	Shochu

We say: If good quality sake and shochu are used then this can be a great drink. However, it lacks the alcoholic bite I associate with a true Martini, so I much prefer this drink when vodka is used in place of shochu.
Origin: Adapted from a drink discovered in 2007 at Shochu Lounge, London, England.

NOT SO COSMO (MOCKTAIL)

★★★⯪☆

Glass: Martini
Garnish: Orange zest twist
Method: SHAKE all ingredients with ice and fine strain into chilled glass.

1	shot	Freshly squeezed orange juice
1	shot	Ocean Spray cranberry juice
1	shot	Freshly squeezed lime juice
1	shot	Freshly squeezed lemon juice

We say: This non-alcoholic cocktail may look like a Cosmo, but it doesn't taste like one.
Origin: Discovered in 2003 at Claridge's Bar, London, England.

NOVARA

★★★☆☆

Glass: Coupette
Garnish: Lemon zest twist
Method: SHAKE all ingredients with ice and strain into chilled glass.

1½	shots	Tanqueray London dry gin
½	shot	Campari Bitter
½	shot	Passion fruit syrup
½	shot	Freshly squeezed lemon juice

We say: This bitter-sweet, orange-pink drink may prove challenging for non-Campari drinkers.
Origin: Created in 2008 by Jamie Boudreau at Vessel, Seattle, USA.

NOVEMBER SEABREEZE (MOCKTAIL)

★★★⯪☆ **Glass:** Collins
Garnish: Lime wedge
Method: SHAKE first three ingredients with ice and strain into ice-filled glass. TOP with soda, gently stir and serve with straws.

2	shots	Ocean Spray cranberry juice
2	shots	Pressed apple juice
1	shot	Freshly squeezed lime juice
Top up with		Soda (club soda)

We say: A superbly refreshing fruity drink, whatever the time of year.

NUCLEAR DAIQUIRI

★★★★☆ **Glass:** Martini
Garnish: Lime wedge
Method: SHAKE all ingredients with ice and fine strain into chilled glass.

1	shot	Wray & Nephew overproof rum
¾	shot	Chartreuse Green liqueur
1	shot	Freshly squeezed lime juice
¼	shot	Taylor's Velvet Falernum liqueur
½	shot	Chilled mineral water

We say: A great way to inflict mutually assured destruction, although there will be fallout the morning after.
Origin: Created in 2005 by Gregor de Gruyther at LAB bar, London, England.

NUEZ DAIQUIRI

★★★★☆ **Glass:** Coupette
Garnish: Walnut
Method: SHAKE all ingredients with ice and fine strain into chilled glass.

2	shots	Bacardi Superior rum
1	shot	Nocello walnut liqueur
¾	shot	Freshly squeezed lime juice
½	shot	Pressed apple juice

We say: A Daiquiri with nutty notes.
Origin: Named after the Spanish for Walnut.

NUTCRACKER SWEET

★★★⯪☆ **Glass:** Martini
Garnish: Dust with chocolate powder
Method: SHAKE all ingredients with ice and fine strain into chilled glass.

2	shots	Ketel One vodka
1	shot	White Crème de Cacao
¾	shot	Amaretto liqueur

We say: After dinner, fortified almond and chocolate.

NUTS & BERRIES

★★★★☆ **Glass:** Martini
Garnish: Raspberries
Method: STIR all ingredients with ice and strain into chilled glass.

1	shot	Raspberry flavoured vodka
1	shot	Ketel One vodka
¼	shot	Hazelnut liqueur
¼	shot	Chambord black raspberry liqueur
1	shot	Lemonade/Sprite/7-Up

We say: The inclusion of a carbonate (lemonade) may annoy some classical bartenders but it adds flavour, sweetness and dilution.
Origin: Created in 2004 by Simon Difford.

NUTTY BERRY'TINI UPDATED

★★★⯪☆ **Glass:** Martini
Garnish: Mint leaf
Method: SHAKE all ingredients with ice and fine strain into chilled glass.

2	shots	Raspberry flavoured vodka
½	shot	Cherry brandy liqueur
½	shot	Hazelnut liqueur
¼	shot	Luxardo maraschino liqueur
1	shot	Ocean Spray cranberry juice
½	shot	Freshly squeezed lime juice

We say: Berry flavoured vodka and cranberry juice, sweetened with hazelnut and cherry liqueurs and dried with lime juice.
Origin: Created by Simon Difford in 2003.

NUTTY NASHVILLE

★★★★☆ **Glass:** Martini
Garnish: Lemon zest twist
Method: STIR honey with bourbon in base of shaker to dissolve honey. Add other ingredients, SHAKE with ice and fine strain into chilled glass.

2	spoons	Runny honey
2	shots	Maker's Mark bourbon
1	shot	Hazelnut liqueur
1	shot	Krupnik spiced honey liqueur

We say: Bourbon and hazelnut smoothed and rounded by honey.
Origin: Created in 2001 by Jason Fendick at The Rockwell, Trafalgar Hotel, London, England.

NUTTY RUSSIAN

★★★⯪☆ **Glass:** Old-fashioned
Garnish: None
Method: SHAKE all ingredients with ice and strain into ice-filled glass.

1½	shots	Ketel One vodka
¾	shot	Hazelnut liqueur
¾	shot	Kahlúa coffee liqueur

We say: A Black Russian with hazelnut liqueur.

NUTTY SUMMER

Glass: Martini
Garnish: Three drops of Angostura bitters
Method: SHAKE all ingredients with ice and fine strain into chilled glass.

1½	shots	Advocaat liqueur
¾	shot	Amaretto liqueur
¾	shot	Malibu coconut rum liqueur
¾	shot	Fresh pressed pineapple juice
½	shot	Double (heavy) cream

We say: This subtle, dessert-style cocktail is packed with flavour. A superb after dinner tipple for summer.
Origin: Created in 2001 by Daniel Spink at Hush Up, London, England.

O'HENRY

Glass: Collins
Garnish: Lemon slice
Method: SHAKE first two ingredients with ice and strain into ice-filled glass. TOP with ginger ale, lightly stir and serve with straws.

2	shots	Maker's Mark bourbon
1	shot	Bénédictine D.O.M.
Top up with		Ginger ale

We say: Herbal whiskey and ginger.
Origin: Discovered in 2006 at Brandy Library, New York City, USA.

OATMEAL COOKIE

Glass: Shot
Garnish: None
Method: SHAKE all ingredients with ice and fine strain into chilled glass.

½	shot	Butterscotch schnapps
¾	shot	Baileys Irish cream liqueur
¼	shot	Goldschläger cinnamon schnapps

We say: A well balanced, creamy shot with hints of butterscotch and cinnamon.

OAXACA OLD-FASHIONED NEW

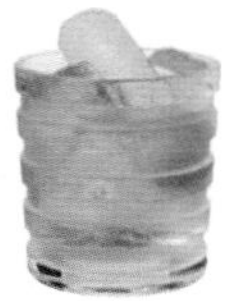

Glass: Old-fashioned
Garnish: Orange zest twist (flamed)
Method: STIR tequila with three ice cubes in a glass. ADD other ingredients and STIR with more ice. Top up ice and STIR some more.

1½	shots	Tequila 100% Agave
½	shot	Mezcal
1	spoon	Agave nectar
1	dash	Angostura aromatic bitters

We say: An agave influenced old-fashioned with a wonderful hit of smokiness from the mezcal.
Origin: Created 2007 by Philip Ward at Death & Co., New York City, USA and now one of many tequila and mezcal-based drinks at Phil's own bar Mayahuel, also in Manhattan.

OAZA

Glass: Old-fashioned
Garnish: Lime wedge
Method: SHAKE all ingredients with ice and fine strain into ice-filled glass.

2	shots	Becherovka liqueur
¾	shot	Freshly squeezed lime juice
¼	shot	Monin Pure Cane 2:1 sugar syrup

We say: Herbal and bittersweet. Not for everyone.
Origin: A popular drink in the Czech Republic where Becerovka, a herbal liquor, is the national drink.

OBITUARY

Glass: Martini
Garnish: Olive
Method: STIR all ingredients with ice and strain into chilled glass.

2	shots	Tanqueray London dry gin
⅛	shot	Absinthe
¼	shot	Martini Extra Dry vermouth

We say: What a way to go. A Dry Martini with a dash of the green fairy.

OCEANBREEZE 🔑

Glass: Collins
Garnish: Lime wedge
Method: POUR cranberry juice into ice-filled glass. SHAKE other ingredients with ice and carefully strain into glass to LAYER over the cranberry juice. Serve with straws.

2	shots	Ketel One vodka
2½	shots	Ocean Spray cranberry juice
1½	shots	Freshly squeezed grapefruit juice
½	shot	Fresh pressed pineapple juice

We say: Refreshingly juicy.
Origin: Created in 2007 by Simon Difford for Ocean Spray.

OCEANS 21

Glass: Martini
Garnish: Orange zest twist (flamed)
Method: SHAKE all ingredients with ice and fine strain into chilled glass.

1	shot	Calvados/Applejack brandy
½	shot	Grand Marnier liqueur
1½	shots	Ocean Spray cranberry juice

We say: Apple, cranberry and orange.

ODDBALL MANHATTAN DRY

★★★★☆

Glass: Martini
Garnish: Maraschino cherry
Method: STIR all ingredients with ice and strain into chilled glass.

2½	shots	Maker's Mark bourbon
½	shot	Chartreuse Yellow liqueur
1	shot	Martini Extra Dry vermouth
3	dashes	Angostura aromatic bitters

We say: Not as oddball as it sounds, the Chartreuse combines harmoniously.

OH CECILIE! NEW

★★★★½

Glass: Old-fashioned
Garnish: Grapefruit zest twist
Method: STIR all ingredients with ice and strain into ice-filled glass.

1½	shots	Tanqueray London dry gin
¾	shot	Aperol
¾	shot	Martini Rosso sweet vermouth
¼	shot	Amer Picon
1	dash	Angostura aromatic bitters

We say: A tasty Danish rift on the Negroni.
Origin: Created in 2010 by Carl Wrangel at the Oak Room, Copenhagen, Denmark and named after his girlfriend.

OH GOSH! ⌐━

★★★★★

Glass: Martini
Garnish: Lemon zest twist
Method: SHAKE all ingredients with ice and fine strain into chilled glass.

1½	shots	Bacardi Superior rum
1	shot	Triple Sec
½	shot	Freshly squeezed lime juice
¼	shot	Monin Pure Cane 2:1 sugar syrup
½	shot	Chilled mineral water

We say: A very subtle orange twist on the classic Daiquiri.
Origin: Created by Tony Conigliaro in 2001 at Isola, London, England. A customer requested a Daiquiri with a difference - when this was served he took one sip and exclaimed "Oh Gosh!".

OIL SLICK

★★½☆☆

Glass: Shot
Garnish: None
Method: Refrigerate ingredients then LAYER in chilled glass by carefully pouring in the order listed.

¾	shot	Baileys Irish cream liqueur
¾	shot	Opal Nera black sambuca

We say: Whiskey, cream and liquorice.

OLD CRYSTAL SHRINE

★★★½☆

Glass: Old-fashioned
Garnish: Lemon & orange zest twists
Method: STIR all ingredients with ice and strain into ice filled glass.

1	spoon	White truffle honey
2	shots	Yamazaki 12yo Japanese whisky
2	dashes	Regan's Orange #6
1	dash	Peychaud's aromatic bitters

We say: Honeyed and spiced whiskey.
Origin: Created in 2008 by Stanislav Vadrna for the Red Monkey Group, Slovakia.

OLD CUBAN

★★★★½

Glass: Martini
Garnish: Mint leaf
Method: Lightly MUDDLE mint in base of shaker (just to bruise). Add next four ingredients, SHAKE with ice and fine strain into chilled glass. TOP with champagne.

6	fresh	Mint leaves
2	shots	Bacardi 8yo aged rum
¾	shot	Freshly squeezed lime juice
½	shot	Monin Pure Cane 2:1 sugar syrup
2	dashes	Angostura aromatic bitters
¾	shot	Brut champagne

We say: A luxurious, minty Daiquiri topped with a splash of champagne.
Origin: Created in 2004 by Audrey Saunders, New York, USA.

OLD FASHIONED #1 (CLASSIC VERSION) ⌐━

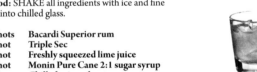

★★★★★

Glass: Old-fashioned
Garnish: Orange zest twist
Method: STIR one shot of bourbon with two ice cubes in a glass. ADD sugar syrup and Angostura and two more ice cubes. STIR some more and add another two ice cubes and the rest of the bourbon. STIR lots more and add more ice.

2½	shots	Maker's Mark bourbon
½	shot	Monin Pure Cane 2:1 sugar syrup
3	dashes	Angostura aromatic bitters

Variant: Old Fashioned #2 (US Version)
We say: The melting and stirring in of ice cubes is essential to the dilution and taste of this sublime classic.
Origin: As with the Martini, the glass this cocktail is served in has taken the name of the drink. The cocktails creation is credited to a bartender called Martin Cuneo at the Pendennis Club in Louisville, Kentucky, USA. He is said to have made the drink for a Kentucky Colonel (and bourbon distiller) named James E. Pepper sometime between 1889 and 1895. In those days the clubhouse was situated at in the old Belknap family mansion located between Third and Fourth Streets on the south side of Walnut Street (now Muhammad Ali Blvd.) in Louisville. This was torn down and replaced by the current opulent Georgian clubhouse, located about a block to the east, at 218 West Walnut Street, which opened in late 1928. A number of sources collaborate the Old Fashioned originating the Pendennis Club, including the 1931 book, '*Old Waldorf Bar Days*', in which it author, Albert Stevens Crocket, writes of this drink, "This was brought to the Old Waldorf in the days of the 'sit-down' Bar, and was introduced by, or in the honor of, Col. James E. Pepper, of Kentucky, a proprietor of a celebrated whiskey of the period. It was said to have been the invention of a bartender at the famous Pendennis Club in Louisville, of which Col. Pepper was a member."

OLD FASHIONED #2 (US VERSION)

★★★★½

Glass: Old-fashioned
Garnish: Orange zest twist & maraschino cherry
Method: MUDDLE orange and cherries in base of shaker. Add other ingredients, SHAKE with ice and fine strain into ice-filled glass.

2	whole	**Maraschino cherries & syrup**
1	slice	**Fresh orange**
2	shots	**Maker's Mark bourbon**
⅛	shot	**Maraschino syrup (from cherry jar)**
¼	shot	**Monin Pure Cane 2:1 sugar syrup**
2	dashes	**Angostura aromatic bitters**

Variant: Old Fashioned #1 (Classic Version)
We say: This drink is often mixed in the glass in which it is to be served. However, shaking better incorporates the flavours produced by muddling and fine straining removes the orange peel and cherry skin.
Origin: In the US, orange segments and sometimes even a maraschino cherry are regularly muddled in this drink: the practice probably originated during Prohibition as a means of disguising rough spirits. This practice is almost unknown in England and as Crosby Gaige wrote in 1944, "Serious-minded persons omit fruit salad from Old Fashioneds."

OLD FASHIONED CADDY

★★★★☆

Glass: Old-fashioned
Garnish: Orange slice & cherry on stick (sail)
Method: SHAKE all ingredients with ice and strain into ice-filled glass.

2	shots	**Dewar's White label Scotch**
½	shot	**De Kuyper Cherry Brandy liqueur**
½	shot	**Martini Rosso sweet vermouth**
2	dashes	**Angostura aromatic bitters**

We say: Rich, red and packed with flavour.
Origin: Created in 2005 by Wayne Collins, London, England.

OLD FLAME

★★★★☆

Glass: Martini
Garnish: Orange zest twist (flamed)
Method: SHAKE all ingredients with ice and fine strain into chilled glass.

1	shot	**Tanqueray London dry gin**
½	shot	**Triple Sec**
½	shot	**Martini Rosso sweet vermouth**
¼	shot	**Campari Bitter**
1½	shots	**Freshly squeezed orange juice**

We say: Bittersweet, orchard fresh orange charged with gin.
Origin: Created by Dale DeGroff, New York, USA

STAR RATINGS EXPLAINED

★★★★★ Excellent

★★★★½ Recommeded	★★★★☆ Praiseworthy
★★★½☆ Commended	★★★☆☆ Mediocre
★★½☆☆ Disappointing	★★☆☆☆ Pretty awful
★½☆☆☆ Shameful	★☆☆☆☆ Disgusting

OLD PAL

★★★½☆

Glass: Old-fashioned
Garnish: Orange slice
Method: STIR all ingredients with ice and strain into ice-filled glass.

1¼	shots	**Canadian whisky**
1¼	shots	**Campari Bitter**
1¼	shots	**Martini Extra Dry vermouth**

We say: A dry, bitter sipper for the more hardened palate.
Origin: Adapted from Harry Craddock's 1930 *'Savoy Cocktail Book'*.

OLE

★★★½☆

Glass: Martini
Garnish: Orange slice
Method: SHAKE all ingredients with ice and fine strain into chilled glass.

2	shots	**Cognac VSOP**
¾	shot	**Cuarenta y Tres (Licor 43) liqueur**
1½	shots	**Freshly squeezed orange juice**

We say: Vanilla, orange and brandy combine well.

OLYMPIC

★★★★½

Glass: Martini
Garnish: Orange zest twist
Method: SHAKE all ingredients with ice and fine strain into chilled glass.

1¼	shots	**Cognac VSOP**
1¼	shots	**Grand Marnier liqueur**
1¼	shots	**Freshly squeezed orange juice**

We say: The perfect balance of cognac and orange juice. One to celebrate the 2012 Games perhaps?
Origin: Adapted from a recipe in Harry Craddock's 1930 *'Savoy Cocktail Book'*.

ONION RING MARTINI

★★★☆☆

Glass: Martini
Garnish: Onion ring
Method: MUDDLE onion in base of shaker. Add other ingredients, SHAKE with ice and fine strain into chilled glass.

2	fresh	**Red onion rings**
1	shot	**Sake**
2	shots	**Tanqueray London dry gin**
3	dashes	**Orange bitters**
⅛	shot	**Monin Pure Cane 2:1 sugar syrup**

We say: Certainly one of the most obscure Martini variations - drinkable, but leaves you with onion breath.
Origin: Reputed to have been created at the Bamboo Bar, Bangkok, Thailand.

OOOH GINGER

★★★★☆

Glass: Martini
Garnish: Candied ginger
Method: STIR all ingredients with ice and fine strain into chilled glass.

2	shots	Tequila 100% Agave
½	shot	Domaine de Canton ginger liqueur
½	shot	Martini Extra Dry vermouth

We say: Subtle ginger spice flavours this dry tequila martini.
Origin: Created in March 2008 by Dick Bradsell and Simon Difford at The Cabinet Room, London, England.

OPAL

★★★★★

Glass: Martini
Garnish: Orange zest twist
Method: SHAKE all ingredients with ice and fine strain into chilled glass.

2	shots	Tanqueray London dry gin
½	shot	Triple Sec
1¼	shots	Freshly squeezed orange juice
¼	shot	Monin Pure Cane 2:1 sugar syrup
⅛	shot	Orange flower water

We say: Fresh, fragrant flavours of orange zest and gin.
Origin: Adapted from the 1920s recipe.

OPAL CAFÉ

★★★★☆

Glass: Shot
Garnish: None
Method: SHAKE first two ingredients with ice and fine strain into chilled glass. FLOAT thin layer of cream over drink.

½	shot	Opal Nera black sambuca
½	shot	Hot espresso coffee
Float		Double (heavy) cream

We say: A great liquorice and coffee drink to sip or shoot.

THE OPENING ACT NEW

★★★★☆

Glass: Collins
Garnish: Mint sprig
Method: SHAKE first four ingredients with ice and strain into ice-filled glass. TOP with tonic water.

2	shots	Domaine de Canton ginger liqueur
½	shot	Campari Bitter
½	shot	Freshly squeezed lime juice
1	dash	Orange bitters
Top up with		Tonic water

We say: Campari and ginger topped with tonic, a surprisingly good combo. Adult and balanced. A great long drink.
Origin: Created by Andrew Pollard for the 2010 Domaine de Canton Bartender of the Year competition winning 'Best Overall Cocktail'

OPENING SHOT

★★★☆☆

Glass: Shot
Garnish: None
Method: SHAKE all ingredients with ice and fine strain into chilled glass.

1	shot	Maker's Mark bourbon
½	shot	Martini Rosso sweet vermouth
⅛	shot	Pomegranate (grenadine) syrup

Variant: Double the quantities and strain into a Martini glass and you have the 1920s classic I based this drink on.
We say: Basically a miserly Sweet Manhattan.

OPERA

★★★★☆

Glass: Martini
Garnish: Orange zest twist
Method: SHAKE all ingredients with ice and fine strain into chilled glass.

2	shots	Tanqueray London dry gin
¼	shot	Luxardo Maraschino liqueur
2	shots	Dubonnet Red (French made)
3	dashes	Orange bitters

We say: Dubonnet smoothes the gin while maraschino adds floral notes.
Origin: Adapted from the classic 1920s cocktail.

ORANG-A-TANG

★★★★☆

Glass: Sling
Garnish: Orange slice
Method: SHAKE first five ingredients with ice and strain into ice-filled glass. FLOAT layer of rum over drink.

1½	shots	Ketel One vodka
¾	shot	Triple Sec
2	shots	Freshly squeezed orange juice
½	shot	Freshly squeezed lime juice
¼	shot	Pomegranate (grenadine) syrup
½	shot	Wood's 100 rum

We say: Orange predominates in this long, tangy, topical cooler.

ORANGE BLOOM MARTINI

★★★★☆

Glass: Martini
Garnish: Maraschino cherry
Method: SHAKE all ingredients with ice and fine strain into chilled glass.

2	shots	Tanqueray London dry gin
1	shot	Triple Sec
1	shot	Martini Rosso sweet vermouth

We say: Strong, fruity, zesty orange laced with gin.
Origin: Adapted from a recipe in the 1930s edition of the *'Savoy Cocktail Book'* by Harry Craddock.

ORANGE BLOSSOM

★★★☆☆

Glass: Old-fashioned
Garnish: Orange zest twist
Method: SHAKE all ingredients with ice and strain into ice-filled glass.

1½	shots	Tanqueray London dry gin
½	shot	Triple Sec
1½	shots	Freshly squeezed orange juice
½	shot	Freshly squeezed lime juice
⅛	shot	Pomegranate (grenadine) syrup

Variant: Served long in a Collins glass this becomes a Harvester.
We say: Gin sweetened with liqueur and grenadine, and soured with lime.

ORANGE BRULÉE

★★★★★

Glass: Martini
Garnish: Dust with chocolate powder
Method: SHAKE first three ingredients with ice and fine strain into chilled glass. FLOAT thin layer of cream over drink and turn glass to spread evenly.

1½	shots	Amaretto liqueur
1½	shots	Grand Marnier liqueur
¾	shot	Cognac VSOP
¼	shot	Double (heavy) cream

We say: A great looking, beautifully balanced after-dinner drink.
Origin: Created in 2005 by Xavier Laigle at Bar le Forum, Paris, France.

ORANGE CUSTARD MARTINI

★★★☆☆

Glass: Martini
Garnish: Orange zest twist
Method: SHAKE all ingredients with ice and fine strain into chilled glass.

2	shots	Advocaat liqueur
1	shot	Tuaca liqueur
½	shot	Grand Marnier liqueur
¼	shot	Monin Vanilla sugar syrup

We say: A smooth creamy orangey dessert cocktail.
Origin: I created this drink in 2002 after rediscovering advocaat on a trip to Amsterdam.

ORANGE DAIQUIRI #1

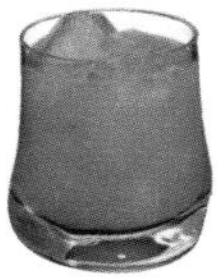

★★★★☆

Glass: Old-fashioned
Garnish: Orange zest twist
Method: SHAKE all ingredients with ice and fine strain into ice-filled glass.

2	shots	Bacardi Superior rum
¾	shot	Freshly squeezed orange juice
½	shot	Freshly squeezed lime juice
¼	shot	Monin Pure Cane 2:1 sugar syrup

AKA: Bolo
We say: Far more serious that it looks. Sweet and sour in harmony.
Origin: My take on a popular drink.

ORANGE DAIQUIRI #2

★★★★☆

Glass: Martini
Garnish: Orange zest twist
Method: SHAKE all ingredients with ice and fine strain into chilled glass.

2	shots	Clément Creole Shrubb liqueur
½	shot	Freshly squeezed lime juice
¾	shot	Chilled mineral water

Variant: Derby Daiquiri
We say: Créole Shrubb is an unusual liqueur made my infusing orange peel in casks of mature Martinique rum.
Origin: I conceived this drink in 1998, after visiting the company which was then importing Créole Shrubb. I took a bottle to London's Met Bar and Ben Reed made me my first Orange Daiquiri.

ORANGE MARTINI

★★★★☆

Glass: Martini
Garnish: Orange zest twist
Method: SHAKE all ingredients with ice and fine strain into chilled glass.

2	shots	Tanqueray London dry gin
1	shot	Freshly squeezed orange juice
½	shot	Martini Rosso sweet vermouth
¼	shot	Monin Pure Cane 2:1 sugar syrup
3	dashes	Orange bitters

We say: A sophisticated, complex balance of orange and gin.
Origin: Adapted from the Orange Cocktail and Orange Martini Cocktail in the 1930s edition of the 'Savoy Cocktail Book' by Harry Craddock.

ORANGE MOJITO

★★★★☆

Glass: Collins
Garnish: Mint sprig
Method: Lightly MUDDLE mint (just to bruise) in base of glass. Add other ingredients and half fill glass with crushed ice. CHURN (stir) with bar spoon. Fill with more crushed ice and churn some more. TOP with soda, stir and serve with straws.

8	fresh	Mint leaves
1½	shots	Ketel One Oranje vodka
½	shot	Mandarine Napoléon liqueur
½	shot	Bacardi Superior rum
1	shot	Freshly squeezed lime juice
½	shot	Monin Pure Cane 2:1 sugar syrup
Top up with		Soda (club soda)

We say: Mint and orange combine to make a wonderfully fresh drink.
Origin: Created in 2001 by Jamie MacDonald while working in Sydney, Australia.

STAR RATINGS EXPLAINED

★★★★★ Excellent

★★★★☆ Recommended	★★★★☆ Praiseworthy
★★★☆☆ Commended	★★★☆☆ Mediocre
★★☆☆☆ Disappointing	★★☆☆☆ Pretty awful
★☆☆☆☆ Shameful	★☆☆☆☆ Disgusting

ORANGE NEGRONI

★★★★☆

Glass: Old-fashioned
Garnish: Orange zest twist
Method: POUR all ingredients into ice-filled glass and stir.

1	shot	Ketel One Oranje vodka
1	shot	Campari Bitter
1	shot	Martini Rosso sweet vermouth

We say: Orange and Campari always combine well especially when supported by sweet vermouth.

ORANGE SPUR

★★★★☆

Glass: Coupette
Garnish: Star anise
Method: STIR all ingredients with ice and strain into chilled glass.

2	shots	Ketel One vodka
½	shot	Marie Brizard anisette liqueur
½	shot	Aperol
2	dashes	Angostura aromatic bitters

We say: Stir well - this bittersweet drink benefits from dilution.
Origin: Created in 2008 by Don Lee at PDT, New York City, USA.

ORANJEY COCKTAIL UPDATED

★★★★☆

Glass: Coupette
Garnish: Orange zest twist
Method: STIR all ingredients with ice and fine strain into chilled glass.

1	shot	Ketel One vodka
1	shot	Ketel One Oranje vodka
½	shot	Triple Sec
¼	shot	Freshly squeezed orange juice
¼	shot	Martini Rosso sweet vermouth
⅛	shot	Campari Bitter

We say: Dry, and yes, very orangey with bittersweet orange complexity.

STAR RATINGS EXPLAINED

★★★★★ **Excellent**

★★★★⯪ Recommended   ★★★★☆ Praiseworthy
★★★⯪☆ Commended   ★★★☆☆ Mediocre
★★⯪☆☆ Disappointing   ★★☆☆☆ Pretty awful
★⯪☆☆☆ Shameful   ★☆☆☆☆ Disgusting

ORANJINIHA

★★★⯪☆

Glass: Collins
Garnish: Orange slice
Method: SHAKE all ingredients with ice and strain into glass filled with crushed ice.

2	shots	Ketel One Oranje vodka
2½	shots	Freshly squeezed orange juice
1	shot	Freshly squeezed lemon juice
½	shot	Monin Pure Cane 2:1 sugar syrup

We say: A tall, richly flavoured orange drink.
Origin: Created in 2002 by Alex Kammerling, London, England.

ORCHARD BREEZE

★★★★⯪

Glass: Collins
Garnish: Apple slice
Method: SHAKE all ingredients with ice and strain into ice-filled glass.

2	shots	Ketel One vodka
1	shot	St-Germain elderflower liqueur
1	shot	Sauvignon blanc wine
2½	shots	Pressed apple juice
¼	shot	Freshly squeezed lime juice

We say: A refreshing, summery combination of white wine, apple, lime and elderflower laced with vodka.
Origin: Created in 2002 by Wayne Collins for Maxximum UK.

ORCHARD CRUSH

★★★★⯪

Glass: Old-fashioned
Garnish: Seasonal berries
Method: SHAKE all ingredients with ice and strain into an ice-filled glass.

1	spoon	Damson jam (preserve)
2	shots	Calvados/Applejack brandy
1	shot	Freshly squeezed lemon juice
¼	shot	Monin Pure Cane 2:1 sugar syrup

We say: Apple brandy and damson jam combine brilliantly in this tangy but not at all sweet cocktail.
Origin: Created in 2008 by Jeffrey Morgenthaler at Bel Ami Lounge, Oregon, USA.

ORIENTAL

★★★★☆

Glass: Martini
Garnish: Orange zest twist
Method: SHAKE all ingredients with ice and fine strain into chilled glass.

2	shots	Straight rye whiskey
1	shot	Martini Rosso sweet vermouth
1	shot	Grand Marnier liqueur
½	shot	Freshly squeezed lime juice

We say: Be warned this dry, orangey bourbon based cocktail packs a punch.
Origin: Adapted from 1930 the *'Savoy Cocktail Book'* in which author Harry Craddock writes of this drink, "In August, 1924, an American Engineer nearly died of fever in the Philippines, and only the extraordinary devotion of Dr. B- saved his life. As an act of gratitude the Engineer gave Dr. B- the recipe of this cocktail."

ORIENTAL GRAPE MARTINI

★★★★☆

Glass: Martini
Garnish: White grapes
Method: MUDDLE grapes in base of shaker. Add other ingredients, SHAKE with ice and fine strain into chilled glass.

2	shots	Ketel One vodka
7	fresh	Seedless white grapes
1½	shots	Sake
⅛	shot	Monin Pure Cane 2:1 sugar syrup

Variant: Double Grape Martini, Grape Martini, Grapple.
We say: Sake adds some oriental intrigue to what would otherwise be a plain old Grape Martini.
Origin: Created by Simon Difford in 2004.

ORIENTAL TART

★★★★☆

Glass: Martini
Garnish: Lychee
Method: SHAKE all ingredients with ice and fine strain into chilled glass.

1½	shots	Tanqueray London dry gin
1	shot	Kwai Feh lychee liqueur
2	shots	Freshly squeezed grapefruit juice

We say: A sour, tart, fruity Martini with more than a hint of lychee.
Origin: Created in 2004 by Simon Difford.

ORIGINAL SIN

★★★★½

Glass: Martini
Garnish: Star anise
Method: POUR absinthe into ice-filled glass and top with water. Leave the mixture to stand in the glass. Separately, STIR all ingredients with ice. Finally discard contents of absinthe-coated glass and fine strain contents of shaker into absinthe washed glass.

½	shot	Absinthe
2	shots	Ketel One vodka
¾	shot	Sake
⅛	shot	Monin Honey syrup

We say: Sake and vodka with a delicate hint of honey.
Origin: Created in 2009 by Spike Marchant and Simon Difford at the Cabinet Room, London, England.

ORIGINS NEW

★★★½☆

Glass: Coupette
Garnish: Fresh ginger slice
Method: MUDDLE ginger in base of shaker. Add other ingredients, SHAKE with ice and fine strain into chilled glass.

1	slice	Fresh root ginger (thumbnail sized)
2	shots	Bacardi Superior rum
⅛	shot	Rioja Red Wine
½	shot	Freshly squeezed lime juice
¼	shot	Pomegranate (grenadine) syrup

We say: A pinky red daiquiri with ginger spice, sweet pomegranate and Rioja wine.
Origin: Created in 2010 by John O'Reilly at the Apartment, Belfast, Northern Ireland. This adaptation of the classic Daiquiri was inspired by the man who created Bacardi rum and his move from Spain to Cuba. The Rioja represents Don Facundo's Spanish homeland, the pomegranate was taken by the Spanish to the New World and so stands for the journey itself, while the ginger represents the heat and spice of the Caribbean.

OSMO

★★★★☆

Glass: Martini
Garnish: Orange zest twist
Method: SHAKE all ingredients with ice and fine strain into chilled glass.

2	shots	Sake
½	shot	Triple Sec
¼	shot	Freshly squeezed lime juice
1½	shots	Ocean Spray cranberry juice

We say: A sake based Cosmopolitan.
Origin: Adapted from a drink discovered in 2005 at Mo Bar, Landmark Mandarin Oriental Hotel, Hong Kong.

OUZI

★★★½☆

Glass: Shot
Garnish: None
Method: SHAKE all ingredients with ice and fine strain into chilled glass.

¾	shot	Ketel One vodka
½	shot	Ouzo 12
¼	shot	Monin Pure Cane 2:1 sugar syrup
¼	shot	Freshly squeezed lemon juice

We say: A lemon and liquorice shooter.

BARTENDER'S TIP ICE

A plentiful supply of fresh ice is essential to making good cocktails. When buying bagged ice look for large, solid cubes of ice. Your ice should be dry, almost sticky to the touch. Avoid 'wet' ice that has started to thaw.

Whenever serving a drink over ice, always fill the glass with ice, rather than just adding a few cubes. Never use ice in a cocktail shaker twice, even if it's to mix the same drink as before.

OYSTER BAY NEW

★★★★☆

Glass: Coupette
Garnish: Olive on stick
Method: STIR all ingredients with ice and strain into chilled glass.

2	shots	Dewar's White Label Scotch
⅓	shot	Martini Extra dry vermouth
⅓	shot	Orange Curaçao liqueur
⅛	shot	Freshly squeezed lemon juice
1	dash	Orange bitters

We say: Citrus notes and dry vermouth subtly influence Scotch in this refined, masculine cocktail.
Origin: Named after Oyster Bay, Long Island. Famous for being the location of Sagamore Hill, US President Theodore Roosevelt's summer White House

P.S. I LOVE YOU

★★★★☆

Glass: Martini
Garnish: Crumbled Cadbury's Flake bar
Method: SHAKE all ingredients with ice and fine strain into chilled glass.

1¼	shots	Baileys Irish cream liqueur
1¼	shots	Amaretto liqueur
¾	shot	Bacardi Oro golden rum
¾	shot	Kahlúa coffee liqueur
1	shot	Double (heavy) cream

We say: P.S. You'll love this creamy flavoursome drink

PABLO ALVAREZ DE CAÑAS SPECIAL

★★★★☆

Glass: Coupette
Garnish: Pineapple cubes, maraschino cherry & orange slice
Method: Place lemon zest in shaker, add other ingredients, SHAKE with ice and strain into ice-filled glass.

1	fresh	Lemon zest twist
1	shot	Cognac VSOP
1	shot	Tio Pepe fino sherry
⅛	shot	De Kuyper Cherry Brandy liqueur
⅛	shot	Monin Pure Cane 2:1 sugar syrup

We say: Sherry is most prevalent on the palate, but all the other ingredients, including the lemon zest, also contribute to this subtle, balanced and altogether a most unusual cocktail.
Origin: Recipe adapted from 1937 Bar Florida (later renamed Floridita) menu.

STAR RATINGS EXPLAINED

★★★★★ **Excellent**

★★★★⯪ Recommended	★★★★☆ Praiseworthy
★★★⯪☆ Commended	★★★☆☆ Mediocre
★★⯪☆☆ Disappointing	★★☆☆☆ Pretty awful
★⯪☆☆☆ Shameful	★☆☆☆☆ Disgusting

PADOVANI UPDATED

★★★★☆

Glass: Old-fashioned
Garnish: Lemon zest twist
Method: STIR all ingredients with ice and strain into ice-filled glass.

| 2 | shots | Dewar's White Label Scotch |
| ¾ | shot | St-Germain elderflower liqueur |

Variant: Single Padovani
We say: Peaty Scotch combines wonderfully with floral, delicate elderflower liqueur.
Origin: Created in 2006 by Simon Difford in London, England and named after a fellow whisky fan, Xavier Padovani. At the time I was working on the launch of St-Germain and Xav was brand ambassador for Monkey Shoulder whisky. The original recipe was equal parts - after all I was trying to sell St-Germain at the time. The reduction of liqueur to allow the Scotch to shine through is the work of the chaps at Le Lion in Hamburg, Germany where they also use single malt and so have appropriately renamed this a 'Single Padovani'.

PAGO PAGO

★★★⯪☆

Glass: Martini
Garnish: Lime wedge
Method: SHAKE all ingredients with ice and fine strain into chilled glass.

2	shots	Bacardi Oro golden rum
¼	shot	Chartreuse Green liqueur
½	shot	White Crème de Cacao
½	shot	Freshly squeezed lime juice
⅛	shot	Monin Pure Cane 2:1 sugar syrup
½	shot	Chilled mineral water

We say: A Daiquiri with a liqueur twist.
Origin: Adapted from Jeff Berry's 'Beachbum Berry Remixed', and according to Jeff originally from a 1940 book called 'The How and When'.

PAINKILLER

★★★★☆

Glass: Collins
Garnish: Pineapple wedge & maraschino cherry
Method: BLEND all ingredients with scoop of ice.

2	shots	Pusser's Navy rum
2	shots	Fresh pressed pineapple juice
1	shot	Freshly squeezed orange juice
1	shot	Coco López cream of coconut

We say: Full-flavoured and fruity.
Origin: From the soggy dollar bar on the island of Jost Van Dyke in the British Virgin Islands. Most of the clientele are sailors and there is no dock so they swim ashore, paying for drinks with wet dollars.

PAISLEY MARTINI ⚷

★★★★☆

Glass: Martini
Garnish: Lemon zest twist
Method: STIR all ingredients with ice and strain into chilled glass.

2½	shots	Tanqueray London dry gin
¼	shot	Dewar's White label Scotch
½	shot	Martini Extra Dry vermouth

We say: A dry Martini for those with a penchant for Scotch.

PALE CHARLIE NEW

★★★★☆

Glass: Collins
Garnish: Grapefruit zest twist
Method: SHAKE first 5 ingredients with ice and strain into ice-filled glass. TOP with ale.

¾	shot	**Sloe Gin liqueur**
¾	shot	**De Kuyper apricot brandy liqueur**
¾	shot	**Freshly squeezed pink grapefruit juice**
¾	shot	**Freshly squeezed lime juice**
2	dashes	**La Fée Parisienne (68%) absinthe**
3	shots	**Pale ale beer**

We say: Zesty, fruity and refreshing with berry and stone fruit accompanying lime and grapefruit with hoppy pale ale.
Origin: Created in 2013 by Michele Mariotti at The American Bar at The Savoy Hotel, London. Michele was one of five finalists in the diffordsguide Beer-tail Competition for London Cocktail Week 2013 held in August 2013 at Simon Difford's Cabinet Room bar in London.

PALE RIDER

★★★☆☆

Glass: Collins
Garnish: Lime wedge
Method: SHAKE all ingredients with ice and strain into ice-filled glass.

2	shots	**Raspberry flavoured vodka**
½	shot	**Peachtree peach schnapps**
2	shots	**Ocean Spray cranberry juice**
1	shot	**Fresh pressed pineapple juice**
1	shot	**Freshly squeezed lime juice**
½	shot	**Monin Pure Cane 2:1 sugar syrup**

We say: Sweet and fruity.
Origin: Created in 1997 by Wayne Collins at Navajo Joe, London, England.

PALERMO

★★★★½

Glass: Martini
Garnish: Vanilla pod
Method: SHAKE all ingredients with ice and fine strain into chilled glass.

1½	shots	**Vanilla-infused Bacardi rum**
1	shot	**Sauvignon blanc wine**
1¼	shots	**Fresh pressed pineapple juice**
¼	shot	**Monin Pure Cane 2:1 sugar syrup**

We say: This smooth cocktail beautifully combines vanilla rum with tart wine and the sweetness of the pineapple juice.
Origin: Adapted from a cocktail discovered in 2001 at Hotel du Vin, Bristol, England.

PALL MALL MARTINI

★★★★☆

Glass: Martini
Garnish: Orange zest twist
Method: SHAKE all ingredients with ice and fine strain into chilled glass.

1	shot	**Tanqueray London dry gin**
1	shot	**Martini Extra Dry vermouth**
1	shot	**Martini Rosso sweet vermouth**
¼	shot	**White Crème de Cacao**
1	dash	**Orange bitters**

We say: A classic Martini served 'perfect' with the tiniest hint of chocolate.

PALM BEACH

★★★½☆

Glass: Martini
Garnish: Maraschino cherry
Method: SHAKE all ingredients with ice and fine strain into chilled glass.

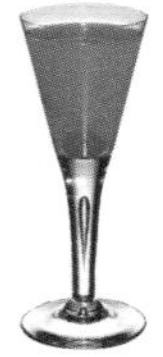

2½	shots	**Tanqueray London dry gin**
½	shot	**Martini Rosso sweet vermouth**
1	shot	**Freshly squeezed grapefruit juice**

We say: Dry, aromatic and packs one hell of a punch.
Origin: A classic from the 1940s.

PALM SPRINGS

★★★½☆

Glass: Collins
Garnish: Apple slice & mint sprig
Method: SHAKE all ingredients with ice and strain into class filled with crushed ice.

4	fresh	**Mint leaves**
1	shot	**Bacardi Oro golden rum**
1	shot	**Passoã passion fruit liqueur**
¼	shot	**Freshly squeezed lime juice**
1	shot	**Pressed apple juice**
2	shots	**Ocean Spray cranberry juice**

We say: Sweet and aromatic.

BARTENDER'S TIP ORDER OF PREPARATION

As in cooking, there is a correct order in which to prepare a drink which, with a few exceptions, runs as follows:

1. Select glass and chill or pre-heat (if required) 2 .Prepare garnish (if required) 3. Pour ingredients. 4. Add ice (if required - add last to minimise melt) 5. Combine ingredients (shake, stir etc.) 6. Add garnish (if required) 7. Consume or serve to guest

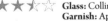

PALMA VIOLET MARTINI

★★★½☆

Glass: Martini
Garnish: Palma Violet sweets
Method: SHAKE all ingredients with ice and fine strain into chilled glass.

1½	shots	Ketel One vodka
¼	shot	Peachtree peach schnapps
1	shot	Benoit Serres créme de violette
½	shot	Freshly squeezed lemon juice
¼	shot	Monin Pure Cane 2:1 sugar syrup
1	dash	Orange bitters
½	shot	Chilled mineral water

We say: A subtly floral drink with a delicate colour.
Origin: Created in 2001 by Jamie Terrell at LAB, London, England.

PALMETTO COCKTAIL NEW

★★★★☆

Glass: Martini or Coupette
Garnish: Orange zest twist
Method: STIR all ingredients with ice and stain into chilled glass.

1½	shots	Rum Aged
1½	shots	Martini Rosso sweet vermouth
2	dashes	Orange bitters

We say: The orange bitters are key to balancing and adding depth to the equal parts aged rum and sweet vermouth. However, go easy with those dashes or bitter orange will dominate this complex cocktail.
Origin: Adapted from Harry Craddock's 1930 *The Savoy Cocktail Book*, which calls for this cocktail to be shaken.

PALOMA (SIMPLE) NEW

★★★★☆

Glass: Collins
Garnish: Lime wedge & salt rim
Method: POUR ingredients into ice-filled glass and gently stir.

2	shots	Olmeca Altos 100% agave tequila
½	shot	Freshly squeezed lime juice
Top up with		Mexican 'Squirt' or Caribbean 'Ting' grapefruit soda

We say: Long, fruity and refreshing.
Origin: Paloma is Spanish for 'dove' and this well-known cocktail in Mexico was created by the legendary Don Javier Delgado Corona, owner/bartender of La Capilla (The Chapel) in Tequila, Mexico. Still mixing, even in his eighties, Don Javier is noted for stirring his drinks with a huge knife.

PALOMA UPDATED

★★★★½

Glass: Collins
Garnish: Lime wedge & salt rim
Method: SHAKE first four ingredients with ice and strain into ice-filled glass. TOP with grapefruit soda, lightly stir and serve with straws.

2	shots	Tequila 100% Agave
2	shots	Freshly squeezed grapefruit juice
½	shot	Freshly squeezed lime juice
¼	shot	Agave nectar
Top up with		Mexican 'Squirt' or Caribbean 'Ting' grapefruit soda

We say: A long, fruity, Margarita.
Origin: The name is Spanish for 'dove' and the cocktail is well-known in Mexico.

PALOMINO FLOR NEW

★★★★½

Glass: Coupette
Garnish: Short pale yellow stalk and leaf from celery heart
Method: MUDDLE celery in base of shaker. Add other ingredients, SHAKE with ice and fine strain into chilled glass.

2	shots	Rum light white/blanco
⅔	shot	Martini Bianco vermouth
⅓	shot	Tio Pepe fino sherry
⅛	shot	St-Germain elderflower liqueur
1	inch	Freshly extracted celery juice

We say: A subtle vegetal note comes from the celery in this unusual aperitif cocktail.
Origin: Jody Monteith at The Liquorists, Manchester, England.

PANACHÉE

★★★☆☆

Glass: Collins
Garnish: None
Method: POUR first two ingredients into glass. Serve iced water separately in a small jug (known in France as a 'broc') so the customer can dilute to their own taste (I recommend four-and-a-half shots). Lastly, add ice to glass.

1	shot	Absinthe
1	shot	Marie Brizard anisette liqueur
Top up with		Chilled mineral water

We say: Anisette sweetens the absinthe and adds a refreshing burst of herbal aniseed.
Origin: This is one of the earliest known absinthe mixtures. Today if you order a 'panachée' at a French café, you will receive beer with lemonade (shandy).

BARTENDER'S TIP FINE STRAIN

Most cocktails that are served 'straight up' without ice benefit from an additional finer strain, over and above the standard strain.

This 'fine strain' removes small fragments of fruit and fine flecks of ice which can spoil the appearance of a drink and is particularly beneficial if the drink has been shaken. Fine straining is achieved by simply holding a fine sieve, like a tea strainer, between the shaker and the glass.

PANCHO VILLA

★★★★☆

Glass: Martini
Garnish: Pineapple wedge
Method: SHAKE all ingredients with ice and fine strain into chilled glass.

1	shot	Bacardi Superior rum
1	shot	Tanqueray London dry gin
1	shot	De Kuyper Apricot Brandy liqueur
¼	shot	De Kuyper Cherry Brandy liqueur
¼	shot	Fresh pressed pineapple juice
½	shot	Chilled mineral water

We say: To quote Victor Bergeron, "This'll tuck you away neatly - and pick you up and throw you right to the floor".
Origin: Adapted from a recipe in the 1942-72 '*Trader Vic's Bartender's Guide*' by Victor Bergeron.

PAPA BEAR

★★★★⯨

Glass: Coupette
Garnish: Honeycomb rim
Method: SHAKE all ingredients with ice and fine strain into chilled glass.

1	spoon	Monin Honey syrup
1½	shots	Cognac VSOP
1½	shots	Krupnik spiced honey liqueur
¾	shot	Freshly squeezed lemon juice

We say: Delicately spiced and honeyed cognac.
Origin: Created in 2008 by Tim Homewood, Dirty Martini Bar, London, England. Named after an old family friend who passed away. He was known to all of his children as 'daddy bear' so Papa Bear seemed appropriate.

PAPA GHIRARDELLI NEW

★★★★⯨☆

Glass: Collins
Garnish: Orange slice
Method: SHAKE first five ingredients with ice and strain into ice-filled glass. TOP with soda.

1½	shots	Macchu pisco
½	shot	Campari Bitter
¾	shot	Martini Rosso sweet vermouth
½	shot	Bénédictine D.O.M.
½	shot	Freshly squeezed lemon juice
Top up with		Soda (club soda)

We say: This cocktail is named after the founder of Ghirardelli Chocolate Company, Domingo Ghirardelli, an Italian-born man who moved to Peru and ran a successful confectioners business and, following the gold rush, ultimately ended up in San Francisco. He went on to found Ghirardely & Girard (later changed to the Ghirardelli Chocolate Company), which has been in continuous operation since 1852. In his own way, Ghirardelli helped build and shape San Francisco, and his company has become synonymous with the city. Ghirardelli Square, which his company-built, has been an official City landmark since 1965.
Origin: Adapted from a drink which was the signature cocktail of San Fanscisco Cocktail Week 21-27 September 2010.

PAPPY HONEYSUCKLE

★★★★⯨

Glass: Martini
Garnish: Physalis (cape gooseberry)
Method: STIR honey with whiskey in base of shaker to dissolve honey. Add other ingredients, SHAKE with ice and fine strain into chilled glass.

1½	shots	Jameson Irish whiskey
1¼	shots	Sauvignon blanc wine
2	spoons	Runny honey
1½	shots	Pressed apple juice
¼	shot	Freshly squeezed lemon juice
¼	shot	Passion fruit syrup

We say: Fresh and fruity with honeyed sweetness.
Origin: Created in 2002 by Shelim Islam at the GE Club, London, England.

PARADISE #1

★★★⯨☆

Glass: Martini
Garnish: Orange zest twist
Method: SHAKE all ingredients with ice and fine strain into chilled glass.

2	shots	Tanqueray London dry gin
1	shot	De Kuyper Apricot Brandy liqueur
1	shot	Freshly squeezed orange juice
¼	shot	Freshly squeezed lemon juice

We say: Orange predominates in this strong complex cocktail.
Origin: Proportioned according to a recipe in the 1930 edition of the '*Savoy Cocktail Book*' by Harry Craddock.

PARADISE #2

★★★⯨☆☆

Glass: Martini
Garnish: Orange zest twist
Method: Cut passion fruit in half and scoop flesh into shaker. Add other ingredients, SHAKE with ice and fine strain into chilled glass.

2	shots	Tanqueray London dry gin
¾	shot	De Kuyper Apricot Brandy liqueur
1¾	shots	Freshly squeezed orange juice
3	dashes	Angostura aromatic bitters

We say: When well made, this wonderfully fruity cocktail beautifully harnesses and balances its ingredients.
Origin: This 1920s recipe has recently been revitalised by Dale DeGroff.

PARADISE #3

★★★★⯨

Glass: Martini
Garnish: Orange zest twist
Method: SHAKE all ingredients with ice and fine strain into chilled glass.

1	fresh	Passion fruit
2	shots	Tanqueray London dry gin
¾	shot	De Kuyper Apricot Brandy liqueur
¾	shot	Freshly squeezed orange juice

We say: Thick, almost syrupy. Rich and fruity.

PARIS MANHATTAN

★★★★⯨

Glass: Martini
Garnish: Maraschino cherry
Method: SHAKE all ingredients with ice and fine strain into chilled glass.

2	shots	Maker's Mark bourbon
1	shot	St~Germain elderflower liqueur
½	shot	Martini Extra Dry vermouth
2	dashes	Angostura aromatic bitters

We say: Elderflower replaces sweet vermouth in this 'perfect' and aromatic Manhattan.
Origin: Created in 2006 by Simon Difford, originally titled 'Elderflower Manhattan'.

PARIS SOUR

★★★★☆

Glass: Old-fashioned
Garnish: Lemon zest twist
Method: SHAKE all ingredients with ice and strain into ice-filled glass.

2	shots	Maker's Mark bourbon
1¼	shots	Dubonnet Red (French made)
¼	shot	Monin Pure Cane 2:1 sugar syrup
½	shot	Freshly squeezed lemon juice
½	fresh	Egg white

We say: A wonderfully accommodating whiskey sour - it's easy to make and a pleasure to drink.
Origin: Created in 2005 by Mark at Match Bar, London, England.

PARISIAN MARTINI #1

★★★★☆

Glass: Martini
Garnish: Lemon zest twist
Method: SHAKE all ingredients with ice and fine strain into chilled glass.

1¼	shots	Tanqueray London dry gin
1¼	shots	Martini Extra Dry vermouth
1¼	shots	Crème de cassis liqueur

We say: Full-on rich cassis is barely tempered by gin and dry vermouth.
Origin: A drink created in the 1920s to promote crème de cassis. This recipe is adapted from one in Harry Craddock's 'Savoy Cocktail Book'.

PARISIAN MARTINI #2

★★★★⯨

Glass: Martini
Garnish: Lime zest twist
Method: SHAKE all ingredients with ice and fine strain into chilled glass.

2	shots	Ketel One vodka
1	shot	St~Germain elderflower liqueur
¼	shot	Martini Extra Dry vermouth

AKA: Can Can
We say: Floral, yet dry and aromatic. The character of the vodka shines through.
Origin: Created in 2006 by Simon Difford.

PARISIAN SIDECAR

★★★★⯨

Glass: Martini
Garnish: Lemon zest twist
Method: SHAKE all ingredients with ice and fine strain into chilled glass.

1½	shots	Cognac VSOP
1½	shots	St~Germain elderflower liqueur
1	shot	Freshly squeezed lemon juice

We say: An elderflower flavoured Sidecar named after the fashionable Left Bank area of Paris.
Origin: Created in 2006 by Simon Difford.

PARISIAN SPRING PUNCH UPDATED

★★★★☆

Glass: Collins
Garnish: Lemon zest twist
Method: SHAKE first four ingredients with ice and strain into ice-filled glass. TOP with champagne and serve with straws.

1	shot	Boulard Grand Solage calvados
½	shot	Martini Extra dry vermouth
¼	shot	Freshly squeezed lemon juice
¼	shot	Monin Pure Cane 2:1 sugar syrup
Top up with		Brut champagne

We say: Dry apple and champagne - like upmarket cider.

PARK AVENUE

★★★★☆

Glass: Martini
Garnish: Maraschino cherry
Method: SHAKE all ingredients with ice and fine strain into chilled glass.

2	shots	Tanqueray London dry gin
½	shot	Grand Marnier liqueur
½	shot	Martini Rosso sweet vermouth
1	shot	Fresh pressed pineapple juice

We say: Very fruity and well-balanced rather than dry or sweet.
Origin: A classic from the 1940s.

PARK LANE

★★★★⯨

Glass: Martini
Garnish: Orange zest twist
Method: SHAKE all ingredients with ice and strain into chilled glass.

2	shots	Tanqueray London dry gin
¾	shot	De Kuyper Apricot Brandy liqueur
¾	shot	Freshly squeezed orange juice
⅛	shot	Pomegranate (grenadine) syrup
½	fresh	Egg white

We say: This smooth, frothy concoction hides a mean kick.

PARLAY PUNCH

★★★☆☆

Glass: Collins
Garnish: Lime wedge
Method: SHAKE all ingredients with ice and strain into ice-filled glass.

1½	shots	Maker's Mark bourbon
1	shot	Southern Comfort liqueur
1	shot	Ocean Spray cranberry juice
½	shot	Freshly squeezed orange juice
½	shot	Freshly squeezed lime juice
1	shot	Fresh pressed pineapple juice

We say: Too many of these tangy punches and you'll be parleying till dawn.
Origin: Adapted from a recipe discovered at Vortex Bar, Atlanta, USA

PARMA NEGRONI

★★★★☆

Glass: Collins
Garnish: Orange slice
Method: SHAKE first five ingredients with ice and strain into ice-filled glass. TOP with tonic water, lightly stir and serve with straws.

1	shot	Tanqueray London dry gin
1	shot	Campari Bitter
1	shot	Freshly squeezed grapefruit juice
½	shot	Monin Pure Cane 2:1 sugar syrup
2	dashes	Angostura aromatic bitters
Top up with		Tonic water

We say: Negroni drinkers will love this fruity adaptation.
Origin: Discovered in 2005 at Club 97, Hong Kong, China.

PASS-ON-THAT

★★★☆☆

Glass: Collins
Garnish: Passion fruit
Method: Cut passion fruit in half and scoop flesh into shaker. Add other ingredients, SHAKE with ice and fine strain into ice-filled glass.

1	fresh	Passion fruit
1	shot	Ketel One vodka
1	shot	Passoã passion fruit liqueur
3	shots	Ocean Spray cranberry juice

We say: Full-on passion fruit and berries.

PASSBOUR COOLER

★★★☆☆

Glass: Collins
Garnish: Orange slice
Method: SHAKE all ingredients with ice and strain into ice-filled glass.

1½	shots	Maker's Mark bourbon
¾	shot	De Kuyper Cherry Brandy liqueur
¾	shot	Passoã passion fruit liqueur
3	shots	Ocean Spray cranberry juice

We say: Cherry and bourbon with passion fruit.

PASSION FRUIT CAIPRINHA

★★★★☆

Glass: Old-fashioned
Method: MUDDLE lime wedges in base of sturdy glass (being careful not to break the glass). Cut the passion fruit in half and scoop out the flesh into the glass. POUR cachaça and sugar syrup into glass, add crushed ice and CHURN (stir) with barspoon. Serve with straws.

1	fresh	Passion fruit
1	fresh	Lime
2	shots	Leblon cachaça
¾	shot	Monin Pure Cane 2:1 sugar syrup

We say: A tasty fruit Caipirinha. You may end up sipping this from the glass as the passion fruit pips tend to clog straws.

PASSION FRUIT COLLINS

★★★★☆

Glass: Collins
Garnish: Lemon slice
Method: Cut passion fruit in half and scoop out flesh into shaker. Add next three ingredients, SHAKE with ice and fine strain into ice-filled glass. TOP with soda, stir and serve with straws.

2	fresh	Passion fruit
2	shots	Tanqueray London dry gin
1½	shots	Freshly squeezed lemon juice
½	shot	Passion fruit syrup
Top up with		Soda (club soda)

We say: This fruity adaptation of the classic Collins may be a tad sharp for some: if so, add a dash more sugar.
Origin: Formula by Simon Difford in 2004.

PASSION FRUIT DAIQUIRI

★★★★☆

Glass: Martini
Garnish: Lime wedge
Method: Cut passion fruit in half and scoop out flesh into shaker. Add other ingredients, SHAKE with ice and fine strain into chilled glass.

2	fresh	Passion fruit
2	shots	Bacardi Superior rum
½	shot	Freshly squeezed lime juice
½	shot	Monin Pure Cane 2:1 sugar syrup

We say: The rum character comes through in this fruity cocktail.
Origin: Formula by Simon Difford in 2004.

PASSION FRUIT MARGARITA

★★★★☆

Glass: Coupette
Garnish: Salt rim & lime wedge
Method: Cut passion fruit in half and scoop out flesh into shaker. Add other ingredients, SHAKE with ice and fine strain into chilled glass.

1	fresh	Passion fruit
2	shots	Tequila 100% Agave
1	shot	Triple Sec
1	shot	Freshly squeezed lime juice
¼	shot	Passion fruit syrup

We say: The flavour of tequila is very evident in this fruity adaptation.
Origin: Formula by Simon Difford in 2004.

PASSION FRUIT MARTINI #1

★★★★☆

Glass: Martini
Garnish: Physalis (cape gooseberry)
Method: Cut passion fruit in half and scoop out flesh into shaker. Add other ingredients, SHAKE with ice and fine strain into chilled glass.

1	fresh	Passion fruit
2	shots	Ketel One vodka
½	shot	Monin Pure Cane 2:1 sugar syrup

We say: A simple but tasty cocktail that wonderfully harnesses the flavour of passion fruit.
Origin: Formula by Simon Difford in 2004.

PASSION FRUIT MARTINI #2

★★★★☆

Glass: Martini
Garnish: Star fruit
Method: Cut passion fruit in half and scoop out flesh into shaker. Add other ingredients, SHAKE with ice and fine strain into chilled glass.

2	fresh	Passion fruit
2	shots	Ketel One vodka
½	shot	Passion fruit syrup

We say: Not for Martini purists, but a fruity, easy drinking concoction for everyone else.
Origin: Formula by Simon Difford in 2004.

PASSION FRUIT MARTINI #3

★★★★☆

Glass: Martini
Garnish: Passion fruit
Method: Cut passion fruit in half and scoop out flesh into shaker. Add other ingredients, SHAKE with ice and fine strain into chilled glass.

2	fresh	Passion fruit
2	shots	Tanqueray London dry gin
½	shot	Triple Sec
¼	shot	Freshly squeezed lemon juice
½	shot	Passion fruit syrup

We say: Full-on passion fruit with gin and citrus hints.
Origin: Formula by Simon Difford in 2004.

PASSION KILLER

★★★☆☆

Glass: Shot
Garnish: None
Method: Refrigerate ingredients then LAYER in chilled glass by carefully pouring in the following order.

½	shot	Midori green melon liqueur
½	shot	Passoã passion fruit liqueur
½	shot	Tequila 100% Agave

We say: Tropical fruit and tequila.

PASSION PUNCH

★★★⯪☆

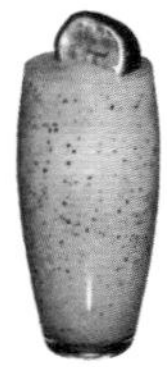

Glass: Collins
Garnish: Passion fruit
Method: Cut passion fruit in half and SCOOP flesh into blender. Add other ingredients and BLEND with 12oz scoop crushed ice. Serve with straws.

1	fresh	Passion fruits
2	shots	Tanqueray London dry gin
¼	shot	Cognac VSOP
¾	shot	Freshly squeezed lime juice
¾	shot	Monin Pure Cane 2:1 sugar syrup
2	dashes	Angostura aromatic bitters

We say: To quote the Trader, "A robust libation with the opulence of 'down under'."
Origin: Adapted from a recipe in the 1947-72 'Trader Vic's Bartender's Guide' by Victor Bergeron.

PASSIONATE RUM PUNCH

★★★★☆

Glass: Collins
Garnish: Passion fruit
Method: Cut passion fruit in half and scoop out flesh into shaker. Add other ingredients, SHAKE with ice and fine strain into glass filled with crushed ice.

3	fresh	Passion fruit
2¼	shots	Wray & Nephew overproof rum
¾	shot	Freshly squeezed lime juice
1	shot	Monin Pure Cane 2:1 sugar syrup
½	shot	Passion fruit syrup

We say: Rum and fruit combine brilliantly in this tropical punch-style drink.
Origin: Formula by Simon Difford in 2004.

PASSOVER

★★★☆☆

Glass: Collins
Garnish: Orange slice
Method: SHAKE all ingredients with ice and strain into ice-filled glass.

2	shots	Ketel One vodka
1	shot	Passoã passion fruit liqueur
3	shots	Freshly squeezed grapefruit juice

We say: Tropical and sweet.

PATRICK GAVIN DUFFY'S PUNCH

★★★⯪☆

Glass: Collins
Garnish: Mint sprig
Method: SHAKE all ingredients with ice and strain into ice-filled glass.

3	shots	Cognac VSOP
1½	shots	Bénédictine D.O.M.
¼	shot	Monin Pure Cane 2:1 sugar syrup
2½	shots	Freshly squeezed orange juice

We say: Over four shots of alcohol per serve means this sure packs a tasty punch.

PAVLOVA SHOT

★★★⯪☆

Glass: Shot
Garnish: None
Method: Refrigerate ingredients the LAYER in chilled glass by carefully pouring in the following order.

¾	shot	Chambord black raspberry liqueur
¾	shot	Ketel One vodka

We say: Pleasant, sweet shot.

PEACH DAIQUIRI

★★★★☆

Glass: Martini
Garnish: Peach slice
Method: SHAKE all ingredients with ice and fine strain into chilled glass.

2	shots	Bacardi Superior rum
1	shot	Peachtree peach schnapps
½	shot	Freshly squeezed lime juice
½	shot	Chilled mineral water

We say: A classic Daiquiri with hint of peach liqueur.
Origin: My take on the Cuban Daiquiri de Melocoton.

PEACH MELBA MARTINI

★★★⯪☆

Glass: Martini
Garnish: Flaked almonds
Method: SHAKE all ingredients with ice and fine strain into chilled glass.

1½	shots	Vanilla-infused Ketel One vodka
¾	shot	Peachtree peach schnapps
¾	shot	Chambord black raspberry liqueur
1	shot	Double (heavy) cream
1	shot	Milk

We say: Not quite Peach Melba dessert, but rich and tasty all the same.
Origin: Melba is a name given to various dishes dedicated to Dame Nellie Melba, the 19th century Australian opera singer. Peach Melba was created in 1892 by the world famous chef Georges-Auguste Escoffier, who was the business partner of César Ritz.

PEANUT BUTTER & JELLY SHOT

★★★☆☆

Glass: Shot
Garnish: None
Method: SHAKE all ingredients with ice and fine strain into a chilled glass.

½	shot	Baileys Irish cream liqueur
½	shot	Chambord black raspberry liqueur
½	shot	Hazelnut liqueur

We say: Does indeed taste a little like peanut butter and jelly (jam in the UK).

PEAR & CARDAMOM SIDECAR

★★★★⯪

Glass: Martini
Garnish: Pear slice
Method: MUDDLE cardamom in base of shaker. Add other ingredients, SHAKE with ice and fine strain into chilled glass.

2	whole	Cardamom pods
1	shot	Cognac VSOP
¾	shot	Triple Sec
¾	shot	Belle de Brillet pear liqueur
¾	shot	Freshly squeezed lemon juice
⅛	shot	Monin Pure Cane 2:1 sugar syrup
½	shot	Chilled mineral water

We say: A wonderful meld of aromatic ingredients.
Origin: Adapted from a drink created in 2002 by Jason Scott at Oloroso, Edinburgh, Scotland.

PEAR & ELDERFLOWER MARTINI

★★★★☆

Glass: Martini
Garnish: Pear slice
Method: SHAKE all ingredients with ice and fine strain into chilled glass.

2	shots	Ketel One vodka
¾	shot	St~Germain elderflower liqueur
1½	shots	Pressed pear juice

We say: Pear and elderflower are a match made in St. Martins Lane.
Origin: Created in 2001 by Angelo Vieira at St. Martins, London, England.

PEAR & VANILLA RICKEY

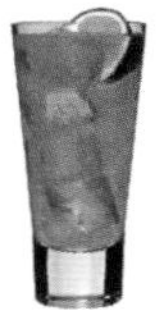

★★★⯪☆

Glass: Collins
Garnish: Lime wedge
Method: SHAKE first three ingredients with ice and strain into ice-filled glass. TOP with lemonade, lightly stir and serve with straws.

1	shot	Vanilla-infused Ketel One vodka
1	shot	Belle de Brillet pear liqueur
1	shot	Freshly squeezed lime juice
Top up with		Lemonade/Sprite/7-Up

We say: Vanilla and pear create a creamy mouthful cut by lime juice.

PEAR DROP

★★★⯪☆

Glass: Shot
Garnish: None
Method: SHAKE all ingredients with ice and fine strain into chilled glass.

½	shot	Ketel One Citroen vodka
½	shot	Kwai Feh lychee liqueur
½	shot	Belle de Brillet pear liqueur

We say: Sweet, sticky and strong.

PEAR DROP MARTINI

★★★★☆

Glass: Martini
Garnish: Pear Drop sweet
Method: SHAKE all ingredients with ice and fine strain into chilled glass.

1¼	shots	Belle de Brillet pear liqueur
1	shot	Poire William eau de vie
1	shot	Limoncello liqueur
1	shot	Pressed pear juice

We say: Not as sticky as the sweet it takes its name from but full-on tangy pear.
Origin: Created in 2002 by Simon Difford.

PEARLINSTRUM NEW

★★★★☆

Glass: Coupette
Garnish: Lime zest twist
Method: SHAKE all ingredients with ice and fine strain into chilled glass.

1½	shots	Ketel One vodka
1½	shot s	Pear flavoured vodka
½	shot	St-Germain elderflower liqueur
½	shot	Martini Extra Dry vermouth

We say: A delicate harmony of pear and elderflower given depth with vermouth and fortified with vodka.
Origin: Created in 2012 by Simon Difford at the Cabinet Room, London, England.

PEAR MARTINI

★★★★☆

Glass: Martini
Garnish: Pear slice
Method: SHAKE all ingredients with ice and fine strain into chilled glass.

1½	shots	Pear flavoured vodka
1½	shots	St~Germain elderflower liqueur
⅛	shot	Martini Extra Dry vermouth

We say: Aromatic pear vodka and floral elderflower liqueur are a match made in heaven. Vermouth adds complexity.

PEAR SHAPED #1 (DELUXE VERSION)

★★★★☆

Glass: Martini
Garnish: Pear slice
Method: Cut passion fruit in half and scoop out flesh into base of shaker. Add other ingredients, SHAKE with ice and fine strain into chilled glass.

1	fresh	Passion fruit
1½	shots	Dewar's White label Scotch
1	shot	Belle de Brillet pear liqueur
1	shot	Pressed apple juice
1	shot	Pressed pear juice
¼	shot	Freshly squeezed lime juice

We say: Wonderful balance of flavours but pear predominates with a dry yet floral finish.

PEAR SHAPED #2 (POPULAR VERSION)

★★★★☆

Glass: Collins
Garnish: Pear slice
Method: SHAKE all ingredients with ice and strain into ice-filled glass.

2	shots	Dewar's White label Scotch
1	shot	Cognac VSOP
3	shots	Pressed apple juice
½	shot	Freshly squeezed lime juice
¼	shot	Monin Vanilla sugar syrup

We say: Scotch, pear and apple combine wonderfully in this medium-sweet long drink.
Origin: Adapted from a drink created in 2003 by Jamie Terrell at Dick's Bar, Atlantic, London, England.

PEAR TREE COCKTAIL

★★★★☆

Glass: Martini
Garnish: Pear slice
Method: SHAKE first two ingredients with ice and fine strain into chilled glass. TOP with champagne.

1½	shots	Pear flavoured vodka
1½	shots	St~Germain elderflower liqueur
Top up with		Brut champagne

We say: Aromatic pear vodka and elderflower liqueur paired with biscuity champagne.

PEDRO COLLINS

★★★★☆

Glass: Collins
Garnish: Orange slice & cherry on stick (sail)
Method: SHAKE first three ingredients with ice and strain into ice-filled glass. TOP with soda, lightly stir and serve with straws.

2	shots	Bacardi Superior rum
1	shot	Freshly squeezed lime juice
½	shot	Monin Pure Cane 2:1 sugar syrup
Top up with		Soda (club soda)

We say: This rum based Tom Collins is basically a long Daiquiri with soda.

PEGGY MARTINI

★★★☆☆

Glass: Martini
Garnish: Orange zest twist
Method: SHAKE all ingredients with ice and fine strain into chilled glass.

2	shots	Tanqueray London dry gin
1	shot	Martini Extra Dry vermouth
¼	shot	Absinthe
¼	shot	Dubonnet Red (French made)
½	shot	Chilled mineral water

We say: Very dry and aromatic.
Origin: Adapted from a reciepe in the 1930s edition of the 'Savoy Cocktail Book' by Harry Craddock

PEGU CLUB #1

★★★★☆

Glass: Martini
Garnish: Lime wedge
Method: SHAKE all ingredients with ice and fine strain into chilled glass.

2	shots	Tanqueray London dry gin
1	shot	Triple Sec
½	shot	Freshly squeezed lime juice
¼	shot	Monin Pure Cane 2:1 sugar syrup
1	dash	Angostura aromatic bitters
1	dash	Orange bitters
½	shot	Chilled mineral water

We say: I've added a dash of sugar to the original recipe to reduce the tartness of this gin based Margarita-like concoction.
Origin: Created in the 1920s at the Pegu Club, an expat gentlemen's club in British colonial Rangoon, Burma. The recipe was first published in Harry MacElhone's 1927 'Barflies and Cocktails'. In his seminal 1930 Savoy Cocktail, Harry Craddock notes of this drink, "The favourite cocktail at the Pegu Club, Burma, and one that has travelled, and is asked for, round the world."

PEGU CLUB #2 NEW

★★★★½

Glass: Martini
Garnish: Lime wedge
Method: SHAKE all ingredients with ice and fine strain into chilled glass.

2	shots	Tanqueray London dry gin
1	shot	Grand Marnier liqueur
½	shot	Freshly squeezed lime juice
1	dash	Angostura aromatic bitters
1	dash	Orange bitters
½	shot	Chilled mineral water

We say: This version of the Burmese classic is richer in orange.

PEGU NUMBER TWO (AKA. PEGU IN PINK)

★★★★☆

Glass: Coupette
Method: POUR absinthe into ice-filled glass, TOP with water and leave to stand. Separately SHAKE rest of ingredients with ice. DISCARD contents of glass (absinthe, water and ice) and fine STRAIN contents of shaker into ice-filled absinthe-coated glass.

½	shot	Absinthe
2	shots	Tanqueray London dry gin
¾	shot	Freshly squeezed lime juice
¾	shot	Curaçao orange liqueur
⅛	shot	Campari Bitter
⅛	shot	Luxardo Maraschino liqueur

We say: Some big, bold, flavours are corralled in this twist on the classic Pegu Club replacing the usual bitters for a Campari/maraschino/absinthe combo.
Origin: Adapted from a drink created in 2008 by Julian de Feral at Bureau, London, England.

STAR RATINGS EXPLAINED

★★★★★ Excellent

★★★★½ Recommended   ★★★★☆ Praiseworthy
★★★½☆ Commended   ★★★☆☆ Mediocre
★★½☆☆ Disappointing   ★★☆☆☆ Pretty awful
★½☆☆☆ Shameful   ★☆☆☆☆ Disgusting

PENDENNIS COCKTAIL

★★★★☆

Glass: Martini
Garnish: Maraschino cherry
Method: SHAKE all ingredients with ice and fine strain into chilled glass.

2	shots	Tanqueray London dry gin
1	shot	De Kuyper Apricot Brandy liqueur
½	shot	Freshly squeezed lime juice
1	dash	Peychaud's aromatic bitters
¾	shot	Chilled mineral water

We say: Tangy, subtle, sweet, and sour.
Origin: This classic is named after the Pendinnis Club in Louisville, Kentucky, which is popularly supposed to be the birthplace of the Old-Fashioned.

PENICILLIN

★★★★½

Glass: Old-fashioned
Garnish: Candied ginger
Method: SHAKE all ingredients with ice and strain into ice-filled glass.

1	shot	Dewar's White label Scotch
1	shot	Lagavulin 16yo malt whisky
¼	shot	Domaine de Canton ginger liqueur
¾	shot	Freshly squeezed lemon juice
½	shot	Monin Honey syrup

We say: Smoke and honey with subtle spice and plenty of Scottish attitude.
Origin: Adapted from a recipe by Sam Ross at Milk & Honey, New York City, USA.

PENTHOUSE COCKTAIL NEW

★★★★☆

Glass: Coupette
Garnish: Maraschino cherry
Method: SHAKE all ingredients with ice and fine strain into chilled glass.

2	shots	Maker's Mark bourbon
¼	shot	Luxardo maraschino liqueur
¾	shot	Freshly squeezed lime juice
½	shot	Monin Pure Cane 2:1 sugar syrup

We say: A bourbon sour with a touch of maraschino adding an almondy cherry note.
Origin: Created by Carl Wrangel at the Oak Room, Copenhagen, Denmark.

PEPIN RIVERO SPECIAL

★★★½☆

Glass: Coupette
Garnish: Chocolate powder rim
Method: SHAKE all ingredients with ice and fine strain into chilled glass.

1½	shots	Tanqueray London dry gin
1	shot	White Crème de Cacao
1	shot	Milk

We say: White chocolate come coconut ice-cream, only vaguely rescued from fluffiness by gin spirit.
Origin: Created by Constantino (Constante) Ribalaigua Vert at the Floridita bar in Havana, Cuba. This recipe is adapted from a 1937 Bar Florida (later renamed Floridita) menu. The name refers to Pepin Rivero, who took over the Cuban El Diario de la Marina newspaper upon the death of his father Don Nicolas Rivero in 1944.

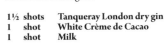

PEPPER & VANILLA'TINI

★★★★⯪

Glass: Martini
Garnish: Yellow pepper strip
Method: SHAKE all ingredients with ice and fine strain into chilled glass.

1	shot	Vanilla-infused Ketel One vodka
¾	shot	Pepper-infused Ketel One vodka
¾	shot	Tuaca liqueur
1	shot	Cuarenta y Tres (Licor 43) liqueur
1	shot	Yellow bell pepper juice

We say: Vanilla and pepper seem to complement each other in a sweet and sour kind of way.
Origin: Formula by Simon Difford in 2002.

PEPPERED MARY

★★★★☆

Glass: Collins
Garnish: Peppered rim & cherry tomato
Method: SHAKE all ingredients with ice and strain into ice-filled glass.

2	shots	Pepper-infused Ketel One vodka
2	shots	Yellow bell pepper juice
2	shots	Tomato juice
½	shot	Freshly squeezed lemon juice
7	drops	Tabasco hot pepper sauce
1	spoon	Worcestershire sauce

We say: Hot and sweet pepper spice in this Bloody Mary.
Origin: Created in 2003 by Simon Difford.

PEPPERMINT VANILLA DAIQUIRI

★★★☆☆

Glass: Old-fashioned
Garnish: Mint sprig
Method: SHAKE all ingredients with ice and strain into glass filled with crushed ice.

2	shots	Bacardi Superior rum
¼	shot	Galliano L'Autentico liqueur
¼	shot	Giffard Menthe Pastille liqueur
½	shot	Freshly squeezed lime juice
⅛	shot	Monin Pure Cane 2:1 sugar syrup

We say: An intriguing combination for folk who want their Daiquiris served 'fresh'.
Origin: Discovered in 2005 at Bellini, Auckland, New Zealand.

PERFECT ALIBI

★★★★☆

Glass: Martini
Garnish: Mint leaf
Method: MUDDLE ginger in base of shaker. Add other ingredients, SHAKE with ice and fine strain into ice-filled glass.

2	inch	Fresh root ginger (thumbnail sized)
½	shot	Krupnik spiced honey liqueur
1½	shots	Bärenjäger honey liqueur
½	shot	Monin Pure Cane 2:1 sugar syrup
3	shots	Cold jasmine tea

We say: A very unusual and pleasant mix of flavours.
Origin: Created in 2001 by Douglas Ankrah for Akbar, London, England.

PERFECT FAIRY NEW

★★★⯪☆

Glass: Wine Glass
Garnish: Freshly grated nutmeg
Method: BLEND all ingredients with one 12oz scoop crushed ice and serve.

1	shot	La Fée Parisienne (68%) absinthe
1	shot	Crème de pêche de vigne liqueur
1	shot	Freshly squeezed lemon juice
1	fresh	Egg white

We say: This white drink with the merest tint of absinthe green balances lemon, peach liqueur and lemon juice, rounded and made fluffy with egg white.
Origin: Adapted from a drink created in 2011 by Charles Vexenat for Pernod Absinthe.

PERFECT GUEST NEW

★★★★⯪

Glass: Coupette
Garnish: Lemon zest twist
Method: STIR all ingredients with ice and strain into chilled glass.

1½	shots	Ketel One vodka
⅔	shot	Lillet Blanc
⅓	shot	St-Germain elderflower liqueur
1	dash	Celery bitters

We say: Clean grainy vodka forms the back bone of this floral and herbal delicate dessert Vodkatini-style drink.
Origin: Created by Giuseppe Santamaria during for the Spanish World Class 2012 bartender's competition.

PERFECT JOHN

★★★★☆

Glass: Martini
Garnish: Orange zest twist
Method: SHAKE all ingredients with ice and fine strain into chilled glass.

1	shot	Ketel One vodka
¾	shot	Triple Sec
¼	shot	Galliano L'Autentico liqueur
1½	shots	Freshly squeezed orange juice

We say: A straight up Harvey Wallbanger with Cointreau.

STAR RATINGS EXPLAINED

★★★★★ Excellent

★★★★⯪ Recommended   ★★★★☆ Praiseworthy
★★★⯪☆ Commended   ★★★☆☆ Mediocre
★★⯪☆☆ Disappointing   ★★☆☆☆ Pretty awful
★⯪☆☆☆ Shameful   ★☆☆☆☆ Disgusting

PERFECT LADY UPDATED

★★★★⯪

Glass: Martini
Garnish: Lemon zest twist (discarded) & peach slice
Method: SHAKE all ingredients with ice and fine strain into chilled glass.

2	shots	Tanqueray London dry gin
¾	shot	Crème de pêche de vigne liqueur
¾	shot	Freshly squeezed lemon juice
½	fresh	Egg white

We say: This twist on a White Lady uses peach liqueur in place of triple sec to make a lighter, fruitier elaboration.
Origin: Created in 1936 by Sidney Cox, a bartender at the Grosvenor House, London for The British Empire Cocktail Competition where it took the 1st Prize. That same year a constitutional crisis in the British Empire was caused by King-Emperor Edward VIII's proposal to marry Wallis Simpson, a twice-divorced American socialite. Religious, legal, political, and moral objections were raised due to Mrs Simpson being twice divorced and the marriage was opposed by the King's governments in the United Kingdom and the autonomous Dominions of the British Commonwealth. Despite the opposition, Edward declared his love for Mrs Simpson and his refusal to give her up led to his abdication in December 1936.

He was succeeded by his brother Albert, who took the regal name George VI. Disgraced due to renouncing the throne, Edward was given the title His Royal Highness the Duke of Windsor. He married Mrs Simpson the following year and they remained married until his death 35 years later. She was obviously his 'Perfect Lady'.

PERFECT REGENT XV

★★★★⯪

Glass: Coupette
Garnish: Seasonal berries
Method: SHAKE all ingredients with ice and fine strain into chilled glass.

2	shots	Cognac VSOP
¼	shot	Martini Rosso sweet vermouth
¼	shot	Martini Extra Dry vermouth
½	shot	Crème de cassis liqueur

We say: Fruity and easy - perhaps not what you would expect.
Origin: Recipe adapted in 2008 by Simon Difford for Courvoisier.

PERFECT SUMMIT MANHATTAN UPDATED

★★★★★

Glass: Coupette
Garnish: Maraschino cherry
Method: STIR all ingredients with ice and strain into a chilled glass.

2½	shot	Maker's Mark bourbon
¾	shot	Noilly Prat dry vermouth
¾	shot	Muscat wine (Chambers preferred)
⅛	shot	Orange curaçao liqueur
2 drops		Fee Brothers Aged Whisky bitters

We say: A riff on a Dry Manhattan given extra depth by the addition of dessert wine and whiskey bitters.
Origin: Adapted from a recipe by Pilar Zeglin, Summit Restaurant Bar, Cincinnati, USA and courtesy of Courtesy of Ardent Spirits.

PERIODISTA DAIQUIRI

★★★★☆

Glass: Martini
Garnish: Lime wedge
Method: SHAKE all ingredients with ice and fine strain into chilled glass.

1½	shots	Bacardi Superior rum
½	shot	Grand Marnier liqueur
½	shot	De Kuyper Apricot Brandy liqueur
½	shot	Freshly squeezed lime juice
½	shot	Chilled mineral water

We say: Basically an orange and apricot Daiquiri.

PERISCOPE

★★★★★

Glass: Martini
Garnish: Grapefruit zest twist
Method: SHAKE all ingredients with ice and fine strain into chilled glass.

1½	shots	Tanqueray London dry gin
1	shot	St~Germain elderflower liqueur
⅛	shot	Freshly squeezed lemon juice
⅛	shot	Freshly squeezed lime juice
½	fresh	Egg white

Variant: Serve in an ice-filled Collins glass and top with soda.
We say: Fabulously light, almost creamy, and refreshing.
Origin: Created by Matt Gee at Milk & Honey, New York City, USA.

PERNELLE

★★★★⯪

Glass: Collins
Garnish: Lemon zest twist & rosemary sprig
Method: SHAKE first four ingredients with ice and strain into glass filled with crushed ice. TOP with soda and serve with straws.

1	shot	Ketel One vodka
1	shot	St~Germain elderflower liqueur
1	shot	Poire William eau de vie
1	shot	Freshly squeezed lemon juice
Top up with		Soda (club soda)

We say: This long clear drink has a grassy, alpine aroma and a fresh pine finish.
Origin: Created in 2007 by Colin Asare-Appiah, London, England for U'Luvka vodka. Named after 14th century alchemist Nicolas Flamel's wife.

PERNOD & BLACK MARTINI

★★★★☆

Glass: Martini
Garnish: Blackberries
Method: MUDDLE blackberries in base of shaker. Add other ingredients, SHAKE with ice and fine strain into a chilled glass.

7	fresh	Blackberries
½	shot	Pernod anise
1½	shots	Ketel One vodka
½	shot	Crème de Mûre liqueur
1	shot	Freshly squeezed lime juice
⅛	shot	Monin Vanilla sugar syrup
¾	shot	Chilled mineral water

We say: Pernod enhances the rich, tart flavours of blackberry.
Origin: Created in 2003 by Simon Difford.

PERONI NEGRONI

★★★½☆

Glass: Shot and Beer
Garnish: None
Method: STIR gin, Campari and vermouth with ice and fine strain into chilled shot glass. Carefully position the shot glass in the beer glass. Then carefully POUR Peroni into beer glass so not quite reaching the top of the shot glass, being careful not to splash any beer into shot glass. Instruct drinker to drink from beer glass and so inevitably also shot glass. Use sturdy glassware.

½	shot	Tanqueray London dry gin
½	shot	Campari Bitter
½	shot	Martini Rosso sweet vermouth
⅛	bottle	Peroni lager

We say: Negroni is a great chaser to beer so why not consume in unison.
Origin: Created by the team at 8 Bar, Falmouth, Cornwall.

PERPETUAL COCKTAIL

★★★★★½

Glass: Coupette
Garnish: Orange zest twist
Method: SHAKE all ingredients with ice and fine strain into chilled glass.

1	shot	Martini Rosso sweet vermouth
1	shot	Martini Extra Dry vermouth
½	shot	Benoit Serres créme de violette
¼	shot	White Crème de Cacao

We say: A tad on the sweet side and flavoured with chocolate, red berries and violets over a base of sweet and dry vermouth.
Origin: Recipe adapted from Hugo R. Ensslin's 1917 book 'Recipes for Mixed Drinks'.

PERROQUET

★★★☆☆

Glass: Collins
Garnish: None
Method: POUR pastis and mint syrup into glass. Serve iced water separately in small jug (known in France as a 'broc') so the customer can dilute to their own taste (I recommend five shots). Lastly, add ice to fill glass.

1	shot	Ricard Pastis
¼	shot	Mint (menthe) syrup
Top up with		Chilled mineral water

We say: The traditional French café drink with a hint of sweet mint.
Origin: Very popular throughout France, this drink is named after the parrot die to the bird's brightly coloured plumage.

PERRY-TINI

★★★★☆

Glass: Martini
Garnish: Pear slice
Method: SHAKE first three ingredients with ice and fine strain into chilled glass. TOP with champagne.

1	shot	Poire William eau de vie
1	shot	Belle de Brillet pear liqueur
2	shots	Pressed pear juice
Top up with		Brut champagne

We say: Pear with a hint of sparkle.
Origin: Created in 2002 by Simon Difford.

PERUVIAN ELDER SOUR

★★★★½

Glass: Martini
Garnish: Lime wedge
Method: SHAKE all ingredients with ice and fine strain into chilled glass.

2	shots	Barsol Quebranta pisco
1	shot	St~Germain elderflower liqueur
½	shot	Freshly squeezed lime juice

We say: This tasty sour combines the aromatics of pisco and elderflower in an intriguing variation on the Margarita. Consider smoothing with fresh egg white.
Origin: Drinks writer Gary Regan created this in 2006 in New York, USA.

PETER PAN MARTINI #1

★★★☆☆

Glass: Martini
Garnish: Orange zest twist
Method: SHAKE all ingredients with ice and fine strain into chilled glass.

1	shot	Tanqueray London dry gin
1	shot	Martini Extra Dry vermouth
1	shot	Freshly squeezed orange juice
3	dashes	Peach bitters

Variant: Substitute Angostura aromatic bitters for peach bitters.
We say: Smoother, lighter and easier than most classic cocktails - perhaps a little too much so.
Origin: Adapted from a recipe in the 1930 edition of the 'Savoy Cocktail Book' by Harry Craddock. The original recipe called for equal parts, including the bitters - surely a mistake

BARTENDER'S TIP DRY SHAKE

It is common practice to first shake drinks containing cream and eggs without ice, then to shake the drink a second time with ice added.

This practice is known as 'dry shaking' and the theory is that first shaking without ice, and so at a higher temperature, better allows the drink to emulsify.

PETER PAN MARTINI #2

★★★☆☆

Glass: Martini
Garnish: Orange zest twist
Method: SHAKE all ingredients with ice and fine strain into chilled glass.

2	shots	**Tanqueray London dry gin**
1	shot	**Martini Extra Dry vermouth**
1	shot	**Freshly squeezed orange juice**
3	dashes	**Peach bitters**

We say: Orange predominates in this complex cocktail.
Origin: Adapted from a recipe in the 1930 edition of the *'Savoy Cocktail Book'* by Harry Craddock.

PETO MARTINI

★★★★½

Glass: Martini
Garnish: Orange zest twist
Method: SHAKE all ingredients with ice and fine strain into chilled glass.

2	shots	**Tanqueray London dry gin**
1	shot	**Martini Extra Dry vermouth**
1	shot	**Martini Rosso sweet vermouth**
¼	shot	**Freshly squeezed orange juice**
⅛	shot	**Luxardo Maraschino liqueur**

We say: An aromatic classic Martini served 'perfect' with a hint of orange juice and maraschino.
Origin: Adapted from a recipe in the 1930 edition of the *'Savoy Cocktail Book'* by Harry Craddock.

PETRUCHIO COCKTAIL

★★★★☆

Glass: Coupette
Garnish: None
Method: SHAKE all ingredients with ice and fine strain into chilled glass.

1	shot	**Tanqueray London dry gin**
1	shot	**Aperol**
½	shot	**Freshly squeezed lemon juice**
¼	shot	**Monin Pure Cane 2:1 sugar syrup**
2	dashes	**Orange bitters**
1	fresh	**Egg white**

We say: Gin-based and bitter-sweet, this bright orange drink has a foamy head which may mislead some into thinking it is sweet and easy.
Origin: Created in 2010 by Jamie Boudreau at Vessel, Seattle, USA

PHARMACEUTICAL STIMULANT

★★★★☆

Glass: Medical cup or Old-fashioned
Garnish: Coffee beans
Method: SHAKE all ingredients with ice and strain into ice-filled glass.

2	shots	**Ketel One vodka**
½	shot	**Kahlúa coffee liqueur**
¼	shot	**Monin Pure Cane 2:1 sugar syrup**
1½	shots	**Hot espresso coffee**

We say: A real wake-up call and the drink that lead to many an Espresso Martini.
Origin: Created in 1998 by Dick Bradsell at The Pharmacy, London, England.

PHISH HOOK NEW

★★★★☆

Glass: Coupette
Garnish: None
Method: STIR all ingredients with ice and fine strain into glass.

2	shots	**Straight rye whiskey**
½	shot	**St~Germain elderflower liqueur**
¼	shot	**Carpano Punt E Mes**
⅛	shot	**Luxardo Maraschino liqueur**

We say: Rye whiskey tamed and flavoured by elderflower, Punt E Mes and maraschino.
Origin: Adapted from a January 2010 recipe courtesy of Jamie Boudreau's spiritsandcocktails.wordpress.com

PIÑA COLADA #1

★★★★½

Glass: Pineapple shell (frozen)
Garnish: Pineapple wedge & maraschino cherry
Method: BLEND all ingredients with one 12oz scoop crushed ice & serve with straws.

2	shots	**Bacardi Oro golden rum**
4	shots	**Fresh pressed pineapple juice**
1	shot	**Coco López cream of coconut**
1	shot	**Double (heavy) cream**
1	pinch	**Salt**

We say: A wonderful creamy, fruity concoction that's not half as sticky as the world would have you believe. Too much ice will detract from the creaminess and kill the drink.
Origin: The name 'Piña Colada' literally means 'strained pineapple', a reference to the freshly pressed and strained pineapple juice used in the drink's preparation.

Three Puerto Rican bartenders contest the ownership of their country's national drink. Ramon 'Monchito' Marrero Pérez claims to have first made it at the Caribe Hilton Hotel's Beachcomber Bar in San Juan on 15th August 1952, using the then newly available Coco Lopez cream of coconut. Ricardo Garcia, who also worked at the Caribe, says that it was he who invented the drink. And Ramon Portas Mingot says he created it

BARTENDER'S TIP LAYER

As the name would suggest, layered drinks include layers of different ingredients, often with contrasting colours.

This effect is achieved by carefully pouring each ingredient into the glass so that it floats on its predecessor. The success of this technique is dependent on the density (specific gravity) of the liquids used. As a rule of thumb, the less alcohol and the more sugar an ingredient contains, the heavier it is. The heaviest ingredients should be poured first and the lightest last.

in 1963 at the Barrachina Restaurant, 104 Fortaleza Street, Old San Juan - the restaurant stands by his claim to this day.

Truth is rum, pineapple and coconut have been mixed together pretty much since rum was first distilled and the first written reference to a Piña Colada was in 1922. However, this recipe did not include coconut and was more a shaken Pineapple Daiquiri made with Bacardi Rum, pineapple juice, lime and sugar - now commonly referred to as a 'Cuban'-style Piña Colada' but perhaps more befitting the name 'strained pineapple' drink than most people consider a 'Piña Colada' today.

So the Puerto Ricans merely added cream of coconut and it is commonly accepted that the modern Piña Colada was adapted from an existing creation at the Caribe Hilton Hotel. Like the Barrachina Restaurant, the hotel has since promoted itself as the home of the Piña Colada and today credits Ramon Marrero Pérez with its invention.

The Caribe Hilton Hotel sits on a 17-acre peninsula outside San Juan and was the first luxury hotel to open in the region, becoming a popular destination for the rich and famous who helped spread word of the drink. Today, the hotel is more 'package tourist' than luxurious and you may prefer the Conrad Hilton across the causeway which traverses the lagoon - we certainly preferred the latter's Piña Colada, which is served Cuban' style.

To make a 'Puerto Rican'-style Piña Colada you'll need a sticky goo called 'cream of coconut', not be confused with coconut cream. Cream of coconut is made by mixing coconut juice, sugar, emulsifier, cellulose, thickeners, citric acid and salt and is sold in 15oz/425ml cans which make 14 to 25 drinks depending on how sweet you like your Piña Coladas. Once opened the can's contents should be stored in a refrigerator: this may thicken the product, so gentle warming may be required prior to use.

The original brand of cream of coconut is Coco Lopez' which was developed in 1948 in Puerto Rico by Don Ramon Lopez-Irizarry - hence the Puerto Rican connection and the believable 1952 date for the creation of the modern day Piña Colada at the Caribe Hilton Hotel. Some say the drink did not acquire its name until the 1960s - perhaps that's where Ramon Portas Mingot and the Barrachina restaurant come into play. It seems there's a day for everything and American readers may want to mark their diaries with National Piña Colada Day which is celebrated each 10th July.

PIÑA COLADA #2 (CUBAN STYLE)

★★★★☆

Glass: Pineapple shell (frozen)
Garnish: Lime wedge
Method: SHAKE all ingredients with ice and strain into ice-filled glass.

2 shots Bacardi 8yo aged rum
4 shots Fresh pressed pineapple juice
¼ shot Freshly squeezed lime juice
¼ shot Monin Pure Cane 2:1 sugar syrup

We say: This Colada has no coconut, but it is smooth, balanced and rather tasty.
Origin: The name 'Piña Colada' literally means 'strained pineapple', a reference to the freshly pressed and strained pineapple juice used in this drink's preparation. The first written reference to a Piña Colada was in 1922 and this recipe was simply shaken Bacardi Rum, pineapple juice, lime and sugar - what we now refer to as a 'Cuban-style Piña Colada' - one without the addition of coconut.

PIÑA COLADA VIRGIN (MOCKTAIL)

★★★☆☆

Glass: Hurricane
Garnish: Pineapple wedge & maraschino cherry
Method: BLEND all ingredients with 18oz of crushed ice and serve with straws.

4 shots Fresh pressed pineapple juice
1½ shots Coco López cream of coconut
¾ shot Double (heavy) cream
¾ shot Milk

AKA: Snow White
We say: A Piña Colada with its guts ripped out.

PIÑA MARTINI

★★★★☆

Glass: Martini
Garnish: Pineapple wedge
Method: SHAKE all ingredients with ice and fine strain into chilled glass.

2 shots Ketel One vodka
1¾ shots Fresh pressed pineapple juice
¼ shot Freshly squeezed lime juice
⅛ shot Monin Pure Cane 2:1 sugar syrup

We say: Rich pineapple but not too sweet.
Origin: Created in 2005 by Simon Difford.

PICADOR

★★★★★

Glass: Martini
Garnish: Lime zest twist
Method: SHAKE all ingredients with ice and fine strain into chilled glass.

2 shots Tequila 100% Agave
1 shot Triple Sec
1 shot Freshly squeezed lime juice

We say: The name might be more masculine but it still tastes just like a classic Margarita.
Origin: Yes, you're right! This drink is exactly the same as a classically proportioned Margarita. It was published in W. J. Tarling's 1937 *Cafe Royal Cocktail Book*, 16 years before the first written reference to a Margarita. Conjecture suggests that this British recipe was copied by whichever American gave the Margarita its name?

PICCA

★★★★☆

Glass: Martini
Garnish: Maraschino cherry
Method: SHAKE all ingredients with ice and fine strain into chilled glass.

1½ shots Dewar's White label Scotch
1 shot Galliano L'Autentico liqueur
1 shot Martini Rosso sweet vermouth
¾ shot Chilled mineral water

We say: Bittersweet whisky.

PICCADILLY MARTINI

★★★★½

Glass: Martini
Garnish: Lemon zest twist
Method: SHAKE all ingredients with ice and fine strain into chilled glass.

2 shots Tanqueray London dry gin
1 shot Martini Extra Dry vermouth
⅛ shot Absinthe
⅛ shot Pomegranate (grenadine) syrup

We say: A classic Martini tempered by a hint of pomegranate and absinthe.
Origin: Adapted from a recipe in the 1930 edition of the *'Savoy Cocktail Book'* by Harry Craddock.

PICHUNCHO MARTINI

Glass: Martini
Garnish: Orange zest twist
Method: SHAKE all ingredients with ice and fine strain into chilled glass.

2¼	shots	Macchu pisco
1½	shots	Martini Rosso sweet vermouth
¼	shot	Monin Pure Cane 2:1 sugar syrup

We say: This drink craves the best pisco and the best sweet vermouth. Find those and measure carefully and it's sublime.
Origin: Based on the traditional Chilean drink: pisco and vermouth served on the rocks.

THE [PICK OF] DESTINY UPDATED

Glass: Martini
Garnish: Orange zest twist
Method: SHAKE all ingredients with ice and fine strain into chilled glass.

2	shots	Bonded straight rye whiskey
1	shot	St-Germain elderflower liqueur
¾	shot	Freshly squeezed orange juice
3 dash Orange bitters		

We say: Fresh floral orange - just picked.
Origin: Adapted from a drink created in 2007 by Amanda Washington at Rye, San Francisco, USA.

PICKLE BACK

Glass: Shot
Garnish: None
Method: POUR ingredients into two separate chilled glasses. Instruct drinker to drink whiskey followed by cucumber chaser.

| 1 | shot | Jameson Irish whiskey |
| 1 | shot | Pickle brine |

We say: Now, I do like a juicy wally (gherkin) with my cod'n'chips but necking the brine in which they are packed is another thing. Our American cousins have some strange habits - drive on the right, carry the ball when playing football and bowl underarm. So these eccentricities should be remembered when I tell you that the drinking of cucumber brine is popular in New York City.
Origin: Created in 2006 at Brooklyn's Bushwick Country Club after the neighbouring business, McClure's Pickles, stored some of their pickles in the bar's basement.

    Apparently this inspired bartender, Reggie Cunningham, to serve Old Crow Bourbon with a shot of McClure's spicy pickle brine. The Ruotolo brother took the drink to their Whiskey Town in New York's East Village with Jameson replacing the Bourbon.

PIERRE COLLINS

Glass: Collins
Garnish: Orange slice & cherry on stick (sail)
Method: SHAKE first three ingredients with ice and strain into ice-filled glass. TOP with soda, lightly stir and serve with straws.

2	shots	Cognac VSOP
1	shot	Freshly squeezed lemon juice
½	shot	Monin Pure Cane 2:1 sugar syrup
Top up with	Soda (club soda)	

We say: A Tom Collins made with cognac. The cognac's character shines through.

PILGRIM COCKTAIL

Glass: Martini
Garnish: Dust with grated nutmeg
Method: SHAKE all ingredients with ice and fine strain into chilled glass.

1½	shots	Bacardi Oro golden rum
½	shot	Grand Marnier liqueur
1	shot	Freshly squeezed orange juice
¾	shot	Freshly squeezed lime juice
¼	shot	Berry Hill pimento allspice liqueur
3	dashes	Angostura aromatic bitters

Variant: Can also be served hot by simmering ingredients gently in a saucepan.
We say: Whether you serve this hot or cold, it's a delicately spiced drink to warm the cockles.

PIMM'S COCKTAIL

Glass: Martini
Garnish: Lemon & orange zest twists
Method: SHAKE first four ingredients with ice and strain into chilled glass. TOP with champagne.

2	shots	Pimm's No.1 Cup
½	shot	Tanqueray London dry gin
¼	shot	Freshly squeezed lemon juice
¼	shot	Monin Pure Cane 2:1 sugar syrup
Top up with	Brut champagne	

We say: Luxuriate in this quintessentially English tipple.

PIMM'S CUP (OR CLASSIC PIMM'S)

Glass: Collins
Garnish: Mint sprig
Method: POUR Pimm's into glass half filled with ice. Add fruit and fill glass with more ice. TOP with lemonade (or ginger ale), lightly stir and serve with straws.

2	shots	Pimm's No.1 Cup
1	slice	Fresh orange
1	slice	Lemon
1	slice	Cucumber (chopped & peeled)
1	fresh	Strawberries (hulled)
Top up with	Lemonade/Sprite/7-Up	

We say: You've not properly experienced an English summer until you've drunk one of these whilst sheltering from the rain.
Origin: This quintessential English summer tipple is usually accredited to James Pimm, who in 1823-4 began trading as a shellfish-monger in London's Lombard Street. He later moved to nearby number 3 Poultry,

also in the City of London, where he established Pimm's Oyster Warehouse. It is here, in 1840, that he is said to have first served this drink. Others dispute this, maintaining that James Pimm only unwittingly lent his name to the drink. They say the true credit lies with his successor, Samuel Morey, who is recorded as having taken out a retail liquor licence in 1860. This would appear to be when the oyster bar first offered its customers spirits. Many establishments of the day mixed house spirits to serve with liqueurs and juices as 'cups', in reference to the tankards in which they were sold. Naturally the 'cup' made at Pimm's Oyster Bar was named after the establishment which retained the goodwill of its founder. Pimm's restaurant became very popular and changed hands a couple more times. Eventually Horatio David Davies, a wine merchant and owner of cafes in London bought the business. He became Sir Horatio, a Member of Parliament and between 1897-1898, Lord Mayor of London. He formed Pimm's into a private company in 1906, which, was controlled by family trusts for another 57 years after his death. The precise date that the drink Pimm's was first sold outside restaurants and bars controlled by the Pimm's company is unknown. However, it is certain that the original product, No.1, was based on gin and flavoured with numerous botanicals including quinine. A second Pimm's product based on Scotch (Pimm's No.2 Cup) was launched and a third (Pimm's No.3 Cup) was based on brandy. Pimm's became popular in Britain in the 1920s and took off internationally after the Second World War. Other versions were then introduced: Pimm's No.4 based on rum, Pimm's No.6 on vodka and Pimm's No.7 on rye whiskey.

PIMM'S ROYALE

★★☆☆☆

Glass: Flute
Garnish: Seasonal berries & cucumber peel
Method: POUR Pimm's into chilled glass and TOP with champagne.

1	shot	Pimm's No.1 Cup
Top up with		Brut champagne

We say: Dry, subtle and refreshing.

PINEAPPLE & CARDAMOM DAIQUIRI

★★★★☆

Glass: Martini
Garnish: Pineapple wedge
Method: MUDDLE cardamom in base of shaker. Add other ingredients, SHAKE with ice and fine strain into chilled glass.

4	whole	Cardamom pods
2	shots	Bacardi Superior rum
1¾	shots	Fresh pressed pineapple juice
¼	shot	Freshly squeezed lime juice
¼	shot	Monin Pure Cane 2:1 sugar syrup

We say: One of the tastiest Daiquiris I've tried.
Origin: Adapted from Herny Besant's Pineapple & Cardamom Martini

PINEAPPLE & CARDAMOM MARTINI

★★★★★

Glass: Martini
Garnish: Pineapple wedge
Method: MUDDLE cardamom in base of shaker. Add other ingredients, SHAKE with ice and fine strain into a chilled glass.

4	whole	Cardamom pods
2	shots	Ketel One vodka
2	shots	Fresh pressed pineapple juice
¼	shot	Monin Pure Cane 2:1 sugar syrup

We say: This is about as good as it gets: a spectacular pairing of fruit and spice.
Origin: Created in 2002 by Henry Besant at The Lonsdale, London, England.

PINEAPPLE & GINGER MARTINI

★★★★☆

Glass: Martini
Garnish: Pineapple wedge
Method: MUDDLE ginger in base of shaker. Add other ingredients, SHAKE with ice and fine strain into chilled glass.

2	slices	Fresh root ginger (thumbnail sized)
2	shots	Ketel One vodka
2	shots	Fresh pressed pineapple juice
⅛	shot	Monin Pure Cane 2:1 sugar syrup

We say: Smooth, rich pineapple flavour with hints of vodka and ginger

PINEAPPLE & SAGE MARGARITA

★★★★☆

Glass: Coupette
Garnish: Pineapple wedge
Method: Lightly MUDDLE sage in base of shaker. Add other ingredients, SHAKE with ice and fine strain into chilled glass.

5	fresh	Sage leaves
2	shots	Tequila 100% Agave
1	shot	Fresh pressed pineapple juice
½	shot	Freshly squeezed lime juice
¼	shot	Agave nectar

We say: Herbal tequila and sweet pineapple in harmony.
Origin: Adapted from a drink created in 2005 at Green & Red Bar London, England.

PINEAPPLE BLOSSOM ⚷

★★★★☆

Glass: Martini
Garnish: Pineapple wedge
Method: SHAKE all ingredients with ice and fine strain into chilled glass.

2	shots	Dewar's White label Scotch
1	shot	Fresh pressed pineapple juice
½	shot	Freshly squeezed lemon juice
½	shot	Monin Pure Cane 2:1 sugar syrup

We say: Richly flavoured but drier than you might expect.
Origin: My interpretation of a classic.

PINEAPPLE DAIQUIRI #1 ⚷
(ON-THE-ROCKS)

★★★★☆

Glass: Old-fashioned
Garnish: Pineapple wedge & maraschino cherry
Method: SHAKE all ingredients with ice and fine strain into ice-filled glass.

2	shots	Bacardi Superior rum
1	shot	Fresh pressed pineapple juice
½	shot	Freshly squeezed lime juice
¼	shot	Monin Pure Cane 2:1 sugar syrup

We say: Rum and pineapple are just meant to go together.
Origin: Formula by Simon Difford.

PINEAPPLE DAIQUIRI #2 (FROZEN)

★★★★½

Glass: Martini (large 10oz)
Garnish: Pineapple wedge & maraschino cherry
Method: BLEND all ingredients with a 12oz scoops crushed ice. Served heaped in the glass and with straws.

2	shots	Bacardi Superior rum
1½	shots	Fresh pressed pineapple juice
½	shot	Freshly squeezed lime juice
¾	shot	Monin Pure Cane 2:1 sugar syrup

We say: Fluffy but very tasty.
Origin: Formula by Simon Difford.

PINEAPPLE FIX

★★★★☆

Glass: Old-fashioned
Garnish: Pineapple wedge
Method: SHAKE all ingredients with ice and strain into ice-filled glass.

2	shots	Bacardi 8yo aged rum
1	shot	Fresh pressed pineapple juice
1	shot	Freshly squeezed lemon juice
½	shot	Monin Pure Cane 2:1 sugar syrup

We say: Rum and pineapple are a match made in heaven, here with lemon adding citrus freshness.

PINEAPPLE FIZZ

★★★★★

Glass: Collins
Garnish: Lime wedge & maraschino cherry
Method: SHAKE first four ingredients with ice and fine strain into chilled glass. TOP with soda, lightly stir and serve with straws.

2	shots	Bacardi Oro golden rum
1½	shots	Fresh pressed pineapple juice
1	shot	Freshly squeezed lime juice
½	shot	Monin Pure Cane 2:1 sugar syrup
Top up with		Soda (club soda)

We say: A Pineapple Daiquiri lengthened with soda. Surprisingly tasty and refreshing.

PINEAPPLE LASSI COCKTAIL NEW

★★★★☆

Glass: Coupette
Garnish: Pineapple wedge
Method: MUDDLE cardamom and then pineapple in base of shaker. ADD other ingredients, SHAKE with ice and fine strain into chilled glass.

3	whole	Cardamom pod
3	wedge	Pineapple (fresh)
1½	shots	Ketel One vodka
1½	shots	Bols Natural Yoghurt liqueur

We say: Creamy yoghurty cardamom and pineapple laced with vodka.
Origin: Created in 2011 by Simon Difford at the Cabinet Room, London, England.

PINEAPPLE MARGARITA

★★★★☆

Glass: Coupette
Garnish: Pineapple wedge
Method: SHAKE all ingredients with ice and fine strain into chilled glass.

2	shots	Tequila 100% Agave
¾	shot	Triple Sec
1½	shots	Fresh pressed pineapple juice

Variant: Add half a shot of pineapple syrup, blend with 12oz scoop of crushed ice and serve frozen.
We say: A Tequila Margarita with a pineapple fruit kick

PINEAPPLE MOJITO

★★★★½

Glass: Collins
Method: Lightly MUDDLE mint (just to bruise) in glass. POUR other ingredients into glass and half fill with crushed ice. CHURN (stir) with barspoon. Fill glass with more crushed ice and churn.

12	fresh	Mint leaves
2	shots	Bacardi Superior rum
¾	shot	Cuarenta y Tres (Licor 43) liqueur
2	shots	Fresh pressed pineapple juice
1	shot	Freshly squeezed lime juice

We say: A fruity, vanilla-ed twist on the classic Mojito
Origin: Discovered in 2003 at Apartment 195, London, England.

PINEAPPLE SMOOTHIE (MOCKTAIL)

★★★½☆

Glass: Collins
Garnish: Pineapple wedge
Method: BLEND all the ingredients with 12oz scoop crushed ice. Serve with straws.

2	spoons	Natural yoghurt
2	spoons	Runny honey
4	shots	Fresh pressed pineapple juice

We say: Fluffy in every sense of the word.

PINI

★★★★½

Glass: Martini
Garnish: Maraschino cherry
Method: SHAKE all ingredients with ice and fine strain into chilled glass.

2	shots	Macchu pisco
½	shot	Cognac VSOP
¼	shot	White Crème de Cacao
¼	shot	Monin Pure Cane 2:1 sugar syrup
½	shot	Chilled mineral water

We say: Use a great pisco and you'll have a wonderfully complex drink.

STAR RATINGS EXPLAINED

★★★★★ Excellent

★★★★½ Recommended	★★★★☆ Praiseworthy
★★★½☆ Commended	★★★☆☆ Mediocre
★★½☆☆ Disappointing	★★☆☆☆ Pretty awful
★½☆☆☆ Shameful	★☆☆☆☆ Disgusting

PINK CHIHUAHUA NEW

★★★★⯨

Glass: Coupette
Garnish: Lime wedge on rim
Method: SHAKE all ingredients with ice and

2	shots	Tequila 100% Agave (blanco)
½	shot	Freshly squeezed lime juice
¼	shot	Freshly squeezed lemon juice
½	shot	Pomegranate (grenadine) syrup
½	fresh	Egg white

We say: Yes, this appropriately named drink is pink and fluffy, due to being sweetened with pomegranate syrup in place of triple sec and given a foamy head by the addition of egg white.
Origin: Created in 2011 by Dick Bradsell at The Pink Chihuahua At El Camion, London, England. This fluffy little pink drink is named after the smallest breed of dog and also referenced the state of Chihuahua in Mexico. At El Camion the front door of the Pink Chihuahua bar is painted with an artist's impression of a Pink Chihuahua.

PINK CLOUD

★★★☆☆

Glass: Martini
Garnish: None
Method: SHAKE all ingredients with ice and fine strain into chilled glass.

1	shot	Amaretto liqueur
1	shot	Pomegranate (grenadine) syrup
1	shot	White Crème de Cacao
¾	shot	Evaporated milk (sweetened)

We say: To make this sweet after dinner drink I've used amaretto and pomegranate syrup in place of créme de noyaux. This almond flavoured liqueur made from apricot and peach stones is not currently available in the UK. US readers should use 2 shots of créme de noyaux in place of the first two ingredients.
Origin: Adapted from a recipe in the 1947-72 'Trader Vic's Bartender's Guide' by Victor Bergeron.

PINK DAIQUIRI

★★★★☆

Glass: Martini
Garnish: Lime wedge
Method: SHAKE all ingredients with ice and fine strain into chilled glass.

2	shots	Bacardi Superior rum
½	shot	Pomegranate (grenadine) syrup
¼	shot	Luxardo Maraschino liqueur
½	shot	Freshly squeezed lime juice
3	dashes	Angostura aromatic bitters
½	shot	Chilled mineral water

AKA: Daiquiri No.5
We say: The quality of the pomegranate syrup will make or break this delicate Daiquiri.
Origin: A classic from the 1930s

PINK FLAMINGO

★★★☆☆

Glass: Collins
Garnish: Apple slice
Method: SHAKE all ingredients with ice and strain into ice-filled glass.

2	shots	Ketel One vodka
1	shot	Sour apple liqueur
½	shot	Freshly squeezed lime juice
1	shot	Ocean Spray cranberry juice

We say: Soapy and citrus flavoured - but in a nice way.
Origin: Created in 2002 by Wayne Collins for Maxxium UK.

PINK GIN UPDATED

★★★★☆

Glass: Martini
Garnish: Lemon zest twist
Method: STIR all ingredients with ice and fine strain into chilled glass.

2	shots	Tanqueray London dry gin
1	shot	Chilled mineral water
2	dashes	Angostura aromatic bitters

We say: Normally I'd advocate liberal use of bitters but this refined and subtle drink benefits from frugality.
Origin: Gin was a favourite of the Royal Navy - along with rum, which was served as a daily ration right up until the 70s. It was often mixed with healthy ingredients to make them more palatable. Pink gin was originally used against stomach upsets, as Angostura aromatic bitters were considered medicinal. Traditionally this drink was made in a bitters swashed glass without the use of ice.

PINK GIN & TONIC

★★★★☆

Glass: Collins
Garnish: Lime slice
Method: POUR gin and Angostura bitters into ice-filled glass, TOP with tonic, lightly STIR and serve with straws.

2	shots	Tanqueray London dry gin
4	dashes	Angostura aromatic bitters
Top up with		Tonic water

We say: Basically a G&T with an extra pep of flavour from Angostura, this has a wider appeal than the original Pink Gin.

PINK GRAPEFRUIT MARGARITA

★★★★☆

Glass: Coupette
Garnish: Lime wedge
Method: SHAKE all ingredients with ice and fine strain into chilled glass

2	shots	Tequila 100% Agave
1	shot	Freshly squeezed grapefruit juice
½	shot	Freshly squeezed lime juice
¼	shot	Monin Pure Cane 2:1 sugar syrup

We say: Delivers exactly what the name promises

PINK HOUND

★★★★☆

Glass: Martini
Garnish: Lemon zest twist
Method: SHAKE all ingredients with ice and fine strain into chilled glass.

2	shots	Tanqueray London dry gin
1½	shots	Freshly squeezed grapefruit juice
¼	shot	Pomegranate (grenadine) syrup

We say: A flavoursome balance of sweet and sour.

PINK LADY

★★★★½

Glass: Martini
Garnish: Maraschino cherry
Method: SHAKE all ingredients with ice and fine strain into chilled glass.

2	shots	Tanqueray London dry gin
½	shot	Freshly squeezed lemon juice
¼	shot	Pomegranate (grenadine) syrup
½	fresh	Egg white

Variant: With the addition of half a shot apple brandy.
We say: Despite the colour, this sharp and alcoholic.
Origin: A classic cocktail named after a successful 1912 stage play.

PINK LEMONADE (MOCKTAIL)

★★★☆☆

Glass: Collins
Garnish: Lemon slice
Method: SHAKE first three ingredients with ice and strain into ice-filled glass. TOP with soda and serve with straws.

2	shots	Freshly squeezed lemon juice
¼	shot	Monin Pure Cane 2:1 sugar syrup
½	shot	Pomegranate (grenadine) syrup
Top up with		Soda (club soda)

We say: A tall, pink, tangy alcohol free cocktail.
Origin: Discovered in 2004 in New York City.

PINK PALACE

★★★★½

Glass: Martini
Garnish: Lemon zest twist
Method: SHAKE all ingredients with ice and fine strain into chilled glass.

2	shots	Tanqueray London dry gin
½	shot	Grand Marnier liqueur
½	shot	Freshly squeezed lime juice
¼	shot	Pomegranate (grenadine) syrup

We say: A great drink but rarely done justice at the Polo Lounge.
Origin: The signature drink at the Polo Lounge, Beverly Hills Hotel, Los Angeles, USA. The hotel, which is lovingly termed the 'Pink Palace' inspired The Eagles' Hotel California and graces the album cover.

PINK SIN MARTINI

★★★☆☆

Glass: Martini
Garnish: Dust with cinnamon powder
Method: SHAKE all ingredients with ice and fine strain into chilled glass.

1½	shots	Ketel One vodka
1	shot	White Crème de Cacao
¾	shot	Goldschläger cinnamon schnapps
1	shot	Ocean Spray cranberry juice

We say: This looks a little like a Cosmo but delivers sweet cinnamon and chocolate.

PINK SQUIRREL

★★★☆☆

Glass: Martini
Garnish: Mint leaf
Method: SHAKE all ingredients with ice and fine strain into chilled glass.

1	shot	Crème de noyaux liqueur
1	shot	White Crème de Cacao
½	shot	Double (heavy) cream
½	shot	Milk

We say: Crème de noyaux, a pink almond liqueur, is now very hard to obtain: if in doubt, substitute with amaretto and grenadine.
Origin: Adapted from Victor Bergeron's '*Trader Vic's Bartender's Guide*' (1972 revised edition).

PINK TUTU

★★★½☆

Glass: Old-fashioned
Garnish: Orange slice
Method: SHAKE all ingredients with ice and strain into ice-filled glass.

1	shot	Peachtree peach schnapps
½	shot	Ketel One vodka
½	shot	Campari Bitter
1½	shots	Freshly squeezed grapefruit juice
¼	shot	Monin Pure Cane 2:1 sugar syrup

We say: A cocktail that's both bitter and sweet.
Origin: Created in 1999 by Dominique of Café Rouge, Leeds, England.

PINKY PINCHER

★★★★☆

Glass: Old-fashioned
Garnish: Mint sprig, orange & lemon slices
Method: SHAKE all ingredients with ice and strain into ice-filled glass.

2	shots	Maker's Mark bourbon
1	shot	Freshly squeezed orange juice
1	shot	Freshly squeezed lemon juice
¼	shot	Monin Pure Cane 2:1 sugar syrup
¼	shot	Monin Almond (orgeat) syrup

We say: Fruity, sweetened bourbon.
Origin: Adapted from a drink created by Victor Bergeron (Trader Vic).

PINO PEPE

★★★★☆

Glass: Pineapple shell (frozen)
Garnish: Mint sprig
Method: BLEND all ingredients with 12oz scoop crushed ice. POUR into glass (or pineapple shell) and serve with straws. If using a pineapple shell, serve with ice cubes.

1	shot	Bacardi Superior rum
1	shot	Ketel One vodka
½	shot	Triple Sec
2	shots	Fresh pressed pineapple juice
½	shot	Freshly squeezed lime juice
¼	shot	Freshly squeezed lemon juice
½	shot	Monin Pure Cane 2:1 sugar syrup

We say: To quote Trader Vic, "Lethal but smooth - pineapple at its best".
Origin: Adapted from a recipe in the 1947-72 '*Trader Vic's Bartender's Guide*' by Victor Bergeron.

PIRATE DAIQUIRI

★★★★☆

Glass: Martini
Garnish: Lime wedge
Method: SHAKE all ingredients with ice and fine strain into chilled glass.

¾	shot	Wray & Nephew overproof rum
¾	shot	Pusser's Navy rum
½	shot	Goldschläger cinnamon schnapps
½	shot	Freshly squeezed lime juice
¼	shot	Pomegranate (grenadine) syrup
¾	shot	Chilled mineral water

We say: Why the name? Well, the rums are hard and nautical, the lime protects against scurvy, the liqueur contains gold and the syrup is red as blood.
Origin: Created in 2004 by Simon Difford.

PISCO BELL RINGER NEW

★★★★☆

Glass: Coupette
Garnish: None
Method: RINSE chilled glass with apricot brandy (swirl liqueur round inside of glass to coat and then shake out excess). SHAKE other ingredients with ice and fine strain into apricot rinsed glass.

⅛	shot	De Kuyper Apricot Brandy liqueur
2	shots	Macchu pisco
½	shot	Freshly squeezed lemon juice
¼	shot	Monin Pure Cane 2:1 sugar syrup
1	dash	Orange bitters
2	dashes	Peychaud's aromatic bitters

We say: Go easy on the bitters and this will be a delicate, aromatic pisco cocktail.
Origin: Yet again I must thanks drinks historian David Wondrich for unearthing this drink and its history. It was created by a bartender named Jim Maloney and first appeared in his 1903 '*How to Mix Drinks*'. Maloney patented the name 'Bell-Ringers' as referring to cocktails served in glasses rinsed with apricot brandy.

PISCO COLLINS

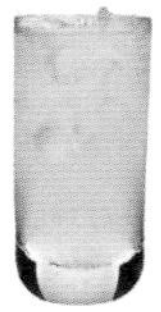

★★★★☆

Glass: Collins
Garnish: Orange slice & cherry on stick (sail)
Method: SHAKE first three ingredients with ice and strain into ice-filled glass. TOP with soda, lightly stir and serve with straws.

2	shots	Macchu pisco
1	shot	Freshly squeezed lime juice
½	shot	Monin Pure Cane 2:1 sugar syrup
Top up with		Soda (club soda)

We say: The most aromatic and flavoursome of the Collins family.

PISCO NARANJA

★★★½☆

Glass: Collins
Garnish: Orange slice
Method: SHAKE all ingredients with ice and strain into ice-filled glass.

2	shots	Macchu pisco
1	shot	Grand Marnier liqueur
3	shots	Freshly squeezed orange juice

We say: Aromatic brandy and orange juice pepped and sweetened with a slug of orange liqueur.
Origin: I based this recipe on the traditional Chilean combination of pisco and orange juice.

PISCO PUNCH #1 (DIFFORD'S FORMULA)

★★★★½

Glass: Collins
Garnish: Pineapple wedge
Method: MUDDLE cloves in base of shaker. ADD other ingredients except for champagne. SHAKE with ice and strain into ice-filled glass. TOP with champagne.

4	dried	Clove
2¼	shots	Macchu pisco
1¾	shots	Fresh pressed pineapple juice
¼	shot	Freshly squeezed orange juice
½	shot	Freshly squeezed lemon juice
½	shot	Monin Pure Cane 2:1 sugar syrup
Top up with		Brut champagne

Variant: This recipe is improved by using the marinade prescribed in Alfredo Micheli's Pisco Punch in place of sugar syrup. If using the marinade drop one of the marinated pineapple wedges and cloves into the drink as the garnish.
We say: A tangy, balanced combination of rich flavours. The quality of pisco used is crucial to the success of a Pisco Punch.
Origin: Created in 2003 by Simon Difford.

PISCO PUNCH #2 (ALFREDO MICHELI'S FORMULA)

★★★★★

Glass: Goblet
Garnish: Pineapple wedge
Method: MUDDLE orange and pineapple in base of shaker. ADD pisco and pineapple marinade. SHAKE with ice and fine strain into ice-filled glass. TOP with no more than two shots of soda water.

2	slices	Fresh orange
3	fresh	Marinated pineapple wedges
2	shots	Macchu pisco
¾	shot	Pineapple marinade
Top up with		Soda (club soda)

We say: This subtly flavoured drink is justifiably legendary.
Recipe for marinade: Core and remove the rind from one ripe pineapple. Cut the pineapple into rings and then into wedges and place in a deep container. Add 30 cloves and one litre of sugar syrup and marinate for 24 hours.
Origin: Alfredo Micheli (who went by the nickname Mike) was employed at the Bank Exchange and spied on Duncan Nichol to learn how to make this legendary drink. After he believed he'd learnt the secret he left to start serving at a newly opened competitor to the Bank Exchange, Paoli's on Montgomery Street.

PISCO PUNCH #3 (LANES' FORMULA)

★★★★☆

Glass: Collins
Garnish: Pineapple wedge
Method: SHAKE first four ingredients with ice and strain into glass filled with crushed ice. TOP with soda, lightly stir and serve with straws.

2½	shots	Macchu pisco
½	shot	Freshly squeezed lemon juice
1	shot	Fresh pressed pineapple juice
½	shot	Monin Pure Cane 2:1 sugar syrup
Top up with		Soda (club soda)

We say: Pisco's character comes through the fruit in this long, refreshing classic.
Origin: This recipe is said to hail from John Lanes, manager of the famous Bank Exchange when it closed in 1919.

PISCO PUNCH #4 (PROSSER'S FORMULA)

★★★★★

Glass: Martini
Garnish: White grapes
Method: MUDDLE grapes in base of shaker. Add other ingredients, SHAKE with ice and fine strain into chilled glass.

20	fresh	Seedless white grapes
2½	shots	Macchu pisco
1	shot	Fresh pressed pineapple juice
⅛	shot	Absinthe

We say: An aromatic take on the Pisco Punch.
Origin: Jack Koeppler, the bartender at the Buena Vista Café in San Francisco who's also famous for being the first bartender in America to serve Irish Coffee, was given this recipe by the son of it's creator, a fellow San Franciscan by the name of Mr Prosser. I've adapted this recipe from his, which originally comprised: 2 shots white grape juice, 2 shots pisco, 1 spoon pineapple juice and 1 spoon absinthe.

PISCO SOUR (DIFFORD'S FORMULA)

★★★★★

Glass: Old-fashioned
Garnish: Three drops of Angostura bitters
Method: SHAKE all ingredients with ice and fine strain into chilled glass.

2½	shots	Macchu pisco
1	shot	Freshly squeezed lime juice
½	shot	Monin Pure Cane 2:1 sugar syrup
½	fresh	Egg white
1	dash	Orange flower water

We say: Traditionally this is drunk is blended with crushed ice, but I prefer it served straight-up. Be sure to drink it quickly while it's cold.
Origin: My adaptation of the Chilean and Peruvian classic.

PISCO SOUR (TRADITIONAL RECIPE)

★★★★⯪

Glass: Goblet
Garnish: Three drops of Angostura bitters
Method: BLEND all ingredients with 12oz scoop crushed ice and serve with straws.

2	shots	Macchu pisco
1	shot	Freshly squeezed lime juice
1	shot	Monin Pure Cane 2:1 sugar syrup
½	fresh	Egg white

Variant: Dust with cinnamon powder.
We say: One of the few really brilliant blended drinks.
Origin: The national drink of both Peru and Chile and both countries lay claim to the origins of the drink and the spirit it is made from. The Pisco Sour is said to have been created in the early 1920s at Bar Morris located, 847 Calle Boza, Jiron de la Union, Lima, Peru. The drinks recent popularity outside of its native Peru and Chile is attributed to Joe Baum who promoted the drink in the 1960s at La Fonda Del Sol in New York.

PISCOLA

★★★⯪☆

Glass: Collins
Garnish: Lime wedge
Method: POUR pisco and bitters into ice-filled glass, top with cola, stir and serve with straws.

2½	shots	Macchu pisco
3	dashes	Angostura aromatic bitters
Top up with		Coca-Cola

We say: A 'brandy' and cola with a hint of angostura bitters. Try and see why the Chileans enjoy it.
Origin: A popular long drink in its native Chile.

STAR RATINGS EXPLAINED

★★★★★ Excellent

★★★★⯪ Recommended	★★★★☆ Praiseworthy
★★★⯪☆ Commended	★★★☆☆ Mediocre
★★⯪☆☆ Disappointing	★★☆☆☆ Pretty awful
★⯪☆☆☆ Shameful	★☆☆☆☆ Disgusting

PLANTATION PUNCH

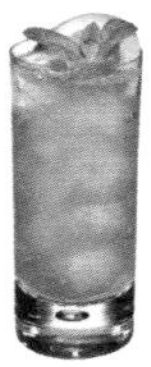

★★★½☆

Glass: Collins
Garnish: Orange slice & mint sprig
Method: SHAKE first five ingredients with ice and strain into ice-filled glass. TOP with soda.

1	shot	Bacardi Superior rum
1½	shots	Southern Comfort liqueur
¾	shot	Freshly squeezed lemon juice
¼	shot	Monin Pure Cane 2:1 sugar syrup
2	dashes	Angostura aromatic bitters
Top up with		Soda (club soda)

We say: Southern Comfort drives this tropical punch.

PLANTER'S PUNCH

★★★★☆

Glass: Collins
Garnish: Orange slice & mint sprig
Method: SHAKE all ingredients with ice and strain into ice-filled glass.

1½	shots	Myer's dark Jamaican rum
1	shot	Freshly squeezed lime juice
½	shot	Monin Pure Cane 2:1 sugar syrup
3	dashes	Angostura aromatic bitters
2	shots	Chilled mineral water

We say: A tangy punch which harnesses the rich flavours of Myers's rum.
Origin: Invented in the late 19th century by the founder of Myers's rum, Fred L. Myers. The recipe on the back of each bottles is known as the 'Old Plantation formula' and uses classic rum punch proportions of 1 sour (lime), 2 sweet (sugar), 3 strong (rum) and 4 weak (water). Rather than this or the American formula (1 sour, 2 sweet, 3 weak, and 4 strong), I've followed David A. Embury's recommendation of 1 sweet, 2 sour, 3 strong and 4 weak.

PLANTER'S PUNCHLESS (MOCKTAIL)

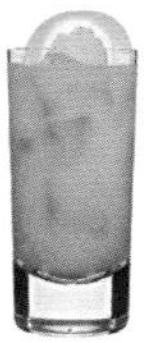

★★★☆☆

Glass: Collins
Garnish: Lime wedge
Method: SHAKE first three ingredients with ice and strain into ice-filled glass. TOP with lemonade, lightly stir and serve with straws.

2	shots	Pressed apple juice
¾	shot	Freshly squeezed lime juice
¼	shot	Pomegranate (grenadine) syrup
Top up with		Lemonade/Sprite/7-Up

We say: A pleasant, if uninspiring, driver's option.

PLANTEUR

★★★★☆

Glass: Collins
Garnish: Orange slice
Method: SHAKE all ingredients with ice and strain into ice-filled glass.

2	shots	Martinique agricole rum
¼	shot	Pomegranate (grenadine) syrup
3½	shots	Freshly squeezed orange juice

We say: Handle with extreme care.

PLATINUM BLONDE

★★★½☆

Glass: Martini
Garnish: Dust with grated nutmeg
Method: SHAKE all ingredients with ice and fine strain into chilled glass.

1½	shots	Bacardi 8yo aged rum
1½	shots	Grand Marnier liqueur
½	shot	Double (heavy) cream
½	shot	Milk

We say: An after dinner sipper.

PLAYA DEL MAR

★★★★☆

Glass: Martini
Garnish: Pineapple wedge
Method: SHAKE all ingredients with ice and fine strain into chilled glass.

1	shot	Tequila 100% Agave
½	shot	Triple Sec
1	shot	Ocean Spray cranberry juice
¾	shot	Fresh pressed pineapple juice
½	shot	Freshly squeezed lime juice
¼	shot	Monin Pure Cane 2:1 sugar syrup

We say: A fruity complex taste with a hint of tequila.
Origin: This cocktail was created in 1997 by Wayne Collins at Navajo Joe, London, England. The name translate as a 'Beach of the Sea'.

PLAYMATE MARTINI

★★★★½

Glass: Martini
Garnish: Orange zest twist
Method: SHAKE all ingredients with ice and fine strain into chilled glass.

1	shot	Cognac VSOP
1	shot	Grand Marnier liqueur
1	shot	De Kuyper Apricot Brandy liqueur
1	shot	Freshly squeezed orange juice
½	fresh	Egg white
3	dashes	Angostura aromatic bitters

We say: Smooth and easy drinking.

PLEASED AS PUNCH NEW

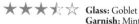

★★★½☆

Glass: Goblet
Garnish: Mint sprig
Method: SHAKE first five ingredients with ice and fine strain into ice-filled glass. TOP with champagne and lightly stir.

1	shot	Ketel One Citroen vodka
½	shot	St-Germain elderflower liqueur
¾	shot	Freshly squeezed lemon juice
¼	shot	Monin Pure Cane 2:1 sugar syrup
5	fresh	Mint leaves
Top up with		Brut champagne

We say: Refreshing lemony citrus with a splash of elderflower liqueur, enlivened with champagne.
Origin: Adapted from a drink created in 2012 by Chris Hopkins, USA.

PLUM COCKTAIL

★★★½☆

Glass: Martini
Garnish: Plum slice
Method: CUT plum into quarters, remove stone and peel. MUDDLE plum in base of shaker. Add other ingredients, SHAKE with ice and fine strain into chilled glass.

1	fresh	Plum (stoned, peeled & chopped)
2	shots	Slivovitz plum brandy
¼	shot	Martini Extra Dry vermouth
¼	shot	Monin Pure Cane 2:1 sugar syrup

We say: The slivovitz adds woody, brandied notes to the plum.
Origin: Formula by Simon Difford in 2004.

PLUM DAIQUIRI

★★★★☆

Glass: Martini
Garnish: Lime wedge
Method: CUT plum into quarters, remove stone and peel. MUDDLE plum in base of shaker. Add other ingredients, SHAKE with ice and fine strain into chilled glass.

1	fresh	Plum (stoned, peeled & chopped)
2	shots	Bacardi Superior rum
½	shot	Freshly squeezed lime juice
½	shot	Monin Pure Cane 2:1 sugar syrup

We say: Depending on the ripeness of the plums, you may need to adjust the quantity of sugar.
Origin: Formula by Simon Difford in 2004.

PLUM MARTINI

★★★★☆

Glass: Martini
Garnish: Plum slice
Method: CUT plum into quarters, remove stone and peel. MUDDLE plum in base of shaker. Add other ingredients, SHAKE with ice and fine strain into chilled glass.

1	fresh	Plum (stoned, peeled & chopped)
2	shots	Ketel One vodka
¾	shot	Martini Extra Dry vermouth
½	shot	Monin Pure Cane 2:1 sugar syrup

Variant: Substitute vanilla sugar syrup for plain sugar syrup.
We say: Fortified plum juice in a Martini glass.
Origin: Formula by Simon Difford in 2004.

PLUM PUDDING MARTINI

★★★½☆

Glass: Martini
Garnish: Dust with grated nutmeg
Method: CUT plum into quarters, remove stone and peel. MUDDLE plum in base of shaker. Add other ingredients, SHAKE with ice and fine strain into chilled glass.

1	fresh	Plum (stoned, peeled & chopped)
1	shot	Raspberry flavoured vodka
1	shot	Vanilla-infused Ketel One vodka
½	shot	Amaretto liqueur
⅛	shot	Goldschläger cinnamon schnapps

We say: Spicy and fruity.
Origin: Created in 2004 by Simon Difford.

PLUM SOUR

★★★★☆

Glass: Old-fashioned
Garnish: Orange zest twist
Method: MUDDLE plum in base of shaker. Add other ingredients, SHAKE with ice and fine strain into ice-filled glass.

1	fresh	Plum (stoned, peeled & chopped)
2	shots	Ketel One vodka
1	shot	Freshly squeezed lemon juice
½	shot	Monin Pure Cane 2:1 sugar syrup
½	fresh	Egg white

We say: Soft, ripe plums are key to this fruity sour.

POET'S DREAM

★★★★½

Glass: Martini
Garnish: Lemon zest twist
Method: STIR all ingredients with ice and strain into chilled glass.

1	shot	Tanqueray London dry gin
1	shot	Bénédictine D.O.M.
1	shot	Martini Extra Dry vermouth
¾	shot	Chilled mineral water

We say: Subtle, honeyed and herbal.
Origin: Adapted from an original recipe in the 1949 edition of 'Esquire's Handbook for Hosts'.

POGO STICK

★★★★☆

Glass: Martini
Garnish: Mint sprig
Method: BLEND all ingredients with 12oz scoop crushed ice. Serve with straws.

2	shots	Tanqueray London dry gin
½	shot	Fresh pressed pineapple juice
½	shot	Freshly squeezed grapefruit juice
½	shot	Freshly squeezed lime juice
½	shot	Monin Pure Cane 2:1 sugar syrup

We say: To quote Trader Vic, "A refreshing blend of gin with pineapple and grapefruit juice... a real romper".
Origin: Adapted from a recipe in the 1947-72 'Trader Vic's Bartender's Guide' by Victor Bergeron.

POINSETTIA

★★★½☆

Glass: Flute
Garnish: Orange slice
Method: POUR first two ingredients into chilled glass. TOP with champagne.

½	shot	Triple Sec
1	shot	Ocean Spray cranberry juice
Top up with		Brut champagne

We say: Fruity champagne.

POLISH MARTINI

★★★★★

Glass: Martini
Garnish: Apple slice
Method: SHAKE all ingredients with ice and fine strain into chilled glass.

¾	shot	Ketel One vodka
¾	shot	Żubrówka bison vodka
¾	shot	Krupnik spiced honey liqueur
¾	shot	Pressed apple juice

We say: Bison vodka and apple juice are a classic comb, here also an additional splash of Polish honey liqueur.
Origin: Created by Dick Bradsell, for his (Polish) father-in-law, Victor Sarge.

POLLY'S SPECIAL

★★★★☆

Glass: Martini
Garnish: Grapefruit wedge
Method: SHAKE all ingredients with ice and fine strain into chilled glass.

2	shots	Dewar's White label Scotch
1	shot	Freshly squeezed grapefruit juice
1	shot	Grand Marnier liqueur
⅛	shot	Monin Pure Cane 2:1 sugar syrup

We say: Sweet, sour, flavoursome and balanced.
Origin: Adapted from a recipe in the 1947-72 *Trader Vic's Bartender's Guide* by Victor Bergeron.

POMEGRANATE BELLINI

★★★½☆

Glass: Flute
Garnish: None
Method: SHAKE first three ingredients with ice and fine strain into chilled glass. TOP with sparkling wine.

1	shot	Pomegranate juice
½	shot	Cuarenta y Tres (Licor 43) liqueur
⅛	shot	Freshly squeezed lemon juice
Top up with		Prosecco sparkling wine

We say: This red drink is drier and more adult than it looks.
Origin: Created in 2005 by Simon Difford.

POMEGRANATE MARGARITA

★★★★½

Glass: Coupette
Garnish: Lime wedge
Method: SHAKE all ingredients with ice and fine strain into chilled glass.

2	shots	Tequila 100% Agave
1	shot	Pomegranate juice
¼	shot	Pomegranate (grenadine) syrup
½	shot	Freshly squeezed lime juice

We say: Pomegranate and tequila combine harmoniously in this Margarita.
Origin: Recipe by Simon Difford in 2006.

POMEGRANATE MARTINI

★★★★½

Glass: Martini
Garnish: Orange zest twist
Method: SHAKE all ingredients with ice and fine strain into chilled glass.

2	shots	Ketel One vodka
1½	shots	Pomegranate juice
½	shot	Pomegranate (grenadine) syrup

We say: This drink was originally based on gin but I find that the juniper and pomegranate clash.
Origin: Adapted from a drink discovered in 2005 at Lotus Bar, Sydney, Australia.

POMME ET SUREAU

★★★★½

Glass: Collins
Garnish: Apple wedge
Method: POUR first two ingredients into ice-filled glass. TOP with soda.

1	shot	Calvados/Applejack brandy
2	shots	St~Germain elderflower liqueur
Top up with		Soda (club soda)

We say: Light, long and refreshing apple and elderflower.
Origin: Created in 2006 by Simon Difford. The name means 'Apple & Elderflower' in French.

POMPANSKI MARTINI

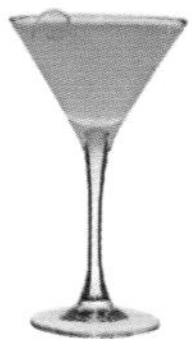

★★★★☆

Glass: Martini
Garnish: Orange zest twist
Method: SHAKE all ingredients with ice and fine strain into chilled glass.

1¾	shots	Ketel One vodka
½	shot	Triple Sec
1½	shots	Freshly squeezed grapefruit juice
¼	shot	Monin Pure Cane 2:1 sugar syrup
1	spoon	Martini Extra Dry vermouth

We say: Dry and zesty with the sharp freshness of grapefruit and a hint of orange.

PONCE DE LEON

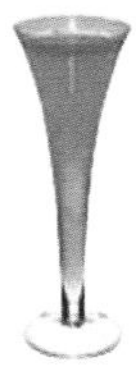

★★★★☆

Glass: Flute
Garnish: None
Method: SHAKE first four ingredients with ice and fine strain into chilled glass. TOP with champagne.

½	shot	Bacardi Superior rum
½	shot	Cognac VSOP
½	shot	Triple Sec
½	shot	Freshly squeezed grapefruit juice
Top up with		Brut champagne

We say: A well-balanced classic champagne cocktail.
Origin: A long lost classic.

PONCHA

Glass: Collins
Garnish: Orange wedge
Method: STIR honey with aguardiente base of shaker to dissolve honey. Add other ingredients, SHAKE with ice and strain into ice filled glass.

2	spoons	Runny honey
2½	shots	Torres Aqua d'Or aguardiente
1	shot	Freshly squeezed lemon juice
¼	shot	Monin Pure Cane 2:1 sugar syrup
1½	shots	Freshly squeezed orange juice
1½	shots	Freshly squeezed grapefruit juice

We say: This citrus refresher is reputedly an excellent cold remedy.
Origin: My adaptation of a traditional drink from the island of Madeira.

PONCHE DE ALGARROBINA

Glass: Goblet
Garnish: Dust with cinnamon powder
Method: BLEND all ingredients with 12oz scoop crushed ice. Serve with straws.

2	shots	Macchu pisco
1	fresh	Egg yolk
1	shot	Condensed milk
1	spoon	Algarrobo extract (or malt extract from health food shops)

We say: A creamy frozen drink with real character. Tip: It pays to add the condensed milk and Algarrobo (or malt extract) after starting the blender.
Origin: A traditional Peruvian drink I discovered at Tito's Restaurant, London, England. Algarrobo is extracted from the fruits of the tree of the same name. It is a sticky honey-like liquid which I find tastes a little like malt extract.

PONTBERRY MARTINI

Glass: Martini
Garnish: Blackberries
Method: SHAKE all ingredients with ice and fine strain into chilled glass.

1½	shots	Ketel One vodka
½	shot	Crème de Mûre liqueur
2	shots	Ocean Spray cranberry juice

We say: A light, fruity, easy drinking cocktail.
Origin: Created by Dick Bradsell in the late 90s for the opening of Agent Provocateur in Pont Street, London, England.

STAR RATINGS EXPLAINED

★★★★★ Excellent

★★★★⯪ Recommended	★★★★☆ Praiseworthy
★★★⯪☆ Commended	★★★☆☆ Mediocre
★★⯪☆☆ Disappointing	★★☆☆☆ Pretty awful
★⯪☆☆☆ Shameful	★☆☆☆☆ Disgusting

POOH'TINI

Glass: Martini
Garnish: Lemon zest twist
Method: STIR honey with vodka in base of shaker to dissolve honey. Add other ingredients, SHAKE with ice and fine strain into chilled glass.

2	spoons	Runny honey
2	shots	Żubrówka bison vodka
1½	shots	Cold camomile tea
½	shot	Krupnik spiced honey liqueur

We say: Grassy honey with spicy, slightly tannic, camomile finish.
Origin: Adapted from a drink discovered in 1999 at Lot 61, New York City.

POP MY CHERRY NEW

Glass: Martini
Garnish: Dust with chocolate powder
Method: SHAKE all ingredients with ice and fine strain into chilled glass.

1	shot	De Kuyper Cherry Brandy liqueur
½	shot	Amaretto liqueur
½	shot	Vanilla-infused Ketel One vodka
1	shot	Milk
1	shot	Double (heavy) cream

We say: A crowd pleasing cherry and almond dessert-style cocktail.
Origin: Adapted from a drink created by in 2010 by Sarah Mason, United Kingdom.

PORN STAR MARTINI

Glass: Coupette
Garnish: Passion fruit
Method: SCOOP the seeds and flesh of passion fruit into base of shaker. Add next four ingredients (all but champagne), SHAKE with ice and fine strain into chilled glass. Separately, POUR champagne into chilled shot glass to serve on the side.

1½	fresh	Passion fruit
2	shots	Vanilla-infused Ketel One vodka
½	shot	Passoã passion fruit liqueur
½	shot	Freshly squeezed lime juice
½	shot	Monin Vanilla sugar syrup
3	shots	Brut champagne

We say: A fruity sweet crowd-pleaser with champagne served on the side.
Origin: Adapted from a drink created by Douglas Ankrah at LAB Bar, London, England.

PORT & MELON MARTINI

★★★★½

Glass: Martini
Garnish: Melon slice
Method: CUT melon into eight segments and de-seed. Cut cubes of flesh from skin of one segment and MUDDLE in base of shaker. Add other ingredients, SHAKE with ice and fine strain into a chilled glass.

⅛	fresh	Cantaloupe melon
1½	shots	Ketel One vodka
1½	shots	Taylor's chip dry white port
1½	shots	Warre's Otima tawny port

We say: The classic seventies starter served as a Martini.
Origin: Created in 2004 by Simon Difford.

PORT & STARBOARD

★★½☆☆

Glass: Shot
Garnish: None
Method: Refrigerate ingredients then LAYER in chilled glass by carefully pouring in the following order.

| ½ | shot | Pomegranate (grenadine) syrup |
| ½ | shot | Giffard Menthe Pastille liqueur |

We say: Easy to layer but hard to drink. Very sweet.
Origin: Named after and inspired by the red and green running lights which respectively mark the 'Port' (left-hand) and 'Starboard' (right-hand) sides of a ship. The red light is called Port side because port wine is red. The original name for the opposite side was Larboard, but over the years was corrupted to Starboard.

PORT FLIP

★★★½☆

Glass: Martini
Garnish: Dust with grated nutmeg
Method: SHAKE all ingredients with ice and fine strain into chilled glass.

1	shot	Cognac VSOP
3	shots	Warre's Otima tawny port
⅛	shot	Monin Pure Cane 2:1 sugar syrup
1	fresh	Egg

We say: Old-school and something of a meal in a glass.

PORT LIGHT

★★★½☆

Glass: Martini
Garnish: Passion fruit
Method: STIR honey with bourbon in base of shaker to dissolve honey. Cut passion fruit in half and scoop flesh into shaker. Add other ingredients, SHAKE with ice and fine strain into chilled glass.

2	spoons	Runny honey
2	shots	Maker's Mark bourbon
2	fresh	Passion fruit
1	shot	Freshly squeezed lemon juice
½	shot	Pomegranate (grenadine) syrup
½	fresh	Egg white

We say: Strong and very fruity. Too many will put your lights out.
Origin: Adapted from a drink created by Victor Bergeron (Trader Vic)

PORT NO.2

★★★½☆

Glass: Martini
Garnish: Orange zest twist
Method: STIR all ingredients with ice and strain into chilled glass.

2	shots	Warre's Otima tawny port
½	shot	Curaçao orange liqueur
2	dashes	Orange bitters
1	dash	Angostura aromatic bitters

We say: Sangria for grown-ups.
Origin: Vintage cocktail of unknown origin.

PORT SANGAREE

★★★½☆

Glass: Martini
Garnish: Orange zest twist
Method: STIR all ingredients with ice and strain into chilled glass.

2	shots	Warre's Otima tawny port
1	shot	Chilled mineral water
¼	shot	Monin Pure Cane 2:1 sugar syrup

We say: Wine-like, light and easy.
Origin: Vintage cocktail of unknown origin.

PORT WINE COCKTAIL

★★★½☆

Glass: Martini
Garnish: Orange zest twist
Method: STIR all ingredients with ice and strain into chilled glass.

| 1 | shot | Cognac VSOP |
| 3 | shots | Warre's Otima tawny port |

We say: Port and brandy served straight-up and dressed-up.
Origin: A classic from the early 1900s.

PORTOBELLO STAR MANHATTAN (PERFECT) NEW

★★★★★

Glass: Coupette
Garnish: Cherry on stick
Method: STIR all ingredients with ice and strain into chilled glass.

2	shots	Straight rye whiskey
½	shot	Martini Extra dry vermouth
½	shot	Carpano Antica Formula
1	dash	Abbott's Bitters

We say: Rye based (originally Jim Beam) perfectly served with dry vermouth and Antica Formula
Origin: Jake Burger introduced his take on the Perfect Manhattan at the Portobello Star, Notting Hill, London, England in 2011 after working with Robert Petrie of Bob's Bitters fame to make a reproduction of Abbott's Bitters. Jake uses Jim Beam rue whiskey, Noilly Prat Blanc Original dry vermouth, Carpano Antica Formula and Abbott's Bitters.

POTTED PARROT

★★★½☆

Glass: Sling
Garnish: Parrot on stick & mint sprig
Method: SHAKE all ingredients with ice and strain into a glass filled with crushed ice.

2 shots Bacardi Superior rum
½ shot Triple Sec
2 shots Freshly squeezed orange juice
1 shot Freshly squeezed lemon juice
¼ shot Monin Pure Cane 2:1 sugar syrup
¼ shot Monin Almond (orgeat) syrup

We say: Tangy orange, not too sweet.
Origin: Adapted from a recipe in the 1947-72 '*Trader Vic's Bartender's Guide*' by Victor Bergeron. Popular in Trader Vic's restaurants.

POUSSE-CAFÉ

★★½☆☆

Glass: Shot
Garnish: None
Method: Refrigerate ingredients then LAYER in chilled glass by carefully pouring in the following order.

¼ shot Pomegranate (grenadine) syrup
¼ shot Kahlúa coffee liqueur
¼ shot Green crème de menthe liqueur
¼ shot Triple Sec
¼ shot Maker's Mark bourbon
¼ shot Wray & Nephew overproof rum

We say: More a test of patience and a steady hand than a drink.
Origin: A pousse-café is now a term for any multi-layered cocktail. The term originally seems to have been a general term for a mixture of liqueurs and/or spirits served after dinner, and most probably originated in France.

PRADO

★★★½☆

Glass: Martini
Garnish: Lime wedge
Method: SHAKE all ingredients with ice and fine strain into chilled glass.

2 shots Tequila 100% Agave
1 shot Freshly squeezed lime juice
½ shot Luxardo Maraschino liqueur
½ shot Egg white

We say: Rather like a cross between an Aviation and a Margarita.

STAR RATINGS EXPLAINED

★★★★★ Excellent

★★★★½ Recommended
★★★½☆ Commended
★★½☆☆ Disappointing
★½☆☆☆ Shameful
★★★★☆ Praiseworthy
★★★☆☆ Mediocre
★★☆☆☆ Pretty awful
★☆☆☆☆ Disgusting

PRAECOCIA COCKTAIL NEW

★★★★½

Glass: Coupette
Garnish: Maraschino cherry
Method: STIR all ingredients with ice and strain into chilled glass.

1½ shots Maker's Mark bourbon
¾ shot Carpano Punt E Mes
¼ shot De Kuyper Apricot Brandy liqueur
1 dash Angostura aromatic bitters

We say: Bourbon and apricot are an established match made in Heaven, and everybody who drinks Manhattan's will recognise how well sweet vermouth and bitters work with bourbon.
Origin: Created in 2010 by Jamie Boudreau at Vessel, Seattle, USA. Jamie describes his 1½ spirit to ¾ vermouth and ¼ modifier as the 'Mister Potato Head of Ratios'.

PRALINE PECAN PIE NEW

★★★★☆

Glass: Coupette
Garnish: Orange zest twist
Method: SHAKE all ingredients with ice and fine strain into chilled glass.

2 shots Maker's Mark bourbon
½ shot Martini Rosso sweet vermouth
½ shot Praline pecan liqueur
2 dashes Angostura aromatic bitters

We say: Reminiscent of a pecan-flavoured Sweet Manhattan.
Origin: Created in December 2010 by Cheri Loughlin, The Intoxicologist, USA.

PRAIRIE OYSTER #1 (MOCKTAIL)

★★½☆☆

Glass: Coupette
Garnish: None
Method: Taking care not to break the egg yolk, PLACE it in the centre of the hollow in the glass. SHAKE the rest of the ingredients with ice and strain over egg. Instruct drinker to down in one.

1 fresh Egg yolk
¼ shot Malt vinegar
1 spoon Worcestershire sauce
1 spoon Tomato ketchup
5 drops Tabasco hot pepper sauce

Variant: Use another spirit such as vodka in place of cognac.
We say: Like many supposed hangover cures, this works on the kill or cure basis. It tastes slightly better than it looks.
Origin: Recipe adapted from Harry Craddock's 1930 '*Savoy Cocktail Book*'. This drink is thought to have originally been created in Germany in the 1870s. Jeeves makes something similar for Bertie Wooster in a P.G. Wodehouse tale.

PRAIRIE OYSTER #2 (MODERN & ALCOHOLIC)

★★★☆☆

Glass: Coupette
Garnish: None
Method: Taking care not to break the egg yolk, PLACE it in the centre of the hollow in the glass. SHAKE the rest of the ingredients with ice and strain over egg. Instruct drinker to down in one.

1	fresh	**Egg yolk**
1	shot	**Cognac VSOP**
¼	shot	**Worcestershire sauce**
¼	shot	**Tomato juice**
5	drops	**Tabasco hot pepper sauce**
2	pinch	**Salt**
2	grind	**Black pepper**
½	shot	**Malt vinegar**

Variant: Use another spirit such as vodka in place of cognac.
We say: This 'pick-me-up' (A.K.A. hangover cure) may be a somewhat daunting prospect irrespective of the present state of your constitution.

PRE SIESTA

★★★★½

Glass: Martini
Garnish: Orange zest twist
Method: SHAKE all ingredients and fine strain into chilled glass.

2	shots	**Tequila 100% Agave**
½	shot	**Aperol**
¾	shot	**Triple Sec**
3	dashes	**Orange bitters**

We say: Orange liqueurs and bitters flavour this tequila-based, salmon-pink, dry and hard cocktail.
Origin: Created in 2007 by Little Rich Hunt at Mahiki, London, England.

PREAKNESS COCKTAIL NEW

★★★★☆

Glass: Coupette
Garnish: Lemon zest twist
Method: STIR all ingredients with ice and strain into chilled glass.

2	shots	**Straight rye whiskey**
1	shot	**Martini Rosso sweet vermouth**
¼	shot	**Bénédictine D.O.M.**
2	dashes	**Angostura aromatic bitters**

We say: A Bénédictine-influenced twist on the Sweet Manhattan.
Origin: Thanks to a 2009 article by Dave Wondrich in The Malt Advocate we know that this cocktail was created in 1936 by a chap called George who was the head bartender at Baltimore's Emerson Hotel. The Preakness Stakes is an American horse race held on the third Saturday in May annually at the Pimlico Race Course in Baltimore. George was the winner of a contest to come up with an official cocktail for the first Preakness Ball held that year. Incidentally, The Pimlico Racetrack is said to be named after "Ben Pimlico's Tavern" which once stood in the area.

PREAKNESS MANHATTAN NEW

★★★★½

Glass: Martini
Garnish: Lemon zest twist
Method: STIR all ingredients with ice and strain into chilled glass.

1½	shots	**Maker's Mark bourbon**
¼	shot	**Cognac VSOP**
½	shot	**Bénédictine D.O.M.**
½	shot	**Martini Rosso sweet vermouth**
3	dashes	**Angostura aromatic bitters**

We say: A Sweet Manhattan with a herbal touch of Bénédictine and cognac.

THE PRECURSORY COCKTAIL

★★★★½

Glass: Coupette
Garnish: Lemon zest twist (discarded) & orange slice
Method: SHAKE all ingredients with ice and fine strain into chilled glass.

1½	shots	**Warre's Otima tawny port**
1½	shots	**Carpano Antica Formula**
¼	shot	**Monin Pure Cane 2:1 sugar syrup**
⅛	shot	**Freshly squeezed lemon juice**
3	dashes	**Angostura aromatic bitters**
3	dashes	**Orange bitters**

We say: The winning cocktail from CLASS magazine Bartender of the Year 2009.
Origin: Adapted from a drink created in 2009 by Tim Philips at Milk & Honey, London, England.

THE PRESERVE COCKTAIL NEW

★★★½☆

Glass: Old-fashioned
Garnish: Mint sprig & raspberries
Method: SHAKE all ingredients with ice and fine strain into chilled glass.

8	fresh	**Raspberries**
1½	shots	**Maker's Mark bourbon**
½	shot	**Crème de Mûre liqueur**
½	shot	**Freshly squeezed lemon juice**
½	shot	**Monin Pure Cane 2:1 sugar syrup**

We say: Slightly sweetened bourbon laced with raspberry jam - at least that's how it tastes.
Origin: Created in 2010 by Gareth Edge at Opal Lounge, Edinburgh, Scotland.

STAR RATINGS EXPLAINED

★★★★★ Excellent

★★★★½	Recommended	★★★★☆	Praiseworthy
★★★½☆	Commended	★★★☆☆	Mediocre
★★½☆☆	Disappointing	★★☆☆☆	Pretty awful
★½☆☆☆	Shameful	★☆☆☆☆	Disgusting

PRESBYTERIAN NEW

★★★⯪☆

Glass: Collins
Garnish: Lemon slice
Method: POUR all ingredients into ice-filled glass and lightly STIR.

2	shots	Dewar's White label Scotch
2	shots	Soda water
Top up with Ginger ale		

We say: Basically a Scotch and soda with a delicate hint of ginger spice.
Origin: A traditional British serve for blended Scotch whisky.

PRESIDENT ⌐🔑

★★★★☆

Glass: Martini
Garnish: Orange zest twist
Method: SHAKE all ingredients with ice and fine strain into chilled glass.

2	shots	Bacardi Superior rum
1	shot	Freshly squeezed orange juice
¼	shot	Freshly squeezed lemon juice
¼	shot	Pomegranate (grenadine) syrup
½	shot	Chilled mineral water

We say: A delicately fruity orange Daiquiri.
Origin: Adapted from a recipe from Harry Craddock's 1930 the *'Savoy Cocktail Book'*.

PRESIDENT VINCENT ⌐🔑

★★★⯪☆

Glass: Martini
Garnish: Lime zest twist
Method: SHAKE all ingredients with ice and fine strain into chilled glass.

2	shots	Bacardi Superior rum
½	shot	Martini Extra Dry vermouth
½	shot	Freshly squeezed lime juice
¼	shot	Monin Pure Cane 2:1 sugar syrup

We say: A dry, spicy take on the Daiquiri.
Origin: Probably originates from the 1930s.

PRESIDENTE ⌐🔑

★★★★☆

Glass: Coupette
Garnish: Orange zest twist (discarded) & maraschino cherry
Method: SHAKE all ingredients with crushed ice and strain into chilled glass.

1½	shots	Bacardi Superior rum
¼	shot	Triple Sec
1½	shots	Martini Extra Dry vermouth

We say: Bone dry, light and delicate. The sweetness and colour of the maraschino cherry garnish makes this drink.
Origin: Thought to have created during the 1920s in Vista Alegre, Havana, Cuba. This recipe is adapted from a 1937 Bar Florida (later renamed Floridita) menu, Havana, Cuba. On page 40 of his 1928 book *'When it's cocktail time in Cuba'*, Basil Woon says of this drink, "It is the aristocrat of cocktails and is the one preferred by the better class of Cuban."

PRESIDENTE MENOCAL SPECIAL ⌐🔑

★★★★☆

Glass: Martini
Garnish: Mint sprig & maraschino cherry
Method: SHAKE all ingredients with ice and fine strain into chilled glass.

7	fresh	Mint leaves
2	shots	Bacardi Superior rum
¼	shot	Monin Pure Cane 2:1 sugar syrup
⅛	shot	Freshly squeezed lime juice

We say: What hot Cuban summers are made for.
Origin: Created by Constantino (Constante) Ribalaigua Vert at the Floridita bar in Havana, Cuba. This recipe is adapted from a 1937 Bar Florida (later renamed Floridita) menu. The name refers to Mario García Menocal, who was president of Cuba from 1912 to 1920.

PRESTIGE COCKTAIL

★★★★⯪

Glass: Martini
Garnish: Pineapple wedge & spiral lime peel
Method: SHAKE all ingredients with ice and strain into chilled glass.

1¾	shots	Bacardi 8yo aged rum
1	shot	Fresh pressed pineapple juice
½	shot	Martini Extra Dry vermouth
½	shot	Taylor's Velvet Falernum liqueur
½	shot	Freshly squeezed lime juice

We say: Slightly sweet but very more-ish. Aged rum, pineapple, clove and lime.
Origin: Created in 2002 by Dale Degroff, New York City, USA.

PRICKLY PEAR MULE

★★★★☆

Glass: Collins
Garnish: Pear slice
Method: SHAKE first five ingredients with ice and strain into ice-filled glass. TOP with ginger beer.

1¼	shots	Belle de Brillet pear liqueur
1¼	shots	Poire William eau de vie
3	shots	Pressed pear juice
¼	shot	Freshly squeezed lemon juice
2	dashes	Angostura aromatic bitters
Top up with Ginger beer		

We say: Subtle pear with ginger spice. Fill the glass with ice and go easy on the ginger beer which can predominate and overpower the pear.
Origin: Created in 2002 by Simon Difford.

PRINCE CHARLIE

★★★★☆

Glass: Martini
Garnish: Lemon zest twist
Method: SHAKE all ingredients with ice and fine strain into chilled glass.

1	shot	Cognac VSOP
1	shot	Drambuie
1	shot	Freshly squeezed lemon juice
¾	shot	Chilled mineral water

We say: Cognac and honey with sweet and sourness in harmony.
Origin: A long lost classic.

PRINCE OF WALES

★★★⯪☆

Glass: Flute
Garnish: Lemon zest twist
Method: RUB sugar cube with lemon zest, coat with bitters and drop into glass. POUR cognac and liqueur over soaked cube and TOP with champagne.

1	cube	Brown sugar
2	dashes	Angostura aromatic bitters
½	shot	Cognac VSOP
½	shot	Grand Marnier liqueur
Top up with		Brut champagne

We say: More interesting than a Classic Champagne Cocktail.

THE PRINCE OF WALES COCKTAIL II NEW

★★★⯪☆

Glass: Coupette
Garnish: Orange slice
Method: MUDDLE pineapple in base of shaker. Add next 5 ingredients (all but champagne), SHAKE with ice and fine strain into chilled glass. TOP with champagne.

1	Wedge	Pineapple
2	shots	Straight rye whiskey
⅛	shot	Luxardo Maraschino liqueur
⅛	shot	Monin Pure Cane 2:1 sugar syrup
1	zest	1 inch Lemon zest
1	dash	Angostura aromatic bitters
Top up with		Brut champagne

We say: Rich whiskey and maraschino with subtle pineapple balanced by a dash of brut champagne.
Origin: Recipe adapted from David Wondrich's 2007 masterpiece 'Imbibe!' in which David tells the story of his Highness Albert Edward, Prince of Wales, son of Queen Victoria and his mastering of this riff on the Improved Whisky Cocktail.

Born 9th November 1841 he was not crowned King Edward VII until 9th August 1902 (ascended 22nd January 1901) and by all accounts made the most of his 60 years as understudy by becoming a playboy and travelling the world – there are worse ways to while away your years. In 1860, he became the first British royal to visit North America and it is thought that this cocktail resulted from that trip.

THE PRINCE OF WALES PUNCH NEW

★★★★☆

Glass: Collins
Garnish: Raspberries
Method: MUDDLE pineapple in base of shaker. Add next five ingredients, SHAKE with ice and fine strain into ice-filled glass. Float the port on drink.

¼	ring	Pineapple (fresh)
1½	shots	Courvoisier VSOP Exclusif
¾	shot	Rum Aged
½	shot	Grand Marnier liqueur
¼	shot	Luxardo maraschino liqueur
1½	shots	Freshly squeezed orange juice
½	shot	Warre's Otima tawny port

We say: Fruity yet complex with the oak maturation of both spirits and liqueurs adding depth of flavour.
Origin: Adapted from Jerry Thomas' 1862 'The Bar-Tender's Guide (How to Mix Drinks or The Bon-Vivant's Companion)'.

PRINCESS MARINA

★★★★☆

Glass: Martini
Garnish: Orange zest twist
Method: SHAKE all ingredients with ice and fine strain into chilled glass.

1	shot	Tanqueray London dry gin
½	shot	Calvados/Applejack brandy
½	shot	Dubonnet Red (French made)
½	shot	Triple Sec
½	shot	Swedish Punch liqueur
¾	shot	Chilled mineral water

We say: Delicate yet loaded with alcohol and flavour.
Origin: Created in the late 1920s/early 1930s and named after the Princess Marina, the late mother of The Duke of Kent, Prince Michael of Kent and Princess Alexandra.

PRINCESS MARY UPDATED

★★★★☆

Glass: Martini
Garnish: Dust with chocolate powder
Method: SHAKE all ingredients with ice and fine strain into chilled glass.

1½	shots	The Bombay Original dry gin
1	shot	Bols white cacao liqueur
1	shot	Double (heavy) cream

We say: Slightly sweet, very creamy - drink after dinner.
Origin: Created in London during 1922 by Scottish bartender Harry MacElhone to celebrate H.R.H. Princess Mary's marriage to Lord Lascelles. The original recipe featured equal parts of all three ingredients: ⅓ gin, ⅓ white crème de cacao and ⅓ fresh cream. The year after, Harry MacElhone purchased his eponymously named bar in Paris.

PRINCESS MARY'S PRIDE

★★★☆☆

Glass: Martini
Garnish: Orange zest twist
Method: SHAKE all ingredients with ice and fine strain into chilled glass.

2	shots	Calvados/Applejack brandy
1	shot	Dubonnet Red (French made)
1	shot	Martini Extra Dry vermouth

We say: Apple brandy to the fore, followed by aromatised wine.
Origin: Created by Harry Craddock on 28th February 1922 to mark the wedding celebrations of H.R.H. Princess Mary. Recipe from 1930s 'Savoy Cocktail Book'.

PRINCESS PRIDE

★★★⯪☆

Glass: Martini
Garnish: Orange zest twist
Method: SHAKE all ingredients with ice and fine strain into chilled glass.

2	shots	Calvados/Applejack brandy
1	shot	Dubonnet Red (French made)
1	shot	Martini Rosso sweet vermouth

We say: Vic's improved version of the Princess Mary's Pride cocktail.
Origin: Adapted from a recipe in the 1947-1972 'Trader Vic's Bartender's Guide' by Victor Bergeron.

PRINCETON

★★★★☆

Glass: Martini
Garnish: Lemon zest twist
Method: SHAKE all ingredients with ice and fine strain into chilled glass.

2	shots	Tanqueray London dry gin
1	shot	Warre's Otima tawny port
¼	shot	Monin Pure Cane 2:1 sugar syrup
2	dashes	Orange bitters

We say: Overproof wine with a herbal orange garnish.
Origin: An old classic originally made with sweet 'Old Tom' gin and without the sugar syrup.

PRINCETON MARTINI

★★★★☆

Glass: Martini
Garnish: Lime zest twist
Method: SHAKE all ingredients with ice and fine strain into chilled glass.

2	shots	Tanqueray London dry gin
½	shot	Martini Extra Dry vermouth
¼	shot	Rose's lime cordial
½	shot	Chilled mineral water

We say: The Dry Martini meets the Gimlet. They should meet more often.

PROCRASTINATION COCKTAIL NEW

★★★★☆

Glass: Coupette
Garnish: Lemon zest twist
Method: STIR all ingredients with ice and strain into chilled glass.

2	shots	Tanqueray London dry gin
½	shot	Martini Extra Dry vermouth
¾	shot	Limoncello liqueur
⅛	shot	Chartreuse Green liqueur

We say: A wet martini flavoured with copious amounts of limoncello (which sweetens and surprisingly on adds subtle lemon favours) and a dash of Chartreuse which shines through.
Origin: Recipe created by Paul Clarke, the Seattle-based cocktail enthusiast behind the excellent cocktailchronicles.com.

PROSPECTOR NEW

★★★★½

Glass: Coupette
Garnish: Orange zest twist (flamed)
Method: STIR all ingredients with ice and strain into chilled glass.

2	shots	Dewar's White label Scotch
¾	shot	Blandy's Alvada madeira
¾	shot	Bénédictine D.O.M.
1	dash	Bitters (whiskey barrel aged)

We say: Complex and strong with all three ingredients balancing and enhancing each other.
Origin: Adapted from a drink created in 2010 by Thomas Waugh at Prospect, San Francisco, USA.

PRUNE FACE

★★★★☆

Glass: Old-fashioned
Garnish: Orange zest twist
Method: POUR bourbon into a glass with four ice cubes and STIR until ice has at least half melted. Add other ingredients and additional ice and stir some more.

2	shots	Maker's Mark bourbon
¾	shot	Vieille de prune eau de vie
¼	shot	Mandarine Napoléon liqueur
¼	shot	Monin Pure Cane 2:1 sugar syrup

We say: Why muddle cherries into your Old Fashioned when you can add a hint of prune?
Origin: Created in 2002 by Dan Warner at Zander, London, England and named after my friend's nickname for his stepmother.

PRUNEAUX

★★★★☆

Glass: Martini
Garnish: Prunes
Method: SHAKE all ingredients with ice and fine strain into chilled glass.

1½	shots	Tanqueray London dry gin
1	shot	Amontillado sherry
½	shot	Pedro Ximénez sherry
¾	shot	Freshly squeezed orange juice
¾	shot	Prune syrup (from tinned fruit)

We say: Sherried prunes further fortified by gin.
Origin: Adapted from a recipe in Harry Craddock's 1930 'Savoy Cocktail Book'.

PUCCINI

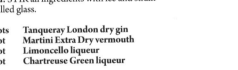

★★★½☆

Glass: Flute
Garnish: Mandarin segment
Method: MUDDLE segments in base of shaker. Add liqueur, SHAKE with ice and fine strain into chilled glass. TOP with prosecco and lightly stir.

8	pieces	Fresh mandarin
¾	shot	Mandarine Napoléon liqueur
Top up with		Prosecco sparkling wine

We say: The use of mandarin makes the Puccini slightly sharper than a simple mimosa.
Origin: Named after the composer of Madame Butterfly, this cocktail id popular in Venice and other areas of northern Italy. It is often made without the mandarin liqueur.

PULP FICTION

★★★★☆

Glass: Collins
Garnish: Apple slice
Method: SHAKE all ingredients with ice and strain into ice-filled glass. TOP with lemonade.

2	shots	Cognac VSOP
2	shots	Pressed apple juice
1	shot	Berentzen Apple schnapps
Top up with		Lemonade/Sprite/7-Up

We say: Originally made with apple pulp, this drink has a zingy apple taste.
Origin: Discovered in 2001 at Teatro, London, UK

PUNCH & JUDY NEW

★★★½☆

Glass: Collins
Garnish: Lime slice & dust with grated nutmeg
Method: SHAKE all ingredients with ice and strain into ice-filled glass.

6	fresh	**Mint leaves**
1	shot	**Courvoisier VSOP Exclusif**
½	shot	**Rum light white/blanco**
½	shot	**Tanqueray London dry gin**
½	shot	**Orange Curaçao liqueur**
1½	shots	**Fresh pressed pineapple juice**
½	shot	**Freshly squeezed lime juice**
½	shot	**Freshly squeezed orange juice**
½	shot	**Agave nectar**
2	dashes	**Angostura aromatic bitters**

We say: A veritable fruit bowl and spirits rail of a punch in a glass.
Origin: Adapted from the official cocktail of the 2008 Tales of the Cocktail created by Charlotte Voisey, USA.

PUNCH (GENERIC NAME)

★★★★★

Glass: Collins
Garnish: Lime slice
Method: SHAKE all ingredients with ice and fine strain into glass filled with crushed ice.

¾	shot	**Freshly squeezed lemon or lime juice**
1½	shots	**Monin Pure Cane 2:1 sugar syrup**
2¼	shots	**Brandy, whisk(e)y, gin, rum etc.**
3	shots	**Sweet fruit juice**
3	dashes	**Angostura aromatic bitters**

We say: Two traditional punches remain on today's cocktail lists, the 'Rum Punch' and the 'Hot Whisky Punch', now better known as the 'Hot Toddy'. Also bear in mind that the Gin Punch probably led to the creation of the Collins.
Origin: Long before the Martini, the V-shaped glass and the cocktail shaker, the drink of choice at society gatherings was punch and the punch bowl was the centre of activity at every party.

Punch had existed in India for centuries before colonialists brought it back to Europe some time in the latter half of the 1600s. The name derives from the Hindi word for five, 'panch', and refers to the five key ingredients: alcohol, citrus, sugar, water and spices. In India, it was made with arrack (the Arabic word for liquor and a local spirit distilled from palm sap or sugar cane). Back in Britain it was common for punches to be spiced with nutmeg or tea.

The classic proportions of a punch follow a mnemonic, 'one of sour, two of sweet, three of strong and four of weak'. It refers to lime juice, sugar, rum and water – the fifth element, spice was added to taste.

The basic punch principle of balancing sweet and sour with spirit and dilution remains key to making a good cocktail. Indeed, the essential punch ingredients - spirit, citrus, sugar and water - lie at the centre of most modern day cocktails including the Daiquiri, Sour, Margarita, Caipirinha and Sidecar. Today's bartenders are now also reintroducing the fifth punch ingredient by muddling or macerating herbs and spices in their cocktails.

STAR RATINGS EXPLAINED

★★★★★ Excellent

★★★★½	Recommended	★★★★☆	Praiseworthy
★★★½☆	Commended	★★★☆☆	Mediocre
★★½☆☆	Disappointing	★★☆☆☆	Pretty awful
★½☆☆☆	Shameful	★☆☆☆☆	Disgusting

PUNCH BACK NEW

★★★★☆

Glass: Collins
Garnish: Pineapple wedge on rim with cherries on stick
Method: SHAKE all ingredients with ice and strain into ice-filled glass.

1½	shots	**Rum Golden**
1	shot	**Leblon cachaça**
¾	shot	**Freshly squeezed lemon juice**
¾	shot	**Monin Pure Cane 2:1 sugar syrup**
2	shots	**Coconut water**
1	dash	**Angostura aromatic bitters**

We say: Cachaça is the raw, spirity love interest in this rum based coconut and lime punch.
Origin: Created in May 2013 by Simon Difford at the Cabinet Room, London, England for the National Aids Trust

PURGATORY

★★★★½

Glass: Martini
Garnish: Lemon zest twist
Method: SHAKE all ingredients with ice and strain into chilled glass.

2½	shots	**Straight rye whiskey**
¾	shot	**Bénédictine D.O.M.**
¾	shot	**Chartreuse Green liqueur**

We say: Too many and you're in it.
Origin: Created in 2007 by Ted Kilgore at Monarch Restaurant, Maplewood, USA. Adapted from an adapted recipe by Gary Regan and first published in his column in The San Francisco Chronicle. Apparently, Kilgore created this drink as a pick-me-up.

PURGATORY A LA FRANÇAISE NEW

★★★★☆

Glass: Old-fashioned
Garnish: Lemon zest twist
Method: STIR all ingredients with ice and strain glass.

1	shot	**Cognac VSOP**
¾	shot	**Lagavulin 16yo malt whisky**
¾	shot	**Chartreuse Yellow liqueur**
¾	shot	**Carpano Punt E Mes**

We say: This Islay smoke influenced drink makes for a great night cap.
Origin: Adapted from a drink discovered in 2010 at Curio Parlour, Paris, France.

THE PURITAN

★★★★★

Glass: Martini
Garnish: Orange zest twist
Method: STIR all ingredients with ice and strain into chilled glass.

1¾	shots	**Tanqueray London dry gin**
½	shot	**Martini Extra Dry vermouth**
¼	shot	**Chartreuse Yellow liqueur**
1	dash	**Orange bitters**
½	shot	**Chilled mineral water**

We say: Vermouth enhances the aromatics; Chartreuse and orange bitters add a hint of sweetness and complexity; gin underpins the whole.
Origin: An often overlooked classic which is thought to have originated at the end of the nineteenth century.

THE PURL

★★★☆☆

Glass: Pint
Garnish: None
Method: POUR ingredients into chilled glass.

| 2 | shots | Old Tom gin |

Top up with British cask conditioned ale

We say: Somebody seems to have spiked my beer!
Origin: In 18th century London Gin tended to be mixed two to one with water and sold by the quarter pint. The Purl, simply gin and ale was another popular mix. Sometimes the beer was warmed first to make a 'hot purl', apparently popular with Thames boatman of the day.

PURPLE HAZE

★★★★☆

Glass: Shot
Garnish: None
Method: SHAKE first three ingredients with ice and strain into glass. POUR liqueur down the inside the glass. This will fall to the bottom and form a purple haze.

1½	shots	Ketel One vodka
½	shot	Freshly squeezed lime juice
¼	shot	Monin Pure Cane 2:1 sugar syrup
⅛	shot	Chambord black raspberry liqueur

We say: A sweet and sour shot with a sweet, berry base.

PURPLE COSMO

★★★★☆

Glass: Martini
Garnish: Orange zest twist
Method: STIR all ingredients with ice and strain into chilled glass.

2	shots	Ketel One Citroen vodka
¾	shot	Parfait Amour liqueur
1½	shots	Ocean Spray cranberry juice
¼	shot	Freshly squeezed lime juice

Variant: Blue Cosmo
We say: If shaken this becomes more of grey cosmo. The flavour and colour make for an interesting twist.

PURPLE HOOTER

★★★★☆

Glass: Collins
Garnish: Lime wedge
Method: SHAKE first three ingredients with ice and strain into ice-filled glass. TOP with soda.

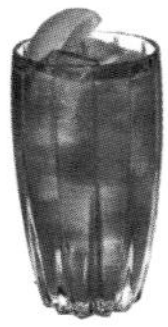

2	shots	Ketel One vodka
1	shot	Chambord black raspberry liqueur
1	shot	Freshly squeezed lime juice

Top up with Soda (club soda)

We say: Tangy, fruity, long and refreshing.

PURPLE FLIRT #1

★★★★☆

Glass: Martini
Garnish: Orange zest twist
Method: SHAKE all ingredients with ice and fine strain into chilled glass.

1½	shots	Ketel One vodka
¾	shot	Opal Nera black sambuca
2	shots	Ocean Spray cranberry juice

We say: This purple drink is surprisingly balanced with subtle hints of liquorice.

PURPLE PEAR MARTINI

★★★★☆

Glass: Martini
Garnish: Pear slice
Method: SHAKE all ingredients with ice and fine strain into chilled glass.

¾	shot	Żubrówka bison vodka
¾	shot	Poire William eau de vie
¾	shot	Benoit Serres créme de violette
1	shot	Lillet Blanc

We say: This floral drink suits its name.
Origin: Created in 2002 by Simon Difford.

PURPLE FLIRT #2

★★★☆☆

Glass: Old-fashioned
Garnish: Orange slice & cherry on stick (sail)
Method: SHAKE all ingredients with ice and strain into ice-filled glass.

1	shot	Gosling's Black Seal rum
¼	shot	Bols Blue Curaçao liqueur
1	shot	Fresh pressed pineapple juice
½	shot	Freshly squeezed lemon juice
¼	shot	Pomegranate (grenadine) syrup
½	fresh	Egg white

We say: This popular drink is more brown than purple. It tastes ok, anyway.

PURPLE TURTLE

★★★★☆

Glass: Shot
Garnish: None
Method: SHAKE all ingredients with ice and fine strain into chilled glass.

½	shot	Tequila 100% Agave
½	shot	Sloe Gin liqueur
½	shot	Bols Blue Curaçao liqueur

We say: The aquamarine shooter goes down a treat

PUSSYFOOT (MOCKTAIL)

★★★★½

Glass: Collins
Garnish: Orange slice
Method: MUDDLE mint in base of shaker. Add other ingredients, SHAKE with ice and fine strain into ice-filled glass.

7	fresh	Mint leaves
4	shots	Freshly squeezed orange juice
½	shot	Freshly squeezed lemon juice
½	shot	Freshly squeezed lime juice
½	shot	Pomegranate (grenadine) syrup
1	fresh	Egg yolk

We say: Probably the best non-alcoholic cocktail ever.
Origin: Created in 1920 by Robert Vermeire at the Embassy Club, London, England. This non-alcoholic is named after 'Pussyfoot' (William E.) Johnson who was an ardent supporter of prohibition.

PYRAMID PUNCH

★★★★★★

Glass: Collins
Garnish: Pineapple wedge
Method: MUDDLE cloves in base of shaker. ADD other ingredients, SHAKE with ice and strain into ice-filled glass.

2	dried	Cloves
2	shots	Macchu pisco
1	shot	St~Germain elderflower liqueur
2	shots	Fresh pressed pineapple juice
½	shot	Freshly squeezed grapefruit juice

We say: Tangy, fruity and packed with flavour. Clove spice, fragrant floral pisco and elderflower with a hint of sweet pineapple and sour grapefruit.
Origin: Simon Difford's 2006 adaptation of the Pisco Punch made famous before Prohibition at San Francisco's legendary Bank Exchange Bar. The Transamerica Pyramid skyscraper now stands on the site of The Bank Exchange, at the corner of Washington & Montgomery Streets, hence this drink's name and garnish.

THE QUAD

★★★★★½

Glass: Coupette
Garnish: Orange zest twist
Method: SHAKE all ingredients with ice and fine strain into chilled glass.

1½	shots	Ketel One Oranje vodka
1	shot	Triple Sec
¼	shot	Campari Bitter
1	shot	Freshly squeezed orange juice

We say: Four different orange flavoured ingredients combine in this complex fruity cocktail.
Origin: Created in 2010 by Simon Difford at the Cabinet Room, London, England.

STAR RATINGS EXPLAINED

★★★★★ Excellent

★★★★½ Recommended	★★★★☆ Praiseworthy
★★★½☆ Commended	★★★☆☆ Mediocre
★★½☆☆ Disappointing	★★☆☆☆ Pretty awful
★½☆☆☆ Shameful	★☆☆☆☆ Disgusting

QUARTER DECK

★★★★☆

Glass: Martini
Garnish: Orange zest twist
Method: SHAKE all ingredients with ice and fine strain into chilled glass.

2	shots	Bacardi Superior rum
1	shot	Pedro Ximénez sherry
¼	shot	Freshly squeezed lemon juice
¾	shot	Chilled mineral water

We say: Hints of prune, toffee and maple syrup. Very complex.
Origin: Long lost classic.

QUARTERBACK

★★★★☆

Glass: Martini
Garnish: Orange zest twist
Method: SHAKE all ingredients with ice and fine strain into chilled glass.

1	shot	Chartreuse Yellow liqueur
1	shot	Triple Sec
1	shot	Double (heavy) cream
1	shot	Milk

We say: This white, creamy drink has a flavoursome bite.

QUEBEC

★★★★☆

Glass: Martini
Garnish: Orange zest twist
Method: STIR all ingredients and strain into chilled glass.

2	shots	Canadian whisky
2	shots	Dubonnet Red (French made)
2	dashes	Orange bitters

We say: Canadian whisky with French accents of aromatised wine - trés Quebecois.
Origin: Created in 2004 by Gonçalo de Sousa Monteiro at Victoria Bar, Berlin, Germany.

QUEEN MARTINI

★★★★☆

Glass: Martini
Garnish: Maraschino cherry
Method: SHAKE all ingredients with ice and fine strain into chilled glass.

1½	shots	Tanqueray London dry gin
½	shot	Martini Extra Dry vermouth
½	shot	Martini Rosso sweet vermouth
½	shot	Freshly squeezed orange juice
½	shot	Fresh pressed pineapple juice

We say: A 'perfectly' fruity Martini that's fit for a....

QUEEN'S PARK SWIZZLE

★★★★☆

Glass: Collins
Garnish: Lime wedge & mint sprig
Method: Lightly MUDDLE mint (just to bruise) in base of glass, add other ingredients and half fill glass with crushed ice. SWIZZLE with a swizzle stick or CHURN (stir) with a bar spoon. Fill glass with more crushed ice and repeat. Serve with straws.

7	fresh	Mint leaves
2	shots	Bacardi 8yo aged rum
¾	shot	Freshly squeezed lime juice
½	shot	Monin Pure Cane 2:1 sugar syrup
3	dashes	Angostura aromatic bitters

We say: This close relation to the Mojito is drier, more complex and less minty than its sibling.
Origin: Created at the Queen's Park Hotel, Port of Spain, Trinidad.

QUELLE VIE

★★★☆☆

Glass: Martini
Garnish: Orange zest twist
Method: STIR all ingredients with ice and fine strain into chilled glass.

2	shots	Cognac VSOP
½	shot	Kümmel
¾	shot	Chilled mineral water

We say: In Craddock's word, "Brandy gives you courage and Kümmel makes you cautious, thus giving you the perfect mixture of bravery and caution, with the bravery predominating."
Origin: Adapted from a recipe in the 1930 *'Savoy Cocktail Book'* by Harry Craddock.

QUINCE MUSTARD MARGARITA

★★★★☆

Glass: Old-fashioned
Garnish: Lime wedge & cracked black pepper
Method: SHAKE all ingredients with ice and fine strain into chilled glass.

1	spoon	Quince mustard jam
2	grinds	Black pepper
1½	shots	Tequila 100% Agave
½	shot	Triple Sec
1	shot	Freshly squeezed lime juice
⅛	shot	Monin Pure Cane 2:1 sugar syrup

We say: A wonderfully quince influenced Margarita.
Origin: Created by Ryan Magarian, Seattle, USA.

QUINCE SOUR

★★★★☆

Glass: Old-fashioned
Garnish: Lemon slice & cherry on stick (sail)
Method: STIR quince jam with vodka in base of shaker to dissolve jam. Add other ingredients, SHAKE with ice and fine strain into ice-filled glass.

3	spoons	Quince mustard jam
2	shots	Ketel One vodka
1	shot	Freshly squeezed lemon juice
½	fresh	Egg white

We say: The sweet quince both flavours and balances the sour.

THE QUINGENTI

★★★★☆

Glass: Martini
Garnish: Lemon zest twist
Method: SHAKE all ingredients with ice and fine strain into chilled glass.

2	shots	Cognac VSOP
½	shot	Berentzen Apple schnapps
½	shot	Martini Extra Dry vermouth
¼	shot	Monin Pure Cane 2:1 sugar syrup

We say: Cognac with apple notes and a touch of herbal complexity by way of dry vermouth.
Origin: A created in 2008 by Simon Difford at the Cabinet Room, London, England to celebrate Courvoisier's Future 500 initiative. As every schoolboy knows, quingenti is Latin for five-hundred.

R U BOBBY MOORE?

★★★★☆

Glass: Martini
Garnish: Apple wedge
Method: STIR honey with Scotch and vodka in base of shaker until honey dissolves. Add other ingredients, SHAKE with ice and fine strain into chilled glass.

3	spoons	Runny honey
1	shot	Dewar's White label Scotch
1	shot	Żubrówka bison vodka
¾	shot	Sauvignon blanc wine
1	shot	Pressed apple juice

We say: It's common to pair Scotch and Żubrówka with apple, but combining all three together with wine and honey really works.
Origin: Created in 2002 by Simon Difford and named after the rhyming slang for 'are you bloody sure?' Bobby Moore was the 60s England football captain and West Ham United defender who regrettably died young in 1993. My dictionary of rhyming slang claims 'Bobby Moore' means 'door' - well, not in East London it doesn't.

BARTENDER'S TIP FLAME

The term ignite, flame or flambé means that the drink should be set alight.

Please exercise extreme care when setting fire to drinks. Be particularly careful not to knock over a lit drink and never attempt to carry a drink which is still alight. Before drinking, cover the glass so as to suffocate the flame and be aware that the rim of the glass may be hot.

RAC COCKTAIL

★★★★☆

Glass: Martini
Garnish: Orange zest twist (discarded) & maraschino cherry
Method: STIR all ingredients with ice and strain into chilled glass.

2	shots	**Tanqueray London dry gin**
1	shot	**Martini Extra Dry vermouth**
1	shot	**Martini Rosso sweet vermouth**
⅛	shot	**Pomegranate (grenadine) syrup**
1	dash	**Orange bitters**

We say: A one to one Perfect Martini with extra grenadine sweetness and orange bitters adding complexity.
Origin: The house cocktail at the Royal Automobile Club in London's Pall Mall. King Edward VII awarded this private members' club its royal title in 1907.

RAGING BULL

★★★½

Glass: Shot
Garnish: None
Method: Refrigerate ingredients then LAYER in chilled glass by carefully pouring in the order listed.

½	shot	**Kahlúa coffee liqueur**
½	shot	**Opal Nera black sambuca**
½	scoop	**Tequila 100% Agave**

We say: Coffee and sambuca make a great combination, as do coffee and tequila.

RAGTIME

★★★★½

Glass: Coupette
Garnish: Orange zest twist
Method: Rinse mixing glass with absinthe (sazerac-style). STIR rest of ingredients with ice and strain into chilled glass.

½	shot	**Absinthe**
1½	shots	**Straight rye whiskey**
1	shot	**Averna Amaro**
1	shot	**Aperol**
1	dash	**Peychaud's aromatic bitters**

We say: This bitter-sweet drink benefits from the strength of bonded rye whiskey and was originally made with Rittenhouse.
Origin: Adapted from a drink created in 2009 by Jeremy James Thompson at Raines Law Rooms, New York City, USA.

RAITA COCKTAIL NEW

★★★★☆

Glass: Coupette
Garnish: Cucumber slices
Method: MUDDLE cardamom, cumin and then cucumber in base of shaker. ADD other ingredients, SHAKE with ice and fine strain into chilled glass.

2	dried	**Cardamom pod**
½	spoon	**Cumin seeds**
1½	inch	**Cucumber (chopped & peeled)**
1½	shots	**Tanqueray London dry gin**
1½	shots	**Bols Natural Yoghurt liqueur**
1	pinch	**Salt**
3	fresh	**Mint leaves**

We say: Fresh cucumber, mint and yoghurt with a hint of cardamom and cumin spice, laced with vodka.
Origin: Created in 2011 by Simon Difford at the Cabinet Room, London, England.

RAMOS GIN FIZZ UPDATED

★★★★★

Glass: Collins
Garnish: Lemon slice & mint sprig
Method: 1/ Flash BLEND first 8 ingredients without ice (to emulsify mix). Then pour contents of blender into shaker and SHAKE with ice. Strain into chilled glass (no ice in glass) and TOP with soda from siphon. ALTERNATIVELY: 2/ Vigorously DRY SHAKE first eight ingredients until bored/tired. Add ice to shaker, SHAKE again and strain into chilled glass (without ice). TOP with soda water from siphon.

2	shots	**Tanqueray London dry gin**
½	shot	**Freshly squeezed lemon juice**
½	shot	**Freshly squeezed lime juice**
¾	shot	**Monin Pure Cane 2:1 sugar syrup**
⅛	shot	**Orange flower water**
3	drops	**Vanilla extract**
1	fresh	**Egg white**
1	shot	**Double (heavy) cream**
Top up with		**Soda from siphon**

AKA: Ramos Fizz or New Orleans Fizz
Variant: Gin Fizz
We say: One of the great classic cocktails. The perfect balance of sweet and sour is enhanced by the incredibly smooth, almost fluffy mouth feel.
Origin: Created in 1888 by Henry C. Ramos at the Imperial Cabinet Saloon on the corner of Gravier and Carondelet Streets in New Orleans. Originally named the New Orleans Fizz the drink was an immediate success, propelling the bar's popularity to the extent that it would often have 20 bartenders and "shaker boys" dedicated to just making Ramos Gin Fizz cocktails, but they would still struggle to meet demand. That's perhaps understandable when you hear that devotees say it takes 12 minutes to shake, requiring several bartenders to shake in relay, not least because the shaker becomes so cold and frosted that it must be wrapped in a cloth to be comfortably held.

The recipe remained a closely guarded secret and, driven by the success of his creation, in 1907 Henry opened his own bar, The Stag, down the street on the corner of St Charles Avenue and Gravier Street, opposite the entrance to the St. Charles Hotel. Incidentally, some say that vanilla extract was the

BARTENDER'S TIP THROWING

Sometimes also referred to as the 'Cuban Roll' after the origin of this method of mixing, 'throwing' offers greater dilution and aeration than stirring but is more gentle than shaking. It is achieved by simply pouring the ingredients from one container to another. To do this, assemble your ingredients in a mixing glass or base of your shaker. Add ice and strain into a second mixing glass with a large diameter lipped rim increasing the distance between the two vessels as you pour. Then pour the partially mixed cocktail back into the first ice-filled container and strain into the second once again. Repeat this process several times and you will have 'thrown' your drink.

secret ingredient which prevented others successfully copying the Ramos Gin Fizz, while others hold it was not originally used.

In his Famous New Orleans Drinks and How to Mix 'Em, Stanley Clisby Arthur writes that at The Stag, "the corps of busy shaker boys behind the bar was one of the sights of the town during Carnival, and in the 1915 Mardi Gras, 35 shaker boys nearly shook their arms off, but were still unable to keep up with the demand."

With the onset of Prohibition in 1920, Henry was forced to close his bar. He died in 1928 believing that his drink would never be served in an American bar again. The recipe to the now legendary Ramos Gin Fizz remained a secret until his brother, Charles Henry Ramos, honoured Henry's memory by publishing the recipe in a full-page advertisement.

In 1935, the Roosevelt (now named the Fairmont) Hotel in New Orleans, just a couple of blocks away from where Henry created the drink, purchased the rights to the Ramos Gin Fizz from Henry's son and trademarked the drink.

The Roosevelt Hotel promoted the drink, the popularity of which was also helped by the governor of Louisiana, Huey P. Long's fondness of it. So much so, that in July 1935, he took a bartender, named Sam Guarino, from the Roosevelt Hotel to the New Yorker Hotel in New York City to train the staff there how to make the drink, so he could have it whenever he stayed in New York. The Museum of the American Cocktail has newsreel footage of this. Bartenders at the Fairmont Hotel's Sazerac Bar continue to proudly make the drink and tell the story of Henry Ramos to this day.

A Ramos Gin Fizz is always served long in a tall, straight-sided glass without ice. To make what is said to be the original style of a Ramos Gin Fizz, use full fat milk in place of cream and shake until the bubbles disappear. Some recipes for a Ramos Gin Fizz call for Old Tom gin, in which case reduce the amount of sugar syrup used.

RANDY

★★★★☆

Glass: Old-fashioned
Garnish: Orange zest twist
Method: STIR all ingredients with ice and strain into ice-filled glass.

1½	**shots**	**Cognac VSOP**
½	**shot**	**Grand Marnier liqueur**
1½	**shots**	**Warre's Otima tawny port**
¼	**shot**	**Monin Vanilla sugar syrup**

We say: Named after the rhyming slang for port and brandy, its base ingredients. Love interest comes courtesy of orange and vanilla.
Origin: Created in 2003 by Simon Difford.

RANGLUM

★★★½☆

Glass: Old-fashioned
Garnish: Lime wedge
Method: SHAKE all ingredients with ice and strain into ice-filled glass.

2	**shots**	**Gosling's Black Seal rum**
½	**shot**	**Wray & Nephew overproof rum**
¾	**shot**	**Taylor's Velvet Falernum liqueur**
1	**shot**	**Freshly squeezed lime juice**
¼	**shot**	**Monin Pure Cane 2:1 sugar syrup**

We say: This Tiki-style drink is rich and tangy with a hint of clove spice.
Origin: Created in 2008 by Gonçalo De Sousa Monteiro at Le Lion, Hamburg, Germany, apparently whilst listening to Ernest Ranglin, hence the name.

RAPSCALLION NEW

★★★★½

Glass: Coupette
Garnish: Lemon zest twist (discarded) and olive on a stick
Method: POUR pastis into chilled glass, TOP with chilled water and leave to stand. Separately STIR other ingredients with ice. DISCARD contents of glass (pastis, water and ice) and STRAIN contents of stirring glass into pastis-coated glass.

¼	**shot**	**Ricard Pastis**
1½	**shots**	**Speyside single malt whisky**
½	**shot**	**Lagavulin 16yo malt whisky**
½	**shot**	**Pedro Ximénez sherry**
¾	**shot**	**Chilled mineral water**

We say: Smoky island malts tamed by the Christmas pudding flavours of Pedro Ximénez with pastis adding notes of enlivening anise. To quote Ruby's menu, "An unabashedly smoky, Scottish version of the Manhattan. Talisker single malt whisky [we used blended Scotch and Lagavulin] and stirred over pedro ximenez sweet sherry with a Ricard pastis rinse. A well-loved signature Ruby Cocktail."
Origin: Adapted from a drink created in 2007 by Adeline Shepard and Craig Harper at Ruby Bar, Co-penhagen.

RASPBERRY ALCOHOLIC SMOOTHIE NEW

★★★★☆

Glass: Sling
Garnish: Raspberries
Method: BLEND ingredients with 12oz scoop of crushed ice. Pour into glass and serve immediately with straws.

2	**shots**	**Ketel One vodka**
1½	**shots**	**Bols Natural Yoghurt liqueur**
3	**spoons**	**Runny honey**
8	**fresh**	**Raspberries**
½	**shot**	**Crème de framboise liqueur**
1	**shot**	**Pressed apple juice**

We say: This soft pink, creamy yoghurt drink is loaded with raspberry fruit and laced with vodka.
Origin: Created in 2011 by Simon Difford at the Cabinet Room, London, England.

RASPBERRY CAIPIRINHA

★★★★☆

Glass: Old-fashioned
Garnish: None
Method: MUDDLE lime and raspberries in base of glass. Add the other ingredients and fill glass with crushed ice. CHURN drink with barspoon and serve with short straws.

¾	**fresh**	**Lime**
8	**fresh**	**Raspberries**
2	**shots**	**Leblon cachaça**
¾	**shot**	**Monin Pure Cane 2:1 sugar syrup**

Variant: Substitute other berries and fruits for raspberries. Add raspberry liqueur in place of sugar. Use rum in place of cachaça to make a Raspberry Caipirissima.
We say: A fruity twist on the popular Caipirinha.

RASPBERRY COLLINS

★★★★☆

Glass: Collins
Garnish: Raspberries & lemon slice
Method: MUDDLE raspberries in base of shaker. Add next five ingredients, SHAKE with ice and strain into ice-filled glass. TOP with soda, lightly stir and serve with straws.

10	fresh	Raspberries
2	shots	Tanqueray London dry gin
½	shot	Crème de framboise liqueur
1½	shots	Freshly squeezed lemon juice
½	shot	Monin Pure Cane 2:1 sugar syrup
3	dashes	Orange bitters
Top up with		Soda (club soda)

Variant: Raspberry Debonnaire
We say: This fruity drink is the most popular modern adaptation of the classic Collins.
Origin: Created in 1999 by Cairbry Hill, London, UK

RASPBERRY COSMO

★★★☆☆

Glass: Martini
Garnish: Raspberries
Method: SHAKE all ingredients with ice and fine strain into chilled glass.

1½	shots	Ketel One Citroen vodka
¾	shot	Crème de framboise liqueur
1	shot	Ocean Spray cranberry juice
½	shot	Freshly squeezed lime juice

We say: Your classic Cosmo but with raspberry liqueur replacing orange liqueur.
Origin: Formula by Simon Difford in 2006.

RASPBERRY DAIQUIRI NEW

★★★☆☆

Glass: Sling
Garnish: 3 Raspberries
Method: BLEND all ingredients with 1/2 scoop (6oz) crushed ice and serve in chilled glass.

1½	shots	Rum light white/blanco
1½	shots	Crème de framboise liqueur
1	shot	Freshly squeezed lime juice

We say: A crowd pleasing, slightly sweet blended fruity Daiquiri.

RASPBERRY DEBONNAIRE

★★★★☆

Glass: Collins
Garnish: Raspberries & lemon slice
Method: MUDDLE raspberries in base of shaker. Add next five ingredients. SHAKE with ice and strain into ice-filled glass. TOP with soda and lightly stir.

10	fresh	Raspberries
2	shots	Ketel One vodka
1½	shots	Freshly squeezed lemon juice
½	shot	Crème de framboise liqueur
½	shot	Monin Pure Cane 2:1 sugar syrup
3	dashes	Orange bitters
Top up with		Soda (club soda)

Variant: Raspberry Collins
We say: If based on gin rather than vodka this would be a Raspberry Collins.

RASPBERRY LASSI COCKTAIL NEW

★★★★☆

Glass: Coupette
Garnish: Raspberries & dust with cracked black pepper
Method: SHAKE all ingredients with ice and fine strain into chilled glass.

8	fresh	Raspberries
1½	shots	Ketel One vodka
1	shot	Bols Natural Yoghurt liqueur
½	shot	Crème de framboise liqueur

We say: Rich creamy vanilla yoghurt with fresh raspberries and raspberry liqueur fortified with vodka.
Origin: Created in 2011 by Simon Difford at the Cabinet Room, London, England.

RASPBERRY LYNCHBERG

★★★☆☆

Glass: Collins
Garnish: Raspberries
Method: SHAKE first three ingredients with ice and strain into ice-filled glass. TOP with lemonade and DRIZZLE liqueur around surface of drink. It will fall through the drink leaving coloured threads.

2	shots	Jack Daniel's Tennessee whiskey
¾	shot	Freshly squeezed lime juice
¼	shot	Monin Pure Cane 2:1 sugar syrup
Top up with		Lemonade/Sprite/7-Up
½	shot	Chambord black raspberry liqueur

We say: This variation on a Lynchburg Lemonade has a sweet and sour flavour laced with whiskey.
Origin: Created in 1992 by Wayne Collins at Road house, London, England.

RASPBERRY MARGARITA

★★★★☆

Glass: Coupette
Garnish: Lime wedge
Method: MUDDLE raspberries in base of shaker. Add other ingredients, SHAKE with ice and fine strain into chilled glass.

7	fresh	Raspberries
2	shots	Tequila 100% Agave
1	shot	Triple Sec
1	shot	Freshly squeezed lime juice
⅛	shot	Monin Pure Cane 2:1 sugar syrup

We say: Just as it says - a raspberry flavoured Margarita.

RASPBERRY MARTINI #1

★★★☆☆

Glass: Martini
Garnish: Raspberries
Method: MUDDLE raspberries in base of shaker. Add other ingredients, SHAKE with ice and fine strain into chilled glass.

10	fresh	Raspberries
2½	shots	Ketel One vodka
½	shot	Monin Pure Cane 2:1 sugar syrup

We say: The simplest of raspberry Martinis but still tastes good.

RASPBERRY MARTINI #2

★★★★☆

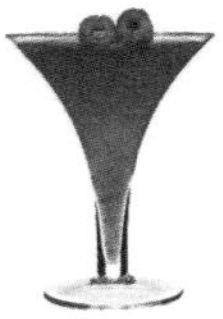

Glass: Martini
Garnish: Raspberries
Method: MUDDLE raspberries in base of shaker. Add other ingredients, SHAKE with ice and fine strain into chilled glass.

7	fresh	**Raspberries**
2	shots	**Tanqueray London dry gin**
1	shot	**Crème de framboise liqueur**
2	dashes	**Orange bitters**

We say: Great raspberry flavour integrated with gin.
Origin: Created in 1997 by Dick Bradsell, London, England.

RASPBERRY MOCHA'TINI

★★★★☆

Glass: Martini
Garnish: Raspberries
Method: SHAKE all ingredients with ice and fine strain into chilled glass.

1½	shots	**Raspberry flavoured vodka**
¾	shot	**Dark Crème de Cacao**
¾	shot	**Crème de framboise liqueur**
1	shot	**Hot espresso coffee**

We say: Sweet chocolate and raspberry tempered by dry coffee and vodka.
Origin: Discovered in 2002 at Lot 61, New York City, USA.

RASPBERRY MULE

★★★★☆

Glass: Collins
Garnish: Lime wedge
Method: MUDDLE raspberries in base of shaker. Add next three ingredients, SHAKE with ice and fine strain into ice-filled glass. TOP with ginger beer, lightly stir and serve with straws.

12	fresh	**Raspberries**
2	shots	**Ketel One vodka**
1	shot	**Freshly squeezed lime juice**
½	shot	**Monin Pure Cane 2:1 sugar syrup**
Top up with		**Ginger beer**

We say: The fruity alternative to a Moscow Mule.

RASPBERRY SAKE'TINI

★★★½☆

Glass: Martini
Garnish: Raspberries
Method: SHAKE all ingredients with ice and fine strain into chilled glass.

1½	shots	**Raspberry flavoured vodka**
½	shot	**Chambord black raspberry liqueur**
1½	shots	**Sake**
½	shot	**Fresh pressed pineapple juice**

We say: Fruity with wafts of sake - reminiscent of a French Martini.

RASPBERRY WATKINS

★★★½☆

Glass: Sling
Garnish: Raspberries
Method: SHAKE first four ingredients with ice and strain into ice-filled glass. TOP with soda, lightly stir and serve with straws.

2	shots	**Ketel One vodka**
½	shot	**Chambord black raspberry liqueur**
½	shot	**Freshly squeezed lime juice**
¼	shot	**Pomegranate (grenadine) syrup**
Top up with		**Soda (club soda)**

We say: A light, long, fizzy and refreshing drink.

RASPUTIN

★★★☆☆

Glass: Collins
Garnish: Lime wedge
Method: SHAKE all ingredients with ice and strain into ice-filled glass.

2	shots	**Raspberry flavoured vodka**
2½	shots	**Ocean Spray cranberry juice**
1½	shots	**Freshly squeezed grapefruit juice**

We say: This fruity adaptation of an Arizona Breeze is raspberry rich.

RAT PACK MANHATTAN

★★★★☆

Glass: Martini
Garnish: Orange zest twist & maraschino cherry
Method: Chill glass, add Grand Marnier, swirl to coat and then DISCARD. STIR other ingredients with ice and strain into liqueur coated glass.

½	shot	**Grand Marnier liqueur**
1½	shots	**Maker's Mark bourbon**
¾	shot	**Martini Rosso sweet vermouth**
¾	shot	**Martini Extra Dry vermouth**
3	dashes	**Angostura aromatic bitters**

We say: A twist on the classic Manhattan.
Origin: Created in 2000 by Wayne Collins at High Holborn, London, England. Originally Wayne used different whiskies to represent each of the Rat Pack crooners. The wash of Grand Marnier was for Sammy Davis, the wild card of the bunch.

RATTLESNAKE

★★★½☆

Glass: Martini
Garnish: Lemon zest twist
Method: SHAKE all ingredients with ice and fine strain into chilled glass.

2	shots	**Maker's Mark bourbon**
¼	shot	**Freshly squeezed lemon juice**
¼	shot	**Monin Pure Cane 2:1 sugar syrup**
⅛	shot	**Absinthe**
½	shot	**Egg white**
½	shot	**Chilled mineral water**

We say: To quote Craddock, "So called because it will either cure rattlesnake bite, or kill rattlesnakes, or make you see them".
Origin: Adapted from a recipe purloined from a 1930 edition of the *'Savoy Cocktail Book'* by Harry Craddock.

RATTLESNAKE SHOT

★★★☆☆

Glass: Shot
Garnish: None
Method: Refrigerate ingredients then LAYER in chilled glass by carefully pouring in the following order.

½ shot   **Kahlúa coffee liqueur**
½ shot   **White Crème de Cacao**
½ shot   **Baileys Irish cream liqueur**

We say: Taste rather like a strong cappuccino.

RAY GUN

★★★☆☆

Glass: Flute
Garnish: Orange zest twist
Method: POUR Chartreuse and blue curaçao into chilled glass. TOP with champagne.

½ shot   **Chartreuse Green liqueur**
¾ shot   **Bols Blue Curaçao liqueur**
Top up with   **Brut champagne**

We say: Not for the faint-hearted.

RAY'S HARD LEMONADE ⚷

★★★★☆

Glass: Collins
Garnish: Mint sprig
Method: Lightly MUDDLE (just to bruise) mint in base of shaker. Add next 4 ingredients, SHAKE with ice and fine strain into ice-filled glass. TOP with soda, lightly stir and serve with straws.

7 fresh   **Mint leaves**
2 shots   **Ketel One vodka**
1 shot   **Freshly squeezed lemon juice**
2 shots   **Freshly squeezed lime juice**
1½ shots   **Monin Pure Cane 2:1 sugar syrup**
Top up with   **Soda (club soda)**

Variant: Hard Lemonade
We say: Alcoholic lemonade with mint? A vodka mojito? However you describe it, it works.
Origin: Discovered in 2004 at Spring Street Natural Restaurant, New York City, USA.

RAZZITINI

★★★★☆

Glass: Martini
Garnish: Raspberries
Method: SHAKE first two ingredients with ice and fine strain into chilled glass. TOP with lemonade.

2½ shots   **Ketel One Citroen vodka**
¾ shot   **Chambord black raspberry liqueur**
Top up with   **Lemonade/Sprite/7-Up**

We say: This citrus and raspberry Martini is a tad on the sweet side.
Origin: Discovered in 2003 at Paramount Hotel, New York City, USA.

RAZZMATAZZ

★★★★☆

Glass: Martini
Garnish: Mint sprig
Method: STIR honey with vodka until honey is dissolved. Add other ingredients, SHAKE all ingredients with ice and fine strain into chilled glass.

3 spoons   **Runny honey**
1½ shots   **Raspberry flavoured vodka**
½ shot   **Triple Sec**
1 shot   **Pressed apple juice**
¼ shot   **Freshly squeezed lime juice**
6 fresh   **Mint leaves**

We say: Fruity with general of razzmatazz
Origin: Created by Wayne Collins, London, England.

RAZZZZZZBERRY MARTINI

★★★★☆

Glass: Martini
Garnish: Raspberries
Method: SHAKE all ingredients with ice and fine strain into chilled glass.

2 shots   **Vanilla-infused Ketel One vodka**
½ shot   **Chambord black raspberry liqueur**
2 shots   **Ocean Spray cranberry juice**

We say: Raspberry and vanilla with characteristic dry cranberry fruit.

REAL LEMONADE (MOCKTAIL) ⚷

★★★★☆

Glass: Collins
Garnish: Lemon slice
Method: POUR ingredients in ice-filled glass and lightly STIR. Serve with straws.

2 shots   **Freshly squeezed lemon juice**
1 shot   **Monin Pure Cane 2:1 sugar syrup**
Top up with   **Soda (club soda)**

We say: The classic English summertime refresher.

STAR RATINGS EXPLAINED

★★★★★ Excellent

★★★★✰ Recommended   ★★★★☆ Praiseworthy
★★★✰☆ Commended   ★★★☆☆ Mediocre
★★✰☆☆ Disappointing   ★★☆☆☆ Pretty awful
★✰☆☆☆ Shameful   ★☆☆☆☆ Disgusting

THE REALITY CHECK NEW

★★★★★

Glass: Beer mug
Garnish: Lime zest twist
Method: MUDDLE raspberries in base of large shaker tin. Add ice and other ingredients then THROW (strain from a height into a second strainer). Repeat four times and then strain into ice-filled glass.

5	fresh	Raspberries
2/3	shot	Ketel One vodka
2/3	shot	Becherovka liqueur
1/4	shot	Lime
2¾	shots	Pilsner lager
1/3	shot	Monin Pure Cane 2:1 sugar syrup
1	shot	Angostura aromatic bitters

We say: Raspberry fruit, herbal complexity and dry hoppy beer with a splash of zesty lime. Fabulously refreshing.
Origin: Created in 2013 by Simone Caporale at the Artesian Bar, Langham Hotel, London. Simone was one of five finalists in the diffordsguide Beer-tail Competition for London Cocktail Week 2013 held in August 2013 at Simon Difford's Cabinet Room bar in London.

RED ANGEL

★★★★☆

Glass: Martini
Garnish: Orange zest twist
Method: SHAKE all ingredients with ice and fine strain into chilled glass.

2	shots	Shiraz red wine
1	shot	Grand Marnier liqueur
1/4	shot	Luxardo Maraschino liqueur
3/4	shot	Chilled mineral water

We say: A subtly flavoured cocktail with a dry, almost tannic edge.
Origin: Created in 2001 by Tony Conigliaro at Isola, Knightsbridge, London, England.

RED APPLE

★★★★☆

Glass: Martini
Garnish: Maraschino cherry
Method: SHAKE all ingredients with ice and fine strain into chilled glass.

1½	shots	Maker's Mark bourbon
1/2	shot	Sour apple liqueur
2	shots	Ocean Spray cranberry juice

Variant: Sour Apple Martini
We say: As Apple Martinis go, this one is rather good.

THE RED ARMY

★★★☆☆

Glass: Old-fashioned
Garnish: Raspberries
Method: MUDDLE raspberries in base of shaker. Add other ingredients, SHAKE with ice and fine strain into chilled glass. MUDDLE raspberries in base of shaker. Add other ingredients, SHAKE with ice and fine strain into glass filled with crushed ice.

12	fresh	Raspberries
2	shots	Raspberry flavoured vodka
1/2	shot	Triple Sec
1	shot	Freshly squeezed lime juice
1/2	shot	Monin Pure Cane 2:1 sugar syrup
1/2	shot	Crème de framboise liqueur

We say: Rather red and rather fruity.
Origin: Created in 2002 by Alex Kammerling, London, England.

RED BREAST

★★★☆☆

Glass: Collins
Garnish: Raspberries
Method: POUR first three ingredients into ice-filled glass and lightly stir. DRIZZLE raspberry liqueur over surface of drink.

2	shots	Dewar's White label Scotch
1/2	shot	Freshly squeezed lime juice
Top up with		Ginger beer
1/2	shot	Crème de framboise liqueur

We say: Long and a tad pink but packs a tasty punch.
Origin: Created in 2004 by Wayne Collins, England.

RED HOOK

★★★★★

Glass: Coupette
Garnish: Maraschino cherry
Method: STIR all ingredient with ice and strain into chilled glass.

2	shots	Straight rye whiskey
1½	shots	Carpano Punt E Mes
1/2	shot	Luxardo Maraschino liqueur

We say: This Manhattan-like drink was inspired by the Brooklyn Cocktail, hence it is named after a neighbourhood of Brooklyn, another of New York City's neighbourhood's. Thought to be the first of many rifts on the Brooklyn to emerge during 2009.
Origin: Created in the early Noughties by Enzo Enrico at Milk and Honey, New York City, USA.

BARTENDER'S TIP MUDDLE

Muddling means pummelling fruits, herbs and/or spices with a muddler (a blunt tool similar to a pestle) so as to crush them and release their flavour. (You can also use a rolling pin.)

As when using a pestle and mortar, push down on the muddler with a twisting action. Never attempt to muddle hard, unripe fruits in a glass as the pressure required could break the glass.

RED HOOKER

Glass: Martini
Garnish: Peach slice
Method: SHAKE all ingredients with ice and fine strain into chilled glass.

1	shot	Boiron peach purée
2	shots	Tequila 100% Agave
¾	shot	Crème de framboise liqueur
¾	shot	Freshly squeezed lemon juice

We say: An appropriately named red, fruity drink with more than a hint of tequila.

RED LION #1 (MODERN FORMULA)

Glass: Martini
Garnish: Orange slice
Method: SHAKE all ingredients with ice and fine strain into chilled glass.

1¼	shots	Tanqueray London dry gin
1¼	shots	Grand Marnier liqueur
1	shot	Freshly squeezed orange juice
1	shot	Freshly squeezed lemon juice
⅛	shot	Pomegranate (grenadine) syrup

We say: The colour of a summer's twilight with a rich tangy orange flavour.
Origin: The classic drink is said to have been created for the Chicago World Fair in 1933. However, it won the British Empire Cocktail Competition that year and was more likely created by W J Tarling for Booth's gin and named after the brand's Red Lion Distillery in London.

RED LION #2 (EMBURY'S FORMULA)

Glass: Martini
Garnish: Orange slice
Method: SHAKE all ingredients with ice and fine strain into chilled glass.

2	shots	Tanqueray London dry gin
¼	shot	Grand Marnier liqueur
½	shot	Freshly squeezed lime juice
¼	shot	Pomegranate (grenadine) syrup
¾	shot	Chilled mineral water

We say: Embury is a Daiquiri fan and this is reminiscent of a Daiquiri in both style and proportions.
Origin: Recipe adapted from one originally published in 'The Fine Art of Mixing Drinks' by David Embury.

RED MANHATTAN NEW

Glass: Coupette
Garnish: Maraschino cherry
Method: STIR all ingredients with ice and strain into chilled glass.

2	shots	Maker's Mark bourbon
1	shot	Martini Rosso sweet vermouth
¼	shot	Claret red wine
⅛	shot	Luxardo maraschino liqueur
2	dashes	Angostura aromatic bitters

We say: The tannins from the splash of red wine add complexity and depth of flavour to this Sweet Manhattan.
Origin: Created in November 2010 by Simon Difford at the Cabinet Room, London, England.

RED MARAUDER

Glass: Martini
Garnish: Raspberries
Method: SHAKE all ingredients with ice and fine strain into chilled glass.

2	shots	Cognac VSOP
½	shot	Chambord black raspberry liqueur
1½	shots	Ocean Spray cranberry juice
¼	shot	Freshly squeezed lime juice

We say: Slightly sweet and fruity with a hint of raspberry and cognac's distinctive flavour.
Origin: Originally created for Martell, long term sponsors of the Grand National, this is named after the horse that won in 2001.

RED MELON'TINI

Glass: Martini
Garnish: Watermelon wedge
Method: Cut watermelon into 16 segments, chop the flesh from one segment into cubes and MUDDLE in base of shaker. Add other ingredients, SHAKE all ingredients with ice and fine strain into chilled glass.

1	segment Fresh watermelon
2	shots	Pepper-infused Ketel One vodka
¼	shot	Monin Pure Cane 2:1 sugar syrup
4	grind	Black pepper

We say: Watermelon peppered with vodka and the subtlest peppery finish.
Origin: Discovered in 2002 at the Fifth Floor Bar, Harvey Nichol's, London, England.

RED NECK MARTINI

Glass: Martini
Garnish: Orange zest twist
Method: SHAKE all ingredients with ice and fine strain into chilled glass.

2	shots	Dewar's White label Scotch
1	shot	Dubonnet Red (French made)
1	shot	De Kuyper Cherry Brandy liqueur

We say: Nicely balanced, aromatic and not too sweet - the flavour of the Scotch shines through.
Origin: Created by Sylvain Solignac in 2002 at Circus Bar, London, England.

RED OR DEAD

Glass: Collins
Garnish: Lime wedge
Method: SHAKE all ingredients with ice and strain into ice-filled glass.

1½	shots	Southern Comfort liqueur
¾	shot	Campari Bitter
¾	shot	Freshly squeezed lime juice
3	shots	Ocean Spray cranberry juice

We say: This long, ruby drink balances sweetness, sourness and bitterness.

RED ROVER

★★★★☆

Glass: Old-fashioned
Garnish: Orange slice
Method: SHAKE all ingredients with ice and strain into ice-filled glass.

3	shots	Shiraz red wine
1	shot	Pusser's Navy rum
½	shot	Chambord black raspberry liqueur

We say: Carpet-scaring red with the body of red wine but the palate of a cocktail.

RED RUM MARTINI

★★★★½

Glass: Martini
Garnish: Redcurrants
Method: MUDDLE redcurrants a base of shaker. Add other ingredients, SHAKE all ingredients with ice and fine strain into chilled glass.

24	fresh	Redcurrants
2	shots	Bacardi 8yo aged rum
½	shot	Sloe Gin liqueur
½	shot	Freshly squeezed lemon juice
½	shot	Monin Vanilla sugar syrup

We say: A beautifully fruity, adult balance of bittersweet flavours.
Origin: Created by Jason Scott in 2002 at Oloroso, Edinburgh, Scotland. This cocktail, which is red and contains rum, is named after 'Red Rum', the only horse in history to win the Grand National three times (on his other two attempts he came second). He became a British hero, made an appearance on the BBC Sports Personality of the Year show and paraded right up to his death at the age 30 in 1995.

RED SNAPPER

★★★★☆

Glass: Collins
Garnish: Salt & pepper rim
Method: SHAKE all ingredients with ice and strain into ice-filled glass. Serve with straws.

2	shots	Tanqueray London dry gin
4	shots	Tomato juice
½	shot	Freshly squeezed lemon juice
7	drops	Tabasco hot pepper sauce
4	dashes	Worcestershire sauce
2	pinch	Celery salt
2	grind	Black pepper

Variant: Bloody Mary
We say: Looks like a Bloody Mary but features gin's aromatic botanicals.
Origin: Today, the term Red Snapper means a Bloody Mary made with gin instead of vodka. But the first known recipes, from the 1940s, describe a 50-50 blend of vodka and tomato juice, with spices, just like an early Bloody Mary: one book even states that the Red Snapper is identical to the Bloody Mary.

Cocktail lore states that the Bloody Mary was officially renamed the Red Snapper at the St. Regis Hotel, at some point after the fabulously wealthy Vincent Astor bought it in 1935. Fernand Petiot, who most likely created the original drink (see 'Bloody Mary'), was working there, but Astor apparently found the title too crude for his clientele and insisted the drink be renamed. Customers, of course, continued to order Bloody Marys, but the Red Snapper found a drink of its own in due course.

REDBACK

★★★☆☆

Glass: Shot
Garnish: Maraschino cherry
Method: POUR sambuca into glass, then pour advocaat down the side of the glass.

½	shot	Advocaat liqueur
1	shot	Opal Nera black sambuca

We say: An impressive looking shot.

REEF JUICE

★★★★☆

Glass: Collins
Garnish: Pineapple wedge
Method: SHAKE all ingredients with ice and strain into ice-filled glass.

1½	shots	Pusser's Navy rum
½	shot	Ketel One vodka
1	shot	Bols Banana liqueur
½	shot	Freshly squeezed lime juice
2½	shots	Fresh pressed pineapple juice
½	shot	Pomegranate (grenadine) syrup

We say: Tangy, fruity and dangerously moreish.
Origin: Charles Tobias, proprietor of Pusser's, created this drink at the Beach Bar in Fort Lauderdale, Florida. It was a favourite of a friend who crashed his boat on the reef.

REGGAE RUM PUNCH

★★★★½

Glass: Collins
Garnish: Pineapple wedge & maraschino cherry
Method: SHAKE all ingredients with ice and strain into glass filled with crushed ice.

1¾	shots	Wray & Nephew overproof rum
½	shot	Crème de framboise liqueur
¾	shot	Freshly squeezed lime juice
¾	shot	Fresh pressed pineapple juice
1½	shots	Freshly squeezed orange juice
¾	shot	Pomegranate (grenadine) syrup

We say: Jamaicans have a sweet tooth and love their rum. This drink combines sweetness, strength and a generous amount of fruit.
Origin: The most popular punch in Jamaica, where it is sold under different names with slightly varying ingredients. It always contains orange, pineapple and most importantly, overproof rum.

RELAJESE CON FACUNDO

★★★★½☆

Glass: Martini
Garnish: Grapefruit slice
Method: SHAKE all ingredients with cubed ice and fine-strain into a chilled glass.

2	shots	Bacardi Superior rum
1	shot	Freshly squeezed grapefruit juice
½	shot	Monin Lavender sugar syrup
2	dashes	Angostura aromatic bitters

We say: Floral but this rum-based drink is far from being a pansy.
Origin: Created in 2008 by Adam Elmegirab at Evolution Bar Consultancy, Aberdeen, Scotland. The name literally translates from Spanish as 'Relax with Facundo'.

REMEMBER THE MAINE

Glass: Old-fashioned
Garnish: Lemon zest twist
Method: POUR the absinthe into ice-filled glass, top up with water and set to one side. Separately, POUR other ingredients into a ice-filled mixing glass and STIR well. DISCARD absinthe, water and ice from serving glass. Finally strain contents of mixing glass into the absinthe rinsed glass.

1	shot	Absinthe
Top up with		Chilled mineral water
2	shots	Maker's Mark bourbon
¾	shot	De Kuyper Cherry Brandy liqueur
¾	shot	Martini Rosso sweet vermouth

We say: Charles H. Baker says of this twist on a Sazerac, "Treat this one with the respect it deserves, gentleman."
Origin: Adapted from a recipe by Charles H. Baker Junior. In his 1939 'The Gentleman's Companion' he writes: "a Hazy Memory of a Night in Havana during the Unpleasantnesses of 1933, when Each Swallow Was Punctuated with Bombs Going off on the Prado, or the Sound of 3" Shells Being Fired at the Hotel NACIONAL, then Haven for Certain Anti-Revolutionary Officers". The drink is named after the press slogan, which allegedly provoked the 1898 Spanish-American War.

REMSEN COOLER

Glass: Collins
Garnish: Lemon peel (whole)
Method: POUR ingredients into ice-filled glass and serve with straws.

2½	shots	Dewar's White label Scotch
Top up with		Soda from siphon

We say: Scotch and soda for the sophisticate.
Origin: Adapted from a recipe purloined from David Embury's classic book, 'The Fine Art of Mixing Drinks', and so named because it was originally made with the now defunct Remsen Scotch whisky. Embury claims this is "the original cooler".

RESOLUTE

Glass: Martini
Garnish: Lemon zest twist
Method: SHAKE all ingredients with ice and fine strain into chilled glass.

2	shots	Tanqueray London dry gin
1	shot	De Kuyper Apricot Brandy liqueur
½	shot	Freshly squeezed lemon juice
¾	shot	Chilled mineral water

We say: All three flavours work in harmony.
Origin: Adapted from a recipe purloined from a 1930 edition of the 'Savoy Cocktail Book' by Harry Craddock.

REVERSE MARTINI

Glass: Martini
Garnish: Chilled olive on stick or lemon zest twist
Method: STIR all ingredients with ice and strain into chilled glass.

2	shots	Martini Extra Dry vermouth
1	shot	Tanqueray London dry gin

We say: Simply a Dry Martini with the proportions reversed to make a dripping Wet Martini.

REVERSED VESPER & TONIC

Glass: Martini
Garnish: Lemon zest twist
Method: SHAKE all ingredients with ice and fine strain into chilled glass.

1	shot	Tanqueray London dry gin
1	shot	Ketel One vodka
1	shot	Lillet Blanc
⅛	shot	Becherovka liqueur
⅛	shot	Pomegranate (grenadine) syrup
½	shot	Tonic water

We say: Martini in style but with the hard edges shaken off and a hint of eastern spice added. Scarily, it took 14 attempts and 13 wasted drinks to arrive at the above formula.
Origin: Created in 2008 by Simon Difford at the Cabinet Room, London, England. James Bond named his favourite style of Martini after the beautiful Russian agent Vesper Lynd. This version is 'Reversed' due to the dramatically increased ratio of Lillet. It mixes east and west ingredients with the introduction of Becherovka, and where there is Becherovka there should be tonic water.

RHETT BUTLER

Glass: Old-fashioned
Garnish: Lime wedge
Method: SHAKE all ingredients with ice and strain into ice-filled glass.

1	shot	Grand Marnier liqueur
1	shot	Southern Comfort liqueur
2	shots	Ocean Spray cranberry juice
1	shot	Freshly squeezed lime juice

We say: A simple and well-balanced classic drink.

BARTENDER'S TIP MEASURING - SHOTS & SPOONS

In this guide measures of each ingredient are expressed in 'shots'. Ideally a shot is 25ml or one US fluid ounce (29.6ml), measured in a standard jigger. (You can also use a clean medicine measure or even a small shot glass.)

Whatever your chosen measure, it should have straight sides to enable you to accurately judge fractions of a shot. Look out for measures which are graduated in ounces and marked with quarter and half ounces.

RHINE WINE COBBLER NEW

★★★★⯨

Glass: Goblet
Garnish: A grape, orange and pineapple slice
Method: MUDDLE grapes and pineapple in base of shaker and fine strain (without shaking) into glass filled with crushed ice. POUR other ingredients into glass and cobble (churn/stir) with barspoon to thoroughly mix.

3	fresh	Seedless white grapes
2	wedge	Pineapple (fresh)
3	shots	Reisling wine (German)
½	shot	Freshly squeezed orange juice
½	shot	Monin Pure Cane 2:1 sugar syrup

We say: Light, grapey, fruit and very refreshing. One for a summer's afternoon.
Origin: Recipe adapted from Harry Johnson's 1882 *'Bartender's Manual'*.

RHINESTONE COWGIRL

★★★⯨☆

Glass: Collins
Garnish: Orange slice
Method: SHAKE all ingredients with ice and strain into chilled glass.

2	shots	Maker's Mark bourbon
2	shots	Ocean Spray cranberry juice
1	shot	Freshly squeezed lemon juice
½	shot	Monin Pure Cane 2:1 sugar syrup
¾	shot	Crème de cassis liqueur

We say: Tangy, citrus, cranberry and berry fruit laced with sweetened bourbon.

RHODE ISLAND RED

★★★★☆

Glass: Collins
Garnish: Lemon & lime zest twists
Method: SHAKE first five ingredients with ice and strain into ice-filled glass. TOP with ginger beer, lightly stir and serve with straws.

2	shots	Tequila 100% Agave
½	shot	Chambord black raspberry liqueur
¾	shot	Freshly squeezed lemon juice
½	shot	Agave nectar
1	dash	Orange bitters
Top up with		Ginger beer

We say: Tequila with a hint of berry fruit, slightly sweetened with agave nectar, spiced and made long with ginger beer.
Origin: Created in 2009 by Vincenzo Marianella at Copa d'Oro, Santa Monica, USA.

RHUBARB & CUSTARD MARTINI

★★★★☆

Glass: Martini
Garnish: Dust with grated nutmeg
Method: SHAKE all ingredients with ice and fine strain into chilled glass.

1¼	shots	Tanqueray London dry gin
1¼	shots	Advocaat liqueur
1¼	shots	Rhubarb syrup (from tinned fruit)

We say: As sharp, sweet, creamy and flavourful as the dessert it imitates.
Origin: We created this drink in 2002. Rhubarb and Custard is a great British dessert and was a cult children's TV cartoon in the 1970s. It featured a naughty pink can called Custard and a dog named Rhubarb who, like many British men, spent a lot of time in his garden shed.

RHUBARB & HONEY BELLINI

★★★★☆

Glass: Flute
Garnish: Orange zest twist
Method: SHAKE rhubarb syrup and honey liqueur with ice and fine strain into chille glass. TOP with Prosecco and gently stir.

1¼	shots	Rhubarb & orange preserve
1¼	shots	Krupnik spiced honey liqueur
Top up with		Prosecco sparkling wine

We say: The implausible combination works surprisingly well.
Origin: A simplified adaptation of a drink created in 2003 by Tony Conigliaro at London's Shumi.

RHUBARB & LEMONGRASS MARTINI

★★★★☆

Glass: Martini
Garnish: Lemongrass
Method: MUDDLE lemongrass in base of shaker. Add other ingredients, SHAKE all ingredients with ice and fine strain into chilled glass.

4	inch	Lemongrass stem (chopped)
2	shots	Tanqueray London dry gin
2	shots	Rhubarb syrup (from tinned fruit)
⅛	shot	Monin Pure Cane 2:1 sugar syrup

We say: Fragrant, exotic lemon flavours combine well with rhubarb to make a surprisingly refreshing long drink.
Origin: I based this cocktail on a drink I discovered in 2003 at Zuma, London, England.

RHUBARB LUCCA NEGRONI NEW

★★★★⯨

Glass: Old-fashioned
Garnish: Orange zest twist (discarded) and rhubarb stirrer
Method: POUR all ingredients into ice-filled glass and STIR.

1	shot	Tanqueray London dry gin
1	shot	Campari Bitter
½	shot	Carpano Antica Formula
½	shot	Rabarbaro

We say: A rhubarb-influenced rift on the classic Negroni.
Origin: Created in 2011 by Jonathan Abarbanel at Quo Vadis, London, England. Jonathan originally used Rhubarb-infused Tanqueray London dry gin.

RHUBARB TRIANGLE NEW

★★★⯪☆

Glass: Martini
Garnish: Float apple slice
Method: SHAKE all ingredients with ice and fine strain into chilled glass.

1½	shots	Rhubarb liqueur
1½	shots	Tanqueray London dry gin
¼	shot	Pressed apple juice
¼	shot	Martini Extra dry vermouth

We say:
Origin: Adapted from a drink created in 2011 by Joseph Cassidy, Surrey, England. The name references Yorkshire's famous rhubarb triangle and also the trio of ingredients.

RIBALAIGUA DAIQUIRI #3

★★★★☆

Glass: Martini
Garnish: Mint leaf
Method: SHAKE all ingredients with ice and fine strain into chilled glass.

2	shots	Bacardi Superior rum
½	shot	Luxardo Maraschino liqueur
1	shot	Freshly squeezed grapefruit juice
½	shot	Chilled mineral water

Variant: With gin in place of rum this becomes Seventh Heaven No.2.
We say: This unusual Daiquiri leads to with sweet maraschino and finishes with sour grapefruit.
Origin: Named for Constantino Ribalaigua, who introduced Hemingway to the Daiquiri at El Floridita, Havana, Cuba.

RICHMOND GIMLET

★★★★☆

Glass: Martini
Garnish: Mint leaf
Method: SHAKE all ingredients with ice and fine strain into chilled glass.

8	fresh	Mint leaves
2	shots	Tanqueray London dry gin
¾	shot	Freshly squeezed lime juice
½	shot	Monin Pure Cane 2:1 sugar syrup
½	shot	Chilled mineral water

We say: A properly grown-up Gimlet.
Origin: Adapted from a recipe created in 2008 by Jeffrey Morgenthaler at Bel Ami Lounge, Oregon, USA.

RITZ COCKTAIL UPDATED

★★★★☆

Glass: Martini
Garnish: Flamed orange zest twist
Method: STIR first four ingredients with ice and strain into chilled glass. TOP with a splash of champagne.

¾	shot	Courvoisier VSOP Exclusif
½	shot	Cointreau triple sec
¼	shot	Luxardo maraschino liqueur
¼	shot	Freshly squeezed lemon juice
Top up with		Brut champagne

We say: Citrus freshness with a cognac backbone, lightened and dried with champagne.
Origin: Created by Dale DeGroff, New York City, USA.

RIVIERA BREEZE

★★★⯪☆

Glass: Old-fashioned
Garnish: Orange slice
Method: POUR pastis and orange juice into glass and then fill with ice. TOP with ginger ale and stir.

1½	shots	Ricard Pastis
2	shots	Freshly squeezed orange juice
Top up with		Ginger ale

We say: An aniseed-rich summertime cooler.
Origin: Created in 2003 by Rool Buckley at Café Lebowitz, New York City, USA.

RIZZO

★★★★☆

Glass: Martini
Garnish: Apple slice
Method: SHAKE all ingredients with ice and fine strain into chilled glass.

1	shot	Calvados/Applejack brandy
1	shot	Tanqueray London dry gin
¾	shot	Freshly squeezed grapefruit juice
½	shot	Freshly squeezed lime juice
¼	shot	Passion fruit syrup
¼	shot	Pomegranate (grenadine) syrup

We say: The tangy, sharp grapefruit reveals hints of apple spirit smoothed by grenadine.
Origin: Created in 2006 by Gregor de Gruyther at Ronnie Scott's, London, England, and named for Betty Rizzo, the leader of the Pink Ladies in the film Grease.

ROA AE

★★★⯪☆

Glass: Collins
Garnish: Pineapple wedge
Method: SHAKE all ingredients with ice and strain into ice-filled glass.

1½	shots	Bacardi Superior rum
½	shot	De Kuyper Apricot Brandy liqueur
½	shot	Grand Marnier liqueur
½	shot	Belle de Brillet pear liqueur
3	shots	Fresh pressed pineapple juice
¾	shot	Freshly squeezed lime juice

We say: Not quite the best, but this long, fruity thirst quencher isn't half bad.
Origin: Discovered in 2003 at Booly Mardy's, Glasgow, Scotland. Cocktail aficionados will be familiar with the Tahitian phase 'Mai Tai - Roa Ae', or 'out of this world - the best', which gave Mai Tai it's name. This cocktail means simply 'the best'.

STAR RATINGS EXPLAINED

★★★★★ Excellent

★★★★⯪ Recommended	★★★★☆ Praiseworthy
★★★⯪☆ Commended	★★★☆☆ Mediocre
★★⯪☆☆ Disappointing	★★☆☆☆ Pretty awful
★⯪☆☆☆ Shameful	★☆☆☆☆ Disgusting

THE ROADRUNNER

★★★★☆

Glass: Martini
Garnish: Lemon zest twist
Method: SHAKE all ingredients with ice and fine strain into chilled glass.

2	shots	**Vanilla-infused tequila**
¾	shot	**Freshly squeezed lemon juice**
2	dashes	**Angostura aromatic bitters**
½	shot	**Maple syrup**
½	fresh	**Egg white**

We say: Citrus and tequila with a hint of maple and vanilla, smoothed with egg white.
Origin: Discovered in 2005 at The Cuckoo Club, London, England.

ROB ROY #1

★★★★☆

Glass: Martini
Garnish: Lemon zest twist (discarded) & maraschino cherry
Method: STIR all ingredients with ice and strain into chilled glass.

2	shots	**Dewar's White label Scotch**
1	shot	**Martini Rosso sweet vermouth**
2	dashes	**Angostura aromatic bitters**
⅛	shot	**Maraschino syrup (from cherry jar)**

Variant: 'Highland', made with orange bitters instead of Angostura.
We say: A Sweet Manhattan made with Scotch in place of bourbon. The dry, peaty whisky and bitters ensure it's not too sweet.
Origin: Created in 1894 at New York's Waldorf-Astoria Hotel (the Empire State Building occupies the site today) and named after the Broadway show that was showing at the time.

ROB ROY #2

★★★★½

Glass: Martini
Garnish: Orange zest twist (discarded) & maraschino cherry
Method: STIR all ingredients with ice and strain into chilled glass.

2	shots	**Dewar's White label Scotch**
1	shot	**Martini Rosso sweet vermouth**
2	dashes	**Peychaud's aromatic bitters**
½	shot	**Chilled mineral water**

We say: The Scotch answer to the Manhattan with added complexity courtesy of Peychaud's aromatic bitters.
Origin: This variation on the classic Rob Roy is recommended by author David Embury in his influential *Fine Art of Mixing Drinks*.

ROBIN HOOD #1

★★★★☆

Glass: Martini
Garnish: Apple wedge
Method: SHAKE all ingredients with ice and fine strain into chilled glass.

1¾	shots	**Bacardi Superior rum**
1¼	shots	**Berentzen Apple schnapps**
¾	shot	**Rose's lime cordial**
½	shot	**Freshly squeezed lime juice**

We say: American readers might consider this a Apple Martini based on rum.
Origin: Adapted from a drink created in 2002 by Tony Conigliaro at The Lonsdale, London, England.

ROC-A-COE UPDATED

★★★½☆

Glass: Martini
Garnish: Maraschino cherry
Method: STIR all ingredients with ice and strain into chilled glass.

1½	shots	**Tanqueray London dry gin**
2	shots	**Amontillado sherry**
⅛	shot	**Monin Pure Cane 2:1 sugar syrup**
½	shot	**Chilled mineral water**

We say: Aromatic and balanced.
Origin: Adapted from a recipe purloined from a 1930 edition of the *'Savoy Cocktail Book'* by Harry Craddock.

ROCK 'N' RYE

★★★★½

Glass: Old-fashioned
Garnish: Orange zest twist (discarded) & maraschino cherry
Method: SHAKE all ingredients with ice and strain into ice-filled glass.

2½	shots	**Straight rye whiskey**
½	shot	**Freshly squeezed orange juice**
⅛	shot	**Freshly squeezed lemon juice**
¼	shot	**Maraschino syrup (from cherry jar)**
¼	shot	**Monin Pure Cane 2:1 sugar syrup**

We say: Great rye whiskey notes with hints of orange and cherry. Slightly sweet but all too easy.
Origin: Created in January 2010 by Simon Difford at the Cabinet Room, London, England.

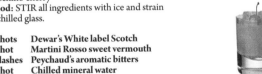

BARTENDER'S TIP FINE STRAIN

Most cocktails that are served 'straight up' without ice benefit from an additional finer strain, over and above the standard strain.

This 'fine strain' removes small fragments of fruit and fine flecks of ice which can spoil the appearance of a drink and is particularly beneficial if the drink has been shaken. Fine straining is achieved by simply holding a fine sieve, like a tea strainer, between the shaker and the glass.

ROCKY LEFT BANK NEW

★★★★½

Glass: Old Fashioned
Garnish: Lime zest twist
Method: SHAKE all ingredients with ice and strain into ice-filled glass.

1½ shots	Tanqueray London dry gin
1½ shots	St-Germain elderflower liqueur
1½ shots	Chablis white wine

We say: Slightly sweet, crowd pleasing combo of gin, elderflower and white wine.
Origin: Created in 2006 by Simon Difford at The Cabinet Room, London, England.

ROCKY MOUNTAIN ROOTBEER

★★★★☆

Glass: Collins
Garnish: Lime wedge
Method: POUR vodka and liqueur into ice-filled glass, TOP up with cola and lightly stir.

2 shots	Ketel One vodka
¾ shot	Galliano L'Autentico liqueur
Top up with	Coca-Cola

We say: Does indeed taste reminiscent of alcoholic root beer.

ROCOCOA

★★★½☆

Glass: Coupette
Garnish: Half vanilla pod
Method: STIR all ingredients with ice and strain into chilled glass.

2 shots	Bacardi Superior rum
⅓ shot	White Crème de Cacao
⅛ shot	Lagavulin 16yo malt whisky
¼ shot	Chilled mineral water
2 dashes	Chocolate bitters

We say: I love this subtly smoky chocolate and light rum. Martini-style cocktail but the in-house tasting panel was more subdued. Please try one for yourself and email with your thoughts.
Origin: Adapted from a drink created by Scott Tyrer at Bibis Italianissimo, Leeds, England.

THE ROFFIGNAC

★★★★☆

Glass: Collins
Garnish: Lime wedge
Method: SHAKE first two ingredients with ice and strain into ice-filled glass. TOP with soda, lightly stir and serve with straws.

2 shots	Cognac VSOP
1 shot	Crème de framboise liqueur
Top up with	Soda (club soda)

We say: This bright red, fruity drink is simple but moreish.
Origin: This classic cocktail is named after Count Louis Philippe Joseph de Roffignac, Mayor of New Orleans 1820-1828. Roffignac is noted for introducing street lights to the city and laying cobblestones on the roads in the French Quarter.

ROGER

★★★½☆

Glass: Martini
Garnish: Peach slice
Method: SHAKE all ingredients with ice and fine strain into chilled glass.

2 shots	Ketel One vodka
2 shots	Boiron peach purée
½ shot	Freshly squeezed lemon juice
¼ shot	Monin Pure Cane 2:1 sugar syrup

We say: Thick and very fruity - one for a summer's afternoon.
Origin: A popular drink in Venice, where it is made using the peach purée mix prepared for bellinis.

ROMAN PUNCH

★★★★☆

Glass: Collins
Garnish: Lemon slice
Method: SHAKE all ingredients with ice and strain into glass filled with crushed ice. Serve with straws.

1½ shots	Bénédictine D.O.M.
1½ shots	Cognac VSOP
¾ shot	Wray & Nephew overproof rum
¾ shot	Freshly squeezed lemon juice
2 shots	Chilled mineral water

We say: Spirited and refreshing with herbal notes.

ROOSEVELT COCKTAIL

★★★★½

Glass: Martini
Garnish: Orange zest twist
Method: SHAKE all ingredients with ice and fine strain into chilled glass.

1¾ shots	Bacardi 8yo aged rum
¾ shot	Martini Extra Dry vermouth
¼ shot	Freshly squeezed orange juice
¼ shot	Monin Pure Cane 2:1 sugar syrup

We say: When right this drink is sublime and hard to improve - we have tried changing proportions but without success.

ROOSEVELT MARTINI ⚬🗝

★★★★½

Glass: Martini
Garnish: Two olives on stick
Method: STIR all ingredients with ice and strain into chilled glass.

| 2½ shots | Tanqueray London dry gin |
| ½ shot | Martini Extra Dry vermouth |

We say: A regular Martini, but garnished with two olives instead of one.
Origin: Named after Franklin Delano Roosevelt (1882-1945), the 32nd President of the United States. Roosevelt is remembered for leading his country into World War II to fight alongside the Allies against Germany and Japan: he died just as victory was in sight.

ROSARITA MARGARITA

★★★★☆

Glass: Martini
Garnish: Lime wedge & salt rim (optional)
Method: SHAKE all ingredients with ice and fine strain into chilled glass.

1½	shots	Tequila 100% Agave
¾	shot	Grand Marnier liqueur
½	shot	Ocean Spray cranberry juice
½	shot	Rose's lime cordial
¾	shot	Freshly squeezed lime juice
½	shot	Monin Pure Cane 2:1 sugar syrup

We say: This peachy coloured Margarita is well balanced and flavoursome.
Origin: Created in 1999 by Robert Plotkin and Raymon Flores of BarMedia, USA.

THE ROSE #1 (ORIGINAL)

★★★★½

Glass: Martini
Garnish: Maraschino cherry
Method: STIR all ingredients with ice and strain into chilled glass.

2	shots	Martini Extra Dry vermouth
1	shot	Kirsch liqueur
½	shot	Raspberry syrup (1 juice to 1 sugar)

We say: This salmon pink drink is wonderfully aromatic.
Origin: Created in 1920 by Johnny Milta at the Chatham Hotel, Paris. This recipe is adapted from one in '*The Fine Art of Mixing Drinks*' by David Embury.

THE ROSE #2

★★★½☆

Glass: Martini
Garnish: Maraschino cherry
Method: STIR all ingredients with ice and fine strain into chilled glass.

2	shots	Tanqueray London dry gin
1	shot	De Kuyper Cherry Brandy liqueur
1	shot	Martini Extra Dry vermouth

We say: Cherry and gin dried with vermouth.
Origin: Adapted from a recipe in Harry Craddock's 1930 '*Savoy Cocktail Book*'.

THE ROSE #3

★★★★½

Glass: Martini
Garnish: Maraschino cherry
Method: SHAKE all ingredients with ice and fine strain into chilled glass.

1½	shots	Kirsch liqueur
1½	shots	Martini Extra Dry vermouth
½	shot	Pomegranate (grenadine) syrup

We say: Delicate, aromatic cherry - not too sweet.
Origin: Adapted from a recipe in Harry Craddock's 1930 '*Savoy Cocktail Book*'.

ROSE PETALINI

★★★★☆

Glass: Martini
Garnish: Rose petal
Method: STIR all ingredients with ice and strain into chilled glass.

1½	shots	Lanique rose petal liqueur
1½	shots	Tanqueray London dry gin
1	shot	Lychee syrup (from tinned fruit)
3	dashes	Peychaud's aromatic bitters

We say: Peychaud's bitters give this fragrant cocktail a delicate pink hue.
Origin: Discovered in 2005 at Rain, Amsterdam, The Netherlands.

ROSE-HYP MARTINI

★★★★★

Glass: Martini
Garnish: Edible flower
Method: THROW all ingredients with ice and strain into chilled glass.

2	shots	Tanqueray London dry gin
¾	shot	St~Germain elderflower liqueur
½	shot	Martini Extra Dry vermouth
¼	shot	Lanique rose petal liqueur

We say: Created in 2006 by Simon Difford in London, England.
Origin: Dry (but not bone dry), aromatic and floral.

BARTENDER'S TIP SWIZZLE

To 'swizzle' a drink is simply to stir it using a particular tool and action.

To swizzle simply immerse the blades of your swizzle stick into the drink, hold the shaft between the palms of both hands and rotate the stick rapidly by sliding your hands back and forth against it. If you do not have a bona fide swizzle stick, use a barspoon in the same manner.

ROSELYN MARTINI

★★★★½

Glass: Martini
Garnish: Maraschino cherry
Method: SHAKE all ingredients with ice and fine strain into chilled glass.

2	shots	**Tanqueray London dry gin**
1	shot	**Martini Extra Dry vermouth**
¼	shot	**Pomegranate (grenadine) syrup**

We say: Subtle and beautifully balanced. A wet Martini made 'easy' by a dash of pomegranate syrup.
Origin: Adapted from a recipe in Harry Craddock's 1930 *'Savoy Cocktail Book'*.

ROSIE LASSI COCKTAIL NEW

★★★★☆

Glass: Coupette
Garnish: Rose petal
Method: SHAKE all ingredients with ice and fine strain into chilled glass.

2	shots	**Ketel One vodka**
1½	shots	**Bols Natural Yoghurt liqueur**
¼	shot	**Lanique rose petal liqueur**

We say: Creamy vanilla yoghurt with floral rose liqueur fortified with vodka.
Origin: Created in 2011 by Simon Difford at the Cabinet Room, London, England.

ROSITA UPDATED

★★★★½

Glass: Old-fashioned
Garnish: Lemon zest twist
Method: POUR ingredients into ice-filled glass and stir.

1½	shots	**Olmeca Altos 100% agave tequila**
1	shot	**Campari Bitter**
½	shot	**Martini Extra dry vermouth**
½	shot	**Martini Rosso sweet vermouth**
1	dash	**Angostura aromatic bitters**

We say: A bittersweet, tequila based, Negroni-like drink.
Origin: The origin of this drink remains unknown, but its popularity (like many things in this industry can be blamed squarely on Gaz Regan, even though for some years he was in denial. The Rosita was introduced to Gaz by a fellow cocktail geek back in 2005; who in turn had discovered the recipe in an article written by Terry Sullivan, a fellow drinks writer. Gaz questioned Sullivan as to where he found the recipe, but he could not remember so Gaz let the matter drop until 2007 when he made the drink as an aperitif for a few friends round for dinner. Gaz's guests asked the origins of the drink and this led Gaz to contact Sullivan again.

This time Sullivan remembered and told Gaz that he had found it in 'The Bartender's Bible'. Now many of you will already be smiling as The Bartender's Bible, published in 1991, was Gary Regan's first book.

Gaz has imbibed and written about thousands of cocktails over the years so it is understandable that he overlooked his own book. After an embarrassed 'oh-yeah' moment he started rummaging around in the back of the closet of his guest room where an oversized envelope still held his working notes for the book. So it transpired that Gaz purloined the recipe from a 1988 edition of 'Mr. Boston Official Bartender's Guide', but he had added a typical Gaz touch, namely a dash of bitters, and predictably a bit more tequila

ROSSINI

★★★★☆

Glass: Flute
Garnish: Strawberry
Method: MUDDLE strawberries in base of shaker. Add liqueur, SHAKE with ice and fine strain into chilled glass. TOP with champagne and gently stir.

4	fresh	**Strawberries (hulled)**
¾	shot	**Crème de fraise liqueur**
Top up with		**Prosecco sparkling wine**

We say: Strawberries seem to complement Prosecco even better than white peaches.
Origin: Named for the 19th century Italian opera composer, Gioachino Antonio Rossini. This is one of the most popular Bellini variants in Venice.

ROSY MARTINI

★★★★☆

Glass: Martini
Garnish: Orange zest twist
Method: STIR all ingredients with ice and strain into chilled glass.

2	shots	**Ketel One Citroen vodka**
¾	shot	**Triple Sec**
¾	shot	**Dubonnet Red (French made)**

We say: An aptly named drink with hints of spice, citrus peel, honey and mulled wine.

ROULETTE

★★★★☆

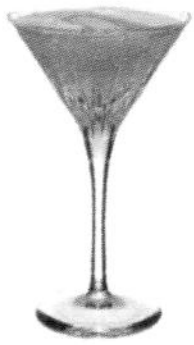

Glass: Martini
Garnish: Orange zest twist
Method: SHAKE all ingredients with ice and fine strain into chilled glass.

1½	shots	**Calvados/Applejack brandy**
¾	shot	**Bacardi Superior rum**
¾	shot	**Swedish Punch liqueur**
½	shot	**Chilled mineral water**

We say: Balanced apple and spice.
Origin: Adapted from a recipe in Harry Craddock's 1930 *'Savoy Cocktail Book'*.

ROUSING CHARLIE

★★★½☆

Glass: Martini
Garnish: Lychee
Method: STIR all ingredients with ice and strain into chilled glass.

¾	shot	**Macchu pisco**
¾	shot	**St~Germain elderflower liqueur**
¾	shot	**Tio Pepe fino sherry**
¾	shot	**Sake**
½	shot	**Lychee syrup (from tinned fruit)**

We say: Subtle with an interesting salty edge, this tastes almost like a wine.
Origin: Adapted from a drink I created in 2002 and named after Charlie Rouse, a very lovely sherry lover.

ROY ROGERS (MOCKTAIL)

★★☆☆☆

Glass: Collins
Garnish: Lime wedge
Method: POUR grenadine and cola into ice-filled glass and stir. Serve with straws.

¼ shot   **Pomegranate (grenadine) syrup**
Top up with Coca-Cola

We say: Cola with an added ingredient - not sure if it makes enough difference.

ROYAL BERMUDA YACHT CLUB DAIQUIRI

★★★★☆

Glass: Martini
Garnish: Lime wedge
Method: SHAKE all ingredients with ice and fine strain into chilled glass.

2½ shots   **Bacardi Oro golden rum**
½ shot   **Taylor's Velvet Falernum liqueur**
¼ shot   **Triple Sec**
¾ shot   **Freshly squeezed lime juice**

We say: A full-flavoured, tangy Daiquiri.
Origin: Created at the eponymous club, established in Bermuda in 1844 and largely frequented by British Army Officers. This recipe is adapted from one in 'Trader Vic's Bartender's Guide'.

ROYAL COSMOPOLITAN

★★★★☆

Glass: Martini
Garnish: Orange zest twist
Method: SHAKE first four ingredients with ice and fine strain into chilled glass. TOP with champagne.

1 shot   **Ketel One Citroen vodka**
½ shot   **Triple Sec**
1 shot   **Ocean Spray cranberry juice**
¼ shot   **Freshly squeezed lime juice**
Top up with Brut champagne

We say: The classic Cosmopolitan with a layer of fizz on top adding a biscuity complexity. Sex And The City meets Ab Fab.
Origin: Created in 2003 by Wayne Collins, London, England.

ROYAL GINGERSNAP

★★★★☆

Glass: Old-fashioned
Garnish: Cinnamon & sugar rim with orange zest twist (flamed)
Method: MUDDLE the cherry in base of shaker. Add other ingredients, SHAKE with ice and fine strain into ice-filled glass.

1 whole   **Maraschino cherries & syrup**
2 shots   **Canadian whisky**
1 spoon   **Orange marmalade**
¼ shot   **Domaine de Canton ginger liqueur**
½ shot   **Freshly squeezed orange juice**
2 dashes   **Angostura aromatic bitters**

We say: Variation on Old-Fashioned
Origin: Created by Dale DeGroff, this recipe is adapted from his 2008 book 'The Essential Cocktail'.

ROYAL MOJITO

★★★★★

Glass: Collins
Garnish: Mint sprig
Method: Lightly MUDDLE mint (just to bruise) in base of glass. Add rum, lime juice and sugar. Half fill glass with crushed ice and CHURN (stir) with bar spoon. Fill glass with more crushed ice and CHURN some more. TOP with champagne, stir and serve with straws.

12 fresh   **Mint leaves**
2 shots   **Bacardi Superior rum**
¾ shot   **Freshly squeezed lime juice**
¼ shot   **Monin Pure Cane 2:1 sugar syrup**
Top up with Brut champagne

AKA: Luxury Mojito
We say: A mojito topped with champagne instead of soda water. There's posh.

ROYAL NAIL

★★★★★

Glass: Old-fashioned
Garnish: Lemon zest twist
Method: STIR ingredients with ice and strain into ice-filled glass.

2 shots   **Dewar's White label Scotch**
1 shot   **Lagavulin 16yo malt whisky**
1 dash   **Peychaud's aromatic bitters**

We say: Two British Royals bittered by a yank.
Origin: Created by Simon Difford at the Cabinet Room, London, England.

ROYAL SMILE

★★★★☆

Glass: Martini
Garnish: Lemon zest twist
Method: SHAKE all ingredients with ice and fine strain into chilled glass.

1 shot   **Tanqueray London dry gin**
1 shot   **Calvados/Applejack brandy**
½ shot   **Freshly squeezed lemon juice**
¼ shot   **Pomegranate (grenadine) syrup**
½ shot   **Chilled mineral water**

We say: This balanced sweet and sour could put a smile on anyone's face. Unless one is not amused!
Origin: Purloined from David Embury's classic book, 'The Fine Art of Mixing Drinks'.

ROYAL TOAST NEW

★★★★☆

Glass: Coupette
Garnish: Maraschino cherry
Method: STIR all ingredients with ice and strain into chilled glass.

1½ shots   **Ketel One vodka**
¾ shot   **Cherry brandy liqueur**
1 shot   **Martini Extra dry vermouth**

We say: Rich cherry liqueur flavours are balanced by dry vermouth and lifted by vodka.
Origin: Adapted from a UKBG recipe from 1937 which was originally equal parts.

ROYAL VELVET MARGARITA

★★★½☆

Glass: Pineapple shell (frozen)
Garnish: Lime wedge
Method: SHAKE all ingredients with ice and fine strain into chilled glass.

2	shots	**Tequila 100% Agave**
½	shot	**Amaretto liqueur**
½	shot	**Chambord black raspberry liqueur**
1	shot	**Freshly squeezed lime juice**

We say: An almond and berry flavoured Margarita.
Origin: Discovered in 2005 at Velvet Margarita Cantina, Los Angeles, USA.

ROYALIST COCKTAIL NEW

★★★★☆

Glass: Coupette
Garnish: Peach slice on rim
Method: STIR all ingredients with ice and strain into chilled glass.

1½	shots	**Martini Extra dry vermouth**
1	shot	**Maker's Mark bourbon**
¾	shot	**Bénédictine D.O.M.**
1	dash	**Peach bitters**

We say: A Manhattan-style cocktail but with dry vermouth and considerably more of it, Bénédictine and peach bitters.
Origin: Adapted from a recipe by W.J. Tarling and featured in his 1937 *The Café Royal Cocktail Book.* Tarling originally called for his drink to be shaken rather than stirred and used ½ Dry Martini vermouth, ¼ bourbon, ¼Bénédictine.

RUBY DAIQUIRI UPDATED

★★★★☆

Glass: Martini
Garnish: Grapefruit wedge
Method: SHAKE all ingredients with ice and fine strain into chilled glass.

2	shots	**Rum light white/blanco**
¼	shot	**Luxardo Amaretto di Saschira**
⅛	shot	**Monin Almond (orgeat) syrup**
¼	shot	**Freshly squeezed lime juice**
¼	shot	**Freshly squeezed pink grapefruit juice**

We say: A well-balanced, almond influenced Daiquiri.
Origin: Created in 2008 by Wrigley (Oz) Osbourne at Goldbrick House, Bristol, England.

THE RUBY GOLD NEW

★★★★½

Glass: Coupette
Garnish: Float raspberry and dust with grated nutmeg
Method: DRY SHAKE (without ice) all ingredients. Add ice, SHAKE again with ice and fine strain into chilled glass.

1¾	shots	**Warre's Otima tawny port**
⅔	shot	**Straight rye whiskey**
½	shot	**Suze gentaine liqueur**
¼	shot	**Monin Pure Cane 2:1 sugar syrup**
1	fresh	**Egg yolk**

We say: A rich after dinner, dessert-style cocktail.
Origin: Created in 2010 by Rufus at the Hide Bar, London. England.

RUBY MARTINI #1

★★★★☆

Glass: Martini
Garnish: Lemon slice
Method: SHAKE all ingredients with ice and fine strain into chilled glass.

1½	shots	**Ketel One Citroen vodka**
1	shot	**Triple Sec**
1	shot	**Freshly squeezed grapefruit juice**
¼	shot	**Monin Pure Cane 2:1 sugar syrup**

We say: A sour, citrus-led variation on the Cosmopolitan.
Origin: Several appearances in episodes of the hit US TV series, Sex And The City, helped this drink become fashionable in 2002, particularly in New York City. It is thought to have originated at the Wave restaurant in Chicago's W Hotel.

RUBY MARTINI #2

★★★½☆

Glass: Martini
Garnish: Lemon zest twist & raspberry
Method: SHAKE all ingredients with ice and fine strain into chilled glass.

1½	shots	**Cognac VSOP**
½	shot	**Triple Sec**
½	shot	**Crème de framboise liqueur**
½	shot	**Martini Rosso sweet vermouth**

We say: Fruity and slightly sweet.
Origin: Created by Wayne Collins, London, England.

RUDE COSMOPOLITAN

★★★★½

Glass: Martini
Garnish: Orange zest twist
Method: SHAKE all ingredients with ice and fine strain into chilled glass.

1	shot	**Tequila 100% Agave**
1	shot	**Triple Sec**
1½	shots	**Ocean Spray cranberry juice**
½	shot	**Freshly squeezed lime juice**
2	dashes	**Orange bitters**

AKA: Mexico City
We say: Don't let the pink appearance of this Cosmopolitan (made with tequila in place of vodka) fool you into thinking it's a fluffy cocktail. It's both serious and superb.

STAR RATINGS EXPLAINED

★★★★★ Excellent

★★★★½ Recommended	★★★★☆ Praiseworthy
★★★½☆ Commended	★★★☆☆ Mediocre
★★½☆☆ Disappointing	★★☆☆☆ Pretty awful
★½☆☆☆ Shameful	★☆☆☆☆ Disgusting

RUDE GINGER COSMOPOLITAN

Glass: Martini
Garnish: Orange zest twist
Method: MUDDLE ginger in base of shaker. Add the other ingredients, SHAKE with ice and fine strain into chilled glass.

2	slices	Fresh root ginger (thumbnail sized)
1½	shots	Tequila 100% Agave
1	shot	Triple Sec
1	shot	Ocean Spray cranberry juice
½	shot	Freshly squeezed lime juice
¼	shot	Rose's lime cordial

We say: To quote Halo's list, "Looks like a cosmo, goes like a Mexican!"
Origin: Created in 2003 by Jeremy Adderley at Halo, Edinburgh, Scotland.

RUDE GYPSY

Glass: Coupette
Garnish: Lime zest twist
Method: STIR all ingredients with ice and strain into chilled glass.

2	shots	Tequila 100% Agave
1	shot	Bénédictine D.O.M.
1	dash	Angostura aromatic bitters

We say: Slightly sweet but wonderfully herbal and slightly spicy.

RUM & RAISIN ALEXANDRA

Glass: Martini
Garnish: Red grapes
Method: MUDDLE grapes in base of shaker. Add other ingredients, SHAKE with ice and fine strain into chilled glass.

7	fresh	Seedless white grapes
1½	shots	Bacardi 8yo aged rum
½	shot	Double (heavy) cream
½	shot	Milk
¼	shot	Monin Pure Cane 2:1 sugar syrup
½	shot	Crème de cassis liqueur

We say: Forgo the ice cream and try this creamy, quaffable, alcoholic dessert.
Origin: Created in 2003 by Ian Morgan, England.

RUM AMANDINE

Glass: Flute
Garnish: Maraschino cherry
Method: SHAKE all ingredients with ice and fine strain into chilled glass.

2	shots	Bacardi Superior rum
⅛	shot	Luxardo Maraschino liqueur
⅛	shot	Absinthe
¾	shot	Freshly squeezed lime juice
¼	shot	Monin Almond (orgeat) syrup
2	dashes	Orange flower water
½	shot	Chilled mineral water

We say: A classic Daiquiri benefiting from the influence of almond and absinthe.
Origin: Marcis Dzelzainis, Quo Vadis, London, England.

RUM OLD FASHIONED

Glass: Old-fashioned
Garnish: Orange zest twist
Method: STIR rum with two ice cubes in a glass. ADD sugar, falernum and Angostura and two more ice cubes. STIR lots more and add more ice.

2	shots	Bacardi 8yo aged rum
½	shot	Wray & Nephew overproof rum
¼	shot	Taylor's Velvet Falernum liqueur
1	dash	Angostura aromatic bitters
⅛	shot	Monin Pure Cane 2:1 sugar syrup

We say: The flavour of the overproof rum greatly adds to the character of this old fashioned.
Origin: Created in 2009 by Goncalo de Sousa Monteiro, Berlin, Germany.

RUM PUNCH

Glass: Collins
Garnish: Orange slice & cherry on stick (sail)
Method: SHAKE all ingredients with ice and fine strain into glass filled with crushed ice.

2¼	shots	Wray & Nephew overproof rum
¾	shot	Freshly squeezed lime juice
1½	shots	Monin Pure Cane 2:1 sugar syrup
3	dashes	Angostura aromatic bitters
3	shots	Chilled mineral water

We say: The classic proportions of this drink are 'one of sour, two of sweet, three of strong and four of weak' - referring to lime juice, sugar syrup, rum and water respectively. In Jamaica, the spiritual home of the Rum Punch, they like their rum overproof (more than 57% alc./vol) and serving over crushed ice dilutes and tames this very strong spirit.

BARTENDER'S TIP FLAME

The term ignite, flame or flambé means that the drink should be set alight.

Please exercise extreme care when setting fire to drinks. Be particularly careful not to knock over a lit drink and never attempt to carry a drink which is still alight. Before drinking, cover the glass so as to suffocate the flame and be aware that the rim of the glass may be hot.

RUM PUNCH-UP

★★★★½☆

Glass: Martini
Garnish: Lime wedge
Method: SHAKE all ingredients with ice and fine strain into chilled glass.

1½	shots	Wray & Nephew overproof rum
½	shot	Freshly squeezed lime juice
½	shot	Monin Pure Cane 2:1 sugar syrup
2	dashes	Angostura aromatic bitters
1	shot	Chilled mineral water

We say: Exactly what the name promises - a rum punch served straight-up, Daiquiri-style.
Origin: Adapted from a drink discovered in 2006 at Albannach, London, England.

RUM SWIZZLE

★★★½☆☆

Glass: Sling
Garnish: Mint sprig & orange slice
Method: POUR all ingredients into glass filled with crushed ice and SWIZZLE (stir).

2	shots	Bacardi 8yo aged rum
½	shot	Taylor's Velvet Falernum liqueur
1	shot	Freshly squeezed lime juice
½	shot	Monin Pure Cane 2:1 sugar syrup
1	dash	Angostura aromatic bitters

We say: Sweet and sour with aged rum base. All too easy.
Origin: This drink emerged in the early 1800s in Guyana when British ex-pats mixed this drink on the terrace of the Georgetown club using a long five-pronged swizzle stick fashioned from a tree branch.

RUM RUNNER

★★★★☆

Glass: Hurricane
Garnish: Pineapple wedge & maraschino cherry
Method: SHAKE all ingredients with ice and strain into glass filled with crushed ice.

1½	shots	Pusser's Navy rum
½	shot	Crème de Mûre liqueur
1	shot	Bols Banana liqueur
1	shot	Freshly squeezed lime juice
2	shots	Fresh pressed pineapple juice
½	shot	Pomegranate (grenadine) syrup

We say: Fruity, sharp and rounded.

RUMBA

★★★★☆

Glass: Old-fashioned
Garnish: Lime wedge
Method: SHAKE all ingredients with ice and strain into glass filled with crushed ice. Serve with straws.

¾	shot	Wray & Nephew overproof rum
1	shot	Tanqueray London dry gin
1	shot	Freshly squeezed lime juice
¼	shot	Monin Pure Cane 2:1 sugar syrup
½	shot	Pomegranate (grenadine) syrup
½	shot	Chilled mineral water

We say: To quote Embury, "Whoever thought up this snootful of liquid dynamite certainly liked his liquor hard!"
Origin: Recipe adapted from David Embury's classic book, '*The Fine Art of Mixing Drinks*'.

RUM SOUR

★★★★☆

Glass: Old-fashioned
Garnish: Orange zest twist
Method: SHAKE all ingredients with ice and strain into ice-filled glass.

2	shots	Bacardi 8yo aged rum
1	shot	Freshly squeezed orange juice
1	shot	Freshly squeezed lime juice
½	shot	Monin Pure Cane 2:1 sugar syrup
½	fresh	Egg white

We say: Smooth and sour - well balanced.

RUSSIAN

★★★½☆

Glass: Martini
Garnish: Orange zest twist
Method: SHAKE all ingredients with ice and fine strain into chilled glass.

1½	shots	Tanqueray London dry gin
1	shot	Ketel One vodka
1	shot	White Crème de Cacao

We say: Gin and vodka with a sweet hint of chocolate.
Origin: Adapted from a recipe in Harry Craddock's 1930 '*Savoy Cocktail Book*'.

BARTENDER'S TIP SWIZZLE

To 'swizzle' a drink is simply to stir it using a particular tool and action.

To swizzle simply immerse the blades of your swizzle stick into the drink, hold the shaft between the palms of both hands and rotate the stick rapidly by sliding your hands back and forth against it. If you do not have a bona fide swizzle stick, use a barspoon in the same manner.

RUSSIAN BRIDE

★★★★☆

Glass: Martini
Garnish: Dust with chocolate powder
Method: SHAKE all ingredients with ice and fine strain into chilled glass.

2	shots	**Vanilla-infused Ketel One vodka**
¾	shot	**Kahlúa coffee liqueur**
¼	shot	**White Crème de Cacao**
½	shot	**Double (heavy) cream**
½	shot	**Milk**

We say: A little on the sweet side for some but vanilla, coffee and chocolate smoothed with cream is a tasty combination.
Origin: Created in 2002 by Miranda Dickson, A.K.A. the Vodka Princess, for the UK's Revolution bar chain, where some 500,000 are sold each year.

RUSSIAN COCKTAIL NEW

★★★½☆

Glass: Coupette
Garnish: Maraschino cherry
Method: SHAKE all ingredients with ice and fine strain into chilled glass.

1½	shots	**Ketel One vodka**
¾	shot	**Cherry brandy liqueur**
¼	shot	**Kirschwasser eau de vie**

We say: Sweet brandy meets dry cherry eau-de-vie in this serious vodka laced cocktail.
Origin: We have David Wondrich to thank for re-discovering this drink, believed to be the first vodka cocktail to appear in print in a 1911 book called 'Beverage Deluxe'. The drink itself is thought to originally come from the St. Charles Hotel in New Orleans, USA.

RUSSIAN NAIL

★★★½☆

Glass: Old-fashioned
Garnish: Dust with grated nutmeg
Method: SHAKE all ingredients with ice and strain into ice-filled glass.

2	shots	**Dewar's White label Scotch**
¾	shot	**Drambuie**
¾	shot	**Kahlúa coffee liqueur**
½	shot	**Double (heavy) cream**
½	shot	**Milk**

We say: A marriage of the Rusty Nail and White Russian cocktails.
Origin: Created in 2010 by a collaboration between Jamie Stephenson and Simon Difford at the Cabinet Room, London, England.

RUSSIAN QUALUUDE SHOT

★★★☆☆

Glass: Shot
Garnish: None
Method: Refrigerate ingredients then LAYER in chilled glass by carefully pouring in the order listed.

½	shot	**Galliano L'Autentico liqueur**
½	shot	**Chartreuse Green liqueur**
½	shot	**Ketel One vodka**

We say: An explosive herb and peppermint shot.

RUSSIAN SPRING PUNCH UPDATED

★★★★½

Glass: Sling
Garnish: Lemon slice & seasonal berries
Method: MUDDLE raspberries in base of shaker. Add next five ingredients, SHAKE with ice and strain into glass filled with crushed ice. TOP with champagne, lightly stir and serve with straws.

7	fresh	**Raspberries**
1	shot	**Ketel One vodka**
¼	shot	**Crème de framboise liqueur**
1	shot	**Freshly squeezed lemon juice**
¼	shot	**Monin Pure Cane 2:1 sugar syrup**
Top up with		**Brut champagne**
¼	shot	**Crème de cassis liqueur**

We say: Well balanced, complex and refreshing.
Origin: Created in the 1990s by Dick Bradsell, London, England.

RUSTY

★★★★☆

Glass: Old-fashioned
Garnish: Orange zest twist
Method: STIR all ingredients with ice and strain into ice-filled glass.

1½	shots	**Bacardi 8yo aged rum**
1½	shots	**Amontillado sherry**
¼	shot	**Lagavulin 16yo malt whisky**
¼	shot	**Monin Pure Cane 2:1 sugar syrup**

We say: The Sherry character of Zacapa is highlighted and its spicy notes built upon with smoky Islay malt.
Origin: Created in December 2008 by Simon Difford at the Cabinet Room, London, England.

RUSTY DAIQUIRI NEW

★★★½☆

Glass: Old-fashioned
Garnish: Lime wedge
Method: SHAKE all ingredients with ice and fine strain into chilled glass.

2	shots	**Bacardi Superior rum**
½	shot	**Drambuie**
¾	shot	**Freshly squeezed lime juice**

We say: Herbal, honeyed Drambuie notes add a Scottish dimension to the classic Cuban cocktail.
Origin: Created in December 2010 by Simon Difford at the Cabinet Room, London, England.

RUSTY MARGARITA NEW

★★★★½

Glass: Old-fashioned
Garnish: Lime wedge
Method: SHAKE all ingredients with ice and strain into ice-filled glass.

2	shots	**Tequila 100% Agave**
1	shot	**Drambuie**
1	shot	**Freshly squeezed lime juice**

We say: The rich honeyed notes from Drambuie combine wonderfully with tequila and add an extra dimension to this this tasty Margarita.
Origin: Created in December 2010 by Simon Difford at the Cabinet Room, London, England.

RUSTY NAIL

★★★★☆ **Glass:** Old-fashioned
Garnish: Lemon zest twist
Method: STIR ingredients with ice and strain into ice-filled glass.

2	shots	**Dewar's White label Scotch**
¾	shot	**Drambuie**

We say: The liqueur smooths and wonderfully combines with the Scotch.
Origin: Created in 1942 at a Hawaiian bar for the artist Theodore Anderson. The proportions of Scotch to Drambuie vary wildly and are a matter of taste. However, the 3:1 proportions used here appear most popular.

THE RUSTY TACK

★★★★☆ **Glass:** Old-fashioned
Garnish: Lemon zest twist
Method: POUR ingredients into ice-filled glass and stir.

2	shots	**Dewar's White label Scotch**
½	shot	**Drambuie**
½	shot	**Domaine de Canton ginger liqueur**

We say: A ginger twist on the rusty nail.
Origin: Adapted from a drink discovered in 2010 in New York City, USA.

RUSTY TO THE CORE NEW

★★★★½ **Glass:** Coupette
Garnish: Apple slice
Method: SHAKE all ingredients with ice and fine strain into chilled glass.

1½	shots	**Calvados/Applejack brandy**
¾	shot	**Drambuie**
¼	shot	**Lagavulin 16yo malt whisky**
1	shot	**Pressed apple juice**
¼	shot	**Freshly squeezed lemon juice**

We say: Honeyed herbal Drambuie with an apple brandy base, freshened with lemon juice and given a wisp of smokiness by a splash of Islay malt.
Origin: Created in 2010 by Julian de Feral at Lutyens Bar, London, England for his autumn menu.

S. TEA G.

★★★½☆ **Glass:** Collins
Garnish: Lemon slice
Method: SHAKE first three ingredients with ice and strain into ice-filled glass. TOP with tonic water.

1½	shots	**Tanqueray London dry gin**
1½	shots	**St~Germain elderflower liqueur**
1	shot	**Cold English breakfast tea**
Top up with		**Tonic water**

We say: Floral, long and refreshing.
Origin: Created in 2006 by Simon Difford.

SANGAREE NEW

★★★★½ **Glass:** Small flute
Garnish: Dust with grated nutmeg
Method: SHAKE gin and sugar with ice and strain into chilled glass. Lastly POUR the port wine which will sink through drink and mix, leaving a thin clear layer.

2	shots	**Bermondsey Old Tom gin**
1	shot	**Taylors 10yo port**
¼	shot	**Monin Pure Cane 2:1 sugar syrup)**

We say: Either drink through the layers of stir before consuming. Fabulously old-school in style, this sweetened port and Old Tom gin drink resembles chilled mulled wine.
Origin: The Sangaree takes its name from the Spanish word for blood 'Sangre'. The drink's origins date back to the early 1700s and it first appears in writing in a 1736 issue of the British Gentleman's Magazine, "... a punch seller in the Strand had devised a new punch made of strong Madeira wine and called Sangre".

SANGAREE #2 NEW

★★★★½ **Glass:** Flute
Garnish: Dust with grated nutmeg
Method: SHAKE gin and sugar with ice and strain into chilled glass. Lastly POUR the port wine which will sink through drink and mix, leaving a thin clear layer.

2	shots	**Old Tom gin**
1	shot	**Warre's Otima tawny port**
¼	shot	**Monin Pure Cane 2:1 sugar syrup**

We say: Either drink through the layers of stir before consuming. Fabulously old-school in style, this sweetened port and Old Tom gin drink resembles chilled mulled wine.
Origin: The Sangaree takes its name from the Spanish word for blood 'Sangre'. The drink's origins date back to the early 1700s and it first appears in writing in a 1736 issue of the British Gentleman's Magazine, "... a punch seller in the Strand had devised a new punch made of strong Madeira wine and called Sangre".

SAÚCO MARGARITA

★★★★½ **Glass:** Margarita
Garnish: Lime wedge & salt rim (optional)
Method: SHAKE all ingredients with ice and fine strain into chilled glass.

1½	shots	**Tequila 100% Agave**
1½	shots	**St~Germain elderflower liqueur**
¾	shot	**Freshly squeezed lime juice**

We say: The floral notes of St-Germain combine wonderfully with the herbaceous tequila and citrussy lime.
Origin: Created in 2006 by Simon Difford and named after 'flor saúco', which is Spanish for elderflower.

STAR RATINGS EXPLAINED

★★★★★ Excellent

★★★★½ Recommeded	★★★★☆ Praiseworthy
★★★½☆ Commended	★★★☆☆ Mediocre
★★½☆☆ Disappointing	★★☆☆☆ Pretty awful
★½☆☆☆ Shameful	★☆☆☆☆ Disgusting

SAGE MARGARITA

★★★★☆

Glass: Coupette
Garnish: Sage leaf
Method: Lightly MUDDLE (just to bruise) sage in base of shaker. Add other ingredients, SHAKE with ice and fine strain into chilled glass.

3	fresh	Sage leaves
2	shots	Tequila 100% Agave
1	shot	Triple Sec
1	shot	Freshly squeezed lime juice
⅛	shot	Monin Pure Cane 2:1 sugar syrup

We say: Exactly as promised - a sage flavoured Margarita.

SAGE MARTINI

★★★★☆

Glass: Martini
Garnish: Sage leaf
Method: Lightly MUDDLE (just to bruise) sage in base of shaker. Add other ingredients, SHAKE with ice and fine strain into chilled glass.

3	fresh	Sage leaves
1½	shots	Ketel One vodka
1½	shots	Martini Extra Dry vermouth
¾	shot	Pressed apple juice

We say: Delicate sage and a hint of apple, dried with vermouth and fortified with vodka.

SAIGON COOLER

★★★★☆

Glass: Collins
Garnish: Raspberries
Method: MUDDLE raspberries in base of shaker. Add other ingredients, SHAKE with ice and fine strain into chilled glass.

7	fresh	Raspberries
2	shots	Tanqueray London dry gin
½	shot	Chambord black raspberry liqueur
3	shots	Ocean Spray cranberry juice
¾	shot	Freshly squeezed lime juice

We say: Well balanced sweet 'n' sour with a rich fruity flavour.
Origin: Created at Bam-Bou, London, England.

SAIGON SLING

★★★★☆

Glass: Sling
Garnish: Pineapple wedge & maraschino cherry
Method: SHAKE first seven ingredients with ice and fine strain into ice-filled glass. TOP with ginger ale.

1½	shots	Tanqueray London dry gin
¾	shot	Ginger & lemongrass cordial
½	shot	Krupnik spiced honey liqueur
¼	shot	Passoã passion fruit liqueur
¾	shot	Freshly squeezed lime juice
1	shot	Fresh pressed pineapple juice
2	dashes	Peychaud's aromatic bitters
Top up with		Ginger ale

We say: A fusion of unusual flavours.
Origin: Created in 2001 by Rodolphe Manor for a London bartending competition.

SAILOR'S COMFORT

★★★☆☆

Glass: Old-fashioned
Garnish: Lime wedge
Method: SHAKE first four ingredients with ice and strain into ice-filled glass. TOP with soda, lightly stir and serve with straws.

1	shot	Sloe Gin liqueur
1	shot	Southern Comfort liqueur
1	shot	Rose's lime cordial
3	dashes	Angostura aromatic bitters
Top up with		Soda (club soda)

We say: Lime, peach and hints of berry make a light, easy drink.
Origin: Discovered in 2002 at Lightship Ten, London.

SAINT CLEMENTS (MOCKTAIL)

★★★☆☆

Glass: Collins
Garnish: Lime wedge
Method: POUR ingredients into ice-filled glass, lightly stir and serve with straws.

| 3 | shots | Freshly squeezed orange juice |
| Top up with | | Bitter lemon |

We say: Slightly more interesting than orange juice.

BARTENDER'S TIP MUDDLE

Muddling means pummelling fruits, herbs and/or spices with a muddler (a blunt tool similar to a pestle) so as to crush them and release their flavour. (You can also use a rolling pin.)

As when using a pestle and mortar, push down on the muddler with a twisting action. Never attempt to muddle hard, unripe fruits in a glass as the pressure required could break the glass.

SAKE MARTINI

★★★★⯪

Glass: Coupette
Garnish: Apple slice
Method: STIR all ingredients with ice and fine strain into chilled glass.

2	shots	Tanqueray London dry gin
2	shots	Sake
⅛	shot	Martini Extra Dry vermouth

We say: Dry, subtle, and depending on your choice of sake, possibly amazing.

SAKE'POLITAN

★★★★☆

Glass: Martini
Garnish: Orange zest twist
Method: SHAKE all ingredients with ice and fine strain into chilled glass.

2¼	shots	Sake
¾	shot	Triple Sec
¾	shot	Ocean Spray cranberry juice
¼	shot	Freshly squeezed lime juice
2	dashes	Orange bitters

We say: A Cosmo with more than a hint of sake.

SAKE-TINI #1

★★★★☆

Glass: Martini
Garnish: Cucumber slices
Method: STIR all ingredients with ice and strain into chilled glass.

1	shot	Tanqueray London dry gin
½	shot	Grand Marnier liqueur
2½	shots	Sake

We say: Sake and a hint of orange liqueur add the perfect aromatic edge to this Martini-style drunk.

SAKE-TINI #2

★★★★☆

Glass: Martini
Garnish: Orange zest twist
Method: SHAKE all ingredients with ice and fine strain into chilled glass.

1½	shots	Ketel One vodka
1	shot	Plum wine
½	shot	Sake
1	shot	Ocean Spray cranberry juice

We say: Salmon-coloured, light and fragrant with plum wine and sake to the fore.
Origin: Discovered at Nobu Berkeley, London, England.

SAKINI

★★★★☆

Glass: Martini
Garnish: Olive on stick
Method: STIR all ingredients with ice and strain into chilled glass.

| 2½ | shots | Ketel One vodka |
| 1 | shot | Sake |

We say: Very dry. The sake creates an almost wine-like delicacy.

SALFLOWER SOUR

★★★★☆

Glass: Martini
Garnish: Orange zest twist
Method: SHAKE all ingredients with ice and fine strain into chilled glass.

2	shots	St~Germain elderflower liqueur
¾	shot	Freshly squeezed orange juice
¾	shot	Freshly squeezed lime juice
1	dash	Orange bitters
½	fresh	Egg white

We say: Classic sweet and sour enhanced by floral notes.
Origin: Created on 12th April 2007 by Salvatore Calabrese at Fifty, London, England.

SALTECCA

★★★☆☆

Glass: Martini
Garnish: Lemon zest twist
Method: STIR all ingredients with ice and fine strain into chilled glass.

2	shots	Tequila 100% Agave
½	shot	Tio Pepe fino sherry
⅛	shot	Caper brine (from jar)
½	shot	Monin Pure Cane 2:1 sugar syrup

We say: Reminiscent of salted water after boiling vegetables but you have got to try these things.

THE SALTY BIRD NEW

★★★★⯪

Glass: Collins
Garnish: Dehydrated pineapple
Method: SHAKE all ingredients with ice and strain into ice-filled glass.

1½	shots	Rum light white/blanco
¾	shot	Campari Bitter
1½	shots	Fresh pressed pineapple juice
½	shot	Freshly squeezed lime juice
¼	shot	Monin Pure Cane 2:1 sugar syrup
1	pinch	Salt

We say: Salty Bird hardly suggests a sweet fruity drink but perfectly befits this bittersweet rum laced pineapple and Campari sipper.
Origin: Created by bartender Lauren Schell and promoted by Campari in 2013

SALTY DOG

★★★★☆

Glass: Martini
Garnish: Salt rim
Method: SHAKE all ingredients with ice and fine strain into chilled glass.

2	shots	Ketel One vodka
⅛	shot	Luxardo Maraschino liqueur
2¼	shots	Freshly squeezed grapefruit juice

We say: For a more interesting drink, try basing this classic on gin rather than vodka.
Origin: Created in the 1960s.

SALTY LYCHEE MARTINI

★★★★☆

Glass: Martini
Garnish: Lychee
Method: STIR all ingredients with ice and strain into chilled glass.

2	shots	Tio Pepe fino sherry
1	shot	Lanique rose petal liqueur
1	shot	Kwai Feh lychee liqueur

We say: Light pink in colour and subtle in flavour with the salty tang of Fino sherry.
Origin: I created this drink in 2002 after trying Dick Bradsell's Lychee & Rose Petal Martini (also in this guide).

SALTY MARTINI NEW

★★★★★

Glass: Martini
Garnish: One large caper berry on pick
Method: STIR all ingredients with ice and strain into chilled glass.

2½	shots	Ketel One vodka
¼	shot	Martini Extra Dry vermouth
¼	shot	Tio Pepe fino sherry
⅛	shot	Caper berry brine

We say: As the name suggests, fino sherry and caper brine add saltiness but this "Salty Martini" also has a distinct nuttiness, so we suggest both a long stir for generous dilution, and serving with grilled almonds.
Origin: Adapted from a drink created in 2009 by Salvatore Calabrese at Fifty, London, England.

SAN FRANCISCO

★★★½☆

Glass: Collins
Garnish: Pineapple wedge
Method: SHAKE all ingredients with ice and strain into ice-filled glass.

2	shots	Ketel One vodka
½	shot	Triple Sec
½	shot	Bols Banana liqueur
1½	shots	Freshly squeezed orange juice
1½	shots	Fresh pressed pineapple juice
¼	shot	Pomegranate (grenadine) syrup

We say: Long, fruity, slightly sweet and laced with vodka.

SANCTUARY

★★★☆☆

Glass: Martini
Garnish: Orange zest twist
Method: STIR all ingredients with ice and strain into chilled glass.

2	shots	Dubonnet Red (French made)
1	shot	Amer Picon
½	shot	Triple Sec

We say: Wine-like with strong hints of bittersweet orange.
Origin: Vintage cocktail of unknown origin.

SANDSTORM

★★★★☆

Glass: Collins
Garnish: Pineapple wedge
Method: SHAKE all ingredients with ice and strain into ice-filled glass.

1½	shots	Tanqueray London dry gin
1	shot	Grand Marnier liqueur
½	shot	Vanilla schnapps
1½	shots	Freshly squeezed grapefruit juice
1½	shots	Fresh pressed pineapple juice
¼	shot	Monin Pure Cane 2:1 sugar syrup
¼	shot	Freshly squeezed lime juice
¼	shot	Rose's lime cordial

We say: A long, fruity drink featuring well balanced sweet and sourness.
Origin: Created in 2003 by James Cunningham at Zinc, Glasgow, Scotland, and is named for its cloudy yellow colour.

SANDY GAFF

★★★½☆

Glass: Boston
Garnish: None
Method: POUR ale into glass, top with ginger ale and lightly stir.

| ⅔ | fill glass with Guinness |
| | Top up with Ginger ale |

AKA: Shandy Gaff
We say: Better than your average lager shandy.
Origin: Adapted from a recipe purloined from David Embury's classic book, 'The Fine Art of Mixing Drinks'
'

SANGAREE (SANGRIA)

★★★★☆

Glass: Collins
Garnish: Dust with grated nutmeg
Method: SHAKE first six ingredients with ice and strain into ice-filled glass. TOP with soda and lightly stir. Serve with straws.

½	shot	Cognac VSOP
½	shot	Grand Marnier liqueur
3	shots	Shiraz red wine
1	shot	Freshly squeezed orange juice
¼	shot	Freshly squeezed lemon juice
½	shot	Monin Pure Cane 2:1 sugar syrup
1	shot	Soda (club soda)

We say: Basically just red wine and orange liqueur, diluted with water, lemon juice and sugar. But tasty!
Origin: This version of the Spanish Sangria was popular in 19th century America. The only real difference is that while a Sangria is usually made in batches, Sangaree are single serve.

STAR RATINGS EXPLAINED

★★★★★ Excellent

★★★★½ Recommended	★★★★☆ Praiseworthy
★★★½☆ Commended	★★★☆☆ Mediocre
★★★½☆ Disappointing	★★☆☆☆ Pretty awful
★½☆☆☆ Shameful	★☆☆☆☆ Disgusting

SANGRIA MARTINI

★★★★☆

Glass: Martini
Garnish: Orange slice
Method: SHAKE all ingredients with ice and fine strain into chilled glass.

1	shot	**Shiraz red wine**
1½	shots	**Cognac VSOP**
¾	shot	**Freshly squeezed orange juice**
½	shot	**Berentzen Apple schnapps**
½	shot	**Crème de framboise liqueur**

We say: Brandy based and fruit laced - just like it's namesake.
Origin: Created in 2003 by Angelo Vieira at The Light Bar, St. Martins Hotel, London, England.

SANGRITA

★★★★½

Glass: Shot
Garnish: None
Method: SHAKE ingredients with ice and strain into shot glass. Serve with a shot of tequila. The drinker can either down the tequila and chase it with sangrita or sip the two drinks alternately.

½	shot	**Tomato juice**
½	shot	**Pomegranate juice**
¼	shot	**Freshly squeezed orange juice**
½	shot	**Freshly squeezed lime juice**
⅛	shot	**Pomegranate (grenadine) syrup**
2	drops	**Tabasco hot pepper sauce**
2	dashes	**Worcestershire sauce**
1	pinch	**Salt**
1	grind	**Black pepper**

We say: In Mexico the quality of the homemade Sangrita can make or break a bar. This recipe is spicey and slightly sweet and perfect for chasing tequila.
Origin: The name means 'little blood' in Spanish and the drink is served with tequila in every bar in Mexico.

SANTIAGO #1

★★★☆☆

Glass: Collins
Garnish: Lime slice
Method: SHAKE first five ingredients with ice and strain into ice-filled glass. TOP with lemonade, lightly stir and serve with straws.

1	shot	**Bacardi Superior rum**
1	shot	**Spiced rum**
½	shot	**Freshly squeezed lime juice**
½	shot	**Freshly squeezed orange juice**
3	dashes	**Angostura aromatic bitters**
Top up with		**Lemonade/Sprite/7-Up**

We say: Light, refreshing and slightly spicy.

STAR RATINGS EXPLAINED

★★★★★ Excellent

★★★★½ Recommeded	★★★★☆ Praiseworthy
★★★½☆ Commended	★★★☆☆ Mediocre
★★½☆☆ Disappointing	★★☆☆☆ Pretty awful
★½☆☆☆ Shameful	★☆☆☆☆ Disgusting

SANTIAGO #2

★★★★☆

Glass: Coupette
Garnish: Raspberries
Method: MUDDLE raspberries in base of shaker. Add other ingredients, SHAKE with ice and fine strain into chilled glass.

3	fresh	**Raspberries**
2	shots	**Bacardi Superior rum**
1¼	shots	**Pomegranate juice**
¾	shot	**Limoncello liqueur**
½	shot	**Freshly squeezed lemon juice**
¼	shot	**Agave nectar**

We say: Lemon fresh pomegranate sweetened with agave nectar and laced with light rum.
Origin: Created in 2008 by Simon Rowe at The Bar at The Dorchester Hotel, London, England.

SANTIAGO AL ANOCHECER

★★★½☆

Glass: Martini
Garnish: Grapefruit zest twist
Method: SHAKE all ingredients with ice and fine strain into chilled glass.

2	shots	**Bacardi Superior rum**
½	shot	**Campari Bitter**
½	shot	**Freshly squeezed grapefruit juice**
½	shot	**Agave nectar**

We say: The same colour as red sky at night. Bitter sweet, Negroni-like and a favourite with shepherd's.
Origin: Created in 2008 by Andrew Coyle at Montpeliers Group, Edinburgh, Scotland. The name literally translates from Spanish as 'Santiago at Dusk'.

SANTIAGO DAIQUIRI

★★★★★

Glass: Martini
Garnish: Maraschino cherry
Method: SHAKE all ingredients with ice and fine strain into chilled glass.

2	shots	**Bacardi Superior rum**
1	shot	**Freshly squeezed lemon juice**
½	shot	**Pomegranate (grenadine) syrup**
½	shot	**Chilled mineral water**

We say: This Daiquiri is particularly delicate in its balance between sweet and sour.
Origin: Adapted from a recipe in Harry Craddock's 1930 '*Savoy Cocktail Book*'. Made with Barardi rum this becomes the Bacardi Cocktail.

SARATOGA COCKTAIL #1

★★★½☆

Glass: Wine
Garnish: Lemon slice
Method: Vigorously SHAKE all ingredients with just two cubes of ice and strain into chilled glass.

1	shot	**Cognac VSOP**
1	shot	**Straight rye whiskey**
1	shot	**Martini Rosso sweet vermouth**
2	dashes	**Angostura aromatic bitters**

We say: Frothy topped yet hardcore.
Origin: Recipe adapted from Jerry Thomas' 1862 '*The Bartenders Guide*'.

SARATOGA COCKTAIL #2

★★★★☆

Glass: Coupette
Garnish: Maraschino cherry
Method: SHAKE all ingredients with ice and fine strain into chilled glass.

2	shots	Cognac VSOP
¼	shot	Luxardo Maraschino liqueur
½	shot	Fresh pressed pineapple juice
½	shot	Freshly squeezed lemon juice
1	dash	Angostura aromatic bitters
½	shot	Chilled mineral water

We say: Dry and robust with cognac character combining well with maraschino and raspberry.

SARGASSO NEW

★★★½☆

Glass: Coupette
Garnish: Orange zest twist
Method: STIR all ingredients with ice and strain into chilled glass.

2	shots	Martinique V.S.O.P rum
¾	shot	Matusalem Oloroso sherry
½	shot	Aperol
2	dashes	Angostura aromatic bitters

We say: This orange-red bitter sweet drink has a dry oaky complexity.
Origin: Created by Don Lee at PDT, New York City, USA.

SATAN'S WHISKERS (CURLED) NEW 🔑

★★★★½

Glass: Martini
Garnish: Orange zest twist
Method: SHAKE all ingredients with ice and fine strain into chilled glass.

1	shot	Tanqueray London dry gin
1	shot	Martini Extra Dry vermouth
1	shot	Martini Rosso sweet vermouth
½	shot	Triple Sec
1	shot	Freshly squeezed orange juice
1	dash	Orange bitters

We say: This variation on the 'Straight' Satan's Whiskers is made curly by the use of triple sec. It seems strangely counter intuitive as you'd think the slightly richer Grand Marnier would be what made it curly.
Origin: Adapted from a recipe in Harry Craddock's 1930 *Savoy Cocktail book*.

SATAN'S WHISKERS (ENROULÉE) NEW

★★★★½

Glass: Martini
Garnish: Orange zest twist
Method: SHAKE all ingredients with ice and fine strain into chilled glass.

1½	shots	Tanqueray London dry gin
½	shot	Martini Extra Dry vermouth
½	shot	Martini Rosso sweet vermouth
½	shot	Mandarine Napoléon liqueur
¼	shot	Freshly squeezed orange juice
2	dashes	Angostura aromatic bitters

Variant: Satan's Whiskers (Straight)
Satan's Whiskers (Curled)
Satan's Whiskers (Marcelled)
We say: Enroulée is the French word for 'curled' and this particular version of Satan's Whiskers is 'curled' by the use of Mandarine Napoléon in place of the Grand Marnier found in the 'straight' version.
Origin: Created in 2011 by Gary (gaz) Regan, New York, USA.

SATAN'S WHISKERS (MARCELLED) NEW

★★★★½

Glass: Martini
Garnish: Orange zest twist
Method: SHAKE all ingredients with ice and fine strain into chilled glass.

1½	shots	Tanqueray London dry gin
¾	shot	Martini Rosso sweet vermouth
1¼	shots	Freshly squeezed orange juice
⅛	shot	Taylor's Velvet Falernum liqueur
2	dashes	Orange bitters

Variant: Satan's Whiskers (Straight)
Satan's Whiskers (Curled)
Satan's Whiskers (Enroulée)
We say: This Variation on the classic Satan's Whiskers calls for it not to be 'curled' (as is the case when you use triple sec), but to be 'marcelled', apparently a deep soft wave in one's hair (for those that still have some) created with curling tongs and popular in the 20s and 30s.
Origin: Adapted from a drink created in 2011 by William "Chili Bill" Eichinger at Finnegan's Wake, San Francisco, USA and courtesy of Gaz Regan's Ardent Spirits.

BARTENDER'S TIP DRY SHAKE

It is common practice to first shake drinks containing cream and eggs without ice, then to shake the drink a second time with ice added.

This practice is known as 'dry shaking' and the theory is that first shaking without ice, and so at a higher temperature, better allows the drink to emulsify.

SATAN'S WHISKERS (STRAIGHT)

★★★★½

Glass: Martini
Garnish: Orange zest twist
Method: SHAKE all ingredients with ice and fine strain into chilled glass.

1	shot	**Tanqueray London dry gin**
1	shot	**Martini Extra Dry vermouth**
1	shot	**Martini Rosso sweet vermouth**
½	shot	**Grand Marnier liqueur**
1	shot	**Freshly squeezed orange juice**
1	shot	**Orange bitters**

Variant: To serve 'Curled' use triple sec in place of Grand Marnier.
We say: A variation on the Bronx. Perfectly balanced tangy orange.
Origin: Adapted from a recipe in Harry Craddock's 1930 '*Savoy Cocktail Book*'.

SATIN SHEET

★★★★☆

Glass: Martini
Garnish: Lime wedge
Method: SHAKE all ingredients with ice and fine strain into chilled glass.

2	shots	**Tequila 100% Agave**
1	shot	**Freshly squeezed lime juice**
½	shot	**Taylor's Velvet Falernum liqueur**
¼	shot	**Monin Pure Cane 2:1 sugar syrup**

We say: A spiced margarita-style drink.

SATSUMA MARTINI

★★★★☆

Glass: Martini
Garnish: Orange zest twist
Method: SHAKE all ingredients with ice and fine strain into chilled glass.

1½	shots	**Ketel One Oranje vodka**
¾	shot	**Grand Marnier liqueur**
1¾	shots	**Pressed apple juice**
1	dash	**Angostura aromatic bitters**

We say: Tastes like its namesake - hard to believe it's almost half apple.
Origin: Adapted from a drink discovered in 2002 at the Fifth Floor Bar, Harvey Nichol's, London, England.

SATURN MARTINI

★★★★½

Glass: Martini
Garnish: White grapes
Method: MUDDLE grapes in base of shaker. STIR honey with vodka and grapes to dissolve honey. Add wine, SHAKE with ice and fine strain into chilled glass.

7	fresh	**Seedless white grapes**
1½	shots	**Ketel One Citroen vodka**
2	shots	**Runny honey**
1½	shots	**Sauvignon blanc wine**

We say: Delicate, beautifully balanced and subtly flavoured.
Origin: Created in 2001 by Tony Conigliaro at Isola, Knightsbridge, London, England.

SAVANNAH

★★★½☆

Glass: Martini
Garnish: Orange zest twist
Method: SHAKE all ingredients with ice and fine strain into chilled glass.

2½	shots	**Tanqueray London dry gin**
¾	shot	**Freshly squeezed orange juice**
½	shot	**White Crème de Cacao**
½	fresh	**Egg white**

We say: Gin and orange with a hint of chocolate - smoothed with egg white.
Origin: Adapted from a recipe in the 1949 edition of '*Esquire's Handbook for Hosts*'.

SAVOY SPECIAL #1

★★★★☆

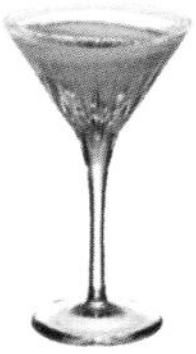

Glass: Martini
Garnish: Orange zest twist
Method: SHAKE all ingredients with ice and fine strain into chilled glass.

2	shots	**Tanqueray London dry gin**
1	shot	**Martini Extra Dry vermouth**
¼	shot	**Pomegranate (grenadine) syrup**
⅛	shot	**Absinthe**
½	shot	**Chilled mineral water**

We say: Wonderfully dry and aromatic.
Origin: Adapted from Harry Craddock's 1930 '*Savoy Cocktail Book*'.

SAY SAY

★★★½☆

Glass: Coupette
Garnish: Lemon zest twist
Method: MUDDLE tomatoes in base of shaker. Add other ingredients, SHAKE with ice and fine strain into chilled glass.

3	fresh	**Cherry tomatoes (chopped)**
1½	shots	**Bacardi Superior rum**
½	shot	**St~Germain elderflower liqueur**
½	shot	**Pomegranate (grenadine) syrup**
¾	shot	**Freshly squeezed lemon juice**

We say: This may have tomatoes in but it is no Bloody Mary. Possibly a tad on the sweet side, but complex none the less.
Origin: Adapted from a drink created in 2008 by J.P. Keating, Saba, Dublin, Republic of Ireland.

STAR RATINGS EXPLAINED

★★★★★ Excellent

★★★★½ Recommended	★★★★☆ Praiseworthy
★★★½☆ Commended	★★★☆☆ Mediocre
★★½☆☆ Disappointing	★★☆☆☆ Pretty awful
★½☆☆☆ Shameful	★☆☆☆☆ Disgusting

SAZERAC UPDATED

★★★★★

Glass: Old-fashioned
Garnish: Lemon zest twist (discarded)
Method: POUR absinthe into ice-filled glass, TOP with water and leave to stand. Separately STIR other ingredients with ice. DISCARD contents of glass (absinthe, water and ice) and STRAIN contents of stirring glass into absinthe-coated glass.

½	shot	La Fée Parisienne (68%) absinthe
Top up with		Chilled mineral water
1½	shots	Courvoisier VSOP Exclusif
1	shot	Maker's Mark bourbon
¼	shot	Monin Pure Cane 2:1 sugar syrup
3	dashes	Angostura aromatic bitters
3	dashes	Peychaud's aromatic bitters

We say: Although considered sacrilege by many and classically apparently a misdemeanour, I believe this drink is better served shaken rather than stirred. The missus agrees! However, bowing to peer pressure I have listed as stirred. Please try for yourself. Don't be concerned about chucking expensive absinthe down the drain - its flavour will be very evident in the finished drink. (The photo is shaken how it should be.)

Origin: The rounded, distinctive flavour of this classic New Orleans cocktail is reliant on one essential ingredient: Peychaud's aromatic bitters created by one Antoine Amedee Peychaud. His story starts in 1795 when he arrives in New Orleans as a refugee in 1795 after his father was forced to flee the island of San Domingo, where his family owned a coffee plantation, after the slaves rebelled.

Antoine grew up to become a pharmacist and bought his own drug and apothecary store at 437 Rue Royale (then No. 123 Royal Street) in 1834. Here he created an 'American Aromatic Bitter Cordial' and marketed it as a medicinal tonic. Such potions were fashionable at the time and there were many similar products.

Antoine also served his bitters mixed with brandy and other liquors. (It has been falsely claimed that the word 'cocktail' originated with Antoine, from a measure known as a 'coquetier' he used to prepare drinks. But it is now undisputed that the term appeared in print in an upstate New York newspaper in 1806, when Antoine was still a child.)

Antoine Peychaud advertised his bitters in local newspapers and many New Orleans bars served drinks prepared with them. One such bar was the Sazerac Coffee House at 13 Exchange Alley, owned by John B. Schiller, also the local agent for a French cognac company 'Sazerac-du-Forge et Fils' of Limoges.

It was here, sometime between 1850 and 1859, that a bartender called Leon Lamothe is thought to have created the Sazerac, probably using Peychaud's aromatic bitters, Sazerac cognac and sugar.

A decade or so later, one Thomas H Handy took over the coffee house and around the same time, Antoine Peychaud fell upon hard times and sold his pharmacy store, along with the formula and brand name of his bitters. A combination of the phylloxera aphid (which devastated French vineyards) and the American Civil War made cognac hard to obtain and Handy was forced to change the recipe of the bar's now established house cocktail. He still used the all-important Peychaud's bitters but substituted Maryland Club rye whiskey, retaining a dash of cognac and adding a splash of the newly fashionable absinthe.

The Sazerac was further adapted in 1912 when absinthe was banned in the US and Herbsaint from Louisiana was substituted. Today the name Sazerac is owned by the Sazerac Company, who licensed the name to the Sazerac Bar at New Orleans' Fairmont Hotel.

SCANDINAVIAN POP

★★★☆☆

Glass: Collins
Garnish: Lime wedge
Method: SHAKE first three ingredients with ice and strain into ice-filled glass. TOP up with ginger ale.

2	shots	Raspberry flavoured vodka
2	shots	Ocean Spray cranberry juice
½	shot	Freshly squeezed lime juice
Top up with		Ginger ale

We say: Berry fruit with a spicy splash of ginger.
Origin: Created by Wayne Collins, London, England.

SCARLETT O'HARA

★★★☆☆

Glass: Martini
Garnish: Lime wedge
Method: SHAKE all ingredients with ice and strain into ice-filled glass.

1½	shots	Southern Comfort liqueur
1½	shots	Ocean Spray cranberry juice
¾	shot	Freshly squeezed lime juice

We say: The tang of lime and the dryness of cranberry balance the apricot sweetness of Southern Comfort.
Origin: This drink helped put Southern Comfort on the proverbial drink map and was created in 1939 and named after the heroine of the film *Gone With The Wind*, released that year.

SCOFFLAW

★★★★☆

Glass: Martini
Garnish: Lemon zest twist
Method: SHAKE all ingredients with ice and fine strain into chilled glass.

1½	shots	Maker's Mark bourbon
1½	shots	Martini Extra Dry vermouth
½	shot	Freshly squeezed lemon juice
¼	shot	Pomegranate (grenadine) syrup
1	dash	Orange bitters

We say: This rust coloured drink is made or broken by the quality of the pomegranate syrup used.
Origin: During the height of Prohibition The Boston Herald ran a competition asking readers to coin a new word for "a lawless drinker of illegally made or illegally obtained liquor". Out of 25,000 entries, 'Scofflaw' was chosen and on 15th January 1924 the $200 prize was shared between two people who had submitted the word. This cocktail was created Jock at Harry's American Bar, Paris, to celebrate the new term.

SCORPION

★★★★☆

Glass: Collins
Garnish: Orange slice & mint sprig
Method: BLEND all ingredients with 12oz crushed ice and serve with straws

1½	shots	Bacardi Superior rum
¾	shot	Cognac VSOP
2	shots	Freshly squeezed orange juice
1	shot	Freshly squeezed lemon juice
½	shot	Monin Almond (orgeat) syrup

Variant: With pisco in the place of cognac.
We say: Well balanced, refreshing spirit and orange. Not sweet.
Origin: Created by Victor Bergeron and this recipe adapted from his '*Trader Vic's Bartender's Guide*' (1972 revised edition).

THE SCOTT

★★★★☆

Glass: Martini
Garnish: Lemon zest twist
Method: STIR all ingredients with ice and strain into chilled glass.

2	shots	Dewar's White label Scotch
½	shot	Drambuie
1	shot	Martini Extra Dry vermouth

We say: This golden drink is dry and sophisticated, yet honeyed and approachable.
Origin: Discovered in 2006 at The Clift Hotel, San Francisco, USA.

SCOTCH BOUNTY MARTINI

★★★★½☆

Glass: Martini
Garnish: Orange zest twist
Method: SHAKE all ingredients with ice and fine strain into chilled glass.

1½	shots	Dewar's White label Scotch
½	shot	White Crème de Cacao
½	shot	Malibu coconut rum liqueur
1½	shots	Freshly squeezed orange juice
⅛	shot	Pomegranate (grenadine) syrup

We say: A medium sweet combination of Scotch, coconut and orange.

SCOTCH MILK PUNCH

★★★½☆

Glass: Martini
Garnish: Dust with grated nutmeg
Method: SHAKE all ingredients with ice and fine strain into chilled glass.

2	shots	Dewar's White label Scotch
½	shot	Monin Pure Cane 2:1 sugar syrup
¾	shot	Double (heavy) cream
¾	shot	Milk

We say: A creamy, malty affair.

SCOTCH NEGRONI

★★★★☆

Glass: Old-fashioned
Garnish: Orange slice
Method: STIR all ingredients and strain into ice-filled glass.

1	shot	Dewar's White label Scotch
1	shot	Campari Bitter
1	shot	Martini Rosso sweet vermouth

We say: Dry, slightly smoky - for palates that appreciate bitterness.

SCOTCH POINT NEW

★★★★★

Glass: Old-fashioned
Garnish: Grapefruit zest twist
Method: STIR all ingredients with ice and strain into ice filled glass.

2½	shots	Dewar's White label Scotch
½	shot	Carpano Punt E Mes
¼	shot	Ruby port
1	dash	Peychaud's aromatic bitters
¼	shot	Chilled mineral water

We say: Scotch, vermouth, fortified wine and bitters. If there is a Manhattan then this is an Aberdeen, Glasgow and Edinburgh rolled into one.
Origin: Created in 2011 by Ian Cameron at the Cabinet Room, London, England.

SCOTCH SOUR

★★★★★

Glass: Old-fashioned
Garnish: Lemon & orange zest twists
Method: DRY SHAKE all ingredients (without ice). Add ice, SHAKE again and strain into ice-filled glass.

2	shots	Dewar's White label Scotch
1	shot	Freshly squeezed lemon juice
½	shot	Monin Pure Cane 2:1 sugar syrup
½	shot	Egg white

We say: This drink is sadly often overlooked in favour of the bourbon based Whiskey Sour.

SCORCHED EARTH

★★★½☆

Glass: Martini
Garnish: Lemon zest twist
Method: STIR all ingredients with ice and fine strain into chilled glass.

1½	shots	Cognac VSOP
½	shot	Martini Rosso sweet vermouth
½	shot	Cynar

We say: Dry, very aromatic and bordering on bitter. Interesting but not to everybody's taste.
Origin: Adapted from a recipe created in 2006 by Nicholas Hearin, at Restaurant Eugene in Atlanta, USA, and first published by Gary Regan.

SCOTTISH BREAKFAST

★★★★☆

Glass: Old-fashioned
Garnish: Dust with cinnamon powder
Method: SHAKE all ingredients with ice and strain into ice-filled glass.

1½	shots	Dewar's White label Scotch
½	shot	Calvados/Applejack brandy
½	shot	Maple syrup
1	shot	Double (heavy) cream
⅛	shot	Monin Pure Cane 2:1 sugar syrup

We say: Scotch sweetened with maple syrup, flavoured with calvados and smoothed with cream.
Origin: Created in 2009 by Erik Castro at Rickhouse, San Francisco, USA.

SCOTTISH GYPSY

★★★★☆

Glass: Coupette
Garnish: Lemon zest twist
Method: STIR all ingredients with ice and strain into chilled glass.

2	shots	Dewar's White label Scotch
1	shot	Bénédictine D.O.M.
3	dashes	Angostura aromatic bitters

We say: Scotch and Bénédictine complement each other in this wonderfully herbal cocktail which is balanced by the addition of bitters.

SCREAMING BANANA BANSHEE

★★★★☆

Glass: Hurricane
Garnish: Banana chunk
Method: BLEND all ingredients with 12oz scoop of crushed ice and serve with straws.

2	shots	Ketel One vodka
1	shot	Bols Banana liqueur
1	shot	White Crème de Cacao
1½	shots	Double (heavy) cream
1½	shots	Milk
½	fresh	Banana (peeled)

We say: An alcoholic milkshake - not too sweet.
Origin: Without the vodka this is a plain 'Banana Banshee'.

SCREAMING ORGASM

★★☆☆☆

Glass: Hurricane
Garnish: Dust with chocolate powder
Method: SHAKE all ingredients with ice and strain into glass filled with crushed ice.

1¼	shots	Ketel One vodka
1¼	shots	Kahlúa coffee liqueur
1¼	shots	Amaretto liqueur
1¼	shots	Baileys Irish cream liqueur
1¼	shots	Double (heavy) cream
1¼	shots	Milk

We say: Probably as fattening as it is alcoholic, this is a huge, creamy dessert in a glass.
Origin: A dodgy drink from the 1980s.

SCREWDRIVER

★★★★☆

Glass: Collins
Garnish: Orange slice
Method: POUR vodka into ice-filled glass and TOP with orange juice. Lightly stir and serve with straws.

| 2½ | shots | Ketel One vodka |
| Top up with | | Freshly squeezed orange juice |

Variant: Harvey Wallbanger
We say: The temperature at which this drink is served and the freshness of the orange juice are crucial to its success but perhaps better made into a Harvey Wallbanger.
Origin: This cocktail first appeared in 1950s in the Middle East. Parched US engineers working in the desert supposedly added orange juice to their vodka and stirred it with the nearest thing to hand, usually a screwdriver.

SEABREEZE #1 (SIMPLE)

★★★☆☆

Glass: Collins
Garnish: Lime slice
Method: SHAKE all ingredients with ice and strain into ice-filled glass.

2	shots	Ketel One vodka
3	shots	Ocean Spray cranberry juice
1½	shots	Freshly squeezed grapefruit juice

We say: Few bartenders bother to shake this simple drink, instead simply pouring and stirring in the glass.
Origin: Thought to have originated in the early 1990s in New York City.

SEABREEZE #2 (LAYERED)

★★★★☆

Glass: Collins
Garnish: Lime wedge
Method: POUR cranberry juice into ice-filled glass. SHAKE other ingredients with ice and carefully strain into glass to LAYER over the cranberry juice.

2	shots	Ketel One vodka
3	shots	Ocean Spray cranberry juice
1½	shots	Freshly squeezed grapefruit juice
½	shot	Freshly squeezed lime juice

We say: This layered version requires mixing with straws before drinking.

SEELBACH UPDATED

★★★★☆

Glass: Flute
Garnish: Orange zest twist
Method: POUR first four ingredients into chilled glass. TOP with champagne.

1	shot	Maker's Mark bourbon
½	shot	Cointreau triple sec
2	dashes	Peychaud's aromatic bitters
2	dashes	Angostura aromatic bitters
Top up with		Brut champagne

We say: A champagne cocktail fortified with bourbon and triple sec liqueur.
Origin: Created circa 1917 and named after its place of origin, the Seelbach Hotel, 500 South 4th Street, Louisville, Kentucky, USA. The original recipe is reputed to have called for seven dashes of each of the aromatic bitters. I find even 7 drops of each a tad excessive. Like many other vintage American whiskey based cocktails, purists often prefer to use rye whiskey in place of bourbon.

The Old Seelbach Bar has been restored to its authentic, early 1900s decor and continues to serve its signature drink to this day. Gary Regan once described the expansive bourbon selection stocked on the bar back here as "one of the finest stretches of mahogany in the country." If visiting the Seelbach be sure to check out the beautiful tiled function room with its vaulted ceiling in the basement.

STAR RATINGS EXPLAINED

★★★★★ Excellent

★★★★☆ Recommended	★★★★☆ Praiseworthy
★★★☆☆ Commended	★★★☆☆ Mediocre
★★☆☆☆ Disappointing	★★☆☆☆ Pretty awful
★☆☆☆☆ Shameful	★☆☆☆☆ Disgusting

SENSATION

★★★★☆

Glass: Martini
Garnish: Maraschino cherry
Method: Lightly MUDDLE mint (just to bruise) in base of shaker. Add other ingredients, SHAKE with ice and fine strain into chilled glass.

12	fresh	**Mint leaves**
2	shots	**Tanqueray London dry gin**
¾	shot	**Luxardo Maraschino liqueur**
¾	shot	**Freshly squeezed lemon juice**
⅛	shot	**Monin Pure Cane 2:1 sugar syrup**
½	shot	**Chilled mineral water**

We say: Fresh, fragrant and balanced.
Origin: Adapted from a recipe in Harry Craddock's 1930 '*Savoy Cocktail Book*'.

SENTIMENTAL MELODY

★★★☆☆

Glass: Martini
Garnish: Orange zest twist (flamed)
Method: STIR preserve and rum in base of a shaker to dissolve the jam. Add other ingredients, SHAKE with ice and fine strain into chilled glass.

2	spoons	**Grapefruit preserve**
2	shots	**Bacardi Superior rum**
¼	shot	**Triple Sec**
½	shot	**St~Germain elderflower liqueur**
¾	shot	**Ocean Spray cranberry juice**
¼	shot	**Pomegranate juice**
½	shot	**Freshly squeezed lime juice**

We say: A twisted Daiquiri with rich berry fruit.
Origin: Adapted from a recipe created in 2008 by Peter Dorelli, London, England.

SERENDIPITY #1

★★★★☆

Glass: Collins
Garnish: Lemon slice
Method: MUDDLE blackberries in in base of shaker. Add other ingredients, SHAKE with ice and strain into glass filled with crushed ice.

6	fresh	**Blackberries**
1	shot	**Tanqueray London dry gin**
½	shot	**Vanilla schnapps**
3	shots	**Ocean Spray cranberry juice**
¼	shot	**Freshly squeezed lemon juice**
¼	shot	**Monin Pure Cane 2:1 sugar syrup**
½	shot	**Crème de cassis liqueur**

We say: Long, red, fruity, vanilla.
Origin: Created in 2002 by Jamie Stephenson, Manchester, England.

STAR RATINGS EXPLAINED

★★★★★ **Excellent**

★★★★⯪ Recommended	★★★★☆ Praiseworthy
★★★⯪☆ Commended	★★★☆☆ Mediocre
★★⯪☆☆ Disappointing	★★☆☆☆ Pretty awful
★⯪☆☆☆ Shameful	★☆☆☆☆ Disgusting

SERENDIPITY #2

★★★★☆

Glass: Old-fashioned
Garnish: Mint sprig
Method: Lightly MUDDLE mint (just to bruise) in base of shaker. Add calvados and apple juice, SHAKE with ice and strain into ice-filled glass. TOP with champagne.

7	fresh	**Mint leaves**
1½	shots	**Calvados/Applejack brandy**
3	shots	**Pressed apple juice**
Top up with		**Brut champagne**

We say: Spirity, minty apple invigorated by a splash of champagne.
Origin: My adaptation of one of Colin Field's drinks. He created it on 31 December 1994 in the Hemingway Bar of the Paris Ritz for Jean-Louis Constanza: upon tasting it, Jean-Louis exclaimed, "Serendipity".

SETTLE PETAL

★★★★☆

Glass: Martini
Garnish: Rose petal
Method: STIR all ingredients with ice and strain into chilled glass.

2	shots	**Tanqueray London dry gin**
1	shot	**Cucumber flavoured vodka**
½	shot	**Rose water**
½	shot	**Monin Vanilla sugar syrup**

We say: An aptly named floral Martini.
Origin: Created in 2003 by Andy Fitzmorris at Eclipse, Notting Hill, London, England.

SEVENTH HEAVEN #2

★★★★⯪

Glass: Martini
Garnish: Mint leaf
Method: SHAKE all ingredients with ice and fine strain into chilled glass.

2¼	shots	**Tanqueray London dry gin**
¾	shot	**Luxardo Maraschino liqueur**
1½	shots	**Freshly squeezed grapefruit juice**

We say: Drink this and you'll be there.
Origin: Adapted from the Seventh Heaven No.2 recipe in Harry Craddock's 1930 '*Savoy Cocktail Book*'.

SEX ON THE BEACH #1

★★⯪☆☆

Glass: Collins
Garnish: Orange slice & cherry on stick (sail)
Method: SHAKE all ingredients with ice and strain into ice-filled glass.

2	shots	**Ketel One vodka**
½	shot	**Peachtree peach schnapps**
½	shot	**Chambord black raspberry liqueur**
1½	shots	**Freshly squeezed orange juice**
1½	shots	**Ocean Spray cranberry juice**

Variant: With melon liqueur in place of peach schnapps.
We say: Sweet fruit laced with vodka.
Origin: An infamous cocktail during the 1980s.

SEX ON THE BEACH #2

Glass: Old-fashioned
Garnish: Orange slice & cherry on stick (sail)
Method: SHAKE all ingredients with ice and strain into ice-filled glass.

2	shots	Ketel One vodka
½	shot	Midori green melon liqueur
½	shot	Chambord black raspberry liqueur
1½	shots	Fresh pressed pineapple juice

We say: Sweeter than most.

SEX ON THE BEACH #3

Glass: Shot
Garnish: None
Method: Refridgerate ingredients then LAYER in chilled glass by carefully pouring in the order listed.

½	shot	Chambord black raspberry liqueur
½	shot	Midori green melon liqueur
½	shot	Freshly squeezed lime juice
½	shot	Fresh pressed pineapple juice

We say: A sweet and sour shot, combining raspberry, melon, lime and pineapple.

SGROPPINO

Glass: Flute
Garnish: Lemon zest twist
Method: BLEND all ingredients without additional ice and serve in chilled glass.

½	shot	Ketel One vodka
¼	shot	Double (heavy) cream
1½	shots	Prosecco sparkling wine
2	scoop	Lemon sorbet

AKA: Sorbetto
We say: Smooth and all too easy to quaff. A great dessert.
Origin: Pronounced 'scroe-pee-noe', this hybrid of cocktail and dessert is often served after meals in Venice. The name comes from a vernacular word meaning 'untie', a reference to the belief that it relaxes your stomach after a hearty meal.

SHADY GROVE COOLER

Glass: Collins
Garnish: Lime wedge
Method: SHAKE first three ingredients with ice and strain into ice-filled glass. TOP with ginger ale, lightly stir and serve with straws.

2	shots	Tanqueray London dry gin
1	shot	Freshly squeezed lime juice
½	shot	Monin Pure Cane 2:1 sugar syrup
Top up with		Ginger ale

We say: Long and refreshing with lime freshness and a hint of ginger.

SHAKERATO

Glass: Martini
Garnish: Lemon zest twist
Method: SHAKE all ingredients with ice and fine strain into chilled glass.

1½	shots	Campari Bitter
¼	shot	Freshly squeezed lemon juice
¼	shot	Monin Pure Cane 2:1 sugar syrup

We say: Campari lovers only need apply.

SHAMROCK #1

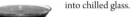

Glass: Martini
Garnish: Orange zest twist (discarded)
Method: STIR all ingredients with ice and strain into chilled glass.

2½	shots	Maker's Mark bourbon
¼	shot	Green crème de menthe liqueur
1	shot	Martini Rosso sweet vermouth
2	dashes	Angostura aromatic bitters

We say: Basically a sweet Manhattan with a dash of green crème de menthe.
Origin: Purloined from David Embury's classic book, 'The Fine Art of Mixing Drinks'.

SHAMROCK #2

Glass: Martini
Garnish: Mint leaf
Method: SHAKE all ingredients with ice and fine strain into chilled glass.

1½	shots	Jameson Irish whiskey
1½	shots	Martini Extra Dry vermouth
½	shot	Chartreuse Green liqueur
½	shot	Green crème de menthe liqueur
½	shot	Chilled mineral water

We say: A great drink for St Patrick's Day.
Origin: Adapted from a recipe in Harry Craddock's 1930 'Savoy Cocktail Book'.

SHAMROCK EXPRESS

Glass: Old-fashioned
Garnish: None
Method: SHAKE all ingredients with ice and strain into ice-filled glass.

1½	shots	Hot espresso coffee
¾	shot	Butterscotch schnapps
1	shot	Ketel One vodka
1	shot	Baileys Irish cream liqueur
¼	shot	Monin Pure Cane 2:1 sugar syrup

We say: Creamy coffee with the sweetness of butterscotch.
Origin: Created in 1999 by Greg Pearson at Mystique, Manchester, England.

SHANDYGAFF

★★★☆☆

Glass: Pint
Garnish: None
Method: POUR ale into glass, TOP with ginger ale.

Fill glass two-thirds full with Lager
Top up with Ginger ale

AKA: Sandygaff
We say: Tastier than your average 'lager shandy'.
Origin: This drink and its name originated in England and dates back to at least the late 19th century. The name comes from the London slang for a pint of beer, 'shant of gatter' (shanty being a public house, gatter meaning water). The ginger ale serves as a flavoursome way to water down the strength of the beer, thus the literal translation, 'pub water'.

In the first chapter of *The History of Mr Polly*, H. G. Wells describes a shandygaff as being, "two pints of beer and two bottles of ginger beer foaming in a huge round-bellied jug." In London the beer is now usually diluted with lemonade and this drink is now simply known as a shandy. When ordering in a pub you are expected to call for 'lager shandy' or 'bitter shandy', the latter specifying the drink should be based on traditional real ale.

Today the term 'Shandygaff' is forgotten in London but popular in the Caribbean where this drink is made with beer and ginger ale or ginger beer.

SHARK BITE

★★★½☆

Glass: Hurricane
Garnish: None
Method: BLEND first three ingredients with 18oz scoop crushed ice and pour into glass. POUR grenadine around edge of the drink. Do not stir before stirring.

2	shots	**Pusser's Navy rum**
3	shots	**Freshly squeezed orange juice**
½	shot	**Freshly squeezed lime juice**
¾	shot	**Pomegranate (grenadine) syrup**

We say: Strong rum and orange juice. A tad sweet but easy to drink.

SHARK'S TOOTH NO.1

★★★½☆

Glass: Sling
Garnish: Lime wedge
Method: SHAKE first five ingredients with ice and strain into ice-filled glass. TOP with soda and serve with straws.

2½	shots	**Wray & Nephew overproof rum**
½	shot	**Freshly squeezed lime juice**
½	shot	**Freshly squeezed lemon juice**
¼	shot	**Monin Pure Cane 2:1 sugar syrup**
¼	shot	**Pomegranate (grenadine) syrup**
Top up with		**Soda (club soda)**

We say: Salmon-pink in colour and heavily influenced by the flavoursome overproof rum.
Origin: Adapted from Victor Bergeron's *'Trader Vic's Bartender's Guide'* (1972 revised edition) where he writes, "One of the first drinks we ever made".

SHARK'S TOOTH NO.3

★★★½☆

Glass: Sling
Garnish: Lime wedge
Method: SHAKE first three ingredients with ice and strain into ice-filled glass. TOP with soda and serve with straws.

2½	shots	**Bacardi Superior rum**
1	shot	**Freshly squeezed lemon juice**
½	shot	**Pomegranate (grenadine) syrup**
Top up with		**Soda (club soda)**

We say: Sounds hard; looks pink. Tastes reminiscent of a dilute Bacardi Cocktail.
Origin: Adapted from Victor Bergeron's *'Trader Vic's Bartender's Guide'* (1972 revised edition).

SHARMAN-COX DAIQUIRI NEW

★★★★☆

Glass: Coupette
Garnish: Orange zest twist (discarded) & lime wedge
Method: DRY SHAKE all ingredients (without ice). SHAKE again with ice and fine strain into chilled glass.

2	shots	**Rum light white/blanco**
⅓	shot	**Bols blue curaçao liqueur**
¼	shot	**Freshly squeezed lime juice**
¼	shot	**Freshly squeezed lemon juice**
¼	shot	**Monin Pure Cane 2:1 sugar syrup**
½	fresh	**Egg white**

We say: A foam-topped blue twist on the classic daiquiri.
Origin: Adapted from a drink created in 2013 at the Rum Kitchen, Notting Hill, London. The name 'Cox' is the common theme to this drink: it is inspired by the Perfect Lady, a classic cocktail created in 1936 by Sidney Cox, a bartender at the Grosvenor House, London for The British Empire Cocktail Competition where it took the 1st Prize; the original Daiquiri, is said to have been created in 1898 by Jennings Cox, an American mining engineer working at a tin mine near the Cuban town of Daiquiri; and most importantly, this drink was created and named to honour our own fabulous Hannah Sharman-Cox.

SHERRY COBBLER

★★★★½

Glass: Collins
Garnish: Lemon & orange wedges
Method: MUDDLE fruit in base of shaker. Add other ingredients, SHAKE with ice and fine strain into a glass filled with crushed ice.

¼	slice	**Pineapple (fresh)**
½	slice	**Fresh orange**
3½	shots	**Tio Pepe fino sherry**
¼	shot	**Luxardo Maraschino liqueur**
¼	shot	**Freshly squeezed lemon juice**
¼	shot	**Monin Pure Cane 2:1 sugar syrup**

We say: This age old cocktail is said to have been the drink for which the waxed paper straw was invented. To quote Harry Johnson, from his 1882 *'Bartender's Manual'*: "It is a very refreshing drink for old and young."
Origin: The origins of this cocktail are unknown but it is one of the original classic cocktails. This recipes is adapted from Jerry Thomas' 1862 book, *'How to Mix Drinks - the Bon Vivant's Companion'*.
In his 1882 *'Bartender's Manual'*, Harry Johnson writes of the Sherry Cobbler, "This drink is without doubt the most popular beverage in the country, with ladies as well as with gentlemen."

SHERRY SOUR

★★★★½

Glass: Old-fashioned
Garnish: Maraschino cherry
Method: SHAKE all ingredients with ice and strain into ice-filled glass.

2	shots	Apostoles palo cortado sherry
¾	shot	Freshly squeezed lemon juice
½	shot	Monin Pure Cane 2:1 sugar syrup
½	fresh	Egg white

We say: The huge flavour of sherry freshened by lemon juice and rounded by egg white.
Origin: Discovered in 2007 at Suba, New York City, USA.

SHIRLEY TEMPLE (MOCKTAIL)

★★★☆☆

Glass: Collins
Garnish: Maraschino cherry & lemon slice
Method: POUR ingredients into ice filled glass, lightly stir and serve with straws.

¼	shot	Pomegranate (grenadine) syrup
¼	shot	Freshly squeezed lemon juice
Top up with		Ginger ale

We say: I've added a splash of lemon juice to the usual recipe. It's still not that exciting.

SHOWBIZ

★★★★☆

Glass: Martini
Garnish: Blackcurrants
Method: SHAKE all ingredients with ice and fine strain into chilled glass.

1¾	shots	Ketel One vodka
1¾	shots	Freshly squeezed grapefruit juice
1	shot	Crème de cassis liqueur

We say: Sweet cassis soured with grapefruit and fortified with vodka.

SI-MAO

★★★½☆

Glass: Shot
Method: SHAKE all ingredients with ice and fine strain into chilled glass.

1	shot	Jack Daniel's Tennessee whiskey
½	fresh	Banana (peeled)
¼	shot	Freshly squeezed orange juice
¼	shot	Freshly squeezed lemon juice

We say: A whiskey laced shot with a hint of banana.
Origin: Adapted from a drink discovered in 2010 at Nobu Berkeley, London, England.

SICILIAN NEGRONI

★★★★☆

Glass: Old-fashioned
Garnish: Orange slice
Method: SHAKE all ingredients with ice and strain into ice-filled glass.

1½	shots	Tanqueray London dry gin
1½	shots	Campari Bitter
1½	shots	Freshly squeezed orange juice

We say: Blood orange juice replaces sweet vermouth in this fruity Negroni.
Origin: Discovered in 2006 at The Last Supper Club, San Francisco, USA.

SIDE ERR NEW

★★★★½

Glass: Old-fashioned
Garnish: Apple slice
Method: POUR ingredients into ice-filled glass and stir.

1	shot	Calvados/Applejack brandy
¼	shot	Żubrówka bison vodka
½	spoon	Lagavulin 16yo malt whisky
2¾	shots	Dry cider

We say: This apple delight combines apple brandy, Bison Grass vodka, dry cider with a smoky whiff of Islay whisky.
Origin: Created in August 2011 by Simon Difford at the Cabinet Room, London, England.

SIDECAR (DIFFORD'S FORMULA)

★★★★½

Glass: Martini
Garnish: Lemon zest twist
Method: SHAKE all ingredients with ice and fine strain into chilled glass.

1½	shots	Cognac VSOP
1	shot	Triple Sec
1	shot	Freshly squeezed lemon juice
½	shot	Chilled mineral water

Variant: Apple Cart

We say: Complex and very slightly on the sour side of balanced. Those with a sweet tooth may prefer with a sugar rim.

There have been periods when it has been fashionable to coat the rim of the glass in which this drink is to be served with sugar. Thankfully sugar rims are now out of vogue and, as Embury writes in his book, "A twist of lemon may be used if desired and the peel dropped into the glass. Otherwise no decoration."

Origin: In his 1948 '*Fine Art of Mixing Drinks*', David A. Embury writes of the Sidecar: "It was invented by a friend of mine at a bar in Paris during World War I and was named after the motorcycle sidecar in which the good captain customarily was driven to and from the little bistro where the drink was born and christened."

Embury doesn't name the bar but it's commonly assumed that he meant Harry's New York Bar and that the cocktail was created by its owner, Harry MacElhone. However, in Harry's own book he credits the drink to Pat MacGarry of Buck's Club, London.

The proportions of this drink are debated as much as its origin. Perhaps due to ease rather than balance, the equal parts formula (1 x brandy, 1 x triple sec and 1 x lemon juice) was the earliest published recipe (Robert Vermeire's 1922 'Cocktails: How to Mix Them' and Harry McElhone's 1922 'ABC of Mixing Cocktails') and still seems popular to this day.

Embury writes of the 'equal parts' Sidecar, "This is the most perfect example of a magnificent drink gone wrong". He argues that "Essentially the Sidecar is nothing but a Daiquiri with brandy in the place of rum and Cointreau in the place of sugar syrup" and so the Daiquiri formula should be followed (2 x brandy, 1/2 x triple sec and 1/4 lemon juice). This may work for a Daiquiri but makes for an overly dry Sidecar.

In his 1930 'The Savoy Cocktail Book', Harry Craddock calls for 2 x brandy; 1 x Cointreau and 1 x lemon juice. The formula I use here takes the middle ground between The Savoy and the 'equal parts' camp. I also find this drink benefits from a little extra dilution.

SIDECAR NAMED DESIRE

Glass: Martini
Garnish: Lemon zest twist
Method: SHAKE all ingredients with ice and fine strain into chilled glass.

2	shots	Calvados/Applejack brandy
1	shot	Berentzen Apple schnapps
1	shot	Freshly squeezed lemon juice

We say: Take a classic Sidecar and add some love interest - apples!

SIDECARRIAGE

Glass: Martini
Garnish: Lemon zest twist
Method: SHAKE all ingredients with ice and fine strain into chilled glass.

1½	shots	Calvados/Applejack brandy
1½	shots	St~Germain elderflower liqueur
1	shot	Freshly squeezed lemon juice

We say: Hints of cider come through in this calvados based Sidecar with an elderflower twist.
Origin: Created in 2006 by Simon Difford.

SIDEKICK

Glass: Martini
Garnish: Orange slice
Method: SHAKE all ingredients with ice and fine strain into chilled glass.

2	shots	Cognac VSOP
¾	shot	Triple Sec
1	shot	Freshly squeezed orange juice
½	shot	Freshly squeezed lime juice

We say: Rich pear and orange with a stabilising hint of sour lime.
Origin: Adapted from a drink discovered in 2003 at Temple Bar, New York City, USA.

SILENT THIRD

Glass: Martini
Garnish: Lemon zest twist
Method: SHAKE all ingredients with ice and fine strain into chilled glass.

1½	shots	Dewar's White label Scotch
1	shot	Triple Sec
¾	shot	Freshly squeezed lemon juice
½	shot	Chilled mineral water

We say: Basically a Sidecar made with Scotch in place of cognac.

SILK PANTIES

Glass: Martini
Garnish: Peach slice
Method: SHAKE all ingredients with ice and fine strain into chilled glass.

2	shots	Ketel One vodka
1	shot	Peachtree peach schnapps
2	dashes	Peach bitters

We say: This drink may be sweet but despite the silly name it is more serious than you might expect.
Origin: Created sometime in the 1980s.

SILK ROAD NEW

Glass: Coupette
Garnish: Grapefruit zest twist
Method: SHAKE all ingredients with ice and fine strain into chilled glass.

1½	shots	Tanqueray London dry gin
⅓	shot	Bénédictine D.O.M.
⅓	shot	De Kuyper apricot brandy liqueur
½	shot	Freshly squeezed lime juice
½	shot	Monin Pure Cane 2:1 sugar syrup
2	dashes	Angostura aromatic bitters

We say: As the name suggests, the Silk Road harnesses the exotic herbs and spices found in the gin and Bénédictine to deliver a harmonious, flavoursome drink with a silky delivery.
Origin: Adapted from a drink created in 2012 by Timothy Carroll at Barrio North, London, England.

SILK STOCKING

Glass: Martini
Garnish: Dust with cinnamon powder
Method: SHAKE all ingredients with ice and fine strain into chilled glass.

2	shots	Tequila 100% Agave
¾	shot	White Crème de Cacao
¼	shot	Pomegranate (grenadine) syrup
¾	shot	Double (heavy) cream

We say: So smooooooth but still retains a tequila bite and a hint of chocolate and fruit.
Origin: We are indebted to Ryan Chetiyawardana from Bramble Bar, Edinburgh, Scotland who shared his recipe for this classic cocktail at The Cabinet Room during the finals of World Class 2009.

SILVER BRONX

Glass: Martini
Garnish: Maraschino cherry
Method: SHAKE all ingredients with ice and fine strain into chilled glass.

2	shots	Tanqueray London dry gin
¼	shot	Martini Extra Dry vermouth
¼	shot	Martini Rosso sweet vermouth
1	shot	Freshly squeezed orange juice
1	fresh	Egg white

We say: A Bronx made 'silver' by the addition of egg white.
Origin: A vintage cocktail adapted from the classic Bronx Cocktail, created in 1906 by Johnny Solon, a bartender at New York's Waldorf-Astoria Hotel, and named after the newly opened Bronx Zoo.

SILVER BULLET MARTINI

★★★★☆

Glass: Martini
Garnish: Lemon zest twist
Method: SHAKE all ingredients with ice and fine strain into chilled glass.

2	shots	Tanqueray London dry gin
1	shot	Kümmel
1	shot	Freshly squeezed lemon juice
¼	shot	Monin Pure Cane 2:1 sugar syrup

Variant: A modern variation is to substitute sambuca for kümmel.
We say: Caraway and fennel flavour this unusual sweet 'n' sour drink.
Origin: Thought to have been created in the 1920s.

SILVER FIZZ

★★★★☆

Glass: Collins (small 8oz)
Garnish: Lemon slice
Method: SHAKE first four ingredients with ice and strain into chilled glass (no ice). TOP with soda from siphon.

2	shots	Brandy, whisk(e)y, gin, rum etc.
1	shot	Freshly squeezed lemon or lime juice
½	shot	Monin Pure Cane 2:1 sugar syrup
½	shot	Egg white
Top up with		Soda from siphon

Variant: Omit the egg white and this is a mere fizz.
We say: I prefer my fizzes with the addition of egg white. Why not try a Derby Fizz, which combines spirits and liqueurs?
Origin: A mid 19th century classic.

SILVER MARTINI

★★★☆☆

Glass: Martini
Garnish: Maraschino cherry
Method: SHAKE all ingredients with ice and fine strain into chilled glass.

1½	shots	Tanqueray London dry gin
1½	shots	Martini Extra Dry vermouth
¼	shot	Luxardo Maraschino liqueur
2	dashes	Orange bitters

We say: Dry and aromatic - for serious imbibers only.
Origin: Adapted from a recipe in Harry Craddock's 1930 '*Savoy Cocktail Book*'

SINGAPORE SLING #1 UPDATED
(BAKER'S FORMULA)

★★★☆☆

Glass: Collins
Garnish: Lemon slice & cherry on stick (sail)
Method: SHAKE first three ingredients with ice and strain into ice-filled glass. TOP with soda, lightly stir and serve with straws.

2	shots	Old Tom gin
¾	shot	Bénédictine D.O.M.
¾	shot	Cherry brandy liqueur
Top up with		Soda (club soda)

Variant: Straits Sling
We say: Lacks the citrus of other Singapore Slings but dilution cuts and so balances the sweetness of the liqueurs.
Origin: Adapted from a recipe by Charles H. Baker Jr. and published in his 1946 'Gentleman's Companion'. This drink was created some time between 1911 and 1915 by Chinese-born Ngiam Tong Boon at the Long Bar in Raffles Hotel, Singapore.

Raffles Hotel is named after the colonial founder of Singapore, Sir Stamford Raffles, and was the Near East's ex-pat central. As Charles H. Baker Jr. wrote in his 1946 book, "Just looking around the terrace porch we've seen Frank Buck, the Sultan of Johor, Aimee Semple McPherson, Somerset Maugham, Dick Halliburton, Doug Fairbanks, Bob Ripley, Ruth Elder and Walker Camp - not that this is any wonder". Raffles still sticks out of modern-day Singapore like a vast, colonial Christmas cake.

Although there is little controversy as to who created the Singapore Sling, where he created it and (roughly) when, there is huge debate over the original name and ingredients. Singapore and the locality was colonially known as the 'Straits Settlements' and it seems certain that Boon's drink was similarly named the 'Straits Sling'. The name appears to have changed sometime between 1922 and 1930.

While contemporary sources are clear that it was cherry brandy that distinguishes the Singapore Sling from another kind of sling, a great debate rages over the type of cherry brandy used. Was it a cherry 'brandy' liqueur or actually a cherry eau de vie? Did fruit juice feature in the original recipe at all? We shall probably never know, but the Raffles Hotel and most other bars today favour cherry brandy.

SINGAPORE SLING #2

★★★★☆

Glass: Sling
Garnish: Lemon slice & cherry on stick (sail)
Method: SHAKE first six ingredients with ice and strain into ice-filled glass. TOP with soda, lightly stir and serve with straws.

2	shots	Tanqueray London dry gin
½	shot	Bénédictine D.O.M.
½	shot	De Kuyper Cherry Brandy liqueur
1	shot	Freshly squeezed lemon juice
2	dashes	Angostura aromatic bitters
2	dashes	Orange bitters
Top up with		Soda (club soda)

We say: On the sour side of dry, this is decidedly more complex than most Singapore Sling recipes.

BARTENDER'S TIP SWIZZLE

To 'swizzle' a drink is simply to stir it using a particular tool and action.

To swizzle simply immerse the blades of your swizzle stick into the drink, hold the shaft between the palms of both hands and rotate the stick rapidly by sliding your hands back and forth against it. If you do not have a bona fide swizzle stick, use a barspoon in the same manner.

SINGAPORE SLING #3 UPDATED
(RAFFLES FORMULA)

★★★½☆

Glass: Sling
Garnish: Lemon slice & cherry on stick (sail)
Method: SHAKE first eight ingredients with ice and strain into ice-filled glass. TOP with soda, lightly stir and serve with straws.

2	shots	**Tanqueray London dry gin**
½	shot	**De Kuyper Cherry Brandy liqueur**
¼	shot	**Bénédictine D.O.M.**
¼	shot	**Triple Sec**
1½	shots	**Fresh pressed pineapple juice**
½	shot	**Freshly squeezed lime juice**
¼	shot	**Pomegranate (grenadine) syrup**
2	dashes	**Angostura aromatic bitters**
Top up with		**Soda (club soda)**

We say: Foaming, tangy and very fruity.

SIR CHARLES PUNCH

★★★★☆

Glass: Old-fashioned
Garnish: Orange zest twist
Method: STIR all ingredients with ice and strain into ice-filled glass.

1	shot	**Warre's Otima tawny port**
½	shot	**Cognac VSOP**
½	shot	**Grand Marnier liqueur**
⅛	shot	**Monin Pure Cane 2:1 sugar syrup**

We say: Short but full of personality.
Origin: Adapted from a recipe in the 1949 edition of *'Esquire's Handbook for Hosts'*, which suggests serving it at Christmas.

SIR THOMAS

★★★★☆

Glass: Martini
Garnish: Maraschino cherry
Method: STIR all ingredients with ice and strain into chilled glass.

2	shots	**Maker's Mark bourbon**
½	shot	**Triple Sec**
½	shot	**De Kuyper Cherry Brandy liqueur**
½	shot	**Martini Rosso sweet vermouth**

We say: Akin to a fruit laced Sweet Manhattan.
Origin: Created in 2005 by Tom Ward, London, England.

STAR RATINGS EXPLAINED

★★★★★ Excellent

★★★★½ Recommeded	★★★★☆ Praiseworthy
★★★½☆ Commended	★★★☆☆ Mediocre
★★½☆☆ Disappointing	★★☆☆☆ Pretty awful
★½☆☆☆ Shameful	★☆☆☆☆ Disgusting

SIR WALTER COCKTAIL

★★★☆☆

Glass: Martini
Garnish: Lemon zest twist
Method: SHAKE all ingredients with ice and fine strain into chilled glass.

¾	shot	**Bacardi Superior rum**
¾	shot	**Cognac VSOP**
¼	shot	**Grand Marnier liqueur**
¼	shot	**Pomegranate (grenadine) syrup**
¾	shot	**Freshly squeezed lemon juice**
2	dashes	**Angostura aromatic bitters**

We say: This blend of rum and cognac has more than a hint of Tiki fruitiness.
Origin: Adapted from Victor Bergeron's *'Trader Vic's Bartender's Guide'* (1972 revised edition).

SKETCHER'S PET

★★★★½

Glass: Flute
Garnish: Orange slice
Method: SHAKE all ingredients with ice and fine strain into chilled glass.

2	shots	**Ketel One vodka**
1	shot	**Freshly squeezed orange juice**
¾	shot	**De Kuyper Apricot Brandy liqueur**
¼	shot	**Passion fruit syrup**
½	shot	**Double (heavy) cream**

We say: A sweet creamy, fruity dessert-style cocktail.
Origin: Created in January 2010 by Zdenek Kestanek at Quo Vadis, London, England for Petek Sketcher.

SKI BREEZE

★★★☆☆

Glass: Collins
Garnish: Apple slice
Method: POUR ingredients into ice-filled glass, lightly stir and serve with straws.

2	shots	**Raspberry flavoured vodka**
3	shots	**Pressed apple juice**
3	shots	**Ginger ale**

We say: A meld of apple and berries with a hint of ginger.

SKID ROW

★★★★☆

Glass: Coupette
Garnish: Orange zest twist (flamed)
Method: STIR all ingredients with ice and strain into chilled glass.

2	shots	**Bols Genever**
½	shot	**De Kuyper Apricot Brandy liqueur**
½	shot	**Chartreuse Yellow liqueur**
1	dash	**Angostura aromatic bitters**
1	dash	**Orange bitters**

We say: Complex and strong in alcohol, bitter-sweet with apricot liqueur and amaro fighting it out over Dutch genever.
Origin: Adapted from a drink created in 2009 by Eric Alperin at The Varnish, Los Angeles, USA.

SLEEPING BISON-TINI

★★★★☆

Glass: Martini
Garnish: Pear slice
Method: SHAKE all ingredients with ice and fine strain into chilled glass.

1½	shots	**Żubrówka bison vodka**
¼	shot	**De Kuyper Apricot Brandy liqueur**
¼	shot	**Belle de Brillet pear liqueur**
1	shot	**Pressed pear juice**
1	shot	**Pressed apple juice**
1	shot	**Cold camomile tea**

We say: A light cocktail featuring a melange of subtle flavours.

SLEEPY HOLLOW

★★★★☆

Glass: Old-fashioned
Garnish: Lemon slice
Method: Lightly MUDDLE mint in base of shaker (just to bruise). Add other ingredients, SHAKE with ice and fine strain into glass filled with crushed ice. Serve with straws.

10	fresh	**Mint leaves**
2	shots	**Tanqueray London dry gin**
½	shot	**De Kuyper Apricot Brandy liqueur**
1	shot	**Freshly squeezed lemon juice**
½	shot	**Monin Pure Cane 2:1 sugar syrup**

We say: Hints of lemon and mint with gin and apricot fruit. Very refreshing.
Origin: An adaptation of a drink created in the early 1930s and named after Washington Irving's novel and its enchanted valley with ghosts, goblins and headless horseman.

SLING (GENERIC NAME)

★★★★☆

Glass: Sling
Garnish: Lemon slice
Method: SHAKE first three ingredients with ice and strain into ice-filled glass. TOP with soda or ginger ale.

2	shots	**Brandy, whisk(e)y, gin, rum etc.**
½	shot	**Freshly squeezed lemon juice**
¼	shot	**Monin Pure Cane 2:1 sugar syrup**
Top up with		**Soda (club soda)**

We say: Sugar balances the citrus juice, the spirit fortifies and the carbonate lengthens.
Origin: The word 'Sling' comes from the German 'schlingen', meaning 'to swallow', and Slings based on a spirit mixed with sugar and water were popularly drunk in the late 1800s.

Slings are similar to Toddies and like Toddies can be served hot. (Toddies, however, are never served cold.) The main difference between a Toddy and a Sling is that Slings are not flavoured by the addition of spices. Also, Toddies tend to be made with plain water, while Slings are charged with water, soda water or ginger ale.

The earliest known definition of 'cocktail' describes it as a bittered sling.

SLIPPERY NIPPLE

★★☆☆☆

Glass: Shot
Garnish: None
Method: LAYER in glass by carefully pouring ingredients in the order listed.

¼	shot	**Pomegranate (grenadine) syrup**
¾	shot	**Luxardo Sambuca dei Cesari**
¾	shot	**Baileys Irish cream liqueur**

We say: The infamous red, clear and brown shot. Very sweet.

SLOE GIN FIZZ

★★★½☆

Glass: Sling
Garnish: Lemon & cucumber slices
Method: SHAKE first five ingredients with ice and strain into ice-filled glass.TOP with soda, stir and serve with straws.

1	shot	**Tanqueray London dry gin**
1½	shots	**Sloe Gin liqueur**
1	shot	**Freshly squeezed lime juice**
¼	shot	**Monin Pure Cane 2:1 sugar syrup**
½	fresh	**Egg white**
Top up with		**Soda (club soda)**

We say: A sour gin fizz with dark, rich sloe gin.

SLOE MOTION

★★★½☆

Glass: Flute
Garnish: Lemon zest twist
Method: POUR liqueur into chilled glass and TOP with champagne.

¾	shot	**Sloe Gin liqueur**
Top up with		**Brut champagne**

We say: Sloe gin proves to be an excellent compliment to champagne.

SLOE TEQUILA

★★★½☆

Glass: Old-fashioned
Garnish: Lime wedge
Method: SHAKE all ingredients with ice and strain into ice-filled glass.

1	shot	**Sloe Gin liqueur**
1	shot	**Tequila 100% Agave**
1	shot	**Rose's lime cordial**

We say: Berry fruit and tequila with a surprisingly tart, bitter finish.

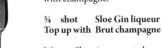

THE SLOPE

★★★★★⯪ **Glass:** Coupette
Garnish: Maraschino cherry
Method: STIR all ingredients with ice and fine strain into chilled glass.

2	shots	Straight rye whiskey
¾	shot	Martini Extra Dry vermouth
¼	shot	De Kuyper Apricot Brandy liqueur
1	dash	Angostura aromatic bitters

We say: An apricot liqueur influenced rift on a classic Manhattan / Brooklyn.
Origin: Created in 2010 by Julie Reiner at Clover Club, Brooklyn, USA.

SLOPPY JOE

★★★★☆ **Glass:** Martini
Garnish: Lime wedge
Method: SHAKE all ingredients with ice and fine strain into chilled glass.

1	shot	Bacardi Superior rum
¼	shot	Triple Sec
1	shot	Martini Extra Dry vermouth
1	shot	Freshly squeezed lime juice
½	shot	Monin Pure Cane 2:1 sugar syrup
¼	shot	Pomegranate (grenadine) syrup

We say: Nicely balances sweet and sourness.

SLOW COMFORTABLE SCREW

★★★⯪☆ **Glass:** Collins
Garnish: Orange slice
Method: SHAKE all ingredients with ice and strain into ice-filled glass.

1	shot	Ketel One Vodka
1	shot	Sloe Gin liqueur
1	shot	Southern Comfort liqueur
3	shots	Freshly squeezed orange juice

We say: A Screwdriver with Sloe gin and Southern Comfort. Fruity and fairly sweet.

SLOW COMFORTABLE SCREW AGAINST THE WALL

★★★⯪☆ **Glass:** Collins
Garnish: None
Method: SHAKE first four ingredients with ice and strain into ice-filled glass. Lastly FLOAT Galliano.

1	shot	Ketel One vodka
1	shot	Sloe Gin liqueur
1	shot	Southern Comfort liqueur
3	shots	Freshly squeezed orange juice
½	shot	Galliano L'Autentico liqueur

We say: Galliano adds the wall (as in Harvey Wallbanger) and some herbal peppermint to this Slow Comfortable Screw.

SLOW SCREW

★★★☆☆ **Glass:** Collins
Garnish: Orange slice
Method: SHAKE all ingredients with ice and strain into ice-filled glass.

1	shot	Sloe Gin liqueur
1	shot	Ketel One vodka
4	shots	Freshly squeezed orange juice

We say: A Screwdriver with sloe gin.

SLUTTY MARY NEW

★★★★★⯪ **Glass:** Collins
Garnish: Salt/pepper rim and garnish with lime, coriander and celery
Method: ROLL (turn shaker over repeatedly rather than shake) all ingredients with ice and strain into ice-filled glass.

2	spoons	Homemade paste
2	shots	Olmeca Altos 100% agave tequila
½	shot	Freshly squeezed lime juice
3	shots	Tomato juice

We say: A Bloody Maria given extra spice with chipotle chilli
Origin: Adapted from a drink created by Carl Wrangel at the Oak Room, Copenhagen, Denmark.
To make paste, blend:
1 can of La Costena Chipotle Chili in Adobo Sauce
2 large bunches of fresh coriander
1 tablespoon of salt
1 tablespoon of black pepper
100ml Agavero tequila liqueur
500ml Worcestershire sauce

SMOKE AND MIRRORS #1 NEW

★★★★★⯪ **Glass:** Coupette
Garnish: Orange zest twist
Method: POUR ingredients into mixing glass, SMOKE (with applewood smoke), then STIR with ice and strain into chilled glass.

1½	shots	Spey malt whisky
½	shot	Bénédictine D.O.M.
½	shot	Byrrh aperitif
3	dashes	Angostura aromatic bitters

We say: his aperitif-style cocktail has subtle smoky peatiness with herbal complexity provided by Bénédictine and Byrrh.
Origin: Created in 2011 by Erik Lorincz at the Savoy's American Bar, London, England where this drink is 'smoked' into a decanter in front of the customer and served at the table.

SMOKE AND MIRRORS #2

★★★★½

Glass: Coupette
Garnish: Lemon zest twist
Method: STIR all ingredients with ice and strain into chilled glass.

2	shots	Lagavulin 16yo malt whisky
¾	shot	De Kuyper Apricot Brandy liqueur
¼	shot	Averna Amaro
2	dashes	Angostura aromatic bitters

We say: A hardcore but sublime drink. Beware - accurate proportions make or break this drink.
Origin: Adapted from a drink discovered in 2010 at Raines Lay Rooms, New York City, USA.

SMOKED MAPLE

★★★★½

Glass: Coupette
Garnish: Orange zest twist
Method: SHAKE all ingredients with ice and fine strain into chilled glass.

2	shots	Lagavulin 16yo malt whisky
¼	shot	De Kuyper Apricot Brandy liqueur
1	spoon	Maple syrup
¼	shot	Freshly squeezed orange juice

We say: This smoky cocktail won't be to everybody's taste but an Islay malt fan will most definatly approve.
Origin: Adapted from a cocktail discovered in 2009 at Dylanbar, Dublin, Ireland.

SMOKE OF SCOTLAND

★★★★☆

Glass: Martini
Garnish: Grapefruit zest twist (flamed)
Method: STIR all ingredients with ice and strain into chilled glass.

2	shots	Lagavulin 16yo malt whisky
½	shot	Martini Extra Dry vermouth
½	shot	St~Germain elderflower liqueur
⅛	shot	Cynar

We say: Smoky, with floral and tropical fruit notes from the elderflower liqueur and added complexity from the vermouth and Cynar.
Origin: Created in 2007 by Vincenzo Marianella at Providence, Los Angeles, USA.

SMOKESTACK LIGHTNING

★★★★½

Glass: Coupette
Garnish: Lime wedge
Method: SHAKE all ingredients with ice and fine strain with ice.

1¾	shots	Tequila 100% Agave
¼	shot	Lagavulin 16yo malt whisky
½	shot	Agave nectar
¾	shot	Freshly squeezed lime juice

We say: Margarita-like with a wisp of Islay smoke.
Origin: Created in 2009 by Simon Difford at the Cabinet Room, London, England for Tales of the Cocktail 2009.

SMOKED APPLETINI NEW

★★★★☆

Glass: Martini
Garnish: None
Method: STIR all ingredients with ice. Smoke with apple and pecan (or other wood) and fine.

1½	shots	Honey flavoured vodka
½	shot	Lagavulin 16yo malt whisky
½	shot	Taylor's Velvet Falernum liqueur
1	shot	Pressed apple juice
⅓	shot	Freshly squeezed lemon juice

We say: Apple and honey with hints of lemon and clove spice.
Origin: Adapted from a drink created in 2012 by Michael Stringer, Flip-It! Mixology, London

SMOKEY JOE

★★★★★

Glass: Martini
Garnish: Beef flavoured hula hoops
Method: STIR all ingredients with ice and strain into chilled glass.

2	shots	Sake
½	shot	Cognac VSOP
¼	shot	Lagavulin 16yo malt whisky
1	shot	Sauternes dessert wine

We say: Sake sweetened with Sauternes and flavoured with cognac and Islay whisky.
Origin: Created in August 2008 by Simon Difford at The Cabinet Room, London, England.

BARTENDER'S TIP LAYER

As the name would suggest, layered drinks include layers of different ingredients, often with contrasting colours.

This effect is achieved by carefully pouring each ingredient into the glass so that it floats on its predecessor. The success of this technique is dependent on the density (specific gravity) of the liquids used. As a rule of thumb, the less alcohol and the more sugar an ingredient contains, the heavier it is. The heaviest ingredients should be poured first and the lightest last.

SMOKEY OLD BASTARD NEW

★★★★½

Glass: Old-fashioned
Garnish: Lemon zest twist
Method: STIR bourbon, tea bag and four ice cubes in glass for 60 seconds. Remove tea bag, add maple syrup and bitters, and STIR some more. Add more ice and the rest of the bourbon. STIR lots more and add more ice.

2	shots	Maker's Mark bourbon
1	shot	Cold Lapsang Souchong tea
¼	shot	Maple syrup
2	dashes	Bokers Bitters

We say: Lapsang souchong flavours and dry tannins are balanced by maple syrup and fortified with bourbon.
Origin: Created in 2011 by Craig Toone at Glovers Bar, Merseyside, England who says of his drink, "Smokey obviously refers to the distinctive tea flavour and the bastard refers to the bastardisation of the classic drink" [Old Fashioned].

SMOKIN ROSE

★★★★☆

Glass: Martini
Garnish: Maraschino cherry
Method: SHAKE all ingredients with ice and strain into chilled glass.

2	shots	Bacardi Superior rum
½	shot	Lanique rose petal liqueur
⅛	shot	Lagavulin 16yo malt whisky
⅛	shot	Monin Pure Cane 2:1 sugar syrup
¼	shot	Pressed apple juice
½	shot	Freshly squeezed lime juice
1	dash	Angostura aromatic bitters

We say: A bizarrely twisted Daiquiri with Islay malt, rose petal liqueur and vanilla.
Origin: Created in 2008 by Simon Difford, The Cabinet Room, London, England.

SMOKING STALLION

★★★★☆

Glass: Martini
Garnish: Dill sprig
Method: STIR all ingredients with ice and fine strain into chilled glass.

1	sprig	Fresh dill
2	shots	Ketel One vodka
½	shot	Martini Extra Dry vermouth
⅛	shot	Lagavulin 16yo malt whisky
⅛	shot	Maple syrup

We say: Subtly herbal and dry with a hint of smokiness.
Origin: Created in 2008 by Bart Van Ween at a Dutch World Class.

SMOKY APPLE MARTINI

★★★½☆

Glass: Martini
Garnish: Maraschino cherry
Method: SHAKE all ingredients with ice and fine strain into chilled glass.

2½	shots	Dewar's White label Scotch
1	shot	Sour apple liqueur
½	shot	Rose's lime cordial

We say: Scotch adds some peaty character to this twist on the Sour Apple Martini.

SMOKY MARTINI #1

★★★★★★

Glass: Martini
Garnish: Olive on stick
Method: STIR all ingredients with ice and strain into chilled glass.

2	shots	Tanqueray London dry gin
¼	shot	Lagavulin 16yo malt whisky
½	shot	Martini Extra Dry vermouth

AKA: Burnt Martini.
Variant: Substitute vodka for gin.
We say: Smoky Islay malt combines with Tanqueray London dry gin to give a smoky, almost sweet character to a traditional Dry Martini.

SMOKY PETE'S GINGER BREW NEW

★★★★☆

Glass: Beer mug
Garnish: None
Method: Blitz BLEND the first three ingredients with two ice cubes for ten seconds. Fine strain into frozen beer mug and TOP with beer. See Origin for Pete's original homemade ginger syrup.

1½	shots	Tanqueray London dry gin
2	shots	Freshly squeezed lemon juice
2	shots	Monin Ginger syrup
4	shots	Dark beer

We say: Imagine a ginger flavoured shandy with a kick – pretty much describes this gin laced lemon and ginger flavoured beer-tail.
Origin: Created in 2012 by Pete Jeary (aka Shaky Pete) at Hawksmoor, Seven Dials, London, England. Pete's original recipe calls for homemade ginger syrup made by blending 1 kg ginger (peeled and chopped), 1 kg caster sugar and 500ml water fine strained into bottles. Pete uses London Pride beer.

SMOOTH & CREAMY'TINI

★★★★☆

Glass: Martini
Garnish: Dust with grated nutmeg
Method: SHAKE all ingredients with ice and fine strain into chilled glass.

1½	shots	Bacardi Oro golden rum
1	shot	Malibu coconut rum liqueur
¼	shot	Bols Banana liqueur
¾	shot	Double (heavy) cream
¾	shot	Milk

We say: Creamy and moreish.

SNAKEBITE

★★★☆☆

Glass: Collins
Garnish: None
Method: POUR lager into glass and TOP with cider.

| ½ | fill glass with Lager |
| | Top up with Dry cider |

Variant: Add a dash of blackcurrant cordial to make a 'Snakebite & Black'.
We say: The students special.

SNOOD MURDEKIN

★★★½☆

Glass: Shot
Garnish: None
Method: SHAKE first three ingredients with ice and strain into chilled glass. FLOAT cream over drink.

½	shot	**Ketel One vodka**
½	shot	**Chambord black raspberry liqueur**
½	shot	**Kahlúa coffee liqueur**
¼	shot	**Double (heavy) cream**

We say: Moreish combination of coffee and raspberries topped with cream.
Origin: Created in the late 90s by Dick Bradsell at Detroit, London, England for Karin Wiklund and named for the sad, flute-playing Moomin Troll.

SNOOPY

★★★★☆

Glass: Old-fashioned
Garnish: Orange zest twist
Method: SHAKE all ingredients with ice and fine strain into ice-filled glass.

1½	shots	**Maker's Mark bourbon**
¾	shot	**Grand Marnier liqueur**
1	shot	**Galliano L'Autentico liqueur**
½	shot	**Campari Bitter**
¼	shot	**Freshly squeezed lemon juice**

We say: Tangy fruit with a balancing hint of citrus and bitterness.

SNOW ON EARTH

★★★☆☆

Glass: Shot
Garnish: None
Method: SHAKE first three ingredients with ice and strain into chilled glass. Carefully FLOAT cream on drink.

½	shot	**Kahlúa coffee liqueur**
½	shot	**Chambord black raspberry liqueur**
½	shot	**Krupnik spiced honey liqueur**
½	shot	**Double (heavy) cream**

We say: A sweet, flavoursome shot.

SNOW WHITE DAIQUIRI

★★★★☆

Glass: Martini
Garnish: Pineapple wedge
Method: SHAKE all ingredients with ice and fine strain into chilled glass.

2	shots	**Bacardi Superior rum**
½	shot	**Fresh pressed pineapple juice**
½	shot	**Freshly squeezed lime juice**
¼	shot	**Monin Pure Cane 2:1 sugar syrup**
½	fresh	**Egg white**

We say: The pineapple and egg white ensure that this delightful Daiquiri has an appropriately white frothy head.
Origin: My adaptation of a classic cocktail.

SNOWBALL

★★★★☆

Glass: Collins
Garnish: Lime zest twist
Method: SHAKE first three ingredients with ice and strain into ice-filled glass. TOP with champagne.

2	shots	**Advocaat liqueur**
1	shot	**Tio Pepe fino sherry**
¾	shot	**Rose's lime cordial**
Top up with		**Brut champagne**

We say: The classic light, frothy concoction. Try it, you may like it.
Origin: This is thought to have originated in Britain in the late 1940s or early 1950s, reaching its peak of popularity in the 1970s.

SNOWFALL MARTINI

★★★★☆

Glass: Martini
Garnish: Vanilla pod
Method: MUDDLE vanilla pod in base of shaker. Add other ingredients, SHAKE with ice and fine strain into chilled glass.

¼	whole	**Vanilla pod**
2	shots	**Vanilla-infused Ketel One vodka**
1¼	unit	**Double (heavy) cream**
1¼	shots	**Milk**
¼	shot	**Monin Pure Cane 2:1 sugar syrup**

We say: An alcoholic version of a vanilla milkshake.
Origin: Discovered in 2002 at Lot 61, New York City, USA.

SNYDER MARTINI

★★★★☆

Glass: Martini
Garnish: Orange zest twist
Method: SHAKE all ingredients with ice and fine strain into chilled glass.

2	shots	**Tanqueray London dry gin**
1	shot	**Martini Extra Dry vermouth**
¼	shot	**Grand Marnier liqueur**

We say: Dry, hardcore and yet mellow.
Origin: Adapted from a recipe in Harry Craddock's 1930 '*Savoy Cocktail Book*'.

SO-SO MARTINI

★★★★☆

Glass: Martini
Garnish: Apple slice
Method: SHAKE all ingredients with ice and fine strain into chilled glass.

1	shot	**Tanqueray London dry gin**
1	shot	**Martini Extra Dry vermouth**
½	shot	**Calvados/Applejack brandy**
½	shot	**Pomegranate (grenadine) syrup**

We say: This beautifully balanced, appley drink is so much more than so-so.
Origin: Adapted from a recipe in Harry Craddock's 1930 '*Savoy Cocktail Book*'. Harry McElhone's 1929 'ABC of Cocktails' credits this drink to "Mr P. Soso, the popular manager of Kit-Kat Club, London."

SOCIALITE

★★★☆☆

Glass: Old-fashioned
Garnish: None
Method: SHAKE all ingredients with ice and strain into glass filled with crushed ice

1	shot	Grand Marnier liqueur
1	shot	Vanilla-infused Ketel One vodka
1	shot	Limoncello liqueur
1	shot	Freshly squeezed lemon juice
½	shot	Monin Vanilla sugar syrup

We say: Rich citrus with lashings of vanilla.
Origin: Discovered in 2001 at Lab Bar, London, England.

SODDEN GRAPE MARTINI

★★★★☆

Glass: Martini
Garnish: White grapes
Method: MUDDLE grapes in base of shaker. Add other ingredients, SHAKE with ice and fine strain into chilled glass.

7	fresh	Seedless white grapes
2	shots	Żubrówka bison vodka
¾	shot	Icewine

We say: A 'sod' is a piece of turf. Here 'sodden' refers to the Bison grass, the flavour of which combines well with the grapes and icewine.
Origin: Created by Simon Difford in 2004.

SOL ARDIENTE

★★★★☆

Glass: Coupette
Garnish: Crushed red peppercorns
Method: MUDDLE peppercorns in base of shaker. Add next four ingredients, SHAKE with ice and fine strain into chilled glass. TOP with splash soda.

1	spoon	Red peppercorns
2	shots	Bacardi Superior rum
1	shot	Fresh pressed pineapple juice
1	shot	Freshly squeezed lime juice
½	shot	Monin Pure Cane 2:1 sugar syrup
Top up with		Soda (club soda)

We say: Red pepper and pineapple influences this twisted Daiquiri.
Origin: Created in 2008 by Anthony Farrell, Sangreal Bartending Ltd, Belfast, Northern Ireland. The name translates from Spanish as 'Burning Sun'.

SOLENT SUNSET

★★★★☆

Glass: Collins
Garnish: Pineapple wedge & maraschino cherry
Method: SHAKE all ingredients with ice and strain into ice-filled glass.

2	shots	Pusser's Navy rum
¼	shot	Pomegranate (grenadine) syrup
¾	shot	Freshly squeezed lime juice
3	shots	Fresh pressed pineapple juice

We say: A Naval-style tropical rum punch for those occasional hot sunny days on the Solent (the stretch of sea which separates the Isle of Wight from mainland Britain).

SOPHISTICATED SAVAGE

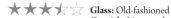

★★★☆☆

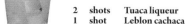

Glass: Old-fashioned
Garnish: Lime wedge
Method: SHAKE all ingredients with ice and strain into ice-filled glass.

2	shots	Tuaca liqueur
1	shot	Leblon cachaça
½	shot	Freshly squeezed lime juice
½	fresh	Egg white

We say: A sour drink with a horse's kick leading into a smooth subtle finish.
Origin: Created by Poul Jensen, Brighton, England.

SORREL RUM PUNCH

★★★★★

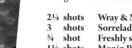

Glass: Collins
Garnish: Lime wedge
Method: SHAKE all ingredients with ice and strain into glass filled with crushed ice. Serve with straws.

2¼	shots	Wray & Nephew overproof rum
3	shots	Sorrelade (see sorrelade recipe)
¾	shot	Freshly squeezed lime juice
1½	shots	Monin Pure Cane 2:1 sugar syrup

We say: This drink harnesses the flavour of sorrelade and combines it with the traditional strength and bitter sweetness of rum punch. Jamaica in a glass.
Origin: A classic Jamaican punch using the classic proportions of 'one of sour, two of sweet, three of strong and four of weak.'

SORRELADE (MOCKTAIL)

★★★☆☆

Glass: Collins
Garnish: Lime wedge
Method: (Bulk recipe.) SOAK dried sorrel in water with ginger, ground cloves, and honey for 12 hours. Bring this mixture to the BOIL then leave to cool and SOAK for a further 12 hours, STRAIN and then keep refrigerated.

70	gram	Sorrel (hibiscus flowers)
1¼	litre	Chilled mineral water
30	gram	Fresh root ginger (thumbnail sized)
12	dried	Clove
3	spoons	Runny honey

We say: Sorrelade looks a little like cranberry juice and like cranberry juice has a bittersweet, slightly spicy taste.
Origin: Jamaican sorrel, also known by it's scientific name 'Hibiscus Sabdariffa', is a plant propagated for its red petals. In Jamaica these are used to make this refreshing drink. (Jamaican sorrel is not related to the English Garden herb of the same name.)

STAR RATINGS EXPLAINED

★★★★★ Excellent

★★★★☆ Recommended	★★★★☆ Praiseworthy
★★★☆☆ Commended	★★★☆☆ Mediocre
★★★☆☆ Disappointing	★★☆☆☆ Pretty awful
★★☆☆☆ Shameful	★☆☆☆☆ Disgusting

SOUR (GENERIC NAME)

★★★½☆

Glass: Old-fashioned
Garnish: Lemon slice & cherry on stick (sail)
Method: SHAKE all ingredients with ice and strain into ice-filled glass.

2	shots	Brandy, whisk(e)y, gin, rum etc.
1	shot	Freshly squeezed lemon juice
½	shot	Monin Pure Cane 2:1 sugar syrup
3	dashes	Angostura aromatic bitters
½	fresh	Egg white

We say: This 4:2:8 formula is a tad sourer than the classic 3:4:8 which translates as: three quarter part of the sour ingredient (lemon juice), one part of the sweet ingredient (sugar syrup) and two parts of the strong ingredient (spirit). So if you find my formula to sour than best follow the classic proportions in future.
Origin: Sours are aptly named drinks. Their flavour comes from either lemon or lime juice, which is balanced with sugar. Sours can be based on practically any spirit but the bourbon based Whiskey Sour is by far the most popular. Many (including myself) believe this drink is only properly made when smoothed with a little egg white.

Sours are served either straight-up in a Sour glass (rather like a small flute) or on the rocks in an old-fashioned glass. They are traditionally garnished with a cherry and an orange slice, or sometimes a lemon slice.

SOUR APPLE MARTINI #1
(POPULAR US VERSION)

★★★½☆

Glass: Martini
Garnish: Maraschino cherry
Method: SHAKE all ingredients with ice and fine strain into chilled glass.

1½	shots	Ketel One vodka
1½	shots	Sour apple liqueur
¼	shot	Rose's lime cordial

Variant: Some bars add sour mix in place of Rose's, others add a dash of fresh lime and sugar.
We say: A hugely popular drink across North America in the Noughties.

SOUR APPLE MARTINI #2 (DELUXE US VERSION)

★★★★½

Glass: Martini
Garnish: Apple slice
Method: SHAKE all ingredients with ice and fine strain into chilled glass.

2	shots	Ketel One vodka
1	shot	Sour apple liqueur
½	shot	Freshly squeezed lime juice
¼	shot	Monin Pure Cane 2:1 sugar syrup
½	fresh	Egg white

We say: A sophisticated version of a contemporary classic.

SOURISE NEW

★★★★½

Glass: Coupette
Garnish: Raspberries
Method: DRY SHAKE all ingredients (without ice). SHAKE again with ice and fine strain into chilled glass.

5	fresh	Raspberries
2	shots	Cognac VSOP
¼	shot	Monin Almond (orgeat) syrup
½	shot	Freshly squeezed lemon juice
¼	shot	Monin Pure Cane 2:1 sugar syrup
½	shot	Egg white

We say: Almond, cognac and raspberry harmoniously sit together to flavour this sour-style cocktail.
Origin: Created in 2010 by David Wondrich and named 'Sourise' after the French for 'smile'.

SOURPUSS MARTINI

★★★★☆

Glass: Martini
Garnish: Physalis (cape gooseberry)
Method: SHAKE all ingredients with ice and fine strain into chilled glass.

1	shot	Ketel One Citroen vodka
½	shot	Midori green melon liqueur
½	shot	Sour apple liqueur
2	shots	Pressed apple juice

We say: A lime-green, flavoursome cocktail that balances sweet and sour.
Origin: Created in 2001 by Colin 'Big Col' Crowden at Time, Leicester, England.

SOUTH BEACH

★★★★☆

Glass: Martini
Garnish: Orange zest twist
Method: SHAKE all ingredients with ice and fine strain into chilled glass.

1	shot	Amaretto liqueur
1	shot	Campari Bitter
2½	shots	Freshly squeezed orange juice
¼	shot	Monin Pure Cane 2:1 sugar syrup

We say: An unusual bittersweet combination with a strong orange and almond flavour.
Origin: Created in 1992 by Dale DeGroff, New York City, USA.

SOUTH CHINA BREEZE

★★★★☆

Glass: Collins
Garnish: Orange slice
Method: SHAKE all ingredients with ice and strain into ice-filled glass.

2	shots	Ketel One vodka
1½	shots	Lychee syrup (from tinned fruit)
3	shots	Freshly squeezed grapefruit juice
3	dashes	Angostura aromatic bitters

We say: Orange and grapefruit with an oriental influence by way of lychee.

SOUTH IRELAND SOUR NEW

★★★★☆

Glass: Coupette
Garnish: Mint leaf
Method: DRY SHAKE all ingredients (without ice). Add ice, SHAKE again and fine strain into chilled glass.

1	shot	Feijoa flavoured vodka
1	shot	Guinness
½	shot	Monin Pure Cane 2:1 sugar syrup
1	shot	Freshly squeezed lemon juice
½	fresh	Egg white

We say: Smells of sticking plasters and uses Feijoa and Guinness. Only a Kiwi could create such a drink. Give it a try, it's not as crazy as it sounds.
Origin: Created by Jacob Briars at Cocktail World Cup 2007 as a reaction to an Irish bartender who said Feijoa was 'undrinkable' to which Jacob responded "in large parts of the world people thought the same about Guinness." So as a joke Jacob made this surprisingly tasty cocktail. The name is a geographical in-joke. The Irishman was from Cork, in southern Ireland. Cork is part of Munster, and they were in Queenstown, in New Zealand's South Island, which was once known as New Munster. With their flat vowel pronunciation, Kiwis say Island and Ireland in exactly the same way.

SOUTH OF THE BORDER

★★★☆☆

Glass: Martini
Garnish: Coffee beans
Method: SHAKE all ingredients with ice and fine strain into chilled glass.

2	shots	Tequila 100% Agave
1	shot	Kahlúa coffee liqueur
¾	shot	Freshly squeezed lime juice
½	fresh	Egg white

We say: A strange mix of lime and coffee.

SOUTH PACIFIC

★★★★☆

Glass: Martini
Garnish: Pineapple wedge
Method: Cut passion fruit in half and scoop flesh in shaker. Add other ingredients, SHAKE with ice and fine strain into chilled glass.

1	fresh	Passion fruit
1	shot	Ketel One Citroen vodka
1	shot	Kwai Feh lychee liqueur
1	shot	Fresh pressed pineapple juice
½	shot	Freshly squeezed lime juice

Origin: Adapted from an original recipe created by Wayne Collins, London, England.

SOUTH PACIFIC BREEZE

★★★★☆

Glass: Collins
Garnish: Pineapple wedge
Method: POUR gin and Galliano into ice-filled glass. TOP with lemonade to just below the rim. DRIZZLE blue curaçao around top of drink (it will sink leaving strings of blue). Serve with straws.

1½ shots	Tanqueray London dry gin
¾ shot	Galliano L'Autentico liqueur
Top up with	Lemonade/Sprite/7-Up
¾ shot	Bols Blue Curaçao liqueur

We say: Quite sweet but flavoursome - looks great.

SOUTHERN CIDER

★★★☆☆

Glass: Martini
Garnish: Lime wedge
Method: SHAKE all ingredients with ice and fine strain into chilled glass.

2	shots	Southern Comfort liqueur
1	shot	Freshly squeezed lime juice
1½	shots	Ocean Spray cranberry juice

We say: Strangely, this cocktail does have a cidery taste.
Origin: Discovered at Opryland Hotel, Nashville, USA.

SOUTHERN MANHATTAN

★★★★☆

Glass: Martini
Garnish: Orange zest twist
Method: STIR all ingredients with ice and strain into chilled glass.

2	shots	Maker's Mark bourbon
1	shot	Southern Comfort liqueur
1	shot	Martini Rosso sweet vermouth
3	dashes	Peychaud's aromatic bitters

We say: A Manhattan with Southern Comfort and Peychaud's adding a hint of southern flavour.
Origin: Created in by Simon Difford in August 2005 for Tales of the Cocktail, New Orleans, USA.

SOUTHERN MINT COBBLER

★★★★☆

Glass: Old-fashioned
Garnish: Mint sprig
Method: Lightly MUDDLE mint (just to bruise) in base of shaker. Add other ingredients, SHAKE with ice and fine strain into glass filled with crushed ice. Serve with straws.

7	fresh	Mint leaves
2	shots	Southern Comfort liqueur
½	shot	Freshly squeezed lemon juice
½	shot	Boiron peach purée

We say: Very fruity and easy to drink.

SOUTHERN MULE

★★★★☆

Glass: Collins
Garnish: Lime wedge
Method: SHAKE first three ingredients with ice and strain into ice filled glass. TOP with ginger beer, lightly stir and serve with straws.

2	shots	Southern Comfort liqueur
½	shot	Freshly squeezed lime juice
3	dashes	Angostura aromatic bitters
Top up with		Ginger beer

We say: Tangy, fruity and spiced with ginger.

SOUTHERN PEACH

★★★☆☆

Glass: Collins
Garnish: Lime wedge
Method: SHAKE all ingredients with ice and strain into ice-filled glass. Serve with straws.

1	shot	Peachtree peach schnapps
1	shot	Southern Comfort liqueur
3	shots	Ocean Spray cranberry juice
1	shot	Freshly squeezed lime juice

We say: Fruity and slightly sweet but far from offensive.

SOUTHERN PUNCH

★★★½☆

Glass: Collins
Garnish: Pineapple wedge
Method: SHAKE all ingredients with ice and strain into ice-filled glass.

½	shot	Maker's Mark bourbon
1½	shots	Southern Comfort liqueur
2	shots	Fresh pressed pineapple juice
1	shot	Freshly squeezed lemon juice
½	shot	Monin Pure Cane 2:1 sugar syrup
½	shot	Pomegranate (grenadine) syrup

We say: Tropical flavours with the warmth of liquor trailed by a fresh lemon finish.

SOUTHERN TEA-KNEE

★★★★½

Glass: Martini
Garnish: Apricot slice
Method: SHAKE all ingredients with ice and fine strain into chilled glass.

½	shot	Tanqueray London dry gin
½	shot	De Kuyper Apricot Brandy liqueur
½	shot	Bols Banana liqueur
1	shot	Southern Comfort liqueur
2	shots	Cold earl gray tea

We say: Sweet fruity flavours balanced by tannic bitterness in the tea.
Origin: Created by Simon Difford in 2002.

SOUTHSIDE ⚷══

★★★★☆

Glass: Martini
Garnish: Mint leaf
Method: SHAKE all ingredients with ice and fine strain into chilled glass.

7	fresh	Mint leaves
2	shots	Tanqueray London dry gin
1	shot	Freshly squeezed lime juice
½	shot	Monin Pure Cane 2:1 sugar syrup

We say: Gin and mint with a splash of lime. Refreshingly balanced.
Origin: This vintage cocktail is purported to have originated at New York's Twenty-One Club. A long version served over crushed ice is said to have come from the southside of Chicago during Prohibition where it was drunk by the Southside mobsters, while on the other side of town hoodlums enjoyed the Northside (gin and ginger ale).

SOUTHSIDE FIZZ ⚷══

★★★½☆

Glass: Collins (small 8oz)
Garnish: Mint sprig
Method: Lightly MUDDLE mint in base of shaker (just to bruise). Add next three ingredients, SHAKE with ice and fine strain into (empty) chilled glass. TOP with soda.

7	fresh	Mint leaves
2	shots	Tanqueray London dry gin
1	shot	Freshly squeezed lemon juice
½	shot	Monin Pure Cane 2:1 sugar syrup
Top up with		Soda from siphon

We say: Recipe adapted from Harry Craddock's 1930 'The Savoy Cocktail Book'.
Origin: A minty Collins.

SOUTHSIDE ROYALE ⚷══

★★★★☆

Glass: Martini
Garnish: Mint leaf
Method: Lightly MUDDLE (just to bruise) mint in base of shaker. Add next three ingredients, SHAKE with ice and fine strain into chilled glass. TOP with a splash of champagne.

7	fresh	Mint leaves
2	shots	Tanqueray London dry gin
1	shot	Freshly squeezed lemon juice
½	shot	Monin Pure Cane 2:1 sugar syrup
Top up with		Brut champagne

Variant: Topped with soda (from a siphon, please) in place of champagne this becomes a mere 'Southside'.
We say: A White Lady with fresh mint and champagne
Origin: Created during Prohibition, either at a New York City speakeasy called Jack & Charlie's, or at Manhattan's Stork Club, or by Chicago's Southside gang to make their bootleg liquor more palatable.

SOYER AU CHAMPAGNE

★★★½☆

Glass: Martini
Garnish: None
Method: PLACE scoop of ice cream in base of glass. SHAKE next three ingredients with ice and strain over ice cream. TOP with champagne and serve while foaming with straws that the drinker should use to mix.

1	scoop	Häagen Dazs vanilla ice cream
½	shot	Cognac VSOP
½	shot	Grand Marnier liqueur
½	shot	Luxardo Maraschino liqueur
Top up with		Brut champagne

We say: A unique dessert of a drink.
Origin: Adapted from a recipe in the 1949 edition of 'Esquire's Handbook For Hosts'. Apparently this was "one of the most popular drinks at Christmas in the continental cafés".

SPARKLING PERRY

★★★★☆

Glass: Flute
Garnish: Pear slice
Method: SHAKE first three ingredients with ice and fine strain into chilled glass. TOP with champagne and lightly stir.

¾	shot	Poire William eau de vie
¾	shot	Belle de Brillet pear liqueur
1	shot	Pressed pear juice
Top up with		Brut champagne

We say: Reminiscent of perry (pear cider).
Origin: Created in December 2002 by Simon Difford.

SPECIAL NEW 🔑

★★★★☆

Glass: Martini
Garnish: Grapefruit wedge
Method: SHAKE all ingredients with ice and fine strain into chilled glass.

1½	shots	Dewar's White label Scotch
1	shot	Freshly squeezed grapefruit juice
1	shot	Grand Marnier liqueur
⅛	shot	Monin Pure Cane 2:1 sugar syrup

We say: Grand Marnier and grapefruit juice provide a flavoursome sweet and sour combination fortified with malty Scotch notes.

SPENCER COCKTAIL 🔑

★★★★☆

Glass: Martini
Garnish: Orange zest twist (discarded) & maraschino cherry
Method: SHAKE all ingredients with ice and fine strain into chilled glass.

2	shots	Tanqueray London dry gin
1	shot	De Kuyper Apricot Brandy liqueur
¼	shot	Freshly squeezed orange juice
1	dash	Angostura aromatic bitters

We say: To quote Craddock, "Very mellifluous: has a fine and rapid action: for morning work."
Origin: Adapted from a recipe in Harry Craddock's 1930 'The Savoy Cocktail Book'.

SPEYSIDE MARTINI 🔑

★★★★☆

Glass: Martini
Garnish: Lemon zest twist
Method: MUDDLE grapes in base of shaker. Add other ingredients, SHAKE with ice and fine strain into chilled glass.

7	fresh	Seedless white grapes
2	shots	Dewar's White label Scotch
¾	shot	De Kuyper Apricot Brandy liqueur
¾	shot	Freshly squeezed grapefruit juice

We say: Scotch, grape juice, apricot liqueur and grapefruit may seem an unlikely combo but they get on well together.
Origin: Discovered in 2004 at Indigo Yard, Edinburgh, Scotland.

SPICED APPLE DAIQUIRI

★★★★☆

Glass: Martini
Garnish: Apple wedge
Method: SHAKE all ingredients with ice and fine strain into chilled glass.

2	shots	Bacardi Superior rum
½	shot	Berentzen Apple schnapps
¼	shot	Goldschläger cinnamon schnapps
½	shot	Freshly squeezed lime juice
¾	shot	Pressed apple juice

We say: Sour apple and cinnamon spice with rum.
Origin: Created in 1999 by Simon Difford.

SPICED CRANBERRY MARTINI

★★★★☆

Glass: Martini
Garnish: Cinnamon & sugar rim
Method: MUDDLE cloves in base of shaker. Add other ingredients, SHAKE with ice and fine strain into chilled glass.

7	dried	Clove
1	shot	Pusser's Navy rum
2	shots	Ocean Spray cranberry juice
½	shot	Monin Pure Cane 2:1 sugar syrup

We say: The cloves and the colour add a festive note to this Martini.
Origin: Created in 2003 by Simon Difford.

SPICED PEAR

★★★★½

Glass: Old-fashioned
Garnish: Pear slice
Method: SHAKE all ingredients with ice and strain into ice-filled glass.

1	shot	Belle de Brillet pear liqueur
1	shot	Spiced rum
1	shot	Pressed pear juice
½	shot	Freshly squeezed lime juice
½	shot	Monin Pure Cane 2:1 sugar syrup

We say: Just as it says on the tin - spiced pear.
Origin: Created in 2002 by James Stewart, Edinburgh, Scotland

SPICY VEGGY

★★★½☆

Glass: Martini
Garnish: Carrot slice
Method: MUDDLE coriander seeds in base of shaker. Add other ingredients, SHAKE with ice and fine strain into chilled glass.

2	spoons	Coriander seeds
2	shots	Tanqueray London dry gin
2	shots	Freshly extracted carrot juice
¼	shot	Monin Pure Cane 2:1 sugar syrup
1	grind	Black pepper
1	pinch	Salt

We say: Reminiscent of alcoholic carrot and coriander soup.
Origin: Created in 2002 by Simon Difford.

SPIKED APPLE CIDER (HOT)

★★★★☆
Glass: Toddy
Garnish: None
Method: MUDDLE cloves in base of shaker. Add cognac and apple juice. SHAKE without ice and fine strain into glass. WARM in microwave then FLOAT double cream over drink.

2	dried	Cloves
2	shots	Cognac VSOP
3	shots	Pressed apple juice
Float		Double (heavy) cream

We say: Warming and lightly spiced under a creamy head.
Origin: Adapted from a drink discovered in 2006 at Double Seven, New York City, USA.

SPITFIRE

★★★★☆
Glass: Martini
Garnish: Lemon zest twist
Method: SHAKE all ingredients with ice and fine strain into chilled glass.

2	shots	Cognac VSOP
½	shot	Sauvignon blanc wine
1	shot	Freshly squeezed lemon juice
½	shot	Monin Pure Cane 2:1 sugar syrup
½	fresh	Egg white

We say: A brandy sour with a splash of dry white wine.
Origin: Created in 2006 by Tony Conigliaro at Shochu Lounge, London, England.

SPORRAN BREEZE

★★★★½
Glass: Collins
Garnish: Apple slice
Method: SHAKE all ingredients with ice and strain into ice-filled glass. Serve with straws.

2	shots	Dewar's White label Scotch
4	shots	Pressed apple juice
½	shot	Passion fruit syrup

We say: As with all simple drinks, the quality and flavour of the three ingredients used greatly affects the end product - choose wisely and you'll have a deliciously fresh blend of malty fruit.
Origin: Phillip Jeffrey created this drink for me in 2002 at the GE Club, London, England. I take credit (if any's due) for the name.

SPRITZ AL BITTER UPDATE

★★★⯪☆
Glass: Old-fashioned
Garnish: Orange zest twist
Method: POUR ingredients into ice-filled glass and lightly stir.

1	shot	Soave wine
1½	shots	Campari Bitter
Top up with		Soda (club soda)

We say: Basically a Spritzer with a generous splash of campari - dry and very refreshing.
Origin: Popular in northern Italy, especially in Venice and the Veneto region where it is pronounced 'Spriss'. (From the German verb Spritzen, meaning spray or splash). This aperitif cocktails origins date back to the end of the 19th century when Venice was still part of the Austrian Empire. During this period German soldiers drunk the local wines of Veneto in taverns where they were billeted but they often diluted these with water to achieve a similar alcohol content to the beer they were more accustomed to drinking. Hence, the Spritzer, a combination of equal parts white wine and soda water.

In Veneto, the Spritz Al Bitter is made with the traditional white wines of the Veneto region, Pinot Grigio or Soave and sometimes with Prosecco. The bitter liqueur used varies according to personal taste with Campari perhaps the driest. Other popular bitter liqueurs used include Aperol, Gran Classico, Select or Cynar. It is usually garnished with a slice of orange but sometimes an olive depending on the liqueur used. According to Gruppo Campari, In Veneto, around 300,000 Spritzes are consumed every day, that's more that's 200 Spritzes a minute.

In the 2000 American comedy film 'Meet the Parents' starring Robert de Niro, Barbra Streisand, and Dustin Hoffman, the latter offers De Niro an Italian Spritz instead of his usual Tom Collins.

SPRITZER UPDATED

★★★☆☆
Glass: Goblet
Garnish: Lemon zest twist
Method: POUR ingredients into chilled glass and lightly stir. No ice!

| 3 | shots | Sauvignon blanc wine |
| Top up with | | Soda (club soda) |

We say: The ultimate 'girlie' drink. To avoid ridicule when diluting a glass of white wine try adding a couple of ice cubes instead.
Origin: The name Spritzer comes from the German verb Spritzen, meaning spray or splash and its origins date back to the end of the 19th century when Venice was still part of the Austrian Empire. During this period German soldiers drunk the local wines of Veneto in the taverns where they were billeted but they often diluted these with water to achieve similar alcohol content to the beer they were more accustomed to drinking. Hence, the Spritzer, a combination of equal parts white wine and soda water.

SPUTNIK #1

★★★⯪☆
Glass: Martini
Garnish: Orange zest twist
Method: SHAKE all ingredients with ice and fine strain into chilled glass.

1	shot	Ketel One vodka
1	shot	Peachtree peach schnapps
1½	shots	Freshly squeezed orange juice
1	shot	Double (heavy) cream

We say: Blasts of fruit cut through this soft creamy drink.

SPUTNIK #2

★★★★☆

Glass: Old-fashioned
Garnish: Orange slice
Method: SHAKE all ingredients with ice and strain into ice filled glass.

1	shot	Bacardi Superior rum
1	shot	Cognac VSOP
2	shots	Freshly squeezed orange juice
½	shot	Monin Pure Cane 2:1 sugar syrup

We say: Orange, cognac and rum meld well.
Origin: A cocktail served in underground clubs all over the former Eastern Bloc. It was originally made with cheap Cuban rum, Georgian brandy and tinned orange juice.

SQUASHED FROG

★★★☆☆

Glass: Shot
Garnish: None
Method: Refrigerate ingredients then LAYER in chilled glass by carefully pouring in the order listed.

½	shot	Pomegranate (grenadine) syrup
½	shot	Midori green melon liqueur
½	shot	Advocaat liqueur

We say: Very sweet. However, the taste is not as offensive as the name might suggest.

ST CROIX SUNSET NEW

★★★☆☆

Glass: Coupette
Garnish: Grapefruit zest twist
Method: SHAKE all ingredients with ice and fine strain into chilled glass.

1½	shots	Rum Aged
1	shot	De Kuyper apricot brandy liqueur
½	shot	Campari Bitter
1	shot	Freshly squeezed orange juice
½	shot	Freshly squeezed lemon juice
¼	shot	Monin Vanilla sugar syrup

We say: Fruity and bitter sweet with flavours of apricot, orange and lemon.
Origin: Adapted from a drink created in 2010 by Fraser Campbell, The Alchemist, Melbourne, Australia.

THE ST-GERMAIN

★★★★☆

Glass: Collins
Garnish: Lime slice
Method: POUR wine and then elderflower liqueur into ice-filled glass. TOP with soda (or champagne), lightly stir and serve with straws.

2	shots	Sauvignon blanc wine
1½	shots	St~Germain elderflower liqueur
Top up with		Soda (club soda)

Variant: Also try 2 shots champagne, 1½ shots St-Germain topped with soda.
We say: A long, easy drinking summer cooler.
Origin: Created in 2006 by Simon Difford, this is the signature drink of St-Germain elderflower liqueur.

ST KITTS (MOCKTAIL)

★★★★☆

Glass: Collins
Garnish: Lime wedge
Method: SHAKE first three ingredients with ice and strain into ice-filled glass. TOP with ginger ale, lightly stir and serve with straws.

3	shots	Fresh pressed pineapple juice
½	shot	Freshly squeezed lime juice
¼	shot	Pomegranate (grenadine) syrup
Top up with		Ginger ale

Variant: Add three dashes Angostura aromatic bitters. This adds a tiny amount of alcohol but greatly improves the drink.
We say: Rust coloured and refreshing.

ST LAWRENCE NEW

★★★☆☆

Glass: Martini
Garnish: Lemon zest twist
Method: SHAKE all ingredients with ice and fine strain into chilled glass.

2½	shots	Maker's Mark bourbon
½	shot	Maple syrup
¾	shot	Freshly squeezed lemon juice

We say: Bourbon soured with lemon juice and sweetened with maple syrup.
Origin: Adapted from a drink discovered in 2011 at Bar Rouge, Copenhagen, Denmark.

ST. PATRICK'S DAY

★★★★☆

Glass: Old-fashioned
Garnish: Mint sprig or shamrock
Method: STIR all ingredients with ice and strain into ice-filled glass.

2	shots	Jameson Irish whiskey
1	shot	Chartreuse Green liqueur
1	shot	Green crème de menthe liqueur
1	dash	Angostura aromatic bitters

We say: Minty, herbal whiskey - a helluva craic.
Origin: Created in 2006 by Simon Difford.

STAFFORDSHIRE DELIGHT NEW

★★★★☆

Glass: Collins
Garnish: Pineapple wedge
Method: SHAKE all ingredients with ice and strain into ice-filled glass.

2	shots	Bacardi Oro golden rum
½	shot	Fernet Branca
½	shot	Monin Almond (orgeat) syrup
½	shot	Freshly squeezed lime juice
1½	shots	Fresh pressed pineapple juice
1	dash	Angostura aromatic bitters

We say: A modern day pick-me-up / hair-of-the-dog with a rich, enlivening bitter sweet bite.
Origin: Adapted from a drink created in 2010 by Thomas Dalloway, United Kingdom.

STAIRS MARTINI

★★★★★

Glass: Martini
Garnish: Pear slice
Method: SHAKE all ingredients with ice and fine strain into chilled glass.

2	shots	Ketel One vodka
1	shot	Pressed pear juice
1	shot	Pressed apple juice
¼	shot	Freshly squeezed lemon juice
¼	shot	Monin Pure Cane 2:1 sugar syrup
2	dashes	Orange bitters

We say: In London's cockney rhyming slang 'apples and pears' means stairs. So this tasty cocktail is appropriately named.
Origin: Created in 2000 by Ian Baldwin at the GE Club, London, England

STANLEY COCKTAIL ⚷

★★★★☆

Glass: Martini
Garnish: Lemon zest twist
Method: SHAKE all ingredients with ice and fine strain into chilled glass.

1½	shots	Tanqueray London dry gin
1½	shots	Bacardi Superior rum
½	shot	Freshly squeezed lemon juice
½	shot	Pomegranate (grenadine) syrup

We say: Salmon pink and reminiscent of a Daiquiri with a splash of gin.
Origin: Adapted from a recipe in Harry Craddock's 1930 '*Savoy Cocktail Book*'.

THE STAR

★★★★☆

Glass: Martini
Garnish: Olive on stick
Method: STIR all ingredients with ice and fine strain into chilled glass.

1½	shots	Calvados/Applejack brandy
1½	shots	Martini Rosso sweet vermouth
1	dash	Angostura aromatic bitters

Variant: T.N.T. Special - with the addition of a dash of sugar.
We say: Like many old classics, this drink needs dilution so stir until you're bored and thirsty.
Origin: Recipe from Harry Craddock's 1930 '*Savoy Cocktail Book*'. Created in the 1870s by a bartender at the Manhattan Club, which once stood at the north corner of 34th Street and 5th Avenue, New York City

STARRY NIGHT

★★★★½

Glass: Coupette
Garnish: Star anise
Method: STIR all ingredients with ice and strain into chilled glass.

2	shots	Chardonnay white wine
½	shot	Poire William eau de vie
½	shot	Luxardo Maraschino liqueur

We say: Delicate pear and aromatic maraschino over a wine base.
Origin: Created in 2008 by Jamie Boudreau at Vessel, Seattle, USA.

STARS & STRIPES SHOT

★★½☆☆

Glass: Shot
Garnish: None
Method: Refrigerate ingredients then LAYER in chilled glass by carefully pouring in the order listed.

½	shot	Chartreuse Green liqueur
½	shot	Luxardo Maraschino liqueur
½	shot	Crème de cassis liqueur

We say: The taste is too sweet and the colours aren't quite right. A shame.
Origin: Adapted from a recipe in Harry Craddock's 1930 *Savoy Cocktail Book*.

STEALTH

★★★½☆

Glass: Shot
Garnish: None
Method: Refrigerate ingredients then LAYER in chilled glass by carefully pouring in the order listed.

½	shot	Kahlúa coffee liqueur
½	shot	Tuaca liqueur
½	shot	Baileys Irish cream liqueur

We say: Reminiscent of a vanilla cappuccino.
Origin: Created by Poul Jensen at St. James', Brighton, England. Another of the B-52 family of drinks, but named after Stealth bombers instead.

STEEL BOTTOM

★★★☆☆

Glass: Collins
Garnish: None
Method: POUR ingredients into glass, lightly stir and serve with straws.

| 1 | shot | Wray & Nephew overproof rum |
| Top up with | | Lager |

We say: For those who like their beer turbo charged.
Origin: A very popular drink in Jamaica.

STEEP FLIGHT

★★★★★

Glass: Martini
Garnish: Apple or pear slice
Method: SHAKE all ingredients with ice and fine strain into ice-filled glass.

1	shot	Calvados/Applejack brandy
1	shot	Ketel One vodka
1	shot	Cognac VSOP
3	shots	Pressed apple juice

We say: 'Apples and pears' is the cockney rhyming slang for stairs, hence the flavours in this particular flight.
Origin: Created in 2005 by Simon Difford. Awarded a Gold in Long Drink category at Drinks International Bartender's Challenge on 31st May 2006.

STEPHEN MARSHALL NEW

★★★★⯪☆

Glass: Old Fashioned
Garnish: Orange zest twist
Method: STIR all ingredients with ice and strain into ice-filled glass.

1	shot	Tanqueray London dry gin
1	shot	Campari Bitter
¾	shot	Hazelnut liqueur
1	shot	Martini Rosso sweet vermouth

We say: A Negroni with hazelnut liqueur. Some will ask: why? Negroni-loving drinkers of hazelnut liqueur might ask: why not?
Origin: Created in 2012 and named for its inventor, the flamboyant, music-loving Senior Global Brand Ambassador of Dewar's Whisky, and a man who likes a Negroni, and, it would appear, hazelnut liqueur.

THE STIG

★★★★★★

Glass: Old-fashioned
Garnish: Lime zest twist
Method: STIR all ingredients with ice and strain into ice-filled glass.

¾	shot	Calvados/Applejack brandy
¾	shot	Macchu pisco
1	shot	St~Germain elderflower liqueur
1	shot	Sauvignon blanc wine

We say: Whiter than white but yet mysterious.
Origin: Created in 2006 by Simon Difford, The Cabinet Room, London, England. Named partly for the 'St-G' on the screw cap of St-Germain and partly after 'The Stig' from the '*Top Gear*' TV series.

STILETTO

★★★★⯪☆

Glass: Collins
Garnish: Lime wedge
Method: SHAKE all ingredients with ice and strain into ice-filled glass.

2	shots	Maker's Mark bourbon
1	shot	Amaretto liqueur
2½	shots	Ocean Spray cranberry juice
½	shot	Freshly squeezed lime juice
¼	shot	Monin Pure Cane 2:1 sugar syrup

We say: Long and fruity with a hint of bourbon and almond.

STINGER

★★★★☆

Glass: Old-fashioned
Garnish: Mint sprig
Method: SHAKE all ingredients with ice and strain into glass filled with crushed ice. Serve with straws.

| 2 | shots | Cognac VSOP |
| ¾ | shot | Giffard Menthe Pastille liqueur |

We say: A refreshing peppermint and cognac digestif.
Origin: In the classic film '*High Society*', Bing Crosby explains to Grace Kelly how the Stinger gained its name. "It's a Stinger. It removes the sting."

STONE & GRAVEL

★★★★⯪☆

Glass: Old-fashioned
Garnish: None
Method: POUR ingredients into glass filled with crushed ice and stir.

| 1 | shot | Wray & Nephew overproof rum |
| 3 | shots | Stone's green ginger wine |

We say: Simple, strong and surprisingly good.
Origin: A popular drink in Jamaica.

STONE FENCE

★★★☆☆

Glass: Pint
Garnish: Apple slice
Method: POUR ingredients into ice-filled glass and stir. Serve with straws.

| 2 | shots | Malibu coconut rum liqueur |
| Top up with | | Dry cider |

Variant: Substitute cognac with calvados, Scotch, bourbon or rum.
We say: Dry cider fortified and made drier by cognac.
Origin: Although the origin of this simple mixed drink and its name are unknown history chronicles its being served at taverns since at least the early 1800s.

THE STONE PLACE NEW

★★★★⯪☆

Glass: Coupette
Garnish: Dust with grated nutmeg
Method: SHAKE all ingredients with ice and fine strain into chilled glass.

2½	shots	Bacardi 8 yo aged rum
¾	shot	Freshly squeezed lemon juice
¾	shot	Freshly squeezed orange juice
¼	shot	Pomegranate (grenadine) syrup

We say: Rum loves fruit and this pink drink has lots of both.
Origin: Adapted from a drink created in 2010 by Willy Shine at Forty Four, New York City, USA. This twist on the Ward 8 is named after the street where Shine's parents, who were big Ward 8 imbibers, used to live.

STORK CLUB

★★★★☆

Glass: Martini
Garnish: Orange zest twist
Method: SHAKE all ingredients with ice and fine strain into chilled glass.

1	shot	Tanqueray London dry gin
1	shot	Triple Sec
1	shot	Freshly squeezed orange juice
½	shot	Freshly squeezed lime juice
2	dashes	Orange bitters

We say: Orange and gin with a souring splash of lime juice.

STRAITS SLING

★★★★☆

Glass: Sling
Garnish: Orange slice & cherry on stick (sail)
Method: SHAKE first six ingredients with ice and strain into ice-filled glass. TOP with soda, lightly stir.

2	shots	Tanqueray London dry gin
½	shot	Bénédictine D.O.M.
½	shot	Kirschwasser eau de vie
1	shot	Freshly squeezed lemon juice
2	dashes	Orange bitters
Top up with		Soda (club soda)

We say: Dry cherry and gin come to the fore in this long refreshing drink.
Origin: Thought to be the original name of the Singapore Sling. Conjecture, partly based on a reference to 'Kirsch' in Embury's *Fine Art of Mixing Drinks*, has it that the drink was originally based on cherry eau de vie and not the cherry liqueur used in most Singapore Sling recipes today.

STRASBERI SLING

★★★½☆

Glass: Sling
Garnish: Mint sprig
Method: SHAKE all ingredients with ice and strain into ice-filled glass.

1½	shots	Raspberry flavoured vodka
1	shot	Pimm's No.1 Cup
½	shot	Monin Pure Cane 2:1 sugar syrup
1	shot	Freshly squeezed lime juice
3	shots	Pressed apple juice

We say: Raspberry and apple combine beautifully in this refreshing drink with its clean citrus tang.
Origin: Created in 2002 by Alex Kammerling, London, England.

STRATOSPHERE

★★★★☆

Glass: Flute
Garnish: Lemon zest twist (discarded) & two cloves
Method: POUR liqueur into glass and TOP with champagne.

| ¼ | shot | Benoit Serres créme de violette |
| Top up with | | Brut champagne |

We say: The thinking woman's Kir Royal.
Origin: Recipe adapted from The Stork Club Bar Book published 1946 in which Lucius Beebe writes, "Leo Spitzel, captain, asserts that a Stratosphere Cocktail will do wonders for you."

STRAWBERRY & BALSAMIC MARTINI

★★★★½

Glass: Martini
Garnish: Strawberry
Method: MUDDLE strawberries in base of shaker. Add other ingredients, SHAKE with ice and fine strain into chilled glass.

5	fresh	Strawberries (hulled)
2½	shots	Ketel One vodka
⅛	shot	Balsamic vinegar of moderna
½	shot	Monin Pure Cane 2:1 sugar syrup

We say: The balsamic adds a little extra interest to the fortified strawberries.
Origin: My version of a drink that became popular in London in 2002 and I believe originated in Che.

STRAWBERRY & BALSAMIC MOJITO #1

★★★★☆

Glass: Martini
Garnish: Strawberry
Method: MUDDLE strawberries in base of shaker. Add other ingredients, SHAKE with ice and fine strain into chilled glass.

5	fresh	Strawberries (hulled)
2	shots	Bacardi Superior rum
¾	shot	Freshly squeezed lime juice
¼	shot	Balsamic vinegar of moderna
½	shot	Monin Pure Cane 2:1 sugar syrup
12	fresh	Mint leaves
Top up with		Soda (club soda)

We say: A fruity twist on the classic Mojito.
Origin: Adapted from a drink created in 2005 by Simon 'Ginge' Warneford at Blanch House, Brighton, England.

STRAWBERRY ALCOHOLIC SMOOTHIE NEW

★★★★☆

Glass: Sling
Garnish: Balsamic covered strawberry
Method: BLEND ingredients with 12oz scoop of crushed ice. Pour into glass and serve immediately with straws.

2	shots	Ketel One vodka
1½	shots	Bols Natural Yoghurt liqueur
3	spoons	Runny honey
5	fresh	Strawberries (hulled)
½	shot	Crème de fraise liqueur
1	shot	Pressed apple juice

We say: This radiantly coloured creamy strawberry yoghurt drink is sweetened with honey and 'hardened' with vodka.
Origin: Created in 2011 by Simon Difford at the Cabinet Room, London, England.

BARTENDER'S TIP SWIZZLE

To 'swizzle' a drink is simply to stir it using a particular tool and action.

To swizzle simply immerse the blades of your swizzle stick into the drink, hold the shaft between the palms of both hands and rotate the stick rapidly by sliding your hands back and forth against it. If you do not have a bona fide swizzle stick, use a barspoon in the same manner.

STRAWBERRY BLONDE

★★★★☆

Glass: Collins
Garnish: Strawberry
Method: MUDDLE strawberries in base of shaker.
Add next three ingredients, SHAKE with ice and
fine strain into ice-filled glass. TOP with soda and
serve with straws.

2	fresh	Strawberries (hulled)
2	shots	Ketel One vodka
1½	shots	Freshly squeezed lemon juice
¾	shot	Monin Pure Cane 2:1 sugar syrup
Top up with		Soda (club soda)

We say: Lurid orange-red in colour and basically
alcoholic strawberry flavoured real lemonade.
Origin: Created in 2008 by Simon Difford at The
Cabinet Room, London, England.

STRAWBERRY BLONDE MARTINI

★★★½☆

Glass: Martini
Garnish: Basil leaf
Method: MUDDLE basil in mixing glass. Add
other ingredients, STIR with ice and fine strain into
chilled glass.

4	fresh	Torn basil leaves
2½	shots	Raspberry flavoured vodka
½	shot	Crème de fraise du bois liqueur
½	shot	Martini Extra Dry vermouth
⅛	shot	Monin Pure Cane 2:1 sugar syrup

We say: Berry vodka dominates with hints of
strawberry and basil.
Origin: Adapted from a recipe discovered in 2003 at
Oxo Tower Bar, London, England

STRAWBERRY COSMO

★★★½☆

Glass: Martini
Garnish: Strawberry
Method: SHAKE all ingredients with ice and fine
strain into chilled glass.

2	shots	Ketel One Citroen vodka
¾	shot	Crème de fraise du bois liqueur
1¼	shots	Ocean Spray cranberry juice
½	shot	Freshly squeezed lime juice

We say: Strawberry liqueur replaces the usual orange
liqueur in this contemporary classic.
Origin: Formula by Simon Difford in 2004.

STRAWBERRY DAIQUIRI

★★★★☆

Glass: Martini
Garnish: Strawberry
Method: MUDDLE strawberries in base of shaker.
Add other ingredients, SHAKE with ice and fine
strain into chilled glass.

7	fresh	Strawberries (hulled)
2	shots	Bacardi Superior rum
½	shot	Freshly squeezed lime juice
¼	shot	Monin Pure Cane 2:1 sugar syrup

We say: Makes strawberries and cream appear very dull.
Origin: A popular drink in Cuba where it is known as
a Daiquiri de Fresa.

THE STRAWBERRY ÉCLAIR

★★★★☆

Glass: Shot
Garnish: None
Method: SHAKE all ingredients with ice and fine
strain into chilled glass.

½	shot	Crème de fraise du bois liqueur
½	shot	Hazelnut liqueur
¼	shot	Freshly squeezed lime juice

We say: Far from sophisticated (some would say like
Australia) but very appropriately named.
Origin: This drink heralds from Australia where it is
a popular shot.

STRAWBERRY FROZEN DAIQUIRI

★★★½☆

Glass: Martini
Garnish: Strawberry
Method: BLEND all ingredients with 6oz scoop of
crushed ice.

2	shots	Bacardi Superior rum
¾	shot	Freshly squeezed lime juice
½	shot	Monin Pure Cane 2:1 sugar syrup
5	fresh	Strawberries (hulled)

We say: A delicious twist on a classic - Strawberry
Mivvi for grown-ups.

STRAWBERRY JIVE

★★★½☆

Glass: Old-fashioned
Garnish: Mint sprig
Method: MUDDLE strawberries in base of shaker.
SHAKE next six ingredients with ice and fine strain
into ice-filled glass. TOP with soda.

2	fresh	Strawberries (hulled)
2	shots	Tanqueray London dry gin
4	fresh	Mint leaves
1	fresh	Torn basil leaves
¼	shot	Monin Pure Cane 2:1 sugar syrup
1	shot	Freshly squeezed orange juice
½	shot	Freshly squeezed lemon juice
Top up with		Soda (club soda)

We say: Strawberry, lemon and orange fruit with
herbal mint and basil, laced with gin and freshened
with soda.
Origin: Adapted from a drink created in 2011 by
Dale DeGroff, New York, USA.

STRAWBERRY MARGARITA

★★★★☆

Glass: Martini
Garnish: Strawberry
Method: MUDDLE strawberries in base of shaker.
Add other ingredients, SHAKE with ice and fine
strain into chilled glass.

2	shots	Tequila 100% Agave
1	shot	Freshly squeezed lime juice
¾	shot	Monin Pure Cane 2:1 sugar syrup
5	fresh	Strawberries (hulled)

We say: Fresh strawberries combine well with
tequila in this fruity margarita.
Origin: Formula by Simon Difford in 2004.

STRAWBERRY MARTINI

★★★★☆

Glass: Martini
Garnish: Strawberry
Method: MUDDLE strawberries in base of shaker. Add other ingredients, SHAKE with ice and fine strain into chilled glass.

5	fresh	Strawberries (hulled)
2½	shots	Ketel One vodka
½	shot	Monin Pure Cane 2:1 sugar syrup
2	grind	Black pepper

We say: Rich strawberries fortified with vodka and a hint of pepper spice.
Origin: Formula by Simon Difford in 2004.

STRAWBERRY ON ACID NEW

★★★★★

Glass: Flute
Garnish: Balsamic covered strawberry
Method: MUDDLE strawberries in base of shaker. Add other ingredients, SHAKE with ice and fine strain into chilled glass. TOP with champagne.

3	fresh	Strawberries (hulled)
1½	shots	Ketel One vodka
¾	shot	Crème de fraise liqueur
⅛	shot	Balsamic vinegar of moderna
1	pinch	Black pepper
Top up with		Brut champagne

We say: Fruity, slightly sweet strawberry, balanced and made interesting by vodka, balsamic vinegar and black pepper tingle.
Origin: Adapted from a drink discovered in 2010 at Bordeaux Quay, Bristol, England.

STRUDEL MARTINI

★★★★★

Glass: Martini
Garnish: Dust with cinnamon powder
Method: SHAKE all ingredients with ice and fine strain into chilled glass.

1½	shots	Ketel One vodka
½	shot	Pedro Ximénez sherry
¾	shot	Pressed apple juice
½	shot	Milk
½	shot	Double (heavy) cream

We say: Still think sherry is just for Granny?
Origin: Created in 2002 by Jason Borthwick, Tiles, Edinburgh, Scotland.

STUPID CUPID

★★★☆☆

Glass: Martini
Garnish: Lemon zest twist
Method: SHAKE all ingredients with ice and fine strain into chilled glass.

2	shots	Ketel One Citroen vodka
½	shot	Sloe Gin liqueur
1	shot	Freshly squeezed lime juice
½	shot	Monin Pure Cane 2:1 sugar syrup

We say: Citrussy with subtle hints of Sloe gin.

SUBMARINE KISS

★★★★★

Glass: Flute
Garnish: Lemon zest twist (discarded)
Method: POUR liqueur into base of chilled glass. DRY SHAKE rest of ingredients (without ice). SHAKE again with ice and fine strain slowly into liqueur primed glass so contents of shaker float over liqueur.

⅓	shot	Benoit Serres créme de violette
2	shots	Tanqueray London dry gin
½	shot	Freshly squeezed lemon juice
¼	shot	Monin Pure Cane 2:1 sugar syrup
½	shot	Egg white

We say: Looks amazing and gives the drinker the option to sip or swirl to mix ingredients and mix the sweet liqueur base.
Origin: In 1915 this drink was reported in the New York 'Day by Day' newspaper as follow, "Sailors who come to Broadway for a touch of high life have invented a new drink called The Submarine Kiss. The liquid combination is a milky white above and purple below and the submarine effect is secured after drinking about three."

SUBOURBON

★★★★☆

Glass: Collins
Garnish: Blackberries
Method: SHAKE all ingredients with ice and fine strain into ice-filled glass.

2	fresh	Blackberries
1½	shots	Maker's Mark bourbon
¾	shot	Carpano Antica Formula
2	shots	Ocean Spray cranberry juice
2	dashes	Angostura aromatic bitters

We say: A fruity (blackberry and cranberry) long bourbon laced drink with a flavour reminiscent of a fruity, sweet manhattan.
Origin: Adapted from a drink created in 2010 by David Steenkamp at Jamie Oliver's Barbecoa, London, England. Originally also with a dash of crème de mûre (blackberry) liqueur so sweeter and fruitier.

SUBURBAN

★★★★☆

Glass: Old-fashioned
Garnish: Orange zest twist
Method: STIR all ingredients with ice and strain into ice-filled glass.

1½	shots	Maker's Mark bourbon
¾	shot	Bacardi 8yo aged rum
¾	shot	Warre's Otima tawny port
1	dash	Angostura aromatic bitters
1	dash	Orange bitters

We say: An interesting alternative to an Old-Fashioned
Origin: Created at New York's old Waldorf-Astoria Hotel (the Empire State Building occupies the site today) for James R Keene, a racehorse owner who's steeds ran in the Suburban Handicap at Brooklyn's Sheepshead Bay track.

SUFFERING BASTARD

★★★⯪☆ **Glass:** Old-fashioned
Garnish: Pineapple cubes, maraschino cherry, lime wedge, cucumber peel & mint sprig
Method: SHAKE all ingredients with ice and strain glass filled with crushed ice.

1	shot	Bacardi Superior rum
2	shots	Martinique agricole rum
1	shot	Freshly squeezed lime juice
½	shot	Curaçao orange liqueur
¼	shot	Monin Almond (orgeat) syrup
½	shot	Monin Pure Cane 2:1 sugar syrup

We say: Pungent, heavily rum laced yet all too easy.
Origin: Adapted from Victor Bergeron's *'Trader Vic's Bartender's Guide'* (1972 revised edition).

SUITABLY FRANK

★★★⯪☆ **Glass:** Shot
Garnish: None
Method: Refrigerate ingredients then LAYER in chilled glass by carefully pouring in the listed order.

½	shot	Cuarenta y Tres (Licor 43) liqueur
½	shot	De Kuyper Cherry Brandy liqueur
½	shot	Ketel One vodka

We say: Frankly - it's a good shot.

SUMMER BREEZE

★★★⯪☆ **Glass:** Collins
Garnish: Apple slice
Method: SHAKE all ingredients with ice and strain into ice-filled glass.

2	shots	Ketel One vodka
1	shot	St~Germain elderflower liqueur
2	shots	Ocean Spray cranberry juice
2	shots	Pressed apple juice

We say: Cranberry, apple and elderflower fortified with vodka.
Origin: Adapted from a drink created in 1998 by Dick Bradsell, London, England.

SUMMER ROSE MARTINI

★★★★☆ **Glass:** Martini
Garnish: Rose petal
Method: STIR first three ingredients with ice and strain into chilled glass. POUR grenadine into the centre of the drink. This should settle to form a red layer in the base of the glass.

1½	shots	Ketel One vodka
¾	shot	White Crème de Cacao
½	shot	Kwai Feh lychee liqueur
½	shot	Pomegranate (grenadine) syrup

We say: This red and white layered drink could have been named War of the Roses. Unless you've a sweet tooth don't mix the factions - sip from the chocolate and lychee top and stop when you hit red.
Origin: Created in 2003 by Davide Lovison at Isola Bar, London, England.

SUMMER TIME MARTINI

★★★⯪☆ **Glass:** Martini
Garnish: Kumquat
Method: SHAKE all ingredients with ice and fine strain into chilled glass.

1½	shots	Tanqueray London dry gin
1	shot	Grand Marnier liqueur
¼	shot	Pomegranate (grenadine) syrup
1½	shots	Freshly squeezed orange juice

We say: Smooth, gin laced fruit for a summer's day.

SUMMIT

★★★☆☆ **Glass:** Old-fashioned
Garnish: Cucumber peel
Method: Lightly MUDDLE lime zest and ginger slices in base of mixing glass. Add other ingredients, STIR with ice and fine strain into ice-filled glass.

1	twist	Lime
1	slice	Fresh root ginger (thumbnail sized)
1½	shots	Cognac VSOP
2	shots	Lemonade/Sprite/7-Up

We say: A cocktail created by a committee rather than any one bartender. "How many bartenders does it take to change a light bulb?" jokes are appropriate.
Origin: Created in January 2008 when around 20 of the world's top mixologists gathered at The International Cognac Summit at the invitation of the BNIC.

SUMO IN A SIDECAR

★★★★⯪ **Glass:** Martini
Garnish: Orange zest twist
Method: SHAKE all ingredients with ice and fine strain into chilled glass.

1	shot	De Kuyper Apricot Brandy liqueur
2½	shots	Sake
½	shot	Freshly squeezed lemon juice

We say: Hints of sake but retains the Sidecar-style.

SUN KISSED VIRGIN

★★★☆☆ **Glass:** Sling
Garnish: Physalis (cape gooseberry)
Method: SHAKE all ingredients with ice and strain into ice-filled glass.

2	shots	Freshly squeezed orange juice
2	shots	Fresh pressed pineapple juice
1	shot	Freshly squeezed lime juice
½	shot	Monin Almond (orgeat) syrup

We say: Golden, slightly sweet and very fruity.

THE SUN SALUTATION

★★★★☆

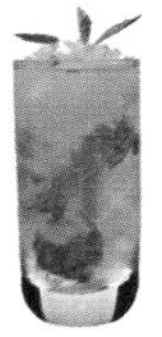

Glass: Collins
Garnish: Mint sprig
Method: MUDDLE mint in base of shaker. Add next three ingredients, SHAKE with ice and fine strain into ice-filled glass. TOP with soda.

10	fresh	Mint leaves
1	shot	Ketel One vodka
1½	shots	Kwai Feh lychee liqueur
¾	shot	Freshly squeezed lemon juice
Top up with		Soda (club soda)

We say: Mint with a hint of lychee - long and refreshing.
Origin: Adapted from a recipe by David Nepove, Enrico's Bar & Restaurant, San Francisco.

SUNDOWNER #1

★★★★☆

Glass: Martini
Garnish: Orange zest twist
Method: SHAKE all ingredients with ice and fine strain into chilled glass.

2	shots	Cognac VSOP
½	shot	Grand Marnier liqueur
½	shot	Freshly squeezed orange juice
½	shot	Freshly squeezed lemon juice
¾	shot	Chilled mineral water

Variant: Red Lion
We say: Cognac and orange served 'up'.
Origin: This cocktail is popular in South Africa where it is made with locally produced brandy and a local orange liqueur called Van der Hum.

SUNDOWNER #2

★★★★☆

Glass: Old-fashioned
Garnish: Mint sprig
Method: SHAKE all ingredients with ice and strain into ice-filled glass.

¾	shot	Grand Marnier liqueur
1½	shots	Southern Comfort liqueur
2	shots	Sauvignon blanc wine

We say: Subtle meld of summer and citrus flavours.
Origin: Adapted from a cocktail created in 2002 by Gary Regis at Bed Bar, London, England.

SUNNY BREEZE

★★★½☆

Glass: Collins
Garnish: Orange slice
Method: SHAKE all ingredients with ice and strain into glass filled with crushed ice.

½	shot	Triple Sec
½	shot	Grand Marnier liqueur
1½	shots	Pernod anise
3	shots	Freshly squeezed grapefruit juice

We say: A suitably named refreshing long drink with an adult dry edge and kick.
Origin: Created in 2003 by Simon Difford.

SUNSHINE COCKTAIL #1

★★★★½

Glass: Martini
Garnish: Pineapple wedge
Method: SHAKE all ingredients with ice and fine strain into chilled glass.

1½	shots	Bacardi Superior rum
1½	shots	Martini Extra Dry vermouth
1½	shots	Fresh pressed pineapple juice
⅛	shot	Pomegranate (grenadine) syrup

We say: Light, fruity and a tad on the sweet side, but could well brighten up your day.
Origin: Adapted from a recipe in my 1949 copy of 'Esquire's Handbook for Hosts'.

SUNSHINE COCKTAIL #2

★★★★☆

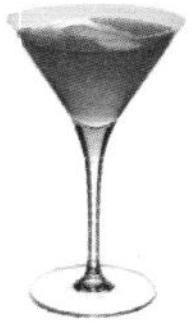

Glass: Martini
Garnish: Lemon zest twist
Method: SHAKE all ingredients with ice and fine strain into chilled glass.

1½	shots	Bacardi Superior rum
¼	shot	
1½	shots	Martini Extra Dry vermouth
¼	shot	Freshly squeezed lemon juice
¼	shot	Crème de cassis liqueur

We say: Fruity, flavoursome and well-balanced.
Origin: Adapted from a recipe in Harry Craddock's 1930 'The Savoy Cocktail Book'.

SUNSTROKE

★★★★☆

Glass: Martini
Garnish: Orange zest twist
Method: SHAKE all ingredients with ice and fine strain into chilled glass.

1	shot	Ketel One vodka
1	shot	Triple Sec
2	shots	Freshly squeezed grapefruit juice

We say: Fruity but balanced. One to sip in the shade.

SUPERMINTY-CHOCOLATINI

★★★½☆

Glass: Martini
Garnish: Chocolate powder rim
Method: SHAKE all ingredients with ice and fine strain into chilled glass.

2	shots	Ketel One vodka
1	shot	White Crème de Cacao
1	shot	Giffard Menthe Pastille liqueur

We say: Obvious but nicely flavoured.

SUPPERTIME DAIQUIRI

★★★★☆ **Glass:** Martini
Garnish: Lime wedge
Method: STIR preserve and rum in base of shaker to dissolve preserve. Add other ingredients, SHAKE with ice and fine strain into chilled glass.

3	spoons	Rhubarb & orange preserve
2	shots	Bacardi Superior rum
¾	shot	Freshly squeezed lime juice

We say: Rhubarb and orange influence this Daiquiri twist.
Origin: Created in 2008 by Jamie MacDonald at Tigerlily, Edinburgh, England in honour of his good friend Sam Kershaw.

THE SURFER

★★★★☆ **Glass:** Collins
Garnish: Lemon slice
Method: POUR lemonade into ice-filled glass to two-thirds full. FLOAT cognac over lemonade. Serve with straws and instruct drinker to stir ingredients before drinking.

| 4 | shots | Lemonade (English-style) |
| 2 | shots | Cognac VSOP |

We say: Good quality lemonade adds lemon freshness and turns cognac into a refreshing afternoons drink.
Origin: A 2008 adaptation of a Cognac Surfer by Simon Difford. The original is made by floating cognac on mineral water.

SURFER ON A.C.D.

★★★☆☆ **Glass:** Shot
Garnish: None
Method: SHAKE first two ingredients with ice and fine strain into chilled glass. FLOAT Jagermeister.

½	shot	Malibu coconut rum liqueur
¼	shot	Jägermeister
¾	shot	Fresh pressed pineapple juice

We say: The spirity herbal topping counters the sweet coconut and pineapple base.

SWAMP WATER

★★★★☆ **Glass:** Collins
Garnish: Lime wedge & mint sprig
Method: SHAKE all ingredients with ice and strain into ice-filled glass.

1½	shots	Chartreuse Green liqueur
4	shots	Fresh pressed pineapple juice
½	shot	Freshly squeezed lime juice

We say: Long and refreshing - the herbal taste of Chartreuse combined with the fruitiness of pineapple.

THE SUZY WONG MARTINI

★★★☆☆ **Glass:** Martini
Garnish: Orange zest twist
Method: SHAKE all ingredients with ice and fine strain into chilled glass.

5	fresh	Torn basil leaves
2	shots	Ketel One Oranje vodka
½	shot	Grand Marnier liqueur
1	shot	Freshly squeezed orange juice
½	shot	Freshly squeezed lime juice
¼	shot	Monin Pure Cane 2:1 sugar syrup

We say: Fresh tasting orange with a hint of basil.
Origin: Discovered in 2005 at Suzy Wong, Amsterdam, The Netherlands.

SWEDISH ALE PUNCH NEW

★★★★☆ **Glass:** Collins
Garnish: Grapefruit slice
Method: SHAKE first three ingredients with ice and fine strain into chilled glass. TOP with beer.

2	shots	Maker's Mark bourbon
1	shot	Swedish Punch liqueur
1	shot	Freshly squeezed pink grapefruit juice
Top up with		British cask conditioned ale

We say: The grapefruit hop notes in the beer are amplified by fresh grapefruit juice while the beers cereal notes are fortified with bourbon. Meanwhile Swedish Punch both sweetens and works its magic.
Origin: Created in 2011 by Simon Difford at the Cabinet Room, London.

SWEDISH BLUE MARTINI

★★★☆☆ **Glass:** Martini
Garnish: Orange zest twist
Method: SHAKE all ingredients with ice and fine strain into chilled glass.

2	shots	Ketel One vodka
½	shot	Bols Blue Curaçao liqueur
½	shot	Peachtree peach schnapps
¼	shot	Freshly squeezed lime juice
¼	shot	Monin Pure Cane 2:1 sugar syrup
2	dashes	Orange bitters
½	shot	Chilled mineral water

We say: A fruity, blue concoction with vodka. Slightly sweet.
Origin: Created in 1999 by Timothy Schofield at Teatro, London, England

---

STAR RATINGS EXPLAINED

★★★★★ Excellent

★★★★⯪ Recommended	★★★★☆ Praiseworthy
★★★⯪☆ Commended	★★★☆☆ Mediocre
★★⯪☆☆ Disappointing	★★☆☆☆ Pretty awful
★⯪☆☆☆ Shameful	★☆☆☆☆ Disgusting

SWEDISH MARGARITA NEW

Glass: Coupette
Garnish: Lime wedge
Method: SHAKE all ingredients with ice and fine strain into chilled glass.

2	shots	Tequila 100% Agave
1	shot	Swedish Punch liqueur
½	shot	Freshly squeezed lime juice
¼	shot	Freshly squeezed lemon juice

We say: A Swedish punch influenced Margarita. Tangy and oily.
Origin: Created in 2010 by Simon Difford at the Cabinet Room, London, England.

SWEDISH RUM PUNCH

Glass: Old-fashioned
Garnish: Lime wedge
Method: SHAKE all ingredients with ice and strain into ice-filled glass.

1½	shots	Bacardi 8yo aged rum
¾	shot	Swedish Punch liqueur
½	shot	Freshly squeezed lime juice

We say: A flavoursome Daiquiri-style with the subtle spice of Swedish punch.
Origin: Created in 2008 by Simon Difford.

SWEET LOUISE

Glass: Martini
Garnish: Blackberries
Method: Cut passion fruit in half and scoop out flesh into shaker. Add other ingredients, SHAKE with ice and fine strain into chilled glass.

1	fresh	Passion fruit
1	shot	Raspberry flavoured vodka
½	shot	Amaretto liqueur
½	shot	Chambord black raspberry liqueur
¾	shot	Freshly squeezed lime juice
¼	shot	Pomegranate (grenadine) syrup

We say: Lots of contrasting flavours but she's a sweet girl.
Origin: Created in 2000 at Monte's Club, London, England.

SWEET MARTINI

Glass: Martini
Garnish: Maraschino cherry
Method: STIR all ingredients with ice and strain into chilled glass.

2½	shots	Tanqueray London dry gin
½	shot	Martini Rosso sweet vermouth

We say: A gin martini made with sweet vermouth - sweet in name but drier than the cherry garnish might indicate.

SWEET SCIENCE

Glass: Martini
Garnish: Orange zest twist
Method: SHAKE all ingredients with ice and fine strain into chilled glass.

2	shots	Dewar's White label Scotch
¾	shot	Drambuie
1½	shots	Freshly squeezed orange juice

We say: Herbal Scotch and orange.
Origin: Created by Charles Schumann, Munich, Germany.

SWEET TART

Glass: Sling
Garnish: Sugar rim & redcurrants
Method: SHAKE first four ingredients with ice and strain into ice-filled glass. TOP with lemonade.

2	shots	Ketel One vodka
¾	shot	Chambord black raspberry liqueur
¾	shot	Amaretto liqueur
1	shot	Freshly squeezed lime juice
Top up with		Lemonade/Sprite/7-Up

We say: As the name suggests, a fruity combination of sweet and sour.

THE SWEETIE PIE

Glass: Coupette
Garnish: Apple wedge
Method: SHAKE all ingredients with ice and fine strain into chilled glass.

2	shots	Bacardi 8yo aged rum
¼	shot	Berry Hill pimento allspice liqueur
1½	shots	Pressed apple juice
2	dashes	Angostura aromatic bitters
1	pinch	Salt

We say: Bitter sweet and most intriguing.
Origin: Adapted from a drink created by Lydia Reissmueller at Eletaria, New York City, USA.

BARTENDER'S TIP FLAME

The term ignite, flame or flambé means that the drink should be set alight.

Please exercise extreme care when setting fire to drinks. Be particularly careful not to knock over a lit drink and never attempt to carry a drink which is still alight. Before drinking, cover the glass so as to suffocate the flame and be aware that the rim of the glass may be hot.

SWIZZLE (GENERIC NAME)

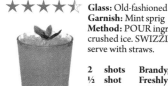

★★★★⯪

Glass: Old-fashioned
Garnish: Mint sprig
Method: POUR ingredients into glass filled with crushed ice. SWIZZLE with a swizzle stick and serve with straws.

2	shots	Brandy, whisk(e)y, gin, rum etc.
½	shot	Freshly squeezed lemon or lime juice
¼	shot	Monin Pure Cane 2:1 sugar syrup

Variant: With rum try orgeat syrup or Velvet Falernum in place of the sugar syrup. With whiskey try Chartreuse.
We say: Match the appropriate citrus juice and sweetener to your spirit and you'll have a superb drink.
Origin: Swizzles originated in the Caribbean. They are sour-style drinks that, distinctively, must be churned with a swizzle stick –originally a twig from a species of tree called Quararibea turbinata which grow in the southern islands of the Caribbean. These trees have forked branches, which make perfect swizzle sticks. Today swizzle sticks are usually made of metal or plastic and have several blades or fingers attached to the base at right angles to the shaft. To use one, simply immerse the blades in the drink, hold the shaft between the palms of both hands and rotate the stick rapidly by sliding your hands back and forth. If you do not have a bona fide swizzle stick, use a barspoon in the same manner. Swizzles can be served as short drinks or lengthened with mineral water.

TABU

★★★⯪☆

Glass: Coconut shell
Garnish: Pineapple cubes, maraschino cherry & mint sprig
Method: BLEND all ingredients with 12oz scoop crushed ice.

1	shot	Bacardi Superior rum
1	shot	Ketel One vodka
1½	shots	Fresh pressed pineapple juice
½	shot	Freshly squeezed lemon juice
¼	shot	Monin Pure Cane 2:1 sugar syrup

We say: Ice-cold fresh pineapple laced with rum and vodka with a splash of citrus.
Origin: Adapted from Victor Bergeron's '*Trader Vic's Bartender's Guide*' (1972 revised edition) where Vic states the drink 'originated in Seattle'.

TABULA RASA NEW

★★★☆☆

Glass: Old-fashioned
Garnish: Orange zest twist
Method: POUR ingredients into ice-filled glass and stir.

1½	shot	Mozart Dry chocolate spirit
1	shot	Campari Bitter
1	shot	Carpano Antica Formula

We say: A chocolate Negroni.
Origin: Created in 2009 by Klaus St Rainer at Schumann's Bar, Munich, Germany.

STAR RATINGS EXPLAINED

★★★★★ **Excellent**

★★★★⯪ Recommended	★★★★☆ Praiseworthy
★★★⯪☆ Commended	★★★☆☆ Mediocre
★★⯪☆☆ Disappointing	★★☆☆☆ Pretty awful
★⯪☆☆☆ Shameful	★☆☆☆☆ Disgusting

TAHITIAN HONEY BEE

★★★★☆

Glass: Martini
Garnish: Lemon zest twist
Method: STIR honey with rum in base of shaker so as to dissolve honey. Add lemon juice, SHAKE with ice and fine strain into chilled glass.

2	shots	Bacardi Superior rum
2	spoons	Runny honey
½	shot	Freshly squeezed lemon juice

We say: Basically a honey Daiquiri - very tasty it is too.
Origin: Adapted from Victor Bergeron's '*Trader Vic's Bartender's Guide*' (1972 revised edition).

TAILOR MADE

★★★★☆

Glass: Martini
Garnish: Grapefruit zest twist
Method: STIR honey with bourbon in base of shaker to dissolve honey. Add other ingredients, SHAKE with ice and fine strain into chilled glass.

1	spoon	Runny honey
1½	shots	Maker's Mark bourbon
¼	shot	Taylor's Velvet Falernum liqueur
1	shot	Freshly squeezed grapefruit juice
1	shot	Ocean Spray cranberry juice

We say: Light, balanced fruit and bourbon.
Origin: Created by Dale DeGroff in New York City, USA.

TAINTED CHERRY

★★★☆☆

Glass: Martini
Garnish: Maraschino cherry
Method: SHAKE all ingredients with ice and fine strain into chilled glass.

1¾	shots	Ketel One vodka
¾	shot	De Kuyper Cherry Brandy liqueur
1¾	shots	Freshly squeezed orange juice

We say: Orange and cherry combine to produce a flavour rather like amaretto.

TANGLEFOOT

★★★★☆

Glass: Coupette
Garnish: Orange zest twist
Method: SHAKE all ingredients with ice and fine strain into chilled glass.

2	shots	Bacardi Superior rum
1	shot	Swedish Punch liqueur
½	shot	Freshly squeezed lemon juice
½	shot	Freshly squeezed orange juice

We say: Light rum, lemon and orange juice served short with a tang of Swedish punch

TANGO MARTINI #1

★★★★½☆

Glass: Martini
Garnish: Orange zest twist
Method: SHAKE all ingredients with ice and fine strain into chilled glass.

1½	shots	Tanqueray London dry gin
½	shot	Triple Sec
½	shot	Martini Rosso sweet vermouth
½	shot	Martini Extra Dry vermouth
1	shot	Freshly squeezed orange juice

We say: Balanced and complex with hints of gin and orange.
Origin: Adapted from a recipe in Harry Craddock's 1930 *Savoy Cocktail Book*. Harry McElhone's 1929 'ABC of Cocktails' credits this drinks creation to Harry, a bartender at Palermo, Rue Fontaine, Paris.

TANGO MARTINI #2

★★★★☆

Glass: Martini
Garnish: Orange zest twist
Method: SHAKE all ingredients with ice and fine strain into chilled glass.

1¾	shots	Tanqueray London dry gin
¾	shot	Passoã passion fruit liqueur
2	shots	Freshly squeezed grapefruit juice
¼	shot	Monin Pure Cane 2:1 sugar syrup

We say: Floral and balanced.
Origin: Adapted from a drink discovered in 2003 at the Bellagio, Las Vegas, USA.

TANTRIS SIDECAR NO.1

★★★★☆

Glass: Martini
Garnish: Lemon zest twist
Method: SHAKE all ingredients with ice and fine strain into chilled glass.

1	shot	Cognac VSOP
½	shot	Calvados/Applejack brandy
½	shot	Triple Sec
¼	shot	Chartreuse Green liqueur
¼	shot	Fresh pressed pineapple juice
½	shot	Freshly squeezed lemon juice
¼	shot	Monin Pure Cane 2:1 sugar syrup

Variant: Omit calvados and replace with an extra half shot cognac. An adaptation demonstrated by Audrey at a Cognac Summit on 22 January 2008.
We say: A Sidecar with extra interest courtesy of Chartreuse, pineapple and Calvados.
Origin: Adapted from a drink created by Audrey Saunders at Bemelmans Bar at The Carlyle Hotel, New York City, USA.

TAPERED NAIL

★★★★½

Glass: Old-fashioned
Garnish: Pineapple wedge
Method: STIR all ingredients with ice and strain into ice-filled glass.

2	shots	Bacardi 8yo aged rum
1	shot	Drambuie
¼	shot	Lagavulin 16yo malt whisky

We say: Rum takes over from Scotch as base spirit in this Nail but Islay malt adds interest and keeps it a true Nail (being any drink with Drambuie and Scotch whiskey).
Origin: Created in 2010 by Simon Difford at the Cabinet Room, London, England.

TARRABERRY'TINI

★★★★☆

Glass: Martini
Garnish: Tarragon sprig
Method: MUDDLE tarragon in base of shaker. Add other ingredients, SHAKE with ice and fine strain into chilled glass.

2	sprig	Fresh tarragon
1¼	shots	Cranberry flavoured vodka
¼	shot	Pernod anise
2	shots	Ocean Spray cranberry juice
¼	shot	Freshly squeezed lemon juice

We say: Cranberry with subtle hints of tarragon and lemon.
Origin: Created in 2003 by Simon Difford.

TARTE AU POMMES

★★★★☆

Glass: Collins
Garnish: Apple fan
Method: SHAKE all ingredients with ice and strain into ice-filled glass.

1	shot	Calvados/Applejack brandy
½	shot	Cranberry flavoured vodka
¼	shot	Goldschläger cinnamon schnapps
4	shots	Ocean Spray cranberry juice
3	dashes	Angostura aromatic bitters

We say: Rich in flavour and well balanced.
Origin: Created in 2001 by Jamie Stephenson at The Lock, Manchester, England.

BARTENDER'S TIP *THROWING*

Sometimes also referred to as the 'Cuban Roll' after the origin of this method of mixing, 'throwing' offers **greater dilution and aeration than stirring but is more gentle than shaking.** It is achieved by simply pouring the ingredients from one container to another. To do this, assemble your ingredients in a mixing glass or base of your shaker. Add ice and strain into a second mixing glass with a large diameter lipped rim increasing the distance between the two vessels as you pour. Then pour the partially mixed cocktail back into the first ice-filled container and strain into the second once again. Repeat this process several times and you will have 'thrown' your drink.

TARTE TATIN MARTINI

★★★★☆

Glass: Martini
Garnish: Dust with cinnamon powder
Method: SHAKE first three ingredients with ice and strain into chilled into chilled glass. SHAKE cream with ice and carefully pour so as to LAYER over drink.

2	shots	Ketel One vodka
¾	shot	Berentzen Apple schnapps
¾	shot	Giffard caramel liqueur
2	shots	Double (heavy) cream

We say: A creamy top hides a vanilla, apple and caramel combo.
Origin: Created in 2003 by Simon Difford. The name means a tart of caramelised apples cooked under a pastry lid, a dish created by the Tatin sisters.

TARTINI ⊙━

★★★★☆

Glass: Martini
Garnish: Raspberries
Method: MUDDLE raspberries in base of shaker. Add other ingredients, SHAKE with ice and fine strain into chilled glass.

2	shots	Ketel One vodka
½	shot	Chambord black raspberry liqueur
1½	shots	Ocean Spray cranberry juice
12	fresh	Raspberries

We say: Rich raspberry flavour, well balanced with bite.
Origin: Adapted from a cocktail I found at Soho Grand, New York City, USA.

TATANKA

★★★★½

Glass: Old-fashioned
Garnish: Apple slice
Method: SHAKE all ingredients with ice and strain into ice-filled glass.

| 2 | shots | Żubrówka bison vodka |
| 2½ | shots | Pressed apple juice |

We say: The taste of this excellent drink (which is equally good served straight-up) is a little reminiscent of Earl Grey tea.
Origin: This Polish drink takes its name from the film 'Dances With Wolves'. Tatanka is a Native American word for buffalo and refers to the Bison grass flavoured vodka the cocktail is based on.

TATANKA ROYALE

★★★★☆

Glass: Flute
Garnish: Apple slice
Method: SHAKE first two ingredients with ice and fine strain into chilled glass. TOP with champagne.

1	shot	Żubrówka bison vodka
1	shot	Pressed apple juice
Top up with		Brut champagne

We say: Champagne with a subtle, grassy hint of apple.
Origin: Discovered in 2004 at Indigo Yard, Edinburgh, Scotland.

TAWNY-TINI

★★★★☆

Glass: Martini
Garnish: Orange zest twist
Method: SHAKE all ingredients with ice and fine strain into chilled glass.

2	shots	Ketel One vodka
2	shots	Warre's Otima tawny port
¼	shot	Maple syrup

We say: Dry yet rich. Port combines wonderfully with the maple syrup and is further fortified by the grainy vodka.

TEAQUILA NEW

★★★★☆

Glass: Glass teacup & saucer (or Collins over ice)
Garnish: Lemon slice on rim
Method: SHAKE all ingredients with ice and fine strain into chilled glass.

2	shots	Cold English breakfast tea
1½	shots	Olmeca Altos 100% agave tequila
½	shot	Honey flavoured vodka
½	shot	Monin Pure Cane 2:1 sugar syrup
½	shot	Freshly squeezed lemon juice
2	dashes	Orange bitters (optional)

We say: A Mexican iced tea sweetened with honey.
Origin: Created in 2011 by Mark Cooke and the rest of the team at North Bar, Leeds, England.

TEDDY BEAR'TINI

★★★★☆

Glass: Martini
Garnish: Pear slice
Method: SHAKE all ingredients with ice and fine strain into chilled glass.

1½	shots	Belle de Brillet pear liqueur
¾	shot	Berentzen Apple schnapps
1½	shots	Pressed apple juice
1	pinch	Ground cinnamon

We say: Beautifully balanced apple and pear with a hint of cinnamon spice.
Origin: Created in 2002 at The Borough, Edinburgh, Scotland. Originally named after a well-known cockney duo but renamed after the cockney rhyming slang for pear.

TENNER MARTINI

★★★★½

Glass: Martini
Garnish: Grapefruit zest twist
Method: STIR all ingredients with ice and strain into chilled glass.

2	shots	Tanqueray London dry gin
1	shot	Martini Extra Dry vermouth
2	dashes	Grapefruit bitters

We say: Very wet, aromatic Martini.

TENNESSEE BERRY MULE

★★★★☆

Glass: Collins
Garnish: Raspberries
Method: MUDDLE raspberries in base of shaker. Add next four ingredients, SHAKE with ice and strain into ice-filled glass. TOP with ginger beer, lightly stir and serve with straws.

8	fresh	Raspberries
1½	shots	Jack Daniel's Tennessee whiskey
1	shot	Amaretto liqueur
1½	shots	Ocean Spray cranberry juice
½	shot	Freshly squeezed lime juice
Top up with		Ginger beer

We say: A berry rich cocktail laced with whiskey, flavoured with Amaretto and topped with ginger beer.
Origin: Adapted in 2003 from a recipe Alex Kammerling created for TGI Friday's UK. Named partly for the ingredients and partly as a reference to Jack Daniel's proprietor (and nephew), Lemuel Motlow, who took up mule trading during Prohibition.

TENNESSEE ICED TEA

★★★★☆

Glass: Sling
Garnish: Lemon wedge
Method: SHAKE first six ingredients with ice and strain into ice-filled glass. TOP with cola and serve with straws.

1	shot	Jack Daniel's Tennessee whiskey
½	shot	Bacardi Superior rum
½	shot	Ketel One vodka
½	shot	Triple Sec
¾	shot	Freshly squeezed lemon juice
¼	shot	Monin Pure Cane 2:1 sugar syrup
Top up with		Coca-Cola

We say: Whiskey and cola with extra interest courtesy of several other spirits and lemon juice.

TENNESSEE RUSH

★★★½☆

Glass: Collins
Garnish: Lime wedge
Method: SHAKE all ingredients with ice and strain into ice-filled glass.

2	shots	Jack Daniel's Tennessee whiskey
1	shot	Mandarine Napoléon liqueur
2½	shots	Ocean Spray cranberry juice
½	shot	Freshly squeezed lime juice

We say: This ruby red cocktail is long, fruity, refreshing and not too sweet.

STAR RATINGS EXPLAINED

★★★★★ Excellent

★★★★½ Recommended	★★★★☆ Praiseworthy
★★★½☆ Commended	★★★☆☆ Mediocre
★★½☆☆ Disappointing	★★☆☆☆ Pretty awful
★½☆☆☆ Shameful	★☆☆☆☆ Disgusting

TEQRONI NEW

★★★★½

Glass: Old-fashioned
Garnish: Orange zest twist
Method: POUR all ingredients into ice-filled glass and stir.

1	shot	Olmeca Altos 100% agave tequila
1	shot	Aperol
1	shot	Martini Rosso sweet vermouth

We say: Lighter and slightly sweeter than a classic gin-based Negroni with Campari. However, this Italian and Mexican trio make for pleasing cross continental bedfellows.
Origin: Unknown, but as the same suggests this is simply a tequila-based Negroni.

TEQUILA BASIL LEMONADE NEW

★★★★½

Glass: Collins
Garnish: Lemon wedge & basil leaf
Method: SHAKE first four ingredients with ice and fine strain into ice-filled glass. Top up with soda and gently stir.

2	shots	Tequila 100% Agave
3	fresh	Torn basil leaves
½	shot	Monin Pure Cane 2:1 sugar syrup
¾	shot	Freshly squeezed lemon juice
Top up with		Soda (club soda)

We say: Just as it says on the tin - tequila charged with lemonade and flavoured with basil.
Origin: Created in 2011 by Chris Stave, a self-professed avid diffordsguide reader. (Thanks Chris.)

TEQUILA FIZZ

★★★★☆

Glass: Sling
Garnish: Orange zest twist
Method: SHAKE first four ingredients with ice and strain into ice-filled glass. TOP with lemonade.

2	shots	Tequila 100% Agave
1	shot	Freshly squeezed orange juice
1	shot	Freshly squeezed lime juice
½	shot	Monin Pure Cane 2:1 sugar syrup
Top up with		Lemonade/Sprite/7-Up

We say: Refreshing with lingering lime.

TEQUILA GIMLET ○━

★★★☆☆

Glass: Martini
Garnish: Lime wedge
Method: STIR all ingredients with ice and strain into chilled glass.

2½	shots	Tequila 100% Agave
¾	shot	Rose's lime cordial

We say: Tequila flavoured and slightly sweetened by lime cordial.

TEQUILA MOCKINGBIRD

★★★☆☆

Glass: Martini
Garnish: Mint leaf
Method: SHAKE all ingredients with ice and fine strain into chilled glass.

2	shots	Tequila 100% Agave
½	shot	Green crème de menthe liqueur
½	shot	Freshly squeezed lime juice
⅛	shot	Monin Pure Cane 2:1 sugar syrup

Variant: With white crème de menthe instead of green crème de menthe.
We say: Minty tequila.
Origin: Named after Harper Lee's 1960 novel 'To Kill a Mockingbird', this is thought to have been created some time in the 1960s. Genius.

TEQUILA SLAMMER

★★★☆☆

Glass: Shot
Garnish: None
Method: POUR tequila into glass and then carefully LAYER with champagne. The drinker should hold and cover the top of the glass with the palm of their hand so as to grip it firmly and seal the contents inside. Then they should briskly pick the glass up and slam it down (not so hard as to break the glass), then quickly gulp the drink down in one while it is still fizzing.

1	shot	Tequila 100% Agave
1	shot	Brut champagne

We say: With cream soda or ginger ale.
Origin: Originally topped with ginger ale and not champagne, this infamous libation is thought to have started out a s a Hell's Angel drink - it needs no ice and can be carried in a bike bag. The simplest slammer is a lick of salt, a shot of tequila and then a bite of lemon (or lime). A Bermuda Slammer involves straight tequila, salt, a slice of lemon and a partner: one has to lick the salt off the other one's neck and bite the lemon (held between their partner's teeth) before downing a shot of tequila. To quote Victor Bergeron (Trader Vic), "You know, this rigmarole with a pinch of salt and lemon juice and tequila - in whatever order - was originally for a purpose: It's hot in Mexico. People dehydrate themselves. And they need more salt. Here, it's not so hot, and we don't need salt in the same way. So you can drink tequila straight right out of the bottle, if you want to."

TEQUILA SMASH

★★★★½

Glass: Old-fashioned
Garnish: Mint sprig
Method: SHAKE all ingredients with ice and fine strain into ice-filled glass.

7	fresh	Mint leaves
2	shots	Tequila 100% Agave
¼	shot	Agave nectar

We say: Simple, not too sweet - a great way to appreciate quality tequila.
Origin: Adapted from the classic Brandy Smash.

TEQUILA SOUR

★★★★½

Glass: Old-fashioned
Garnish: Lime zest twist
Method: SHAKE all ingredients with ice and fine strain into ice-filled glass.

2	shots	Tequila 100% Agave
1	shot	Freshly squeezed lime juice
½	shot	Monin Pure Cane 2:1 sugar syrup
½	fresh	Egg white

We say: A standard sour but with tequila zing.

TEQUILA SUNRISE

★★★½☆

Glass: Collins
Garnish: Orange slice
Method: SHAKE first two ingredients with ice and strain into ice-filled glass. POUR grenadine in a circle around the top of the drink (it will sink to create a sunrise effect).

2	shots	Tequila 100% Agave
¾	shot	Pomegranate (grenadine) syrup
3	shots	Freshly squeezed orange juice

We say: Everyone has heard of this drink, but those who have tried it will wonder why it's so famous.

TEQUILA SUNSET

★★★★☆

Glass: Sling
Garnish: Lemon slice
Method: STIR honey with tequila in base of shaker until honey dissolves. Add other ingredients, SHAKE with ice and strain into ice-filled glass. TOP with soda.

7	spoons	Runny honey
2	shots	Tequila 100% Agave
2	shots	Freshly squeezed lemon juice

We say: A good sweet and sour balance with subtle honey hints.

TEQUILA'TINI

★★★½☆

Glass: Martini
Garnish: Lime zest twist
Method: SHAKE all ingredients with ice and fine strain into chilled glass.

2	shots	Tequila 100% Agave
1	shot	Martini Extra Dry vermouth
½	shot	Monin Pure Cane 2:1 sugar syrup
3	dashes	Angostura aromatic bitters

We say: If you like tequila and strong drinks - this is for you.

TERESA

★★★☆☆

Glass: Martini
Garnish: Lime wedge
Method: SHAKE all ingredients with ice and fine strain into chilled glass.

2	shots	**Campari Bitter**
1	shot	**Freshly squeezed lime juice**
¾	shot	**Crème de cassis liqueur**

We say: Bold, sweet and sour.
Origin: Created by Rafael Ballesteros of Spain, this recipe is taken from 'The *Joy of Mixology*' by Gary Regan.

TEST PILOT

★★★★☆

Glass: Old-fashioned
Garnish: Lime zest twist
Method: SHAKE all ingredients with ice and fine strain into ice-filled glass.

1½	shots	**Bacardi 8yo aged rum**
¾	shot	**Bacardi Superior rum**
¼	shot	**Triple Sec**
¼	shot	**Taylor's Velvet Falernum liqueur**
¼	shot	**Freshly squeezed lemon juice**

We say: A fruity, sophisticated Daiquiri with hints of almond and spicy clove, served short over ice.
Origin: Adapted from a recipe in the *1947-72 Trader Vic's Bartender's Guide* by Victor Bergeron.

TESTAROSSA

★★★½☆

Glass: Collins
Garnish: Orange slice
Method: POUR all ingredients into ice-filled glass, lightly stir and serve with straws.

1½	shots	**Ketel One vodka**
1½	shots	**Campari Bitter**
Top up with		**Soda (club soda)**

We say: Campari and soda with some oomph.

TEX COLLINS

★★★½☆

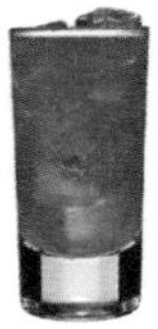

Glass: Collins
Garnish: Lemon slice
Method: STIR honey with gin in base of shaker to dissolve honey. Add grapefruit juice, SHAKE with ice and strain into ice-filled glass. TOP with soda water.

2	shots	**Tanqueray London dry gin**
2	spoons	**Runny honey**
2	shots	**Freshly squeezed grapefruit juice**
Top up with		**Soda (club soda)**

We say: A dry, tart blend of grapefruit and gin.
Origin: Adapted from a recipe in the 1949 edition of '*Esquire's Handbook for Hosts*'.

TEXAS ICED TEA

★★★½☆

Glass: Sling
Garnish: Lemon wedge
Method: SHAKE first six ingredients with ice and strain into ice-filled glass. TOP with cola.

1	shot	**Tequila 100% Agave**
½	shot	**Bacardi Superior rum**
½	shot	**Ketel One vodka**
½	shot	**Triple Sec**
¾	shot	**Freshly squeezed lemon juice**
¼	shot	**Monin Pure Cane 2:1 sugar syrup**
Top up with		**Coca-Cola**

We say: My favourite of the Iced Tea family of drinks. The tequila shines through.

TEXSUN

★★★½☆

Glass: Martini
Garnish: Lemon zest twist
Method: SHAKE all ingredients with ice and fine strain into chilled glass.

1½	shots	**Maker's Mark bourbon**
1½	shots	**Martini Extra Dry vermouth**
1½	shots	**Freshly squeezed grapefruit juice**

We say: Bone dry with fruity herbal hints.
Origin: Adapted from a recipe in the 1949 edition of '*Esquire's Handbook for Hosts*'.

THAI LADY

★★★½☆

Glass: Martini
Garnish: Lemon zest twist
Method: MUDDLE lemongrass in base of shaker. Add other ingredients, SHAKE with ice and fine strain into chilled glass.

2	inch	**Lemongrass stem (chopped)**
2	shots	**Tanqueray London dry gin**
½	shot	**Triple Sec**
1	shot	**Freshly squeezed lemon juice**
¼	shot	**Monin Pure Cane 2:1 sugar syrup**

We say: A White Lady with the added flavour of lemongrass.
Origin: Adapted from a recipe by Jamie Terrell, London, England.

THAI LEMONADE

★★★★☆

Glass: Collins
Garnish: Lime wedge
Method: MUDDLE coriander in base of shaker. Add next two ingredients, SHAKE with ice and fine strain into ice-filled glass. TOP with ginger beer.

5	inch	**Freshly squeezed lemon juice**
2	shots	**Freshly squeezed lime juice**
½	shot	**Monin Almond (orgeat) syrup**
Top up with		**Ginger beer**

We say: Lime lemonade with Thai influences courtesy of ginger, almond and coriander.
Origin: Adapted from a drink created in 2005 by Charlotte Voisey, London, England.

THAI RED DAIQUIRI

★★★★☆

Glass: Old-fashioned
Garnish: Lime zest twist
Method: MUDDLE pepper in base of shaker. Add other ingredients, SHAKE with ice and fine strain into chilled glass.

½	slice	Red pepper slice
3	fresh	Torn basil leaves
2	shots	Bacardi 8yo aged rum
½	fresh	Coconut water
½	shot	Freshly squeezed lime juice
¼	sprig	Monin Pure Cane 2:1 sugar syrup

We say: Created in December 2008 by Simon Difford at the Cabinet Room, London, England.
Origin: Aged rum, delicately spiced by red pepper and basil.

THE [PICK OF] DESTINY

★★★★☆

Glass: Martini
Garnish: Orange zest twist
Method: SHAKE all ingredients with ice and fine strain into chilled glass.

2	shots	Straight rye whiskey
1	shot	St~Germain elderflower liqueur
¾	shot	Freshly squeezed orange juice
3	shots	Orange bitters

We say: Fresh floral orange - just picked.
Origin: Adapted from a drink created in 2007 by Amanda Washington at Rye, San Francisco, USA.

THOMAS BLOOD MARTINI

★★★½☆

Glass: Martini
Garnish: Apple wedge
Method: STIR honey with vodka in base of shaker until honey dissolves. Add other ingredients, SHAKE with ice and fine strain into chilled glass.

2	spoons	Runny honey
1	shot	Ketel One vodka
1	shot	Krupnik spiced honey liqueur
1	shot	Berentzen Apple schnapps
1	shot	Freshly squeezed lemon juice

We say: An appealing, honey led melange of sweet and sour.

THREE MILER

★★★★☆

Glass: Martini
Garnish: Lemon zest twist
Method: SHAKE all ingredients with ice and fine strain into chilled glass.

1½	shots	Cognac VSOP
1½	shots	Bacardi Superior rum
½	shot	Pomegranate (grenadine) syrup
½	shot	Freshly squeezed lemon juice

We say: A seriously strong drink, in flavour and in alcohol.
Origin: Adapted from the Three Miller Cocktail in the 1930 '*Savoy Cocktail Book*'.

THREESOME

★★★½☆

Glass: Martini
Garnish: Pineapple wedge
Method: SHAKE all ingredients with ice and fine strain into chilled glass.

1½	shots	Calvados/Applejack brandy
1	shot	Triple Sec
½	shot	Pernod anise
1½	shots	Fresh pressed pineapple juice

We say: Why stop at three when you can have a foursome? An interesting meld of apple, orange, anise and pineapple.
Origin: Adapted from a drink discovered in 2002 at Circus Bar, London, England.

THRILLER FROM VANILLA

★★★★☆

Glass: Martini
Garnish: Half vanilla pod
Method: SHAKE all ingredients with ice and fine strain into chilled glass.

¾	shot	Vanilla-infused Ketel One vodka
¾	shot	Tanqueray London dry gin
½	shot	Triple Sec
2	shots	Freshly squeezed orange juice

We say: Orange and creamy vanilla fortified with a hint of gin.
Origin: Adapted from a drink discovered in 2003 at Oporto, Leeds, England. The 'Thriller in Manila' was the name given to the 1975 heavyweight fight between Muhammad Ali and Smokin' Joe Frazier.

THRILLER MARTINI

★★★★☆

Glass: Martini
Garnish: Orange zest twist
Method: SHAKE all ingredients with ice and fine strain into chilled glass.

2½	shots	Dewar's White label Scotch
¾	shot	Tanqueray London dry gin
¾	shot	Freshly squeezed orange juice
⅛	shot	Monin Pure Cane 2:1 sugar syrup

We say: Spiced Scotch with a hint of orange.

THUNDERBIRD

★★★★☆

Glass: Martini
Garnish: Pineapple wedge
Method: SHAKE all ingredients with ice and fine strain into chilled glass.

1½	shots	Maker's Mark bourbon
¾	shot	Amaretto liqueur
1	shot	Fresh pressed pineapple juice
1	shot	Freshly squeezed orange juice

We say: Tangy bourbon with fruity almond.

TI PUNCH

Glass: Old-fashioned
Garnish: Lime zest twist
Method: POUR the rum and sugar into glass. Then SQUEEZE the lime disc between finger and thumb before dropping into the drink. This expresses the oil from the skin and little of the juice into the Ti Punch. Lastly STIR and consider adding two or three ice cubes.

1½	shots	Martinique agricole rum
¼	shot	Martinique cane sugar syrup
1	slice	Lime

We say: This drink only works with authentic agricole rum and sugar cane juice. On its native islands it is usual to use rhum blanc (unaged white agricole rum) during the day and rhum vieux (aged agricole rum) during the evening. Note: Traditionally the limes used to make this drink are not cut into slices or wedges. Instead a round disc is cut from the side of the fruit. These are cut large enough that some of the fruits pulp backs the peel on the disc.
Origin: Named Ti from the French word 'Petit', this is literally a small rum punch: unlike most rum punches, it is not lengthened with water or juice. It is popular in the French islands of Martinique, Guadeloupe, Réunion and Maurice where it's often drunk straight down without adding ice and chased by a large glass of chilled water (called a 'crase' in Martinique). These islands are also home to Rhum Agricole (a style of rum distilled only from sugar cane juice and usually bottled at 50% alc./vol.)

TICK-TACK MARTINI

Glass: Martini
Garnish: Tic-Tac mints
Method: STIR all ingredients with ice and strain into chilled glass.

2	shots	Ketel One vodka
½	shot	Luxardo Sambuca dei Cesari
½	shot	Giffard Menthe Pastille liqueur

We say: Strangely enough, tastes like a Tic-Tac mint.
Origin: Created in 2001 by Rodolphe Sorel.

TIGER'S MILK

Glass: Old-fashioned
Garnish: Dust with grated nutmeg
Method: SHAKE all ingredients with ice and strain into ice-filled glass.

2	shots	Cognac VSOP
2	drops	Vanilla extract
1	pinch	Ground cinnamon
¼	shot	Monin Pure Cane 2:1 sugar syrup
¾	shot	Milk
¾	shot	Double (heavy) cream
½	fresh	Egg white

We say: Creamy cognac and spice.
Origin: Adapted from a recipe purloined from Charles H. Baker Jr's classic book, 'The Gentleman's Companion'. He first discovered this drink in April 1931 at Gerber's Snug Bar, Beijing, China.

TIJUANA BRASS

Glass: Old-fashioned
Garnish: Cucumber foam
Method: SHAKE first three ingredients with ice and fine strain into ice-filled glass. Top with cucumber foam (fill a cream whipper two-thirds full with equal parts liquefied cucumber juice, 1:1 simple syrup and egg white, charge with two CO2 cartridges and chill).

2	shots	Tequila 100% Agave
¾	shot	Agave nectar
1	shot	Freshly squeezed lime juice

We say: Pronounced "Tea-You-One-Na" this is basically a Tommy's Margarita topped with cucumber foam.
Origin: Created in 2009 by Damian Windsor at The Roger Room, Los Angeles, USA.

TIKI BAR MARGARITA

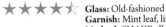

Glass: Old-fashioned
Garnish: Mint leaf, lime & pineapple wedges
Method: SHAKE all ingredients with ice and strain into glass filled with crushed ice.

2	shots	Tequila 100% Agave
½	shot	Monin Almond (orgeat) syrup
1	shot	Freshly squeezed lime juice

We say: A simple almond twist on the classic Margarita - fantastic.
Origin: Created in 2005 by Crispin Somerville and Jasper Eyears at Bar Tiki, Mexico City.

TIKI MAX

Glass: Old-fashioned
Garnish: Mint sprig & lime wedge
Method: SHAKE first nine ingredients with ice and strain into glass filled with crushed ice. FLOAT overproof rum on drink.

1	shot	Pusser's Navy rum
1	shot	Bacardi Superior rum
½	shot	Grand Marnier liqueur
½	shot	De Kuyper Apricot Brandy liqueur
¾	shot	Monin Almond (orgeat) syrup
¾	shot	Freshly squeezed lime juice
1½	shots	Fresh pressed pineapple juice
½	shot	Freshly squeezed orange juice
6	dashes	Angostura aromatic bitters
½	shot	Wood's 100 rum

We say: This drink breaks the golden rule - simple is beautiful. However, it's tasty and packs a punch.
Origin: Created in 2008 by Simon Difford at the Cabinet Room, London, England.
The inspiration for this drink came not from the similarly named discount clothing retailer but the venerable Tiki cocktail itself. Tiki drinks, otherwise known as 'exotics' originated in 1934 when Ernest Raymond Beaumont Gantt, a Louisiana native who had made some money bootlegging rum during Prohibition, opened a bar called Don's Beachcomber in Hollywood and began serving rum based, fruity cocktails. Soon after, Victor 'Trader Vic' Bergeron transformed his restaurant Hinky Dinks into a similar faux Polynesian style. These founding fathers spawned many Tiki imitators and despite a dip in popularity from the 1970s, happily the Noughties saw a revival in the fortunes of Tiki.

TILT

★★★★☆

Glass: Sling
Garnish: Pineapple leaf
Method: SHAKE first five ingredients with ice and strain into glass filled with crushed ice. TOP with bitter lemon.

1½	shots	**Pineapple flavoured vodka**
½	shot	**Malibu coconut rum liqueur**
1½	shots	**Fresh pressed pineapple juice**
1	shot	**Freshly squeezed grapefruit juice**
¼	shot	**Monin Vanilla sugar syrup**
Top up with		**Bitter lemon**

We say: Totally tropical taste.

TIP TOP COCKTAIL

★★★★½

Glass: Coupette
Garnish: Lemon zest twist
Method: STIR all ingredients with ice and strain into chilled glass.

2	shots	**Martini Extra Dry vermouth**
¾	shot	**Bénédictine D.O.M.**
2	dashes	**Angostura aromatic bitters**

We say: The lemon zest twist is essential to the fine balance of this vermouth (note; no spirit) cocktail.
Origin: Recipe adapted from Albert S. Crockett's 1935 '*Old Waldorf Bar Days*'.

TIPPERARY #1

★★★★½

Glass: Martini
Garnish: Maraschino cherry
Method: SHAKE all ingredients with ice and fine strain into chilled glass.

2	shots	**Jameson Irish whiskey**
½	shot	**Chartreuse Green liqueur**
1	shot	**Martini Rosso sweet vermouth**
½	shot	**Chilled mineral water**

We say: Chartreuse fans will love this serious drink. The uninitiated will hate it.
Origin: Adapted from a recipe in Harry Craddock's 1930 '*Savoy Cocktail Book*', which called for equal parts.

TIPPERARY #2

★★★★½

Glass: Martini
Garnish: Mint leaf
Method: Lightly MUDDLE mint in base in shaker (just to bruise). Add other ingredients, SHAKE with ice and fine strain into chilled glass.

7	fresh	**Mint leaves**
2	shots	**Tanqueray London dry gin**
1	shot	**Martini Extra Dry vermouth**
¼	shot	**Freshly squeezed orange juice**
¼	shot	**Pomegranate (grenadine) syrup**

We say: Delicate with subtle hints of mint, orange and gin.
Origin: Adapted from a drink purloined from David Embury's classic book, '*The Fine Art of Mixing Drinks*'.

TIRAMISU MARTINI

★★★★☆

Glass: Martini
Garnish: Dust with chocolate powder
Method: SHAKE all ingredients with ice and fine strain into chilled glass.

1	shot	**Cognac VSOP**
½	shot	**Kahlúa coffee liqueur**
½	shot	**Dark Crème de Cacao**
½	shot	**Milk**
½	shot	**Double (heavy) cream**
1	fresh	**Egg yolk**
1	spoon	**Mascarpone cheese**

We say: The chef meets the bartender in the rich dessert cocktail.
Origin: Created by Adam Ennis in 2001 at Isola, London, England.

TIZIANO

★★★½☆

Glass: Flute
Garnish: Black grapes
Method: MUDDLE grapes in base of shaker. Add Dubbonet, SHAKE with ice and fine strain into chilled glass. Slowly TOP with Prosecco and lightly stir.

10	fresh	**Seedless white grapes**
1	shot	**Dubonnet Red (French made)**
Top up with		**Prosecco sparkling wine**

We say: Not dissimilar to a sparkling Shiraz wine.
Origin: Named for the 15th century Venetian painter Titian, who was celebrated for his use of auburn red, this cocktail is commonplace in his home town, where it is made without the Dubbonet.

TNT (TEQUILA 'N' TONIC)

★★★★☆

Glass: Collins
Garnish: Lime wedge
Method: POUR all ingredients into ice-filled glass and STIR.

1½	shots	**Tequila 100% Agave**
½	shot	**Freshly squeezed lime juice**
Top up with		**Tonic water**

We say: A simple but very tasty way to enjoy tequila.
Origin: Adapted from Victor Bergeron's '*Trader Vic's Bartender's Guide*' (1972 revised edition).

TOAST & ORANGE MARTINI

★★★★☆

Glass: Martini
Garnish: Orange zest twist
Method: SHAKE all ingredients with ice and fine strain into chilled glass.

2	shots	**Maker's Mark bourbon**
1	spoon	**Orange marmalade**
3	dashes	**Peychaud's aromatic bitters**
⅛	shot	**Monin Pure Cane 2:1 sugar syrup**

We say: Bourbon rounded and enhanced by bitter orange and Peychaud's bitters.

TOASTED ALMOND

★★★★☆

Glass: Martini
Garnish: Dust with chocolate powder
Method: SHAKE all ingredients with ice and fine strain into chilled glass.

1	shot	Ketel One vodka
1	shot	Amaretto liqueur
¾	shot	Kahlúa coffee liqueur
¾	shot	Double (heavy) cream
¾	shot	Milk

We say: Slightly sweet but smooth, creamy and definitely toasted.

TODDY MARTINI

★★★½☆

Glass: Martini
Garnish: Lemon zest twist
Method: SHAKE all ingredients with ice and fine strain into chilled glass.

1½	shots	Dewar's White label Scotch
1	shot	Bärenjäger honey liqueur
¾	shot	Freshly squeezed lemon juice

We say: An ice cold but warming combo of Scotch, honey and lemon.
Origin: Created in 2001 by Jamie Terrell at LAB, London, England.

TOFFEE APPLE

★★★★☆

Glass: Sling
Garnish: Apple wedge
Method: SHAKE all ingredients with ice and strain into ice-filled glass.

1	shot	Calvados/Applejack brandy
2	shots	Giffard caramel liqueur
1	shot	Pressed apple juice
¼	shot	Freshly squeezed lime juice

We say: The taste is just as the name suggests.
Origin: Created in 2002 by Nick Strangeway, London, England.

TOFFEE APPLE MARTINI

★★★★☆

Glass: Martini
Garnish: Apple slice & fudge
Method: SHAKE all ingredients with ice and fine strain into chilled glass.

1	shot	Calvados/Applejack brandy
1	shot	Ketel One vodka
1	shot	Toffee liqueur
1½	shots	Pressed apple juice

We say: This amber, liquid toffee apple is almost creamy on the palate.
Origin: Created in 2003 by Simon Difford.

TOKYO BLOODY MARY

★★★★☆

Glass: Collins
Garnish: Celery stick
Method: SHAKE all ingredients with ice and strain into ice-filled glass.

2	shots	Sake
3½	shots	Tomato juice
½	shot	Freshly squeezed lemon juice
¼	shot	Warre's Otima tawny port
7	drops	Tabasco hot pepper sauce
3	dashes	Worcestershire sauce
1	pinch	Celery salt
1	grind	Black pepper

We say: Sake adds an interesting dimension to the traditionally vodka based Bloody Mary.

TOKYO ICED TEA

★★★½☆

Glass: Sling
Garnish: Lemon slice
Method: SHAKE first seven ingredients with ice and strain into ice-filled glass. TOP with lemonade, lightly stir and serve with straws.

½	shot	Bacardi Superior rum
½	shot	Tanqueray London dry gin
½	shot	Ketel One vodka
½	shot	Tequila 100% Agave
½	shot	Triple Sec
½	shot	Midori green melon liqueur
1	shot	Freshly squeezed lime juice
Top up with		Lemonade/Sprite/7-Up

We say: You will be surprised how the half shot of melon liqueur shows through the other ingredients

TOKYO TEA

★★★★☆

Glass: Collins
Garnish: Lychee
Method: SHAKE first three ingredients with ice and fine strain into ice-filled glass. TOP with cola, lightly stir and serve with straws.

2	shots	Tanqueray London dry gin
1½	shots	Kwai Feh lychee liqueur
1	shot	Cold jasmine tea
Top up with		Coca-Cola

We say: Light, floral and, due to the tannins in the jasmine tea, refreshingly dry.
Origin: Created by Simon Difford in 2004.

TOLLEYTOWN PUNCH

★★★½☆

Glass: Collins
Garnish: Orange & lemon slices
Method: SHAKE first four ingredients with ice and strain into ice-filled glass. TOP with ginger ale.

2	shots	Jack Daniel's Tennessee whiskey
2	shots	Ocean Spray cranberry juice
½	shot	Fresh pressed pineapple juice
½	shot	Freshly squeezed orange juice
Top up with		Ginger ale

We say: A fruity long drink with a dry edge that also works well made in bulk and served from a punch bowl.
Origin: Tolleytown is close to Lynchburg.

TOM & JERRY NEW

★★★★½

Glass: Toddy
Garnish: Dust with freshly grated nutmeg
Method: BEAT egg yolk and egg white separately in mixing bowls, then fold the yolk and white together with caster sugar. Stir in cognac and rum and pour into glass(es). Top up with hot (not boiling) water, STIR and serve.

1	fresh	Egg white
1	fresh	Egg yolk
2	spoons	Powdered sugar
1	shot	Bacardi 8yo aged rum
1	shot	Courvoisier Exclusif VSOP cognac
Top up with hot water		

We say: A warming and filling winter's meal in itself. This recipe will fill two small glasses and given the faff involved in its making you might as well treble the recipe and make for 5 or 6 people.
Origin: Reputedly created by Professor Jerry Thomas at the Planter's House Hotel in St Louis but many believe this drinks real origins predate him. This recipe is adapted from William J. Tarling's 1937 '*Café Royal Cocktail Book* Coronation Edition'.

TOM ARNOLD ⊙━━

★★★★☆

Glass: Collins
Garnish: Lemon slice
Method: SHAKE all ingredients with ice and strain into ice-filled glass.

1½	shots	Ketel One vodka
1½	shots	Freshly squeezed lemon juice
¾	shot	Monin Pure Cane 2:1 sugar syrup
2	shots	Cold English breakfast tea

Variant: Arnold Palmer, John Daly
We say: Traditional lemonade laced with vodka and lengthened with tea to make a light and refreshing drink.
Origin: This is one of a series of tea-based drinks that were originally named after golfers. It takes its name from the actor and comedian who starred in '*National Lampoon's Golf Punk*'.

TOM COLLINS

★★★★☆

Glass: Collins
Garnish: Orange slice & cherry on stick (sail)
Method: SHAKE first three ingredients with ice and strain into ice-filled glass. TOP with soda, lightly stir and serve with straws.

2	shots	Old Tom gin
1	shot	Freshly squeezed lemon juice
¾	shot	Monin Pure Cane 2:1 sugar syrup
Top up with		**Soda (club soda)**

We say: A medium-sweet gin Collins.
Origin: In England, this drink is traditionally credited to John Collins, a bartender who worked at Limmer's Hotel, Conduit Street, London. The 'coffee house' of this hotel, a true dive bar, was popular with sporting types during the 19th century, and famous, according to the 1860s memoirs of a Captain Gronow, for its gin-punch as early as 1814.

John (or possibly Jim) Collins, head waiter of Limmer's, is immortalised in a limerick, which was apparently first printed in an 1892 book entitled 'Drinks of the World'. In 1891 a Sir Morell Mackenzie had identified John Collins as the creator of the Tom Collins, using this limerick,

although both the words of the rhyme and the conclusions he drew from it were disputed. But, according to this version of the story, the special gin-punch for which John Collins of Limmer's was famous went on to become known as the Tom Collins when it was made using Old Tom gin.

Others say that the Tom Collins originated in New York, and takes its name from the Great Tom Collins Hoax of 1874, a practical joke which involved telling a friend that a man named Tom Collins had been insulting them, and that he could be found in a bar some distance away, and took the city by storm. This is supported by the fact that the first known written occurrence of a Tom Collins cocktail recipe is found in the 1876 edition of Jerry Thomas' 'The Bartender's Guide'. Three drinks titled Tom Collins are listed: Tom Collins Whiskey, Tom Collins Brandy and Tom Collins Gin.

An alternative story attributes the drink to a Collins who started work at a New York tavern called the Whitehouse in 1873 and started pouring a thirst quencher made with gin. Another identifies a different Tom Collins, who worked as a bartender in New Jersey and New York area. There are apparently also versions of its creation in San Francisco and Australia, and it is not impossible that the drink evolved in two or more places independently.

TOMAHAWK ⊙━━

★★★½☆

Glass: Collins
Garnish: Pineapple wedge
Method: SHAKE all ingredients with ice and strain into ice-filled glass.

1	shot	Tequila 100% Agave
1	shot	Triple Sec
2	shots	Ocean Spray cranberry juice
2	shots	Fresh pressed pineapple juice

We say: A simple recipe and an effective drink.

TOMATE

★★★☆☆

Glass: Collins
Garnish: None
Method: POUR pastis and grenadine into glass. SERVE iced water separately in a small jug (known in France as a 'broc') so the customer can dilute to their own taste (I recommend five shots). Lastly ADD ICE to fill glass.

1	shot	Ricard Pastis
¼	shot	Pomegranate (grenadine) syrup
Top up with		**Chilled mineral water**

We say: The traditional aniseed and liquorice French café drink with a sweet hint of fruit.
Origin: Very popular throughout France. Pronounced 'Toh-Maht', the name literally means 'tomato' and refers to the drink's colour.

TOMATINI

Glass: Coupette
Garnish: Peppered cherry tomato
Method: MUDDLE tomato in base of shaker. Add other ingredients, SHAKE with ice and fine strain into chilled glass.

1	fresh	Cherry tomatoes (chopped)
2	shots	Ketel One vodka
½	shot	White balsamic vinegar
½	shot	Freshly squeezed lemon juice
⅓	shot	Monin Pure Cane 2:1 sugar syrup
1	pinch	Black pepper

We say: A sweet and sour sipper that has to be tried. Delicate and yet assertive, this is an 'out there' recipe!
Origin: Created by Jimmy Barrat, Dubai for World Class 2012 bartender's competition.

TOMMY'S MARGARITA

Glass: Margarita
Garnish: Lime wedge
Method: SHAKE all ingredients with ice and fine strain into chilled glass.

2	shots	Tequila 100% Agave
1	shot	Freshly squeezed lime juice
½	shot	Agave nectar

We say: The flavour of agave is king in this simple Margarita, made without the traditional orange liqueur.
Origin: Created by Julio Bermejo and named after his family's Mexican restaurant and bar in San Francisco. Julio is legendary for his Margaritas and his knowledge of tequila.

TONGA

Glass: Hurricane
Garnish: Orange, lime & lemon slices
Method: SHAKE all ingredients with ice and strain into ice-filled glass.

2	shots	Bacardi Superior rum
½	shot	Cognac VSOP
¼	shot	Bacardi 8yo aged rum
½	shot	Pomegranate (grenadine) syrup
2	shots	Freshly squeezed orange juice
¾	shot	Freshly squeezed lemon juice
¾	shot	Freshly squeezed lime juice
¼	shot	Monin Pure Cane 2:1 sugar syrup

We say: The rum and cognac flavours are masked by zesty orange.

TONGUE TWISTER

Glass: Old-fashioned
Garnish: Maraschino cherry
Method: SHAKE all ingredients with ice and strain into glass filled with crushed ice.

¾	shot	Bacardi Superior rum
¾	shot	Tequila 100% Agave
¾	shot	Ketel One vodka
½	shot	Coco López cream of coconut
3	shots	Fresh pressed pineapple juice
½	shot	Milk
½	shot	Double (heavy) cream
¼	shot	Pomegranate (grenadine) syrup

We say: This creamy, sweet Tiki number is laced with three different spirits.
Origin: Adapted from a drink featured in May 2006 on www.tikibartv.com

TONIC BOOM

Glass: Old-fashioned
Garnish: None
Method: POUR tonic water into old-fashioned glass. Then POUR gin into shot glass. Instruct drinker to hold gin-filled shot glass directly over surface of tonic water and drop shot into old-fashioned glass and consume.

6	shots	Tonic water
1	shot	Tanqueray London dry gin

We say: Essentially a gin and tonic bomb. To quote a Portobello Star regular, "the thinking man's Jager Bomb".
Origin: Created in 2010 by Edward 'Teddy' McPartland at The Portobello Star, London, England

TONKA NEW

Glass: Martini
Garnish: Orange zest twist (flamed)
Method: STIR all ingredients with ice and strain into chilled glass.

2	shots	Yamazaki 12yo Japanese whisky
1	shot	Carpano Antica Formula
½	shot	Mozart Dry chocolate spirit
2	dashes	Orange bitters

We say: A chocolaty, Japanese whisky-based Manhattan-like drink served on the rocks.
Origin: Created in 2010 by Klaus St. Rainer at Schumann's Bar Munich, Germany.

BARTENDER'S TIP MUDDLE

Muddling means pummelling fruits, herbs and/or spices with a muddler (a blunt tool similar to a pestle) so as to crush them and release their flavour. (You can also use a rolling pin.)

As when using a pestle and mortar, push down on the muddler with a twisting action. Never attempt to muddle hard, unripe fruits in a glass as the pressure required could break the glass.

TOO ACHE SIDECAR

★★★★☆

Glass: Coupette
Garnish: Lemon zest twist
Method: SHAKE all ingredients with ice and fine strain into chilled glass.

1½	shots	**Cognac VSOP**
1½	shots	**Tuaca liqueur**
1	shot	**Freshly squeezed lemon juice**

We say: Tuaca replaces Cointreau in this twist on the Sidecar.
Origin: Created in 2009 by Simon Difford at the Cabinet Room, London, England at the insistence of Charlotte Ashburner, UK Tuaca Brand Manager.

TOO CLOSE FOR COMFORT

★★★½☆

Glass: Martini
Garnish: Lemon zest twist
Method: SHAKE all ingredients with ice and fine strain into chilled glass.

1½	shots	**Ketel One vodka**
1	shot	**Southern Comfort liqueur**
1	shot	**Freshly squeezed lemon juice**
½	shot	**Monin Pure Cane 2:1 sugar syrup**

We say: Sweet and sour with the distinctive flavour of Southern Comfort.
Origin: Adapted from a drink discovered in 2005 at Mezza9, Singapore.

TOOTIE FRUITY LIFESAVER

★★★½☆

Glass: Pineapple shell (frozen)
Garnish: Lemon zest twist
Method: SHAKE all ingredients with ice and strain into ice-filled glass. Serve with straws.

1½	shots	**Ketel One vodka**
¾	shot	**Bols Banana liqueur**
¾	shot	**Galliano L'Autentico liqueur**
1	shot	**Ocean Spray cranberry juice**
1	shot	**Fresh pressed pineapple juice**
1	shot	**Freshly squeezed orange juice**

We say: Aptly named fruity drink.

TOP BANANA SHOT

★★★½☆

Glass: Shot
Garnish: None
Method: Refrigerate ingredients then LAYER in chilled glass by carefully pouring in the order listed.

½	shot	**Kahlúa coffee liqueur**
½	shot	**White Crème de Cacao**
½	shot	**Bols Banana liqueur**
½	shot	**Ketel One vodka**

We say: Banana, chocolate and coffee.

TOREADOR

★★★★☆

Glass: Martini
Garnish: Lime zest twist
Method: SHAKE all ingredients with ice and fine strain into chilled glas.

2	shots	**Tequila 100% Agave**
1	shot	**De Kuyper Apricot Brandy liqueur**
1	shot	**Freshly squeezed lime juice**

We say: Apricot brandy replaces triple sec in what otherwise follows the same recipe to a classic Margarita.
Origin: This twist in the Margarita was published in W. J. Tarling's 1937 *'Cafe Royal Cocktail Book'*, 16 years before the first written reference to a Margarita. He also lists another drink called a Picador which is identical to the later Margarita.

TOTAL RECALL

★★★½☆

Glass: Collins
Garnish: Lime wedge
Method: SHAKE all ingredients with ice and strain into ice-filled glass.

¾	shot	**Tequila 100% Agave**
¾	shot	**Bacardi Oro golden rum**
¾	shot	**Southern Comfort liqueur**
1½	shots	**Ocean Spray cranberry juice**
1½	shots	**Freshly squeezed orange juice**
¾	shot	**Freshly squeezed lime juice**

We say: A long, burgundy coloured drink with a taste reminiscent of blood orange.

LA TOUR EIFFEL NEW

★★★★½

Glass: Flute
Garnish: Lemon zest twist
Method: STIR all ingredients with ice and fine strain into chilled glass.

2½	shots	**Courvoisier VSOP cognac**
½	shot	**Triple Sec**
½	shot	**Suze**
4	drops	**Absinthe**

We say: Bitter sweet cognac-influenced palate with lingering flavours of liquorice root, honey, pine and eucalyptus from the Suze.
Origin: Adapted from a drink created in 2007 by Gary Regan after a Sazerac-fuelled trip to New Orleans. He was inspired by how the Sazerac might have been if it had originally been created in France rather than New Orleans.

STAR RATINGS EXPLAINED

★★★★★ Excellent

★★★★½	Recommended	★★★★☆	Praiseworthy
★★★½☆	Commended	★★★☆☆	Mediocre
★★½☆☆	Disappointing	★★☆☆☆	Pretty awful
★½☆☆☆	Shameful	★☆☆☆☆	Disgusting

TRANSYLVANIAN MARTINI

★★★☆☆

Glass: Martini
Garnish: Pineapple wedge
Method: SHAKE all ingredients with ice and fine strain into chilled glass.

2	shots	Ketel One vodka
1	shot	Passoã passion fruit liqueur
1	shot	Fresh pressed pineapple juice

We say: A tad sweet and a tad dull.
Origin: Created for the 1994 International Bartenders cocktail competition.

TRE MARTINI ⚷

★★★★☆

Glass: Martini
Garnish: Lemon zest twist
Method: SHAKE all ingredients with ice and fine strain into chilled glass.

2	shots	Bacardi Superior rum
½	shot	Chambord black raspberry liqueur
1½	shots	Pressed apple juice

We say: A simple, well balanced, fruity drink, laced with rum.
Origin: Created in 2002 by Asa Nevestveit at Sosho, London, England.

TREACLE NO.1

★★★★½

Glass: Old-fashioned
Garnish: Lemon zest twist
Method: STIR sugar syrup and bitters with two ice cubes in glass. Add rest of rum, another couple of ice cubes and STIR again. Fill glass with ice and STIR again. Finally FLOAT apple juice.

2	shots	Myer's dark Jamaican rum
¼	shot	Monin Pure Cane 2:1 sugar syrup
½	shot	Pressed apple juice
2	dashes	Angostura aromatic bitters

We say: Richly flavoured, almost like molasses.
Origin: This twist on the Old-Fashioned was created by Dick Bradsell. Like the original, it takes about five minutes to make and there are no shortcuts.

TREACLE NO.2 NEW

★★★★☆

Glass: Old-fashioned
Garnish: Orange zest twist
Method: STIR one shot of rum with two ice cubes in a glass. ADD sugar syrup, bitters and two more ice cubes. STIR some more and add another two ice cubes and the rest of the rum. STIR lots more and add more ice.

2	shots	Bacardi 8yo aged rum
⅓	shot	Pedro Ximénez sherry
¼	shot	Demerara sugar syrup (2:1)
1	dash	Angostura aromatic bitters

We say: Made to appeal to drinkers who actually want a cocktail that tastes like Treacle. And it does.
Origin: Adapted from a 2011 reworking on Bradsell's original recipe by Fraser Campbell at the The Alchemist Bar, Melbourne, Australia.

TRES AMIGOS DAIQUIRI NEW

★★★★½

Glass: Coupette
Garnish: Lime wedge
Method: SHAKE all ingredients with ice and fine strain into chilled glass.

1	shot	Tequila 100% Agave
1	shot	Tequila 100% Agave
¼	shot	Pusser's Navy rum
½	shot	Freshly squeezed lime juice
¼	shot	Monin Pure Cane 2:1 sugar syrup

We say: Actually this is a navy rum influenced Margarita made to Daiquiri proportions, but whatever it's called, its damn good.
Origin: Adapted from Craig Toone's (8:2:1) interoperation of a cocktail that was doing the rounds in Manchester in 2003, originally under the name 'Triple Rum Daiquiri'.

TRES COMPADRES MARGARITA ⚷

★★★★½

Glass: Coupette
Garnish: Lime wedge & salt rim (optional)
Method: SHAKE ingredients with ice and fine strain into chilled glass.

1¼	shots	Tequila 100% Agave
½	shot	Triple Sec
½	shot	Chambord black raspberry liqueur
½	shot	Rose's lime cordial
¾	shot	Freshly squeezed lime juice
¾	shot	Freshly squeezed orange juice
¾	shot	Freshly squeezed grapefruit juice

We say: A well balanced, tasty twist on the s tandard Margarita.
Origin: Created in 1999 by Robert Plotkin and Raymon Flores of BarMedia, USA.

TRIANGULAR MARTINI

★★★★☆

Glass: Martini
Garnish: Toblerone chocolate
Method: STIR honey with vodka in base of shaker until honey dissolves. Add other ingredients, SHAKE with ice and fine strain into chilled glass.

2	spoons	Runny honey
1½	shots	Vanilla-infused Ketel One vodka
½	shot	Amaretto liqueur
1¼	shots	Dark Crème de Cacao
¾	shot	Double (heavy) cream
½	fresh	Egg white

We say: Nibble at the garnish as you sip honeyed, chocolate and almond flavoured liquid candy.
Origin: Created by Simon Difford in 2003. The famous triangular Toblerone chocolate bar was invented in 1908 by the Swiss chocolate maker Theodor Tobler. The name is a blend of Tobler with Torrone, the Italian word for honey-almond nougat, one of its main ingredients.

TRIBBBLE

Glass: Shot
Garnish: None
Method: Refrigerate ingredients then LAYER in chilled glass by carefully pouring in the following order.

½	shot	Butterscotch schnapps
½	shot	Bols Banana liqueur
½	shot	Baileys Irish cream liqueur

We say: Named Tribbble with three 'B's' due to its three layers: butterscotch, banana and Baileys.
Origin: A drink created by bartenders at TGI Friday's UK in 2002.

TRIFLE MARTINI

Glass: Martini
Garnish: Hundreds & Thousands
Method: SHAKE all ingredients with ice and fine strain into chilled glass.

2	shots	Raspberry flavoured vodka
½	shot	Chambord black raspberry liqueur
2	shots	Drambuie

We say: A cocktail that tastes like its namesake.
Origin: Created by Ian Baldwin at GE Club, London, England.

TRIFLE'TINI

Glass: Martini
Garnish: Crumbled Cadbury's Flake bar
Method: MUDDLE raspberries and strawberries in base of shaker. Add next four ingredients, SHAKE with ice and fine strain into chilled glass. Lightly WHIP cream and FLOAT over drink.

10	fresh	Raspberries
2	fresh	Strawberries (hulled)
2	shots	Cognac VSOP
¾	shot	Amaretto liqueur
½	shot	Crème de fraise du bois liqueur
1	shot	Pedro Ximénez sherry
1½	shots	Double (heavy) cream

We say: Very rich - looks and taste like a trifle.
Origin: Created in 2000 by Ian Baldwin at the GE Club, London, England.

TRILBY #1

Glass: Martini
Garnish: Orange zest twist
Method: STIR all ingredients with ice and strain into chilled glass.

1	shot	Dewar's White label Scotch
⅛	shot	Absinthe
1	shot	Parfait Amour liqueur
1	shot	Martini Rosso sweet vermouth
¾	shot	Chilled mineral water
2	dashes	Orange bitters

We say: An aromatic old classic of unknown origin.

TRILBY #2

Glass: Martini
Garnish: Lemon zest twist
Method: STIR all ingredients with ice and strain into chilled glass.

3	shots	Martini Extra Dry vermouth
¼	shot	Triple Sec
1	dash	Peychaud's aromatic bitters
½	shot	Dewar's White label Scotch

We say: Salmon pink in colour and distinctly different in style. One of those drinks you just have to try.

TRINITY

Glass: Martini
Garnish: Orange zest twist (discarded) & maraschino cherry
Method: STIR all ingredients with ice and strain into chilled glass.

2½	shots	Dewar's White label Scotch
¼	shot	De Kuyper Apricot Brandy liqueur
1	shot	Martini Extra Dry vermouth
¼	shot	Giffard Menthe Pastille liqueur
1	dash	Orange bitters

We say: A Dry Manhattan based on Scotch with a dash of apricot liqueur and a touch of crème de menthe.
Origin: Recipe purloined from David Embury's classic book, 'The Fine Art of Mixing Drinks'.

TRIPLE 'C' MARTINI

Glass: Martini
Garnish: Chocolate powder rim
Method: SHAKE all ingredients with ice and fine strain into chilled glass.

2	shots	Vanilla-infused Ketel One vodka
1	shot	Dark Crème de Cacao
1¼	shots	Ocean Spray cranberry juice

We say: Rich vanilla, dark chocolate and cranberry juice.
Origin: We created this drink and originally called it the Chocolate Covered Cranberry Martini.

TRIPLE ORANGE UPDATED

Glass: Martini
Garnish: Orange zest twist
Method: SHAKE all ingredients with ice and fine strain into chilled glass.

1	shot	Ketel One vodka
1	shot	Grand Marnier liqueur
¼	shot	Campari Bitter
1½	shots	Freshly squeezed orange juice
½	fresh	Egg white

We say: This aperitif cocktail has a trio of orange flavours with the bitter orange of Campari adding character and balance.
Origin: Created in 1998 by Simon Difford.

TRIPLEBERRY

★★★★☆

Glass: Martini
Garnish: Seasonal berries
Method: MUDDLE raspberries in base of shaker. Add other ingredients, SHAKE with ice and fine strain into chilled glass.

7	fresh	Raspberries
2	shots	Ketel One vodka
½	shot	Crème de fraise du bois liqueur
¼	shot	Shiraz red wine
½	shot	Crème de cassis liqueur

We say: Rich berry fruit fortified with vodka and tamed by the tannins from a splash of red wine.
Origin: Created in 2006 by Simon Difford.

TROPIC

★★★★☆

Glass: Collins
Garnish: Lemon slice
Method: SHAKE all ingredients with ice and strain into ice-filled glass.

1	shot	Bénédictine D.O.M.
2	shots	Sauvignon blanc wine
2	shots	Freshly squeezed grapefruit juice
½	shot	Freshly squeezed lemon juice

We say: A light, satisfying cooler.
Origin: Based on a recipe believed to date back to the 1950s.

TROPIC THUNDER NEW

★★★★☆

Glass: Coupette
Garnish: Dust with freshly ground black pepper
Method: SHAKE all ingredients with ice and fine strain into chilled glass.

1½	shots	Tanqueray London dry gin
¾	shot	Crème de pêche de vigne liqueur
½	shot	Freshly squeezed lemon juice
1	shot	Fresh pressed pineapple juice

We say: Gin, peach, lemon juice and pineapple juice may not seem the most obvious combination but it's a combo that works.
Origin: Created by Sean Henry at Epernay Champagne Bar, Leeds, England and to quote Sean is "named Tropic Thunder as it aptly describes what to expect on the palate."

TROPICAL BREEZE

★★★☆☆

Glass: Collins
Garnish: Lime wedge
Method: SHAKE all ingredients with ice and strain into ice-filled glass.

1½	shots	Ketel One vodka
1	shot	Passoã passion fruit liqueur
2½	shots	Ocean Spray cranberry juice
1½	shots	Freshly squeezed grapefruit juice

We say: A sweet, fruity Seabreeze.

TROPICAL CAIPIRINHA

★★★★☆

Glass: Old-fashioned
Garnish: Lime wedge
Method: SHAKE all ingredient with ice and strain into glass filled crushed ice.

1	shot	Leblon cachaça
1	shot	Malibu coconut rum liqueur
1	shot	Fresh pressed pineapple juice
1	shot	Freshly squeezed lime juice
¼	shot	Monin Pure Cane 2:1 sugar syrup

We say: In drink circles, tropical usually spells sweet. This drink has a tropical flavour but a definite adult sourness.
Origin: Created by Simon Difford in 2003.

TROPICAL DAIQUIRI

★★★★☆

Glass: Martini
Garnish: Pineapple wedge
Method: SHAKE all ingredients with ice and fine strain into chilled glass.

2	shots	Gosling's Black Seal rum
¼	shot	Pomegranate (grenadine) syrup
1	shot	Fresh pressed pineapple juice
½	shot	Freshly squeezed lime juice

We say: A seriously tangy Daiquiri.
Origin: Adapted from a recipe in David Embury's classic book 'The Fine Art of Mixing Drinks'.

TULIP COCKTAIL

★★★★☆

Glass: Martini
Garnish: Lemon zest twist
Method: SHAKE all ingredients with ice and fine strain into chilled glass.

1	shot	Calvados/Applejack brandy
½	shot	De Kuyper Apricot Brandy liqueur
1	shot	Martini Rosso sweet vermouth
½	shot	Freshly squeezed lemon juice
½	shot	Chilled mineral water

We say: Rich but balanced with bags of fruit: apple, apricot and lemon.
Origin: Adapted from a recipe in Harry Craddock's 1930 'Savoy Cocktail Book'.

TURF MARTINI

★★★★☆

Glass: Martini
Garnish: Orange zest twist
Method: SHAKE all ingredients with ice and fine strain into chilled glass.

1½	shots	Tanqueray London dry gin
1½	shots	Martini Rosso sweet vermouth
⅛	shot	Luxardo Maraschino liqueur
⅛	shot	Absinthe
2	dashes	Orange bitters

We say: Old-school, full flavoured, aromatic and dry.
Origin: Created before 1900 at the Ritz Hotel, Paris, France.

TURKISH COFFEE MARTINI

★★★★☆

Glass: Martini
Garnish: Coffee beans
Method: MUDDLE cardamom pods in base of shaker. Add other ingredients, SHAKE with ice and fine strain into chilled glass.

8	whole	Cardamom pods
2	shots	Ketel One vodka
2	shots	Hot espresso coffee
½	shot	Monin Pure Cane 2:1 sugar syrup

We say: Coffee is often made with cardomom in Arab countries. This drinks harnesses the aromatic, eucalyptus, citrus flavour of cardomom coffee and adds a little vodka zing.
Origin: Created this in 2003 by Simon Difford.

TURKISH DELIGHT MARTINI

★★★★☆

Glass: Martini
Garnish: Turkish Delight
Method: STIR honey and vodka in base of shaker until honey dissolves. Add other ingredients, SHAKE with ice and fine strain into chilled glass.

2	spoons	Runny honey
1	shot	Ketel One vodka
1	shot	Vanilla-infused Ketel One vodka
½	shot	White Crème de Cacao
⅛	shot	Rose water
¾	shot	Chilled mineral water
½	fresh	Egg white

We say: Rosewater, honey, chocolate and vanilla provide a distinct flavour of Turkish Delight - fortified with vodka.
Origin: Created in 2003 by Simon Difford.

TURQUOISE DAIQUIRI

★★★½☆

Glass: Martini
Garnish: Lime wedge
Method: SHAKE all ingredients with ice and fine strain into chilled glass.

1½	shots	Bacardi Superior rum
½	shot	Triple Sec
½	shot	Bols Blue Curaçao liqueur
¾	shot	Freshly squeezed lime juice
1	shot	Fresh pressed pineapple juice

We say: A blue-rinsed Daiquiri with orange and pineapple - with tequila instead of rum it would be a twisted Margarita.

TUSCAN MULE

★★★★½☆

Glass: Collins
Garnish: Lime wedge
Method: SHAKE first two ingredients with ice and strain into ice-filled glass. TOP with ginger beer, lightly stir and serve with straws.

2	shots	Tuaca liqueur
¾	shot	Freshly squeezed lime juice
Top up with		Ginger beer

We say: A spicy long drink smoothed with vanilla.
Origin: Adapted from a drink created in 2003 by Sammy Berry, Brighton, England.

TUTTI FRUTTI

★★★☆☆

Glass: Collins
Garnish: Lime wedge
Method: SHAKE all ingredients with ice and strain into ice-filled glass.

1	shot	Tequila 100% Agave
1	shot	Midori green melon liqueur
1	shot	Passoã passion fruit liqueur
3	shots	Ocean Spray cranberry juice

We say: A berry drink with a tropical tinge.

TUXEDO COCKTAIL UPDATED

★★★★½

Glass: Martini
Garnish: Lemon zest twist & maraschino cherry
Method: STIR all ingredients with ice and fine strain into chilled glass.

1¾	shots	Old Tom gin
1¾	shots	Martini Extra dry vermouth
3	dashes	Orange bitters
1	dash	La Fée Parisienne (68%) absinthe
⅛	shot	Luxardo maraschino liqueur

We say: Equal pars old tom gin and vermouth flavoured with the merest hint of maraschino, absinthe and orange bitters.
Origin: Recipe adapted from Harry Johnson's 'Bartenders' Manual' first published in 1882. The drink was not created at the Tuxedo Club as is often suspected as this did not open until 1886. The Tuxedo Club is a private member-owned country club near the village of Tuxedo Park, Orange County, New York State.

While the club can't claim to have created this cocktail, it is credited with being the birthplace of the tuxedo jacket - well at least where its American name originated. The origins of black tie dinner dress dates from 1860, when Henry Poole & Co. of London's Savile Row made a short smoking jacket for the Prince of Wales (later Edward VII) as an informal alternative to white tie dress, then the standard formal wear.

In the spring of 1886, the Prince invited James Potter, a rich New Yorker to Sandringham. When Potter sort the Prince's advice on dinner dress, he sent Potter to his tailor's, Henry Poole. Back in New York Potter wore his newly acquired dinner suit at the Tuxedo Park Club which had recently opened. Other members of the club copied him and so the tailless dinner jacket acquired the club's name.

TVR

★★★☆☆

Glass: Collins
Garnish: Lime wedge
Method: POUR ingredients into ice-filled glass. Lightly stir and serve with straws.

1	shot	Tequila 100% Agave
1	shot	Ketel One vodka
Top up with		Red Bull

Variant: Served as a shot.
We say: Very much 'driven' by the flavour of Red Bull. Use an anejo tequila to balance the initial sweetness on the palate.
Origin: A 90s drink named after its ingredients (tequila, vodka, Red Bull), and which is also the name of a British sports car.

TWENTIETH CENTURY MARTINI

★★★½☆

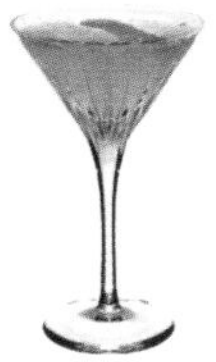

Glass: Martini
Garnish: Lemon zest twist
Method: SHAKE all ingredients with ice and fine strain into chilled glass.

1½	**shots**	**Tanqueray London dry gin**
½	**shot**	**White Crème de Cacao**
¾	**shot**	**Martini Extra Dry vermouth**
½	**shot**	**Freshly squeezed lemon juice**

We say: Chocolate and lemon juice. 21st century tastes have definitely moved on.
Origin: Thought to have been created in 1939 by one C.A. Tuck and named after the express train that travelled between New York City and Chicago.

TWINKLE

★★★★½

Glass: Martini
Garnish: Lemon zest twist
Method: SHAKE first two ingredients with ice and fine strain into chilled glass. TOP with Prosecco (or champagne).

3	**shots**	**Ketel One vodka**
¾	**shot**	**St~Germain elderflower liqueur**
Top up with		**Brut champagne**

We say: Its hard to believe this floral, dry, golden tipple contains three whole shots of vodka.
Origin: Created in 2002 by Tony Conigliaro at The Lonsdale, London, England.

TWISTED SOBRIETY

★★★★☆

Glass: Flute
Garnish: None
Method: SHAKE first two ingredients with ice and fine strain into chilled glass. TOP with champagne.

1	**shot**	**Cognac VSOP**
1	**shot**	**Poire William eau de vie**
Top up with		**Brut champagne**

We say: Fortified champagne with a hint of pear.

TWO 'T' FRUITY

★★★★☆

Glass: Martini
Garnish: Tooty Frooties
Method: SHAKE all ingredients with ice and fine strain into chilled glass.

2½	**shots**	**Ketel One vodka**
3	**dashes**	**Orange bitters**
¾	**shot**	**Passion fruit syrup**

We say: Simple is beautiful - this drink is both. The rawness of vodka is balanced with sweet passion fruit and hints of orange bitters.
Origin: Created in 2002 at Hush, London, England.

TWO-ONE-TWO (212)

★★★½☆

Glass: Collins
Garnish: Grapefruit zest twist
Method: SHAKE all ingredients with ice and fine strain into chilled glass.

2	**shots**	**Ruby grapefruit juice**
1	**shot**	**Aperol**
2	**shots**	**Tequila 100% Agave**

We say: Earthy taste with freshness coming fro the grapefruit.
Origin: Created in 2008 by Willy Shine at Contemporary Cocktails Inc. in New York City. The name is a reference to NYC's 212 area code as well as the ounces in the recipe. Willy is also the Partida Tequila Ambassador for NYC so I should point out that this is the brand originally called for in his recipe.

TYPHOON

★★★☆☆

Glass: Old-fashioned
Garnish: None
Method: STIR all ingredients with ice and strain into ice-filled glass.

1¾	**shots**	**Tanqueray London dry gin**
½	**shot**	**Luxardo Sambuca dei Cesari**
½	**shot**	**Rose's lime cordial**

We say: Great if you love Sambuca.

U.S. MARTINI

★★★★★

Glass: Martini
Garnish: Vanilla pod
Method: SHAKE all ingredients with ice and fine strain into chilled glass.

1½	**shots**	**Vanilla-infused Courvoisier cognac**
1¼	**shots**	**Sauvignon blanc wine**
1½	**shots**	**Fresh pressed pineapple juice**
¼	**shot**	**Monin Pure Cane 2:1 sugar syrup**

We say: A relatively dry cocktail where the vanilla combines beautifully with the cognac and the acidity of the wine balances the sweetness of the pineapple juice.
Origin: Adapted from the Palermo cocktail discovered in 2001 at Hotel du Vin, Bristol, England. I created this drink in 2003 and named it after the grape varieties Ugni and Sauvignon. Ugni Blanc is the most common grape in Cognac, and Sauvignon Blanc is the grape used in the wine.

UGURUNDU

★★★½☆

Glass: Shot
Garnish: None
Method: Lightly MUDDLE mint in base of shaker (just to bruise). Add other ingredients, SHAKE with ice and fine strain into chilled glass.

3	**fresh**	**Mint leaves**
½	**shot**	**Cranberry flavoured vodka**
½	**shot**	**Rose's lime cordial**

We say: Fresh tasting and all too easy to knock back.
Origin: Created by Peter Kubista at Bugsy's Bar, Prague, Czech Republic.

UMBONGO

★★★☆☆

Glass: Collins
Garnish: Orange slice
Method: Cut passion fruit in half and scoop out flesh into shaker. Add next three ingredients, SHAKE with ice and fine strain into ice-filled glass. TOP with ginger ale.

1	fresh	Passion fruit
1	shot	Ketel One vodka
1	shot	Passoã passion fruit liqueur
1	shot	Freshly squeezed orange juice
Top up with		Ginger ale

We say: Pleasant, light and medium sweet tropical-style drink.

UNCLE VANYA

★★★★☆

Glass: Martini
Garnish: Lime wedge
Method: SHAKE all ingredients with ice and fine strain into chilled glass.

1¾	shots	Ketel One Vodka
1	shot	Crème de Mûre liqueur
1	shot	Freshly squeezed lime juice
½	shot	Monin Pure Cane 2:1 sugar syrup
½	fresh	Egg white

We say: Simple but great - smooth, sweet 'n' sour blackberry, although possibly a tad on the sweet side for some.
Origin: Named after Anton Chekhov's greatest play - a cheery tale of envy and despair. A popular drink in Britain's TGI Friday bars, its origins are unknown.

UNICAR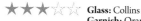

★★★★☆

Glass: Coupette
Garnish: Orange zest twist
Method: SHAKE all ingredients with ice and fine strain into chilled glass.

2½	shots	Cognac VSOP
¾	shot	Freshly squeezed lemon juice
½	shot	Monin Pure Cane 2:1 sugar syrup

We say: A miss-made but fabulously balanced Sidecar inspired this drink.
Origin: Inspired by a drink discovered in May 2010 at Babel Bar, Hotel du Rome, Berlin, Germany. Named after a combination of 'Sidecar' and 'Ugni-blanc', the grape from which cognac is most commonly made.

UNION CLUB

★★★★☆

Glass: Martini
Garnish: Orange zest twist
Method: SHAKE all ingredients with ice and fine strain into chilled glass.

2	shots	Maker's Mark bourbon
¼	shot	Triple Sec
½	shot	Freshly squeezed lime juice
⅛	shot	Monin Almond (orgeat) syrup
⅛	shot	Pomegranate (grenadine) syrup
½	fresh	Egg white

We say: Balanced sweet and sour with bourbon to the fore.
Origin: Adapted from a recipe purloined from David Embury's classic book, 'The Fine Art of Mixing Drinks'.

UNION CLUB COCKTAIL

★★★★☆

Glass: Coupette
Garnish: Orange zest twist
Method: SHAKE all ingredients with ice and fine strain into chilled glass.

2	shots	Maker's Mark bourbon
½	shot	Luxardo Maraschino liqueur
½	shot	Campari Bitter
1½	shots	Freshly squeezed orange juice

We say: Maraschino and Campari balance perfectly. Fruity yet dry and complex.
Origin: Created in 2008 by Jamie Boudreau at Tini Bigs, Seattle, USA and named after a gambling joint Wyatt Earp opened in Seattle in 1899.

UNIVERSAL SHOT

★★★☆☆

Glass: Shot
Garnish: None
Method: Refrigerate ingredients then LAYER in chilled glass by carefully pouring in the order listed.

½	shot	Midori green melon liqueur
½	shot	Freshly squeezed grapefruit juice
½	shot	Ketel One vodka

We say: Sweet melon liqueur toned down by grapefruit and fortified by vodka.

UNUSUAL NEGRONI COCKTAIL NEW

★★★☆☆

Glass: Old-fashioned
Garnish: Orange zest twist
Method: STIR all ingredients with ice and strain into ice filled glass.

1	shot	Tanqueray London dry gin
1	shot	Aperol
1	shot	Lillet Blanc

We say: A very soft rendition of a classic Negroni.
Origin: Adapted from a drink created in 2011 by Charlotte Voisey, USA.

UP IN THE AIR NEW

★★★★☆

Glass: Coupette
Garnish: Lemon slice
Method: SHAKE all ingredients with ice and fine strain into chilled glass.

2	shots	Ketel One vodka
½	shot	Pressed apple juice
½	shot	Freshly squeezed lemon juice
¼	shot	Monin Almond (orgeat) syrup

We say: Apple, almond and lemon juice fortified with vodka in this richly flavoured sweet and sour cocktail.
Origin: Adapted from a drink discovered in 2011 at the Chapel Bar, Berlin, Germany.

UPSIDE-DOWN RASPBERRY CHEESCAKE

★★★★☆

Glass: Martini
Garnish: Crumbled Digestive biscuit
Method: First Layer: MUDDLE raspberries in base of shaker. Add Chambord, SHAKE with ice and fine strain into centre of glass. Second Layer: Grate lemon zest into shaker. Add rest of ingredients, SHAKE all ingredients with ice and strain into glass over spoon so as to LAYER over raspberry base.

First Layer:
4	fresh	Raspberries
½	shot	Chambord black raspberry liqueur

Second Layer:
½	fresh	Lemon zest twist
2	shots	Vanilla-infused Ketel One vodka
½	shot	Vanilla schnapps
½	shot	Monin Pure Cane 2:1 sugar syrup
5	spoon	Mascarpone cheese
1	shot	Double (heavy) cream

We say: Surprisingly, the biscuity top continues to float as you sip the vanilla cream layer right down to the point when you hit the raspberry base.
Origin: I created this in 2003 after adapting Wayne Collins' original cheesecake recipe.

URBAN HOLISTIC

★★★☆☆

Glass: Martini
Garnish: Lemon zest twist
Method: SHAKE first two ingredients with ice and fine strain into chilled glass. TOP with ginger ale.

2	shots	Sake
1	shot	Martini Extra Dry vermouth
Top up with		Ginger ale

We say: East meets West in this dry refreshing cocktail.
Origin: Adapted from a drink discovered in 2005 at Mo Bar, Landmark Mandarin Oriental Hotel, Hong Kong..

URBAN OASIS

★★★☆☆

Glass: Martini
Garnish: Orange zest twist
Method: SHAKE all ingredients with ice and fine strain into chilled glass.

1½	shots	Ketel One Oranje vodka
½	shot	Raspberry flavoured vodka
¼	shot	Chambord black raspberry liqueur
1½	shots	Fresh pressed pineapple juice

We say: Alcoholic orange and raspberry sherbet - how bad is that? A crowd pleasing drink.
Origin: Discovered in 2003 at Paramount Hotel, New York City, USA.

UTTERLY BUTTERLY

★★★☆☆

Glass: Collins
Garnish: Apple wedge
Method: STIR peanut butter with vodka in base of shaker. Add other ingredients, SHAKE with ice and fine strain into ice-filled glass.

1	spoon	Smooth peanut butter
2	shots	Ketel One vodka
¼	shot	Goldschläger cinnamon schnapps
½	shot	Malibu coconut rum liqueur
1½	shots	Pressed apple juice
1½	shots	Fresh pressed pineapple juice
¾	shot	Freshly squeezed lime juice

We say: Yup, your eyes are not deceiving you and nor will your taste buds - it's made with peanut butter. Refreshingly different.

VACATION

★★★☆☆

Glass: Martini
Garnish: Orange slice
Method: SHAKE first five ingredients with ice and fine strain into chilled glass. Then POUR your favoured final liqueur into the centre of the drink. It should sink.

2	shots	Vanilla-infused Ketel One vodka
½	shot	Malibu coconut rum liqueur
½	shot	Freshly squeezed lime juice
1	shot	Fresh pressed pineapple juice
¼	fresh	Egg white
¼	shot	Chambord black raspberry liqueur

Variant: This drink can be finished with your choice of three different coloured and flavoured liqueurs. Substitute blue curaçao (blue) for either Midori (green) or Chambord (red).
We say: A great looking, fairly sweet cocktail with hints of vanilla, coconut and pineapple.
Origin: My adaptation (in 2003) of the signature drink at the Merc Bar, New York City, USA.

VALENCIA COCKTAIL NO. 2

★★★★☆

Glass: Flute
Garnish: Orange zest twist
Method: POUR first three ingredients into chilled glass. TOP with champagne.

½	shot	De Kuyper Apricot Brandy liqueur
¼	shot	Freshly squeezed orange juice
4	dashes	Orange bitters
Top up with		Brut champagne

Variant: Also served as a Martini with gin in place of champagne.
We say: Floral and fruity - makes Bucks Fizz look a tad sad.
Origin: Adapted from the Valencia Cocktail No. 2 in *The Savoy Cocktail Book*.

VALENCIA MARTINI

★★★★½☆

Glass: Martini
Garnish: Orange zest twist
Method: STIR all ingredients with ice and strain into chilled glass.

| 2½ | shots | Tanqueray London dry gin |
| ½ | shot | Tio Pepe fino sherry |

AKA: Spanish Martini
Variant: Flame of Love Martini
We say: A Martini-style drink but using fino sherry instead of vermouth. Crisp and dry.

VALENTINO

★★★★☆

Glass: Martini
Garnish: Lemon zest twist
Method: STIR all ingredients with ice and strain into a chilled glass.

2	shots	Tanqueray London dry gin
½	shot	Campari Bitter
1	shot	Martini Rosso sweet vermouth

We say: A variation on the Negroni. More gin and less Campari, make for an unusual bittersweet Martini.

VALKYRIE

★★★½☆

Glass: Old-fashioned
Garnish: Lemon zest twist
Method: SHAKE all ingredients with ice and strain into glass filled with crushed ice. Serve with straws.

2	shots	Vanilla-infused Ketel One vodka
½	shot	Freshly squeezed lemon juice
½	shot	Monin Vanilla sugar syrup

We say: This sipping drink has a rich vanilla sweet 'n' sour flavour.
Origin: Created in 2003 by Simon Difford. The name comes from Norse mythology and literally translates as 'chooser of the slain'.

VAMPIRO

★★★★☆

Glass: Old-fashioned
Garnish: Lime wedge
Method: SHAKE all ingredients with ice and strain into ice-filled glass.

2	shots	Tequila 100% Agave
1	shot	Tomato juice
1	shot	Freshly squeezed orange juice
½	shot	Freshly squeezed lime juice
½	shot	Pomegranate (grenadine) syrup
7	drops	Tabasco hot pepper sauce
1	pinch	Salt
1	grind	Black pepper

We say: Something of a supercharged Bloody Mary with tequila and a hint of sweet grenadine.
Origin: The national drink of Mexico where it's often made with pomegranate juice in place of tomato juice and without the grenadine.

VANCOUVER

★★★½☆

Glass: Martini
Garnish: Lemon zest twist
Method: STIR all ingredients with ice and fine strain into chilled glass.

1½	shots	Tanqueray London dry gin
¾	shot	Martini Rosso sweet vermouth
¼	shot	Bénédictine D.O.M.
1	dash	Orange bitters

We say: A herbal medium dry Martini.

VANDERBILT

★★★★½

Glass: Martini
Garnish: Lemon zest twist
Method: SHAKE all ingredients with ice and fine strain into chilled glass.

2¼	shots	Cognac VSOP
¾	shot	De Kuyper Cherry Brandy liqueur
⅛	shot	Monin Pure Cane 2:1 sugar syrup (2:1)
2	dashes	Angostura aromatic bitters

We say: Tangy, rich cherry and hints of vanilla fortified with brandy.
Origin: Adapted from a recipe in Harry Craddock's 1930 'Savoy Cocktail Book'.

VANILLA & GRAPEFRUIT DAIQUIRI

★★★★½

Glass: Martini
Garnish: Grapefruit zest twist (discarded) & vanilla pod
Method: SHAKE all ingredients with ice and fine strain into chilled glass.

2½	shots	Vanilla-infused Bacardi rum
½	shot	Freshly squeezed lime juice
½	shot	Monin Pure Cane 2:1 sugar syrup
1	shot	Freshly squeezed grapefruit juice

We say: Reminiscent of a Hemingway Special, this flavoursome, vanilla laced Daiquiri has a wonderfully tangy bittersweet finish.
Origin: Created in 2003 by Simon Difford.

VANILLA & RASPBERRY MARTINI

★★★★☆

Glass: Martini
Garnish: Raspberries
Method: MUDDLE raspberries in base of shaker. Add other ingredients, SHAKE with ice and fine strain into chilled glass.

12	fresh	Raspberries
2	shots	Vanilla-infused Ketel One vodka
¼	shot	Shiraz red wine
¼	shot	Monin Pure Cane 2:1 sugar syrup
½	shot	Chilled mineral water

We say: Exactly that - vanilla and raspberries.
Origin: Created in 2006 by Simon Difford.

VANILLA DAIQUIRI UPDATED

★★★★⯪ **Glass:** Martini
Garnish: Lime wedge
Method: SHAKE all ingredients with ice and fine strain into chilled glass.

2	shots	Vanilla-infused Bacardi rum
½	shot	Freshly squeezed lime juice
¼	shot	Monin Pure Cane 2:1 sugar syrup
¾	shot	Chilled mineral water

We say: The classic 'Natural Daiquiri' with a hint of vanilla.

VANILLA LAIKA

★★★⯪☆ **Glass:** Collins
Garnish: Seasonal berries
Method: SHAKE all ingredients with ice and strain into glass filled with crushed ice.

1½	shots	Vanilla-infused Ketel One vodka
¾	shot	Crème de Mûre liqueur
¼	shot	Freshly squeezed lemon juice
¾	shot	Monin Pure Cane 2:1 sugar syrup
4	shots	Pressed apple juice

We say: Vanilla berry fruit in a tall, refreshing drink.
Origin: Created by Jake Burger in 2002 at Townhouse, Leeds, England. Laika was a Russian dog and the first canine in space.

VANILLA MARGARITA

★★★★☆ **Glass:** Old-fashioned
Garnish: Lime wedge
Method: SHAKE all ingredients with ice and fine strain into ice-filled chilled glass.

2	shots	Vanilla-infused tequila
1	shot	Triple Sec
1	shot	Freshly squeezed lemon juice

We say: A classic Margarita with a hint of vanilla.
Origin: I first discovered this drink in 1998 at Café Pacifico, London, England.

VANILLA SENSATION

★★★★☆ **Glass:** Martini
Garnish: Apple slice
Method: SHAKE all ingredients with ice and fine strain into chilled glass.

2	shots	Vanilla-infused Ketel One vodka
1	shot	Sour apple liqueur
½	shot	Martini Extra Dry vermouth

We say: A pleasing vanilla twist on an Apple Martini.
Origin: Created in 2003 but by whom is unknown.

VANILLA VODKA SOUR

★★★★☆ **Glass:** Flute
Garnish: Lemon & orange zest twists
Method: SHAKE all ingredients with ice and fine strain into chilled glass.

2	shots	Vanilla-infused Ketel One vodka
¾	shot	Cuarenta y Tres (Licor 43) liqueur
¾	shot	Freshly squeezed lemon juice
½	fresh	Egg white

We say: A Vodka Sour with a blast of spicy vanilla.

VANILLA'TINI

★★★⯪☆ **Glass:** Martini
Garnish: Half vanilla pod
Method: STIR all ingredients with ice and strain into chilled glass.

2½	shots	Vanilla-infused Ketel One vodka
½	shot	Hazelnut liqueur
1½	shots	Lemonade/Sprite/7-Up

We say: Vanilla, hazelnut and a hint of creamy citrus.
Origin: Discovered in 2003 at Paramount Hotel, New York City, USA.

VANITINI

★★★⯪☆ **Glass:** Martini
Garnish: Pineapple wedge
Method: SHAKE all ingredients with ice and fine strain into chilled glass.

2	shots	Vanilla-infused Ketel One vodka
2	shots	Sauvignon blanc wine
¾	shot	Sour pineapple liqueur
¼	shot	Crème de Mûre liqueur

We say: Vanilla and pineapple dried by the acidity of the wine, and sweetened and flavoured by blackberry liqueur.

VANTE MARTINI

★★★★⯪ **Glass:** Martini
Garnish: Orange zest twist
Method: MUDDLE cardamom in base of shaker. Add other ingredients, SHAKE with ice and fine strain into chilled glass.

4	fresh	Cardamom pods
1½	shots	Vanilla-infused Ketel One vodka
1½	shots	Sauvignon blanc wine
1	shot	Cuarenta y Tres (Licor 43) liqueur
¼	shot	Fresh pressed pineapple juice

We say: Bold, aromatic and complex flavours.
Origin: Created in 2003 by Simon Difford.

VAVAVOOM

★★★★☆

Glass: Flute
Garnish: None
Method: POUR ingredients into chilled glass. TOP with champagne.

½	shot	Triple Sec
½	shot	Freshly squeezed lemon juice
½	shot	Monin Pure Cane 2:1 sugar syrup
Top up with		Brut champagne

We say: This drink does indeed give champagne that vavavoom.
Origin: Adapted from a drink created in 2002 by Yannick Misieriaux at The Fifth Floor Bar, Harvey Nichols, London, England, and named after the Renault television advertisements.

VELVET ELVIS

★★★½☆

Glass: Old-fashioned
Garnish: Lime wedge
Method: SHAKE first three ingredients with ice and strain into ice-filled glass. TOP with lemon-lime soda.

1½	shots	Jack Daniel's Tennessee whiskey
1	shot	Chambord black raspberry liqueur
½	shot	Freshly squeezed lime juice
Top up with		Lemonade/Sprite/7-Up

We say: The merest bit on the sweet side, fruity with a hint of whiskey.

VELVET FOG

★★★★½

Glass: Martini
Garnish: Orange zest twist (discarded) & dust with grated nutmeg
Method: SHAKE all ingredients with ice and fine strain into chilled glass.

1½	shots	Ketel One vodka
¾	shot	Taylor's Velvet Falernum liqueur
1¼	shots	Freshly squeezed lime juice
¾	shot	Freshly squeezed orange juice
2	dashes	Angostura aromatic bitters

We say: Tangy, fresh and bittersweet.
Origin: Created by Dale DeGroff, New York City, USA.

VELVET HAMMER

★★★½☆

Glass: Martini
Garnish: Dust with grated nutmeg
Method: SHAKE all ingredients with ice and fine strain into chilled glass.

1	shot	Ketel One vodka
¾	shot	Triple Sec
¾	shot	White Crème de Cacao
¾	shot	Double (heavy) cream
¾	shot	Milk
¼	shot	Pomegranate (grenadine) syrup

Variant: With apricot brandy and coffee liqueur in place of cacao and grenadine.
We say: Lots of velvet with a little bit of hammer courtesy of a shot of vodka.

VELVET THREESOME

★★★★½

Glass: Coupette
Garnish: Orange zest twist
Method: STIR all ingredients with ice and fine strain into chilled glass.

¾	shot	Calvados/Applejack brandy
¾	shot	Cognac VSOP
¾	shot	Macchu pisco
½	shot	Cuarenta y Tres (Licor 43) liqueur
¼	shot	Martini Extra Dry vermouth

We say: A trio of brandies with a dash of herbal vanilla, rounded with vermouth.
Origin: Created in 2010 by Simon Difford at the Cabinet Room, London, England.

VENETIAN UPDATED

★★★★☆

Glass: Old-fashioned
Garnish: Orange zest twist (discarded)
Method: STIR all ingredients with ice and fine strain into ice filled glass.

2	shots	Aperol
2	shots	Sauvignon blanc wine
1	spoon	Cartron No. 7
1	spoon	Elderflower cordial
1	spoon	Picon Biere

We say: Burnished copper red and bitter sweet with Aperol, wine and a dash of elderflower, fruit liqueur and bitters.
Origin: Created in 2009 by Rich Hunt at Quo Vadis, London, England. It is based on the flavours of the spritz, but there are no bubbles of any kind.

VENETO

★★★½☆

Glass: Martini
Garnish: Lemon zest twist
Method: SHAKE all ingredients with ice and fine strain into chilled glass.

2	shots	Cognac VSOP
½	shot	Luxardo Sambuca dei Cesari
½	shot	Freshly squeezed lemon juice
⅛	shot	Monin Pure Cane 2:1 sugar syrup
½	shot	Egg white

We say: A serious, Stinger-like drink.

VENUS IN FURS

★★★½☆

Glass: Collins
Garnish: Seasonal berries & lemon slice
Method: SHAKE all ingredients with ice and strain into ice-filled glass.

1	shot	Raspberry flavoured vodka
1	shot	Ketel One Citroen vodka
3½	shots	Pressed apple juice
3	dashes	Angostura aromatic bitters

We say: Juicy flavours with a hint of spice make for a refreshing, quaffable drink.
Origin: A cocktail which emerged in London's bars early in 2002.

VENUS MARTINI

★★★★☆

Glass: Martini
Garnish: Raspberries
Method: MUDDLE raspberries in base of shaker. Add other ingredients, SHAKE with ice and fine strain into chilled glass.

7	fresh	Raspberries
2	shots	Tanqueray London dry gin
1	shot	Triple Sec
¼	shot	Monin Pure Cane 2:1 sugar syrup
3	dashes	Peychaud's aromatic bitters

We say: Raspberry with hints of bitter orange and gin - surprisingly dry.

VERDANT MARTINI

★★★★☆

Glass: Martini
Garnish: Mint leaf
Method: SHAKE all ingredients with ice and fine strain into chilled glass.

2	shots	Żubrówka bison vodka
⅛	shot	Chartreuse Green liqueur
2	shots	Pressed apple juice
½	shot	Freshly squeezed lime juice

We say: A herbal apple pie of a drink.
Origin: This drink was created in 2003 and named after the hue of its ingredients.

VERDI MARTINI

★★★★☆

Glass: Martini
Garnish: Pineapple wedge
Method: SHAKE all ingredients with ice and fine strain into chilled glass.

1¾	shots	Ketel One vodka
½	shot	Midori green melon liqueur
½	shot	Peachtree peach schnapps
1	shot	Fresh pressed pineapple juice
1	shot	Pressed apple juice
¼	shot	Freshly squeezed lime juice

We say: A melange of fruits combine in a gluggable short drink.
Origin: Adapted from a drink discovered in 2002 at the Fifth Floor Bar, Harvey Nichols, London, England.

VERT'ICAL BREEZE

★★★★☆

Glass: Collins
Garnish: Lemon wedge
Method: SHAKE all ingredients with ice and strain into ice-filled glass.

1½	shots	Absinthe
3	shots	Ocean Spray cranberry juice
3	shots	Freshly squeezed grapefruit juice

We say: For those who don't speak French, 'vert' means green - the colour of absinthe. Vertical suggests take-off - try it and see.

VERY RUSTY DAIQUIRI

★★★★☆

Glass: Coupette
Garnish: Lime wedge
Method: SHAKE all ingredients with ice and fine strain into chilled glass.

2	shots	Bacardi 8yo aged rum
½	shot	Drambuie
½	shot	Freshly squeezed lime juice

We say: Honey and spice notes from Drambuie add interest to this 'aged daiquiri'.
Origin: Created in December 2010 by Simon Difford at the Cabinet Room, London, England.

VESPER DRY MARTINI

★★★★★

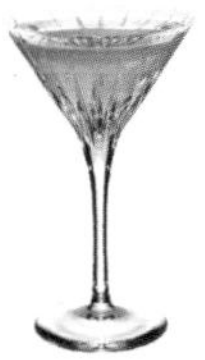

Glass: Martini
Garnish: Lemon zest twist
Method: SHAKE all ingredients with ice and fine strain into chilled glass.

3	shots	Tanqueray London dry gin
1	shot	Ketel One vodka
½	shot	Lillet Blanc

We say: Many bartenders advocate that a Martini should be stirred and not shaken, some citing the ridiculous argument that shaking will "bruise the gin." If you like your Martinis shaken (as I do) then avoid the possible look of distaste from your server and order a Vesper. This Martini is always shaken, an action that aerates the drink, and makes it colder and more dilute than simply stirring. It also gives the drink a slightly clouded appearance and can leave small shards of ice on the surface of the drink. This is easily prevented by the use of a fine strainer when pouring.

Origin: This variation on the Dry Martini is said to have been created by Gilberto Preti at Duke's Hotel, London, for the author Ian Fleming. He liked it so much that he included it in his first James Bond novel, '*Casino Royale*', published in 1953.

In chapter seven Bond explains to a Casino bartender exactly how to make and serve the drink: "In a deep champagne goblet. Three measures of Gordon's, one of vodka, half a measure of Kina Lillet [now called Lillet Blanc]. Shake it very well until it's ice-cold, then add a large slice of lemon peel."

When made, 007 compliments the bartender, but tells him it would be better made with a grain-based vodka. He also explains his Martini to Felix Leiter, the CIA man, saying, "This drink's my own invention. I'm going to patent it when I can think of a good name."

In chapter eight, Bond meets the beautiful agent Vesper Lynd. She explains why her parents named her Vesper and Bond asks if she'd mind if he called his favourite Martini after her. Like so many of Bond's love interests Vesper turns out to be a double agent and the book closes with his words, "The bitch is dead now.'"

VIAGRA FALLS

★★★½☆

Glass: Martini
Garnish: Orange zest twist
Method: SHAKE all ingredients with ice and fine strain into chilled glass.

¾	shot	Absinthe
1½	shots	Sour apple liqueur
1¾	shots	Chilled mineral water
2	dashes	Orange bitters

We say: Aniseed and apple - sure to get your pecker up.
Origin: Created by Jack Leuwens, London, England.

VICTORIA'S SECRET

★★★☆☆

Glass: Collins
Garnish: Seasonal berries
Method: SHAKE first four ingredients with ice and strain into ice-filled glass. SHAKE other ingredients with ice and carefully strain into glass so this second layer floats on first.

1	shot	Sloe Gin liqueur
½	shot	Bottlegreen Cox's Apple & Plum Cordial
½	shot	Freshly squeezed lemon juice
1	shot	Pressed apple juice
1½	shots	Bacardi Superior rum
½	shot	Boiron mango purée
½	shot	Passion fruit syrup
¾	shot	Freshly squeezed orange juice

We say: Amber and red layer easily in this fruity drink.
Origin: Created in 2008 by Jamie Stephenson at The Bar Academy, Manchester, England.

VICTORIAN LEMONADE

★★★½☆

Glass: Collins
Garnish: Lemon slice
Method: Lightly MUDDLE mint (just to bruise) in base of shaker. Add other ingredients, SHAKE with ice and fine strain into ice-filled glass.

12	fresh	Mint leaves
1½	shots	Tanqueray London dry gin
1	shot	Freshly squeezed lemon juice
¾	shot	Monin Pure Cane 2:1 sugar syrup
2½	shots	Chilled mineral water

We say: Gin laced, mint flavoured, traditional lemonade.

VIEJO MARTINI NEW

★★★★☆

Glass: Martini
Garnish: None
Method: STIR all ingredients with ice and strain into chilled glass.

2½	shots	Ketel One vodka
⅛	shot	Tequila 100% Agave (añejo)
¼	shot	Martini Extra Dry vermouth

We say: A 'Dry Martini' influenced by a hint of aged tequila.
Origin: Created in 2011 by Ian Cameron at the Cabinet Room, London, England.

STAR RATINGS EXPLAINED

★★★★★ Excellent

★★★★½ Recommended   ★★★★☆ Praiseworthy
★★★½☆ Commended   ★★★☆☆ Mediocre
★★½☆☆ Disappointing   ★★☆☆☆ Pretty awful
★½☆☆☆ Shameful   ★☆☆☆☆ Disgusting

VIEUX CARRÉ COCKTAIL

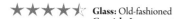

★★★★½

Glass: Old-fashioned
Garnish: Lemon zest twist
Method: STIR all ingredients with ice and strain into ice-filled glass.

1	shot	Maker's Mark bourbon
1	shot	Cognac VSOP
¼	shot	Bénédictine D.O.M.
1	shot	Martini Rosso sweet vermouth
1	dash	Angostura aromatic bitters
1	dash	Peychaud's aromatic bitters

We say: Like an ultra-smooth and complex Sweet Manhattan served on the rocks.
Origin: Created in 1938 by Walter Bergeron, the then head bartender at what is now the Carousel bar at the Monteleone Hotel, New Orleans, USA. Pronounced 'Voo-Ka-Ray', it is named after the French term for New Orlean's French Quarter and literally translates as 'old square'.

VIEUX MOT

★★★☆☆

Glass: Coupette
Garnish: Maraschino cherry
Method: SHAKE all ingredients with ice and fine strain into chilled glass.

1½	shots	Tanqueray London dry gin
¾	shot	St~Germain elderflower liqueur
¾	shot	Freshly squeezed lemon juice
¼	shot	Monin Pure Cane 2:1 sugar syrup

We say: The ingredients combine to taste like lychee. Very fresh.
Origin: Created in 2007 by Don Lee at PDT, New York City, USA.

VIEUX NAVINE NEW

★★★★☆

Glass: Coupette
Garnish: Maraschino cherry
Method: STIR all ingredients with ice and strain into chilled glass.

1	shot	Calvados/Applejack brandy
1	shot	Maker's Mark bourbon
1	shot	Martini Rosso sweet vermouth
1	dash	Bitters (whiskey barrel aged)
1	dash	Maple bitters (optional)

We say: An apple spirit influenced Sweet Manhattan-style cocktail.
Origin: Adapted from a drink created in 2010 by Patrick Brennan at Prospect, San Francisco, USA.

VIOLET AFFINITY

★★★★½

Glass: Martini
Garnish: Lemon zest twist
Method: STIR all ingredients with ice and strain into chilled glass.

2	shots	Benoit Serres créme de violette
1	shot	Martini Rosso sweet vermouth
1	shot	Martini Extra Dry vermouth

We say: Amazingly delicate and complex for such a simple drink.
Origin: An adaptation of the classic Affinity.

VODKA COLLINS  UPDATED

★★★★☆

Glass: Collins
Garnish: Orange slice & cherry on stick (sail)
Method: SHAKE first three ingredients with ice and strain into ice-filled glass. TOP with soda, lightly stir and serve with straws.

2	shots	Ketel One vodka
1	shot	Freshly squeezed lemon juice
½	shot	Monin Pure Cane 2:1 sugar syrup
Top up with		Soda (club soda)

AKA: Joe Collins
We say: A Tom Collins with vodka - a refreshing balance of sweet and sour.
Origin: The exact origins of this drink are unknown but it is certain that Vodka Collins' were being served in New York after the repeal of Prohibition in 1933.

VODKA DAISY NEW

★★★☆☆

Glass: Goblet
Garnish: Lemon wedge
Method: SHAKE all ingredients with ice and strain into glass filled with crushed ice. CHURN (stir) drink with ice and serve with straws.

2	shots	Ketel One vodka
1	shot	Freshly squeezed lemon juice
½	shot	Pomegranate (grenadine) syrup
½	shot	Monin Pure Cane 2:1 sugar syrup

We say: Slightly sweet with gentle fruitiness.

VODKA ESPRESSO UPDATED

★★★★½

Glass: Old-fashioned
Garnish: loat 3 coffee beans
Method: SHAKE all ingredients with ice and fine strain into ice-filled glass.

2	shots	Ketel One vodka
1½	shots	Hot espresso coffee
½	shot	Kahlúa coffee liqueur
¼	shot	Monin Pure Cane 2:1 sugar syrup

Variant: Pharmaceutical Stimulant, Espresso Martini.
We say: Vodka and coffee combine in this tasty wake up call.
Origin: Created in 1983 by Dick Bradsell at the Soho Brasserie, London, England and originally created for a customer who had asked for a drink to "wake her up, and f*** her up." When asked as to exactly why he settled on that drink, that day, Dick says: "The coffee machine at the Soho Brasserie was right next to the station where I served drinks. It was a nightmare, as there were coffee grounds everywhere, so coffee was very much on my mind. And it was all about vodka back then - it was all people were drinking."

VODKA GIMLET

★★★★☆

Glass: Martini
Garnish: Lime wedge
Method: STIR all ingredients with ice and strain into chilled glass.

| 2½ | shots | Ketel One vodka |
| 1¼ | shots | Rose's lime cordial |

Variant: Shaken. The original Gimlet is based on gin.
We say: Sweetened lime fortified with vodka.

VODKA RICKEY

★★★½☆

Glass: Collins (small 8oz)
Garnish: Length of lime peel
Method: SHAKE first three ingredients with ice and strain into ice-filled glass. TOP with soda.

2	shots	Ketel One vodka
½	shot	Freshly squeezed lime juice
¼	shot	Monin Pure Cane 2:1 sugar syrup
Top up with		Soda (club soda)

We say: Lacks interest but balanced and hard to fault as a simple and refreshing drink.

VODKA SOUR

★★★★☆

Glass: Old-fashioned
Garnish: Lemon slice & cherry on stick (sail)
Method: SHAKE all ingredients with ice and strain into ice-filled glass.

2	shots	Ketel One vodka
1	shot	Freshly squeezed lemon juice
½	shot	Monin Pure Cane 2:1 sugar syrup
3	dashes	Angostura aromatic bitters
½	fresh	Egg white

We say: A great vodka based drink balancing sweet and sour.

VODKATINI (VODKA DRY MARTINI) UPDATED

★★★★½

Glass: Martini
Garnish: Chilled olive on stick or lemon zest twist
Method: SHAKE all ingredients with ice and fine strain into chilled glass.

| 2½ | shots | Ketel One vodka |
| ¼ | shot | Martini Extra Dry vermouth |

AKA: Kangaroo
Variant: Stir rather than shake.
We say: Temperature is key to the enjoyment of this modern classic. Consume while icy cold.
Origin: Exactly where the Vodkatini fits in the vexed question of the origins of the Dry Martini are unknown but it is certain that 'Vodka Martinis' were being served in New York after the repeal of Prohibition in 1933.

VOLGA BOATMAN

★★★½☆

Glass: Martini
Garnish: Orange zest twist
Method: SHAKE all ingredients with ice and fine strain into chilled glass.

1½	shots	Ketel One vodka
¾	shot	Kirschwasser eau de vie
1½	shots	Freshly squeezed orange juice

We say: Basically a Screwdriver with a cherry twist.
Origin: Adapted from David Embury's classic 'Fine Art of Mixing Drinks'. Named after the Cecil b. De Mille movie, it references Europe's longest river.

VOODOO

★★★★☆

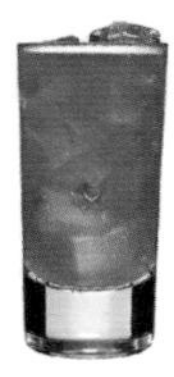

Glass: Collins
Garnish: Dust with cinnamon powder (sprinkled through flame)
Method: SHAKE all ingredients with ice and strain into ice-filled glass.

2	shots	**Bacardi 8yo aged rum**
¾	shot	**Martini Rosso sweet vermouth**
2½	shots	**Pressed apple juice**
½	shot	**Freshly squeezed lime juice**
¼	shot	**Monin Pure Cane 2:1 sugar syrup**

We say: The rich flavour of the aged rum marries well with apple and lime juice.
Origin: Created in 2002 by Alex Kammerling, London, England.

VOODOO I DO

★★★★☆

Glass: Old-fashioned
Garnish: Pineapple wedge & maraschino cherry
Method: MUDDLE pineapple in base of shaker. Add other ingredients, SHAKE with ice and fine strain into ice-filled glass.

1	ring	**Pineapple (fresh)**
2	shots	**Tequila 100% Agave**
¼	shot	**Triple Sec**
½	shot	**De Kuyper Apricot Brandy liqueur**
½	shot	**Freshly squeezed lime juice**

We say: A harmonious Tiki-style concoction.
Origin: Adapted from a drink created in 2011 by Michael Layer at the Chapel Bar, Berlin, Germany.

VOYAGER VODKA MARTINI NEW

★★★★½

Glass: Coupette or Martini
Garnish: Frozen green grape on stick (place on stick then freeze)
Method: STIR all ingredients with ice and fine strain into chilled glass.

2½	shots	**Ketel One vodka**
½	shot	**Martini Extra dry vermouth**
½	shot	**Sake**
⅛	shot	**Macchu pisco**

We say: Why have your Martini dampened by just vermouth, when the Japanese and South Americans have so much to give?
Origin: Created in 2013 by Simon Difford at the Cabinet Room, London, England.

VOWEL COCKTAIL

★★★★½

Glass: Martini
Garnish: Orange zest twist
Method: SHAKE all ingredients with ice and fine strain into chilled glass.

1¼	shots	**Dewar's White label Scotch**
1	shot	**Kümmel**
1	shot	**Martini Rosso sweet vermouth**
¾	shot	**Freshly squeezed orange juice**
2	dashes	**Angostura aromatic bitters**

We say: Caraway from the Kümmel subtly dominates this aromatic drink.
Origin: Adapted from a recipe in *'Vintage Spirits & Forgotten Cocktails'* by Ted Haigh (AKA Dr Cocktail).

WAGON WHEEL

★★★☆☆

Glass: Old-fashioned
Garnish: Lemon slice
Method: SHAKE all ingredients with ice and fine strain into glass filled with crushed ice.

1½	shots	**Cognac VSOP**
1½	shots	**Southern Comfort liqueur**
¾	shot	**Freshly squeezed lemon juice**
¼	shot	**Pomegranate (grenadine) syrup**

We say: This classic cocktail will be best appreciated by lovers of Southern Comfort.
Origin: Adapted from a recipe purloined from David Embury's *'Fine Art of Mixing Drinks'*.

WAH-WAH

★★★★☆

Glass: Martini
Garnish: Orange zest twist
Method: SHAKE all ingredients with ice and fine strain into chilled glass.

1½	shots	**Macchu pisco**
1	shot	**St~Germain elderflower liqueur**
¾	shot	**Aperol**
¾	shot	**Freshly squeezed grapefruit juice**
1	dash	**Angostura aromatic bitters**

We say: Bittersweet and complex with hints of elderflower and grapefruit.
Origin: Created in 2007 at Range, San Francisco, USA.

WALDORF COCKTAIL NO.1

★★★★☆

Glass: Martini
Garnish: Lemon zest twist
Method: STIR all ingredients with ice and strain into chilled glass

2	shots	**Maker's Mark bourbon**
1	shot	**Martini Rosso sweet vermouth**
⅛	shot	**Absinthe**
2	dashes	**Angostura aromatic bitters**

We say: A Sweet Manhattan dried by the merest hint of bitter absinthe.
Origin: The eponymous cocktail from the Waldorf Hotel which stood on Fifth Avenue. The Empire State Building now occupies the hotel's original site and what is known as the Waldorf-Astoria Hotel is now at 301 Park Avenue. Consisting of equal parts whiskey (probably originally rye), sweet vermouth and absinthe with a dash of bitters. This is the earlier of the two classic versions of this vintage cocktail which appeared in Jacques Straub's 1914 book *'Drinks'* and later in A. S. Crockett's 1935 *'The Old Waldorf-Astoria Bar Book'*. The recipe above is adapted to better suit modern palates and ingredients.

STAR RATINGS EXPLAINED

★★★★★ Excellent

★★★★½ Recommended	★★★★☆ Praiseworthy
★★★½☆ Commended	★★★☆☆ Mediocre
★★½☆☆ Disappointing	★★☆☆☆ Pretty awful
★½☆☆☆ Shameful	★☆☆☆☆ Disgusting

WALDORF COCKTAIL NO.2

★★★★☆

Glass: Martini
Garnish: Lemon zest twist
Method: SHAKE all ingredients with ice and fine strain into chilled glass.

2	shots	Swedish Punch liqueur
1½	shots	Tanqueray London dry gin
¾	shot	Freshly squeezed lime juice

Variant: Astor
We say: Lime works better than lemon but like the Astor, using a combination of lime and lemon makes for a better drink.
Origin: This is the later of two versions of this vintage cocktail from New York's Waldorf-Astoria. It appears in the 1939 *Café Royale book* and in the 1955 '*United Kingdom Bartender's Book*'. Both offer a choice between using lemon or lime. The original recipe calls for two parts Swedish punch to one part gin but with this makes for an overly sweet drink.

WALDORF DAIQUIRI NEW

★★★★½

Glass: Martini
Garnish: A walnut, apple wedge and chunk of blue cheese on the side
Method: MUDDLE celery in base of shaker. Add other ingredients, SHAKE with ice and fine strain into chilled glass.

2	inch	Freshly extracted celery juice
2	shots	Rum Aged
½	shot	Bols Cacao White
¼	shot	Monin Pure Cane 2:1 sugar syrup
½	shot	Freshly squeezed lemon juice
½	shot	Pressed apple juice

We say: Walnut, celery and apple are essential elements to both a Waldorf Salad and this tasty Daiquiri.
Origin: Adapted from a drink created in 2010 by Julian de Feral at Lutyens Bar, London, England.

WALNUT ALEXANDER

★★★★☆

Glass: Martini
Garnish: Dust with grated nutmeg
Method: SHAKE all ingredients with ice and fine strain into chilled glass.

2	shots	Cognac VSOP
½	shot	Nocello walnut liqueur
¼	shot	Monin Pure Cane 2:1 sugar syrup
½	shot	Milk
½	shot	Double (heavy) cream

We say: One to accompany the nutty chocolates from the after-dinner selection box.
Origin: Created in 2008 by Simon Difford at The Cabinet Room, London, England.

WALNUT MARTINI

★★★★☆

Glass: Martini
Garnish: Walnut
Method: STIR all ingredients with ice and strain into chilled glass.

2	shots	Ketel One vodka
¾	shot	Tuaca liqueur
¾	shot	Nocello walnut liqueur
¾	shot	Martini Extra Dry vermouth

We say: Nutty but nice.
Origin: Created in 2005 by Simon Difford.

WALTZING MATILDA

★★★★☆

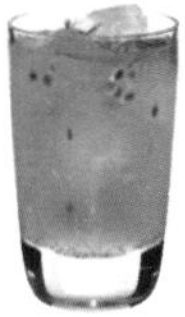

Glass: Collins
Garnish: Orange slice
Method: Cut passion fruit in half and scoop out flesh into shaker. Add next three ingredients, SHAKE with ice and fine strain into ice-filled glass. TOP with ginger ale.

1	fresh	Passion fruit
1	shot	Tanqueray London dry gin
2	shots	Sauvignon blanc wine
⅛	shot	Grand Marnier liqueur
Top up with		Ginger ale

We say: Passion fruit, gin, wine and ginger ale all combine well in this refreshing drink.
Origin: Adapted from a recipe from David Embury's classic book, '*The Fine Art of Mixing Drinks*'.

WANTON ABANDON

★★★★☆

Glass: Martini
Garnish: Strawberry
Method: MUDDLE strawberries in shaker. Add next three ingredients, SHAKE with ice and fine strain into chilled glass. TOP with champagne.

5	fresh	Strawberries (hulled)
2	shots	Ketel One vodka
¾	shot	Freshly squeezed lemon juice
½	shot	Monin Pure Cane 2:1 sugar syrup
Top up with		Brut champagne

We say: A crowd-pleaser - looks great and its fruity, balanced flavour will offend few.

BARTENDER'S TIP FINE STRAIN

Most cocktails that are served 'straight up' without ice benefit from an additional finer strain, over and above the standard strain.

This 'fine strain' removes small fragments of fruit and fine flecks of ice which can spoil the appearance of a drink and is particularly beneficial if the drink has been shaken. Fine straining is achieved by simply holding a fine sieve, like a tea strainer, between the shaker and the glass.

WARD EIGHT

★★★★☆

Glass: Martini
Garnish: Orange slice & cherry on stick (sail)
Method: SHAKE all ingredients with ice and fine strain into chilled glass.

2¼	shots	Maker's Mark bourbon
¾	shot	Freshly squeezed lemon juice
¾	shot	Freshly squeezed orange juice
¼	shot	Pomegranate (grenadine) syrup
½	shot	Chilled mineral water

We say: This is a spirited, sweet and sour combination - like most politicians.
Origin: Ward Eight was a voting district of Boston famed for its political corruption. This drink was first served by Tom Hussion in November 1898 at Boston's Locke-Ober Café, in honour of Martin Lomasney, its owner who was running for election.

WARSAW

★★★☆☆

Glass: Martini
Garnish: Orange zest twist
Method: STIR all ingredients with ice and fine strain into chilled glass.

2	shots	Ketel One vodka
½	shot	Polska Wisniowka cherry liqueur
¼	shot	Triple Sec
2	dashes	Angostura aromatic bitters
¾	shot	Chilled mineral water

We say: Subtle cherry notes with orange.

WARSAW COOLER

★★★★☆

Glass: Collins
Garnish: Mint sprig & orange zest twist
Method: STIR honey with vodka in base of shaker until honey dissolves. Add other ingredients, SHAKE with ice and strain into ice-filled glass.

2	spoons	Runny honey
1½	shots	Żubrówka bison vodka
½	shot	Spiced rum
¼	shot	Triple Sec
½	shot	Monin Pure Cane 2:1 sugar syrup
¾	shot	Freshly squeezed lemon juice
2	shots	Pressed apple juice

Origin: Created in 2002 by Morgan Watson of Apartment, Belfast, Northern Ireland.

WARSAW PACT

★★★★☆

Glass: Martini
Garnish: Mint leaf
Method: SHAKE all ingredients with ice and fine strain into chilled glass.

5	fresh	Mint leaves
2	shots	Żubrówka bison vodka
½	shot	Amaretto liqueur
1½	shots	Pressed apple juice

We say: Fruit and mint flavours combine in this beautifully balanced complex yet easy cocktail.
Origin: Adapted from a drink discovered in 2007 at Paparazzi, Warsaw, Poland.

WASABI MARTINI

★★★★☆

Glass: Martini
Garnish: Yaki nori seaweed
Method: Squeeze a pea-sized quantity of wasabi paste onto a barspoon and STIR with vodka until wasabi dissolves. Add other ingredients, SHAKE with ice and fine strain into chilled glass.

2	shots	Ketel One vodka
1	pea	Wasabi paste
¾	shot	Freshly squeezed lemon juice
½	shot	Monin Pure Cane 2:1 sugar syrup

We say: Wonderfully balanced with spicy heat and a zesty finish.
Origin: Created in 2004 by Philippe Guidi at Morton's, London, England.

WASH HOUSE

★★★★☆

Glass: Martini
Garnish: Thyme sprig
Method: Lightly MUDDLE basil (just to bruise) in base of shaker. Add other ingredients, SHAKE with ice and fine strain into chilled glass.

4	fresh	Torn basil leaves
2	shots	Ketel One vodka
½	shot	Freshly squeezed lime juice
½	shot	Monin Pure Cane 2:1 sugar syrup
½	shot	Chilled mineral water

We say: Delicately herbal - simple but refreshing.
Origin: Adapted from a recipe by Neyah White at Nopa, San Francisco, USA. The building that now houses Nopa was once a laundry, hence the name.

WASHINGTON APPLE

★★★★☆

Glass: Collins
Garnish: Apple slice
Method: SHAKE first four ingredients with ice and fine strain into ice-filled glass. DRIZZLE grenadine over drink. Serve with straws.

2	shots	Ketel One vodka
½	shot	Sour apple liqueur
3	shots	Pressed apple juice
¼	shot	Freshly squeezed lime juice
¼	shot	Pomegranate (grenadine) syrup

We say: A long version of the popular Sour Apple Martini.
Origin: Created by Wayne Collins, London, England.

WATERLOO SUNSET

★★★★☆

Glass: Flute
Garnish: Raspberries
Method: STIR first two ingredients with ice and strain into chilled glass. TOP with champagne. Add raspberry liqueur.

1	shot	Tanqueray London dry gin
½	shot	St~Germain elderflower liqueur
¼	shot	Chambord black raspberry liqueur

We say: Fruity, pink champagne.
Origin: Created in 2008 by Dan Warner, then Beefeater Global Ambassador, hence originally made using Beefeater gin.

WATERMELON & BASIL MARTINI

★★★★☆

Glass: Martini
Garnish: Watermelon wedge
Method: Cut watermelon into 16 segments, chop the flesh from one segment into cubes and MUDDLE in base of skater. Add other ingredients, SHAKE with ice and fine strain into chilled glass.

1	slice	Fresh watermelon
7	fresh	Torn basil leaves
2	shots	Tanqueray London dry gin
½	shot	Monin Pure Cane 2:1 sugar syrup

We say: Refreshing watermelon with interesting herbal hints from the basil and gin.

WATERMELON & BASIL SMASH

★★★★☆

Glass: Collins
Garnish: Watermelon wedge
Method: Cut watermelon into 16 segments, chop the flesh from one segment into cubes and MUDDLE in base of skater. Add other ingredients, SHAKE with ice and fine strain into ice-filled glass. TOP with ginger ale.

1	slice	Fresh watermelon
8	fresh	Torn basil leaves
2	shots	Tequila 100% Agave
¾	shot	Limoncello liqueur
Top up with		Ginger ale

We say: Sweet and sour, long and refreshing with subtle hints of basil, ginger and tequila amongst the fruit.

WATERMELON COOLER

★★★½☆

Glass: Collins
Garnish: Watermelon wedge
Method: SHAKE all ingredients with ice and strain into ice-filled glass.

1½	shots	Bacardi Superior rum
½	shot	Midori green melon liqueur
3½	shots	Ocean Spray cranberry juice
¼	shot	Freshly squeezed lime juice

We say: Summery, refreshing and light.

WATERMELON COSMO

★★★½☆

Glass: Martini
Garnish: Watermelon wedge
Method: Cut watermelon into 16 segments, chop the flesh from one segment into cubes and MUDDLE in base of skater. Add other ingredients, SHAKE with ice and fine strain into chilled glass.

1	slice	Fresh watermelon
2	shots	Ketel One Citroen vodka
¾	shot	Freshly squeezed lime juice
¾	shot	Ocean Spray cranberry juice
⅛	shot	Rose's lime cordial
½	shot	Midori green melon liqueur
2	dashes	Orange bitters

We say: Looks like a standard Cosmo but tastes just as the name suggests.
Origin: Created in 2003 by Eric Fossard at Cecconi's, London, England.

WATERMELON MAN

★★★½☆

Glass: Collins
Garnish: Lime wedge
Method: SHAKE first four ingredients with ice and strain into ice-filled glass. Top with lemonade and serve with straws.

2	shots	Ketel One vodka
1	shot	Watermelon liqueur
¼	shot	Monin Pure Cane 2:1 sugar syrup
½	shot	Freshly squeezed lime juice
1	shot	Pomegranate (grenadine) syrup
Top up with		Soda (club soda)

We say: Sweet and far from sophisticated, but better than the fodder peddled at most clubs.
Origin: Named after the Herbie Hancock track and popularised by a club night promoter called Cookie in Berlin during the mid-1990s. He started serving this cocktail at his club nights and now practically every bar in Berlin offers it. Try the original at his Cookie Club.

WATERMELON MARTINI

★★★★☆

Glass: Martini
Garnish: Watermelon wedge
Method: Cut watermelon into 16 segments, chop the flesh from one segment into cubes and MUDDLE in base of skater. Add other ingredients, SHAKE with ice and fine strain into chilled glass.

1	slice	Fresh watermelon
2	shots	Ketel One vodka
½	shot	Monin Pure Cane 2:1 sugar syrup

We say: So fruity, you could almost convince yourself this is a health drink.

WATERS OF CHAOS

★★★★☆

Glass: Old-fashioned
Garnish: Ti-Punch style lime slice
Method: SHAKE all ingredients with ice and strain into ice-filled glass.

1½	shots	Bols Genever
¼	shot	Wray & Nephew overproof rum
¼	shot	Chartreuse Green liqueur
¾	shot	Freshly squeezed lime juice
½	shot	Monin Pure Cane 2:1 sugar syrup
½	shot	Chilled mineral water

We say: Overproof rum and Chartreuse do indeed have the potential to be waters of chaos.
Origin: Created by Simon Difford at the Cabinet Room, London, England and named after the words of the track Argha Noah by Nightmares on Wax.

STAR RATINGS EXPLAINED

★★★★★ Excellent

★★★★½ Recommeded	★★★★☆ Praiseworthy
★★★½☆ Commended	★★★☆☆ Mediocre
★★½☆☆ Disappointing	★★☆☆☆ Pretty awful
★½☆☆☆ Shameful	★☆☆☆☆ Disgusting

WEBSTER MARTINI

★★★⯪☆

Glass: Martini
Garnish: Lime zest twist
Method: SHAKE all ingredients with ice and fine strain into chilled glass.

2	shots	Tanqueray London dry gin
½	shot	De Kuyper Apricot Brandy liqueur
1	shot	Martini Extra Dry vermouth
½	shot	Freshly squeezed lime juice

We say: Balanced rather than sweet. The old-school Dry Martini meets the contemporary fruit driven Martini.
Origin: Adapted form a recipe in Harry Craddock's 1930 'Savoy Cocktail Book'. Craddock wrote of this drink "A favourite cocktail at the bar of the S.S. Mauretania."

WEEPING JESUS

★★★⯪☆

Glass: Old-fashioned
Garnish: None
Method: SHAKE first three ingredients with ice and strain into glass with crushed ice. TOP up with lemonade.

1	shot	Absinthe
1	shot	Peachtree peach schnapps
1	shot	Pomegranate (grenadine) syrup
Top up with		Lemonade/Sprite/7-Up

We say: This bright red cocktail makes the strong aniseed flavours of absinthe approachable.
Origin: Created in 2002 by Andy Jones at Yates's, London, England.

WEISSEN SOUR NEW

★★★★⯪

Glass: Collins
Garnish: Lemon slice
Method: STIR marmalade with bourbon in base of shaker to dissolve marmalade. Add lemon juice and bitters, SHAKE with ice and fine strain into ice-filled glass. TOP with beer.

2	shots	Maker's Mark bourbon
1	spoon	Orange marmalade
¾	shot	Freshly squeezed lemon juice
2	dashes	Orange bitters
Top up with		Weisse (wheat) beer

We say: Wheaty bourbon with wheat beer and marmaladey citrus notes - they all go hand in hand and so work harmoniously in this unusual long drink.
Origin: Adapted from a recipe created in 2010 by Kevin Diedrich at the Burritt Room, San Francisco, USA.

WELL OILED MAI TAI NEW

★★★⯪☆

Glass: Old-fashioned
Garnish: Half lime shell, cherry, pineapple cube & mint sprig
Method: SHAKE all ingredients with ice and strain into glass filled with crushed ice.

2	shots	Bacardi 8yo aged rum
¼	shot	Taylor's Velvet Falernum liqueur
½	shot	Monin Almond (orgeat) syrup
¾	shot	Freshly squeezed lime juice
2	dashes	Angostura aromatic bitters

We say: A heavily lime spiced riff on the classic Mai Tai.
Origin: Adapted from a drink created in 2011 by Craig Toone at Kuckoo Boutique Bar, Newton-le-Willows, England. Craig's drink was inspired by the Tiki Margarita and he told us, "I looked at 'cross breeding' two other well-known classics. Therefore I present the love child of a Mai Tai and Corn & Oil...genes carried forwards are falernum in place of triple sec and a dash of angostura to the basic Trader Mai Tai recipe."

THE WENTWORTH

★★★★☆

Glass: Martini
Garnish: Orange zest twist
Method: SHAKE all ingredients with ice and fine strain into chilled glass.

1¼	shots	Maker's Mark bourbon
1¼	shots	Dubonnet Red (French made)
1¼	shots	Ocean Spray cranberry juice

We say: The pleasing tang of bourbon adds backbone to this fruity herbal cocktail.
Origin: Created in 2003 by Sharon Cooper at the Harvest Restaurant, Pomfret, Connecticut, USA.

THE WET SPOT

★★★★☆

Glass: Martini
Garnish: Lemon zest twist
Method: SHAKE all ingredients with ice and fine strain into chilled glass.

1½	shots	Tanqueray London dry gin
½	shot	De Kuyper Apricot Brandy liqueur
1	shot	St~Germain elderflower liqueur
1	shot	Pressed apple juice
¾	shot	Freshly squeezed lemon juice

We say: Sharp but fresh tasting and moreish.
Origin: Adapted from a drink created by Willy Shine and Aisha Sharpe at Bed Bar, New York City, USA.

WHAT THE HELL

★★★★☆

Glass: Martini
Garnish: Lime wedge
Method: SHAKE all ingredients with ice and fine strain into chilled glass.

2	shots	Tanqueray London dry gin
1	shot	De Kuyper Apricot Brandy liqueur
¾	shot	Martini Extra Dry vermouth
¼	shot	Freshly squeezed lime juice
⅛	shot	Monin Pure Cane 2:1 sugar syrup

We say: Gin and dry apricots.

WHIP ME & BEAT ME

Glass: Shot
Garnish: None
Method: SHAKE all ingredients with ice and fine strain into chilled glass.

½	shot	Absinthe
½	shot	Double (heavy) cream
½	shot	Malibu coconut rum liqueur
½	shot	Milk

We say: A creamy, coconut, absinthe laden shot

WHISKEY COBBLER

Glass: Goblet
Garnish: Lemon slice & mint sprig
Method: SHAKE all ingredients with ice and strain into glass filled with crushed ice.

2	shots	Dewar's White label Scotch
½	shot	Cognac VSOP
½	shot	Grand Marnier liqueur

We say: A hardcore yet sophisticated drink.

WHISKEY COLLINS

Glass: Collins
Garnish: Orange slice & cherry on stick (sail)
Method: SHAKE first four ingredients with ice and strain into ice-filled glass. TOP with soda water, lightly stir and serve with straws.

2	shots	Maker's Mark bourbon
¾	shot	Freshly squeezed lemon juice
½	shot	Monin Pure Cane 2:1 sugar syrup
3	dashes	Angostura aromatic bitters
Top up with		Soda (club soda)

We say: A whiskey based twist on the classic Tom Collins.

WHISKEY DAISY #1

Glass: Martini
Garnish: Lemon zest twist
Method: SHAKE all ingredients with ice and fine strain into chilled glass.

1¾	shots	Maker's Mark bourbon
½	shot	Triple Sec
¼	shot	Pomegranate (grenadine) syrup
¾	shot	Freshly squeezed lemon juice

We say: This venerable, bourbon led classic has a strong citrus flavour.

WHISKEY DAISY #2

Glass: Goblet
Garnish: Lemon & orange zest twists
Method: SHAKE first four ingredients with ice and fine strain into glass filled with crushed ice. TOP with small dash soda.

1½	shots	Maker's Mark bourbon
1	spoon	Monin Honey syrup
½	shot	Grand Marnier liqueur
¾	shot	Freshly squeezed lemon juice
Top up with		Soda (club soda)

We say: Light, fresh and fruity. Perfect for a summer's afternoon.
Origin: Recipe adapted from Harry Johnson's 1888 'Bartender's Manual'.

WHISKEY SOUR #1 (CLASSIC FORMULA)

Glass: Old-fashioned
Garnish: Lemon slice & cherry on stick (sail)
Method: SHAKE all ingredients with ice and strain into ice-filled glass.

2	shots	Maker's Mark bourbon
¾	shot	Freshly squeezed lemon juice
1	shot	Monin Pure Cane 2:1 sugar syrup
3	dashes	Angostura aromatic bitters
½	fresh	Egg white

We say: I find the classic formulation more sweet than sour and prefer the 4:2:8 ratio.
Origin: This recipe follows the classic sour proportions (3:4:8) three quarter part of the sour ingredient (lemon juice) one part of the sweet ingredient (sugar syrup) and two parts of the strong ingredient (whiskey).

WHISKEY SOUR #2 (DIFFORD'S FORMULA)

Glass: Old-fashioned
Garnish: Lemon slice & cherry on stick (sail)
Method: SHAKE all ingredients with ice and strain into ice-filled glass.

2	shots	Maker's Mark bourbon
1	shot	Freshly squeezed lemon juice
½	shot	Monin Pure Cane 2:1 sugar syrup
3	dashes	Angostura aromatic bitters
½	fresh	Egg white

We say: Smooth with a hint of citrus sourness and an invigorating blast of whiskey.
Origin: A 4:2:8 sour formula.

BARTENDER'S TIP DRY SHAKE

It is common practice to first shake drinks containing cream and eggs without ice, then to shake the drink a second time with ice added.

This practice is known as 'dry shaking' and the theory is that first shaking without ice, and so at a higher temperature, better allows the drink to emulsify.

WHISKEY SQUIRT

★★★★☆

Glass: Collins
Garnish: Peach slice
Method: SHAKE first three ingredients with ice and strain into ice-filled glass. TOP with soda from a siphon. Serve with straws.

2	shots	Boiron peach purée
2	shots	Maker's Mark bourbon
¼	shot	Grand Marnier liqueur
Top up with		Soda from siphon

We say: Peach combines wonderfully with bourbon and this drink benefits from that marriage.
Origin: Adapted from a recipe purloined from David Embury's classic book, 'The Fine Art of Mixing Drinks'.

WHISKEY TEA HIGHBALL NEW

★★★★☆

Glass: Collins
Garnish: Orange zest twist
Method: STIR all ingredients with ice and strain into ice-filled glass.

1½	shots	Maker's Mark bourbon
½	shot	Lagavulin 16yo Islay malt
½	shot	Lapsang souchong tea syrup (2:1)
2	shots	Lapsang souchong tea

AKA: Smoky Whiskey Highball
We say: Smoky lapsang souchong tea, smoky Islay malt and sweet bourbon served long and refreshing.
Origin: Recipe adapted from a drink created in 2011 by Andrew Noye at the Barn Bar at Blackberry Farm, Walland, Tennessee, USA.

WHISKY FIZZ

★★★★☆

Glass: Collins
Garnish: Lemon slice
Method: SHAKE first three ingredients with ice and strain into ice-filled glass. TOP with soda, lightly stir and serve with straws.

2	shots	Dewar's White label Scotch
1	shot	Freshly squeezed lemon juice
½	shot	Monin Pure Cane 2:1 sugar syrup
Top up with		Soda from siphon

We say: The character of the whisky shines through this refreshing, balanced, sweet and sour drink.

WHISKY FLOWER NEW

★★★★☆

Glass: Old-fashioned
Garnish: Lemon zest twist
Method: DRY SHAKE all ingredients (without ice) SHAKE again with ice and strain into ice-filled glass.

2	shots	Lagavulin 16yo malt whisky
1½	shots	St~Germain elderflower liqueur
1	shot	Freshly squeezed lemon juice
½	fresh	Egg white

We say: Basically an elderflower whisky sour with added interest due to the use of an Islay malt.
Origin: Created by Robert Williams at Mamasan, Glasgow, Scotland.

WHISKY MAC

★★★★☆

Glass: Old-fashioned
Method: POUR ingredients into ice-filled glass and lightly stir.

| 2 | shots | Dewar's White label Scotch |
| 1 | shot | Stone's green ginger wine |

We say: Ginger wine smoothes and spices the Scotch.

WHITE CARGO

★★★★★

Glass: Martini
Garnish: Dust with grated nutmeg
Method: SHAKE all ingredients with ice and fine strain into chilled glass.

2	shots	Tanqueray London dry gin
1	scoop	Häagen Dazs vanilla ice cream
¼	shot	Chardonnay white wine

We say: A delicious dessert-style drink.
Origin: Adapted from Harry Craddock's 1930 'The Savoy Cocktail Book'.

WHITE COSMO

★★★★☆

Glass: Martini
Garnish: Orange zest twist
Method: SHAKE all ingredients with ice and fine strain into chilled glass.

1	shot	Ketel One Citroen vodka
1	shot	Triple Sec
1½	shots	Ocean spray white cranberry
½	shot	Freshly squeezed lime juice

AKA: Cosmo Blanco
We say: Just what it says on the tin.
Origin: Emerged during 2002 in New York City.

BARTENDER'S TIP LAYER

As the name would suggest, layered drinks include layers of different ingredients, often with contrasting colours.

This effect is achieved by carefully pouring each ingredient into the glass so that it floats on its predecessor. The success of this technique is dependent on the density (specific gravity) of the liquids used. As a rule of thumb, the less alcohol and the more sugar an ingredient contains, the heavier it is. The heaviest ingredients should be poured first and the lightest last.

WHITE ELEPHANT

★★★½☆

Glass: Martini
Garnish: Dust with chocolate powder
Method: SHAKE all ingredients with ice and fine strain into chilled glass.

2	shots	**Ketel One vodka**
¾	shot	**White Crème de Cacao**
¾	shot	**Double (heavy) cream**
¾	shot	**Milk**

AKA: White Beach
We say: Smooth and creamy with a hint of chocolate.

WHITE GIN FIZZ

★★★½☆

Glass: Collins
Garnish: Lemon wedge
Method: SHAKE first four ingredients with ice and strain into ice-filled glass. TOP with soda from a siphon.

2	shots	**Tanqueray London dry gin**
1	shot	**Freshly squeezed lemon juice**
¼	shot	**Monin Pure Cane 2:1 sugar syrup**
2	scoop	**Lemon sorbet**
Top up with		**Soda from siphon**

We say: Almost creamy in consistency, this gin fizz reminds us of the Sgroppino found in Venice.
Origin: Created in 2003 by Tony Conigliaro at Shumi, London, England.

WHITE KNIGHT

★★★½☆

Glass: Martini
Garnish: Dust with grated nutmeg
Method: SHAKE all ingredients with ice and fine strain into chilled glass.

¾	shot	**Dewar's White label Scotch**
¾	shot	**Kahlúa coffee liqueur**
¾	shot	**Drambuie**
¾	shot	**Milk**
¾	shot	**Double (heavy) cream**

We say: This creamy after-dinner drink features Scotch and honey with a hint of coffee. Not too sweet.

WHITE LADY

★★★★½

Glass: Martini
Garnish: Lemon zest twist
Method: SHAKE all ingredients with ice and fine strain into chilled glass.

1¾	shots	**Tanqueray London dry gin**
1	shot	**Triple Sec**
1	shot	**Freshly squeezed lemon juice**
1	fresh	**Egg white**

Variant: Chelsea Sidecar, Boxcar
We say: A simple but lovely classic drink with a sour finish.
Origin: In 1919 Harry MacElhone, while working at Ciro's Club, London, England, created his first White Lady with 2 shots triple sec, 1 shot white crème de menthe and 1 shot lemon juice. In 1923, he created the White Lady above at his own Harry's New York Bar in Paris, France.

WHITE LION

★★★★☆

Glass: Martini
Garnish: Lime wedge
Method: SHAKE all ingredients with ice and fine strain into chilled glass.

2	shots	**Bacardi Superior rum**
¼	shot	**Triple Sec**
¼	shot	**Pomegranate (grenadine) syrup**
½	shot	**Freshly squeezed lime juice**

We say: This fruity Daiquiri is superb when made with quality pomegranate syrup and rum.
Origin: Adapted from a recipe purloined from David Embury's classic book, '*The Fine Art of Mixing Drinks*'.

WHITE RUSSIAN

★★★★☆

Glass: Old-fashioned
Garnish: Dust with grated nutmeg
Method: SHAKE all ingredients with ice and strain into ice-filled glass.

2	shots	**Ketel One vodka**
1	shot	**Kahlúa coffee liqueur**
½	shot	**Milk**
½	shot	**Double (heavy) cream**

Variant: Shake and strain vodka and coffee liqueur, then float cream.
We say: A Black Russian smoothed with cream.
Origin: Unknown but popularised by the 1998 film '*The Big Lebowski*' in which this drink is the favoured tipple of 'The Dude' character.

WHITE SANGRIA

★★★½☆

Glass: Old-fashioned
Garnish: Seasonal fruit
Method: SHAKE first three ingredients with ice and strain into ice-filled glass. TOP with lemonade.

1	shot	**Grand Marnier liqueur**
2	shots	**Sauvignon blanc wine**
1	shot	**Ocean spray white cranberry**
Top up with		**Lemonade/Sprite/7-Up**

We say: A twist on the traditional Spanish and Portuguese punch.

STAR RATINGS EXPLAINED

★★★★★ Excellent

★★★★½	Recommended	★★★★☆	Praiseworthy
★★★½☆	Commended	★★★☆☆	Mediocre
★★½☆☆	Disappointing	★★☆☆☆	Pretty awful
★½☆☆☆	Shameful	★☆☆☆☆	Disgusting

WHITE SATIN

★★★☆☆
Glass: Martini
Garnish: Dust with chocolate powder
Method: SHAKE all ingredients with ice and fine strain into chilled glass.

1½	shots	Galliano L'Autentico liqueur
1	shot	Kahlúa coffee liqueur
¾	shot	Milk
¾	shot	Double (heavy) cream

We say: Smoother than a cashmere codpiece!

WHITE STINGER

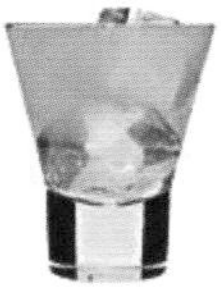

★★★½☆
Glass: Old-fashioned
Garnish: None
Method: SHAKE all ingredients with ice and strain into ice-filled glass.

2	shots	Ketel One vodka
½	shot	Giffard Menthe Pastille liqueur
½	shot	White Crème de Cacao

We say: A liquid After Eight.

WHITE TIGERS

★★★½☆
Glass: Martini
Garnish: Dust with cinnamon powder
Method: SHAKE all ingredients with ice and strain into chilled glass.

2	shots	Calvados/Applejack brandy
¾	shot	Cuarenta y Tres (Licor 43) liqueur
½	fresh	Egg white
1	dash	Angostura aromatic bitters

We say: Vanilla and apple pie with an almost creamy mouth feel.

WHOOP IT UP NEW

★★★★☆
Glass: Coupette
Garnish: Lemon zest twist
Method: SHAKE all ingredients with ice and fine strain into chilled glass.

1	shot	Honey flavoured vodka
1	shot	Rum light white/blanco
½	shot	Domaine de Canton ginger liqueur
½	shot	Bénédictine D.O.M.
½	shot	Freshly squeezed lemon juice
3	drops	Difford's Daiquiri Bitters

We say: Honey, ginger, warm spices and lemon juice. A chilled winter warmer.
Origin: Created in 2010 by Simon Difford at The Cabinet Room, London, England.

WIBBLE

★★★★½
Glass: Martini
Garnish: Lemon zest twist
Method: SHAKE all ingredients with ice and fine strain into chilled glass.

1	shot	Tanqueray London dry gin
1	shot	Sloe Gin liqueur
1	shot	Freshly squeezed grapefruit juice
¼	shot	Freshly squeezed lemon juice
⅛	shot	Monin Pure Cane 2:1 sugar syrup
⅛	shot	Crème de Mûre liqueur

We say: As Dick once said to me, "It may make you wobble, but it won't make you fall down." Complex and balanced.
Origin: Created in 1999 by Dick Bradsell at The Player, London, England for Nick Blacknell - a conspicuous lover of gin.

WIDOW'S KISS

★★★★★
Glass: Martini
Garnish: Mint leaf
Method: STIR all ingredients with ice and fine strain into chilled glass.

1½	shots	Calvados/Applejack brandy
¾	shot	Bénédictine D.O.M.
¾	shot	Chartreuse Yellow liqueur
2	dashes	Angostura aromatic bitters

We say: Fantastically herbal with hints of apple, mint and eucalyptus. This classic is often made with green Chartreuse - We prefer ours with half yellow and half green and dare we say shaken.
Origin: Created before 1895 by George Kappeler at New York City's Holland House.

WILD BLOSSOM UPDATED

★★★★☆
Glass: Martini
Garnish: Grapefruit zest twist
Method: SHAKE all ingredients with ice and fine strain into chilled glass.

2	shots	Tanqueray London dry gin
¾	shot	St-Germain elderflower liqueur
¾	shot	Freshly squeezed grapefruit juice
1	shot	Ocean Spray cranberry juice

We say: Aptly named - it is indeed blossom-like, yet also dry and serious.
Origin: Adapted from a drink created in 2007 by James Scarito at BLT Market, New York City, USA.

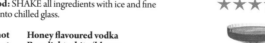

BARTENDER'S TIP SWIZZLE

To 'swizzle' a drink is simply to stir it using a particular tool and action.

To swizzle simply immerse the blades of your swizzle stick into the drink, hold the shaft between the palms of both hands and rotate the stick rapidly by sliding your hands back and forth against it. If you do not have a bona fide swizzle stick, use a barspoon in the same manner.

WILD HONEY

★★★½☆

Glass: Martini
Garnish: Dust with grated nutmeg
Method: SHAKE all ingredients with ice and fine strain into chilled glass.

1½	shots	Dewar's White label Scotch
½	shot	Vanilla-infused Ketel One vodka
¾	shot	Drambuie
½	shot	Galliano L'Autentico liqueur
½	shot	Milk
½	shot	Double (heavy) cream

We say: A serious yet creamy after dinner cocktail with whisky and honey.
Origin: Created in 2001 by James Price at Bar Red, London, England.

WILD IRISH ROSE UPDATED

★★★★½

Glass: Coupette
Garnish: Lemon zest twist & maraschino cherry
Method: SHAKE first four ingredients with ice and fine strain into chilled glass. TOP with soda.

2	shots	Jameson Irish whiskey
½	shot	Freshly squeezed lemon juice
¼	shot	Monin Pure Cane 2:1 sugar syrup
¼	shot	Pomegranate (grenadine) syrup
½	shot	Soda (club soda)

We say: The gentle bite of Irish whisky soured with lemon and sweetened with pomegranate syrup. The splash of soda which crowns this drink serves to lighten and add a touch of sparkle.
Origin: An adaptation on Dale DeGroff's twist on the classic Jack Rose.

WILD PROMENADE MARTINI

★★★★☆

Glass: Martini
Garnish: Raspberries
Method: MUDDLE cucumber and raspberries in base of shaker. Add other ingredients, SHAKE with ice and fine strain into chilled glass.

2	inch	Cucumber (chopped & peeled)
5	fresh	Raspberries
1½	shots	Ketel One vodka
½	shot	Raspberry flavoured vodka
½	shot	Crème de framboise liqueur
¼	shot	Monin Pure Cane 2:1 sugar syrup

We say: Rich raspberry with green hints of cucumber.
Origin: Created in 2002 by Mehdi Otmann at The Player, London, England.

STAR RATINGS EXPLAINED

★★★★★ Excellent

★★★★½ Recommended	★★★★☆ Praiseworthy
★★★½☆ Commended	★★★☆☆ Mediocre
★★½☆☆ Disappointing	★★☆☆☆ Pretty awful
★½☆☆☆ Shameful	★☆☆☆☆ Disgusting

WILL OF ALAN

★★★★½

Glass: Old-fashioned
Garnish: Lime wedge
Method: DRY SHAKE all ingredients without ice. Add ice, SHAKE again and strain into ice-filled glass.

2	shots	Bacardi 8yo aged rum
½	shot	Taylor's Velvet Falernum liqueur
¾	shot	Pineapple (fresh)
¾	shot	Freshly squeezed lime juice
2	dashes	Old-fashioned bitters
¼	fresh	Egg white

We say: Fantastic, spiced, tiki-style twisted Daiquiri.
Origin: Discovered in 2008 at Tonic, Edinburgh, Scotland.

WILLIAM PORTER NEW

★★★★½

Glass: Coupette
Garnish: None
Method: STIR all ingredients with ice and strain into chilled glass.

2	shots	Dewar's White Label Scotch
½	shot	Martini Rosso sweet vermouth
¼	shot	Cointreau triple sec
⅛	shot	Freshly squeezed lime juice
1	dash	Orange bitters

We say: A delicate, Manhattan-like combo of Scotch, sweet vermouth and triple sec.
Origin: Named after William Trotter Porter (1809–1858), an American journalist and editor who founded the Spirit of the Times, a newspaper devoted to sports.

WILTON MARTINI

★★★★☆

Glass: Martini
Garnish: Cinnamon dusted apple slice
Method: SHAKE all ingredients with ice and fine strain into chilled glass.

1	shot	Ketel One vodka
1	shot	Calvados/Applejack brandy
½	shot	Berentzen Apple schnapps
⅛	shot	Goldschläger cinnamon schnapps
1½	shots	Pressed apple juice

We say: Refined cinnamon and apple.
Origin: A 2003 adaptation of the signature cocktail at The Blue Bar, The Berkeley Hotel, London, England.

WIMBLEDON MARTINI

★★★★☆

Glass: Martini
Garnish: Strawberry
Method: MUDDLE strawberries in base of shaker. Add other ingredients, SHAKE with ice and fine strain into chilled glass.

6	fresh	Strawberries (hulled)
1½	shots	Bacardi Superior rum
1½	shots	Crème de fraise du bois liqueur
¼	shot	Monin Pure Cane 2:1 sugar syrup
½	shot	Milk
½	shot	Double (heavy) cream

We say: Takes some getting through the strainer, but when you do it's simply strawberries and cream.

THE WINDSOR ROSE

★★★★☆

Glass: Martini
Garnish: Rose petal
Method: SHAKE all ingredients with ice and fine strain into chilled glass.

1¼	shots	Ketel One Oranje vodka
1	shot	Triple Sec
1	shot	Ocean Spray cranberry juice
½	shot	Freshly squeezed lime juice
⅛	shot	Rose water

We say: An orange vodka and rosewater Cosmo.
Origin: Adapted from a drink discovered in 2005 at The Polo Club Lounge, New Orleans, USA.

WINDY MILLER

★★★★☆

Glass: Collins
Garnish: Lemon slice
Method: SHAKE first three ingredients with ice and strain into glass filled with crushed ice. TOP with lemonade.

1	shot	Ketel One Citroen vodka
½	shot	Absinthe
1	shot	Mandarine Napoléon liqueur
Top up with		Lemonade/Sprite/7-Up

We say: British readers over 40 may remember the children's TV series Trumpton, Chigley and Camberwick Green. If you do, then sing between sips, 'Pugh, Pugh, Barney McGrew, Cuthbert, Dibble and Grubb.'
Origin: Discovered in 2000 at Teatro, London, England.

WINE COOLER

★★★☆☆

Glass: Collins
Garnish: None
Method: POUR first four ingredients into ice-filled glass. TOP with lemonade, lightly stir and serve with straws.

4	shots	Sauvignon blanc wine
½	shot	Ketel One Citroen vodka
½	shot	Freshly squeezed lemon juice
½	shot	Freshly squeezed orange juice
Top up with		Lemonade/Sprite/7-Up

We say: Like a citrussy white wine Spritzer.

WINK

★★★★☆

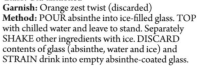

Glass: Old-fashioned
Garnish: Orange zest twist (discarded)
Method: POUR absinthe into ice-filled glass. TOP with chilled water and leave to stand. Separately SHAKE other ingredients with ice. DISCARD contents of glass (absinthe, water and ice) and STRAIN drink into empty absinthe-coated glass.

½	shot	Absinthe
2	shots	Tanqueray London dry gin
¼	shot	Triple Sec
⅛	shot	Monin Pure Cane 2:1 sugar syrup
2	dashes	Peychaud's aromatic bitters

We say: Reminiscent of a Sazerac but with gin and triple sec. Delicate, remarkably fruity and very sippable.
Origin: Created in 2002 by Tony Conigliaro at The Lonsdale, London, England.

WINTER MARTINI

★★★★☆

Glass: Martini
Garnish: Lemon zest twist
Method: STIR all ingredients with ice and strain into chilled glass.

2	shots	Cognac VSOP
½	shot	Sour apple liqueur
½	shot	Martini Extra Dry vermouth
¼	shot	Monin Pure Cane 2:1 sugar syrup

We say: Reminiscent of an Apple Cart (a Calvados Sidecar), this is simple, balanced and tastes great.

WISECRACK FIZZ

★★★★☆

Glass: Collins
Garnish: Lemon zest twist
Method: SHAKE first four ingredients with ice and strain into an ice-filled glass. TOP with soda and serve with straws.

1½	shots	Macchu pisco
1	shot	St-Germain elderflower liqueur
1	shot	Freshly squeezed grapefruit juice
½	shot	Freshly squeezed lemon juice
Top up with		Soda (club soda)

We say: Light, balanced and refreshing. The pisco character shines through.
Origin: Created in 2007 by Matt Gee at Milk & Honey, New York City, USA.

WOLF TICKET NEW

★★★★☆

Glass: Sour or Martini/Coupette
Garnish: Lemon zest twist
Method: MUDDLE peach in base of shaker. Add other ingredients, SHAKE with ice and fine strain into chilled glass.

½	fresh	Ripe peach (skinned and diced)
1½	shots	Maker's Mark bourbon
¼	shot	Crème de pêche de vigne liqueur
½	shot	Freshly squeezed lemon juice
½	shot	Monin Pure Cane 2:1 sugar syrup
1	dash	Angostura aromatic bitters

We say: The ripeness and quality of the peach will make or break this drink. If in season white peaches are preferable.
Origin: Adapted from a drink created in 2013 by Eric Johnson at the Sycamore Den, a 1970s-inspired cocktail lounge in San Diego's Normal Heights neighbourhood, USA

WONKY MARTINI

★★★★☆

Glass: Martini
Garnish: Orange zest twist
Method: STIR all ingredients with ice and strain into chilled glass.

1½	shots	Vanilla-infused Ketel One vodka
1½	shots	Tuaca liqueur
1½	shots	Martini Rosso sweet vermouth
2	shots	Orange bitters

We say: A sweet, wet Vodkatini invigorated with orange and vanilla.
Origin: Created in 2003 by Simon Difford.

WOO WOO

★★★☆☆

Glass: Old-fashioned
Garnish: Lime wedge
Method: SHAKE all ingredients with ice and strain into ice-filled glass.

2	shots	**Ketel One vodka**
1	shot	**Peachtree peach schnapps**
2	shots	**Ocean Spray cranberry juice**

We say: Fruity, dry cranberry laced with vodka and peach. Not nearly as bad as its reputation but still lost in the eighties.

WOODLAND PUNCH

★★★½☆

Glass: Collins
Garnish: Lime wedge
Method: SHAKE first four ingredients with ice and strain into ice-filled glass. TOP with soda, lightly stir and serve with straws.

2	shots	**Southern Comfort liqueur**
¼	shot	**De Kuyper Cherry Brandy liqueur**
½	shot	**Freshly squeezed lime juice**
2	shots	**Fresh pressed pineapple juice**
Top up with		**Soda (club soda)**

We say: Tart, tangy and refreshing.
Origin: Adapted from a drink created in 1997 by Foster Creppel. This is the signature at his Woodland Plantation, the great house in the west bank of the Mississippi that features on every bottle of Southern Comfort.

WOODSIDE NEW

★★★★☆

Glass: Coupette
Garnish: None
Method: MUDDLE pineapple in base of shaker and add other ingredients. DRY SHAKE (without ice), then SHAKE again with ice and fine strain into chilled glass.

½	ring	**Pineapple (fresh)**
¾	shot	**Rum light white/blanco**
½	shot	**Ruby port**
¾	shot	**Martini Extra dry vermouth**
½	shot	**Freshly squeezed lemon juice**
½	shot	**Monin Pure Cane 2:1 sugar syrup**
2	dashes	**Angostura aromatic bitters**
½	fresh	**Egg white**

We say: Delicately fruity, light and fluffy.
Origin: Created in 2009 by Darren Thrower at The Kenilworth, Warwickshire, England and named after Count Basie's "*Jumpin' at the Woodside*".

WOXUM NEW

★★★½☆

Glass: Coupette
Garnish: Lemon zest twist
Method: STIR all ingredients with ice and strain into chilled glass.

1½	shots	**Laird's Applejack brandy**
½	shot	**Martini Rosso sweet vermouth**
½	shot	**Chartreuse Yellow liqueur**

We say: The flavour of Chartreuse shines through in this slightly sweet, spirit cocktail.
Origin: Recipe is adapted from Albert Stevens Crockett's 1935 '*The Old Waldorf-Astoria Bar Book*'.

YACHT CLUB

★★★½☆

Glass: Martini
Garnish: Lemon zest twist
Method: STIR all ingredients with ice and strain into chilled glass.

2	shots	**Bacardi Oro golden rum**
¼	shot	**De Kuyper Apricot Brandy liqueur**
1	shot	**Martini Rosso sweet vermouth**

We say: Rich and slightly sweet with hints of apricot fruit.
Origin: Adapted from a recipe purloined form David Embury's classic book, *The Fine Art of Mixing Drinks*.

YELLOW BELLY MARTINI

★★★★☆

Glass: Martini
Garnish: Lemon zest twist
Method: SHAKE all ingredients with ice and fine strain into chilled glass.

1	shot	**Ketel One Citroen vodka**
1	shot	**Limoncello liqueur**
1	shot	**Freshly squeezed lemon juice**
⅛	shot	**Monin Pure Cane 2:1 sugar syrup**
½	shot	**Chilled mineral water**

We say: Lemon, lemon, lemon. Nice though!

YELLOW BIRD

★★★☆☆

Glass: Martini
Garnish: Banana chunk
Method: SHAKE all ingredients with ice and fine strain into chilled glass.

1½	shots	**Bacardi Oro golden rum**
½	shot	**Bols Banana liqueur**
¼	shot	**De Kuyper Apricot Brandy liqueur**
¼	shot	**Galliano L'Autentico liqueur**
1½	shots	**Fresh pressed pineapple juice**
¼	shot	**Freshly squeezed lime juice**

We say: A sweet and sour cocktail four different fruits, rum and a splash of Galliano

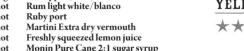

STAR RATINGS EXPLAINED

★★★★★ Excellent

★★★★½ Recommended	★★★★☆ Praiseworthy
★★★½☆ Commended	★★★☆☆ Mediocre
★★½☆☆ Disappointing	★★☆☆☆ Pretty awful
★½☆☆☆ Shameful	★☆☆☆☆ Disgusting

YELLOW FEVER MARTINI

★★★½☆

Glass: Martini
Garnish: Pineapple wedge
Method: SHAKE all ingredients with ice and fine strain into chilled glass.

2½	shots	**Ketel One vodka**
1½	shots	**Fresh pressed pineapple juice**
½	shot	**Galliano L'Autentico liqueur**
½	shot	**Freshly squeezed lime juice**
⅛	shot	**Monin Pure Cane 2:1 sugar syrup**

We say: Fortified pineapple with a subtle hint of cooling peppermint.

YELLOW PARROT

★★★★☆

Glass: Martini
Garnish: Orange zest twist
Method: SHAKE all ingredients with ice and fine strain into chilled glass.

¼	shot	**Absinthe**
1	shot	**Chartreuse Yellow liqueur**
1	shot	**De Kuyper Apricot Brandy liqueur**
1	shot	**Chilled mineral water**

We say: The aniseed of the absinthe combines well with the other ingredients. A bit of a sweety but a strong old bird.
Origin: Some say this was created in 1935 by Albert Coleman at The Stork Club, New York City, but the drink featured in Harry Craddock's *Savoy Cocktail Book* five years before that.

YOKOHAMA

★★★½☆

Glass: Martini
Garnish: Orange zest twist
Method: SHAKE all ingredients and fine strain into chilled glass.

½	shot	**Ketel One vodka**
1	shot	**Freshly squeezed orange juice**
1	shot	**Tanqueray London dry gin**
¼	shot	**Absinthe**
½	shot	**Pomegranate (grenadine) syrup**

We say: Gin and orange with a hint of absinthe.
Origin: One of the earliest published vodka recipes and credited to Harry McElhone who also created the Monkey Gland #1 to which this cocktail is practically identical, albeit a splash of vodka.

STAR RATINGS EXPLAINED

★★★★★ Excellent

★★★★½ Recommeded	★★★★☆ Praiseworthy
★★★½☆ Commended	★★★☆☆ Mediocre
★★½☆☆ Disappointing	★★☆☆☆ Pretty awful
★½☆☆☆ Shameful	★☆☆☆☆ Disgusting

YOUNG MAN COCKTAIL NEW

★★★★☆

Glass: Coupette
Garnish: Maraschino cherry
Method: STIR all ingredients with ice and strain into chilled glass.

1½	shots	**Courvoisier VSOP Exclusif**
½	shot	**Martini Rosso sweet vermouth**
½	shot	**Grand Marnier liqueur**
2	dashes	**Angostura aromatic bitters**

We say: This particular Young Man is essentially a cognac-based Sweet Manhattan with a splash of orange curaçao – unsurprisingly, the result is slightly sweetened cognac with a hint of orange.
Origin: Adapted from a drink in Harry Craddock's 1930 *The Savoy Cocktail Book*.

YOU'VE GOT MAIL

★★★★☆

Glass: Collins
Garnish: Orange slice
Method: SHAKE first four ingredients with ice and fine strain into ice-filled glass. TOP with champagne.

2	shots	**Leblon cachaça**
¼	shot	**Monin Pure Cane 2:1 sugar syrup**
½	shot	**Freshly squeezed lime juice**
½	shot	**Freshly squeezed orange juice**
¼	shot	**Monin Honey syrup**
Top up with		**Brut champagne**

We say: Cachaça and citrus balanced by honey and topped with champagne.
Origin: An adaptation of Dave Wondrich's adaptation of the classic Airmail.

YULE LUVIT

★★★½☆

Glass: Shot
Garnish: Dust with grated nutmeg
Method: Refrigerate ingredients then LAYER in chilled glass by carefully pouring in the following order.

¾	shot	**Maker's Mark bourbon**
¾	shot	**Hazelnut liqueur**

We say: Actually, 'yule' find it strongly nutty and sweet

YUM

★★★☆☆

Glass: Collins
Garnish: Lemon wedge
Method: SHAKE all ingredients with ice and strain into ice-filled glass.

½	shot	**Peachtree peach schnapps**
1½	shots	**Mandarine Napoléon liqueur**
¼	shot	**Chambord black raspberry liqueur**
1	shot	**Freshly squeezed lemon juice**
3	shots	**Pressed apple juice**

We say: If you like sweet, fruity 'disco drinks' then this is indeed yummy

Z MARTINI

★★★★★

Glass: Martini
Garnish: Blue cheese stuffed olives
Method: STIR all ingredients with ice and strain into chilled glass.

| 2½ | shots | Ketel One vodka |
| 1¼ | shots | Warre's Otima tawny port |

We say: Grainy vodka with dry, wine-like notes. Top marks for the garnish alone.
Origin: Discovered in 2004 at Les Zygomates, Boston, USA.

ZABAGLIONE MARTINI

★★★½☆

Glass: Martini
Garnish: None
Method: Separately BEAT egg white until stiff and frothy and yolk until this is as liquid as water, then pour into shaker. Add other ingredients, SHAKE with ice and fine strain into chilled glass.

1	fresh	Egg white
1	fresh	Egg yolk
1½	shots	Advocaat liqueur
½	shot	Cognac VSOP
1	shot	Marsala wine
¾	shot	Freshly squeezed lemon juice

We say: Like the dessert, this is sweet and rich with flavours of egg and fortified wine.
Origin: Created by Simon Difford in 2003 after the classic Italian dessert, which incidentally derives its name form the Neapolitan dialect word 'zapillare', meaning 'to foam'.

ZAC'S DAIQUIRI

★★★★☆

Glass: Martini
Garnish: Lemon zest twist
Method: SHAKE all ingredients with ice and strain into chilled glass.

2	shots	Bacardi 8yo aged rum
½	shot	Freshly squeezed lemon juice
½	shot	Pressed apple juice
¼	shot	Monin Pure Cane 2:1 sugar syrup

We say: Zacapa has whiskey hints, which suit lemon rather than lime in a Daiquiri. Daiquiris benefit from dilution and here a dash of apple juice adds a barely perceptible amount of fruit as well.
Origin: Created in January 2009 by Simon Difford at the Cabinet Room, London, England.

ZAKUSKI MARTINI

★★★★☆

Glass: Martini
Garnish: Cucumber peel
Method: MUDDLE cucumber in base of shaker. Add other ingredients, SHAKE with ice and fine strain into chilled glass.

1	inch	Cucumber (chopped & peeled)
2	shots	Ketel One Citroen vodka
½	shot	Triple Sec
½	shot	Freshly squeezed lemon juice
¼	shot	Monin Pure Cane 2:1 sugar syrup

We say: Appropriately named after the Russian snack.
Origin: Created in 2002 by Alex Kammerling, London, England.

THE ZAMBOANGA 'ZEINIE' COCKTAIL

★★★★☆

Glass: Martini
Garnish: Lime zest twist (discarded) & cherry
Method: SHAKE all ingredients with ice and fine strain into chilled glass.

2	shots	Cognac VSOP
¼	shot	Maraschino syrup (from cherry jar)
1	shot	Fresh pressed pineapple juice
½	shot	Freshly squeezed lime juice
2	dashes	Angostura aromatic bitters

We say: Reminiscent of a tropical Sidecar.
Origin: Adapted from a recipe purloined from Charles H. Baker Jr's classic book, *The Gentleman's Companion*. He describes this as "another palate twister from the land where the Monkeys Have No Tails. This drink found its way down through the islands to Mindanao from Manila..."

ZANZIBAR

★★★½☆

Glass: Old-fashioned
Garnish: Lime zest twist
Method: SHAKE all ingredients with ice and strain into ice-filled glass.

2	shots	Gosling's Black Seal rum
¼	shot	De Kuyper Apricot Brandy liqueur
¼	shot	Grand Marnier liqueur
⅛	shot	Monin Almond (orgeat) syrup
½	shot	Freshly squeezed orange juice
½	shot	Freshly squeezed lime juice

Origin: Discovered in 2005 at Zanzi Bar, Prague, Czech Republic.

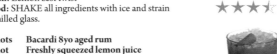

BARTENDER'S TIP MEASURING - SHOTS & SPOONS

In this guide measures of each ingredient are expressed in 'shots'. Ideally a shot is 25ml or one US fluid ounce (29.6ml), measured in a standard jigger. (You can also use a clean medicine measure or even a small shot glass.)

Whatever your chosen measure, it should have straight sides to enable you to accurately judge fractions of a shot. Look out for measures which are graduated in ounces and marked with quarter and half ounces.

ZAZA

★★★★☆

Glass: Martini
Garnish: Orange zest twist
Method: SHAKE all ingredients with ice and fine strain into chilled glass.

| 2 | shots | Tanqueray London dry gin |
| 2 | shots | Dubonnet Red (French made) |

AKA: Dubbonet Cocktail
Variant: Substitute Sloe gin or Fino sherry in place of gin.
We say: Zaza is a diminutive of Isabelle. But there is nothing diminutive about this simple, yet fantastic drink.
Origin: Adapted from a recipe in Harry Craddock's 1930 '*Savoy Cocktail Book*'. It is named after a French play which was a hit around the verge of the 20th century and was followed by opera and film versions.

ZEE DEE

★★★★☆

Glass: Martini
Garnish: Lemon zest twist
Method: STIR all ingredients with ice and strain into chilled glass.

1½	shots	Bacardi 8yo aged rum
1½	shots	Pressed apple juice
1½	shots	Amontillado sherry

Origin: Created in January 2009 by Simon Difford at the Cabinet Room, London, England.

ZELDA MARTINI

★★★★☆

Glass: Martini
Garnish: Mint sprig
Method: Lightly MUDDLE mint (just to bruise) in base of shaker. Add other ingredients, SHAKE with ice and fine strain into chilled glass.

5	fresh	Mint leaves
2	shots	Żubrówka bison vodka
1	shot	Freshly squeezed lime juice
¾	shot	Monin Almond (orgeat) syrup
½	shot	Chilled mineral water

We say: Bison grass vodka combines brilliantly with mint and almond.
Origin: Created in May 2002 by Phillip Jeffrey at the GE Club, London, England. He made it for a friend called Zelda - the name really wouldn't have worked if she'd been called Tracy.

ZESTY

★★★½☆

Glass: Old-fashioned
Garnish: Lime zest twist
Method: SHAKE all ingredients with ice and strain into glass filled with crushed ice.

| 2 | shots | Hazelnut liqueur |
| ½ | shot | Freshly squeezed lime juice |

We say: Citrus fresh with a nutty touch.

ZEUS MARTINI

★★★★½

Glass: Martini
Garnish: Coffee beans
Method: POUR Fernet Branca into frozen glass, swirl round and DISCARD. MUDDLE raisins with cognac in base of shaker. Add other ingredients, SHAKE with ice and fine strain into chilled glass.

1	shot	Fernet Branca
24	dried	Raisins
2	shots	Cognac VSOP
⅛	shot	Kahlúa coffee liqueur
¼	shot	Maple syrup
1	shot	Chilled mineral water

We say: Rich, pungent and not too sweet.
Origin: Adapted from Dr Zeus, a cocktail created by Adam Ennis in 2001 at Isola, London, England.

ZHIVAGO MARTINI

★★★★☆

Glass: Martini
Garnish: Apple slice
Method: SHAKE all ingredients with ice and fine strain into chilled glass.

1½	shots	Vanilla-infused Ketel One vodka
½	shot	Maker's Mark bourbon
½	shot	Sour apple liqueur
1	shot	Freshly squeezed lime juice
¾	shot	Monin Pure Cane 2:1 sugar syrup

We say: Perfectly balanced sweet and sour - sweet apple, vanilla and bourbon balanced by lime juice.
Origin: Created in 2002 by Alex Kammerling, London, England.

ZINGY GINGER MARTINI

★★★★☆

Glass: Martini
Garnish: Lemon zest twist
Method: SHAKE all ingredients with ice and fine strain into chilled glass.

2½	shots	Ketel One Citroen vodka
½	shot	Monin Ginger syrup
½	shot	Freshly squeezed lemon juice
½	shot	Chilled mineral water

We say: It sure is both zingy and gingery.
Origin: Created in 2001 by Reece Clark at Hush Up, London, England.

STAR RATINGS EXPLAINED

★★★★★ Excellent

★★★★⯨ Recommended	★★★★☆ Praiseworthy
★★★⯨☆ Commended	★★★☆☆ Mediocre
★★⯨☆☆ Disappointing	★★☆☆☆ Pretty awful
★⯨☆☆☆ Shameful	★☆☆☆☆ Disgusting

ZOMBIE #1 (INTOXICA! RECIPE)

★★★★☆

Glass: Hurricane
Garnish: Mint sprig
Method: STIR brown sugar with lemon juice in base of shaker until it dissolves. Add other ingredients, SHAKE with ice and strain into ice-filled glass.

1	spoon	Brown sugar
1	shot	Bacardi Oro golden rum
1	shot	Demerara 151° overproof rum
1	shot	Bacardi Superior rum
1	shot	Freshly squeezed lemon juice
1	shot	Fresh pressed pineapple juice
1	shot	Freshly squeezed lime juice
1	dash	Angostura aromatic bitters
1	shot	Passion fruit syrup

We say: Plenty of flavour and alcohol with tangy rum and fruit.
Origin: The above recipe for Don the Beachcomber's classic cocktail is based on one published in Intoxica! by Jeff Berry.

ZOMBIE #2 (VIC'S FORMULA)

★★★½☆

Glass: Collins
Garnish: Mint sprig
Method: BLEND all ingredients with one 12oz scoop crushed ice. Serve with straws.

¾	shot	Bacardi Superior rum
¾	shot	Bacardi 8yo aged rum
½	shot	Grand Marnier liqueur
¼	shot	Pomegranate (grenadine) syrup
1½	shots	Freshly squeezed orange juice
2½	shots	Fresh pressed pineapple juice
1	shot	Freshly squeezed lemon juice
½	shot	Freshly squeezed lime juice

We say: More fruit than alcohol but tangy not sweet.
Origin: Adapted from a recipe in the *1947-72 Trader Vic's Bartender's Guide* by Victor Bergeron.

ZOMBIE #3 (MODERN FORMULA)

★★★★☆

Glass: Hurricane
Garnish: Pineapple wedge
Method: SHAKE first nine ingredients with ice & strain into glass filled with crushed ice. FLOAT overproof rum.

¾	shot	Bacardi Superior rum
¾	shot	Pusser's Navy rum
¾	shot	Bacardi Oro golden rum
½	shot	De Kuyper Apricot Brandy liqueur
½	shot	Grand Marnier liqueur
2½	shots	Freshly squeezed orange juice
2½	shots	Fresh pressed pineapple juice
1	shot	Freshly squeezed lime juice
½	shot	Pomegranate (grenadine) syrup
½	shot	Wray & Nephew overproof rum

We say: A heady mix of four different rums.

ZOOM

★★★★✦

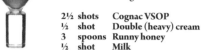

Glass: Martini
Garnish: Dust with chocolate powder
Method: SHAKE all ingredients with ice and fine strain into chilled glass.

2½	shots	Cognac VSOP
½	shot	Double (heavy) cream
3	spoons	Runny honey
½	shot	Milk

We say: Cognac is smoothed with honey and softened with milk and cream in this classic cocktail.

ŽUBRÓWKA COCKTAIL NEW

★★★★✦

Glass: Coupette
Garnish: Lemon zest twist
Method: POUR absinthe into ice-filled glass, top with water and stand to one side. Separately STIR all ingredients with ice. Dump contents of glass and strain stirred drink into the now absinthe washed glass.

½	shot	Absinthe
1½	shots	Žubrówka bison vodka
¼	shot	Goldschläger cinnamon schnapps
1½	shots	Martini Rosso sweet vermouth
1	dash	Angostura aromatic bitters

We say: The grassy notes of Žubrówka and delicate cinnamon shine through in this well balanced and delicately spicy vintage cocktail.
Origin: Adapted from W. J. Tarling's (Bill Tarling) 1937 '*Café Royal Cocktail Book*', the invention of this drink is credited to S. T. Yakimovitch.

ZUBWAY

★★★★☆

Glass: Collins
Garnish: Raspberries
Method: Chop watermelon and MUDDLE in base of shaker with raspberries. Add other ingredients, SHAKE with ice and fine strain into ice-filled glass.

1	slice	Fresh watermelon
2½	shots	Žubrówka bison vodka
½	shot	Monin Pure Cane 2:1 sugar syrup
3	fresh	Raspberries

Origin: Created in 1999 by Jamie Terrell, London, England.

BARTENDER'S TIP MEASURING - SHOTS & SPOONS

In this guide measures of each ingredient are expressed in 'shots'. Ideally a shot is 25ml or one US fluid ounce (29.6ml), measured in a standard jigger. (You can also use a clean medicine measure or even a small shot glass.)

Whatever your chosen measure, it should have straight sides to enable you to accurately judge fractions of a shot. Look out for measures which are graduated in ounces and marked with quarter and half ounces.

Our partners

Everything for the well-stocked bar – brands we believe in

Each year I taste thousands of products brought to market – you can see my ratings and reviews of them all at diffordsguide.com – and I am in the unique position of having made and rated every drink recipe contained in this cocktail encyclopedia.

You'll notice that I have chosen specific brands for some spirits category throughout the book. I have chosen these brands because, in my opinion, they make great drinks and are available globally at most good liquor stores or supermarkets. None of them are esoteric or expensive, and all represent well-made products that offer good value for money.

In fact, in the speed-rail of The Cabinet Room – my private bar in Bermondsey, London – you'll find these very products that have been included here.

Cheers,
Simon Difford.
simon@diffordsguide.com

ANGOSTURA AROMATIC BITTERS

The most famous and most used brand of herbal bitters in the world. First created in 1824 by Johann Gottlieb Benjamin Siegert, a German doctor, to treat stomach disorders and indigestion a military hospital in the town of Angostura, Venezuela.

★★★★★

BENTON'S OLD FASHIONED
MANHATTAN SWEET
MINT JULEP
OLD FASHIONED #1
PUNCH (GENERIC NAME)
WHISKEY SOUR #2
WIDOW'S KISS

★★★★⯪

APPLE BRANDY SOUR
BUENA VIDA
THE COMET
DANDY COCKTAIL
FINO FLIP
OLD CUBAN
THE PRECURSORY COCKTAIL
ROSITA
SMOKE AND MIRRORS #2
TIP TOP COCKTAIL
TREACLE NO.1
VELVET FOG
WHISKEY COLLINS

BACARDI 8YO

Bacardi '8', as it is better known, is said to be made to an original recipe from 1862 and is a blend of rums aged in American charred oak casks for between 8 and 16 years. Bacardi 8 is made from molasses, is quadruple distilled in continuous column stills and is charcoal filtered.

★★★★★

DAIQUIRI NATURAL NO.1 #2
RUM OLD FASHIONED

★★★★⯪

DAIQUIRI NOIR
DARK DAIQUIRI
DOCTOR #1
FLIPPING GOOD
FOSBURY FLIP
HAROLD AND MAUDE

LOVE ME FLIP
MOTHER RUIN
MULATA DAIQUIRI
OLD CUBAN
PRESTIGE COCKTAIL
RED RUM MARTINI
ROOSEVELT COCKTAIL
TAPERED NAIL
WILL OF ALAN

★★★★☆

MAI TAI (VIC'S FORMULA)
PIÑA COLADA #2 (CUBAN STYLE)
QUEEN'S PARK SWIZZLE

BACARDI OAKHEART

Bacardi Oakheart is a "spiced spirit drink" - it's below 37.5% alcohol by volume so while it may be a 'flavoured rum' in the US it is technically not a rum in Europe, hence the 'spirit drink' descriptor.

★★★★⯪

SPICED PEAR
WARSAW COOLER

★★★★☆

BOMBER
CABLE CAR

★★★⯪☆

JAMAICAN MULE
LONG ISLAND SPICED TEA

BACARDI SUPERIOR

Bacardi Superior is a 'light white' rum first made in 1862 by Don Facundo Bacardi Massó in Santiago de Cuba. It is a blend of heavy-bodied and drier light-bodied rums aged separately in lightly charred ex-bourbon casks for a minimum of 12 months. These rums are charcoal filtrated and blended.

★★★★★

AGED HONEY DAIQUIRI
BREAKFAST CLUB
DAIQUIRI NATURAL NO.1 #1
EL PRESIDENTE NO.1 #2
HONEYSUCKLE DAIQUIRI
MARY PICKFORD
MISSIONARY'S DOWNFALL

MOJITO #1
OH GOSH!
SANTIAGO DAIQUIRI

★★★★⯪

AKU AKU
ANGEL'S DRAFT
BAJITO
DERBY DAIQUIRI
GIN CLUB PUNCH NO.1
FLORIDA DAIQUIRI
FOUR LEAF CLOVER
HEMINGWAY SPECIAL DAIQUIRI
PALOMINO FLOR
SOL ARDIENTE

BOLS BANANA LIQUEUR

Bols Banana is based on a rum distillate rather than neutral spirit to provide extra character and is flavoured with banana extract enhanced by a touch of vanilla and a hint of almonds.

★★★★⯪

SOUTHERN TEA-KNEE

★★★★☆

BANANA BOOMER
BANANA COLADA
BANANAS & CREAM
BANOFFEE MARTINI
BEJA FLOR
CARIBBEAN BREEZE
FUNKY MONKEY
DIRTY BANANA
GULF COAST SEX ON THE BEACH
JUMPING JACK FLASH
RUM RUNNER
REEF JUICE
TRIBBBLE
SMOOTH & CREAMY'TINI
BANANA ALCOHOLIC SMOOTHIE

★★★⯪☆

BANANA BLISS
BANANA DAIQUIRI
CHICLET DAIQUIRI
FLAMINGO #1

BOLS BLUE CURACAO

Bols Blue is the original and remains the world's best-selling Blue Curaçao. It is one of the oldest flavours in the modern Bols liqueur range and in the 19th century was known as "Crème de Ciel". It is prepared with a distillate of especially aromatic bitter orange peel.

★★★★☆

LOTUS MARTINI
BIKINI MARTINI
BLUE PASSION
BLUE VELVET MARGARITA
CHINA BLUE MARTINI
INK MARTINI
CORPSE REVIVER NO. BLUE
BLUE LASSI

★★★⯪☆

SWEDISH BLUE MARTINI
TURQUOISE DAIQUIRI
ALEXANDER'S BIG BROTHER
BABY BLUE MARTINI
BLACK MUSSEL
BLUE COSMO
BLUE KAMIKAZE
BLUE MARGARITA
BLUE MONDAY

BOLS BUTTERSCOTCH

Butterscotch is a type of confectionery dating back to the 1850s whose primary ingredients are brown sugar and butter, although other ingredients such as corn syrup, cream, vanilla, and salt are part of some recipes. Bols Butterscotch is a secret blend of quality butterscotch syrup and spices.

★★★★☆

BANOFFEE MARTINI
BON BON
BUTTERSCOTCH MARTINI
GINGERBREAD MARTINI
GIVE ME A DIME
GOLD MEMBER
MET MANHATTAN
TRIBBBLE
BOURBON COOKIE

★★★⯪☆

APPLE CRUMBLE MARTINI #1
BUTTERSCOTCH DAIQUIRI

BUTTERSCOTCH DELIGHT
OATMEAL COOKIE
SHAMROCK EXPRESS
DOUGHNUT MARTINI
BARTENDER'S MUM

BOLS CACAO BROWN

Bols started making 'Bols Huile de Cacao' liqueur in the 19th century using cacao, then a new exotic ingredient. Bols still flavours this liqueur with a hot percolation of cacao beans giving it the taste of dark chocolate compared to that of white chocolate for Bols Crème de Cacao White.

★★★★★

MOO'LATA

★★★★⯪

BLACK MARTINI
BRANDY ALEXANDER
MOCHA MARTINI
TRIPLE 'C' MARTINI
MIDNIGHT OVER TENNESSEE
MULATA DAIQUIRI

★★★★☆

CHOCOLATE PUFF
CHOCOLATE SIDECAR
CHOCOLARITA DIVINO'S
HAZELNUT ALEXANDER
HONEY WALL
RASPBERRY MOCHA'TINI
TIRAMISU MARTINI
TRIANGULAR MARTINI
BLACK STRAP
MULATA DAISY
CHATHAM HOTEL SPECIAL
DEATH BY CHOCOLATE

BOLS GENEVER

Flavoured with a whisky-like triple grain distillate made of corn, wheat and rye, which the Dutch call maltwine. This flavoursome distillate is blended with a juniper-berry distillate and a separate botanical distillate, including coriander, caraway and aniseed. The recipe contains over 50% maltwine.

★★★★★

MARTINEZ #1
MARTINEZ #2
DUTCH COUNT NEGRONI

★★★★⯪

ALAMAGOOZLUM COCKTAIL
COLLINS

★★★★☆

I B DAMM'D
NEW AMSTERDAM
AMSTERDAM COCKTAIL
FLYING DUTCH MARTINI
JENEVER SOUR
DEATH IN THE GULF STREAM
DUTCH MARTINI
GIN DAISY #2
GIN PUNCH #2
THE HOLLAND HOUSE COCKTAIL

★★★⯪☆

WATERS OF CHAOS
IMPROVED HOLLAND GIN
COCKTAIL
SKID ROW
DUTCH WORD

BOLS CACAO WHITE

The recipe contains over 50% maltwine Bols has been making chocolate distillates since the 19th century and it continues to infuse and then distil the best quality cacao beans to give this liqueur a creamy, milk chocolate flavour when compared to the dark chocolate flavour of Bols Cacao Brown liqueur.

★★★★★

SILK STOCKING
MOO'LATA

★★★★⯪

ACE OF CLUBS DAQUIRI
ALEXANDER
BRANDY ALEXANDER
EASTER MARTINI
PINI
MULATA DAIQUIRI
DELMARVA COCKTAIL #2
MOTHER RUM
PERPETUAL COCKTAIL
BÈNÈDICTINE CONVERSION
COESSENTIAL

★★★★☆

BEHEMOTH
BUTTERSCOTCH MARTINI

CHERRY ALEXANDER
CHOCOLATE MARTINI
CHOCOLATE & CRANBERRY
MARTINI
CHOCOLATE MINT MARTINI
CHOCOLATE SAZERAC

BOLS NATURAL YOGHURT LIQUEUR

Launched in 2010, Bols Natural Yoghurt is made from fresh yoghurt and is the world's first and only yoghurt liqueur. The specially coated creamy white bottle with its blue livery protects the sensitive natural contents from ultra-violet light damage and also gives it considerable back bar standout.

★★★★★

JASMINE LASSI COCKTAIL

★★★★★☆

CREAMY VANILLA COLADA

★★★★☆

LOVE ME FLIP
BLUE LASSI
BOMBAY LASSI COCKTAIL
PINEAPPLE LASSI COCKTAIL
RAITA COCKTAIL
ROSIE LASSI COCKTAIL
RASPBERRY LASSI COCKTAIL
BANANA ALCOHOLIC SMOOTHIE
RASPBERRY ALCOHOLIC SMOOTHIE
STRAWBERRY ALCOHOLIC SMOOTHIE
GREEK PIÑA COLADA

TANQUERAY LONDON DRY GIN

London dry gin is a classic style of juniper-led gin which, as the name suggests, has a dry taste profile. Classic examples include Tanqueray, Beefeater and Bombay Original. Look for brands which describe themselves as being 'distilled' London dry gins.

★★★★★

BREAKFAST MARTINI
CHANTICLEER
DRY MARTINI #1
NEGRONI
NEGRONI SPUMANTE

THE MONEY PENNY
THE LAST WORD
THE PURITAN
RAMOS GIN FIZZ
REVERSE MARTINI

★★★★☆

ALEXANDER
AVIATION #2
BEE'S KNEES
CASINO #2
CLOVER CLUB NO.3 #1
EARL GREY MAR-TEA-NI
FOGCUTTER
GIMLET #2 (SCHUMANN'S RECIPE)
PERFECT LADY
SATAN'S WHISKERS (CURLED)

CHAMBORD LIQUEUR ROYALE DE FRANCE

Chambord is a rich framboise-style liqueur based on neutral spirit with blackberries and raspberries flavoured with herbs and honey. It is named after Chambord, the largest chateau in France's Loire Valley.

★★★★☆

CHARLIE
ECLIPSE
FRENCH DAIQUIRI
IVO
TRES COMPADRES MARGARITA

★★★★☆

BLACK CHERRY MARTINI
ENCANTADO
ESTES
FIRST OF JULY
FLIRTINI #1
FRENCH BISON-TINI
FRENCH MARTINI
HOT TUB
JA-MORA
MARQUEE
NUTS & BERRIES
RHODE ISLAND RED
TARTINI
TRE MARTINI
WATERLOO SUNSET

COCO LÓPEZ CREAM OF COCONUT

Coco López Cream of Coconut is a non-alcoholic sticky goo made with coconut milk from coconuts harvested in the Dominican Republic, cane sugar, emulsifier, cellulose, thickeners, citric acid and salt and is sold in 15oz/425ml cans. No heat is used in the process.

★★★★⯪

PIÑA COLADA #1

★★★★☆

FUNKY MONKEY
BANANA COLADA
PAINKILLER

★★★⯪☆

BUZZARD'S BREATH
BAHIA
NEW PORT CODEBREAKER
TONGUE TWISTER
CARIBBEAN PIÑA COLADA
BATIDA DE COCO

COURVOISIER

Exclusif is a blend of eaux-de-vie from all of the four top cognac regions: Grande Champagne, Petite Champagne (6 to 10 years old), Fins Bois (minimum 5 years old) and around 20% Borderies (10 to 15 years old). Thus Exclusif has an average age of 7 to 12 years.

★★★★★

BOLERO SOUR
COGNAC JULEP
CLASSIC COCKTAIL
BETWEEN THE SHEETS #2
EAST INDIA #1
FISH HOUSE PUNCH #1

★★★★⯪

A.B.C. COCKTAIL
AMERICAN BEAUTY #1
BOMBAY NO.2
BRANDY ALEXANDER
BRANDY FLIP
BRANDY SOUR
CHAMPS-ELYSÉES
COFFEE COCKTAIL
SIDECAR (DIFFORD'S FORMULA)
VIEUX CARRÉ
IN-SEINE

DE KUYPER APRICOT BRANDY

Also known as 'apry' in French, these liqueurs are produced either by infusing apricots in brandy and sweetening, or by infusing apricots in neutral spirit. The best examples are distilled from apricots. In the United States the term 'apricot brandy' refers to a flavoured brandy that is based on grape brandy.

★★★★⯪

ALGERIA
ANGEL FACE
DULCHIN
FOSBURY FLIP
MULE'S HIND LEG
NACIONAL DAIQUIRI #1
NACIONAL DAIQUIRI #2
PARK LANE
PLAYMATE MARTINI
PARADISE
SUMO IN A SIDECAR
TIKI MAX
CLARIDGE COCKTAIL
SKETCHER'S PET
THE SLOPE
SMOKE AND MIRRORS #2
SMOKED MAPLE
PRAECOCIA COCKTAIL

★★★★☆

AUNT EMILY
BANANA BOOMER

DE KUYPER CHERRY BRANDY

A rich fruit liqueur made from dark red cherries blended with brandy and distillates of ingredients such as cinnamon and cloves. The kernels are crushed for an enhanced almond flavour.

★★★★⯪

BLOOD & SAND #2
CUNNINGHAM
FOG CUTTER #2
MYRTLE BANK SPECIAL RUM PUNCH
VANDERBILT

★★★★☆

BANANA BOOMER
CHERRUTE
CHERRY ALEXANDER

CHERRY MARINER
CHERRY MARTINI
DIMI-TINI
HORSESHOE SLING
I'LL TAKE MANHATTAN
THE LEAVENWORTH
OLD FASHIONED CADDY
PABLO ALVAREZ DE CAÑAS SPECIAL
PANCHO VILLA
ROYAL TOAST

DEWAR'S WHITE LABEL SCOTCH WHISKY

Created in 1899 by Master Blender A.J. Cammeron, the first master blender at John Dewar and Sons Ltd. Heavily influenced by Aberfeldy single Highland malt which is central to the blend. Dewar's White Label is the Number 1 selling Scotch whisky in the USA.

★★★★★

MIZU WARI
ROYAL NAIL
SCOTCH SOUR
SCOTCH POINT

★★★★☆

AFFINITY
BOBBY BURNS #1
THE BROADMOOR
CHIN CHIN
HEATHER JULEP
HONEY & MARMALADE DRAM
HOT TODDY #1
ISLANDER
LIQUORICE WHISKY SOUR
PENICILLIN

GALLIANO L'AUTENTICO

Galliano is a vibrant, golden, vanilla-flavoured liqueur from Italy, easily recognised by its tall, fluted bottle, inspired by Roman columns.
Galliano was invented in 1896 by Arturo Vaccari, a distiller from Livorno in Tuscany, and is flavoured with more than 25 botanicals.

★★★★☆

HARVEY WALLBANGER
DAIQUIRI AUTHENTICO
☆

★★★★☆

ADAM & EVE
BARTENDER'S ROOT BEER
BOSSA NOVA #1
CARIBBEAN PUNCH
GUISEPPE'S HABIT
GOLDEN DREAM
HIGHLAND SLING
JUMPING JACK FLASH
MAXIM'S COFFEE (HOT)
MILANO SOUR
PERFECT JOHN
PICCA
ROCKY MOUNTAIN ROOTBEER
SNOOPY
FERNANDO
G.G AND G
LE DIJONNAIS MARTINI
ITALIAN MILK PUNCH #2

GRAND MARNIER CORDON ROUGE

Cordon Rouge (literally 'red ribbon') is the original Grand Marnier liqueur created in 1880 by Louis-Alexandre Marnier-Lapostolle and was first served at receptions given by Edward VII and Emperor Franz Joseph before becoming a favourite of the Russian Court.

★★★★☆

AMPERSAND
CLASSIC COCKTAIL
EAST INDIA #1
ORANGE BRULÉE
THE COMET
DULCHIN
EAST INDIA #2
GRAND COSMOPOLITAN
MANDARINTINI
MARNY COCKTAIL
MEXICO COCKTAIL
MEXICANO (HOT)
MILLION DOLLAR MARGARITA
OLYMPIC
PINK PALACE
PLAYMATE MARTINI
RED LION #1 (MODERN FORMULA)
TIKI MAX
LARCHMONT
SATAN'S WHISKERS (STRAIGHT)

JAMESON IRISH WHISKEY

The world's best-selling Irish whiskey, Jameson is made from a blend of malted and unmalted barley pot still whisky and column distilled grain whiskey. Jameson (standard or 'unreserved') is aged for an average of 5-6 years in casks previously used to age Bourbon and Oloroso Sherry.

★★★★⯪

IRISH COFFEE
IRISH COFFEE MARTINI
PAPPY HONEYSUCKLE
TIPPERARY #1
DETROIT ATHLETIC CLUB
WILD IRISH ROSE

★★★★☆

CAMERON'S KICK
DONEGAL
GLOOM LIFTER
JAMES JOYCE
ST. PATRICK'S DAY
SHAMROCK #2
DUBLINER
LAVENDER HONEY SOUR
MOLLY'S MILK

★★★⯪☆⯪

BLACKTHORN IRISH
CAUSEWAY
BLACK EYE
PICKLE BACK
EVERY-BODY'S IRISH COCKTAIL

KETEL ONE

The Dutch refer to their pot stills as 'ketels', thus this vodka is named after the Nolet's original 'Distilleerketel #1', which dates back to 1864. Made by blending highly rectified column still wheat neutral spirit with the same spirit redistilled in a copper alembic.

★★★★★

ESPRESSO MARTINI
JASMINE LASSI COCKTAIL
PINEAPPLE & CARDAMOM MARTINI
POLISH MARTINI
REVERSED VESPER & TONIC
SALTY MARTINI
STEEP FLIGHT
STAIRS MARTINI
VESPER DRY MARTINI

★★★★⯪

CUCUMBER MARTINI
COSMOPOLITAN #1
GRAND COSMOPOLITAN
GRAPEFRUIT JULEP
ICEWINE MARTINI
KANGAROO DRY MARTINI
MILANO
SGROPPINO

KWAI FEH LYCHEE

Named after Lady Yang Kuei Fei, the beautiful concubine of the last emperor of the T'ang dynasty, Hsuan Tsung (A.D. 712-756). Lady Yang Kuei Fei loved fresh lychee fruit and the emperor had the fruit brought from Canton, Southern China 600 miles to his northern palace by guards on fast horses.

★★★★☆

CHINESE COSMOPOLITAN
CHINESE WHISPER MARTINI
LYCHEE & BLACKCURRANT
MARTINI
LYCHEE & SAKE MARTINI
LYCHEE MARTINI
ORIENTAL TART
SUMMER ROSE MARTINI
TOKYO TEA

★★★⯪☆

CHINA BLUE
CHINA MARTINI
ENCHANTED
LYCHEE MAC
LYCHEE RICKEY
MELLOW MARTINI
PEAR DROP
SOUTH PACIFIC

LA FÉE PARISIENNE ABSINTHE (68%)

La Fée is made in Paris to a 19th century recipe containing wormwood (Artemisia absinthium) and flavoured with anise, hyssop and other aromatic herbs.

★★★★★

CAJUN NAIL
PISCO PUNCH #4
SAZERAC

★★★★⯪

BOBBY BURNS #2
BOMBAY NO.2
LA LOUISIANE COCKTAIL
LINSTEAD
MOONSHINE MARTINI
ORIGINAL SIN
PICADILLY MARTINI
RAGTIME

LUXARDO AMARETTO DI SASCHIRA LIQUEUR

The Luxardo family have been distilling fine liqueurs in the Veneto region of Italy for six generations. They make their amaretto with the pure paste of the finest almonds, from Avola in southern Sicily, and age it for eight months in Larchwood vats.

★★★★⯪

ALMOND OLD FASHIONED
BELLA DONNA DAIQUIRI
DON'S DELIGHT
NUTTY SUMMER

★★★★☆

ATHOLL BROSE
BROOKLYN #2
CHAS
DOWNHILL RACER
JOCKEY CLUB
MAE WEST MARTINI
HAWAIIAN COCKTAIL
ITALIAN MILK PUNCH
LOCH ALMOND
P.S. I LOVE YOU
RUBY DAIQUIRI
THUNDERBIRD
TOASTED ALMOND
TRIANGULAR MARTINI
WARSAW PACT

LUXARDO LIMONCELLO LIQUEUR

Luxardo has been making Limoncello since 1906 but with the new bottle introduced in May 2010 came a new formulation with a more intense lemon flavour. This new Luxardo Limoncello has around 25 percent more fresh lemon juice and essential oils from the peel of Sicilian lemons.

★★★★☆

BON BON
CUBAN HEAL
ITALIAN SUN
LEMON SORBET
LEMONY
MOTOX
NAVIGATOR
PEAR DROP MARTINI
PROCRASTINATION COCKTAIL
SANTIAGO #2
WATERMELON & BASIL SMASH
YELLOW BELLY MARTINI

★★★⯪☆

THE AMALFI
BASILICO
GRAPPARITA
GREEN BEETLE
LIMONCELLO MARTINI
SOCIALITE

LUXARDO MARASCHINO ORIGINALE

Luxardo Maraschino is aged for two years in white Finnish ashwood vats before being put in bottles encased in hand-plaited straw - originally to make transportation safe and now a trade mark exported to over 60 countries.

★★★★★

AMATITAN TWIST
CASINO #1
DAIQUIRI NO.1 FROZEN
KING'S JUBILEE
MARTINEZ #2 (MODERN GENEVER)

★★★★⯪

AVIATION NO.1
BRANDY CRUSTA
BOOKLYN COCKTAIL
BUSHWICK
CARROLL GARDENS
CLARA ASTIE COCKTAIL
CORONATION COCKTAIL NO.1
THE ELDER AVIATOR
FLORIDA DAIQUIRI
MOONSHINE MARTINI
MARTINEZ #3 (OLD TOM)
PETO MARTINI
RED HOOK
SHERRY COBBLER

LUXARDO SAMBUCA DEI CESARI

Luxardo Sambuca is a sweet and strong liqueur made from green Sicilian aniseed. The essential oils of the star anise are extracted by steam distilling and are soluble in pure alcohol. Uniquely, Luxardo's Sambuca is macerated in pure spirit and matured in Finnish ash wood vats.

★★★⯪☆

ALL WHITE FRAPPÉ
BUMBLE BEE
LIQUORICE SHOT
VENETO
CRÈME DE CAFÉ

MAKER'S MARK (RED TOP)

Maker's Mark is regarded by many as being the first Kentucky Straight Bourbon to market itself as a 'premium' brand. It is also noted for its high corn content and being blended in batches of 150 casks which fill around 3,000 cases.

★★★★★

BOILERMAKER
MANHATTAN PERFECT
OLD FASHIONED #1
MINT JULEP
WHISKEY SOUR #2
IN-SEINE
SAZERAC
PERFECT SUMMIT MANHATTAN
BENTON'S OLD FASHIONED

★★★★⯪

BOURBON BLUSH
BOURBON MILK PUNCH
BRAINSTORM
CARAMEL MANHATTAN
BOURBON CRUSTA
DANDY COCKTAIL
DIXIE DEW
FANCY FREE
GEORGIA MINT JULEP
JULEP MARTINI
KENTUCKY PEAR

MARTINI EXTRA DRY

Launched on New Year's Day 1900, Martini Extra Dry is made from a blend of wines, flavoured with botanicals (leaves, flowers, fruits, seeds, roots and barks) whose properties have been extracted by maceration in ethyl alcohol and mixed with the result of some botanical macerations that have been distilled.

★★★★★

ADDINGTON
MANHATTAN PERFECT
SMOKY MARTINI

★★★★⯪

AMBER ROOM #2
BAMBOO #1
BUCKEYE
CLOVER CLUB NO.3 #2
DICKENS' DRY MARTINI
DON DAISY
EL TORADO
NICK & NORA
PARIS MANHATTAN
PEAR MARTINI
PERFECT REGENT VX
PERPETUAL COCKTAIL
PICADILLY MARTINI
POET'S DREAM
THE QUINGENTI
ROOSEVELT COCKTAIL
THE SLOPE

MARTINI ROSSO

Made to Rossi's original recipe developed in the 1860s, this recipe has been passed down through each of the company's Master Herbalists. Several aromatic herbs are used, with a large proportion of Italian herbs providing the core flavours.

★★★★★

CUBAN LIBERAL
THE DEFENDER
MARTINEZ #1
NEGRONI

★★★★⯪

AMPERSAND
CARAMEL MANHATTAN
DELMONICO

DUTCH COUNT NEGRONI
LITTLE VENICE
MEXICAN MANHATTAN
THE MILLION DOLLAR COCKTAIL
PICHUNCHO MARTINI

★★★★☆

FRUIT CUP
NOON
ORIENTAL
PALL MALL MARTINI
PARK AVENUE
QUEEN MARTINI
SILVER BRONX
VALENTINO

MIDORI GREEN MELON LIQUEUR

Midori is made with Japanese Yubari and Musk melons - Yubari melons are similar to cantaloupe melons and are a traditional Japanese gift during the summer. The melons are grown in an area where the soil is rich in volcanic ash, which warms the melons during growth.

★★★★☆

AWOL
ENVY
E.T.
ILLUSION
JAPANESE SLIPPER
KOOLAID
MAE WEST MARTINI
MELON COLLIE MARTINI
MELON DAIQUIRI #1
MELON DAIQUIRI #2
MELON MARGARITA #1
SOURPUSS MARTINI
VERDI MARTINI

★★★⯪☆

COCO CABANA
CONGO BLUE
COOL MARTINI
ALIAN SECRETION
EVITA
GRATEFUL DEAD

MONIN ORGEAT/ ALMOND SYRUP

Monin's Almond Syrup uses no artificial flavourings - only good quality almonds to capture a truly authentic flavour, and makes it to a precise sweetness of 61.30 brix (meaning there's 61.3g of sugar to every 100g of syrup).

★★★★⯪

TIKI BAR MARGARITA
SOURISE

★★★★☆

COSMOPOLITAN DELIGHT
JAPANESE COCKTAIL
LEMON BUTTER COOKIE
MENEHUNE JUICE
COOL ORCHARD
MARAMA RUM PUNCH
THAI LEMONADE
MAI TAI (VIC'S)
MARKET DAIQUIRI
SCORPION
ALMOND MARTINI #1
ARMY & NAVY
CAMERON'S KICK
DAIQUIRI DE LUXE
FOG CUTTER #1
KIWI CRUSH
MAUREQUE
MOMISETTE

OLMECA TEQUILA

A reposado mixto tequila from the highland region of Los Altos, aged 5-6 months in ex-bourbon casks.

★★★★★

LAVENDER MARGARITA
TOMMY'S MARGARITA
PICADOR
AMATITAN TWIST
LA PERLA

★★★★⯪

ALMOND OLD FASHIONED
BALD EAGLE
BUENA VIDA
EL TORADO
ELEGANTE MARGARITA
ESTILO VIEJO
FLUTTER

JALISCO ESPRESSO
LOLITA MARGARITA
LUCKY LILY MARGARITA
MARGARITA-ON-THE-ROCKS
MEXICAN MARTINI
MEXICAN MULE

PEACHTREE PEACH SCHNAPPS

The world's best-selling peach schnapps, relaunched at the end of 2010 with a new bottle design. One of the leading products among the De Kuyper stable.

★★★★★

MISSIONARY'S DOWNFALL

★★★★⯪

BOHEMIAN ICED TEA
AKU AKU

★★★★☆

GEORGIA MINT JULEP
APPLE SPRITZ
BELLINI-TINI
BERMUDA COCKTAIL
CUSTARD TART
ENVY
JELLY BELLY BEANY
JEREZ
PEACH DAIRUIRI
VERDI MARTINI
MITCH MARTINI

★★★⯪☆

CREAM CAKE
INK MARTINI
JACUZZI

WARNINKS ADVOCAAT LIQUEUR

Warninks is an entirely natural product made only using brandy, egg yolks, sugar and vanilla without any preservatives or artificial thickeners. Warninks is the best-selling advocaat in the UK with a 50% share of the market.

★★★★⯪

CANARY FLIP

★★★★☆

CRÈME ANGLAISE MARTINI
CUSTARD TART
DUTCH BREAKFAST MARTINI
DUTCH COURAGE
RHUBARB & CUSTARD MARTINI
SNOWBALL

★★★⯪☆

AMBROSIA COCKTAIL
APPLE & CUSTARD COCKTAIL
BESSIE & JESSIE
EGG CUSTARD MARTINI
FLUFFY DUCK
GRANNY'S MARTINI
NEW PORT CODEBREAKER
ORANGE CUSTARD MARTINI
ZABAGLIONE MARTINI